DRAMA IN THE MODERN WORLD:

Plays and Essays

DRAMA IN THE

MODERN WORLD:

Plays and Essays ❧ SAMUEL A. WEISS

UNIVERSITY OF ILLINOIS, CHICAGO

D. C. Heath and Company, Boston

Preface

FROM REALISM TO absurdist anti-theatre, modern drama is a complex of
styles, genres, themes and forms exceptional in scope and variety. Without
attempting any mechanical representation of dramatic trends, I have selected
fourteen plays from the modern repertory—ranging from Ibsen to the
current Soviet playwright Arbuzov—which stand out as masterworks of their
kind. Inevitably, an international spread of major figures and tendencies
appears. The near classic status of Ibsen, Strindberg, Shaw, Chekhov, and
Synge needs no arguing. No more does the high achievement (regardless of
one's personal predilections) of Pirandello, O'Neill, Brecht, Lorca, and
Giraudoux. In recent years, the "theatre of the absurd," notably that of
Beckett and Ionesco, has been the most challenging development in the
theatre along with the epic drama of Brecht and his followers. From contemporary American playwrights I have chosen Tennessee Williams, who
(however one judges his limitations) commands sure theatrical instincts and
sensitivity. Only one dramatist perhaps needs introducing—Alexei Arbuzov,
at the moment the leading Soviet playwright. The liberalizing trend in post-
Stalin Russia is evident in Arbuzov's tentative and modest departures from a
narrowly conceived Socialist realism. His recent work is a superior example
of contemporary Soviet culture which it would be ostrich-like to ignore.

In selecting plays from the above writers I have been guided by the
principles of taste and merit, since any search for the "typical" play would
be artificial and futile. From Beckett's works I have chosen *All That Fall,*
quite possibly the greatest radio drama written.

Instead of lengthy editorial introduction and commentary, I have appended
to each play a stimulating critical essay written by the playwright or some
suitable critic. The ideal sought was a vivid and lucid essay, arguing a point
of view and instinct with style as well as intelligence. Strindberg, Synge and

Pirandello comment importantly on their own work. Ionesco debates with Kenneth Tynan, and both go to the heart of contemporary dramatic controversy. Gorki brilliantly recalls Chekhov; Yeats discusses Synge; and O'Casey pays warm but pungent tribute to Shaw. In addition to penetrating and provocative essays by Mary McCarthy, Eric Bentley, Joseph Wood Krutch, Arturo Barea and Maurice Valency, I have included a fascinating interview with Samuel Beckett and two pieces of high journalistic reviewing: Roy Walker on *All That Fall* and Stark Young on *The Glass Menagerie*. A. Korneichuk officially interprets "socialist realism."

Editorial apparatus is deliberately brief and unobtrusive. Succinct introductions before the plays give enough background and biographical information to orient the reader without prejudicing his approach and appreciation. The bibliography is highly selective on the basis of readability and usefulness. Wherever possible I have included outstanding articles which can be read in reasonably short time. Finally, the dates accompanying the plays refer to time of final composition except where otherwise indicated.

S.A.W.

Contents

DRAMA IN THE MODERN WORLD:

Plays and Essays

IBSEN WAS BORN IN THE TOWN OF SKIEN IN SOUTHERN

Henrik
Ibsen
1828-1906

Norway, into a merchant family that suffered a humiliating bankruptcy when he was eight. Thus he experienced the destructive effects of narrow provincial values early in life, and throughout his career he was to inveigh against stultifying convention and to champion the re-bellious spirit. At fifteen he left his family and moved to Grimstad, a neighboring small town where he was apprenticed to a pharmacist; there, at eighteen, he fathered an illegitimate child. At Grimstad, too, Ibsen found provincial life intolerable and expressed his revolt in wild and riotous pranks. Finally he set out for Christiania to study medicine, but his bent for philosophy and literature soon won out. Caught up in the revolutionary currents of 1848, he had written a verse drama, *Catiline,* idealizing the Roman traitor as a champion of liberty. He now joined a liberal weekly and a secret revolutionary group, but renounced political activity when the group's leaders were seized and imprisoned. A turning point in his life came when he was invited to become stage manager of the state theatre in Bergen, and from 1851 to 1862 he was associated with theatres in Bergen and Christiania, producing, directing, and writing. In 1864, however, he became depressed and embittered by Norway's failure to defend Denmark against Prussia, and left for a self-imposed exile in Rome. Not until 1891 did he return to Norway. In Italy he wrote his finest poetic dramas, *Brand* (1866) and *Peer Gynt* (1867). But it was his realistic prose plays in which he grappled with contemporary social and moral issues that made a profound impression on European culture and drama; he was hailed as a liberator by some and denounced as a subverter of morality by others. Ibsen struck out against hypocrisy and social conformity and called for creative self-realization in such plays as *A Doll's House* (1879), *Ghosts* (1881), and *An Enemy of the People* (1882). He met the central issue of the individual in society with a slashing attack on the "compact majority." Yet he recognized the limits of his own iconoclasm, as is evident in the subtle studies of neurotic idealists and destructive pseudo-Ibsenites in *The Wild Duck* (1884), *Rosmersholm* (1886), and *Hedda Gabler* (1890). With *The Master Builder* (1892) Ibsen turned to the tragedy of the aging artist. A deepening note of frustration and failure now entered his work; his plays withdrew into ever more obscure symbolism, dealing with autobiographical and metaphysical matters. He died in 1906, after a series of strokes had broken his once-powerful mind.

THE WILD DUCK ❦ BY HENRIK IBSEN

English Adaptation by Max Faber

CHARACTERS

HAAKON WERLE, a prosperous merchant and manufacturer in his sixties

GREGERS WERLE, his son—in his late thirties

OLD EKDAL,—in his seventies

HJALMAR EKDAL, his son—a photographer, in his late thirties

GINA EKDAL, Hjalmar's wife—in her early forties

HEDVIG EKDAL, their daughter, aged fourteen

A FLABBY GENTLEMAN

A BALD GENTLEMAN

A SHORT-SIGHTED GENTLEMAN

SIX OTHER GENTLEMEN

MRS. BERTHA SÖRBY, Haakon Werle's housekeeper—in her middle forties

DOCTOR RELLING, in his middle forties

MOLVIK, an ex-student of theology—in his middle thirties

GRAABERG, Haakon Werle's book-keeper —in his sixties

PETTERSEN, Haakon Werle's manservant —in his late fifties

JENSEN, a hired waiter

SEVERAL OTHER HIRED WAITERS

Guests at Haakon Werle's dinner-party

The action of the play takes place in a Norwegian provincial town during three consecutive days of the winter of 1884.

❦ Act I

Evening. HAAKON WERLE'S *study— well and comfortably appointed. There are well-fitted bookcases and handsomely upholstered furniture. Centre, a writing-table with papers and documents on it. The lighted lamps have green shades giving a soft light. Centre Back, large folding doors stand wide open with the curtains drawn back so that the inner room can be seen, beautifully furnished and brilliantly lit by lamps and branched candlesticks. Down Right, a small baize-covered door leads to* HAAKON WERLE'S *office. Above it a large fireplace in which a bright fire is burning. Right a double door leading into the dining-room.*

JENSEN *is moving about the study, putting things in order, while two or three other hired* WAITERS *can be seen lighting candles, etc., in the inner room under* PETTERSEN'S *supervision. The noise of talking and laughter from the dinner-party in the dining-room is interrupted by a knife rapped on a glass, followed by* the sound of a toast being proposed, followed by loud approval and the resumption of conversation. PETTERSEN *comes into the study, runs his eye over the activities of* JENSEN, *then crosses to fireplace, lights the lamp on the mantelpiece and puts the shade on.*

PETTERSEN. D'you hear that, Jensen? The old man's got himself on to his legs and is toasting Mrs. Sörby in a fine old speech this time!

JENSEN (*moving an armchair*). I suppose it's true wot they say—about 'im and 'er being—pretty well in with each other . . . ?

PETTERSEN. I'm sure I don't know.

JENSEN. They also say 'e was pretty 'ot stuff in 'is young days, wasn't 'e?

PETTERSEN. I dare say.

JENSEN. And they also say 'e's really giving this beano in honour of 'is son— that's wot I 'eard, any'ow.

PETTERSEN. It's quite true. The young master came home yesterday.

JENSEN. First time I ever 'eard Mr. Werle 'ad a son.

PETTERSEN. Oh yes, he's got a son all right. But he never leaves the works at Höidal—at least, he's never been in this house all the years I've been here.

(*Enter a* WAITER (*not one of those*

The Wild Duck by Henrik Ibsen. Adapted by Max Faber. Copyright © 1958 by Max Faber. Reprinted by permission of Heinemann Educational Books Ltd.

already visible) from Left in the inner room.)

WAITER. Excuse me, Mr. Pettersen—but there's an old fellow here who wants to——

PETTERSEN (*to himself*). Now, who the devil can this be . . . ?

(*Enter* OLD EKDAL *by the same way as the* WAITER. *He wears a shabby overcoat with a high collar and woollen mittens. He carries a stick and a fur cap and has a paper parcel under his arm. His dingy reddish-brown hair is obviously a wig; his moustache is grey.*)

PETTERSEN. Good Lord—what are you doing here?

OLD EKDAL (*hovering*). I've got to get into the office, Pettersen—got to get into the office. . . .

PETTERSEN. The office was closed an hour ago, you know that.

OLD EKDAL. Yes, I know. That's what they told me at the front door on my way in. But Graaberg's still up there. Be a good chap, Pettersen, and let me through this way (*pointing to baize-covered door*). After all, it wouldn't be the first time. . . .

PETTERSEN. Oh, all right then. (*Crossing and opening baize-covered door.*) But see you go out the proper way, that's all. We've got company this evening.

OLD EKDAL (*following*). Oh, but I know all about that—all about it! H'm. . . . Thanks, Pettersen—you're a good old friend—I shan't forget you! (*To himself.*) Blithering old fool . . . !

(*Exit* OLD EKDAL. PETTERSEN *closes door behind him.*)

JENSEN. 'E's one o' the office lot, isn't 'e?

PETTERSEN. Oh, no. They just give him odd jobs of copying to do sometimes. All the same, believe it or not, he's been a regular swell in his time, has old Ekdal.

JENSEN. Yes, you can see he's 'ad 'is troubles. . . .

PETTERSEN. He was an officer in the army once, y'know—a lieutenant.

JENSEN. Was 'e now? Only goes to show. . . .

PETTERSEN. Yes. After that he got into the timber trade somehow. Eventually he went into partnership with old Mr. Werle at the Höidal works and, by all accounts, played him a very dirty trick. . . . Oh, I know Old Ekdal backwards—many's the

beer and bitters we've had together down at Ma Eriksen's!

JENSEN. He'd never strike me as 'aving the money to stand anybody a drink!

PETTERSEN. Of course he hasn't, Jensen—I always do the paying. I never think there's any harm in doing a good turn to folk who've seen better days.

JENSEN. Why? Did he go bankrupt, then?

PETTERSEN. Far worse than that—he went to gaol.

JENSEN. Did 'e now? Gaol too!

PETTERSEN. Or perhaps it was the penitentiary—(*listening*). Sssh! That's them. They're getting up from table. . . .

(*The dining-room doors are thrown open from inside by two* WAITERS. *Enter* MRS. SÖRBY *from dining-room in conversation with two male guests. The remaining guests follow with* HAAKON WERLE *among them.* HJALMAR EKDAL *and* GREGERS WERLE *enter last.*)

MRS. SÖRBY. Oh—coffee in the music-room, please, Pettersen.

PETTERSEN. Very good, madam.

(MRS. SÖRBY *and the two gentleman pass into the inner room and exeunt to left, followed by* PETTERSEN *and* JENSEN.)

FLABBY GENT. (*to* BALD GENT.). Phew —bit of a labour of Hercules getting through that dinner, wasn't it?

BALD GENT. Oh, I don't know—it's surprising what you can eat out of mere politeness in three hours!

FLABBY GENT. Yes, but the aftermath, my dear Chamberlain, the aftermath—(*belches*).

ANOTHER GENT. Did I hear somebody say coffee and maraschino in the music-room?

FLABBY GENT. Splendid! Then I daresay Mrs. Sörby will play us something—(*belches*).

BALD GENT. (*significantly*). So long as dear Mrs. Sörby doesn't play something we don't like . . . !

FLABBY GENT. Not on your life! Bertha would never go back on her old friends! (*Belches.*)

(*Group passes into inner room.*)

WERLE (*quietly and a little anxiously*). Gregers, I don't believe any of them noticed it.

GREGERS (*turning to him*). Noticed what, Father?

WERLE. Then you didn't notice it, either?

GREGERS. Notice what?

WERLE. We were thirteen at table. . . .

GREGERS. Thirteen. Were we?

WERLE. Yes. (*Glancing towards* HJALMAR.) We're usually twelve. (*To the company.*) Well, gentlemen—there's coffee and maraschino in the music-room. . . .

(*All except* HJALMAR *and* GREGERS *exeunt to music-room.*)

HJALMAR (*a little uncomfortably*). You shouldn't have asked me, Gregers. . . .

GREGERS. What? Not ask my best and one and only friend to a dinner supposed to be in my honour?

HJALMAR. Well—I don't think your father's too pleased about it. You see . . . I never do come here. . . .

GREGERS. So I gather. But I shan't be staying very long, and I felt I wanted to see you and talk to you again. . . . After all, we were at school together and—well —it must be sixteen or seventeen years since we saw each other.

HJALMAR. Is it all that time?

GREGERS. It certainly is. And how have things been with you? You're looking very well. What's more you've put on weight——

HJALMAR. Oh, I wouldn't say that. I've probably filled out a little—and look a bit more of a man than I did.

GREGERS. There's no doubt about that —the outer man looks very promising.

HJALMAR (*gloomily*). Ah, but what about the inner man, Gregers! Believe me, that's a very different story! Of course, you know all about the terrible and tragic misfortune which I and my family have had to bear since you and I last met . . . ?

GREGERS (*gently*). How *is* your father now?

HJALMAR. I'd much rather we didn't talk about it, Gregers. Of course, my poor unhappy father lives with me now—he hasn't another soul in the world to cling to. Oh, it's so painful for me to talk about it. Tell me about yourself—how have you been getting on up there?

GREGERS. Oh, I've enjoyed the most excellent solitude! I've had ample time in which to reflect upon the nature of things. . . . However, why shouldn't we sit down and make ourselves comfortable . . . ?

(*Crosses to armchairs by fire, gestures* HJALMAR *to one, and as* HJALMAR *takes it settles himself in the other.*)

HJALMAR (*rather emotionally*). All the same, I do thank you for asking me to your father's table—it makes me feel that you no longer think badly of me. . . .

GREGERS (*surprised*). Where on earth did you get the idea that I ever thought badly of you?

HJALMAR. You did at first, you know . . .

GREGERS. At first?

HJALMAR. Yes, when the blow fell. And, after all, I suppose it was perfectly natural that you should—when your own father was within an inch of being drawn into that—er—terrible business.

GREGERS. Why should *that* have made me think badly of you? Or did somebody put the idea into your head?

HJALMAR. As a matter of fact, Gregers, I know you did. (*Changing his tone.*) Your father told me.

GREGERS (*with a slight start*). My father? So that was it! That explains why you never wrote to me—not a word. . . .

HJALMAR. Yes.

GREGERS. Not even when you decided to become a photographer?

HJALMAR. Your father said it would be better if I didn't write to you about anything.

GREGERS (*staring straight in front of him*). Yes . . . yes . . . that was understandable, perhaps. . . . Tell me, Hjalmar —d'you find your life as it is . . . reasonably satisfactory?

HJALMAR (*with a slight sigh*). Yes— yes, of course I do. . . . I've little enough to complain of, really. It felt a bit strange at first, I admit—it was such a completely different life. But then, of course, all the circumstances were different. . . My father's hopeless ruin . . . and the shame and degradation of it, Gregers——

GREGERS (*touched*). Yes—yes, I know.

HJALMAR. Naturally, I couldn't go on with my studies. There wasn't a shilling to spare—on the contrary, we were up to our eyes in debt—mostly to your father, I believe.

GREGERS. H'm. . . .

HJALMAR. And so it seemed best to make a clean break with the old life. As a matter of fact, it was largely on your father's advice that I did; and since he was so generously concerned to help me——

GREGERS. My father was?

HJALMAR. Surely you knew that? Where else could I have got the money to study photography, equip a studio and go into business? It costs a tidy bit, you know. . . .

GREGERS. And my father paid for all that?

HJALMAR. But I thought you knew, Gregers? He gave me to understand he'd written and told you all about it.

GREGERS. He never said a word about it to *me*. Perhaps he forgot. Although our correspondence has always been confined to business matters. . . . So it was all my father's doing?

HJALMAR. Yes—it certainly was. He didn't want it to be known—but, all the same, it was he. And it was really he who enabled me to get married. Or didn't you know anything about that, either?

GREGERS (*touching* HJALMAR'S *arm for a moment*). Not a word! Anyhow, Hjalmar, I can't tell you how pleased I am to hear all this . . . but I'm not altogether pleased with myself. . . . It occurs to me that perhaps I've misjudged my father in some things. . . . This at least suggests he has a heart . . . even a conscience. . . .

HJALMAR. A conscience?

GREGERS. Yes—or whatever you like to call it. All the same, I can't tell you how glad I am to hear all this about father. . . . So you're a married man, eh, Hjalmar? Well, that's more than I shall ever be able to say for myself! Are you *happily* married?

HJALMAR. Yes, very. I've as cheerful and hard-working a wife as any man could wish for—and she's by no means uneducated, you know.

GREGERS (*a little surprised*). No—of course not.

HJALMAR. Well, life itself is an education. You see. In her daily intercourse with me—or with some of our very cultured friends—you'd hardly know her for the same Gina.

GREGERS. Gina?

HJALMAR. Yes—had you forgotten that was her name?

GREGERS. Gina, you said? What Gina?

HJALMAR. Surely you remember her? She used to work here.

GREGERS (*eyeing him*). D'you mean Gina Hansen?

HJALMAR. Of course—Gina Hansen.

GREGERS. Who kept house for us during mother's last illness?

HJALMAR. Yes, I believe so. But, you know, Gregers, I could have sworn your father wrote to you about our marriage.

GREGERS (*rising*). Yes, that's right, he did—but I don't think he . . . (*pacing*). Wait a moment, though—yes, he did mention it now I come to think of it. But then my father always writes so briefly. (*Sitting on chair-arm.*) But tell me, Hjalmar—this is extraordinarily interesting—how did you come to know Gina?

HJALMAR. Oh, quite simply. Gina, as you know, didn't stay very long—everything was in such a muddle, owing to your mother's illness, and so on, that—well, I suppose Gina felt she couldn't cope with it; so she gave notice and left. I believe that was about a year before your mother died—or perhaps it was the same year.

GREGERS. It was the same year—I remember distinctly; I was up at the works at the time. What happened then?

HJALMAR. Oh, Gina went back to live with her mother—the Mrs. Hansen who used to keep the little restaurant—a very respectable and hard-working woman. She had a room to let—rather a pretty room it was, and quite comfortable. . . .

GREGERS. And, as luck would have it, I suppose you got it, eh?

HJALMAR. Yes—luck in the guise of your father again; that is, he suggested my going there. . . . Well, there you are, that's how I got to know Gina!

GREGERS. And before you knew it you were engaged, eh?

HJALMAR. Well—it's never very difficult for young people to fall in love, is it?

GREGERS (*rising and pacing*). Tell me —when you got engaged—was it then that my fa—I mean, that you decided to take up photography?

HJALMAR. That's right—I was naturally very anxious to get settled in something, and have a home of my own as quickly as possible. And both your father and I thought photography the best thing —so did Gina. You see—by a fortunate

chance Gina knew a little bit about retouching photographs.

GREGERS. A very happy coincidence.

HJALMAR (*rising: happily*). Yes,
wasn't it? An extraordinary piece of luck!

GREGERS. As you say—quite extraordinary. In fact, my father seems to have
been a sort of Fairy Godmother to
you. . . .

HJALMAR (*warmly*). Well, at any
rate, he didn't desert his old friend's son
in his hour of need. He's certainly got a
heart—you see!

(*Enter* MRS. SÖRBY *on* HAAKON
WERLE'S *arm.*)

MRS. SÖRBY. No—I'm not going to let
you have your own way any longer! Now
come along, Mr. Werle, there's a dear. It's
so much better for you not to be in there
with all those bright lights; you'll only
strain your eyes again—and it's very bad
for them.

WERLE (*slipping his arm from hers
and passing his hand across his eyes*).
Yes . . . I think perhaps you're right. . . .

(*Enter* PETTERSEN *with a punch-bowl
on a tray and* JENSEN *in his wake.*)

MRS. SÖRBY (*pausing in inner room
doorway*). Now gentlemen, if you'd like
some punch, you must please come in
here and get it. . . .

FLABBY GENT. (*joining her*). Come
now, Mrs. Sörby, you don't seriously intend to deny us our precious smoking
rights?

MRS. SÖRBY. Yes, I do—in *here!* No
smoking in Mr. Werle's own private sanc-
tum . . . I'm sorry, Chamberlain!

BALD GENT. And when did you decree
this harsh embargo, Mrs. Sörby?

MRS. SÖRBY. After our last dinner, my
dear Mr. Balle, when certain of our
honoured guests allowed themselves to
go a little too far.

BALD GENT. And are we never to go a
little too far, Mrs. Sörby?

MRS. SÖRBY. Not the least bit—in any
direction. . . .

(*Most of the guests have come into
the study from the inner room, and*
WAITERS *are handing round punch.*)

WERLE (*crossing to* HJALMAR). You
seem to be very absorbed, Ekdal. Have
you found something to interest you?

HJALMAR. I was just looking at this
album, Mr. Werle.

BALD GENT. (*wandering about*). Ah—
photographs! But, of course, that's very
much in your line nowadays, isn't it?

FLABBY GENT. (*seated in armchair*).
Yes—haven't you brought any of your
own with you?

HJALMAR. No—I haven't.

FLABBY GENT. Well, I think you
should have. Photographs enjoyed in a
sitting position are very good for the
digestion! (*Belches.*)

BALD GENT. And they can often contribute handsomely to an evening's entertainment, y'know.

SHORT-SIGHTED GENT. And all con-
tributions thankfully received, what?

MRS. SÖRBY: What they really mean,
Hjalmar, is that when one is asked out to
dinner one should always be prepared to
do something in return for it afterwards.

FLABBY GENT. Specially after a *good*
dinner—why, bless me, it should be a
pleasure!

BALD GENT. And when it's a matter of
eating to live——

MRS. SÖRBY. You're quite right about
that!

(*They take punch and go on laughing
and joking.*)

GREGERS (*quietly*). You really must
join in, Hjalmar.

HJALMAR. How on earth can I?

FLABBY GENT. (*turning in his chair*).
Don't you think, Mr. Werle, that Tokay
is always a remarkably sound wine?

WERLE (*standing with his back to the
fire*). I can safely vouch for the one you
had tonight—one of the finest vintages,
as I'm quite sure you noticed.

FLABBY GENT. I did, indeed! It had a
remarkably delicate flavour. But then, of
course, that *was* a good year.

HJALMAR (*shyly*). Does the year
matter with Tokay, then?

FLABBY GENT. (*laughing*). Well—
that's a good one! (*Belches.*)

WERLE (*smiling*). Well, well—I'm
sadly afraid a good wine is wasted on
you. . . .

BALD GENT. Tokay and photographs,
Mr. Ekdal, have something in common:
they both need sunshine! Isn't that so?

HJALMAR. Yes—no doubt—light—is
—very—important.

MRS. SÖRBY (*glancing round*). And it's
very important to some others too . . . the

sunshine of Court favour! Chamberlains as well, they also like to bask in the sunlight of Court favour.

BALD GENT. Oh, Mrs. Sörby! That's a very ancient jest!

SHORT-SIGHTED GENT. Mrs. Sörby's coming out!

FLABBY GENT. But at our expense, remember. (*With mock menace.*) Oh, you naughty Madame Bertha! Naughty!

MRS. SÖRBY. And *their* vintages differ too, you know—the older ones are the best!

SHORT-SIGHTED GENT. Oh, I say! Am I one of the older ones, Mrs. Sörby?

MRS. SÖRBY. Oh, far from it!

BALD GENT. There you are! And what about me, dear, sweet Mrs. Sörby?

FLABBY GENT. Yes, and me! Come along—tell us *our* vintage!

MRS. SÖRBY. Both very sweet, gentlemen.

(*Sips her punch to them, and the men laugh and flirt with her*).

WERLE. Mrs. Sörby can always contrive to slip out of the net—if she's a mind to. . . . Fill your glasses, gentlemen! Pettersen! Gregers—come and have a glass with me. . . . (GREGERS doesn't move.) Ekdal, won't you join us? I had no chance of drinking with you at dinner. . . .

(*The baize-covered door opens and* GRAABERG *puts his head round the edge of it.*)

GRAABERG. Excuse me, sir—I'm sorry to trouble you—but I can't get out.

WERLE. Are you locked in again?

GRAABERG. I'm very sorry, sir—but I'm afraid Flagstad's gone off with the keys.

WERLE. Very well, then—you can come through this way.

GRAABERG (*apologetically*). But . . . I—I have someone with me, sir.

WERLE. Well then, hurry up, both of you. You needn't pay any attention to us.

(*Enter* GRAABERG *followed by* OLD EKDAL. WERLE *registers annoyance and disgust. The talk and laughter suddenly cease.* HJALMAR *starts on seeing his father, quickly puts down his glass, and turns away to the fireplace.*)

OLD EKDAL (*without raising his eyes, and bowing to right and left as he goes*). So sorry—very sorry for coming the wrong way—door's locked—they've locked up—so sorry——

(*Exeunt* GRAABERG *and* OLD EKDAL *by inner room and off right.*)

WERLE (*through his teeth*). Confound that Graaberg!

GREGERS (*staring after them in amazement: to* HJALMAR): But . . . surely that couldn't have been——

FLABBY GENT. (*testily*). What's happened? Who was that?

GREGERS. Oh, nobody—only the bookkeeper and someone.

SHORT-SIGHTED GENT. (*to* HJALMAR). Did you know that man?

HJALMAR. I don't know—I didn't notice. . . .

FLABBY GENT. What *is* all this about? (*Rises and crosses to some others who are conversing in low tones.*)

MRS. SÖRBY (*to* PETTERSEN, *quietly*). Give him something to take home with him—something nice.

PETTERSEN (*nodding*). I'll see to it, madam.

(*Exit* PETTERSEN *into inner room and off right.*)

GREGERS (*to* HJALMAR, *somewhat moved*). So it was really he?

HJALMAR. Yes.

GREGERS. And yet you stood there and denied knowing him?

HJALMAR (*whispering vehemently*). But how could I——

GREGERS. —Acknowledge your own father?

HJALMAR (*desperately*). If you were in my place. . . .

(*The low-toned general conversation rises quickly to an artificial vivacity. The* BALD GENT. *crosses to* HJALMAR *and* GREGERS.)

BALD GENT. (*genially*). Ah! Talking over old times, eh? The good old college days! Cigar, Mr. Ekdal? I can give you a light. . . . Ah, but I forgot—smoking is strictly prohibited!

HJALMAR. Anyhow—I'd rather not smoke just now, thank you.

FLABBY GENT. (*turning to them*). Ekdal, how about giving us a recitation? You had quite a gift for that sort of thing at one time.

HJALMAR. I'm sorry. I'm afraid I can't remember anything.

FLABBY GENT. Great pity! What would you like to do, Balle?

HJALMAR. I think I'll go now, Gregers.

When fate deals a man such blows as I've had. . . . You'll say good night to your father and thank him for me, won't you?

GREGERS. Yes, of course. . . . Are you going straight home?

HJALMAR. Yes, why?

GREGERS. I thought perhaps I might look in later, that's all.

HJALMAR. No, I'd much rather you didn't. Don't come to my house. Mine is a dreary house, Gregers—especially after all this—abundance. . . . We can always meet somewhere in town.

MRS. SÖRBY (*going up to him: quietly*). You're not going, Hjalmar?

HJALMAR. Yes.

MRS. SÖRBY. Very well then, but remember me to Gina.

HJALMAR. I will.

MRS. SÖRBY. And tell her I'm coming to see her before very long.

HJALMAR. Thank you—I will.

(MRS. SÖRBY *smiles and crosses to* PETTERSEN *who is entering from the inner room.*)

HJALMAR. You stay with your guests, Gregers—I'll slip out quietly.

(*Exit* HJALMAR *by inner room and off right.* PETTERSEN *comes in.*)

MRS. SÖRBY (*to* PETTERSEN). Well—did you look after him?

PETTERSEN. Yes, Madam—I sent him off with a bottle of cognac.

MRS. SÖRBY. Oh—couldn't you have done better than that?

PETTERSEN. I don't think so, madam—it's what he likes best. . . .

FLABBY GENT. (*standing in inner room doorway with sheet-music in his hand*). Are you ready, Mrs. Sörby? Shall we play our duet now?

MRS. SÖRBY (*crossing*). Yes—by all means—a good idea!

OMNES. Bravo! Bravo! (*Etc.*)

(*Exeunt* MRS. SÖRBY *and* FLABBY GENT. *into inner room and off left, followed by all except* GREGERS *and* HAAKON WERLE. GREGERS *stands by the fire; his father makes a show of looking for something on the writing-table, and seems to expect his son to follow the others. When it becomes obvious that* GREGERS *is not going to move,* HAAKON WERLE *crosses towards inner room.*)

GREGERS. Just a moment, Father.

WERLE (*halting*). Well, what is it?

GREGERS. I must have a word with you.

WERLE. Can't it wait for some more private occasion?

GREGERS. I think not. There may never be such an occasion. . . .

WERLE (*eyeing him*). What d'you mean?

(*The distant sound of a piano is faintly audible from the inner room; beginning gently, it increases in volume as the scene proceeds.*)

GREGERS. How could you allow that family to go to the dogs like that?

WERLE. Presumably, you mean the Ekdals?

GREGERS. Yes, I mean the Ekdals. Lieutenant Ekdal was one of your closest friends.

WERLE. Far too close, as it turned out. I've been paying for it for years. Thanks to him my reputation—yes, *mine!*—has been permanently damaged.

GREGERS (*quietly*). Are you quite sure that it was entirely his doing?

WERLE. You don't suppose there was anyone else——

GREGERS. You and he were acting together in that forestry deal. . . .

WERLE. But Ekdal did the survey and drew the map—that deceptive map. It was he alone who ordered the illegal felling of timber on Government property. The whole business was in his hands from first to last. I never for one moment suspected what Lieutenant Ekdal was actually doing.

GREGERS. Nor, I fancy, did Lieutenant Ekdal.

WERLE. H'm—I wonder. . . . However, the fact remains that he was found guilty and I was acquitted.

GREGERS. Yes, I know there was nothing proved against you.

WERLE. Acquittal, my dear boy, is acquittal. Anyhow, why are you digging up these old troubles that have turned my hair prematurely grey? Is that what you've been brooding over up at Höidal all these years? Because I can assure you, Gregers, that here in the town, *my* connection with that affair was entirely forgotten long ago.

GREGERS. But not that unfortunate family's!

WERLE. Now what would you have had me do for these people? Ekdal came out of prison a broken man, past helping. There are some creatures that, when they get a couple of shots in the body, dive straight to the bottom and never come up again. . . . I give you my word, Gregers, I've done everything I could—short of laying myself open to suspicion and gossip.

GREGERS. Suspicion . . . ? Oh, yes—I see. . . .

WERLE. I've gone so far as to give Ekdal copying to do for the office—and I pay him far more than the job is worth.

GREGERS (*avoiding his look*). I've no doubt about that.

WERLE. You smile as if you had! Naturally, I can't show it to you on the books—as I never enter payments of that kind.

GREGERS (*smiling coldly*). No—there are certain disbursements which are best not recorded.

WERLE (*with a slight start*). What d'you mean by that?

GREGERS (*with sudden resolution*). Did you enter the amount you paid to have Hjalmar Ekdal taught photography?

WERLE. Why should *I* have entered it?

GREGERS. Because you paid for it. I also happen to know that you enabled him to set up house and start his business.

WERLE. And yet you can say I've done nothing for the Ekdals! In one way or another they've cost me a pretty penny, I can tell you!

GREGERS. And have you entered any of *those* expenses in the books?

WERLE. Why d'you ask?

GREGERS. Oh, I have my reasons. I believe I'm right in saying that your charitable interest in the son of your old friend began just before his marriage. . . . ?

WERLE. Really, Gregers, after all these years, how can you possibly expect me to——

GREGERS. You wrote to me about that time—a business letter, naturally—and in a brief postscript you mentioned that Hjalmar Ekdal had married a Miss Hansen.

WERLE. Well, that was perfectly correct. That was her name!

GREGERS. Yes, but you omitted to mention that this Miss Hansen was in fact our former housekeeper—Gina Hansen.

WERLE (*with an ill-managed cynical laugh*). It certainly never occurred to me that you would be passionately interested in our former housekeeper.

GREGERS. I wasn't. (*Lowering his tone.*) But apparently there was somebody else in the house who *was.* . . .

WERLE (*sharply*). What d'you mean? (*Angrily.*) D'you mean me?

GREGERS (*quietly*). Yes . . . weren't you?

WERLE (*blustering*). And you——! You actually dare——! It's . . . it's that barefaced ingrate! That damned photographer! Crawling in here with his vile insinuations . . . !

GREGERS. Hjalmar never even implied such a thing. In fact, I'd almost swear he doesn't even so much as suspect anything.

WERLE. Then where did you get such an idea? Who put it into your head?

GREGERS. My mother—my poor, unhappy mother—she told me—the last time I saw her. . . .

WERLE. Your mother! I might have guessed it. You two always stuck together! It was she who first turned you against me.

GREGERS. Not she, but what she had to endure—all the suffering and humiliation that wore her down and brought her to such a miserable end.

WERLE. She didn't suffer shame or humiliation—not more than others, anyhow. But you can't do anything with morbid and neurotic people. I know all about that! And you can harbour a suspicion like that—and go digging up all sorts of ancient rumours and slander against your own father! Really, Gregers, at your age, I should have thought you could have found something better to do!

GREGERS. I agree. It's time I did.

WERLE. In that case you might take things a bit more easily than you do! What *is* your idea of staying up at the works, year in and year out, slogging away like some common clerk, and refusing to accept a shilling more than the ordinary monthly wage? It's downright foolishness.

GREGERS. Ah, I wish I could feel so sure about that. . . .

WERLE. I know you better than you think. *You* want to be independent—you don't want to be indebted to me for anything. Well then, there happens to be an opportunity for you to gain that independence and become once and for all your own master.

GREGERS. Indeed? And how, exactly?

WERLE. When I wrote and asked you to return home immediately——

GREGERS. Yes—just why did you do that? I've been waiting all day to find out.

WERLE. I propose to offer you a partnership in the firm.

GREGERS. I? A partner? In *your* firm?

WERLE. Yes. It needn't involve our seeing a lot of each other. You could take charge of the business here in town, and I should move up to the works.

GREGERS. You? at Höidal?

WERLE. Yes, to tell you the truth, Gregers, I'm not so well equipped for work as I was: I have to spare my eyes as much as possible—they've been troubling me a lot lately——

GREGERS. They always have.

WERLE. But they're a lot worse now. And besides, circumstances might conceivably make it desirable for me to live there . . . at any rate, for a time.

GREGERS. It all sounds slightly incredible to me.

WERLE. Listen to me, Gregers—I know we disagree profoundly about many things. All the same, we *are* father and son. And I do think it should be possible for us to come to some sort of understanding.

GREGERS. You mean ostensibly, of course. . . ?

WERLE. Well—even that would be something. . . . What d'you say, Gregers? Don't you think it might be possible?

GREGERS (*eyeing him coldly*). There's something behind all this.

WERLE. What d'you mean?

GREGERS. I think you want to make use of me.

WERLE. Two men so closely connected can always be of use to each other.

GREGERS. That's what they say.

WERLE. The fact is, Gregers, I should greatly appreciate having you at home with me for a time. I'm a lonely man, my boy. Indeed, I've been lonely all my life—I feel it more than ever now that I'm getting on in years. . . . I need companionship.

GREGERS. You have Mrs. Sörby.

WERLE. True—I have. And in many ways she's grown almost indispensable to me. She's cheerful and good-tempered—the house is a brighter place because of her—and that's just what I need.

GREGERS. In that case, surely, you've already found what you want?

WERLE. Unfortunately, I'm afraid it can't last. In such circumstances a woman easily finds herself in a false position in the eyes of the world. Indeed, it's not very much better for the man.

GREGERS. Oh, I don't know. When a man gives such excellent dinner-parties as you do, such risks should mean nothing to him.

WERLE. That's all very well, Gregers; but what about her? I'm afraid she's got to the point where she won't put up with it much longer. And even if, out of her regard for me, she's ready to endure all the gossip and scandal and so on, would you, Gregers, with your strong sense of justice, say that——

GREGERS. Why be diplomatic? Are you thinking of marrying her?

WERLE. And supposing I were—what then?

GREGERS. Yes—what then?

WERLE. Would you be entirely opposed to it?

GREGERS. Oh, no—I certainly shouldn't.

WERLE (*hesitantly*). I wasn't sure whether . . . perhaps . . . your devotion to your mother's memory——

GREGERS. *I'm* not neurotic.

WERLE. Well, whether you are or not, at any rate you've taken a great weight off my mind. I'm relieved to think that I have your approval.

GREGERS (*eyeing him steadily*). Now I understand what use you have for me.

WERLE. Use for you? What an expression!

GREGERS. Oh, surely we needn't be too genteel in our choice of words—not when we're alone, at any rate. (*With a short laugh.*) So that's it! That was why it was so urgently necessary for me to come to town. To help you provide a family background for the benefit of Mrs. Sörby! A realistic little tableau of father and son! How very original!

WERLE (*furiously*). How dare you adopt that tone?

GREGERS. When was there ever any

family life in this house? Never, so far as I can remember. But now, oh yes, something of the sort is just what we want! How very reassuring for the anxious gossips, when the absent son returns on the wings of filial piety, in nice time for his ageing papa's wedding breakfast! *Then* what happens to those inconvenient rumours about the poor dead mother—and all that she had to put up with? The action of the son has stamped them out!

WERLE. I don't believe there's anyone on earth you dislike as much as me, Gregers. . . .

GREGERS (*quietly*). I've seen you at too close quarters.

WERLE. But through your mother's eyes. (*Lowering his tone.*) And remember—her vision was not always unclouded.

GREGERS (*only just controlling himself*). I know what you're trying to suggest. And who was to blame for mother's state of mind? Only you and your——! The last of them was that woman you palmed off on to Hjalmar Ekdal, after you'd done with her. . . . Ach!

WERLE (*shrugging*). That's your mother—almost word for word!

GREGERS (*ignoring the point*). And there he is, with the simple trust of a child, in the middle of all that deceit, living under the same roof with a creature like that, little suspecting that what he calls his home is built upon a lie! (*Taking a step towards his father.*) When I look back on all you've done, I see only a battlefield strewn with broken lives!

WERLE. I'm beginning to think the gulf that separates us is too wide——

GREGERS (*self-controlled and with a slight bow*). I think so too—and that's why I'm going.

WERLE. You're going? You mean leaving the house?

GREGERS. Yes. At last I've found a mission in life.

WERLE. Really? And what is it?

GREGERS. You'd laugh if I told you.

WERLE. A lonely man doesn't laugh so easily, Gregers.

GREGERS (*pausing on threshold of inner room*). Look, Father—can you see what game Mrs. Sörby's playing with your guests? Blind Man's Buff! Good night—goodbye.

(*Exit off right. For a moment the only sound is that of the guests at their game.*)

WERLE (*muttering contemptuously*). Poor devil! And then he says he's not neurotic!

(*Crosses towards inner room.*)

Medium Curtain

🌺 Act II

Later the same evening.

HJALMAR EKDAL'S *studio—a large room at the top of the house. Up right a sloping glass roof with a blue curtain running on wires half drawn. Up left door leading to landing. Left a door, below it a stove, and down left another door. Down right a door leading to the sittingroom. Centre back a pair of sliding doors. The studio is simply but comfortably furnished. Right a sofa somewhat away from the wall. Centre a table and chairs. Beside the stove a large shabby armchair. Various items of photographic apparatus are scattered about the room. Left of the sliding doors a bookcase containing a few books, boxes of photographic plates, bottles of chemicals, a miscellany of photographer's implements and carpenter's tools. On the table a lighted lamp with a shade, a litter of photographs and retouching impedimenta—paper, brushes, etc.*

GINA *sits by the table sewing and, from time to time, glances anxiously at* HEDVIG, *who sits on the sofa reading a book with her thumbs in her ears and her hands shading her eyes.*

GINA. Hedvig, dear. . . . (*Pauses. When it is plain that* HEDVIG *hasn't heard, more loudly.*) Hedvig . . . Hedvig!

HEDVIG (*putting down her hands and looking up*). Yes, Mother?

GINA. Now, dear—you've done quite enough reading for one evening.

HEDVIG. Oh, Mother, let me go on a little more, please—just a tiny bit.

GINA. No, dear, you must put the book away now—you know Father doesn't like you reading too much. Besides, he never reads himself in the evening.

HEDVIG (*shutting book*). No—but then Father doesn't like reading.

GINA (*putting down sewing and tak-*

ing up a small account book and a pencil). Can you remember how much we paid for that butter this morning?

HEDVIG. One and eight, I think.

GINA. So it was. (*Makes an entry.*) We do seem to get through an awful lot of butter in this house. Then there was the breakfast sausage—and cheese. . . . Let's see now (*Writing*)—oh, yes, and then the ham—'m, yes (*Adding up*)—that makes—

HEDVIG. And don't forget the beer, Mother.

GINA. Oh, yes, of course, the beer. (*Writing.*) It does mount up something shocking. . . . Still, we can't manage on no less, I suppose.

HEDVIG. Well, we didn't need anything hot for dinner, as Father was out.

GINA. Yes, we're that much in hand. And on top of it I took eight and six for photographs. . . .

HEDVIG. Did you really, Mother—all that?

GINA. Yes, eight and six!

(*Pause.* GINA *resumes her sewing.* HEDVIG *takes paper and pencil and begins drawing, shading her eyes with her left hand.*)

HEDVIG. Isn't it lovely to think of Father's having dinner at a dinner-party at Mr. Werle's?

GINA. Yes, but Mr. Werle didn't ask him. It was his son, Mr. Gregers, who did that. (*A slight pause.*) We don't have nothing to do with Mr. Werle.

HEDVIG. Well, I do hope Father won't be long—because he promised he'd ask Mrs. Sörby for something nice for me.

GINA. Well, there's plenty of good things going in that house—believe me, I know!

HEDVIG (*drawing*). As a matter of fact, I believe I'm just a little bit hungry.

(*Enter* OLD EKDAL *by the landing door. He still carries the paper parcel and has another bulging from his overcoat pocket.*)

GINA. You *are* late tonight, Grandfather, whatever's happened?

OLD EKDAL. They'd locked the office. I had to wait for Graaberg to finish. Then I had to come through the—ach . . . !

HEDVIG. Did they give you some more copying to do, Grandfather?

OLD EKDAL. Yes—all this! Look here!

GINA. Now isn't that nice!

HEDVIG. And you've got another parcel in your pocket, Grandfather.

OLD EKDAL. In my pocket? Oh—that's nothing—nothing at all—just nothing (*Putting his stick in a corner.*) Well, I've plenty to keep me occupied now, Gina—this'll keep me busy for some time. (*Chuckles, pulls sliding door open a little.*) Sssh! (*Peeps in.*) Look at 'em! (*Shutting door carefully, chuckling.*) All fast asleep, every one of 'em! She's even found her way into her basket! There now! What d'you think of that?

HEDVIG. Are you sure the basket'll be warm enough for her, Grandfather?

OLD EKDAL. Warm enough? (*Chuckles.*) My goodness me! She's warm enough in all that straw!

(*Crosses to bedroom door and exit. After a few moments he opens the door again and puts his head into the room.*)

No matches anywhere, Gina?

GINA. There's a box on the mantelpiece. . . .

(OLD EKDAL *withdraws his head again and shuts the door.*)

HEDVIG. Isn't it nice that Grandfather's got all that copying?

GINA. Yes, poor old gentleman—at least he'll make himself a little pocket money.

HEDVIG. And he won't be able to spend all morning down at that horrid Mrs. Eriksen's.

GINA. Yes—there's that as well.

(*A slight pause.*)

HEDVIG. D'you suppose they're still sitting down eating their dinner?

GINA. Goodness knows—I dare say. . . .

HEDVIG. Just think of all the nice things Father must be eating. And he'll come home feeling so wonderful inside, won't he, Mother?

GINA. Yes—and if only we could tell him we'd let the room.

HEDVIG. Oh, we needn't worry about that this evening.

GINA. We'd be better off if we had, though, wouldn't we? As it is, it's just standing there empty doing nothing.

HEDVIG. What I mean was we don't *need* it this evening—Father'll be in such a good mood anyhow. Like this we can save the room for another time.

GINA (*looking up*). You like having some good news for Father when he gets home of an evening, don't you?

HEDVIG. Oh yes—because we have such a very much nicer time then.

GINA (*thoughtfully*). Yes—there's something in that, I suppose.

(*Enter* OLD EKDAL *and crosses to kitchen.*)

(*Turning.*) Is there anything you want in the kitchen, Grandfather?

OLD EKDAL. Yes, yes—I can manage—you stay where you are. (*Exit into kitchen.*)

GINA (*after a short pause*). Surely he isn't raking out the fire in there? (*Pause.*) Go and see what he's up to, Hedvig—there's a good girl.

(*Enter* OLD EKDAL *with a small jug of steaming water.*)

HEDVIG. Oh, did you want some hot water, Grandfather?

OLD EKDAL. Of course I want some hot water, m'dear. . . . Got some writing to do. . . . That ink's as thick as porridge—h'm—thicker. . . . (*Crossing to bedroom.*)

GINA. All right—only do eat your supper first, Grandfather, it's all ready for you on the tray.

OLD EKDAL. Supper—what's that? I've no time for supper, Gina. I tell you, I've enough to do without . . . (*entering bedroom*). And see I'm not interrupted.

(*Exit and shuts the door.* GINA *and* HEDVIG *exchange glances.*)

GINA (*quietly*). Now I wonder where he got the money from. . . ?

HEDVIG. D'you think Mr. Graaberg let him have it?

GINA. No—he'd never do that. Not Graaberg—he always sends the money to me.

HEDVIG. Perhaps somebody let him have a bottle without paying.

GINA. Well, I can't imagine who! Poor old Grandfather! Who'd give *him* credit?

(*Enter* HJALMAR *by landing door. He wears a heavy overcoat and a grey felt hat.*)

(*Putting down sewing and rising.*) Why, Hjalmar—you're not back already?

HEDVIG (*simultaneously and jumping up*). Fancy you being home so early, Father!

HJALMAR (*taking off his hat*). Oh, most of the other guests were leaving, so I——

HEDVIG. But it's ever so early. . . .

HJALMAR. It was only a dinner-party, you know. (*Starts removing his overcoat.*)

GINA. Here—let me give you a hand.

HEDVIG. Me too! Were there lots of people there, Father?

HJALMAR. Oh no—not so very many. We were twelve or fourteen at table, I should think.

GINA. And did you talk to all of them?

HJALMAR. Oh yes, I had something to say to each; but Gregers wanted me to himself most of the time.

GINA. Has he still got that ugly face of his?

HJALMAR. Well, he hasn't changed very much. . . . Has—er—has Father come in yet?

HEDVIG. Yes—Grandfather's in there—writing.

HJALMAR. Did he have anything to say?

GINA. No, nothing in particular. Why?

HJALMAR. He didn't mention that—er—well, I heard something about his being with Graaberg, that's all. . . . I think I'll go in and see him for a minute.

GINA. I don't think I should, if I were you, Hjalmar. . . .

HJALMAR. Why—why not? Did he actually say he didn't want me to?

GINA. I don't think he wants anybody in there tonight.

HEDVIG (*making signs to* HJALMAR). He's——

GINA (*not seeing* HEDVIG'S *signals*). He came out and got himself some hot water just now.

HJALMAR. Ah! so that's it?

GINA (*after a moment's hesitation*). Yes—same old story.

HJALMAR. Oh—good heavens! Poor old white-haired Father! Oh, well—I suppose he may as well enjoy himself while he can. . . .

(*Enter* OLD EKDAL, *wearing an old jacket, smoking a large pipe, and just noticeably less sober.*)

OLD EKDAL. Ah! So you've come home to roost! I thought I heard your voice in there!

HJALMAR. Yes—I've just got back.

OLD EKDAL. You didn't see me, I don't suppose?

HJALMAR. No—but they told me you'd just gone—and so I thought I might as well come along after you.

OLD EKDAL. H'm. That was very considerate of you, Hjalmar. What were all those people supposed to be?

HJALMAR. Oh, they were a very mixed bag. There were Chamberlains Flor and Balle—and Chamberlain Kaspersen—and Chamberlain somebody else—and several other gentlemen of the Court. . . . Oh, I can't remember them all.

OLD EKDAL (*nodding*). Are you listening to this, Gina? Here's our Hjalmar in the middle of all those Chamberlains!

GINA. Yes—they're very grand up at the house nowadays.

HEDVIG. Did the Chamberlains sing, Father—or give recitations?

HJALMAR. No—they simply talked a lot of rubbish most of the time. They wanted me to recite—but I refused!

OLD EKDAL (*approvingly*). You refused to be drawn, eh?

GINA. Oh, but I do think you might have, really, Hjalmar.

HJALMAR. Of course not—one doesn't always do as one's asked. (*Pacing.*) At least, I don't.

OLD EKDAL. That's Hjalmar all over—a mind of his own!

HJALMAR. Well, I don't see why I should bother to entertain half society because I happen to go out once in a while. Why should *I* exert myself the whole time? Let them exert themselves! They've nothing better to do than go from house to house, from table to table, every night. They should be grateful for all the free meals they get and do something in return for them!

GINA. Surely you didn't tell them that, Hjalmar?

HJALMAR (*humming and hawing*). Oh, they had to hear a good deal—I can tell you!

OLD EKDAL. Even the Chamberlains?

HJALMAR. They were there, weren't they? (*Easily.*) Oh, yes—and later on we had quite an amusing little discussion about Tokay. . . .

OLD EKDAL. Tokay! Now that's a wine worth drinking!

HJALMAR (*judicially*). No . . . not always, Father! Sometimes it is—it all depends on the vintage—it depends entirely on how much *sunshine* the grapes have had.

GINA. Why, Hjalmar, you know everything!

OLD EKDAL. And didn't they disagree with you about that?

HJALMAR. Ah—they tried to; but they were told it's just the same with Chamberlains—some are of a good vintage, others indifferent. . . .

GINA. The things you do think of!

OLD EKDAL. So you made 'em put that in their pipes and smoke it, too, eh?

HJALMAR. Straight to their faces!

OLD EKDAL. D'you hear that, Gina? Straight to their faces! Chamberlains' faces!

GINA. He is a one! Just fancy—straight to their faces. Oh, Hjalmar!

HJALMAR. Yes, but that's between ourselves. One doesn't repeat things like that, y'know. For, of course, the whole thing was extremely friendly from first to last. They're really decent people. *I'd* no wish to hurt their feelings—certainly not!

OLD EKDAL (*to no one in particular*). Straight to their faces. Well . . . I don't know!

HEDVIG (*affectionately*). It's wonderful to see you in a dress-coat, Father—and it suits you splendidly, too!

HJALMAR. You think so? (*Admiring himself in the mirror on the wall behind the sofa.*) I don't think it's too bad—and it's a perfect fit, of course! Might almost have been made for me—a trifle tight under the arms, perhaps. . . . (*Beginning to take off coat.*) Give me a hand, Hedvig—I think I may as well get into my old jacket. . . . D'you know where it is, Gina?

GINA (*fetching it*). Here you are, dear. (*Helps him on with it.*)

HJALMAR. That's better! (*Handing dress coat to* GINA.) And remember it's to go back to Molvik first thing in the morning.

GINA (*carefully folding coat and laying it aside*). Of course, dear—I'll see to it.

HJALMAR (*stretching himself*). Ah! That's more like it! Besides, I think loose-fitting clothes are more suited to my easy-going personality. Don't you, Hedvig?

HEDVIG. Yes, Father, I do really.

HJALMAR. Especially when I loosen my tie like this (*does so*) and leave the ends free, eh?

HEDVIG (*gravely*). Yes—that's perfect—and it goes so much better with your moustache and those nice curly bits. . . .

HJALMAR. I should think "wavy" would describe them better.

HEDVIG. Yes, wavy . . . or curly. . . .

HJALMAR. Wavy?

HEDVIG (*after a brief pause, touching his arm*). Father. . . ?

HJALMAR. Well, what is it?

HEDVIG. You know quite well what it is.

HJALMAR. Indeed, I don't.

HEDVIG (*laughing and protesting*). Oh, Father, do stop teasing me!

HJALMAR. Why? What *is* the matter?

HEDVIG (*shaking him*). Oh, Father, stop pretending! Where are they? All the nice things you promised to bring me? Remember? Where did you put them?

HJALMAR. Well, bless me, if I haven't gone and forgotten all about them!

HEDVIG. Now you know you're only teasing me, Father. It's naughty of you. Where did you hide them?

HJALMAR. No—truly I forgot. Well, perhaps I didn't quite forget, after all. I'll have a look. I think I may have *something* for you, Hedvig.

(*Crosses and searches in pockets of dress coat.*)

HEDVIG (*jubilantly*). Oh, Mother, Mother. . . !

GINA. There now! You see? If you only give him time. . . .

HJALMAR (*producing a folded card*). Ah, here it is.

HEDVIG. But that's only an old piece of card!

HJALMAR. Ah, it's very much more than that, Hedvig. It's the bill of fare—the menu. See, here it is written—"Menu" —right across the top—that means bill of fare—what there is to eat.

HEDVIG. But . . . didn't you bring anything else?

HJALMAR. I tell you I forgot the other things—and, anyhow, you may take my word for it, such delicacies are generally very unsatisfying—hardly worth eating. . . . Now you come and sit at the table and read out the names of the dishes, and I'll try to remember how each of them tasted. . . . You'll like that. . . .

HEDVIG (*gulping*). Th-thank you.

(*Sits down but does not read.* GINA *makes signs to her which* HJALMAR *sees.*)

HJALMAR (*pacing*). It's fantastic the number of things the father of a family is expected to remember—he's only to forget the most insignificant item and he's treated to nothing but black looks and long faces. Well, one can get used

to that, too, I suppose. (*Stopping beside* OLD EKDAL *by the stove.*) Did you have a look in there this evening, Father?

OLD EKDAL. Oh yes, I did—the moment I got home. She's gone to bed in her basket.

HJALMAR. Really? In her basket, eh? (*After glancing at* HEDVIG.) H'm—that shows she must be getting used to it!

OLD EKDAL. I told you she would! But, you know, Hjalmar, there's still quite a few things we——

HJALMAR. Ah, yes—the little improvements. . . .

OLD EKDAL. They've got to be done, y'know.

HJALMAR. Well, then, why shouldn't we go over them now? Let's make ourselves comfortable on the sofa.

OLD EKDAL. Oh—yes, I—all right—just wait till I fill me pipe (*crossing to bedroom*) and I'd better give it a good clean, too, while I'm about it. . . . H'm!

(*Exit into bedroom and shuts the door.*)

GINA (*to* HJALMAR, *smiling*). Cleaning his pipe!

HJALMAR. Yes, yes, I know. Gina—leave him to it. . . . Poor shipwrecked old father. . . . Yes, I suppose we had better get those little improvements out of the way tomorrow.

GINA. I don't see where you're going to get the time tomorrow, Hjalmar——

HEDVIG (*interrupting*). Oh, yes he will, Mother!

GINA. But there's all them photographs have to be retouched—they've been sending round for them again time out of number.

HJALMAR. Oh yes—those infernal prints—everlasting prints! Oh, I'll soon get those done. That reminds me—any new orders this afternoon?

GINA. No such luck. And tomorrow I've only got those two coming I told you about.

HJALMAR. That's all, eh? Well, I suppose if people won't make a little effort——

GINA. But what more can I do? Advertising costs money! As it is I put more in the paper than we can really afford!

HJALMAR. Oh yes, of course, the papers! Always the papers! Well, you can see how much good they do. I suppose nobody's called to look at the room, either?

GINA. Not so far, they haven't.

HJALMAR. Well, what else d'you expect? If people don't keep their wits about them what's——You really must make an effort, Gina.

HEDVIG (*rising*). Shall I get your flute, Father?

HJALMAR. Flute? No, Hedvig, I don't think you better. The pleasures of this world are not for me! (*Pacing.*) Work—that's my lot—nothing but work! Well, tomorrow I'll work—you see if I don't! I'll work as long as my strength will let me!

GINA. But, Hjalmar dear, I didn't mean it like that.

HEDVIG. Father, shall I get you a bottle of beer, then?

HJALMAR. No—I can do without it. I require nothing for myself—nothing—absolutely nothing. (*Coming to a halt.*) Did you say beer?

HEDVIG (*coaxingly*). Yes, Father—lovely, cool, beautiful, bubbly beer. . . .

HJALMAR. Well, since you're so pressing . . . just one bottle, eh?

GINA. Yes, do that, dear—then we'll make ourselves nice and comfy.

(HEDVIG *darts towards the kitchen but, as she passes close to* HJALMAR *he puts out his hand and stops her, looks at her for a moment, then clasps her to him.*)

HJALMAR. Hedvig! My own little Hedvig!

HEDVIG (*with tears of joy*). Oh, dear, darling Father!

HJALMAR. No, you musn't call me that —I don't deserve it. Here have I been sitting at the rich man's table—gorging myself at the festive board—and I couldn't even remember to——

GINA (*settling herself at the table*). Oh, don't talk so silly, Hjalmar.

HJALMAR. But it isn't silly. (*To* HEDVIG.) For all that you musn't think too badly of me, Hedvig—after all, I do love you, you know—dearly. . . .

HEDVIG (*throwing her arms around him*). And we love you, too, Father—oh, so much—so very much!

HJALMAR. And if sometimes I seem to be a little unreasonable—you must remember that I'm a man beset by a host of cares. Ah, well—(*wipes his eyes*)—never mind. No beer at a moment like this— get me the flute.

(HEDVIG *runs to the bookcase and returns with the flute.*)

Thank you, dear. That's it—with my flute in my hand, and you two beside me—Ah. . . .

(HEDVIG *sits on the sofa with* GINA. HJALMAR *walks up and down, then puts the flute to his lips and breaks resolutely into a Bohemian dance—but too slowly, and with exaggerated pathos. After a few bars he stops, stretches out his left hand, and speaks with great feeling.*)

The place may be poor and humble, Gina—but it is home. And I want you to know that my real happiness is always here. . . . (*Resumes playing.*)

(*A knock on the landing door.*)

GINA (*rising*). Sssh! Hjalmar—I think there's somebody at the door.

HJALMAR (*removing the flute from his lips: exasperatedly*). There's always something!

(GINA *crosses to landing door and opens it.*)

GREGERS (*offstage*). I beg your pardon, but——

GINA (*recoiling slightly*). Oh!

GREGERS. Doesn't Mr. Ekdal the photographer live here?

GINA. Yes—yes, he lives here.

HJALMAR (*laying down flute and crossing*). Why, Gregers! It's you! I thought I recognized your voice—come in! This is a pleasant surprise!

(*Enter* GREGERS *wearing an overcoat over a plain grey country suit.*)

GREGERS. Well, I told you I might come along.

HJALMAR. Yes, but I hardly expected you this evening—Have you left the party, then?

GREGERS. Not only the party—I've left my father's house. Oh, good evening, Mrs. Ekdal—I don't suppose you recognize me?

GINA. Oh, you're not all that easy to forget, Mr. Gregers.

GREGERS. I resemble my mother, I believe—and, of course, you remember her.

HJALMAR. Did you say you've left the house?

GREGERS. Yes, I've gone to an hotel.

HJALMAR. Really . . . Well, now you're here—take off your coat and sit down. . . .

GREGERS. Thank you, I will.

(*Removes overcoat, which* GINA *takes and hangs up beside* HJALMAR'S.)

HJALMAR. Take the sofa——

(GREGERS *sits on the sofa and* HJALMAR *takes a chair by the table.*)

GREGERS (*glancing round*). So this is where you live, eh, Hjalmar—this is your home . . . ?

HJALMAR. It's also the studio, as you can see.

GINA. And, we generally use it as a sort of sitting-room as well, as it's the biggest room in the maisonette.

HJALMAR. We had a more luxurious place, but this one has the enormous advantage of having such first-class anterooms.

GINA. Yes, and we've even got a nice one to let across the passage!

GREGERS (*to* HJALMAR). Ah—so you let rooms as well, do you?

HJALMAR. Well, not so far. Good tenants aren't so easy to come by these days—in fact, if you want them, you've got to be prepared to make an effort. (*To* HEDVIG.) What happened to that beer, Hedvig?

(HEDVIG *nods and exits into kitchen.*)

GREGERS. Your daughter?

HJALMAR. Yes, that's Hedvig.

GREGERS. Your only child?

HJALMAR. Yes, our one and only. Our greatest joy, Gregers—(*lowering his tone*)—and, I grieve to say, our deepest sorrow.

GREGERS. Oh? In what way?

HJALMAR. She's in immediate danger of losing her sight.

GREGERS. She's going blind?

HJALMAR. Yes. But it's only in the early stages so far; and it may be some time before she realizes it for herself, poor child. However, according to the doctor—and he's warned us—it's quite inevitable.

GREGERS. How terrible for you both! But how did it happen?

HJALMAR (*sighing*). Oh—it's hereditary, I'm afraid. . . .

GREGERS (*with a slight start*). Hereditary?

GINA. Yes, y'know—Hjalmar's mother suffered something chronic with her poor eyes. . . .

HJALMAR. At least, so my father told me—I don't remember her.

GREGERS. Poor child! And how does she take it?

HJALMAR. Well, naturally, we haven't had the heart to tell her anything. She hasn't the slightest inkling of it. She's as happy as a lark, singing about the place all day . . . and fluttering her way into never-ending night. (*Overcome.*) It's a terrible cross for me to bear, Gregers.

(*Enter* HEDVIG *with a tray of glasses and beer which she puts on the table.* HJALMAR *strokes her hair.*)

Ah, thank you, my darling!

(HEDVIG *puts an arm round his neck and whispers in his ear.*)

No, dear, thank you—I don't think we need any bread and butter just now. (*Looking round.*) Unless, of course, you'd care for some, Gregers?

GREGERS (*shaking his head*). No, not for me, thank you.

HJALMAR (*in the same melancholy tone*). Well, perhaps a couple of slices, then. Or, if you have just a crust, that'll do nicely for me. And—Hedvig—plenty of butter.

(HEDVIG *nods gaily and exits into kitchen.*)

GREGERS (*who has been watching her*). She seems quite well in other respects.

GINA. Oh yes—everything else about her's all right, thank goodness!

GREGERS. She looks as if she'll be very like you, Mrs. Ekdal. How old is she now?

GINA. Fourteen, as near as no matter—it's her birthday the day after tomorrow.

GREGERS. She's tall for her age.

GINA. Yes—she's shot up something wonderful these last twelve months. . . .

GREGERS. It certainly makes one realize one's age, to see these youngsters growing up. You two have been married—oh, let me see now . . . it must be——

GINA. Well now . . . we were married in . . . why, it's fifteen years!

GREGERS. Is it really as long as that?

GINA (*eyeing him*). Yes—it is.

HJALMAR. Yes, it must be. Fifteen years all but a few months. (*Changing his tone.*) I should think they must have seemed very long years to you up at the works, Gregers.

GREGERS. They seemed so indeed at the time; but, looking back on them, I hardly know how they've gone.

(*Enter* OLD EKDAL *from his room, walking unsteadily. He is without his pipe and wearing an old-fashioned military cap.*)

OLD EKDAL. Here I am, Hjalmar! Ready to sit down and discuss the orders of the day for tomorrow.

HJALMAR (*crossing to him*). Father, we've a visitor! I don't know if you remember him? Gregers Werle.

OLD EKDAL (*staring blearily at* GREGERS). Werle? Nonsense, boy! That's not Werle—it must be the son. What's he want me for?

HJALMAR. Not you, Father—he's come to see me.

OLD EKDAL. Does he? Then nothing's the matter again?

HJALMAR. No, Father—there's nothing wrong.

OLD EKDAL (*with an expansive gesture*). Not that it would rout me if there was. I'm afraid of nothing, only——

GREGERS (*crossing to him*). I bring you greetings from your old hunting-grounds—that's all, Lieutenant Ekdal.

OLD EKDAL (*bewildered*). Hunting-grounds? Where?

GREGERS. At Höidal. . . . You remember the forests? And the works?

OLD EKDAL. Oh, them! Yes! I knew every stick of those forests at one time!

GREGERS. Yes—you were a great sportsman in those days.

OLD EKDAL. 's fact. I quite believe you. What's that—my cap you're eyeing. I can wear it at home if nobody wants me to—so long as I don't take it out with me, then nobody can see me in it. . . . What's that matter?

(*Enter* HEDVIG *with a plate of bread and butter which she puts on the table.*)

HJALMAR. Now, Father—why not sit down and have a glass of beer? Help yourself, Gregers.

(OLD EKDAL *mumbles and staggers to the sofa.* GREGERS *takes a chair beside him,* HJALMAR *one on the other side of* GREGERS. GINA *sits at the table, sewing.* HEDVIG *stands beside her father.*)

GREGERS. D'you remember, Lieutenant Ekdal, how Hjalmar and I used to come up and visit you during the summer holidays, and sometimes at Christmas?

OLD EKDAL. No, I don't! I remember the bears—used to shoot 'em all hours of the day and night! Hundreds of 'em—I was a very good shot—I've shot nine bears.

GREGERS (*sympathetically*). And now I don't suppose you ever get any shooting?

OLD EKDAL. Oh, you don't know! Don't I? I still get a bit of shooting—not the old way, though. . . . Forests . . . (*drinks*) . . . yes, that's it—forests. . . . What's yours like up there now?

GREGERS. I'm afraid the forest is not what it was—it's been thinned out a good deal since your time. . . .

OLD EKDAL. Thinned out? Thinned out. . . . (*More softly—nervously.*) It's dangerous to do that—to thin out trees in a forest. Things come of it. . . . Forests get their own back.

HJALMAR (*filling* OLD EKDAL'S *glass*). Come now, Father—a little more beer.

GREGERS. I can't think how an open-air man like you, Lieutenant Ekdal, can bear to live cooped up in four walls in the middle of a stuffy town like this.

OLD EKDAL (*chuckling quietly and glancing at* HJALMAR). Oh, here's not bad. Not bad at all, sir. I can tell you that.

GREGERS. Yes, but what about all those things that used to mean so much to you? The cool breezes, the spacious life of the woods and hills, the animals and birds——

OLD EKDAL (*grinning and winking*). Hjalmar—shall we let him see it?

HJALMAR (*quietly and slightly embarrassed*). No, Father—not this evening.

GREGERS. Why, what does he want me to see?

HJALMAR. Oh, it's nothing really—some other time, perhaps. . . .

GREGERS. You know, Lieutenant Ekdal, it suddenly occurs to me that I'm bound to be going back to the works fairly soon—now why shouldn't you come along with me? I'm sure there'd be plenty of copying up there for you. After all, for a man like you, it's not very lively here—you've nothing much to interest you——

OLD EKDAL (*taken aback*). Not very lively? *I'm* not interested in them.

GREGERS. Oh, I know you have Hjalmar; but then he's got his family to think of. . . . And a man like you, who's always answered the call of the wild——

OLD EKDAL (*thumping the table*). Hjalmar—now he's *got* to see it!

HJALMAR. But Father, is there any point in it? It's all dark in there now.

OLD EKDAL. Dark? Bosh! What's

wrong with the moon? (*Rising unsteadily.*) I say he's *got* to see it! Out of my way, Hjalmar. (*Lurching past him towards sliding doors.*) Here—come and help me, Hjalmar.

HEDVIG. Oh, do, Father, please!

HJALMAR (*rising*). Very well, then.

GREGERS (*to* GINA). What have they got in there?

GINA. Oh, you musn't expect marvels.

(OLD EKDAL—*with* HEDVIG'S *help—and* HJALMAR *each pull back one of the sliding doors.* GREGERS *remains standing by the sofa.* GINA *continues to sit and sew. The open doorway reveals a large irregular attic with odd nooks and corners and two stove-pipes rising through the floor and up to the roof. Parts of the attic are lit by bright moonlight shining through the skylights, other parts are in deep shadow.*)

OLD EKDAL (*to* GREGERS). Now, sir! Step right up! You can't see from where I was!

GREGERS (*crossing*). What have you got?

OLD EKDAL (*beckoning*). Look close and you'll see better—eh?

HJALMAR (*slightly awkwardly*). Of course, this is all my father's department —you appreciate that?

GREGERS (*on the threshold of attic and looking in*). You keep poultry, Lieutenant Ekdal?

OLD EKDAL. I shouldn't be at all surprised! *And* chickens! (*Chuckling.*) They're having a good roost now—you ought to see them in the mornings!

HEDVIG. And we've got a——

OLD EKDAL. Sssh! Not so fast! Keep him waiting!

GREGERS. You've pigeons too, I see. . . .

OLD EKDAL. You do. I believe we have! Only they like nesting up as high as they can get—in the roof-tree—the top branch!

HJALMAR. And they're not all the ordinary kind of pigeon, either.

OLD EKDAL. Ordinary! Certainly not— they're jolly extraordinary! There's some pouter and a few tumblers—but come over here and have a look. . . . See those hutches against the fence?

GREGERS. Yes—what are they for?

OLD EKDAL. That's where the rabbits roost, young feller-me-lad.

GREGERS. D'you mean to say you keep rabbits, too?

OLD EKDAL. Of course—what d'you think we keep hutches for? Where'd you be without rabbits? Fancy asking if we keep rabbits, Hjalmar? H'm—but now for the real thing! Out of the light, Hedvig! Take your stand here, sir—that's better. Now look down there—straight ahead of you. . . . I see a basket filled with straw—can you?

GREGERS. Yes. There's a bird in it, isn't there?

OLD EKDAL (*indignantly*). H'm—a bird he calls it!

GREGERS. Isn't it a duck?

OLD EKDAL. Of course it's a duck!

HJALMAR. Yes, but what *sort* of duck, Gregers?

HEDVIG. It's not just an ordinary sort of duck—

OLD EKDAL. Sssh! Quiet there!

GREGERS. Well, it's certainly not a Turkish duck.

OLD EKDAL. No, Mr. . . . Werle, my boy—it's certainly not a Turkish duck, either. It's a wild duck!

GREGERS. What, really? A wild duck?

OLD EKDAL. The same! That bird—as you called it—is a live wild duck . . . *our* wild duck, my Mr. Werle.

HEDVIG. *My* wild duck. She's mine.

GREGERS. And it actually manages to thrive up here, does it?

OLD EKDAL. Why not? She's got her own water-trough to splash about in whenever she likes. . . .

HJALMAR. The water's changed every other day.

GINA. Hjalmar, dear, it's getting so cold. . . .

OLD EKDAL. H'm. That means lights out! Well, better they get a good night's sleep. . . . Push, Hedvig!

(HJALMAR *and* HEDVIG *push the doors to.*)

Ah—never mind. (*To* GREGERS.) The next time you shall have a proper look at her. (*Sitting in armchair by stove.*) Ah, they're queer fish, wild duck . . . I give you my word, sir. . . .

GREGERS. But how on earth did you catch it, Lieutenant Ekdal?

OLD EKDAL. I never did. There's one particular man we've got to be thankful for for her in this town. . . .

GREGERS (*with a slight start*). Not my father, by any chance?

OLD EKDAL (*drowsily*). Hit him on

the nail! That one and the same particular man was none other than your father himself.

HJALMAR. It's very odd you should guess that, Gregers.

GREGERS. Well, you told me you owed so many things to my father, and I wondered whether——

GINA. But we didn't really get it from Mr. Werle—only in a manner of speaking. . . .

OLD EKDAL. It's old Haakon Werle we've got to thank for it all the same, Gina. . . . (*To* GREGERS.) He went out for a shoot in his boat and missed her! His sight—he's losing it, y'know. And he winged her. . . .

GREGERS. Oh, I see—a stray shot in the body, eh?

HJALMAR. Yes—a couple of shots, I rather think.

HEDVIG. One of them was under the wing—so she couldn't fly away.

GREGERS. But . . . didn't she dive straight to the bottom?

OLD EKDAL (*sleepily*). Always do—wild duck . . . dive straight to the bottom . . . hook themselves into the weeds—and all the other muck that grows down there—and make sure they never come up again. . . .

GREGERS. But your wild duck came up again, Lieutenant Ekdal?

OLD EKDAL (*yawning*). Your father's dog brought it up—very clever dog, that! Dived right in after her and brought her to the surface again. . . .

GREGERS (*to* HJALMAR). And so you took her in?

HJALMAR. Not quite like that. Your father took her home with him, but somehow she didn't seem to thrive; so he ordered Pettersen to destroy her——

OLD EKDAL (*half asleep*). Pettersen . . . that Pettersen . . blithering old fish-face. . . .

HJALMAR. And that's how it happened. Father knows Pettersen slightly and, when he heard about it, got Pettersen to hand her over.

GREGERS. But she manages to thrive up here apparently?

HJALMAR. Oh yes, she does. She's even got fat. She's grown so used to it in there by now that she's entirely forgotten about the old life out of doors . . . and that's all that matters.

GREGERS. Yes, of course, you're quite right. And so long as she never gets a glimpse of the sea or the sky—well, I don't think I'd better stay any longer—I think your father's asleep. . . .

HJALMAR. Oh, don't take any notice of that. . . .

GREGERS. By the way, didn't I hear you say something about having a room to let? Across the passage, wasn't it?

HJALMAR. Yes, why? D'you know of anybody?

GREGERS. Can I have that room?

HJALMAR. You?

GINA. Oh no, not *you*, Mr. Gregers, I—well, I mean . . .

GREGERS (*quietly*). I'd like the room, if you've no objection . . . and I'd like to move in first thing in the morning.

HJALMAR. By all means—it'll be a pleasure to have you in the house, Gregers.

GINA. Oh, but, Mr. Gregers, it's nothing like the sort of room you'd be accustomed to. . . .

HJALMAR. Why, Gina—how can you say that?

GINA. Well, you know for yourself how pokey and dark it is in there. . . .

GREGERS. That doesn't matter in the least, I assure you, Mrs. Ekdal.

HJALMAR. I should call it quite a nice room, decently furnished and with a charm of its own.

GINA. But what about them two he'll have underneath him?

GREGERS. What two are they?

GINA. Well, one of them's been a tutor. . . .

HJALMAR. He's got some sort of degree, I think. His name's Molvik.

GINA. And the other's a doctor and his name's Relling.

GREGERS. Relling? I believe I used to know him—he practised for a bit up at Höidal.

GINA. They're a proper pair of good-for-nothings, they are. Out on the tiles all night, and coming in at all hours, and then like as not——

GREGERS. Oh, one soon gets accustomed to that sort of thing. I shall try to emulate the wild duck. . . .

GINA. Well, I'd sleep on it first if I were you.

GREGERS. I do believe you're reluctant to have me in the house, Mrs. Ekdal.

GINA. Oh, no. Now whatever gave you that idea?

HJALMAR. Well, you haven't been exactly cordial about it, Gina. (*To Gregers.*) Are you thinking of staying in town for some time, then?

GREGERS (*putting on his overcoat*). Yes—now I *am* thinking of remaining. . . .

HJALMAR. But not in your father's house? What d'you intend to do?

GREGERS. Ah—now if only I knew that, I'd have very little to worry about! But when one's had the misfortune to be called "Gregers"—"Gregers" with "Werle" tacked on to it—well, did you ever hear anything more revolting?

HJALMAR. Oh, I don't think it's so bad. What's wrong with it?

GREGERS. Ach! I should feel like spitting on a fellow with a name like that! But once you're already in the world with the handicap of being "Gregers Werle," as I am——

HJALMAR (*laughing*). And if you weren't Gregers Werle, who else would you like to be?

GREGERS. If I *could* have my choice . . . a very clever dog.

GINA. A dog!

HEDVIG (*involuntarily*). Oh no—not a dog!

GREGERS. Yes—a very, very clever dog. One that dives straight to the bottom after wild duck, when they dive in and hook themselves into the weeds and muck. . . .

HJALMAR. Quite frankly, Gregers, I haven't the least idea what you mean.

GREGERS. Oh—I don't think it means very much, anyhow. It's agreed then—I move in first thing tomorrow morning. (*To* GINA.) You won't find me any trouble to you—I'm quite used to doing for myself! (*To* HJALMAR.) We can go into the sordid details in the morning. . . . Good night, Mrs. Ekdal. (*To* HEDVIG.) Good night. . . .

GINA. Good night, Mr. Werle.

HEDVIG. Good night.

HJALMAR (*lighting a candle*). Just a moment, I'll light you down—it's rather dark on the stairs. . . .

(*Exeunt* HJALMAR *and* GREGERS *by landing door.*)

GINA (*staring ahead of her with her sewing in her lap*). Well . . . of all the funny things—fancy wanting to be a dog. . . .

HEDVIG. You know, Mother—I don't think he really meant that at all. . . .

GINA. Well then, what *did* he mean?

HEDVIG. I don't know, Mother—all I know is that he made me feel as if he didn't mean *any* of it . . . as if he was really saying something different all the time. . . .

GINA. D'you really think so? But what a funny thing to say. . . .

(*Enter* HJALMAR.)

HJALMAR. The lamp was still on downstairs. (*Blowing out candle and putting it down.*) Now at last one can get something to eat. (*Starting to eat bread and butter.*) Well, you see, Gina? You've only to keep your wits about you——

GINA. How d'you mean—wits?

HJALMAR. Well, anyhow, we've let that room at last. And to an old friend like Gregers. . . .

GINA. Well, I don't know what to say about it, I'm sure. . . .

HEDVIG. Oh, Mother—it'll be such fun. You see!

HJALMAR (*to* GINA). You are extraordinary. At first you were so anxious about letting the room, and now it *is* let, you don't like it.

GINA. Yes, I do . . . but if only it had been somebody else. . . . And what d'you think Mr. Werle's going to say about it when he hears?

HJALMAR. It's none of his business.

GINA. I dare say. But you don't need glasses to see that something's up between them two again? Why's he leaving home? You know as well as I do what they think of each other. . . .

HJALMAR. Maybe so, but——

GINA. And now Mr. Werle may get it into his head that you're at the bottom of it. . . .

HJALMAR. I can't help it if he does. Oh, I don't say that Mr. Werle hasn't occasionally rendered me considerable assistance—but that doesn't make me dependent upon him for the rest of my days.

GINA. That's all very well, Hjalmar: but supposing he goes and vents it on Grandpa, and makes him suffer for it? So as he loses what little bit of extra he gets from Graaberg. . . .

HJALMAR. I could find it in my heart to say "All the better if he did!" Isn't it humiliating enough for a man like me to see his grey-haired old father made an outcast? However, I fancy the time for that to be over and done with isn't very far off. (*Taking another piece of bread and butter.*) I know my mission in life—and now I intend to fulfil it!

HEDVIG. Oh, Father! Yes—you must!

GINA. Sssh! You don't want to wake Grandpa!

HJALMAR (*softly*). And I shall fulfil it, let me tell you! The day will come when . . . yes, and that's why it's such a good thing I've let that room! Don't you see how much more independent it makes me? And that's as it should be! A man with a mission in life has to be independent! (*Emotionally and looking towards* OLD EKDAL.) Poor Father! Poor, white-haired, old Father! You can depend on your Hjalmar! He'll carry your burden—never fear! His shoulders are broad enough—well, strong enough, at all events. . . . One fine day you'll wake up —You believe it, don't you, Gina?

GINA. Yes, of course, dear. (*Putting down sewing.*) Don't you think we ought to be getting him to bed? (*Rises.*)

HJALMAR (*with a sigh*). Yes—I suppose so. . . .

(*They cross to* OLD EKDAL *and, as* GINA *begins gently moving a cushion, which she hands to* HJALMAR, HEDVIG *crosses to* OLD EKDAL's *bedroom door and opens it. As she crosses towards arm-chair——*)

Medium Curtain

🌸 Act III

As before. The following morning. The blue curtain is wholly drawn back and the sun shines in through the glass roof. HJALMAR *sits at the table, laboriously retouching a photograph: several others lie before him. After a few moments enter* GINA *by landing door. She wears a hat and cloak and has a large covered shopping basket over her arm.*

HJALMAR (*looking up and stretching himself*). Back already, Gina?

GINA. Yes. There's so much to be done. I haven't had a minute to breathe this morning. (*Puts down basket on chair and sets about taking off hat and coat.*)

HJALMAR. Have you been to see how Gregers is getting on?

GINA. Yes. And it's a good thing I did! He certainly didn't waste any time about getting untidy. You never saw such a mess in all your life!

HJALMAR. Why—what's the matter?

GINA. And him a dab at doing for himself! Tried to light the stove with the damper in! Talk about smoke! Enough to smell you out of house and home!

HJALMAR. Poor Gregers!

GINA. Oh, but that was only the beginning! Next thing is he wants to douse the fire, so he goes and pours his jug over it—floor's like a pond in there!

HJALMAR. Oh well, never mind.

GINA. I got the porter's wife to go in and clear up after him—the pig! The room won't be fit to live in for hours.

HJALMAR. What's he going to do in the meantime, then?

GINA. I don't know. He said he was going out for a breath of air. He could do with some, I shouldn't wonder. . . .

HJALMAR. As a matter of fact I looked in to see him myself for a few minutes just after you left.

GINA. So he said. And you had to go and ask him to dinner.

HJALMAR. *Luncheon*, Gina—luncheon, not dinner. Just for a bite of something, that's all. After all, it's his first day here—we couldn't very well do otherwise. You've got something in the house, I suppose?

GINA. Oh, I'll manage to scrape up a bit of something, I dare say.

HJALMAR. Well, it had better be more than a bit of something. I shouldn't be surprised if Relling and Molvik didn't come up. I met Relling on the stairs just now, and I felt I had to——

GINA. Oh, you did! So we're to have those two as well, are we?

HJALMAR. Good heavens! A couple more or less can't possibly make all that difference.

(OLD EKDAL *puts his head round his bedroom door.*)

OLD EKDAL. I say, Hjalmar . . . (*sees* GINA). Oh, I—er——

GINA (*briskly*). Now what is it, Grandpa? Is there anything you want?

OLD EKDAL. No—no, nothing—it doesn't matter. . . . H'm. . . .

(*Withdraws head and shuts door.*)

GINA (*taking up basket*). And whatever you do, don't let *him* go sneaking out again.

HJALMAR. Yes, yes all right—I know. ... Oh, and Gina—I think a little herring salad might be a good idea. I believe Relling and Molvik made rather a night of it. ...

GINA. Well, so long as they don't come before I'm ready, that's all.

HJALMAR. Oh, they won't. You've plenty of time.

GINA. Well, that's something. Meantime it wouldn't hurt *you* to do a bit o' work!

HJALMAR. What else am I doing? I'm working as hard as I can.

GINA. Well then, you'll get it done all the sooner.

(*Exit* GINA *into kitchen.* HJALMAR *resumes his work with a total lack of energy.* OLD EKDAL *looks in again and glances warily round the studio.*)

OLD EKDAL (*softly*). Hey! Hjalmar! Are you still busy?

HJALMAR. Yes, I'm still slaving away at these—photographs.

OLD EKDAL. Oh, all right, then—never mind. If you're such a slave as all that, I'll——(*Draws in his head but leaves door open.*)

(HJALMAR *works silently for a few moments before stealing a glance at the kitchen door. Then lays down his brush, rises and crosses to bedroom door.*)

HJALMAR. Are you busy, Father?

OLD EKDAL (*offstage, morosely*). If you're slaving away, Hjalmar—then *I'm* slaving away.

HJALMAR. Oh, all right, then.

(*Crosses to table and resumes work. After a few moments enter* OLD EKDAL.)

OLD EKDAL. Look here, Hjalmar—I'm not really so very busy, I find.

HJALMAR. I thought you were doing that copying.

OLD EKDAL. Oh, to hell with it! Graaberg, too! He can wait a couple of days, can't he? It's not a matter of life and death, I imagine. ...

HJALMAR. No. Besides, you're not his servant.

OLD EKDAL. And there's all that work in there. We've got to get on with it, y'know. ...

HJALMAR. Yes—just what *I* was thinking. Shall I open the door for you?

OLD EKDAL. Well ... I think you might just as well. ...

HJALMAR (*rising*). At least it'll be one job done.

OLD EKDAL. That's the spirit. And we haven't much time—if it's to be ready by the morning. It *is* tomorrow, isn't it? Eh?

HJALMAR. Yes, that's right—it's tomorrow.

(*Joins* OLD EKDAL *in pushing back the sliding doors. The sun shines through the skylights. Some pigeons are fluttering about, others are cooing on the rafters. Hens can be heard clucking.*)

There you are, Father, now you can get to work.

OLD EKDAL (*entering attic*). Aren't *you* coming?

HJALMAR. Yes—I think so——

(*Sees* GINA *at kitchen door.*)

No, I'd better not. I've got too much to do. All these photographs ... but look —I'll just show you how it works.

(*Pulls a cord and a curtain slips down inside the doorway. It is made of old fishing net for most of its length; but about the lowest two feet of it is made of old sail-cloth—enough, that is, to mask the floor of the attic.*)

It's perfectly simple ... there you are. (*Crossing to table.*) Now perhaps I can get some peace and quiet for a few minutes—and get on with my work!

(*Enter* GINA *from kitchen as* OLD EKDAL *begins vigorously breaking up a crate with a hammer.*)

GINA. Is he messing about in there again? He's not going to keep that up all morning, is he?

HJALMAR. Well, of course ... if you'd rather he slipped out to Mrs. Eriksen's. ... (*Sitting.*) Now is there anything you particularly want? You know you said——

GINA. I was only wondering whether you'd like me to lay dinner in here, that's all—luncheon, I mean. ...

HJALMAR. I don't see why not. We've no early sittings, have we?

GINA. No—nobody at all today except those two love-birds who want to be taken together again.

HJALMAR. Oh, those! Why on earth couldn't they have made it some other day.

GINA (*patiently*). But, Hjalmar dear, I arranged it specially yesterday so as I could do them this afternoon while you was having your nap.

HJALMAR. Ah! Splendid! Then, by all means, let us have lunch in here. (*Rises and begins clearing his work from the table.*)

GINA. Well, there's no need to be in such a hurry—there's plenty of time to lay the cloth. You can have the table for a long while yet.

HJALMAR. You don't suppose I *want* to stop work, do you? Just as I'm getting on nicely?

GINA (*sweetly*). That's right, dear. The sooner you finish the more time you'll have afterwards, y'know. . . .

(*Exit into kitchen.*)

OLD EKDAL (*coming up to the net*). Hey! (*Whistles.*) Hjalmar!

HJALMAR. Well?

OLD EKDAL (*with an eye on the kitchen door*). Afraid we shall have to move that water-trough after all.

HJALMAR. That's what I've been saying all along.

OLD EKDAL (*thoughtfully*). H'm—well. . . .

(*Vanishes.* HJALMAR *resumes work for a few moments, then gives a longing glance at the attic and begins to rise. Enter* HEDVIG *from kitchen.* HJALMAR *promptly sits down again.*)

HJALMAR. Now what do *you* want?

HEDVIG. Only to be with you, Father.

HJALMAR (*after a slight pause*). Have you been sent in here to keep an eye on me, or something?

HEDVIG. Oh, of course not.

HJALMAR. What's your mother doing out there?

HEDVIG. She's making some herring salad. (*Crossing to table.*) Isn't there something I could do, Daddy?

HJALMAR. No, I'd much rather do it alone, as long as I am able to. . . . You needn't bother, Hedvig. . . . If only your father can manage to keep his health. . . .

HEDVIG. Oh, Father, please, you musn't say such horrible things.

(*She wanders about for a little, then comes to a stand at the net curtain and looks into the attic.*)

HJALMAR. What's Grandfather doing in there?

HEDVIG. I think he's laying a new path up to the water-trough.

HJALMAR. He'll never manage that by himself. And I have to sit here and. . . .

HEDVIG (*crossing to table*). Give me the brush, Father. I can do it. I know just how to.

HJALMAR. Nonsense—you'll only hurt your eyes.

HEDVIG. No, I shan't—not a bit, Father, really. Please let me have the brush.

HJALMAR (*rising*). Well, after all . . . it wouldn't take me more than two or three minutes.

HEDVIG. Well, then, what harm can it possibly do? (*Taking brush.*) Now. . . . (*Sitting.*) Why, they've only got to be copied from this one!

HJALMAR. But see you don't hurt your eyes, d'you hear? Because *I* won't be answerable. You're doing it on your own responsibility, d'you understand that?

HEDVIG (*busy*). Yes—yes, of course I do.

HJALMAR (*watching her*). H'm—you work quickly, Hedvig. You're good at it. But only for a few minutes, mind.

(*Slips carefully into the attic past the edge of the net.* HEDVIG *goes on working, screwing up her eyes and with her head bowed low over the photographs, while from the attic the voices of* HJALMAR *and* OLD EKDAL *are heard in indistinct argument, punctuated by vague, heavy noises.* HJALMAR, *his jacket off, comes up to the net.*)

Pass me the pincers, will you, Hedvig? They're over there on the bookshelf. Oh, and the chisel. (*Turning away.*) Now, Father—just let me show you what I meant. (*Taking tools from* HEDVIG.) Ah, thank you, that's what I want. It's a good thing I came—he'd never have managed.

(*Vanishes.*)

(*Offstage.*) Now, Father. . . .

(*Renewed sounds of talking and carpentering.* HEDVIG *stands looking through the net. After a few moments a knock on landing door, which* HEDVIG *does not hear. Then the door opens and enter* GREGERS, *dressed as for indoors. He pauses for a second and then coughs.*)

HEDVIG (*turning and crossing*). Oh, good morning. Do please come in.

GREGERS. Thank you. (*Glancing towards attic.*) I didn't know you'd got the workmen in the house.

HEDVIG. No, it's only Father and Grandfather. I'll tell them you're here.

GREGERS. Oh no—no, don't do that.

Let me wait till they've finished. (*Sits on sofa.*)

HEDVIG (*beginning to clear away photographs, etc.*). It's dreadfully untidy in here, I'm afraid. . . .

GREGERS. Oh, don't move them on my account. They're prints in process of being finished, aren't they?

HEDVIG. Yes—a few I was helping my father with.

GREGERS. Then you mustn't let me disturb you.

HEDVIG. Well . . . I would like to get on, if you don't mind.

(*Sits down and resumes work as before.*)

(GREGERS *watches her closely for a few moments.*)

GREGERS. And how's the wild duck this morning? Did she sleep well?

HEDVIG. Yes, thank you, I think so.

GREGERS (*looking towards attic*). It looks very different in there by daylight, doesn't it?

HEDVIG. Yes, but it's always changing, you know. It looks quite different in the morning from what it does in the afternoon—and different again when it's sunny, and when it rains.

GREGERS. You've noticed that?

HEDVIG. You can't help noticing it.

GREGERS. And do *you* like being in there with the wild duck?

HEDVIG. Yes, when I can manage it. . . .

GREGERS. No, I don't suppose you get a lot of spare time. You're still at school, I expect, aren't you?

HEDVIG. No—Father took me away. You see, he's afraid of it hurting my eyes.

GREGERS. Oh, I see. Then I suppose he reads with you himself.

HEDVIG. He's promised to, but so far he hasn't had time—he's been so busy.

GREGERS. Isn't there anyone else who could help you?

HEDVIG. Yes, there's Mr. Molvik—only he's always—well sometimes he's——

GREGERS. Not quite sober, eh?

HEDVIG. Yes, I expect that's what it is.

GREGERS. Then you must have plenty of time to do as you like. And in there—I suppose it's a sort of world in itself?

HEDVIG. Oh, yes, it is—and it has such wonderful things in it!

GREGERS. Really?

HEDVIG. Yes—there are whole cup-boards full of books, and a lot of the books have got pictures in them.

GREGERS. A-ha!

HEDVIG. Yes, and there's an old bureau with drawers and flaps and things, and a great big clock with little men and women that go running in and out whenever it strikes—that is, when it did strike—it doesn't now—because it doesn't go.

GREGERS. So time has stood still in there with the wild duck?

HEDVIG. Yes. And then there's an old paint-box and—oh, all kinds of things! And, of course, all the books.

GREGERS. Which I suppose you like reading?

HEDVIG. Yes—when I can get the chance. But most of them are in English—and I can't make head or tail of English. But I look at the pictures—especially one book—a huge one called "Harrison's History of London." It must be quite a hundred years old, and there are dozens of pictures in it. At the beginning there's one of Death with an hour-glass and a young girl. I don't like that one. But there's all the others—pictures of churches, and castles and streets and ships sailing on the high seas. . . .

GREGERS. But tell me, where did all these treasures come from?

HEDVIG. Oh, they belonged to an old sea captain, who once lived here. He brought them home with him. They used to call him the Flying Dutchman—which is funny, really, because he wasn't a Dutchman at all.

GREGERS. Wasn't he, now?

HEDVIG. No, he wasn't. Then one day he didn't come back again—and, well, he hadn't taken these things with him. . . .

GREGERS. I see. Tell me, when you're sitting in there looking at the pictures, don't you wish you could really go sailing round the world, and see all those wonderful sights for yourself?

HEDVIG. Oh, no. I want to stay at home always, and help Mother and Father.

GREGERS. And retouch photographs?

HEDVIG. Well, not only that. What I should like to do most of all would be to engrave pictures like those in the English books.

GREGERS. H'm. And what does your father think about that?

HEDVIG. I don't think Father likes it

very much. He's funny about things like that. Can you imagine? He wants me to learn basket-making and straw-plaiting. I don't see what use that is.

GREGERS. No, nor do I.

HEDVIG. But, of course, Father's quite right when he says that if I'd learnt to make baskets I could have made the new one for the wild duck.

GREGERS. Yes—that's true. And, after all, you'd have been the proper person to do it.

HEDVIG. Yes, because she's *my* wild duck.

GREGERS. Of course she is.

HEDVIG. Yes, she's all mine. But I do lend her to Father and Grandfather some-times —when they want her.

GREGERS. I see. And what do they want her for?

HEDVIG. Oh, they look after her, and build things for her . . . all that sort of thing.

GREGERS. In fact, your wild duck is obviously the most distinguished resident in the attic. . . .

HEDVIG. Oh, yes, indeed she is. You see, she's a real wild bird. And she's got no one to love now. . . . Poor thing—it's such a shame.

GREGERS. Unlike the rabbits, she's no family, eh?

HEDVIG. Exactly! She's no friends, either. I mean, after all, most of the hens were chicks together; but she hasn't any-body. That's what's so queer about the wild duck—no one knows anything about her, or where she came from——

GREGERS. And she's been down to the ocean-bed.

HEDVIG (*with a sudden smile*). Why d'you say "ocean-bed"?

GREGERS. What else should I say?

HEDVIG. Well, you might have said "the bottom of the sea."

GREGERS. Oh—isn't it the same if I say "ocean-bed," then?

HEDVIG. Oh, it's not that; but it seems so odd to hear somebody else talking about "the ocean-bed". . . .

GREGERS. Why? Why is it so odd? Tell me.

HEDVIG. No, I can't—it's all so silly. . . .

GREGERS. Oh, I'm sure it isn't. Why did you smile just now?

HEDVIG. Well, you know, it was be-cause whenever it suddenly comes home to me what really *is* in there. I always think of the whole place and everything in it as "the ocean-bed"—and that's just silly!

GREGERS. Oh—I don't think I'd go as far as that!

HEDVIG. But, of course, it's silly—it's only an attic, really.

GREGERS (*eying her steadily*). Are you so sure?

HEDVIG (*astonished*). What? That it's an attic?

GREGERS. Yes. Are you quite certain of it?

(HEDVIG *gapes at him, dumbfounded. Enter* GINA *from kitchen with things for laying the table.*)

(*Rising.*) I'm afraid I've come too early.

GINA. Well, you've got to be some-where, haven't you? Besides, we shan't be long now. Clear those things off the table, Hedvig, there's a dear.

(HEDVIG *clears away the photographs, etc., and during the following dialogue [i.e. down to* "Exeunt GINA *and* HEDVIG *into the kitchen"] helps* GINA *to lay the table.* GREGERS *sits in the armchair and turns the pages of an album.*)

GREGERS. I hear that *you* can do re-touching, Mrs. Ekdal. . . .

GINA (*shooting him a glance*). H'm—yes, I can.

GREGERS. That was rather fortunate, wasn't it?

GINA. How d'you mean—fortunate?

GREGERS. Well, wasn't it? Since Hjalmar was to be a photographer. . . .

HEDVIG. Oh, Mummy can take photo-graphs too, you know.

GINA. Yes, I had to learn to do that as well.

GREGERS. In other words—it's really you who are carrying on the business. Isn't that it?

GINA. Well, when Hjalmar hasn't time to attend to it himself, I——

GREGERS. Yes, I expect his old father claims a good deal of his time, doesn't he?

GINA. You don't suppose a man like Hjalmar's going to give his time to tak-ing just anybody who comes here and wants to be took?

GREGERS. Oh, I entirely agree with you; but, surely, having once gone in for the thing——

GINA. I shouldn't have thought you needed telling, Mr. Gregers, that my Hjalmar isn't just one of your tupp'ny-ha'p'ny photographers. . . .

GREGERS. Oh, no, of course not; but——

(*Sound of a shot in the attic.*)

Good lord! What's that?

GINA. It's them—they're shooting again!

GREGERS. *Shooting—in there?*

HEDVIG. Oh yes—you see, that's how they go out shooting.

GREGERS. *What!* (*Rising and crossing to attic doorway.*) What are you shooting in there, Hjalmar?

HJALMAR (*coming up to the net*). Oh, it's you. I'd no idea—I was so taken up. And you didn't tell us, Hedvig. (*Reaches for jacket; enters round side of net and begins putting on jacket.*)

GREGERS. Do you go shooting in the attic?

HJALMAR (*showing a double-barrelled pistol*). Oh, only with this.

GINA. You mark my words, one of these fine days you and Grandpa'll have a nasty accident with that there resolver.

HJALMAR (*sharply*). Revolver, Gina —not "resolver." And, anyhow, I've told you before this type of weapon is a pistol.

GINA. Well, I can't see that that makes it any better.

GREGERS. So you've become a sports-man as well, eh, Hjalmar?

HJALMAR. Oh, I join Father in potting at a few rabbits now and then—just to please him.

GINA. That's men all over—they must always have something to amuse themselves with.

HJALMAR (*irritably*). Exactly. We must always have something to *amuse* us.

GINA. Well, that's just what I said, didn't I?

HJALMAR. H'm. (*To* GREGERS.) Fortunately, the attic is so situated that the other people in the house can't hear us firing. (*Putting pistol on top shelf of bookcase.*) And you're not to touch it, Hedvig—one barrel's loaded. So don't forget.

GREGERS (*looking into attic*). Ah, you've a shotgun, too, I see.

HJALMAR. Oh, that's one of Father's old guns. It's no good now—the lock's gone wrong. We amuse ourselves by tak-

ing it to pieces sometimes—cleaning and oiling it, and then putting it together again. I say "we," but it's mostly Father —he likes messing about with things like that.

HEDVIG (*crossing to* GREGERS). Now you can see the wild duck properly.

GREGERS. I was just looking. That wing seems to droop a bit, doesn't it?

HEDVIG. Well—no wonder! That's where she was hit.

GREGERS (*nodding*). She appears to drag one leg a little, too. . . .

HJALMAR. Only a very little.

HEDVIG. You see, that was the leg the dog caught her by when he rescued her.

HJALMAR. Otherwise she's in perfect condition. And that's no mean feat for a bird that's been riddled with shot and clamped between a retriever's teeth——

GREGERS (*glancing at* HEDVIG). And been down on the ocean-bed for so long.

HEDVIG (*smiling*). Yes.

GINA (*finishing laying the table*). That blessed wild duck! All that fuss over a bird! You wouldn't think there was any-one else in the house!

HJALMAR. H'm—is luncheon nearly ready?

GINA. It's almost on the table. Hedvig, you can come into the kitchen and give a hand.

(*Exeunt* GINA *and* HEDVIG *into kitchen.*)

HJALMAR (*quietly*). I don't think you'd better stand there staring at Father, if you don't mind, Gregers. He doesn't like being watched.

(GREGERS *moves away.*)

Besides, I'd better shut the doors before the others come. (*Clapping his hands and shooing the fowls back from the net.*) Shoo! Sha! In there you go! Go on! Get back! Shoo! (*Pulling the cord and raising the net.*) Useful little dodge, eh? I invented it myself. In fact, I invented most of our little devices. (*Shutting doors.*) I always enjoy improvising gadgets and having the fun of repairing them when they go wrong. That one, of course, is really necessary—as Gina won't have rabbits and fowls running loose in the studio.

GREGERS. I can well believe it. After all, the studio is very much your wife's concern. . . .

HJALMAR. Well, I generally leave the

more pedestrian details of the business to her—so that I can segregate myself in the parlour and give my mind to more important things.

GREGERS. What things, Hjalmar?

HJALMAR. I'm surprised you didn't ask me that before. But then, I dare say you haven't heard about my new invention. . . .

GREGERS. Invention? No, I can't really say I have.

HJALMAR. Really? *Haven't* you? Oh well—living off the map, as you've been doing, I suppose——

GREGERS. Do you mean to tell me you've actually invented something?

HJALMAR. Well, I haven't quite finished it yet; but I'm resolutely pursuing it. As I'm sure you'll understand, when I made up my mind to devote my life exclusively to photography, it wasn't with the intention of taking ordinary photographs of ordinary people. . . .

GREGERS. No, your wife was telling me something of the sort just now.

HJALMAR. I vowed that, if I were to dedicate my powers to this trade, I would raise it to the level of an art and a science. And so I decided to apply my whole mind to perfecting this great invention.

GREGERS. And what *is* the invention? I mean, what does it do?

HJALMAR. Oh, my dear Gregers, you mustn't ask me for details yet. These things take time, y'know. And you mustn't run away with the idea that I'm actuated by vanity. I'm not working for my own sake. Oh, no—it's my mission in life that beckons me forward day and night.

GREGERS. And what is that mission?

HJALMAR. Have you forgotten that silver-haired old man in there?

GREGERS. Your poor old father? But what exactly can you hope to do for him?

HJALMAR. At the very least, I can revive his self-respect, by restoring honour and dignity to the name of Ekdal.

GREGERS. I see. So that's your mission in life?

HJALMAR. Just that. I must save that shipwrecked old warrior—for he was shipwrecked. As soon as those ghastly investigations were made, he began to falter. That pistol—the one we use for

the rabbits—has played its part in the tragedy of the house of Ekdal.

GREGERS. That pistol? Indeed?

HJALMAR. Yes. When the sentence was pronounced, and he was to go to prison, he was found with that pistol in his hand——

GREGERS (*sympathetically*). Was he really?

HJALMAR. Yes—but he couldn't bring himself to it. His courage failed him—so demoralized, so broken in spirit was he. Can *you* understand that, Gregers? A man like that—a soldier—a big-game hunter with nine bears to his credit—descended from two lieutenant-colonels —one after the other, of course. Can you understand it, Gregers?

GREGERS. Oh yes, I can—quite easily.

HJALMAR. Well, I can't. But that pistol played yet another part in the history of our family. When he was put into prison-grey and under lock and key, then came my own hour of agony. I remember I drew down all the blinds. And when at last I peeped out and saw the sun shining as usual, I couldn't understand it. And when I saw the people laughing and chattering in the street as usual, I couldn't understand that, either . . . I felt as one does in a total eclipse—as if the universe was standing still.

GREGERS. I know. I felt like that when my mother died.

HJALMAR. And in that same hour Hjalmar Ekdal turned the pistol upon his own breast. . . .

GREGERS. But . . . d'you mean to say that you, too . . . ?

HJALMAR. Yes.

GREGERS. But you didn't pull the trigger.

HJALMAR. No. At the crucial moment I gained the victory over myself—and chose life. And—believe me, Gregers— it takes a certain amount of courage to choose *life* in such circumstances.

GREGERS. It rather depends upon which way you look at it.

HJALMAR. Oh, of *course*. But I don't regret my decision, because my invention is getting on beautifully and will soon be finished. And, by the way, Dr. Relling thinks, as I do, that when that happens Father may well be allowed to wear his uniform again. And I ask for no other reward. . . .

GREGERS. Ah! So that's what he meant when he was talking about his old cap?

HJALMAR. Yes—that little privilege is what he longs for more than anything else in the world. You can't imagine how deeply touching it can be sometimes. For instance—whenever we have some little family celebration, such as our wedding anniversary, a birthday—or something of that sort—in comes the old gentleman splendid in the lieutenant's uniform of happier days. But he's only to hear a knock at the door—he daren't show himself to strangers, y'know—and he hurries back into his room as fast as his poor old legs'll carry him. . . . It hurts a son to have to stand by and see things like that.

GREGERS. How soon d'you suppose your invention will be ready?

HJALMAR. My dear Gregers, these things can never be tied down to any particular date. It's entirely a matter of intuition.

GREGERS. At any rate, it's progressing satisfactorily.

HJALMAR. Oh yes, by leaps and bounds. And not a day passes without my giving my mind to it. Every afternoon after lunch I lock myself in the parlour and concentrate—without fear of interruption. But I can't be driven to it—*that's* not the way. Dr. Relling says exactly the same.

GREGERS. Yes, but don't you think that all these very ingenious little things for the attic rather tend to deflect you from the big thing?

HJALMAR. Not a bit of it—most certainly not. You mustn't say that. No one could possibly follow *that* exacting train of thought all day long. I must have some form of relaxation—something to fill the empty hours whilst I'm waiting for inspiration to return. It comes when it will —and that's all there is to be said about it.

GREGERS. You know, my dear Hjalmar, I'm inclined to think there's something of the wild duck in you.

HJALMAR. The wild duck? What on earth d'you mean by that?

GREGERS. You've dived straight to the bottom and hooked yourself into the muck.

HJALMAR. Are you thinking of the well-nigh fatal shot that winged both Father and me?

GREGERS. Not entirely. I wouldn't say you've been winged exactly; you've been trapped in a poisonous marsh, Hjalmar. And there you've contracted an insidious disease and, because of it, you've dived straight to the bottom to die in the dark.

HJALMAR. I? Die in the dark? Really, Gregers! How can you talk such nonsense?

GREGERS. Oh, don't be alarmed—I'll bring you to the surface again somehow. You see, I, too, have a mission in life—I came upon it yesterday.

HJALMAR. I dare say—but kindly leave me out of it. I can assure you that —apart from a certain very natural melancholy—no man could be healthier than I am.

GREGERS. That sort of complacency is only an effect of the miasma.

HJALMAR. Now, my dear, good Gregers, please stop talking about disease and miasma, I'm not used to it. In my house nobody ever *mentions* such distasteful subjects.

GREGERS. I can well believe that!

HJALMAR. They don't do me any good. And there's no miasma here, as you put it. The poor photographer's home is humble, I know—and his means are slender—but he *is* an inventor, as well as the breadwinner of his family. And that in itself lifts me above my humble surroundings. . . . Ah, here they are with luncheon!

(*Enter* GINA *and* HEDVIG *from kitchen with trays of bottles of beer, a decanter of brandy, glasses, etc. At the same time enter* DR. RELLING *and* MOLVIK *by landing door. They are dressed for indoors—* MOLVIK *in black.*)

GINA (*crossing to table*). Oh, there you are, you two—just at the piscological moment!

RELLING. Once Molvik got it into his nose that there was herring-salad, there was no holding him! Good morning once again, Ekdal.

HJALMAR. Gregers, let me introduce Mr. Molvik . . . and Doctor—oh, but, of course, you and Relling have met before. . . .

RELLING. Ah, Mr. Werle junior, isn't it? Yes, we've crossed swords more than once up at Höidal. You've just moved in, haven't you.

GREGERS. Yes, I moved in this morning.

RELLING. Molvik and I have the room

under yours; so when you need the Doctor and the Priest, you haven't far to send!

GREGERS. Stranger things have happened. Last night we were thirteen at table, I remember. . . .

HJALMAR. Now Gregers, please don't let us indulge in any more uncomfortable topics!

RELLING. I don't think you need have the slightest anxiety, Ekdal. The Devil isn't very likely to be after you!

HJALMAR. I should hope not, indeed—if only for the sake of my family. But let's sit down and eat, drink and be merry!

GREGERS. Aren't we going to wait for your father?

HJALMAR. No, he'll have his in his room later on. Well, shall we begin?

(*The men sit down at table and* GINA *and* HEDVIG *wait on them.*)

RELLING (*helping himself*). Molvik was revoltingly drunk again yesterday, Mrs. Ekdal.

GINA. Not again, surely! Tch-tch!

RELLING. Didn't you hear me getting the body upstairs at the midnight hour?

GINA. Can't say I did.

RELLING. Good thing too! Molvik was disgusting last night!

GINA. Oh, you weren't really—were you, Mr. Molvik?

MOLVIK. Let us draw a veil over the doings of last night. Such behaviour is not the product of my better self.

RELLING (*to* GREGERS). It takes him by storm, y'know. He's like a man possessed—so much so that I daren't let him out of my sight! You see, Mr. Molvik is a demoniac.

GREGERS. Demoniac?

RELLING. Oh, dear, yes—Molvik's a demoniac.

GREGERS. Oh.

RELLING. And demoniacs aren't built for walking on a straight line—they have to sway a little now and then. . . . So you still grind away at those unsavoury works of yours up at horrible Höidal?

GREGERS. I've done so up to now.

RELLING. And did you ever get a hearing for that claim you used to go about making?

GREGERS. Claim? (*Comprehending.*) Oh, I see.

HJALMAR. What claim was that, Gregers?

GREGERS. Oh—it's all nonsense!

RELLING. Don't you believe him! For months he canvassed every workman's cottage in the district with something he called "the claim of the ideal."

GREGERS. Ah, I was very young then.

RELLING. You certainly were! Puerile, I should have said. And as for the claim of the ideal—well, nobody ever acknowledged it while I was up there.

GREGERS. Nobody has since, either.

RELLING. Ah! That sounds as if you've learnt a certain amount of sense and begun—shall we say?—asking rather less. . . .

GREGERS. Never when I have to deal with a man who's worthy of the name.

HJALMAR. That sounds reasonable enough. Bring some more butter, Gina.

RELLING (*over his shoulder*). And a nice fat slice of pork for Molvik.

MOLVIK. Ugh! Not pork!

(*A knock on the attic door.*)

HJALMAR. Open the door, Hedvig—I think Grandfather wants to come out.

(HEDVIG *crosses to attic doors and pulls one aside a little.* OLD EKDAL *squeezes sideways round the edge of it into the room. He has a fresh rabbit-skin in one hand and his jacket over the other arm.* HEDVIG *shuts the door after him.*)

OLD EKDAL. Good morning, gentlemen! Excellent sport today! (*Displaying rabbit-skin.*) Shot a real beauty—a whopper.

HJALMAR. Oh, Father—and you skinned it without waiting for me!

OLD EKDAL. Yes, and salted it, too! Lovely tender meat, rabbit is. Sweet as sugar. Well, eat hearty, gentlemen!

(*Exit into bedroom.*)

MOLVIK (*rising hastily*). Excuse me, but—I don't . . . I think I . . . I shall have to go downstairs at once. . . .

RELLING. Have some soda-water, you ass!

MOLVIK (*crossing hurriedly to landing door*). Ugh—ugh, I . . . ugh!

Exit.

RELLING (*to* HJALMAR). I think that calls for a toast to the old hunter, don't you?

HJALMAR (*clinking glasses with* RELLING). To the hardy old hunter who's been face to face with death!

RELLING. To the grey-haired—(*drinks*)

—by the way, what *is* the colour of his hair? Grey or white?

HJALMAR. I'm not sure—it's between the two, I think. He's got precious little hair, anyhow.

RELLING. Which proves you can get through life perfectly well with a wig. . . . You know, Ekdal—fundamentally, you're a happy man. You've this great mission in life to work for—

HJALMAR. And I *do* work, believe me. (*Enter* GINA, *from kitchen with butter, which she sets before* HJALMAR.)

RELLING. That you've a wife in a million, padding about in comfortable felt slippers, with that homely gait of hers, waiting on you hand and foot—

HJALMAR. Yes, Gina. (*Nodding to her.*) I could have chosen no truer companion for the rough roads of life. . . .

GINA. Oh, go on with you, Hjalmar—don't sit there catechizing me.

RELLING. And then you've your Hedvig.

HJALMAR. My little girl—yes, my baby comes first! Hedvig, come to me, darling. . . .

(HEDVIG *crosses.*)

My little angel. . . . (*Stroking her hair.*) What day is it tomorrow, eh?

HEDVIG (*shaking him*). Oh, no, Daddy —you mustn't tell them, please!

HJALMAR. It's like a knife in my heart to think what a meagre business it will have to be—just a little party in there in the attic. . . .

HEDVIG. But Daddy—that's just what I want!

RELLING. You wait until your father's great invention is given to the world, Hedvig. . . .

HJALMAR. Yes, then—then you shall see! Hedvig—I've decided to provide for your future—so that you can live in comfort for the rest of your days. Yes— all I shall ask will be something for *you!* That'll be the poor inventor's sole reward!

HEDVIG (*throwing her arms round his neck: softly*). Oh, you—dear—darling— Daddy!

RELLING. Well, Mr. Werle, don't you find it very pleasant, once in a while, to sit at a well-furnished table in the bosom of a happy family?

HJALMAR. Yes, these little occasions mean very much to me.

GREGERS. For my part, I don't thrive in the odours of the marsh.

RELLING. Odours of the marsh!

HJALMAR. Oh, don't start that all over again!

GINA. Good gracious me! There's no odours marching round *this* house, Mr. Werle! The place gets a thorough good airing every day of the week, let me tell you. . . .

GREGERS (*rising*). Not all the airing in the world will clear away the odour I have in mind.

GINA. Well, you heard what he said, Hjalmar!

RELLING. Excuse me—but might not you yourself be carrying the infection with you—from the mines up there?

GREGERS. I should expect *you* to call what I bring into this house infection.

RELLING (*crossing to him*). Now you just listen to me, young Mr. Werle: I've a strong suspicion that you're still going about with that unreduced claim of the ideal in your coat-tail pocket.

GREGERS. I carry it in my breast.

RELLING. Well, wherever you carry it, I advise you not to start playing the dun here with it whilst I'm about.

GREGERS. And what if I do?

RELLING. Then you'll go head first down the stairs. Now you know.

HJALMAR (*rising*). Oh, come now, Relling, really—

GREGERS. All right, Relling—just try— try and throw me out—

GINA (*coming between them*). Now please, Doctor—not in here, we don't want anything like that. And, as for you, Mr. Werle, you're a fine one, I must say, talking about odours in other people's houses, after the way you behaved with that stove.

(*A knock on the landing door.*)

HEDVIG. There's someone at the door, Mummy.

HJALMAR. And now we're to have visitors!

GINA. I'd better go and see who it is. (*Crossing to landing door, opening it, and recoiling slightly.*) Oh—oh dear!

(*Enter* HAAKON WERLE. *He is wearing a fur coat and stops just inside the door.*)

WERLE. I beg your pardon—but I understand my son is staying here.

GINA (*gulping*). Yes. . . .

HJALMAR (*crossing to* HAAKON

WERLE). Oh, Mr. Werle, won't you come in, sir?

WERLE. Thank you. I only wish to speak to my son.

GREGERS. Well—here I am. . . .

WERLE. I should prefer to speak with you in the privacy of your room.

GREGERS. My room? Very well. (*He turns to door.*)

GINA. Oh, but you can't possibly—not in the state it's in. . . .

WERLE. In that case the passage here will do very well. I must speak to you alone.

HJALMAR. Why not in here, Mr. Werle? We can easily go into the parlour. . . . Come along, Relling.

(*Exeunt* GINA *and* HEDVIG *into kitchen:* RELLING *and* HJALMAR *by door right.*)

GREGERS (*after a slight pause*). Well? We're alone now—

WERLE. In the light of your sudden move into this house I've been reconsidering certain things you let fall last night, and I'm forced to the conclusion that you intend me some mischief.

GREGERS. I intend opening Hjalmar Ekdal's eyes. It's high time he realised his position—that's all.

WERLE. Is that what you meant last night by your mission in life?

GREGERS. Yes. You've left me no other.

WERLE. Is it I that have warped your mind, Gregers?

GREGERS. You've warped my whole life. Oh, I'm not thinking of all that about mother. It's entirely thanks to you that I'm the prey and victim of a guilty conscience.

WERLE. Ah! So it's your conscience that's the trouble?

GREGERS. I should have stood up to you when you laid your trap for Lieutenant Ekdal. I should have warned him—I'd a pretty shrewd notion of what was happening.

WERLE (*scathingly*). That would have been the time to speak. What a pity you didn't!

GREGERS. I couldn't. I'd neither the moral nor the physical courage. I was too afraid of you—not only then, but for years afterwards.

WERLE. However—you seem to have made an excellent recovery.

GREGERS. Fortunately, I have. The wrong done to Lieutenant Ekdal, both by me and by—others, can never be undone; but I can at least deliver Hjalmar from the lies and deceit that are strangling him.

WERLE. And d'you think that will be helping him?

GREGERS. I'm quite sure of it.

WERLE. And do you consider this respectable photographer the kind of man to be grateful for such a service?

GREGERS. I do.

WERLE. H'm. We shall see.

GREGERS. Besides, if I am to go on living, I must find some cure for my sick conscience.

WERLE. You never will. You suffered from the disease as a child. You got it from your mother, Gregers—it's all you did get from her.

GREGERS (*smiling bitterly*). Haven't you forgiven her yet for the mistake you made in marrying her for the money she hadn't got?

WERLE. Don't let us waste time on irrelevancies. Am I to take it that you are determined to put young Ekdal on what you fondly imagine to be the right scent?

GREGERS. Yes—you may.

WERLE. In that case, I might have spared myself the journey. Obviously there is no point in my asking you to return home with me.

GREGERS. None whatever.

WERLE. And I suppose you won't come into the firm, either?

GREGERS. No.

WERLE. Very well. But now that I am about to re-marry, your share of the estate will come to you at once.

GREGERS (*quickly*). No! I don't want it.

WERLE. You don't want it?

GREGERS. No. My conscience forbids it.

WERLE (*after a slight pause*). D'you mean to go back to the works?

GREGERS. No. I consider myself no longer in your employ.

WERLE. What are you going to do, then?

GREGERS (*quietly*). Fulfil my mission in life—only that.

WERLE. Yes, yes—but after that? What are you going to live on?

GREGERS. I've saved a little out of my salary.

WERLE. And how long do you think *that'll* last you?

GREGERS. I think it will last my time.

WERLE. And what exactly do you mean by that?

GREGERS. I don't propose to answer any more questions. . . .

WERLE. Goodbye, then, Gregers.

GREGERS. Goodbye.

(*Exit* HAAKON WERLE *by landing door. A moment later the door right opens and* HJALMAR *peeps in.*)

HJALMAR. Has your father gone?

GREGERS. Yes.

(*Enter* HJALMAR *and* RELLING *by door right,* GINA *and* HEDVIG *from the kitchen.*)

RELLING. That lunch was a failure.

GREGERS. Get your hat and coat, Hjalmar—I want you to come out for a long walk with me.

HJALMAR. Why, of course, Gregers. What did your father want? Anything to do with me?

GREGERS. Oh, come along. I've a lot to say to you. I'll get my coat and meet you downstairs.

(*Exit by landing door.*)

GINA. I shouldn't go out with him, if I were you, Hjalmar.

RELLING. No! Don't you! Stay where you are!

HJALMAR. What nonsense! When my oldest friend feels the wish to confide in me. . . . (*Takes down coat and puts it on, then his hat.*)

RELLING. But hang it all, man! Can't you see the fellow's mad—deranged—out of his mind—barmy!

GINA. The Doctor's right, Hjalmar. He's not all there, like his mother was. She used to have whatsanames *just* like him. . . .

HJALMAR. Then he has all the more need for a friend's watchful eye. . . . (*To* GINA.) See that dinner's ready in good time. Goodbye for the present.

(*Exit by landing door.*)

RELLING. It's a great pity that fellow didn't go to hell via one of the mines at Höidal.

GINA. Gracious! Whatever makes you say that?

RELLING (*muttering*). Oh, I have my reasons.

GINA. And d'you really think young Mr. Gregers's wrong in his head?

RELLING. No, worse luck. He's no madder than most. But he's certainly suffering from *one* complaint. . . .

GINA. What's that, then?

RELLING. Well, I'll tell you, Mrs. Ekdal. He's suffering from an acute attack of probity fever.

GINA. Probity fever?

HEDVIG. Is that a kind of disease?

RELLING. Yes—it's a national disease; but it only crops up sporadically. (*Nodding to* GINA.) Well—thank you for your hospitality.

(*Exit by landing door.*)

GINA (*pacing*). Ugh, that Gregers Werle—he always was a nasty sort!

HEDVIG (*standing by table and looking enquiringly at* GINA). But it's all so confusing, Mother. . . .

Medium Curtain

Act IV

As before. Late the same afternoon.

Centre right a camera with a cloth over it and a pedestal, a small table, some chairs, etc., carefully arranged before it (as though for the taking of a photograph.) It is near sunset and, as the action proceeds, the light diminishes to dusk.

GINA *stands at the open landing door with a small box and a wet photographic plate in her hands.*

GINA (*speaking offstage*). Yes—without fail. If I promise a thing I always keep it. The first dozen'll be ready for you Monday morning. Good afternoon.

(*The sound of footsteps going downstairs.* GINA *shuts door, crosses to camera, puts plate in box and box in camera as enter* HEDVIG *from kitchen.*)

HEDVIG. Have they gone, Mother?

GINA (*tidying up*). Yes, thank the Lord—and a fine job I had getting rid of 'em, too.

HEDVIG. I wonder what's happened to Father. He should have been home a long time ago.

GINA. I suppose he isn't down there yarning away with Doctor Relling, is he?

HEDVIG. No, he isn't, Mother. I went down the back way just now and asked.

GINA. And his supper getting cold, an' all!

HEDVIG. I know. And it's so unlike Father—he's always so particular about being in time for dinner.

GINA. Oh—he won't be long now—you see!

HEDVIG. Well, I do wish he'd hurry up —everything seems so different today, somehow. . . .

GINA (*listening*). Hold your noise. I think that's him now.

(*Enter* HJALMAR *by landing door*.)

HEDVIG (*running to him*). Oh, Father —we thought you were never coming! We've been waiting *such* a time. . . .

GINA (*glancing at him*). You have been gone a long while, Hjalmar. . . .

HJALMAR (*avoiding her eyes*). Longer than usual, I agree.

(*Takes off coat.* GINA *and* HEDVIG *move to help him, but he waves them off.*)

GINA. Did you have some sup—dinner with Mr. Gregers, then?

HJALMAR (*hanging up his coat*). No.

GINA (*crossing to kitchen*). Then I'll get it for you.

HJALMAR. No. Leave it now—I don't want anything.

HEDVIG (*crossing to him*). Aren't you feeling very well, Father?

HJALMAR. Yes—I'm all right, I suppose. Gregers took me for rather a long walk.

GINA. Well, you shouldn't have gone with him in the first place, Hjalmar. You never were much of a one for walking. You're not used to it, that's what it is.

HJALMAR. One has to get used to a great many things in this world. (*Pacing.*) Has anybody been whilst I was out?

GINA. Only the two love-birds, that's all.

HJALMAR. No new orders?

GINA. No, not today.

HEDVIG. Never mind, Father! There'll be some tomorrow! You see if there aren't!

HJALMAR. I sincerely hope so—as tomorrow I intend to start work in real earnest.

HEDVIG. Tomorrow! Oh, *not* tomorrow. . . .

HJALMAR. Ah . . . yes—well, the day after, then. In future, I'm resolved to do all the work myself. I want no assistance from anyone.

GINA. And what good'll that do, Hjalmar? It'll only make your life a misery again. Like this I can look after the photograph side while you get on with the invention.

HEDVIG. And don't forget the wild duck, Daddy—and the chickens—and the rabbits——

HJALMAR. Don't talk to me about all that rubbish! From tomorrow I shall never set foot in that attic again.

HEDVIG. Oh, but Father—you promised me—we were going to have a party. . . .

HJALMAR. That's right, so I did. Well then, from the day *after* tomorrow. And as for that damned wild duck—I could almost wring its neck!

HEDVIG (*shrieking*). The wild duck.

GINA. Well! What a thing to say!

HEDVIG (*shaking his arm*). But, Father —it's *my* wild duck!

HJALMAR. I know, and that's why I shan't do it—only for your sake—I haven't the heart to. But something deep down inside me tells me that I ought to. I oughtn't to allow anything that has passed through *those* hands to remain under my roof.

GINA. Just because Grandpa happened to go and get it off that Pettersen, it doesn't mean——

HJALMAR (*pacing*). There are certain claims—what can I call them?—claims of the ideal—certain moral obligations which a man cannot disregard except to the detriment of his own soul.

HEDVIG (*following him*). But think of the wild duck, Father—the poor wild duck!

HJALMAR (*halting*). I have said that I will spare it—for your sake. However, there are far greater and more important problems to be considered. I think you'd better go out for your evening walk now, Hedvig—it's about dark enough for you. You needn't stay out too long.

HEDVIG. I don't think I want to go out now. . . .

HJALMAR. Now run along. Your eyes look as if they've been watering again. It's the atmosphere in here—it's bad for you. . . . Like all the air in the house. . . .

HEDVIG. Oh, all right then. I'll go out the back way. I'll just get my cloak and hat—they're in my bedroom. And Father —you mustn't hurt the wild duck whilst I'm out. . . .

HJALMAR. Not so much as a feather of its head. (*Drawing her to him.*) You and I, Hedvig—we two . . . well, run along now.

(HEDVIG *glances a little anxiously at* HJALMAR *and* GINA, *then exit by kitchen door.*)

(*Pacing, without raising his eyes.*) Gina!

GINA. Yes?

HJALMAR. From tomorrow—or shall we say from the day after tomorrow?—I should like to keep the household accounts myself.

GINA. Keep the household accounts?

HJALMAR. At least, I want to keep an account of what comes in.

GINA. Lord! That wouldn't take you long!

HJALMAR (*slowly*). I'm not so sure . . . you seem to make the money go a surprisingly long way. . . . (*Stopping and looking at her.*) How d'you manage it?

GINA. That's only because Hedvig and I manage on so little.

HJALMAR. Is it true that Father's very liberally paid for the copying he does for Mr. Werle?

GINA. I'm sure I don't know about it being liberal—I don't rightly know what they do pay for that sort of work.

HJALMAR. Well, how much *does* he get—approximately?

GINA. Oh, it's all according. . . . I'd say it's just enough to cover his keep—with a little over for pocket-money.

HJALMAR. Enough to cover his keep! And why did you never tell me this?

GINA. How could I, when you were always so proud to think that everything he got came from you?

HJALMAR. Whereas in fact it came from Mr. Werle!

GINA. Oh, well—he's got plenty, goodness knows!

HJALMAR. You'd better light the lamp.

GINA (*lighting lamp*). And besides, we don't know for certain it *is* Mr. Werle —it might be that Graaberg——

HJALMAR. Why try to put it on to Graaberg?

GINA. Oh, I don't know, I only thought——

HJALMAR. H'm!

GINA. Well, anyhow, it wasn't me got Grandpa the copying—you might as well remember that—it was Bertha Sörby did —soon after she went to work there. . . .

HJALMAR. Your voice seems to me to be trembling a little, Gina.

GINA (*putting shade on lamp*). Does it?

HJALMAR. And your hands are trembling.

GINA (*firmly*). You may as well come straight out with it, Hjalmar. What's he been saying to you about me?

HJALMAR. Is it true—can it *possibly* be true—that there was something between you and Mr. Werle when you were in service there?

GINA. No, it isn't—it's not true—not while I was working there, anyhow. Oh, Mr. Werle was after me, all right. And his wife soon saw it—and she didn't half create. She took to making things as hard as ever she could for me—used to knock me about too. . . . Well, it got to such a pitch it drove me out of the house—so I give notice. . . .

HJALMAR. It was afterwards, then?

GINA. I went home. And my mother—well, she wasn't at all the nice woman you took her for, Hjalmar—she kept on at me and kept on at me about one thing and another—and Mr. Werle was a widower by then. . . .

HJALMAR. Well? Go on.

GINA. Well, it's best for you to be told, I suppose. He wouldn't let me alone —he never gave me a moment's peace, till he got what he wanted. . . .

HJALMAR. And this is the mother of my child!

GINA. Oh, I know it was wrong of me. I ought to have told you about it long ago. . . .

HJALMAR. You ought to have told me at the outset—then I should have known the sort of woman you were.

GINA. And would you have married me all the same?

HJALMAR. How can you imagine such a thing!

GINA. No. And that's just why I never dared say anything. You see, I'd come to care for you so much . . . *you* know that —and I couldn't face making myself miserable. . . .

HJALMAR (*pacing*). And this is the mother of my Hedvig! And to think that everything I see around me (*kicks a chair*)—everything I thought was my home—I owe to your ex-lover. Ah! that rake Werle!

GINA. D'you regret the fourteen—I mean, fifteen years we've been together?

HJALMAR (*standing in front of her*). Tell me: haven't you repented every day, every hour, the web of lies and deceit you were spinning round me? *Haven't* you? Answer me! Haven't you gone about in an agony of regret and remorse?

GINA. How could I, Hjalmar—with all the housework and that to think of?

HJALMAR. And you never spared so much as a thought for your past?

GINA. No. Lord knows, I'd almost forgotten all about that old story.

HJALMAR. Ah—this calm indifference —this complacency! I find it almost revolting! Not even a twinge of remorse!

GINA. Now just you tell me this, Hjalmar Ekdal: where would you have been if you hadn't found a wife like me?

HJALMAR. Like you.

GINA. Yes, like me. Haven't I always been more practical than you? Yes, and more business-like than you? But then, of course, I'm a little bit older than you. . . .

HJALMAR. Well, and where *would* I have been?

GINA. A nice sort of life you were leading when you first met me! You'd got into downright bad habits—and you can't deny it!

HJALMAR. You haven't the faintest idea what a man suffers when he's miserable and desperate——

GINA. Perhaps I haven't. And I don't suppose I've much to complain of, seeing that you turned out quite the model husband once you got a home of your own. And now just as we'd got everything nice and cosy, and me and Hedvig was just thinking we could divulge ourselves a bit more in the way of food and clothes——

HJALMAR. Yes—in the middle of a morass of deceit.

GINA. Oh, how I wish that hateful creature had never come here, that I do!

HJALMAR. Yes—I felt too I had a happy home. That was a delusion. Now where am I to find that buoyant flexibility of spirit so vital to me if I am to put my invention into terms of reality. Perhaps it'll die with me—and it'll be your past, Gina, that'll have killed it.

GINA (*tearfully*). Don't talk like that, Hjalmar . . . I who have never wanted

anything more than to do what was best for you as long as I lived. . . .

HJALMAR. And what—I ask you— becomes of the breadwinner's dreams *now?* Lying in there on the sofa, brooding over the invention, I always had the feeling that it would consume my last ounce of strength. I felt, even, that the day when I held the patent in my hand would be my last. But I was happy in the dream that you would live on as the dead inventor's rich and honoured widow!

GINA (*drying her tears*). Oh, don't talk so silly, Hjalmar. Please God I'll never see the day when *I'm* a widow!

HJALMAR. Well, the dream's over now . . . all over. It was only a dream—it doesn't matter. . . .

(*Enter* GREGERS *by landing door. He hesitates on the threshold for a moment.*)

GREGERS. May I come in?

HJALMAR. Yes—yes, come in—do.

GREGERS (*advancing beaming and with outstretched hands*). Well, my good friends! (*Looks from one to the other, then whispers to* HJALMAR.) Haven't you done it yet?

HJALMAR (*aloud*). Yes—it's done.

GREGERS. It is?

HJALMAR. I've just lived through the bitterest moments of my life.

GREGERS. But also the noblest, I hope.

HJALMAR. Well, at least it's over now —for the time being, at any rate.

GINA. May God forgive you, Mr. Gregers.

GREGERS (*astonished*). But I don't understand. . . .

HJALMAR. What don't you understand?

GREGERS. That after such a great moment of redemption—a moment which was to initiate a completely new life—a real companionship based on truth and purified of falsehood——

HJALMAR. Yes, I know—I know all about that.

GREGERS. I came into this room convinced that I should see faces shining with a new transfiguration, but all I see is apathy, and depression.

GINA. Well—if that's what it is—— (*Lifts shade from lamp.*)

GREGERS. You wilfully misunderstand me, Mrs. Ekdal. However, *you* need time —that I can realize. But you, Hjalmar— surely you must feel yourself newly consecrated after the supreme moment. . . ?

HJALMAR. Oh, I do, Gregers—yes, of course, I do—in some ways, that is—I do, indeed.

GREGERS. For there's nothing finer in the world than to forgive one who has erred, and then to raise her up to you in love. . . .

HJALMAR. D'you think it so easy for a man to recover when he has drunk from such a bitter cup?

GREGERS. Not for an *ordinary* man, perhaps. But a man like you——

HJALMAR. Good heavens, Gregers— I know that well enough. But you must give me time.

GREGERS. There's a lot of the wild duck in you, Hjalmar.

(*Enter* RELLING *by landing door.*)

RELLING. Ah! So the wild duck's still on the agenda?

HJALMAR. Yes—Mr. Werle's badly winged victim.

RELLING. Old Werle? Is *he* the burning topic?

HJALMAR. He—and us.

RELLING (*sotto voce, to* GREGERS). Why don't you go to the Devil?

HJALMAR. What was that?

RELLING. I was merely expressing the fervent wish that this quack would take himself off before he has time to make a mess of both your lives—as he certainly will.

GREGERS. No mess will be made of their lives, Doctor Relling. Hjalmar I needn't speak for—we know him. And I've no doubt that, at the bottom of her heart, she too is honourable and sincere.

GINA (*tearfully*). Then you might have let me go on as I was.

RELLING (*to* GREGERS). Would it be unpardonably rude to enquire what you really want in this house, Mr. Werle?

GREGERS. I want to lay the foundations of a true marriage.

RELLING. Then you don't consider the Ekdals' marriage good enough as it is?

GREGERS. Oh, I dare say it's as satisfactory as most—unfortunately. But it has yet to be a *true* marriage.

HJALMAR. You've never been moved by the claims of the ideal, Relling. . . .

RELLING. Nonsense, my dear fellow! But with all respect, Mr. Werle, how many true marriages—approximately, of course—have you actually observed since you began to notice such things?

GREGERS. Scarcely a single one.

RELLING. Nor have I.

GREGERS. But I have observed a great number of the opposite kind. And it has also been my lot to observe at close quarters the terrible harm such a marriage can do to a couple.

HJALMAR. He's right, Relling. A man's whole moral support may collapse under him—*that's* the terrible part of it.

RELLING. Well, I can't say I've ever been married, not exactly—so I can't very well be dogmatic. But this I do know: the child is an *integral* part of the marriage: and, as such, this child in particular must be protected.

HJALMAR. Ah, Hedvig! Yes—my poor little Hedvig.

RELLING. Exactly. You must be good enough to keep Hedvig out of all this. You two are grown-up people—and whatever ghastly mess you choose to make of your own lives is—God knows! —your own business. But—and I am warning you—go carefully where Hedvig's concerned, or you may do *her* a "terrible harm."

HJALMAR. Harm?

RELLING. *Yes*—or she may harm herself—and possibly others as well.

GINA. But how can you know that, Doctor?

HJALMAR. Her sight was in no immediate danger, I thought?

RELLING. I'm not referring to her sight. Hedvig's at a critical age. She may take it into her head to get up to anything.

GINA. That's true—you can see it already. She's taken to playing about with the kitchen fire—"playing house-afire" she calls it. I'm only afraid that one of these days she'll set the place alight. . . .

RELLING. There you are, you see.

GREGERS (*to* RELLING). Well, but how d'you account for it? What's the cause?

RELLING (*impatiently*). My dear sir —the girl's growing up!

HJALMAR. So long as she has me! So long as there's breath in my body.

(*A knock on the landing door.*)

GINA. Sssh, Hjalmar—there's someone come. (*Calling.*) Come in!

(*Enter* MRS. SÖRBY *in outdoor clothes.*)

MRS. SÖRBY. Good evening.

GINA (*crossing to her*). Why—Bertha —it's you. . . .

MRS. SÖRBY. Of course it's me, dear. I hope this isn't an inconvenient moment?

HJALMAR. Not at all—as an emissary from *that* house——

MRS. SÖRBY (*to* GINA). To tell you the truth I was rather hoping to find you alone at this time. I just wanted to run in and have a little chat with you . . . and say goodbye.

GINA. Why? Are you going away, then?

MRS. SÖRBY. Yes—first thing tomorrow morning—up to Höidal. Mr. Werle left this afternoon. (*To* GREGERS.) He sent you his kind regards. . . .

GINA. Well, fancy that now.

HJALMAR. So Mr. Werle's left, and you're going after him?

MRS. SÖRBY. Yes. And what d'you say to that, Hjalmar?

HJALMAR. I say, take care—that's all.

GREGERS. Perhaps I'd better explain. Mrs. Sörby and my father are going to be married.

HJALMAR. Married!

GINA. Oh, Bertha! So it's come to that at last!

RELLING (*his voice slightly trembling*). Surely this can't be true?

MRS. SÖRBY. Yes, my dear Doctor, it's perfectly true.

RELLING. You're going to marry again?

MRS. SÖRBY. Yes, it certainly looks like it. Mr. Werle's got a special license—and we're going to be married very quietly up at the works.

GREGERS. Then, as a dutiful stepson, I suppose I must offer you my felicitations.

MRS. SÖRBY. That's very nice of you, I'm sure—if you really mean it. I hope we shall *both* be very happy.

RELLING. I think you may reasonably hope for that. To the best of my belief, Mr. Werle never gets drunk; and I doubt very much if he ever beats his wives— like the late lamented horsedoctor.

MRS. SÖRBY. Oh, Sörby's dead—let him rest in peace. He had his good points too, you know.

RELLING. I shouldn't think Mr. Werle could help having better ones.

MRS. SÖRBY. At any rate, he hasn't dissipated all that was best in him. A man who does that must take the consequences.

RELLING. Tonight I shall go out with Molvik.

MRS. SÖRBY. No—you mustn't do that. . . . Don't do that—please—for my sake. . . .

RELLING. There's nothing else for it. (*To* HJALMAR.) Why not join us, Hjalmar?

GINA. Thank you all the same, Doctor Relling, but Hjalmar doesn't care for esplanades of that sort.

HJALMAR (*exasperatedly, and louder than he intends*). Oh, be quiet!

RELLING. Well, goodbye . . . Mrs. Werle.

(*Exit by landing door.*)

GREGERS (*to* MRS. SÖRBY, *smoothly*). I had no idea that you and Doctor Relling were such old friends, Mrs. Sörby.

MRS. SÖRBY. Oh yes—we've known each other for years. Indeed, at one time, it looked as if our friendship might have ripened into something.

GREGERS. But, luckily for you, it didn't.

MRS. SÖRBY. You can put it that way, if you like. You see—I was always cautious about acting on impulse. After all, you can't expect a woman to *throw* herself away.

GREGERS. Aren't you just a little bit afraid that I might mention this old acquaintance of yours to my father?

MRS. SÖRBY (*sweetly*). Oh, but he's heard all about it long ago—from me.

GREGERS. Really?

MRS. SÖRBY. Your father knows *everything* that could truthfully be said about me by anyone. I told him all. It was the very first thing I did when I realized what his intentions were.

GREGERS. Then you acted with what I imagine must be quite uncommon candour.

MRS. SÖRBY. I've always been candid, Mr. Werle. I find it's the best policy for us women.

HJALMAR. What have you to say to that, Gina?

GINA. All women aren't made alike, you know. Some get on best like that— and others don't.

MRS. SÖRBY. Well, Gina, *I* believe it's the wisest thing to do as I've done. And, on his side, Mr. Werle's been perfectly frank with me too. And that's what makes the real bond between us. Now he can sit and talk to me as frankly as a child—and

that's something he's never been able to
do before. All through his youth and manhood he'd had to *listen*—a man full of
strength and vitality—listen to sermons
about sins he never committed! Or so
I've heard.

GINA. Yes, that's right enough.

GREGERS (*coldly*). If you ladies intend
to pursue this subject, I trust you'll excuse
me.

MRS. SÖRBY. Oh, you needn't go on
that account. I've nothing more to say
about it. I only wanted you to know that
I've done nothing sly or underhand. It
may seem to you I've done rather well for
myself—and so I have, in a way. All the
same, I don't think I'm getting any more
than I'm giving. At least, I shall never
leave him, and I can look after him and
care for him as nobody else can—now
that he'll soon be helpless.

HJALMAR. Helpless?

GREGERS. You needn't mention that
here, Mrs. Sörby.

MRS. SÖRBY. It's no use trying to conceal it any longer—much as he'd like to.
Mr. Werle's going blind.

HJALMAR (*with start*). Going blind?
That's . . . extraordinary. He's going
blind, too!

GINA. Lots of people do.

MRS. SÖRBY. And you can imagine
what *that* means to a business man. Well,
I shall have to be his eyes—as far as I
can. But I must really be going now—
I've such a lot to do. Oh, and I was to
tell you, Hjalmar, that if there was anything Mr. Werle could do for you, you
have only to apply to Graaberg.

GREGERS. An offer which I'm sure Mr.
Ekdal will decline with thanks.

MRS. SÖRBY. Indeed? Times have
changed, then. He never used to——

GINA. It's quite true, Bertha—Hjalmar
doesn't want any more from Mr. Werle
now.

HJALMAR (*slowly and pompously*).
Kindly convey my compliments to your
future husband, and tell him that I intend
to take an early opportunity of calling
upon this Mr. Graaberg——

GREGERS. What! You're going to do
that?

HJALMAR. —Of calling upon this Mr.
Graaberg, I say, and desiring him to fur-
nish me with an accurate account of my
financial liability to his employer. I shall

pay this debt of honour—debt of honour!
(*Laughs.*) That's rather funny . . . but let
us call it a debt of honour. However, it
shall be paid in full—and with five per
cent. interest.

GINA. But Hjalmar—we haven't got
the money for that—God knows!

HJALMAR. You may also inform your
future husband that I am labouring night
and day at the development of my invention. And be kind enough to add that
what alone bolsters up my mental
strength in this exhausting task is the desire to rid myself of an agonising burden
of debt—the money advanced to me by
your fiancé.

MRS. SÖRBY (*thoughtfully*). Something
has happened in this house. . . .

HJALMAR. Yes . . . that's quite right.

MRS. SÖRBY (*after a slight pause*).
Very well, then. There was something
else I wanted to talk to you about, Gina
—but it must wait till some other time.
Goodbye.

(*Turns to landing door.* HJALMAR *and*
GREGERS *bow slightly.* GINA *follows* MRS.
SÖRBY *to the door.*)

HJALMAR. Not beyond the threshold,
Gina!

(*Exit* MRS. SÖRBY. GINA *shuts the door
after her.*)

Well—there it is, Gregers. At last I've
lifted the burden of debt from my
shoulders.

GREGERS. Anyhow, you soon will, I'm
sure.

HJALMAR. I think my attitude may be
called correct.

GREGERS. You're the man I've always
taken you for.

HJALMAR. There are certain times, my
dear Gregers, when it's impossible to disregard the claims of the ideal. And yet, as
the breadwinner of a family, I can't help
wincing and fretting under it. It's no
joke, I can tell you, for a man of limited
means to undertake the discharge of a
debt which has accumulated over a long
period of years, and over which the dust
of oblivion has settled—so to speak.
However, be that as it may—the man in
me demands his rights.

GREGERS (*putting a hand on* HJAL-
MAR'S *shoulder*). Now, my dear Hjalmar, wasn't it a good thing I came?

HJALMAR. Yes, it certainly was.

GREGERS. And isn't it a good thing that

at last you are able to realize your true position?

HJALMAR (*impatiently*). Yes, of course it is. But there's one thing that worries me, Gregers. . . .

GREGERS. What's that?

HJALMAR. It's—but I don't know whether I ought to express myself so freely about your father. . . .

GREGERS. You can say what you like, so far as I'm concerned.

HJALMAR. Well . . . I can't help feeling how bitterly unjust it is that it should be he and not I who will realise the true marriage.

GREGERS. How can you possibly say that?

HJALMAR. I say it because it's true. This marriage between your father and Mrs. Sörby will be based on complete confidence. They conceal nothing, and have no reservations. They build their house, so to speak, on the rock of mutual forgiveness.

GREGERS. Well—and what about it?

HJALMAR. But isn't that the crux of the whole matter? Didn't you say yourself that such conditions are the only foundation of a true marriage?

GREGERS. But the two situations are hardly the same, Hjalmar. Surely you don't compare either yourself or your wife with those two—well, I needn't say more than that.

HJALMAR. Gregers, there's something in all this that offends my sense of justice. It makes me wonder if there *is* such a thing as a just Providence in the world. . . .

GINA. Hjalmar! How in God's name can you say such a thing!

GREGERS. H'm. . . . I think perhaps we'd better not go into that question.

HJALMAR. All the same, I seem to see the hand of fate in all this. Isn't *he* going blind?

GINA. Well—you can't be sure.

HJALMAR. Oh yes, we can—it has all the marks of a divine retribution. Hasn't he, in his time, blinded the eyes of a trusting fellow-creature?

GREGERS. He's done that to a good many, I'm afraid.

HJALMAR. And now Fate steps in—inexorable and mysterious—and demands the man's own eyes.

GINA. How can you go on saying such

awful things, Hjalmar? You frighten the life out of me—you really do. . . .

HJALMAR. It's good and wholesome to sound the deeps of life's darker side, sometimes.

(*Enter* HEDVIG *by landing door. She is wearing her hat and cloak, and is happy and out of breath.*)

GINA. You haven't been very long, Hedvig.

HEDVIG. I didn't feel like staying out long, Mother; and it was a good thing I didn't because I met someone at the door.

HJALMAR. Mrs. Sörby, I suppose.

HEDVIG. Yes.

HJALMAR (*pacing*). Well—I hope you've seen her for the last time.

(*A slight pause.* HEDVIG *looks from one to the other, a little disconcerted and as if trying to get her bearings, then crosses to* HJALMAR.)

HEDVIG (*coaxingly*). Father. . . .

HJALMAR. Well—what is it?

HEDVIG. Mrs. Sörby brought me something. . . .

HJALMAR (*halting*). You?

HEDVIG. Yes—something for tomorrow. . . .

GINA. Bertha always does give you something for your birthday.

HJALMAR. What is it?

HEDVIG. Oh, you're not to see it yet! Mother's to give it me in bed tomorrow morning.

HJALMAR. A conspiracy to keep me in the dark—is that it?

HEDVIG (*quickly*). No—you can see it if you like. It's a big letter. (*Takes letter from her cloak pocket.*)

HJALMAR. A letter, eh?

HEDVIG. Yes—only the letter—the other's coming on later, I expect. But just think of it, Father—a letter! I've never had a letter before. And look—it's addressed to me—it's got Miss on the envelope. (*Reading.*) "Miss Hedvig Ekdal." That's *me!*

HJALMAR. Let me see it.

HEDVIG (*giving it to him*). Here you are.

HJALMAR. This is Mr. Werle's handwriting.

GINA. Are you sure, Hjalmar?

HJALMAR. Well, look at it!

GINA. Now what would I know about it?

HJALMAR. Hedvig—may I open this letter and read it?

HEDVIG. Yes, of course—if you want to.

GINA. No, Hjalmar, not tonight. It's for tomorrow.

HEDVIG (*softly*). Oh, please let him read it! It's bound to be something nice, and that'll put Father in a good temper, and then everything'll be all right again.

HJALMAR. Then I may open it?

HEDVIG. Yes—go on, Father. I'm longing to know what it says!

HJALMAR. Very well, then. (*Opens the envelope, takes out a paper and reads it with growing astonishment.*) What in the world. . . .

GINA. What's it say?

HEDVIG (*after a slight pause*). What does it *say*, Father?

HJALMAR. Be quiet for a minute. (*Re-reads paper, appears disturbed, but says with self-control.*) Hedvig, this is a deed of gift.

HEDVIG. Gift? A present? What is it?

HJALMAR (*thrusting it into her hands*). See for yourself.

(HEDVIG *takes it over to the lamp, and shading her eyes, reads with difficulty.*)

(*To* GREGERS, *breathlessly*). Her eyes! And now this. . . .

HEDVIG (*looking up*). But it says it's for Grandfather.

HJALMAR (*taking the paper*). Gina—can you understand this?

GINA. No. I can't. What's it all about?

HJALMAR. Mr. Werle writes to Hedvig that her old grandfather need no longer concern himself with the copying, as, for the future, he may draw five pounds a month from the office——

GREGERS. A-ha!

HEDVIG. Five pounds, Mother! I read that.

GINA. How nice for Grandfather!

HJALMAR. Five pounds a month for so long as he needs it—that means as long as he lives.

GINA. Well, then he's provided for, poor old gentleman.

HJALMAR. But that's not all. You didn't read far enough, Hedvig. Afterwards the gift passes on to you.

HEDVIG. To me! What—all of it?

HJALMAR. Yes—it says here it's to be the same sum, and for the rest of your life. D'you hear that, Gina?

GINA. Yes—I heard.

HEDVIG. Just think of it! All that money for me! (*Shaking him.*) Oh, Father, Father—aren't you *pleased?*

HJALMAR (*drawing away*). Pleased? (*Pacing.*) What a perspective it reveals —what a scene it unrolls before me! It's Hedvig—*Hedvig* for whom he provides so generously!

GINA. Well—it's Hedvig's birthday. . . .

HEDVIG. And you'll get it, all the same, Father. I shall give it all to you and Mother—every penny!

HJALMAR. To your mother, yes. That's just it. . . .

GREGERS. Hjalmar, this is some sort of trap he's setting for you.

HJALMAR. What? *Another!*

GREGERS. When he was here this morning he said: "Hjalmar Ekdal is not at all the man you take him for."

HJALMAR. Not the man. . . ?

GREGERS. Yes. He said "You'll see."

HJALMAR. He thought you would see that I could be bought off!

HEDVIG. Oh, Mother—what is it all about?

GINA (*kindly*). Now you just run along and take your things off.

(*Exit* HEDVIG, *almost in tears, into kitchen.*)

GREGERS. Yes, Hjalmar—now we shall *see* who was right, he or I.

HJALMAR (*tearing the paper slowly in half and putting the pieces on the table*). There's my answer.

GREGERS. That's what I expected.

HJALMAR (*crossing to* GINA, *who is by the stove, and speaking quietly*). Now I want the truth, Gina. If it *was* all over between you and him when—as you put it—you came to care for me, why did he do so much to help us get married?

GINA. I don't know, perhaps he thought he'd always find a welcome here. . . .

HJALMAR. Is that all? Wasn't he afraid of a certain eventuality?

GINA. I don't know what you mean.

HJALMAR. I want to know whether—your child . . . has the right to live under my roof.

GINA (*drawing herself up, her eyes flashing*). You ask me *that!*

HJALMAR. And you've got to answer. Is Hedvig my child, or——? Well——?

GINA (*defiantly*). I don't know.

HJALMAR (*his voice shaking*). You don't know!

GINA. How should I know . . . a woman like me. . . .

HJALMAR (*turning from her, quietly*). Then there's nothing to keep me in this house. . . .

GREGERS. Don't be too hasty, Hjalmar —think what you're doing.

HJALMAR (*taking down his overcoat*). There's nothing here for a man like me to think twice about.

GREGERS. Oh, yes there is—there's a good deal! The three of you must be together if you're to achieve the crowning self-sacrifice—forgiveness.

HJALMAR. I don't care—I don't *want* it! Where's my hat? (*Takes up his hat.*) My home is in ruins. . . . (*Breaking down in tears.*) Gregers—I have no child now. . . .

(*Enter* HEDVIG *by kitchen door. She remains standing in doorway.*)

HEDVIG. What are you saying, Father? (*Starts towards him.*) Father. . . .

GINA. Now see what you've——

HJALMAR. Stay where you are, Hedvig! Don't come near me! I can't bear to see you! (*Turning away.*) Her eyes. . . . (*Just audibly.*) Goodbye. . . . (*Crosses to landing door.*)

HEDVIG (*clinging to him, screaming*). No—no. . . . Don't . . . don't leave me. . . .

GINA (*urgently*). Look at the child, Hjalmar! *Look* at the child!

HJALMAR. I won't! I tell you I can't! I must get out of here—get out of all this——

(*Tears himself away from* HEDVIG *and exit by landing door.*)

HEDVIG (*in despair*). He's going away from us! He's going away . . . and he'll never come back—never. . . .

GINA. Don't cry, Hedvig. Father'll come back, he'll come back, dear—you'll see. . . .

HEDVIG (*throwing herself on sofa and sobbing*). No! No, he won't! He won't! He'll never come back!

GREGERS. Will you believe I meant it all for the best, Mrs. Ekdal?

GINA. Yes, I suppose so. But all the same—God forgive you, Gregers Werle. . . .

HEDVIG (*sobbing*). I can't bear it! I shall die if he doesn't come back! What have I done to Father? Mother, go after him—fetch him home again . . . you must fetch him. . . .

GINA. Yes, dear—I will. Only you must stop crying. I'll go and see if I can find him. (*Putting on cloak.*) Perhaps he's gone down to Doctor Relling's. I shall find him. But you must stop crying first. No more tears now—promise me?

HEDVIG (*sobbing*). Yes—I promise. I will stop . . . if only Father comes back again. . . .

(GINA *crosses to landing door.*)

GREGERS (*to* GINA). Hadn't you better leave him to fight his battle by himself?

GINA. He'll have plenty of time for that afterwards. The first thing's the child. . . .

(*Exit. A slight pause.*)

HEDVIG (*sitting up and wiping her eyes*). What—what is it all about? Why doesn't Father want me any more?

GREGERS. You mustn't ask that till you're a big girl—till you're grown up.

HEDVIG (*gulping*). But I can't go on being miserable like this till I'm grown up. I believe I know what it is—perhaps I don't really belong to Father, after all.

GREGERS (*uneasily*). But how could that be?

HEDVIG. Mother might have found me. And Father's only just heard about it. I know things like that happen in books. . . .

GREGERS. Well, and supposing it were true. . . .

HEDVIG. I think he might love me just as well, all the same—even more, perhaps. After all, the wild duck was found —and given to us as a present—and I love her very much indeed.

GREGERS. Ah, yes—the wild duck. (*In a light tone.*) Tell me more about her, Hedvig——

HEDVIG. The poor wild duck! He can't bear to see her, either. Why—just think! —he wanted to wring her neck!

GREGERS. Oh, he'd never do that, I'm sure.

HEDVIG. No, but he said he'd like to. And I think it's horrid of Father even to say it, because I pray for the wild duck every night—that her days may be long and that she may be delivered from evil.

GREGERS (*eyeing her*). Do you say your prayers every night?

HEDVIG. Oh, yes.

GREGERS. Who taught you to do that?

HEDVIG. I taught myself. It all started when Father was very ill and had leeches on his neck—and told us he was wrestling with death.

GREGERS. Really?

HEDVIG. Yes—that night, while I was lying in bed, I prayed for him. And since then I've always said my prayers every night when I go to bed.

GREGERS. And now you pray for the wild duck too, eh?

HEDVIG. Yes. You see, I thought it best to put the wild duck in, because she was so poorly at first.

GREGERS. And d'you say your prayers in the morning as well?

HEDVIG. No, of course not.

GREGERS. And why not in the morning?

HEDVIG. Because it's light in the morning—and there's nothing to be afraid of.

GREGERS. And yet your father was going to wring the neck of the wild duck you love so much.

HEDVIG. No—he said he could almost, but that he wouldn't for my sake. I think that was very nice of Father.

GREGERS (*sitting a little nearer to her*). But supposing you were to sacrifice the wild duck—of your own free will—and for *his* sake . . . ?

HEDVIG (*rising*). The wild duck!

GREGERS. Yes. Supposing you were to sacrifice for his sake the greatest treasure you have in the world?

HEDVIG. Do you really think that would help?

GREGERS. Try it, Hedvig.

HEDVIG (*softly and with shining eyes*). Yes—I will try it!

GREGERS. Are you really brave enough to do it, d'you think?

HEDVIG. I'll ask Grandfather to shoot the wild duck for me.

GREGERS. Yes—do that. But not a word to your mother, remember.

HEDVIG. Why not?

GREGERS. She doesn't understand us.

HEDVIG (*softly*). The wild duck! Yes, I will—I'll try first thing tomorrow morning!

(*Enter* GINA *by landing door.*)

(*Going towards her.*) Did you find him, Mother?

GINA. No, but I heard he looked in on Doctor Relling, and took him along with him.

GREGERS. Are you quite sure of that?

GINA. Yes, the porter's wife told me. That Molvik went with 'em, too, she said.

GREGERS. At a time like this . . . when he should be fighting it out alone. . . .

GINA (*taking off her things*). When men get like that you can't do much with 'em, I suppose. And Lord knows where that Doctor Relling won't take him. I ran over to Mrs. Eriksen's—but they weren't there, either of 'em.

HEDVIG (*choking back her tears*). Supposing—supposing he never comes home any more?

GREGERS. But he *will*—he'll come home. Besides, I shall have something to tell him tomorrow, and *then* you'll see how quickly he'll come. Believe that, Hedvig, and sleep peacefully. Good night.

(*Exit by landing door.*)

HEDVIG (*throwing herself into* GINA'S *arms and sobbing*). Mother . . . Oh, Mother. . . . !

GINA (*patting her and sighing*). Yes, Doctor Relling knew what he was talking about. This is what comes of cranky people going round and making out claims on the—whatsaname. . . .

Medium Curtain

🌿 Act V

As before. Early the following morning.

The light coming through the falling snow which smears the panes of the glass roof is cold and grey.

Enter GINA *from kitchen wearing a bibbed apron and carrying a duster and brush. She crosses stolidly towards sitting-room door as* HEDVIG *enters excitedly by landing door.*

GINA (*stopping*). Well?

HEDVIG. Oh, Mother—I believe he's down with Doctor Relling——

GINA. There—now what did I tell you!

HEDVIG. Because the porter's wife said she was sure there were two people with Doctor Relling when he came home last night. . . .

GINA. Just as I thought!

HEDVIG. But that's not much good if he won't come up to us.

GINA. I'll go down to him, I think, and have a word with him.

(*Enter* OLD EKDAL *from his bedroom,*

wearing a shabby dressing gown and slippers, and smoking his pipe.)

OLD EKDAL. Hjalmar, are you—? (*Crossing.*) What? Isn't Hjalmar at home?

GINA. No, he's gone out.

OLD EKDAL. So early? And while it's snowing? Well, I suppose he knows his own business best. I shall have to go the rounds myself, that's all.

(*Exit by attic door, which* HEDVIG *helps him to open and closes after him.*)

HEDVIG (*quietly*). Whatever will Grandfather say, Mother, when he hears that Father wants to leave us?

GINA. Nonsense! Grandfather must never hear anything about it. It's a mercy he wasn't in yesterday when there was all that commotion!

HEDVIG. Yes, but——

(*Enter* GREGERS *by landing door.*)

GREGERS. Well—any news of him yet?

GINA. So far as I can make out, he's downstairs with Doctor Relling.

GREGERS. Relling! You mean he actually went out with that pair.

GINA. I shouldn't be at all surprised.

GREGERS. When he should have given the night to searching his heart and coming to terms with himself!

GINA. Oh, yes—I dare say.

(*Enter* RELLING *by landing door.*)

HEDVIG (*crossing to him*). Is Father in your room, Doctor Relling?

GINA (*simultaneously*). Is he with you?

RELLING. Yes, of course he is.

HEDVIG. And you never told us!

RELLING. Yes—I'm a brute! But, you see, I had to deal with the other brute first—I mean the demoniac one, of course! And after that, well, I couldn't keep awake—I slept like a log——

GINA. And what does Hjalmar say this morning?

RELLING. He doesn't say anything!

HEDVIG. Doesn't he speak?

RELLING. Not a blessed word.

GREGERS. No—well, I can quite understand that. . . .

GINA. What is he doing?

RELLING. Lying on the sofa having a heartfelt snore.

GINA (*indignantly*). Isn't that just like him? He always *did* snore.

HEDVIG. He's asleep? How *can* he sleep?

RELLING. Well, it certainly sounds as if he can, Hedvig.

GREGERS. It's hardly surprising after the spiritual conflict he's passed through——

GINA. But, of course, he's not used to being out on the tiles all night.

HEDVIG. Perhaps it's a good thing for him to get some sleep, Mother?

GINA. I know—I'm sure it is—and we mustn't wake him up too soon. Well, thank you ever so much, Doctor Relling. And now I really must get on with my housework, else I shall be all behind like a donkey's tail. You come and help me, Hedvig.

(*Exeunt* GINA *and* HEDVIG *into parlour.*)

GREGERS. What's your opinion of the spiritual conflict that's rending Hjalmar Ekdal?

RELLING. I must confess I've never detected any spiritual conflict in progress *there.*

GREGERS. Not at such a critical moment, when his whole life has been re-orientated. How can you imagine for one moment that a man of Hjalmar's personality——

RELLING. Personality—that fellow? If he ever had any tendency towards the abnormal condition you call "personality," it was squashed out of him when he was a boy.

GREGERS. That's rather odd—considering all the care and affection with which he was brought up.

RELLING. What, by those two dotty, hysterical maiden aunts of his?

GREGERS. Let me tell you that they were two ladies who never at any time allowed themselves to ignore the claims of the ideal. Oh, I know that will only make you sneer. . . .

RELLING. No, I'm in no mood for that. I know all about those two ladies—he's deluged me with rhetoric on the subject of his "two soul-mothers." And, if you ask me, he's very little to thank them for. It's Hjalmar Ekdal's misfortune that, in his own circle, he's always been looked up to as a shining light——

GREGERS. And isn't he? With his depth of mind?

RELLING. I've never noticed it. The mere fact that his father believed it hardly surprises me. The poor old Lieutenant never was very bright.

GREGERS. He has a truly childlike mind —and always has had. That's something you could never understand.

RELLING. Have it your own way. But when our adorable little Hjalmar was packed off to college, his fellow-students promptly united in seeing him as the coming man. A handsome young rascal he was, too—pink and white, a typical housemaid's Adonis—with his shallow emotionalism, his sympathetic voice, and his ability to spout other people's verses and other people's ideas——

GREGERS (*indignantly*). Is it Hjalmar Ekdal you're describing in such terms?

RELLING. Yes, with your permission. I'm simply turning your precious idol inside out so that you can see what you bow down to.

GREGERS. I doubt if I was ever as blind as that.

RELLING. Well, you're not far off it. You see, you, too, are a sick man. . . .

GREGERS (*after a slight pause*). You're quite right, I am.

RELLING. Exactly. Your case is a complicated one. Firstly, there's this troublesome probity fever of yours. And then— even worse—you're constantly in a delirium of hero-worship. You must always have something outside yourself which you can deify.

GREGERS. Yes—it must be something outside myself.

RELLING. But you always make such preposterous mistakes about these shining half-gods you think you've discovered. Here again you've come to a workman's cottage and presented your claim of the ideal, but the tenants are bankrupt.

GREGERS. If you've so poor an opinion of Hjalmar Ekdal, what possible satisfaction can you derive from spending so much time in his company?

RELLING. It's really quite simple. You see, for my sins, I'm supposed to be a kind of doctor. And therefore I feel bound to do what I can for the sick who happen to be living in the same house.

GREGERS. Really! So Hjalmar Ekdal is sick too, is he?

RELLING. Most people are, I'm afraid.

GREGERS. And what sort of treatment are you giving him?

RELLING. Oh, my usual one—helping him to keep up his own special fantasy —what I call a "life-lie."

GREGERS. A "life-lie," did you say?

RELLING. Yes, I said "life-lie." You see, the "life-lie" is the actuating principle.

GREGERS. May I ask by what "life-lie" Hjalmar has to be sustained?

RELLING. No *thank you!* I don't share professional secrets with quacks. You'd only get my patient into a more unholy mess than he is already. But my method is infallible. I've even applied it successfully to Molvik. I set him up in life as a "demoniac." That's the blue pill I gave *him!*

GREGERS. Then he's not demoniac?

RELLING. What the devil does "demoniac" mean, anyhow? That's only a piece of mumbo-jumbo I cooked up to give the fellow something to live for. If I hadn't, the poor, harmless muggins would have succumbed to self-contempt and despair years ago. And then the old lieutenant—he's another. But he found his cure for himself.

GREGERS. You've diagnosed him as well, have you?

RELLING. Imagine it—an ex-bear-hunter shutting himself up in a gloomy attic to shoot rabbits! And yet there's no happier sportsman in the world than that old man fiddling about in there amongst all that rubbish. The four or five withered Christmas trees he's collected in there are the same to him as the whole green forest of Höidal; the few fowls are the game in the tree-tops; and the rabbits hopping about the floor are the bears he has to encounter. Yes—how is the mighty hunter fallen!

GREGERS. Poor old Ekdal. He's certainly had to temper the ideals of his youth.

RELLING. And, while I think of it, Mr. Werle junior—don't use the foreign word "ideals"—we have a perfectly satisfactory native word—"lies."

GREGERS. And d'you think the two things are connected?

RELLING. Yes—exactly like typhus and putrid fever!

GREGERS. Doctor Relling—I shan't rest until I've got Hjalmar Ekdal out of your clutches.

RELLING. So much the worse for him! Dock the average man of his life-lie and you take his happiness.

(*Enter* HEDVIG *from parlour.*)

(*To* HEDVIG.) Ah—and how's the wild duck's little mother? I think I'll just slip downstairs for a minute, and see if Father's still sleeping on that wonderful invention of his. . . .

(*Exit by landing door.*)

GREGERS (*crossing to* HEDVIG). I can see by your face that you haven't done it.

HEDVIG. Done what? Oh, you mean about the wild duck. . . . N-no.

GREGERS. I suppose your courage failed at the last minute?

HEDVIG. No—not exactly. You see, when I woke up this morning, I thought about all we'd been saying, and—well, it all seemed so silly. . . .

GREGERS. Silly?

HEDVIG. Yes. I don't know—last night, at the time, it sounded so beautiful; but after I'd been asleep and thought about it again, somehow it didn't seem to make sense.

GREGERS. H'm . . . I ought not to have expected that you could grow up in this household without having something spoiled in you.

HEDVIG. Oh, I don't care about that— if only Father would come up. . . .

GREGERS. What a pity your eyes have never been opened to the really valuable things in life. If you had the true, joyous, brave spirit of sacrifice in you, you'd soon see how quickly he'd come. . . . But I still have faith in you, Hedvig.

(*Exit by landing door.* HEDVIG *wanders about the room for a few moments. She is about to go into the kitchen when there is a knock on the attic door. She crosses to it and opens it enough for* OLD EKDAL *to squeeze through, and pushes it to behind him.*)

OLD EKDAL. H'm—there's not much fun, I can tell you, in having to go the morning rounds by yourself.

HEDVIG. Aren't you going shooting this morning, then, Grandfather?

OLD EKDAL. It's not shooting weather, m'dear; it's so overcast in there you can hardly see an inch in front of your nose.

HEDVIG. Don't you ever feel you'd like to shoot something besides rabbits?

OLD EKDAL. And what's wrong with rabbits—aren't they good enough?

HEDVIG. Yes—but the wild duck——

OLD EKDAL. A-ha! Are you afraid I

shall shoot your wild duck? Not on your life, little one! Never!

HEDVIG (*thoughtfully*). They say wild duck are very difficult to shoot. Perhaps you couldn't.

OLD EKDAL. Couldn't I? I should jolly well think I could.

HEDVIG. How would you do it, Grandfather? Not with my wild duck, of course, but somebody else's?

OLD EKDAL. I should take care to shoot it in the right place— that's always the breast—that's the way! The only other thing you've got to be careful about is seeing that you shoot *against* the lie of the feathers—not *with* the lie of the feathers. See?

HEDVIG. Do they die then, Grandfather?

OLD EKDAL. Yes, of course, so long as you shoot straight! Well, after all that, I think I'll go and have a wash and brush up. . . . H'm—well, now you know all about it—H'm!

(*Exit into bedroom.* HEDVIG *waits a moment, glances towards parlour door, then crosses to bookcase and takes the double-barrelled pistol down from the shelf and looks at it. Enter* GINA *with brush and duster from the parlour.* HEDVIG *replaces the pistol unobserved.*)

GINA. Now, Hedvig—don't stand there rummaging about among your father's things; you know he doesn't like it.

HEDVIG (*moving away from bookcase*). I was only going to tidy up a little.

GINA. Well, you'd do far better to go into the kitchen and see that the milk for the coffee doesn't boil over. I'll take him some breakfast down on a tray when I go.

(*Exit* HEDVIG *by kitchen door.* GINA *begins sweeping and dusting. After a few moments the landing door is opened gingerly and* HJALMAR *looks in. He wears his overcoat but no hat. He has an unwashed appearance, his hair is dishevelled and his eyes are dull and heavy.*)

(*Stopping work and looking at him*). Oh. So you have come back then, Hjalmar?

HJALMAR (*coming further in, tonelessly*). Yes, I've come—but only to go away again. . . .

GINA. Yes—yes, I suppose so. But— lumme! What a sight you do look!

HJALMAR. A sight?

GINA. And all in your nice winter coat, too! Just look at it! Ruined—that's what it is!

(*Enter* HEDVIG *by kitchen door, but remaining in doorway.*)

HEDVIG. Mother, hadn't I better—— (*Seeing* HJALMAR, *crying out joyfully and running to him.*) Daddy! Oh, Father!

HJALMAR (*turning from her and warding her off*). No! Go away! Go away! (*To* GINA.) Keep her away from me!

GINA (*quietly*). You'd better go into the other room, Hedvig.

(*Exit* HEDVIG, *chagrined and bewildered, by parlour door.*)

HJALMAR (*pulling out table-drawer; fussily*). Where are my books? I *must* have them.

GINA. What books?

HJALMAR. My scientific books, of course. The technical periodicals I need for my invention.

GINA (*looking in bookcase*). Are these the ones—with the paper covers on?

HJALMAR. Of course they are.

GINA (*putting a pile of magazines on the table*). Shall I get Hedvig to cut the pages for you?

HJALMAR. I don't want them cut.

(*A slight pause.*)

GINA. You're really going, then, Hjalmar?

HJALMAR (*crossing to bookcase and picking out books*). I should have thought that was obvious.

GINA. Oh—well. . . .

HJALMAR (*returning to table with books and dumping them down vehemently*). I can't live here and get a knife in my heart every hour of the day!

GINA. God forgive you for the hard things you think of me, that's all.

HJALMAR. Prove that——

GINA (*hotly*). I think you're the one to do the proving.

HJALMAR. What? With *your* past? There are certain claims—I might almost call them claims of the ideal—that——

GINA. But what about Grandfather? What's to become of him, poor old chap?

HJALMAR. I require no one to teach me my duty, thank you. My helpless father goes with me. I shall go into town and make the necessary arrangements.

H'm—(*hesitantly*)—I suppose nobody found my hat on the stairs?

GINA. No—why? Have you been and lost it, then?

HJALMAR. I was wearing it when I came in last night, of course. There's no doubt about that. But this morning it seems to have disappeared.

GINA. My goodness! Wherever did you go last night with those two rowdies?

HJALMAR. Don't bother me with trivialities. D'you think I can remember details in *my* state?

GINA (*crossing to kitchen*). Well—so long as you haven't caught cold, Hjalmar. . . .

(*Exit.*)

HJALMAR (*emptying table-drawer; muttering angrily*). Blast you, Relling! Damn you! You're a swine and a loafer! Egging people on! I wish I could get someone to murder you.

(*Puts some old letters on one side, then comes across the torn deed of gift, takes it up and examines the torn edges. Then, as* GINA *enters with breakfast tray, hurriedly puts down pieces and fusses with other papers.*)

GINA (*putting tray on table*). I've brought you a cup of something hot, in case you feel like it—some bread and butter, and a nice bit of cold meat.

HJALMAR (*hungrily eyeing tray*). Cold meat? Food? No. Not another mouthful under this roof! It's true I haven't had so much as a bite of solid food for the last twenty-four hours—but that doesn't matter. . . . My notes! The opening sections of my autobiography! And where are my diaries? And all my important papers? Where are they? (*Crossing to parlour door, opening it and drawing back*) She's in there now!

GINA. Good gracious! The child must be *somewhere.*

HJALMAR. Come out of there!

(*Stands aside as enter* HEDVIG, *looking scared. With his hand on the door knob, to* GINA:)

During the last few minutes I spend in my former home, I wish to be spared the presence of interlopers.

(*Exit into parlour.*)

HEDVIG (*running to* GINA: *in a low trembling voice*). Does he mean me, Mother?

GINA. You go into the kitchen, Hedvig—no, better go to your own room. (*Crossing to open parlour door.*) Wait a minute, Hjalmar. You needn't start turning those drawers upside down. I know where everything is.

(*Exit into parlour.* HEDVIG *stands motionless for a moment, frightened and miserable and biting her lips to keep back the tears, while the voices of* HJALMAR *and* GINA *are heard through the open parlour door. Then, clenching her hands, softly:*)

HEDVIG. The wild duck!

(*Crosses on tiptoe to the bookcase, takes down pistol, crosses to attic door, pushes it aside a little, slips in and shuts it after her. Enter* HJALMAR *from parlour carrying notebooks and papers which he puts on the table, and followed by* GINA *carrying a portmanteau.*)

HJALMAR. That portmanteau's no earthly use—I've a hundred and one things to drag round with me.

GINA. Well, surely you needn't take it all in one go? You could call back for the rest later on—and make do with a clean shirt and pants just for the time being. . . .

HJALMAR (*puffing*). Phew! All this ghastly packing! I'm exhausted! (*Pulls off overcoat and throws it on sofa.*)

GINA. That coffee must be stone cold by now.

HJALMAR (*picking up cup and drinking absently*). H'm—yes. . . . (*Gulps more coffee.*)

GINA (*dusting chairs*). You won't half have a job getting another attic big enough to take all them rabbits.

HJALMAR. What? Have I got to take all those rabbits with me?

GINA. Well, I'm sure Grandpa'll never be able to do without his rabbits.

HJALMAR. He'll have to, that's all. *I'm* sacrificing far greater things than rabbits.

GINA (*dusting bookcase*). D'you want your flute put in your portwhatsaname?

HJALMAR. Flute? No. But give me the pistol.

GINA. D'you want to take the resolver along with you?

HJALMAR. Yes. My loaded pistol.

GINA (*looking for it*). I can't see it —it's not here. He must have taken it in there with him.

HJALMAR. Is he in the attic?

GINA. Yes, of course he is.

HJALMAR. H'm—poor, lonely old man. (*Eats a piece of bread and butter and finishes the coffee.*)

GINA. If only we hadn't let that room you could have moved in there.

HJALMAR. And gone on living under the same roof with——! No—never!

GINA. Come to that, I daresay you could manage in the parlour for a couple of days. You'd have it all to yourself.

HJALMAR. Never within these walls!

GINA (*briskly*). Well then, downstairs with Doctor Relling and Molvik?

HJALMAR. Don't mention their names to me! The mere thought of them takes away my appetite! No, I must go out into the storm and the snow, and trudge from door to door, begging shelter for my helpless father and myself.

GINA. But you've got no hat, Hjalmar. You went and lost it. . . .

HJALMAR. Oh, those two unspeakable blackguards! Those vice-ridden wasters! Well, a hat will have to be found! (*Taking another slice of bread and butter.*) Something'll have to be done—I can't afford to risk my life. (*Looks for something on the tray.*)

GINA. What is it you want?

HJALMAR. Butter.

GINA. I'll get you some—it won't take a minute.

(*Exit into kitchen.*)

HJALMAR (*calling after her*). Oh, it doesn't matter. Dry bread is good enough for me.

(*Enter* GINA *from kitchen with butter dish.*)

GINA. Here you are—it's nice and fresh too. (*Pours more coffee.*)

(HJALMAR *sits on the sofa, puts more butter on a slice of bread and butter, then eats for a few moments in silence.*)

HJALMAR (*between mouthfuls*). Could I—if I *did* have it all to myself—without intrusion from anyone—*anyone*—manage in the parlour for a couple of days?

GINA. You know very well you could if you wanted to.

HJALMAR. Because, as it is, I can't see the remotest possibility of moving all *father's* things out at such short notice.

GINA. Besides, you've still got to tell him you don't reckon to live with us no more.

HJALMAR (*pushing his cup away*). Yes—of course—there's that too. I have somehow to make him understand all the intricate ramifications of this business. . . . I must consider. I must have time to think. I can't possibly shoulder all these burdens in one day.

GINA. No—and especially in such terrible weather as it is outside.

HJALMAR (touching the torn deed). I see this document is still lying about.

GINA. Yes, I haven't touched it.

HJALMAR. It's so much waste paper so far as I'm concerned——

GINA. Well, I'm sure I've no intention of using it.

HJALMAR. At the same time it might be better not to lose it—and, what with all this moving, it might easily——

GINA. I'll see it's put away, Hjalmar.

HJALMAR. After all, the gift is, in the first instance, made to Father—and it's entirely for him to decide whether he will avail himself of it.

GINA. Yes, poor old gentleman——

HJALMAR. Just to be on the safe side —where did you put the gum?

(GINA crosses to bookcase and fetches gum-bottle and gum.)

GINA. Here you are.

HJALMAR. And the brush?

GINA (patiently). Here. (Hands it to him.)

HJALMAR (taking up scissors). Now just a strip of paper down the back. . . . (Cutting and gumming.) Far be it from me to lay hands on other people's property, least of all a poor, destitute old man's, or—anyone else's for that matter. There now—that'll do, I think. Better leave it there, and when it's dry put it away. I never wish to set eyes on that paper again—never!

(Enter GREGERS by landing door.)

GREGERS (surprised). Why, Hjalmar —what are you sitting there for?

HJALMAR (rising hurriedly). I was so exhausted I had to sit down for a minute.

GREGERS. You've had some breakfast too, I see.

HJALMAR. The claims of the body have to be met sometimes. . . .

GREGERS. What have you decided to do?

HJALMAR. For a man like me, there's only one thing to do. I'm just running through my most important papers. But, as you know it's exacting work and it takes time.

GINA (a little impatiently). Now am I to get the room ready for you? Or am I to pack that portwhatsaname?

HJALMAR (glancing irritably at GREGERS). Pack . . . and get the room ready!

GINA (picking up the portmanteau). All right, then—I'll get your shirt and things.

(Exit into parlour and shuts door. A slight pause.)

GREGERS. Hjalmar, I never imagined it would end like this. D'you feel bound to leave house and home?

HJALMAR (pacing restlessly). What else would you have me do? I'm not built for bearing unhappiness, Gregers. I must have peace and a sense of security in my life.

GREGERS. But can't you have that here? Why not try it? It seems to me that at last you have solid foundations on which to build, and can make a fresh start. And remember, there's the invention to live for.

HJALMAR. Oh, don't talk to me about my invention! It may well be years before it matures.

GREGERS. Really?

HJALMAR. Heavens above! What d'you want me to invent? Almost everything's already been invented by someone or other. It's getting more difficult every day——

GREGERS. But you've worked so hard and so long. . . .

HJALMAR. It was that swine Relling who started me on it.

GREGERS. Relling?

HJALMAR. Yes, it was he who first revealed to me my ability to make some outstanding scientific discovery in the realm of photography.

GREGERS. Aha! Relling!

HJALMAR. And I've known such great happiness in the work. Not so much on account of the invention itself as because Hedvig believed in it—believed in it with all a child's utter enthusiasm. At least I was fool enough to think so.

GREGERS. You can't really believe that Hedvig was being disingenuous?

HJALMAR. I can believe anything now. It's Hedvig who stands in my way. She'll blot out the sun for me always now.

GREGERS. Hedvig? . . . Hedvig? How could she ever blot out the sun for you?

HJALMAR. I've loved that child so unspeakably. I've been so unspeakably happy whenever I came into this poor room and she ran to meet me, looking at me with her sweet short-sighted eyes. What a fool I've been! Loving her unspeakably, I surrendered to the delusion that she loved me unspeakably in return.

GREGERS. Can you call that a delusion?

HJALMAR. How can I possibly tell? I can get nothing out of Gina—the ideal side of these questions has no existence for her. But with you, Gregers, I feel compelled to be honest: I am haunted by the terrible doubt that Hedvig has never really and truly loved me.

GREGERS. But supposing she could prove to you that she did love you? (*Listening.*) What's that? It sounded like the wild duck. . . .

HJALMAR. Yes . . . (*listening*) . . . that's the wild duck. Father's in there.

GREGERS. Is he? (*Eagerly.*) I tell you, you may yet have proof that your poor, misunderstood little Hedvig really loves you.

HJALMAR. What proof could *she* give me?

GREGERS. Hedvig doesn't know the meaning of deceit, Hjalmar.

HJALMAR. Ah, if I could only be sure of that! How do *we* know what has passed between Gina and that Mrs. Sörby when they've sat here of an afternoon whispering and gossiping? And Hedvig's all ears, I can tell you! Perhaps that deed of gift wasn't such a surprise-packet, after all. In fact, I believe I overheard something of the sort.

GREGERS. What's come over you?

HJALMAR. I've had my eyes opened. You've only to wait a little longer, and you'll see that the deed of gift is only the beginning. Mrs. Sörby has always made much of Hedvig. And now she's in a position to do whatever she likes for the child. They can take her away from me at any moment they choose.

GREGERS. Hedvig would never leave you.

HJALMAR. Don't be too sure of that. If they come with their hands full of gold and beckon her. . . . And I have loved her so unspeakably! I should have counted it my greatest blessing to take her tenderly by the hand and lead her, as one leads a frightened child through some great, dark, empty room. But now I feel so bitterly sure that the poor photographer in his humble attic has never been anything to her. She has only been cunning enough to keep on the right side of him until the time was ripe.

GREGERS. You don't really believe that, Hjalmar.

HJALMAR. That's the terrifying part of it—I don't know what to believe—I never shall know. But how can it be otherwise? Why, they've only to come laden with gifts and say to her: "Leave him—the right life for you is with us——"

GREGERS (*quickly*). Well, what then?

HJALMAR. And if I were to ask her: Hedvig, are you willing to forgo that life for me? (*Laughing derisively.*) No, thank you! You'd soon hear what I'd get for an answer!

(*Sound of a shot in the attic.*)

GREGERS (*joyfully*). Hjalmar!

HJALMAR. Yes, listen to him! Shooting—at a time like this!

(*Enter GINA from parlour.*)

GINA. Oh, Hjalmar, there's Grandpa shooting away in there again—and all by himself too.

HJALMAR. I'd better just go and have a look. (*Starts towards the attic.*)

GREGERS (*quickly and emotionally*). Wait a moment: d'you know what that was?

HJALMAR. Yes, of course I do.

GREGERS. No, you don't. But I do. That was the proof you wanted.

HJALMAR. Proof? What proof?

GREGERS. It was a child's sacrifice. She's got your father to shoot the wild duck.

HJALMAR. Shoot the wild duck?

GINA. Well, of all things!

HJALMAR. But what for?

GREGERS. She wanted to sacrifice her greatest treasure for you—and then, she thought, surely you would come to love her again.

HJALMAR (*emotionally*). Oh—poor child!

GINA. The things she thinks of!

GREGERS. She wanted only your love again, Hjalmar—without it she felt she couldn't live.

GINA (*tearfully*). There—now you can see for yourself, Hjalmar.

HJALMAR. Gina—where is she?

GINA. Poor little soul—sitting out there

all alone in the kitchen, I shouldn't wonder.

HJALMAR (*crossing quickly to kitchen door and flinging it open*). Hedvig—come here. Come to me! (*Looking round.*) She's not here.

GINA. Then she must be in her own little room.

(*Exit* HJALMAR *into kitchen.*)

HJALMAR (*offstage*). No, she's not here either.

(*Entering.*) She must have gone out.

GINA. Yes—you know you wouldn't have her anywhere in the house.

HJALMAR. If only she'd come back now, so that I could tell her—everything'll be all right now, Gregers—now I believe we *can* make a fresh start.

GREGERS (*quietly*). I knew it. I knew all along the child would bring it about.

(*Enter* OLD EKDAL *from bedroom. He is in full uniform and buckling on his sword.*)

HJALMAR (*astonished*). Father! Are you in there?

GINA. Have you been shooting in your room?

OLD EKDAL (*crossing, reproachfully*). So you go shooting on your own—eh, Hjalmar?

HJALMAR (*anxious and bewildered*). Then it wasn't you who fired that shot in the attic?

OLD EKDAL. *I* fired?—H'm.

GREGERS (*almost shouting to* HJALMAR). She shot the wild duck herself?

HJALMAR. What's that? (*Rushing to attic door, pulling it aside, looking in and calling*). Hedvig!

GINA (*joining* HJALMAR). Oh God! What's happened?

HJALMAR (*entering attic*). She's lying on the floor!

GREGERS. Hedvig—on the floor? (*Joins* HJALMAR.)

GINA (*simultaneously*). Hedvig! (*In attic.*) Oh no! no—no. . . !

OLD EKDAL. Ah-ha! So she had to go shooting too!

(HJALMAR *and* GREGERS *bring* HEDVIG *into the studio. The pistol is still gripped in her right hand, which is hanging down. They lay her on the sofa.*)

HJALMAR. The pistol must have gone off in her hand. She's hurt. Get help quickly—be quick!

(GINA *runs out by landing door.*)

GINA (*calling*). Doctor Relling! Doctor Relling! Quickly! Come quickly, Doctor Relling!

OLD EKDAL (*quietly*). Forests get their own back.

HJALMAR (*on his knees beside* HEDVIG). She'll come round in a minute, you'll see—she'll be all right—I'm sure she will—she'll——

(*Enter* GINA *by landing door.*)

GINA (*crossing quickly to them*). Is she badly hurt? Where? I can't see——

(*Enter* RELLING *hurriedly followed by* MOLVIK, *whose open coat reveals that he has neither waistcoat nor tie.*)

RELLING. What's wrong?

GINA. Hedvig's hurt herself shooting.

HJALMAR. Quickly, Relling——

RELLING. Shooting?

(*Moves table a little, stoops over* HEDVIG *and begins to examine her.*)

HJALMAR (*looking anxiously up at* RELLING). It's not serious, is it, Relling? Is it? She's hardly bleeding at all. There's no danger is there?

RELLING. How did it happen?

HJALMAR. I've no idea.

GINA. She wanted to shoot the wild duck.

RELLING. The wild duck?

HJALMAR. The pistol must have gone off in her hand.

RELLING. H'm—I see.

OLD EKDAL. Forests get their own back. . . . Well—I'm not afraid of 'em. . . .

(*Exit into attic, pulling door to behind him.*)

HJALMAR. Well, Relling—why don't you speak?

RELLING. She's shot in the breast.

HJALMAR. Yes, but she's coming to!

RELLING. Surely you can see that Hedvig's dead?

GINA (*bursting into tears*). Oh, my baby—my little girl . . . Hedvig. . . .

GREGERS (*huskily*). On the ocean-bed. . . .

HJALMAR (*jumping up*). No—no, she must live! She *must* live! Oh—Relling—for God's sake! Just so that I can tell her now I loved her all the time!

RELLING. The shot must have entered the heart. There's internal haemorrhage. Death must have been instantaneous.

HJALMAR. And I! I drove her away from me as if she were an animal! And then, frightened, she crept into the attic and died for love of me! (*Sobbing.*) Never to be able to make it up to her! Never to be able to tell her—— (*Clenching his fists.*) Oh thou who art in heaven —if thou *art* there—why hast thou done this to me!

GINA. Sssh! Sssh! Don't say such things. Perhaps, when all's said and done —we'd no right to keep her. . . .

MOLVIK. The maid is not dead, but sleepeth.

RELLING. Bosh!

HJALMAR (*crossing calmly to sofa, folding his arms and looking down at* HEDVIG). She lies there so stiff and still. . . .

RELLING (*trying to take the pistol from her hand*). She's got hold of it very tight—very tight. . . .

GINA. No—no, Doctor, don't break her fingers—leave it.

HJALMAR. She shall take it with her.

GINA. Yes, leave it. But the child mustn't lie here to be made a show of. She shall go into her own little room. Help me with her, Hjalmar.

(GINA *and* HJALMAR *lift* HEDVIG *and cross with her towards kitchen.*)

HJALMAR. Oh, Gina—Gina—can you bear it?

GINA. We must help each other. Now, at any rate, she belongs to both of us.

MOLVIK (*stretching out his arms and mumbling*). Blessed be the Lord—earth to earth—ashes to ashes—dust——

RELLING (*in a fierce undertone*). Be quiet, you fool—you're drunk.

(*Exit* HJALMAR *and* GINA *by kitchen door with* HEDVIG. RELLING *follows them with his eyes, then crosses and shuts the door after them.*

Exit MOLVIK *stealthily by landing door.*)

(*Turning to* GREGERS.) Nothing will ever induce me to believe that that shot was an accident.

GREGERS (*his self-possession gone: hoarsely*). No one can say how this terrible thing happened.

RELLING. There are powder marks on her dress. She must have put the muzzle to her breast and fired.

GREGERS. Hedvig hasn't died in vain. Didn't you see how sorrow brought out all that is noble in him?

RELLING. Most people show a certain nobility in the presence of death. But how long d'you suppose it'll last with him?

GREGERS. It will last all his life—and grow greater.

RELLING. Six months from now little Hedvig will be no more to him than an exquisite theme for declamation.

GREGERS. And you dare to say that of Hjalmar Ekdal?

RELLING. We'll talk about it again when the first grass has withered on her grave. Then you'll hear him holding forth about "the beloved child untimely ripped from her father's heart." Then you'll see him soaking himself in warm floods of sentimentality, self-admiration and self-pity. You wait and see!

GREGERS. If you're right and I'm wrong, then life's not worth living.

RELLING. Oh, life wouldn't be so bad really, if we could only get rid of those infernal duns, who keep on badgering us poor folk with the claims of the ideal.

GREGERS (*staring in front of him*). In that case, I'm glad my destiny is what it is.

RELLING. Pardon me—but what *is* your destiny?

GREGERS (*turning to landing door*). To be the thirteenth at table.

RELLING. I can well believe it!

Curtain

MARY McCARTHY: *The Will and Testament of Ibsen*

Reprinted from *Sights and Spectacles* by Mary McCarthy, by permission of Farrar, Straus & Cudahy, Inc. Copyright © 1956 by Mary McCarthy.

GINA. Wasn't that a queer thing to say—that he'd like to be a dog?
HEDWIG. I tell you what, Mother. I think he meant something else by that.
GINA. What else could he mean?
HEDWIG. Well, I don't know; but it was as though he meant something else all the time—and not what he said.

THIS SHORT CATECHISM—FROM THE SECOND ACT OF *THE WILD Duck*—is at first sight only a sort of road sign to the audience to look out for curves ahead. Hjalmar Ekdal's wife and daughter are discussing his friend, Gregers, the

meddling fanatic who has inserted himself into the family speaking a dark language and pressing what he calls the claim of the ideal. In the scene just before he has expressed the wish to be a dog—an "extraordinarily clever dog. The kind that goes to the bottom after wild duck when they dive down and bite fast hold of the weeds and the tangle down in the mud." Translated out of this idiom into plain speech, this means that Gregers sees himself as the rescuer of the household which his father (the hunter) has wounded and sent down into the depths. These depths, ironically, are located in an attic, where Hjalmar, who plays the flute and has a windy, "artistic" personality, also plays at being a professional photographer and inventor while his wife does the hard work. In the neighboring garret room, behind a curtain, Hjalmar's disgraced, drunken old father, wearing a brown wig and his lieutenant's uniform, plays at being a hunter with an old double-barreled pistol, some barnyard fowls, pigeons, rabbits, and a real wild duck. Father and son "go hunting" in this make-believe forest, which is rather like photographers' scenery. Hedwig, the percipient little girl, who is not Hjalmar's real daughter but the illegitimate child of Gregers' father, is going blind. This blindness is a metaphor for the state of darkened self-deception in which the little family lives. Gregers believes that he has the duty to *open Hjalmar's eyes* to the true facts of his marriage. At the house of Gregers' father, who is also los-

ing his sight, they are drinking Tokay wine and playing Blind Man's Buff.

In short, as Hedwig indicates to her uninstructed mother, the dramatist means something else all the time and not what he says. Everything, Hedwig precociously understands, is symbolic. The real wild duck is the child, Hedwig, who picks up Gregers' "loaded" suggestion and shoots herself. The tragic climax of *The Wild Duck* is brought about, thus, by an act of over-interpretation. Gregers, for once, was speaking literally when he said to the little girl: "But suppose, now, that you of your own free will, sacrificed the wild duck for *his* sake?" But Hedwig, confused and terrified the next morning by her supposed father's harshness (for Hjalmar's eyes have at last been opened), thinks that she has finally grasped Gregers' under-meaning and, presuming that she is the "sacrifice" alluded to, goes into the garret room and puts the pistol to her breast.

This ending, like so many of Ibsen's dramatic finales ("The mill race! The mill race!"), seems a little heavy and strained, like the last crashing chords of movie music. Yet it is utterly just. The child's suggestibility has a semantic grounding. She has been led by the Higher Critics around her to look for the real reality under the surface of language—that is, to schematize her life as she lives it. Gregers, with his "claim of the ideal," Hjalmar, with his talk of "a task in life," are both inveterate schematizers, one a truth-speaker, the other an aesthetician. As his wife says of Hjalmar, "Surely you realize, Mr. Werle, that my husband isn't one of those ordinary photographers." Everything has conspired to make Hedwig distrust the *ordinary* way of looking at things. In a peculiarly sinister scene in the third act, Gregers has been talking to Hedwig about the garret room where the wild duck lives. She tells him that sometimes the whole room and all the things in it seem to her like "the ocean's depths," and then she adds: "But that's so silly."

GREGERS. No, you mustn't say that.
HEDWIG. It is; because it's only an attic.
GREGERS. (*looking hard at her*). Are you so sure of that?
HEDWIG. (*astonished*). That it's an attic?
GREGERS. Yes. Do you know that for certain?
(*Hedwig is silent, looking at him with an open mouth.*)

Gregers preaches mysteries. Hjalmar's daily conversation is a flow of oratory. He always speaks of his brown-wigged bald father as "the white-haired old man." And his pretended "purpose in life" is a sort of parody of Gregers' "purpose to live for." Hjalmar too conceives of himself as a savior, the rescuer of his father. "Yes, I will rescue that ship-wrecked man. For he was ship-wrecked when the storm broke loose on him. . . . That pistol there, my friend—the one we use to shoot rabbits with—it has played its part in the tragedy of the House of Ekdal." Again, a flight of metaphors, more disjointed and *ad libitum* in Hjalmar's case, a fact which points to the difference between the two rhetoricians. Hjalmar improvises idly on the instrument of language, but Gregers is in earnest, with his single unifying metaphor of the duck and the bird dog and the hunter, which he pursues to the fearful end.

The men are poet-idealists; Hedwig is a budding poetess. Gina, the uneducated wife, belongs to the prosy multitude that was patronized earlier in the century by Wordsworth: "A primrose by the river's brim, A yellow primrose was to him. And it was nothing more." "That there blessed wild duck," she exclaims. "The fuss there is over it!" When Gregers, true to his metaphor, speaks of the "swamp vapor" that is morally poisoning the Ekdal household, Gina retorts: "Lord knows there's no smell of swamps here, Mr. Werle; I air the place out every blessed day."

The Wild Duck was written in the middle of Ibsen's career, after *Pillars of Society, A Doll's House, Ghosts, An Enemy of the People* and before the sequence of plays beginning with *Rosmersholm*. Ibsen regarded it as a departure from his earlier work, and it is often taken to be a satiric repudiation of "the Ibsenites" or even of Ibsen himself as a crusading social dramatist. In the figure of Gregers Werle, an ugly man in a countrified gray suit who appears on his mission of truth to rip the veil of illusion from a satisfied household, it is certainly possible to see a cruel self-portrait of the dramatic author who sought to "let in the air" on the stuffy Norwegian community, to expose its hypocrisy and commercial chicanery, its enslavement to a notion of duty and to a sentimentalized picture of family life. Gregers Werle's harping on the concept of "a true marriage," which shall not be based on lies and concealment, is certainly a mocking echo of the doctrines of *Ghosts* and *A Doll's House*. Moreover, Gregers Werle has been a radical before the opening of the play, and Ibsen, though he was a stock figure of respectability in private life, looked upon himself as a radical, even an anarchist, and throughout his plays, up to the very end, there is a doctrinal insistence on freedom and the necessity of self-realization that today has a somewhat period and moralistic flavor, as though the notion of duty, reappearing in the guise of Duty to Oneself, had become, if anything, more puritan, more rigid, more sternly forbidding, than the notion of duty to God or family or bourgeois custom. If Gregers Werle is Ibsen in his tendentious and polemical aspect, then indeed he is a demon that Ibsen is trying to cast out through the exorcism of this play—a grotesque and half-pathetic demon, in that he will never understand anything concrete, a demon, in fact, of abstraction who bursts into the play with his ugly face and ugly name like some parochial incorruptible Robespierre whose activities are circumscribed by a sad fate to the reform of a single bohemian family. But if Gregers Werle represents the demand for truth in its ultimate, implacable form, then the message of the play is, as some critics have said, cynical and nihilistic, since the converse of Gregers is a Dr. Relling, a lodger downstairs who believes that lies and illusions are necessary to human survival.

A softer reading of Ibsen's intention suggests that Gregers represents only the eternal interfering busybody, but this reduces the play to a platitude—an object-lesson in what happens when an outsider tries to tell married people how to run their lives. Shaw's opinion was that Gregers is simply a particularly dangerous case of idealism and duty on the rampage, and according to Shaw's thesis Ibsen spent his life doing doughty battle against the joint forces of duty and idealism—the vested interests of the day. But Ibsen was a more divided nature than Shaw allowed for, and the battle was within.

Ibsen is not an attractive personality, and his work has, intermittently, a curious confessional closet-smell, as though he were using his play-writing as a form of psychotherapy. This is especially noticeable in *The Master Builder,* where the hero is Ibsen in a symbolic disguise. The master builder (read sound dramatic craftsman) has first built churches (the early poetic plays), then houses for people to live in (the social dramas), and is finally erecting houses with steeples (the late, symbolic plays). This hero, Master Solness, is very darkly motivated; there has been a fire, years ago, through which, indirectly, he and his wife lost their children, but which, at the same time, permitted him to start on his successful career as a builder and real-estate developer. Now he is obsessed with jealousy of younger men in his profession, and he is suffering from a failure of nerve, which is connected with the fire, perhaps, or with his wife's compulsive sense of duty and her invalidism or with his abandonment of church architecture. The play is strangely thin, more like a scenario with several writers contributing suggestions in a story conference than like a finished play, and throughout its jerky development, there is a sense of something elusive, as though Ibsen, again, like Gregers Werle, meant something else all the time and not what he said. There is the same odd feeling in *Rosmersholm,* which is full of disjointed references, like the talk of an insane person—what are those white

horses, really, and what is the mill race, and what is that quest for total innocence, on which the play seems to turn and yet not to turn?

The idea of guilt for some sin of the past, a sin, even, of the fathers, plays a great part in Ibsen. Like many of his characters, he has a secret in his early life—a poor girl whom he got in trouble and left to fend for herself. Hereditary disease, illegitimacy, the death of children haunt the Ibsen world; they are all in *The Wild Duck.* In the early plays, the guilt or the sin is localized; we know what the protagonist has done, in the past, which will spring the trap on him. But in the later plays, starting with *Rosmersholm,* the guilt has become diffuse, and it is no longer clear what is the matter. A kind of corny symbolism replaces the specific fact in the mechanism of the plot—white horses, steeples, trolls, a sailor, a mermaid, and the sea and a ring. And these symbols, which are only vague portents, correspond to a vague ache or yearning in the breasts of the principal characters, who talk about themselves distractedly, as though they were relating their symptoms in a session of group analysis. *Hedda Gabler* is an exception; next to *The Wild Duck,* it is Ibsen's most successful play. Hedda does not discuss herself; the General's daughter is too haughty for that. Instead, she behaves, and the subject of the play is visibly present, as it was in *The Doll's House,* as it still is in *The Wild Duck.* Her suicide at the end is less convincing than her burning of the manuscript, and her burning of the manuscript is less convincing than the transfixing moment in the first act when she pretends to think that the aunt's new hat, lying on the sofa, is the servant's old bonnet. But Ibsen is not very good at making big events happen; he is better at the small shocking event, the psychopathology of everyday life: Hedda and her husband's aunt's hat, Nora, when she nonchalantly pushes off the sewing on her poor widowed friend, Christine, Hjalmar, when he talks himself into letting Hedwig with her half-blind eyes do his retouching for him so that he can go off and play hunter with his father in the attic, Hjalmar cutting his father at the Werle soirée, Hjalmar eating butter obliviously while his hungry daughter watches him. These are the things one knows oneself to be capable of. If the larger gestures are less credible in Ibsen, this is possibly because of his very success in the realistic convention, which implies a norm of behavior on the part of its guilty citizens within their box-like living rooms. The realistic convention requires credibility, that is, a statistical norm; the audience must believe that the people on the stage are more or less like themselves, no worse and no better, in short, they are ordinary, restrained by cowardice or public opinion from stooping too low or rising too high. The faculty for determining likelihood or credibility becomes more and more highly developed—a sensitized measuring instrument—as a society becomes more homogeneous and parochial and less stratified in terms of class.

But this very ordinariness, this exaction of truth to life, is a limitation on an artist, especially on one with "titanic" ambitions, like Ibsen. And this is where symbolism enters, as a device to deepen or heighten the realistic drama while keeping it within the frame of the three-wall stage. Symbolic thinking was already natural to him, as *Peer Gynt* and *Brand* indicate. Here, however, it was used in the old-fashioned way, to sustain a philosophical argument, that is, to make abstractions concrete and visible, with the text of the play serving as a kind of libretto to the music of the thought behind it. But starting with *Pillars of Society,* Ibsen began to reverse the process—to make the concrete abstract, in the "coffin-ships," whose rotting hulls are supposed to symbolize the whole of Norwegian society. But the temptation of this new, allusive method (the method described by Hedwig in the passage quoted) was that it led to grandiosity and cunning or more precisely, to the kind of schematic thinking exemplified by Gregers Werle; this schematic thinking being really a form of God-identification, in which the symbolist imposes on the concrete, created world his own private design and lays open to question the most primary facts of existence, i.e., whether an attic is "really" an attic or is not in fact a swamp or something else. The allusive, hinting language employed by Gregers is the language of all messianic individuals and interfering, paranoid prophets. And like Hjalmar's

sentimental flow of metaphor, it is the language of bad art, art that is really religion or edification. This type of symbolism is often found in sermons and in addresses by college presidents, who liken the institution to a ship, themselves to the pilot at the helm, etc.

Ibsen sees all this in Gregers, and he sees, furthermore, that Gregers is incurable. In his last speech of the play, Gregers has merely shifted metaphors: "GREGERS (*looking in front of him*). In that case, I am glad my destiny is what it is. RELLING. May I ask—what *is* your destiny? GREGERS (*on the point of going*). To be thirteenth at table." This cryptic and portentous remark means something more than it says, evidently—either that the speaker is going to commit suicide or that he sees himself from henceforth as the odd, unassimilable man, the bird of ill omen, and that he finds a mysterious satisfaction in the picture.

Odious, baneful creature. And yet one cannot throw off the feeling that Gregers is something more than a repudiation of an earlier stage in the author's development. As in *The Master Builder,* where Solness is fond of likening himself fatly to a troll, there is a sense of confession here which lingers in that last remark and far from rounding off the play leaves it hanging, like an unanswered doubt. The fact is, in any case, that Ibsen, if he did unburden himself of a certain amount of self-dislike through the medium of Gregers, did not follow this up with any reforms. Quite the contrary. In the light of the later plays, this confession appears as a sort of indulgence bought for all future sins. The wild duck in the attic is revived as the carp in the pond of *The Lady from the Sea,* and here it is the *sympathetic* characters who hint that the carp is "really" a symbol of themselves in their brackish village. The pietistic talk of a "task" or a "purpose in life," which has already been heard in *A Doll's House,* is not silenced by the pistol shot in *The Wild Duck;* it breaks out again, irrepressibly, in *Rosmersholm,* in *The Lady from the Sea,* and even in *Hedda Gabler;* once more it is the sympathetic characters who voice the notions of Gregers and Hjalmar and who allegorize themselves as instruments of a hidden Will. The plays grow more grandiose as the symbolic content inflates them, and the scenery changes to cliffs and mountain tops that evoke the painted canvas settings of Hjalmar's photographic studio.

No doubt there is a good deal of bathetic "studio" art in all the great late nineteenth-century writers, with the exception of Tolstoy. It is in Dickens and George Eliot and Dostoevsky, certainly; they paid for being titans and for the power to move a mass audience by a kind of auto-intoxication or self-hypnosis that allowed them to manipulate their emotions like a stage hand cranking out a snowstorm from a machine containing bits of paper. This effect of false snow falling on a dramatic scene is more noticeable in Ibsen than in any of his great coevals, and he left it as his legacy to the American school of playwrights, to O'Neill and now Tennessee Williams, Arthur Miller, and William Inge. (Shaw, who considered himself indebted to Ibsen, never learned anything from him, for he did not work in the realistic convention,

though he may not always have been aware of the fact.) If Ibsen's followers are not better than they are, this may be partly because the master, compared to the great architect-novelists of his period, was only a master builder. The "Freudian" character of his symbols has often been remarked upon, and perhaps his most important contribution was clinical: he was the first to put a neurotic woman—Hedda, Ellida Wangel, Mrs. Solness, Nora—on the stage.

But his work, viewed as a whole, seems at once repetitive and inchoate. Twice, in *Hedda Gabler* and *The Wild Duck,* he created a near-masterpiece. The rest of his career appears as a series of false starts and reverses in an interior conversation that keeps lapsing into reverie. The goal of all Ibsen's heroes and heroines—self-realization—looms throughout his plays like one of his symbolic mountain peaks, which the toiling author himself could never reach.

FROM HIS BIRTH, STRINDBERG'S EXISTENCE SEEMS TO

August Strindberg 1849-1912

have been haunted. His father, a bankrupt Stockholm manufacturer of aristocratic descent, and his mother, an ex-barmaid, had lived together without benefit of marriage until shortly before August was born. His home life was one of poverty, overcrowding, and neglect, tinctured with the religious fanaticism of a grandmother. The death of his mother when August was thirteen and his father's rapid remarriage further aggravated Strindberg's hypersensitivity. In later years he was obsessed with a savage anti-feminism, hating women yet hopelessly dependent on them. His instability became apparent early in his life. Beginning as a lay preacher, he then turned to private tutoring; discharged as a tutor, he enrolled in the University at Upsala. Here financial difficulties forced his withdrawal, and he became a public-school teacher. He took to alcohol, and further instability followed as he tried first the study of medicine, then acting, and finally writing. Success with a verse drama earned him a University scholarship, but he failed his examinations; he returned to Stockholm and a variety of odd jobs. In 1875 he began an affair with an older married woman, Baroness Wrangel, who obtained a divorce and married Strindberg. This was the first of his three tormented marriages and ended in divorce fourteen years later. A second marriage failed, and Strindberg now began to suffer from delusions of persecution and grandeur. He was already famous as the author of plays, novels, and stories and had written his powerful realistic dramas depicting the deadly struggle between men and women: *The Father* (1887), *Miss Julie* (1888), and *Creditors* (1888). For a period Strindberg was genuinely insane, but friendly care led to his recovery, and he returned to writing in another great burst of energy. In plays such as *To Damascus* (Parts I, II–1898; Part III–1904), *The Dream Play* (1902), and *The Ghost Sonata* (1907), Strindberg turned from realism to experimental techniques of symbolism. His misfortunes continued as his third marriage ended in divorce and his attempt to run a theatre failed. In 1911 he discovered that he had cancer. His countrymen now rallied to him with a celebration for his sixty-third birthday, and when he died the following year they honored him with a great public demonstration.

MISS JULIE A Tragedy in One Act

BY AUGUST STRINDBERG ❧ *Translated by Elizabeth Sprigge*

CHARACTERS

MISS JULIE, *aged 25*
JEAN, *the valet, aged 30*
KRISTIN, *the cook, aged 35*

Scene: The large kitchen of a Swedish manor house in a country district in the eighties.

Midsummer eve.

The kitchen has three doors, two small ones into Jean's and Kristin's bedrooms, and a large, glass-fronted double one, opening on to a courtyard. This is the only way to the rest of the house.

Through these glass doors can be seen part of a fountain with a cupid, lilac bushes in flower and the tops of some Lombardy poplars. On one wall are shelves edged with scalloped paper on which are kitchen utensils of copper, iron and tin.

To the left is the corner of a large tiled range and part of its chimney-hood, to the right the end of the servants' dinner table with chairs beside it.

The stove is decorated with birch boughs, the floor strewn with twigs of juniper. On the end of the table is a large Japanese spice jar full of lilac.

There are also an ice-box, a scullery table and a sink. Above the double door hangs a big old-fashioned bell; near it is a speaking-tube.

A fiddle can be heard from the dance in the barn near-by. Kristin is standing at the stove, frying something in a pan. She wears a light-coloured cotton dress and a big apron.

Jean enters, wearing livery and carrying a pair of large riding-boots with spurs, which he puts in a conspicuous place.

JEAN. Miss Julie's crazy again to-night, absolutely crazy.

KRISTIN. Oh, so you're back, are you?

JEAN. When I'd taken the Count to the station, I came back and dropped in at the Barn for a dance. And who did I see there but our young lady leading off with the gamekeeper. But the moment she sets eyes on me, up she rushes and invites me to waltz with her. And how she waltzed—I've never seen anything like it! She's crazy.

KRISTIN. Always has been, but never so bad as this last fortnight since the engagement was broken off.

JEAN. Yes, that was a pretty business, to be sure. He's a decent enough chap, too, even if he isn't rich. Oh, but they're choosy! (*Sits down at the end of the table.*) In any case, it's a bit odd that our young—er—lady would rather stay at home with the yokels than go with her father to visit her relations.

KRISTIN. Perhaps she feels a bit awkward, after that bust-up with her fiancé.

JEAN. Maybe. That chap had some guts, though. Do you know the sort of thing that was going on, Kristin? I saw it with my own eyes, though I didn't let on I had.

KRISTIN. You saw them . . . ?

JEAN. Didn't I just! Came across the pair of them one evening in the stable-yard. Miss Julie was doing what she called "training" him. Know what that was? Making him jump over her riding-whip—the way you teach a dog. He did it twice and got a cut each time for his pains, but when it came to the third go, he snatched the whip out of her hand and broke it into smithereens. And then he cleared off.

KRISTIN. What goings on! I never did!

JEAN. Well, that's how it was with that little affair . . . Now, what have you got for me, Kristin? Something tasty?

KRISTIN (*serving from the pan to his plate*). Well, it's just a little bit of kidney I cut off their joint.

JEAN (*smelling it*). Fine! That's my special delice. (*Feels the plate.*) But you might have warmed the plate.

KRISTIN. When you choose to be finicky you're worse than the Count himself. (*Pulls his hair affectionately.*)

JEAN (*crossly*). Stop pulling my hair. You know how sensitive I am.

KRISTIN. There, there! It's only love, you know.

(JEAN *eats.* KRISTIN *brings a bottle of beer.*)

JEAN. Beer on Midsummer Eve? No thanks! I've got something better than that. (*From a drawer in the table brings out a bottle of red wine with a yellow seal.*) Yellow seal, see! Now get me a glass. You use a glass with a stem, of course, when you're drinking it straight.

KRISTIN (*giving him a wine-glass*). Lord help the woman who gets you for a husband, you old fusser! (*She puts the beer in the ice-box and sets a small saucepan on the stove.*)

JEAN. Nonsense! You'll be glad enough to get a fellow as smart as me. And I don't think it's done you any harm people calling me your fiancé. (*Tastes the wine.*) Good. Very good indeed. But not quite warmed enough. (*Warms the glass in his hand.*) We bought this in Dijon. Four francs the litre without the bottle, and duty on top of that. What are you cooking now? It stinks.

KRISTIN. Some bloody muck Miss Julie wants for Diana.

JEAN. You should be more refined in your speech, Kristin. But why should you spend a holiday cooking for that bitch? Is she sick or what?

KRISTIN. Yes, she's sick. She sneaked out with the pug at the lodge and got in the usual mess. And that, you know, Miss Julie won't have.

JEAN. Miss Julie's too high-and-mighty in some respects, and not enough in others, just like her mother before her. The Countess was more at home in the kitchen and cowsheds than anywhere else, but would she ever go driving with only one horse? She went round with her cuffs filthy, but she had to have the coronet on the cuff-links. Our young lady—to come back to her—hasn't any proper respect for herself or her position. I mean she isn't refined. In the Barn just now she dragged the gamekeeper away from Anna and made him dance with her—no waiting to be asked. We wouldn't do a thing like that. But that's what happens when the gentry try to behave like the common people—they become common . . . Still, she's a fine girl. Smashing! What shoulders! And what—er etcetera!

KRISTIN. Oh come off it! I know what Clara says, and she dresses her.

JEAN. Clara? Pooh, you're all jealous! But I've been out riding with her . . . and as for her dancing!

KRISTIN. Listen, Jean. You will dance with me, won't you, as soon as I'm through?

JEAN. Of course I will.

KRISTIN. Promise?

JEAN. Promise? When I say I'll do a thing I do it. Well, thanks for the supper. It was a real treat. (*Corks the bottle.*)

(JULIE *appears in the doorway, speaking to someone outside.*)

JULIE. I'll be back in a moment. Don't wait.

(JEAN *slips the bottle into the drawer and rises respectfully.* JULIE *enters and joins* KRISTIN *at the stove.*)

Well, have you made it? (KRISTIN *signs that* JEAN *is near them.*)

JEAN (*gallantly*). Have you ladies got some secret?

JULIE (*flipping his face with her handkerchief*). You're very inquisitive.

JEAN. What a delicious smell! Violets!

JULIE (*coquettishly*). Impertinence! Are you an expert of scent too? I must say you know how to dance. Now don't look. Go away. (*The music of a schottische begins.*)

JEAN (*with impudent politeness*). Is it some witches' brew you're cooking on Midsummer Eve? Something to tell your stars by, so you can see your future?

JULIE (*sharply*). If you could see that you'd have good eyes. (*To* KRISTIN.) Put it in a bottle and cork it tight. Come and dance this schottische with me, Jean.

JEAN (*hesitating*). I don't want to be rude, but I've promised to dance this one with Kristin.

JULIE. Well, she can have another,

can't you, Kristin? You'll lend me Jean, won't you?

KRISTIN (*bottling*). It's nothing to do with me. When you're so condescending, Miss, it's not his place to say no. Go on, Jean, and thank Miss Julie for the honour.

JEAN. Frankly speaking, Miss, and no offence meant, I wonder if it's wise for you to dance twice running with the same partner, specially as those people are so ready to jump to conclusions.

JULIE (*flaring up*). What did you say? What sort of conclusions? What do you mean?

JEAN (*meekly*). As you choose not to understand, Miss Julie, I'll have to speak more plainly. It looks bad to show a preference for one of your retainers when they're all hoping for the same unusual favour.

JULIE. Show a preference! The very idea! I'm surprised at you. I'm doing the people an honour by attending their ball when I'm mistress of the house, but if I'm really going to dance, I mean to have a partner who can lead and doesn't make me look ridiculous.

JEAN. If those are your orders, Miss, I'm at your service.

JULIE (*gently*). Don't take it as an order. To-night we're all just people enjoying a party. There's no question of class. So now give me your arm. Don't worry, Kristin. I shan't steal your sweetheart.

(JEAN *gives* JULIE *his arm and leads her out.*

Left alone, KRISTIN *plays her scene in an unhurried, natural way, humming to the tune of the schottische, played on a distant violin. She clears* JEAN's *place, washes up and puts things away, then takes off her apron, brings out a small mirror from a drawer, props it against the jar of lilac, lights a candle, warms a small pair of tongs and curls her fringe. She goes to the door and listens, then turning back to the table finds* MISS JULIE's *forgotten handkerchief. She smells it, then meditatively smooths it out and folds it.*

Enter JEAN.)

JEAN. She really *is* crazy. What a way to dance! With people standing grinning at her too from behind the doors. What's got into her, Kristin?

KRISTIN. Oh, it's just her time coming on. She's always queer then. Are you going to dance with me now?

JEAN. Then you're not wild with me for cutting that one?

KRISTIN. You know I'm not—for a little thing like that. Besides, I know my place.

JEAN (*putting his arm round her waist*). You're a sensible girl, Kristin, and you'll make a very good wife . . .

(*Enter* JULIE, *unpleasantly surprised.*)

JULIE (*with forced gaiety*). You're a fine beau—running away from your partner.

JEAN. Not away, Miss Julie, but as you see, back to the one I deserted.

JULIE (*changing her tone*). You really can dance, you know. But why are you wearing your livery on a holiday? Take it off at once.

JEAN. Then I must ask you to go away for a moment, Miss. My black coat's here. (*Indicates it hanging on the door to his room.*)

JULIE. Are you so shy of me—just over changing a coat? Go into your room then—or stay here and I'll turn my back.

JEAN. Excuse me then, Miss. (*He goes to his room and is partly visible as he changes his coat.*)

JULIE. Tell me, Kristin, is Jean your fiancé? You seem very intimate.

KRISTIN. My fiancé? Yes, if you like. We call it that.

JULIE. Call it?

KRISTIN. Well, you've had a fiancé yourself, Miss, and . . .

JULIE. But we really were engaged.

KRISTIN. All the same it didn't come to anything.

(JEAN *returns in his black coat.*)

JULIE. Très gentil, Monsieur Jean. Très gentil.

JEAN. Vous voulez plaisanter, Madame.

JULIE. Et vous voulez parler français. Where did you learn it?

JEAN. In Switzerland, when I was sommelier at one of the biggest hotels in Lucerne.

JULIE. You look quite the gentleman in that get-up. Charming. (*Sits at the table.*)

JEAN. Oh, you're just flattering me!

JULIE (*annoyed*). Flattering you?

JEAN. I'm too modest to believe you would pay real compliments to a man like me, so I must take it you are exaggerating—that this is what's known as flattery.

JULIE. Where on earth did you learn to make speeches like that? Perhaps you've been to the theatre a lot.

JEAN. That's right. And travelled a lot too.

JULIE. But you come from this neighbourhood, don't you?

JEAN. Yes, my father was a labourer on the next estate—the District Attorney's place. I often used to see you, Miss Julie, when you were little, though you never noticed me.

JULIE. Did you really?

JEAN. Yes. One time specially I remember . . . but I can't tell you about that.

JULIE. Oh do! Why not? This is just the time.

JEAN. No, I really can't now. Another time, perhaps.

JULIE. Another time means never. What harm in now?

JEAN. No harm, but I'd rather not. (*Points to* KRISTIN, *now fast asleep.*) Look at her.

JULIE. She'll make a charming wife, won't she? I wonder if she snores.

JEAN. No, she doesn't, but she talks in her sleep.

JULIE (*cynically*). How do you know she talks in her sleep?

JEAN (*brazenly*). I've heard her. (*Pause. They look at one another.*)

JULIE. Why don't you sit down?

JEAN. I can't take such a liberty in your presence.

JULIE. Supposing I order you to.

JEAN. I'll obey.

JULIE. Then sit down. No, wait a minute. Will you get me a drink first?

JEAN. I don't know what's in the icebox. Only beer, I expect.

JULIE. There's no only about it. My taste is so simple I prefer it to wine.

(JEAN *takes a bottle from the ice-box, fetches a glass and plate and serves the beer.*)

JEAN. At your service.

JULIE. Thank you. Won't you have some yourself?

JEAN. I'm not really a beer-drinker, but if it's an order . . .

JULIE. Order? I should have thought it was ordinary manners to keep your partner company.

JEAN. That's a good way of putting it. (*He opens another bottle and fetches a glass.*)

JULIE. Now, drink my health. (*He hesitates.*) I believe the man really is shy.

(JEAN *kneels and raises his glass with mock ceremony.*)

JEAN. To the health of my lady!

JULIE. Bravo! Now kiss my shoe and everything will be perfect. (*He hesitates, then boldly takes hold of her foot and lightly kisses it.*) Splendid. You ought to have been an actor.

JEAN (*rising*). We can't go on like this, Miss Julie. Someone might come in and see us.

JULIE. Why would that matter?

JEAN. For the simple reason that they'd talk. And if you knew the way their tongues were wagging out there just now, you . . .

JULIE. What were they saying? Tell me. Sit down.

JEAN (*sitting*). No offence meant, Miss, but . . . well, their language wasn't nice, and they were hinting . . . oh, you know quite well what. You're not a child, and if a lady's seen drinking alone at night with a man—and a servant at that —then . . .

JULIE. Then what? Besides, we're not alone. Kristin's here.

JEAN. Yes, asleep.

JULIE. I'll wake her up. (*Rises.*) Kristin, are you asleep? (KRISTIN *mumbles in her sleep.*) Kristin! Goodness, how she sleeps!

KRISTIN (*in her sleep*). The Count's boots are cleaned—put the coffee on— yes, yes, at once . . . (*Mumbles incoherently.*)

JULIE (*tweaking her nose*). Wake up, can't you!

JEAN (*sharply*). Let her sleep.

JULIE. What?

JEAN. When you've been standing at the stove all day you're likely to be tired at night. And sleep should be respected.

JULIE (*changing her tone*). What a nice idea. It does you credit. Thank you for it. (*Holds out her hand to him.*) Now come out and pick some lilac for me.

(*During the following,* KRISTIN *goes sleepily into her bedroom.*)

JEAN. Out with you, Miss Julie?

JULIE. Yes.

JEAN. It wouldn't do. It really wouldn't.

JULIE. I don't know what you mean. You can't possibly imagine that . . .

JEAN. I don't, but others do.

JULIE. What? That I'm in love with the valet?

JEAN. I'm not a conceited man, but such a thing's been known to happen, and to these rustics nothing's sacred.

JULIE. You, I take it, are an aristocrat.

JEAN. Yes, I am.

JULIE. And I am coming down in the world.

JEAN. Don't come down, Miss Julie. Take my advice. No one will believe you came down of your own accord. They'll all say you fell.

JULIE. I have a higher opinion of our people than you. Come and put it to the test. Come on. (*Gazes into his eyes.*)

JEAN. You're very strange, you know.

JULIE. Perhaps I am, but so are you. For that matter everything is strange. Life, human beings, everything, just scum drifting about on the water until it sinks —down and down. That reminds me of a dream I sometimes have, in which I'm on top of a pillar and can't see any way of getting down. When I look down I'm dizzy; I have to get down but I haven't the courage to jump. I can't stay there and I long to fall, but I don't fall. There's no respite. There can't be any peace at all for me until I'm down, right down on the ground. And if I did get to the ground I'd want to be under the ground . . . Have you ever felt like that?

JEAN. No. In my dream I'm lying under a great tree in a dark wood. I want to get up, up to the top of it, and look out over the bright landscape where the sun is shining and rob that high nest of its golden eggs. And I climb and climb, but the trunk is so thick and smooth and it's so far to the first branch. But I know if I can once reach that first branch I'll go to the top just as if I'm on a ladder. I haven't reached it yet, but I shall get there, even if only in my dreams.

JULIE. Here I am chattering about dreams with you. Come on. Only into the park. (*She takes his arm and they go towards the door.*)

JEAN. We must sleep on nine midsummer flowers tonight; then our dreams will come true, Miss Julie. (*They turn at the door. He has a hand to his eye.*)

JULIE. Have you got something in your eye? Let me see.

JEAN. Oh, it's nothing. Just a speck of dust. It'll be gone in a minute.

JULIE. My sleeve must have rubbed against you. Sit down and let me see to it. (*Takes him by the arm and makes him sit down, bends his head back and tries to get the speck out with the corner of her handkerchief.*) Keep still now, quite still. (*Slaps his hand.*) Do as I tell you. Why, I believe you're trembling, big, strong man though you are! (*Feels his biceps.*) What muscles!

JEAN (*warning*). Miss Julie!

JULIE. Yes, Monsieur Jean?

JEAN. Attention. Je ne suis qu'un homme.

JULIE. Will you stay still! There now. It's out. Kiss my hand and say thank you.

JEAN (*rising*). Miss Julie, listen. Kristin's gone to bed now. Will you listen?

JULIE. Kiss my hand first.

JEAN. Very well, but you'll have only yourself to blame.

JULIE. For what?

JEAN. For what! Are you still a child at twenty-five? Don't you know it's dangerous to play with fire?

JULIE. Not for me. I'm insured.

JEAN (*bluntly*). No, you're not. And even if you are, there's still stuff here to kindle a flame.

JULIE. Meaning yourself?

JEAN. Yes. Not because I'm me, but because I'm a man and young and . . .

JULIE. And good-looking? What incredible conceit! A Don Juan perhaps? Or a Joseph? Good Lord, I do believe you are a Joseph!

JEAN. Do you?

JULIE. I'm rather afraid so.

(*JEAN goes boldly up and tries to put his arms round her and kiss her. She boxes his ears.*)

How dare you!

JEAN. Was that in earnest or a joke?

JULIE. In earnest.

JEAN. Then what went before was in earnest too. You take your games too seriously and that's dangerous. Anyhow, I'm tired of playing now and beg leave to return to my work. The Count will want his boots first thing and it's past midnight now.

JULIE. Put those boots down.

JEAN. No. This is my work, which it's my duty to do. But I never undertook to be your playfellow and I never will be. I consider myself too good for that.

JULIE. You're proud.

JEAN. In some ways—not all.

JULIE. Have you ever been in love?

JEAN. We don't put it that way, but I've been gone on quite a few girls. And once I went sick because I couldn't have the one I wanted. Sick, I mean, like those princes in the Arabian Nights who couldn't eat or drink for love.

JULIE. Who was she? (*No answer.*) Who was she?

JEAN. You can't force me to tell you that.

JULIE. If I ask as an equal, ask as a —friend? Who was she?

JEAN. You.

JULIE (*sitting*). How absurd!

JEAN. Yes, ludicrous, if you like. That's the story I wouldn't tell you before, see, but now I will . . . Do you know what the world looks like from below? No, you don't. No more than the hawks and falcons do whose backs one hardly ever sees because they're always soaring up aloft. I lived in a labourer's hovel with seven other children and a pig, out in the grey fields where there isn't a single tree. But from the window I could see the wall round the Count's park with apple-trees above it. That was the Garden of Eden, guarded by many terrible angels with flaming swords. All the same I and the other boys managed to get to the tree of life. Does all this make you despise me?

JULIE. Goodness, all boys steal apples!

JEAN. You say that now, but all the same you do despise me. However, one time I went into the Garden of Eden with my mother to weed the onion beds. Close to the kitchen garden there was a Turkish pavilion hung all over with jasmine and honeysuckle. I hadn't any idea what it was used for, but I'd never seen such a beautiful building. People used to go in and then come out again, and one day the door was left open. I crept up and saw the walls covered with pictures of kings and emperors, and the windows had red curtains with fringes— you know now what the place was, don't you? I . . . (*Breaks off a piece of lilac and holds it for* JEAN *to smell. As he talks,*

she takes it from him.) I had never been inside the manor, never seen anything but the church, and this was more beautiful. No matter where my thoughts went, they always came back—to that place. The longing went on growing in me to enjoy it fully, just once. Enfin, I sneaked in, gazed and admired. Then I heard someone coming. There was only one way out for the gentry, but for me there was another and I had no choice but to take it. (JULIE *drops the lilac on the table.*) Then I took to my heels, plunged through the raspberry canes, dashed across the strawberry beds and found myself on the rose terrace. There I saw a pink dress and a pair of white stockings —it was you. I crawled into a weed pile and lay there right under it among prickly thistles and damp rank earth. I watched you walking among the roses and said to myself: "If it's true that a thief can get to heaven and be with the angels, it's pretty strange that a labourer's child here on God's earth mayn't come in the park and play with the Count's daughter."

JULIE (*sentimentally*). Do you think all poor children feel the way you did?

JEAN (*taken aback, then rallying*). *All* poor children? . . . Yes, of course they do. Of course.

JULIE. It must be terrible to be poor.

JEAN (*with exaggerated distress*). Oh yes, Miss Julie, yes. A dog may lie on the Countess's sofa, a horse may have his nose stroked by a young lady, but a servant . . . (*change of tone*) well, yes, now and then you meet one with guts enough to rise in the world, but how often? Anyhow, do you know what I did? Jumped in the millstream with my clothes on, was pulled out and got a hiding. But the next Sunday, when Father and all the rest went to Granny's, I managed to get left behind. Then I washed with soap and hot water, put my best clothes on and went to church so as to see you. I did see you and went home determined to die. But I wanted to die beautifully and peacefully, without any pain. Then I remembered it was dangerous to sleep under an elder bush. We had a big one in full bloom, so I stripped it and climbed into the oats-bin with the flowers. Have you ever noticed how smooth oats are? Soft to touch as human skin . . . Well, I closed the lid and shut my eyes, fell asleep, and when they woke me I was very ill. But I didn't die, as you see. What I meant by all that, I don't know. There was no hope of winning you—you were simply a symbol of the hopelessness of ever getting out of the class I was born in.

JULIE. You put things very well, you know. Did you go to school?

JEAN. For a while. But I've read a lot of novels and been to the theatre. Besides, I've heard educated folk talking—that's what's taught me most.

JULIE. Do you stand round listening to what we're saying?

JEAN. Yes, of course. And I've heard quite a bit too! On the carriage box or rowing the boat. Once I heard you, Miss Julie, and one of your young lady friends . . .

JULIE. Oh! Whatever did you hear?

JEAN. Well, it wouldn't be nice to repeat it. And I must say I was pretty startled. I couldn't think where you had learnt such words. Perhaps, at bottom, there isn't as much difference between people as one's led to believe.

JULIE. How dare you! We don't behave as you do when we're engaged.

JEAN (looking hard at her). Are you sure? It's no use making out so innocent to me.

JULIE. The man I gave my love to was a rotter.

JEAN. That's what you always say—afterwards.

JULIE. Always?

JEAN. I think it must be always. I've heard the expression several times in similar circumstances.

JULIE. What circumstances?

JEAN. Like those in question. The last time . . .

JULIE (rising). Stop. I don't want to hear any more.

JEAN. Nor did she—curiously enough. May I go to bed now, please?

JULIE (gently). Go to bed on Midsummer Eve?

JEAN. Yes. Dancing with that crowd doesn't really amuse me.

JULIE. Get the key of the boathouse and row me out on the lake. I want to see the sun rise.

JEAN. Would that be wise?

JULIE. You sound as though you're frightened for your reputation.

JEAN. Why not? I don't want to be made a fool of, nor to be sent packing without a character when I'm trying to better myself. Besides, I have Kristin to consider.

JULIE. So now it's Kristin.

JEAN. Yes, but it's you I'm thinking about too. Take my advice and go to bed.

JULIE. Am I to take orders from you?

JEAN. Just this once, for your own sake. Please. It's very late and sleepiness goes to one's head and makes one rash. Go to bed. What's more, if my ears don't deceive me, I hear people coming this way. They'll be looking for me, and if they find us here, you're done for.

(The CHORUS approaches, singing. During the following dialogue the song is heard in snatches, and in full when the peasants enter.)

Out of the wood two women came,
Tridiri-ralla, tridiri-ra.
The feet of one were bare and cold,
Tridiri-ralla-la.

The other talked of bags of gold,
Tridiri-ralla, tridiri-ra.
But neither had a sou to her name,
Tridiri-ralla-la.

The bridal wreath I give to you,
Tridiri-ralla, tridiri-ra.
But to another I'll be true,
Tridiri-ralla-la.

JULIE. I know our people and I love them, just as they do me. Let them come. You'll see.

JEAN. No, Miss Julie, they don't love you. They take your food, then spit at it. You must believe me. Listen to them, just listen to what they're singing . . . No, don't listen.

JULIE (listening). What are they singing?

JEAN. They're mocking—you and me.

JULIE. Oh no! How horrible! What cowards!

JEAN. A pack like that's always cowardly. But against such odds there's nothing we can do but run away.

JULIE. Run away? Where to? We can't get out and we can't go into Kristin's room.

JEAN. Into mine, then. Necessity knows no rules. And you can trust me. I really am your true and devoted friend.

JULIE. But supposing . . . supposing they were to look for you in there?

JEAN. I'll bolt the door, and if they try to break in I'll shoot. Come on. (*Pleading.*) Please come.

JULIE (*tensely*). Do you promise . . . ?

JEAN. I swear!

(*Julie goes quickly into his room and he excitedly follows her.*

Led by the fiddler, the peasants enter in festive attire with flowers in their hats. They put a barrel of beer and a keg of spirits, garlanded with leaves, on the table, fetch glasses and begin to carouse. The scene becomes a ballet. They form a ring and dance and sing and mime: "Out of the wood two women came." Finally they go out, still singing.

JULIE *comes in alone. She looks at the havoc in the kitchen, wrings her hands, then takes out her powder puff and powders her face.*

JEAN *enters in high spirits.*)

JEAN. Now you see! And you heard, didn't you? Do you still think it's possible for us to stay here?

JULIE. No, I don't. But what can we do?

JEAN. Run away. Far away. Take a journey.

JULIE. Journey? But where to?

JEAN. Switzerland. The Italian lakes. Ever been there?

JULIE. No. Is it nice?

JEAN. Ah! Eternal summer, oranges, evergreens . . . ah!

JULIE. But what would we do there?

JEAN. I'll start a hotel. First-class accommodation and first-class customers.

JULIE. Hotel?

JEAN. There's life for you. New faces all the time, new languages—no time for nerves or worries, no need to look for something to do—work rolling up of its own accord. Bells ringing night and day, trains whistling, buses coming and going, and all the time gold pieces rolling on to the counter. There's life for you!

JULIE. For *you*. And I?

JEAN. Mistress of the house, ornament of the firm. With your looks, and your style . . . oh, it's bound to be a success! Terrific! You'll sit like a queen in the office and set your slaves in motion by pressing an electric button. The guests will file past your throne and nervously lay their treasure on your table. You've no idea the way people tremble when they get their bills. I'll salt the bills and you'll sugar them with your sweetest smiles. Ah, let's get away from here! (*Produces a time-table.*) At once, by the next train. We shall be at Malmö at six-thirty, Hamburg eight-forty next morning, Frankfurt-Basle the following day, and Como by the St. Gothard pass in—let's see—three days. Three days!

JULIE. That's all very well. But Jean, you must give me courage. Tell me you love me. Come and take me in your arms.

JEAN (*reluctantly*). I'd like to, but I daren't. Not again in this house. I love you—that goes without saying. You can't doubt that, Miss Julie, can you?

JULIE (*shyly, very feminine*). Miss? Call me Julie. There aren't any barriers between us now. Call me Julie.

JEAN (*uneasily*). I can't. As long as we're in this house, there *are* barriers between us. There's the past and there's the Count. I've never been so servile to anyone as I am to him. I've only got to see his gloves on a chair to feel small. I've only to hear his bell and I shy like a horse. Even now, when I look at his boots, standing there so proud and stiff, I feel my back beginning to bend. (*Kicks the boots.*) It's those old, narrow-minded notions drummed into us as children . . . but they can soon be forgotten. You've only got to get to another country, a republic, and people will bend themselves double before my porter's livery. Yes, double they'll bend themselves, but I shan't. I wasn't born to bend. I've got guts, I've got character, and once I reach that first branch, you'll watch me climb. Today I'm valet, next year I'll be proprietor, in ten years I'll have made a fortune, and then I'll go to Roumania, get myself decorated and I may, I only say *may*, mind you, end up as a Count.

JULIE (*sadly*). That would be very nice.

JEAN. You see in Roumania one can buy a title, and then you'll be a Countess after all. My Countess.

JULIE. What do I care about all that? I'm putting those things behind me. Tell me you love me, because if you don't . . . if you don't, what am I?

JEAN. I'll tell you a thousand times over—later. But not here. No sentimentality now or everything will be lost. We must consider this thing calmly like reasonable people. (*Takes a cigar, cuts and lights it.*) You sit down there and I'll sit here and we'll talk as if nothing has happened.

JULIE. My God, have you no feelings at all?

JEAN. Nobody has more. But I know how to control them.

JULIE. A short time ago you were kissing my shoe. And now . . .

JEAN (*harshly*). Yes, that was then. Now, we have something else to think about.

JULIE. Don't speak to me so brutally.

JEAN. I'm not. Just sensibly. One folly's been committed, don't let's have more. The Count will be back at any moment and we've got to settle our future before that. Now, what do you think of my plans? Do you approve?

JULIE. It seems a very good idea—but just one thing. Such a big undertaking would need a lot of capital. Have you got any?

JEAN (*chewing his cigar*). I certainly have. I've got my professional skill, my wide experience and my knowledge of foreign languages. That's capital worth having, it seems to me.

JULIE. But it won't buy even one railway ticket.

JEAN. Quite true. That's why I need a backer to advance some ready cash.

JULIE. How could you get that at a moment's notice?

JEAN. You must get it, if you want to be my partner.

JULIE. I can't. I haven't any money of my own. (*Pause.*)

JEAN. Then the whole thing's off.

JULIE. And . . . ?

JEAN. We go on as we are.

JULIE. Do you think I'm going to stay under this roof as your mistress? With everyone pointing at me? Do you think I can face my father after this? No. Take me away from here, away from this shame, this humiliation. Oh my God, what have I done? My God, my God! (*Weeps.*)

JEAN. So that's the tune now, is it? What have you done? Same as many before you.

JULIE (*hysterically*). And now you despise me. I'm falling, I'm falling.

JEAN. Fall as far as me and I'll lift you up again.

JULIE. Why was I so terribly attracted to you? The weak to the strong, the falling to the rising? Or was it love? Is that love? Do you know what love is?

JEAN. Do I? You bet I do. Do you think I never had a girl before?

JULIE. The things you say, the things you think!

JEAN. That's what life's taught me, and that's what I am. It's no good getting hysterical or giving yourself airs. We're both in the same boat now. Here, my dear girl, let me give you a glass of something special. (*Opens the drawer, takes out the bottle of wine and fills two used glasses.*)

JULIE. Where did you get that wine?

JEAN. From the cellar.

JULIE. My father's burgundy.

JEAN. Why not, for his son-in-law?

JULIE. And I drink beer.

JEAN. That only shows your taste's not so good as mine.

JULIE. Thief!

JEAN. Are you going to tell on me?

JULIE. Oh God! The accomplice of a petty thief! Was I blind drunk? Have I dreamt this whole night? Midsummer Eve, the night for innocent merrymaking.

JEAN. Innocent, eh?

JULIE. Is anyone on earth as wretched as I am now?

JEAN. Why should *you* be? After such a conquest. What about Kristin in there? Don't you think she has any feelings?

JULIE. I did think so, but I don't any longer. No. A menial is a menial . . .

JEAN. And a whore is a whore.

JULIE (*falling to her knees, her hands clasped*). O God in heaven, put an end to my miserable life! Lift me out of this filth in which I'm sinking. Save me! Save me!

JEAN. I must admit I'm sorry for you. When I was in the onion bed and saw you up there among the roses, I . . . yes, I'll tell you now . . . I had the same dirty thoughts as all boys.

JULIE. You, who wanted to die because of me?

JEAN. In the oats-bin? That was just talk.

JULIE. Lies, you mean.

JEAN (*getting sleepy*). More or less. I think I read a story in some paper about a chimney-sweep who shut himself up in a chest full of lilac because he'd been summonsed for not supporting some brat . . .

JULIE. So this is what you're like.

JEAN. I had to think up something. It's always the fancy stuff that catches the women.

JULIE. Beast!

JEAN. Merde!

JULIE. Now you have seen the falcon's back.

JEAN. Not exactly its *back*.

JULIE. I was to be the first branch.

JEAN. But the branch was rotten.

JULIE. I was to be a hotel sign.

JEAN. And I the hotel.

JULIE. Sit at your counter, attract your clients and cook their accounts.

JEAN. I'd have done that myself.

JULIE. That any human being can be so steeped in filth!

JEAN. Clean it up, then.

JULIE. Menial! Lackey! Stand up when I speak to you.

JEAN. Menial's whore, lackey's harlot, shut your mouth and get out of here! Are you the one to lecture me for being coarse? Nobody of my kind would ever be as coarse as you were tonight. Do you think any servant girl would throw herself at a man that way? Have you ever seen a girl of my class asking for it like that? I haven't. Only animals and prostitutes.

JULIE (*broken*). Go on. Hit me, trample on me—it's all I deserve. I'm rotten. But help me! If there's any way out at all, help me.

JEAN (*more gently*). I'm not denying myself a share in the honour of seducing you, but do you think anybody in my place would have dared look in your direction if you yourself hadn't asked for it? I'm still amazed . . .

JULIE. And proud.

JEAN. Why not? Though I must admit the victory was too easy to make me lose my head.

JULIE. Go on hitting me.

JEAN (*rising*). No. On the contrary, I apologise for what I've said. I don't hit a person who's down—least of all a woman. I can't deny there's a certain satisfaction in finding that what dazzled

one below was just moonshine, that that falcon's back is grey after all, that there's powder on the lovely cheek, that polished nails can have black tips, that the handkerchief is dirty although it smells of scent. On the other hand, it hurts to find that what I was struggling to reach wasn't high and isn't real. It hurts to see you fallen so low you're far lower than your own cook. Hurts like when you see the last flowers of summer lashed to pieces by rain and turned to mud.

JULIE. You're talking as if you're already my superior.

JEAN. I am. I might make you a Countess, but you could never make me a Count, you know.

JULIE. But I am the child of a Count, and you could never be that.

JEAN. True, but I might be the father of Counts if . . .

JULIE. You're a thief. I'm not.

JEAN. There are worse things than being a thief—much lower. Besides, when I'm in a place I regard myself as a member of the family to some extent, as one of the children. You don't call it stealing when children pinch a berry from overladen bushes. (*His passion is roused again.*) Miss Julie, you're a glorious woman, far too good for a man like me. You were carried away by some kind of madness, and now you're trying to cover up your mistake by persuading yourself you're in love with me. You're not, although you may find me physically attractive, which means your love's no better than mine. But I wouldn't be satisfied with being nothing but an animal for you, and I could never make you love me.

JULIE. Are you sure?

JEAN. You think there's a chance? Of my loving you, yes, of course. You're beautiful, refined (*takes her hand*) educated, and you can be nice when you want to be. The fire you kindle in a man isn't likely to go out. (*Puts his arm round her.*) You're like mulled wine, full of spices, and your kisses . . . (*He tries to pull her to him, but she breaks away.*)

JULIE. Let go of me! You won't win me that way.

JEAN. Not that way, how then? Not by kisses and fine speeches, not by planning the future and saving you from shame? How then?

JULIE. How? How? I don't know.
There isn't any way. I loathe you—loathe
you as I loathe rats, but I can't escape
from you.

JEAN. Escape with me.

JULIE (*pulling herself together*).
Escape? Yes, we must escape. But I'm so
tired. Give me a glass of wine. (*He pours
it out. She looks at her watch.*) First we
must talk. We still have a little time.
(*Empties the glass and holds it out for
more.*)

JEAN. Don't drink like that. You'll get
tipsy.

JULIE. What's that matter?

JEAN. What's it matter? It's vulgar
to get drunk. Well, what have you got to
say?

JULIE. We've got to run away, but we
must talk first—or rather, I must, for so
far you've done all the talking. You've
told me about your life, now I want to
tell you about mine, so that we really
know each other before we begin this
journey together.

JEAN. Wait. Excuse my saying so, but
don't you think you may be sorry afterwards if you give away your secrets to
me?

JULIE. Aren't you my friend?

JEAN. On the whole. But don't rely on
me.

JULIE. You can't mean that. But anyway, everyone knows my secrets. Listen.
My mother wasn't well-born; she came of
quite humble people, and was brought up
with all those new ideas of sex-equality
and women's rights and so on. She
thought marriage was quite wrong. So
when my father proposed to her, she said
she would never become his *wife* . . .
but in the end she did. I came into the
world, as far as I can make out, against
my mother's will, and I was left to run
wild, but I had to do all the things a boy
does—to prove women are as good as
men. I had to wear boys' clothes; I was
taught to handle horses—and I wasn't
allowed in the dairy. She made me groom
and harness and go out hunting; I even
had to try to plough. All the men on the
estate were given the women's jobs, and
the women the men's, until the whole
place went to rack and ruin and we were
the laughing-stock of the neighbourhood.
At last my father seems to have come to
his senses and rebelled. He changed

everything and ran the place his own way.
My mother got ill—I don't know what
was the matter with her, but she used to
have strange attacks and hide herself in
the attic or the garden. Sometimes she
stayed out all night. Then came the great
fire which you have heard people talking
about. The house and the stables and the
barns—the whole place burnt to the
ground. In very suspicious circumstances.
Because the accident happened the very
day the insurance had to be renewed, and
my father had sent the new premium, but
through some carelessness of the mes-
senger it arrived too late. (*Refills her
glass and drinks.*)

JEAN. Don't drink any more.

JULIE. Oh, what does it matter? We
were destitute and had to sleep in the
carriages. My father didn't know how to
get money to rebuild, and then my mother
suggested he should borrow from an old
friend of hers, a local brick manufacturer.
My father got the loan and, to his surprise, without having to pay interest. So
the place was rebuilt. (*Drinks.*) Do you
know who set fire to it?

JEAN. Your lady mother.

JULIE. Do you know who the brick
manufacturer was?

JEAN. Your mother's lover?

JULIE. Do you know whose the money
was?

JEAN. Wait . . . no, I don't know that.

JULIE. It was my mother's.

JEAN. In other words, the Count's,
unless there was a settlement.

JULIE. There wasn't any settlement.
My mother had a little money of her own
which she didn't want my father to control, so she invested it with her—friend.

JEAN. Who grabbed it.

JULIE. Exactly. He appropriated it. My
father came to know all this. He couldn't
bring an action, couldn't pay his wife's
lover, nor prove it was his wife's money.
That was my mother's revenge because
he made himself master in his own house.
He nearly shot himself then—at least
there's a rumour he tried and didn't bring
it off. So he went on living, and my
mother had to pay dearly for what she'd
done. Imagine what those five years were
like for me. My natural sympathies were
with my father, yet I took my mother's
side, because I didn't know the facts. I'd
learnt from her to hate and distrust men

—you know how she loathed the whole male sex. And I swore to her I'd never become the slave of any man.

JEAN. And so you got engaged to that attorney.

JULIE. So that he should be my slave.

JEAN. But he wouldn't be.

JULIE. Oh yes, he wanted to be, but he didn't have the chance. I got bored with him.

JEAN. Is that what I saw—in the stable-yard?

JULIE. What did you see?

JEAN. What I saw was him breaking off the engagement.

JULIE. That's a lie. It was I who broke it off. Did he say it was him? The cad.

JEAN. He's not a cad. Do you hate men, Miss Julie?

JULIE. Yes . . . most of the time. But when that weakness comes, oh . . . the shame!

JEAN. Then, do you hate me?

JULIE. Beyond words. I'd gladly have you killed like an animal.

JEAN. Quick as you'd shoot a mad dog, eh?

JULIE. Yes.

JEAN. But there's nothing here to shoot with—and there isn't a dog. So what do we do now?

JULIE. Go abroad.

JEAN. To make each other miserable for the rest of our lives?

JULIE. No, to enjoy ourselves for a day or two, for a week, for as long as enjoyment lasts, and then—to die . . .

JEAN. Die? How silly! I think it would be far better to start a hotel.

JULIE (without listening) . . . die on the shores of Lake Como, where the sun always shines and at Christmas time there are green trees and glowing oranges.

JEAN. Lake Como's a rainy hole and I didn't see any oranges outside the shops. But it's a good place for tourists. Plenty of villas to be rented by—er—honeymoon couples. Profitable business, that. Know why? Because they all sign a lease for six months and all leave after three weeks.

JULIE (naively). After three weeks? Why?

JEAN. They quarrel, of course. But the rent has to be paid just the same. And then it's let again. So it goes on and on,

for there's plenty of love although it doesn't last long.

JULIE. You don't want to die with me?

JEAN. I don't want to die at all. For one thing I like living and for another I consider suicide's a sin against the Creator who gave us life.

JULIE. You believe in God—you?

JEAN. Yes, of course. And I go to church every Sunday. Look here, I'm tired of all this. I'm going to bed.

JULIE. Indeed! And do you think I'm going to leave things like this? Don't you know what you owe the woman you've ruined?

JEAN (taking out his purse and throwing a silver coin on the table). There you are. I don't want to be in anybody's debt.

JULIE (pretending not to notice the insult). Don't you know what the law is?

JEAN. There's no law unfortunately that punishes a woman for seducing a man.

JULIE. But can you see anything for it but to go abroad, get married and then divorce?

JEAN. What if I refuse this mésalliance?

JULIE. Mésalliance?

JEAN. Yes, for me. I'm better bred than you, see! Nobody in my family committed arson.

JULIE. How do you know?

JEAN. Well, you can't prove otherwise, because we haven't any family records outside the Registrar's office. But I've seen your family tree in that book on the drawing-room table. Do you know who the founder of your family was? A miller who let his wife sleep with the King one night during the Danish war. I haven't any ancestors like that. I haven't any ancestors at all, but I might become one.

JULIE. This is what I get for confiding in someone so low, for sacrificing my family honour . . .

JEAN. Dishonour! Well, I told you so. One shouldn't drink, because then one talks. And one shouldn't talk.

JULIE. Oh, how ashamed I am, how bitterly ashamed! If at least you loved me!

JEAN. Look here—for the last time— what do you want? Am I to burst into tears? Am I to jump over your riding whip? Shall I kiss you and carry you off to Lake Como for three weeks, after which . . . What am I to do? What do you want? This is getting unbearable, but that's what comes of playing around with women. Miss Julie, I can see how miserable you are; I know you're going through hell, but I don't understand you. We don't have scenes like this; we don't go in for hating each other. We make love for fun in our spare time, but we haven't all day and all night for it like you. I think you must be ill. I'm sure you're ill.

JULIE. Then you must be kind to me. You sound almost human now.

JEAN. Well, be human yourself. You spit at me, then won't let me wipe it off —on you.

JULIE. Help me, help me! Tell me what to do, where to go.

JEAN. Jesus, as if I knew!

JULIE. I've been mad, raving mad, but there must be a way out.

JEAN. Stay here and keep quiet. Nobody knows anything.

JULIE. I can't. People do know. Kristin knows.

JEAN. They don't know and they wouldn't believe such a thing.

JULIE (hesitating). But—it might happen again.

JEAN. That's true.

JULIE. And there might be—consequences.

JEAN (in panic). Consequences! Fool that I am I never thought of that. Yes, there's nothing for it but to go. At once. I can't come with you. That would be a complete giveaway. You must go alone— abroad—anywhere.

JULIE. Alone? Where to? I can't.

JEAN. You must. And before the Count gets back. If you stay, we know what will happen. Once you've sinned you feel you might as well go on, as the harm's done. Then you get more and more reckless and in the end you're found out. No. You must go abroad. Then write to the Count and tell him everything, except that it was me. He'll never guess that—and I don't think he'll want to.

JULIE. I'll go if you come with me.

JEAN. Are you crazy, woman? "Miss Julie elopes with valet." Next day it would be in the headlines, and the Count would never live it down.

JULIE. I can't go. I can't stay. I'm so tired, so completely worn out. Give me orders. Set me going. I can't think any more, can't act . . .

JEAN. You see what weaklings you are. Why do you give yourselves airs and turn up your noses as if you're the lords of creation? Very well, I'll give you your orders. Go upstairs and dress. Get money for the journey and come down here again.

JULIE (softly). Come up with me.

JEAN. To your room? Now you've gone crazy again. (Hesitates a moment.) No! Go along at once. (Takes her hand and pulls her to the door.)

JULIE (as she goes). Speak kindly to me, Jean.

JEAN. Orders always sound unkind. Now you know. Now you know.

(Left alone, JEAN sighs with relief, sits down at the table, takes out a notebook and pencil and adds up figures, now and then aloud. Dawn begins to break. KRISTIN enters dressed for church, carrying his white dickey and tie.)

KRISTIN. Lord Jesus, look at the state the place is in! What have you been up to? (Turns out the lamp.)

JEAN. Oh, Miss Julie invited the crowd in. Did you sleep through it? Didn't you hear anything?

KRISTIN. I slept like a log.

JEAN. And dressed for church already.

KRISTIN. Yes, you promised to come to Communion with me today.

JEAN. Why, so I did. And you've got my bib and tucker, I see. Come on then. (Sits. KRISTIN begins to put his things on. Pause. Sleepily.) What's the lesson today?

KRISTIN. It's about the beheading of John the Baptist, I think.

JEAN. That's sure to be horribly long. Hi, you're choking me! Oh Lord, I'm so sleepy, so sleepy!

KRISTIN. Yes, what have you been doing up all night? You look absolutely green.

JEAN. Just sitting here talking with Miss Julie.

KRISTIN. She doesn't know what's proper, that one. (Pause.)

JEAN. I say, Kristin.

KRISTIN. What?

JEAN. It's queer really, isn't it, when you come to think of it? Her.

KRISTIN. What's queer?

JEAN. The whole thing. (*Pause.*)

KRISTIN (*looking at the half-filled glasses on the table*). Have you been drinking together too?

JEAN. Yes.

KRISTIN. More shame you. Look me straight in the face.

JEAN. Yes.

KRISTIN. Is it possible? Is it possible?

JEAN (*after a moment*). Yes, it is.

KRISTIN. Oh! This I would never have believed. How low!

JEAN. You're not jealous of her, surely?

KRISTIN. No, I'm not. If it had been Clara or Sophie I'd have scratched your eyes out. But not of her. I don't know why; that's how it is, though. But it's disgusting.

JEAN. You're angry with her, then.

KRISTIN. No. With you. It was wicked of you, very very wicked. Poor girl. And, mark my words, I won't stay here any longer now—in a place where one can't respect one's employers.

JEAN. Why should one respect them?

KRISTIN. You should know since you're so smart. But you don't want to stay in the service of people who aren't respectable, do you? I wouldn't demean myself.

JEAN. But it's rather a comfort to find out they're no better than us.

KRISTIN. I don't think so. If they're no better there's nothing for us to live up to. Oh and think of the Count! Think of him. He's been through so much already. No, I won't stay in the place any longer. A fellow like you too! If it had been that attorney, now, or somebody of her own class . . .

JEAN. Why, what's wrong with . . .

KRISTIN. Oh, you're all right in your own way, but when all's said and done there is a difference between one class and another. No, this is something I'll never be able to stomach. That our young lady who was so proud and so down on men you'd never believe she'd let one come near her should go and give herself to one like you. She who wanted to have poor Diana shot for running after the lodge-keeper's pug. No, I must say . . . ! Well, I won't stay here any longer. On the twenty-fourth of October I quit.

JEAN. And then?

KRISTIN. Well, since you mention it, it's about time you began to look around, if we're ever going to get married.

JEAN. But what am I to look for? I shan't get a place like this when I'm married.

KRISTIN. I know you won't. But you might get a job as porter or caretaker in some public institution. Government rations are small but sure, and there's a pension for the widow and children.

JEAN. That's all very fine, but it's not in my line to start thinking at once about dying for my wife and children. I must say I had rather bigger ideas.

KRISTIN. You and your ideas! You've got obligations too, and you'd better start thinking about them.

JEAN. Don't *you* start pestering me about obligations. I've had enough of that. (*Listens to a sound upstairs.*) Anyway, we've plenty of time to work things out. Go and get ready, now, and we'll be off to church.

KRISTIN. Who's that walking about upstairs?

JEAN. Don't know—unless it's Clara.

KRISTIN (*going*). You don't think the Count could have come back without our hearing him?

JEAN (*scared*). The Count? No, he can't have. He'd have rung for me.

KRISTIN. God help us! I've never known such goings on.

(*Exit.*)

(*The sun has now risen and is shining on the treetops. The light gradually changes until it slants in through the windows.* JEAN *goes to the door and beckons.* JULIE *enters in travelling clothes, carrying a small bird-cage covered with a cloth which she puts on a chair.*)

JULIE. I'm ready.

JEAN. Hush! Kristin's up.

JULIE (*in a very nervous state*). Does she suspect anything?

JEAN. Not a thing. But, my God, what a sight you are!

JULIE. Sight? What do you mean?

JEAN. You're white as a corpse and—pardon me—your face is dirty.

JULIE. Let me wash, then. (*Goes to the sink and washes her face and hands.*) There. Give me a towel. Oh! The sun is rising!

JEAN. And that breaks the spell.

JULIE. Yes. The spell of Midsummer

Eve . . . But listen, Jean. Come with me. I've got the money.

JEAN (*skeptically*). Enough?

JULIE. Enough to start with. Come with me. I can't travel alone today. It's Midsummer Day, remember. I'd be packed into a suffocating train among crowds of people who'd all stare at me. And it would stop at every station while I yearned for wings. No, I can't do that, I simply can't. There will be memories too; memories of Midsummer Days when I was little. The leafy church—birch and lilac—the gaily spread dinner table, relatives, friends—evening in the park—dancing and music and flowers and fun. Oh, however far you run away—there'll always be memories in the baggage car—and remorse and guilt.

JEAN. I will come with you, but quickly now then, before it's too late. At once.

JULIE. Put on your things. (*Picks up the cage.*)

JEAN. No luggage, mind. That would give us away.

JULIE. No, only what we can take with us in the carriage.

JEAN (*fetching his hat*). What on earth have you got there? What is it?

JULIE. Only my greenfinch. I don't want to leave it behind.

JEAN. Well, I'll be damned! We're to take a bird-cage along, are we? You're crazy. Put that cage down.

JULIE. It's the only thing I'm taking from my home. The only living creature who cares for me since Diana went off like that. Don't be cruel. Let me take it.

JEAN. Put that cage down, I tell you —and don't talk so loud. Kristin will hear.

JULIE. No, I won't leave it in strange hands. I'd rather you killed it.

JEAN. Give the little beast here, then, and I'll wring its neck.

JULIE. But don't hurt it, don't . . . no, I can't.

JEAN. Give it here. I *can*.

JULIE (*taking the bird out of the cage and kissing it*). Dear little Serena, must you die and leave your mistress?

JEAN. Please don't make a scene. It's *your* life and future we're worrying about. Come on, quick now!

(*He snatches the bird from her, puts it on a board and picks up a chopper. JULIE turns away.*)

You should have learnt how to kill chickens instead of target-shooting. Then you wouldn't faint at a drop of blood.

JULIE (*screaming*). Kill me too! Kill me! You who can butcher an innocent creature without a quiver. Oh, how I hate you, how I loathe you! There is blood between us now. I curse the hour I first saw you. I curse the hour I was conceived in my mother's womb.

JEAN. What's the use of cursing? Let's go.

JULIE (*going to the chopping-block as if drawn against her will*). No, I won't go yet. I can't . . . I must look. Listen! There's a carriage. (*Listens without taking her eyes off the board and chopper.*) You don't think I can bear the sight of blood. You think I'm so weak. Oh, how I should like to see your blood and your brains on a chopping-block! I'd like to see the whole of your sex swimming like that in a sea of blood. I think I could drink out of your skull, bathe my feet in your broken breast and eat your heart roasted whole. You think I'm weak. You think I love you, that my womb yearned for your seed and I want to carry your offspring under my heart and nourish it with my blood. You think I want to bear your child and take your name. By the way, what is your name? I've never heard your surname. I don't suppose you've got one. I should be "Mrs. Hovel" or "Madam Dunghill." You dog wearing my collar, you lackey with my crest on your buttons! I share you with my cook; I'm my own servant's rival! Oh! Oh! Oh! . . . You think I'm a coward and will run away. No, now I'm going to stay—and let the storm break. My father will come back . . . find his desk broken open . . . his money gone. Then he'll ring that bell— twice for the valet—and then he'll send for the police . . . and I shall tell everything. Everything. Oh how wonderful to make an end of it all—a real end! He has a stroke and dies and that's the end of all of us. Just peace and quietness . . . eternal rest. The coat of arms broken on the coffin and the Count's line extinct . . . But the valet's line goes on in an orphanage, wins laurels in the gutter and ends in jail.

JEAN. There speaks the noble blood!

Bravo, Miss Julie. But now, don't let the cat out of the bag.

(KRISTIN *enters dressed for church, carrying a prayer-book.* JULIE *rushes to her and flings herself into her arms for protection.*)

JULIE. Help me, Kristin! Protect me from this man!

KRISTIN (*unmoved and cold*). What goings-on for a feast day morning! (*Sees the board.*) And what a filthy mess. What's it all about? Why are you screaming and carrying on so?

JULIE. Kristin, you're a woman and my friend. Beware of that scoundrel!

JEAN (*embarrassed*). While you ladies are talking things over, I'll go and shave. (*Slips into his room.*)

JULIE. You must understand. You must listen to me.

KRISTIN. I certainly don't understand such loose ways. Where are you off to in those travelling clothes? And he had his hat on, didn't he, eh?

JULIE. Listen, Kristin. Listen, I'll tell you everything.

KRISTIN. I don't want to know anything.

JULIE. You must listen.

KRISTIN. What to? Your nonsense with Jean? I don't care a rap about that; it's nothing to do with me. But if you're thinking of getting him to run off with you, we'll soon put a stop to that.

JULIE (*very nervously*). Please try to be calm, Kristin, and listen. I can't stay here, nor can Jean—so we must go abroad.

KRISTIN. Hm, hm!

JULIE (*brightening*). But you see, I've had an idea. Supposing we all three go—abroad—to Switzerland and start a hotel together . . . I've got some money, you see . . . and Jean and I could run the whole thing—and I thought you would take charge of the kitchen. Wouldn't that be splendid? Say yes, do. If you come with us everything will be fine. Oh do say yes! (*Puts her arms round* KRISTIN.)

KRISTIN (*coolly thinking*). Hm, hm.

JULIE (*presto tempo*). You've never travelled, Kristin. You should go abroad and see the world. You've no idea how nice it is travelling by train—new faces all the time and new countries. On our way through Hamburg we'll go to the zoo—you'll love that—and we'll go to the theatre and the opera too . . . and when we get to Munich there'll be the museums, dear, and pictures by Rubens and Raphael—the great painters, you know . . . You've heard of Munich, haven't you? Where King Ludwig lived —you know, the king who went mad. . . . We'll see his castles—some of his castles are still just like in fairy-tales . . . and from there it's not far to Switzerland— and the Alps. Think of the Alps, Kristin dear, covered with snow in the middle of summer . . . and there are oranges there and trees that are green the whole year round . . .

(JEAN *is seen in the door of his room, sharpening his razor on a strop which he holds with his teeth and his left hand. He listens to the talk with satisfaction and now and then nods approval.* JULIE *continues, tempo prestissimo.*)

And then we'll get a hotel . . . and I'll sit at the desk, while Jean receives the guests and goes out marketing and writes letters . . . There's life for you! Trains whistling, buses driving up, bells ringing upstairs and downstairs . . . and I shall make out the bills—and I shall cook them too . . . you've no idea how nervous travellers are when it comes to paying their bills. And you—you'll sit like a queen in the kitchen . . . of course there won't be any standing at the stove for you. You'll always have to be nicely dressed and ready to be seen, and with your looks—no, I'm not flattering you— one fine day you'll catch yourself a husband . . . some rich Englishman, I shouldn't wonder—they're the ones who are easy (*slowing down*) to catch . . . and then we'll get rich and build ourselves a villa on Lake Como . . . of course it rains there a little now and then—but —(*dully*)—the sun must shine there too sometimes—even though it seems gloomy —and if not—then we can come home again—come back—(*pause*)—here—or somewhere else . . .

KRISTIN. Look here, Miss Julie, do you believe all that yourself?

JULIE (*exhausted*). Do I believe it?

KRISTIN. Yes.

JULIE (*wearily*). I don't know. I don't believe anything any more. (*Sinks down on the bench; her head in her arms on the table.*) Nothing. Nothing at all.

KRISTIN (*turning to* JEAN). So you meant to beat it, did you?

JEAN (*disconcerted, putting the razor on the table*). Beat it? What are you talking about? You've heard Miss Julie's plan, and though she's tired now with being up all night, it's a perfectly sound plan.

KRISTIN. Oh, is it? If you thought I'd work for that . . .

JEAN (*interrupting*). Kindly use decent language in front of your mistress. Do you hear?

KRISTIN. Mistress?

JEAN. Yes.

KRISTIN. Well, well, just listen to that!

JEAN. Yes, it would be a good thing if you did listen and talked less. Miss Julie is your mistress and what's made you lose your respect for her now ought to make you feel the same about yourself.

KRISTIN. I've always had enough self-respect——

JEAN. To despise other people.

KRISTIN. —not to go below my own station. Has the Count's cook ever gone with the groom or the swineherd? Tell me that.

JEAN. No, you were lucky enough to have a high-class chap for your beau.

KRISTIN. High-class all right—selling the oats out of the Count's stable.

JEAN. You're a fine one to talk—taking a commission on the groceries and bribes from the butcher.

KRISTIN. What the devil . . . ?

JEAN. And now you can't feel any respect for your employers. You, you!

KRISTIN. Are you coming to church with me? I should think you need a good sermon after your fine deeds.

JEAN. No, I'm not going to church today. You can go alone and confess your own sins.

KRISTIN. Yes, I'll do that and bring back enough forgiveness to cover yours too. The Saviour suffered and died on the cross for all our sins, and if we go to Him with faith and a penitent heart, He takes all our sins upon Himself.

JEAN. Even grocery thefts?

JULIE. Do you believe that, Kristin?

KRISTIN. That is my living faith, as sure as I stand here. The faith I learnt as a child and have kept ever since, Miss Julie. "But where sin abounded, grace did much more abound."

JULIE. Oh, if I had your faith! Oh, if . . .

KRISTIN. But you see you can't have it without God's special grace, and it's not given to all to have that.

JULIE. Who is it given to then?

KRISTIN. That's the great secret of the workings of grace, Miss Julie. God is no respecter of persons, and with Him the last shall be first . . .

JULIE. Then I suppose He does respect the last.

KRISTIN (*continuing*) . . . and it is easier for a camel to go through the eye of a needle than for a rich man to enter into the kingdom of God. That's how it is, Miss Julie. Now I'm going—alone, and on my way I shall tell the groom not to let any of the horses out, in case anyone should want to leave before the Count gets back. Goodbye.

(*Exit.*)

JEAN. What a devil! And all on account of a greenfinch.

JULIE (*wearily*). Never mind the greenfinch. Do you see any way out of this, any end to it?

JEAN (*pondering*). No.

JULIE. If you were in my place, what would you do?

JEAN. In your place? Wait a bit. If I was a woman—a lady of rank who had —fallen. I don't know. Yes, I do know now.

JULIE (*picking up the razor and making a gesture*). This?

JEAN. Yes. But *I* wouldn't do it, you know. There's a difference between us.

JULIE. Because you're a man and I'm a woman? What is the difference?

JEAN. The usual difference—between man and woman.

JULIE (*holding the razor*). I'd like to. But I can't. My father couldn't either, that time he wanted to.

JEAN. No, he didn't want to. He had to be revenged first.

JULIE. And now my mother is revenged again, through me.

JEAN. Didn't you ever love your father, Miss Julie?

JULIE. Deeply, but I must have hated him too—unconsciously. And he let me be brought up to despise my own sex, to be half woman, half man. Whose fault is what's happened? My father's, my mother's or my own? My own? I haven't anything that's my own. I haven't one single thought that I didn't get from my father, one emotion that didn't come from my mother, and as for this last idea —about all people being equal—I got that from him, my fiancé—that's why I call him a cad. How can it be my fault? Push the responsibility on to Jesus, like Kristin does? No, I'm too proud and— thanks to my father's teaching—too intelligent. As for all that about a rich person not being able to get into heaven, it's just a lie, but Kristin, who has money in the savings-bank, will certainly not get in. Whose fault is it? What does it matter whose fault it is? In any case I must take the blame and bear the consequences.

JEAN. Yes, but . . . (*There are two sharp rings on the bell.* JULIE *jumps to her feet.* JEAN *changes into his livery.*) The Count is back. Supposing Kristin . . . (*Goes to the speaking-tube, presses it and listens.*)

JULIE. Has he been to his desk yet?

JEAN. This is Jean, sir. (*Listens.*) Yes, sir. (*Listens.*) Yes, sir, very good, sir. (*Listens.*) At once, sir? (*Listens.*) Very good, sir. In half an hour.

JULIE (*in panic*). What did he say? My God, what did he say?

JEAN. He ordered his boots and his coffee in half an hour.

JULIE. Then there's half an hour . . . Oh, I'm so tired! I can't do anything. Can't be sorry, can't run away, can't stay, can't live—can't die. Help me. Order me, and I'll obey like a dog. Do me this last service—save my honour, save his name. You know what I ought to do, but haven't the strength to do. Use your strength and order me to do it.

JEAN. I don't know why—I can't now —I don't understand . . . It's just as if this coat made me—I can't give you orders—and now that the Count has spoken to me—I can't quite explain, but . . . well, that devil of a lackey is bending my back again. I believe if the Count came down now and ordered me to cut my throat, I'd do it on the spot.

JULIE. Then pretend you're him and I'm you. You did some fine acting before, when you knelt to me and played the aristocrat. Or . . . Have you ever seen a hypnotist at the theatre? (*He nods.*) He says to the person "Take the broom," and he takes it. He says "Sweep," and he sweeps . . .

JEAN. But the person has to be asleep.

JULIE (*as if in a trance*). I am asleep already . . . the whole room has turned to smoke—and you look like a stove— a stove like a man in black with a tall hat—your eyes are glowing like coals when the fire is low—and your face is a white patch like ashes. (*The sunlight has now reached the floor and lights up* JEAN.) How nice and warm it is! (*She holds out her hands as though warming them at a fire.*) And so light—and so peaceful.

JEAN (*putting the razor in her hand*). Here is the broom. Go now while it's light—out to the barn—and . . . (*Whispers in her ear.*)

JULIE (*waking*). Thank you. I am going now—to rest. But just tell me that even the first can receive the gift of grace.

JEAN. The first? No, I can't tell you that. But wait . . . Miss Julie, I've got it! You aren't one of the first any longer. You're one of the last.

JULIE. That's true. I'm one of the very last. I *am* the last. Oh! . . . But now I can't go. Tell me again to go.

JEAN. No, I can't now, either. I can't.

JULIE. And the first shall be last.

JEAN. Don't think, don't think. You're taking my strength away too and making me a coward. What's that? I thought I saw the bell move . . . To be so frightened of a bell! Yes, but it's not just a bell. There's somebody behind it—a hand moving it—and something else moving the hand—and if you stop your ears—if you stop your ears—yes, then it rings louder than ever. Rings and rings until you answer—and then it's too late. Then the police come and . . . and . . . (*The bell rings twice loudly.* JEAN *flinches, then straightens himself up.*) It's horrible. But there's no other way to end it . . . Go!

(JULIE *walks firmly out through the door.*)

Curtain

AUGUST STRINDBERG: *Foreword to* Miss Julie

THEATRE HAS LONG SEEMED TO ME — IN COMMON WITH MUCH other art—a *Biblia Pauperum,* a Bible in pictures for those who cannot read what is written or printed; and I see the playwright as a lay preacher peddling the ideas of his time in popular form, popular enough for the middle-classes, mainstay of theatre audiences, to grasp the gist of the matter without troubling their brains too much. For this reason theatre has always been an elementary school for the young, the semi-educated and for women who still have a primitive capacity for deceiving themselves and letting themselves be deceived—who, that is to say, are susceptible to illusion and to suggestion from the author. I have therefore thought it not unlikely that in these days, when that rudimentary and immature thought-process operating through fantasy appears to be developing into reflection, research and analysis, that theatre, like religion, might be discarded as an outworn form for whose appreciation we lack the necessary conditions. This opinion is confirmed by the major crisis still prevailing in the theatres of Europe, and still more by the fact that in those countries of culture, producing the greatest thinkers of the age, namely England and Germany, drama —like other fine arts—is dead.

Some countries, it is true, have attempted to create a new drama by using the old forms with up-to-date contents, but not only has there been insufficient time for these new ideas to be popularized, so that the audience can grasp them, but also people have been so wrought up by the taking of sides that pure, disinterested appreciation has become impossible. One's deepest impressions are upset when an applauding or a hissing majority dominates as forcefully and openly as it can in the theatre. Moreover, as no new form has been devised for these new contents, the new wine has burst the old bottles.

In this play I have not tried to do anything new, for this cannot be done, but only to modernize the form to meet the demands which may, I think, be made on this art today. To this end I chose—or surrendered myself to—a theme which claims to be outside the controversial issues of today, since questions of social climbing or falling, of higher or lower, better or worse, of man and woman, are, have been and will be of lasting interest. When I took this theme from a true story told me some years ago, which made a deep impression, I saw it as a subject for tragedy, for as yet it is tragic to see one favoured by fortune go under, and still more to see a family heritage die out, although a time may come when we have grown so developed and enlightened that we shall view with indifference life's spectacle, now seeming so brutal, cynical and heartless. Then we shall have dispensed with those inferior, unreliable instruments of thought called feelings, which become harmful and superfluous as reasoning develops.

The fact that my heroine rouses pity is solely due to weakness; we cannot resist fear of the same fate overtaking us. The hyper-sensitive spectator may, it is true, go beyond this kind of pity, while the man with belief in the future may actually demand some suggestion for remedying the evil—in other words some kind of policy. But, to begin with, there is no such thing as absolute evil; the downfall of one family is the good fortune of another, which thereby gets a chance to rise, and, fortune being only comparative, the alternation of rising and falling is one of life's principal charms. Also, to the man of policy, who wants to remedy the painful fact that the bird of prey devours the dove, and lice the bird of prey, I should like to put the question: why should it be remedied? Life is not so mathematically idiotic as only to permit the big to eat the small; it happens just as often that the bee kills the lion or at least drives it mad.

That my tragedy depresses many people is their own fault. When we have grown strong as the pioneers of the French revolution, we shall be happy and relieved to see the national parks cleared of ancient rotting trees which have stood too long in the way of others equally entitled to a period of growth—as relieved as we are when an incurable invalid dies.

My tragedy "The Father" was recently criticised for being too sad—as if one wants cheerful tragedies! Everybody is clamouring for this supposed "joy of life," and theatre managers demand farces, as if the joy of life consisted in being ridiculous and portraying all human beings as suffering from St. Vitus's dance or total idiocy. I myself find the joy of life in its strong and cruel struggles, and my pleasure in learning, in adding to my knowledge. For this reason I have chosen for this play an unusual situation, but an instructive one—an exception, that is to say, but a great exception, one proving the rule, which will no doubt annoy all lovers of the commonplace. What will offend simple minds is that my plot is not simple, nor its point of view single. In real life an action—this, by the way, is a somewhat new discovery—is generally caused by a whole series of motives, more or less fundamental, but as a rule the spectator chooses just one of these—the one which his mind can most easily grasp or that does most credit to his intelligence. A suicide is committed. Business troubles, says the man of affairs. Unrequited love, say the women. Sickness, says the invalid. Despair, says the down-and-out. But it is possible that the motive lay in all or none of these directions, or that the dead man concealed his actual motive by revealing quite another, likely to reflect more to his glory.

I see Miss Julie's tragic fate to be the result of many circumstances: the mother's character, the father's mistaken upbringing of the girl, her own nature, and the influence of her fiancé on a weak, degenerate mind. Also, more directly, the festive mood of Midsummer Eve, her father's absence, her monthly indisposi-

tion, her pre-occupation with animals, the excitement of dancing, the magic of dusk, the strongly aphrodisiac influence of flowers, and finally the chance that drives the couple into a room alone—to which must be added the urgency of the excited man.

My treatment of the theme, moreover, is neither exclusively physiological nor psychological. I have not put the blame wholly on the inheritance from her mother, nor on her physical condition at the time, nor on immorality. I have not even preached a moral sermon; in the absence of a priest I leave this to the cook.

I congratulate myself on this multiplicity of motives as being up-to-date, and if others have done the same thing before me, then I congratulate myself on not being alone in my "paradoxes," as all innovations are called.

In regard to the drawing of the characters, I have made my people somewhat "characterless" for the following reasons. In the course of time the word character has assumed manifold meanings. It must have originally signified the dominating trait of the soul-complex, and this was confused with temperament. Later it became the middle-class term for the automaton, one whose nature had become fixed or who had adapted himself to a particular rôle in life. In fact a person who had ceased to grow was called a character, while one continuing to develop—the skilful navigator of life's river, sailing not with sheets set fast, but veering before the wind to luff again—was called characterless, in a derogatory sense, of course, because he was so hard to catch, classify and keep track of. This middle-class conception of the immobility of the soul was transferred to the stage where the middle-class has always ruled. A character came to signify a man fixed and finished: one who invariably appeared either drunk or jocular or melancholy, and characterization required nothing more than a physical defect such as a club-foot, a wooden leg, a red nose; or the fellow might be made to repeat some such phrase as: "That's capital!" or: "Barkis is willin'!" This simple way of regarding human beings still survives in the great Molière. Harpagon is nothing but a miser, although Harpagon might have been not only a miser, but also a first-rate financier, an excellent father and a good citizen. Worse still, his "failing" is a distinct advantage to his son-in-law and his daughter, who are his heirs, and who therefore cannot criticise him, even if they have to wait a while to get to bed. I do not believe, therefore, in simple stage characters; and the summary judgments of authors—this man is stupid, that one brutal, this jealous, that stingy, and so forth—should be challenged by the Naturalists who know the richness of the soul-complex and realise that vice has a reverse side very much like virtue.

Because they are modern characters, living in a period of transition more feverishly hysterical than its predecessor at least, I have drawn my figures vacillating, disintegrated, a blend of old and new. Nor does it seem to me unlikely that, through newspapers and conversations, modern ideas may have filtered down to the level of the domestic servant.

My souls (characters) are conglomerations of past and present stages of civilization, bits from books and newspapers, scraps of humanity, rags and tatters of fine clothing, patched together as is the human soul. And I have added a little evolutionary history by making the weaker steal and repeat the words of the stronger, and by making the characters borrow ideas or "suggestions" from one another.

Miss Julie is a modern character, not that the half-woman, the man-hater, has not existed always, but because now that she has been discovered she has stepped to the front and begun to make a noise. The half-woman is a type who thrusts herself forward, selling herself nowadays for power, decorations, distinctions, diplomas, as formerly for money. The type implies degeneration; it is not a good type and it does not endure; but it can unfortunately transmit its misery, and degenerate men seem instinctively to choose their mates from among such women, and so they breed, producing offspring of indeterminate sex to whom life is torture. But fortunately they perish, either because they cannot come to terms with reality, or because their repressed instincts break out uncontrollably, or again because their hopes of catching up with men are shattered. The type is tragic, revealing a desperate fight against nature, tragic too in its Romantic inheritance now dissipated by Naturalism, which wants nothing but happiness—and for happiness strong and sound species are required.

But Miss Julie is also a relic of the old warrior nobility now giving way to the new nobility of nerve and brain. She is a victim of the discord which a mother's "crime" has produced in a family, a victim too of the day's complaisance, of circumstances, of her own defective constitution, all of which are equivalent to the Fate or Universal Law of former days. The Naturalist has abolished guilt with God, but the consequences of the action—punishment, imprisonment or the fear of it—he cannot abolish, for the simple reason that they remain whether he is acquitted or not. An injured fellow-being is not so complacent as outsiders, who have not been injured, can afford to be. Even if the father had felt impelled to take no vengeance, the daughter would have taken vengeance on herself, as she does here, from that innate or acquired sense of honour which the upper-classes inherit—whether from Barbarism or Aryan forebears, or from the chivalry of the Middle Ages, who knows? It is a very beautiful thing, but it has become a danger nowadays to the preservation of the race. It is the nobleman's *hara-kiri*, the Japanese law of inner conscience which compels him to cut his own stomach open at the insult of another, and which survives in modified form in the duel, a privilege of the nobility. And so the valet Jean lives on, but Miss Julie cannot live without honour. This is the thrall's advantage over the nobleman, that he lacks this fatal preoccupation with honour. And in all of us Aryans there is something of the nobleman, or the Don Quixote, which makes us sympathize with the man who commits suicide because he has done something ignoble and lost his honour. And we are noblemen enough to suffer at the sight of fallen greatness littering the earth like a corpse—yes, even if the fallen rise again and make restitution by honourable deeds. Jean, the valet, is a race-builder, a man of marked characteristics. He was a labourer's son who has educated himself towards becoming a gentleman. He has learnt easily, through his well-developed senses (smell, taste, vision)—and he also has a sense of beauty. He has already bettered himself, and is thick-skinned enough to have no scruples about using other people's services. He is already foreign to his associates, despising them as part of the life he has turned his back on, yet also fearing and fleeing from them because they know his secrets, pry into his plans, watch his rise with envy, and look forward with pleasure to his fall. Hence his dual, indeterminate character, vacillating between love of the heights and hatred of those who have already achieved them. He is, he says himself, an aristocrat; he has learned the secrets of good society. He is polished, but vulgar within; he already wears his tails with taste, but there is no guarantee of his personal cleanliness.

He has some respect for his young lady, but he is frightened of Kristin, who knows his dangerous secrets, and he is sufficiently callous not to allow the night's events to wreck his plans for the future. Having both the slave's brutality and the master's lack of squeamishness, he can see blood without fainting and take disaster by the horns. Consequently he emerges from the battle unscathed, and probably ends his days as a hotel-keeper. And even if *he* does not become a Roumanian Count, his son will doubtless go to the university and perhaps become a county attorney.

The light which Jean sheds on a lower-class conception of life, life seen from below, is on the whole illuminating— when he speaks the truth, which is not often, for he says what is favourable to himself rather than what is true. When Miss Julie suggests that the lower-classes must be oppressed by the attitude of their superiors, Jean naturally agrees, as his object is to gain her sympathy; but when he perceives the advantage of separating himself from the common herd, he at once takes back his words.

It is not because Jean is now rising that he has the upper hand of Miss Julie, but because he is a man. Sexually he is the aristocrat because of his virility, his keener senses and his capacity for taking the initiative. His inferiority is mainly due to the social environment in which he lives, and he can probably shed it with his valet's livery.

The slave mentality expresses itself in his worship of the Count (the boots), and his religious superstition; but he worships the Count chiefly because he holds that higher position for which Jean himself is striving. And this worship remains even when he has won the daughter of the house and seen how empty is that lovely shell.

I do not believe that a love relationship in the "higher" sense could exist between two individuals of such different quality, but I have made Miss Julie imagine that she is in love, so as to lessen her sense of guilt, and I let Jean suppose that if his social position were altered he would truly love her. I think love is like the hyacinth which has to strike roots in darkness *before* it can produce a vigorous flower. In this case it shoots up quickly, blossoms and goes to seed all at the same time, which is why the plant dies so soon.

As for Kristin, she is a female slave, full of servility and sluggishness acquired in front of the kitchen fire, and stuffed full of morality and religion, which are her cloak and scape-goat. She goes to church as a quick and easy way of unloading her household thefts on to Jesus and taking on a fresh cargo of guiltlessness. For the rest she is a minor character, and I have therefore sketched her in the same manner as the Pastor and the Doctor in "The Father," where I wanted ordinary human beings, as are most country pastors and provincial doctors. If these minor characters seem abstract to some people this is due to the fact that ordinary people are to a certain extent abstract in pursuit of their work; that is to say, they are without individuality, showing, while working, only one side of themselves. And as long as the spectator does not feel a need to see them from other sides, there is nothing wrong with my abstract presentation.

In regard to the dialogue, I have departed somewhat from tradition by not making my characters catechists who ask stupid questions in order to elicit a smart reply. I have avoided the symmetrical, mathematical construction of French dialogue, and let people's minds work irregularly, as they do in real life where, during a conversation, no topic is drained to the dregs, and one mind finds in another a chance cog to engage in. So too the dialogue wanders, gathering in the opening scenes material which is later picked up, worked over, repeated, expounded and developed like the theme in a musical composition.

The plot speaks for itself, and as it really only concerns two people, I have concentrated on these, introducing only one minor character, the cook, and keeping the unhappy spirit of the father above and behind the action. I have done this because it seems to me that the psychological process is what interests people most today. Our inquisitive souls are no longer satisfied with seeing a thing happen; we must also know how it happens. We want to see the wires themselves, to watch the machinery, to examine the box with the false bottom, to take hold of the magic ring in order to find the join, and look at the cards to see how they are marked.

In this connection I have had in view the documentary novels of the brothers de Goncourt, which appeal to me more than any other modern literature.

As far as the technical side of the work is concerned I have made the experiment of abolishing the division into acts. This is because I have come to the conclusion that our capacity for illusion is disturbed by the intervals, during which the audience has time to reflect and escape from the suggestive influence of the author-hypnotist. My play will probably take an hour and a half, and as one can listen to a lecture, a sermon or a parliamentary debate for as long as that or longer, I do not think a theatrical performance will be fatiguing in the same length of time. As early as 1872, in one of my first dramatic attempts, "The Outlaw," I tried this concentrated form, although with scant success. The play was written in five acts, and only when finished did I become aware of the restless, disjointed effect that it produced. The script was burnt and from the ashes rose a single well-knit act—fifty pages of print, playable in one hour. The form of the present play is, therefore, not new, but it appears to be my own, and changing tastes may make it timely. My hope is one day to have an audience educated enough to sit through a whole evening's entertainment in one act, but one would have to try this out to see. Meanwhile, in order to provide respite for the audience and the players, without allowing the audience to escape from the illusion, I have introduced three art forms: monologue, mime and ballet. These are all part of drama, having their origins in classic tragedy, monody having become monologue and the chorus, ballet.

Monologue is now condemned by our realists as unnatural, but if one provides motives for it one makes it natural, and then can use it to advantage. It is, surely, natural for a public speaker to walk up and down the room practicing his speech, natural for an actor to read his part aloud, for a servant girl to talk to her cat, a mother to prattle to her child, an old maid to chatter to her parrot, and a sleeper to talk in his sleep. And in order that the actor may have a chance, for once, of working independently, free from the author's direction, it is better that the monologue should not be written, but only indicated. For since it is of small importance what is said in one's sleep or to the parrot or to the cat—none of it influences the action—a talented actor, identifying himself with the atmosphere and the situation, may improvise better than the author, who cannot calculate ahead how much may be said or how long taken without waking the audience from the illusion.

Some Italian theatres have, as we know, returned to improvisation, thereby producing actors who are creative, although within the bounds set by the author. This may well be a step forward, or even the beginning of a new art-form worthy to be called *productive*.

In places where monologue would be unnatural I have used mime, leaving here an even wider scope for the actor's imagination, and more chance for him to win independent laurels. But so as not to try the audience beyond endurance, I have introduced music—fully justified by the Midsummer Eve dance—to exercise its powers of persuasion during the dumb show. But I beg the musical director to consider carefully his choice of compositions, so that conflicting moods are not induced by selections from the current operetta or dance show, or by folk-tunes of too local a character.

The ballet I have introduced cannot be replaced by the usual kind of "crowd-scene," for such scenes are too badly played—a lot of grinning idiots seizing the opportunity to show off and thus destroying the illusion. And as peasants cannot improvise their taunts, but use ready-made phrases with a double meaning, I have not composed their lampoon, but taken a little-known song and dance which I myself noted down in the Stockholm district. The words are not quite to the point, but this too is intentional, for the cunning, i.e. weakness, of the slave prevents him from direct attack. Nor can there be clowning in a serious action, or coarse joking in a situation which nails the lid on a family coffin.

As regards the scenery, I have borrowed from impressionist painting its asymmetry and its economy; thus, I think, strengthening the illusion. For the fact that one does not see the whole room and all the furniture leaves scope for conjecture—that is to say imagination is roused and complements what is seen. I have succeeded too in getting rid of those tiresome exits through doors, since scenery doors are made of canvas, and rock at the slightest touch. They cannot even express the wrath of an irate head of the family who, after a bad dinner, goes out slamming the door behind him, "so that the whole house shakes." On the stage it rocks. I have also kept to a single set, both in order to let the characters develop in their métier and to break away from over-decoration. When one has only one set, one may expect it to be realistic; but as a matter of fact nothing is harder than to get a stage room that looks something like a room, however easily the scene painter can produce flaming volcanoes and water-falls. Presumably the walls must be of canvas; but it seems about time to dispense with painted shelves and cooking utensils. We are asked to accept so many stage conventions that we might at least be spared the pain of painted pots and pans.

I have set the back wall and the table diagonally so that the actors may play full-face and in half-profile when they are sitting opposite one another at the table. In the opera Aïda I saw a diagonal background, which led the eye to unfamiliar perspectives and did not look like mere reaction against boring straight lines.

Another much needed innovation is the abolition of foot-lights. This lighting from below is said to have the purpose of making the actors' faces fatter. But why, I ask, should all actors have fat faces? Does not this underlighting flatten out all the subtlety of the lower part of the face, specially the jaw, falsify the shape of the nose and throw shadows up over the eyes? Even if this were not so, one thing is certain: that the lights hurt the performers' eyes, so that the full play of their expression is lost. The foot-lights strike part of the retina usually protected —except in sailors who have to watch sunlight on water—and therefore one seldom sees anything other than a crude rolling of the eyes, either sideways or up towards the gallery, showing their whites. Perhaps this too causes that tiresome blinking of the eyelashes, especially by actresses. And when anyone on the stage wants to speak with his eyes, the only thing he can do is to look straight at the audience, with whom he or she then gets into direct communication, outside the framework of the set—a habit called, rightly or wrongly, "greeting one's friends."

Would not sufficiently strong side-lighting, with some kind of reflectors, add to the actor's powers of expression by allowing him to use the face's greatest asset:—the play of the eyes?

I have few illusions about getting the actors to play to the audience instead of with it, although this is what I want. That I shall see an actor's back throughout a critical scene is beyond my dreams, but I do wish crucial scenes could be played, not in front of the prompter's box, like duets expecting applause, but in the place required by the action. So, no revolutions, but just some small modifications, for to make the stage into a real room with the fourth wall missing would be too upsetting altogether.

I dare not hope that the actresses will listen to what I have to say about make-up, for they would rather be beautiful than life-like, but the actor might consider whether it is to his advantage to create an abstract character with grease-paints, and cover his face with it like a mask. Take the case of a man who draws a choleric charcoal line between his eyes and then, in this fixed state of wrath, has to smile at some repartee. What a frightful grimace the result is! And equally, how is that false forehead, smooth as a billiard ball, to wrinkle when the old man loses his temper?

In a modern psychological drama, where the subtlest reactions of a character need to be mirrored in the face rather than expressed by sound and gesture, it would be worth while experimenting with powerful side-lighting on a small stage and a cast without make-up, or at least with the minimum.

If, in addition, we could abolish the visible orchestra, with its distracting lamps and its faces turned toward the audience; if we could have the stalls raised so that the spectators' eyes were higher than the players' knees; if we could get rid of the boxes (the centre of my target), with their tittering diners and supper-parties, and have total darkness in the auditorium during the performance; and if, first and foremost, we could have a *small* stage and a *small* house, then perhaps a new dramatic art might arise, and theatre once more become a place of entertainment for educated people. While waiting for such a theatre it is as well for us to go on writing so as to stock that repertory of the future.

I have made an attempt. If it has failed, there is time enough to try again.

". . . TO JUDGE BETWEEN GOOD AND BAD, BETWEEN

Anton Chekhov 1860-1904

successful and unsuccessful, would need the eye of God," Chekhov wrote. Yet it would be false to suppose that this kindliest of writers was indifferent to human weakness or considered vulgarity and idleness on a par with sensitivity and hard work. Responsibilities settled early upon Chekhov when his father, facing the bankruptcy of his shop, escaped to Moscow with his family, leaving Anton in Taganrog to complete his preparatory studies. When some years later Chekhov joined his family in Moscow, he found it necessary not only to finance his medical studies at the University but to support the family as well. To do so he took to writing brief comic sketches which he published under pseudonyms. In 1884 he received his medical degree and thereafter devoted himself to his two callings, medicine ("my lawful spouse") and literature ("my mistress"). He had also contracted tuberculosis, the disease that was to cut his life short. The success of his first volume of stories gave Chekhov the freedom to write more seriously, and there followed the great tales which establish him as the unsurpassed master of the short story. After writing some short farces for vaudeville performance, Chekhov tried a full-length play, *Ivanov* (1887). It was a failure, and Chekhov was so discouraged that not until 1896 did he attempt another play, *The Sea Gull*. It too failed, and Chekhov vowed never again to write for the theatre; but the founding of the Moscow Art Theatre by Nemirovitch-Dantchenko and Constantin Stanislavsky induced him to change his mind. To the Moscow Art Theatre we owe the successful revival of *The Sea Gull* and Chekhov's succeeding masterpieces: *Uncle Vanya* (1897), *The Three Sisters* (1900), and *The Cherry Orchard* (1904). Chekhov knew well the ineffectual lives of the unproductive classes and the ignorance that prevailed over much of Russia. He wrote about the loneliness of his characters, their unfulfilled or wasted lives, their follies, strivings, dreams, and frustrations, with rare compassion and humor. To escape stagnation through purposeful labor was Chekhov's guiding principle. In addition to his literary work, he continued to practice medicine, studied peasant life, and investigated the barbarous conditions in Russian prisons in the hope of aiding those who suffered. His health soon failed, however, and he died at the early age of forty-four.

THE CHERRY ORCHARD

BY ANTON CHEKHOV ❧ *Translated by Constance Garnett*

CHARACTERS

MADAME RANEVSKY (LYUBOV ANDRE-
YEVNA), *the owner of the Cherry
Orchard*
ANYA, *her daughter, aged 17*
VARYA, *her adopted daughter, aged 24*
GAEV (LEONID ANDREYEVITCH), *brother
of Madame Ranevsky*
LOPAHIN (YERMOLAY ALEXEYEVITCH),
a Merchant
TROFIMOV (PYOTR SERGEYEVITCH), *a
Student*

SEMYONOV-PISHTCHIK, *a Landowner*
CHARLOTTA IVANOVNA, *a Governess*
EPIHODOV (SEMYON PANTALEYEVITCH),
a Clerk
DUNYASHA, *a Maid*
FIRS, *an old Valet, aged 87*
YASHA, *a young Valet*
A VAGRANT
THE STATION MASTER
A POST-OFFICE CLERK
VISITORS, SERVANTS

The action takes place on the estate of
MADAME RANEVSKY.

❧ Act I

*A room, which has always been called
the nursery. One of the doors leads into*
ANYA's *room. Dawn, sun rises during
the scene. May, the cherry trees in flower,
but it is cold in the garden with the frost
of early morning. Windows closed.*

Enter DUNYASHA *with a candle and
Lopahin with a book in his hand.*

LOPAHIN. The train's in, thank God.
What time is it?

DUNYASHA. Nearly two o'clock (*puts
out the candle*). It's daylight already.

LOPAHIN. The train's late! Two hours,
at least (*yawns and stretches*). I'm a
pretty one; what a fool I've been. Came
here on purpose to meet them at the
station and dropped asleep. . . . Dozed
off as I sat in the chair. It's annoying. . . .
You might have waked me.

DUNYASHA. I thought you had gone
(*listens*). There, I do believe they're
coming!

LOPAHIN (*listens*). No, what with the
luggage and one thing and another (*a
pause*). Lyubov Andreyevna has been
abroad five years; I don't know what she
is like now. . . . She's a splendid woman.
A good-natured, kind-hearted woman. I

remember when I was a lad of fifteen,
my poor father—he used to keep a little
shop here in the village in those days—
gave me a punch in the face with his fist
and made my nose bleed. We were in
the yard here, I forget what we'd come
about—he had had a drop. Lyubov Andreyevna—I can see her now—she was a
slim young girl then—took me to wash
my face, and then brought me into this
very room, into the nursery. "Don't cry,
little peasant," says she, "it will be well
in time for your wedding day" . . . (*a
pause*). Little peasant. . . . My father
was a peasant, it's true, but here am I in
a white waistcoat and brown shoes, like
a pig in a bun shop. Yes, I'm a rich man,
but for all my money, come to think, a
peasant I was, and a peasant I am (*turns
over the pages of the book*). I've been
reading this book and I can't make head
or tail of it. I fell asleep over it (*a pause*).

DUNYASHA. The dogs have been awake
all night, they feel that the mistress is
coming.

LOPAHIN. Why, what's the matter with
you, Dunyasha?

DUNYASHA. My hands are all of a
tremble. I feel as though I should faint.

LOPAHIN. You're a spoilt soft creature,

From *The Cherry Orchard and Other Plays* by Anton Tchekhov from the Russian by Constance Garnett. London, Chatto & Windus, 1923, (half title, *The Plays of Anton Tchekov*;
trans. by Constance Garnett; New York, The Modern Library, 1930).

Dunyasha. And dressed like a lady too, and your hair done up. That's not the thing. One must know one's place.

(*Enter* EPIHODOV *with a nosegay; he wears a pea-jacket and highly polished creaking topboots; he drops the nosegay as he comes in.*)

EPIHODOV (*picking up the nosegay*). Here! the gardener's sent this, says you're to put it in the dining-room (*gives* DUNYASHA *the nosegay*).

LOPAHIN. And bring me some kvass.

DUNYASHA. I will (*goes out*).

EPIHODOV. It's chilly this morning, three degrees of frost, though the cherries are all in flower. I can't say much for our climate (*sighs*). I can't. Our climate is not often propitious to the occasion. Yermolay Alexeyevitch, permit me to call your attention to the fact that I purchased myself a pair of boots the day before yesterday, and they creak, I venture to assure you, so that there's no tolerating them. What ought I to grease them with?

LOPAHIN. Oh, shut up! Don't bother me.

EPIHODOV. Every day some misfortune befalls me. I don't complain, I'm used to it, and I wear a smiling face.

(DUNYASHA *comes in, hands* LOPAHIN *the kvass.*)

EPIHODOV. I am going (*stumbles against a chair, which falls over*). There! (*As though triumphant*) There you see now, excuse the expression, an accident like that among others. . . . It's positively remarkable (*goes out*).

DUNYASHA. Do you know, Yermolay Alexeyevitch, I must confess, Epihodov has made me a proposal.

LOPAHIN. Ah!

DUNYASHA. I'm sure I don't know. . . . He's a harmless fellow, but sometimes when he begins talking, there's no making anything of it. It's all very fine and expressive, only there's no understanding it. I've a sort of liking for him too. He loves me to distraction. He's an unfortunate man; every day there's something. They tease him about it—two and twenty misfortunes they call him.

LOPAHIN (*listening*). There! I do believe they're coming.

DUNYASHA. They are coming! What's the matter with me? . . . I'm cold all over.

LOPAHIN. They really are coming. Let's go and meet them. Will she know me? It's five years since I saw her.

DUNYASHA (*in a flutter*). I shall drop this very minute. . . . Ah, I shall drop.

(*There is a sound of two carriages driving up to the house.* LOPAHIN *and* DUNYASHA *go out quickly. The stage is left empty. A noise is heard in the adjoining rooms.* FIRS, *who has driven to meet* MADAME RANEVSKY, *crosses the stage hurriedly, leaning on a stick. He is wearing old-fashioned livery and a high hat. He says something to himself, but not a word can be distinguished. The noise behind the scenes goes on increasing. A voice: "Come, let's go in here."* Enter LYUBOV ANDREYEVNA, ANYA, *and* CHARLOTTA IVANOVNA *with a pet dog on a chain, all in travelling dresses,* VARYA *in an out-door coat with a kerchief over her head,* GAEV, SEMYONOV-PISHTCHIK, LOPAHIN, DUNYASHA *with bag and parasol, servants with other articles. All walk across the room.*)

ANYA. Let's come in here. Do you remember what room this is, mamma?

LYUBOV (*joyfully, through her tears*). The nursery!

VARYA. How cold it is, my hands are numb. (*To* LYUBOV ANDREYEVNA) Your rooms, the white room and the lavender one, are just the same as ever, mamma.

LYUBOV. My nursery, dear delightful room. . . . I used to sleep here when I was little . . . (*cries*). And here I am, like a little child . . . (*kisses her brother and* VARYA, *and then her brother again*). Varya's just the same as ever, like a nun. And I knew Dunyasha (*kisses* DUNYASHA).

GAEV. The train was two hours late. What do you think of that? Is that the way to do things?

CHARLOTTA (*to* PISHTCHIK). My dog eats nuts, too.

PISHTCHIK (*wonderingly*). Fancy that!

(*They all go out except* ANYA *and* DUNYASHA.)

DUNYASHA. We've been expecting you so long (*takes* ANYA's *hat and coat*).

ANYA. I haven't slept for four nights on the journey. I feel dreadfully cold.

DUNYASHA. You set out in Lent, there was snow and frost, and now? My darling! (*Laughs and kisses her*) I have missed you, my precious, my joy. I must tell you . . . I can't put it off a minute. . . .

ANYA (*wearily*). What now?

DUNYASHA. Epihodov, the clerk, made me a proposal just after Easter.

ANYA. It's always the same thing with you . . . (*straightening her hair*). I've lost all my hairpins . . . (*she is staggering from exhaustion*).

DUNYASHA. I don't know what to think, really. He does love me, he does love me so!

ANYA (*looking towards her door, tenderly*). My own room, my windows just as though I had never gone away. I'm home! Tomorrow morning I shall get up and run into the garden. . . . Oh, if I could get to sleep! I haven't slept all the journey, I was so anxious and worried.

DUNYASHA. Pyotr Sergeyevitch came the day before yesterday.

ANYA (*joyfully*). Petya!

DUNYASHA. He's asleep in the bath house, he has settled in there. I'm afraid of being in their way, says he. (*Glancing at her watch*) I was to have waked him, but Varvara Mihalovna told me not to. Don't you wake him, says she.

(*Enter* VARYA *with a bunch of keys at her waist.*)

VARYA. Dunyasha, coffee, and make haste. . . . Mamma's asking for coffee.

DUNYASHA. This very minute (*goes out*).

VARYA. Well, thank God, you've come. You're home again (*petting her*). My little darling has come back! My precious beauty has come back again!

ANYA. I have had a time of it!

VARYA. I can fancy.

ANYA. We set off in Holy Week—it was so cold then, and all the way Charlotta would talk and show off her tricks. What did you want to burden me with Charlotta for?

VARYA. You couldn't have travelled all alone, darling. At seventeen!

ANYA. We got to Paris at last, it was cold there—snow. I speak French shockingly. Mamma lives on the fifth floor, I went up to her and there were a lot of French people, ladies, an old priest with a book. The place smelt of tobacco and so comfortless. I felt sorry, oh! so sorry for mamma all at once, I put my arms round her neck, and hugged her and wouldn't

let her go. Mamma was as kind as she could be, and she cried. . . .

VARYA (*through her tears*). Don't speak of it, don't speak of it!

ANYA. She had sold her villa at Mentone, she had nothing left, nothing. I hadn't a farthing left either, we only just had enough to get here. And mamma doesn't understand! When we had dinner at the stations, she always ordered the most expensive things and gave the waiters a whole rouble. Charlotta's just the same. Yasha too must have the same as we do; it's simply awful. You know Yasha is mamma's valet now, we brought him here with us.

VARYA. Yes, I've seen the young rascal.

ANYA. Well, tell me—have you paid the arrears on the mortgage?

VARYA. How could we get the money?

ANYA. Oh, dear! Oh, dear!

VARYA. In August the place will be sold.

ANYA. My goodness!

LOPAHIN (*peeps in at the door and moos like a cow*). Moo! (*Disappears.*)

VARYA (*weeping*). There, that's what I could do to him (*shakes her fist*).

ANYA (*embracing* VARYA, *softly*). Varya, has he made you an offer? (VARYA *shakes her head*) Why, but he loves you. Why is it you don't come to an understanding? What are you waiting for?

VARYA. I believe that there never will be anything between us. He has a lot to do, he has no time for me . . . and takes no notice of me. Bless the man, it makes me miserable to see him. . . . Everyone's talking of our being married, everyone's congratulating me, and all the while there's really nothing in it; it's all like a dream! (*In another tone*) You have a new brooch like a bee.

ANYA (mournfully). Mamma bought it. (*Goes into her own room and in a light-hearted childish tone*) And you know, in Paris I went up in a balloon!

VARYA. My darling's home again! My pretty is home again!

(DUNYASHA *returns with the coffee-pot and is making the coffee.*)

VARYA (*standing at the door*). All day long, darling, as I go about looking after the house, I keep dreaming all the time. If only we could marry you to a rich man, then I should feel more at rest. Then I would go off by myself on a pilgrimage

to Kiev, to Moscow . . . and so I would
spend my life going from one place to
another. . . . I would go on and on. . . .
What bliss!

ANYA. The birds are singing in the
garden. What time is it?

VARYA. It must be nearly three. It's
time you were asleep, darling (*going into*
ANYA's *room*). What bliss!

(YASHA *enters with a rug and a travelling bag.*)

YASHA (*crosses the stage, mincingly*).
May one come in here, pray?

DUNYASHA. I shouldn't have known
you, Yasha. How you have changed
abroad.

YASHA. H'm! . . . And who are you?

DUNYASHA. When you went away, I
was that high (*shows distance from
floor*). Dunyasha, Fyodor's daughter. . . .
You don't remember me!

YASHA. H'm! . . . You're a peach!
(*Looks round and embraces her: she
shrieks and drops a saucer.* YASHA *goes
out hastily.*)

VARYA (*in the doorway, in a tone of
vexation*). What now?

DUNYASHA (*through her tears*). I
have broken a saucer.

VARYA. Well, that brings good luck.

ANYA (*coming out of her room*). We
ought to prepare mamma: Petya is here.

VARYA. I told them not to wake him.

ANYA (*dreamily*). It's six years since
father died. Then only a month later little
brother Grisha was drowned in the river,
such a pretty boy he was, only seven. It
was more than mamma could bear, so
she went away, went away without looking back (*shuddering*). . . . How well
I understand her, if only she knew! (*A
pause*) And Petya Trofimov was Grisha's
tutor, he may remind her.

(*Enter* FIRS: *he is wearing a pea-jacket
and a white waistcoat.*)

FIRS (*goes up to the coffee-pot,
anxiously*). The mistress will be served
here (*puts on white gloves*). Is the coffee
ready? (*Sternly to* DUNYASHA) Girl!
Where's the cream?

DUNYASHA. Ah, mercy on us! (*Goes
out quickly.*)

FIRS (*fussing round the coffee-pot*).
Ech! you good-for-nothing! (*Muttering
to himself*) Come back from Paris. And
the old master used to go to Paris too . . .
horses all the way (*laughs*).

VARYA. What is it, Firs?

FIRS. What is your pleasure? (*Gleefully*) My lady has come home! I have
lived to see her again! Now I can die
(*weeps with joy*).

(*Enter* LYUBOV ANDREYEVNA, GAEV
and SEMYONOV-PISHTCHIK; *the latter is
in a short-waisted full coat of fine cloth,
and full trousers.* GAEV, *as he comes in,
makes a gesture with his arms and his
whole body, as though he were playing
billiards.*)

LYUBOV. How does it go? Let me
remember. Cannon off the red!

GAEV. That's it—in off the white!
Why, once, sister, we used to sleep together in this very room, and now I'm
fifty-one, strange as it seems.

LOPAHIN. Yes, time flies.

GAEV. What do you say?

LOPAHIN. Time, I say, flies.

GAEV. What a smell of patchouli!

ANYA. I'm going to bed. Good-night,
mamma (*kisses her mother*).

LYUBOV. My precious darling (*kisses
her hands*). Are you glad to be home? I
can't believe it.

ANYA. Good-night, uncle.

GAEV (*kissing her face and hands*).
God bless you! How like you are to
your mother! (*To his sister*) At her age
you were just the same, Lyuba.

(ANYA *shakes hands with* LOPAHIN
and PISHTCHIK, *then goes out, shutting
the door after her.*)

LYUBOV. She's quite worn out.

PISHTCHIK. Aye, it's a long journey,
to be sure.

VARYA (*to* LOPAHIN *and* PISHTCHIK).
Well, gentlemen? It's three o'clock and
time to say good-bye.

LYUBOV (*laughs*). You're just the
same as ever, Varya (*draws her to her
and kisses her*). I'll just drink my coffee
and then we will all go and rest. (FIRS
puts a cushion under her feet) Thanks,
friend. I am so fond of coffee, I drink
it day and night. Thanks, dear old man
(*kisses* FIRS).

VARYA. I'll just see whether all the
things have been brought in (*goes out*).

LYUBOV. Can it really be me sitting
here? (*Laughs*) I want to dance about
and clap my hands. (*Covers her face
with her hands*) And I could drop asleep
in a moment! God knows I love my
country, I love it tenderly; I couldn't

look out of the window in the train, I kept crying so. (*Through her tears*) But I must drink my coffee, though. Thank you, Firs, thanks, dear old man. I'm so glad to find you still alive.

FIRS. The day before yesterday.

GAEV. He's rather deaf.

LOPAHIN. I have to set off for Harkov directly, at five o'clock. . . . It is annoying! I wanted to have a look at you, and a little talk. . . . You are just as splendid as ever.

PISHTCHIK (*breathing heavily*). Handsomer, indeed. . . . Dressed in Parisian style . . . completely bowled me over.

LOPAHIN. Your brother, Leonid Andreyevitch here, is always saying that I'm a low-born knave, that I'm a money-grubber, but I don't care one straw for that. Let him talk. Only I do want you to believe in me as you used to. I do want your wonderful tender eyes to look at me as they used to in the old days. Merciful God! My father was a serf of your father and of your grandfather, but you—you—did so much for me once, that I've forgotten all that; I love you as though you were my kin . . . more than my kin.

LYUBOV. I can't sit still, I simply can't . . . (*jumps up and walks about in violent agitation*). This happiness is too much for me. . . . You may laugh at me, I know I'm silly. . . . My own bookcase (*kisses the bookcase*). My little table.

GAEV. Nurse died while you were away.

LYUBOV (*sits down and drinks coffee*). Yes, the Kingdom of Heaven be hers! You wrote me of her death.

GAEV. And Anastasy is dead. Squinting Petruchka has left me and is in service now with the police captain in the town (*takes a box of caramels out of his pocket and sucks one*).

PISHTCHIK. My daughter, Dashenka, wishes to be remembered to you.

LOPAHIN. I want to tell you something very pleasant and cheering (*glancing at his watch*). I'm going directly . . . there's no time to say much . . . well, I can say it in a couple of words. I needn't tell you your cherry orchard is to be sold to pay your debts; the 22nd of August is the date fixed for the sale; but don't you worry, dearest lady, you may sleep in peace, there is a way of saving it. . . . This is what I propose. I beg your atten-

tion! Your estate is not twenty miles from the town, the railway runs close by it, and if the cherry orchard and the land along the river bank were cut up into building plots and then let on lease for summer villas, you would make an income of at least 25,000 roubles a year out of it.

GAEV. That's all rot, if you'll excuse me.

LYUBOV. I don't quite understand you, Yermolay Alexeyevitch.

LOPAHIN. You will get a rent of at least 25 roubles a year for a three-acre plot from summer visitors, and if you say the word now, I'll bet you what you like there won't be one square foot of ground vacant by the autumn, all the plots will be taken up. I congratulate you; in fact, you are saved. It's a perfect situation with that deep river. Only, of course, it must be cleared—all the old buildings, for example, must be removed, this house too, which is really good for nothing and the old cherry orchard must be cut down.

LYUBOV. Cut down? My dear fellow, forgive me, but you don't know what you are talking about. If there is one thing interesting—remarkable indeed—in the whole province, it's just our cherry orchard.

LOPAHIN. The only thing remarkable about the orchard is that it's a very large one. There's a crop of cherries every alternate year, and then there's nothing to be done with them, no one buys them.

GAEV. This orchard is mentioned in the "Encyclopædia."

LOPAHIN (*glancing at his watch*). If we don't decide on something and don't take some steps, on the 22nd of August the cherry orchard and the whole estate too will be sold by auction. Make up your minds! There is no other way of saving it, I'll take my oath on that. No, No!

FIRS. In the old days, forty or fifty years ago, they used to dry the cherries, soak them, pickle them, make jam too, and they used . . .

GAEV. Be quiet, Firs.

FIRS. And they used to send the preserved cherries to Moscow and to Harkov by the waggon-load. That brought the money in! And the preserved cherries in those days were soft and juicy, sweet and fragrant. . . . They knew the way to do them then. . . .

LYUBOV. And where is the recipe now?

FIRS. It's forgotten. Nobody remembers it.

PISHTCHIK (to LYUBOV ANDREY-EVNA). What's it like in Paris? Did you eat frogs there?

LYUBOV. Oh, I ate crocodiles.

PISHTCHIK. Fancy that now!

LOPAHIN. There used to be only the gentlefolks and the peasants in the country, but now there are these summer visitors. All the towns, even the small ones, are surrounded nowadays by these summer villas. And one may say for sure, that in another twenty years there'll be many more of these people and that they'll be everywhere. At present the summer visitor only drinks tea in his verandah, but maybe he'll take to working his bit of land too, and then your cherry orchard would become happy, rich and prosperous. . . .

GAEV (indignant). What rot!

(Enter VARYA and YASHA.)

VARYA. There are two telegrams for you, mamma (takes out keys and opens an old-fashioned bookcase with a loud crack). Here they are.

LYUBOV. From Paris (tears the telegrams, without reading them). I have done with Paris.

GAEV. Do you know, Lyuba, how old that bookcase is? Last week I pulled out the bottom drawer and there I found the date branded on it. The bookcase was made just a hundred years ago. What do you say to that? We might have celebrated its jubilee. Though it's an inanimate object, still it is a book case.

PISHTCHIK (amazed). A hundred years! Fancy that now.

GAEV. Yes. . . . It is a thing . . . (feeling the bookcase). Dear, honoured bookcase! Hail to thee who for more than a hundred years hast served the pure ideals of good and justice; thy silent call to fruitful labour has never flagged in those hundred years, maintaining (in tears) in the generations of man, courage and faith in a brighter future and fostering in us ideals of good and social consciousness (a pause).

LOPAHIN. Yes. . . .

LYUBOV. You are just the same as ever, Leonid.

GAEV (a little embarrassed). Cannon off the right into the pocket!

LOPAHIN (looking at his watch). Well, it's time I was off.

YASHA (handing LYUBOV ANDREY-EVNA medicine). Perhaps you will take your pills now.

PISHTCHIK. You shouldn't take medicines, my dear madam . . . they do no harm and no good. Give them here . . . honoured lady (takes the pill-box, pours the pills into the hollow of his hand, blows on them, puts them in his mouth and drinks off some kvass). There!

LYUBOV (in alarm). Why, you must be out of your mind!

PISHTCHIK. I have taken all the pills.

LOPAHIN. What a glutton! (All laugh.)

FIRS. His honour stayed with us in Easter week, ate a gallon and a half of cucumbers . . . (mutters).

LYUBOV. What is he saying?

VARYA. He has taken to muttering like that for the last three years. We are used to it.

YASHA. His declining years!

(CHARLOTTA IVANOVNA, a very thin, lanky figure in a white dress with a lorgnette in her belt, walks across the stage.)

LOPAHIN. I beg your pardon, Charlotta Ivanovna, I have not had time to greet you (tries to kiss her hand).

CHARLOTTA (pulling away her hand). If I let you kiss my hand, you'll be wanting to kiss my elbow, and then my shoulder.

LOPAHIN. I've no luck today! (All laugh) Charlotta Ivanovna, show us some tricks!

LYUBOV. Charlotta, do show us some tricks!

CHARLOTTA. I don't want to. I'm sleepy (goes out).

LOPAHIN. In three weeks' time we shall meet again (kisses LYUBOV ANDREYEVNA's hand). Good-bye till then —I must go. (To GAEV) Good-bye. (Kisses PISHTCHIK) Good-bye. (Gives his hand to VARYA, then to FIRS and YASHA) I don't want to go. (To LYUBOV ANDREYEVNA) If you think over my plan for the villas and make up your mind, then let me know; I will lend you 50,000 roubles. Think of it seriously.

VARYA (angrily). Well, do go, for goodness sake.

LOPAHIN. I'm going, I'm going (*goes out*).

GAEV. Low-born knave! I beg pardon, though . . . Varya is going to marry him, he's Varya's fiancé.

VARYA. Don't talk nonsense, uncle.

LYUBOV. Well, Varya, I shall be delighted. He's a good man.

PISHTCHIK. He is, one must acknowledge, a most worthy man. And my Dashenka . . . says too that . . . she says . . . various things (*snores, but at once wakes up*). But all the same, honoured lady, could you oblige me . . . with a loan of 240 roubles . . . to pay the interest on my mortgage tomorrow?

VARYA (*dismayed*). No, no.

LYUBOV. I really haven't any money.

PISHTCHIK. It will turn up (*laughs*). I never lose hope. I thought everything was over, I was a ruined man, and lo and behold—the railway passed through my land and . . . they paid me for it. And something else will turn up again, if not today, then tomorrow . . . Dashenka'll win two hundred thousand . . . she's got a lottery ticket.

LYUBOV. Well, we've finished our coffee, we can go to bed.

FIRS (*brushes* GAEV, *reprovingly*). You have got on the wrong trousers again! What am I to do with you?

VARYA (*softly*). Anya's asleep. (*Softly opens the window*) Now the sun's risen, it's not a bit cold. Look, mamma, what exquisite trees! My goodness! And the air! The starlings are singing!

GAEV (*opens another window*). The orchard is all white. You've not forgotten it, Lyuba? That long avenue that runs straight, straight as an arrow, how it shines on a moonlight night. You remember? You've not forgotten?

LYUBOV (*looking out of the window into the garden*). Oh, my childhood, my innocence! It was in this nursery I used to sleep, from here I looked out into the orchard, happiness waked with me every morning and in those days the orchard was just the same, nothing has changed (*laughs with delight*). All, all white! Oh, my orchard! After the dark gloomy autumn, and the cold winter; you are young again, and full of happiness, the heavenly angels have never left you. . . . If I could cast off the burden that weighs on my heart, if I could forget the past!

GAEV. H'm! and the orchard will be sold to pay our debts; it seems strange. . . .

LYUBOV. See, our mother walking . . . all in white, down the avenue! (*Laughs with delight*) It is she!

GAEV. Where?

VARYA. Oh, don't, mamma!

LYUBOV. There is no one. It was my fancy. On the right there, by the path to the arbour, there is a white tree bending like a woman. . . .

(*Enter* TROFIMOV *wearing a shabby student's uniform and spectacles.*)

LYUBOV. What a ravishing orchard! White masses of blossoms, blue sky. . . .

TROFIMOV. Lyubov Andreyevna! (*She looks round at him*) I will just pay my respects to you and then leave you at once (*kisses her hand warmly*). I was told to wait until morning, but I hadn't the patience to wait any longer. . . .

(LYUBOV ANDREYEVNA *looks at him in perplexity.*)

VARYA (*through her tears*). This is Petya Trofimov.

TROFIMOV. Petya Trofimov, who was your Grisha's tutor. . . . Can I have changed so much?

(LYUBOV ANDREYEVNA *embraces him and weeps quietly.*)

GAEV (*in confusion*). There, there, Lyuba.

VARYA (*crying*). I told you, Petya, to wait till tomorrow.

LYUBOV. My Grisha . . . my boy . . . Grisha . . . my son!

VARYA. We can't help it, mamma, it is God's will.

TROFIMOV (*softly through his tears*). There . . . there.

LYUBOV (*weeping quietly*). My boy was lost . . . drowned. Why? Oh, why, dear Petya? (*More quietly*) Anya is asleep in there, and I'm talking loudly . . . making this noise. . . . But, Petya? Why have you grown so ugly? Why do you look so old?

TROFIMOV. A peasant-woman in the train called me a mangy-looking gentleman.

LYUBOV. You were quite a boy then, a pretty little student, and now your hair's thin—and spectacles. Are you really a student still? (*Goes towards the door.*)

TROFIMOV. I seem likely to be a perpetual student.

LYUBOV (*kisses her brother, then*

VARYA). Well, go to bed. . . . You are older too, Leonid.

PISHTCHIK (*follows her*). I suppose it's time we were asleep. . . . Ugh! my gout. I'm staying the night! Lyubov Andreyevna, my dear soul, if you could . . . tomorrow morning . . . 240 roubles.

GAEV. That's always his story.

PISHTCHIK. 240 roubles . . . to pay the interest on my mortgage.

LYUBOV. My dear man, I have no money.

PISHTCHIK. I'll pay it back, my dear . . . a trifling sum.

LYUBOV. Oh, well, Leonid will give it to you. . . . You give him the money, Leonid.

GAEV. Me give it him! Let him wait till he gets it!

LYUBOV. It can't be helped, give it him. He needs it. He'll pay it back.

(LYUBOV ANDREYEVNA, TROFIMOV, PISHTCHIK *and* FIRS *go out.* GAEV, VARYA *and* YASHA *remain.*)

GAEV. Sister hasn't got out of the habit of flinging away her money. (*To* YASHA) Get away, my good fellow, you smell of the hen-house.

YASHA (*with a grin*). And you, Leonid Andreyevitch, are just the same as ever.

GAEV. What's that? (*To* VARYA) What did he say?

VARYA (*to* YASHA). Your mother has come from the village; she has been sitting in the servants' room since yesterday, waiting to see you.

YASHA. Oh, bother her!

VARYA. For shame!

YASHA. What's the hurry? She might just as well have come tomorrow (*goes out*).

VARYA. Mamma's just the same as ever, she hasn't changed a bit. If she had her own way, she'd give away everything.

GAEV. Yes (*a pause*). If a great many remedies are suggested for some disease, it means that the disease is incurable. I keep thinking and racking my brains; I have many schemes, a great many, and that really means none. If we could only come in for a legacy from somebody, or marry our Anya to a very rich man, or we might go to Yaroslavl and try our luck with our old aunt, the Countess. She's very, very rich, you know.

VARYA (*weeps*). If God would help us.

GAEV. Don't blubber. Aunt's very rich, but she doesn't like us. First, sister married a lawyer instead of a nobleman. . . .

(ANYA *appears in the doorway.*)

GAEV. And then her conduct, one can't call it virtuous. She is good, and kind, and nice, and I love her, but, however one allows for extenuating circumstances, there's no denying that she's an immoral woman. One feels it in her slightest gesture.

VARYA (*in a whisper*). Anya's in the doorway.

GAEV. What do you say? (*A pause*) It's queer, there seems to be something wrong with my right eye. I don't see as well as I did. And on Thursday when I was in the district Court. . . .

(*Enter* ANYA.)

VARYA. Why aren't you asleep, Anya?

ANYA. I can't get to sleep.

GAEV. My pet (*kisses* ANYA'S *face and hands*). My child (*weeps*). You are not my niece, you are my angel, you are everything to me. Believe me, believe. . . .

ANYA. I believe you, uncle. Everyone loves you and respects you . . . but, uncle dear, you must be silent . . . simply be silent. What were you saying just now about my mother, about your own sister? What made you say that?

GAEV. Yes, yes . . . (*puts his hand over his face*). Really, that was awful! My God, save me! And today I made a speech to the bookcase . . . so stupid! And only when I had finished, I saw how stupid it was.

VARYA. It's true, uncle, you ought to keep quiet. Don't talk, that's all.

ANYA. If you could keep from talking, it would make things easier for you, too.

GAEV. I won't speak (*kisses* ANYA'S *and* VARYA'S *hands*). I'll be silent. Only this is about business. On Thursday I was in the district Court; well, there was a large party of us there and we began talking of one thing and another, and this and that, and do you know, I believe that it will be possible to raise a loan on an I.O.U. to pay the arrears on the mortgage.

VARYA. If the Lord would help us!

GAEV. I'm going on Tuesday; I'll talk of it again. (*To* VARYA) Don't blubber. (*To* ANYA) Your mamma will talk to Lopahin; of course, he won't refuse her. And as soon as you're rested you shall go to Yaroslavl to the Countess, your great-aunt. So we shall all set to work in three directions at once, and the business is done. We shall pay off arrears, I'm convinced of it (*puts a caramel in his mouth*). I swear on my honour, I swear by anything you like, the estate shan't be sold (*excitedly*). By my own happiness, I swear it! Here's my hand on it, call me the basest, vilest of men, if I let it come to an auction! Upon my soul I swear it!

ANYA (*her equanimity has returned, she is quite happy*). How good you are, uncle, and how clever! (*Embraces her uncle*) I'm at peace now! Quite at peace! I'm happy!

(*Enter* FIRS.)

FIRS (*reproachfully*). Leonid Andreyevitch, have you no fear of God? When are you going to bed?

GAEV. Directly, directly. You can go, Firs. I'll . . . yes, I will undress myself. Come, children, bye-bye. We'll go into details tomorrow, but now go to bed (*kisses* ANYA *and* VARYA). I'm a man of the eighties. They run down that period, but still I can say I have had to suffer not a little for my convictions in my life. It's not for nothing that the peasant loves me. One must know the peasant! One must know how . . .

ANYA. At it again, uncle!

VARYA. Uncle dear, you'd better be quiet!

FIRS (*angrily*). Leonid Andreyevitch!

GAEV. I'm coming. I'm coming. Go to bed. Potted the shot—there's a shot for you! A beauty! (*Goes out,* FIRS *hobbling after him.*)

ANYA. My mind's at rest now. I don't want to go to Yaroslavl, I don't like my great-aunt, but still my mind's at rest. Thanks to uncle (*sits down*).

VARYA. We must go to bed. I'm going. Something unpleasant happened while you were away. In the old servants' quarters there are only the old servants, as you know—Efimyushka, Polya and Yevstigney—and Karp too. They began letting stray people in to spend the night —I said nothing. But all at once I heard they had been spreading a report that I gave them nothing but pease pudding to eat. Out of stinginess, you know. . . . And it was all Yevstigney's doing. . . . Very well, I said to myself. . . . If that's how it is, I thought, wait a bit. I sent for Yevstigney . . . (*yawns*). He comes. . . .

"How's this, Yevstigney," I said, "you could be such a fool as to? . . ." (*Looking at* ANYA) Anitchka! (*a pause*). She's asleep (*puts her arm round* ANYA). Come to bed . . . come along! (*Leads her*) My darling has fallen asleep! Come . . . (*They go.*)

(*Far away beyond the orchard a shepherd plays on a pipe.* TROFIMOV *crosses the stage and, seeing* VARYA *and* ANYA, *stands still.*)

VARYA. Sh! asleep, asleep. Come, my own.

ANYA (*softly, half asleep*). I'm so tired. Still those bells. Uncle . . . dear . . . mamma and uncle. . . .

VARYA. Come, my own, come along.

(*They go into* ANYA'S *room.*)

TROFIMOV (*tenderly*). My sunshine! My spring.

The Curtain Falls.

❦ Act II

The open country. An old shrine, long abandoned and fallen out of the perpendicular; near it a well, large stones that have apparently once been tombstones, and an old garden seat. The road to GAEV'S *house is seen. On one side rise dark poplars; and there the cherry orchard begins. In the distance a row of telegraph poles and far, far away on the horizon there is faintly outlined a great town, only visible in very fine clear weather. It is near sunset.* CHARLOTTA, YASHA *and* DUNYASHA *are sitting on the seat.* EPIHODOV *is standing near, playing something mournful on a guitar. All sit plunged in thought.* CHARLOTTA *wears an old forage cap; she has taken a gun from her shoulder and is tightening the buckle on the strap.*

CHARLOTTA (*musingly*). I haven't a real passport of my own, and I don't know how old I am, and I always feel that I'm a young thing. When I was a little girl, my father and mother used to travel about to fairs and give performances—very good ones. And I used to dance *salto-mortale* and all sorts of things. And when papa and mamma died, a German lady took me and had me educated. And so I grew up and became a

governess. But where I came from, and
who I am, I don't know. . . . Who my
parents were, very likely they weren't
married . . . I don't know (takes a cu-
cumber out of her pocket and eats). I
know nothing at all (a pause). One
wants to talk and has no one to talk to
. . . I have nobody.

EPIHODOV (plays on the guitar and
sings). "What care I for the noisy world!
What care I for friends or foes!" How
agreeable it is to play on the mandolin!

DUNYASHA. That's a guitar, not a
mandolin (looks in a hand-mirror and
powders herself).

EPIHODOV. To a man mad with love, it's
a mandolin. (Sings) "Were her heart but
aglow with love's mutual flame." (YASHA
joins in.)

CHARLOTTA. How shockingly these
people sing! Foo! Like jackals!

DUNYASHA (to YASHA). What happiness, though, to visit foreign lands.

YASHA. Ah, yes! I rather agree with
you there (yawns, then lights a cigar).

EPIHODOV. That's comprehensible. In
foreign lands everything has long since
reached full completion.

YASHA. That's so, of course.

EPIHODOV. I'm a cultivated man, I read
remarkable books of all sorts, but I can
never make out the tendency I am myself
precisely inclined for, whether to live or
to shoot myself, speaking precisely, but
nevertheless I always carry a revolver.
Here it is . . . (shows revolver).

CHARLOTTA. I've had enough, and now
I'm going (puts on the gun). Epihodov,
you're a very clever fellow, and a very
terrible one too, all the women must be
wild about you. Br-r-r! (Goes) These
clever fellows are all so stupid; there's not
a creature for me to speak to. . . . Always alone, alone, nobody belonging to
me . . . and who I am, and why I'm on
earth, I don't know (walks away slowly).

EPIHODOV. Speaking precisely, not
touching upon other subjects, I'm bound
to admit about myself, that destiny behaves mercilessly to me, as a storm to a
little boat. If, let us suppose, I am
mistaken, then why did I wake up this
morning, to quote an example, and look
round, and there on my chest was a spider
of fearful magnitude . . . like this
(shows with both hands). And then I
take up a jug of kvass, to quench my

thirst, and in it there is something in the
highest degree unseemly, of the nature of
a cockroach (a pause). Have you read
Buckle? (A pause) I am desirous of
troubling you, Dunyasha, with a couple
of words.

DUNYASHA. Well, speak.

EPIHODOV. I should be desirous to
speak with you alone (sighs).

DUNYASHA (embarrassed). Well—
only bring me my mantle first. It's by
the cupboard. It's rather damp here.

EPIHODOV. Certainly. I will fetch it.
Now I know what I must do with my
revolver (takes guitar and goes off playing on it).

YASHA. Two and twenty misfortunes!
Between ourselves, he's a fool (yawns).

DUNYASHA. God grant he doesn't shoot
himself! (A pause) I am so nervous, I'm
always in a flutter. I was a little girl when
I was taken into our lady's house, and
now I have quite grown out of peasant
ways, and my hands are white, as white
as a lady's. I'm such a delicate, sensitive
creature, I'm afraid of everything. I'm so
frightened. And if you deceive me, Yasha,
I don't know what will become of my
nerves.

YASHA (kisses her). You're a peach!
Of course a girl must never forget herself; what I dislike more than anything is
a girl being flighty in her behaviour.

DUNYASHA. I'm passionately in love
with you, Yasha; you are a man of culture—you can give your opinion about
anything (a pause).

YASHA (yawns). Yes, that's so. My
opinion is this: if a girl loves anyone,
that means that she has no principles
(a pause). It's pleasant smoking a cigar
in the open air (listens). Someone's
coming this way . . . it's the gentlefolk
(DUNYASHA embraces him impulsively).
Go home, as though you had been to the
river to bathe; go by that path, or else
they'll meet you and suppose I have made
an appointment with you here. That I
can't endure.

DUNYASHA (coughing softly). The
cigar has made my head ache . . . (goes
off).

(YASHA remains sitting near the shrine.
Enter LYUBOV ANDREYEVNA, GAEV and
LOPAHIN.)

LOPAHIN. You must make up your
mind once for all—there's no time to

lose. It's quite a simple question, you know. Will you consent to letting the land for building or not? One word in answer: Yes or no? Only one word!

LYUBOV. Who is smoking such horrible cigars here? (*Sits down.*)

GAEV. Now the railway line has been brought near, it's made things very convenient (*sits down*). Here we have been over and lunched in town. Cannon off the white! I should like to go home and have a game.

LYUBOV. You have plenty of time.

LOPAHIN. Only one word! (*Beseechingly*) Give me an answer!

GAEV (*yawning*). What do you say?

LYUBOV (*looks in her purse*). I had quite a lot of money here yesterday, and there's scarcely any left today. My poor Varya feeds us all on milk soup for the sake of economy; the old folks in the kitchen get nothing but pease pudding, while I waste my money in a senseless way (*drops purse, scattering gold pieces*). There, they have all fallen out! (*Annoyed.*)

YASHA. Allow me, I'll soon pick them up (*collects the coins*).

LYUBOV. Pray do, Yasha. And what did I go off to the town to lunch for? Your restaurant's a wretched place with its music and the tablecloth smelling of soap. . . . Why drink so much, Leonid? And eat so much? And talk so much? Today you talked a great deal again in the restaurant, and all so inappropriately. About the era of the 'seventies, about the decadents. And to whom? Talking to waiters about decadents!

LOPAHIN. Yes.

GAEV (*waving his hand*). I'm incorrigible; that's evident. (*Irritably to* YASHA) Why is it you keep fidgeting about in front of us!

YASHA (*laughs*). I can't help laughing when I hear your voice.

GAEV (*to his sister*). Either I or he. . . .

LYUBOV. Get along! Go away, Yasha.

YASHA (*gives* LYUBOV ANDREYEVNA *her purse*). Directly (*hardly able to suppress his laughter*). This minute . . . (*goes off*).

LOPAHIN. Deriganov, the millionaire, means to buy your estate. They say he is coming to the sale himself.

LYUBOV. Where did you hear that?

LOPAHIN. That's what they say in town.

GAEV. Our aunt in Yaroslavl has promised to send help; but when, and how much she will send, we don't know.

LOPAHIN. How much will she send? A hundred thousand? Two hundred?

LYUBOV. Oh, well! . . . Ten or fifteen thousand, and we must be thankful to get that.

LOPAHIN. Forgive me, but such reckless people as you are—such queer, unbusiness-like people—I never met in my life. One tells you in plain Russian your estate is going to be sold, and you seem not to understand it.

LYUBOV. What are we to do? Tell us what to do.

LOPAHIN. I do tell you every day. Every day I say the same thing. You absolutely must let the cherry orchard and the land on building leases; and do it at once, as quick as may be—the auction's close upon us! Do understand! Once make up your mind to build villas, and you can raise as much money as you like, and then you are saved.

LYUBOV. Villas and summer visitors—forgive me saying so—it's so vulgar.

GAEV. There I perfectly agree with you.

LOPAHIN. I shall sob, or scream, or fall into a fit. I can't stand it! You drive me mad! (*To* GAEV) You're an old woman!

GAEV. What do you say?

LOPAHIN. An old woman! (*Gets up to go.*)

LYUBOV (*in dismay*). No, don't go! Do stay, my dear friend! Perhaps we shall think of something.

LOPAHIN. What is there to think of?

LYUBOV. Don't go, I entreat you! With you here it's more cheerful, anyway (*a pause*). I keep expecting something, as though the house were going to fall about our ears.

GAEV (*in profound dejection*). Potted the white! It fails—a kiss.

LYUBOV. We have been great sinners. . . .

LOPAHIN. You have no sins to repent of.

GAEV (*puts a caramel in his mouth*). They say I've eaten up my property in caramels (*laughs*).

LYUBOV. Oh, my sins! I've always thrown my money away recklessly like a lunatic. I married a man who made nothing but debts. My husband died of champagne—he drank dreadfully. To my misery I loved another man, and immediately—it was my first punishment—the blow fell upon me, here, in the river . . . my boy was drowned and I went abroad—went away for ever, never to return, not to see that river again . . . I shut my eyes, and fled, distracted, and *he* after me . . . pitilessly, brutally. I bought a villa at Mentone, for *he* fell ill there, and for three years I had no rest day or night. His illness wore me out, my soul was dried up. And last year, when my villa was sold to pay my debts, I went to Paris and there he robbed me of everything and abandoned me for another woman; and I tried to poison myself. . . . So stupid, so shameful! . . . And suddenly I felt a yearning for Russia, for my country, for my little girl . . . (*dries her tears*). Lord, Lord, be merciful! Forgive my sins! Do not chastise me more! (*Takes a telegram out of her pocket*) I got this today from Paris. He implores forgiveness, entreats me to return (*tears up the telegram*). I fancy there is music somewhere (*listens*).

GAEV. That's our famous Jewish orchestra. You remember, four violins, a flute and a double bass.

LYUBOV. That still in existence? We ought to send for them one evening, and give a dance.

LOPAHIN (*listens*). I can't hear. . . . (*Hums softly*) "For money the Germans will turn a Russian into a Frenchman." (*Laughs*) I did see such a piece at the theatre yesterday! It was funny!

LYUBOV. And most likely there was nothing funny in it. You shouldn't look at plays, you should look at yourselves a little oftener. How grey your lives are! How much nonsense you talk.

LOPAHIN. That's true. One may say honestly, we live a fool's life (*pause*). My father was a peasant, an idiot; he knew nothing and taught me nothing, only beat me when he was drunk, and always with his stick. In reality I am just such another blockhead and idiot. I've learnt nothing properly. I write a wretched hand. I write so that I feel ashamed before folks, like a pig.

LYUBOV. You ought to get married, my dear fellow.

LOPAHIN. Yes . . . that's true.

LYUBOV. You should marry our Varya, she's a good girl.

LOPAHIN. Yes.

LYUBOV. She's a good-natured girl, she's busy all day long, and what's more, she loves you. And you have liked her for ever so long.

LOPAHIN. Well? I'm not against it. . . . She's a good girl (*pause*).

GAEV. I've been offered a place in the bank: 6,000 roubles a year. Did you know?

LYUBOV. You would never do for that! You must stay as you are.

(*Enter* FIRS *with overcoat.*)

FIRS. Put it on, sir, it's damp.

GAEV (*putting it on*). You bother me, old fellow.

FIRS. You can't go on like this. You went away in the morning without leaving word (*looks him over*).

LYUBOV. You look older, Firs!

FIRS. What is your pleasure?

LOPAHIN. You look older, she said.

FIRS. I've had a long life. They were arranging my wedding before your papa was born . . . (*laughs*). I was the head footman before the emancipation came. I wouldn't consent to be set free then; I stayed on with the old master . . . (*a pause*). I remember what rejoicings they made and didn't know themselves what they were rejoicing over.

LOPAHIN. Those were fine old times. There was flogging, anyway.

FIRS (*not hearing*). To be sure! The peasants knew their place, and the masters knew theirs; but now they're all at sixes and sevens, there's no making it out.

GAEV. Hold your tongue, Firs. I must go to town tomorrow. I have been promised an introduction to a general, who might let us have a loan.

LOPAHIN. You won't bring that off. And you won't pay your arrears, you may rest assured of that.

LYUBOV. That's all his nonsense. There is no such general.

(*Enter* TROFIMOV, ANYA *and* VARYA.)

GAEV. Here come our girls.

ANYA. There's mamma on the seat.

LYUBOV (*tenderly*). Come here, come along. My darlings! (*Embraces* ANYA *and* VARYA) If you only knew how I love you both. Sit beside me, there, like that. (*All sit down.*)

LOPAHIN. Our perpetual student is always with the young ladies.

TROFIMOV. That's not your business.

LOPAHIN. He'll soon be fifty, and he's still a student.

TROFIMOV. Drop your idiotic jokes.

LOPAHIN. Why are you so cross, you queer fish?

TROFIMOV. Oh, don't persist!

LOPAHIN (*laughs*). Allow me to ask you what's your idea of me?

TROFIMOV. I'll tell you my idea of you, Yermolay Alexeyevitch: you are a rich man, you'll soon be a millionaire. Well, just as in the economy of nature a wild beast is of use, who devours everything that comes in his way, so you too have your use.

(*All laugh.*)

VARYA. Better tell us something about the planets, Petya.

LYUBOV. No, let us go on with the conversation we had yesterday.

TROFIMOV. What was it about?

GAEV. About pride.

TROFIMOV. We had a long conversation yesterday, but we came to no conclusion. In pride, in your sense of it, there is something mystical. Perhaps you are right from your point of view; but if one looks at it simply, without subtlety, what sort of pride can there be, what sense is there in it, if man in his physiological formation is very imperfect, if in the immense majority of cases he is coarse, dull-witted, profoundly unhappy? One must give up glorification of self. One should work, and nothing else.

GAEV. One must die in any case.

TROFIMOV. Who knows? And what does it mean—dying? Perhaps man has a hundred senses, and only the five we know are lost at death, while the other ninety-five remain alive.

LYUBOV. How clever you are, Petya!

LOPAHIN (*ironically*). Fearfully clever!

TROFIMOV. Humanity progresses, perfecting its powers. Everything that is beyond its ken now will one day become familiar and comprehensible; only we must work, we must with all our powers aid the seeker after truth. Here among us in Russia the workers are few in number as yet. The vast majority of the intellectual people I know, seek nothing, do nothing, are not fit as yet for work of any kind. They call themselves intellectual, but they treat their servants as inferiors, behave to the peasants as though they were animals, learn little, read nothing seriously, do practically nothing, only talk about science and know very little about art. They are all serious people, they all have severe faces, they all talk of weighty matters and air their theories, and yet the vast majority of us—ninety-nine per cent.—live like savages, at the least thing fly to blows and abuse, eat piggishly, sleep in filth and stuffiness, bugs everywhere, stench and damp and moral impurity. And it's clear all our fine talk is only to divert our attention and other people's. Show me where to find the crèches there's so much talk about, and the reading-rooms? They only exist in novels: in real life there are none of them. There is nothing but filth and vulgarity and Asiatic apathy. I fear and dislike very serious faces. I'm afraid of serious conversations. We should do better to be silent.

LOPAHIN. You know, I get up at five o'clock in the morning, and I work from morning to night; and I've money, my own and other people's, always passing through my hands, and I see what people are made of all round me. One has only to begin to do anything to see how few honest, decent people there are. Sometimes when I lie awake at night, I think: "Oh! Lord, thou hast given us immense forests, boundless plains, the widest horizons, and living here we ourselves ought really to be giants."

LYUBOV. You ask for giants! They are no good except in story-books; in real life they frighten us.

(EPIHODOV *advances in the background, playing on the guitar.*)

LYUBOV (*dreamily*). There goes Epihodov.

ANYA (*dreamily*). There goes Epihodov.

GAEV. The sun has set, my friends.

TROFIMOV. Yes.

GAEV (*not loudly, but, as it were, declaiming*). O nature, divine nature, thou art bright with eternal lustre, beautiful and indifferent! Thou, whom we call mother, thou dost unite within thee life and death! Thou dost give life and dost destroy!

VARYA (*in a tone of supplication*). Uncle!

ANYA. Uncle, you are at it again!

TROFIMOV. You'd much better be cannoning off the red!

GAEV. I'll hold my tongue, I will.

(*All sit plunged in thought. Perfect stillness. The only thing audible is the muttering of* FIRS. *Suddenly there is a sound in the distance, as it were from the sky—the sound of a breaking harp-string, mournfully dying away.*)

LYUBOV. What is that?

LOPAHIN. I don't know. Somewhere far away a bucket fallen and broken in the pits. But somewhere very far away.

GAEV. It might be a bird of some sort —such as a heron.

TROFIMOV. Or an owl.

LYUBOV (*shudders*). I don't know why, but it's horrid (*a pause*).

FIRS. It was the same before the calamity—the owl hooted and the samovar hissed all the time.

GAEV. Before what calamity?

FIRS. Before the emancipation (*a pause*).

LYUBOV. Come, my friends, let us be going; evening is falling. (*To* ANYA) There are tears in your eyes. What is it, darling? (*Embraces her.*)

ANYA. Nothing, mamma; it's nothing.

TROFIMOV. There is somebody coming.

(*The wayfarer appears in a shabby white forage cap and an overcoat; he is slightly drunk.*)

WAYFARER. Allow me to inquire, can I get to the station this way?

GAEV. Yes. Go along that road.

WAYFARER. I thank you most feelingly (*coughing*). The weather is superb. (*Declaims*) My brother, my suffering brother! . . . Come out to the Volga! Whose groan do you hear? . . . (*To* VARYA) Mademoiselle, vouchsafe a hungry Russian thirty kopeks.

(VARYA *utters a shriek of alarm.*)

LOPAHIN (*angrily*). There's a right and a wrong way of doing everything!

LYUBOV (*hurriedly*). Here, take this (*looks in her purse*). I've no silver. No matter—here's gold for you.

WAYFARER. I thank you most feelingly! (*Goes off.*)

(*Laughter.*)

VARYA (*frightened*). I'm going home —I'm going . . . Oh, mamma, the servants have nothing to eat, and you gave him gold!

LYUBOV. There's no doing anything with me. I'm so silly! When we get home, I'll give you all I possess. Yermolay Alexeyevitch, you will lend me some more . . . !

LOPAHIN. I will.

LYUBOV. Come, friends, it's time to be going. And Varya, we have made a match of it for you. I congratulate you.

VARYA (*through her tears*). Mamma, that's not a joking matter.

LOPAHIN. "Ophelia, get thee to a nunnery!"

GAEV. My hands are trembling; it's a long while since I had a game of billiards.

LOPAHIN. "Ophelia! Nymph, in thy orisons be all my sins remember'd.'"

LYUBOV. Come, it will soon be suppertime.

VARYA. How he frightened me! My heart's simply throbbing.

LOPAHIN. Let me remind you, ladies and gentlemen: on the 22nd of August the cherry orchard will be sold. Think about that! Think about it!

(*All go off, except* TROFIMOV *and* ANYA.)

ANYA (*laughing*). I'm grateful to the wayfarer! He frightened Varya and we are left alone.

TROFIMOV. Varya's afraid we shall fall in love with each other, and for days together she won't leave us. With her narrow brain she can't grasp that we are above love. To eliminate the petty and transitory which hinders us from being free and happy—that is the aim and meaning of our life. Forward! We go forward irresistibly towards the bright star that shines yonder in the distance. Forward! Do not lag behind, friends.

ANYA (*claps her hands*). How well you speak! (*A pause*) It is divine here today.

TROFIMOV. Yes, it's glorious weather.

ANYA. Somehow, Petya, you've made me so that I don't love the cherry orchard as I used to. I used to love it so dearly. I used to think that there was no spot on earth like our garden.

TROFIMOV. All Russia is our garden. The earth is great and beautiful—there are many beautiful places in it (*a pause*). Think only, Anya, your grandfather, and great-grandfather, and all your ancestors were slave-owners—the owners of living souls—and from every cherry in the orchard, from every leaf, from every trunk there are human creatures looking at you. Cannot you hear their voices? Oh, it is awful! Your orchard is a fearful thing, and when in the evening or at night one walks about the orchard, the old bark on the trees glimmers dimly in the dusk, and the old cherry trees seem to be dreaming of centuries gone by and tortured by fearful visions. Yes! We are at least two hundred years behind, we have really gained nothing yet, we have no definite attitude to the past, we do nothing but theorise or complain of depression or drink vodka. It is clear that to begin to live in the present we must first expiate our past, we must break with it; and we can expiate it only by suffering, by extraordinary unceasing labour. Understand that, Anya.

ANYA. The house we live in has long ceased to be our own, and I shall leave it, I give you my word.

TROFIMOV. If you have the house keys, fling them into the well and go away. Be free as the wind.

ANYA. (*in ecstasy*). How beautifully you said that!

TROFIMOV. Believe me, Anya, believe me! I am not thirty yet, I am young, I am still a student, but I have gone through so much already! As soon as winter comes I am hungry, sick, careworn, poor as a beggar, and what ups and downs of fortune have I not known! And my soul was always, every minute, day and night, full of inexplicable forebodings. I have a foreboding of happiness, Anya. I see glimpses of it already.

ANYA (*pensively*). The moon is rising.

(EPIHODOV *is heard playing still the same mournful song on the guitar. The moon rises. Somewhere near the poplars* VARYA *is looking for* ANYA *and calling* "Anya! Where are you?")

TROFIMOV. Yes, the moon is rising (*a pause*). Here is happiness—here it comes! It is coming nearer and nearer; already I can hear its footsteps. And if we never see it—if we may never know it—what does it matter? Others will see it after us.

VARYA'S VOICE. Anya! Where are you?

TROFIMOV. That Varya again! (*Angrily*) It's revolting!

ANYA. Well, let's go down to the river. It's lovely there.

TROFIMOV. Yes, let's go. (*They go.*)

VARYA'S VOICE. Anya! Anya!

The Curtain Falls.

Act III

A drawing-room divided by an arch from a larger drawing-room. A chandelier burning. The Jewish orchestra, the same that was mentioned in Act II, is heard playing in the ante-room. It is evening. In the larger drawing-room they are dancing the grand chain. The voice of SEMYONOV-PISHTCHIK: *"Promenade à une paire!" Then enter the drawing-room in couples first* PISHTCHIK *and* CHARLOTTA IVANOVNA, *then* TROFIMOV *and* LYUBOV ANDREYEVNA, *thirdly* ANYA *with the Post-Office Clerk, fourthly* VARYA *with the Station Master, and other guests.* VARYA *is quietly weeping and wiping away her tears as she dances. In the last couple is* DUNYASHA. *They move across the drawing-room.* PISHTCHIK *shouts:* Grand rond, balancez!" *and* "Les Cavaliers à genou et remerciez vos dames."

FIRS *in a swallow-tail coat brings in seltzer water on a tray.* PISHTCHIK *and* TROFIMOV *enter the drawing-room.*

PISHTCHIK. I am a full-blooded man; I have already had two strokes. Dancing's hard work for me, but as they say, if you're in the pack, you must bark with the rest. I'm as strong, I may say, as a horse. My parent, who would have his joke—may the Kingdom of Heaven be his!—used to say about our origin that the ancient stock of the Semyonov-Pishtchiks was derived from the very horse that Caligula made a member of the senate (*sits down*). But I've no money, that's where the mischief is. A hungry dog believes in nothing but meat. . . . (*snores, but at once wakes up*). That's like me . . . I can think of nothing but money.

TROFIMOV. There really is something horsy about your appearance.

PISHTCHIK. Well . . . a horse is a fine beast . . . a horse can be sold.

(*There is the sound of billiards being played in an adjoining room.* VARYA *appears in the arch leading to the larger drawing-room.*)

TROFIMOV (*teasing*). Madame Lopahin! Madame Lopahin!

VARYA (*angrily*). Mangy-looking gentleman!

TROFIMOV. Yes, I am a mangy-looking gentleman, and I'm proud of it!

VARYA (*pondering bitterly*). Here we have hired musicians and nothing to pay them! (*Goes out.*)

TROFIMOV (*to* PISHTCHIK). If the energy you have wasted during your lifetime in trying to find the money to pay your interest, had gone to something else, you might in the end have turned the world upside down.

PISHTCHIK. Nietzsche, the philosopher, a very great and celebrated man . . . of enormous intellect . . . says in his works, that one can make forged bank-notes.

TROFIMOV. Why, have you read Nietzsche?

PISHTCHIK. What next . . . Dashenka told me. . . . And now I am in such a position, I might just as well forge bank-notes. The day after tomorrow I must pay 310 roubles—130 I have procured (*feels in his pockets, in alarm*). The money's gone! I have lost my money! (*Through his tears*) Where's the money? (*Gleefully*) Why, here it is behind the lining. . . . It has made me hot all over.

(*Enter* LYUBOV ANDREYEVNA *and* CHARLOTTA IVANOVNA.)

LYUBOV (*hums the Lezginka*). Why is Leonid so long? What can he be doing in town? (*To* DUNYASHA) Offer the musicians some tea.

TROFIMOV. The sale hasn't taken place, most likely.

LYUBOV. It's the wrong time to have the orchestra, and the wrong time to give a dance. Well, never mind (*sits down and hums softly*).

CHARLOTTA (*gives* PISHTCHIK *a pack of cards*). Here's a pack of cards. Think of any card you like.

PISHTCHIK. I've thought of one.

CHARLOTTA. Shuffle the pack now. That's right. Give it here, my dear Mr. Pishtchik. Ein, zwei, drei—now look, it's in your breast pocket.

PISHTCHIK (*taking a card out of his breast pocket*). The eight of spades! Perfectly right! (*Wonderingly*) Fancy that now!

CHARLOTTA (*holding pack of cards in her hands, to* TROFIMOV). Tell me quickly which is the top card.

TROFIMOV. Well, the queen of spades.

CHARLOTTA. It is! (*To* PISHTCHIK) Well, which card is uppermost?

PISHTCHIK. The ace of hearts.

CHARLOTTA. It is! (*Claps her hands, pack of cards disappears*) Ah! what lovely weather it is today!

(*A mysterious feminine voice which seems coming out of the floor answers her.* "Oh, yes, it's magnificent weather, madam.")

CHARLOTTA. You are my perfect ideal.

VOICE. And I greatly admire you too, madam.

STATION MASTER (*applauding*). The lady ventriloquist—bravo!

PISHTCHIK (*wonderingly*). Fancy that now! Most enchanting, Charlotta Ivanovna. I'm simply in love with you.

CHARLOTTA. In love? (*Shrugging shoulders*) What do you know of love, guter Mensch, aber schlechter Musikant.

TROFIMOV (*pats* PISHTCHIK *on the shoulder*). You dear old horse. . . .

CHARLOTTA. Attention, please! Another trick! (*Takes a travelling rug from a chair*) Here's a very good rug; I want to sell it (*shaking it out*). Doesn't anyone want to buy it?

PISHTCHIK (*wonderingly*). Fancy that!

CHARLOTTA. Ein, zwei, drei! (*Quickly picks up rug she has dropped; behind the rug stands* ANYA; *she makes a curtsey, runs to her mother, embraces her and runs back into the larger drawing-room amidst general enthusiasm.*)

LYUBOV (*applauds*). Bravo! Bravo!

CHARLOTTA. Now again! Ein, zwei, drei! (*Lifts up the rug; behind the rug stands* VARYA, *bowing.*)

PISHTCHIK (*wonderingly*). Fancy that now!

CHARLOTTA. That's the end (*throws the rug at* PISHTCHIK, *makes a curtsey, runs into the larger drawing-room*).

PISHTCHIK (*hurries after her*). Mischievous creature! Fancy! (*Goes out.*)

LYUBOV. And still Leonid doesn't come. I can't understand what he's doing in the town so long! Why, everything must be over by now. The estate is sold, or the sale has not taken place. Why keep us so long in suspense?

VARYA (*trying to console her*). Uncle's bought it. I feel sure of that.

TROFIMOV (*ironically*). Oh, yes!

VARYA. Great-aunt sent him an author-isation to buy it in her name, and transfer the debt. She's doing it for Anya's sake, and I'm sure God will be merciful. Uncle will buy it.

LYUBOV. My aunt in Yaroslavl sent fifteen thousand to buy the estate in her name, she doesn't trust us—but that's not enough even to pay the arrears (*hides her face in her hands*). My fate is being sealed today, my fate. . . .

TROFIMOV (*teasing* VARYA). Madame Lopahin.

VARYA (*angrily*). Perpetual student! Twice already you've been sent down from the University.

LYUBOV. Why are you angry, Varya? He's teasing you about Lopahin. Well, what of that? Marry Lopahin if you like, he's a good man, and interesting; if you don't want to, don't! Nobody compels you, darling.

VARYA. I must tell you plainly, mamma, I look at the matter seriously; he's a good man, I like him.

LYUBOV. Well, marry him. I can't see what you're waiting for.

VARYA. Mamma. I can't make him an offer myself. For the last two years, every-one's been talking to me about him. Everyone talks; but he says nothing or else makes a joke. I see what it means. He's growing rich, he's absorbed in business, he has no thoughts for me. If I had money, were it ever so little, if I had only a hundred roubles, I'd throw every-thing up and go far away. I would go into a nunnery.

TROFIMOV. What bliss!

VARYA (*to* TROFIMOV). A student ought to have sense! (*In a soft tone with tears*) How ugly you've grown, Petya! How old you look! (*To* LYUBOV ANDRE-YEVNA, *no longer crying*) But I can't do without work, mamma; I must have something to do every minute.

(*Enter* YASHA.)

YASHA (*hardly restraining his laugh-ter*). Epihodov has broken a billiard cue! (*Goes out.*)

VARYA. What is Epihodov doing here? Who gave him leave to play billiards? I can't make these people out (*goes out*).

LYUBOV. Don't tease her, Petya. You see she has grief enough without that.

TROFIMOV. She is so very officious, meddling in what's not her business. All the summer she's given Anya and me no peace. She's afraid of a love affair be-tween us. What's it to do with her? Besides, I have given no grounds for it. Such triviality is not in my line. We are above love!

LYUBOV. And I suppose I am beneath love. (*Very uneasily*) Why is it Leonid's not here? If only I could know whether the estate is sold or not! It seems such an incredible calamity that I really don't know what to think. I am distracted . . . I shall scream in a minute . . . I shall do something stupid. Save me, Petya, tell me something, talk to me!

TROFIMOV. What does it matter whether the estate is sold today or not? That's all done with long ago. There's no turning back, the path is overgrown. Don't worry yourself, dear Lyubov Andre-yevna. You mustn't deceive yourself; for once in your life you must face the truth!

LYUBOV. What truth? You see where the truth lies, but I seem to have lost my sight, I see nothing. You settle every great problem so boldly, but tell me, my dear boy, isn't it because you're young—because you haven't yet understood one of your problems through suffering? You look forward boldly, and isn't it that you don't see and don't expect anything dreadful because life is still hidden from your young eyes? You're bolder, more honest, deeper than we are, but think, be just a little magnanimous, have pity on me. I was born here, you know, my father and mother lived here, my grandfather lived here, I love this house. I can't con-ceive of life without the cherry orchard, and if it really must be sold, then sell me with the orchard (*embraces* TROFIMOV, *kisses him on the forehead*). My boy was drowned here (*weeps*). Pity me, my dear kind fellow.

TROFIMOV. You know I feel for you with all my heart.

LYUBOV. But that should have been said differently, so differently (*takes out her handkerchief, telegram falls on the floor*). My heart is so heavy today. It's so noisy here, my soul is quivering at every sound, I'm shuddering all over, but I can't go away; I'm afraid to be quiet and alone. Don't be hard on me, Petya . . . I love you as though you were one of ourselves. I would gladly let you marry Anya—I swear I would—only, my dear boy, you must take your degree, you do nothing—you're simply tossed by fate from place to place. That's so strange. It is, isn't it? And you must do something with your beard to make it grow somehow (*laughs*). You look so funny!

TROFIMOV (*picks up the telegram*). I've no wish to be a beauty.

LYUBOV. That's a telegram from Paris. I get one every day. One yesterday and one today. That savage creature is ill again, he's in trouble again. He begs forgiveness, beseeches me to go, and really I ought to go to Paris to see him. You look shocked, Petya. What am I to do, my dear boy, what am I to do? He is ill, he is alone and unhappy, and who'll look after him, who'll keep him from doing the wrong thing, who'll give him his medicine at the right time? And why hide it or be silent? I love him, that's clear. I love him! I love him! He's a millstone about my neck, I'm going to the bottom with him, but I love that stone and can't live without it (*presses* TROFIMOV's *hand*). Don't think ill of me, Petya, don't tell me anything, don't tell me. . . .

TROFIMOV (*through his tears*). For God's sake forgive my frankness: why, he robbed you!

LYUBOV. No! No! No! You mustn't speak like that (*covers her ears*).

TROFIMOV. He is a wretch! You're the only person that doesn't know it! He's a worthless creature! A despicable wretch!

LYUBOV (*getting angry, but speaking with restraint*). You're twenty-six or twenty-seven years old, but you're still a schoolboy.

TROFIMOV. Possibly.

LYUBOV. You should be a man at your age! You should understand what love means! And you ought to be in love yourself. You ought to fall in love! (*Angrily*) Yes, yes, and it's not purity in you, you're simply a prude, a comic fool, a freak.

TROFIMOV (*in horror*). The things she's saying!

LYUBOV. I am above love! You're not above love, but simply as our Firs here says, "You are a good-for-nothing." At your age not to have a mistress!

TROFIMOV (*in horror*). This is awful! The things she is saying! (*Goes rapidly* into the larger drawing-room clutching his head) This is awful! I can't stand it! I'm going. (*Goes off, but at once returns*) All is over between us! (*Goes off into the ante-room.*)

LYUBOV (*shouts after him*). Petya! Wait a minute! You funny creature! I was joking! Petya! (*There is a sound of somebody running quickly downstairs and suddenly falling with a crash.* ANYA *and* VARYA *scream, but there is a sound of laughter at once.*)

LYUBOV. What has happened?

(ANYA *runs in.*)

ANYA (*laughing*). Petya's fallen downstairs! (*Runs out.*)

LYUBOV. What a queer fellow that Petya is!

(*The Station Master stands in the middle of the larger room and reads "The Magdalene," by Alexey Tolstoy. They listen to him, but before he has recited many lines strains of a waltz are heard from the ante-room and the reading is broken off. All dance.* TROFIMOV, ANYA, VARYA *and* LYUBOV ANDREYEVNA *come in from the ante-room.*)

LYUBOV. Come, Petya—come, pure heart! I beg your pardon. Let's have a dance! (*Dances with* PETYA.)

(ANYA *and* VARYA *dance.* FIRS *comes in, puts his stick down near the side door.* YASHA *also comes into the drawing-room and looks on at the dancing.*)

YASHA. What is it, old man?

FIRS. I don't feel well. In old days we used to have generals, barons and admirals dancing at our balls, and now we send for the post-office clerk and the station master and even they're not over-anxious to come. I am getting feeble. The old master, the grandfather, used to give sealing-wax for all complaints. I have been taking sealing-wax for twenty years or more. Perhaps that's what's kept me alive.

YASHA. You bore me, old man! (*Yawns*) it's time you were done with.

FIRS. Ach, you're a good-for-nothing! (*Mutters.*)

(TROFIMOV *and* LYUBOV ANDREYEVNA *dance in larger room and then on to the stage*).

LYUBOV. *Merci.* I'll sit down a little (*sits down*). I'm tired.

(*Enter* ANYA.)

ANYA (*excitedly*). There's a man in

the kitchen has been saying that the cherry orchard's been sold today.

LYUBOV. Sold to whom?

ANYA. He didn't say to whom. He's gone away.

(*She dances with* TROFIMOV, *and they go off into the larger room.*)

YASHA. There was an old man gossiping there, a stranger.

FIRS. Leonid Andreyevitch isn't here yet, he hasn't come back. He has his light overcoat on, *demi-saison,* he'll catch cold for sure. Ach! Foolish young things!

LYUBOV. I feel as though I should die. Go, Yasha, find out to whom it has been sold.

YASHA. But he went away long ago, the old chap (*laughs*).

LYUBOV (*with slight vexation*). What are you laughing at? What are you pleased at?

YASHA. Epihodov is so funny. He's a silly fellow, two and twenty misfortunes.

LYUBOV. Firs, if the estate is sold, where will you go?

FIRS. Where you bid me, there I'll go.

LYUBOV. Why do you look like that? Are you ill? You ought to be in bed.

FIRS. Yes (*ironically*). Me go to bed and who's to wait here? Who's to see to things without me? I'm the only one in all the house.

YASHA (*to* LYUBOV ANDREYEVNA). Lyubov Andreyevna, permit me to make a request of you; if you go back to Paris again, be so kind as to take me with you. It's positively impossible for me to stay here (*looking about him; in an undertone*). There's no need to say it, you see for yourself—an uncivilised country, the people have no morals, and then the dullness! The food in the kitchen's abominable, and then Firs runs after one muttering all sorts of unsuitable words. Take me with you, please do!

(*Enter* PISHTCHIK.)

PISHTCHIK. Allow me to ask you for a waltz, my dear lady. (LYUBOV ANDREYEVNA *goes with him*) Enchanting lady, I really must borrow of you just 180 roubles (*dances*), only 180 roubles. (*They pass into the larger room.*)

YASHA (*hums softly*). "Knowest thou my soul's emotion."

(*In the larger drawing-room, a figure in a gray top hat and in check trousers is gesticulating and jumping about. Shouts of "Bravo, Charlotta Ivanovna."*)

DUNYASHA (*she has stopped to powder herself*). My young lady tells me to dance. There are plenty of gentlemen, and too few ladies, but dancing makes me giddy and makes my heart beat. Firs, the post-office clerk said something to me just now that quite took my breath away.

(*Music becomes more subdued.*)

FIRS. What did he say to you?

DUNYASHA. He said I was like a flower.

YASHA (*yawns*). What ignorance! (*Goes out.*)

DUNYASHA. Like a flower. I am a girl of such delicate feelings, I am awfully fond of soft speeches.

FIRS. Your head's being turned.

(*Enter* EPIHODOV.)

EPIHODOV. You have no desire to see me, Dunyasha. I might be an insect (*sighs*). Ah! life!

DUNYASHA. What is it you want?

EPIHODOV. Undoubtedly you may be right (*sighs*). But of course, if one looks at it from that point of view, if I may so express myself, you have, excuse my plain speaking, reduced me to a complete state of mind. I know my destiny. Every day some misfortune befalls me and I have long ago grown accustomed to it, so that I look upon my fate with a smile. You gave me your word, and though I . . .

DUNYASHA. Let us have a talk later, I entreat you, but now leave me in peace, for I am lost in reverie (*plays with her fan*).

EPIHODOV. I have a misfortune every day, and if I may venture to express myself, I merely smile at it, I even laugh.

(VARYA *enters from the larger drawing-room.*)

VARYA. You still have not gone, Epihodov. What a disrespectful creature you are, really! (*To* DUNYASHA) Go along, Dunyasha! (*To* EPIHODOV) First you play billiards and break the cue, then you go wandering about the drawing-room like a visitor!

EPIHODOV. You really cannot, if I may so express myself, call me to account like this.

VARYA. I'm not calling you to account, I'm speaking to you: You do nothing but wander from place to place and don't do your work. We keep you as a counting-house clerk, but what use you are I can't say.

EPIHODOV (*offended*). Whether I work or whether I walk, whether I eat or whether I play billiards, is a matter to be judged by persons of understanding and my elders.

VARYA. You dare to tell me that! (*Firing up*) You dare! You mean to say I've no understanding. Begone from here! This minute!

EPIHODOV (*intimidated*). I beg you to express yourself with delicacy.

VARYA (*beside herself with anger*). This moment! get out! away! (*He goes towards the door, she following him*) Two and twenty misfortunes! Take yourself off! Don't let me set eyes on you! (EPIHODOV *has gone out, behind the door his voice,* "I shall lodge a complaint against you") What! You're coming back? (*Snatches up the stick* FIRS *has put down near the door*) Come! Come! Come! I'll show you! What! you're coming? Then take that! (*She swings the stick, at the very moment that* LOPAHIN *comes in.*)

LOPAHIN. Very much obliged to you!

VARYA (*angrily and ironically*). I beg your pardon!

LOPAHIN. Not at all! I humbly thank you for your kind reception!

VARYA. No need of thanks for it. (*Moves away, then looks round and asks softly*) I haven't hurt you?

LOPAHIN. Oh, no! Not at all! There's an immense bump coming up, though!

VOICES FROM LARGER ROOM: Lopahin has come! Yermolay Alexeyevitch!

PISHTCHIK. What do I see and hear? (*Kisses* LOPAHIN) There's a whiff of cognac about you, my dear soul, and we're making merry here too!

(*Enter* LYUBOV ANDREYEVNA.)

LYUBOV. Is it you, Yermolay Alexeyevitch? Why have you been so long? Where's Leonid?

LOPAHIN. Leonid Andreyevitch arrived with me. He is coming.

LYUBOV (*in agitation*). Well! Well! Was there a sale? Speak!

LOPAHIN (*embarrassed, afraid of betraying his joy*). The sale was over at four o'clock. We missed our train—had to wait till half-past nine. (*Sighing heavily*) Ugh! I feel a little giddy.

(*Enter* GAEV. *In his right hand he has purchases, with his left hand he is wiping away his tears.*)

LYUBOV. Well, Leonid? What news? (*Impatiently, with tears*) Make haste, for God's sake!

GAEV (*makes her no answer, simply waves his hand. To* FIRS, *weeping*). Here, take them; there's anchovies, Kertch herrings. I have eaten nothing all day. What I have been through! (*Door into the billiard room is open. There is heard a knocking of balls and the voice of* YASHA *saying* "Eighty-seven." GAEV's *expression changes, he leaves off weeping*) I am fearfully tired. Firs, come and help me change my things (*goes to his own room across the larger drawing-room*).

PISHTCHIK. How about the sale? Tell us, do!

LYUBOV. Is the cherry orchard sold?

LOPAHIN. It is sold.

LYUBOV. Who has bought it?

LOPAHIN. I have bought it. (*A pause.* LYUBOV *is crushed; she would fall down if she were not standing near a chair and table.*)

(VARYA *takes keys from her waistband, flings them on the floor in middle of drawing-room and goes out.*)

LOPAHIN. I have bought it! Wait a bit, ladies and gentlemen, pray. My head's a bit muddled, I can't speak (*laughs*). We came to the auction. Deriganov was there already. Leonid Andreyevitch only had 15,000 and Deriganov bid 30,000, besides the arrears, straight off. I saw how the land lay. I bid against him. I bid 40,000, he bid 45,000, I said 55, and so he went on, adding 5 thousands and I adding 10. Well . . . So it ended. I bid 90, and it was knocked down to me. Now the cherry orchard's mine! Mine! (*chuckles*) My God, the cherry orchard's mine! Tell me that I'm drunk, that I'm out of my mind, that it's all a dream (*stamps with his feet*). Don't laugh at me! If my father and my grandfather could rise from their graves and see all that has happened! How their Yermolay, ignorant, beaten Yermolay, who used to run about barefoot in winter, how that very Yermolay has bought the finest estate in the world! I have bought the estate where my father and grandfather were slaves, where they weren't even admitted into the kitchen. I am asleep, I am dreaming! It is all fancy, it is the work of your imagination plunged in the darkness of ignorance (*picks up keys, smiling fondly*). She threw away the keys; she means to show she's not the house-wife now (*jingles the keys*). Well, no matter. (*The orchestra is heard tuning up*) Hey, musicians! Play! I want to hear you. Come, all of you, and look how Yermolay Lopahin will take the axe to the cherry orchard, how the trees will fall to the ground! We will build houses on it and our grandsons and great-grandsons will see a new life springing up there. Music! Play up!

(*Music begins to play.* LYUBOV ANDRE-YEVNA *has sunk into a chair and is weeping bitterly.*)

LOPAHIN (*reproachfully*). Why, why didn't you listen to me? My poor friend! Dear lady, there's no turning back now. (*With tears*) Oh, if all this could be over, oh, if our miserable disjointed life could somehow soon be changed!

PISHTCHIK (*takes him by the arm, in an undertone*). She's weeping, let us go and leave her alone. Come (*takes him by the arm and leads him into the larger drawing-room*).

LOPAHIN. What's that? Musicians, play up! All must be as I wish it. (*With irony*) Here comes the new master, the owner of the cherry orchard! (*Accidentally tips over a little table, almost upsetting the candelabra*) I can pay for everything! (*Goes out with* PISHTCHIK. *No one remains on the stage or in the larger drawing-room except* LYUBOV, *who sits huddled up, weeping bitterly. The music plays softly.* ANYA *and* TROFIMOV *come in quickly.* ANYA *goes up to her mother and falls on her knees before her.* TROFIMOV *stands at the entrance to the larger drawing-room*).

ANYA. Mamma! Mamma, you're cry-ing, dear, kind, good mamma! My pre-cious! I love you! I bless you! The cherry orchard is sold, it is gone, that's true, that's true! But don't weep, mamma! Life is still before you, you have still your good, pure heart! Let us go, let us go, darling, away from here! We will make a new garden, more splendid than this one; you will see it, you will understand. And joy, quiet, deep joy, will sink into your soul like the sun at evening! And

you will smile, mamma! Come, darling, let us go!

The Curtain Falls.

🌿 Act IV

SCENE: *Same as in First Act. There are neither curtains on the windows nor pictures on the walls: only a little furniture remains piled up in a corner as if for sale. There is a sense of desolation; near the outer door and in the background of the scene are packed trunks, travelling bags, etc. On the left the door is open, and from here the voices of* VARYA *and* ANYA *are audible.* LOPAHIN *is standing waiting.* YASHA *is holding a tray with glasses full of champagne. In front of the stage* EPIHODOV *is tying up a box. In the background behind the scene a hum of talk from the peasants who have come to say good-bye. The voice of* GAEV: "Thanks, brothers, thanks!"*

YASHA. The peasants have come to say good-bye. In my opinion, Yermolay Alexeyevitch, the peasants are good-natured, but they don't know much about things.

(*The hum of talk dies away. Enter across front of stage* LYUBOV ANDRE-YEVNA *and* GAEV. *She is not weeping, but is pale; her face is quivering—she cannot speak.*)

GAEV. You gave them your purse, Lyuba. That won't do—that won't do!

LYUBOV. I couldn't help it! I couldn't help it!

(*Both go out.*)

LOPAHIN (*in the doorway, calls after them*). You will take a glass at parting? Please do. I didn't think to bring any from the town, and at the station I could only get one bottle. Please take a glass. (*A pause*) What? You don't care for any? (*Comes away from the door*) If I'd known, I wouldn't have bought it. Well, and I'm not going to drink it. (YASHA *carefully sets the tray down on a chair*) You have a glass, Yasha, anyway.

YASHA. Good luck to the travellers, and luck to those that stay behind! (*Drinks*) This champagne isn't the real thing, I can assure you.

LOPAHIN. It cost eight roubles the bottle (*a pause*). It's devilish cold here.

YASHA. They haven't heated the stove today—it's all the same since we're going (*laughs*).

LOPAHIN. What are you laughing for?

YASHA. For pleasure.

LOPAHIN. Though it's October, it's as still and sunny as though it were summer. It's just right for building! (*Looks at his watch; says in doorway*) Take note, ladies and gentlemen, the train goes in forty-seven minutes; so you ought to start for the station in twenty minutes. You must hurry up!

(TROFIMOV *comes in from out of doors wearing a great-coat.*)

TROFIMOV. I think it must be time to start, the horses are ready. The devil only knows what's become of my goloshes; they're lost. (*In the doorway*) Anya! My goloshes aren't here. I can't find them.

LOPAHIN. And I'm getting off to Harkov. I am going in the same train with you. I'm spending all the winter at Harkov. I've been wasting all my time gossiping with you and fretting with no work to do. I can't get on without work. I don't know what to do with my hands, they flap about so queerly, as if they didn't belong to me.

TROFIMOV. Well, we're just going away, and you will take up your profitable labours again.

LOPAHIN. Do take a glass.

TROFIMOV. No, thanks.

LOPAHIN. Then you're going to Moscow now?

TROFIMOV. Yes. I shall see them as far as the town, and tomorrow I shall go on to Moscow.

LOPAHIN. Yes, I daresay, the professors aren't giving any lectures, they're waiting for your arrival.

TROFIMOV. That's not your business.

LOPAHIN. How many years have you been at the University?

TROFIMOV. Do think of something newer than that—that's stale and flat (*hunts for goloshes*). You know we shall most likely never see each other again, so let me give you one piece of advice at parting: don't wave your arms about—get out of the habit. And another thing, building villas, reckoning up that the summer visitors will in time become independent farmers—reckoning like that, that's not the thing to do either. After all, I am fond of you: you have fine

delicate fingers like an artist, you've a fine delicate soul.

LOPAHIN (*embraces him*). Good-bye, my dear fellow. Thanks for everything. Let me give you money for the journey, if you need it.

TROFIMOV. What for? I don't need it.

LOPAHIN. Why, you haven't got a halfpenny.

TROFIMOV. Yes, I have, thank you. I got some money for a translation. Here it is in my pocket, (*anxiously*) but where can my goloshes be?

VARYA (*from the next room*). Take the nasty things! (*Flings a pair of goloshes onto the stage.*)

TROFIMOV. Why are you so cross, Varya? h'm! . . . but those aren't my goloshes.

LOPAHIN. I sowed three thousand acres with poppies in the spring, and now I have cleared forty thousand profit. And when my poppies were in flower, wasn't it a picture! So here, as I say, I made forty thousand, and I'm offering you a loan because I can afford to. Why turn up your nose? I am a peasant—I speak bluntly.

TROFIMOV. Your father was a peasant, mine was a chemist—and that proves absolutely nothing whatever. (LOPAHIN *takes out his pocketbook*) Stop that—stop that. If you were to offer me two hundred thousand I wouldn't take it. I am an independent man, and everything that all of you, rich and poor alike, prize so highly and hold so dear, hasn't the slightest power over me—it's like so much fluff fluttering in the air. I can get on without you. I can pass by you. I am strong and proud. Humanity is advancing towards the highest truth, the highest happiness, which is possible on earth, and I am in the front ranks.

LOPAHIN. Will you get there?

TROFIMOV. I shall get there (*a pause*). I shall get there, or I shall show others the way to get there.

(*In the distance is heard the stroke of an axe on a tree.*)

LOPAHIN. Good-bye, my dear fellow; it's time to be off. We turn up our noses at one another, but life is passing all the while. When I am working hard without resting, then my mind is more at ease, and it seems to me as though I too know what I exist for; but how many people there are in Russia, my dear boy, who exist, one doesn't know what for. Well, it doesn't matter. That's not what keeps things spinning. They tell me Leonid Andreyevitch has taken a situation. He is going to be a clerk at the bank—6,000 roubles a year. Only, of course, he won't stick to it—he's too lazy.

ANYA (*in doorway*). Mamma begs you not to let them chop down the orchard until she's gone.

TROFIMOV. Yes, really, you might have the tact (*walks out across the front of the stage*).

LOPAHIN. I'll see to it! I'll see to it! Stupid fellows! (*Goes out after him.*)

ANYA. Has Firs been taken to the hospital?

YASHA. I told them this morning. No doubt they have taken him.

ANYA (*to* EPIHODOV, *who passes across the drawing-room*). Semyon Pantaleye-vitch, inquire, please, if Firs has been taken to the hospital.

YASHA (*in a tone of offense*). I told Yegor this morning—why ask a dozen times?

EPIHODOV. Firs is advanced in years. It's my conclusive opinion no treatment would do him good; it's time he was gathered to his fathers. And I can only envy him (*puts a trunk down on a card-board hat-box and crushes it*). There now, of course—I knew it would be so.

YASHA (*jeeringly*). Two and twenty misfortunes!

VARYA (*through the door*). Has Firs been taken to the hospital?

ANYA. Yes.

VARYA. Why wasn't the note for the doctor taken too?

ANYA. Oh, then, we must send it after them (*goes out*).

VARYA (*from the adjoining room*). Where's Yasha? Tell him his mother's come to say good-bye to him.

YASHA (*waves his hand*). They put me out of all patience!

(DUNYASHA *has all this time been busy about the luggage. Now, when* YASHA *is left alone, she goes up to him.*)

DUNYASHA. You might just give me one look, Yasha. You're going away. You're leaving me (*weeps and throws herself on his neck*).

YASHA. What are you crying for? (*Drinks the champagne*) In six days I

shall be in Paris again. Tomorrow we shall get into the express train and roll away in a flash. I can scarcely believe it! *Vive la France!* It doesn't suit me here—it's not the life for me; there's no doing anything. I have seen enough of the ignorance here. I have had enough of it (*drinks champagne*). What are you crying for? Behave yourself properly, and then you won't cry.

DUNYASHA (*powders her face, looking in a pocket-mirror*). Do send me a letter from Paris. You know how I loved you, Yasha—how I loved you! I am a tender creature, Yasha.

YASHA. Here they are coming! (*Busies himself about the trunks, humming softly. Enter* LYUBOV ANDREYEVNA, GAEV, ANYA *and* CHARLOTTA IVA-NOVNA.)

GAEV. We ought to be off. There's not much time now (*looking at* YASHA). What a smell of herrings!

LYUBOV. In ten minutes we must get into the carriage (*casts a look about the room*). Farewell, dear house, dear old home of our fathers! Winter will pass and spring will come, and then you will be no more; they will tear you down! How much those walls have seen! (*Kisses her daughter passionately*) My treasure, how bright you look! Your eyes are sparkling like diamonds! Are you glad? Very glad?

ANYA. Very glad! A new life is beginning, mamma.

GAEV. Yes, really, everything is all right now. Before the cherry orchard was sold, we were all worried and wretched, but afterwards, when once the question was settled conclusively, irrevocably, we all felt calm and even cheerful. I am a bank clerk now—I am a financier—cannon off the red. And you, Lyuba, after all, you are looking better; there's no question of that.

LYUBOV. Yes. My nerves are better, that's true. (*Her hat and coat are handed to her*) I'm sleeping well. Carry out my things, Yasha. It's time. (*To* ANYA) My darling, we shall soon see each other again. I am going to Paris. I can live there on the money your Yaroslavl auntie sent us to buy the estate with—hurrah for auntie!—but that money won't last long.

ANYA. You'll come back soon, mamma,

won't you? I'll be working up for my examination in the high school, and when I have passed that, I shall set to work and be a help to you. We will read all sorts of things together, mamma, won't we? (*Kisses her mother's hands*) We will read in the autumn evenings. We'll read lots of books, and a new wonderful world will open out before us (*dreamily*). Mamma, come soon.

LYUBOV. I shall come, my precious treasure (*embraces her*).

(*Enter* LOPAHIN. CHARLOTTA *softly hums a song.*)

GAEV. Charlotta's happy; she's singing!

CHARLOTTA (*picks up a bundle like a swaddled baby*). Bye, bye, my baby. (*A baby is heard crying: "Ooah! ooah!"*) Hush, hush, my pretty boy! (*Ooah! ooah!*) Poor little thing! (*Throws the bundle back*) You must please find me a situation. I can't go on like this.

LOPAHIN. We'll find you one, Charlotta Ivanovna. Don't you worry yourself.

GAEV. Everyone's leaving us. Varya's going away. We have become of no use all at once.

CHARLOTTA. There's nowhere for me to be in the town. I must go away. (*Hums*) What care I. . . .

(*Enter* PISHTCHIK.)

LOPAHIN. The freak of nature!

PISHTCHIK (*gasping*). Oh! . . . let me get my breath. . . . I'm worn out . . . my most honoured . . . Give me some water.

GAEV. Want some money, I suppose? Your humble servant! I'll go out of the way of temptation (*goes out*).

PISHTCHIK. It's a long while since I have been to see you . . . dearest lady. (*To* LOPAHIN) You are here . . . glad to see you . . . a man of immense intellect . . . take . . . here (*gives* LOPAHIN) 400 roubles. That leaves me owing 840.

LOPAHIN (*shrugging his shoulders in amazement*). It's like a dream. Where did you get it?

PISHTCHIK. Wait a bit . . . I'm hot . . . a most extraordinary occurrence! Some Englishmen came along and found in my land some sort of white clay. (*To* LYUBOV ANDREYEVNA) And 400 for you . . . most lovely . . . wonderful (*gives money*). The rest later (*sips water*). A young man in the train was telling me just now that a great philosopher advises jumping off a house-top. "Jump!" says he; "the whole gist of the problem lies in that." (*Wonderingly*) Fancy that, now! Water, please!

LOPAHIN. What Englishmen?

PISHTCHIK. I have made over to them the rights to dig the clay for twenty-four years . . . and now, excuse me . . . I can't stay . . . I must be trotting on. I'm going to Znoikovo . . . to Kardamanovo. . . . I'm in debt all round (*sips*) . . . To your very good health! . . . I'll come in on Thursday.

LYUBOV. We are just off to the town, and tomorrow I start for abroad.

PISHTCHIK. What! (*In agitation*) Why to the town? Oh, I see the furniture . . . the boxes. No matter . . . (*through his tears*) . . . no matter . . . men of enormous intellect . . . these Englishmen. Never mind . . . be happy. God will succour you . . . no matter . . . everything in this world must have an end (*kisses* LYUBOV ANDREYEVNA'S *hand*). If the rumour reaches you that my end has come, think of this . . . old horse, and say: "There once was such a man in the world . . . Semyonov-Pishtchik . . . the Kingdom of Heaven be his!" . . . most extraordinary weather . . . yes. (*Goes out in violent agitation, but at once returns and says in the doorway*) Dashenka wishes to be remembered to you (*goes out*).

LYUBOV. Now we can start. I leave with two cares in my heart. The first is leaving Firs ill. (*Looking at her watch*) We still have five minutes.

ANYA. Mamma, Firs has been taken to the hospital. Yasha sent him off this morning.

LYUBOV. My other anxiety is Varya. She is used to getting up early and working; and now, without work, she's like a fish out of water. She is thin and pale, and she's crying, poor dear! (*A pause*) You are well aware, Yermolay Alexeyevitch, I dreamed of marrying her to you, and everything seemed to show that you would get married (*whispers to* ANYA *and motions to* CHARLOTTA *and both go out*). She loves you—she suits you. And I don't know—I don't know why it is you seem, as it were, to avoid each other. I can't understand it!

LOPAHIN. I don't understand it myself, I confess. It's queer somehow, altogether.

If there's still time, I'm ready now at once. Let's settle it straight off, and go ahead; but without you, I feel I shan't make her an offer.

LYUBOV. That's excellent. Why, a single moment's all that's necessary. I'll call her at once.

LOPAHIN. And there's champagne all ready too (*looking into the glasses*). Empty! Someone's emptied them already. (YASHA *coughs*) I call that greedy.

LYUBOV (*eagerly*). Capital! We will go out. Yasha, *allez!* I'll call her in. (*At the door*) Varya, leave all that; come here. Come along! (*Goes out with* YASHA.)

LOPAHIN (*looking at his watch*). Yes.

(*A pause. Behind the door, smothered laughter and whispering, and, at last, enter* VARYA.)

VARYA (*looking a long while over the things*). It is strange, I can't find it anywhere.

LOPAHIN. What are you looking for?

VARYA. I packed it myself, and I can't remember (*a pause*).

LOPAHIN. Where are you going now, Varvara Mihailova?

VARYA. I? To the Ragulins. I have arranged to go to them to look after the house—as a housekeeper.

LOPAHIN. That's in Yashnovo? It'll be seventy miles away (*a pause*). So this is the end of life in this house!

VARYA (*looking among the things*). Where is it? Perhaps I put it in the trunk. Yes, life in this house is over—there will be no more of it.

LOPAHIN. And I'm just off to Harkov —by this next train. I've a lot of business there. I'm leaving Epihodov here, and I've taken him on.

VARYA. Really!

LOPAHIN. This time last year we had snow already, if you remember; but now it's so fine and sunny. Though it's cold, to be sure—three degrees of frost.

VARYA. I haven't looked (*a pause*). And besides, our thermometer's broken (*a pause*).

(*Voice at the door from the yard:* "Yermolay Alexeyevitch!")

LOPAHIN (*as though he had long been expecting this summons*). This minute!

(LOPAHIN *goes out quickly.* VARYA *sitting on the floor and laying her head on a bag full of clothes, sobs quietly. The*

door opens. LYUBOV ANDREYEVNA *comes in cautiously.*)

LYUBOV. Well? (*A pause*) We must be going.

VARYA (*has wiped her eyes and is no longer crying*). Yes, mamma, it's time to start. I shall have time to get to the Ragulins today, if only you're not late for the train.

LYUBOV (*in the doorway*). Anya, put your things on.

(*Enter* ANYA, *then* GAEV *and* CHARLOTTA IVANOVA. GAEV *has on a warm coat with a hood. Servants and cabmen come in.* EPIHODOV *bustles about the luggage.*)

LYUBOV. Now we can start on our travels.

ANYA (*joyfully*). On our travels!

GAEV. My friends—my dear, my precious friends! Leaving this house for ever, can I be silent? Can I refrain from giving utterance at leave-taking to those emotions which now flood all my being?

ANYA (*supplicatingly*). Uncle!

VARYA. Uncle, you mustn't!

GAEV (*dejectedly*). Cannon and into the pocket . . . I'll be quiet . . . (*Enter* TROFIMOV *and afterwards* LOPAHIN.)

TROFIMOV. Well, ladies and gentlemen, we must start.

LOPAHIN. Epihodov, my coat!

LYUBOV. I'll stay just one minute. It seems as though I have never seen before what the walls, what the ceilings in this house were like, and now I look at them with greediness, with such tender love.

GAEV. I remember when I was six years old sitting in that window on Trinity Day watching my father going to church.

LYUBOV. Have all the things been taken?

LOPAHIN. I think all. (*Putting on overcoat, to* EPIHODOV) You, Epihodov, mind you see everything is right.

EPIHODOV (*in a husky voice*). Don't you trouble, Yermolay Alexeyevitch.

LOPAHIN. Why, what's wrong with your voice?

EPIHODOV. I've just had a drink of water, and I choked over something.

YASHA (*contemptuously*). The ignorance!

LYUBOV. We are going—and not a soul will be left here.

LOPAHIN. Not till the spring.

VARYA (*pulls a parasol out of a bundle, as though about to hit someone with it.*

LOPAHIN *makes a gesture as though alarmed*). What is it? I didn't mean anything.

TROFIMOV. Ladies and gentlemen, let us get into the carriage. It's time. The train will be in directly.

VARYA. Petya, here they are, your goloshes, by that box. (*With tears*) And what dirty old things they are!

TROFIMOV (*putting on his goloshes*). Let us go, friends!

GAEV (*greatly agitated, afraid of weeping*). The train—the station! Double baulk, ah!

LYUBOV. Let us go!

LOPAHIN. Are we all here? (*Locks the side-door on left*) The things are all here. We must lock up. Let us go!

ANYA. Good-bye, home! Good-bye to the old life!

TROFIMOV. Welcome to the new life!

(TROFIMOV *goes out with* ANYA. VARYA *looks round the room and goes out slowly.* YASHA *and* CHARLOTTA IVANOVNA, *with her dog, go out.*)

LOPAHIN. Till the spring, then! Come, friends, till we meet! (*Goes out.*)

(LYUBOV ANDREYEVNA *and* GAEV *remain alone. As though they had been waiting for this, they throw themselves on each other's necks, and break into subdued smothered sobbing, afraid of being overheard.*)

GAEV (*in despair*). Sister, my sister!

LYUBOV. Oh, my orchard!—my sweet, beautiful orchard! My life, my youth, my happiness, good-bye! good-bye!

VOICE OF ANYA (*calling gaily*). Mamma!

VOICE OF TROFIMOV (*gaily, excitedly*). Aa—oo!

LYUBOV. One last look at the walls, at the windows. My dear mother loved to walk about this room.

GAEV. Sister, sister!

VOICE OF ANYA. Mamma!

VOICE OF TROFIMOV. Aa—oo!

LYUBOV. We are coming. (*They go out.*)

(*The stage is empty. There is the sound of the doors being locked up, then of the carriages driving away. There is silence. In the stillness there is the dull stroke of an axe in a tree, clanging with a mournful lonely sound. Footsteps are heard.* FIRS *appears in the doorway on the right. He is dressed as always—in a pea-jacket and white waistcoat, with slippers on his feet. He is ill.*)

FIRS (*goes up to the doors, and tries the handles*). Locked! They have gone . . . (*sits down on sofa*). They have forgotten me. . . . Never mind . . . I'll sit here a bit. . . . I'll be bound Leonid Andreyevitch hasn't put his fur coat on and has gone off in his thin overcoat (*sighs anxiously*). I didn't see after him. . . . These young people . . . (*mutters something that can't be distinguished*). Life has slipped by as though I hadn't lived. (*Lies down*) I'll lie down a bit. . . . There's no strength in you, nothing left you—all gone! Ech! I'm good for nothing (*lies motionless*).

(*A sound is heard that seems to come from the sky, like a breaking harp-string, dying away mournfully. All is still again, and there is heard nothing but the strokes of the axe far away in the orchard.*)

The Curtain Falls.

MAXIM GORKY: *Anton Chekhov*

From *Literary Portraits* in *On Literature* by Maxim Gorky. Moscow: Foreign Languages Publishing House, n.d.

HE ONCE INVITED ME TO VISIT HIM IN THE VILLAGE OF KUCHUK-KOI, where he had a tiny plot of ground and a white, two-storey house. He showed me over his "estate," talking animatedly all the time:

"If I had lots of money I would build a sanitorium here for sick village teachers. A building full of light, you know, very light, with big windows and high ceilings. I'd have a splendid library, all sorts of musical instruments, an apiary, a vegetable garden, an orchard. I'd have lectures on agronomy, meteorology, and so on—teachers ought to know everything, old man—everything!"

He broke off suddenly, coughed, cast an oblique glance at me, and smiled his sweet, gentle smile, a smile which had an irresistible charm, forcing one to follow his words with the keenest attention.

"Does it bore you to listen to my dreams? I love talking about this. If you only knew the absolute necessity for the Russian countryside of good, clever, educated teachers! In Russia we have simply got to create exceptional conditions for teachers, and that as soon as possible, since we realize that unless the people get an all-round education the state will collapse like a house built from insufficiently baked bricks. The teacher must be an actor, an artist, passionately in love with his work, and our teachers are navvies, half-educated individuals, who go to the village to teach children about as willingly as they would go to exile. They are famished, downtrodden, they live in perpetual fear of losing their livelihood. And the teacher ought to be the first man in the village, able to answer all the questions put to him by the peasants, to instil in the peasants a respect for his power worthy of attention and respect, whom no one will dare to shout at . . . to lower his dignity, as in our country everybody does—the village policeman, the rich shopkeeper, the priest, the school patron, the elder and that official who, though he is called a school inspector, busies himself, not over the improvement of conditions for education, but simply and

solely over the carrying out of district circulars to the letter. It's absurd to pay a niggardly pittance to one who is called upon to educate the people—to educate the people, mind! It is intolerable that such a one should go about in rags, shiver in a damp, dilapidated school, be poisoned by fumes from badly ventilated stoves, be always catching cold, and by the age of thirty be a mass of disease—laryngitis, rheumatism, tuberculosis. It's a disgrace to us! For nine or ten months in the year our teachers live the lives of hermits, without a soul to speak to, they grow stupid from loneliness, without books or amusements. And if they venture to invite friends to come and see them, people think they are disaffected—that idiotic word with which cunning folk terrify fools. . . . All this is disgusting . . . a kind of mockery of human beings doing a great and terribly important work. I tell you, when I meet a teacher I feel quite awkward in front of him—for his timidity, and his shabbiness. I feel as if I myself were somehow to blame for the teacher's wretched state—I do, really!"

Pausing for a moment, he threw out his arm and said softly:

"What an absurd, clumsy country our Russia is!"

A shadow of profound sorrow darkened his fine eyes, and a fine network of wrinkles showed at the corners, deepening his glance. He looked around him and began making fun of himself.

"There you are—I've treated you to a full-length leading article from a liberal newspaper. Come on, I'll give you some tea as a reward for your patience. . . ."

This was often the way with him. One moment he would be talking with warmth, gravity and sincerity, and the next, he would be laughing at himself and his own words. And beneath this gentle, sorrowful laughter could be felt the subtle scepticism of a man who knew the value of words, the value of dreams. There was a shade of his attractive modesty, his intuitive delicacy in this laughter, too.

We walked back to the house in silence. It was a warm, bright day; the sound of waves sparkling in the vivid rays of the sun, could be heard. In the valley, a dog was squealing its delight about something. Chekhov took me by the arm and said slowly, his speech interrupted by coughs:

"It's disgraceful and very sad, but it is true—there are many people who envy dogs. . . ."

And then he added, laughing:

"Everything I say today sounds senile —I must be getting old." . . .

It seems to me that in the presence of Anton Pavlovich everyone felt an unconscious desire to be simpler, more truthful, more himself, and I had many opportunities of observing how people threw off their attire of grand bookish phrases, fashionable expressions, and all the rest of the cheap trifles with which Russians, in their anxiety to appear Europeans, adorn themselves, as savages deck themselves with shells and fishes' teeth. Anton Pavlovich was not fond of fishes' teeth and cocks' feathers; all that is tawdry, tinkling, alien, donned by human beings for the sake of an "imposing appearance," embarrassed him, and I noticed that whenever he met with one of these dressed-up individuals he felt an overmastering impulse to free him from his ponderous and superfluous trappings, distorting the true face and living soul of his interlocutor. All his life Anton Pavlovich lived the life of the soul, was always himself, inwardly free, and took no notice of what some expected, and others—less delicate —demanded of Anton Chekhov. He did not like conversations on "lofty" subjects —conversations which Russians, in the simplicity of their hearts, find so amusing, forgetting that it is absurd, and not in the least witty, to talk about the velvet apparel of the future, while not even possessing in the present a decent pair of trousers.

Of a beautiful simplicity himself, he loved all that was simple, real, sincere, and he had a way of his own of making others simple. . . .

He had the art of exposing vulgarity everywhere, an art which can only be mastered by one whose own demands on life are very high, and which springs from the ardent desire to see simplicity, beauty and harmony in man. He was a severe and merciless judge of vulgarity.

Someone said in his presence that the editor of a popular magazine, a man perpetually talking about the necessity for love and sympathy for others, had insulted a railway guard without the slightest provocation, and was in the habit of treating his subordinates roughly.

"Naturally," said Anton Pavlovich, with a grim chuckle. "He's an aristocrat, a cultivated man . . . he went to a seminary. His father went about in bast shoes, but *he* wears patent leather boots."

And the tone in which these words were spoken at once dismissed the "aristocrat" as a mediocre and ridiculous individual.

"A very gifted person," he said of a certain journalist. "His writing is always so lofty, so humane . . . saccharine. He calls his wife a fool in front of people. His servants sleep in a damp room, and they all develop rheumatism. . . ."

"Do you like So-and-So, Anton Pavlovich?"

"Oh, yes. A nice man," replies Anton Pavlovich, coughing. "He knows everything. He reads a lot. He took three books of mine and never returned them. A bit absent-minded, tells you one day that you're a fine fellow, and the next tells someone else that you stole the black silk socks with blue stripes of your mistress's husband." . . .

A subtle mockery almost always twinkled gently in his grey mournful eyes, but occasionally these eyes would become cold, keen, harsh, and at such moments a hard note would creep into the smooth, cordial tones of his voice, and then I felt that this modest, kindly man could stand up against any hostile force, stand up firmly, without knuckling under to it.

It sometimes seemed to me that there was a shade of hopelessness in his attitude to others, something akin to a cold, still despair.

"The Russian is a strange being," he said once. "He is like a sieve, he can hold nothing for long. In his youth he crams himself eagerly with everything that comes his way, and by the time he is thirty nothing is left of it all but a heap of colourless rubbish. If one wants to lead a good life, a human life, one must work. Work with love and with faith. And we don't know how to do that in our country. An architect, having built two or three decent houses, sits down to play cards for the rest of his life or hangs about the backstage of a theatre. As soon as a doctor acquires a practice he stops keeping up with science, never reads anything but *Novosti Terapii* (*Therapeutical News*) and by the age of forty is firmly convinced that all diseases come from colds. I have never met a single official who had even the slightest idea of the significance of his work—they usually dig themselves in in the capital, or some provincial town, and invent papers which they dispatch to Zmiyev and Smorgon for fulfilment. And whose freedom of movement is impeded in Zmiyev or Smorgon by these documents the official no more cares than an atheist does about the torments of hell. Having made a name by a successful defence the barrister ceases to bother about the defence of truth and does nothing but defend the rights of property, put money on horses, eat oysters, and pass himself off as a connoisseur of all the arts. An actor, having performed two or three parts with fair success, no longer learns his parts, but puts on a top hat and considers himself a genius. Russia is a land of greedy idlers. People eat and drink enormously, love to sleep in the daytime, and snore in their sleep. They marry for the sake of order in their homes, and take a mistress for the sake of social prestige. Their psychology is a dog's psychology. Beat them and they squeal meekly and sneak off to their kennels. Caress them, and they lie on their backs with their paws up, wagging their tails."

A cold, sorrowful contempt underlay these words. But while despising, he could pity, and when anyone was abused in his presence, Anton Pavlovich was sure to stick up for him.

"Come now! He's an old man, he's seventy. . . ."

Or:

"He's still young, it's just his stupidity. . . ."

And when he spoke like this I could see no signs of disgust in his face. . . .

When one is young, vulgarity seems to be simply amusing and insignificant, but it gradually surrounds the individual, its grey mist creeping into his brains and blood, like poison or charcoal fumes, till he becomes like an old tavern-sign, eaten up with rust—there seems to be something depicted on it, but what, it is impossible to make out.

From the very first Anton Pavlovich managed to reveal, in the grey ocean of vulgarity, its tragically sombre jokes. One only has to read his "humorous" stories carefully, to realize how much that was cruel was seen and shamefacedly concealed by the author in comic narrative and situations.

He had an almost virginal modesty, he could never bring himself to challenge people loudly and openly: "Be more decent—can't you!" vainly trusting that they would themselves realize the urgent necessity for being more decent. Detesting all that was vulgar and unclean, he described the seamy side of life in the lofty language of the poet, with the gentle smile of the humorist, and the bitter inner reproach beneath the polished surface of his stories is scarcely noticeable. . . .

No one ever understood the tragic nature of life's trifles so clearly and intuitively as Chekhov did, never before has a writer been able to hold up to human beings such a ruthlessly truthful picture of all that was shameful and pitiable in the dingy chaos of middle-class life.

His enemy was vulgarity. All his life he fought against it, held it up to scorn, depicted it with a keen impartial pen, discovering the fungus of vulgarity even where, at first glance, everything seemed to be ordered for the best, the most convenient, and even brilliant. And vulgarity got back on him with an ugly trick when his dead body—the body of a poet—was sent to Moscow in an oyster wagon.

This dingy green wagon strikes me as the broad triumphant grin of vulgarity at its weary foe, and the innumerable "reminiscences" of the yellow press—mere hypocritical grief, behind which I seem to feel the cold, stinking breath of that very vulgarity which secretly rejoiced in the death of its enemy.

Reading the works of Chekhov makes

one feel as if it were a sad day in late
autumn, when the air is transparent, the
bare trees stand out in bold relief against
the sky, the houses are huddled together,
and people are dim and dreary. Everything is so strange, so lonely, motionless,
powerless. The remote distances are blue
and void, merging with the pale sky,
breathing a dreary cold on the half-frozen
mud. But the mind of the author, like
the autumn sunshine, lights up the well-
trodden roads, the crooked streets, the
dirty, cramped houses in which pitiful
"little" people gasp out their lives in boredom and idleness, filling their dwellings
with a meaningless, drowsy bustle. There
goes "the darling," as nervous as a little
grey mouse, a sweet, humble woman, who
loves so indiscriminately and so slavishly.
Strike her a blow on the cheek and she
will not even dare, meek slave, to cry out.
Beside her stands the melancholy Olga
from *The Three Sisters;* she, too, is capable of loving and submits patiently to the
whims of the depraved, vulgar wife of
her fainéant brother; the lives of her
sisters fall in ruins around her and she
only cries, incapable of doing anything
about it, while not a single living, strong
word of protest against vulgarity is
formed within her.

And there go the tearful Ranevskaya
and the rest of the former owners of
The Cherry Orchard—selfish as children,
and flabby as old people. They, who
should have been dead long ago, whine
and snivel, blind to what is going on
around them, comprehending nothing,
parasites unable to fasten their suckers
into life again. The worthless student
Trofimov holds forth eloquently on the
need for working, and fritters away his
time, amusing himself by dull-witted
taunts at Varya, who works unceasingly
for the welfare of the idlers.

Vershinin [the hero of *The Three
Sisters*] dreams of the good life to come
in three hundred years, and in the meantime does not notice that everything
around him is falling to pieces, that before his very eyes Solyony is ready, out
of boredom and stupidity, to kill the
pitiable Baron Tusenbach.

A long procession of slaves to love,
to their own stupidity and laziness, to
their greed for earthly blessings passes
before the reader's eyes. Here are the
slaves to the obscure fear of life, moving
in vague anxiety and filling the air with
inarticulate ravings about the future, feeling that there is no place for them in
the present. . . .

Sometimes the report of a gun is heard
from the grey mass—this is Ivanov or
Treplev, who, having suddenly discovered
the only thing to do, has given up the
ghost.

Many of them indulge in beautiful
dreams of the glorious life to come in
two hundred years, and nobody thinks of
asking the simple question: who is to
make it glorious, if we do nothing but
dream?

And now a great, wise man passes by
this dull, dreary crowd of impotent creatures, casting an attentive glance on them
all, these dreary inhabitants of his native
land, and says, with his sad smile, in tones
of gentle but profound reproach, with
despairing grief on his face and in his
heart, in a voice of exquisite sincerity:

"What a dull life you lead, gentlemen!"

I have never met anyone who felt the
importance of work as the basis of culture so profoundly and diversely as A. P.
This feeling showed itself in all the trifles
of his home life, in the selection of things
for the home, in that love for things in
themselves, and, while quite untainted by
the desire to collect, he never wearied of
admiring them as the product of man's
creative spirit. He loved building, plant-
ing gardens, adorning the earth, he felt
the poetry of work. With what touching
care he watched the growth of the fruit-
trees and shrubs he had himself planted.
In the midst of the innumerable cares
connected with the building of his house
at Autko, he said:

"If everyone in the world did all he
was capable of on his own plot of land,
what a beautiful world it would be!" . . .

He spoke little and reluctantly about
his literary work. I had almost said with
the same virginal reserve with which
he spoke about Lev Tolstoi. Very occasionally, when in spirits, he would re-
late the plot of a story, chuckling—it
was always a humorous story.

"I say, I'm going to write a story about
a schoolmistress, an atheist—she adores
Darwin, is convinced of the necessity for
fighting the prejudices and superstitions
of the people, and herself goes to the

bath-house at midnight to scald a black cat to get a wishbone for attracting a man and arousing his love—there is such a bone, you know. . . ."

He always spoke of his plays as "amusing," and really seemed to be sincerely convinced that he wrote "amusing plays." No doubt Savva Morozov was repeating Chekhov's own words when he stubbornly maintained: "Chekhov's plays must be produced as lyrical comedies." . . .

His disease sometimes called into being a hypochondriac, or even a misanthropical, mood. At such times he would be extremely critical, and very hard to get on with.

One day, lying on the sofa, giving dry coughs, and playing with the thermometer, he said:

"To live simply to die is by no means amusing, but to live with the knowledge that you will die before your time, that really is idiotic. . . ."

Another time, seated at the open window and gazing out into the distance, at the sea, he suddenly said peevishly:

"We are accustomed to live in hopes of good weather, a good harvest, a nice love-affair, hopes of becoming rich or getting the office of chief of police, but I've never noticed anyone hoping to get wiser. We say to ourselves: it'll be better under a new tsar, and in two hundred years it'll be still better, and nobody tries to make this good time come tomorrow. On the whole, life gets more and more complex every day and moves on at its own sweet will, and people get more and more stupid, and get isolated from life in ever-increasing numbers."

After a pause he added, wrinkling up his forehead:

"Like crippled beggars in a religious procession."

He was a doctor, and the illness of a doctor is always worse than the illnesses of his patients. The patients only feel, but the doctor, as well as feeling, has a pretty good idea of the destructive effect of the disease on his constitution. This is a case in which knowledge brings death nearer. . . .

I once heard Tolstoi praise a story of Chekhov's—*The Darling*, I think it was.

"It's like lace woven by a virtuous maiden," he said. "There used to be girl lace-makers in the old days, who, their whole lives long, wove their dreams of happiness into the pattern. They wove their fondest dreams, their lace was saturated with vague, pure aspirations of love." Tolstoi spoke with true emotion, with tears in his eyes.

But that day Chekhov had a temperature, and sat with his head bent, vivid spots of colour on his cheeks, carefully wiping his pince-nez. He said nothing for some time, and at last, sighing, said softly and awkwardly: "There are misprints in it."

Much could be written of Chekhov, but this would require close, precise narration, and that is what I'm no good at. He should be written about as he himself wrote *The Steppe*, a fragrant, open-air, very Russian story, pensive and wistful. A story for one's self.

It does one good to remember a man like that, it is like a sudden visitation of cheerfulness, it gives a clear meaning to life again.

Man is the axis of the Universe.

And his vices, you ask, his shortcomings?

We all hunger for the love of our fellow creatures, and when one is hungry, even a half-baked loaf tastes sweet.

AS PAMPHLETEER, WIT, CONTROVERSIALIST, CRITIC,

George Bernard Shaw

1856-1950

and playwright, Shaw challenged cant and con- vention throughout a long lifetime of activity. Shaw was born in Dublin into an impecunious Irish Protestant family with pretensions to gen- tility; his father was an alcoholic ex-civil serv- ant, his mother a musician. After some perfunc- tory schooling he was apprenticed to a Dublin real-estate agent, but in 1876 he moved to Lon- don, where his mother had been living for some time. There fol- lowed years of unemployment, study, and unsuccessful novel-writing. In- fluenced by Henry George and Karl Marx, Shaw threw himself into the Socialist movement. He helped to found the Fabian Society, and turned to pamphleteering and speech-making. In 1885 he found a job as a music critic and later also wrote drama and art criticism. He championed the music of Wagner and the drama of Ibsen, and finally offered to write a play for the Independent Theatre. His play *Widowers' Houses,* written when he was thirty-six, provoked a storm of comment, and Shaw's career as a dramatist was launched. Among his subjects for bold and iconoclastic treatment were conventional religious thinking (*Androcles and the Lion,* 1912, and *Back to Methuselah,* 1921), relations between the sexes (*Mrs. Warren's Profes- sion,* 1893; *Candida,* 1894; *Man and Superman,* 1903), romantic military heroics (*Arms and the Man,* 1894), and philanthropy (*Major Barbara,* 1905). Shaw brought to his dramatic work a wide knowledge of comic techniques, an acute and fearlessly independent intellect, a precise and scintillating prose style, and a profound moral sense that sought through laughter and logic to expel human folly and cowardice. Personally timid ("he was always afraid of intimacy—physical, emotional, and spiritual," wrote his friend R. Ellis Roberts), Shaw fought his own nature and donned a mask of aggressive cockiness and occasional clowning. The world saw him as jaunty, confident, and unafraid up to his death at the age of ninety-four.

MAJOR BARBARA

BY GEORGE BERNARD SHAW

❧ Act I

It is after dinner in January 1906, in the library in Lady Britomart Undershaft's house in Wilton Crescent. A large and comfortable settee is in the middle of the room, upholstered in dark leather. A person sitting on it (it is vacant at present) would have, on his right, Lady Britomart's writing table, with the lady herself busy at it; a smaller writing table behind him on his left; the door behind him on Lady Britomart's side; and a window with a window seat directly on his left. Near the window is an armchair.

Lady Britomart is a woman of fifty or thereabouts, well dressed and yet careless of her dress, well bred and quite reckless of her breeding, well mannered and yet appallingly outspoken and indifferent to the opinion of her interlocutors, amiable and yet peremptory, arbitrary, and high-tempered to the last bearable degree, and withal a very typical managing matron of the upper class, treated as a naughty child until she grew into a scolding mother, and finally settling down with plenty of practical ability and worldly experience, limited in the oddest way with domestic and class limitations, conceiving the universe exactly as if it were a large house in Wilton Crescent, though handling her corner of it very effectively on that assumption, and being quite enlightened and liberal as to the books in the library, the pictures on the walls, the music in the portfolios, and the articles in the papers.

Her son, Stephen, comes in. He is a gravely correct young man under 25, taking himself very seriously, but still in some awe of his mother, from childish habit and bachelor shyness rather than from any weakness of character.

STEPHEN. Whats the matter?

LADY BRITOMART. Presently, Stephen. (Stephen submissively walks to the settee and sits down. He takes up a Liberal weekly called The Speaker.)

LADY BRITOMART. Dont begin to read, Stephen. I shall require all your attention.

STEPHEN. It was only while I was waiting——

LADY BRITOMART. Dont make excuses, Stephen. (He puts down The Speaker.) Now! (She finishes her writing; rises; and comes to the settee.) I have not kept you waiting very long, I think.

STEPHEN. Not at all, mother.

LADY BRITOMART. Bring me my cushion. (He takes the cushion from the chair at the desk and arranges it for her as she sits down on the settee.) Sit down. (He sits down and fingers his tie nervously.) Dont fiddle with your tie, Stephen: there is nothing the matter with it.

STEPHEN. I beg your pardon. (He fiddles with his watch chain instead.)

LADY BRITOMART. Now are you attending to me, Stephen?

STEPHEN. Of course, mother.

LADY BRITOMART. No: it's not of course. I want something much more than your everyday matter-of-course attention. I am going to speak to you very seriously, Stephen. I wish you would let that chain alone.

STEPHEN (hastily relinquishing the chain). Have I done anything to annoy you, mother? If so, it was quite unintentional.

LADY BRITOMART (astonished). Nonsense! (With some remorse) My poor boy, did you think I was angry with you?

STEPHEN. What is it, then, mother? You are making me very uneasy.

LADY BRITOMART (squaring herself at him rather aggressively). Stephen: may I ask you how soon you intend to realize that you are a grown-up man, and that I am only a woman?

STEPHEN (amazed). Only a——

LADY BRITOMART. Dont repeat my words, please: it is a most aggravating habit. You must learn to face life seriously, Stephen. I really cannot bear the whole burden of our family affairs any longer. You must advise me: you must assume the responsibility.

STEPHEN. I!

LADY BRITOMART. Yes, you, of course. You were 24 last June. Youve been at Harrow and Cambridge. Youve been to India and Japan. You must know a lot of things, now; unless you have wasted your time most scandalously. Well, advise me.

STEPHEN (*much perplexed*). You know I have never interfered in the household——

LADY BRITOMART. No: I should think not. I dont want you to order the dinner.

STEPHEN. I mean in our family affairs.

LADY BRITOMART. Well, you must interfere now; for they are getting quite beyond me.

STEPHEN (*troubled*). I have thought sometimes that perhaps I ought; but really, mother, I know so little about them; and what I do know is so painful! it is so impossible to mention some things to you—(*he stops, ashamed*).

LADY BRITOMART. I suppose you mean your father.

STEPHEN (*almost inaudibly*). Yes.

LADY BRITOMART. My dear: we cant go on all our lives not mentioning him. Of course you were quite right not to open the subject until I asked you to; but you are old enough now to be taken into my confidence, and to help me to deal with him about the girls.

STEPHEN. But the girls are all right. They are engaged.

LADY BRITOMART (*complacently*). Yes: I have made a very good match for Sarah. Charles Lomax will be a millionaire at 35. But that is ten years ahead; and in the meantime his trustees cannot under the terms of his father's will allow him more than £800 a year.

STEPHEN. But the will says also that if he increases his income by his own exertions, they may double the increase.

LADY BRITOMART. Charles Lomax's exertions are much more likely to decrease his income than to increase it. Sarah will have to find at least another £800 a year for the next ten years; and even then they will be as poor as church mice. And what about Barbara? I thought Barbara was going to make the most brilliant career of all of you. And what does she do? Joins the Salvation Army; discharges her maid; lives on a pound a week; and walks in one evening with a professor of Greek whom she has picked up in the street, and who pretends to be a Salvationist, and actually plays the big drum for her in public because he has fallen head over ears in love with her.

STEPHEN. I was certainly rather taken aback when I heard they were engaged. Cusins is a very nice fellow, certainly: nobody would ever guess that he was born in Australia; but——

LADY BRITOMART. Oh, Adolphus Cusins will make a very good husband. After all, nobody can say a word against Greek: it stamps a man at once as an educated gentleman. And my family, thank Heaven, is not a pig-headed Tory one. We are Whigs, and believe in liberty. Let snobbish people say what they please: Barbara shall marry, not the man they like, but the man *I* like.

STEPHEN. Of course I was thinking only of his income. However, he is not likely to be extravagant.

LADY BRITOMART. Dont be too sure of that, Stephen. I know your quiet, simple, refined, poetic people like Adolphus: quite content with the best of everything! They cost more than your extravagant people, who are always as mean as they are second rate. No: Barbara will need at least £2000 a year. You see it means two additional households. Besides, my dear, you must marry soon. I dont approve of the present fashion of philandering bachelors and late marriages; and I am trying to arrange something for you.

STEPHEN. It's very good of you, mother; but perhaps I had better arrange that for myself.

LADY BRITOMART. Nonsense! you are much too young to begin matchmaking: you would be taken in by some pretty little nobody. Of course I dont mean that you are not to be consulted: you know that as well as I do. (*Stephen closes his lips and is silent.*) Now dont sulk, Stephen.

STEPHEN. I am not sulking, mother. What has all this got to do with—with —with my father?

LADY BRITOMART. My dear Stephen: where is the money to come from? It is easy enough for you and the other children to live on my income as long as we are in the same house; but I cant keep four families in four separate houses. You know how poor my father is: he has barely seven thousand a year now; and really, if he were not the Earl of Stevenage, he would have to give up society. He can do nothing for us. He says, naturally enough, that it is absurd that he should be asked to provide for the children of a man who is rolling in money. You see, Stephen, your father must be fabulously wealthy, because there is always a war going on somewhere.

STEPHEN. You need not remind me of that, mother. I have hardly ever opened a newspaper in my life without seeing our name in it. The Undershaft torpedo! The Undershaft quick firers! The Undershaft ten inch! the Undershaft disappearing rampart gun! the Undershaft submarine! and now the Undershaft aerial battleship! At Harrow they called me the Woolwich Infant. At Cambridge it was the same. A little brute at King's who was always trying to get up revivals, spoilt my Bible —your first birthday present to me—by writing under my name, "Son and heir to Undershaft and Lazarus, Death and Destruction Dealers: address Christendom and Judea." But that was not so bad as the way I was kowtowed to everywhere because my father was making millions by selling cannons.

LADY BRITOMART. It is not only the cannons, but the war loans that Lazarus arranges under cover of giving credit for the cannons. You know, Stephen, it's perfectly scandalous. Those two men, Andrew Undershaft and Lazarus, positively have Europe under their thumbs. That is why your father is able to behave as he does. He is above the law. Do you think Bismarck or Gladstone or Disraeli could have openly defied every social and moral obligation all their lives as your father has? They simply wouldnt have dared. I asked Gladstone to take it up. I asked The Times to take it up. I asked the Lord Chamberlain to take it up. But it was just like asking them to declare war on the Sultan. They wouldnt. They said they couldnt touch him. I believe they were afraid.

STEPHEN. What could they do? He does not actually break the law.

LADY BRITOMART. Not break the law! He is always breaking the law. He broke the law when he was born: his parents were not married.

STEPHEN. Mother! Is that true?

LADY BRITOMART. Of course it's true: that was why we separated.

STEPHEN. He married without letting you know this!

LADY BRITOMART (*rather taken aback by this inference*). Oh no. To do Andrew justice, that was not the sort of thing he did. Besides, you know the Undershaft motto: Unashamed. Everybody knew.

STEPHEN. But you said that was why you separated.

LADY BRITOMART. Yes, because he was not content with being a foundling himself: he wanted to disinherit you for another foundling. That was what I couldnt stand.

STEPHEN (*ashamed*). Do you mean for—for—for——

LADY BRITOMART. Dont stammer, Stephen. Speak distinctly.

STEPHEN. But this is so frightful to me, mother. To have to speak to you about such things!

LADY BRITOMART. It's not pleasant for me, either, especially if you are still so childish that you must make it worse by a display of embarrassment. It is only in the middle classes, Stephen, that people get into a state of dumb helpless horror when they find that there are wicked people in the world. In our class, we have to decide what is to be done with wicked people; and nothing should disturb our self-possession. Now ask your question properly.

STEPHEN. Mother: have you no consideration for me? For Heaven's sake either treat me as a child, as you always do, and tell me nothing at all; or tell me everything and let me take it as best I can.

LADY BRITOMART. Treat you as a child! What do you mean? It is most unkind and ungrateful of you to say such a thing. You know I have never treated any of you as children. I have always made you my companions and friends, and allowed you perfect freedom to do and say whatever you liked, so long as you liked what I could approve of.

STEPHEN (*desperately*). I daresay we have been the very imperfect children of a very perfect mother; but I do beg you to let me alone for once, and tell me about this horrible business of my father wanting to set me aside for another son.

LADY BRITOMART (*amazed*). Another son! I never said anything of the kind. I never dreamt of such a thing. This is what comes of interrupting me.

STEPHEN. But you said——

LADY BRITOMART (*cutting him short*). Now be a good boy, Stephen, and listen to me patiently. The Undershafts are descended from a foundling in the parish of St Andrew Undershaft in the city. That was long ago, in the reign of James the First. Well, this foundling was adopted by an armorer and gun-maker. In the course of time the foundling succeeded to the business; and from some notion of gratitude, or some vow or something, he adopted another foundling, and left the business to him. And that foundling did the same. Ever since that, the cannon business has always been left to an adopted foundling named Andrew Undershaft.

STEPHEN. But did they never marry? Were there no legitimate sons?

LADY BRITOMART. Oh yes: they married just as your father did; and they were rich enough to buy land for their own children and leave them well provided for. But they always adopted and trained some foundling to succeed them in the business; and of course they always quarrelled with their wives furiously over it. Your father was adopted in that way; and he pretends to consider himself bound to keep up the tradition and adopt somebody to leave the business to. Of course I was not going to stand that. There may have been some reason for it when the Undershafts could only marry women in their own class, whose sons were not fit to govern great estates. But there could be no excuse for passing over my son.

STEPHEN (*dubiously*). I am afraid I should make a poor hand of managing a cannon foundry.

LADY BRITOMART. Nonsense! you could easily get a manager and pay him a salary.

STEPHEN. My father evidently had no great opinion of my capacity.

LADY BRITOMART. Stuff, child! you were only a baby: it had nothing to do with your capacity. Andrew did it on principle, just as he did every perverse and wicked thing on principle. When my father remonstrated, Andrew actually told him to his face that history tells us of only two successful institutions: one the Undershaft firm, and the other the Roman Empire under the Antonines. That was because the Antonine emperors all adopted their successors. Such rubbish! The Stevenages are as good as the Antonines, I hope; and you are a Stevenage. But that was Andrew all over. There you have the man! Always clever and unanswerable when he was defending nonsense and wickedness: always awkward and sullen when he had to behave sensibly and decently!

STEPHEN. Then it was on my account that your home life was broken up, mother. I am sorry.

LADY BRITOMART. Well, dear, there were other differences. I really cannot bear an immoral man. I am not a Pharisee, I hope; and I should not have minded his merely doing wrong things: we are none of us perfect. But your father didnt exactly do wrong things: he said them and thought them: that was what was so dreadful. He really had a sort of religion of wrongness. Just as one doesnt mind men practising immorality so long as they own that they are in the wrong by preaching morality; so I couldnt forgive Andrew for preaching immorality while he practised morality. You would all have grown up without principles, without any knowledge of right and wrong, if he had been in the house. You know, my dear, your father was a very attractive man in some ways. Children did not dislike him; and he took advantage of it to put the wickedest ideas into their heads, and make them quite unmanageable. I did not dislike him myself: very far from it; but nothing can bridge over moral disagreement.

STEPHEN. All this simply bewilders me, mother. People may differ about matters of opinion, or even about religion; but how can they differ about right and wrong? Right is right; and wrong is wrong; and if a man cannot distinguish them properly, he is either a fool or a rascal: thats all.

LADY BRITOMART (*touched*). Thats my own boy (*she pats his cheek*)! Your father never could answer that: he used to laugh and get out of it under cover of some affectionate nonsense. And now that you understand the situation, what do you advise me to do?

STEPHEN. Well, what can you do?

LADY BRITOMART. I must get the money somehow.

STEPHEN. We cannot take money from him. I had rather go and live in some cheap place like Bedford Square or even Hampstead than take a farthing of his money.

LADY BRITOMART. But after all, Stephen, our present income comes from Andrew.

STEPHEN (*shocked*). I never knew that.

LADY BRITOMART. Well, you surely didnt suppose your grandfather had anything to give me. The Stevenages could not do everything for you. We gave you social position. Andrew had to contribute something. He had a very good bargain, I think.

STEPHEN (*bitterly*). We are utterly dependent on him and his cannons, then?

LADY BRITOMART. Certainly not: the money is settled. But he provided it. So you see it is not a question of taking money from him or not: it is simply a question of how much. I dont want any more for myself.

STEPHEN. Nor do I.

LADY BRITOMART. But Sarah does; and Barbara does. That is, Charles Lomax and Adolphus Cusins will cost them more. So I must put my pride in my pocket and ask for it, I suppose. That is your advice, Stephen, is it not?

STEPHEN. No.

LADY BRITOMART (*sharply*). Stephen!

STEPHEN. Of course if you are determined——

LADY BRITOMART. I am not determined: I ask your advice; and I am waiting for it. I will not have all the responsibility thrown on my shoulders.

STEPHEN (*obstinately*). I would die sooner than ask him for another penny.

LADY BRITOMART (*resignedly*). You mean that *I* must ask him. Very well, Stephen: it shall be as you wish. You will be glad to know that your grandfather concurs. But he thinks I ought to ask Andrew to come here and see the girls. After all, he must have some natural affection for them.

STEPHEN. Ask him here!!!

LADY BRITOMART. Do not repeat my words, Stephen. Where else can I ask him?

STEPHEN. I never expected you to ask him at all.

LADY BRITOMART. Now dont tease, Stephen. Come! you see that it is necessary that he should pay us a visit, dont you?

STEPHEN (*reluctantly*). I suppose so, if the girls cannot do without his money.

LADY BRITOMART. Thank you, Stephen: I knew you would give me the right advice when it was properly explained to you. I have asked your father to come this evening. (*Stephen bounds from his seat.*) Dont jump, Stephen: it fidgets me.

STEPHEN (*in utter consternation*). Do you mean to say that my father is coming here tonight—that he may be here at any moment?

LADY BRITOMART (*looking at her watch*). I said nine. (*He gasps. She rises.*) Ring the bell, please. (*Stephen goes to the smaller writing table; presses a button on it; and sits at it with his elbows on the table and his head in his hands, outwitted and overwhelmed.*) It is ten minutes to nine yet; and I have to prepare the girls. I asked Charles Lomax and Adolphus to dinner on purpose that they might be here. Andrew had better see them in case he should cherish any delusions as to their being capable of supporting their wives. (*The butler enters: Lady Britomart goes behind the settee to speak to him.*) Morrison: go up to the drawing room and tell everybody to come down here at once. (*Morrison withdraws. Lady Britomart turns to Stephen.*) Now remember, Stephen: I shall need all your countenance and authority. (*He rises and tries to recover some vestige of these attributes.*) Give me a chair, dear. (*He pushes a chair forward from the wall to where she stands, near the smaller writing table. She sits down; and he goes to the armchair, into which he throws himself.*) I dont know how Barbara will take it. Ever since they made her a major in the Salvation Army she has developed a propensity to have her own way and order people about which quite cows me sometimes. It's not ladylike: I'm sure I dont know where she picked it up. Anyhow, Barbara shant bully me; but still it's just as well that your father should be here before she has time to refuse to meet him or make a fuss. Dont look nervous, Stephen: it will only encourage Barbara to make difficulties. *I* am nervous enough, goodness knows; but I dont shew it.

(*Sarah and Barbara come in with their respective young men, Charles Lomax and Adolphus Cusins. Sarah is slender, bored, and mundane. Barbara is robuster, jollier, much more energetic. Sarah is fashionably dressed: Barbara is in Salvation Army uniform. Lomax, a young man about town, is like many other young men about town. He is afflicted with a frivolous sense of humor which plunges him at the most inopportune moments into paroxysms of imperfectly suppressed laughter. Cusins is a spectacled student, slight, thin haired, and sweet voiced, with a more complex form of Lomax's complaint. His sense of humor is intellectual and subtle, and is complicated by an appalling temper. The lifelong struggle of a benevolent temperament and a high conscience against impulses of inhuman ridicule and fierce impatience has set up a chronic strain which has visibly wrecked his constitution. He is a most implacable, determined, tenacious, intolerant person who by mere force of character presents himself as—and indeed actually is—considerate, gentle, explanatory, even mild and apologetic, capable possibly of murder, but not of cruelty or coarseness. By the operation of some instinct which is not merciful enough to blind him with the illusions of love, he is obstinately bent on marrying Barbara. Lomax likes Sarah and thinks it will be rather a lark to marry her. Consequently he has not attempted to resist Lady Britomart's arrangements to that end.*

All four look as if they had been having a good deal of fun in the drawing room. The girls enter first, leaving the swains outside. Sarah comes to the settee. Barbara comes in after her and stops at the door.)

BARBARA. Are Cholly and Dolly to come in?

LADY BRITOMART (*forcibly*). Barbara: I will not have Charles called Cholly: the vulgarity of it positively makes me ill.

BARBARA. It's all right, mother: Cholly is quite correct nowadays. Are they to come in?

LADY BRITOMART. Yes, if they will behave themselves.

BARBARA (*through the door*). Come in, Dolly; and behave yourself.

(*Barbara comes to her mother's writing table. Cusins enters smiling, and wanders towards Lady Britomart.*)

SARAH (*calling*). Come in, Cholly. (*Lomax enters, controlling his features very imperfectly, and places himself vaguely between Sarah and Barbara.*)

LADY BRITOMART (*peremptorily*). Sit down, all of you. (*They sit. Cusins crosses to the window and seats himself there. Lomax takes a chair. Barbara sits at the writing table and Sarah on the settee.*) I dont in the least know what you are laughing at, Adolphus. I am surprised at you, though I expected nothing better from Charles Lomax.

CUSINS (*in a remarkably gentle voice*). Barbara has been trying to teach me the West Ham Salvation March.

LADY BRITOMART. I see nothing to laugh at in that; nor should you if you are really converted.

CUSINS (*sweetly*). You were not present. It was really funny, I believe.

LOMAX. Ripping.

LADY BRITOMART. Be quiet, Charles. Now listen to me, children. Your father is coming here this evening.

(*General stupefaction. Lomax, Sarah, and Barbara rise: Sarah scared, and Barbara amused and expectant.*)

LOMAX (*remonstrating*). Oh I say!

LADY BRITOMART. You are not called on to say anything, Charles.

SARAH. Are you serious, mother?

LADY BRITOMART. Of course I am serious. It is on your account, Sarah, and also on Charles's. (*Silence. Sarah sits, with a shrug. Charles looks painfully unworthy.*) I hope you are not going to object, Barbara.

BARBARA. I! why should I? My father has a soul to be saved like anybody else. He's quite welcome as far as I am concerned. (*She sits on the table, and softly whistles "Onward, Christian Soldiers."*)

LOMAX (*still remonstrant*). But really, dont you know! Oh I say!

LADY BRITOMART (*frigidly*). What do you wish to convey, Charles?

LOMAX. Well, you must admit that this is a bit thick.

LADY BRITOMART (*turning with ominous suavity to Cusins*). Adolphus: you are a professor of Greek. Can you translate Charles Lomax's remarks into reputable English for us?

CUSINS (*cautiously*). If I may say so, Lady Brit, I think Charles has rather happily expressed what we all feel. Homer, speaking of Autolycus, uses the same phrase. πυκινὸν δόμον ἐλθεῖν means a bit thick.

LOMAX (*handsomely*). Not that I mind, you know, if Sarah dont. (*He sits.*)

LADY BRITOMART (*crushingly*). Thank you. Have I your permission, Adolphus, to invite my own husband to my own house?

CUSINS (*gallantly*). You have my unhesitating support in everything you do.

LADY BRITOMART. Tush! Sarah: have you nothing to say?

SARAH. Do you mean that he is coming regularly to live here?

LADY BRITOMART. Certainly not. The spare room is ready for him if he likes to stay for a day or two and see a little more of you; but there are limits.

SARAH. Well, he cant eat us, I suppose. *I* dont mind.

LOMAX (*chuckling*). I wonder how the old man will take it.

LADY BRITOMART. Much as the old woman will, no doubt, Charles.

LOMAX (*abashed*). I didnt mean—at least——

LADY BRITOMART. You didnt think, Charles. You never do; and the result is, you never mean anything. And now please attend to me, children. Your father will be quite a stranger to us.

LOMAX. I suppose he hasnt seen Sarah since she was a little kid.

LADY BRITOMART. Not since she was a little kid, Charles, as you express it with that elegance of diction and refinement of thought that seem never to desert you. Accordingly—er—(*impatiently*) Now I have forgotten what I was going to say. That comes of your provoking me to be sarcastic, Charles. Adolphus: will you kindly tell me where I was.

CUSINS (*sweetly*). You were saying that as Mr Undershaft has not seen his children since they were babies, he will form his opinion of the way you have brought them up from their behavior tonight, and that therefore you wish us all to be particularly careful to conduct ourselves well, especially Charles.

LADY BRITOMART (*with emphatic approval*). Precisely.

LOMAX. Look here, Dolly: Lady Brit didnt say that.

LADY BRITOMART (*vehemently*). I did, Charles. Adolphus's recollection is perfectly correct. It is most important that you should be good; and I do beg you for once not to pair off into opposite corners and giggle and whisper while I am speaking to your father.

BARBARA. All right, mother. We'll do you credit. (*She comes off the table, and sits in her chair with ladylike elegance.*)

LADY BRITOMART. Remember, Charles, that Sarah will want to feel proud of you instead of ashamed of you.

LOMAX. Oh I say! theres nothing to be exactly proud of, dont you know.

LADY BRITOMART. Well, try and look as if there was.

(*Morrison, pale and dismayed, breaks into the room in unconcealed disorder.*)

MORRISON. Might I speak a word to you, my lady?

LADY BRITOMART. Nonsense! Shew him up.

MORRISON. Yes, my lady. (*He goes.*)

LOMAX. Does Morrison know who it is?

LADY BRITOMART. Of course. Morrison has always been with us.

LOMAX. It must be a regular corker for him, dont you know.

LADY BRITOMART. Is this a moment to get on my nerves, Charles, with your outrageous expressions?

LOMAX. But this is something out of the ordinary, really——

MORRISON (*at the door*). The—er—Mr Undershaft. (*He retreats in confusion.*)

(*Andrew Undershaft comes in. All rise. Lady Britomart meets him in the middle of the room behind the settee.*

Andrew is, on the surface, a stoutish, easygoing elderly man, with kindly patient manners, and an engaging simplicity of character. But he has a watchful, deliberate, waiting, listening face, and formidable reserves of power, both bodily and mental, in his capacious chest and long head. His gentleness is partly that of a strong man who has learnt by experience that his natural grip hurts ordinary people unless he handles them very carefully, and partly the mellowness of age and success. He is also a little shy in his present very delicate situation.)

LADY BRITOMART. Good evening, Andrew.

UNDERSHAFT. How d'ye do, my dear.

LADY BRITOMART. You look a good deal older.

UNDERSHAFT (*apologetically*). I am somewhat older. (*Taking her hand with a touch of courtship*) Time has stood still with you.

LADY BRITOMART (*throwing away his hand*). Rubbish! This is your family.

UNDERSHAFT (*surprised*). Is it so large? I am sorry to say my memory is failing very badly in some things. (*He offers his hand with paternal kindness to Lomax.*)

LOMAX (*jerkily shaking his hand*). Ahdedoo.

UNDERSHAFT. I can see you are my eldest. I am very glad to meet you again, my boy.

LOMAX (*remonstrating*). No, but look here dont you know—(*Overcome*) Oh I say!

LADY BRITOMART (*recovering from momentary speechlessness*). Andrew: do you mean to say that you dont remember how many children you have?

UNDERSHAFT. Well, I am afraid I—. They have grown so much—er. Am I making any ridiculous mistake? I may as well confess: I recollect only one son. But so many things have happened since, of course—er—

LADY BRITOMART (*decisively*). Andrew: you are talking nonsense. Of course you have only one son.

UNDERSHAFT. Perhaps you will be good enough to introduce me, my dear.

LADY BRITOMART. That is Charles Lomax, who is engaged to Sarah.

UNDERSHAFT. My dear sir, I beg your pardon.

LOMAX. Notatall. Delighted, I assure you.

LADY BRITOMART. This is Stephen.

UNDERSHAFT (*bowing*). Happy to make your acquaintance, Mr Stephen. Then (*going to Cusins*) you must be my son. (*Taking Cusins' hands in his*) How are you, my young friend? (*To Lady Britomart*) He is very like you, my love.

CUSINS. You flatter me, Mr Undershaft. My name is Cusins: engaged to Barbara. (*Very explicitly*) That is Major Barbara Undershaft, of the Salvation Army. That is Sarah, your second daughter. This is Stephen Undershaft, your son.

UNDERSHAFT. My dear Stephen, I beg your pardon.

STEPHEN. Not at all.

UNDERSHAFT. Mr Cusins: I am much indebted to you for explaining so precisely. (*Turning to Sarah*) Barbara, my dear—

SARAH (*prompting him*). Sarah.

UNDERSHAFT. Sarah, of course. (*They shake hands. He goes over to Barbara*) Barbara—I am right this time, I hope?

BARBARA. Quite right. (*They shake hands.*)

LADY BRITOMART (*resuming command*). Sit down, all of you. Sit down, Andrew. (*She comes forward and sits on the settee. Cusins also brings his chair forward on her left. Barbara and Stephen resume their seats. Lomax gives his chair to Sarah and goes for another.*)

UNDERSHAFT. Thank you, my love.

LOMAX (*conversationally, as he brings a chair forward between the writing table and the settee, and offers it to Undershaft*). Takes you some time to find out exactly where you are, dont it?

UNDERSHAFT (*accepting the chair, but remaining standing*). That is not what embarrasses me, Mr Lomax. My difficulty is that if I play the part of a father, I shall produce the effect of an intrusive stranger; and if I play the part of a discreet stranger, I may appear a callous father.

LADY BRITOMART. There is no need for you to play any part at all, Andrew. You had much better be sincere and natural.

UNDERSHAFT (*submissively*). Yes, my dear: I daresay that will be best. (*He sits down comfortably.*) Well, here I am. Now what can I do for you all?

LADY BRITOMART. You need not do anything, Andrew. You are one of the family. You can sit with us and enjoy yourself.

(*A painfully conscious pause. Barbara makes a face at Lomax, whose too long suppressed mirth immediately explodes in agonized neighings.*)

LADY BRITOMART (*outraged*). Charles

Lomax: if you can behave yourself, behave yourself. If not, leave the room.

LOMAX. I'm awfully sorry, Lady Brit; but really you know, upon my soul! (*He sits on the settee between Lady Britomart and Undershaft, quite overcome.*)

BARBARA. Why dont you laugh if you want to, Cholly? It's good for your inside.

LADY BRITOMART. Barbara: you have had the education of a lady. Please let your father see that; and dont talk like a street girl.

UNDERSHAFT. Never mind me, my dear. As you know, I am not a gentleman; and I was never educated.

LOMAX (*encouragingly*). Nobody'd know it, I assure you. You look all right, you know.

CUSINS. Let me advise you to study Greek, Mr. Undershaft. Greek scholars are privileged men. Few of them know Greek; and none of them know anything else; but their position is unchallengeable. Other languages are the qualifications of waiters and commercial travellers: Greek is to a man of position what the hallmark is to silver.

BARBARA. Dolly: dont be insincere. Cholly: fetch your concertina and play something for us.

LOMAX (*jumps up eagerly, but checks himself to remark doubtfully to Undershaft*). Perhaps that sort of thing isnt in your line, eh?

UNDERSHAFT. I am particularly fond of music.

LOMAX (*delighted*). Are you? Then I'll get it. (*He goes upstairs for the instrument.*)

UNDERSHAFT. Do you play, Barbara?

BARBARA. Only the tambourine. But Cholly's teaching me the concertina.

UNDERSHAFT. Is Cholly also a member of the Salvation Army?

BARBARA. No: he says it's bad form to be a dissenter. But I dont despair of Cholly. I made him come yesterday to a meeting at the dock gates, and take the collection in his hat.

UNDERSHAFT (*looks whimsically at his wife*)!!

LADY BRITOMART. It is not my doing, Andrew. Barbara is old enough to take her own way. She has no father to advise her.

BARBARA. Oh yes she has. There are no orphans in the Salvation Army.

UNDERSHAFT. Your father there has a great many children and plenty of experience, eh?

BARBARA (*looking at him with quick interest and nodding*). Just so. How did you come to understand that? (*Lomax is heard at the door trying the concertina.*)

LADY BRITOMART. Come in, Charles. Play us something at once.

LOMAX. Righto! (*He sits down in his former place, and preludes.*)

UNDERSHAFT. One moment, Mr Lomax. I am rather interested in the Salvation Army. Its motto might be my own: Blood and Fire.

LOMAX (*shocked*). But not your sort of blood and fire, you know.

UNDERSHAFT. My sort of blood cleanses: my sort of fire purifies.

BARBARA. So do ours. Come down tomorrow to my shelter—the West Ham shelter—and see what we're doing. We're going to march to a great meeting in the Assembly Hall at Mile End. Come and see the shelter and then march with us: it will do you a lot of good. Can you play anything?

UNDERSHAFT. In my youth I earned pennies, and even shillings occasionally, in the streets and in public house parlors by my natural talent for stepdancing. Later on, I became a member of the Undershaft orchestral society, and performed passably on the tenor trombone.

LOMAX (*scandalized—putting down the concertina*). Oh I say!

BARBARA. Many a sinner has played himself into heaven on the trombone, thanks to the Army.

LOMAX (*to Barbara, still rather shocked*). Yes; but what about the cannon business, dont you know? (*To Undershaft*) Getting into heaven is not exactly in your line, is it?

LADY BRITOMART. Charles!!!

LOMAX. Well; but it stands to reason, dont it? The cannon business may be necessary and all that: we cant get on without cannons; but it isnt right, you know. On the other hand, there may be a certain amount of tosh about the Salvation Army—I belong to the Established Church myself—but still you cant deny that it's religion; and you cant go against religion, can you? At least unless youre downright immoral, dont you know.

UNDERSHAFT. You hardly appreciate my position, Mr Lomax—

LOMAX (*hastily*). I'm not saying anything against you personally—

UNDERSHAFT. Quite so, quite so. But consider for a moment. Here I am, a profiteer in mutilation and murder. I find myself in a specially amiable humor just now because, this morning, down at the foundry, we blew twenty-seven dummy soldiers into fragments with a gun which formerly destroyed only thirteen.

LOMAX (*leniently*). Well, the more destructive war becomes, the sooner it will be abolished, eh?

UNDERSHAFT. Not at all. The more destructive war becomes the more fascinating we find it. No, Mr Lomax: I am obliged to you for making the usual excuse for my trade; but I am not ashamed of it. I am not one of those men who keep their morals and their business in watertight compartments. All the spare money my trade rivals spend on hospitals, cathedrals, and other receptacles for conscience money, I devote to experiments and researches in improved methods of destroying life and property. I have always done so; and I always shall. Therefore your Christmas card moralities of peace on earth and goodwill among men are of no use to me. Your Christianity, which enjoins you to resist not evil, and to turn the other cheek, would make me a bankrupt. My morality—my religion—must have a place for cannons and torpedoes in it.

STEPHEN (*coldly—almost sullenly*). You speak as if there were half a dozen moralities and religions to choose from, instead of one true morality and one true religion.

UNDERSHAFT. For me there is only one true morality; but it might not fit you, as you do not manufacture aerial battleships. There is only one true morality for every man; but every man has not the same true morality.

LOMAX (*overtaxed*). Would you mind saying that again? I didnt quite follow it.

CUSINS. It's quite simple. As Euripides says, one man's meat is another man's poison morally as well as physically.

UNDERSHAFT. Precisely.

LOMAX. Oh, that! Yes, yes, yes. True. True.

STEPHEN. In other words, some men are honest and some are scoundrels.

BARBARA. Bosh! There are no scoundrels.

UNDERSHAFT. Indeed? Are there any good men?

BARBARA. No. Not one. There are neither good men nor scoundrels: there are just children of one Father; and the sooner they stop calling one another names the better. You neednt talk to me: I know them. Ive had scores of them through my hands: scoundrels, criminals, infidels, philanthropists, missionaries, county councillors, all sorts. Theyre all just the same sort of sinner; and theres the same salvation ready for them all.

UNDERSHAFT. May I ask have you ever saved a maker of cannons?

BARBARA. No. Will you let me try?

UNDERSHAFT. Well, I will make a bargain with you. If I go to see you tomorrow in your Salvation Shelter, will you come the day after to see me in my cannon works?

BARBARA. Take care. It may end in your giving up the cannons for the sake of the Salvation Army.

UNDERSHAFT. Are you sure it will not end in your giving up the Salvation Army for the sake of the cannons?

BARBARA. I will take my chance of that.

UNDERSHAFT. And I will take my chance of the other. (*They shake hands on it.*) Where is your shelter?

BARBARA. In West Ham. At the sign of the cross. Ask anybody in Canning Town. Where are your works?

UNDERSHAFT. In Perivale St Andrews. At the sign of the sword. Ask anybody in Europe.

LOMAX. Hadnt I better play something?

BARBARA. Yes. Give us Onward, Christian Soldiers.

LOMAX. Well, thats rather a strong order to begin with, dont you know. Suppose I sing Thourt passing hence, my brother. It's much the same tune.

BARBARA. It's too melancholy. You get saved, Cholly; and youll pass hence, my brother, without making such a fuss about it.

LADY BRITOMART. Really, Barbara, you go on as if religion were a pleasant subject. Do have some sense of propriety.

UNDERSHAFT. I do not find it an unpleasant subject, my dear. It is the only one that capable people really care for.

LADY BRITOMART (*looking at her watch*). Well, if you are determined to have it, I insist on having it in a proper and respectable way. Charles: ring for prayers.

(*General amazement. Stephen rises in dismay.*)

LOMAX (*rising*). Oh I say!

UNDERSHAFT (*rising*). I am afraid I must be going.

LADY BRITOMART. You cannot go now, Andrew: it would be most improper. Sit down. What will the servants think?

UNDERSHAFT. My dear: I have conscientious scruples. May I suggest a compromise? If Barbara will conduct a little service in the drawing room, with Mr Lomax as organist, I will attend it willingly. I will even take part, if a trombone can be procured.

LADY BRITOMART. Dont mock, Andrew.

UNDERSHAFT (*shocked—to Barbara*). You dont think I am mocking, my love, I hope.

BARBARA. No, of course not; and it wouldn't matter if you were: half the Army came to their first meeting for a lark. (*Rising*) Come along. (*She throws her arm round her father and sweeps him out, calling to the others from the threshold*) Come, Dolly. Come, Cholly.

(*Cusins rises.*)

LADY BRITOMART. I will not be disobeyed by everybody. Adolphus: sit down. (*He does not.*) Charles: you may go. You are not fit for prayers: you cannot keep your countenance.

LOMAX. Oh I say! (*He goes out.*)

LADY BRITOMART (*continuing*). But you, Adolphus, can behave yourself if you choose to. I insist on your staying.

CUSINS. My dear Lady Brit: there are things in the family prayer book that I couldnt bear to hear you say.

LADY BRITOMART. What things, pray?

CUSINS. Well, you would have to say before all the servants that we have done things we ought not to have done, and left undone things we ought to have done, and that there is no health in us. I cannot bear to hear you doing yourself such an injustice, and Barbara such an injustice. As for myself, I flatly deny it: I

have done my best. I shouldnt dare to marry Barbara—I couldnt look you in the face—if it were true. So I must go to the drawing room.

LADY BRITOMART (*offended*). Well, go. (*He starts for the door.*) And remember this, Adolphus (*he turns to listen*): I have a very strong suspicion that you went to the Salvation Army to worship Barbara and nothing else. And I quite appreciate the very clever way in which you systematically humbug me. I have found you out. Take care Barbara doesnt. Thats all.

CUSINS (*with unruffled sweetness*). Dont tell on me. (*He steals out.*)

LADY BRITOMART. Sarah: if you want to go, go. Anything's better than to sit there as if you wished you were a thousand miles away.

SARAH (*languidly*). Very well, mamma. (*She goes.*)

(*Lady Britomart, with a sudden flounce, gives way to a little gust of tears.*)

STEPHEN (*going to her*). Mother: whats the matter?

LADY BRITOMART (*swishing away her tears with her handkerchief*). Nothing. Foolishness. You can go with him, too, if you like, and leave me with the servants.

STEPHEN. Oh, you mustnt think that, mother. I—I dont like him.

LADY BRITOMART. The others do. That is the injustice of a woman's lot. A woman has to bring up her children; and that means to restrain them, to deny them things they want, to set them tasks, to punish them when they do wrong, to do all the unpleasant things. And then the father, who has nothing to do but pet them and spoil them, comes in when all her work is done and steals their affection from her.

STEPHEN. He has not stolen our affection from you. It is only curiosity.

LADY BRITOMART (*violently*). I wont be consoled, Stephen. There is nothing the matter with me. (*She rises and goes towards the door.*)

STEPHEN. Where are you going, mother?

LADY BRITOMART. To the drawing room, of course. (*She goes out. Onward, Christian Soldiers, on the concertina, with tambourine accompaniment, is heard when the door opens.*) Are you coming, Stephen?

STEPHEN. No. Certainly not. (*She goes. He sits down on the settee, with compressed lips and an expression of strong dislike.*)

🌱 Act II

The yard of the West Ham shelter of the Salvation Army is a cold place on a January morning. The building itself, an old warehouse, is newly whitewashed. Its gabled end projects into the yard in the middle, with a door on the ground floor, and another in the loft above it without any balcony or ladder, but with a pulley rigged over it for hoisting sacks. Those who come from this central gable end into the yard have the gateway leading to the street on their left, with a stone horse-trough just beyond it, and, on the right, a penthouse shielding a table from the weather. There are forms at the table; and on them are seated a man and a woman, both much down on their luck, finishing a meal of bread (one thick slice each, with margarine and golden syrup) and diluted milk.

The man, a workman out of employment, is young, agile, a talker, a poser, sharp enough to be capable of anything in reason except honesty or altruistic considerations of any kind. The woman is a commonplace old bundle of poverty and hard-worn humanity. She looks sixty and probably is forty-five. If they were rich people, gloved and muffed and well wrapped up in furs and overcoats, they would be numbed and miserable; for it is a grindingly cold raw January day; and a glance at the background of grimy warehouses and leaden sky visible over the whitewashed walls of the yard would drive any idle rich person straight to the Mediterranean. But these two, being no more troubled with visions of the Mediterranean than of the moon, and being compelled to keep more of their clothes in the pawnshop, and less on their persons, in winter than in summer, are not depressed by the cold: rather are they stung into vivacity, to which their meal has just now given an almost jolly turn. The man takes a pull at his mug, and then gets up and moves about the yard with his hands deep in his pockets, occasionally breaking into a stepdance.

THE WOMAN. Feel better arter your meal, sir?

THE MAN. No. Call that a meal! Good enough for you, praps; but wot is it to me, an intelligent workin man.

THE WOMAN. Workin man! Wot are you?

THE MAN. Painter.

THE WOMAN (*skeptically*). Yus, I dessay.

THE MAN. Yus, you dessay! I know. Every loafer that cant do nothink calls isself a painter. Well, I'm a real painter: grainer, finisher, thirty-eight bob a week when I can get it.

THE WOMAN. Then why dont you go and get it?

THE MAN. I'll tell you why. Fust: I'm intelligent—fffff! it's rotten cold here (*he dances a step or two*)—yes: intelligent beyond the station o life into which it has pleased the capitalists to call me; and they dont like a man that sees through em. Second, an intelligent bein needs a doo share of appiness; so I drink somethink cruel when I get the chawnce. Third, I stand by my class and do as little as I can so's to leave arf the job for me fellow workers. Fourth, I'm fly enough to know wots inside the law and wots outside it; and inside it I do as the capitalists do: pinch wot I can lay me ands on. In a proper state of society I am sober, industrious and honest: in Rome, so to speak, I do as the Romans do. Wots the consequence? When trade is bad—and it's rotten bad now—and the employers az to sack arf their men, they generally start on me.

THE WOMAN. Whats your name?

THE MAN. Price. Bronterre O'Brien Price. Usually called Snobby Price, for short.

THE WOMAN. Snobby's a carpenter, aint it? You said you was a painter.

PRICE. Not that kind of snob, but the genteel sort. I'm too uppish, owing to my intelligence, and my father being a Chartist and a reading, thinking man: a stationer, too. I'm none of your common hewers of wood and drawers of water; and dont you forget it. (*He returns to his seat at the table, and takes up his mug.*) Wots your name?

THE WOMAN. Rummy Mitchens, sir.

PRICE (*quaffing the remains of his milk to her*). Your elth, Miss Mitchens.

RUMMY (*correcting him*). Missis Mitchens.

PRICE. Wot! Oh Rummy, Rummy! Respectable married woman, Rummy, gittin rescued by the Salvation Army by pretendin to be a bad un. Same old game!

RUMMY. What am I to do? I cant starve. Them Salvation lasses is dear good girls; but the better you are, the worse they likes to think you were before they rescued you. Why shouldnt they have a bit o credit, poor loves? theyre worn to rags by their work. And where would they get the money to rescue us if we was to let on we're no worse than other people? You know what ladies and gentlemen are.

PRICE. Thievin swine! Wish I ad their job, Rummy, all the same. Wot does Rummy stand for? Pet name praps?

RUMMY. Short for Romola.

PRICE. For wot!?

RUMMY. Romola. It was out of a new book. Somebody me mother wanted me to grow up like.

PRICE. We're companions in misfortune, Rummy. Both on us got names that nobody cawnt pronounce. Consequently I'm Snobby and youre Rummy because Bill and Sally wasnt good enough for our parents. Such is life!

RUMMY. Who saved you, Mr Price? Was it Major Barbara?

PRICE. No: I come here on my own. I'm going to be Bronterre O'Brien Price, the converted painter. I know wot they like. I'll tell em how I blasphemed and gambled and wopped my poor old mother—

RUMMY (*shocked*). Used you to beat your mother?

PRICE. Not likely. She used to beat me. No matter: you come and listen to the converted painter, and youll hear how she was a pious woman that taught me me prayers at er knee, an how I used to come home drunk and drag her out o bed be er snow white airs, an lam into er with the poker.

RUMMY. Thats whats so unfair to us women. Your confessions is just as big lies as ours: you dont tell what you really done no more than us; but you men can tell your lies right out at the meetins and be made much of for it; while the sort o confessions we az to make az to be wispered to one lady at a time. It aint right, spite of all their piety.

PRICE. Right! Do you s'pose the Army'd be allowed if it went and did right? Not much. It combs our air and makes us good little blokes to be robbed and put upon. But I'll play the game as good as any of em. I'll see somebody struck by lightnin, or hear a voice saying "Snobby Price: where will you spend eternity?" I'll av a time of it, I tell you.

RUMMY. You wont be let drink, though.

PRICE. I'll take it out in gorspellin, then. I dont want to drink if I can get fun enough any other way.

(*Jenny Hill, a pale, overwrought, pretty Salvation lass of 18, comes in through the yard gate, leading Peter Shirley, a half hardened, half worn-out elderly man, weak with hunger.*)

JENNY (*supporting him*). Come! pluck up. I'll get you something to eat. Youll be all right then.

PRICE (*rising and hurrying officiously to take the old man off Jenny's hands*). Poor old man! Cheer up, brother: youll find rest and peace and appiness ere. Hurry up with the food, miss: e's fair done. (*Jenny hurries into the shelter.*) Ere, buck up, daddy! she's fetching y'a thick slice of breadn treacle, an a mug o skyblue. (*He seats him at the corner of the table.*)

RUMMY (*gaily*). Keep up your old art! Never say die!

SHIRLEY. I'm not an old man. I'm ony 46. I'm as good as ever I was. The grey patch come in my hair before I was thirty. All it wants is three pennorth o hair dye: am I to be turned on the streets to starve for it? Holy God! Ive worked ten to twelve hours a day since I was thirteen, and paid my way all through; and now am I to be thrown into the gutter and my job given to a young man that can do it no better than me because Ive black hair that goes white at the first change?

PRICE (*cheerfully*). No good jawrin about it. Youre ony a jumped-up, jerked-off, orspittle-turned-out incurable of an old workin man: who cares about you? Eh? Make the thievin swine give you a meal: theyve stole many a one from you. Get a bit o your own back. (*Jenny returns with the usual meal.*) There you are, brother. Awsk a blessin an tuck that into you.

SHIRLEY (*looking at it ravenously but not touching it, and crying like a child*). I never took anything before.

JENNY (*petting him*). Come, come! the Lord sends it to you: he wasnt above taking bread from his friends; and why should you be? Besides, when we find you a job you can pay us for it if you like.

SHIRLEY (*eagerly*). Yes, yes: thats true. I can pay you back: it's only a loan. (*Shivering*) Oh Lord! oh Lord! (*He turns to the table and attacks the meal ravenously.*)

JENNY. Well, Rummy, are you more comfortable now?

RUMMY. God bless you, lovey! youve fed my body and saved my soul, havent you? (*Jenny, touched, kisses her.*) Sit down and rest a bit: you must be ready to drop.

JENNY. Ive been going hard since morning. But theres more work than we can do. I mustnt stop.

RUMMY. Try a prayer for just two minutes. Youll work all the better after.

JENNY (*her eyes lighting up*). Oh isnt it wonderful how a few minutes prayer revives you! I was quite lightheaded at twelve o'clock, I was so tired; but Major Barbara just sent me to pray for five minutes; and I was able to go on as if I had only just begun. (*To Price*) Did you have a piece of bread?

PRICE (*with unction*). Yes, miss; but Ive got the piece that I value more; and thats the peace that passeth hall hannerstennin.

RUMMY (*fervently*). Glory Hallelujah!

(*Bill Walker, a rough customer of about 25, appears at the yard gate and looks malevolently at Jenny.*)

JENNY. That makes me so happy. When you say that, I feel wicked for loitering here. I must get to work again.

(*She is hurrying to the shelter, when the new-comer moves quickly up to the door and intercepts her. His manner is so threatening that she retreats as he comes at her truculently, driving her down the yard.*)

BILL. Aw knaow you. Youre the one that took awy maw girl. Youre the one that set er agen me. Well, I'm gowin to ev er aht. Not that Aw care a carse for er or you: see? Bat Aw'll let er knaow; and Aw'll let you knaow. Aw'm gowing to give her a doin thatll teach er to cat awy from me. Nah in wiv you and tell er to cam aht afore Aw cam in and kick er aht. Tell er Bill Walker wants er. She'll knaow wot thet means; and if she keeps me witing itll be worse. You stop to jawr beck at me; and Aw'll stawt on you: d'ye eah? Theres your wy. In you gow. (*He takes her by the arm and slings her towards the door of the shelter. She falls on her hand and knee. Rummy helps her up again.*)

PRICE (*rising, and venturing irresolutely toward Bill*). Easy there, mate. She aint doin you no arm.

BILL. Oo are you callin mite? (*Standing over him threateningly*) Youre gowin to stend ap for er, aw yer? Put ap your ends.

RUMMY (*running indignantly to him to scold him*). Oh, you great brute— (*He instantly swings his left hand back against her face. She screams and reels back to the trough, where she sits down, covering her bruised face with her hands and rocking herself and moaning with pain.*)

JENNY (*going to her*). Oh, God forgive you! How could you strike an old woman like that?

BILL (*seizing her by the hair so violently that she also screams, and tearing her away from the old woman*). You Gawd forgimme again an Aw'll Gawd forgive you one on the jawr thetll stop you pryin for a week. (*Holding her and turning fiercely on Price*) Ev you ennything to sy agen it?

PRICE (*intimidated*). No, matey: she aint anything to do with me.

BILL. Good job for you! Aw'd pat two meals into you and fawt you with one finger arter, you stawved cur. (*To Jenny*) Nah are you gowin to fetch aht Mog Ebbijem; or em Aw to knock your fice off you and fetch her meself?

JENNY (*writhing in his grasp*). Oh please someone go in and tell Major Barbara— (*she screams again as he wrenches her head down; and Price and Rummy flee into the shelter.*)

BILL. You want to gow in and tell your Mijor of me, do you?

JENNY. Oh please dont drag my hair. Let me go.

BILL. Do you or downt you? (*She stifles a scream*). Yus or nao?

JENNY. God give me strength—

BILL (*striking her with his fist in the face*). Gow an shaow her thet, and tell her if she wants one lawk it to cam and interfere with me. (*Jenny, crying with pain, goes into the shed. He goes to the form and addresses the old man.*) Eah: finish your mess; an git aht o maw wy.

SHIRLEY (*springing up and facing him fiercely, with the mug in his hand*). You take a liberty with me, and I'll smash you over the face with the mug and cut your eye out. Aint you satisfied—young whelps like you—with takin the bread out o the mouths of your elders that have brought you up and slaved for you, but you must come shovin and cheekin and bullyin in here, where the bread o charity is sickenin in our stummicks?

BILL (*contemptuously, but backing a little*). Wot good are you, you aold palsy mag? Wot good are you?

SHIRLEY. As good as you and better. I'll do a day's work agen you or any fat young soaker of your age. Go and take my job at Horrockses, where I worked for ten year. They want young men there: they cant afford to keep men over forty-five. Theyre very sorry—give you a character and happy to help you to get anything suited to your years—sure a steady man wont be long out of a job. Well, let em try you. Theyll find the differ. What do you know? Not as much as how to beeyave yourself—layin your dirty fist across the mouth of a respectable woman!

BILL. Downt provowk me to ly it acrost yours: d'ye eah?

SHIRLEY (*with blighting contempt*). Yes: you like an old man to hit, dont you, when youve finished with the women. I aint seen you hit a young one yet.

BILL (*stung*). You loy, you aold soup-kitchener, you. There was a yang menn eah. Did Aw offer to itt him or did Aw not?

SHIRLEY. Was he starvin or was he not? Was he a man or only a crosseyed thief an a loafer? Would you hit my son-in-law's brother?

BILL. Oo's ee?

SHIRLEY. Todger Fairmile o Balls Pond. Him that won £20 off the Japanese

wrastler at the music hall by standin out 17 minutes 4 seconds agen him.

BILL (*sullenly*). Aw'm nao music awl wrastler. Ken he box?

SHIRLEY. Yes: an you cant.

BILL. Wot! Aw cawnt, cawnt Aw? Wots thet you sy (*threatening him*)?

SHIRLEY (*not budging an inch*). Will you box Todger Fairmile if I put him on to you? Say the word.

BILL (*subsiding with a slouch*). Aw'll stend ap to enny menn alawv, if he was ten Todger Fairmawls. But Aw dont set ap to be a perfeshnal.

SHIRLEY (*looking down on him with unfathomable disdain*). You box! Slap an old woman with the back o your hand! You hadnt even the sense to hit her where a magistrate couldn't see the mark of it, you silly young lump of conceit and ignorance. Hit a girl in the jaw and ony make her cry! If Todger Fairmile'd done it, she wouldnt a got up inside o ten minutes, no more than you would if he got to you. Yah! I'd set about you myself if I had a week's feedin in me instead o two months' starvation. (*He turns his back on him and sits down moodily at the table.*)

BILL (*following him and stooping over him to drive the taunt in*). You loy! youve the bread and treacle in you that you cam eah to beg.

SHIRLEY (*bursting into tears*). Oh God! it's true: I'm only an old pauper on the scrap heap. (*Furiously*) But youll come to it yourself; and then youll know. Youll come to it sooner than a teetotaller like me, fillin yourself with gin at this hour o the mornin!

BILL. Aw'm nao gin drinker, you aold lawr; bat wen Aw want to give my girl a bloomin good awdin Aw lawk to ev a bit o devil in me: see? An eah Aw emm, talkin to a rotten aold blawter like you sted o givin her wot for. (*Working himself into a rage*) Aw'm gowin in there to fetch her aht. (*He makes vengefully for the shelter door.*)

SHIRLEY. Youre going to the station on a stretcher, more likely; and theyll take the gin and the devil out of you there when they get you inside. You mind what youre about: the major here is the Earl o Stevenage's granddaughter.

BILL (*checked*). Garn!

SHIRLEY. Youll see.

BILL (*his resolution oozing*). Well, Aw aint dan nathin to er.

SHIRLEY. Spose she said you did! who'd believe you?

BILL (*very uneasy, skulking back to the corner of the penthouse*). Gawd! theres no jastice in this cantry. To think wot them people can do! Aw'm as good as er.

SHIRLEY. Tell her so. It's just what a fool like you would do.

(*Barbara, brisk and businesslike, comes from the shelter with a note book, and addresses herself to Shirley. Bill, cowed, sits down in the corner on a form, and turns his back on them.*)

BARBARA. Good morning.

SHIRLEY (*standing up and taking off his hat*). Good morning, miss.

BARBARA. Sit down: make yourself at home. (*He hesitates; but she puts a friendly hand on his shoulder and makes him obey.*) Now then! since youve made friends with us, we want to know all about you. Names and addresses and trades.

SHIRLEY. Peter Shirley. Fitter. Chucked out two months ago because I was too old.

BARBARA (*not at all surprised*). Youd pass still. Why didnt you dye your hair?

SHIRLEY. I did. Me age come out at a coroner's inquest on me daughter.

BARBARA. Steady?

SHIRLEY. Teetotaller. Never out of a job before. Good worker. And sent to the knackers like an old horse!

BARBARA. No matter: if you did your part God will do his.

SHIRLEY (*suddenly stubborn*). My religion's no concern of anybody but myself.

BARBARA (*guessing*). I know. Secularist?

SHIRLEY (*hotly*). Did I offer to deny it?

BARBARA. Why should you? My own father's a Secularist, I think. Our Father —yours and mine—fulfils himself in many ways; and I daresay he knew what he was about when he made a Secularist of you. So buck up, Peter! we can always find a job for a steady man like you. (*Shirley, disarmed and a little bewildered, touches his hat. She turns from him to Bill.*) Whats your name?

BILL (*insolently*). Wots thet to you?

BARBARA (*calmly making a note*). Afraid to give his name. Any trade?

BILL. Oo's afride to give is name? (*Doggedly, with a sense of heroically defying the House of Lords in the person of Lord Stevenage*) If you want to bring a chawge agen me, bring it. (*She waits, unruffled.*) Moy nime's Bill Walker.

BARBARA (*as if the name were familiar: trying to remember how*). Bill Walker? (*Recollecting*) Oh, I know: youre the man that Jenny Hill was praying for inside just now. (*She enters his name in her note book.*)

BILL. Oo's Jenny Ill? And wot call as she to pry for me?

BARBARA. I dont know. Perhaps it was you that cut her lip.

BILL (*defiantly*). Yus, it was me that cat her lip. Aw aint afride o you.

BARBARA. How could you be, since youre not afraid of God? Youre a brave man, Mr Walker. It takes some pluck to do our work here; but none of us dare lift our hand against a girl like that, for fear of her father in heaven.

BILL (*sullenly*). I want nan o your kentin jawr. I spowse you think Aw cam eah to beg from you, like this demmiged lot eah. Not me. Aw downt want your bread and scripe and ketlep. Aw dont blieve in your Gawd, no more than you do yourself.

BARBARA (*sunnily apologetic and ladylike, as on a new footing with him*). Oh, I beg your pardon for putting your name down, Mr Walker. I didnt understand. I'll strike it out.

BILL (*taking this as a slight, and deeply wounded by it*). Eah! you let maw nime alown. Aint it good enaff to be in your book?

BARBARA (*considering*). Well, you see, theres no use putting down your name unless I can do something for you, is there? Whats your trade?

BILL (*still smarting*). Thets nao concern o yours.

BARBARA. Just so. (*Very businesslike*) I'll put you down as (*writing*) the man who—struck—poor little Jenny Hill—in the mouth.

BILL (*rising threateningly*). See eah. Awve ed enaff o this.

BARBARA (*quite sunny and fearless*). What did you come to us for?

BILL. Aw cam for maw gel, see? Aw

cam to tike her aht o this and to brike er jawr for er.

BARBARA (*complacently*). You see I was right about your trade. (*Bill, on the point of retorting furiously, finds himself, to his great shame and terror, in danger of crying instead. He sits down again suddenly.*) Whats her name?

BILL (*dogged*). Er nime's Mog Ebbijem: thets wot her nime is.

BARBARA. Mog Habbijam! Oh, she's gone to Canning Town, to our barracks there.

BILL (*fortified by his resentment of Mog's perfidy*). Is she? (*Vindictively*) Then Aw'm gowin to Kennintahn arter her. (*He crosses to the gate; hesitates; finally comes back at Barbara.*) Are you loyin to me to git shat o me?

BARBARA. I dont want to get shut of you. I want to keep you here and save your soul. Youd better stay: youre going to have a bad time today, Bill.

BILL. Oo's gowin to give it to me? You, preps?

BARBARA. Someone you dont believe in. But youll be glad afterwards.

BILL (*slinking off*). Aw'll gow to Kennintahn to be aht o reach o your tangue. (*Suddenly turning on her with intense malice*) And if Aw downt fawnd Mog there, Aw'll cam beck and do two years for you, selp me Gawd if Aw downt!

BARBARA (*a shade kindlier, if possible*). It's no use, Bill. She's got another bloke.

BILL. Wot!

BARBARA. One of her own converts. He fell in love with her when he saw her with her soul saved, and her face clean, and her hair washed.

BILL (*surprised*). Wottud she wash it for, the carroty slat? It's red.

BARBARA. It's quite lovely now, because she wears a new look in her eyes with it. It's a pity youre too late. The new bloke has put your nose out of joint, Bill.

BILL. Aw'll put his nowse aht o joint for him. Not that Aw care a carse for er, mawnd thet. But Aw'll teach her to drop me as if Aw was dirt. And Aw'll teach him to meddle with maw judy. Wots iz bleedin nime?

BARBARA. Sergeant Todger Fairmile.

SHIRLEY (*rising with grim joy*). I'll go with him, miss. I want to see them two

meet. I'll take him to the infirmary when it's over.

BILL (*to Shirley, with undissembled misgiving*). Is thet im you was speakin on?

SHIRLEY. Thats him.

BILL. Im that wrastled in the music awl?

SHIRLEY. The competitions at the National Sportin Club was worth nigh a hundred a year to him. He's gev em up now for religion; so he's a bit fresh for want of the exercise he was accustomed to. He'll be glad to see you. Come along.

BILL. Wots is wight?

SHIRLEY. Thirteen four. (*Bill's last hope expires.*)

BARBARA. Go and talk to him, Bill. He'll convert you.

SHIRLEY. He'll convert your head into a mashed potato.

BILL (*sullenly*). Aw aint afride of im. Aw aint afride of ennybody. Bat e can lick me. She's dan me. (*He sits down moodily on the edge of the horse trough.*)

SHIRLEY. You aint going. I thought not. (*He resumes his seat.*)

BARBARA (*calling*). Jenny!

JENNY (*appearing at the shelter door with a plaster on the corner of her mouth*). Yes, Major.

BARBARA. Send Rummy Mitchens out to clear away here.

JENNY. I think she's afraid.

BARBARA (*her resemblance to her mother flashing out for a moment*). Nonsense! she must do as she's told.

JENNY (*calling into the shelter*). Rummy: the Major says you must come.

(*Jenny comes to Barbara, purposely keeping on the side next Bill, lest he should suppose that she shrank from him or bore malice.*)

BARBARA. Poor little Jenny! Are you tired? (*Looking at the wounded cheek*) Does it hurt?

JENNY. No: it's all right now. It was nothing.

BARBARA (*critically*). It was as hard as he could hit, I expect. Poor Bill! You dont feel angry with him, do you?

JENNY. Oh no, no, no: indeed I dont, Major, bless his poor heart! (*Barbara kisses her; and she runs away merrily into the shelter. Bill writhes with an agonizing return of his new and alarming symp-*

toms, but says nothing. Rummy Mitchens comes from the shelter.)

BARBARA (*going to meet Rummy*). Now Rummy, bustle. Take in those mugs and plates to be washed; and throw the crumbs about for the birds.

(*Rummy takes the three plates and mugs; but Shirley takes back his mug from her, as there is still some milk left in it.*)

RUMMY. There aint any crumbs. This aint a time to waste good bread on birds.

PRICE (*appearing at the shelter door*). Gentleman come to see the shelter, Major. Says he's your father.

BARBARA. All right. Coming. (*Snobby goes back into the shelter, followed by Barbara.*)

RUMMY (*stealing across to Bill and addressing him in a subdued voice, but with intense conviction*). I'd av the lor of you, you flat eared pignosed potwalloper, if she'd let me. Youre no gentleman, to hit a lady in the face. (*Bill, with greater things moving in him, takes no notice.*)

SHIRLEY (*following her*). Here! in with you and dont get yourself into more trouble by talking.

RUMMY (*with hauteur*). I aint ad the pleasure o being hintroduced to you, as I can remember. (*She goes into the shelter with the plates.*)

SHIRLEY. Thats the—

BILL (*savagely*). Downt you talk to me, d'ye eah? You lea me alown, or Aw'll do you a mischief. Aw'm not dirt under your feet, ennywy.

SHIRLEY (*calmly*). Dont you be afeerd. You aint such prime company that you need expect to be sought after. (*He is about to go into the shelter when Barbara comes out, with Undershaft on her right.*)

BARBARA. Oh, there you are, Mr. Shirley! (*Between them*) This is my father. I told you he was a Secularist, didn't I? Perhaps youll be able to comfort one another.

UNDERSHAFT (*startled*). A Secularist! Not the least in the world: on the contrary, a confirmed mystic.

BARBARA. Sorry, I'm sure. By the way, papa, what is your religion? in case I have to introduce you again.

UNDERSHAFT. My religion? Well, my dear, I am a Millionaire. That is my religion.

BARBARA. Then I'm afraid you and Mr Shirley wont be able to comfort one another after all. Youre not a Millionaire, are you, Peter?

SHIRLEY. No; and proud of it.

UNDERSHAFT (*gravely*). Poverty, my friend, is not a thing to be proud of.

SHIRLEY (*angrily*). Who made your millions for you? Me and my like. Whats kep us poor? Keepin you rich. I wouldnt have your conscience, not for all your income.

UNDERSHAFT. I wouldnt have your income, not for all your conscience, Mr Shirley. (*He goes to the penthouse and sits down on a form.*)

BARBARA (*stopping Shirley adroitly as he is about to retort*). You wouldnt think he was my father, would you, Peter? Will you go into the shelter and lend the lasses a hand for a while: we're worked off our feet.

SHIRLEY (*bitterly*). Yes: I'm in their debt for a meal, aint I?

BARBARA. Oh, not because youre in their debt, but for love of them, Peter, for love of them. (*He cannot understand, and is rather scandalized*) There! dont stare at me. In with you; and give that conscience of yours a holiday (*bustling him into the shelter*).

SHIRLEY (*as he goes in*). Ah! it's a pity you never was trained to use your reason, miss. Youd have been a very taking lecturer on Secularism.

(*Barbara turns to her father.*)

UNDERSHAFT. Never mind me, my dear. Go about your work; and let me watch it for a while.

BARBARA. All right.

UNDERSHAFT. For instance, whats the matter with that outpatient over there?

BARBARA (*looking at Bill, whose attitude has never changed, and whose expression of brooding wrath has deepened*). Oh, we shall cure him in no time. Just watch. (*She goes over to Bill and waits. He glances up at her and casts his eyes down again, uneasy, but grimmer than ever.*) It would be nice to just stamp on Mog Habbijam's face, wouldn't it, Bill?

BILL (*starting up from the trough in consternation*). It's a loy: Aw never said so. (*She shakes her head.*) Oo taold you wot was in moy mawnd?

BARBARA. Only your new friend.

BILL. Wot new friend?

BARBARA. The devil, Bill. When he gets round people they get miserable, just like you.

BILL (*with a heartbreaking attempt at devil-may-care cheerfulness*). Aw aint miserable. (*He sits down again, and stretches his legs in an attempt to seem indifferent.*)

BARBARA. Well, if youre happy, why dont you look happy, as we do?

BILL (*his legs curling back in spite of him*). Aw'm eppy enaff, Aw tell you. Woy cawnt you lea me alown? Wot ev I dan to you? Aw aint smashed your fice, ev Aw?

BARBARA (*softly: wooing his soul*). It's not me thats getting at you, Bill.

BILL. Oo else is it?

BARBARA. Somebody that doesnt intend you to smash women's faces, I suppose. Somebody or something that wants to make a man of you.

BILL (*blustering*). Mike a menn o me! Aint Aw a menn? eh? Oo sez Aw'm not a menn?

BARBARA. Theres a man in you somewhere, I suppose. But why did he let you hit poor little Jenny Hill? That wasnt very manly of him, was it?

BILL (*tormented*). Ev dan wiv it, Aw tell you. Chack it. Aw'm sick o your Jenny Ill and er silly little fice.

BARBARA. Then why do you keep thinking about it? Why does it keep coming up against you in your mind? Youre not getting converted, are you?

BILL (*with conviction*). Not ME. Not lawkly.

BARBARA. Thats right, Bill. Hold out against it. Put out your strength. Dont lets get you cheap. Todger Fairmile said he wrestled for three nights against his salvation harder than he ever wrestled with the Jap at the music hall. He gave in to the Jap when his arm was going to break. But he didn't give in to his salvation until his heart was going to break. Perhaps youll escape that. You havent any heart, have you?

BILL. Wot d'ye mean? Woy aint Aw got a awt the sime as ennybody else?

BARBARA. A man with a heart wouldnt have bashed poor little Jenny's face, would he?

BILL (*almost crying*). Ow, will you lea me alown? Ev Aw ever offered to meddle with you, that you cam neggin and provowkin me lawk this? (*He writhes convulsively from his eyes to his toes.*)

BARBARA (*with a steady soothing hand on his arm and a gentle voice that never lets him go*). It's your soul thats hurting you, Bill, and not me. Weve been through it all ourselves. Come with us, Bill (*He looks wildly round.*) To brave manhood on earth and eternal glory in heaven. (*He is on the point of breaking down.*) Come. (*A drum is heard in the shelter; and Bill, with a gasp, escapes from the spell as Barbara turns quickly. Adolphus enters from the shelter with a big drum.*) Oh! there you are, Dolly. Let me introduce a new friend of mine, Mr Bill Walker. This is my bloke, Bill: Mr. Cusins. (*Cusins salutes with his drumstick.*)

BILL. Gowin to merry im?

BARBARA. Yes.

BILL (*fervently*). Gawd elp im! Gaw-aw-aw-awd elp im!

BARBARA. Why? Do you think he wont be happy with me?

BILL. Awve aony ed to stend it for a mawnin: e'll ev to stend it for a lawftawm.

CUSINS. That is a frightful reflection, Mr. Walker. But I cant tear myself away from her.

BILL. Well, Aw ken (*To Barbara*) Eah! do you knaow where Aw'm gowin to, and wot Aw'm gowin to do?

BARBARA. Yes: youre going to heaven; and youre coming back here before the week's out to tell me so.

BILL. You loy. Aw'm gowin to Kennintahn, to spit in Todger Fairmawl's eye. Aw beshed Jenny Ill's fice; an nar Aw'll git me aown fice beshed and cam beck and shaow it to er. Ee'll itt me ardern Aw itt her. Thatll mike us square. (*To Adolphus*) Is thet fair or is it not? Youre a genlmn: you oughter knaow.

BARBARA. Two black eyes wont make one white one, Bill.

BILL. Aw didnt awst you. Cawnt you never keep your mahth shat? Oy awst the genlmn.

CUSINS (*reflectively*). Yes: I think youre right, Mr Walker. Yes: I should do it. It's curious: it's exactly what an ancient Greek would have done.

BARBARA. But what good will it do?

CUSINS. Well, it will give Mr. Fairmile

some exercise; and it will satisfy Mr. Walker's soul.

BILL. Rot! there aint nao sach a thing as a saoul. Ah kin you tell wevver Awve a saoul or not? You never seen it.

BARBARA. Ive seen it hurting you when you went against it.

BILL (*with compressed aggravation*). If you was maw gel and took the word aht o me mahth lawk thet, Aw'd give you sathink youd feel urtin, Aw would. (*To Adolphus*) You tike maw tip, mite. Stop er jawr; or youll doy afoah your tawm. (*With intense expression*) Wore aht: thets wot youll be: wore aht. (*He goes away through the gate.*)

CUSINS (*looking after him*). I wonder!

BARBARA. Dolly! (*indignant, in her mother's manner.*)

CUSINS. Yes, my dear, it's very wearing to be in love with you. If it lasts, I quite think I shall die young.

BARBARA. Should you mind?

CUSINS. Not at all. (*He is suddenly softened, and kisses her over the drum, evidently not for the first time, as people cannot kiss over a big drum without practice. Undershaft coughs.*)

BARBARA. It's all right, papa, weve not forgotten you. Dolly: explain the place to papa: I havnt time. (*She goes busily into the shelter.*)

(*Undershaft and Adolphus now have the yard to themselves. Undershaft, seated on a form, and still keenly attentive, looks hard at Adolphus. Adolphus looks hard at him.*)

UNDERSHAFT. I fancy you guess something of what is in my mind, Mr. Cusins. (*Cusins flourishes his drumsticks as if in the act of beating a lively rataplan, but makes no sound.*) Exactly so. But suppose Barbara finds you out!

CUSINS. You know, I do not admit that I am imposing on Barbara. I am quite genuinely interested in the views of the Salvation Army. The fact is, I am a sort of collector of religions; and the curious thing is that I find I can believe them all. By the way, have you any religion?

UNDERSHAFT. Yes.

CUSINS. Anything out of the common?

UNDERSHAFT. Only that there are two things necessary to Salvation.

CUSINS (*disappointed, but polite*). Ah,

the Church Catechism. Charles Lomax also belongs to the Established Church.

UNDERSHAFT. The two things are—

CUSINS. Baptism and—

UNDERSHAFT. No. Money and gunpowder.

CUSINS (*surprised, but interested*). That is the general opinion of our governing classes. The novelty is in hearing any man confess it.

UNDERSHAFT. Just so.

CUSINS. Excuse me: is there any place in your religion for honor, justice, truth, love, mercy and so forth?

UNDERSHAFT. Yes: they are the graces and luxuries of a rich, strong, and safe life.

CUSINS. Suppose one is forced to choose between them and money or gunpowder?

UNDERSHAFT. Choose money and gunpowder; for without enough of both you cannot afford the others.

CUSINS. That is your religion?

UNDERSHAFT. Yes.

(*The cadence of this reply makes a full close in the conversation. Cusins twists his face dubiously and contemplates Undershaft. Undershaft contemplates him.*)

CUSINS. Barbara wont stand that. You will have to choose between your religion and Barbara.

UNDERSHAFT. So will you, my friend. She will find out that that drum of yours is hollow.

CUSINS. Father Undershaft: you are mistaken: I am a sincere Salvationist. You do not understand the Salvation Army. It is the army of joy, of love, of courage: it has banished the fear and remorse and despair of the old hell-ridden evangelical sects: it marches to fight the devil with trumpet and drum, with music and dancing, with banner and palm, as becomes a sally from heaven by its happy garrison. It picks the waster out of the public house and makes a man of him: it finds a worm wriggling in a back kitchen, and lo! a woman! Men and women of rank too, sons and daughters of the Highest. It takes the poor professor of Greek, the most artificial and self-suppressed of human creatures, from his meal of roots, and lets loose the rhapsodist in him; reveals the true worship of Dionysos to him; sends him down the public street drumming dithyrambs. (*He plays a thundering flourish on the drum.*)

UNDERSHAFT. You will alarm the shelter.

CUSINS. Oh, they are accustomed to these sudden ecstasies. However, if the drum worries you—(*he pockets the drumsticks; unhooks the drum; and stands it on the ground opposite the gateway.*)

UNDERSHAFT. Thank you.

CUSINS. You remember what Euripides says about your money and gunpowder?

UNDERSHAFT. No.

CUSINS (*declaiming*).

One and another
In money and guns may outpass his
    brother;
And men in their millions float and flow
And seethe with a million hopes as
    leaven;
And they win their will; or they miss
    their will;
And their hopes are dead or are pined for
    still;
        But who'er can know
        As the long days go
That to live is happy, has found his
    heaven.

My translation: what do you think of it?

UNDERSHAFT. I think, my friend, that if you wish to know, as the long days go, that to live is happy, you must first acquire money enough for a decent life, and power enough to be your own master.

CUSINS. You are damnably discouraging. (*He resumes his declamation.*)

Is it so hard a thing to see
That the spirit of God—whate'er it
    be—
The law that abides and changes not, ages
    long,
The Eternal and Nature-born: these
    things be strong?
What else is Wisdom? What of Man's
    endeavor,
Or God's high grace so lovely and so
    great?
To stand from fear set free? to breathe
    and wait?
To hold a hand uplifted over Fate?
And shall not Barbara be loved for ever?

UNDERSHAFT. Euripides mentions Barbara, does he?

CUSINS. It is a fair translation. The word means Loveliness.

UNDERSHAFT. May I ask—as Barbara's father—how much a year she is to be loved for ever on?

CUSINS. As for Barbara's father, that is more your affair than mine. I can feed her by teaching Greek: that is about all.

UNDERSHAFT. Do you consider it a good match for her?

CUSINS (*with polite obstinacy*). Mr. Undershaft: I am in many ways a weak, timid, ineffectual person; and my health is far from satisfactory. But whenever I feel that I must have anything, I get it, sooner or later. I feel that way about Barbara. I dont like marriage: I feel intensely afraid of it; and I dont know what I shall do with Barbara or what she will do with me. But I feel that I and nobody else must marry her. Please regard that as settled.—Not that I wish to be arbitrary; but why should I waste your time in discussing what is inevitable?

UNDERSHAFT. You mean that you will stick at nothing: not even the conversion of the Salvation Army to the worship of Dionysos.

CUSINS. The business of the Salvation Army is to save, not to wrangle about the name of the pathfinder. Dionysos or another: what does it matter?

UNDERSHAFT (*rising and approaching him*). Professor Cusins: you are a young man after my own heart.

CUSINS. Mr. Undershaft: you are, as far as I am able to gather, a most infernal old rascal; but you appeal very strongly to my sense of ironic humor.

(*Undershaft mutely offers his hand. They shake.*)

UNDERSHAFT (*suddenly concentrating himself*). And now to business.

CUSINS. Pardon me. We are discussing religion. Why go back to such an uninteresting and unimportant subject as business?

UNDERSHAFT. Religion is our business at present, because it is through religion alone that we can win Barbara.

CUSINS. Have you, too, fallen in love with Barbara?

UNDERSHAFT. Yes, with a father's love.

CUSINS. A father's love for a grown-up daughter is the most dangerous of all infatuations. I apologize for mentioning my own pale, coy, mistrustful fancy in the same breath with it.

UNDERSHAFT. Keep to the point. We have to win her; and we are neither of us Methodists.

CUSINS. That doesnt matter. The power Barbara wields here—the power that wields Barbara herself—is not Calvinism, not Presbyterianism, not Methodism—

UNDERSHAFT. Not Greek Paganism either, eh?

CUSINS. I admit that. Barbara is quite original in her religion.

UNDERSHAFT (*triumphantly*). Aha! Barbara Undershaft would be. Her inspiration comes from within herself.

CUSINS. How do you suppose it got there?

UNDERSHAFT (*in towering excitement*). It is the Undershaft inheritance. I shall hand on my torch to my daughter. She shall make my converts and preach my gospel—

CUSINS. What! Money and gunpowder!

UNDERSHAFT. Yes, money and gunpowder. Freedom and power. Command of life and command of death.

CUSINS (*urbanely: trying to bring him down to earth*). This is extremely interesting, Mr Undershaft. Of course you know that you are mad.

UNDERSHAFT (*with redoubled force*). And you?

CUSINS. Oh, mad as a hatter. You are welcome to my secret since I have discovered yours. But I am astonished. Can a madman make cannons?

UNDERSHAFT. Would anyone else than a madman make them? And now (*with surging energy*) question for question. Can a sane man translate Euripides?

CUSINS. No.

UNDERSHAFT (*seizing him by the shoulder*). Can a sane woman make a man of a waster or a woman of a worm?

CUSINS (*reeling before the storm*). Father Colossus—Mammoth Millionaire—

UNDERSHAFT (*pressing him*). Are there two mad people or three in this Salvation shelter today?

CUSINS. You mean Barbara is as mad as we are?

UNDERSHAFT (*pushing him lightly off and resuming his equanimity suddenly and completely*). Pooh, Professor! let us

call things by their proper names. I am a millionaire; you are a poet: Barbara is a savior of souls. What have we three to do with the common mob of slaves and idolators? (*He sits down again with a shrug of contempt for the mob.*)

CUSINS. Take care! Barbara is in love with the common people. So am I. Have you never felt the romance of that love?

UNDERSHAFT (*cold and sardonic*). Have you ever been in love with Poverty, like St Francis? Have you ever been in love with Dirt, like St Simeon! Have you ever been in love with disease and suffering, like our nurses and philanthropists? Such passions are not virtues, but the most unnatural of all the vices. This love of the common people may please an earl's granddaughter and a university professor; but I have been a common man and a poor man; and it has no romance for me. Leave it to the poor to pretend that poverty is a blessing: leave it to the coward to make a religion of his cowardice by preaching humility: we know better than that. We three must stand together above the common people: how else can we help their children to climb up beside us? Barbara must belong to us, not to the Salvation Army.

CUSINS. Well, I can only say that if you think you will get her away from the Salvation Army by talking to her as you have been talking to me, you dont know Barbara.

UNDERSHAFT. My friend: I never ask for what I can buy.

CUSINS (*in a white fury*). Do I understand you to imply that you can buy Barbara?

UNDERSHAFT. No; but I can buy the Salvation Army.

CUSINS. Quite impossible.

UNDERSHAFT. You shall see. All religious organizations exist by selling themselves to the rich.

CUSINS. Not the Army. That is the Church of the poor.

UNDERSHAFT. All the more reason for buying it.

CUSINS. I dont think you quite know what the Army does for the poor.

UNDERSHAFT. Oh yes I do. It draws their teeth: that is enough for me as a man of business.

CUSINS. Nonsense! It makes them sober—

UNDERSHAFT. I prefer sober workmen. The profits are larger.

CUSINS. honest—

UNDERSHAFT. Honest workmen are the most economical.

CUSINS. attached to their homes—

UNDERSHAFT. So much the better: they will put up with anything sooner than change their shop.

CUSINS. happy—

UNDERSHAFT. An invaluable safeguard against revolution.

CUSINS. unselfish—

UNDERSHAFT. Indifferent to their own interests, which suits me exactly.

CUSINS. with their thoughts on heavenly things—

UNDERSHAFT (*rising*). And not on Trade Unionism nor Socialism. Excellent.

CUSINS (*revolted*). You really are an infernal old rascal.

UNDERSHAFT (*indicating Peter Shirley, who has just come from the shelter and strolled dejectedly down the yard between them*). And this is an honest man!

SHIRLEY. Yes; and what av I got by it? (*He passes on bitterly and sits on the form, in the corner of the penthouse.*)

(*Snobby Price, beaming sanctimoniously, and Jenny Hill, with a tambourine full of coppers, come from the shelter and go to the drum, on which Jenny begins to count the money.*)

UNDERSHAFT (*replying to Shirley*). Oh, your employers must have got a good deal by it from first to last. (*He sits on the table, with one foot on the side form, Cusins, overwhelmed, sits down on the same form nearer the shelter. Barbara comes from the shelter to the middle of the yard. She is excited and a little overwrought.*)

BARBARA. Weve just had a splendid experience meeting at the other gate in Cripps's lane. Ive hardly ever seen them so much moved as they were by your confession, Mr Price.

PRICE. I could almost be glad of my past wickedness if I could believe that it would elp to keep hathers stright.

BARBARA. So it will, Snobby. How much, Jenny?

JENNY. Four and tenpence, Major.

BARBARA. Oh Snobby, if you had given your poor mother just one more kick, we should have got the whole five shillings!

PRICE. If she heard you say that, miss, she'd be sorry I didnt. But I'm glad. Oh what a joy it will be to her when she hears I'm saved!

UNDERSHAFT. Shall I contribute the odd twopence, Barbara? The millionaire's mite, eh? (*He takes a couple of pennies from his pocket.*)

BARBARA. How did you make that twopence?

UNDERSHAFT. As usual. By selling cannons, torpedoes, submarines, and my new patent Grand Duke hand grenade.

BARBARA. Put it back in your pocket. You cant buy your salvation here for twopence: you must work it out.

UNDERSHAFT. Is twopence not enough? I can afford a little more, if you press me.

BARBARA. Two million millions would not be enough. There is bad blood on your hands; and nothing but good blood can cleanse them. Money is no use. Take it away. (*She turns to Cusins.*) Dolly: you must write another letter for me to the papers. (*He makes a wry face.*) Yes: I know you dont like it; but it must be done. The starvation this winter is beating us: everybody is unemployed. The General says we must close this shelter if we cant get more money. I force the collections at the meetings until I am ashamed: dont I, Snobby?

PRICE. It's a fair treat to see you work it, miss. The way you got them up from three-and-six to four-and-ten with that hymn, penny by penny and verse by verse, was a caution. Not a Cheap Jack on Mile End Waste could touch you at it.

BARBARA. Yes; but I wish we could do without it. I am getting at last to think more of the collection than of the people's souls. And what are those hatfuls of pence and halfpence? We want thousands! tens of thousands! hundreds of thousands! I want to convert people, not to be always begging for the Army in a way I'd die sooner than beg for myself.

UNDERSHAFT (*in profound irony*). Genuine unselfishness is capable of anything, my dear.

BARBARA (*unsuspectingly, as she turns away to take the money from the drum and put it in a cash bag she carries*). Yes, isnt it? (*Undershaft looks sardonically at Cusins.*)

CUSINS (*aside to Undershaft*). Mephistopheles! Machiavelli!

BARBARA (*tears coming into her eyes as she ties the bag and pockets it*). How are we to feed them? I cant talk religion to a man with bodily hunger in his eyes. (*Almost breaking down*) It's frightful.

JENNY (*running to her*). Major, dear—

BARBARA (*rebounding*). No: dont comfort me. It will be all right. We shall get the money.

UNDERSHAFT. How?

JENNY. By praying for it, of course. Mrs Baines says she prayed for it last night; and she has never prayed for it in vain: never once. (*She goes to the gate and looks out into the street.*)

BARBARA (*who has dried her eyes and regained her composure*). By the way, dad, Mrs Baines has come to march with us to our big meeting this afternoon; and she is very anxious to meet you, for some reason or other. Perhaps she'll convert you.

UNDERSHAFT. I shall be delighted, my dear.

JENNY (*at the gate: excitedly*). Major! Major! heres that man back again.

BARBARA. What man?

JENNY. The man that hit me. Oh, I hope he's coming back to join us.

(*Bill Walker, with frost on his jacket, comes through the gate, his hands deep in his pockets and his chin sunk between his shoulders, like a cleaned-out gambler. He halts between Barbara and the drum.*)

BARBARA. Hullo, Bill! Back already!

BILL (*nagging at her*). Bin talkin ever sence, ev you?

BARBARA. Pretty nearly. Well, has Todger paid you out for poor Jenny's jaw?

BILL. Nao e aint.

BARBARA. I thought your jacket looked a bit snowy.

BILL. Sao it is snaowy. You want to knaow where the snaow cam from, downt you?

BARBARA. Yes.

BILL. Well, it cam from orf the grahnd in Pawkinses Corner in Kennintahn. It got rabbed orf be maw shaoulders: see?

BARBARA. Pity you didnt rub some off with your knees, Bill! That would have done you a lot of good.

BILL (*with sour mirthless humor*). Aw was sivin anather menn's knees at the tawm. E was kneelin on moy ed, e was.

JENNY. Who was kneeling on your head?

BILL. Todger was. E was pryin for me: pryin camfortable wiv me as a cawpet. Sow was Mog. Sao was the aol bloomin meetin. Mog she sez "Ow Lawd brike is stabborn sperrit; bat downt urt is dear art." Thet was wot she said. "Downt urt is dear art!" An er blowk—thirteen stun four!—kneelin wiv all is wight on me. Fanny, aint it?

JENNY. Oh no. We're so sorry, Mr Walker.

BARBARA (*enjoying it frankly*). Nonsense! of course it's funny. Served you right, Bill! You must have done something to him first.

BILL (*doggedly*). Aw did wot Aw said Aw'd do. Aw spit in is eye. E looks ap at the skoy and sez, "Ow that Aw should be fahnd worthy to be spit upon for the gospel's sike!" e sez; an Mog sez "Glaory Allelloolier!"; an then e called me Braddher, an dahned me as if Aw was a kid and e was me mather worshin me a Setterda nawt. Aw ednt jast nao shaow wiv im at all. Arf the street pryed; an the tather arf larfed fit to split theirselves. (*To Barbara*) There! are you settisfawd nah?

BARBARA (*her eyes dancing*). Wish I'd been there, Bill.

BILL. Yus: youd a got in a hextra bit o talk on me, wouldnt you?

JENNY. I'm so sorry, Mr. Walker.

BILL (*fiercely*). Downt you gow bein sorry for me: youve no call. Listen eah. Aw browk your jawr.

JENNY. No, it didnt hurt me: indeed it didnt, except for a moment. It was only that I was frightened.

BILL. Aw downt want to be forgive be you, or be ennybody. Wot Aw did Aw'll py for. Aw trawd to gat me aown jawr browk to settisfaw you—

JENNY (*distressed*). Oh no—

BILL (*impatiently*). Tell y' Aw did: cawnt you listen to wots bein taold you? All Aw got be it was bein mide a sawt of in the pablic street for me pines. Well, if Aw cawnt settisfaw you one wy, Aw ken anather. Listen eah! Aw ed two quid sived agen the frost; an Awve a pahnd of it left. A mite o mawn last week ed words with the judy e's gowin to merry.

E give er wot-for; an e's bin fawned fifteen bob. E ed a rawt to itt er cause they was gowin to be merrid; but Aw ednt nao rawt to itt you; sao put anather fawv bob on an call it a pahnd's worth. (*He produces a sovereign.*) Eahs the manney. Tike it; and lets ev no more o your forgivin an pryin and your Mijor jawrin me. Let wot Aw dan be dan an pide for; and let there be a end of it.

JENNY. Oh, I couldnt take it, Mr. Walker. But if you would give a shilling or two to poor Rummy Mitchens! you really did hurt her; and she's old.

BILL (*contemptuously*). Not lawkly. Aw'd give her anather as soon as look at er. Let her ev the lawr o me as she threatened! She aint forgiven me: not mach. Wot Aw dan to er is not on me mawnd—wot she (*indicating Barbara*) mawt call on me conscience—no more than stickin a pig. It's this Christian gime o yours that Aw wownt ev plyed agen me: this bloomin forgivin an neggin an jawrin that mikes a menn thet sore that iz lawf's a burdn to im. Aw wownt ev it, Aw tell you; sao tike your manney and stop thraowin your silly beshed fice hap agen me.

JENNY. Major: may I take a little of it for the Army?

BARBARA. No: the Army is not to be bought. We want your soul, Bill; and we'll take nothing less.

BILL (*bitterly*). Aw knaow. Me an maw few shillins is not good enaff for you. Youre a earl's grendorter, you are. Nathink less than a andered pahnd for you.

UNDERSHAFT. Come, Barbara! you could do a great deal of good with a hundred pounds. If you will set this gentleman's mind at ease by taking his pound, I will give the other ninety-nine. (*Bill, dazed by such opulence, instinctively touches his cap.*)

BARBARA. Oh, youre too extravagant, papa. Bill offers twenty pieces of silver. All you need offer is the other ten. That will make the standard price to buy anybody who's for sale. I'm not; and the Army's not. (*To Bill*) Youll never have another quiet moment, Bill, until you come round to us. You cant stand out against your salvation.

BILL (*sullenly*). Aw cawnt stend aht agen music awl wrastlers and awtful tangued women. Awve offered to py. Aw can do no more. Tike it or leave it. There it is. (*He throws the sovereign on the drum, and sits down on the horse-trough. The coin fascinates Snobby Price, who takes an early opportunity of dropping his cap on it.*)

(*Mrs Baines comes from the shelter. She is dressed as a Salvation Army Commissioner. She is an earnest looking woman of about 40, with a caressing, urgent voice, and an appealing manner.*)

BARBARA. This is my father, Mrs Baines. (*Undershaft comes from the table, taking his hat off with marked civility.*) Try what you can do with him. He wont listen to me, because he remembers what a fool I was when I was a baby. (*She leaves them together and chats with Jenny.*)

MRS BAINES. Have you been shewn over the shelter, Mr Undershaft? You know the work we're doing, of course.

UNDERSHAFT (*very civilly*). The whole nation knows it, Mrs Baines.

MRS BAINES. No, sir: the whole nation does not know it, or we should not be crippled as we are for want of money to carry our work through the length and breadth of the land. Let me tell you that there would have been rioting this winter in London but for us.

UNDERSHAFT. You really think so?

MRS BAINES. I know it. I remember 1886, when you rich gentlemen hardened your hearts against the cry of the poor. They broke the windows of your clubs in Pall Mall.

UNDERSHAFT (*gleaming with approval of their method*). And the Mansion House Fund went up next day from thirty thousand pounds to seventy-nine thousand! I remember quite well.

MRS BAINES. Well, wont you help me to get at the people? They wont break windows then. Come here, Price. Let me shew you to this gentleman. (*Price comes to be inspected.*) Do you remember the window breaking?

PRICE. My ole father thought it was the revolution, maam.

MRS BAINES. Would you break windows now?

PRICE. Oh no, maam. The windows of eaven av bin opened to me. I know now that the rich man is a sinner like myself.

RUMMY (*appearing above at the loft door*). Snobby Price!

SNOBBY. Wot is it?

RUMMY. Your mother's askin for you at the other gate in Cripps's Lane. She's heard about your confession. (*Price turns pale.*)

MRS. BAINES. Go, Mr Price; and pray with her.

JENNY. You can go through the shelter, Snobby.

PRICE (*to Mrs Baines*). I couldnt face her now, maam, with all the weight of my sins fresh on me. Tell her she'll find her son at ome, waitin for her in prayer. (*He skulks off through the gate, incidentally stealing the sovereign on his way out by picking up his cap from the drum.*)

MRS BAINES (*with swimming eyes*). You see how we take the anger and the bitterness against you out of their hearts, Mr Undershaft.

UNDERSHAFT. It is certainly most convenient and gratifying to all large employers of labor, Mrs Baines.

MRS BAINES. Barbara: Jenny: I have good news: most wonderful news. (JENNY *runs to her.*) My prayers have been answered. I told you they would, Jenny, didnt I?

JENNY. Yes, yes.

BARBARA (*moving nearer to the drum*). Have we got money enough to keep the shelter open?

MRS BAINES. I hope we shall have enough to keep all the shelters open. Lord Saxmundham has promised us five thousand pounds—

BARBARA. Hooray!

JENNY. Glory!

MRS BAINES. —if—

BARBARA. "If!" If what?

MRS BAINES. —if five other gentlemen will give a thousand each to make it up to ten thousand.

BARBARA. Who is Lord Saxmundham? I never heard of him.

UNDERSHAFT (*who has pricked up his ears at the peer's name, and is now watching Barbara curiously*). A new creation, my dear. You have heard of Sir Horace Bodger?

BARBARA. Bodger! Do you mean the distiller? Bodger's whisky!

UNDERSHAFT. That is the man. He is one of the greatest of our public bene-factors. He restored the cathedral at Hakington. They made him a baronet for that. He gave half a million to the funds of his party: they made him a baron for that.

SHIRLEY. What will they give him for the five thousand?

UNDERSHAFT. There is nothing left to give him. So the five thousand, I should think, is to save his soul.

MRS BAINES. Heaven grant it may! Oh Mr Undershaft, you have some very rich friends. Cant you help us towards the other five thousand? We are going to hold a great meeting this afternoon at the Assembly Hall in the Mile End Road. If I could only announce that one gentleman had come forward to support Lord Saxmundham, others would follow. Dont you know somebody? couldnt you? wouldnt you? (*her eyes fill with tears*) oh, think of those poor people, Mr Undershaft: think of how much it means to them, and how little to a great man like you.

UNDERSHAFT (*sardonically gallant*). Mrs Baines: you are irresistible. I cant dissappoint you; and I cant deny myself the satisfaction of making Bodger pay up. You shall have your five thousand pounds.

MRS BAINES. Thank God!

UNDERSHAFT. You dont thank me?

MRS BAINES. Oh sir, dont try to be cynical: dont be ashamed of being a good man. The Lord will bless you abundantly; and our prayers will be like a strong fortification round you all the days of your life. (*With a touch of caution*) You will let me have the cheque to shew at the meeting, wont you? Jenny: go in and fetch a pen and ink. (*Jenny runs to the shelter door.*)

UNDERSHAFT. Do not disturb Miss Hill: I have a fountain pen. (*Jenny halts. He sits at the table and writes the cheque. Cusins rises to make room for him. They all watch him silently.*)

BILL (*cynically, aside to Barbara, his voice and accent horribly debased*). Wot prawce selvytion nah?

BARBARA. Stop. (*Undershaft stops writing: they all turn to her in surprise.*) Mrs Baines: are you really going to take this money?

MRS BAINES (*astonished*). Why not, dear?

BARBARA. Why not! Do you know what my father is? Have you forgotten that Lord Saxmundham is Bodger the whisky man? Do you remember how we implored the County Council to stop him from writing Bodger's Whisky in letters of fire against the sky; so that the poor drink-ruined creatures on the Embankment could not wake up from their snatches of sleep without being reminded of their deadly thirst by that wicked sky sign? Do you know that the worst thing I have had to fight here is not the devil, but Bodger, Bodger, Bodger, with his whisky, his distilleries, and his tied houses? Are you going to make our shelter another tied house for him, and ask me to keep it?

BILL. Rotten dranken whisky it is too.

MRS BAINES. Dear Barbara: Lord Saxmundham has a soul to be saved like any of us. If heaven has found the way to make a good use of his money, are we to set ourselves up against the answer to our prayers?

BARBARA. I know he has a soul to be saved. Let him come down here; and I'll do my best to help him to his salvation. But he wants to send his cheque down to buy us, and go on being as wicked as ever.

UNDERSHAFT (with a reasonableness which Cusins alone perceives to be ironical). My dear Barbara: alcohol is a very necessary article. It heals the sick—

BARBARA. It does nothing of the sort.

UNDERSHAFT. Well, it assists the doctor: that is perhaps a less questionable way of putting it. It makes life bearable to millions of people who could not endure their existence if they were quite sober. It enables Parliament to do things at eleven at night that no sane person would do at eleven in the morning. Is it Bodger's fault that this inestimable gift is deplorably abused by less than one per cent of the poor?

(He turns again to the table; signs the cheque; and crosses it.)

MRS BAINES. Barbara: will there be less drinking or more if all those poor souls we are saving come tomorrow and find the doors of our shelters shut in their faces? Lord Saxmundham gives us the money to stop drinking—to take his own business from him.

CUSINS (impishly). Pure self-sacrifice on Bodger's part, clearly! Bless dear Bodger! (Barbara almost breaks down as Adolphus, too, fails her.)

UNDERSHAFT (tearing out the cheque and pocketing the book as he rises and goes past Cusins to Mrs Baines). I also, Mrs Baines, may claim a little disinterestedness. Think of my business! think of the widows and orphans! the men and lads torn to pieces with shrapnel and poisoned with lyddite! (Mrs Baines shrinks; but he goes on remorselessly) the oceans of blood, not one drop of which is shed in a really just cause! the ravaged crops! the peaceful peasants forced, women and men, to till their fields under the fire of opposing armies on pain of starvation! the bad blood of the fierce little cowards at home who egg on others to fight for the gratification of their national vanity! All this makes money for me: I am never richer, never busier than when the papers are full of it. Well, it is your work to preach peace on earth and good will to men. (Mrs Baines's face lights up again.) Every convert you make is a vote against war. (Her lips move in prayer.) Yet I give you this money to help you to hasten my own commercial ruin. (He gives her the cheque.)

CUSINS (mounting the form in an ecstasy of mischief). The millennium will be inaugurated by the unselfishness of Undershaft and Bodger. Oh be joyful! (He takes the drum-sticks from his pocket and flourishes them.)

MRS BAINES (taking the cheque). The longer I live the more proof I see that there is an Infinite Goodness that turns everything to the work of salvation sooner or later. Who would have thought that any good could have come out of war and drink? And yet their profits are brought today to the feet of salvation to do its blessed work. (She is affected to tears.)

JENNY (running to Mrs Baines and throwing her arms round her). Oh dear! how blessed, how glorious it all is!

CUSINS (in a convulsion of irony). Let us seize this unspeakable moment. Let us march to the great meeting at once. Excuse me just an instant. (He rushes into the shelter. Jenny takes her tambourine from the drum head.)

MRS BAINES. Mr Undershaft: have you

ever seen a thousand people fall on their knees with one impulse and pray? Come with us to the meeting. Barbara shall tell them that the Army is saved, and saved through you.

CUSINS (*returning impetuously from the shelter with a flag and a trombone, and coming between Mrs Baines and Undershaft*). You shall carry the flag down the first street, Mrs Baines (*he gives her the flag*). Mr Undershaft is a gifted trombonist: he shall intone an Olympian diapason to the West Ham Salvation March. (*Aside to Undershaft, as he forces the trombone on him*) Blow, Machiavelli, blow.

UNDERSHAFT (*aside to him, as he takes the trombone*). The trumpet in Zion! (*Cusins rushes to the drum, which he takes up and puts on. Undershaft continues, aloud*) I will do my best. I could vamp a bass if I knew the tune.

CUSINS. It is a wedding chorus from one of Donizetti's operas; but we have converted it. We convert everything to good here, including Bodger. You remember the chorus. "For thee immense rejoicing—immenso giubilo—immenso giubilo." (*With drum obbligato*) Rum tum ti tum tum, tum tum ti ta—

BARBARA. Dolly: you are breaking my heart.

CUSINS. What is a broken heart more or less here? Dionysos Undershaft has descended. I am possessed.

MRS BAINES. Come, Barbara: I must have my dear Major to carry the flag with me.

JENNY. Yes, yes, Major darling.

CUSINS (*snatches the tambourine out of Jenny's hand and mutely offers it to Barbara.*)

BARBARA (*coming forward a little as she puts the offer behind her with a shudder, whilst Cusins recklessly tosses the tambourine back to Jenny and goes to the gate*). I cant come.

JENNY. Not come!

MRS BAINES (*with tears in her eyes*). Barbara: do you think I am wrong to take the money?

BARBARA (*impulsively going to her and kissing her*). No, no: God help you, dear, you must: you are saving the Army. Go; and may you have a great meeting!

JENNY. But arnt you coming?

BARBARA. No. (*She begins taking off the silver S brooch from her collar.*)

MRS BAINES. Barbara: what are you doing?

JENNY. Why are you taking your badge off? You cant be going to leave us, Major.

BARBARA (*quietly*). Father: come here.

UNDERSHAFT (*coming by her*). My dear! (*Seeing that she is going to pin the badge on his collar, he retreats to the penthouse in some alarm.*)

BARBARA (*following him*). Dont be frightened. (*She pins the badge on and steps back towards the table, shewing him to the others*) There! It's not much for £5000, is it?

MRS BAINES. Barbara: if you wont come and pray with us, promise me you will pray for us.

BARBARA. I cant pray now. Perhaps I shall never pray again.

MRS BAINES. Barbara!

JENNY. Major!

BARBARA (*almost delirious*). I cant bear any more. Quick march!

CUSINS (*calling to the procession in the street outside*). Off we go. Play up, there! Immenso giubilo. (*He gives the time with his drum; and the band strikes up the march, which rapidly becomes more distant as the procession moves briskly away.*)

MRS BAINES. I must go, dear. Youre overworked: you will be all right tomorrow. We'll never lose you. Now Jenny: step out with the old flag. Blood and Fire! (*She marches out through the gate with her flag.*)

JENNY. Glory Hallelujah! (*flourishing her tambourine and marching*).

UNDERSHAFT (*to Cusins, as he marches out past him easing the slide of his trombone*). "My ducats and my daughter!"

CUSINS (*following him out*). Money and gunpowder!

BARBARA. Drunkenness and Murder! My God: why hast thou forsaken me? (*She sinks on the form with her face buried in her hands. The march passes away into silence. Bill Walker steals across to her.*)

BILL (*taunting*). Wot prawce selvytion nah?

SHIRLEY. Dont you hit her when she's down.

BILL. She itt me wen aw wiz dahn. Waw shouldnt Aw git a bit o me aown beck?

BARBARA (*raising her head*). I didnt take your money, Bill. (*She crosses the yard to the gate and turns her back on the two men to hide her face from them.*)

BILL (*sneering after her*). Naow, it warnt enaff for you. (*Turning to the drum, he misses the money*) Ellow! If you aint took it sammun else ez. Weres it gorn? Bly me if Jenny Ill didnt tike it arter all!

RUMMY (*screaming at him from the loft*). You lie, you dirty blackguard! Snobby Price pinched it off the drum when he took up his cap. I was up here all the time an see im do it.

BILL. Wot! Stowl maw manney! Waw didnt you call thief on him, you silly aold macker you?

RUMMY. To serve you aht for ittin me acrost the fice. It's cost y'pahnd, that az. (*Raising a pæn of squalid triumph*) I done you. I'm even with you. Uve ad it aht o y—(*Bill snatches up Shirley's mug and hurls it at her. She slams the loft door and vanishes. The mug smashes against the door and falls in fragments.*)

BILL (*beginning to chuckle*). Tell us, aol menn, wot o'clock this mawnin was it wen im as they call Snobby Prawce was sived?

BARBARA (*turning to him more composedly, and with unspoiled sweetness*). About half past twelve, Bill. And he pinched your pound at a quarter to two. I know. Well, you cant afford to lose it. I'll send it to you.

BILL (*his voice and accent suddenly improving*). Not if Aw wiz to stawve for it. Aw aint to be bought.

SHIRLEY. Aint you? Youd sell yourself to the devil for a pint o beer; only there aint no devil to make the offer.

BILL (*unashamed*). Sao Aw would, mite, and often ev, cheerful. But she cawnt baw me. (*Approaching Barbara*) You wanted maw saoul, did you? Well, you aint got it.

BARBARA. I nearly got it, Bill. But weve sold it back to you for ten thousand pounds.

SHIRLEY. And dear at the money!

BARBARA. No, Peter: it was worth more than money.

BILL (*salvationproof*). It's nao good: you cawnt get rahnd me nah. Aw downt blieve in it; and Awve seen tody that Aw was rawt. (*Going*) Sao long, aol soup-kitchener! Ta, ta, Mijor Earl's Grendorter! (*Turning at the gate*) Wot prawce selvytion nah? Snobby Prawce! Ha! Ha!

BARBARA (*offering her hand*). Goodbye, Bill.

BILL (*taken aback, half plucks his cap off; then shoves it on again defiantly*). Git aht. (*Barbara drops her hand, discouraged. He has a twinge of remorse*). But thets aw rawt, you knaow. Nathink pasnl. Naow mellice. Sao long, Judy. (*He goes.*)

BARBARA. No malice. So long, Bill.

SHIRLEY (*shaking his head*). You make too much of him, miss, in your innocence.

BARBARA (*going to him*). Peter: I'm like you now. Cleaned out, and lost my job.

SHIRLEY. Youve youth an hope. Thats two better than me.

BARBARA. I'll get you a job, Peter. Thats hope for you: the youth will have to be enough for me. (*She counts her money.*) I have just enough left for two teas at Lockharts, a Rowton doss for you, and my tram and bus home. (*He frowns and rises with offended pride. She takes his arm.*) Dont be proud, Peter: it's sharing between friends. And promise me youll talk to me and not let me cry. (*She draws him towards the gate.*)

SHIRLEY. Well, I'm not accustomed to talk to the like of you—

BARBARA (*urgently*). Yes, yes: you must talk to me. Tell me about Tom Paine's books and Bradlaugh's lectures. Come along.

SHIRLEY. Ah, if you would only read Tom Paine in the proper spirit, miss! (*They go out through the gate together.*)

❧ Act III

Next day after lunch Lady Britomart is writing in the library in Wilton Crescent. Sarah is reading in the armchair near the window. Barbara, in ordinary fashionable dress, pale and brooding, is on the settee. Charles Lomax enters. He starts on seeing

Barbara fashionably attired and in low spirits.

LOMAX. Youve left off your uniform!

(*Barbara says nothing; but an expression of pain passes over her face.*)

LADY BRITOMART (*warning him in low tones to be careful*). Charles!

LOMAX (*much concerned, coming behind the settee and bending sympathetically over Barbara*). I'm awfully sorry, Barbara. You know I helped you all I could with the concertina and so forth. (*Momentously*) Still, I have never shut my eyes to the fact that there is a certain amount of tosh about the Salvation Army. Now the claims of the Church of England—

LADY BRITOMART. Thats enough, Charles. Speak of something suited to your mental capacity.

LOMAX. But surely the Church of England is suited to all our capacities.

BARBARA (*pressing his hand*). Thank you for your sympathy, Cholly. Now go and spoon with Sarah.

LOMAX (*dragging a chair from the writing table and seating himself affectionately by Sarah's side*) How is my ownest today?

SARAH. I wish you wouldnt tell Cholly to do things, Barbara. He always comes straight and does them. Cholly: we're going to the works this afternoon.

LOMAX. What works?

SARAH. The cannon works.

LOMAX. What? your governor's shop!

SARAH. Yes.

LOMAX. Oh I say!

(*Cusins enters in poor condition. He also starts visibly when he sees Barbara without her uniform.*)

BARBARA. I expected you this morning, Dolly. Didnt you guess that?

CUSINS (*sitting down beside her*). I'm sorry. I have only just breakfasted.

SARAH. But weve just finished lunch.

BARBARA. Have you had one of your bad nights?

CUSINS. No: I had rather a good night: in fact, one of the most remarkable nights I have ever passed.

BARBARA. The meeting?

CUSINS. No: after the meeting.

LADY BRITOMART. You should have gone to bed after the meeting. What were you doing?

CUSINS. Drinking.

LADY BRITOMART.	⎫	⎧	Adolphus!
SARAH.			Dolly!
BARBARA.			Dolly!
LOMAX.	⎭	⎩	Oh I say!

LADY BRITOMART. What were you drinking, may I ask?

CUSINS. A most devilish kind of Spanish burgundy, warranted free from added alcohol: a Temperance burgundy in fact. Its richness in natural alcohol made any addition superfluous.

BARBARA. Are you joking, Dolly?

CUSINS (*patiently*). No. I have been making a night of it with the nominal head of this household: that is all.

LADY BRITOMART. Andrew made you drunk!

CUSINS. No: he only provided the wine. I think it was Dionysos who made me drunk. (*To Barbara*) I told you I was possessed.

LADY BRITOMART. Youre not sober yet. Go home to bed at once.

CUSINS. I have never before ventured to reproach you, Lady Brit; but how could you marry the Prince of Darkness?

LADY BRITOMART. It was much more excusable to marry him than to get drunk with him. That is a new accomplishment of Andrew's, by the way. He usent to drink.

CUSINS. He doesnt now. He only sat there and completed the wreck of my moral basis, the rout of my convictions, the purchase of my soul. He cares for you, Barbara. That is what makes him so dangerous to me.

BARBARA. That has nothing to do with it, Dolly. There are larger loves and diviner dreams than the fireside ones. You know that, dont you?

CUSINS. Yes: that is our understanding. I know it. I hold to it. Unless he can win me on that holier ground he may amuse me for a while; but he can get no deeper hold, strong as he is.

BARBARA. Keep to that; and the end will be right. Now tell me what happened at the meeting?

CUSINS. It was an amazing meeting. Mrs Baines almost died of emotion. Jenny Hill simply gibbered with hysteria. The Prince of Darkness played his trombone like a madman: its brazen roarings were like the laughter of the damned. 117 conversions took place then and there. They prayed with the most touching sincerity and gratitude for Bodger, and for the anonymous donor of the £5000. Your father would not let his name be given.

LOMAX. That was rather fine of the old man, you know. Most chaps would have wanted the advertisement.

CUSINS. He said all the charitable institutions would be down on him like kites on a battle-field if he gave his name.

LADY BRITOMART. Thats Andrew all over. He never does a proper thing without giving an improper reason for it.

CUSINS. He convinced me that I have all my life been doing improper things for proper reasons.

LADY BRITOMART. Adolphus: now that Barbara has left the Salvation Army, you had better leave it too. I will not have you playing that drum in the streets.

CUSINS. Your orders are already obeyed, Lady Brit.

BARBARA. Dolly: were you ever really in earnest about it? Would you have joined if you had never seen me?

CUSINS (disingenuously). Well—er—well, possibly, as a collector of religions—

LOMAX (cunningly). Not as a drummer, though, you know. You are a very clearheaded brainy chap, Dolly; and it must have been apparent to you that there is a certain amount of tosh about—

LADY BRITOMART. Charles: if you must drivel, drivel like a grown-up man and not like a schoolboy.

LOMAX (out of countenance). Well, drivel is drivel, dont you know, whatever a man's age.

LADY BRITOMART. In good society in England, Charles, men drivel at all ages by repeating silly formulas with an air of wisdom. Schoolboys make their own formulas out of slang, like you. When they reach your age, and get political private secretaryships and things of that sort, they drop slang and get their formulas out of the Spectator or The Times. You had better confine yourself to The Times. You will find that there is a certain amount of tosh about The Times; but at least its language is reputable.

LOMAX (overwhelmed). You are so awfully strong-minded, Lady Brit—

LADY BRITOMART. Rubbish! (Morrison comes in.) What is it?

MORRISON. If you please, my lady, Mr Undershaft has just drove up to the door.

LADY BRITOMART. Well, let him in. (Morrison hesitates.) Whats the matter with you?

MORRISON. Shall I announce him, my lady; or is he at home here, so to speak, my lady?

LADY BRITOMART. Announce him.

MORRISON. Thank you, my lady. You wont mind my asking, I hope. The occasion is in a manner of speaking new to me.

LADY BRITOMART. Quite right. Go and let him in.

MORRISON. Thank you, my lady. (He withdraws.)

LADY BRITOMART. Children: go and get ready. (Sarah and Barbara go upstairs for their out-of-door wraps.) Charles: go and tell Stephen to come down here in five minutes: you will find him in the drawing room. (Charles goes.) Adolphus: tell them to send round the carriage in about fifteen minutes. (Adolphus goes.)

MORRISON (at the door). Mr Undershaft.

(Undershaft comes in. Morrison goes out.)

UNDERSHAFT. Alone! How fortunate!

LADY BRITOMART (rising). Dont be sentimental, Andrew. Sit down. (She sits on the settee: he sits beside her, on her left. She comes to the point before he has time to breathe). Sarah must have £800 a year until Charles Lomax comes into his property. Barbara will need more, and need it permanently, because Adolphus hasnt any property.

UNDERSHAFT (resignedly). Yes, my dear: I will see to it. Anything else? for yourself, for instance?

LADY BRITOMART. I want to talk to you about Stephen.

UNDERSHAFT (rather wearily). Dont, my dear. Stephen doesnt interest me.

LADY BRITOMART. He does interest me. He is our son.

UNDERSHAFT. Do you really think so? He has induced us to bring him into the world; but he chose his parents very incongruously, I think. I see nothing of myself in him, and less of you.

LADY BRITOMART. Andrew: Stephen is

an excellent son, and a most steady, capable, highminded young man. You are simply trying to find an excuse for disinheriting him.

UNDERSHAFT. My dear Biddy: the Undershaft tradition disinherits him. It would be dishonest of me to leave the cannon foundry to my son.

LADY BRITOMART. It would be most unnatural and improper of you to leave it to anyone else, Andrew. Do you suppose this wicked and immoral tradition can be kept up for ever? Do you pretend that Stephen could not carry on the foundry just as well as all the other sons of the big business houses?

UNDERSHAFT. Yes: he could learn the office routine without understanding the business, like all the other sons; and the firm would go on by its own momentum until the real Undershaft—probably an Italian or a German—would invent a new method and cut him out.

LADY BRITOMART. There is nothing that any Italian or German could do that Stephen could not do. And Stephen at least has breeding.

UNDERSHAFT. The son of a foundling! Nonsense!

LADY BRITOMART. My son, Andrew! And even you may have good blood in your veins for all you know.

UNDERSHAFT. True. Probably I have. That is another argument in favour of a foundling.

LADY BRITOMART. Andrew: dont be aggravating. And dont be wicked. At present you are both.

UNDERSHAFT. This conversation is part of the Undershaft tradition, Biddy. Every Undershaft's wife has treated him to it ever since the house was founded. It is mere waste of breath. If the tradition be ever broken it will be for an abler man than Stephen.

LADY BRITOMART (*pouting*). Then go away.

UNDERSHAFT (*deprecatory*). Go away!

LADY BRITOMART. Yes: go away. If you will do nothing for Stephen, you are not wanted here. Go to your foundling, whoever he is; and look after him.

UNDERSHAFT. The fact is, Biddy—

LADY BRITOMART. Dont call me Biddy. I dont call you Andy.

UNDERSHAFT. I will not call my wife Britomart: it is not good sense. Seriously,

my love, the Undershaft tradition has landed me in a difficulty. I am getting on in years; and my partner Lazarus has at last made a stand and insisted that the succession must be settled one way or the other; and of course he is quite right. You see, I havent found a fit successor yet.

LADY BRITOMART (*obstinately*). There is Stephen.

UNDERSHAFT. Thats just it: all the foundlings I can find are exactly like Stephen.

LADY BRITOMART. Andrew!!

UNDERSHAFT. I want a man with no relations and no schooling: that is, a man who would be out of the running altogether if he were not a strong man. And I cant find him. Every blessed foundling nowadays is snapped up in his infancy by Barnardo homes, or School Board officers, or Boards of Guardians; and if he shews the least ability he is fastened on by schoolmasters; trained to win scholarships like a racehorse; crammed with secondhand ideas; drilled and disciplined in docility and what they call good taste; and lamed for life so that he is fit for nothing but teaching. If you want to keep the foundry in the family, you had better find an eligible foundling and marry him to Barbara.

LADY BRITOMART. Ah! Barbara! Your pet! You would sacrifice Stephen to Barbara.

UNDERSHAFT. Cheerfully. And you, my dear, would boil Barbara to make soup for Stephen.

LADY BRITOMART. Andrew: this is not a question of our likings and dislikings: it is a question of duty. It is your duty to make Stephen your successor.

UNDERSHAFT. Just as much as it is your duty to submit to your husband. Come, Biddy! these tricks of the governing class are of no use with me. I am one of the governing class myself; and it is waste of time giving tracts to a missionary. I have the power in this matter; and I am not to be humbugged into using it for your purposes.

LADY BRITOMART. Andrew: you can talk my head off; but you cant change wrong into right. And your tie is all on one side. Put it straight.

UNDERSHAFT (*disconcerted*). It wont

stay unless it's pinned (*he fumbles at it with childish grimaces*)—

(*Stephen comes in.*)

STEPHEN (*at the door*). I beg your pardon (*about to retire*).

LADY BRITOMART. No: come in, Stephen. (*Stephen comes forward to his mother's writing table.*)

UNDERSHAFT (*not very cordially*). Good afternoon.

STEPHEN (*coldly*). Good afternoon.

UNDERSHAFT (*to Lady Britomart*). He knows all about the tradition, I suppose?

LADY BRITOMART. Yes. (*To Stephen*) It is what I told you last night, Stephen.

UNDERSHAFT (*sulkily*). I understand you want to come into the cannon business.

STEPHEN. *I* go into trade! Certainly not.

UNDERSHAFT (*opening his eyes, greatly eased in mind and manner*). Oh! in that case—

LADY BRITOMART. Cannons are not trade, Stephen. They are enterprise.

STEPHEN. I have no intention of becoming a man of business in any sense. I have no capacity for business and no taste for it. I intend to devote myself to politics.

UNDERSHAFT (*rising*). My dear boy: this is an immense relief to me. And I trust it may prove an equally good thing for the country. I was afraid you would consider yourself disparaged and slighted. (*He moves towards Stephen as if to shake hands with him.*)

LADY BRITOMART (*rising and interposing*). Stephen: I cannot allow you to throw away an enormous property like this.

STEPHEN (*stiffly*). Mother: there must be an end of treating me as a child, if you please. (*Lady Britomart recoils, deeply wounded by his tone.*) Until last night I did not take your attitude seriously, because I did not think you meant it seriously. But I find now that you left me in the dark as to matters which you should have explained to me years ago. I am extremely hurt and offended. Any further discussion of my intentions had better take place with my father, as between one man and another.

LADY BRITOMART. Stephen! (*She sits down again, her eyes filling with tears.*)

UNDERSHAFT (*with grave compassion*). You see, my dear, it is only the big men who can be treated as children.

STEPHEN. I am sorry, mother, that you have forced me—

UNDERSHAFT (*stopping him*). Yes, yes, yes, yes: thats all right, Stephen. She wont interfere with you any more: your independence is achieved: you have won your latchkey. Dont rub it in; and above all, dont apologize. (*He resumes his seat.*) Now what about your future, as between one man and another—I beg your pardon, Biddy: as between two men and a woman.

LADY BRITOMART (*who has pulled herself together strongly*). I quite understand, Stephen. By all means go your own way if you feel strong enough. (*Stephen sits down magisterially in the chair at the writing table with an air of affirming his majority.*)

UNDERSHAFT. It is settled that you do not ask for the succession to the cannon business.

STEPHEN. I hope it is settled that I repudiate the cannon business.

UNDERSHAFT. Come, come! dont be so devilishly sulky: it's boyish. Freedom should be generous. Besides, I owe you a fair start in life in exchange for disinheriting you. You cant become prime minister all at once. Havent you a turn for something? What about literature, art, and so forth?

STEPHEN. I have nothing of the artist about me, either in faculty or character, thank Heaven!

UNDERSHAFT. A philosopher, perhaps? Eh?

STEPHEN. I make no such ridiculous pretension.

UNDERSHAFT. Just so. Well, there is the army, the navy, the Church, the Bar. The Bar requires some ability. What about the Bar?

STEPHEN. I have not studied law. And I am afraid I have not the necessary push—I believe that is the name barristers give to their vulgarity—for success in pleading.

UNDERSHAFT. Rather a difficult case, Stephen. Hardly anything left but the stage, is there? (*Stephen makes an impatient movement.*) Well, come! is there anything you know or care for?

STEPHEN (*rising and looking at him*

steadily). I know the difference between right and wrong.

UNDERSHAFT (*hugely tickled*). You dont say so! What! no capacity for business, no knowledge of law, no sympathy with art, no pretension to philosophy; only a simple knowledge of the secret that has puzzled all the philosophers, baffled all the lawyers, muddled all the men of business, and ruined most of the artists: the secret of right and wrong. Why, man, youre a genius, a master of masters, a god! At twentyfour, too!

STEPHEN (*keeping his temper with difficulty*). You are pleased to be facetious. I pretend to nothing more than any honorable English gentleman claims as his birthright (*he sits down angrily*).

UNDERSHAFT. Oh, thats everybody's birthright. Look at poor little Jenny Hill, the Salvation lassie! she would think you were laughing at her if you asked her to stand up in the street and teach grammar or geography or mathematics or even drawing room dancing; but it never occurs to her to doubt that she can teach morals and religion. You are all alike, you respectable people. You cant tell me the bursting strain of a ten-inch gun, which is a very simple matter; but you all think you can tell me the bursting strain of a man under temptation. You darent handle high explosives; but youre all ready to handle honesty and truth and justice and the whole duty of man, and kill one another at that game. What a country! What a world!

LADY BRITOMART (*uneasily*). What do you think he had better do, Andrew?

UNDERSHAFT. Oh, just what he wants to do. He knows nothing and he thinks he knows everything. That points clearly to a political career. Get him a private secretaryship to someone who can get him an Under Secretaryship; and then leave him alone. He will find his natural and proper place in the end on the Treasury Bench.

STEPHEN (*springing up again*). I am sorry, sir, that you force me to forget the respect due to you as my father. I am an Englishman and I will not hear the Government of my country insulted. (*He thrusts his hands in his pockets, and walks angrily across to the window.*)

UNDERSHAFT (*with a touch of brutality*). The government of your country!

I am the government of your country: I, and Lazarus. Do you suppose that you and half a dozen amateurs like you, sitting in a row in that foolish gabble shop, can govern Undershaft and Lazarus? No, my friend: you will do what pays us. You will make war when it suits us, and keep peace when it doesnt. You will find out that trade requires certain measures when we have decided on those measures. When I want anything to keep my dividends up, you will discover that my want is a national need. When other people want something to keep my dividends down, you will call out the police and military. And in return you shall have the support and applause of my newspapers, and the delight of imagining that you are a great statesman. Government of your country! Be off with you, my boy, and play with your caucuses and leading articles and historic parties and great leaders and burning questions and the rest of your toys. *I* am going back to my counting-house to pay the piper and call the tune.

STEPHEN (*actually smiling, and putting his hand on his father's shoulder with indulgent patronage*). Really, my dear father, it is impossible to be angry with you. You dont know how absurd all this sounds to me. You are very properly proud of having been industrious enough to make money; and it is greatly to your credit that you have made so much of it. But it has kept you in circles where you are valued for your money and deferred to for it, instead of in the doubtless very old-fashioned and behind-the-times public school and university where I formed my habits of mind. It is natural for you to think that money governs England; but you must allow me to think I know better.

UNDERSHAFT. And what does govern England, pray?

STEPHEN. Character, father, character.

UNDERSHAFT. Whose character? Yours or mine?

STEPHEN. Neither yours nor mine, father, but the best elements in the English national character.

UNDERSHAFT. Stephen: Ive found your profession for you. Youre a born journalist. I'll start you with a high-toned weekly review. There!

(*Before Stephen can reply, Sarah, Barbara, Lomax, and Cusins come in ready for walking. Barbara crosses the room to the window and looks out. Cusins drifts amiably to the armchair. Lomax remains near the door, whilst Sarah comes to her mother.*

Stephen goes to the smaller writing table and busies himself with his letters.)

SARAH. Go and get ready, mamma: the carriage is waiting. (*Lady Britomart leaves the room.*)

UNDERSHAFT (*to Sarah*). Good day, my dear. Good afternoon, Mr Lomax.

LOMAX (*vaguely*). Ahdedoo.

UNDERSHAFT (*to Cusins*). Quite well after last night, Euripides, eh?

CUSINS. As well as can be expected.

UNDERSHAFT. Thats right (*To Barbara*) So you are coming to see my death and devastation factory, Barbara?

BARBARA (*at the window*). You came yesterday to see my salvation factory. I promised you a return visit.

LOMAX (*coming forward between Sarah and Undershaft*). Youll find it awfully interesting. Ive been through the Woolwich Arsenal; and it gives you a ripping feeling of security, you know, to think of the lot of beggars we could kill if it came to fighting. (*To Undershaft, with sudden solemnity*) Still, it must be rather an awful reflection for you, from the religious point of view as it were. Youre getting on, you know, and all that.

SARAH. You dont mind Cholly's imbecility, papa, do you?

LOMAX (*much taken aback*). Oh I say!

UNDERSHAFT. Mr Lomax looks at the matter in a very proper spirit, my dear.

LOMAX. Just so. Thats all I meant, I assure you.

SARAH. Are you coming, Stephen?

STEPHEN. Well, I am rather busy—er —(*Magnanimously*) Oh well, yes: I'll come. That is, if there is room for me.

UNDERSHAFT. I can take two with me in a little motor I am experimenting with for field use. You wont mind its being rather unfashionable. It's not painted yet; but it's bullet proof.

LOMAX (*appalled at the prospect of confronting Wilton Crescent in an unpainted motor*). Oh I say!

SARAH. The carriage for me, thank you. Barbara doesnt mind what she's seen in.

LOMAX. I say, Dolly, old chap: do you really mind the car being a guy? Because of course if you do I'll go in it. Still—

CUSINS. I prefer it.

LOMAX. Thanks awfully, old man. Come, my ownest. (*He hurries out to secure his seat in the carriage. Sarah follows him.*)

CUSINS (*moodily walking across to Lady Britomart's writing table*). Why are we two coming to this Works Department of Hell? that is what I ask myself.

BARBARA. I have always thought of it as a sort of pit where lost creatures with blackened faces stirred up smoky fires and were driven and tormented by my father. Is it like that, dad?

UNDERSHAFT (*scandalized*). My dear! It is a spotlessly clean and beautiful hillside town.

CUSINS. With a Methodist chapel? Oh do say theres a Methodist chapel.

UNDERSHAFT. There are two: a Primitive one and a sophisticated one. There is even an Ethical Society; but it is not much patronized, as my men are all strongly religious. In the High Explosives Sheds they object to the presence of Agnostics as unsafe.

CUSINS. And yet they dont object to you!

BARBARA. Do they obey all your orders?

UNDERSHAFT. I never give them any orders. When I speak to one of them it is "Well, Jones, is the baby doing well? and has Mrs Jones made a good recovery?" "Nicely, thank you, sir." And thats all.

CUSINS. But Jones has to be kept in order. How do you maintain discipline among your men?

UNDERSHAFT. I dont. They do. You see, the one thing Jones wont stand is any rebellion from the man under him, or any assertion of social equality between the wife of the man with 4 shillings a week less than himself, and Mrs Jones! Of course they all rebel against me, theoretically. Practically, every man of them keeps the man just below him in his place. I never meddle with them. I never bully them. I dont even bully Lazarus. I say that certain things are to be done; but I dont order anybody to do them. I dont say, mind you, that there is no ordering about and snubbing and even bullying. The men snub the boys and order them about; the carmen snub the sweepers; the artisans snub the unskilled laborers; the foremen drive and bully both the laborers and artisans; the assistant engineers find fault with the foremen; the chief engineers drop on the assistants; the departmental managers worry the chiefs; and the clerks have tall hats and hymnbooks and keep up the social tone by refusing to associate on equal terms with anybody. The result is a colossal profit, which comes to me.

CUSINS (*revolted*). You really are a —well, what I was saying yesterday.

BARBARA. What was he saying yesterday?

UNDERSHAFT. Never mind, my dear. He thinks I have made you unhappy. Have I?

BARBARA. Do you think I can be happy in this vulgar silly dress? I! who have worn the uniform. Do you understand what you have done to me? Yesterday I had a man's soul in my hand. I set him in the way of life with his face to salvation. But when we took your money he turned back to drunkenness and derision. (*With intense conviction*) I will never forgive you that. If I had a child, and you destroyed its body with your explosives—if you murdered Dolly with your horrible guns—I could forgive you if my forgiveness would open the gates of heaven to you. But to take a human soul from me, and turn it into the soul of a wolf! that is worse than any murder.

UNDERSHAFT. Does my daughter despair so easily? Can you strike a man to the heart and leave no mark on him?

BARBARA (*her face lighting up*). Oh, you are right: he can never be lost now: where was my faith?

CUSINS. Oh, clever clever devil!

BARBARA. You may be a devil; but God speaks through you sometimes. (*She takes her father's hands and kisses them.*) You have given me back my happiness: I feel it deep down now, though my spirit is troubled.

UNDERSHAFT. You have learnt something. That always feels at first as if you had lost something.

BARBARA. Well, take me to the factory of death; and let me learn something more. There must be some truth or other behind all this frightful irony. Come, Dolly. (*She goes out.*)

CUSINS. My guardian angel! (*To Undershaft*) Avaunt! (*He follows Barbara.*)

STEPHEN (*quietly, at the writing table*). You must not mind Cusins, father. He is a very amiable good fellow; but he is a Greek scholar and naturally a little eccentric.

UNDERSHAFT. Ah, quite so. Thank you, Stephen. Thank you. (*He goes out.*)

(*Stephen smiles patronizingly; buttons his coat responsibly; and crosses the room to the door. Lady Britomart, dressed for out-of-doors, opens it before he reaches it. She looks round for others; looks at Stephen; and turns to go without a word.*)

STEPHEN (*embarrassed*). Mother—

LADY BRITOMART. Dont be apologetic, Stephen. And dont forget that you have outgrown your mother. (*She goes out.*)

(*Perivale St Andrews lies between two Middlesex hills, half climbing the northern one. It is an almost smokeless town of white walls, roofs of narrow green slates or red tiles, tall trees, domes, campaniles, and slender chimney shafts, beautifully situated and beautiful in itself. The best view of it is obtained from the crest of a slope about half a mile to the east, where the high explosives are dealt with. The foundry lies hidden in the depths between, the tops of its chimneys sprouting like huge skittles into the middle distance. Across the crest runs an emplacement of concrete, with a firestep, and a parapet which suggests a fortification, because there is a huge cannon of the obsolete Woolwich Infant pattern peering across it at the town. The cannon is mounted on an experimental gun carriage: possibly the original model of the Undershaft disappearing rampart gun alluded to by Stephen. The firestep, being a convenient place to sit, is furnished here and there with straw disc cushions; and at one place there is the additional luxury of a fur rug.*

Barbara is standing on the firestep, looking over the parapet towards the town. On her right is the cannon; on her left the end of a shed raised on piles, with a ladder of three or four steps up to the door, which opens outwards and has a little wooden landing at the threshold, with a fire bucket in the corner of the landing. Several dummy soldiers more or less mutilated, with straw protruding from their gashes, have been shoved out of the way under the landing. A few others are nearly upright against the shed;

and one has fallen forward and lies, like a grotesque corpse, on the emplacement. The parapet stops short of the shed, leaving a gap which is the beginning of the path down the hill through the foundry to the town. The rug is on the firestep near this gap. Down on the emplacement behind the cannon is a trolley carrying a huge conical bombshell with a red band painted on it. Further to the right is the door of an office, which, like the sheds, is of the lightest possible construction.

Cusins arrives by the path from the town.)

BARBARA. Well?

CUSINS. Not a ray of hope. Everything perfect! wonderful! real! It only needs a cathedral to be a heavenly city instead of a hellish one.

BARBARA. Have you found out whether they have done anything for old Peter Shirley?

CUSINS. They have found him a job as gatekeeper and timekeeper. He's frightfully miserable. He calls the time-keeping brainwork, and says he isnt used to it; and his gate lodge is so splendid that he's ashamed to use the rooms, and skulks in the scullery.

BARBARA. Poor Peter!

(*Stephen arrives from the town. He carries a fieldglass.*)

STEPHEN (*enthusiastically*). Have you two seen the place? Why did you leave us?

CUSINS. I wanted to see everything I was not intended to see; and Barbara wanted to make the men talk.

STEPHEN. Have you found anything discreditable?

CUSINS. No. They call him Dandy Andy and are proud of his being a cunning old rascal; but it's all horribly, frightfully, immorally, unanswerably perfect.

(*Sarah arrives.*)

SARAH. Heavens! what a place! (*She crosses to the trolley.*) Did you see the nursing home!? (*She sits down on the shell.*)

STEPHEN. Did you see the libraries and schools!?

SARAH. Did you see the ball room and the banqueting chamber in the Town Hall!?

STEPHEN. Have you gone into the insurance fund. the pension fund, the build-

ing society, the various applications of cooperation!?

(*Undershaft comes from the office, with a sheaf of telegrams in his hand.*)

UNDERSHAFT. Well, have you seen everything? I'm sorry I was called away. (*Indicating the telegrams*) Good news from Manchuria.

STEPHEN. Another Japanese victory?

UNDERSHAFT. Oh, I dont know. Which side wins does not concern us here. No: the good news is that the aerial battleship is a tremendous success. At the first trial it has wiped out a fort with three hundred soldiers in it.

CUSINS (*from the platform*). Dummy soldiers?

UNDERSHAFT (*striding across to Stephen and kicking the prostrate dummy brutally out of his way*). No: the real thing.

(*Cusins and Barbara exchange glances. Then Cusins sits on the step and buries his face in his hands. Barbara gravely lays her hand on his shoulder. He looks up at her in whimsical desperation.*)

UNDERSHAFT. Well, Stephen, what do you think of the place?

STEPHEN. Oh, magnificent. A perfect triumph of modern industry. Frankly, my dear father, I have been a fool: I had no idea of what it all meant: of the wonderful forethought, the power of organization, the administrative capacity, the financial genius, the colossal capital it represents. I have been repeating to myself as I came through your streets "Peace hath her victories no less renowned than War." I have only one misgiving about it all.

UNDERSHAFT. Out with it.

STEPHEN. Well, I cannot help thinking that all this provision for every want of your workmen may sap their independence and weaken their sense of responsibility. And greatly as we enjoyed our tea at that splendid restaurant—how they gave us all that luxury and cake and jam and cream for threepence I really cannot imagine!—still you must remember that restaurants break up home life. Look at the continent, for instance! Are **you sure so much pampering is really** good for the men's characters?

UNDERSHAFT. Well you see, my dear **boy, when you are organizing civilization** you have to make up your mind whether trouble and anxiety are good things or not. If you decide that they are, then, I take it, you simply dont organize civilization; and there you are, with trouble and anxiety enough to make us all angels! But if you decide the other way, you may as well go through with it. However, Stephen, our characters are safe here. A sufficient dose of anxiety is always provided by the fact that we may be blown to smithereens at any moment.

SARAH. By the way, papa, where do you make the explosives?

UNDERSHAFT. In separate little sheds, like that one. When one of them blows up, it costs very little; and only the people quite close to it are killed.

(*Stephen, who is quite close to it, looks at it rather scaredly, and moves away quickly to the cannon. At the same moment the door of the shed is thrown abruptly open; and a foreman in overalls and list slippers comes out on the little landing and holds the door for Lomax, who appears in the doorway.*)

LOMAX (*with studied coolness*). My good fellow: you neednt get into a state of nerves. Nothing's going to happen to you; and I suppose it wouldnt be the end of the world if anything did. A little bit of British pluck is what you want, old chap. (*He descends and strolls across to Sarah.*)

UNDERSHAFT (*to the foreman*). Anything wrong, Bilton?

BILTON (*with ironic calm*). Gentleman walked into the high explosives shed and lit a cigaret, sir: thats all.

UNDERSHAFT. Ah, quite so. (*Going over to Lomax*) Do you happen to remember what you did with the match?

LOMAX. Oh come! I'm not a fool. I took jolly good care to blow it out before I chucked it away.

BILTON. The top of it was red hot inside, sir.

LOMAX. Well, suppose it was! I didn't chuck it into any of your messes.

UNDERSHAFT. Think no more of it, Mr Lomax. By the way, would you mind lending me your matches.

LOMAX (*offering his box*). Certainly.

UNDERSHAFT. Thanks. (*He pockets the matches.*)

LOMAX (*lecturing to the company generally*). You know, these high explosives dont go off like gunpowder, ex-cept when theyre in a gun. When theyre spread loose, you can put a match to them without the least risk: they just burn quietly like a bit of paper. (*Warming to the scientific interest of the subject*) Did you know that, Undershaft? Have you ever tried?

UNDERSHAFT. Not on a large scale, Mr Lomax. Bilton will give you a sample of gun cotton when you are leaving if you ask him. You can experiment with it at home. (*Bilton looks puzzled.*)

SARAH. Bilton will do nothing of the sort, papa. I suppose it's your business to blow up the Russians and Japs; but you might really stop short of blowing up poor Cholly. (*Bilton gives it up and retires into the shed.*)

LOMAX. My ownest, there is no danger. (*He sits beside her on the shell.*)

(*Lady Britomart arrives from the town with a bouquet.*)

LADY BRITOMART (*impetuously*). Andrew: you shouldnt have let me see this place.

UNDERSHAFT. Why, my dear?

LADY BRITOMART. Never mind why: you shouldnt have: thats all. To think of all that (*indicating the town*) being yours! and that you have kept it to yourself all these years!

UNDERSHAFT. It does not belong to me. I belong to it. It is the Undershaft inheritance.

LADY BRITOMART. It is not. Your ridiculous cannons and that noisy banging foundry may be the Undershaft inheritance; but all that plate and linen, all that furniture and those houses and orchards and gardens belong to us. They belong to me: they are not a man's business. I wont give them up. You must be out of your senses to throw them all away; and if you persist in such folly, I will call in a doctor.

UNDERSHAFT (*stooping to smell the bouquet*). Where did you get the flowers, my dear?

LADY BRITOMART. Your men presented them to me in your William Morris Labor Church.

CUSINS. Oh! It needed only that. A Labor Church! (*He mounts the firestep distractedly, and leans with his elbows on the parapet, turning his back to them.*)

LADY BRITOMART. Yes, with Morris's words in mosaic letters ten feet high round the dome. NO MAN IS GOOD ENOUGH TO

BE ANOTHER MAN'S MASTER. The cynicism of it!

UNDERSHAFT. It shocked the men at first, I am afraid. But now they take no more notice of it than of the ten commandments in church.

LADY BRITOMART. Andrew: you are trying to put me off the subject of the inheritance by profane jokes. Well, you shant. I dont ask it any longer for Stephen: he has inherited far too much of your perversity to be fit for it. But Barbara has rights as well as Stephen. Why should not Adolphus succeed to the inheritance? I could manage the town for him; and he can look after the cannons, if they are really necessary.

UNDERSHAFT. I should ask nothing better if Adolphus were a foundling. He is exactly the sort of new blood that is wanted in English business. But he's not a foundling; and theres an end of it. (*He makes for the office door.*)

CUSINS (*turning to them*). Not quite. (*They all turn and stare at him*). I think—Mind! I am not committing myself in any way as to my future course— but I think the foundling difficulty can be got over. (*He jumps down to the emplacement.*)

UNDERSHAFT (*coming back to him*). What do you mean?

CUSINS. Well, I have something to say which is in the nature of a confession.

SARAH.
LADY BRITOMART. } Confession!
BARBARA.
STEPHEN.

LOMAX. Oh I say!

CUSINS. Yes, a confession. Listen, all. Until I met Barbara I thought myself in the main an honorable, truthful man, because I wanted the approval of my conscience more than I wanted anything else. But the moment I saw Barbara, I wanted her far more than the approval of my conscience.

LADY BRITOMART. Adolphus!

CUSINS. It is true. You accused me yourself, Lady Brit, of joining the Army to worship Barbara; and so I did. She bought my soul like a flower at a street corner; but she bought it for herself.

UNDERSHAFT. What! Not for Dionysos or another?

CUSINS. Dionysos and all the others are in herself. I adored what was divine in her, and was therefore a true worshipper. But I was romantic about her too. I thought she was a woman of the people, and that a marriage with a professor of Greek would be far beyond the wildest social ambitions of her rank.

LADY BRITOMART. Adolphus!!

LOMAX. Oh I say!!!

CUSINS. When I learnt the horrible truth—

LADY BRITOMART. What do you mean by the horrible truth, pray?

CUSINS. That she was enormously rich; that her grandfather was an earl; that her father was the Prince of Darkness—

UNDERSHAFT. Chut!

CUSINS. —and that I was only an adventurer trying to catch a rich wife, then I stooped to deceive her about my birth.

BARBARA (*rising*). Dolly!

LADY BRITOMART. Your birth! Now Adolphus, dont dare to make up a wicked story for the sake of these wretched cannons. Remember: I have seen photographs of your parents; and the Agent General for South Western Australia knows them personally and has assured me that they are most respectable married people.

CUSINS. So they are in Australia; but here they are outcasts. Their marriage is legal in Australia, but not in England. My mother is my father's deceased wife's sister; and in this island I am consequently a foundling. (*Sensation.*)

BARBARA. Silly! (*She climbs to the cannon, and leans, listening, in the angle it makes with the parapet.*)

CUSINS. Is the subterfuge good enough, Machiavelli?

UNDERSHAFT (*thoughtfully*). Biddy: this may be a way out of the difficulty.

LADY BRITOMART. Stuff! A man cant make cannons any the better for being his own cousin instead of his proper self. (*She sits down on the rug with a bounce that expresses her downright contempt for their casuistry.*)

UNDERSHAFT (*to Cusins*). You are an educated man. That is against the tradition.

CUSINS. Once in ten thousand times it happens that the schoolboy is a born master of what they try to teach him. Greek has not destroyed my mind: it has nourished it. Besides, I did not learn it at an English public school.

UNDERSHAFT. Hm! Well, I cannot afford to be too particular: you have cornered the foundling market. Let it pass. You are eligible, Euripides: you are eligible.

BARBARA. Dolly: yesterday morning, when Stephen told us all about tradition, you became very silent; and you have been strange and excited ever since. Were you thinking of your birth then?

CUSINS. When the finger of Destiny suddenly points at a man in the middle of his breakfast, it makes him thoughtful.

UNDERSHAFT. Aha! You have had your eye on the business, my young friend, have you?

CUSINS. Take care! There is an abyss of moral horror between me and your accursed aerial battleships.

UNDERSHAFT. Never mind the abyss for the present. Let us settle the practical details and leave your final decision open. You know that you will have to change your name. Do you object to that?

CUSINS. Would any man named Adolphus—any man called Dolly!—object to be called something else?

UNDERSHAFT. Good. Now, as to money! I propose to treat you handsomely from the beginning. You shall start at a thousand a year.

CUSINS (with sudden heat, his spectacles twinkling with mischief). A thousand! You dare offer a miserable thousand to the son-in-law of a millionaire! No, by Heavens, Machiavelli! you shall not cheat me. You cannot do without me; and I can do without you. I must have two thousand five hundred a year for two years. At the end of that time, if I am a failure, I go. But if I am a success, and stay on, you must give me the other five thousand.

UNDERSHAFT. What other five thousand?

CUSINS. To make the two years up to five thousand a year. The two thousand five hundred is only half pay in case I should turn out a failure. The third year I must have ten per cent on the profits.

UNDERSHAFT (taken aback). Ten per cent! Why, man, do you know what my profits are?

CUSINS. Enormous, I hope: otherwise I shall require twenty-five per cent.

UNDERSHAFT. But, Mr Cusins, this is a serious matter of business. You are not bringing any capital into the concern.

CUSINS. What! no capital! Is my mastery of Greek no capital? Is my access to the subtlest thought, the loftiest poetry yet attained by humanity, no capital? My character! my intellect! my life! my career! what Barbara calls my soul! are these no capital? Say another word; and I double my salary.

UNDERSHAFT. Be reasonable—

CUSINS (peremptorily). Mr Undershaft: you have my terms. Take them or leave them.

UNDERSHAFT (recovering himself). Very well. I note your terms; and I offer you half.

CUSINS (disgusted). Half!

UNDERSHAFT (firmly). Half.

CUSINS. You call yourself a gentleman; and you offer me half!!

UNDERSHAFT. I do not call myself a gentleman; but I offer you half.

CUSINS. This to your future partner! your successor! your son-in-law!

BARBARA. You are selling your own soul, Dolly, not mine. Leave me out of the bargain, please.

UNDERSHAFT. Come! I will go a step further for Barbara's sake. I will give you three fifths; but that is my last word.

CUSINS. Done!

LOMAX. Done in the eye! Why, I get only eight hundred, you know.

CUSINS. By the way, Mac, I am a classical scholar, not an arithmetical one. Is three fifths more than half or less?

UNDERSHAFT. More, of course.

CUSINS. I would have taken two hundred and fifty. How you can succeed in business when you are willing to pay all that money to a University don who is obviously not worth a junior clerk's wages!—well! What will Lazarus say?

UNDERSHAFT. Lazarus is a gentle romantic Jew who cares for nothing but string quartets and stalls at fashionable theatres. He will be blamed for your rapacity in money matters, poor fellow! as he has hitherto been blamed for mine. You are a shark of the first order, Euripides. So much the better for the firm!

BARBARA. Is the bargain closed, Dolly? Does your soul belong to him now?

CUSINS. No: the price is settled: that is all. The real tug of war is still to come. What about the moral question?

LADY BRITOMART. There is no moral question in the matter at all, Adolphus. You must simply sell cannons and weapons to people whose cause is right and just, and refuse them to foreigners and criminals.

UNDERSHAFT (*determinedly*). No: none of that. You must keep the true faith of an Armorer, or you dont come in here.

CUSINS. What on earth is the true faith of an Armorer?

UNDERSHAFT. To give arms to all men who offer an honest price for them, without respect of persons or principles: to aristocrat and republican, to Nihilist and Tsar, to Capitalist and Socialist, to Protestant and Catholic, to burglar and policeman, to black man, white man and yellow man, to all sorts and conditions, all nationalities, all faiths, all follies, all causes and all crimes. The first Undershaft wrote up in his shop IF GOD GAVE THE HAND, LET NOT MAN WITHHOLD THE SWORD. The second wrote up ALL HAVE THE RIGHT TO FIGHT: NONE HAVE THE RIGHT TO JUDGE. The third wrote up TO MAN THE WEAPON: TO HEAVEN THE VICTORY. The fourth had no literary turn; so he did not write up anything; but he sold cannons to Napoleon under the nose of George the Third. The fifth wrote up PEACE SHALL NOT PREVAIL SAVE WITH A SWORD IN HER HAND. The sixth, my master, was the best of all. He wrote up NOTHING IS EVER DONE IN THIS WORLD UNTIL MEN ARE PREPARED TO KILL ONE ANOTHER IF IT IS NOT DONE. After that, there was nothing left for the seventh to say. So he wrote up, simply, UNASHAMED.

CUSINS. My good Machiavelli, I shall certainly write something up on the wall; only, as I shall write it in Greek, you wont be able to read it. But as to your Armorer's faith, if I take my neck out of the noose of my own morality I am not going to put it into the noose of yours. I shall sell cannons to whom I please and refuse them to whom I please. So there!

UNDERSHAFT. From the moment when you become Andrew Undershaft, you will never do as you please again. Dont come here lusting for power, young man.

CUSINS. If power were my aim I should not come here for it. You have no power.

UNDERSHAFT. None of my own, certainly.

CUSINS. I have more power than you, more will. You do not drive this place: it drives you. And what drives the place?

UNDERSHAFT (*enigmatically*). A will of which I am a part.

BARBARA (*startled*). Father! Do you know what you are saying; or are you laying a snare for my soul?

CUSINS. Dont listen to his metaphysics, Barbara. The place is driven by the most rascally part of society, the money hunters, the pleasure hunters, the military promotion hunters; and he is their slave.

UNDERSHAFT. Not necessarily. Remember the Armorer's Faith. I will take an order from a good man as cheerfully as from a bad one. If you good people prefer preaching and shirking to buying my weapons and fighting the rascals, dont blame me. I can make cannons: I cannot make courage and conviction. Bah! you tire me, Euripides, with your morality mongering. Ask Barbara: she understands. (*He suddenly reaches up and takes Barbara's hands, looking powerfully into her eyes*) Tell him, my love, what power really means.

BARBARA (*hypnotized*). Before I joined the Salvation Army, I was in my own power; and the consequence was that I never knew what to do with myself. When I joined it, I had not time enough for all the things I had to do.

UNDERSHAFT (*approvingly*). Just so. And why was that, do you suppose?

BARBARA. Yesterday I should have said, because I was in the power of God. (*She resumes her self-possession, withdrawing her hands from his with a power equal to his own.*) But you came and shewed me that I was in the power of Bodger and Undershaft. Today I feel—oh! how can I put it into words? Sarah: do you remember the earthquake at Cannes, when we were little children?—how little the surprise of the first shock mattered compared to the dread and horror of waiting for the second? That is how I feel in this place today. I stood on the rock I thought eternal; and without a word of warning it reeled and crumbled under me. I was safe with an infinite wisdom watching me, an army marching to Salvation with me; and in a moment, at a stroke of your pen in a cheque book, I stood alone; and the heavens were empty. That was the first shock of the earthquake: I am waiting for the second.

UNDERSHAFT. Come, come, my daughter! dont make too much of your little tinpot tragedy. What do we do here when we spend years of work and thought and thousands of pounds of solid cash on a new gun or an aerial battleship that turns out just a hairsbreadth wrong after all? Scrap it. Scrap it without wasting another hour or another pound on it. Well, you have made for yourself something that you call a morality or a religion or what not. It doesnt fit the facts. Well, scrap it. Scrap it and get one that does fit. That is what is wrong with the world at present. It scraps its obsolete steam engines and dynamos; but it wont scrap its old prejudices and its old moralities and its old religions and its old political constitutions. Whats the result? In machinery it does very well; but in morals and religion and politics it is working at a loss that brings it nearer bankruptcy every year. Dont persist in that folly. If your old religion broke down yesterday, get a newer and a better one for tomorrow.

BARBARA. Oh how gladly I would take a better one to my soul! But you offer me a worse one. (*Turning on him with sudden vehemence.*) Justify yourself: shew me some light through the darkness of this dreadful place, with its beautifully clean workshops, and respectable workmen, and model homes.

UNDERSHAFT. Cleanliness and respectability do not need justification, Barbara: they justify themselves. I see no darkness here, no dreadfulness. In your Salvation shelter I saw poverty, misery, cold and hunger. You gave them bread and treacle and dreams of heaven. I give from thirty shillings a week to twelve thousand a year. They find their own dreams; but I look after the drainage.

BARBARA. And their souls?

UNDERSHAFT. I save their souls just as I saved yours.

BARBARA (*revolted*). You saved my soul! What do you mean?

UNDERSHAFT. I fed you and clothed you and housed you. I took care that you should have money enough to live handsomely—more than enough; so that you could be wasteful, careless, generous. That saved your soul from the seven deadly sins.

BARBARA (*bewildered*). The seven deadly sins!

UNDERSHAFT. Yes, the deadly seven. (*Counting on his fingers*) Food, clothing, firing, rent, taxes, respectability and children. Nothing can lift those seven millstones from Man's neck but money; and the spirit cannot soar until the millstones are lifted. I lifted them from your spirit. I enabled Barbara to become Major Barbara; and I saved her from the crime of poverty.

CUSINS. Do you call poverty a crime?

UNDERSHAFT. The worst of crimes. All the other crimes are virtues beside it: all the other dishonors are chivalry itself by comparison. Poverty blights whole cities; spreads horrible pestilences; strikes dead the very souls of all who come within sight, sound, or smell of it. What you call crime is nothing: a murder here and a theft there, a blow now and a curse then: what do they matter? they are only the accidents and illnesses of life: there are not fifty genuine professional criminals in London. But there are millions of poor people, abject people, dirty people, ill fed, ill clothed people. They poison us morally and physically: they kill the happiness of society: they force us to do away with our own liberties and to organize unnatural cruelties for fear they should rise against us and drag us down into their abyss. Only fools fear crime: we all fear poverty. Pah! (*turning on Barbara*) you talk of your half-saved ruffian in West Ham: you accuse me of dragging his soul back to perdition. Well, bring him to me here; and I will drag his soul back again to salvation for you. Not by words and dreams; but by thirtyeight shillings a week, a sound house in a handsome street, and a permanent job. In three weeks he will have a fancy waistcoat; in three months a tall hat and a chapel sitting; before the end of the year he will shake hands with a duchess at a Primrose League meeting, and join the Conservative Party.

BARBARA. And will he be the better for that?

UNDERSHAFT. You know he will. Dont be a hypocrite, Barbara. He will be better fed, better housed, better clothed, better behaved; and his children will be pounds heavier and bigger. That will be better than an American cloth mattress in a shelter, chopping firewood, eating bread and treacle, and being forced to kneel down from time to time to thank heaven for it: knee drill, I think you call it. It is cheap work converting starving men with a Bible in one hand and a slice of bread in the other. I will undertake to convert West Ham to Mahometanism on the same terms. Try your hand on my men: their souls are hungry because their bodies are full.

BARBARA. And leave the east end to starve?

UNDERSHAFT (*his energetic tone dropping into one of bitter and brooding remembrance*). I was an east ender. I moralized and starved until one day I swore that I would be a full-fed free man at all costs; that nothing should stop me except a bullet, neither reason nor morals nor the lives of other men. I said "Thou shalt starve ere I starve"; and with that word I became free and great. I was a dangerous man until I had my will: now I am a useful, beneficent, kindly person. That is the history of most self-made millionaires, I fancy. When it is the history of every Englishman we shall have an England worth living in.

LADY BRITOMART. Stop making speeches, Andrew. This is not the place for them.

UNDERSHAFT (*punctured*). My dear: I have no other means of conveying my ideas.

LADY BRITOMART. Your ideas are nonsense. You got on because you were selfish and unscrupulous.

UNDERSHAFT. Not at all. I had the strongest scruples about poverty and starvation. Your moralists are quite unscrupulous about both: they make virtues of them. I had rather be a thief than a pauper. I had rather be a murderer than a slave. I dont want to be either; but if you force the alternative on me, then, by Heaven, I'll choose the braver and more moral one. I hate poverty and slavery worse than any other crimes whatsoever. And let me tell you this. Poverty and slavery have stood up for centuries to your sermons and leading articles: they will not stand up to my machine guns. Dont preach at them: dont reason with them. Kill them.

BARBARA. Killing. Is that your remedy for everything?

UNDERSHAFT. It is the final test of conviction, the only lever strong enough to overturn a social system, the only way of saying Must. Let six hundred and seventy fools loose in the streets; and three policemen can scatter them. But huddle them together in a certain house in Westminster; and let them go through certain ceremonies and call themselves certain names until at last they get the courage to kill; and your six hundred and seventy fools become a government. Your pious mob fills up ballot papers and imagines it is governing its masters; but the ballot paper that really governs is the paper that has a bullet wrapped up in it.

CUSINS. That is perhaps why, like most intelligent people, I never vote.

UNDERSHAFT. Vote! Bah! When you vote, you only change the names of the cabinet. When you shoot, you pull down governments, inaugurate new epochs, abolish old orders and set up new. Is that historically true, Mr Learned Man, or is it not?

CUSINS. It is historically true. I loathe having to admit it. I repudiate your sentiments. I abhor your nature. I defy you in every possible way. Still, it is true. But it ought not to be true.

UNDERSHAFT. Ought! ought! ought! ought! ought! Are you going to spend your life saying ought, like the rest of our moralists? Turn your oughts into shalls, man. Come and make explosives with me. Whatever can blow men up can blow society up. The history of the world is the history of those who had courage enough to embrace this truth. Have you the courage to embrace it, Barbara?

LADY BRITOMART. Barbara: I positively forbid you to listen to your father's abominable wickedness. And you, Adolphus, ought to know better than to go about saying that wrong things are true. What does it matter whether they are true if they are wrong?

UNDERSHAFT. What does it matter whether they are wrong if they are true?

LADY BRITOMART (*rising*). Children: come home instantly. Andrew: I am exceedingly sorry I allowed you to call on us. You are wickeder than ever. Come at once.

BARBARA (*shaking her head*). It's no use running away from wicked people, mamma.

LADY BRITOMART. It is every use. It shews your disapprobation of them.

BARBARA. It does not save them.

LADY BRITOMART. I can see that you are going to disobey me. Sarah: are you coming home or are you not?

SARAH. I daresay it's very wicked of papa to make cannons; but I dont think I shall cut him on that account.

LOMAX (*pouring oil on the troubled waters*). The fact is, you know, there is a certain amount of tosh about this notion of wickedness. It doesnt work. You must look at facts. Not that I would say a word in favor of anything wrong; but then, you see, all sorts of chaps are always doing all sorts of things; and we have to fit them in somehow, dont you know. What I mean is that you cant go cutting everybody; and thats about what it comes to. (*Their rapt attention to his eloquence makes him nervous.*) Perhaps I dont make myself clear.

LADY BRITOMART. You are lucidity itself, Charles. Because Andrew is successful and has plenty of money to give to Sarah, you will flatter him and encourage him in his wickedness.

LOMAX (*unruffled*). Well, where the carcase is, there will the eagles be gathered, dont you know. (*To Undershaft*) Eh? What?

UNDERSHAFT. Precisely. By the way, may I call you Charles?

LOMAX. Delighted. Cholly is the usual ticket.

UNDERSHAFT (*to Lady Britomart*). Biddy—

LADY BRITOMART (*violently*). Dont dare call me Biddy. Charles Lomax: you are a fool. Adolphus Cusins: you are a Jesuit. Stephen: you are a prig. Barbara: you are a lunatic. Andrew: you are a vulgar tradesman. Now you all know my opinion; and my conscience is clear, at all events (*she sits down with a vehemence that the rug fortunately softens*).

UNDERSHAFT. My dear: you are the incarnation of morality. (*She snorts.*) Your conscience is clear and your duty done when you have called everybody names. Come, Euripides! it is getting late; and we all want to go home. Make up your mind.

CUSINS. Understand this, you old demon—

LADY BRITOMART. Adolphus!

UNDERSHAFT. Let him alone, Biddy. Proceed, Euripides.

CUSINS. You have me in a horrible dilemma. I want Barbara.

UNDERSHAFT. Like all young men, you greatly exaggerate the difference between one young woman and another.

BARBARA. Quite true, Dolly.

CUSINS. I also want to avoid being a rascal.

UNDERSHAFT (*with biting contempt*). You lust for personal righteousness, for self-approval, for what you call a good conscience, for what Barbara calls salvation, for what I call patronizing people who are not so lucky as yourself.

CUSINS. I do not: all the poet in me recoils from being a good man. But there are things in me that I must reckon with. Pity—

UNDERSHAFT. Pity! The scavenger of misery.

CUSINS. Well, love.

UNDERSHAFT. I know. You love the needy and the outcast: you love the oppressed races, the negro, the Indian ryot, the underdog everywhere. Do you love the Japanese? Do you love the French? Do you love the English?

CUSINS. No. Every true Englishman detests the English. We are the wickedest nation on earth; and our success is a moral horror.

UNDERSHAFT. That is what comes of your gospel of love, is it?

CUSINS. May I not love even my father-in-law?

UNDERSHAFT. Who wants your love, man? By what right do you take the liberty of offering it to me? I will have your due heed and respect, or I will kill you. But your love! Damn your impertinence!

CUSINS (*grinning*). I may not be able to control my affections, Mac.

UNDERSHAFT. You are fencing, Euripides. You are weakening: your grip is slipping. Come! try your last weapon. Pity and love have broken in your hand: forgiveness is still left.

CUSINS. No: forgiveness is a beggar's refuge. I am with you there: we must pay our debts.

UNDERSHAFT. Well said. Come! you will suit me. Remember the words of Plato.

CUSINS (*starting*). Plato! You dare quote Plato to me!

UNDERSHAFT. Plato says, my friend, that society cannot be saved until either the Professors of Greek take to making gunpowder, or else the makers of gunpowder become Professors of Greek.

CUSINS. Oh, tempter, cunning tempter!

UNDERSHAFT. Come! choose, man, choose.

CUSINS. But perhaps Barbara will not marry me if I make the wrong choice.

BARBARA. Perhaps not.

CUSINS (*desperately perplexed*). You hear!

BARBARA. Father: do you love nobody?

UNDERSHAFT. I love my best friend.

LADY BRITOMART. And who is that, pray?

UNDERSHAFT. My bravest enemy. That is the man who keeps me up to the mark.

CUSINS. You know, the creature is really a sort of poet in his way. Suppose he is a great man, after all!

UNDERSHAFT. Suppose you stop talking and make up your mind, my young friend.

CUSINS. But you are driving me against my nature. I hate war.

UNDERSHAFT. Hatred is the coward's revenge for being intimidated. Dare you make war on war? Here are the means: my friend Mr Lomax is sitting on them.

LOMAX (*springing up*). Oh I say! You dont mean that this thing is loaded, do you? My ownest: come off it.

SARAH (*sitting placidly on the shell*). If I am to be blown up, the more thoroughly it is done the better. Dont fuss, Cholly.

LOMAX (*to Undershaft, strongly remonstrant*). Your own daughter, you know!

UNDERSHAFT. So I see. (*To Cusins*) Well, my friend, may we expect you here at six tomorrow morning?

CUSINS (*firmly*). Not on any account. I will see the whole establishment blown up with its own dynamite before I will get up at five. My hours are healthy, rational hours: eleven to five.

UNDERSHAFT. Come when you please: before a week you will come at six and stay until I turn you out for the sake of your health. (*Calling*) Bilton! (*He turns to Lady Britomart, who rises.*) My dear: let us leave these two young people to

themselves for a moment. (*Bilton comes from the shed.*) I am going to take you through the gun cotton shed.

BILTON (*barring the way*). You cant take anything explosive in here, sir.

LADY BRITOMART. What do you mean? Are you alluding to me?

BILTON (*unmoved*). No, maam. Mr. Undershaft has the other gentleman's matches in his pocket.

LADY BRITOMART (*abruptly*). Oh! I beg your pardon. (*She goes into the shed.*)

UNDERSHAFT. Quite right, Bilton, quite right: here you are. (*He gives Bilton the box of matches.*) Come, Stephen. Come, Charles. Bring Sarah. (*He passes into the shed.*)

(*Bilton opens the box and deliberately drops the matches into the fire-bucket.*)

LOMAX. Oh! I say. (*Bilton stolidly hands him the empty box.*) Infernal nonsense! Pure scientific ignorance! (*He goes in.*)

SARAH. Am I all right, Bilton?

BILTON. Youll have to put on list slippers, miss: thats all. Weve got em inside. (*She goes in.*)

STEPHEN (*very seriously to Cusins*). Dolly, old fellow, think. Think before you decide. Do you feel that you are a sufficiently practical man? It is a huge undertaking, an enormous responsibility. All this mass of business will be Greek to you.

CUSINS. Oh, I think it will be much less difficult than Greek.

STEPHEN. Well, I just want to say this before I leave you to yourselves. Dont let anything I have said about right and wrong prejudice you against this great chance in life. I have satisfied myself that the business is one of the highest character and a credit to our country. (*Emotionally*) I am very proud of my father. I—(*Unable to proceed, he presses Cusins' hand and goes hastily into the shed, followed by Bilton.*)

(*Barbara and Cusins, left alone together, look at one another silently.*)

CUSINS. Barbara: I am going to accept this offer.

BARBARA. I thought you would.

CUSINS. You understand, dont you, that I had to decide without consulting you. If I had thrown the burden of the choice on you, you would sooner or later have despised me for it.

BARBARA. Yes: I did not want you to sell your soul for me any more than for this inheritance.

CUSINS. It is not the sale of my soul that troubles me: I have sold it too often to care about that. I have sold it for a professorship. I have sold it for an income. I have sold it to escape being imprisoned for refusing to pay taxes for hangmen's ropes and unjust wars and things that I abhor. What is all human conduct but the daily and hourly sale of our soul for trifles? What I am now selling it for is neither money nor position nor comfort, but for reality and for power.

BARBARA. You know that you will have no power, and that he has none.

CUSINS. I know. It is not for myself alone. I want to make power for the world.

BARBARA. I want to make power for the world too; but it must be spiritual power.

CUSINS. I think all power is spiritual: these cannons will not go off by themselves. I have tried to make spiritual power by teaching Greek. But the world can never be really touched by a dead language and a dead civilization. The people must have power; and the people cannot have Greek. Now the power that is made here can be wielded by all men.

BARBARA. Power to burn women's houses down and kill their sons and tear their husbands to pieces.

CUSINS. You cannot have power for good without having power for evil too. Even mother's milk nourishes murderers as well as heroes. This power which only tears men's bodies to pieces has never been so horribly abused as the intellectual power, the imaginative power, the poetic, religious power that can enslave men's souls. As a teacher of Greek I gave the intellectual man weapons against the common man. I now want to give the common man weapons against the intellectual man. I love the common people. I want to arm them against the lawyers, the doctors, the priests, the literary men, the professors, the artists, and the politicians, who, once in authority, are more disastrous and tyrannical than all the fools, rascals, and impostors. I want a

power simple enough for common men to use, yet strong enough to force the intellectual oligarchy to use its genius for the general good.

BARBARA. Is there no higher power than that (*pointing to the shell*)?

CUSINS. Yes; but that power can destroy the higher powers just as a tiger can destroy a man: therefore Man must master that power first. I admitted this when the Turks and Greeks were last at war. My best pupil went out to fight for Hellas. My parting gift to him was not a copy of Plato's Republic, but a revolver and a hundred Undershaft cartridges. The blood of every Turk he shot—if he shot any—is on my head as well as on Undershaft's. That act committed me to this place for ever. Your father's challenge has beaten me. Dare I make war on war? I must. I will. And now, is it all over between us?

BARBARA (*touched by his evident dread of her answer*). Silly baby Dolly! How could it be!

CUSINS (*overjoyed*). Then you—you —you—Oh for my drum! (*He flourishes imaginary drumsticks.*)

BARBARA (*angered by his levity*). Take care, Dolly, take care. Oh, if only I could get away from you and from father and from it all! if I could have the wings of a dove and fly away to heaven!

CUSINS. And leave me!

BARBARA. Yes, you, and all the other naughty mischievous children of men. But I cant. I was happy in the Salvation Army for a moment. I escaped from the world into a paradise of enthusiasm and prayer and soul saving; but the moment our money ran short, it all came back to Bodger: it was he who saved our people: he, and the Prince of Darkness, my papa. Undershaft and Bodger: their hands stretch everywhere: when we feed a starving fellow creature, it is with their bread, because there is no other bread; when we tend the sick, it is in the hospitals they endow; if we turn from the churches they build, we must kneel on the stones of the streets they pave. As long as that lasts, there is no getting away from them. Turning our backs on Bodger and Undershaft is turning our backs on life.

CUSINS. I thought you were determined

to turn your back on the wicked side of life.

BARBARA. There is no wicked side: life is all one. And I never wanted to shirk my share in whatever evil must be endured, whether it be sin or suffering. I wish I could cure you of middle-class ideas, Dolly.

CUSINS (gasping). Middle cl—! A snub! A social snub to me! from the daughter of a foundling!

BARBARA. That is why I have no class, Dolly: I come straight out of the heart of the whole people. If I were middle-class I should turn my back on my father's business; and we should both live in an artistic drawing room, with you reading the reviews in one corner, and I in the other at the piano, playing Schumann: both very superior persons, and neither of us a bit of use. Sooner than that, I would sweep out the guncotton shed, or be one of Bodger's barmaids. Do you know what would have happened if you had refused papa's offer?

CUSINS. I wonder!

BARBARA. I should have given you up and married the man who accepted it. After all, my dear old mother has more sense than any of you. I felt like her when I saw this place—felt that I must have it—that never, never, never could I let it go; only she thought it was the houses and the kitchen ranges and the linen and china, when it was really all the human souls to be saved: not weak souls in starved bodies, sobbing with gratitude for a scrap of bread and treacle, but fullfed, quarrelsome, snobbish, uppish creatures, all standing on their little rights and dignities, and thinking that my father ought to be greatly obliged to them for making so much money for him—and so he ought. That is where salvation is really wanted. My father shall never throw it in my teeth again that my converts were bribed with bread. (She is transfigured.) I have got rid of the bribe of bread. I have got rid of the bribe of heaven. Let God's work be done for its own sake: the work he had to create us to do because it cannot be done except by living men and women. When I die, let him be in my debt, not I in his; and let me forgive him as becomes a woman of my rank.

CUSINS. Then the way of life lies through the factory of death?

BARBARA. Yes, through the raising of hell to heaven and of man to God, through the unveiling of an eternal light in the Valley of The Shadow. (Seizing him with both hands) Oh, did you think my courage would never come back? did you believe that I was a deserter? that I, who have stood in the streets, and taken my people to my heart, and talked of the holiest and greatest things with them, could ever turn back and chatter foolishly to fashionable people about nothing in a drawing room? Never, never, never, never: Major Barbara willl die with the colors. Oh! and I have my dear little Dolly boy still; and he has found me my place and my work. Glory Hallelujah! (She kisses him.)

CUSINS. My dearest: consider my delicate health. I cannot stand as much happiness as you can.

BARBARA. Yes: it is not easy work being in love with me, is it? But it's good for you. (She runs to the shed, and calls, childlike) Mamma! Mamma! (Bilton comes out of the shed, followed by Undershaft.) I want Mamma.

UNDERSHAFT. She is taking off her list slippers, dear. (He passes on to Cusins.) Well? What does she say?

CUSINS. She has gone right up into the skies.

LADY BRITOMART (coming from the shed and stopping on the steps, obstructing Sarah, who follows with Lomax. Barbara clutches like a baby at her mother's skirt). Barbara: when will you learn to be independent and to act and think for yourself? I know as well as possible what that cry of "Mamma, Mamma," means. Always running to me!

SARAH (touching Lady Britomart's ribs with her finger tips and imitating a bicycle horn). Pip! pip!

LADY BRITOMART (highly indignant). How dare you say Pip! pip! to me, Sarah? You are both very naughty children. What do you want, Barbara?

BARBARA. I want a house in the village to live in with Dolly. (Dragging at the skirt) Come and tell me which one to take.

UNDERSHAFT (to Cusins). Six o'clock tomorrow morning, Euripides.

SEAN O'CASEY: *A Whisper About Bernard Shaw*

A WHISPER IS ALL A SHORT ARTICLE CAN BE ABOUT SUCH A ONE as Shaw. A wonderful man, he was born ninety years ago in the wonderful city of Dublin, capital of Eire. Seer, saint, and sage, he was usually to be found teaching through a laugh among the community of publicans and sinners. A leader who carried a flag of rebellion against every wrong, every pious fraud, every stupidity that institutional and conventional interest used to keep themselves up and the mass of the people down. A leader who went forward, not with a threat, not even with a frown, but with a laugh flying like a pennon from his pointed spear of thought. He showed to the self-satisfied bourgeois the indecent pictures of themselves, naked of every new thought or idea; he went on dancing round the strongroom of a bank, as David had done before the Ark of the Covenant, not as the Israelite did, to worship, but as a sure and sensible man, to mock. He showed how many of them got the money out of the corruption and degradation of the people, enabling them to be most respectable, and to give a grandiloquent worship to their God. The piercing barbs he hurled at the self-righteous possessors of wealth, of inherited power, of superior education, prostrate before their gods of stale ideas and outworn creeds, were half-hidden in the curled-up, colored tissue of a mischievous laugh; but when the colored tissue fell away, the barb was often deep in the resentful and quivering flesh of the victim, forcing the placid, self-satisfied voice to yell; and on the way Shaw laid many of the bourgeois low, saving the best of them, when their wounds had healed, from their own conceit, stupidity, and self-satisfaction, proving to them that two birds in a bush are often more beautiful and more useful to man than one bird in the hand.

Shaw's main fight, armed with all his logical art and wit, was to force forward a system of bare thought that would, in the long or short run, evolve a sane and sensible life for all. Poverty was the gigantic foe, the black Apollyon, that Shaw met on his long pilgrimage through life; and this demon he set out to kill. Wounding him sorely, Shaw didn't succeed in destroying him, though he may yet have the joy of seeing him laid low forever; for on this demon, in this land, Shaw's clenched fist has dealt the hardiest blows, and he has had no small part in bringing a Labor Movement into power. The Lady Poverty of St. Francis is a slovenly, unhandsome dame to St. Bernard. So far from fondling her, or even honoring her, he does not even stoop to pity her. Kick her out of the house of life! He says himself, "In the guise of plays, I contended that poverty should be neither pitied as an inevitable misfortune, nor tolerated as a just retribution for misconduct; but resolutely stamped out and prevented from recurring as a disease fatal to human society." Fatal to human society! That slogan holds the highest lettering of all the slogans on Shaw's banner. He found poverty to be in the way of an honest religion, of a decent life, of sound politics, and the creation of color and form and line in art. And now, after ninety years of a laboring life, there are few intelligent people left in the world who will dare to disagree with him. That is the main reason that made Shaw—a born communist, as he calls himself—into a practical and energetic Socialist; "for under Socialism no one would be allowed to be poor. You would be forcibly fed, clothed, lodged, taught, and employed, whether you liked it or not; and if it were discovered you had neither character nor industry enough to deserve the trouble taken with you, you might possibly be executed in a kindly manner." In other words, while you lived, you'd be made to live well, and made to work well to make the good life last. All this to Shaw was a necessary postulate to permament civilization; and the world seemed to be going his way now. These major claims, supported with all their correlations—freedom for thought, worship, or antagonism to belief, self-expression, sex, and brotherhood—Shaw unceasingly preached, and fought for them, too, on council, on platform, and in play. He fought for education grimly at times, and again with a laughing violence; education for all; not only for instruction in reading, writing, and arithmetic—so long the trinity of the working class—to make them fit for the toil of field, factory, and workshop; but an education fitting them to educate themselves, and become genial, civilized human beings; education that gave them a grand chance of enjoying music, of scenting out the flowers of literature, of tracing the line and feeling the color and form of painting, and of hearing Shakespeare's voice speaking out loud.

Though Shaw spoke many times to meetings of the workers, influencing them powerfully and making them feel proud of having such a fine mind as friend and leader, it was the solid, respectable, serene middle class that Shaw reached and affected most, by preface and play, by puzzling them, by teasing them, and laughing at them, even by frightening them; but eventually convincing influential numbers of them that Socialism was not only not dangerous, but acceptable to fine and intelligent minds, and a movement to be supported by intelligent and conscientious men and women. This was, indeed, a great achievement, for among the middle class were many fine and sensitive minds, writers, men of law and learning, officers of army and navy, managers in bank and business house, in factory and storehouse, with ministers of religion, forming a substantial group of thought and action, giving weight and importance to the Labor Movement and to progressive thought everywhere. This forward step of the big middle class helped greatly to bring about the decline of the great Liberal Party; and even those left of it, who elect still to cling to the old name, are being impelled to put forward stronger ideas of an active democracy than they had held before the great power of Shaw's ideas, in his writing and his talk, collided with their power and influence. It is now desperately trying to revive its disheartened remnants, to rally its scattered forces, and, if it is to succeed in any way, it must enfold ideas and recommend action, which would have frightened, if not appalled, the soft-stepping, sure-stepping Liberals of a generation ago; and the merciless hunter in the woodpile was the veteran, Bernard Shaw.

It is on the stage that Shaw's effective influence did most work, work, in a great way, for God (should God exist), work for man, and work for the Theater (though Shaw's influence cannot be measured anywhere or at any time). He set down a lamp in the Theater that has ever since been a light to our feet and a guide to our path. Long before he started to write plays, Shaw had been known to many as a Socialist preacher, and a damn good one, too; not quite so well known as a critic of music and of painting; but it is, I think, as a playwright that Shaw stands pre-eminent in the recognition of the people. Occasionally, he is quoted as a philosopher, a social reformer, a sage; but, first and foremost, in all talk about him, in fervent approval or cynical rejection, he appears in spirit before us all as a dramatist. As a critic of painting, he seems to be forgotten; as a critic of music, his reception of Brahms as a musical prodigy, but, compared with his great predecessors, an addlehead, is still resented by the old brahmins; and his criticism of Shakespeare, whom he knew by heart, in comparison with Ibsen, is quoted, not unreasonably, as outrageous; but the fact remains that his ephemeral weekly articles of fifty years ago, written to boil his pot, are still alive in seven fat volumes which sell freely and are taken as models by his latest successors. Though most of the plays mentioned are so old-fashioned as to be forgotten forever, the criticisms remain potent and vivid opinions of the drama of that day, and, at times, of the drama of the future; but it is his position as a playwright in the world of drama that is a never-ending delight and a frigid or fiery controversy.

And a hard fight he had to get on to the stage at all. He says himself, "I had to cut my own way into it at the point of the pen, and then throw some of its defenders into the moat." A fine fighter against enemies of the people, against enemies of the stage. With him, the Theater in England began to wear again the dignity and grandeur of a proper place for earnest and hilarious men and women. Shaw claims that the Theater "is as important today as the Church was in the Middle Ages; having its own apostolic succession, from Aeschylus onwards, as serious and as continuously inspired as that younger institution, the apostolic succession of the Christian Church." Even more important now, he goes on, "for in that Church you can no longer laugh, whereas in the church of the Theater the oftener you laugh the better, because by laughter only can you destroy evil without malice, and affirm good fellowship without mawkishness"; though, to me, the philosophy of regarding evil without hating it, even maliciously, must ever be without effective fulfillment of its destruction.

What kind of a dramatist is Shaw? To what other dramatist does he correspond? None of the eminent, save perhaps Ibsen in his first polemical plays; with Ibsen, the poet, he has little to do; and with the far less eminent Brieux—who wrote one fine play, *The Three Daughters of M. Dupont*—he but exchanges a handshake and a genial nod of the head. He is nearer the Russian than he is to the German or the Frenchman, I think. By some cynical critics, Shaw has been called "a poet without the poetry," but that remark isn't at all fair, and true only within its own pontifical cleverness; for a lot of his plays are musical, and gleams of a poetical imagination stream out of them for all sensitive eyes to see. After some argumentative dispute with Shaw, Yeats, the Irish poet, wrote to Lady Gregory, one of the founders of the Abbey Theater, saying, "Shaw seems to have no poetical sense. He is a logician, and a logician is a fool when life, which is a thing of emotion, is in question. It is as if a watch were to understand a bullock." Well, first, I'd say that Shaw understood more about a bullock than Yeats did. Emotion is part of life, but it isn't the whole of life; and logic comes well into life, too: the logic of growth, the infant, the child, the adolescent, the man; first the leaf, then the ear, then the corn in the ear. Christ was something of a logi-

cian, and something of a poet, too; and so was Shaw. Yeats was wrong, for it is poetical emotion to be sensitive to all the phases of life, its sorrow, its joy, success and failure, the wonder of children, the splendor of animated nature; all of which Shaw had in full, but Yeats only in part; for he thought as much of Sato's sword as he did of an evening full of the linnets' wings.

Undoubtedly, there is poetry in the scene showing the death of Dubedat, between the young poet and Candida; poetry in many parts of the prophetic *Heartbreak House,* in the banks of the Loire scene between the Page, Dunois, and Joan of Arc; a comical poetry in the ending of the first act of the same play; there is poetry in the greeting of the tumultuous Roman soldiers, falling into a dressed front, hailing Caesar, quietly dominant on the throne of Egypt; and think of the lovely lyrical philosophy of Father Keegan, the silenced priest in *John Bull's Other Island;* and many, many more poetical instances for those who have eyes to see and ears to hear them. Let those who write plays today throw a wider chest than Shaw's, in either poetry or prose—if they can!

He was a great playwright, but the shy, poetic urge in Shaw was often restrained by the dominant urge of the thinker; and it is as a thinker that Shaw takes his place, in the opinion of many, among the great men of the world. He is, to many more, an odd thinker—different from those who seem to sit at huge dark desks, poised on important purpose, elegantly posed, surrounded by candles of knowledge, who drop granite thoughts, polished like pearls, into the bemazed ear of life; like Herbert Read etching his esthetic and philosophic views on stylish tablets: no loud word, not a one; no snatch of a song, not a tap of a taradiddle on the desk; perfect serenity, pure candle light; not a flicker from the flame.

Shaw was a gay one, a demonic democrat; full of courage, vigor, animated by a buoyant wit, devastating to sham and humbug everywhere, thrusting hypocrisy and cruel conduct out of the doorway of life. Hardly a creed, no institution of thought or manners, no gilded nonsense on the stage, in pulpit or press escaped the pointed remarks of this amiable, lovable, fearless philosopher who loved and fought for, above all things, "the golden heresy of truth." Apart from Shaw's belief in Socialism, which is but a commonsense way of life, it would be hard to pin down Shaw to any decisive creed on what the activities of life should be, or may become; of what the stage should show in scene or say in dialogue; or what the manners of men should be in the deeper things concerning man; for he ventured as far as thought could reach, and looked further; and he, a communist, born one, he tells us himself, is the rarest and biggest individualist in the British Isles. But one not out for profits, but rather for the gain of his own integrity; a gain that is bound to grow into a wider display of the same grand virtue by the people who come into contact with his brave and pure ideas.

By many, too, Shaw was thought to be "an irresponsible joker"; but his kind of joking is a characteristic of the Irish; and Shaw in his temperament is Irish of the Irish. We Irish, when we think, and we often do this, are just as serious and sober as the Englishman; but we never hesitate to give a serious thought the benefit and halo of a laugh. That is why we are so often thought to be irresponsible, whereas, in point of fact, we are critical realists, while Englishmen often mistake sentimental mutterings for everlasting truths. This silvery thread of laughter runs through all of Shaw's plays, and most of his writing, weaving a delightful decoration into his keen thought and thrusting satire. This joking sage has been a godsend to England (and to Ireland, too), for his wisdom, his love of truth and freedom, his gay spirit and fearless conduct have been a banner before us, a banner and a bugle band leading the slow, the certain, the glorious ascent of man.

THE POET AND DRAMATIST JOHN MILLINGTON SYNGE

John Millington Synge 1871-1909

was born in a Dublin suburb to a well-established Irish Protestant family of English descent. His father died shortly after the child's birth, but despite the family's straitened circumstances Synge received a good education and took a B.A. at Trinity College, Dublin in 1892. His chief interest at the time was in music, and to pursue further study he went to Germany. Gradually, Synge turned from music to literature and set up in Paris to study the new trends in French letters. While there he met William Butler Yeats and briefly joined the Paris branch of the Young Ireland Society, a nationalist movement for Irish independence and cultural revival. But the revolutionary goals of Young Ireland were not for the quiet and withdrawn Synge. Upon Yeats' advice Synge returned to Ireland and spent six weeks among the peasants of the primitive Aran Islands. During the next few years, he drifted between France and Ireland and became more and more absorbed in studying Irish speech, legend and folkways. In 1902 Synge wrote two one-act plays, the ironic comedy *In the Shadow of the Glen* and the powerful symbolist tragedy *Riders to the Sea*. The first was produced in 1903 by the Irish National Theatre Society (later the famous Abbey Theatre), founded by Yeats, Lady Gregory and Edward Martyn, and was poorly received by the nationalist press that found the play's theme of loveless marriage a libel on Irish womanhood. *Riders to the Sea* fared somewhat better, and Synge's next play, *The Well of the Saints* (1905) was ignored. But with the production of *The Playboy of the Western World* (1907) nationalist fury broke forth. For two acts the audience sat tensely quiet, but when in the third act Christy used the word *shifts* (female underclothes) violent hissing erupted countered by applause. Hypersensitive to any criticism of Irish life and morals, the nationalists denounced the comedy as a slander of the Irish peasant, a "squalid, offensive production," and for the remaining week police were required to control the audience. Synge, by then seriously ill with cancer, had but two years to live. Rejecting the "joyless and pallid words" of naturalistic drama, he had drawn on the eloquent dialects of Irish speech to fashion a drama rooted in Irish folk life and tinged with fancy, romance and irony. Synge died at thirty-eight without having completed his last tragic play, *Deirdre of the Sorrows*.

GLOSSARY

banbhs farmlands left fallow

banns public announcement in church of a proposed marriage

blackthorn a walking cane

boreen a narrow lane or path

cess stop

cleeve a basket

cnuceen a small hill

cockles burrs growing in grain fields

cockshot man the man who runs the shooting gallery at a fair

conceit idea

creel cart a cart with a wickerwork basket

curragh a small boat made by covering a wicker frame with hide or tarpaulin; a coracle

da dad

droughty thirsty

frish-frash slops.

gaffer fellow

gallous strange, wonderful

gob beak

hop'orth a half-penny's worth

jobbing cheating

liefer preferably

loy a long, narrow spade

lug ear

mitch off sneak away

moiling drudging

pandied struck

parlatic paralyzed.

peeler a policeman

pike spike

porter a weak, rather sweet stout, originally a mixture of ale and stout

pot-boy a boy who carries pots of ale in a pub

poteen a strong Irish whiskey, illicitly made

scribes ditches

scruff the nape of the neck

shaving cheating

shebeen a tavern where taxable liquors are sold without the license required by law

skelping whipping

slate thrash

spavindy crippled

streeleen a stream

streeler a wanderer

supeen a small drink

swiggling swinging

thraneen a very small coin

trick-o'-the-loop man the operator of a concession at a carnival

turbary peat turf, used for fuel

wattle a walking stick

whisht be quiet

winkered wearing blinders

THE PLAYBOY OF THE WESTERN WORLD ❧ BY JOHN M. SYNGE

PREFACE

January 21, 1907

IN WRITING *THE PLAYBOY OF THE WESTERN WORLD,* AS IN MY other plays, I have used one or two words only that I have not heard among the country people of Ireland, or spoken in my own nursery before I could read the newspapers. A certain number of the phrases I employ I have heard also from herds and fishermen along the coast from Kerry to Mayo or from beggar-women and ballad-singers nearer Dublin; and I am glad to acknowledge how much I owe to the folk-imagination of these fine people. Anyone who has lived in real intimacy with the Irish peasantry will know that the wildest sayings and ideas in this play are tame indeed, compared with the fancies one may hear in any little hillside cabin in Geesala, or Carraroe, or Dingle Bay. All art is a collaboration; and there is little doubt that in the happy ages of literature, striking and beautiful phrases were as ready to the story-teller's or the play-wright's hand, as the rich cloaks and dresses of his time. It is probable that when the Elizabethan dramatist took his ink-horn and sat down to his work he used many phrases that he had just heard, as he sat at dinner, from his mother or his children. In Ireland, those of us who know the people have the same privilege. When I was writing *The Shadow of the Glen,* some years ago, I got more aid than any learning could have given me from a chink in the floor of the old Wicklow house where I was staying, that let me hear what was being said by the servant girls in the kitchen. This matter, I think, is of importance, for in countries where the imagination of the people, and the language they use, is rich and living, it is possible for a writer to be rich and copious in his words, and at the same time to give the reality, which is the root of all poetry, in a comprehensive and natural form. In the modern literature of towns, however, richness is found only in sonnets, or prose poems, or in one or two elaborate books that are far away from the profound and common interests of life. One has, on one side, Mallarmé and Huysmans producing this literature; and on the other, Ibsen and Zola dealing with the reality of life in joyless and pallid words. On the stage one must have reality, and one must have joy; and that is why the intellectual modern drama has failed, and people have grown sick of the false joy of the musical comedy, that has been given them in place of the rich joy found only in what is superb and wild in reality. In a good play every speech should be as fully flavoured as a nut or apple, and such speeches cannot be written by anyone who works among people who have shut their lips on poetry. In Ireland, for a few years more, we have a popular imagination that is fiery, and magnificent, and tender; so that those of us who wish to write start with a chance that is not given to writers in places where the spring-time of the local life has been forgotten, and the harvest is a memory only, and the straw has been turned into bricks.

CHARACTERS

CHRISTOPHER MAHON
OLD MAHON (*his father, a squatter*)
MICHAEL JAMES FLAHERTY, *called* MICHAEL JAMES (*a publican*)
MARGARET FLAHERTY, *called* PEGEEN MIKE (*his daughter*)
WIDOW QUIN (*a woman of about thirty*)
SHAWN KEOGH (*her cousin, a young farmer*)
PHILLY CULLEN and JIMMY FARRELL (*small farmers*)
SARA TANSEY, SUSAN BRADY, and HONOR BLAKE (*village girls*)
A BELLMAN
SOME PEASANTS

The action takes place near a village, on a wild coast of Mayo. The first Act passes on an evening of autumn, the other two Acts on the following day.

Act I

SCENE: *Country public-house or shebeen, very rough and untidy. There is a sort of counter on the right with shelves, holding many bottles and jugs, just seen above it. Empty barrels stand near the counter. At back, a little to left of counter, there is a door into the open air, then, more to the left, there is a settle with shelves above it, with more jugs, and a table beneath a window. At the left there is a large open fire-place, with turf fire, and a small door into inner room. Pegeen, a wild-looking but fine girl of about twenty, is writing at table. She is dressed in the usual peasant dress.*

PEGEEN (*slowly as she writes*). Six yards of stuff for to make a yellow gown. A pair of lace boots with lengthy heels on them and brassy eyes. A hat is suited for a wedding-day. A fine tooth comb. To be sent with three barrels of porter in Jimmy Farrell's creel cart on the evening of the coming Fair to Mister Michael James Flaherty. With the best compliments of this season. Margaret Flaherty.

SHAWN KEOGH (*a fat and fair young man comes in as she signs, looks around awkwardly, when he sees she is alone*). Where's himself?

PEGEEN (*without looking at him*). He's coming. (*She directs the letter*) To Master Sheamus Mulroy, Wine and Spirit Dealer, Castlebar.

SHAWN (*uneasily*). I didn't see him on the road.

PEGEEN. How would you see him (*licks stamp and puts it on letter*) and it dark night this half hour gone by?

SHAWN (*turning towards the door again*). I stood a while outside wondering would I have a right to pass on or to walk in and see you, Pegeen Mike (*comes to fire*), and I could hear the cows breathing, and sighing in the stillness of the air, and not a step moving any place from this gate to the bridge.

PEGEEN (*putting letter in envelope*). It's above at the cross-roads he is, meeting Philly Cullen; and a couple more are going along with him to Kate Cassidy's wake.

SHAWN (*looking at her blankly*). And he's going that length in the dark night?

PEGEEN (*impatiently*). He is surely, and leaving me lonesome on the scruff of the hill. (*She gets up and puts envelope on dresser, then winds clock*) Isn't it long the nights are now, Shawn Keogh, to be leaving a poor girl with her own self counting the hours to the dawn of day?

SHAWN (*with an awkward humour*). If it is, when we're wedded in a short while you'll have no call to complain, for I've little will to be walking off to wakes or weddings in the darkness of the night.

PEGEEN (*with rather scornful good humour*). You're making mighty certain, Shaneen, that I'll wed you now.

SHAWN. Aren't we after making a good bargain, the way we're only waiting these days on Father Reilly's dispensation from the bishops, or the Court of Rome?

PEGEEN (*looking at him teasingly, washing up at dresser*). It's a wonder,

Shaneen, the Holy Father'd be taking notice of the likes of you; for if I was him I wouldn't bother with this place where you'll meet none but Red Linahan, has a squint in his eye, and Patcheen is lame in his heel, or the mad Mulrannies were driven from California and they lost in their wits. We're a queer lot these times to go troubling the Holy Father on his sacred seat.

SHAWN (*scandalized*). If we are, we're as good this place as another, maybe, and as good these times as we were for ever.

PEGEEN (*with scorn*). As good, is it? Where now will you meet the like of Daneen Sullivan knocked the eye from a peeler, or Marcus Quin, God rest him, got six months for maiming ewes, and he a great warrant to tell stories of holy Ireland till he'd have the old women shedding down tears about their feet. Where will you find the like of them, I'm saying?

SHAWN (*timidly*). If you don't, it's a good job, maybe; for (*with peculiar emphasis on the words*) Father Reilly has small conceit to have that kind walking around and talking to the girls.

PEGEEN (*impatiently, throwing water from basin out of the door*). Stop tormenting me with Father Reilly (*imitating his voice*) when I'm asking only what way I'll pass these twelve hours of dark, and not take my death with the fear. (*Looking out of door.*)

SHAWN (*timidly*). Would I fetch you the Widow Quin, maybe?

PEGEEN. Is it the like of that murderer? You'll not, surely.

SHAWN (*going to her, soothingly*). Then I'm thinking himself will stop along with you when he sees you taking on, for it'll be a long night-time with great darkness, and I'm after feeling a kind of fellow above in the furzy ditch, groaning wicked like a maddening dog, the way it's good cause you have, maybe, to be fearing now.

PEGEEN (*turning on him sharply*). What's that? Is it a man you seen?

SHAWN (*retreating*). I couldn't see him at all; but I heard him groaning out, and breaking his heart. It should have been a young man from his words speaking.

PEGEEN (*going after him*). And you never went near to see was he hurted or what ailed him at all?

SHAWN. I did not, Pegeen Mike. It was a dark, lonesome place to be hearing the like of him.

PEGEEN. Well, you're a daring fellow, and if they find his corpse stretched above in the dews of dawn, what'll you say then to the peelers, or the Justice of the Peace?

SHAWN (*thunderstruck*). I wasn't thinking of that. For the love of God, Pegeen Mike, don't let on I was speaking of him. Don't tell your father and the men is coming above; for if they heard that story, they'd have great blabbing this night at the wake.

PEGEEN. I'll maybe tell them, and I'll maybe not.

SHAWN. They are coming at the door. Will you whisht, I'm saying?

PEGEEN. Whisht yourself. (*She goes behind counter.* MICHAEL JAMES, *fat jovial publican, comes in followed by* PHILLY CULLEN, *who is thin and mistrusting, and* JIMMY FARRELL, *who is fat and amorous, about forty-five.*)

MEN (*together*). God bless you. The blessing of God on this place.

PEGEEN. God bless you kindly.

MICHAEL (*to men who go to the counter*). Sit down now, and take your rest. (*Crosses to* SHAWN *at the fire*) And how is it you are, Shawn Keogh? Are you coming over the sands to Kate Cassidy's wake?

SHAWN. I am not, Michael James. I'm going home the short cut to my bed.

PEGEEN (*speaking across the counter*). He's right too, and have you no shame, Michael James, to be quitting off for the whole night, and leaving myself lonesome in the shop?

MICHAEL (*good-humouredly*). Isn't it the same whether I go for the whole night or a part only? and I'm thinking it's a queer daughter you are if you'd have me crossing backward through the Stooks of the Dead Women, with a drop taken.

PEGEEN. If I am a queer daughter, it's a queer father'd be leaving me lonesome these twelve hours of dark, and I piling the turf with the dogs barking, and the calves mooing, and my own teeth rattling with the fear.

JIMMY (*flatteringly*). What is there to hurt you, and you a fine, hardy girl would knock the head of any two men in the place?

PEGEEN (*working herself up*). Isn't there the harvest boys with their tongues red for drink, and the ten tinkers is camped in the east glen, and the thousand militia—bad cess to them!—walking idle through the land. There's lots surely to hurt me, and I won't stop alone in it, let himself do what he will.

MICHAEL. If you're that afeard, let Shawn Keogh stop along with you. It's the will of God, I'm thinking, himself should be seeing to you now.

(*They all turn on* SHAWN.)

SHAWN (*in horrified confusion*). I would and welcome, Michael James, but I'm afeard of Father Reilly; and what at all would the Holy Father and the Cardinals of Rome be saying if they heard I did the like of that?

MICHAEL (*with contempt*). God help you! Can't you sit in by the hearth with the light lit and herself beyond in the room? You'll do that surely, for I've heard tell there's a queer fellow above, going mad or getting his death, maybe, in the gripe of the ditch, so she'd be safer this night with a person here.

SHAWN (*with plaintive despair*). I'm afeard of Father Reilly, I'm saying. Let you not be tempting me, and we near married itself.

PHILLY (*with cold contempt*). Lock him in the west room. He'll stay then and have no sin to be telling to the priest.

MICHAEL (*to* SHAWN, *getting between him and the door*). Go up now.

SHAWN (*at the top of his voice*). Don't stop me, Michael James. Let me out of the door, I'm saying, for the love of the Almighty God. Let me out. (*Trying to dodge past him*) Let me out of it, and may God grant you His indulgence in the hour of need.

MICHAEL (*loudly*). Stop your noising, and sit down by the hearth. (*Gives him a push and goes to counter laughing.*)

SHAWN (*turning back, wringing his hands*). Oh, Father Reilly and the saints of God, where will I hide myself today? Oh, St. Joseph and St. Patrick and St. Brigid, and St. James, have mercy on me now! (SHAWN *turns round, sees door clear, and makes a rush for it.*)

MICHAEL (*catching him by the coat-tail*). You'd be going, is it?

SHAWN (*screaming*). Leave me go, Michael James, leave me go, you old Pagan, leave me go, or I'll get the curse of the priests on you, and of the scarlet-coated bishops of the courts of Rome. (*With a sudden movement he pulls himself out of his coat, and disappears out of the door, leaving his coat in* MICHAEL'S *hands.*)

MICHAEL (*turning round, and holding up coat*). Well, there's the coat of a Christian man. Oh, there's sainted glory this day in the lonesome west; and by the will of God I've got you a decent man, Pegeen, you'll have no call to be spying after if you've a score of young girls, maybe, weeding in your fields.

PEGEEN (*taking up the defense of her property*). What right have you to be making game of a poor fellow for minding the priest, when it's your own the fault is, not paying a penny pot-boy to stand along with me and give me courage in the doing of my work? (*She snaps the coat away from him, and goes behind counter with it.*)

MICHAEL (*taken aback*). Where would I get a pot-boy? Would you have me send the bellman screaming in the streets of Castlebar?

SHAWN (*opening the door a chink and putting in his head, in a small voice*). Michael James!

MICHAEL (*imitating him*). What ails you?

SHAWN. The queer dying fellow's beyond looking over the ditch. He's come up, I'm thinking, stealing your hens. (*Looks over his shoulder*) God help me, he's following me now (*he runs into room*) and if he's heard what I said, he'll be having my life, and I going home lonesome in the darkness of the night.

(*For a perceptible moment they watch the door with curiosity. Some one coughs outside. Then* CHRISTY MAHON, *a slight young man, comes in very tired and frightened and dirty.*)

CHRISTY (*in a small voice*). God save all here!

MEN. God save you kindly.

CHRISTY (*going to the counter*). I'd trouble you for a glass of porter, woman of the house. (*He puts down coin.*)

PEGEEN (*serving him*). You're one of the tinkers, young fellow, is beyond camped in the glen?

CHRISTY. I am not; but I'm destroyed walking.

MICHAEL (*patronizingly*). Let you come up then to the fire. You're looking famished with the cold.

CHRISTY. God reward you. (*He takes up his glass and goes a little way across to the left, then stops and looks about him*) Is it often the police do be coming into this place, master of the house?

MICHAEL. If you'd come in better hours, you'd have seen "Licensed for the sale of Beer and Spirits, to be consumed on the premises," written in white letters above the door, and what would the polis want spying on me, and not a decent house within four miles, the way every living Christian is a bona fide, saving one widow alone?

CHRISTY (*with relief*). It's a safe house, so. (*He goes over to the fire, sighing and moaning. Then he sits down, putting his glass beside him and begins gnawing a turnip, too miserable to feel the others staring at him with curiosity.*)

MICHAEL (*going after him*). Is it yourself is fearing the polis? You're wanting, maybe?

CHRISTY. There's many wanting.

MICHAEL. Many surely, with the broken harvest and the ended wars. (*He picks up some stockings, etc., that are near the fire, and carries them away furtively*) It should be larceny, I'm thinking.

CHRISTY (*dolefully*). I had it in my mind it was a different word and a bigger.

PEGEEN. There's a queer lad. Were you never slapped in school, young fellow, that you don't know the name of your deed?

CHRISTY (*bashfully*). I'm slow at learning, a middling scholar only.

MICHAEL. If you're a dunce itself, you'd have a right to know that larceny's robbing and stealing. Is it for the like of that you're wanting?

CHRISTY (*with a flash of family pride*). And I the son of a strong farmer (*with a sudden qualm*), God rest his soul, could have bought up the whole of your old house awhile since, from the butt of his tailpocket, and not have missed the weight of it gone.

MICHAEL (*impressed*). If it's not stealing, it's maybe something big.

CHRISTY (*flattered*). Aye; it's maybe something big.

JIMMY. He's a wicked-looking young fellow. Maybe he followed after a young woman on a lonesome night.

CHRISTY (*shocked*). Oh, the saints forbid, mister; I was all times a decent lad.

PHILLY (*turning on* JIMMY). You're a silly man, Jimmy Farrell. He said his father was a farmer a while since, and there's himself now in a poor state. Maybe the land was grabbed from him, and he did what any decent man would do.

MICHAEL (*to* CHRISTY, *mysteriously*). Was it bailiffs?

CHRISTY. The divil a one.

MICHAEL. Agents?

CHRISTY. The divil a one.

MICHAEL. Landlords?

CHRISTY (*peevishly*). Ah, not at all, I'm saying. You'd see the like of them stories on any little paper of a Munster town. But I'm not calling to mind any person, gentle, simple, judge or jury, did the like of me.

(*They all draw nearer with delighted curiosity.*)

PHILLY. Well, that lad's a puzzle-the-world.

JIMMY. He'd beat Dan Davies' circus, or the holy missioners making sermons on the villainy of man. Try him again, Philly.

PHILLY. Did you strike golden guineas out of solder, young fellow, or shilling coins itself?

CHRISTY. I did not, mister, not sixpence nor a farthing coin.

JIMMY. Did you marry three wives maybe? I'm told there's a sprinkling have done that among the holy Luthers of the preaching north.

CHRISTY (*shyly*). I never married with one, let alone with a couple or three.

PHILLY. Maybe he went fighting for the Boers, the like of the man beyond, was judged to be hanged, quartered and drawn. Were you off east, young fellow, fighting bloody wars for Kruger and the freedom of the Boers?

CHRISTY. I never left my own parish till Tuesday was a week.

PEGEEN (*coming from counter*). He's done nothing, so. (*To* CHRISTY) If you didn't commit murder or a bad, nasty thing, or false coining, or robbery, or butchery, or the like of them, there isn't anything that would be worth your troubling for to run from now. You did nothing at all.

CHRISTY (*his feelings hurt*). That's an unkindly thing to be saying to a poor orphaned traveller, has a prison behind him, and hanging before, and hell's gap gaping below.

PEGEEN (*with a sign to the men to be quiet*). You're only saying it. You did nothing at all. A soft lad the like of you wouldn't slit the windpipe of a screeching sow.

CHRISTY (*offended*). You're not speaking the truth.

PEGEEN (*in mock rage*). Not speaking the truth, it is? Would you have me knock the head off you with the butt of the broom?

CHRISTY (*twisting round on her with a sharp cry of horror*). Don't strike me. I killed my poor father, Tuesday was a week, for doing the like of that.

PEGEEN (*with blank amazement*). Is it killed your father?

CHRISTY (*subsiding*). With the help of God I did surely, and that the Holy Immaculate Mother may intercede for his soul.

PHILLY (*retreating with* JIMMY). There's a daring fellow.

JIMMY. Oh, glory be to God!

MICHAEL (*with great respect*). That was a hanging crime, mister honey. You should have had good reason for doing the like of that.

CHRISTY (*in a very reasonable tone*). He was a dirty man, God forgive him, and he getting old and crusty, the way I couldn't put up with him at all.

PEGEEN. And you shot him dead?

CHRISTY (*shaking his head*). I never used weapons. I've no license, and I'm a law-fearing man.

MICHAEL. It was with a hilted knife maybe? I'm told, in the big world it's bloody knives they use.

CHRISTY (*loudly, scandalized*). Do you take me for a slaughter-boy?

PEGEEN. You never hanged him, the way Jimmy Farrell hanged his dog from the license, and had it screeching and wriggling three hours at the butt of a string, and himself swearing it was a dead dog, and the peelers swearing it had life?

CHRISTY. I did not then. I just riz the loy and let fall the edge of it on the ridge of his skull, and he went down at my feet like an empty sack, and never let a grunt or groan from him at all.

MICHAEL (*making a sign to* PEGEEN *to fill* CHRISTY'S *glass*). And what way weren't you hanged, mister? Did you bury him then?

CHRISTY (*considering*). Aye. I buried him then. Wasn't I digging spuds in the field?

MICHAEL. And the peelers never followed after you the eleven days that you're out?

CHRISTY (*shaking his head*). Never a one of them, and I walking forward facing hog, dog, or divil on the highway of the road.

PHILLY (*nodding wisely*). It's only with a common week-day kind of a murderer them lads would be trusting their carcase, and that man should be a great terror when his temper's roused.

MICHAEL. He should then. (*To* CHRISTY) And where was it, mister honey, that you did the deed?

CHRISTY (*looking at him with suspicion*). Oh, a distant place, master of the house, a windy corner of high, distant hills.

PHILLY (*nodding with approval*). He's a close man, and he's right, surely.

PEGEEN. That'd be a lad with the sense of Solomon to have for a pot-boy, Michael James, if it's the truth you're seeking one at all.

PHILLY. The peelers is fearing him, and if you'd that lad in the house there isn't one of them would come smelling around if the dogs itself were lapping poteen from the dung-pit of the yard.

JIMMY. Bravery's a treasure in a lonesome place, and a lad would kill his father, I'm thinking, would face a foxy divil with a pitchpike on the flags of hell.

PEGEEN. It's the truth they're saying, and if I'd that lad in the house, I wouldn't be fearing the loosed kharki cut-throats, or the walking dead.

CHRISTY (*swelling with surprise and triumph*). Well, glory be to God!

MICHAEL (*with deference*). Would you think well to stop here and be pot-boy, mister honey, if we gave you good wages, and didn't destroy you with the weight of work?

SHAWN (*coming forward uneasily*). That'd be a queer kind to bring into a decent quiet household with the like of Pegeen Mike.

PEGEEN (*very sharply*). Will you whisht? Who's speaking to you?

SHAWN (*retreating*). A bloody-handed murderer the like of . . .

PEGEEN (*snapping at him*). Whisht I am saying; we'll take no fooling from your like at all. (*To* CHRISTY *with a honeyed voice*) And you, young fellow, you'd have a right to stop, I'm thinking, for we'd do our all and utmost to content your needs.

CHRISTY (*overcome with wonder*). And I'd be safe in this place from the searching law?

MICHAEL. You would, surely. If they're not fearing you, itself, the peelers in this place is decent droughty poor fellows, wouldn't touch a cur dog and not give warning in the dead of night.

PEGEEN (*very kindly and persuasively*). Let you stop a short while anyhow. Aren't you destroyed walking with your feet in bleeding blisters, and your whole skin needing washing like a Wicklow sheep?

CHRISTY (*looking round with satisfaction*). It's a nice room, and if it's not humbugging me you are, I'm thinking that I'll surely stay.

JIMMY (*jumps up*). Now, by the grace of God, herself will be safe this night, with a man killed his father holding danger from the door, and let you come on, Michael James, or they'll have the best stuff drunk at the wake.

MICHAEL (*going to the door with men*). And begging your pardon, mister, what name will we call you, for we'd like to know?

CHRISTY: Christopher Mahon.

MICHAEL. Well, God bless you, Christy, and a good rest till we meet again when the sun'll be rising to the noon of day.

CHRISTY. God bless you all.

MEN. God bless you.

(*They go out except* SHAWN, *who lingers at door.*)

SHAWN (*to* PEGEEN). Are you wanting me to stop along with you and keep you from harm?

PEGEEN (*gruffly*). Didn't you say you were fearing Father Reilly?

SHAWN. There'd be no harm staying now, I'm thinking, and himself in it too.

PEGEEN. You wouldn't stay when there was need for you, and let you step off nimble this time when there's none.

SHAWN. Didn't I say it was Father Reilly . . .

PEGEEN. Go on, then, to Father Reilly (*in a jeering tone*), and let him put you in the holy brotherhoods, and leave that lad to me.

SHAWN. If I meet the Widow Quin. . . .

PEGEEN. Go on, I'm saying, and don't be waking this place with your noise. (*She hustles him out and bolts the door*) That lad would wear the spirits from the saints of peace. (*Bustles about, then takes off her apron and pins it up in the window as a blind,* CHRISTY *watching her timidly. Then she comes to him and speaks with bland good-humour*) Let you stretch out now by the fire, young fellow. You should be destroyed travelling.

CHRISTY (*shyly again, drawing off his boots*). I'm tired, surely, walking wild eleven days, and waking fearful in the night. (*He holds up one of his feet, feeling his blisters, and looking at them with compassion.*)

PEGEEN (*standing beside him, watching him with delight*). You should have had great people in your family, I'm thinking, with the little, small feet you have, and you with a kind of a quality name, the like of what you'd find on the great powers and potentates of France and Spain.

CHRISTY (*with pride*). We were great, surely, with wide and windy acres of rich Munster land.

PEGEEN. Wasn't I telling you, and you a fine, handsome young fellow with a noble brow?

CHRISTY (*with a flash of delighted surprise*). Is it me?

PEGEEN. Aye. Did you never hear that from the young girls where you come from in the west or south?

CHRISTY (*with venom*). I did not then. Oh, they're bloody liars in the naked parish where I grew a man.

PEGEEN. If they are itself, you've heard it these days, I'm thinking, and you walking the world telling out your story to young girls or old.

CHRISTY. I've told my story no place till this night, Pegeen Mike, and it's foolish I was here, maybe, to be talking free, but you're decent people, I'm thinking, and yourself a kindly woman, the way I wasn't fearing you at all.

PEGEEN (*filling a sack with straw*). You've said the like of that, maybe, in every cot and cabin where you've met a young girl on your way.

CHRISTY (*going over to her, gradually raising his voice*). I've said it nowhere till this night, I'm telling you, for I've seen none the like of you the eleven long days I am walking the world, looking over a low ditch or a high ditch on my north or my south, into stony scattered fields, or scribes of bog, where you'd see young, limber girls, and fine prancing women making laughter with the men.

PEGEEN. If you weren't destroyed travelling, you'd have as much talk and streeleen, I'm thinking, as Owen Roe O'Sullivan or the poets of the Dingle Bay, and I've heard all times it's the poets are your like, fine fiery fellows with great rages when their temper's roused.

CHRISTY (*drawing a little nearer to her*). You've a power of rings, God bless you, and would there be any offense if I was asking are you single now?

PEGEEN. What would I want wedding so young?

CHRISTY (*with relief*). We're alike, so.

PEGEEN (*she puts sack on settle and beats it up*). I never killed my father. I'd be afeard to do that, except I was the like of yourself with blind rages tearing me within, for I'm thinking you should have had great tussling when the end was come.

CHRISTY (*expanding with delight at the first confidential talk he has ever had with a woman*). We had not then. It was a hard woman was come over the hill, and if he was always a crusty kind when he'd a hard woman setting him on, not the divil himself or his four fathers could put up with him at all.

PEGEEN (*with curiosity*). And isn't it a great wonder that one wasn't fearing you?

CHRISTY (*very confidentially*). Up to the day I killed my father, there wasn't a person in Ireland knew the kind I was, and I there drinking, waking, eating, sleeping, a quiet, simple poor fellow with no man giving me heed.

PEGEEN (*getting a quilt out of the cupboard and putting it on the sack*). It was the girls were giving you heed maybe,

and I'm thinking it's most conceit you'd have to be gaming with their like.

CHRISTY (*shaking his head, with simplicity*). Not the girls itself, and I won't tell you a lie. There wasn't anyone heeding me in that place saving only the dumb beasts of the field. (*He sits down at fire.*)

PEGEEN (*with disappointment*). And I thinking you should have been living the like of a king of Norway or the Eastern world. (*She comes and sits beside him after placing bread and mug of milk on the table.*)

CHRISTY (*laughing piteously*). The like of a king, is it? And I after toiling, moiling, digging, dodging from the dawn till dusk with never a sight of joy or sport saving only when I'd be abroad in the dark night poaching rabbits on hills, for I was a divil to poach, God forgive me, (*very naïvely*) and I near got six months for going with a dung fork and stabbing a fish.

PEGEEN. And it's that you'd call sport, is it, to be abroad in the darkness with yourself alone?

CHRISTY. I did, God help me, and there I'd be as happy as the sunshine of St. Martin's Day, watching the light passing the north or the patches of fog, till I'd hear a rabbit starting to screech and I'd go running in the furze. Then when I'd my full share I'd come walking down where you'd see the ducks and geese stretched sleeping on the highway of the road, and before I'd pass the dunghill, I'd hear himself snoring out, a loud lonesome snore he'd be making all times, the while he was sleeping, and he a man 'd be raging all times, the while he was waking, like a gaudy officer you'd hear cursing and damning and swearing oaths.

PEGEEN. Providence and Mercy, spare us all!

CHRISTY. It's that you'd say surely if you seen him and he after drinking for weeks, rising up in the red dawn, or before it maybe, and going out into the yard as naked as an ash tree in the moon of May, and shying clods against the visage of the stars till he'd put the fear of death into the banbhs and the screeching sows.

PEGEEN. I'd be well-nigh afeard of that lad myself, I'm thinking. And there was no one in it but the two of you alone?

CHRISTY. The divil a one, though he'd sons and daughters walking all great states and territories of the world, and not a one of them, to this day, but would say their seven curses on him, and they rousing up to let a cough or sneeze, maybe, in the deadness of the night.

PEGEEN (*nodding her head*). Well, you should have been a queer lot. I never cursed my father the like of that, though I'm twenty and more years of age.

CHRISTY. Then you'd have cursed mine, I'm telling you, and he a man never gave peace to any, saving when he'd get two months or three, or be locked in the asylums for battering peelers or assaulting men (*with depression*) the way it was a bitter life he led me till I did up a Tuesday and halve his skull.

PEGEEN (*putting her hand on his shoulder*). Well, you'll have peace in this place, Christy Mahon, and none to trouble you, and it's near time a fine lad like you should have your good share of the earth.

CHRISTY. It's time surely, and I a seemly fellow with great strength in me and bravery of. . . .

(*Someone knocks.*)

CHRISTY (*clinging to* PEGEEN). Oh, glory! it's late for knocking, and this last while I'm in terror of the peelers, and the walking dead.

(*Knocking again.*)

PEGEEN. Who's there?

VOICE (*outside*). Me.

PEGEEN. Who's me?

VOICE. The Widow Quin.

PEGEEN (*jumping up and giving him the bread and milk*). Go on now with your supper, and let on to be sleepy, for if she found you were such a warrant to talk, she'd be stringing gabble till the dawn of day. (*He takes bread and sits shyly with his back to the door.*)

PEGEEN (*opening door, with temper*). What ails you, or what is it you're wanting at this hour of the night?

WIDOW QUIN (*coming in a step and peering at* CHRISTY). I'm after meeting Shawn Keogh and Father Reilly below, who told me of your curiosity man, and they fearing by this time he was maybe roaring, romping on your hands with drink.

PEGEEN (*pointing to* CHRISTY). Look now is he roaring, and he stretched away drowsy with his supper and his mug of milk. Walk down and tell that to Father Reilly and to Shaneen Keogh.

WIDOW QUIN (*coming forward*). I'll not see them again, for I've their word to lead that lad forward for to lodge with me.

PEGEEN (*in blank amazement*). This night, is it?

WIDOW QUIN (*going over*). This night. "It isn't fitting," says the priesteen, "to have his likeness lodging with an orphaned girl." (*To* CHRISTY) God save you, mister!

CHRISTY (*shyly*). God save you kindly.

WIDOW QUIN (*looking at him with half-amazed curiosity*). Well, aren't you a little smiling fellow? It should have been great and bitter torments did rouse your spirits to a deed of blood.

CHRISTY (*doubtfully*). It should, maybe.

WIDOW QUIN. It's more than "maybe" I'm saying, and it'd soften my heart to see you sitting so simple with your cup and cake, and you fitter to be saying your catechism than slaying your da.

PEGEEN (*at counter, washing glasses*). There's talking when any'd see he's fit to be holding his head high with the wonders of the world. Walk on from this, for I'll not have him tormented and he destroyed travelling since Tuesday was a week.

WIDOW QUIN (*peaceably*). We'll be walking surely when his supper's done, and you'll find we're great company, young fellow, when it's of the like of you and me you'd hear the penny poets singing in an August Fair.

CHRISTY (*innocently*). Did you kill your father?

PEGEEN (*contemptuously*). She did not. She hit himself with a worn pick, and the rusted poison did corrode his blood the way he never overed it, and died after. That was a sneaky kind of murder did win small glory with the boys itself. (*She crosses to* CHRISTY'S *left.*)

WIDOW QUIN (*with good-humour*). If it didn't, maybe all knows a widow woman has buried her children and destroyed her man is a wiser comrade for a young lad than a girl, the like of you, who'd go helter-skeltering after any man would let you a wink upon the road.

PEGEEN (*breaking out into wild rage*). And you'll say that, Widow Quin, and you gasping with the rage you had racing the hill beyond to look on his face.

WIDOW QUIN (*laughing derisively*). Me, is it? Well, Father Reilly has cuteness to divide you now. (*She pulls* CHRISTY *up*) There's great temptation in a man did slay his da, and we'd best be going, young fellow; so rise up and come with me.

PEGEEN (*seizing his arm*). He'll not stir. He's pot-boy in this place, and I'll not have him stolen off and kidnabbed while himself's abroad.

WIDOW QUIN. It'd be a crazy pot-boy'd lodge him in the shebeen where he works by day, so you'd have a right to come on, young fellow, till you see my little houseen, a perch off on the rising hill.

PEGEEN. Wait till morning, Christy Mahon. Wait till you lay eyes on her leaky thatch is growing more pasture for her buck goat than her square of fields, and she without a tramp itself to keep in order her place at all.

WIDOW QUIN. When you see me contriving in my little gardens, Christy Mahon, you'll swear the Lord God formed me to be living lone, and that there isn't my match in Mayo for thatching, or mowing, or shearing a sheep.

PEGEEN (*with noisy scorn*). It's true the Lord God formed you to contrive indeed. Doesn't the world know you reared a black lamb at your own breast, so that the Lord Bishop of Connaught felt the elements of a Christian, and he eating it after in a kidney stew? Doesn't the world know you've been seen shaving the foxy skipper from France for a three-penny bit and a sop of grass tobacco would wring the liver from a mountain goat you'd meet leaping the hills?

WIDOW QUIN (*with amusement*). Do you hear her now, young fellow? Do you hear the way she'll be rating at your own self when a week is by?

PEGEEN (*to* CHRISTY). Don't heed her. Tell her to go into her pigsty and not plague us here.

WIDOW QUIN. I'm going; but he'll come with me.

PEGEEN (*shaking him*). Are you dumb, young fellow?

CHRISTY (*timidly, to* WIDOW QUIN). God increase you; but I'm pot-boy in this place, and it's here I'd liefer stay.

PEGEEN (*triumphantly*). Now you have heard him, and go on from this.

WIDOW QUIN (*looking round the room*). It's lonesome this hour crossing the hill, and if he won't come along with me, I'd have a right maybe to stop this night with yourselves. Let me stretch out on the settle, Pegeen Mike; and himself can lie by the hearth.

PEGEEN (*short and fiercely*). Faith, I won't. Quit off or I will send you now.

WIDOW QUIN (*gathering her shawl up*). Well, it's a terror to be aged a score. (*To* CHRISTY) God bless you now, young fellow, and let you be wary, or there's right torment will await you here if you go romancing with her like, and she waiting only, as they bade me say, on a sheepskin parchment to be wed with Shawn Keogh of Killakeen.

CHRISTY (*going to* PEGEEN *as she bolts the door*). What's that she's after saying?

PEGEEN. Lies and blather, you've no call to mind. Well, isn't Shawn Keogh an impudent fellow to send up spying on me? Wait till I lay hands on him. Let him wait, I'm saying.

CHRISTY. And you're not wedding him at all?

PEGEEN. I wouldn't wed him if a bishop came walking for to join us here.

CHRISTY. That God in glory may be thanked for that.

PEGEEN. There's your bed now. I've put a quilt upon you I'm after quilting a while since with my own two hands, and you'd best stretch out now for your sleep, and may God give you a good rest till I call you in the morning when the cocks will crow.

CHRISTY (*as she goes to inner room*). May God and Mary and St. Patrick bless you and reward you, for your kindly talk. (*She shuts the door behind her. He settles his bed slowly, feeling the quilt with immense satisfaction*) Well, it's a clean bed and soft with it, and it's great luck and company I've won me in the end of time—two fine women fighting for the likes of me—till I'm thinking this night wasn't I a foolish fellow not to kill my father in the years gone by.

The Curtain Falls.

✤ Act II

SCENE, *as before. Brilliant morning light.* CHRISTY, *looking bright and cheerful, is cleaning a girl's boots.*

CHRISTY (*to himself, counting jugs on dresser*). Half a hundred beyond. Ten there. A score that's above. Eighty jugs. Six cups and a broken one. Two plates. A power of glasses. Bottles, a schoolmaster'd be hard set to count, and enough in them, I'm thinking, to drunken all the wealth and wisdom of the County Clare. (*He puts down the boot carefully*) There's her boots now, nice and decent for evening use, and isn't it grand brushes she has? (*He puts them down and goes by degrees to the looking-glass*) Well, this'd be a fine place to be my whole life talking out with swearing Christians, in place of my old dogs and cat, and I stalking around, smoking my pipe and drinking my fill, and never a day's work but drawing a cork an odd time, or wiping a glass, or rinsing out a shiny tumbler for a decent man. (*He takes the looking-glass from the wall and puts it on the back of a chair; then sits down in front of it and begins washing his face*) Didn't I know rightly I was handsome, though it was the divil's own mirror we had beyond, would twist a squint across an angel's brow; and I'll be growing fine from this day, the way I'll have a soft lovely skin on me and won't be the like of the clumsy young fellows do be ploughing all times in the earth and dung. (*He starts*) Is she coming again? (*He looks out*) Stranger girls. God help me, where'll I hide myself away and my long neck naked to the world? (*He looks out*) I'd best go to the room maybe till I'm dressed again. (*He gathers up his coat and the looking-glass, and runs into the inner room. The door is pushed open, and* SUSAN BRADY *looks in, and knocks on door.*)

SUSAN. There's nobody in it. (*Knocks again*)

NELLY (*pushing her in and following her, with* HONOR BLAKE *and* SARA TANSEY). It'd be early for them both to be out walking the hill.

SUSAN. I'm thinking Shawn Keogh was making game of us and there's no such man in it at all.

HONOR (*pointing to straw and quilt*). Look at that. He's been sleeping there in the night. Well, it'll be a hard case if he's gone off now, the way we'll never set eyes on a man killed his father, and we after rising early and destroying ourselves running fast on the hill.

NELLY. Are you thinking them's his boots?

SARA (*taking them up*). If they are, there should be his father's track on them. Did you never read in the papers the way murdered men do bleed and drip?

SUSAN. Is that blood there, Sara Tansey?

SARA (*smelling it*). That's bog water, I'm thinking, but it's his own they are surely, for I never seen the like of them for whity mud, and red mud, and turf on them, and the fine sands of the sea. That man's been walking, I'm telling you. (*She goes down right, putting on one of his boots.*)

SUSAN (*going to window*). Maybe he's stolen off to Belmullet with the boots of Michael James, and you'd have a right so to follow after him, Sara Tansey, and you the one yoked the ass cart and drove ten miles to set your eyes on the man bit the yellow lady's nostril on the northern shore. (*She looks out.*)

SARA (*running to window with one boot on*). Don't be talking, and we fooled to-day. (*Putting on other boot*) There's a pair do fit me well, and I'll be keeping them for walking to the priest, when you'd be ashamed this place, going up winter and summer with nothing worth while to confess at all.

HONOR (*who has been listening at the door*). Whisht! there's someone inside the room. (*She pushes door a chink open*) It's a man.

(SARA *kicks off boots and puts them where they were. They all stand in a line looking through chink.*)

SARA. I'll call him. Mister! Mister! (*He puts in his head*) Is Pegeen within?

CHRISTY (*coming in as meek as a mouse, with the looking-glass held behind his back*). She's above on the cnuceen, seeking the nanny-goats, the way she'd have a sup of goat's milk for to colour my tea.

SARA. And asking your pardon, is it you's the man killed his father?

CHRISTY (*sidling toward the nail where the glass was hanging*). I am, God help me!

SARA (*taking eggs she has brought*). Then my thousand welcomes to you, and I've run up with a brace of duck's eggs for your food today. Pegeen's ducks is no use, but these are the real rich sort. Hold out your hand and you'll see it's no lie I'm telling you.

CHRISTY (*coming forward shyly, and holding out his left hand*). They're a great and weighty size.

SUSAN. And I run up with a pat of butter, for it'd be a poor thing to have you eating your spuds dry, and you after running a great way since you did destroy your da.

CHRISTY. Thank you kindly.

HONOR. And I brought you a little cut of cake, for you should have a thin stomach on you, and you that length walking the world.

NELLY. And I brought you a little laying pullet—boiled and all she is—was crushed at the fall of night by the curate's car. Feel the fat of that breast, mister.

CHRISTY. It's bursting, surely. (*He feels it with the back of his hand, in which he holds the presents.*)

SARA. Will you pinch it? Is your right hand too sacred for to use at all? (*She slips round behind him*) It's a glass he has. Well, I never seen to this day a man with a looking-glass held to his back. Them that kills their fathers is a vain lot surely.

(*Girls giggle.*)

CHRISTY (*smiling innocently and piling presents on glass*). I'm very thankful to you all today. . . .

WIDOW QUIN (*coming in quickly, at door*). Sara Tansey, Susan Brady, Honor Blake! What in glory has you here at this hour of day?

GIRLS (*giggling*). That's the man killed his father.

WIDOW QUIN (*coming to them*). I know well it's the man; and I'm after putting him down in the sports below for racing, leaping, pitching, and the Lord knows what.

SARA (*exuberantly*). That's right, Widow Quin. I'll bet my dowry that he'll lick the world.

WIDOW QUIN. If you will, you'd have a right to have him fresh and nourished in place of nursing a feast. (*Taking presents*) Are you fasting or fed, young fellow?

CHRISTY. Fasting, if you please.

WIDOW QUIN (*loudly*). Well, you're the lot. Stir up now and give him his breakfast. (*To* CHRISTY) Come here to me (*she puts him on bench beside her while the girls make tea and get his breakfast*) and let you tell us your story before Pegeen will come, in place of grinning your ears off like the moon of May.

CHRISTY (*beginning to be pleased*). It's a long story; you'd be destroyed listening.

WIDOW QUIN. Don't be letting on to be shy, a fine, gamey, treacherous lad the like of you. Was it in your house beyond you cracked his skull?

CHRISTY (*shy but flattered*). It was not. We were digging spuds in his cold, sloping, stony, divil's patch of a field.

WIDOW QUIN. And you went asking money of him, or making talk of getting a wife would drive him from his farm?

CHRISTY. I did not, then; but there I was, digging and digging, and "You squinting idiot," says he, "let you walk down now and tell the priest you'll wed the Widow Casey in a score of days."

WIDOW QUIN. And what kind was she?

CHRISTY (*with horror*). A walking terror from beyond the hills, and she two score and five years, and two hundred-weights and five pounds in the weighing scales, with a limping leg on her, and a blinded eye, and she a woman of noted misbehavior with the old and young.

GIRLS (*clustering round him, serving him*). Glory be.

WIDOW QUIN. And what did he want driving you to wed with her? (*She takes a bit of the chicken.*)

CHRISTY (*eating with growing satisfaction*). He was letting on I was wanting a protector from the harshness of the world, and he without a thought the whole while but how he'd have her hut to live in and her gold to drink.

WIDOW QUIN. There's maybe worse than a dry hearth and a widow woman and your glass at night. So you hit him then?

CHRISTY (*getting almost excited*). I did not. "I won't wed her," says I, "when all know she did suckle me for six weeks when I came into the world, and she a hag this day with a tongue on her has the crows and seabirds scattered, the way they would cast a shadow on her garden with the dread of her curse."

WIDOW QUIN (*teasingly*). That one should be right company.

SARA (*eagerly*). Don't mind her. Did you kill him then?

CHRISTY. "She's too good for the like of you," says he, "and go on now or I'll flatten you out like a crawling beast has passed under a dray." "You will not if I can help it," says I. "Go on," says he, "or I'll have the divil making garters of your limbs tonight." "You will not if I can help it," says I. (*He sits up, brandishing his mug.*)

SARA. You were right surely.

CHRISTY (*impressively*). With that the sun came out between the cloud and the hill, and it shining green in my face. "God have mercy on your soul," says he, lifting a scythe; "or on your own," says I, raising the loy.

SUSAN. That's a grand story.

HONOR. He tells it lovely.

CHRISTY (*flattered and confident, waving bone*). He gave a drive with the scythe, and I gave a lep to the east. Then I turned around with my back to the north, and I hit a blow on the ridge of his skull, laid him stretched out, and he split to the knob of his gullet. (*He raises the chicken bone to his Adam's apple.*)

GIRLS (*together*). Well, you're a marvel! Oh, God bless you! You're the lad surely!

SUSAN. I'm thinking the Lord God sent him this road to make a second husband to the Widow Quin, and she with a great yearning to be wedded, though all dread her here. Lift him on her knee, Sara Tansey.

WIDOW QUIN. Don't tease him.

SARA (*going over to dresser and counter very quickly, and getting two glasses and porter*). You're heroes surely, and let you drink a supeen with your arms linked like the outlandish lovers in the sailor's song. (*She links their arms and gives them the glasses*) There now. Drink a health to the wonders of the western world, the pirates, preachers, poteenmakers, with the jobbing jockies; parching peelers, and the juries fill their stomachs selling judgments of the English law. (*Brandishing the bottle.*)

WIDOW QUIN. That's a right toast, Sara Tansey. Now, Christy.

(*They drink with their arms linked, he drinking with his left hand, she with her right. As they are drinking,* PEGEEN MIKE *comes in with a milk can and stands aghast. They all spring away from* CHRISTY. *He goes down left.* WIDOW QUIN *remains seated.*)

PEGEEN (*angrily, to* SARA). What is it you're wanting?

SARA (*twisting her apron*). An ounce of tobacco.

PEGEEN. Have you tuppence?

SARA. I've forgotten my purse.

PEGEEN. Then you'd best be getting it and not fooling us here. (*To the* WIDOW QUIN, *with more elaborate scorn*) And what is it you're wanting, Widow Quin?

WIDOW QUIN (*insolently*). A penn'orth of starch.

PEGEEN (*breaking out*). And you without a white shift or a shirt in your whole family since the drying of the flood. I've no starch for the like of you, and let you walk on now to Killamuck.

WIDOW QUIN (*turning to* CHRISTY, *as she goes out with the girls*). Well, you're mighty huffy this day, Pegeen Mike, and, you young fellow, let you not forget the sports and racing when the noon is by.

(*They go out.*)

PEGEEN (*imperiously*). Fling out that rubbish and put them cups away. (CHRISTY *tidies away in great haste*) Shove in the bench by the wall. (*He does so*) And hang that glass on the nail. What disturbed it at all?

CHRISTY (*very meekly*). I was making myself decent only, and this a fine country for young lovely girls.

PEGEEN (*sharply*). Whisht your talking of girls. (*Goes to counter—right.*)

CHRISTY. Wouldn't any wish to be decent in a place. . . .

PEGEEN. Whisht I'm saying.

CHRISTY (*looks at her face for a moment with great misgivings, then as a last effort, takes up a loy, and goes towards her, with feigned assurance*). It was with a loy the like of that I killed my father.

PEGEEN (*still sharply*). You've told me that story six times since the dawn of day.

CHRISTY (*reproachfully*). It's a queer thing you wouldn't care to be hearing it and them girls after walking four miles to be listening to me now.

PEGEEN (*turning around astonished*). Four miles.

CHRISTY (*apologetically*). Didn't himself say there were only four bona fides living in the place?

PEGEEN. It's bona fides by the road they are, but that lot came over the river lepping the stones. It's not three perches when you go like that, and I was down this morning looking on the papers the postboy does have in his bag. (*With meaning and emphasis*) For there was great news this day, Christopher Mahon. (*She goes into room left.*)

CHRISTY (*suspiciously*). Is it news of my murder?

PEGEEN (*inside*). Murder, indeed.

CHRISTY (*loudly*). A murdered da?

PEGEEN (*coming in again and crossing right*). There was not, but a story filled half a page of the hanging of a man. Ah, that should be a fearful end, young fellow, and it worst of all for a man who destroyed his da, for the like of him would get small mercies, and when it's dead he is, they'd put him in a narrow grave, with cheap sacking wrapping him round, and pour down quicklime on his head, the way you'd see a woman pouring any frish-frash from a cup.

CHRISTY (*very miserably*). Oh, God help me. Are you thinking I'm safe? You were saying at the fall of night, I was shut of jeopardy and I here with yourselves.

PEGEEN (*severely*). You'll be shut of jeopardy in no place if you go talking with a pack of wild girls the like of them do be walking abroad with the peelers, talking whispers at the fall of night.

CHRISTY (*with terror*). And you're thinking they'd tell?

PEGEEN (*with mock sympathy*). Who knows, God help you.

CHRISTY (*loudly*). What joy would they have to bring hanging to the likes of me?

PEGEEN. It's queer joys they have, and who knows the thing they'd do, if it'd make the green stones cry itself to think of you swaying and swiggling at the butt of a rope, and you with a fine, stout neck, God bless you! the way you'd be a half an hour, in great anguish, getting your death.

CHRISTY (*getting his boots and putting them on*). If there's that terror of them, it'd be best, maybe, I went on wandering like Esau or Cain and Abel on the other sides of Neifin or the Erris plain.

PEGEEN (*beginning to play with him*). It would, maybe, for I've heard the Circuit Judges this place is a heartless crew.

CHRISTY (*bitterly*). It's more than Judges this place is a heartless crew. (*Looking up at her*) And isn't it a poor thing to be starting again and I a lonesome fellow will be looking out on women and girls the way the needy fallen spirits do be looking on the Lord?

PEGEEN. What call have you to be that lonesome when there's poor girls walking Mayo in their thousands now?

CHRISTY (*grimly*). It's well you know what call I have. It's well you know it's a lonesome thing to be passing small towns with the lights shining sideways when the night is down, or going in strange places with a dog noising before you and a dog noising behind, or drawn to the cities where you'd hear a voice kissing and talking deep love in every shadow of the ditch, and you passing on with an empty, hungry stomach failing from your heart.

PEGEEN. I'm thinking you're an odd man, Christy Mahon. The oddest walking fellow I ever set my eyes on to this hour today.

CHRISTY. What would any be but odd men and they living lonesome in the world?

PEGEEN. I'm not odd, and I'm my whole life with my father only.

CHRISTY (*with infinite admiration*). How would a lovely handsome woman the like of you be lonesome when all men should be thronging around to hear the sweetness of your voice, and the little infant children should be pestering your steps I'm thinking, and you walking the roads.

PEGEEN. I'm hard set to know what way a coaxing fellow the like of yourself should be lonesome either.

CHRISTY. Coaxing?

PEGEEN. Would you have me think a man never talked with the girls would have the words you've spoken today? It's only letting on you are to be lonesome, the way you'd get around me now.

CHRISTY. I wish to God I was letting

on; but I was lonesome all times, and born lonesome, I'm thinking, as the moon of dawn. (*Going to door.*)

PEGEEN (*puzzled by his talk*). Well, it's a story I'm not understanding at all why you'd be worse than another, Christy Mahon, and you a fine lad with the great savagery to destroy your da.

CHRISTY. It's little I'm understanding myself, saving only that my heart's scalded this day, and I am going off stretching out the earth between us, the way I'll not be walking near you another dawn of the year till the two of us do arise to hope or judgment with the saints of God, and now I'd best be going with my wattle in my hand, for hanging is a poor thing (*turning to go*), and it's little welcome only is left me in this house today.

PEGEEN (*sharply*). Christy! (*He turns round*) Come here to me. (*He goes towards her*) Lay down that switch and throw some sods on the fire. You're potboy in this place, and I'll not have you mitch off from us now.

CHRISTY. You were saying I'd be hanged if I stay.

PEGEEN (*quite kindly at last*). I'm after going down and reading the fearful crimes of Ireland for two weeks or three, and there wasn't a word of your murder. (*Getting up and going over to the counter*) They've likely not found the body. You're safe so with ourselves.

CHRISTY (*astonished, slowly*). It's making game of me you were (*following her with fearful joy*), and I can stay so, working at your side, and I not lonesome from this mortal day.

PEGEEN. What's to hinder you from staying, except the widow woman or the young girls would inveigle you off?

CHRISTY (*with rapture*). And I'll have your words from this day filling my ears, and that look is come upon you meeting my two eyes, and I watching you loafing around in the warm sun, or rinsing your ankles when the night is come.

PEGEEN (*kindly, but a little embarrassed*). I'm thinking you'll be a loyal young lad to have working around, and if you vexed me a while since with your leaguing with the girls, I wouldn't give a thraneen for a lad hadn't a mighty spirit in him and a gamey heart.

(SHAWN KEOGH *runs in carrying a cleeve on his back, followed by the* WIDOW QUIN.)

SHAWN (*to* PEGEEN). I was passing below, and I seen your mountainy sheep eating cabbages in Jimmy's field. Run up or they'll be bursting surely.

PEGEEN. Oh, God mend them! (*She puts a shawl over her head and runs out.*)

CHRISTY (*looking from one to the other, still in high spirits*). I'd best go to her aid maybe. I'm handy with ewes.

WIDOW QUIN (*closing the door*). She can do that much, and there is Shaneen has long speeches for to tell you now. (*She sits down with an amused smile.*)

SHAWN (*taking something from his pocket and offering it to* CHRISTY). Do you see that, mister?

CHRISTY (*looking at it*). The half of a ticket to the Western States!

SHAWN (*trembling with anxiety*). I'll give it to you and my new hat (*pulling it out of hamper*); and my breeches with the double seat (*pulling it off*); and my new coat is woven from the blackest shearings for three miles around (*giving him the coat*); I'll give you the whole of them, and my blessing, and the blessing of Father Reilly itself, maybe, if you'll quit from this and leave us in the peace we had till last night at the fall of dark.

CHRISTY (*with a new arrogance*). And for what is it you're wanting to get shut of me?

SHAWN (*looking to the* WIDOW *for help*). I'm a poor scholar with middling faculties to coin a lie, so I'll tell you the truth, Christy Mahon. I'm wedding with Pegeen beyond, and I don't think well of having a clever fearless man the like of you dwelling in her house.

CHRISTY (*almost pugnaciously*). And you'd be using bribery for to banish me?

SHAWN (*in an imploring voice*). Let you not take it badly, mister honey, isn't beyond the best place for you where you'll have golden chains and shiny coats and you riding upon hunters with the ladies of the land? (*He makes an eager sign to the* WIDOW QUIN *to come to help him.*)

WIDOW QUIN (*coming over*). It's true for him, and you'd best quit off and not have that poor girl setting her mind on you, for there's Shaneen thinks she wouldn't suit you though all is saying that she'll wed you now.

(CHRISTY *beams with delight.*)

SHAWN (*in terrified earnest*). She wouldn't suit you, and she with the divil's own temper the way you'd be strangling one another in a score of days. (*He makes the movement of strangling with his hands*) It's the like of me only that she's fit for, a quiet simple fellow wouldn't raise a hand upon her if she scratched itself.

WIDOW QUIN (*putting SHAWN's hat on CHRISTY*). Fit them clothes on you anyhow, young fellow, and he'd maybe loan them to you for the sports. (*Pushing him towards inner door*) Fit them on and you can give your answer when you have them tried.

CHRISTY (*beaming, delighted with the clothes*). I will then. I'd like herself to see me in them tweeds and hat. (*He goes into room and shuts the door.*)

SHAWN (*in great anxiety*). He'd like herself to see them. He'll not leave us, Widow Quin. He's a score of divils in him the way it's well nigh certain he will wed Pegeen.

WIDOW QUIN (*jeeringly*). It's true all girls are fond of courage and do hate the like of you.

SHAWN (*walking about in desperation*). Oh, Widow Quin, what'll I be doing now? I'd inform again him, but he'd burst from Kilmainham and he'd be sure and certain to destroy me. If I wasn't so God-fearing, I'd near have courage to come behind him and run a pike into his side. Oh, it's a hard case to be an orphan and not to have your father that you're used to, and you'd easy kill and make yourself a hero in the sight of all. (*Coming up to her*) Oh, Widow Quin, will you find me some contrivance when I've promised you a ewe?

WIDOW QUIN. A ewe's a small thing, but what would you give me if I did wed him and did save you so?

SHAWN (*with astonishment*). You?

WIDOW QUIN. Aye. Would you give me the red cow you have and the mountainy ram, and the right of way across your rye path, and a load of dung at Michaelmas, and turbary upon the western hill?

SHAWN (*radiant with hope*). I would surely, and I'd give you the wedding-ring I have, and the loan of a new suit, the way you'd have him decent on the wedding-day. I'd give you two kids for your dinner, and a gallon of poteen, and I'd call the piper on the long car to your wedding from Crossmolina or from Ballina. I'd give you. . . .

WIDOW QUIN. That'll do so, and let you whisht, for he's coming now again.

(CHRISTY *comes in very natty in the new clothes.* WIDOW QUIN *goes to him admiringly.*)

WIDOW QUIN. If you seen yourself now, I'm thinking you'd be too proud to speak to us at all, and it'd be a pity surely to have your like sailing from Mayo to the Western World.

CHRISTY (*as proud as a peacock*). I'm not going. If this is a poor place itself, I'll make myself contented to be lodging here.

(WIDOW QUIN *makes a sign to SHAWN to leave them.*)

SHAWN. Well, I'm going measuring the race-course while the tide is low, so I'll leave you the garments and my blessing for the sports today. God bless you! (*He wriggles out.*)

WIDOW QUIN (*admiring CHRISTY*). Well, you're mighty spruce, young fellow. Sit down now while you're quiet till you talk with me.

CHRISTY (*swaggering*). I'm going abroad on the hillside for to seek Pegeen.

WIDOW QUIN. You'll have time and plenty for to seek Pegeen, and you heard me saying at the fall of night the two of us should be great company.

CHRISTY. From this out I'll have no want of company when all sorts is bringing me their food and clothing (*he swaggers to the door, tightening his belt*), the way they'd set their eyes upon a gallant orphan cleft his father with one blow to the breeches belt. (*He opens door, then staggers back*) Saints of glory! Holy angels from the throne of light!

WIDOW QUIN (*going over*). What ails you?

CHRISTY. It's the walking spirit of my murdered da!

WIDOW QUIN (*looking out*). Is it that tramper?

CHRISTY (*wildly*). Where'll I hide my poor body from that ghost of hell?

(*The door is pushed open, and OLD MAHON appears on threshold. CHRISTY darts in behind door.*)

WIDOW QUIN (*in great amusement*). God save you, my poor man.

MAHON (*gruffly*). Did you see a young lad passing this way in the early morning or the fall of night?

WIDOW QUIN. You're a queer kind to walk in not saluting at all.

MAHON. Did you see the young lad?

WIDOW QUIN (*stiffly*). What kind was he?

MAHON. An ugly young streeler with a murderous gob on him, and a little switch in his hand. I met a tramper seen him coming this way at the fall of night.

WIDOW QUIN. There's harvest hundreds do be passing these days for the Sligo boat. For what is it you're wanting him, my poor man?

MAHON. I want to destroy him for breaking the head on me with the clout of a loy. (*He takes off a big hat, and shows his head in a mass of bandages and plaster, with some pride*) It was he did that, and amn't I a great wonder to think I've traced him ten days with that rent in my crown?

WIDOW QUIN (*taking his head in both hands and examining it with extreme delight*). That was a great blow. And who hit you? A robber maybe?

MAHON. It was my own son hit me, and he the divil a robber, or anything else, but a dirty, stuttering lout.

WIDOW QUIN (*letting go his skull and wiping her hands in her apron*). You'd best be wary of a mortified scalp, I think they call it, lepping around with that wound in the splendour of the sun. It was a bad blow surely, and you should have vexed him fearful to make him strike that gash in his da.

MAHON. Is it me?

WIDOW QUIN (*amusing herself*). Aye. And isn't it a great shame when the old and hardened do torment the young?

MAHON (*raging*). Torment him, it is? And I after holding out with the patience of a martyred saint till there's nothing but destruction on, and I'm driven out in my old age with none to aid me.

WIDOW QUIN (*greatly amused*). It's a sacred wonder the way that wickedness will spoil a man.

MAHON. My wickedness, is it? Amn't I after saying it is himself has me destroyed, and he a lier on walls, a talker of folly, a man you'd see stretched the half of the day in the brown ferns with his belly to the sun.

WIDOW QUIN. Not working at all?

MAHON. The divil a work, or if he did itself, you'd see him raising up a haystack like the stalk of a rush, or driving our last cow till he broke her leg at the hip, and when he wasn't at that he'd be fooling over little birds he had—finches and felts—or making mugs at his own self in the bit of a glass we had hung on the wall.

WIDOW QUIN (*looking at* CHRISTY). What way was he so foolish? It was running wild after the girls maybe?

MAHON (*with a shout of derision*). Running wild, is it? If he seen a red petticoat coming swinging over the hill, he'd be off to hide in the sticks, and you'd see him shooting out his sheep's eyes between the little twigs and the leaves, and his two ears rising like a hare looking out through a gap. Girls, indeed!

WIDOW QUIN. It was drink maybe?

MAHON. And he a poor fellow would get drunk on the smell of a pint. He'd a queer rotten stomach, I'm telling you, and when I gave him three pulls from my pipe a while since, he was taken with contortions till I had to send him in the ass cart to the females' nurse.

WIDOW QUIN (*clasping her hands*). Well, I never till this day heard tell of a man the like of that!

MAHON. I'd take a mighty oath you didn't surely, and wasn't he the laughing joke of every female woman where four baronies meet, the way the girls would stop their weeding if they seen him coming the road to let a roar at him, and call him the looney of Mahon's.

WIDOW QUIN. I'd give the world and all to see the like of him. What kind was he?

MAHON. A small, low fellow.

WIDOW QUIN. And dark?

MAHON. Dark and dirty.

WIDOW QUIN (*considering*). I'm thinking I seen him.

MAHON (*eagerly*). An ugly young blackguard.

WIDOW QUIN. A hideous, fearful villain, and the spit of you.

MAHON. What way is he fled?

WIDOW QUIN. Gone over the hills to catch a coasting steamer to the north or south.

MAHON. Could I pull up on him now?

WIDOW QUIN. If you'll cross the sands below where the tide is out, you'll be in it as soon as himself, for he had to go round ten miles by the top of the bay. (*She points to the door*) Strike down by the head beyond and then follow on the roadway to the north and east.

(MAHON *goes abruptly.*)

WIDOW QUIN (*shouting after him*). Let you give him a good vengeance when you come up with him, but don't put yourself in the power of the law, for it'd be a poor thing to see a judge in his black cap reading out his sentence on a civil warrior the like of you. (*She swings the door to and looks at* CHRISTY, *who is cowering in terror, for a moment, then she bursts into a laugh.*)

WIDOW QUIN. Well, you're the walking Playboy of the Western World, and that's the poor man you had divided to his breeches belt.

CHRISTY (*looking out: then, to her*). What'll Pegeen say when she hears that story? What'll she be saying to me now?

WIDOW QUIN. She'll knock the head of you, I'm thinking, and drive you from the door. God help her to be taking you for a wonder, and you a little schemer making up the story you destroyed your da.

CHRISTY (*turning to the door, nearly speechless with rage, half to himself*). To be letting on he was dead, and coming back to his life, and following after me like an old weasel tracing a rat, and coming in here laying desolation between my own self and the fine women of Ireland, and he a kind of carcase that you'd fling upon the sea . . .

WIDOW QUIN (*more soberly*). There's talking for a man's one only son.

CHRISTY (*breaking out*). His one son, is it? May I meet him with one tooth and it aching, and one eye to be seeing seven and seventy divils in the twists of the road, and one old timber leg on him to limp into the scalding grave. (*Looking out*) There he is now crossing the strands, and that the Lord God would send a high wave to wash him from the world.

WIDOW QUIN (*scandalized*). Have you no shame? (*Putting her hand on his shoulder and turning him round*) What ails you? Near crying, is it?

CHRISTY (*in despair and grief*). Amn't I after seeing the lovelight of the star of knowledge shining from her brow, and hearing words would put you thinking on the holy Brigid speaking to the infant saints, and now she'll be turning again, and speaking hard words to me, like an old woman with a spavindy ass she'd have, urging on a hill.

WIDOW QUIN. There's poetry talk for a girl you'd see itching and scratching, and she with a stale stink of poteen on her from selling in the shop.

CHRISTY (*impatiently*). It's her like is fitted to be handling merchandise in the heavens above, and what'll I be doing now, I ask you, and I a kind of wonder was jilted by the heavens when a day was by.

(*There is a distant noise of girls' voices.* WIDOW QUIN *looks from window and comes to him, hurriedly.*)

WIDOW QUIN. You'll be doing like myself, I'm thinking, when I did destroy my man, for I'm above many's the day, odd times in great spirits, abroad in the sunshine, darning a stocking or stitching a shift; and odd times again looking out on the schooners, hookers, trawlers is sailing the sea, and I thinking on the gallant hairy fellows are drifting beyond, and myself long years living alone.

CHRISTY (*interested*). You're like me, so.

WIDOW QUIN. I am your like, and it's for that I'm taking a fancy to you, and I with my little houseen above where there'd be myself to tend you, and none to ask were you a murderer or what at all.

CHRISTY. And what would I be doing if I left Pegeen?

WIDOW QUIN. I've nice jobs you could be doing, gathering shells to make a whitewash for our hut within, building up a little goose-house, or stretching a new skin on an old curragh I have, and if my hut is far from all sides, it's there you'll meet the wisest old men, I tell you, at the corner of my wheel, and it's there yourself and me will have great times whispering and hugging. . . .

VOICES (*outside, calling far away*). Christy! Christy Mahon! Christy!

CHRISTY. Is it Pegeen Mike?

WIDOW QUIN. It's the young girls, I'm thinking, coming to bring you to the sports below, and what is it you'll have me to tell them now?

CHRISTY. Aid me for to win Pegeen. It's herself only that I'm seeking now. (WIDOW QUIN *gets up and goes to window*) Aid me for to win her, and I'll be asking God to stretch a hand to you in the hour of death, and lead you short cuts through the Meadows of Ease, and up the floor of Heaven to the Footstool of the Virgin's Son.

WIDOW QUIN. There's praying.

VOICES (*nearer*). Christy! Christy Mahon!

CHRISTY (*with agitation*). They're coming. Will you swear to aid and save me for the love of Christ?

WIDOW QUIN (*looks at him for a moment*). If I aid you, will you swear to give me a right of way I want, and a mountainy ram, and a load of dung at Michaelmas, the time that you'll be master here?

CHRISTY. I will, by the elements and stars of night.

WIDOW QUIN. Then we'll not say a word of the old fellow, the way Pegeen won't know your story till the end of time.

CHRISTY. And if he chances to return again?

WIDOW QUIN. We'll swear he's a maniac and not your da. I could take an oath I seen him raving on the sands today.

(*Girls run in.*)

SUSAN. Come on to the sports below. Pegeen says you're to come.

SARA TANSEY. The lepping's beginning, and we've a jockey's suit to fit upon you for the mule race on the sands below.

HONOR. Come on, will you?

CHRISTY. I will then if Pegeen's beyond.

SARA TANSEY. She's in the boreen making game of Shaneen Keogh.

CHRISTY. Then I'll be going to her now. (*He runs out, followed by the girls.*)

WIDOW QUIN. Well, if the worst comes in the end of all, it'll be great game to see there's none to pity him but a widow woman, the like of me, has buried her children and destroyed her man. (*She goes out.*)

The Curtain Falls.

Act III

SCENE, *as before. Later in the day.* JIMMY *comes in, slightly drunk.*

JIMMY (*calls*). Pegeen! (*Crosses to inner door*) Pegeen Mike! (*Comes back again into the room*) Pegeen! (PHILLY *comes in in the same state*) (*To* PHILLY) Did you see herself?

PHILLY. I did not; but I sent Shawn Keogh with the ass cart for to bear him home. (*Trying cupboards, which are locked*) Well, isn't he a nasty man to get into such staggers at a morning wake? and isn't herself the divil's daughter for locking, and she so fussy after that young gaffer, you might take your death with drought and none to heed you?

JIMMY. It's little wonder she'd be fussy, and he after bringing bankrupt ruin on the roulette man, and the trick-o'-the-loop man, and breaking the nose of the cockshot-man, and winning all in the sports below, racing, lepping, dancing, and the Lord knows what! He's right luck, I'm telling you.

PHILLY. If he has, he'll be rightly hobbled yet, and he not able to say ten words without making a brag of the way he killed his father, and the great blow he hit with the loy.

JIMMY. A man can't hang by his own informing, and his father should be rotten by now.

(OLD MAHON *passes window slowly.*)

PHILLY. Supposing a man's digging spuds in that field with a long spade, and supposing he flings up the two halves of that skull, what'll be said then in the papers and the courts of law?

JIMMY. They'd say it was an old Dane, maybe, was drowned in the flood. (OLD MAHON *comes in and sits down near door listening*) Did you never hear tell of the skulls they have in the city of Dublin, ranged out like blue jugs in a cabin of Connaught?

PHILLY. And you believe that?

JIMMY (*pugnaciously*). Didn't a lad see them and he after coming from harvesting in the Liverpool boat? "They have them there," says he, "making a show of the great people there was one time walking the world. White skulls and black skulls and yellow skulls, and some with full teeth, and some haven't only but one."

PHILLY. It was no lie, maybe, for when I was a young lad there was a graveyard beyond the house with the remnants of a man who had thighs as long as your arm. He was a horrid man, I'm telling you, and there was many a fine Sunday I'd put him together for fun, and he with shiny bones, you wouldn't meet the like of these days in the cities of the world.

MAHON (*getting up*). You wouldn't, is it? Lay your eyes on that skull, and tell me where and when there was another the like of it, is splintered only from the blow of a loy.

PHILLY. Glory be to God! And who hit you at all?

MAHON (*triumphantly*). It was my own son hit me. Would you believe that?

JIMMY. Well, there's wonders hidden in the heart of man!

PHILLY (*suspiciously*). And what way was it done?

MAHON (*wandering about the room*). I'm after walking hundreds and long scores of miles, winning clean beds and the fill of my belly four times in the day, and I doing nothing but telling stories of that naked truth. (*He comes to them a little aggressively*) Give me a supeen and I'll tell you now.

(WIDOW QUIN *comes in and stands aghast behind him. He is facing* JIMMY *and* PHILLY, *who are on the left.*)

JIMMY. Ask herself beyond. She's the stuff hidden in her shawl.

WIDOW QUIN (*coming to* MAHON *quickly*). You here, is it? You didn't go far at all?

MAHON. I seen the coasting steamer passing, and I got a drought upon me and a cramping leg, so I said, "The divil go along with him," and turned again. (*Looking under her shawl*) And let you give me a supeen, for I'm destroyed travelling since Tuesday was a week.

WIDOW QUIN (*getting a glass, in a cajoling tone*). Sit down then by the fire and take your ease for a space. You've a right to be destroyed indeed, with your walking, and fighting, and facing the sun. (*Giving him poteen from a stone jar she has brought in*) There now is a drink for you, and may it be to your happiness and length of life.

MAHON (*taking glass greedily and sitting down by fire*). God increase you!

WIDOW QUIN (*taking men to the right stealthily*). Do you know what? That man's raving from his wound today, for I met him a while since telling a rambling tale of a tinker had him destroyed. Then he heard of Christy's deed, and he up and says it was his son had cracked his skull. O isn't madness a fright, for he'll go killing someone yet, and he thinking it's the man has struck him so?

JIMMY (*entirely convinced*). It's a fright, surely. I knew a party was kicked in the head by a red mare, and he went killing horses a great while, till he eat the insides of a clock and died after.

PHILLY (*with suspicion*). Did he see Christy?

WIDOW QUIN. He didn't. (*With a warning gesture*) Let you not be putting him in mind of him, or you'll be likely summoned if there's murder done. (*Looking round at* MAHON) Whisht! He's listening. Wait now till you hear me taking him easy and unravelling all. (*She goes to* MAHON) And what way are you feeling, mister? Are you in contentment now?

MAHON (*slightly emotional from his drink*). I'm poorly only, for it's a hard story the way I'm left today, when it was I did tend him from his hour of birth, and he a dunce never reached his second book, the way he'd come from school, many's the day, with his legs lamed under him, and he blackened with his beatings like a tinker's ass. It's a hard story, I'm saying, the way some do have their next and nighest raising up a hand of murder on them, and some is lonesome getting their death with lamentation in the dead of night.

WIDOW QUIN (*not knowing what to say*). To hear you talking so quiet, who'd know you were the same fellow we seen pass today?

MAHON. I'm the same surely. The wrack and ruin of three score years; and it's a terror to live that length, I tell you, and to have your sons going to the dogs against you, and you wore out scolding them, and skelping them, and God knows what.

PHILLY (*to* JIMMY). He's not raving. (*To* WIDOW QUIN) Will you ask him what kind was his son?

WIDOW QUIN (*to* MAHON, *with a peculiar look*). Was your son that hit you a lad of one year and a score maybe, a great hand at racing and lepping and licking the world?

MAHON (*turning on her with a roar of rage*). Didn't you hear me say he was the fool of men, the way from this out he'll know the orphan's lot with old and young making game of him and they swearing, raging, kicking at him like a mangy cur.

(*A great burst of cheering outside, some way off.*)

MAHON (*putting his hands to his ears*). What in the name of God do they want roaring below?

WIDOW QUIN (*with the shade of a smile*). They're cheering a young lad, the champion Playboy of the Western World.

(*More cheering.*)

MAHON (*going to window*). It'd split my heart to hear them, and I with pulses in my brain-pan for a week gone by. Is it racing they are?

JIMMY (*looking from door*). It is then. They are mounting him for the mule race will be run upon the sands. That's the playboy on the winkered mule.

MAHON (*puzzled*). That lad, is it? If you said it was a fool he was, I'd have laid a mighty oath he was the likeness of my wandering son. (*Uneasily, putting his hand to his head*) Faith, I'm thinking I'll go walking for to view the race.

WIDOW QUIN (*stopping him, sharply*). You will not. You'd best take the road to Belmullet, and not be dilly-dallying in this place where there isn't a spot you could sleep.

PHILLY (*coming forward*). Don't mind her. Mount there on the bench and you'll have a view of the whole. They're hurrying before the tide will rise, and it'd be near over if you went down the pathway through the crags below.

MAHON (*mounts on bench, WIDOW QUIN beside him*). That's a right view again the edge of the sea. They're coming now from the point. He's leading. Who is he at all?

WIDOW QUIN. He's the champion of the world, I tell you, and there isn't a hop'orth isn't falling lucky to his hands today.

PHILLY (*looking out, interested in the race*). Look at that. They're pressing him now.

JIMMY. He'll win it yet.

PHILLY. Take your time, Jimmy Farrell. It's too soon to say.

WIDOW QUIN (*shouting*). Watch him taking the gate. There's riding.

JIMMY (*cheering*). More power to the young lad!

MAHON. He's passing the third.

JIMMY. He'll lick them yet!

WIDOW QUIN. He'd lick them if he was running races with a score itself.

MAHON. Look at the mule he has, kicking the stars.

WIDOW QUIN. There was a lep! (*Catching hold of MAHON in her excitement*) He's fallen! He's mounted again! Faith, he's passing them all!

JIMMY. Look at him skelping her!

PHILLY. And the mountain girls hooshing him on!

JIMMY. It's the last turn! The post's cleared for them now!

MAHON. Look at the narrow place. He'll be into the bogs! (*With a yell*) Good rider! He's through it again!

JIMMY. He's neck and neck!

MAHON. Good boy to him! Flames, but he's in!

(*Great cheering, in which all join.*)

MAHON (*with hesitation*). What's that? They're raising him up. They're coming this way. (*With a roar of rage and astonishment*) It's Christy, by the stars of God! I'd know his way of spitting and he astride the moon.

(*He jumps down and makes for the door, but WIDOW QUIN catches him and pulls him back.*)

WIDOW QUIN. Stay quiet, will you? That's not your son. (*To JIMMY*) Stop him, or you'll get a month for the abetting of manslaughter and be fined as well.

JIMMY. I'll hold him.

MAHON (*struggling*). Let me out! Let me out, the lot of you, till I have my vengeance on his head today.

WIDOW QUIN (*shaking him, vehemently*). That's not your son. That's a man is going to make a marriage with the daughter of this house, a place with fine trade, with a license, and with poteen too.

MAHON (*amazed*). That man marrying a decent and a moneyed girl! Is it mad yous are? Is it in a crazy-house for females that I'm landed now?

WIDOW QUIN. It's mad yourself is with

the blow upon your head. That lad is the wonder of the Western World.

MAHON. I seen it's my son.

WIDOW QUIN. You seen that you're mad. (*Cheering outside*) Do you hear them cheering him in the zig-zags of the road? Aren't you after saying that your son's a fool, and how would they be cheering a true idiot born?

MAHON (*getting distressed*). It's maybe out of reason that that man's himself. (*Cheering again*) There's none surely will go cheering him. Oh, I'm raving with a madness that would fright the world! (*He sits down with his hand to his head*) There was one time I seen ten scarlet divils letting on they'd cork my spirit in a gallon can; and one time I seen rats as big as badgers sucking the life blood from the butt of my lug; but I never till this day confused that dribbling idiot with a likely man. I'm destroyed surely.

WIDOW QUIN. And who'd wonder when it's your brain-pan that is gaping now?

MAHON. Then the blight of the sacred drought upon myself and him, for I never went mad to this day, and I not three weeks with the Limerick girls drinking myself silly, and parlatic from the dusk to dawn. (*To* WIDOW QUIN, *suddenly*) Is my visage astray?

WIDOW QUIN. It is then. You're a sniggering maniac, a child could see.

MAHON (*getting up more cheerfully*). Then I'd best be going to the union beyond, and there'll be a welcome before me, I tell you (*with great pride*), and I a terrible and fearful case, the way that there I was one time, screeching in a straitened waistcoat, with seven doctors writing out my sayings in a printed book. Would you believe that?

WIDOW QUIN. If you're a wonder itself, you'd best be hasty, for them lads caught a maniac one time and pelted the poor creature till he ran out, raving and foaming, and was drowned in the sea.

MAHON (*with philosophy*). It's true mankind is the divil when your head's astray. Let me out now and I'll slip down the boreen, and not see them so.

WIDOW QUIN (*showing him out*). That's it. Run to the right, and not a one will see.

(*He runs off.*)

PHILLY (*wisely*). You're at some gaming, Widow Quin; but I'll walk after him and give him his dinner and a time to rest, and I'll see then if he's raving or as sane as you.

WIDOW QUIN (*annoyed*). If you go near that lad, let you be wary of your head, I'm saying. Didn't you hear him telling he was crazed at times?

PHILLY. I heard him telling a power; and I'm thinking we'll have right sport, before night will fall. (*He goes out.*)

JIMMY. Well, Philly's a conceited and foolish man. How could that madman have his senses and his brain-pan slit? I'll go after them and see him turn on Philly now.

(*He goes;* WIDOW QUIN *hides poteen behind counter. Then hubbub outside.*)

VOICES. There you are! Good jumper! Grand lepper! Darlint boy! He's the racer! Bear him on, will you!

(CHRISTY *comes in, in jockey's dress, with* PEGEEN MIKE, SARA, *and other girls, and men.*)

PEGEEN (*to crowd*). Go on now and don't destroy him and he drenching with sweat. Go along, I'm saying, and have your tug-of-warring till he's dried his skin.

CROWD. Here's his prizes! A bagpipes! A fiddle was played by a poet in the years gone by! A flat and three-thorned blackthorn would lick the scholars out of Dublin town!

CHRISTY (*taking prizes from the men*). Thank you kindly, the lot of you. But you'd say it was little only I did this day if you'd seen me a while since striking my one single blow.

TOWN CRIER (*outside, ringing a bell*). Take notice, last event of this day! Tug-of-warring on the green below! Come on, the lot of you! Great achievement for all Mayo men!

PEGEEN. Go on, and leave him for to rest and dry. Go on, I tell you, for he'll do no more. (*She hustles crowd out;* WIDOW QUIN *following them.*)

MEN (*going*). Come on, then. Good luck for the while!

PEGEEN (*radiantly, wiping his face with her shawl*). Well, you're the lad, and you'll have great times from this out when you could win that wealth of prizes, and you sweating in the heat of noon!

CHRISTY (*looking at her with delight*). I'll have great times if I win the crowning prize I'm seeking now, and that's your promise that you'll wed me in a fortnight, when our banns is called.

PEGEEN (*backing away from him*). You've right daring to go ask me that, when all knows you'll be starting to some girl in your own townland, when your father's rotten in four months, or five.

CHRISTY (*indignantly*). Starting from you, is it? (*He follows her*) I will not, then, and when the airs is warming in four months, or five, it's then yourself and me should be pacing Neifin in the dews of night, the times sweet smells do be rising, and you'd see a little shiny new moon, maybe, sinking on the hills.

PEGEEN (*looking at him playfully*). And it's that kind of a poacher's love you'd make, Christy Mahon, on the sides of Neifin, when the night is down?

CHRISTY. It's little you'll think if my love's a poacher's, or an earl's itself, when you'll feel my two hands stretched around you, and I squeezing kisses on your puckered lips, till I'd feel a kind of pity for the Lord God in all ages sitting lonesome in his golden chair.

PEGEEN. That'll be right fun, Christy Mahon, and any girl would walk her heart out before she'd meet a young man was your like for eloquence, or talk, at all.

CHRISTY (*encouraged*). Let you wait, to hear me talking, till we're astray in Erris, when Good Friday's by, drinking a sup from a well, and making mighty kisses with our wetted mouths, or gaming in a gap of sunshine, with yourself stretched back unto your necklace, in the flowers of the earth.

PEGEEN (*in a lower voice, moved by his tone*). I'd be nice so, is it?

CHRISTY (*with rapture*). If the mitred bishops seen you that time, they'd be the like of the holy prophets, I'm thinking, do be straining the bars of Paradise to lay eyes on the Lady Helen of Troy, and she abroad, pacing back and forward, with a nosegay in her golden shawl.

PEGEEN (*with real tenderness*). And what is it I have, Christy Mahon, to make me fitting entertainment for the like of you, that has such poet's talking, and such bravery of heart?

CHRISTY (*in a low voice*). Isn't there the light of seven heavens in your heart alone, the way you'll be an angel's lamp to me from this out, and I abroad in the darkness, spearing salmons in the Owens, or the Carrowmore?

PEGEEN. If I was your wife, I'd be along with you those nights, Christy Mahon, the way you'd see I was a great hand at coaxing bailiffs, or coining funny nick-names for the stars of night.

CHRISTY. You, is it? Taking your death in the hailstones, or in the fogs of dawn.

PEGEEN. Yourself and me would shelter easy in a narrow bush, (*with a qualm of dread*) but we're only talking, maybe, for this would be a poor, thatched place to hold a fine lad is the like of you.

CHRISTY (*putting his arm around her*). If I wasn't a good Christian, it's on my naked knees I'd be saying my prayers and paters to every jackstraw you have roofing your head, and every stony pebble is paving the laneway to your door.

PEGEEN (*radiantly*). If that's the truth, I'll be burning candles from this out to the miracles of God that have brought you from the south today, and I, with my gowns bought ready, the way that I can wed you, and not wait at all.

CHRISTY. It's miracles, and that's the truth. Me there toiling a long while, and walking a long while, not knowing at all I was drawing all times nearer to this holy day.

PEGEEN. And myself, a girl, was tempted often to go sailing the seas till I'd marry a Jew-man, with ten kegs of gold, and I not knowing at all there was the like of you drawing nearer, like the stars of God.

CHRISTY. And to think I'm long years hearing women talking that talk, to all bloody fools, and this the first time I've heard the like of your voice talking sweetly for my own delight.

PEGEEN. And to think it's me is talking sweetly, Christy Mahon, and I the fright of seven townlands for my biting tongue. Well, the heart's a wonder; and, I'm thinking, there won't be our like in Mayo, for gallant lovers, from this hour, today. (*Drunken singing is heard outside*) There's my father coming from the wake, and when he's had his sleep we'll tell him, for he's peaceful then.

(*They separate.*)

MICHAEL (*singing outside*).
The jailor and the turnkey
    They quickly ran us down,
And brought us back as prisoners

Once more to Cavan town.

(*He comes in supported by* SHAWN.)
There we lay bewailing
All in a prison bound. . . .

(*He sees* CHRISTY. *Goes and shakes
him drunkenly by the hand, while* PEGEEN
and SHAWN *talk on the left.*)

MICHAEL (*to* CHRISTY). The blessing
of God and the holy angels on your head,
young fellow. I hear tell you're after
winning all in the sports below; and
wasn't it a shame I didn't bear you along
with me to Kate Cassidy's wake, a fine,
stout lad, the like of you, for you'd never
see the match of it for flows of drink, the
way when we sunk her bones at noonday
in her narrow grave, there were five men,
aye, and six men, stretched out retching
speechless on the holy stones.

CHRISTY (*uneasily, watching* PEGEEN).
Is that the truth?

MICHAEL. It is then, and aren't you a
louty schemer to go burying your poor
father unbeknownst when you'd a right
to throw him on the crupper of a Kerry
mule and drive him westwards, like holy
Joseph in the days gone by, the way we
could have given him a decent burial,
and not have him rotting beyond, and
not a Christian drinking a smart drop to
the glory of his soul?

CHRISTY (*gruffly*). It's well enough
he's lying, for the likes of him.

MICHAEL (*slapping him on the back*).
Well, aren't you a hardened slayer? It'll
be a poor thing for the household man
where you go sniffing for a female wife;
and (*pointing to* SHAWN) look beyond
at that shy and decent Christian I have
chosen for my daughter's hand, and I
after getting the gilded dispensation this
day for to wed them now.

CHRISTY. And you'll be wedding them
this day, is it?

MICHAEL (*drawing himself up*). Aye.
Are you thinking, if I'm drunk itself, I'd
leave my daughter living single with a
little frisky rascal is the like of you?

PEGEEN (*breaking away from* SHAWN).
Is it the truth the dispensation's come?

MICHAEL (*triumphantly*). Father
Reilly's after reading it in gallous Latin,
and "It's come in the nick of time," says
he; "so I'll wed them in a hurry, dread-
ing that young gaffer who'd capsize the
stars."

PEGEEN (*fiercely*). He's missed his

nick of time, for it's that lad, Christy
Mahon, that I'm wedding now.

MICHAEL (*loudly, with horror*). You'd
be making him a son to me, and he wet
and crusted with his father's blood?

PEGEEN. Aye. Wouldn't it be a bitter
thing for a girl to go marrying the like
of Shaneen, and he a middling kind of a
scarecrow, with no savagery or fine words
in him at all?

MICHAEL (*gasping and sinking on a
chair*). Oh, aren't you a heathen daughter
to go shaking the fat of my heart, and I
swamped and drownded with the weight
of drink? Would you have them turning
on me the way that I'd be roaring to the
dawn of day with the wind upon my
heart? Have you not a word to aid me,
Shaneen? Are you not jealous at all?

SHAWN (*in great misery*). I'd be afeard
to be jealous of a man did slay his da.

PEGEEN. Well, it'd be a poor thing to
go marrying your like. I'm seeing there's
a world of peril for an orphan girl, and
isn't it a great blessing I didn't wed you,
before himself came walking from the
west or south?

SHAWN. It's a queer story you'd go
picking a dirty tramp up from the highways of the world.

PEGEEN (*playfully*). And you think
you're a likely beau to go straying along
with, the shiny Sundays of the opening
year, when it's sooner on a bullock's liver
you'd put a poor girl thinking than on
the lily or the rose?

SHAWN. And have you no mind of my
weight of passion, and the holy dispensation, and the drift of heifers I am giving,
and the golden ring?

PEGEEN. I'm thinking you're too fine
for the like of me, Shawn Keogh of
Killakeen, and let you go off till you'd
find a radiant lady with droves of bullocks
on the plains of Meath, and herself be-
dizened in the diamond jewelries of
Pharaoh's ma. That'd be your match,
Shaneen. So God save you now! (*She
retreats behind* CHRISTY.)

SHAWN. Won't you hear me telling
you . . . ?

CHRISTY (*with ferocity*). Take yourself
from this, young fellow, or I'll maybe
add a murder to my deeds today.

MICHAEL (*springing up with a shriek*).
Murder is it? Is it mad yous are? Would
you go making murder in this place, and

it piled with poteen for our drink to-night? Go on to the foreshore if it's fighting you want, where the rising tide will wash all traces from the memory of man. (*Pushing* SHAWN *towards* CHRISTY.)

SHAWN (*shaking himself free, and getting behind* MICHAEL). I'll not fight him, Michael James. I'd liefer live a bachelor, simmering in passions to the end of time, than face a lepping savage the like of him has descended from the Lord knows where. Strike him yourself, Michael James, or you'll lose my drift of heifers and my blue bull from Sneem.

MICHAEL. Is it me fight him, when it's father-slaying he's bred to now? (*Pushing* SHAWN) Go on, you fool, and fight him now.

SHAWN (*coming forward a little*). Will I strike him with my hand?

MICHAEL. Take the loy is on your western side.

SHAWN. I'd be afeard of the gallows if I struck him with that.

CHRISTY (*taking up the loy*). Then I'll make you face the gallows or quit off from this.

(SHAWN *flies out of the door.*)

CHRISTY. Well, fine weather be after him, (*going to* MICHAEL, *coaxingly*) and I'm thinking you wouldn't wish to have that quaking blackguard in your house at all. Let you give us your blessing and hear her swear her faith to me, for I'm mounted on the springtide of the stars of luck, the way it'll be good for any to have me in the house.

PEGEEN (*at the other side of* MICHAEL). Bless us now, for I swear to God I'll wed him, and I'll not renege.

MICHAEL (*standing up in the centre, holding on to both of them*). It's the will of God, I'm thinking, that all should win an easy or a cruel end, and it's the will of God that all should rear up lengthy families for the nurture of the earth. What's a single man, I ask you, eating a bit in one house and drinking a sup in another, and he with no place of his own, like an old braying jackass strayed upon the rocks? (*To* CHRISTY) It's many would be in dread to bring your like into their house for to end them, maybe, with a sudden end; but I'm a decent man of Ireland, and I liefer face the grave untimely and I seeing a score of grandsons growing up little gallant swearers by the name of

God, than go peopling my bedside with puny weeds the like of what you'd breed, I'm thinking, out of Shaneen Keogh. (*He joins their hands*) A daring fellow is the jewel of the world, and a man did split his father's middle with a single clout, should have the bravery of ten, so may God and Mary and St. Patrick bless you, and increase you from this mortal day.

CHRISTY *and* PEGEEN. Amen, O Lord! (*Hubbub outside.*)

(OLD MAHON *rushes in, followed by all the crowd, and* WIDOW QUIN. *He makes a rush at* CHRISTY, *knocks him down, and begins to beat him.*)

PEGEEN (*dragging back his arm*). Stop that, will you? Who are you at all?

MAHON. His father, God forgive me!

PEGEEN (*drawing back*). Is it rose from the dead?

MAHON. Do you think I look so easy quenched with the tap of a loy? (*Beats* CHRISTY *again.*)

PEGEEN (*glaring at* CHRISTY). And it's lies you told, letting on you had him slitted, and you nothing at all.

CHRISTY (*catching* MAHON's *stick*). He's not my father. He's a raving maniac would scare the world. (*Pointing to* WIDOW QUIN) Herself knows it's true.

CROWD. You're fooling Pegeen! The Widow Quin seen him this day, and you likely knew! You're a liar!

CHRISTY (*dumbfounded*). It's himself was a liar, lying stretched out with an open head on him, letting on he was dead.

MAHON. Weren't you off racing the hills before I got my breath with the start I had seeing you turn on me at all?

PEGEEN. And to think of the coaxing glory we had given him, and he after doing nothing but hitting a soft blow and chasing northward in a sweat of fear. Quit off from this.

CHRISTY (*piteously*). You've seen my doings this day, and let you save me from the old man; for why would you be in such a scorch of haste to spur me to destruction now?

PEGEEN. It's there your treachery is spurring me, till I'm hard set to think you're the one I'm after lacing in my heart-strings half-an-hour gone by. (*To* MAHON) Take him on from this, for I think bad the world should see me raging for a Munster liar, and the fool of men.

MAHON. Rise up now to retribution, and come on with me.

CROWD (*jeeringly*). There's the playboy! There's the lad thought he'd rule the roost in Mayo. Slate him now, mister.

CHRISTY (*getting up in shy terror*). What is it drives you to torment me here, when I'd asked the thunders of the might of God to blast me if I ever did hurt to any saving only that one single blow?

MAHON (*loudly*). If you didn't, you're a poor good-for-nothing, and isn't it by the like of you the sins of the whole world are committed?

CHRISTY (*raising his hands*). In the name of the Almighty God. . . .

MAHON. Leave troubling the Lord God. Would you have him sending down droughts, and fevers, and the old hen and the cholera morbus?

CHRISTY (*to* WIDOW QUIN). Will you come between us and protect me now?

WIDOW QUIN. I've tried a lot, God help me, and my share is done.

CHRISTY (*looking round in desperation*). And I must go back into my torment is it, or run off like a vagabond straying through the Unions with the dusts of August making mud-stains in the gullet of my throat, or the winds of March blowing on me till I'd take an oath I felt them making whistles of my ribs within?

SARA. Ask Pegeen to aid you. Her like does often change.

CHRISTY. I will not then, for there's torment in the splendour of her like, and she a girl any moon of midnight would take pride to meet, facing southwards on the heaths of Keel. But what did I want crawling forward to scorch my understanding at her flaming brow?

PEGEEN (*to* MAHON, *vehemently, fearing she will break into tears*). Take him on from this or I'll set the young lads to destroy him here.

MAHON (*going to him, shaking his stick*). Come on now if you wouldn't have the company to see you skelped.

PEGEEN (*half laughing, through her tears*). That's it, now the world will see him pandied, and he an ugly liar was playing off the hero, and the fright of men.

CHRISTY (*to* MAHON, *very sharply*). Leave me go!

CROWD. That's it. Now, Christy. If them two set fighting, it will lick the world.

MAHON (*making a grab at Christy*). Come here to me.

CHRISTY (*more threateningly*). Leave me go, I'm saying.

MAHON. I will maybe, when your legs is limping, and your back is blue.

CROWD. Keep it up, the two of you. I'll back the old man. Now the playboy.

CHRISTY (*in low and intense voice*). Shut your yelling, for if you're after making a mighty man of me this day by the power of a lie, you're setting me now to think if it's a poor thing to be lonesome, it's worse maybe to go mixing with the fools of earth.

(MAHON *makes a movement towards him.*)

CHRISTY (*almost shouting*). Keep off . . . lest I do show a blow unto the lot of you would set the guardian angels winking in the clouds above. (*He swings round with a sudden rapid movement and picks up a loy.*)

CROWD (*half frightened, half amused*). He's going mad! Mind yourselves! Run from the idiot!

CHRISTY. If I am an idiot, I'm after hearing my voice this day saying words would raise the topknot on a poet in a merchant's town. I've won your racing, your lepping, and. . . .

MAHON. Shut your gullet and come on with me.

CHRISTY. I'm going, but I'll stretch you first.

(*He runs at* OLD MAHON *with the loy, chases him out of the door, followed by crowd and* WIDOW QUIN. *There is a great noise outside, then a yell, and dead silence for a moment.* CHRISTY *comes in, half dazed, and goes to fire.*)

WIDOW QUIN (*coming in, hurriedly, and going to him*). They're turning again you. Come on, or you'll be hanged, indeed.

CHRISTY. I'm thinking, from this out, Pegeen'll be giving me praises the same as in the hours gone by.

WIDOW QUIN (*impatiently*). Come by the back-door. I'd think bad to have you stifled on the gallows tree.

CHRISTY (*indignantly*). I will not, then. What good'd be my lifetime, if I left Pegeen?

WIDOW QUIN. Come on, and you'll be no worse than you were last night; and you with a double murder this time to be telling to the girls.

CHRISTY. I'll not leave Pegeen Mike.

WIDOW QUIN (*impatiently*). Isn't there the match of her in every parish public, from Binghamstown until the plain of Meath? Come on, I tell you, and I'll find you finer sweethearts at each waning moon.

CHRISTY. It's Pegeen I'm seeking only, and what'd I care if you brought me a drift of chosen females, standing in their shifts itself, maybe, from this place to the Eastern World?

SARA (*runs in, pulling off one of her petticoats*). They're going to hang him. (*Holding out petticoat and shawl*) Fit these upon him, and let him run off to the east.

WIDOW QUIN. He's raving now; but we'll fit them on him, and I'll take him, in the ferry, to the Achill boat.

CHRISTY (*struggling feebly*). Leave me go, will you? when I'm thinking of my luck today, for she will wed me surely, and I a proven hero in the end of all.

(*They try to fasten petticoat round him.*)

WIDOW QUIN. Take his left hand, and we'll pull him now. Come on, young fellow.

CHRISTY (*suddenly starting up*). You'll be taking me from her? You're jealous, is it, of her wedding me? Go on from this. (*He snatches up a stool, and threatens them with it.*)

WIDOW QUIN (*going*). It's in the madhouse they should put him, not in jail, at all. We'll go by the back-door, to call the doctor, and we'll save him so.

(*She goes out, with* SARA, *through inner room. Men crowd in the doorway.* CHRISTY *sits down again by the fire.*)

MICHAEL (*in a terrified whisper*). Is the old lad killed surely?

PHILLY. I'm after feeling the last gasps quitting his heart.

(*They peer in at* CHRISTY.)

MICHAEL (*with a rope*). Look at the way he is. Twist a hangman's knot on it, and slip it over his head, while he's not minding at all.

PHILLY. Let you take it, Shaneen. You're the soberest of all that's here.

SHAWN. Is it me to go near him, and he the wickedest and worst with me? Let you take it, Pegeen Mike.

PEGEEN. Come on, so.

(*She goes forward with the others, and they drop the double hitch over his head.*)

CHRISTY. What ails you?

SHAWN (*triumphantly, as they pull the rope tight on his arms*). Come on to the peelers, till they stretch you now.

CHRISTY. Me!

MICHAEL. If we took pity on you, the Lord God would, maybe, bring us ruin from the law today, so you'd best come easy, for hanging is an easy and a speedy end.

CHRISTY. I'll not stir. (*To* PEGEEN) And what is it you'll say to me, and I after doing it this time in the face of all?

PEGEEN. I'll say, a strange man is a marvel, with his mighty talk; but what's a squabble in your back-yard, and the blow of a loy, have taught me that there's a great gap between a gallous story and a dirty deed. (*To* MEN) Take him on from this, or the lot of us will be likely put on trial for his deed today.

CHRISTY (*with horror in his voice*). And it's yourself will send me off, to have a horny-fingered hangman hitching his bloody slip-knots at the butt of my ear.

MEN (*pulling rope*). Come on, will you?

(*He is pulled down on the floor.*)

CHRISTY (*twisting his legs round the table*). Cut the rope, Pegeen, and I'll quit the lot of you, and live from this out, like the madmen of Keel, eating muck and green weeds, on the faces of the cliffs.

PEGEEN. And leave us to hang, is it, for a saucy liar, the like of you? (*To* MEN) Take him on, out from this.

SHAWN. Pull a twist on his neck, and squeeze him so.

PHILLY. Twist yourself. Sure he cannot hurt you, if you keep your distance from his teeth alone.

SHAWN. I'm afeard of him. (*To* PEGEEN) Lift a lighted sod, will you, and scorch his leg.

PEGEEN (*blowing the fire, with a bellows*). Leave go now, young fellow, or I'll scorch your shins.

CHRISTY. You're blowing for to torture me. (*His voice rising and growing stronger*) That's your kind, is it? Then let the lot of you be wary, for, if I've to face the gallows, I'll have a gay march down, I tell you, and shed the blood of some of you before I die.

SHAWN (*in terror*). Keep a good hold, Philly. Be wary, for the love of God. For I'm thinking he would liefest wreak his pains on me.

CHRISTY (*almost gaily*). If I do lay my hands on you, it's the way you'll be at the fall of night, hanging as a scarecrow for the fowls of hell. Ah, you'll have a gallous jaunt I'm saying, coaching out through Limbo with my father's ghost.

SHAWN (*to* PEGEEN). Make haste, will you? Oh, isn't he a holy terror, and isn't it true for Father Reilly, that all drink's a curse that has the lot of you so shaky and uncertain now?

CHRISTY. If I can wring a neck among you, I'll have a royal judgment looking on the trembling jury in the courts of law. And won't there be crying out in Mayo the day I'm stretched upon the rope with ladies in their silks and satins snivelling in their lacy kerchiefs, and they rhyming songs and ballads on the terror of my fate? (*He squirms round on the floor and bites* SHAWN's *leg.*)

SHAWN (*shrieking*). My leg's bit on me. He's the like of a mad dog, I'm thinking, the way that I will surely die.

CHRISTY (*delighted with himself*). You will then, the way you can shake out hell's flags of welcome for my coming in two weeks or three, for I'm thinking Satan hasn't many have killed their da in Kerry, and in Mayo too.

(OLD MAHON *comes in behind on all fours and looks on unnoticed.*)

MEN (*to* PEGEEN). Bring the sod, will you?

PEGEEN (*coming over*). God help him so. (*Burns his leg.*)

CHRISTY (*kicking and screaming*). O glory be to God!

(*He kicks loose from the table, and they all drag him towards the door.*)

JIMMY (*seeing* OLD MAHON). Will you look what's come in?

(*They all drop* CHRISTY *and run left.*)

CHRISTY (*scrambling on his knees face to face with old* MAHON). Are you coming to be killed a third time, or what ails you now?

MAHON. For what is it they have you tied?

CHRISTY. They're taking me to the peelers to have me hanged for slaying you.

MICHAEL (*apologetically*). It is the will of God that all should guard their little cabins from the treachery of law, and what would my daughter be doing if I was ruined or was hanged itself?

MAHON (*grimly, loosening* CHRISTY). It's little I care if you put a bag on her neck, and went picking cockles till the hour of death; but my son and myself will be going our own way, and we'll have great times from this out telling stories of the villainy of Mayo, and the fools is here. (*To* CHRISTY, *who is freed*) Come on now.

CHRISTY. Go with you, is it? I will then, like a gallant captain with his heathen slave. Go on now and I'll see you from this day stewing my oatmeal and washing my spuds, for I'm master of all fights from now. (*Pushing* MAHON) Go on, I'm saying.

MAHON. Is it me?

CHRISTY. Not a word out of you. Go on from this.

MAHON (*walking out and looking back at* CHRISTY *over his shoulder*). Glory be to God! (*With a broad smile*) I am crazy again! (*Goes.*)

CHRISTY. Ten thousand blessings upon all that's here, for you've turned me a likely gaffer in the end of all, the way I'll go romancing through a romping lifetime from this hour to the dawning of the judgment day. (*He goes out.*)

MICHAEL. By the will of God, we'll have peace now for our drinks. Will you draw the porter, Pegeen?

SHAWN (*going up to her*). It's a miracle Father Reilly can wed us in the end of all, and we'll have none to trouble us when his vicious bite is healed.

PEGEEN (*hitting him a box on the ear*). Quit my sight. (*Putting her shawl over her head and breaking out into wild lamentations*) Oh my grief, I've lost him surely. I've lost the only Playboy of the Western World.

The Curtain Falls.

Extracts from Note Books of J. M. Synge

From *Plays,* by John M. Synge. London, George Allen & Unwin, n.d.

(1907)

THE ARTISTIC VALUE OF ANY WORK OF ART IS MEASURED BY ITS *uniqueness.* Its human value is given largely by its intensity and its richness, for if it is rich it is many-sided or universal, and, for this reason, sane—another word for wholesome, since all insanities are due to a one-sided excitement.

No personal originality is enough to make a rich work unique, unless it has also the characteristic of a particular time and locality and the life that is in it. For this reason all historical plays and novels and poems—except a very few that continue the tradition of a country—or like *Faust* and *Don Juan* renew some stock type—are relatively worthless. Every healthy mind is more interested in *Tit-Bits* than in *Idylls of the King,* or any of the other more or less artificial retellings of classical or saga stories. The most that one can claim for work of this kind—such as Keats's *Isabella*—when it is beautiful, is that it is made for a Utopia of art.

All Utopian work is unsatisfying, first because it is weak and therefore vague and therefore wanting in uniqueness, and also because it is only the catastrophes of life that give substance and power to the tragedy and humour which are the true poles of art. The religious art is a thing of the past only—a vain and foolish regret—and its place has been taken by our quite modern feeling for the beauty and mystery of nature, an emotion that has gradually risen up as religion in the dogmatic sense has gradually died. Our pilgrimages are not to Canterbury or Jerusalem, but to Killarney, Cumberland and the Alps.

In my plays and topographical books I have tried to give humanity and this mysterious external world.

Man has gradually grown up in this world that is about us, and I think that while Tolstoy is wrong in claiming that art should be intelligible to the peasant, he is right in seeking a criterion for the arts, and I think this is to be found in testing art by its compatibility with the outside world and the peasants or people who live near it. A book, I mean, that one feels ashamed to read in a cottage of Dingle Bay one may fairly call a book that is not healthy—or universal.

All theorizing is bad for the artist, because it makes him live in the intelligence instead of in the half-subconscious faculties by which all real creation is performed. This is one reason why hostile criticism is harmful to an artist, because it forces him to construct systems and defend and explain his own work.

Young and therefore living truths, views, what you will, have a certain diffidence or tenderness that makes it impossible to state them without the accompanying emotional or imaginative life in which they naturally arise. That is, they are stated in the arts when they are dead, only the flesh is cleared away and the naked skeletons are shown by essayists and metaphysicians.

Humour is the test of morals, as no vice is humorous. Bestial is, in its very essence, opposed to the idea of humour. All decadence is opposed to true humour. The heartiness of real and frank laughter is a sign that cannot be mistaken that what we laugh at is not out of harmony with that instinct of sanity that we call by so many names.

The shopman says that a work of art is not artistic if it is unwholesome, which is foolish; the fashionable critic says that it is absurd to say a work of art is unwholesome if it is good art, which is foolish also. There are beautiful and interesting plants which are deadly, and others that are kindly. It is absurd to say a flower is not beautiful nor admire its beauty because it is deadly, but it is absurd also to deny its deadliness.

(1908)

No one is less fond of theories and divisions in the arts than I am, and yet they cannot altogether be gone without. In these matters we need not expect to say anything very new, but in applying, for ourselves, to our own life, what is thought in different ways by many, we are likely to hit on matters of some value. For a long time I have felt that Poetry roughly is of two kinds, the poetry of real life—the poetry of Burns and Shakespeare and Villon, and the poetry of a land of fancy—the poetry of Spenser and Keats and Ronsard. That is obvious enough, but what is highest in poetry is always reached where the dreamer is leaning out to reality, or where the man of real life is lifted out of it, and in all the poets the greatest have both these elements, that is, they are supremely engrossed with life, and yet with the wildness of their fancy they are always passing out of what is simple and plain. Such is the case with Dante and Chaucer and Goethe and Shakespeare. In Ireland Mr. Yeats, one of the poets of the fancy land, has interests in the world and, for this reason, his poetry has had a lifetime in itself, but A. E., on the other hand, who is of the fancy land only, ended his career of poetry in his first volume.

It would be easy to carry this division a long way, to compare the romances of the Arthurian style with the modern realistic novel. Gottfried of Strassburg and Malory become real here and there—suddenly a real voice seems to speak out of their golden and burning words—and they are then extraordinarily powerful. So, on the other hand, it is only with Huysmans that the realistic becomes of interest.

W. B. YEATS: *Preface to The Well of the Saints*

SIX YEARS AGO I WAS STAYING IN A STUDENTS' HOTEL IN THE LATIN Quarter, and somebody, whose name I cannot recollect, introduced me to an Irishman, who, even poorer than myself, had taken a room at the top of the house. It was J. M. Synge, and I, who thought I knew the name of every Irishman who was working at literature, had never heard of him. He was a graduate of Trinity College, Dublin, too, and Trinity College does not, as a rule, produce artistic minds. He told me that he had been living in France and Germany, reading French and German literature, and that he wished to become a writer. He had, however, nothing to show but one or two poems and impressionistic essays, full of that kind of morbidity that has its root in too much brooding over methods of expression, and ways of looking upon life, which come, not out of life, but out of literature, images reflected from mirror to mirror. He had wandered among people whose life is as picturesque as the Middle Ages, playing his fiddle to Italian sailors, and listening to stories in Bavarian woods, but life had cast no light into his writings. He had learned Irish years ago, but had begun to forget it, for the only language that interested him was that conventional language of modern poetry which has begun to make us all weary. I was very weary of it, for I had finished *The Secret Rose,* and felt how it had separated my imagination from life, sending my Red Hanrahan, who should have trodden the same roads with myself, into some undiscoverable country.[1] I said: "Give up Paris. You will never create anything by reading Racine, and Arthur Symons will always be a better critic of French literature. Go to the Aran Islands. Live there as if you were one of the people themselves; express a life that has never found expression." I had just come from Aran, and my imagination was full of those grey islands where men must reap with knives because of the stones.

He went to Aran and became a part of its life, living upon salt fish and eggs, talking Irish for the most part, but listening also to the beautiful English which has grown up in Irish-speaking districts, and takes its vocabulary from the time of Malory and of the translators of the Bible, but its idiom and its vivid metaphor from Irish. When Mr. Synge began to write in this language, Lady Gregory had already used it finely in her translations of Dr. Hyde's lyrics and plays, or of old Irish literature, but she had listened with different ears. He made his own selection of word and phrase, choosing what would express his own personality. Above all, he made word and phrase dance to a very strange rhythm, which will always, till his plays have created their own tradition, be difficult to actors who have not learned it from his lips. It is essential, for it perfectly fits the drifting emotion, the dreaminess, the vague yet measureless desire, for which he would create a dramatic form. It blurs definition, clear edges, everything that comes from the will, it turns imagination from all that is of the present, like a gold background in a religious picture, and it strengthens in every emotion whatever comes to it from far off, from brooding memory and dangerous hope. When he brought *The Shadow of the Glen,* his first play, to the Irish National Theatre Society, the players were puzzled by the rhythm, but gradually they became certain that his Woman of the Glen, as melancholy as a curlew, driven to distraction by her own sensitiveness, her own fineness, could not speak with any other tongue, that all his people would change their life if the rhythm changed. Perhaps no Irish countryman had ever that exact

[1] Since writing this I have, with Lady Gregory's help, put *Red Hanrahan* into the common speech.—W. B. Y.

rhythm in his voice, but certainly if Mr. Synge had been born a countryman, he would have spoken like that. It makes the people of his imagination a little disembodied; it gives them a kind of innocence even in their anger and their cursing. It is part of its maker's attitude towards the world, for while it makes the clash of wills among his persons indirect and dreamy, it helps him to see the subject-matter of his art with wise, clear-seeing, unreflecting eyes; to preserve the integrity of art in an age of reasons and purposes. Whether he write of old beggars by the roadside, lamenting over the misery and ugliness of life, or of an old Aran woman mourning her drowned sons, or of a young wife married to an old husband, he has no wish to change anything, to reform anything; all these people pass by as before an open window, murmuring strange, exciting words.

If one has not fine construction, one has not drama, but if one has not beautiful or powerful and individual speech, one has not literature, or, at any rate, one has not great literature. Rabelais, Villon, Shakespeare, William Blake, would have known one another by their speech. Some of them knew how to construct a story, but all of them had abundant, resonant, beautiful, laughing, living speech. It is only the writers of our modern dramatic movement, our scientific dramatists, our naturalists of the stage, who have thought it possible to be like the greatest, and yet to cast aside even the poor persiflage of the comedians, and to write in the impersonal language that has come, not out of individual life, nor out of life at all, but out of necessities of commerce, of Parliament, of Board Schools, of hurried journeys by rail.

If there are such things as decaying art and decaying institutions, their decay must begin when the element they receive into their care from the life of every man in the world begins to rot. Literature decays when it no longer makes more beautiful, or more vivid, the language which unites it to all life, and when one finds the criticism of the student, and the purpose of the reformer, and the logic of the man of science, where there should have been the reveries of the common heart, ennobled into some raving Lear or unabashed Don Quixote. One must not forget that the death of language, the substitution of phrases as nearly impersonal as algebra for words and rhythms varying from man to man, is but a part of the tyranny of impersonal things. I have been reading through a bundle of German plays, and have found everywhere a desire, not to express hopes and alarms common to every man that ever came into the world, but politics or social passion, a veiled or open propaganda. Now it is duelling that has need of reproof; now it is the ideas of an actress, returning from the free life of the stage, that must be contrasted with the prejudice of an old-fashioned town; now it is the hostility of Christianity and Paganism in our own day that is to find an obscure symbol in a bell thrown from its tower by spirits of the wood. I compare the work of these dramatists with the greater plays of their Scandinavian master, and remember that even he, who has made so many clear-drawn characters, has made us no abundant character, no man of genius in whom we could believe, and that in him also, even when it is Emperor and Galilean that are face to face, even the most momentous figures are subordinate to some tendency, to some movement, to some inanimate energy, or to some process of thought whose very logic has changed it into mechanism—always to "something other than human life."

We must not measure a young talent, whether we praise or blame, with that of men who are among the greatest of our time, but we may say of any talent, following out a definition, that it takes up the tradition of great drama as it came from the hands of the Masters who are acknowledged by all time, and turns away from a dramatic movement which, though it has been served by fine talent, has been imposed upon us by science, by artificial life, by a passing order.

When the individual life no longer delights in its own energy, when the body is not made strong and beautiful by the activities of daily life, when men have no delight in decorating the body, one may be certain that one lives in a passing order, amid the inventions of a fading vitality. If Homer were alive to-day, he would only resist, after a deliberate struggle, the temptation to find his subject not in Helen's beauty, that every man has desired, nor in the wisdom and endurance of Odysseus that has been the desire of every woman that has come into the world, but in what somebody would describe, perhaps, as "the inevitable contest," arising out of economic causes, between the country-places and small towns on the one hand, and, upon the other, the great city of Troy, representing one knows not what "tendency to centralisation."

Mr. Synge has in common with the great theatre of the world, with that of Greece and that of India, with the creator of Falstaff, with Racine, a delight in language, a preoccupation with the individual life. He resembles them also by a preoccupation with what is lasting and noble, that came to him, not, as I think, from books, but while he listened to old stories in the cottages, and contrasted what they remembered with reality. The only literature of the Irish countrypeople is their songs, full often of extravagant love, and their stories of kings and of kings' children. "I will cry my fill, but not for God, but because Finn and the Fianna are not living," says Oisin in the story. Every writer, even every small writer, who has belonged to the great tradition, has had his dream of an impossibly noble life, and the greater he is, the more does it seem to plunge him into some beautiful or bitter reverie. Some, and of these are all the earliest poets of the world, gave it direct expression; others mingle it so subtly with reality that it is a day's work to disentangle it; others bring it near by showing us whatever is most its contrary. Mr. Synge, indeed, sets before us ugly, deformed or sinful people, but his people, moved by no practical ambition, are driven by a dream of that impossible life. That we may feel how intensely his Woman of the Glen dreams of days that shall be entirely alive, she that is "a hard woman to please" must spend her days between a sour-faced old husband, a man who goes mad upon the hills, a craven lad and a drunken tramp; and those two

blind people of *The Well of the Saints* are so transformed by the dream that they choose blindness rather than reality. He tells us of realities, but he knows that art has never taken more than its symbols from anything that the eye can see or the hand measure.

It is the preoccupation of his characters with their dream that gives his plays their drifting movement, their emotional subtlety. In most of the dramatic writing of our time, and this is one of the reasons why our dramatists do not find the need for a better speech, one finds a simple motive lifted, as it were, into the full light of the stage. The ordinary student of drama will not find anywhere in *The Well of the Saints* that excitement of the will in the presence of attainable advantages, which he is accustomed to think the natural stuff of drama, and if he see it played he will wonder why act is knitted to act so loosely, why it is all like a decoration on a flat surface, why there is so much leisure in the dialogue, even in the midst of passion. If he see *The Shadow of the Glen,* he will ask, Why does this woman go out of her house? Is it because she cannot help herself, or is she content to go? Why is it not all made clearer? And yet, like everybody when caught up into great events, she does many things without being quite certain why she does them. She hardly understands at moments why her action has a certain form, more clearly than why her body is tall or short, fair or brown. She feels an emotion that she does not understand. She is driven by desires that need for their expression, not "I admire this man," or "I must go, whether I will or no," but words of suggestion, rhythms of voice, movements that escape analysis. In addition to all this, she has something that she shares with none but the children of one man's imagination. She is intoxicated by a dream which is hardly understood by herself, but possesses her like something half remembered on a sudden wakening. . . .

PIRANDELLO WAS BORN IN SICILY, THE SON OF A RICH

Luigi Pirandello 1867-1936

mine-owner, a powerful man able to use his fists, and a gentle mother. At the University of Rome, to which he went after his early schooling, Pirandello fought outmoded methods of teaching and was attracted to the study of philology, a subject he further pursued at the University of Bonn. After receiving his doctor's degree, Pirandello published several volumes of verse, and in 1893 he settled into an abandoned convent near Rome and joined the literary life of the capital. The following year he entered into a marriage—arranged by his father—with a girl whom he had never seen before. For ten years the couple lived in Rome on allowances contributed by their parents, but in 1904 the family fortunes suddenly declined and Pirandello was forced to take up teaching. At about the same time his wife's mind gave way, and for fourteen years Pirandello underwent the agony of coping with an insane woman. The focus of his writing now shifted from the local color of Sicilian life to probing into states of mind and preoccupation with old age, death, and insanity. His work took on the marks of a morbidly obsessed intellect, of a grim humor tragically oriented, and of an attraction for the grotesque. In 1916 he won European acclaim with his play *Right You Are If You Think You Are*. His recurrent theme was of illusion and reality, of the true self behind the social mask, a theme which he explored in such plays as *Six Characters in Search of an Author* (1921) and *Henry IV* (1922). Pirandello's earlier liberalism had been replaced by a cynical evaluation of society's sham respectability. Though his writings indicate that he was basically anarchistic, he nevertheless defended Italy's attack on Ethiopia in 1935 and accepted a decoration from Italy's Fascist dictator, Mussolini. Late in life Pirandello attempted to establish a national theatre, but failed. In 1934, two years before his death, he received the Nobel Prize.

SIX CHARACTERS IN SEARCH OF AN AUTHOR ❦ BY LUIGI PIRANDELLO

Translated from the Italian by Edward Storer

CHARACTERS OF THE COMEDY IN THE MAKING:

THE FATHER
THE MOTHER
THE STEPDAUGHTER
THE SON

MADAME PACE
THE BOY ⎫
THE CHILD ⎭ *(These two do not speak)*

ACTORS OF THE COMPANY:

THE MANAGER
LEADING LADY
LEADING MAN
SECOND LADY
LEAD
L'INGÉNUE
JUVENILE LEAD

OTHER ACTORS AND ACTRESSES
PROPERTY MAN
PROMPTER
MACHINIST
MANAGER'S SECRETARY
DOOR-KEEPER
SCENE-SHIFTERS

DAYTIME: *The Stage of a Theater.*

❦ Act I

N.B. *The Comedy is without acts or scenes. The performance is interrupted once, without the curtain being lowered, when* THE MANAGER *and the chief characters withdraw to arrange the scenario. A second interruption of the action takes place when, by mistake the stage hands let the curtain down.*

The spectators will find the curtain raised and the stage as it usually is during the daytime. It will be half dark, and empty, so that from the beginning the public may have the impression of an impromptu performance.

PROMPTER'S *box and a small table and chair for* THE MANAGER.

Two other small tables and several chairs scattered about as during rehearsals.

The ACTORS *and* ACTRESSES *of the company enter from the back of the stage:*

First one, then another, then two together: nine or ten in all. They are about to rehearse a Pirandello play: Mixing It Up. *Some of the company move off towards their dressing rooms. The* PROMPTER, *who has the "book" under his arm, is waiting for* THE MANAGER *in order to begin the rehearsal.*

The ACTORS *and* ACTRESSES, *some standing, some sitting, chat and smoke. One perhaps reads a paper; another cons his part.*

Finally, THE MANAGER *enters and goes to the table prepared for him. His* SECRETARY *brings him his mail, through which he glances. The* PROMPTER *takes his seat, turns on a light, and opens the "book."*

THE MANAGER *(Throwing a letter down on the table).* I can't see. *(To* PROPERTY MAN*)* Let's have a little light, please!

PROPERTY MAN. Yes sir, yes, at once. *(A light comes down on to the stage)*

THE MANAGER *(Clapping his hands).* Come along! Come along! Second act of *Mixing it Up. (Sits down)*

(*The* ACTORS *and* ACTRESSES *go from the front of the stage to the wings, all except the three who are to begin the rehearsal*)

THE PROMPTER (*Reading the "book"*). "Leo Gala's house. A curious room serving as dining-room and study."

THE MANAGER (*To* PROPERTY MAN). Fix up the old red room.

PROPERTY MAN (*Noting it down*). Red set. All right!

THE PROMPTER (*Continuing to read from the "book"*). "Table already laid and writing desk with books and papers. Bookshelves. Exit rear to Leo's bedroom. Exit left to kitchen. Principal exit to right."

THE MANAGER (*Energetically*). Well, you understand: The principal exit over there; here, the kitchen. (*Turning to* ACTOR *who is to play the part of Socrates*) You make your entrances and exits here. (*To* PROPERTY MAN) The baize doors at the rear, and curtains.

PROPERTY MAN (*Noting it down*). Right-o!

PROMPTER (*Reading as before*). "When the curtain rises, Leo Gala, dressed in cook's cap and apron is busy beating an egg in a cup. Philip, also dressed as a cook, is beating another egg. Guido Venanzi is seated and listening."

LEADING MAN (*To* MANAGER). Excuse me, but must I absolutely wear a cook's cap?

THE MANAGER (*Annoyed*). I imagine so. It says so there anyway. (*Pointing to the "book"*)

LEADING MAN. But it's ridiculous!

THE MANAGER. Ridiculous? Ridiculous? Is it my fault if France won't send us any more good comedies, and we are reduced to putting on Pirandello's works where nobody understands anything, and where the author plays the fool with us all? (*The* ACTORS *grin.* THE MANAGER *goes to* LEADING MAN *and shouts*) Yes sir, you put on the cook's cap and beat eggs. Do you suppose that with all this egg-beating business you are on an ordinary stage? Get that out of your head. You represent the shell of the eggs you are beating! (*Laughter and comments among the* ACTORS) Silence! and listen to my explanations, please! (*To* LEADING MAN): "The empty form of reason without the fullness of instinct, which is blind"—You stand

for reason, your wife is instinct. It's a mixing up of the parts, according to which you who act your own part become the puppet of yourself. Do you understand?

LEADING MAN. I'm hanged if I do.

THE MANAGER. Neither do I. But let's get on with it. It's sure to be a glorious failure anyway. (*Confidentially*): But I say, please face three-quarters. Otherwise, what with the abstruseness of the dialogue, and the public that won't be able to hear you, the whole thing will go to hell. Come on! come on!

PROMPTER. Pardon sir, may I get into my box? There's a bit of a draught.

THE MANAGER. Yes, yes, of course!

At this point, the DOOR-KEEPER *has entered from the stage door and advances towards* THE MANAGER'S *table, taking off his braided cap. During this manœuver, the* SIX CHARACTERS *enter, and stop by the door at back of stage, so that when the* DOOR-KEEPER *is about to announce their coming to* THE MANAGER, *they are already on the stage. A tenuous light surrounds them, almost as if irradiated by them— the faint breath of their fantastic reality.*

This light will disappear when they come forward towards the ACTORS. *They preserve, however, something of the dream lightness in which they seem almost suspended; but this does not detract from the essential reality of their forms and expressions.*

He who is known as THE FATHER *is a man of about 50: hair, reddish in color, thin at the temples; he is not bald, however; thick moustaches, falling over his still fresh mouth, which often opens in an empty and uncertain smile. He is fattish, pale; with an especially wide forehead. He has blue, oval-shaped eyes, very clear and piercing. Wears light trousers and a dark jacket. He is alternatively melifluous and violent in his manner.*

THE MOTHER *seems crushed and terrified as if by an intolerable weight of shame and abasement. She is dressed in modest black and wears a thick widow's veil of crêpe. When she lifts this, she reveals a wax-like face. She always keeps her eyes downcast.*

THE STEPDAUGHTER *is dashing, almost impudent, beautiful. She wears mourning too, but with great elegance. She shows contempt for the timid half-frightened manner of the wretched* BOY (*14 years old, and also dressed in black*); *on the other hand, she displays a lively tenderness for her little sister,* THE CHILD (*about four*), *who is dressed in white, with a black silk sash at the waist.*

THE SON (22) *tall, severe in his attitude of contempt for* THE FATHER, *supercilious and indifferent to* THE MOTHER. *He looks as if he had come on the stage against his will.*

DOORKEEPER (*Cap in hand*). Excuse me, sir. . . .

THE MANAGER (*Rudely*). Eh? What is it?

DOORKEEPER (*Timidly*). These people are asking for you, sir.

THE MANAGER (*Furious*). I am rehearsing, and you know perfectly well no one's allowed to come in during rehearsals! (*Turning to the* CHARACTERS): Who are you, please? What do you want?

THE FATHER (*Coming forward a little, followed by the others, who seem embarrassed*). As a matter of fact . . . we have come here in search of an author. . . .

THE MANAGER (*Half angry, half amazed*). An author? What author?

THE FATHER. Any author, sir.

THE MANAGER. But there's no author here. We are not rehearsing a new piece.

THE STEPDAUGHTER (*Vivaciously*). So much the better, so much the better! We can be your new piece.

AN ACTOR (*Coming forward from the others*). Oh, do you hear that?

THE FATHER (*To* STEPDAUGHTER). Yes, but if the author isn't here . . . (*To* MANAGER) . . . unless you would be willing. . . .

THE MANAGER. You are trying to be funny.

THE FATHER. No, for Heaven's sake, what are you saying? We bring you a drama, sir.

THE STEPDAUGHTER. We may be your fortune.

THE MANAGER. Will you oblige me by going away? We haven't time to waste with mad people.

THE FATHER (*Mellifluously*). Oh sir, you know well that life is full of infinite absurdities, which, strangely enough, do not even need to appear plausible, since they are true.

THE MANAGER. What the devil is he talking about?

THE FATHER. I say that to reverse the ordinary process may well be considered a madness: that is, to create credible situations, in order that they may appear true. But permit me to observe that if this be madness, it is the sole *raison d'être* of your profession, gentlemen. (*The* ACTORS *look hurt and perplexed*)

THE MANAGER (*Getting up and looking at him*). So our profession seems to you one worthy of madmen then?

THE FATHER. Well, to make seem true that which isn't true . . . without any need . . . for a joke as it were . . . Isn't that your mission, gentlemen: to give life to fantastic characters on the stage?

THE MANAGER (*Interpreting the rising anger of the* COMPANY). But I would beg you to believe, my dear sir, that the profession of the comedian is a noble one. If today, as things go, the playwrights give us stupid comedies to play and puppets to represent instead of men, remember we are proud to have given life to immortal works here on these very boards! (*The* ACTORS, *satisfied, applaud their* MANAGER)

THE FATHER (*Interrupting furiously*). Exactly, perfectly, to living beings more alive than those who breathe and wear clothes: being less real perhaps, but truer! I agree with you entirely. (*The* ACTORS *look at one another in amazement*)

THE MANAGER. But what do you mean? Before, you said . . .

THE FATHER. No, excuse me, I meant it for you, sir, who were crying out that you had no time to lose with madmen, while no one better than yourself knows that nature uses the instrument of human fantasy in order to pursue her high creative purpose.

THE MANAGER. Very well—but where does all this take us?

THE FATHER. Nowhere! It is merely to show you that one is born to life in many forms, in many shapes, as tree, or as stone, as water, as butterfly, or as woman. So one may also be born a character in a play.

THE MANAGER (*With feigned comic dismay*). So you and these other friends of yours have been born characters?

THE FATHER. Exactly, and alive as you

see! (MANAGER *and* ACTORS *burst out laughing*)

THE FATHER (*Hurt*). I am sorry you laugh, because we carry in us a drama, as you can guess from this woman here, veiled in black.

THE MANAGER (*Losing patience at last and almost indignant*). Oh, chuck it! Get away please! Clear out of here! (*To* PROPERTY MAN) For Heaven's sake, turn them out!

THE FATHER (*Resisting*). No, no, look here, we. . . .

THE MANAGER (*Roaring*). We come here to work, you know.

LEADING ACTOR. One cannot let oneself be made such a fool of.

THE FATHER (*Determined, coming forward*). I marvel at your incredulity, gentlemen. Are you not accustomed to see the characters created by an author spring to life in yourselves and face each other? Just because there is no "book" (*Pointing to the* PROMPTER'S *box*) which contains us, you refuse to believe. . . .

THE STEPDAUGHTER (*Advances towards* MANAGER, *smiling and coquettish*). Believe me, we are really six most interesting characters, sir; side-tracked however.

THE FATHER. Yes, that is the word! (*To* MANAGER *all at once*) In the sense, that is, that the author who created us alive no longer wished, or was no longer able, materially to put us into a work of art. And this was a real crime, sir; because he who has had the luck to be born a character can laugh even at death. He cannot die. The man, the writer, the instrument of the creation will die, but his creation does not die. And to live for ever, it does not need to have extraordinary gifts or to be able to work wonders. Who was Sancho Panza? Who was Don Abbondio? Yet they live eternally because—live germs as they were—they had the fortune to find a fecundating matrix, a fantasy which could raise and nourish them: make them live for ever!

THE MANAGER. That is quite all right. But what do you want here, all of you?

THE FATHER. We want to live.

THE MANAGER (*Ironically*). For Eternity?

THE FATHER. No, sir, only for a moment . . . in you.

AN ACTOR. Just listen to him!

LEADING LADY. They want to live, in us! . . .

JUVENILE LEAD (*Pointing to the* STEPDAUGHTER). I've no objection, as far as that one is concerned!

THE FATHER. Look here! Look here! The comedy has to be made. (*To the* MANAGER) But if you and your actors are willing, we can soon concert it among ourselves.

THE MANAGER (*Annoyed*). But what do you want to concert? We don't go in for concerts here. Here we play dramas and comedies!

THE FATHER. Exactly! That is just why we have come to you.

THE MANAGER. And where is the "book"?

THE FATHER. It is in us! (*The* ACTORS *laugh*) The drama is in us, and we are the drama. We are impatient to play it. Our inner passion drives us on to this.

THE STEPDAUGHTER (*Disdainful, alluring, treacherous, full of impudence*). My passion, sir! Ah, if you only knew! My passion for him! (*Points to the* FATHER *and makes a pretence of embracing him. Then she breaks out into a loud laugh*)

THE FATHER (*Angrily*). Behave yourself! And please don't laugh in that fashion.

THE STEPDAUGHTER. With your permission, gentlemen, I, who am a two months' orphan, will show you how I can dance and sing.

(*Sings and then dances* Prenez garde à Tchou-Tchin-Tchou)

Les chinois sont un peuple malin,
De Shanghaî à Pékin,
Ils ont mis des écriteaux partout:
Prenez garde à Tchou-Tchin-Tchou.

ACTORS *and* ACTRESSES. Bravo! Well done! Tip-top!

THE MANAGER. Silence! This isn't a café concert, you know! (*Turning to the* FATHER *in consternation*) Is she mad?

THE FATHER. Mad? No, she's worse than mad.

THE STEPDAUGHTER (*To* MANAGER). Worse? Worse? Listen! Stage this drama for us at once! Then you will see that at a certain moment I . . . when this little darling here . . . (*Takes the* CHILD *by the hand and leads her to the* MANAGER)

Isn't she a dear? (*Takes her up and kisses her*) Darling! Darling! (*Puts her down again and adds feelingly*) Well, when God suddenly takes this dear little child away from that poor mother there; and this imbecile here (*seizing hold of the* BOY *roughly and pushing him forward*) does the stupidest things, like the fool he is, you will see me run away. Yes, gentlemen, I shall be off. But the moment hasn't arrived yet. After what has taken place between him and me (*indicates the* FATHER *with a horrible wink*) I can't remain any longer in this society, to have to witness the anguish of this mother here for that fool . . . (*Indicates the* SON) Look at him! Look at him! See how indifferent, how frigid he is, because he is the legitimate son. He despises me, despises him (*pointing to the* BOY), despises this baby here; because . . . we are bastards. (*Goes to the* MOTHER *and embraces her*) And he doesn't want to recognize her as his mother—she who is the common mother of us all. He looks down upon her as if she were only the mother of us three bastards. Wretch! (*She says all this very rapidly, excitedly. At the word "bastards" she raises her voice, and almost spits out the final "Wretch!"*)

THE MOTHER (*To the* MANAGER, *in anguish*). In the name of these two little children, I beg you . . . (*She grows faint and is about to fall*) Oh God!

THE FATHER (*Coming forward to support her as do some of the* ACTORS). Quick, a chair, a chair for this poor widow!

THE ACTORS. Is it true? Has she really fainted?

THE MANAGER. Quick, a chair! Here!

(*One of the* ACTORS *brings a chair, the others proffer assistance. The* MOTHER *tries to prevent the* FATHER *from lifting the veil which covers her face*)

THE FATHER. Look at her! Look at her!

THE MOTHER. No, stop; stop it please!

THE FATHER (*Raising her veil*). Let them see you!

THE MOTHER (*Rising and covering her face with her hands, in desperation*). I beg you, sir, to prevent this man from carrying out his plan which is loathsome to me.

THE MANAGER (*Dumbfounded*). I don't understand at all. What is the situation? Is this lady your wife? (*To the* FATHER)

THE FATHER. Yes, gentlemen: my wife!

THE MANAGER. But how can she be a widow if you are alive? (*The* ACTORS *find relief for their astonishment in a loud laugh*)

THE FATHER. Don't laugh! Don't laugh like that, for Heaven's sake. Her drama lies just here in this: she has had a lover, a man who ought to be here.

THE MOTHER (*With a cry*). No! No!

THE STEPDAUGHTER. Fortunately for her, he is dead. Two months ago as I said. We are mourning, as you see.

THE FATHER. He isn't here you see, not because he is dead. He isn't here—look at her a moment and you will understand—because her drama isn't a drama of the love of two men for whom she was incapable of feeling anything except possibly a little gratitude—gratitude not for me but for the other. She isn't a woman, she is a mother, and her drama —powerful, sir, I assure you—lies, as a matter of fact, all in these four children she has had by two men.

THE MOTHER. I had them? Have you got the courage to say that I wanted them? (*To the* COMPANY) It was his doing. It was he who gave me that other man, who forced me to go away with him.

THE STEPDAUGHTER. It isn't true.

THE MOTHER (*Startled*). Not true, isn't it?

THE STEPDAUGHTER. No, it isn't true, it just isn't true.

THE MOTHER. And what can you know about it?

THE STEPDAUGHTER. It isn't true. Don't believe it. (*To* MANAGER) Do you know why she says so? For that fellow there. (*Indicates the* SON) She tortures herself, destroys herself on account of the neglect of that son there; and she wants him to believe that if she abandoned him when he was only two years old, it was because he (*indicates the* FATHER) made her do so.

THE MOTHER (*Vigorously*). He forced me to it, and I call God to witness it. (*To the* MANAGER) Ask him (*indicates the* FATHER) if it isn't true. Let him speak. You (*to* DAUGHTER) are not in a position to know anything about it.

THE STEPDAUGHTER. I know you lived in peace and happiness with my father while he lived. Can you deny it?

THE MOTHER. No, I don't deny it . . .

THE STEPDAUGHTER. He was always full of affection and kindness for you. (*To the* BOY, *angrily*) It's true, isn't it? Tell them! Why don't you speak, you little fool?

THE MOTHER. Leave the poor boy alone. Why do you want to make me appear ungrateful, daughter? I don't want to offend your father. I have answered him that I didn't abandon my house and my son through any fault of mine, nor from any wilful passion.

THE FATHER. It is true. It was my doing.

LEADING MAN (*To the* COMPANY). What a spectacle!

LEADING LADY. We are the audience this time.

JUVENILE LEAD. For once, in a way.

THE MANAGER (*Beginning to get really interested*). Let's hear them out. Listen!

THE SON. Oh yes, you're going to hear a fine bit now. He will talk to you of the Demon of Experiment.

THE FATHER. You are a cynical imbecile. I've told you so already a hundred times. (*To the* MANAGER) He tries to make fun of me on account of this expression which I have found to excuse myself with.

THE SON (*With disgust*). Yes, phrases! phrases!

THE FATHER. Phrases! Isn't everyone consoled when faced with a trouble or fact he doesn't understand, by a word, some simple word, which tells us nothing and yet calms us?

THE STEPDAUGHTER. Even in the case of remorse. In fact, especially then.

THE FATHER. Remorse? No, that isn't true. I've done more than use words to quieten the remorse in me.

THE STEPDAUGHTER. Yes, there was a bit of money too. Yes, yes, a bit of money. There were the hundred lire he was about to offer me in payment, gentlemen. . . . (*Sensation of horror among the* ACTORS)

THE SON (*To the* STEPDAUGHTER). This is vile.

THE STEPDAUGHTER. Vile? There they were in a pale blue envelope on a little mahogany table in the back of Madame Pace's shop. You know Madame Pace— one of those ladies who attract poor girls of good family into their ateliers, under the pretext of their selling *robes et manteaux.*

THE SON. And he thinks he has bought the right to tyrannize over us all with those hundred lire he was going to pay; but which, fortunately—note this, gentlemen—he had no chance of paying.

THE STEPDAUGHTER. It was a near thing, though, you know! (*Laughs ironically*)

THE MOTHER (*Protesting*). Shame, my daughter, shame!

THE STEPDAUGHTER. Shame indeed! This is my revenge! I am dying to live that scene. . . . The room . . . I see it . . . Here is the window with the mantles exposed, there the divan, the looking-glass, a screen, there in front of the window the little mahogany table with the blue envelope containing one hundred lire. I see it. I see it. I could take hold of it. . . But you, gentlemen, you ought to turn your backs now: I am almost nude, you know. But I don't blush: I leave that to him. (*Indicating* FATHER)

THE MANAGER. I don't understand this at all.

THE FATHER. Naturally enough. I would ask you, sir, to exercise your authority a little here, and let me speak before you believe all she is trying to blame me with. Let me explain.

THE STEPDAUGHTER. Ah yes, explain it in your own way.

THE FATHER. But don't you see that the whole trouble lies here. In words, words. Each one of us has within him a whole world of things, each man of us his own special world. And how can we ever come to an understanding if I put in the words I utter the sense and value of things as I see them; while you who listen to me must inevitably translate them according to the conception of things each one of you has within himself. We think we understand each other, but we never really do. Look here! This woman (*indicating the* MOTHER) takes all my pity for her as a specially ferocious form of cruelty.

THE MOTHER. But you drove me away.

THE FATHER. Do you hear her? I

drove her away! She believes I really sent her away.

THE MOTHER. You know how to talk, and I don't; but, believe me sir (*To* MANAGER), after he had married me . . . who knows why? . . . I was a poor insignificant woman. . . .

THE FATHER. But, good Heaven! it was just for your humility that I married you. I loved this simplicity in you. (*He stops when he sees she makes signs to contradict him, opens his arms wide in sign of desperation, seeing how hopeless it is to make himself understood*) You see she denies it. Her mental deafness, believe me, is phenomenal, the limit (*touches his forehead*): deaf, deaf, mentally deaf! She had plenty of feeling. Oh yes, a good heart for the children; but the brain—deaf, to the point of desperation—!

THE STEPDAUGHTER. Yes, but ask him how his intelligence has helped us.

THE FATHER. If we could see all the evil that may spring from good, what should we do? (*At this point the* LEADING LADY *who is biting her lips with rage at seeing the* LEADING MAN *flirting with the* STEPDAUGHTER, *comes forward and says to the* MANAGER)

LEADING LADY. Excuse me, but are we going to rehearse today?

MANAGER. Of course, of course; but let's hear them out.

JUVENILE LEAD. This is something quite new.

L'INGÉNUE. Most interesting!

LEADING LADY. Yes, for the people who like that kind of thing. (*Casts a glance at* LEADING MAN)

THE MANAGER (*To* FATHER). You must please explain yourself quite clearly. (*Sits down*)

THE FATHER. Very well then: listen! I had in my service a poor man, a clerk, a secretary of mine, full of devotion, who became friends with her. (*Indicating the* MOTHER) They understood one another, were kindred souls in fact, without, however, the least suspicion of any evil existing. They were incapable even of thinking of it.

THE STEPDAUGHTER. So he thought of it—for them!

THE FATHER. That's not true. I meant to do good to them—and to myself, I confess, at the same time. Things had come to the point that I could not say a

word to either of them without their making a mute appeal, one to the other, with their eyes. I could see them silently asking each other how I was to be kept in countenance, how I was to be kept quiet. And this, believe me, was just about enough of itself to keep me in a constant rage, to exasperate me beyond measure.

THE MANAGER. And why didn't you send him away then—this secretary of yours?

THE FATHER. Precisely what I did, sir. And then I had to watch this poor woman drifting forlornly about the house like an animal without a master, like an animal one has taken in out of pity.

THE MOTHER. Ah yes! . . .

THE FATHER (*Suddenly turning to the* MOTHER). It's true about the son anyway, isn't it?

THE MOTHER. He took my son away from me first of all.

THE FATHER. But not from cruelty. I did it so that he should grow up healthy and strong by living in the country.

THE STEPDAUGHTER (*Pointing to him ironically*). As one can see.

THE FATHER (*Quickly*). Is it my fault if he has grown up like this? I sent him to a wet nurse in the country, a peasant, as *she* did not seem to me strong enough, though she is of humble origin. That was, anyway, the reason I married her. Unpleasant all this may be, but how can it be helped? My mistake possibly, but there we are! All my life I have had these confounded aspirations towards a certain moral sanity. (*At this point the* STEPDAUGHTER *bursts out into a noisy laugh*) Oh, stop it! Stop it! I can't stand it.

THE MANAGER. Yes, please stop it, for Heaven's sake.

THE STEPDAUGHTER. But imagine moral sanity from him, if you please—the client of certain ateliers like that of Madame Pace!

THE FATHER. Fool! That is the proof that I am a man! This seeming contradiction, gentlemen, is the strongest proof that I stand here a live man before you. Why, it is just for this very incongruity in my nature that I have had to suffer what I have. I could not live by the side of that woman (*indicating the* MOTHER) any longer; but not so much for the boredom she inspired me with as for the pity I felt for her.

THE MOTHER. And so he turned me out—.

THE FATHER. —well provided for! Yes, I sent her to that man, gentlemen . . . to let her go free of me.

THE MOTHER. And to free himself.

THE FATHER. Yes, I admit it. It was also a liberation for me. But great evil has come of it. I meant well when I did it; and I did it more for her sake than mine. I swear it. (*Crosses his arms on his chest; then turns suddenly to the* MOTHER) Did I ever lose sight of you until that other man carried you off to another town, like the angry fool he was? And on account of my pure interest in you . . . my pure interest, I repeat, that had no base motive in it . . . I watched with the tenderest concern the new family that grew up around her. She can bear witness to this. (*Points to the* STEPDAUGHTER)

THE STEPDAUGHTER. Oh yes, that's true enough. When I was a kiddie, so so high, you know, with plaits over my shoulders and knickers longer than my skirts, I used to see him waiting outside the school for me to come out. He came to see how I was growing up.

THE FATHER. This is infamous, shameful!

THE STEPDAUGHTER. No. Why?

THE FATHER. Infamous! Infamous! (*Then excitedly to* MANAGER, *explaining*) After she (*indicating* MOTHER) went away, my house seemed suddenly empty. She was my incubus, but she filled my house. I was like a dazed fly alone in the empty rooms. This boy here (*indicating the* SON) was educated away from home, and when he came back, he seemed to me to be no more mine. With no mother to stand between him and me, he grew up entirely for himself, on his own, apart, with no tie of intellect or affection binding him to me. And then—strange but true—I was driven, by curiosity at first and then by some tender sentiment, towards her family, which had come into being through my will. The thought of her began gradually to fill up the emptiness I felt all around me. I wanted to know if she were happy in living out the simple daily duties of life. I wanted to think of her as fortunate and happy because far away from the complicated

torments of my spirit. And so, to have proof of this, I used to watch that child coming out of school.

THE STEPDAUGHTER. Yes, yes. True. He used to follow me in the street and smiled at me, waved his hand, like this. I would look at him with interest, wondering who he might be. I told my mother, who guessed at once. (*The* MOTHER *agrees with a nod*) Then she didn't want to send me to school for some days; and when I finally went back, there he was again—looking so ridiculous—with a paper parcel in his hands. He came close to me, caressed me, and drew out a fine straw hat from the parcel, with a bouquet of flowers—all for me!

THE MANAGER. A bit discursive this, you know!

THE SON (*Contemptuously*). Literature! Literature!

THE FATHER. Literature indeed! This is life, this is passion!

THE MANAGER. It may be, but it won't act.

THE FATHER. I agree. This is only the part leading up. I don't suggest this should be staged. She (*pointing to the* STEPDAUGHTER), as you see, is no longer the flapper with plaits down her back—.

THE STEPDAUGHTER. —and the knickers showing below the skirt!

THE FATHER. The drama is coming now, sir; something new, complex, most interesting.

THE STEPDAUGHTER. As soon as my father died. . . .

THE FATHER. —there was absolute misery for them. They came back here, unknown to me. Through her stupidity! (*Pointing to the* MOTHER) It is true she can barely write her own name; but she could anyhow have got her daughter to write to me that they were in need. . . .

THE MOTHER. And how was I to divine all this sentiment in him?

THE FATHER. That is exactly your mistake, never to have guessed any of my sentiments.

THE MOTHER. After so many years apart, and all that had happened. . . .

THE FATHER. Was it my fault if that fellow carried you away? It happened quite suddenly; for after he had obtained some job or other, I could find no trace of them; and so, not unnaturally, my interest in them dwindled. But the drama culminated unforeseen and violent on their return, when I was impelled by my miserable flesh that still lives. . . . Ah! what misery, what wretchedness is that of the man who is alone and disdains debasing *liaisons!* Not old enough to do without women, and not young enough to go and look for one without shame. Misery? It's worse than misery; it's a horror; for no woman can any longer give him love; and when a man feels this. . . . One ought to do without, you say? Yes, yes, I know. Each of us when he appears before his fellows is clothed in a certain dignity. But every man knows what unconfessable things pass within the secrecy of his own heart. One gives way to the temptation, only to rise from it again, afterwards, with a great eagerness to reestablish one's dignity, as if it were a tombstone to place on the grave of one's shame, and a monument to hide and sign the memory of our weaknesses. Everybody's in the same case. Some folks haven't the courage to say certain things, that's all!

THE STEPDAUGHTER. All appear to have the courage to do them though.

THE FATHER. Yes, but in secret. Therefore, you want more courage to say these things. Let a man but speak these things out, and folks at once label him a cynic. But it isn't true. He is like all the others, better indeed, because he isn't afraid to reveal with the light of the intelligence the red shame of human bestiality on which most men close their eyes so as not to see it. Woman—for example, look at her case! She turns tantalizing inviting glances on you. You seize her. No sooner does she feel herself in your grasp than she closes her eyes. It is the sign of her mission, the sign by which she says to man: "Blind yourself, for I am blind."

THE STEPDAUGHTER. Sometimes she can close them no more: when she no longer feels the need of hiding her shame to herself, but dry-eyed and dispassionately, sees only that of the man who has blinded himself without love. Oh, all these intellectual complications make me sick, disgust me—all this philosophy that uncovers the beast in man, and then seeks to save him, excuse him . . . I can't stand it, sir. When a man seeks to "simplify" life bestially, throwing aside every relic of humanity, every chaste aspiration, every pure feeling, all sense of ideality, duty, modesty, shame . . . then nothing is more revolting and nauseous than a certain kind of remorse—crocodiles' tears, that's what it is.

THE MANAGER. Let's come to the point. This is only discussion.

THE FATHER. Very good, sir! But a fact is like a sack which won't stand up when it is empty. In order that it may stand up, one has to put into it the reason and sentiment which have caused it to exist. I couldn't possibly know that after the death of that man, they had decided to return here, that they were in misery, and that she (*pointing to the* MOTHER) had gone to work as a modiste, and at a shop of the type of that of Madame Pace.

THE STEPDAUGHTER. A real high-class modiste, you must know, gentlemen. In appearance, she works for the leaders of the best society; but she arranges matters so that these elegant ladies serve her purpose . . . without prejudice to other ladies who are . . . well . . . only so so.

THE MOTHER. You will believe me, gentlemen, that it never entered my mind that the old hag offered me work because she had her eye on my daughter.

THE STEPDAUGHTER. Poor mamma! Do you know, sir, what that woman did when I brought her back the work my mother had finished? She would point out to me that I had torn one of my frocks, and she would give it back to my mother to mend. It was I who paid for it, always I; while this poor creature here believed she was sacrificing herself for me and these two children here, sitting up at night sewing Madame Pace's robes.

THE MANAGER. And one day you met there. . . .

THE STEPDAUGHTER. Him, him. Yes, sir, an old client. There's a scene for you to play! Superb!

THE FATHER. She, the Mother arrived just then. . . .

THE STEPDAUGHTER (*Treacherously*). Almost in time!

THE FATHER (*Crying out*). No, in time! in time! Fortunately I recognized her . . . in time. And I took them back home with me to my house. You can imagine now her position and mine: she, as you see her; and I who cannot look her in the face.

THE STEPDAUGHTER. Absurd! How

can I possibly be expected—after that—to be a modest young miss, a fit person to go with his confounded aspirations for "a solid moral sanity"?

THE FATHER. For the drama lies all in this—in the conscience that I have, that each one of us has. We believe this conscience to be a single thing, but it is many-sided. There is one for this person, and another for that. Diverse consciences. So we have this illusion of being one person for all, of having a personality that is unique in all our acts. But it isn't true. We perceive this when, tragically perhaps, in something we do, we are, as it were, suspended, caught up in the air on a kind of hook. Then we perceive that all of us was not in that act, and that it would be an atrocious injustice to judge us by that action alone, as if all our existence were summed up in that one deed. Now do you understand the perfidy of this girl? She surprised me in a place where she ought not to have known me, just as I could not exist for her; and she now seeks to attach to me a reality such as I could never suppose I should have to assume for her in a shameful and fleeting moment of my life. I feel this above all else. And the drama, you will see, acquires a tremendous value from this point. Then there is the position of the others . . . his . . . (Indicating the SON)

THE SON (Shrugging his shoulders scornfully). Leave me alone! I don't come into this.

THE FATHER. What? You don't come into this?

THE SON. I've got nothing to do with it, and don't want to have; because you know well enough I wasn't made to be mixed up in all this with the rest of you.

THE STEPDAUGHTER. We are only vulgar folk! He is the fine gentleman. You may have noticed, Mr. Manager, that I fix him now and again with a look of scorn while he lowers his eyes—for he knows the evil he has done me.

THE SON (Scarcely looking at her). I?

THE STEPDAUGHTER. You! you! I owe my life on the streets to you. Did you or did you not deny us, with your behavior, I won't say the intimacy of home, but even that mere hospitality which makes guests feel at their ease? We were intruders who had come to disturb the kingdom of your legitimacy. I should like to have you witness, Mr. Manager, certain scenes between him and me. He says I have tyrannized over everyone. But it was just his behavior which made me insist on the reason for which I had come into the house—this reason he calls "vile" —into his house, with my mother, who is his mother too. And I came as mistress of the house.

THE SON. It's easy for them to put me always in the wrong. But imagine, gentlemen, the position of a son, whose fate it is to see arrive one day at his home a young woman of impudent bearing, a young woman who inquires for his father, with whom who knows what business she has. This young man has then to witness her return bolder than ever, accompanied by that child there. He is obliged to watch her treat his father in an equivocal and confidential manner. She asks money of him in a way that lets one suppose he must give it her, must, do you understand, because he has every obligation to do so.

THE FATHER. But I have, as a matter of fact, this obligation. I owe it to your mother.

THE SON. How should I know? When had I ever seen or heard of her? One day there arrive with her (indicating STEP-DAUGHTER) that lad and this baby here. I am told: "This is your mother too, you know." I divine from her manner (indicating STEPDAUGHTER again) why it is they have come home. I had rather not say what I feel and think about it. I shouldn't even care to confess to myself. No action can therefore be hoped for from me in this affair. Believe me, Mr. Manager, I am an "unrealized" character, dramatically speaking; and I find myself not at all at ease in their company. Leave me out of it, I beg you.

THE FATHER. What? It is just because you are so that . . .

THE SON. How do you know what I am like? When did you ever bother your head about me?

THE FATHER. I admit it. I admit it. But isn't that a situation in itself? This aloofness of yours which is so cruel to me and to your mother, who returns home and sees you almost for the first time grown up, who doesn't recognize you but knows you are her son . . . (*Pointing out the* MOTHER *to the* MANAGER) See, she's crying!

THE STEPDAUGHTER (*Angrily, stamping her foot*). Like a fool!

THE FATHER (*Indicating* STEPDAUGHTER). She can't stand him, you know. (*Then referring again to the* SON): He says he doesn't come into the affair, whereas he is really the hinge of the whole action. Look at that lad who is always clinging to his mother, frightened and humiliated. It is on account of this fellow here. Possibly his situation is the most painful of all. He feels himself a stranger more than the others. The poor little chap feels mortified, humiliated at being brought into a home out of charity as it were. (*In confidence*)—: He is the image of his father. Hardly talks at all. Humble and quiet.

THE MANAGER. Oh, we'll cut him out. You've no notion what a nuisance boys are on the stage . . .

THE FATHER. He disappears soon, you know. And the baby too. She is the first to vanish from the scene. The drama consists finally in this: when that mother re-enters my house, her family born outside of it, and shall we say superimposed on the original, ends with the death of the little girl, the tragedy of the boy and the flight of the elder daughter. It cannot go on, because it is foreign to its surroundings. So after much torment, we three remain: I, the mother, that son. Then, owing to the disappearance of that extraneous family, we too find ourselves strange to one another. We find we are living in an atmosphere of mortal desolation which is the revenge, as he (*indicating* SON) scornfully said of the Demon of Experiment, that unfortunately hides in me. Thus, sir, you see when faith is lacking, it becomes impossible to create certain states of happiness, for we lack the necessary humility. Vaingloriously, we try to substitute ourselves for this faith, creating thus for the rest of the world a reality which we believe after their fashion, while, actually, it doesn't exist. For each one of us has his own reality to be respected before God, even when it is harmful to one's very self.

THE MANAGER. There is something in what you say. I assure you all this interests me very much. I begin to think there's the stuff for a drama in all this, and not a bad drama either.

THE STEPDAUGHTER (*Coming forward*). When you've got a character like me.

THE FATHER (*Shutting her up, all excited to learn the decision of the* MANAGER). You be quiet!

THE MANAGER (*Reflecting, heedless of interruption*). It's new . . . hem . . . yes . . .

THE FATHER. Absolutely new!

THE MANAGER. You've got a nerve though, I must say, to come here and fling it at me like this . . .

THE FATHER. You will understand, sir, born as we are for the stage . . .

THE MANAGER. Are you amateur actors then?

THE FATHER. No, I say born for the stage, because . . .

THE MANAGER. Oh, nonsense. You're an old hand, you know.

THE FATHER. No sir, no. We act that rôle for which we have been cast, that rôle which we are given in life. And in my own case, passion itself, as usually happens, becomes a trifle theatrical when it is exalted.

THE MANAGER. Well, well, that will do. But you see, without an author . . . I could give you the address of an author if you like . . .

THE FATHER. No, no. Look here! You must be the author.

THE MANAGER. I? What are you talking about?

THE FATHER. Yes, you, you! Why not?

THE MANAGER. Because I have never been an author: that's why.

THE FATHER. Then why not turn author now? Everybody does it. You don't want any special qualities. Your task is made much easier by the fact that we are all here alive before you . . .

THE MANAGER. It won't do.

THE FATHER. What? When you see us live our drama . . .

THE MANAGER. Yes, that's all right. But you want someone to write it.

THE FATHER. No, no. Someone to take it down, possibly, while we play it, scene by scene! It will be enough to sketch it out at first, and then try it over.

THE MANAGER. Well . . . I am almost

tempted. It's a bit of an idea. One might have a shot at it.

THE FATHER. Of course. You'll see what scenes will come out of it. I can give you one, at once . . .

THE MANAGER. By Jove, it tempts me. I'd like to have a go at it. Let's try it out. Come with me to my office. (*Turning to the* ACTORS) You are at liberty for a bit, but don't stop out of the theater for long. In a quarter of an hour, twenty minutes, all back here again! (*To the* FATHER). We'll see what can be done. Who knows if we don't get something really extraordinary out of it?

THE FATHER. There's no doubt about it. They (*indicating the* CHARACTERS) had better come with us too, hadn't they?

THE MANAGER. Yes, yes. Come on! come on! (*Moves away and then turning to the* ACTORS). Be punctual, please! (MANAGER *and the* SIX CHARACTERS *cross the stage and go off. The other* ACTORS *remain, looking at one another in astonishment*)

LEADING MAN. Is he serious? What the devil does he want to do?

JUVENILE LEAD. This is rank madness.

THIRD ACTOR. Does he expect to knock up a drama in five minutes?

JUVENILE LEAD. Like the improvisers!

LEADING LADY. If he thinks I'm going to take part in a joke like this . . .

JUVENILE LEAD. I'm out of it anyway.

FOURTH ACTOR. I should like to know who they are. (*Alludes to* CHARACTERS)

THIRD ACTOR. What do you suppose? Madmen or rascals!

JUVENILE LEAD. And he takes them seriously!

L'INGÉNUE. Vanity! He fancies himself as an author now.

LEADING MAN. It's absolutely unheard of. If the stage has come to this . . . well I'm . . .

FIFTH ACTOR. It's rather a joke.

THIRD ACTOR. Well, we'll see what's going to happen next.

(*Thus talking, the* ACTORS *leave the stage; some going out by the little door at the back; others retiring to their dressing-rooms.*

The curtain remains up.

The action of the play is suspended for twenty minutes)

Act II

The stage call-bells ring to warn the company that the play is about to begin again.

THE STEPDAUGHTER *comes out of the* MANAGER*'s office along with The* CHILD *and the* BOY. *As she comes out of the office, she cries:*

Nonsense! Nonsense! Do it yourselves! I'm not going to mix myself up in this mess. (*Turning to the* CHILD *and coming quickly with her on to the stage*) Come on, Rosetta, let's run!

(THE BOY *follows them slowly, remaining a little behind and seeming perplexed*)

THE STEPDAUGHTER (*Stops, bends over the* CHILD *and takes the latter's face between her hands*). My little darling! You're frightened, aren't you? You don't know where we are, do you? (*Pretending to reply to a question of the* CHILD) What is the stage? It's a place, baby, you know, where people play at being serious, a place where they act comedies. We've got to act a comedy now, dead serious, you know; and you're in it also, little one. (*Embraces her, pressing the little head to her breast, and rocking the* CHILD *for a moment*) Oh darling, darling, what a horrid comedy you've got to play! What a wretched part they've found for you! A garden . . . a fountain . . . look . . . just suppose, kiddie, it's here. Where, you say? Why, right here in the middle. It's all pretence you know. That's the trouble, my pet: it's all make-believe here. It's better to imagine it though, because if they fix it up for you, it'll only be painted cardboard, painted cardboard for the rockery, the water, the plants . . . Ah, but I think a baby like this one would sooner have a make-believe fountain than a real one, so she could play with it. What a joke it'll be for the others! But for you, alas! not quite such a joke: you who are real, baby dear, and really play by a real fountain that is big and green and beautiful, with ever so many bamboos around it that are reflected in the water, and a whole lot of little ducks swimming about . . . No, Rosetta, no, your mother doesn't bother about you on account of that wretch of a son there. I'm in the devil of a temper, and as for that lad . . . (*Seizes* BOY *by the arm to force him to take one of his hands out of his pockets*) What have you got there? What are you hiding? (*Pulls his hand out of his pocket, looks into it and catches the glint of a revolver*) Ah, where did you get this?

(THE BOY, *very pale in the face, looks at her, but does not answer*) Idiot! If I'd been in your place, instead of killing myself, I'd have shot one of those two, or both of them: father and son.

(THE FATHER *enters from the office, all excited from his work.* THE MANAGER *follows him*)

THE FATHER. Come on, come on, dear! Come here for a minute! We've arranged everything. It's all fixed up.

THE MANAGER (*Also excited*). If you please, young lady, there are one or two points to settle still. Will you come along?

THE STEPDAUGHTER (*Following him towards the office*). Ouff! what's the good, if you've arranged everything.

(THE FATHER, MANAGER *and* STEP-DAUGHTER *go back into the office again* [*off*] *for a moment. At the same time, THE* SON, *followed by* THE MOTHER, *comes out*)

THE SON (*Looking at the three entering office*). Oh this is fine, fine! And to think I can't even get away!

(THE MOTHER *attempts to look at him, but lowers her eyes immediately when he turns away from her. She then sits down.* THE BOY *and* THE CHILD *approach her. She casts a glance again at the* SON, *and speaks with humble tones, trying to draw him into conversation*)

THE MOTHER. And isn't my punishment the worst of all? (*Then seeing from the* SON'S *manner that he will not bother himself about her*) My God! Why are you so cruel? Isn't it enough for one person to support all this torment? Must you then insist on others seeing it also?

THE SON (*Half to himself, meaning the* MOTHER *to hear, however*). And they want to put it on the stage! If there was at least a reason for it! He thinks he has got at the meaning of it all. Just as if each one of us in every circumstance of life couldn't find his own explanation of it! (*Pauses*) He complains he was discovered in a place where he ought not to have been seen, in a moment of his life

which ought to have remained hidden and kept out of the reach of that convention which he has to maintain for other people. And what about my case? Haven't I had to reveal what no son ought ever to reveal: how father and mother live and are man and wife for themselves quite apart from that idea of father and mother which we give them? When this idea is revealed, our life is then linked at one point only to that man and that woman; and as such it should shame them, shouldn't it?

(THE MOTHER *hides her face in her hands. From the dressing-rooms and the little door at the back of the stage the* ACTORS *and* STAGE MANAGER *return, followed by the* PROPERTY MAN, *and the* PROMPTER. *At the same moment, THE* MANAGER *comes out of his office, accompanied by the* FATHER *and the* STEP-DAUGHTER)

THE MANAGER. Come on, come on, ladies and gentlemen! Heh! you there, machinist!

MACHINIST. Yes sir?

THE MANAGER. Fix up the white parlor with the floral decorations. Two wings and a drop with a door will do. Hurry up!

(THE MACHINIST *runs off at once to prepare the scene, and arranges it while* THE MANAGER *talks with the* STAGE MAN-AGER, *the* PROPERTY MAN, *and the* PROMPTER *on matters of detail*).

THE MANAGER (*To* PROPERTY MAN). Just have a look, and see if there isn't a sofa or divan in the wardrobe . . .

PROPERTY MAN. There's the green one.

THE STEPDAUGHTER. No, no! Green won't do. It was yellow, ornamented with flowers—very large! and most comfortable!

PROPERTY MAN. There isn't one like that.

THE MANAGER. It doesn't matter! Use the one we've got.

THE STEPDAUGHTER. Doesn't matter? It's most important!

THE MANAGER. We're only trying it now. Please don't interfere. (*To* PROP-ERTY MAN) See if we've got a shop window—long and narrowish.

THE STEPDAUGHTER. And the little table! The little mahogany table for the pale blue envelope!

PROPERTY MAN (*To* MANAGER). There's that little gilt one.

THE MANAGER. That'll do fine.

THE FATHER. A mirror.

THE STEPDAUGHTER. And the screen! We must have a screen. Otherwise how can I manage?

PROPERTY MAN. That's all right, Miss. We've got any amount of them.

THE MANAGER (*To the* STEPDAUGHTER). We want some clothes pegs too, don't we?

THE STEPDAUGHTER. Yes, several, several!

THE MANAGER. See how many we've got and bring them all.

PROPERTY MAN. All right!

(*The* PROPERTY MAN *hurries off to obey his orders. While he is putting the things in their places, the* MANAGER *talks to the* PROMPTER *and then with the* CHARACTERS *and the* ACTORS)

THE MANAGER (*To* PROMPTER). Take your seat. Look here: this is the outline of the scenes, act by act. (*Hands him some sheets of paper*) And now I'm going to ask you to do something out of the ordinary.

PROMPTER. Take it down in shorthand?

THE MANAGER (*Pleasantly surprised*). Exactly! Can you do shorthand?

PROMPTER. Yes, a little.

MANAGER. Good! (*Turning to a stage hand*) Go and get some paper from my office, plenty, as much as you can find.

(*The* STAGE HAND *goes off, and soon returns with a handful of paper which he gives to the* PROMPTER)

THE MANAGER (*To* PROMPTER). You follow the scenes as we play them, and try and get the points down, at any rate the most important ones. (*Then addressing the* ACTORS) Clear the stage, ladies and gentlemen! Come over here (*Pointing to the Left*) and listen attentively.

LEADING LADY. But, excuse me, we . . .

THE MANAGER. (*Guessing her thought*). Don't worry! You won't have to improvise.

LEADING MAN. What have we to do then?

THE MANAGER. Nothing. For the moment you just watch and listen. Everybody will get his part written out afterwards. At present we're going to try the thing as best we can. They're going to act now.

THE FATHER (*As if fallen from the clouds into the confusion of the stage*). We? What do you mean, if you please, by a rehearsal?

THE MANAGER. A rehearsal for them. (*Points to the* ACTORS)

THE FATHER. But since we are the characters . . .

THE MANAGER. All right: "characters" then, if you insist on calling yourselves such. But here, my dear sir, the characters don't act. Here the actors do the acting. The characters are there, in the "book"— (*Pointing towards* PROMPTER'S box) when there is a "book"!

THE FATHER. I won't contradict you; but excuse me, the actors aren't the characters. They want to be, they pretend to be, don't they? Now if these gentlemen here are fortunate enough to have us alive before them . . .

THE MANAGER. Oh this is grand! You want to come before the public yourselves then?

THE FATHER. As we are . . .

THE MANAGER. I can assure you it would be a magnificent spectacle!

LEADING MAN. What's the use of us here anyway then?

THE MANAGER. You're not going to pretend that you can act? It makes me laugh! (*The* ACTORS *laugh*) There, you see, they are laughing at the notion. But, by the way, I must cast the parts. That won't be difficult. They cast themselves. (*To the* SECOND LADY LEAD) You play the Mother. (*To the* FATHER) We must find her a name.

THE FATHER. Amalia, sir.

THE MANAGER. But that is the real name of your wife. We don't want to call her by her real name.

THE FATHER. Why ever not, if it is her name? . . . Still, perhaps, if that lady must . . . (*Makes a slight motion of the hand to indicate the* SECOND LADY LEAD) I see this woman here (*means the* MOTHER) as Amalia. But do as you like. (*Gets more and more confused*) I don't know what to say to you. Already, I begin to hear my own words ring false, as if they had another sound . . .

THE MANAGER. Don't you worry about it. It'll be our job to find the right tones. And as for her name, if you want her Amalia, Amalia it shall be; and if you don't like it, we'll find another! For the moment though, we'll call the characters in this way: (*to* JUVENILE LEAD) You are the Son; (*to the* LEADING LADY) You naturally are the Stepdaughter . . .

THE STEPDAUGHTER (*Excitedly*). What? what? I, that woman there? (*Bursts out laughing*)

THE MANAGER (*Angry*). What is there to laugh at?

LEADING LADY (*Indignant*). Nobody has ever dared to laugh at me. I insist on being treated with respect; otherwise I go away.

THE STEPDAUGHTER. No, no, excuse me . . . I am not laughing at you . . .

THE MANAGER (*To* STEPDAUGHTER). You ought to feel honored to be played by . . .

LEADING LADY (*At once, contemptuously*). "That woman there" . . .

THE STEPDAUGHTER. But I wasn't speaking of you, you know. I was speaking of myself—whom I can't see at all in you! That is all. I don't know . . . but . . . you . . . aren't in the least like me . . .

THE FATHER. True. Here's the point. Look here, sir, our temperaments, our souls . . .

THE MANAGER. Temperament, soul, be hanged. Do you suppose the spirit of the piece is in you? Nothing of the kind!

THE FATHER. What, haven't we our own temperaments, our own souls?

THE MANAGER. Not at all. Your soul or whatever you like to call it takes shape here. The actors give body and form to it, voice and gesture. And my actors—I may tell you—have given expression to much more lofty material than this little drama of yours, which may or may not hold up on the stage. But if it does, the merit of it, believe me, will be due to my actors.

THE FATHER. I don't dare contradict you, sir; but, believe me, it is a terrible suffering for us who are as we are, with these bodies of ours, these features to see . . .

THE MANAGER (*Cutting him short and out of patience*). Good heavens! The make-up will remedy all that, man, the make-up . . .

THE FATHER. Maybe. But the voice, the gestures . . .

THE MANAGER. Now, look here! On the stage, you as yourself, cannot exist. The actor here acts you, and that's an end to it!

THE FATHER. I understand. And now I think I see why our author who conceived us as we are, all alive, didn't want to put us on the stage after all. I haven't the least desire to offend your actors. Far from it! But when I think that I am to be acted by . . . I don't know by whom . . .

LEADING MAN (*On his dignity*). By me, if you've no objection!

THE FATHER (*Humbly, mellifluously*). Honored, I assure you, sir. (*Bows*) Still, I must say that try as this gentleman may, with all his good will and wonderful art, to absorb me into himself . . .

LEADING MAN. Oh chuck it! "Wonderful art!" Withdraw that, please!

THE FATHER. The performance he will give, even doing his best with make-up to look like me . . .

LEADING MAN. It will certainly be a bit difficult! (*The* ACTORS *laugh*)

THE FATHER. Exactly! It will be difficult to act me as I really am. The effect will be rather—apart from the make-up—according as to how he supposes I am, as he senses me—if he does sense me—and not as I inside of myself feel myself to be. It seems to me then that account should be taken of this by everyone whose duty it may become to criticize us . . .

THE MANAGER. Heavens! The man's starting to think about the critics now! Let them say what they like. It's up to us to put on the play if we can. (*Looking around*) Come on! come on! Is the stage set? (*To the* ACTORS *and* CHARACTERS) Stand back—stand back! Let me see, and don't let's lose any more time! (*To the* STEPDAUGHTER) Is it all right as it is now?

THE STEPDAUGHTER. Well, to tell the truth, I don't recognize the scene.

THE MANAGER. My dear lady, you can't possibly suppose that we can construct that shop of Madame Pace piece by piece here? (*To the* FATHER) You said a white room with flowered wall paper, didn't you?

THE FATHER. Yes.

THE MANAGER. Well then. We've got the furniture right, more or less. Bring that little table a bit further forward. (*The* STAGE HANDS *obey the order. To* PROPERTY MAN) You go and find an envelope, if possible, a pale blue one; and give it to that gentleman. (*Indicates* FATHER)

PROPERTY MAN. An ordinary envelope?

MANAGER *and* FATHER. Yes, yes, an ordinary envelope.

PROPERTY MAN. At once, sir. (*Exit*)

THE MANAGER. Ready, everyone! First scene—the Young Lady. (*The* LEADING LADY *comes forward*) No, no, you must wait. I meant her. (*Indicating the* STEP-DAUGHTER) You just watch—

THE STEPDAUGHTER (*Adding at once*). How I shall play it, how I shall live it! . . .

LEADING LADY (*Offended*). I shall live it also, you may be sure, as soon as I begin!

THE MANAGER (*With his hands to his head*). Ladies and gentlemen, if you please! No more useless discussions! Scene I: the young lady with Madame Pace: Oh! (*Looks around as if lost*) And this Madame Pace, where is she?

THE FATHER. She isn't with us, sir.

THE MANAGER. Then what the devil's to be done?

THE FATHER. But she is alive too.

THE MANAGER. Yes, but where is she?

THE FATHER. One minute. Let me speak! (*Turning to the* ACTRESSES) If these ladies would be so good as to give me their hats for a moment . . .

THE ACTRESSES (*Half surprised, half laughing, in chorus*). What?
Why?
Our hats?
What does he say?

THE MANAGER. What are you going to do with the ladies' hats? (*The* ACTORS *laugh*)

THE FATHER. Oh nothing. I just want to put them on these pegs for a moment. And one of the ladies will be so kind as to take off her mantle . . .

THE ACTORS. Oh, what d'you think of that? Only the mantle?
He must be mad.

SOME ACTRESSES. But why?
Mantles as well?

THE FATHER. To hang them up here for a moment. Please be so kind, will you?

THE ACTRESSES. (*Taking off their hats, one or two also their cloaks, and going to hang them on the racks*) After all, why not?

There you are!
This is really funny.
We've got to put them on show.

THE FATHER. Exactly; just like that, on show.

THE MANAGER. May we know why?

THE FATHER. I'll tell you. Who knows if, by arranging the stage for her, she does not come here herself, attracted by the very articles of her trade? (*Inviting the* ACTORS *to look towards the exit at back of stage*) Look! Look!

(*The door at the back of stage opens and* MADAME PACE *enters and takes a few steps forward. She is a fat, oldish woman with puffy oxygenated hair. She is rouged and powdered, dressed with a comical elegance in black silk. Round her waist is a long silver chain from which hangs a pair of scissors. The* STEPDAUGHTER *runs over to her at once amid the stupor of the* ACTORS)

THE STEPDAUGHTER (*Turning towards her*). There she is! There she is!

THE FATHER (*Radiant*). It's she! I said so, didn't I? There she is!

THE MANAGER (*Conquering his surprise, and then becoming indignant*). What sort of a trick is this?

LEADING MAN (*Almost at the same time*). What's going to happen next?

JUVENILE LEAD. Where does *she* come from?

L'INGÉNUE. They've been holding her in reserve, I guess.

LEADING LADY. A vulgar trick!

THE FATHER (*Dominating the protests*). Excuse me, all of you! Why are you so anxious to destroy in the name of a vulgar, commonplace sense of truth, this reality which comes to birth attracted and formed by the magic of the stage itself, which has indeed more right to live here than you, since it is much truer than you—if you don't mind my saying so? Which is the actress among you who is to play Madame Pace? Well, here is Madame Pace herself. And you will allow, I fancy, that the actress who acts her will be less true than this woman here, who is herself in person. You see my daughter recognized her and went over to her at once. Now you're going to witness the scene!

(*But the scene between the* STEPDAUGH-TER *and* MADAME PACE *has already begun despite the protest of the* ACTORS *and the reply of* THE FATHER. *It has begun quietly, naturally, in a manner impossible for the stage. So when the* ACTORS, *called to attention by* THE FATHER, *turn round and see* MADAME PACE, *who has placed one hand under the* STEPDAUGHTER'S *chin to raise her head, they observe her at first with great attention, but hearing her speak in an unintelligible manner their interest begins to wane)*

THE MANAGER. Well? well?

LEADING MAN. What does she say?

LEADING LADY. One can't hear a word.

JUVENILE LEAD. Louder! Louder please!

THE STEPDAUGHTER (*Leaving* MADAME PACE, *who smiles a Sphinx-like smile, and advancing towards the* ACTORS). Louder? Louder? What are you talking about? These aren't matters which can be shouted at the top of one's voice. If I have spoken them out loud, it was to shame him and have my revenge. (*Indicates* FATHER) But for Madame it's quite a different matter.

THE MANAGER. Indeed? indeed? But here, you know, people have got to make themselves heard, my dear. Even we who are on the stage can't hear you. What will it be when the public's in the theater? And anyway, you can very well speak up now among yourselves, since we shan't be present to listen to you as we are now. You've got to pretend to be alone in a room at the back of a shop where no one can hear you.

(THE STEPDAUGHTER *coquettishly and with a touch of malice makes a sign of disagreement two or three times with her finger*)

THE MANAGER. What do you mean by no?

THE STEPDAUGHTER (*Sotto voce, mysteriously*). There's someone who will hear us if she (*indicating* MADAME PACE) speaks out loud.

THE MANAGER (*In consternation*). What? Have you got someone else to spring on us now? (*The* ACTORS *burst out laughing*)

THE FATHER. No, no sir. She is alluding to me. I've got to be here—there behind that door, in waiting; and Madame Pace knows it. In fact, if you will allow me, I'll go there at once, so I can be quite ready. (*Moves away*)

THE MANAGER (*Stopping him*). No! wait! wait! We must observe the conventions of the theater. Before you are ready . . .

THE STEPDAUGHTER (*Interrupting him*). No, get on with it at once! I'm just dying, I tell you, to act this scene. If he's ready, I'm more than ready.

THE MANAGER (*Shouting*). But, my dear young lady, first of all, we must have the scene between you and this lady . . . (*Indicates* MADAME PACE) Do you understand? . . .

THE STEPDAUGHTER. Good Heavens! She's been telling me what you know already: that Mamma's work is badly done again, that the material's ruined; and that if I want her to continue to help us in our misery I must be patient . . .

MADAME PACE (*Coming forward with an air of great importance*). Yes indeed, sir, I no wanta take advantage of her, I no wanta be hard . . .

(*Note:* MADAME PACE *is supposed to talk in a jargon half Italian, half English*)

THE MANAGER (*Alarmed*). What? What? she talks like that? (*The* ACTORS *burst out laughing again*)

THE STEPDAUGHTER (*Also laughing*). Yes, yes, that's the way she talks, half English, half Italian! Most comical it is!

MADAME PACE. Itta seem not verra polite gentlemen laugha atta me eef I trya best speaka English.

THE MANAGER. *Diamine!* Of course! Of course! Let her talk like that! Just what we want. Talk just like that, Madame, if you please! The effect will be certain. Exactly what was wanted to put a little comic relief into the crudity of the situation. Of course she talks like that! Magnificent!

THE STEPDAUGHTER. Magnificent? Certainly! When certain suggestions are made to one in language of that kind, the effect is certain, since it seems almost a joke. One feels inclined to laugh when one hears her talk about an "old signore" "who wanta talka nicely with you." Nice old signore, eh, Madame?

MADAME PACE. Not so old, my dear, not so old! And even if you no lika him, he won't make any scandal!

THE MOTHER (*Jumping up amid the amazement and consternation of the* ACTORS *who had not been noticing her. They move to restrain her*). You old devil! You murderess!

THE STEPDAUGHTER (*Running over*

to calm her MOTHER). Calm yourself, mother, calm yourself! Please don't . . .

THE FATHER (*Going to her also at the same time*). Calm yourself! Don't get excited! Sit down now!

THE MOTHER. Well then, take that woman away out of my sight!

THE STEPDAUGHTER (*To* MANAGER). It is impossible for my mother to remain here.

THE FATHER (*To* MANAGER). They can't be here together. And for this reason, you see: that woman there was not with us when we came . . . If they are on together, the whole thing is given away inevitably, as you see.

THE MANAGER. It doesn't matter. This is only a first rough sketch—just to get an idea of the various points of the scene, even confusedly . . . (*Turning to* the MOTHER *and leading her to her chair*) Come along, my dear lady, sit down now, and let's get on with the scene . . .

(*Meanwhile, the* STEPDAUGHTER, *coming forward again, turns to* MADAME PACE)

THE STEPDAUGHTER. Come on, Madame, come on!

MADAME PACE (*Offended*). No, no, grazie. I not do anything witha your mother present.

THE STEPDAUGHTER. Nonsense! Introduce this "old signore" who wants to talk nicely to me. (*Addressing the company imperiously*) We've got to do this scene one way or another, haven't we? Come on! (*To* MADAME PACE) You can go!

MADAME PACE. Ah yes! I go'way! I go'way! Certainly! (*Exits furious*)

THE STEPDAUGHTER (*To the* FATHER). Now you make your entry. No, you needn't go over there. Come here. Let's suppose you've already come in. Like that, yes! I'm here with bowed head, modest-like. Come on! Out with your voice! Say "Good morning, Miss" in that peculiar tone, that special tone . . .

THE MANAGER. Excuse me, but are you the Manager, or am I? (*To the* FATHER, *who looks undecided and perplexed*) Get on with it, man! Go down there to the back of the stage. You needn't go off. Then come right forward here.

(THE FATHER *does as he is told, looking troubled and perplexed at first. But as soon as he begins to move, the reality of*

the action affects him, and he begins to smile and to be more natural. The ACTORS *watch intently*)

THE MANAGER (*Sotto voce, quickly to the* PROMPTER *in his box*). Ready! ready? Get ready to write now.

THE FATHER (*Coming forward and speaking in a different tone*). Good afternoon, Miss!

THE STEPDAUGHTER (*Head bowed down slightly, with restrained disgust*). Good afternoon!

THE FATHER (*Looks under her hat which partly covers her face. Perceiving she is very young, he makes an exclamation, partly of surprise, partly of fear lest he compromise himself in a risky adventure*). Ah . . . but . . . ah . . . I say . . . this is not the first time that you have come here, is it?

THE STEPDAUGHTER (*Modestly*). No sir.

THE FATHER. You've been here before, eh? (*Then seeing her nod agreement*) More than once? (*Waits for her to answer, looks under her hat, smiles, and then says*) Well then, there's no need to be so shy, is there? May I take off your hat?

THE STEPDAUGHTER (*Anticipating him and with veiled disgust*). No sir . . . I'll do it myself. (*Takes it off quickly*)

(THE MOTHER, *who watches the progress of the scene with* THE SON *and the other two* CHILDREN *who cling to her, is on thorns; and follows with varying expressions of sorrow, indignation, anxiety, and horror the words and actions of the other two. From time to time she hides her face in her hands and sobs*)

THE MOTHER. Oh, my God, my God!

THE FATHER (*Playing his part with a touch of gallantry*). Give it to me! I'll put it down. (*Takes hat from her hands*) But a dear little head like yours ought to have a smarter hat. Come and help me choose one from the stock, won't you?

L'INGÉNUE (*Interrupting*). I say . . . those are our hats, you know.

THE MANAGER (*Furious*). Silence! silence! Don't try and be funny, if you please . . . We're playing the scene now, I'd have you notice. (*To the* STEPDAUGHTER) Begin again, please!

THE STEPDAUGHTER (*Continuing*). No thank you, sir.

THE FATHER. Oh, come now. Don't

talk like that. You must take it. I shall be upset if you don't. There are some lovely little hats here; and then—Madame will be pleased. She expects it, anyway, you know.

THE STEPDAUGHTER. No, no! I couldn't wear it!

THE FATHER. Oh, you're thinking about what they'd say at home if they saw you come in with a new hat? My dear girl, there's always a way round these little matters, you know.

THE STEPDAUGHTER (*All keyed up*). No, it's not that. I couldn't wear it because I am . . . as you see . . . you might have noticed . . . (*Showing her black dress*)

THE FATHER. . . . in mourning! Of course: I beg your pardon: I'm frightfully sorry . . .

THE STEPDAUGHTER (*Forcing herself to conquer her indignation and nausea*). Stop! Stop! It's I who must thank you. There's no need for you to feel mortified or specially sorry. Don't think any more of what I've said. (*Tries to smile*) I must forget that I am dressed so . . .

THE MANAGER (*Interrupting and turning to the* PROMPTER). Stop a minute! Stop! Don't write that down. Cut out that last bit. (*Then to the* FATHER *and* STEPDAUGHTER) Fine! it's going fine! (*To the* FATHER *only*) And now you can go on as we arranged. (*To the* ACTORS) Pretty good that scene, where he offers her the hat, eh?

THE STEPDAUGHTER. The best's coming now. Why can't we go on?

THE MANAGER. Have a little patience! (*To the* ACTORS) Of course, it must be treated rather lightly.

LEADING MAN. Still, with a bit of go in it!

LEADING LADY. Of course! It's easy enough! (*To* LEADING MAN) Shall you and I try it now?

LEADING MAN. Why, yes! I'll prepare my entrance. (*Exit in order to make his entrance*)

THE MANAGER (*To* LEADING LADY). See here! The scene between you and Madame Pace is finished. I'll have it written out properly after. You remain here . . . oh, where are you going?

LEADING LADY. One minute. I want to put my hat on again. (*Goes over to hatrack and puts her hat on her head*).

THE MANAGER. Good! You stay here with your head bowed down a bit.

THE STEPDAUGHTER. But she isn't dressed in black.

LEADING LADY. But I shall be, and much more effectively than you.

THE MANAGER (*To* STEPDAUGHTER). Be quiet please, and watch! You'll be able to learn something. (*Clapping his hands*) Come on! come on! Entrance, please!

(*The door at rear of stage opens, and the* LEADING MAN *enters with the lively manner of an old gallant. The rendering of the scene by the* ACTORS *from the very first words is seen to be quite a different thing, though it has not in any way the air of a parody. Naturally, the* STEPDAUGHTER *and the* FATHER, *not being able to recognize themselves in the* LEADING LADY *and the* LEADING MAN, *who deliver their words in different tones and with a different psychology, express, sometimes with smiles, sometimes with gestures, the impression they receive*)

LEADING MAN. Good afternoon, Miss . . .

THE FATHER (*At once unable to contain himself*). No! no!

(THE STEPDAUGHTER, *noticing the way the* LEADING MAN *enters, bursts out laughing*)

THE MANAGER (*Furious*). Silence! And you, please, just stop that laughing. If we go on like this, we shall never finish.

THE STEPDAUGHTER. Forgive me, sir, but it's natural enough. This lady (*indicating* LEADING LADY) stands there still; but if she is supposed to be me, I can assure you that if I heard anyone say "Good afternoon" in that manner and in that tone, I should burst out laughing as I did.

THE FATHER. Yes, yes, the manner, the tone . . .

THE MANAGER. Nonsense! Rubbish! Stand aside and let me see the action.

LEADING MAN. If I've got to represent an old fellow who's coming into a house of an equivocal character . . .

THE MANAGER. Don't listen to them, for Heaven's sake! Do it again! It goes fine. (*Waiting for the* ACTORS *to begin again*) Well?

LEADING MAN. Good afternoon, Miss.

LEADING LADY. Good afternoon.

LEADING MAN (*Imitating the gesture*

of the FATHER *when he looked under the hat, and then expressing quite clearly first satisfaction and then fear).* Ah, but . . . I say . . . this is not the first time that you have come here, is it?

THE MANAGER. Good, but not quite so heavily. Like this. (*Acts himself*) "This isn't the first time that you have come here" . . . (*To* LEADING LADY) And you say: "No, sir."

LEADING LADY. No, sir.

LEADING MAN. You've been here before, more than once.

THE MANAGER. No, no, stop! Let her nod "yes" first. "You've been here before, eh?" (*The* LEADING LADY *lifts up her head slightly and closes her eyes as though in disgust. Then she inclines her head twice*)

THE STEPDAUGHTER (*Unable to contain herself*) Oh my God! (*Puts a hand to her mouth to prevent herself from laughing*)

THE MANAGER (*Turning round*). What's the matter?

THE STEPDAUGHTER. Nothing, nothing!

THE MANAGER (*To* LEADING MAN). Go on!

LEADING MAN. You've been here before, eh? Well then, there's no need to be so shy, is there? May I take off your hat?

(*The* LEADING MAN *says this last speech in such a tone and with such gestures that the* STEPDAUGHTER, *though she has her hand to her mouth, cannot keep from laughing*)

LEADING LADY (*Indignant*). I'm not going to stop here to be made a fool of by that woman there.

LEADING MAN. Neither am I! I'm through with it!

THE MANAGER (*Shouting to* STEPDAUGHTER). Silence! for once and all, I tell you!

THE STEPDAUGHTER. Forgive me! forgive me!

THE MANAGER. You haven't any manners: that's what it is! You go too far.

THE FATHER (*Endeavoring to intervene*). Yes, it's true, but excuse her . . .

THE MANAGER. Excuse what? It's absolutely disgusting.

THE FATHER. Yes, sir, but believe me, it has such a strange effect when . . .

THE MANAGER. Strange? Why strange? Where is it strange?

THE FATHER. No, sir; I admire your actors—this gentleman here, this lady; but they are certainly not us!

THE MANAGER. I should hope not. Evidently they cannot be you, if they are actors.

THE FATHER. Just so: actors! Both of them act our parts exceedingly well. But, believe me, it produces quite a different effect on us. They want to be us, but they aren't, all the same.

THE MANAGER. What is it then anyway?

THE FATHER. Something that is . . . that is theirs—and no longer ours . . .

THE MANAGER. But naturally, inevitably. I've told you so already.

THE FATHER. Yes, I understand . . . I understand . . .

THE MANAGER. Well then, let's have no more of it! (*Turning to the* ACTORS) We'll have the rehearsals by ourselves, afterwards, in the ordinary way. I never could stand rehearsing with the author present. He's never satisfied! (*Turning to* FATHER *and* STEPDAUGHTER) Come on! Let's get on with it again; and try and see if you can't keep from laughing.

THE STEPDAUGHTER. Oh, I shan't laugh any more. There's a nice little bit coming from me now: you'll see.

THE MANAGER. Well then: when she says "Don't think any more of what I've said. I must forget, etc.," you (*addressing the* FATHER) come in sharp with "I understand, I understand"; and then you ask her . . .

THE STEPDAUGHTER (*Interrupting*). What?

THE MANAGER. Why she is in mourning.

THE STEPDAUGHTER. Not at all! See here: when I told him that it was useless for me to be thinking about my wearing mourning, do you know how he answered me? "Ah well," he said, "then let's take off this little frock."

THE MANAGER. Great! Just what we want, to make a riot in the theater!

THE STEPDAUGHTER. But its the truth!

THE MANAGER. What does that matter? Acting is our business here. Truth up to a certain point, but no further.

THE STEPDAUGHTER. What do you want to do then?

THE MANAGER. You'll see, you'll see! Leave it to me.

THE STEPDAUGHTER. No sir! What you want to do is to piece together a little romantic sentimental scene out of my disgust, out of all the reasons, each more cruel and viler than the other, why I am what I am. He is to ask me why I'm in mourning; and I'm to answer with tears in my eyes, that it is just two months since papa died. No sir, no! He's got to say to me; as he did say: "Well, let's take off this little dress at once." And I; with my two months' mourning in my heart, went there behind that screen, and with these fingers tingling with shame . . .

THE MANAGER (*Running his hands through his hair*). For Heaven's sake! What are you saying?

THE STEPDAUGHTER (*Crying out excitedly*). The truth! The truth!

THE MANAGER. It may be. I don't deny it, and I can understand all your horror; but you must surely see that you can't have this kind of thing on the stage. It won't go.

THE STEPDAUGHTER. Not possible, eh? Very well! I'm much obliged to you— but I'm off!

THE MANAGER. Now be reasonable! Don't lose your temper!

THE STEPDAUGHTER. I won't stop here! I won't! I can see you've fixed it all up with him in your office. All this talk about what is possible for the stage . . . I understand! He wants to get at his complicated "cerebral drama," to have his famous remorses and torments acted; but I want to act my part, *my part!*

THE MANAGER (*Annoyed, shaking his shoulders*) Ah! Just *your* part! But, if you will pardon me, there are other parts than yours: his (*indicating the* FATHER) and hers! (*Indicating the* MOTHER) On the stage you can't have a character becoming too prominent and overshadowing all the others. The thing is to pack them all into a neat little framework and then act what is actable. I am aware of the fact that everyone has his own interior life which he wants very much to put forward. But the difficulty lies in this fact: to set out just so much as is necessary for the stage, taking the other characters into consideration, and at the same time hint at the unrevealed interior life of each. I am willing to admit, my dear young lady, that from your point of view it would be a fine idea if each character could tell the public all his troubles in a nice monologue or a regular one-hour lecture. (*Good-humoredly*) You must restrain yourself, my dear, and in your own interest, too; because this fury of yours, this exaggerated disgust you show, may make a bad impression, you know. After you have confessed to me that there were others before him at Madame Pace's and more than once . . .

THE STEPDAUGHTER (*Bowing her head, impressed*). It's true. But remember those others mean him for me all the same.

THE MANAGER (*Not understanding*). What? The others? What do you mean?

THE STEPDAUGHTER. For one who has gone wrong, sir, he who was responsible for the first fault is responsible for all that follow. He is responsible for my faults, was, even before I was born. Look at him, and see if it isn't true!

THE MANAGER. Well, well! And does the weight of so much responsibility seem nothing to you? Give him a chance to act it, to get it over!

THE STEPDAUGHTER. How? How can he act all his "noble remorses," all his "moral torments," if you want to spare him the horror of being discovered one day—after he had asked her what he did ask her—in the arms of her, that already fallen woman, that child, sir, that child he used to watch come out of school? (*She is moved*)

(THE MOTHER *at this point is overcome with emotion, and breaks out into a fit of crying.*

All are touched. A long pause)

THE STEPDAUGHTER (*As soon as the* MOTHER *becomes a little quieter, adds resolutely and gravely*). At present, we are unknown to the public. Tomorrow, you will act us as you wish, treating us in your own manner. But do you really want to see drama, do you want to see it flash out as it really did?

THE MANAGER. Of course! That's just what I do want, so I can use as much of it as is possible.

THE STEPDAUGHTER. Well then, ask that Mother there to leave us.

THE MOTHER (*Changing her low plaint*

into a sharp cry). No! No! Don't permit it, sir, don't permit it!

THE MANAGER. But it's only to try it.

THE MOTHER. I can't bear it. I can't.

THE MANAGER. But since it has happened already . . . I don't understand!

THE MOTHER. It's taking place now. It happens all the time. My torment isn't a pretended one. I live and feel every minute of my torture. Those two children there—have you heard them speak? They can't speak any more. They cling to me to keep my torment actual and vivid for me. But for themselves, they do not exist, they aren't any more. And she (*indicating* STEPDAUGHTER) has run away, she has left me, and is lost. If I now see her here before me, it is only to renew for me the tortures I have suffered for her too.

THE FATHER. The eternal moment! She (*indicating the* STEPDAUGHTER) is here to catch me, fix me, and hold me eternally in the stocks for that one fleeting and shameful moment of my life. She can't give it up! And you sir, cannot either fairly spare me it.

THE MANAGER. I never said I didn't want to act it. It will form, as a matter of fact, the nucleus of the whole first act right up to her surprise. (*Indicating the* MOTHER)

THE FATHER. Just so! This is my punishment: the passion in all of us that must culminate in her final cry.

THE STEPDAUGHTER. I can hear it still in my ears. It's driven me mad, that cry— You can put me on as you like; it doesn't matter. Fully dressed, if you like —provided I have at least the arm bare; because, standing like this (*she goes close to the* FATHER *and leans her head on his breast*) with my head so, and my arms round his neck, I saw a vein pulsing in my arm here; and then, as if that live vein had awakened disgust in me, I closed my eyes like this, and let my head sink on his breast. (*Turning to the* MOTHER) Cry out, mother! Cry out! (*Buries head in* FATHER's *breast, and with her shoulders raised as if to prevent her hearing the cry, adds in tones of intense emotion*) Cry out as you did then!

THE MOTHER (*Coming forward to separate them*). No! My daughter, my daughter! (*And after having pulled her away from him*) You brute! you brute!

She is my daughter! Don't you see she's my daughter?

THE MANAGER (*Walking backwards towards footlights*). Fine! fine! Damned good! And then, of course—curtain!

THE FATHER (*Going towards him excitedly*). Yes, of course, because that's the way it really happened.

THE MANAGER (*Convinced and pleased*). Oh, yes, no doubt about it. Curtain here, curtain!

(*At the reiterated cry of* THE MANAGER, THE MACHINIST *lets the curtain down, leaving* THE MANAGER *and* THE FATHER *in front of it before the footlights*)

THE MANAGER. The darned idiot! I said "curtain" to show the act should end there, and he goes and lets it down in earnest. (*To the* FATHER, *while he pulls the curtain back to go onto the stage again*) Yes, yes, it's all right. Effect certain! That's the right ending. I'll guarantee the first act, at any rate.

🌱 *Act III*

When the curtain goes up again, it is seen that the stage hands have shifted the bit of scenery used in the last part, and have rigged up instead at the back of the stage a drop, with some trees, and one or two wings. A portion of a fountain basin is visible. THE MOTHER *is sitting on the* Right *with the two children by her side.* THE SON *is on the same side, but away from the others. He seems bored, angry, and full of shame.* THE FATHER *and* THE STEPDAUGHTER *are also seated towards the* Right *front. On the other side* (Left) *are the* ACTORS, *much in the positions they occupied before the curtain was lowered. Only* THE MANAGER *is standing up in the middle of the stage, with his hand closed over his mouth, in the act of meditating.*

THE MANAGER (*Shaking his shoulders after a brief pause*). Ah yes: the second act! Leave it to me, leave it all to me as we arranged, and you'll see! It'll go fine!

THE STEPDAUGHTER. Our entry into his house (*indicates* FATHER) in spite of him... (*indicates the* SON)

THE MANAGER (*Out of patience*). Leave it to me, I tell you!

THE STEPDAUGHTER. Do let it be clear, at any rate, that it is in spite of my wishes.

THE MOTHER (*From her corner, shaking her head*). For all the good that's come of it . . .

THE STEPDAUGHTER (*Turning towards her quickly*). It doesn't matter. The more harm done us, the more remorse for him.

THE MANAGER (*Impatiently*). I understand! Good Heavens! I understand! I'm taking it into account.

THE MOTHER (*Supplicatingly*). I beg you, sir, to let it appear quite plain that for conscience' sake I did try in every way . . .

THE STEPDAUGHTER (*Interrupting indignantly and continuing for the* MOTHER). . . . to pacify me, to dissuade me from spiting me. (*To* MANAGER) Do as she wants: satisfy her, because it is true! I enjoy it immensely. Anyhow, as you can see, the meeker she is, the more she tries to get at his heart, the more distant and aloof does he become.

THE MANAGER. Are we going to begin this second act or not?

THE STEPDAUGHTER. I'm not going to talk any more now. But I must tell you this: you can't have the whole action take place in the garden, as you suggest. It isn't possible!

THE MANAGER. Why not?

THE STEPDAUGHTER. Because he (*indicates the* SON *again*) is always shut up alone in his room. And then there's all the part of that poor dazed-looking boy there which takes place indoors.

THE MANAGER. Maybe! On the other hand, you will understand—we can't change scenes three or four times in one act.

THE LEADING MAN. They used to once.

THE MANAGER. Yes, when the public was up to the level of that child there.

THE LEADING LADY. It makes the illusion easier.

THE FATHER (*Irritated*). The illusion! For Heaven's sake, don't say illusion. Please don't use that word, which is particularly painful for us.

THE MANAGER (*Astounded*). And why, if you please?

THE FATHER. It's painful, cruel, really cruel; and you ought to understand that.

THE MANAGER. But why? What ought we to say then? The illusion, I tell you, sir, which we've got to create for the audience . . .

THE LEADING MAN. With our acting.

THE MANAGER. The illusion of a reality.

THE FATHER. I understand; but you, perhaps, do not understand us. Forgive me! You see . . . here for you and your actors, the thing is only—and rightly so . . . a kind of game . . .

THE LEADING LADY (*Interrupting indignantly*). A game! We're not children here, if you please! We are serious actors.

THE FATHER. I don't deny it. What I mean is the game, or play, of your art, which has to give, as the gentleman says, a perfect illusion of reality.

THE MANAGER. Precisely——!

THE FATHER. Now, if you consider the fact that we (*indicates himself and the other five* CHARACTERS), as we are, have no other reality outside of this illusion . . .

THE MANAGER (*Astonished, looking at his* ACTORS, *who are also amazed*). And what does that mean?

THE FATHER (*After watching them for a moment with a wan smile*). As I say, sir, that which is a game of art for you is our sole reality. (*Brief pause. He goes a step or two nearer the* MANAGER *and adds*) But not only for us, you know, by the way. Just you think it over well. (*Looks him in the eyes*) Can you tell me who you are?

THE MANAGER (*Perplexed, half smiling*). What? Who am I? I am myself.

THE FATHER. And if I were to tell you that that isn't true, because you are I? . . .

THE MANAGER. I should say you were mad——! (*The* ACTORS *laugh*)

THE FATHER. You're quite right to laugh: because we are all making believe here. (*To* MANAGER) And you can therefore object that it's only for a joke that that gentleman there (*indicates the* LEADING MAN), who naturally is himself, has to be me, who am on the contrary myself—this thing you see here. You see I've caught you in a trap! (*The* ACTORS *laugh*)

THE MANAGER (*Annoyed*). But we've had all this over once before. Do you want to begin again?

THE FATHER. No, no! that wasn't my meaning! In fact, I should like to request you to abandon this game of art (*Looking at the* LEADING LADY *as if anticipating her*) which you are accustomed to play here with your actors, and to ask you seriously once again: who are you?

THE MANAGER (*Astonished and irritated, turning to his* ACTORS). If this fellow here hasn't got a nerve! A man who calls himself a character comes and asks me who I am!

THE FATHER (*With dignity, but not offended*). A character, sir, may always ask a man who he is. Because a character has really a life of his own, marked with his especial characteristics; for which reason he is always "somebody." But a man—I'm not speaking of you now—may very well be "nobody."

THE MANAGER. Yes, but you are asking these questions of me, the boss, the manager! Do you understand?

THE FATHER. But only in order to know if you, as you really are now, see yourself as you once were with all the illusions that were yours then, with all the things both inside and outside of you as they seemed to you—as they were then indeed for you. Well, sir, if you think of all those illusions that mean nothing to you now, of all those things which don't even *seem* to you to exist any more, while once they *were* for you, don't you feel that—I won't say these boards—but the very earth under your feet is sinking away from you when you reflect that in the same way this *you* as you feel it today—all this present reality of yours—is fated to seem a mere illusion to you tomorrow?

THE MANAGER (*Without having understood much, but astonished by the specious argument*). Well, well! And where does all this take us anyway?

THE FATHER. Oh, nowhere! It's only to show you that if we (*indicating the* CHARACTERS) have no other reality beyond illusion, you too must not count overmuch on your reality as you feel it today, since, like that of yesterday, it may prove an illusion for you tomorrow.

THE MANAGER (*Determining to make fun of him*). Ah, excellent! Then you'll be saying next that you, with this comedy of yours that you brought here to act, are truer and more real than I am.

THE FATHER (*With the greatest seriousness*). But of course; without doubt!

THE MANAGER. Ah, really?

THE FATHER. Why, I thought you'd understand that from the beginning.

THE MANAGER. More real than I?

THE FATHER. If your reality can change from one day to another . . .

THE MANAGER. But everyone knows it can change. It is always changing, the same as anyone else's.

THE FATHER (*With a cry*). No, sir, not ours! Look here! That is the very difference! Our reality doesn't change: it can't change! It can't be other than what it is, because it is already fixed for ever. It's terrible. Ours is an immutable reality which should make you shudder when you approach us if you are really conscious of the fact that your reality is a mere transitory and fleeting illusion, taking this form today and that tomorrow, according to the conditions, according to your will, your sentiments, which in turn are controlled by an intellect that shows them to you today in one manner and tomorrow . . . who knows how? . . . Illusions of reality represented in this fatuous comedy of life that never ends, nor can ever end! Because if tomorrow it were to end . . . then why, all would be finished.

THE MANAGER. Oh for God's sake, will you *at least* finish with this philosophizing and let us try and shape this comedy which you yourself have brought me here? You argue and philosophize a bit too much, my dear sir. You know you seem to me almost, almost . . . (*Stops and looks him over from head to foot*) Ah, by the way, I think you introduced yourself to me as a—what shall . . . we say—a "character," created by an author who did not afterwards care to make a drama of his own creations.

THE FATHER. It is the simple truth, sir.

THE MANAGER. Nonsense! Cut that out, please! None of us believes it, because it isn't a thing, as you must recognize yourself, which one can believe seriously. If you want to know, it seems to me you are trying to imitate the manner of a certain author whom I heartily detest—I warn you—although I have unfortunately bound myself to put on one of his works. As a matter of fact, I was just starting to rehearse it, when you arrived. (*Turning to the* ACTORS) And this is what we've gained—out of the frying-pan into the fire!

THE FATHER. I don't know to what author you may be alluding, but believe me I feel what I think; and I seem to be philosophizing only for those who do not think what they feel, because they blind themselves with their own sentiment. I know that for many people this self-blinding seems much more "human"; but the contrary is really true. For man never reasons so much and becomes so introspective as when he suffers; since he is anxious to get at the cause of his sufferings, to learn who has produced them, and whether it is just or unjust that he should have to bear them. On the other hand, when he is happy, he takes his happiness as it comes and doesn't analyze it, just as if happiness were his right. The animals suffer without reasoning about their sufferings. But take the case of a man who suffers and begins to reason about it. Oh no! it can't be allowed! Let him suffer like an animal, and then—ah yes, he is "human!"

THE MANAGER. Look here! Look here! You're off again, philosophizing worse than ever.

THE FATHER. Because I suffer, sir! I'm not philosophizing: I'm crying aloud the reason of my sufferings.

THE MANAGER (*Makes brusque movement as he is taken with a new idea*). I should like to know if anyone has ever heard of a character who gets right out of his part and perorates and speechifies as you do. Have you ever heard of a case? I haven't.

THE FATHER. You have never met such a case, sir, because authors, as a rule, hide the labor of their creations. When the characters are really alive before their author, the latter does nothing but follow them in their action, in their words, in the situations which they suggest to him; and he has to will them the way they will themselves—for there's trouble if he doesn't. When a character is born, he acquires at once such an independence, even of his own author, that he can be imagined by everybody even in many other situations where the author never dreamed of placing him; and so he acquires for himself a meaning which the author never thought of giving him.

THE MANAGER. Yes, yes, I know this.

THE FATHER. What is there then to marvel at in us? Imagine such a misfortune for characters as I have described to you: to be born of an author's fantasy, and be denied life by him; and then answer me if these characters left alive, and yet without life, weren't right in doing what they did do and are doing now, after they have attempted everything in their power to persuade him to give them their stage life. We've all tried him in turn, I, she (*indicating the* STEPDAUGHTER) *and she.* (*Indicating the* MOTHER)

THE STEPDAUGHTER. It's true. I too have sought to tempt him, many, many times, when he had been sitting at his writing table, feeling a bit melancholy, at the twilight hour. He would sit in his armchair too lazy to switch on the light, and all the shadows that crept into his room were full of our presence coming to tempt him. (*As if she saw herself still there by the writing table, and was annoyed by the presence of the* ACTORS) Oh, if you would only go away, go away and leave us alone—mother here with that son of hers—I with that Child—that Boy there always alone—and then I with him—(*just hints at the* FATHER)—and then I alone, alone . . . in those shadows! (*Makes a sudden movement as if in the vision she has of herself illuminating those shadows she wanted to seize hold of herself*) Ah! my life! my life! Oh, what scenes we proposed to him—and I tempted him more than any of the others!

THE FATHER. Maybe. But perhaps it was your fault that he refused to give us life: because you were too insistent, too troublesome.

THE STEPDAUGHTER. Nonsense! Didn't he make me so himself? (*Goes close to the* MANAGER *to tell him as if in confidence*) In my opinion he abandoned us in a fit of depression, of disgust for the ordinary theater as the public knows it and likes it.

THE SON. Exactly what it was, sir; exactly that!

THE FATHER. Not at all! Don't believe it for a minute. Listen to me! You'll be doing quite right to modify, as you suggest, the excesses both of this girl here, who wants to do too much, and of this young man, who won't do anything at all.

THE SON. No, nothing!

THE MANAGER. You too get over the mark occasionally, my dear sir, if I may say so.

THE FATHER. I? When? Where?

THE MANAGER. Always! Continuously! Then there's this insistence of yours in trying to make us believe you are a character. And then too, you must really argue and philosophize less, you know, much less.

THE FATHER. Well, if you want to take away from me the possibility of representing the torment of my spirit which never gives me peace, you will be suppressing me: that's all. Every true man, sir, who is a little above the level of the beasts and plants does not live for the sake of living, without knowing how to live; but he lives so as to give a meaning and a value of his own to life. For me this is *everything*. I cannot give up this, just to represent a mere fact as she (*indicating the* STEPDAUGHTER) wants. It's all very well for her, since her "vendetta" lies in the "fact." I'm not going to do it. It destroys my *raison d'être*.

THE MANAGER. Your *raison d'être!* Oh, we're going ahead fine! First she starts off, and then you jump in. At this rate, we'll never finish.

THE FATHER. Now, don't be offended! Have it your own way—provided, however, that within the limits of the parts you assign us each one's sacrifice isn't too great.

THE MANAGER. You've got to understand that you can't go on arguing at your own pleasure. Drama is action, sir, action and not confounded philosophy.

THE FATHER. All right. I'll do just as much arguing and philosophizing as everybody does when he is considering his own torments.

THE MANAGER. If the drama permits! But for Heaven's sake, man, let's get along and come to the scene.

THE STEPDAUGHTER. It seems to me we've got too much action with our coming into his house. (*Indicating* FATHER) You said, before, you couldn't change the scene every five minutes.

THE MANAGER. Of course not. What we've got to do is to combine and group up all the facts in one simultaneous, close-knit action. We can't have it as you want, with your little brother wandering like a ghost from room to room, hiding behind doors and meditating a project which—what did you say it did to him?

THE STEPDAUGHTER. Consumes him, sir, wastes him away!

THE MANAGER. Well, it may be. And then at the same time, you want the little girl there to be playing in the garden . . . one in the house, and the other in the garden: isn't that it?

THE STEPDAUGHTER. Yes, in the sun, in the sun! That is my only pleasure: to see her happy and careless in the garden after the misery and squalor of the horrible room where we all four slept together. And I had to sleep with her—I, do you understand?—with my vile contaminated body next to hers; with her folding me fast in her loving little arms. In the garden, whenever she spied me, she would run to take me by the hand. She didn't care for the big flowers, only the little ones; and she loved to show me them and pet me.

THE MANAGER. Well then, we'll have it in the garden. Everything shall happen in the garden; and we'll group the other scenes there. (*Calls a* STAGE HAND) Here, a back-cloth with trees and something to do as a fountain basin. (*Turning round to look at the back of the stage*) Ah, you've fixed it up. Good! (*To* STEPDAUGHTER) This is just to give an idea, of course. The Boy, instead of hiding behind the doors, will wander about here in the garden, hiding behind the trees. But it's going to be rather difficult to find a child to do that scene with you where she shows you the flowers. (*Turning to the* YOUTH) Come forward a little, will you please? Let's try it now! Come along! come along! (*Then seeing him come shyly forward, full of fear and looking lost*) It's a nice business, this lad here. What's the matter with him? We'll have to give him a word or two to say. (*Goes close to him, puts a hand on his shoulders, and leads him behind one of the trees*) Come on! come on! Let me see you a little! Hide here . . . yes, like that. Try and show your head just a little as if you were looking for someone . . . (*Goes back to observe the effect, when the* BOY *at once goes through the action*) Excellent! fine! (*Turning to* STEPDAUGHTER) Suppose the little girl there were to surprise him as he looks round, and run over to him, so we could give him a word or two to say?

THE STEPDAUGHTER. It's useless to hope he will speak, as long as that fellow there is here . . . (*Indicates the* SON) You must send him away first.

THE SON (*Jumping up*). Delighted!

delighted! I don't ask for anything better. (*Begins to move away*)

THE MANAGER (*At once stopping him*) No! No! Where are you going? Wait a bit!

(*The* MOTHER *gets up, alarmed and terrified at the thought that he is really about to go away. Instinctively she lifts her arms to prevent him, without, however, leaving her seat*)

THE SON (*To* MANAGER, *who stops him*). I've got nothing to do with this affair. Let me go please! Let me go!

THE MANAGER. What do you mean by saying you've got nothing to do with this?

THE STEPDAUGHTER (*Calmly, with irony*). Don't bother to stop him: he won't go away.

THE FATHER. He has to act the terrible scene in the garden with his mother.

THE SON (*Suddenly resolute and with dignity*). I shall act nothing at all. I've said so from the very beginning. (*To the* MANAGER) Let me go!

THE STEPDAUGHTER (*Going over to the* MANAGER) Allow me? (*Puts down the* MANAGER's *arm which is restraining the* SON) Well, go away then, if you want to! (*The* SON *looks at her with contempt and hatred. She laughs and says*) You see, he can't, he can't go away! He is obliged to stay here, indissolubly bound to the chain. If I, who fly off when that happens which has to happen, because I can't bear him—if I am still here and support that face and expression of his, you can well imagine that he is unable to move. He has to remain here, has to stop with that nice father of his, and that mother whose only son he is. (*Turning to the* MOTHER) Come on, mother, come along! (*Turning to* MANAGER *to indicate her*) You see, she was getting up to keep him back. (*To the* MOTHER, *beckoning her with her hand*) Come on! come on! (*Then to* MANAGER) You can imagine how little she wants to show these actors of yours what she really feels; but so eager is she to get near him that . . . There, you see? She is willing to act her part. (*And in fact, the* MOTHER *approaches him; and as soon as the* STEPDAUGHTER *has finished speaking, opens her arms to signify that she consents*)

THE SON (*Suddenly*). No! No! If I can't go away, then I'll stop here; but I repeat: I act nothing!

THE FATHER (*To* MANAGER *excitedly*). You can force him, sir.

THE SON. Nobody can force me.

THE FATHER. I can.

THE STEPDAUGHTER. Wait a minute, wait . . . First of all, the baby has to go to the fountain . . . (*Runs to take the* CHILD *and leads her to the fountain*)

THE MANAGER. Yes, yes of course; that's it. Both at the same time.

(*The second* LADY LEAD *and the* JUVENILE LEAD *at this point separate themselves from the group of* ACTORS. *One watches the* MOTHER *attentively; the other moves about studying the movements and manner of the* SON *whom he will have to act*)

THE SON (*To* MANAGER). What do you mean by both at the same time? It isn't right. There was no scene between me and her. (*Indicates the* MOTHER) Ask her how it was!

THE MOTHER. Yes, it's true. I had come into his room . . .

THE SON. Into my room, do you understand? Nothing to do with the garden.

THE MANAGER. It doesn't matter. Haven't I told you we've got to group the action?

THE SON (*Observing the* JUVENILE LEAD *studying him*). What do you want?

THE JUVENILE LEAD. Nothing! I was just looking at you.

THE SON (*Turning towards the* SECOND LADY LEAD). Ah! she's at it too: to re-act her part! (*Indicating the* MOTHER)

THE MANAGER. Exactly! And it seems to me that you ought to be grateful to them for their interest.

THE SON. Yes, but haven't you yet perceived that it isn't possible to live in front of a mirror which not only freezes us with the image of ourselves, but throws our likeness back at us with a horrible grimace?

THE FATHER. That is true, absolutely true. You must see that.

THE MANAGER (*To* SECOND LADY LEAD *and* JUVENILE LEAD). He's right! Move away from them!

THE SON. Do as you like. I'm out of this!

THE MANAGER. Be quiet, you, will you? And let me hear your mother! (*To*

MOTHER) You were saying you had entered . . .

THE MOTHER. Yes, into his room, because I couldn't stand it any longer. I went to empty my heart to him of all the anguish that tortures me . . . But as soon as he saw me come in . . .

THE SON. Nothing happened! There was no scene. I went away, that's all! I don't care for scenes!

THE MOTHER. It's true, true. That's how it was.

THE MANAGER. Well now, we've got to do this bit between you and him. It's indispensable.

THE MOTHER. I'm ready . . . when you are ready. If you could only find a chance for me to tell him what I feel here in my heart.

THE FATHER (*Going to* SON *in a great rage*). You'll do this for your mother, for your mother, do you understand?

THE SON (*Quite determined*). I do nothing!

THE FATHER (*Taking hold of him and shaking him*). For God's sake, do as I tell you! Don't you hear your mother asking you for a favor? Haven't you even got the guts to be a son?

THE SON (*Taking hold of the* FATHER). No! No! And for God's sake stop it, or else . . . (*General agitation. The* MOTHER, *frightened, tries to separate them*)

THE MOTHER (*Pleading*). Please! please!

THE FATHER (*Not leaving hold of the* SON). You've got to obey, do you hear?

THE SON (*Almost crying from rage*). What does it mean, this madness you've got? (*They separate*) Have you no decency, that you insist on showing everyone our shame? I won't do it! I won't! And I stand for the will of our author in this. He didn't want to put us on the stage, after all!

THE MANAGER. Man alive! You came here . . .

THE SON (*Indicating* FATHER). *He* did! I didn't!

THE MANAGER. Aren't you here now?

THE SON. It was his wish, and he dragged us along with him. He's told you not only the things that did happen, but also things that have never happened at all.

THE MANAGER. Well, tell me then what did happen. You went out of your room without saying a word?

THE SON. Without a word, so as to avoid a scene!

THE MANAGER. And then what did you do?

THE SON. Nothing . . . walking in the garden . . . (*Hesitates for a moment with expression of gloom*)

THE MANAGER (*Coming closer to him, interested by his extraordinary reserve*). Well, well . . . walking in the garden . . .

THE SON (*Exasperated*). Why on earth do you insist? It's horrible! (*The* MOTHER *trembles, sobs, and looks towards the fountain*)

THE MANAGER (*Slowly observing the glance and turning towards the* SON *with increasing apprehension*). The baby?

THE SON. There in the fountain . . .

THE FATHER (*Pointing with tender pity to the* MOTHER). She was following him at the moment . . .

THE MANAGER (*To the* SON, *anxiously*). And then you . . .

THE SON. I ran over to her; I was jumping in to drag her out when I saw something that froze my blood . . . the boy there, standing stock still, with eyes like a madman's, watching his little drowned sister, in the fountain! (*The* STEPDAUGHTER *bends over the fountain to hide the* CHILD. *She sobs*) Then . . . (*A revolver shot rings out behind the trees where the* BOY *is hidden*)

THE MOTHER (*With a cry of terror runs over in that direction together with several of the* ACTORS *amid general confusion*). My son! My son! (*Then amid the cries and exclamations one hears her voice*) Help! Help!

THE MANAGER (*Pushing the* ACTORS *aside while they lift up the* BOY *and carry him off*). Is he really wounded?

SOME ACTORS. He's dead! dead!

OTHER ACTORS. No, no, it's only make believe, it's only pretence!

THE FATHER (*With a terrible cry*). Pretence? Reality, sir, reality!

THE MANAGER. Pretence? Reality? To hell with it all! Never in my life has such a thing happened to me. I've lost a whole day over these people, a whole day!

Curtain

LUIGI PIRANDELLO: *Six Characters in Search of an Author (1925)*

Translated by Eric Bentley. From the book *Naked Masks: Five Plays* by Luigi Pirandello. Copyright, 1922, 1952 by E. P. Dutton & Co., Inc. Renewal, 1950 by Stefano, Fausto and Lietta Pirandello. Reprinted by permission of the publishers.

IT SEEMS LIKE YESTERDAY BUT IS ACTUALLY MANY YEARS AGO THAT a nimble little maidservant entered the service of my art. However, she always comes fresh to the job.

She is called Fantasy.

A little puckish and malicious, if she likes to dress in black no one will wish to deny that she is often positively bizarre and no one will wish to believe that she always does everything in the same way and in earnest. She sticks her hand in her pocket, pulls out a cap and bells, sets it on her head, red as a cock's comb, and dashes away. Here today, there tomorrow. And she amuses herself by bringing to my house—since I derive stories and novels and plays from them—the most disgruntled tribe in the world, men, women, children, involved in strange adventures which they can find no way out of; thwarted in their plans; cheated in their hopes; with whom, in short, it is often torture to deal.

Well, this little maidservant of mine, Fantasy, several years ago, had the bad inspiration or ill-omened caprice to bring a family into my house. I wouldn't know where she fished them up or how, but, according to her, I could find in them the subject for a magnificent novel.

I found before me a man about fifty years old, in a dark jacket and light trousers, with a frowning air and ill-natured, mortified eyes; a poor woman in widow's weeds leading by one hand a little girl of four and by the other a boy of rather more than ten; a cheeky and "sexy" girl, also clad in black but with an equivocal and brazen pomp, all atremble with a lively, biting contempt for the mortified old man and for a young fellow of twenty who stood on one side closed in on himself as if he despised them all. In short, the six characters who are seen coming on stage at the beginning of the play. Now one of them and now another —often beating down one another—embarked on the sad story of their adventures, each shouting his own reasons, and projecting in my face his disordered passions, more or less as they do in the play to the unhappy Manager.

What author will be able to say how and why a character was born in his fantasy? The mystery of artistic creation is the same as that of birth. A woman who loves may desire to become a mother; but the desire by itself, however intense, cannot suffice. One fine day she will find herself a mother without having any precise intimation when it began. In the same way an artist imbibes very many germs of life and can never say how and why, at a certain moment, one of these vital germs inserts itself into his fantasy, there to become a living creature on a plane of life superior to the changeable existence of every day.

I can only say that, without having made any effort to seek them out, I found before me, alive—you could touch them and even hear them breathe—the six characters now seen on the stage. And they stayed there in my presence, each with his secret torment and all bound together by the one common origin and mutual entanglement of their affairs, while I had them enter the world of art, constructing from their persons, their passions, and their adventures a novel, a drama, or at least a story.

Born alive, they wished to live.

To me it was never enough to present a man or a woman and what is special and characteristic about them simply for the pleasure of presenting them; to narrate a particular affair, lively or sad, simply for the pleasure of narrating it;

to describe a landscape simply for the pleasure of describing it.

There are some writers (and not a few) who do feel this pleasure and, satisfied, ask no more. They are, to speak more precisely, historical writers.

But there are others who, beyond such pleasure, feel a more profound spiritual need on whose account they admit only figures, affairs, landscapes which have been soaked, so to speak, in a particular sense of life and acquire from it a universal value. These are, more precisely, philosophical writers.

I have the misfortune to belong to these last.

I hate symbolic art in which the presentation loses all spontaneous movement in order to become a machine, an allegory —a vain and misconceived effort because the very fact of giving an allegorical sense to a presentation clearly shows that we have to do with a fable which by itself has no truth either fantastic or direct; it was made for the demonstration of some moral truth. The spiritual need I speak of cannot be satisfied—or seldom, and that to the end of a superior irony, as for example in Ariosto—by such allegorical symbolism. This latter starts from a concept, and from a concept which creates or tries to create for itself an image. The former, on the other hand, seeks in the image—which must remain alive and free throughout—a meaning to give it value.

Now, however much I sought, I did not succeed in uncovering this meaning in the six characters. And I concluded therefore that it was no use making them live.

I thought to myself: "I have already afflicted my readers with hundreds and hundreds of stories. Why should I afflict them now by narrating the sad entanglements of these six unfortunates?"

And, thinking thus, I put them away from me. Or rather I did all I could to put them away.

But one doesn't give life to a character for nothing.

Creatures of my spirit, these six were already living a life which was their own and not mine any more, a life which it was not in my power any more to deny them.

Thus it is that while I persisted in desiring to drive them out of my spirit, they, as if completely detached from every narrative support, characters from a novel miraculously emerging from the pages of the book that contained them, went on living on their own, choosing certain moments of the day to reappear before me in the solitude of my study and coming—now one, now the other, now two together—to tempt me, to propose that I present or describe this scene or that, to explain the effects that could be secured with them, the new interest which a certain unusual situation could provide, and so forth.

For a moment I let myself be won over. And this condescension of mine, thus letting myself go for a while, was enough, because they drew from it a new increment of life, a greater degree of clarity and addition, consequently a greater degree of persuasive power over me. And thus as it became gradually harder and harder for me to go back and free myself from them, it became easier and easier for them to come back and tempt me. At a certain point I actually became obsessed with them. Until, all of a sudden, a way out of the difficulty flashed upon me.

"Why not," I said to myself, "present this highly strange fact of an author who refuses to let some of his characters live though they have been born in his fantasy, and the fact that these characters, having by now life in their veins, do not resign themselves to remaining excluded from the world of art? They are detached from me; live on their own; have acquired voice and movement; have by themselves—in this struggle for existence that they have had to wage with me—become dramatic characters, characters that can move and talk on their own initiative; already see themselves as such; have learned to defend themselves against me; will even know how to defend themselves against others. And so let them go where dramatic characters do go to have life: on a stage. And let us see what will happen."

That's what I did. And, naturally, the result was what it had to be: a mixture of tragic and comic, fantastic and realistic, in a humorous situation that was quite new and infinitely complex, a drama which is conveyed by means of the characters, who carry it within them and suffer it, a drama, breathing, speaking, self-propelled, which seeks at all costs to find the means of its own presentation; and the comedy of the vain attempt at an improvised realization of the drama on stage. First, the surprise of the poor actors in a theatrical company rehearsing a play by day on a bare stage (no scenery, no flats). Surprise and incredulity at the sight of the six characters announcing themselves as such in search of an author. Then, immediately afterward, through that sudden fainting fit of the Mother veiled in black, their instinctive interest in the drama of which they catch a glimpse in her and in the other members of the strange family, an obscure, ambiguous drama, coming about so unexpectedly on a stage that is empty and unprepared to receive it. And gradually the growth of this interest to the bursting forth of the contrasting passions of Father, of Stepdaughter, of Son, of that poor Mother, passions seeking, as I said, to overwhelm each other with a tragic, lacerating fury.

And here is the universal meaning at first vainly sought in the six characters, now that, going on stage of their own accord, they succeed in finding it within themselves in the excitement of the desperate struggle which each wages against the other and all wage against the Manager and the actors, who do not understand them.

Without wanting to, without knowing it, in the strife of their bedeviled souls, each of them, defending himself against the accusations of the others, expresses as his own living passion and torment the passion and torment which for so many years have been the pangs of my spirit: the deceit of mutual understanding irremediably founded on the empty abstraction of the words, the multiple personality of everyone corresponding to the possibilities of being to be found in each of us, and finally the inherent tragic conflict between life (which is always moving and changing) and form (which fixes it, immutable).

Two above all among the six characters, the Father and the Stepdaughter, speak of that outrageous, unalterable fixity of their form in which he and she see their essential nature expressed perma-

nently and immutably, a nature that for one means punishment and for the other revenge; and they defend it against the factitious affectations and unaware volatility of the actors, and they try to impose it on the vulgar Manager who would like to change it and adapt it to the so-called exigencies of the theatre.

If the six characters don't all seem to exist on the same plane, it is not because some are figures of first rank and others of the second, that is, some are main characters and others minor ones—the elementary perspective necessary to all scenic or narrative art—nor is it that any are not completely created—for their purpose. They are all six at the same point of artistic realization and on the same level of reality, which is the fantastic level of the whole play. Except that the Father, the Stepdaughter, and also the Son are realized as mind; the Mother as nature; the Boy as a presence watching and performing a gesture and the Baby unaware of it all. This fact creates among them a perspective of a new sort. Unconsciously I had had the impression that some of them needed to be fully realized (artistically speaking), others less so, and others merely sketched in as elements in a narrative or presentational sequence: the most alive, the most completely created, are the Father and the Stepdaughter who naturally stand out more and lead the way, dragging themselves along beside the almost dead weight of the others —first, the Son, holding back; second, the Mother, like a victim resigned to her fate, between the two children who have hardly any substance beyond their appearance and who need to be led by the hand.

And actually! actually they had each to appear in that stage of creation which they had attained in the author's fantasy at the moment when he wished to drive them away.

If I now think about these things, about having intuited that necessity, having unconsciously found the way to resolve it by means of a new perspective, and about the way in which I actually obtained it, they seem like miracles. The fact is that the play was really conceived in one of those spontaneous illuminations of the fantasy when by a miracle all the elements of the mind answer to each other's call and work in divine accord. No human brain, working "in the cold," however stirred up it might be, could ever have succeeded in penetrating far enough, could ever have been in a position to satisfy all the exigencies of the play's form. Therefore the reasons which I will give to clarify the values of the play must not be thought of as intentions that I conceived beforehand when I prepared myself for the job and which I now undertake to defend, but only as discoveries which I have been able to make afterward in tranquillity.

I wanted to present six characters seeking an author. Their play does not manage to get presented—precisely because the author whom they seek is missing. Instead is presented the comedy of their vain attempt with all that it contains of tragedy by virtue of the fact that the six characters have been rejected.

But can one present a character while rejecting him? Obviously, to present him one needs, on the contrary, to receive him into one's fantasy before one can express him. And I have actually accepted and realized the six characters: I have, however, accepted and realized them as rejected: in search of *another* author.

What have I rejected of them? Not themselves, obviously, but their drama, which doubtless is what interests them above all but which did not interest me —for the reasons already indicated.

And what is it, for a character—his drama?

Every creature of fantasy and art, in order to exist, must have his drama, that is, a drama in which he may be a character and for which he *is* a character. This drama is the character's *raison d'être,* his vital function, necessary for his existence.

In these six, then, I have accepted the "being" without the reason for being. I have taken the organism and entrusted to it, not its own proper function, but another more complex function into which its own function entered, if at all, only as a datum. A terrible and desperate situation especially for the two—Father and Stepdaughter—who more than the others crave life and more than the others feel themselves to be characters, that is, absolutely need a drama and therefore their own drama—the only one which they can envisage for themselves yet which meantime they see rejected: an "impossible" situation from which they feel they must escape at whatever cost; it is a matter of life and death. True, I have given them another *raison d'être,* another function: precisely that "impossible" situation, the drama of being in search of an author and rejected. But that this should be a *raison d'être,* that it should have become their real function, that it should be necessary, that it should suffice, they can hardly suppose; for they have a life of their own. If someone were to tell them, they wouldn't believe him. It is not possible to believe that the sole reason for our living should lie in a torment that seems to us unjust and inexplicable.

I cannot imagine, therefore, why the charge was brought against me that the character of the Father was not what it should have been because it stepped out of its quality and position as a character and invaded at times the author's province and took it over. I who understand those who don't quite understand me see that the charge derives from the fact that the character expresses and makes his own a torment of spirit which is recognized as mine. Which is entirely natural and of absolutely no significance. Aside from the fact that this torment of spirit in the character of the Father derives from causes, and is suffered and lived for reasons that have nothing to do with the drama of my personal experience, a fact which alone removes all substance from the criticism, I want to make it clear that the inherent torment of my spirit is one thing, a torment which I can legitimately —provided that it be organic—reflect in a character, and that the activity of my spirit as revealed in the realized work, the activity that succeeds in forming a drama out of the six characters in search of an author is another thing. If the Father participated in this latter activity, if he competed in forming the drama of the six characters without an author, then and only then would it by all means be justified to say that he was at times the author himself and therefore not the man he should be. But the Father suffers and does not create his existence as a character in search of an author. He suffers it as an inexplicable fatality and as a situation which he tries with all his powers to rebel against, which he tries to remedy; hence it is that he is a character in search of an author and nothing more, even if he expresses as his own the torment of my spirit. If he, so to speak, assumed some of the author's responsibilities, the fatality would be completely explained. He would, that is to say, see himself accepted, if only as a rejected character, accepted in the poet's heart of hearts, and he would no longer have any reason to suffer the despair of not finding someone to construct and affirm his life as a character. I mean that he would quite willingly accept the *raison d'être* which the author gives him and without regrets would forgo his own, throwing over the Manager and the actors to whom in fact he runs as his only recourse.

There is one character, that of the Mother, who on the other hand does not care about being alive (considering being alive as an end in itself). She hasn't the least suspicion that she is *not* alive. It has never occurred to her to ask how and why and in what manner she lives. In short, she is not aware of being a character inasmuch as she is never, even for a moment, detached from her role. She doesn't know she has a role.

This makes her perfectly organic. Indeed, her role of Mother does not of itself, in its natural essence, embrace mental activity. And she does not exist as a mind. She lives in an endless continuum of feeling, and therefore she cannot acquire awareness of her life—that is, of her existence as a character. But with all this, even she, in her own way and for her own ends, seeks an author, and at a certain stage seems happy to have been brought before the Manager. Because she hopes to take life from him, perhaps? No: because she hopes the Manager will have her present a scene with the Son in which she would put so much of her own life. But it is a scene which does not exist, which never has and never could take place. So unaware is she of being a character, that is, of the life that is possible to her, all fixed and determined, moment by moment, in every action, every phrase.

She appears on stage with the other characters but without understanding what the others make her do. Obviously, she imagines that the itch for life with which the husband and the daughter are afflicted and for which she herself is to be found on stage is no more than one of the usual incomprehensible extravagances of this man who is both tortured and torturer and—horrible, most horrible —a new equivocal rebellion on the part of that poor erring girl. The Mother is completely passive. The events of her own life and the values they assume in her eyes, her very character, are all things which are "said" by the others and which she only once contradicts, and that because the maternal instinct rises up and rebels within her to make it clear that she didn't at all wish to abandon either the son or the husband: the Son was taken from her and the husband forced her to abandon him. She is only correcting data; she explains and knows nothing.

In short, she is nature. Nature fixed in the figure of a mother.

This character gave me a satisfaction of a new sort, not to be ignored. Nearly all my critics, instead of defining her, after their habit, as "unhuman"—which seems to be the peculiar and incorrigible characteristic of all my creatures without exception—had the goodness to note "with real pleasure" that at last a *very human* figure had emerged from my fantasy. I explain this praise to myself in the following way: since my poor Mother is entirely limited to the natural attitude of a Mother with no possibility of free mental activity, being, that is, little more than a lump of flesh completely alive in all its functions—procreation, lactation, caring for and loving its young—without any need therefore of exercising her brain, she realizes in her person the true and complete "human type." That must be how it is, since in a human organism nothing seems more superfluous than the mind.

But the critics have tried to get rid of the Mother with this praise without bothering to penetrate the nucleus of poetic values which the character in the play represents. A very human figure, certainly, because mindless, that is, unaware of being what she is or not caring to explain it to herself. But not knowing that she is a character doesn't prevent her from being one. That is her drama in my play. And the most living expression of it comes spurting out in her cry to the Manager, who wants her to think all these things have happened already and therefore cannot now be a reason for renewed lamentations: "No, it's happening now, it's happening always! My torture is not a pretense, signore! I am alive and present, always, in every moment of my torture: it is renewed, alive, and present always!" This she *feels,* without being conscious of it, and feels it therefore as something inexplicable: but she feels it so terribly that she doesn't think it *can* be something to explain either to herself or to others. She feels it and that is that. She feels it as pain and this pain is immediate; she cries it out. Thus she reflects the growing fixity of life in a form— the same thing, which in another way, tortures the Father and the Stepdaughter. In them, mind. In her, nature. The mind rebels and, as best it may, seeks an advantage; nature, if not aroused by sensory stimuli, weeps.

Conflict between life-in-movement and form is the inexorable condition not only of the mental but also of the physical order. The life which in order to exist has become fixed in our corporeal form little by little kills that form. The tears of a nature thus fixed lament the irreparable, continuous aging of our bodies. Hence the tears of the Mother are passive and perpetual. Revealed in three faces, made significant in three distinct and simultaneous dramas, this inherent conflict finds in the play its most complete expression. More: the Mother declares also the particular value of artistic form— a form which does not delimit or destroy its own life and which life does not consume—in her cry to the Manager. If the Father and Stepdaughter began their scene a hundred thousand times in succession, always, at the appointed moment, at the instant when the life of the work of art must be expressed with that cry, it would always be heard, unaltered and unalterable in its form, not as a mechanical repetition, not as a return determined by external necessities, but, on the contrary, alive every time and as new, suddenly born *thus forever!* embalmed alive in its incorruptible form. Hence, always, as we open the book, we shall find Francesca alive and confessing to Dante her sweet sin, and if we turn to the passage

a hundred thousand times in succession, Francesca will speak her words, never repeating them mechanically, but saying them as though each time were the first time with such living and sudden passion that Dante every time will turn faint. All that lives, by the fact of living, has a form, and by the same token must die— except the work of art which lives forever in so far as it *is* form.

The birth of a creature of human fantasy, a birth which is a step across the threshold between nothing and eternity, can also happen suddenly, occasioned by some necessity. An imagined drama needs a character who does or says a certain necessary thing; accordingly this character is born and is precisely what he had to be. In this way Madame Pace is born among the six characters and seems a miracle, even a trick, realistically portrayed on the stage. It is no trick. The birth is real. The new character is alive not because she was alive already but because she is now happily born as is required by the fact of her being a character —she is obliged to be as she is. There is a break here, a sudden change in the level of reality of the scene, because a character can be born in this way only in the poet's fancy and not on the boards of a stage. Without anyone's noticing it, I have all of a sudden changed the scene: I have gathered it up again into my own fantasy without removing it from the spectator's eyes. That is, I have shown them, instead of the stage, my own fantasy in the act of creating—my own fantasy in the form of this same stage. The sudden and uncontrollable changing of a visual phenomenon from one level of reality to another is a miracle comparable to those of the saint who sets his own statue in motion: it is neither wood nor stone at such a moment. But the miracle is not arbitrary. The stage —a stage which accepts the fantastic reality of the six characters—is no fixed, immutable datum. Nothing in this play exists as given and preconceived. Everything is in the making, is in motion, is a sudden experiment: even the place in which this unformed life, reaching after its own form, changes and changes again, contrives to shift position organically. The level of reality changes. When I had the idea of bringing Madame Pace to birth right there on the stage, I felt I could do it and I did it. Had I noticed that this birth was unhinging and silently, unnoticed, in a second, giving another shape, another reality to my scene, I certainly wouldn't have brought it about. I would have been afraid of the apparent lack of logic. And I would have committed an ill-omened assault on the beauty of my work. The fervor of my mind saved me from doing so. For, despite appearances, with their specious logic, this fantastic birth is sustained by a real necessity in mysterious, organic relation with the whole life of the work.

That someone now tells me it hasn't all the value it could have because its expression is not constructed but chaotic, because it smacks of romanticism, makes me smile.

I understand why this observation was made to me: because in this work of mine the presentation of the drama in which the six characters are involved appears tumultuous and never proceeds in an orderly manner. There is no logical development, no concatenation of the events. Very true. Had I hunted it with a lamp I couldn't have found a more disordered, crazy, arbitrary, complicated, in short, romantic way of presenting "the drama in which the six characters are involved." Very true. But I have not presented that drama. I have presented another—and I won't undertake to say again what!—in which, among the many fine things that everyone, according to his tastes, can find, there is a discreet satire on romantic procedures: in the six characters thus excited to the point where they stifle themselves in the roles which each of them plays in a certain drama while I present them as characters in another play which they don't know and don't suspect the existence of, so that this inflammation of their passions—which belongs to the realm of romantic procedures—is humorously "placed," located in the void. And the drama of the six characters presented not as it would have been organized by my fantasy had it been accepted but in this way, as a rejected drama, could not exist in the work except as a "situation," with some little development, and could not come out ex-

cept in indications, stormily, disorderedly, in violent foreshortenings, in a chaotic manner: continually interrupted, sidetracked, contradicted (by one of its characters), denied, and (by two others) not even seen.

There is a character indeed—he who denies the drama which makes him a character, the Son—who draws all his importance and value from being a character not of the comedy in the making —which as such hardly appears—but from the presentation that I made of it. In short, he is the only one who lives solely as "a character in search of an author"—inasmuch as the author he seeks is not a dramatic author. Even this could not be otherwise. The character's attitude is an organic product of my conception, and it is logical that in the situation it should produce greater confusion and disorder and another element of romantic contrast.

But I had precisely to *present* this organic and natural chaos. And to present a chaos is not at all to present chaotically, that is, romantically. That my presentation is the reverse of confused, that it is quite simple, clear, and orderly, is proved by the clarity which the intrigue, the characters, the fantastic and realistic, dramatic and comic levels of the work have had for every public in the world and by the way in which, for those with more searching vision, the unusual values enclosed within it come out.

Great is the confusion of tongues among men if criticisms thus made find words for their expression. No less great than this confusion is the intimate law of order which, obeyed in all points, makes this work of mine classical and typical and at its catastrophic close forbids the use of words. Though the audience eventually understands that one does not create life by artifice and that the drama of the six characters cannot be presented without an author to give them value with his spirit, the Manager remains vulgarly anxious to know how the thing turned out, and the "ending" is remembered by the Son in its sequence of actual moments, but without any sense and therefore not needing a human voice for its expression. It happens stupidly, uselessly, with the going off of a mechanical weapon on stage. It breaks up and disperses the sterile experiment of the characters and the actors, which has apparently been made without the assistance of the poet.

The poet, unknown to them, as if looking on at a distance during the whole period of the experiment, was at the same time busy creating—with it and of it—his own play.

O'NEILL WAS ALOOF, SHY, AND BROODING; HIS LIFE WAS

Eugene O'Neill 1888-1953

full of pain and frustration. His father, a rich and successful actor, was pathologically tight-fisted; his mother was the victim of drugs; an older brother was alcoholic; O'Neill himself was twice divorced; his eldest child committed suicide in 1950. His early years were divided between traveling with his family on theatrical tours and boarding in various Catholic schools. After an unsuccessful year at Princeton, O'Neill turned briefly to business, but soon left to prospect for gold in Honduras. He failed to find it, returned to business, failed at that, and in 1910 shipped as a merchant seaman. After a rough, heavy-drinking, vagabond life, O'Neill joined his father's acting company for a time; presently, however, he took a job on a newspaper in New London, Connecticut. Then his strained health broke, and O'Neill found himself hospitalized with tuberculosis. During his convalescence he thought seriously about drama and apparently began to write. In 1914, he was enrolled in George Pierce Baker's playwriting course at Harvard, and the following year he was living in New York among the artists of Greenwich Village. O'Neill's first play was produced in 1916 in the summer art colony at Provincetown, Massachusetts, and when the Provincetown Players moved to New York, O'Neill provided them with other one-act dramas of the sea. His full-length play *Beyond the Horizon* was produced in 1920, and from then on O'Neill's reputation was secured as play followed play during the nineteen-twenties and established him as America's leading dramatist. From realistic drama O'Neill turned restlessly to more experimental forms in plays such as *The Hairy Ape* (1921) and *The Great God Brown* (1925). An increasing interest in metaphysical and psycho-analytical themes now directed his work—notably in *Desire under the Elms* (1924)—as O'Neill, grappling with man's tragic relation to the universe, broke through conventional dramaturgy in the massive forms of *Strange Interlude* (1927) and *Mourning Becomes Electra* (1931), his transformation of the Oresteian trilogy of Aeschylus. In the mid-thirties O'Neill withdrew from the stage to work on a cycle of nine plays encompassing the history of an American family, but the project never materialized. His absence from the theater was broken in 1946 with the appearance of *The Iceman Cometh* (written in 1939), a naturalistic play that echoed O'Neill's past. His powerful autobiographical play, *Long Day's Journey into Night* (1956) was composed from 1939 to 1941, but in accordance with the playwright's wishes it was not produced until after his death in 1953.

DESIRE UNDER THE ELMS

❦ BY EUGENE O'NEILL

CHARACTERS

EPHRAIM CABOT.

SIMEON ⎫
PETER ⎬ *his sons.*
EBEN   ⎭

ABBIE PUTNAM.

Young GIRL, *two* FARMERS, *the* FIDDLER, *a* SHERIFF, *and other folk from the neighboring farms.*

(*The action of the entire play takes place in, and immediately outside of, the Cabot farmhouse in New England, in the year 1850. The south end of the house faces front to a stone wall with a wooden gate at center opening on a country road. The house is in good condition but in need of paint. Its walls are a sickly grayish, the green of the shutters faded. Two enormous elms are on each side of the house. They bend their trailing branches down over the roof. They appear to protect and at the same time subdue. There is a sinister maternity in their aspect, a crushing, jealous absorption. They have developed from their intimate contact with the life of man in the house an appalling humaneness. They brood oppressively over the house. They are like exhausted women resting their sagging breasts and hands and hair on its roof, and when it rains their tears trickle down monotonously and rot on the shingles.*

There is a path running from the gate around the right corner of the house to the front door. A narrow porch is on this side. The end wall facing us has two windows in its upper story, two larger ones on the floor below. The two upper are those of the father's bedroom and that of the brothers. On the left, ground floor, is the kitchen—on the right, the parlor, the shades of which are always drawn down.)

❦ *Part I*

Scene I

(*Exterior of the farmhouse. It is sunset of a day at the beginning of summer in the year 1850. There is no wind and everything is still. The sky above the roof is suffused with deep colors, the green of the elms glows, but the house is in shadow, seeming pale and washed out by contrast.*

A door opens and EBEN CABOT *comes to the end of the porch and stands looking down the road to the right. He has a large bell in his hand and this he swings mechanically, awakening a deafening clangor. Then he puts his hands on his hips and stares up at the sky. He sighs with a puzzled awe and blurts out with halting appreciation.*)

EBEN. God! Purty! (*His eyes fall and he stares about him frowningly. He is twenty-five, tall and sinewy. His face is well formed, good-looking, but its expression is resentful and defensive. His defiant, dark eyes remind one of a wild animal's in captivity. Each day is a cage in which he finds himself trapped but inwardly unsubdued. There is a fierce repressed vitality about him. He has black hair, mustache, a thin curly trace of beard. He is dressed in rough farm clothes.*

He spits on the ground with intense disgust, turns and goes back into the house.)

SIMEON *and* PETER *come in from their work in the fields. They are tall men, much older than their half-brother* (SIMEON *is thirty-nine and* PETER *thirty-seven*), *built on a squarer, simpler model, fleshier in body, more bovine and homelier in face, shrewder and more practical. Their shoulders stoop a bit from years of farm work. They clump heavily along in their clumsy thick-soled boots caked with earth. Their clothes, their faces, hands, bare arms and throats are earth-stained. They smell of earth. They stand together for a moment in front of the house and, as if with the one impulse, stare dumbly up at the sky, leaning on their hoes. Their faces have a compressed, unresigned expression. As they look upward, this softens.*)

SIMEON (*grudgingly*). Purty.

PETER. Ay-eh.

SIMEON (*suddenly*). Eighteen year ago.

PETER. What?

SIMEON. Jenn. My woman. She died.

PETER. I'd fergot.

SIMEON. I rec'lect—now an' agin. Makes it lonesome. She'd hair long's a hoss' tail—an' yaller like gold!

PETER. Waal—she's gone. (*This with indifferent finality—then after a pause*) They's gold in the West, Sim.

SIMEON (*still under the influence of sunset—vaguely*). In the sky?

PETER. Waal—in a manner o' speakin' —thar's the promise. (*Growing excited*) Gold in the sky—in the West—Golden Gate—Californi-a!—Goldest West!— fields o' gold!

SIMEON (*excited in his turn*). Fortunes layin' just atop o' the ground waitin' t' be picked! Solomon's mines, they says! (*For a moment they continue looking up at the sky—then their eyes drop.*)

PETER (*with sardonic bitterness*). Here —it's stones atop o' the ground—stones atop o' stones—makin' stone walls— year atop o' year—him 'n' yew 'n' me 'n' then Eben—makin' stone walls fur him to fence us in!

SIMEON. We've wuked. Give our strength. Give our years. Plowed 'em under in the ground—(*he stamps rebelliously*)—rottin'—makin' soil for his crops! (*A pause.*) Waal—the farm pays good for hereabouts.

PETER. If we plowed in Californi-a, they'd be lumps o' gold in the furrow!

SIMEON. Californi-a's t'other side o' earth, a'most. We got t' calc'late—

PETER (*after a pause*). 'Twould be hard fur me, too, to give up what we've 'arned here by our sweat. (*A pause,* EBEN *sticks his head out of the dining-room window, listening.*)

SIMEON. Ay-eh. (*A pause.*) Mebbe— he'll die soon.

PETER (*doubtfully*). Mebbe.

SIMEON. Mebbe—fur all we knows— he's dead now.

PETER. Ye'd need proof.

SIMEON. He's been gone two months —with no word.

PETER. Left us in the fields an evenin' like this. Hitched up an' druv off into the West. That's plum onnateral. He hain't never been off this farm 'ceptin' t' the village in thirty year or more, not since he married Eben's maw. (*A pause. Shrewdly*) I calc'late we might git him declared crazy by the court.

SIMEON. He skinned 'em too slick. He got the best o' all on 'em. They'd never b'lieve him crazy. (*A pause*) We got t' wait—till he's under ground.

EBEN (*with a sardonic chuckle*). Honor thy father! (*They turn, startled, and stare at him. He grins, then scowls.*) I pray he's died. (*They stare at him. He continues matter-of-factly*) Supper's ready.

SIMEON *and* PETER (*together*). Ay-eh.

EBEN (*gazing up at the sky*). Sun's downin' purty.

SIMEON *and* PETER (*together*). Ay-eh. They's gold in the West.

EBEN. Ay-eh. (*Pointing*) Yonder atop o' the hill pasture, ye mean?

SIMEON *and* PETER (*together*). In Californi-a!

EBEN. Hunh? (*Stares at them indifferently for a second, then drawls*) Waal —supper's gittin' cold. (*He turns back into kitchen.*)

SIMEON (*startled—smacks his lips*). I air hungry!

PETER (*sniffing*). I smells bacon!

SIMEON (*with hungry appreciation*). Bacon's good!

PETER (*in same tone*). Bacon's bacon! (*They turn, shouldering each other, their bodies bumping and rubbing together as they hurry clumsily to their food, like two friendly oxen toward their evening meal. They disappear around the right corner of house and can be heard entering the door.*)

Curtain

Scene II

(*The color fades from the sky. Twilight begins. The interior of the kitchen is now visible. A pine table is at center, a cook-stove in the right rear corner, four rough wooden chairs, a tallow candle on the table. In the middle of the rear wall is fastened a big advertising poster with a ship in full sail and the word "California" in big letters. Kitchen utensils hang from nails. Everything is neat and in order but the atmosphere is of a men's camp kitchen rather than that of a home.*

Places for three are laid. EBEN *takes boiled potatoes and bacon from the stove and puts them on the table, also a loaf of bread and a crock of water.* SIMEON *and* PETER *shoulder in, slump down in their chairs without a word.* EBEN *joins them. The three eat in silence for a moment, the two elder as naturally unrestrained as beasts of the field,* EBEN *picking at his food without appetite, glancing at them with a tolerant dislike.*)

SIMEON (*suddenly turns to* EBEN). Looky here! Ye'd oughtn't t' said that, Eben.

PETER. 'Twa'n't righteous.

EBEN. What?

SIMEON. Ye prayed he'd died.

EBEN. Waal—don't yew pray it? (*A pause.*)

PETER. He's our Paw.

EBEN (*violently*). Not mine!

SIMEON (*dryly*). Ye'd not let no one else say that about yer Maw! Ha! (*He gives one abrupt sardonic guffaw.* PETER *grins.*)

EBEN (*very pale*). I meant—I hain't his'n—I hain't like him—he hain't me!

PETER (*dryly*). Wait till ye've growed his age!

EBEN (*intensely*). I'm Maw—every drop o' blood! (*A pause. They stare at him with indifferent curiosity.*)

PETER (*reminiscently*). She was good t' Sim 'n' me. A good Stepmaw's scurse.

SIMEON. She was good t' everyone.

EBEN (*greatly moved, gets to his feet and makes an awkward bow to each of them—stammering*). I be thankful t'ye. I'm her—her heir. (*He sits down in confusion.*)

PETER (*after a pause—judicially*). She was good even t' him.

EBEN (*fiercely*). An' fur thanks he killed her!

SIMEON (*after a pause*). No one never kills nobody. It's allus somethin'. That's the murderer.

EBEN. Didn't he slave Maw t' death?

PETER. He slaved himself t' death. He's slaved Sim 'n' me 'n' yew t' death—on'y none o' us hain't died—yit.

SIMEON. It's somethin'—drivin' him—t' drive us!

EBEN (*vengefully*). Waal—I hold him t' jedgment! (*Then scornfully*) Somethin'! What's somethin'?

SIMEON. Dunno.

EBEN (*sardonically*). What's drivin' yew to Californi-a, mebbe? (*They look at him in surprise.*) Oh, I've heerd ye! (*Then, after a pause*) But ye'll never go t' the gold fields!

PETER (*assertively*). Mebbe!

EBEN. Whar'll ye git the money?

PETER. We kin walk. It's an a'mighty ways—Californi-a—but if yew was t' put all the steps we've walked on this farm end t' end we'd be in the moon!

EBEN. The Injuns'll skulp ye on the plains.

SIMEON (*with grim humor*). We'll mebbe make 'em pay a hair fur a hair!

EBEN (*decisively*). But t'ain't that. Ye won't never go because ye'll wait here fur yer share o' the farm, thinkin' allus he'll die soon.

SIMEON (*after a pause*). We've a right.

PETER. Two-thirds belongs t' us.

EBEN (*jumping to his feet*). Ye've no right! She wa'n't yewr Maw! It was her farm! Didn't he steal it from her? She's dead. It's my farm.

SIMEON (*sardonically*). Tell that t' Paw—when he comes! I'll bet ye a dollar he'll laugh—fur once in his life. Ha! (*He laughs himself in one single mirthless bark.*)

PETER (*amused in turn, echoes his brother*). Ha!

SIMEON (*after a pause*). What've ye got held agin us, Eben? Year after year it's skulked in yer eye—somethin'.

PETER. Ay-eh.

EBEN. Ay-eh. They's somethin'. (*Suddenly exploding*) Why didn't ye never stand between him 'n' my Maw when he was slavin' her to her grave—t' pay her back fur the kindness she done t' yew?

(*There is a long pause. They stare at him in surprise.*)

SIMEON. Waal—the stock'd got t' be watered.

PETER. 'R they was woodin' t' do.

SIMEON. 'R plowin'.

PETER. 'R hayin'.

SIMEON. 'R spreadin' manure.

PETER. 'R weedin'.

SIMEON. 'R prunin'.

PETER. 'R milkin'.

EBEN (*breaking in harshly*). An' makin' walls—stone atop o' stone—makin' walls till yer heart's a stone ye heft up out o' the way o' growth onto a stone wall t' wall in yer heart!

SIMEON (*matter-of-factly*). We never had no time t' meddle.

PETER (*to* EBEN). Yew was fifteen afore yer Maw died—an' big fur yer age. Why didn't ye never do nothin'?

EBEN (*harshly*). They was chores t' do, wa'n't they? (*A pause—then slowly*) It was on'y arter she died I come to think o' it. Me cookin'—doin' her work —that made me know her, suffer her sufferin'—she'd come back t' help—come back t' bile potatoes—come back t' fry bacon—come back t' bake biscuits—come back all cramped up t' shake the fire, an' carry ashes, her eyes weepin' an' bloody with smoke an' cinders same's they used t' be. She still comes back—stands by the stove thar in the evenin'— she can't find it nateral sleepin' an' restin' in peace. She can't git used t' bein' free—even in her grave.

SIMEON. She never complained none.

EBEN. She'd got too tired. She'd got too used t' bein' too tired. That was what he done. (*With vengeful passion*) An' sooner 'r later, I'll meddle. I'll say the thin's I didn't say then t' him! I'll yell 'em at the top o' my lungs. I'll see t' it my Maw gits some rest an' sleep in her grave! (*He sits down again, relapsing into a brooding silence. They look at him with a queer indifferent curiosity.*)

PETER (*after a pause*). Whar in tarnation d'ye s'pose he went, Sim?

SIMEON. Dunno. He druv off in the buggy, all spick an' span, with the mare all breshed an' shiny, druv off clackin' his tongue an' wavin' his whip. I remember it right well. I was finishin' plowin', it was spring an' May an' sunset, an' gold in the West, an' he druv off into it. I yells "Whar ye goin', Paw?" an' he hauls up by the stone wall a jiffy. His old snake's eyes was glitterin' in the sun like he'd been drinkin' a jugful an' he says with a mule's grin: "Don't ye run away till I come back!"

PETER. Wonder if he knowed we was wantin' fur Californi-a?

SIMEON. Mebbe. I didn't say nothin' and he says, lookin' kinder queer an' sick: "I been hearin' the hens cluckin' an' the roosters crowin' all the durn day. I been listenin' t' the cows lowin' an' everythin' else kickin' up till I can't stand it no more. It's spring an' I'm feelin' damned," he says. "Damned like an old bare hickory tree fit on'y fur burnin'," he says. An' then I calc'late I must've looked a mite hopeful, fur he adds real spry and vicious: "But don't git no fool idee I'm dead. I've sworn t' live a hundred an' I'll do it, if on'y t' spite yer sinful greed! An' now I'm ridin' out t' learn God's message t' me in the spring, like the prophets done. An' yew git back t' yer plowin'," he says. An' he druv off singin' a hymn. I thought he was drunk—'r I'd stopped him goin'.

EBEN (*scornfully*). No, ye wouldn't! Ye're scared o' him. He's stronger—inside —than both o' ye put together!

PETER (*sardonically*). An' yew—be yew Samson?

EBEN. I'm gittin' stronger. I kin feel it growin' in me—growin' an' growin' —till it'll bust out—! (*He gets up and puts on his coat and a hat. They watch him, gradually breaking into grins. EBEN avoids their eyes sheepishly.*) I'm goin' out fur a spell—up the road.

PETER. T' the village?

SIMEON. T' see Minnie?

EBEN (*defiantly*). Ay-eh!

PETER (*jeeringly*). The Scarlet Woman!

SIMEON. Lust—that's what's growin' in ye!

EBEN. Waal—she's purty!

PETER. She's been purty fur twenty year!

SIMEON. A new coat o' paint'll make a heifer out of forty.

EBEN. She hain't forty!

PETER. If she hain't, she's teeterin' on the edge.

EBEN (desperately). What d'yew know—

PETER. All they is . . . Sim knew her —an' then me arter—

SIMEON. An' Paw kin tell yew somethin' too! He was fust!

EBEN. D'ye mean t' say he . . . ?

SIMEON (with a grin). Ay-eh! We air his heirs in everythin'!

EBEN (intensely). That's more to it! That grows on it! It'll bust soon! (Then violently) I'll go smash my fist in her face! (He pulls open the door in rear violently.)

SIMEON (with a wink at PETER— drawlingly). Mebbe—but the night's wa'm—purty—by the time ye get thar mebbe ye'll kiss her instead!

PETER. Sart'n he will! (They both roar with coarse laughter. EBEN rushes out and slams the door—then the outside front door—comes around the corner of the house and stands still by the gate, staring up at the sky.)

SIMEON (looking after him). Like his Paw.

PETER. Dead spit an' image!

SIMEON. Dog'll eat dog!

PETER. Ay-eh. (Pause. With yearning) Mebbe a year from now we'll be in Californi-a.

SIMEON. Ay-eh. (A pause. Both yawn.) Let's git t'bed. (He blows out the candle. They go out door in rear. EBEN stretches his arms up to the sky—rebelliously.)

EBEN. Waal—thar's a star, an' somewhar's they's him, an' here's me, an' thar's Min up the road—in the same night. What if I does kiss her? She's like t'night, she's soft 'n' wa'm, her eyes kin wink like a star, her mouth's wa'm, her arms're wa'm, she smells like a wa'm plowed field, she's purty . . . Ay-eh! By God A'mighty she's purty, an' I don't give a damn how many sins she's sinned afore mine or who she's sinned 'em with, my sin's as purty as any one on 'em! (He strides off down the road to the left.)

Scene III

(It is the pitch darkness just before dawn. EBEN comes in from the left and goes around to the porch, feeling his way, chuckling bitterly and cursing half-aloud to himself.)

EBEN. The cussed old miser! (He can be heard going in the front door. There is a pause as he goes upstairs, then a loud knock on the bedroom door of the brothers.) Wake up!

SIMEON (startledly). Who's thar?

EBEN (pushing open the door and coming in, a lighted candle in his hand. The bedroom of the brothers is revealed. Its ceiling is the sloping roof. They can stand upright only close to the center dividing wall of the upstairs. SIMEON and PETER are in a double bed, front. EBEN's cot is to the rear. EBEN has a mixture of silly grin and vicious scowl on his face). I be!

PETER (angrily). What in hell's-fire . . . ?

EBEN. I got news fur ye! Ha! (He gives one abrupt sardonic guffaw.)

SIMEON (angrily). Couldn't ye hold it 'til we'd got our sleep?

EBEN. It's nigh sunup. (Then explosively) He's gone an' married agen!

SIMEON and PETER (explosively). Paw?

EBEN. Got himself hitched to a female 'bout thirty-five—an' purty, they says . . .

SIMEON (aghast). It's a durn lie!

PETER. Who says?

SIMEON. They been stringin' ye!

EBEN. Think I'm a dunce, do ye? The hull village says. The preacher from New Dover, he brung the news—told it t'our preacher—New Dover, that's whar the old loon got himself hitched—that's whar the woman lived—

PETER (no longer doubting—stunned). Waal . . . !

SIMEON (the same). Waal . . . !

EBEN (sitting down on a bed—with vicious hatred). Ain't he a devil out o' hell? It's jest t' spite us—the damned old mule!

PETER (after a pause). Everythin'll go t' her now.

SIMEON. Ay-eh (A pause—dully) Waal—if it's done—

PETER. It's done us. (Pause—then per-

suasively) They's gold in the fields o' Californi-a, Sim. No good a-stayin' here now.

SIMEON. Jest what I was a-thinkin'. (*Then with decision*) S'well fust's last! Let's light out and git this mornin'.

PETER. Suits me.

EBEN. Ye must like walkin'.

SIMEON (*sardonically*). If ye'd grow wings on us we'd fly thar!

EBEN. Ye'd like ridin' better—on a boat, wouldn't ye? (*Fumbles in his pocket and takes out a crumpled sheet of foolscap.*) Waal, if ye sign this ye kin ride on a boat. I've had it writ out an' ready in case ye'd ever go. It says fur three hundred dollars t' each ye agree yewr shares o' the farm is sold t' me. (*They look supiciously at the paper. A pause.*)

SIMEON (*wonderingly*). But if he's hitched agen—

PETER. An' whar'd yew git that sum o' money, anyways?

EBEN (*cunningly*). I know whar it's hid. I been waitin'—Maw told me. She knew whar it lay fur years, but she was waitin' . . . It's her'n—the money he hoarded from her farm an' hid from Maw. It's my money by rights now.

PETER. Whar's it hid?

EBEN (*cunningly*). Whar yew won't never find it without me. Maw spied on him—'r she'd never knowed. (*A pause. They look at him suspiciously, and he at them.*) Waal, is it fa'r trade?

SIMEON. Dunno.

PETER. Dunno.

SIMEON (*looking at window*). Sky's grayin'.

PETER. Ye better start the fire, Eben.

SIMEON. An' fix some vittles.

EBEN. Ay-eh. (*Then with a forced jocular heartiness*) I'll git ye a good one. If ye're startin' t' hoof it t' Californi-a ye'll need somethin' that'll stick t' yer ribs. (*He turns to the door, adding meaningly*) But ye kin ride on a boat if ye'll swap. (*He stops at the door and pauses. They stare at him.*)

SIMEON (*suspiciously*). Whar was ye all night?

EBEN (*defiantly*). Up t' Min's. (*Then slowly*) Walkin' thar, fust I felt 's if I'd kiss her; then I got a-thinkin' o' what ye'd said o' him an' her an' I says, I'll bust her nose fur that! Then I got t' the village an' heerd the news an' I got mad-

der'n hell an' run all the way t' Min's not knowin' what I'd do— (*He pauses—then sheepishly but more defiantly*) Waal—when I seen her, I didn't hit her—nor I didn't kiss her nuther—I begun t' beller like a calf an' cuss at the same time, I was so durn mad—an' she got scared—an' I jest grabbed holt an' tuk her! (*Proudly*) Yes, sirree! I tuk her. She may've been his'n—an' your'n, too—but she's mine now!

SIMEON (*dryly*). In love, air yew?

EBEN (*with lofty scorn*). Love! I don't take no stock in sech slop!

PETER (*winking at* SIMEON). Mebbe Eben's aimin' t' marry, too.

SIMEON. Min'd make a true faithful he'pmeet! (*They snicker.*)

EBEN. What do I care fur her—'ceptin' she's round an' wa'm? The p'int is she was his'n—an' now she belongs t' me! (*He goes to the door—then turns—rebelliously.*) An' Min hain't sech a bad un. They's worse'n Min in the world, I'll bet ye! Wait'll we see this cow the Old Man's hitched t'! She'll beat Min, I got a notion! (*He starts to go out.*)

SIMEON (*suddenly*). Mebbe ye'll try t' make her your'n, too?

PETER. Ha! (*He gives a sardonic laugh of relish at this idea.*)

EBEN (*spitting with disgust*). Her—here—sleepin' with him—stealin' my Maw's farm! I'd as soon pet a skunk 'r kiss a snake! (*He goes out. The two stare after him suspiciously. A pause. They listen to his steps receding.*)

PETER. He's startin' the fire.

SIMEON. I'd like t' ride t' Californi-a —but—

PETER. Min might o' put some scheme in his head.

SIMEON. Mebbe it's all a lie 'bout Paw marryin'. We'd best wait an' see the bride.

PETER. An' don't sign nothin' till we does!

SIMEON. Nor till we've tested it's good money! (*Then with a grin*) But if Paw's hitched we'd be sellin' Eben somethin' we'd never git nohow!

PETER. We'll wait an' see. (*Then with sudden vindictive anger*) An' till he comes, let's yew 'n' me not wuk a lick, let Eben tend to thin's if he's a mind t', let's us jest sleep an' eat an' drink likker, an' let the hull damned farm go t' blazes!

SIMEON (*excitedly*). By God, we've 'arned a rest! We'll play rich fur a change. I hain't a-goin' to stir outa bed till breakfast's ready.

PETER. An' on the table!

SIMEON (*after a pause—thoughtfully*). What d' ye calc'late she'll be like—our new Maw? Like Eben thinks?

PETER. More'n likely.

SIMEON (*vindictively*). Waal—I hope she's a she-devil that'll make him wish he was dead an' living in the pit o' hell fur comfort!

PETER (*fervently*). Amen!

SIMEON (*imitating his father's voice*). "I'm ridin' out t' learn God's message t' me in the spring like the prophets done," he says. I'll bet right then an' thar he knew plumb well he was goin' whorin', the stinkin' old hypocrite!

Scene IV

(*Same as Scene II—shows the interior of the kitchen with a lighted candle on table. It is gray dawn outside.* SIMEON *and* PETER *are just finishing their breakfast.* EBEN *sits before his plate of untouched food, brooding frowningly.*)

PETER (*glancing at him rather irritably*). Lookin' glum don't help none.

SIMEON (*sarcastically*). Sorrowin' over his lust o' the flesh!

PETER (*with a grin*). Was she yer fust?

EBEN (*angrily*). None o' yer business. (*A pause.*) I was thinkin' o' him. I got a notion he's gittin' near—I kin feel him comin' on like yew kin feel malaria chill afore it takes ye.

PETER. It's too early yet.

SIMEON. Dunno. He'd like t' catch us nappin'—jest t' have somethin' t' hoss us 'round over.

PETER (*mechanically gets to his feet.* SIMEON *does the same*). Waal—let's git t' wuk. (*They both plod mechanically toward the door before they realize. Then they stop short.*)

SIMEON (*grinning*). Ye're a cussed fool, Pete—and I be wuss! Let him see we hain't wukin'! We don't give a durn!

PETER (*as they go back to the table*). Not a damned durn! It'll serve t' show him we're done with him. (*They sit down again.* EBEN *stares from one to the other with surprise.*)

SIMEON (*grins at him*). We're aimin' t' start bein' lilies o' the field.

PETER. Nary a toil 'r spin 'r lick o' wuk do we put in!

SIMEON. Ye're sole owner—till he comes—that's what ye wanted. Waal, ye got t' be sole hand, too.

PETER. The cows air bellerin'. Ye better hustle at the milkin'.

EBEN (*with excited joy*). Ye mean ye'll sign the paper?

SIMEON (*dryly*). Mebbe.

PETER. Mebbe.

SIMEON. We're considerin'. (*Peremptorily*) Ye better git t' wuk.

EBEN (*with queer excitement*). It's Maw's farm agen! It's my farm! Them's my cows! I'll milk my durn fingers off fur cows o' mine! (*He goes out door in rear, they stare after him indifferently.*)

SIMEON. Like his Paw.

PETER. Dead spit 'n' image!

SIMEON. Waal—let dog eat dog! (EBEN *comes out of front door and around the corner of the house. The sky is beginning to grow flushed with sunrise.* EBEN *stops by the gate and stares around him with glowing, possessive eyes. He takes in the whole farm with his embracing glance of desire.*)

EBEN. It's purty! It's damned purty! It's mine! (*He suddenly throws his head back boldly and glares with hard, defiant eye at the sky.*) Mine, d'ye hear? Mine! (*He turns and walks quickly off left, rear, toward the barn. The two brothers light their pipes.*)

SIMEON (*putting his muddy boots up on the table, tilting back his chair, and puffing defiantly*). Waal—this air solid comfort—fur once.

PETER. Ay-eh. (*He follows suit. A pause. Unconsciously they both sigh.*)

SIMEON (*suddenly*). He never was much o' a hand at milkin', Eben wa'n't.

PETER (*with a snort*). His hands air like hoofs! (*A pause.*)

SIMEON. Reach down the jug thar! Let's take a swaller. I'm feelin' kind o' low.

PETER. Good idee! (*He does so—gets two glasses—they pour out drinks of whisky.*) Here's t' the gold in Californi-a!

SIMEON. An' luck t' find it! (*They drink—puff resolutely—sigh—take their feet down from the table.*)

PETER. Likker don't 'pear t' sot right.

SIMEON. We hain't used t' it this early. (*A pause. They become very restless.*)

PETER. Gittin' close in this kitchen.

SIMEON (*with immense relief*). Let's git a breath o' air. (*They arise briskly and go out rear—appear around house and stop by the gate. They stare up at the sky with a numbed appreciation.*)

PETER. Purty!

SIMEON. Ay-eh. Gold's t' the East now.

PETER. Sun's startin' with us fur the Golden West.

SIMEON (*staring around the farm, his compressed face tightened, unable to conceal his emotion*). Waal—it's our last mornin'—mebbe.

PETER (*the same*). Ay-eh.

SIMEON (*stamps his foot on the earth and addresses it desperately*). Waal—ye've thirty year o' me buried in ye—spread out over ye—blood an' bone an' sweat—rotted away—fertilizin' ye—richin' yer soul—prime manure, by God, that's what I been t' ye!

PETER. Ay-eh! An' me!

SIMEON. An' yew, Peter. (*He sighs—then spits.*) Waal—no use'n cryin' over spilt milk.

PETER. They's gold in the West—an' freedom, mebbe. We been slaves t' stone walls here.

SIMEON (*defiantly*). We hain't nobody's slaves from this out—nor no thin's slaves nuther. (*A pause—restlessly*) Speakin' o' milk, wonder how Eben's managin'?

PETER. I s'pose he's managin'.

SIMEON. Mebbe we'd ought t' help—this once.

PETER. Mebbe. The cows knows us.

SIMEON. An' likes us. They don't know him much.

PETER. An' the hosses, an' pigs, an' chickens. They don't know him much.

SIMEON. They knows us like brothers—an' likes us! (*Proudly*) Hain't we raised 'em t' be fust-rate, number one prize stock?

PETER. We hain't—not no more.

SIMEON (*dully*). I was fergittin'. (*Then resignedly*) Waal, let's go help Eben a spell an' git waked up.

PETER. Suits me. (*They are starting off down left, rear, for the barn when EBEN appears from there hurrying toward them, his face excited.*)

EBEN (*breathlessly*). Waal—har they be! The old mule an' the bride! I seen 'em from the barn down below at the turnin'.

PETER. How could ye tell that far?

EBEN. Hain't I as far-sight as he's nearsight? Don't I know the mare 'n' buggy, an' two people settin' in it? Who else . . . ? An' I tell ye I kin feel 'em a-comin', too! (*He squirms as if he had the itch.*)

PETER (*beginning to be angry*). Waal—let him do his own unhitchin'!

SIMEON (*angry in his turn*). Let's hustle in an' git our bundles an' be a-goin' as he's a-comin'. I don't want never t' step inside the door agen arter he's back. (*They both start back around the corner of the house. EBEN follows them.*)

EBEN (*anxiously*). Will ye sign it afore ye go?

PETER. Let's see the color o' the old skinflint's money an' we'll sign. (*They disappear left. The two brothers clump upstairs to get their bundles. EBEN appears in the kitchen, runs to the window, peers out, comes back and pulls up a strip of flooring in under stove, takes out a canvas bag and puts it on table, then sets the floorboard back in place. The two brothers appear a moment after. They carry old carpet bags.*)

EBEN (*puts his hand on bag guardingly*). Have ye signed?

SIMEON (*shows paper in his hand*). Ay-eh (*Greedily*) Be that the money?

EBEN (*opens bag and pours out pile of twenty-dollar gold pieces*). Twenty-dollar pieces—thirty on 'em. Count 'em. (*PETER does so, arranging them in stacks of five, biting one or two to test them.*)

PETER. Six hundred. (*He puts them in bag and puts it inside his shirt, carefully.*)

SIMEON (*handing paper to EBEN*). Har ye be.

EBEN (*after a glance, folds it carefully and hides it under his shirt—gratefully*). Thank yew.

PETER. Thank yew fur the ride.

SIMEON. We'll send ye a lump o' gold fur Christmas. (*A pause. EBEN stares at them and they at him.*)

PETER (*awkwardly*). Waal—we're a-goin'.

SIMEON. Comin' out t' the yard?

EBEN. No. I'm waitin' in here a spell. (*Another silence. The brothers edge awkwardly to the door in rear—then turn and stand.*)

SIMEON. Waal—good-by.

PETER. Good-by.

EBEN. Good-by. (*They go out. He sits down at the table, faces the stove and pulls out the paper. He looks from it to the stove. His face, lighted up by the shaft of sunlight from the windows, has an expression of trance. His lips move. The two brothers come out to the gate.*)

PETER (*looking off toward barn*). Thar he be—unhitchin'.

SIMEON (*with a chuckle*). I'll bet ye he's riled!

PETER. An' thar she be.

SIMEON. Let's wait 'n' see what our new Maw looks like.

PETER (*with a grin*). An' give him our partin' cuss!

SIMEON (*grinning*). I feel like raisin' fun. I feel light in my head an' feet.

PETER. Me, too. I feel like laffin' till I'd split up the middle.

SIMEON. Reckon it's the likker?

PETER. No. My feet feel itchin' t' walk an' walk—an' jump high over thin's—an'. . . .

SIMEON. Dance? (*A pause.*)

PETER (*puzzled*). It's plumb onnateral.

SIMEON (*a light coming over his face*). I calc'late it's 'cause school's out. It's holiday. Fur once we're free!

PETER (*dazedly*). Free?

SIMEON. The halter's broke—the harness is busted—the fence bars is down—the stone walls air crumblin' an' tumblin'! We'll be kickin' up an' tearin' away down the road!

PETER (*drawing a deep breath—oratorically*). Anybody that wants this stinkin' old rock-pile of a farm kin hev it. 'Tain't our'n, no sirree!

SIMEON (*takes the gate off its hinges and puts it under his arm*). We harby 'bolishes shet gates an' open gates, an' all gates, by thunder!

PETER. We'll take it with us fur luck an' let 'er sail free down some river.

SIMEON (*as a sound of voices comes from left, rear*). Har they comes! (*The two brothers congeal into two stiff, grim-visaged statues. EPHRAIM CABOT and ABBIE PUTNAM come in. CABOT is seventy-five, tall and gaunt, with great, wiry, concentrated power, but stoop-shouldered from toil. His face is as hard as if it were hewn out of a boulder, yet there is a weakness in it, a petty pride in its own narrow strength. His eyes are small, close together, and extremely near-sighted, blinking continually in the effort to focus on objects, their stare having a straining, ingrowing quality. He is dressed in his dismal black Sunday suit. ABBIE is thirty-five, buxom, full of vitality. Her round face is pretty but marred by its rather gross sensuality. There is strength and obstinacy in her jaw, a hard determination in her eyes, and about her whole personality the same unsettled, untamed, desperate quality which is so apparent in EBEN.*)

CABOT (*as they enter—a queer strangled emotion in his dry cracking voice*). Har we be t' hum, Abbie.

ABBIE (*with lust for the word*). Hum! (*Her eyes gloating on the house without seeming to see the two stiff figures at the gate.*) It's purty—purty! I can't b'lieve it's r'ally mine.

CABOT (*sharply*). Yewr'n? Mine! (*He stares at her penetratingly. She stares back. He adds relentingly.*) Our'n—mebbe! It was lonesome too long. I was growin' old in the spring. A hum's got t' hev a woman.

ABBIE (*her voice taking possession*). A woman's got t' hev a hum!

CABOT (*nodding uncertainly*). Ay-eh. (*Then irritably*) Whar be they? Ain't thar nobody about—'r wukin'—'r nothin'?

ABBIE (*sees the brothers. She returns their stare of cold appraising contempt with interest—slowly*). Thar's two men loafin' at the gate an' starin' at me like a couple o' strayed hogs.

CABOT (*straining his eyes*). I kin see 'em—but I can't make out. . . .

SIMEON. It's Simeon.

PETER. It's Peter.

CABOT (*exploding*). Why hain't ye wukin'?

SIMEON (*dryly*). We're waitin' t' welcome ye hum—yew an' the bride!

CABOT (*confusedly*). Huh? Waal—this be yer new Maw, boys. (*She stares at them and they at her.*)

SIMEON (*turns away and spits contemptuously*). I see her!

PETER (*spits also*). An' I see her!

ABBIE (*with the conqueror's conscious superiority*). I'll go in an' look at *my* house. (*She goes slowly around to porch.*)

SIMEON (*with a snort*). Her house!

PETER (*calls after her*). Ye'll find Eben inside. Ye better not tell him it's *yewr* house.

ABBIE (*mouthing the name*). Eben. (*Then quietly*) I'll tell Eben.

CABOT (*with a contemptuous sneer*). Ye needn't heed Eben. Eben's a dumb fool—like his Maw—soft an' simple!

SIMEON (*with his sardonic burst of laughter*). Ha! Eben's a chip o' yew— spit 'n' image—hard 'n' bitter's a hickory tree! Dog'll eat dog. He'll eat ye yet, old man!

CABOT (*commandingly*). Ye git t' wuk!

SIMEON (*as* ABBIE *disappears in house —winks at* PETER *and says tauntingly*). So that thar's our new Maw, be it? Whar in hell did ye dig her up? (*He and* PETER *laugh*.)

PETER. Ha! Ye'd better turn her in the pen with the other sows. (*They laugh uproariously, slapping their thighs*.)

CABOT (*so amazed at their effrontery that he stutters in confusion*). Simeon! Peter! What's come over ye? Air ye drunk?

SIMEON. We're free, old man—free o' yew an' the hull damned farm! (*They grow more and more hilarious and excited*.)

PETER. An' we're startin' out fur the gold fields o' Californi-a!

SIMEON. Ye kin take this place an' burn it!

PETER. An' bury it—fur all we cares!

SIMEON. We're free, old man! (*He cuts a caper*.)

PETER. Free! (*He gives a kick in the air*.)

SIMEON (*in a frenzy*). Whoop!

PETER. Whoop! (*They do an absurd Indian war dance about the old man, who is petrified between rage and the fear that they are insane*.)

SIMEON. We're free as Injuns! Lucky we don't skulp ye!

PETER. An' burn yer barn an' kill the stock!

SIMEON. An' rape yer new woman! Whoop! (*He and* PETER *stop their dance, holding their sides, rocking with wild laughter*.)

CABOT (*edging away*). Lust fur gold— fur the sinful, easy gold o' Californi-a! It's made ye mad!

SIMEON (*tauntingly*). Wouldn't ye like us to send ye back some sinful gold, ye old sinner?

PETER. They's gold besides what's in Californi-a! (*He retreats back beyond the vision of the old man and takes the bag of money and flaunts it in the air above his head, laughing*.)

SIMEON. And sinfuller, too!

PETER. We'll be voyagin' on the sea! Whoop! (*He leaps up and down*.)

SIMEON. Livin' free! Whoop! (*He leaps in turn*.)

CABOT (*suddenly roaring with rage*). My cuss on ye!

SIMEON. Take our'n in trade fur it! Whoop!

CABOT. I'll hev ye both chained up in the asylum!

PETER. Ye old skinflint! Good-by!

SIMEON. Ye old blood sucker! Good-by!

CABOT. Go afore I . . . !

PETER. Whoop! (*He picks a stone from the road.* SIMEON *does the same*.)

SIMEON. Maw'll be in the parlor.

PETER. Ay-eh! One! Two!

CABOT (*frightened*). What air ye . . . ?

PETER. Three! (*They both throw, the stones hitting the parlor window with a crash of glass, tearing the shade*.)

SIMEON. Whoop!

PETER. Whoop!

CABOT (*in a fury now, rushing toward them*). If I kin lay hands on ye—I'll break yer bones fur ye! (*But they beat a capering retreat before him,* SIMEON *with the gate still under his arm.* CABOT *comes back, panting with impotent rage. Their voices as they go off take up the song of the gold-seekers to the old tune of "Oh, Susannah!"*)

"I jumped aboard the Liza ship,
  And traveled on the sea,
  And every time I thought of home
  I wished it wasn't me!
  Oh! Californi-a,
  That's the land fur me!
  I'm off to Californi-a!
  With my wash bowl on my knee."

(*In the meantime, the window of the upper bedroom on right is raised and* ABBIE *sticks her head out. She looks down at* CABOT—*with a sigh of relief*.)

ABBIE. Waal—that's the last o' them two, hain't it? (*He doesn't answer. Then in possessive tones*) This here's a nice bedroom, Ephraim. It's a r'al nice bed. Is it my room, Ephraim?

CABOT (*grimly—without looking up*). Our'n! (*She cannot control a grimace of aversion and pulls back her head slowly and shuts the window. A sudden horrible thought seems to enter* CABOT'S *head.*) They been up to somethin'! Mebbe— mebbe they've pizened the stock—'r somethin'! (*He almost runs off down toward the barn. A moment later the kitchen door is slowly pushed open and* ABBIE *enters. For a moment she stands looking at* EBEN. *He does not notice her at first. Her eyes take him in penetratingly with a calculating appraisal of his strength as against hers. But under this her desire is dimly awakened by his youth and good looks. Suddenly he becomes conscious of her presence and looks up. Their eyes meet. He leaps to his feet, glowering at her speechlessly.*)

ABBIE (*in her most seductive tones, which she uses all through this scene*). Be you—Eben? I'm Abbie—(*She laughs.*) I mean, I'm yer new Maw.

EBEN (*viciously*). No, damn ye!

ABBIE (*as if she hadn't heard—with a queer smile*). Yer Paw's spoke a lot o' yew. . . .

EBEN. Ha!

ABBIE. Ye mustn't mind him. He's an old man. (*A long pause. They stare at each other.*) I don't want t' pretend playin' Maw t' ye, Eben. (*Admiringly*) Ye're too big an' strong fur that. I want t' be frens with ye. Mebbe with me fur a fren ye'd find ye'd like livin' here better. I kin make it easy fur ye with him, mebbe. (*With a scornful sense of power*) I calc'late I kin git him t' do most anythin' fur me.

EBEN (*with bitter scorn*). Ha! (*They stare again,* EBEN *obscurely moved, physically attracted to her—in forced stilted tones*) Yew kin go t' the devil!

ABBIE (*calmly*). If cussin' me does ye good, cuss all ye've a mind t'. I'm all prepared t' have ye agin me—at fust. I don't blame ye nuther. I'd feel the same at any stranger comin' t' take my Maw's place. (*He shudders. She is watching him carefully.*) Yew must've cared a lot fur yewr Maw, didn't ye? My Maw died afore I'd growed. I don't remember her none. (*A pause.*) But yew won't hate me long, Eben. I'm not the wust in the world—an'

yew an' me've got a lot in common. I kin tell that by lookin' at ye. Waal—I've had a hard life, too—oceans o' trouble an' nuthin' but wuk fur reward. I was a orphan early an had t' wuk fur others in other folks' hums. Then I married an' he turned out a drunken spreer an' so he had to wuk fur others an' me too agen in other folks' hums, an' the baby died, an' my husband got sick an' died too, an' I was glad, sayin' now I'm free fur once, on'y I diskivered right away all I was free fur was t' wuk agen in other folks' hums, doin' other folks' wuk till I'd most give up hope o' ever doin' my own wuk in my own hum, an' then your Paw come. . . . (CABOT *appears returning from the barn. He comes to the gate and looks down the road the brothers have gone. A faint strain of their retreating voices is heard:*) "*Oh, Californi-a! That's the place for me.*" *He stands glowering, his fist clenched, his face grim with rage.*)

EBEN (*fighting against his growing attraction and sympathy—harshly*). An' bought yew—like a harlot! (*She is stung and flushes angrily. She has been sincerely moved by the recital of her troubles. He adds furiously:*) An' the price he's payin' ye—this farm—was my Maw's, damn ye!—an' mine now!

ABBIE (*with a cool laugh of confidence*). Yewr'n? We'll see 'bout that! (*Then strongly*) Waal—what if I did need a hum? What else'd I marry an old man like him fur?

EBEN (*maliciously*). I'll tell him ye said that!

ABBIE (*smiling*). I'll say ye're lyin' a-purpose—an' he'll drive ye off the place!

EBEN. Ye devil!

ABBIE (*defying him*). This be my farm—this be my hum—this be my kitchen—!

EBEN (*furiously, as if he were going to attack her*). Shut up, damn ye!

ABBIE (*walks up to him—a queer coarse expression of desire in her face and body—slowly*). An' upstairs—that be my bedroom—an' my bed! (*He stares into her eyes, terribly confused and torn. She adds softly:*) I hain't bad nor mean— 'ceptin' fur an enemy—but I got t' fight fur what's due me out o' life, if I ever 'spect t' git it. (*Then putting her hand on his arm—seductively)* Let's yew 'n' me be frens, Eben.

EBEN (*stupidly—as if hypnotized*). Ay-eh. (*Then furiously flinging off her arm*) No, ye durned old witch! I hate ye! (*He rushes out the door.*)

ABBIE (*looks after him smiling satisfiedly—then half to herself, mouthing the word*). Eben's nice. (*She looks at the table, proudly.*) I'll wash up *my* dishes now. (EBEN *appears outside, slamming the door behind him. He comes around corner, stops on seeing his father, and stands staring at him with hate.*)

CABOT (*raising his arms to heaven in the fury he can no longer control*). Lord God o' Hosts, smite the undutiful sons with Thy wust cuss!

EBEN (*breaking in violently*). Yew 'n' yewr God! Allus cussin' folks—allus naggin' 'em!

CABOT (*oblivious to him—summoningly*). God o' the old! God o' the lonesome!

EBEN (*mockingly*). Naggin' His sheep t' sin! T' hell with yewr God! (CABOT *turns. He and* EBEN *glower at each other.*)

CABOT (*harshly*). So it's yew. I might've knowed it. (*Shaking his finger threateningly at him*) Blasphemin' fool! (*Then quickly*) Why hain't ye t' wuk?

EBEN. Why hain't yew? They've went. I can't wuk it all alone.

CABOT (*contemptuously*). Nor noways! I'm wuth ten o' ye yit, old's I be! Ye'll never be more'n half a man! (*Then, matter-of-factly*) Waal—let's git t' the barn. (*They go. A last faint note of the "Californi-a" song is heard from the distance.* ABBIE *is washing her dishes.*)

Curtain

❧ Part II

Scene I

(*The exterior of the farmhouse, as in Part I—a hot Sunday afternoon two months later.* ABBIE, *dressed in her best, is discovered sitting in a rocker at the end of the porch. She rocks listlessly, enervated by the heat, staring in front of her with bored, half-closed eyes.*)

EBEN *sticks his head out of his bedroom window. He looks around furtively and tries to see—or hear—if anyone is on the porch, but although he has been careful to make no noise,* ABBIE *has sensed his movement. She stops rocking, her face grows animated and eager, she waits attentively.* EBEN *seems to feel her presence, he scowls back his thoughts of her and spits with exaggerated disdain—then withdraws back into the room.* ABBIE *waits, holding her breath as she listens with passionate eagerness for every sound within the house.*

EBEN *comes out. Their eyes meet. His falter, he is confused, he turns away and slams the door resentfully. At this gesture,* ABBIE *laughs tantalizingly, amused but at the same time piqued and irritated. He scowls, strides off the porch to the path and starts to walk past her to the road with a grand swagger of ignoring her existence. He is dressed in his store suit, spruced up, his face shines from soap and water.* ABBIE *leans forward on her chair, her eyes hard and angry now, and, as he passes her, gives a sneering, taunting chuckle.*)

EBEN (*stung—turns on her furiously*). What air yew cacklin' 'bout?

ABBIE (*triumphant*). Yew!

EBEN. What about me?

ABBIE. Ye look all slicked up like a prize bull.

EBEN (*with a sneer*). Waal—ye hain't so durned purty yerself, be ye? (*They stare into each other's eyes, his held by hers in spite of himself, hers glowingly possessive. Their physical attraction becomes a palpable force quivering in the hot air.*)

ABBIE (*softly*). Ye don't mean that, Eben. Ye may think ye mean it, mebbe, but ye don't. Ye can't. It's agin nature, Eben. Ye been fightin' yer nature ever since the day I come—tryin' t' tell yerself I hain't purty t'ye. (*She laughs a low humid laugh without taking her eyes from his. A pause—her body squirms desirously—she murmurs languorously.*) Hain't the sun strong an' hot? Ye kin feel it burnin' into the earth—Nature—makin' thin's grow—bigger 'n' bigger—burnin' inside ye—makin' ye want t' grow—into somethin' else—till ye're jined with it—an' it's your'n—but it owns ye, too—an' makes ye grow bigger—like a tree—like them elums—(*She laughs again softly, holding his eyes. He takes a step toward her, compelled against his will.*) Nature'll beat ye, Eben. Ye might's well own up t' it fust 's last.

EBEN (*trying to break from her spell—confusedly*). If Paw'd hear ye goin' on. . . . (*Resentfully*) But ye've made such a damned idjit out o' the old devil . . . ! (ABBIE *laughs.*)

ABBIE. Waal—hain't it easier fur yew with him changed softer?

EBEN (*defiantly*). No. I'm fightin' him—fightin' yew—fightin' fur Maw's rights t' her hum! (*This breaks her spell for him. He glowers at her.*) An' I'm onto ye. Ye hain't foolin' me a mite. Ye're aimin' t' swaller up everythin' an' make it your'n. Waal, you'll find I'm a heap sight bigger hunk nor yew kin chew! (*He turns from her with a sneer.*)

ABBIE (*trying to regain her ascendancy—seductively*). Eben!

EBEN. Leave me be! (*He starts to walk away.*)

ABBIE (*more commandingly*). Eben!

EBEN (*stops—resentfully*). What d'ye want?

ABBIE (*trying to conceal a growing excitement*). Whar air ye goin'?

EBEN (*with malicious nonchalance*). Oh—up the road a spell.

ABBIE. T' the village?

EBEN (*airily*). Mebbe.

ABBIE (*excitedly*). T' see that Min, I s'pose?

EBEN. Mebbe.

ABBIE (*weakly*). What d'ye want t' waste time on her fur?

EBEN (*revenging himself now—grinning at her*). Ye can't beat Nature, didn't ye say? (*He laughs and again starts to walk away.*)

ABBIE (*bursting out*). An ugly old hake!

EBEN (*with a tantalizing sneer*). She's purtier'n yew be!

ABBIE. That every wuthless drunk in the county has. . . .

EBEN (*tauntingly*). Mebbe—but she's better'n yew. She owns up fa'r 'n' squar' t' her doin's.

ABBIE (*furiously*). Don't ye dare compare. . . .

EBEN. She don't go sneakin' an' stealin'—what's mine.

ABBIE (*savagely seizing on his weak point*). Your'n? Yew mean—my farm?

EBEN. I mean the farm yew sold yerself fur like any other old whore—my farm!

ABBIE (*stung—fiercely*). Ye'll never live t' see the day when even a stinkin' weed on it'll belong t' ye! (*Then in a scream*) Git out o' my sight! Go on t' yer slut—disgracin' yer Paw 'n' me! I'll git yer Paw t' horsewhip ye off the place if I want t'! Ye're only livin' here 'cause I tolerate ye! Git along! I hate the sight o' ye! (*She stops, panting and glaring at him.*)

EBEN (*returning her glance in kind*). An' I hate the sight o' yew! (*He turns and strides off up the road. She follows his retreating figure with concentrated hate. Old* CABOT *appears coming up from the barn. The hard, grim expression of his face has changed. He seems in some queer way softened, mellowed. His eyes have taken on a strange, incongruous dreamy quality. Yet there is no hint of physical weakness about him—rather he looks more robust and younger.* ABBIE *sees him and turns away quickly with unconcealed aversion. He comes slowly up to her.*)

CABOT (*mildly*). War yew an' Eben quarrelin' agen?

ABBIE (*shortly*). No.

CABOT. Ye was talkin' a'mighty loud. (*He sits down on the edge of porch.*)

ABBIE (*snappishly*). If ye heerd us they hain't no need askin' questions.

CABOT. I didn't hear what ye said.

ABBIE (*relieved*). Waal—it wa'n't nothin' t' speak on.

CABOT (*after a pause*). Eben's queer.

ABBIE (*bitterly*). He's the dead spit 'n' image o' yew!

CABOT (*queerly interested*). D'ye think so, Abbie? (*After a pause, ruminatingly*) Me 'n' Eben's allus fit 'n' fit. I never could b'ar him noways. He's so thunderin' soft—like his Maw.

ABBIE (*scornfully*). Ay-eh! 'Bout as soft as yew be!

CABOT (*as if he hadn't heard*). Mebbe I been too hard on him.

ABBIE (*jeeringly*). Waal—ye're gettin' soft now—soft as slop! That's what Eben was sayin'.

CABOT (*his face instantly grim and ominous*). Eben was sayin'? Waal, he'd best not do nothin' t' try me 'r he'll soon diskiver. . . . (*A pause. She keeps her face turned away. His gradually softens. He stares up at the sky.*) Purty, hain't it?

ABBIE (*crossly*). I don't see nothin' purty.

CABOT. The sky. Feels like a wa'm field up thar.

ABBIE (*sarcastically*). Air yew aimin' t' buy up over the farm too? (*She snickers contemptuously.*)

CABOT (*strangely*). I'd like t' own my place up thar. (*A pause.*) I'm gittin' old Abbie, I'm gittin' ripe on the bough. (*A pause. She stares at him mystified. He goes on.*) It's allus lonesome cold in the house—even when it's bilin' hot outside. Hain't yew noticed?

ABBIE. No.

CABOT. It's wa'm down t' the barn—nice smellin' an' warm—with the cows. (*A pause.*) Cows is queer.

ABBIE. Like yew?

CABOT. Like Eben. (*A pause.*) I'm gittin' t' feel resigned t' Eben—jest as I got t' feel 'bout his Maw. I'm gittin' t' learn to b'ar his softness—jest like her'n. I calc'late I c'd a'most take t' him—if he wa'n't sech a dumb fool! (*A pause.*) I s'pose it's old age a-creepin' in my bones.

ABBIE (*indifferently*). Waal—ye hain't dead yet.

CABOT (*roused*). No, I hain't, yew bet —not by a hell of a sight!—I'm sound 'n' tough as hickory! (*Then moodily*) But arter three score and ten the Lord warns ye t' prepare. (*A pause.*) That's why Eben's come in my head. Now that his cussed sinful brothers is gone their path t' hell, they's no one left but Eben.

ABBIE (*resentfully*). They's me, hain't they? (*Agitatedly*) What's all this sudden likin' ye tuk to Eben? Why don't ye say nothin' 'bout me? Hain't I yer lawful wife?

CABOT (*simply*). Ay-eh. Ye be. (*A pause—he stares at her desirously—his eyes grow avid—then with a sudden movement he seizes her hands and squeezes them, declaiming in a queer camp meeting preacher's tempo:*) Yew air my Rose o' Sharon! Behold, yew air fair; yer eyes air doves; yer lips air like scarlet; yer two breasts air like two fawns; yer navel be like a round goblet; yer belly be like a heap o' wheat. . . . (*He covers her hand with kisses. She does not seem to notice. She stares before her with hard angry eyes.*)

ABBIE (*jerking her hands away—*

harshly). So ye're plannin' t' leave the farm t' Eben, air ye?

CABOT (*dazedly*). Leave . . . ? (*Then with resentful obstinacy*) I hain't a-givin' it t' no one!

ABBIE (*remorselessly*). Ye can't take it with ye.

CABOT (*thinks a moment—then reluctantly*). No, I calc'late not. (*After a pause—with a strange passion*) But if I could, I would, by the Etarnal! 'R if I could, in my dyin' hour, I'd set it afire an' watch it burn—this house an' every ear o' corn an' every tree down t' the last blade o' hay! I'd sit an' know it was all a-dying with me an' no one else'd ever own what was mine, what I'd made out o' nothin' with my own sweat 'n' blood! (*A pause—then he adds with a queer affection.*) 'Ceptin' the cows. Them I'd turn free.

ABBIE (*harshly*). An' me?

CABOT (*with a queer smile*). Ye'd be turned free, too.

ABBIE (*furiously*). So that's the thanks I git fur marryin' ye—t' have ye change kind to Eben who hates ye, an' talk o' turnin' me out in the road.

CABOT (*hastily*). Abbie! Ye know I wa'n't. . . .

ABBIE (*vengefully*). Just let me tell ye a thing or two 'bout Eben. Whar's he gone? T' see that harlot, Min! I tried fur t' stop him. Disgracin' yew an' me—on the Sabbath, too!

CABOT (*rather guiltily*). He's a sinner —nateral-born. It's lust eatin' his heart.

ABBIE (*enraged beyond endurance—wildly vindictive*). An' his lust fur me! Kin ye find excuses fur that?

CABOT (*stares at her—after a dead pause*). Lust—fur yew?

ABBIE (*defiantly*). He was tryin' t' make love t' me—when ye heerd us quarrelin'.

CABOT (*stares at her—then a terrible expression of rage comes over his face—he springs to his feet shaking all over*). By the A'mighty God—I'll end him!

ABBIE (*frightened now for* EBEN). No! Don't ye!

CABOT (*violently*). I'll git the shotgun an' blow his soft brains t' the top o' them elums!

ABBIE (*throwing her arms around him*). No, Ephraim!

knowin' what it meant. It made me bitter 'n wormwood. It aged me—them coveting what I'd made fur mine. Then this spring the call come—the voice o' God cryin' in my wilderness, in my lonesomeness—t' go out an' seek an' find! (*Turning to her with strange passion*) I sought ye an' I found ye! Yew air my Rose o' Sharon! Yer eyes air like. . . . (*She has turned a blank face, resentful eyes to his. He stares at her for a moment —then harshly*) Air ye any the wiser fur all I've told ye?

ABBIE (*confusedly*). Mebbe.

CABOT (*pushing her away from him— angrily*). Ye don't know nothin'—nor never will. If ye don't hev a son t' redeem ye . . . (*This in a tone of cold threat.*)

ABBIE (*resentfully*). I've prayed, hain't I?

CABOT (*bitterly*). Pray agen—fur understandin'!

ABBIE (*a veiled threat in her tone*). Ye'll have a son out o' me, I promise ye.

CABOT. How kin ye promise?

ABBIE. I got second-sight mebbe. I kin foretell. (*She gives a queer smile.*)

CABOT. I believe ye have. Ye give me the chills sometimes. (*He shivers.*) It's cold in this house. It's oneasy. They's thin's pokin' about in the dark—in the corners. (*He pulls on his trousers, tucking in his night shirt, and pulls on his boots.*)

ABBIE (*surprised*). Whar air ye goin'?

CABOT (*queerly*). Down whar it's restful—whar it's warm—down t' the barn. (*Bitterly*) I kin talk t' the cows. They know. They know the farm an' me. They'll give me peace. (*He turns to go out the door.*)

ABBIE (*a bit frightenedly*). Air ye ailin' tonight, Ephraim?

CABOT. Growin'. Growin' ripe on the bough. (*He turns and goes, his boots clumping down the stairs. EBEN sits up with a start, listening. ABBIE is conscious of his movement and stares at the wall. CABOT comes out of the house around the corner and stands by the gate, blinking at the sky. He stretches up his hands in a tortured gesture*) God A'mighty, call from the dark! (*He listens as if expecting an answer. Then his arms drop, he shakes his head and plods off toward the barn. EBEN and ABBIE stare at each other through the wall. EBEN sighs heavily and ABBIE echoes it. Both become terribly nervous, uneasy. Finally ABBIE gets up and listens, her ear to the wall. He acts as if he saw every move she was making, he becomes resolutely still. She seems driven into a decision—goes out the door in rear determinedly. His eyes follow her. Then as the door of his room is opened softly, he turns away, waits in an attitude of strained fixity. ABBIE stands for a second staring at him, her eyes burning with desire. Then with a little cry she runs over and throws her arms about his neck, she pulls his head back and covers his mouth with kisses. At first, he submits dumbly; then he puts his arms about her neck and returns her kisses, but finally, suddenly aware of his hatred, he hurls her away from him, springing to his feet. They stand speechless and breathless, panting like two animals.*)

ABBIE (*at last—painfully.*) Ye shouldn't, Eben—ye shouldn't—I'd make ye happy!

EBEN (*harshly*). I don't want t' be happy—from yew!

ABBIE (*helplessly*). Ye do, Eben! Ye do! Why d'ye lie?

EBEN (*viciously*). I don't take t' ye, I tell ye! I hate the sight o' ye!

ABBIE (*with an uncertain troubled laugh*). Waal, I kissed ye anyways—an' ye kissed back—yer lips was burnin'—ye can't lie 'bout that! (*Intensely*) If ye don't care, why did ye kiss me back—why was yer lips burnin'?

EBEN (*wiping his mouth*). It was like pizen on 'em (*Then tauntingly*) When I kissed ye back, mebbe I thought 'twas someone else.

ABBIE (*wildly*). Min?

EBEN. Mebbe.

ABBIE (*torturedly*). Did ye go t' see her? Did ye r'ally go? I thought ye mightn't. Is that why ye throwed me off jest now?

EBEN (*sneeringly*). What if it be?

ABBIE (*raging*). Then ye're a dog, Eben Cabot!

EBEN (*threateningly*). Ye can't talk that way t' me!

ABBIE (*with a shrill laugh*). Can't I? Did ye think I was in love with ye—a weak thin' like yew? Not much! I on'y wanted ye fur a purpose o' my own—an' I'll hev ye fur it yet 'cause I'm stronger'n yew be!

EBEN (*resentfully*). I knowed well it

was on'y part o' yer plan t' swaller everythin'!

ABBIE (*tauntingly*). Mebbe!

EBEN (*furious*). Git out o' my room!

ABBIE. This air my room an' ye're on'y hired help!

EBEN (*threateningly*). Git out afore I murder ye!

ABBIE (*quite confident now*). I hain't a mite afeerd. Ye want me, don't ye? Yes, ye do! An' yer Paw's son'll never kill what he wants! Look at yer eyes! They's lust fur me in 'em, burnin' 'em up! Look at yer lips now! They're tremblin' an' longin' t' kiss me, an' yer teeth t' bite (*He is watching her now with a horrible fascination. She laughs a crazy triumphant laugh.*) I'm a-goin' t' make all o' this hum my hum! They's one room hain't mine yet, but it's a-goin' t' be tonight. I'm a-goin' down now an light up! (*She makes him a mocking bow.*) Won't ye come courtin' me in the best parlor, Mister Cabot?

EBEN (*staring at her—horribly confused—dully*). Don't ye dare! It hain't been opened since Maw died an' was laid out thar! Don't ye . . . ! (*But her eyes are fixed on his so burningly that his will seems to wither before hers. He stands swaying toward her helplessly.*)

ABBIE (*holding his eyes and putting all her will into her words as she backs out the door*). I'll expect ye afore long, Eben.

EBEN (*stares after her for a while, walking toward the door. A light appears in the parlor window. He murmurs*). In the parlor? (*This seems to arouse connotations for he comes back and puts on his white shirt, collar, half ties the tie mechanically, puts on coat, takes his hat, stands barefooted looking about him in bewilderment, mutters wonderingly:*) Maw! Whar air yew? (*Then goes slowly toward the door in rear.*)

Scene III

(*A few minutes later. The interior of the parlor is shown. A grim, repressed room like a tomb in which the family has been interred alive.* ABBIE *sits on the edge of the horsehair sofa. She has lighted all the candles and the room is revealed in all its preserved ugliness. A change*

has come over the woman. She looks awed and frightened now, ready to run away.

The door is opened and EBEN *appears. His face wears an expression of obsessed confusion. He stands staring at her, his arms hanging disjointedly from his shoulders, his feet bare, his hat in his hand.*)

ABBIE (*after a pause—with a nervous, formal politeness*). Won't ye set?

EBEN (*dully*). Ay-eh. (*Mechanically he places his hat carefully on the floor near the door and sits stiffly beside her on the edge of the sofa. A pause. They both remain rigid, looking straight ahead with eyes full of fear.*)

ABBIE. When I fust came in—in the dark—they seemed somethin' here.

EBEN (*simply*). Maw.

ABBIE. I kin still feel—somethin'. . . .

EBEN. It's Maw.

ABBIE. At fust I was feerd o' it. I wanted t' yell an' run. Now—since yew come—seems like it's growin' soft an' kind t' me. (*Addressing the air—queerly*) Thank yew.

EBEN. Maw allus loved me.

ABBIE. Mebbe it knows I love yew too. Mebbe that makes it kind t' me.

EBEN (*dully*). I dunno. I should think she'd hate ye.

ABBIE (*with certainty*). No. I kin feel it don't—not no more.

EBEN. Hate ye fur stealin' her place—here in her hum—settin' in her parlor whar she was laid— (*He suddenly stops, staring stupidly before him.*)

ABBIE. What is it, Eben?

EBEN (*in a whisper*). Seems like Maw didn't want me t' remind ye.

ABBIE (*excitedly*). I knowed, Eben! It's kind t' me! It don't b'ar me no grudges fur what I never knowed an' couldn't help!

EBEN. Maw b'ars him a grudge.

ABBIE. Waal, so does all o' us.

EBEN. Ay-eh. (*With passion*) I does, by God!

ABBIE (*taking one of his hands in hers and patting it*). Thar! Don't git riled thinkin' o' him. Think o' yer Maw who's kind t' us. Tell me about yer Maw, Eben.

EBEN. They hain't nothin' much. She was kind. She was good.

ABBIE (*putting one arm over his shoulder. He does not seem to notice—passionately*). I'll be kind an' good t' ye!

EBEN. Sometimes she used t' sing fur me.

ABBIE. I'll sing fur ye!

EBEN. This was her hum. This was her farm.

ABBIE. This is my hum! This is my farm!

EBEN. He married her t' steal 'em. She was soft an' easy. He couldn't 'preciate her.

ABBIE. He can't 'preciate me!

EBEN. He murdered her with his hardness.

ABBIE. He's murderin' me!

EBEN. She died. (*A pause.*) Sometimes she used to sing fur me. (*He bursts into a fit of sobbing.*)

ABBIE (*both her arms around him—with wild passion*). I'll sing fur ye! I'll die fur ye! (*In spite of her overwhelming desire for him, there is a sincere maternal love in her manner and voice—a horribly frank mixture of lust and mother love.*) Don't cry, Eben! I'll take yer Maw's place! I'll be everythin' she was t' ye! Let me kiss ye, Eben! (*She pulls his head around. He makes a bewildered pretense of resistance. She is tender.*) Don't be afeerd! I'll kiss ye pure, Eben—same 's if I was a Maw t' ye—an' ye kin kiss me back 's if yew was my son—my boy—sayin' good-night t' me! Kiss me, Eben. (*They kiss in restrained fashion. Then suddenly wild passion overcomes her. She kisses him lustfully again and again and he flings his arms about her and returns her kisses. Suddenly, as in the bedroom, he frees himself from her violently and springs to his feet. He is trembling all over, in a strange state of terror. ABBIE strains her arms toward him with fierce pleading.*) Don't ye leave me, Eben! Can't ye see it hain't enuf—lovin' ye like a Maw—can't ye see it's got t' be that an' more—much more—a hundred times more—fur me t' be happy—fur yew t' be happy?

EBEN (*to the presence he feels in the room*). Maw! Maw! What d'ye want? What air ye tellin' me?

ABBIE. She's tellin' ye t' love me. She knows I love ye an' I'll be good t' ye. Can't ye feel it? Don't ye know? She's tellin' ye t' love me, Eben!

EBEN. Ay-eh. I feel—mebbe she—but—I can't figger out—why—when ye've stole

her place—here in her hum—in the parlor whar she was—

ABBIE (*fiercely*). She knows I love ye!

EBEN (*his face suddenly lighting up with a fierce triumphant grin*). I see it! I see why. It's her vengeance on him—so's she kin rest quiet in her grave!

ABBIE (*wildly*). Vengeance o' God on the hull o' us. What d'we give a durn? I love ye, Eben! God knows I love ye! (*She stretches out her arms for him.*)

EBEN (*throws himself on his knees beside the sofa and grabs her in his arms—releasing all his pent-up passion*). An' I love yew, Abbie!—now I kin say it! I been dyin' fur want o' ye—every hour since ye come! I love ye! (*Their lips meet in a fierce, bruising kiss.*)

Scene IV

(*Exterior of the farmhouse. It is just dawn. The front door at right is opened and* EBEN *comes out and walks around to the gate. He is dressed in his working clothes. He seems changed. His face wears a bold and confident expression, he is grinning to himself with evident satisfaction. As he gets near the gate, the window of the parlor is heard opening and the shutters are flung back and* ABBIE *sticks her head out. Her hair tumbles over her shoulders in disarray, her face is flushed, she looks at* EBEN *with tender, languorous eyes and calls softly.*)

ABBIE. Eben. (*As he turns—playfully*) Jest one more kiss afore ye go. I'm goin' to miss ye fearful all day.

EBEN. An' me yew, ye kin bet! (*He goes to her. They kiss several times. He draws away, laughingly.*) Thar. That's enuf, hain't it? Ye won't hev none left fur next time.

ABBIE. I got a million o' 'em left fur yew! (*Then a bit anxiously*) D'ye r'ally love me, Eben?

EBEN (*emphatically*). I like ye better'n any gal I ever knowed! That's gospel!

ABBIE. Likin' hain't lovin'.

EBEN. Waal then—I love ye. Now air yew satisfied?

ABBIE. Ay-eh, I be. (*She smiles at him adoringly.*)

EBEN. I better git t' the barn. The old critter's liable t' suspicion an' come sneakin' up.

ABBIE (*with a confident laugh*). Let him! I kin allus pull the wool over his eyes. I'm goin' t' leave the shutters open and let in the sun 'n' air. This room's been dead long enuf. Now it's goin' t' be my room!

EBEN (*frowning*). Ay-eh.

ABBIE (*hastily*). I meant—our room.

EBEN. Ay-eh.

ABBIE. We made it our'n last night, didn't we? We give it life—our lovin' did. (*A pause.*)

EBEN (*with a strange look*). Maw's gone back t' her grave. She kin sleep now.

ABBIE. May she rest in peace! (*Then tenderly rebuking*) Ye oughtn't t' talk o' sad thin's—this mornin'.

EBEN. It jest come up in my mind o' itself.

ABBIE. Don't let it. (*He doesn't answer. She yawns.*) Waal, I'm a-goin' t' steal a wink o' sleep. I'll tell the Old Man I hain't feelin' pert. Let him git his own vittles.

EBEN. I see him comin' from the barn. Ye better look smart an' git upstairs.

ABBIE. Ay-eh. Good-by. Don't fergit me. (*She throws him a kiss. He grins— then squares his shoulders and awaits his father confidently.* CABOT *walks slowly up from the left, staring up at the sky with a vague face.*)

EBEN (*jovially*). Mornin', Paw. Stargazin' in daylight?

CABOT. Purty, hain't it?

EBEN (*looking around him possessively*). It's a durned purty farm.

CABOT. I mean the sky.

EBEN (*grinning*). How d'ye know? Them eyes o' your'n can't see that fur. (*This tickles his humor and he slaps his thigh and laughs.*) Ho-ho! That's a good un!

CABOT (*grimly sarcastic*). Ye're feelin' right chipper, hain't ye? Whar'd ye steal the likker?

EBEN (*good-naturedly*). 'Tain't likker. Jest life. (*Suddenly holding out his hand —soberly*) Yew 'n' me is quits. Let's shake hands.

CABOT (*suspiciously*). What's come over ye?

EBEN. Then don't. Mebbe it's jest as well. (*A moment's pause.*) What's come over me? (*Queerly*) Didn't ye feel her passin'—goin' back t' her grave?

CABOT (*dully*). Who?

EBEN. Maw. She kin rest now an' sleep content. She's quits with ye.

CABOT (*confusedly*). I rested. I slept good—down with the cows. They know how t' sleep. They're teachin' me.

EBEN (*suddenly jovial again*). Good fur the cows! Waal—ye better git t' work.

CABOT (*grimly amused*). Air ye bossin' me, ye calf?

EBEN (*beginning to laugh*). Ay-eh! I'm bossin' yew! Ha-ha-ha! see how ye like it! Ha-ha-ha! I'm the prize rooster o' this roost. Ha-ha-ha! (*He goes off toward the barn laughing.*)

CABOT (*looks after him with scornful pity*). Soft-headed. Like his Maw. Dead spit 'n' image. No hope in him! (*He spits with contemptuous disgust.*) A born fool! (*Then matter-of-factly*) Waal—I'm gittin' peckish. (*He goes toward door.*)

Curtain

❦ Part III

Scene I

(*A night in late spring the following year. The kitchen and the two bedrooms upstairs are shown. The two bedrooms are dimly lighted by a tallow candle in each.* EBEN *is sitting on the side of the bed in his room, his chin propped on his fists, his face a study of the struggle he is making to understand his conflicting emotions. The noisy laughter and music from below where a kitchen dance is in progress annoy and distract him. He scowls at the floor.*

In the next room a cradle stands beside the double bed.

In the kitchen all is festivity. The stove has been taken down to give more room to the dancers. The chairs, with wooden benches added, have been pushed back against the walls. On these are seated, squeezed in tight against one another, farmers and their wives and their young folks of both sexes from the neighboring farms. They are all chattering and laughing loudly. They evidently have some secret joke in common. There is no end of winking, of nudging, of meaning nods of the head toward CABOT *who, in a state of extreme hilarious excitement increased by the amount he has drunk, is standing near the rear door where there is a small keg of whisky and serving drinks to all the men. In the left corner, front, dividing the attention with her husband,* ABBIE *is sitting in a rocking chair, a shawl wrapped about her shoulders. She is very pale, her face is thin and drawn, her eyes are fixed anxiously on the open door in rear as if waiting for someone.*

The musician is tuning up his fiddle, seated in the far right corner. He is a lanky young fellow with a long, weak face. His pale eyes blink incessantly and he grins about him slyly with a greedy malice.)

ABBIE (*suddenly turning to a young girl on her right*). Whar's Eben?

YOUNG GIRL (*eying her scornfully*). I dunno, Mrs. Cabot. I hain't seen Eben in ages. (*Meaningly*) Seems like he's spent most o' his time t' hum since yew come.

ABBIE (*vaguely*). I tuk his Maw's place.

YOUNG GIRL. Ay-eh. So I heerd. (*She turns away to retail this bit of gossip to her mother sitting next to her.* ABBIE *turns to her left to a big stoutish middle-aged man whose flushed face and staring eyes show the amount of "likker" he has consumed.*)

ABBIE. Ye hain't see Eben, hev ye?

MAN. No, I hain't. (*Then he adds with a wink*) If yew hain't, who would?

ABBIE. He's the best dancer in the county. He'd ought t' come an' dance.

MAN (*with a wink*). Mebbe he's doin' the dutiful an' walkin' the kid t' sleep. It's a boy, hain't it?

ABBIE (*nodding vaguely*). Ay-eh—born two weeks back—purty's a picter.

MAN. They all is—t' their Maws. (*Then in a whisper, with a nudge and a leer*) Listen, Abbie—if ye ever git tired o' Eben, remember me! Don't fergit now! (*He looks at her uncomprehending face for a second—then grunts disgustedly.*) Waal—guess I'll likker agin. (*He goes over and joins* CABOT, *who is arguing noisily with an old farmer over cows. They all drink.*)

ABBIE (*this time appealing to nobody in particular*). Wonder what Eben's a-doin'? (*Her remark is repeated down the line with many a guffaw and titter until it reaches the fiddler. He fastens his blinking eyes on* ABBIE.)

FIDDLER (*raising his voice*). Bet I kin tell ye, Abbie, what Eben's doin'! He's down t' the church offerin' up prayers o' thanksgivin'. (*They all titter expectantly.*)

MAN. What fur? (*Another titter.*)

FIDDLER. 'Cause unto him a—(*he hesitates just long enough*)—brother is born! (*A roar of laughter. They all look from* ABBIE *to* CABOT. *She is oblivious, staring at the door.* CABOT, *although he hasn't heard the words, is irritated by the laughter and steps forward, glaring about him. There is an immediate silence.*)

CABOT. What're ye all bleatin' about—like a flock o' goats? Why don't ye dance, damn ye? I axed ye here t' dance—t' eat, drink an' be merry—an' thar ye set cacklin' like a lot o' wet hens with the pip! Ye've swilled my likker an' guzzled my vittles like hogs, hain't ye? Then dance fur me, can't ye? That's fa'r an' squar', hain't it? (*A grumble of resentment goes around but they are all evidently in too much awe of him to express it openly.*)

FIDDLER (*slyly*). We're waitin' fur Eben. (*A suppressed laugh.*)

CABOT (*with a fierce exultation*). T'hell with Eben! Eben's done fur now! I got a new son! (*His mood switching with drunken suddenness*) But ye needn't t' laugh at Eben, none o' ye! He's my blood, if he be a dumb fool. He's better nor any o' yew! He kin do a day's work a'most up t' what I kin—an' that'd put any o' yew pore critters t' shame!

FIDDLER. An' he kin do a good night's work, too! (*A roar of laughter.*)

CABOT. Laugh, ye damn fools! Ye're right jist the same, Fiddler. He kin work day an' night too, like I kin, if need be!

OLD FARMER (*from behind the keg where he is weaving drunkenly back and forth—with great simplicity*). They hain't many t' touch ye, Ephraim—a son at seventy-six. That's a hard man fur ye! I be on'y sixty-eight an' I couldn't do it. (*A roar of laughter in which* CABOT *joins uproariously.*)

CABOT (*slapping him on the back*). I'm sorry fur ye, Hi. I'd never suspicion sech weakness from a boy like yew!

OLD FARMER. An' I never reckoned yew had it in ye nuther, Ephraim. (*There is another laugh.*)

CABOT (*suddenly grim*). I got a lot in me—a hell of a lot—folks don't know on. (*Turning to the* FIDDLER) Fiddle 'er up, durn ye! Give 'em somethin' t' dance t'! What air ye, an ornament? Hain't this a celebration? Then grease yer elbow an' go it!

FIDDLER (*seizes a drink which the* OLD FARMER *holds out to him and downs it*). Here goes! (*He starts to fiddle "Lady of the Lake." Four young fellows and four girls form in two lines and dance a square dance. The* FIDDLER *shouts directions for the different movements, keeping his words in the rhythm of the music and interspersing them with jocular personal remarks to the dancers themselves. The people seated along the walls stamp their feet and clap their hands in unison.* CABOT *is especially active in this respect. Only* ABBIE *remains apathetic, staring at the door as if she were alone in a silent room.*)

FIDDLER. Swing your partner t' the right! That's it, Jim! Give her a b'ar hug! Her Maw hain't lookin'. (*Laughter.*) Change partners! That suits ye, don't it, Essie, now ye got Reub afore ye? Look at her redden up, will ye! Waal, life is short an' so's love, as the feller says. (*Laughter.*)

CABOT (*excitedly, stamping his foot*). Go it, boys! Go it, gals!

FIDDLER (*with a wink at the others*). Ye're the spryest seventy-six ever I sees, Ephraim! Now if ye'd on'y good eyesight . . . ! (*Suppressed laughter. He gives* CABOT *no chance to retort but roars.*) Promenade! Ye're walkin' like a bride down the aisle, Sarah! Waal, while they's life they's allus hope. I've heerd tell. Swing your partner to the left! Gosh A'mighty, look at Johnny Cook high-steppin'! They hain't goin' t' be much strength left fur hoein' in the corn lot t'morrow. (*Laughter.*)

CABOT. Go it! Go it! (*Then suddenly, unable to restrain himself any longer, he prances into the midst of the dancers, scattering them, waving his arms about wildly.*) Ye're all hoofs! Git out o' my road! Give me room! I'll show ye dancin'. Ye're all too soft! (*He pushes them roughly away. They crowd back toward the walls, muttering, looking at him resentfully.*)

FIDDLER (*jeeringly*). Go it, Ephraim! Go it! (*He starts "Pop Goes the Weasel," increasing the tempo with every verse until at the end he is fiddling crazily as fast as he can go.*)

CABOT (*starts to dance, which he does very well and with tremendous vigor. Then he begins to improvise, cuts incredibly grotesque capers, leaping up and cracking his heels together, prancing around in a circle with body bent in an Indian war dance, then suddenly straightening up and kicking as high as he can with both legs. He is like a monkey on a string. And all the while he intersperses his antics with shouts and derisive comments*). Whoop! Here's dancin' fur ye! Whoop! See that! Seventy-six, if I'm a day! Hard as iron yet! Beatin' the young 'uns like I allus done! Look at me! I'd invite ye t' dance on my hundredth birthday on'y ye'll all be dead by then. Ye're a sickly generation! Yer hearts air pink, not red! Yer veins is full o' mud an' water! I be the on'y man in the county! Whoop! See that! I'm a Injun! I've killed Injuns in the West afore ye was born— an' skulped 'em too! They's a arrer wound on my backside I c'd show ye! The hull tribe chased me. I outrun 'em all—with the arrer stuck in me! An' I tuk vengeance on 'em. Ten eyes fur an eye, that was my motter! Whoop! Look at me! I kin kick the ceilin' off the room! Whoop!

FIDDLER (*stops playing—exhaustedly*). God A'mighty, I got enuf. Ye got the devil's strength in ye.

CABOT (*delightedly*). Did I beat yew, too? Wa'al, ye played smart. Hev a swig. (*He pours whisky for himself and* FIDDLER. *They drink. The others watch* CABOT *silently with cold, hostile eyes. There is a dead pause. The* FIDDLER *rests.* CABOT *leans against the keg, panting, glaring around him confusedly. In the room above,* EBEN *gets to his feet and tiptoes out the door in rear, appearing a moment later in the other bedroom. He moves silently, even frightenedly, toward the cradle and stands there looking down at the baby. His face is as vague as his reactions are confused, but there is a trace of tenderness, of interested discovery. At the same moment that he reaches the cradle,* ABBIE *seems to sense something. She gets up weakly and goes to* CABOT.)

ABBIE. I'm goin' up t' the baby.

CABOT (*with real solicitude*). Air ye able fur the stairs? D'ye want me t' help ye, Abbie?

ABBIE. No. I'm able. I'll be down agen soon.

CABOT. Don't ye git wore out! He needs ye, remember—our son does! (*He grins affectionately, patting her on the back. She shrinks from his touch.*) ABBIE (*dully*). Don't—tech me. I'm goin'—up. (*She goes.* CABOT *looks after her. A whisper goes around the room.* CABOT *turns. It ceases. He wipes his forehead streaming with sweat. He is breathing pantingly.*)

CABOT. I'm a-goin' out t' git fresh air. I'm feelin' a mite dizzy. Fiddle up thar! Dance, all o' ye! Here's likker fur them as wants it. Enjoy yerselves. I'll be back. (*He goes, closing the door behind him.*)

FIDDLER (*sarcastically*). Don't hurry none on our account! (*A suppressed laugh. He imitates* ABBIE.) Whar's Eben? (*More laughter.*)

A WOMAN (*loudly*). What's happened in this house is plain as the nose on yer face! (ABBIE *appears in the doorway upstairs and stands looking in surprise and adoration at* EBEN, *who does not see her.*)

A MAN. Ssshh! He's li'ble t' be listenin' at the door. That'd be like him. (*Their voices die to an intensive whispering. Their faces are concentrated on this gossip. A noise as of dead leaves in the wind comes from the room.* CABOT *has come out from the porch and stands by the gate, leaning on it, staring at the sky blinkingly.* ABBIE *comes across the room silently.* EBEN *does not notice her until she is quite near.*)

EBEN (*starting*). Abbie!

ABBIE. Ssshh! (*She throws her arms around him. They kiss—then bend over the cradle together.*) Ain't he purty?— dead spit 'n' image o' yew!

EBEN (*pleased*). Air he? I can't tell none.

ABBIE. E-zactly like!

EBEN (*frowningly*). I don't like this. I don't like lettin' on what's mine's his'n. I been doin' that all my life. I'm gittin' t' the end o' b'arin' it!

ABBIE (*putting her finger on his lips*). We're doin' the best we kin. We got t' wait. Somethin's bound t' happen. (*She puts her arms around him.*) I got t' go back.

EBEN. I'm goin' out. I can't b'ar it with the fiddle playin' an' the laughin'.

ABBIE. Don't git feelin' low. I love ye, Eben. Kiss me. (*He kisses her. They remain in each other's arms.*)

CABOT (*at the gate, confusedly*). Even the music can't drive it out—somethin'. Ye kin feel it droppin' off the elums, climbin' up the roof, sneakin' down the chimney, pokin' in the corners! They's no peace in houses, they's no rest livin' with folks. Somethin's always livin' with ye. (*With a deep sigh*) I'll go t' the barn an' rest a spell. (*He goes wearily toward the barn.*)

FIDDLER (*tuning up*). Let's celebrate the old skunk gittin' fooled! We kin have some fun now he's went. (*He starts to fiddle "Turkey in the Straw." There is real merriment now. The young folks get up to dance.*)

Scene II

(*A half hour later—exterior—*EBEN *is standing by the gate looking up at the sky, an expression of dumb pain bewildered by itself on his face.* CABOT *appears, returning from the barn, walking wearily, his eyes on the ground. He sees* EBEN *and his whole mood immediately changes. He becomes excited, a cruel, triumphant grin comes to his lips, he strides up and slaps* EBEN *on the back. From within comes the whining of the fiddle and the noise of stamping feet and laughing voices.*)

CABOT. So har ye be!

EBEN (*startled, stares at him with hatred for a moment—then dully*). Ay-eh.

CABOT (*surveying him jeeringly*). Why hain't ye been in t' dance? They was all axin' fur ye.

EBEN. Let 'em ax!

EBEN. They's a hull passel o' purty gals.

EBEN. T' hell with 'em!

CABOT. Ye'd ought t' be marryin' one o' 'em soon.

EBEN. I hain't marryin' no one.

CABOT. Ye might 'arn a share o' a farm that way.

EBEN (*with a sneer*). Like yew did, ye mean? I hain't that kind.

CABOT (*stung*). Ye lie! 'Twas yer Maw's folks aimed t' steal my farm from me.

EBEN. Other folks don't say so. (*After a pause—defiantly*) An' I got a farm, anyways!

CABOT (*derisively*). Whar?

EBEN (*stamps a foot on the ground*). Har!

CABOT (*throws his head back and laughs coarsely*). Ho-ho! Ye hev, hev ye? Waal, that's a good un!

EBEN (*controlling himself—grimly*). Ye'll see!

CABOT (*stares at him suspiciously, trying to make him out—a pause—then with scornful confidence*). Ay-eh. I'll see. So'll ye. It's ye that's blind—blind as a mole underground. (EBEN *suddenly laughs, one short sardonic bark: "Ha." A pause.* CABOT *peers at him with renewed suspicion.*) What air ye hawin' 'bout? (EBEN *turns away without answering.* CABOT *grows angry.*) God A'mighty, yew air a dumb dunce! They's nothin' in that thick skull o' your'n but noise—like a empty keg it be! (EBEN *doesn't seem to hear*—CABOT'S *rage grows.*) Yewr farm! God A'mighty! If ye wa'n't a born donkey ye'd know ye'll never own stick nor stone on it, specially now arter him bein' born. It's his'n, I tell ye—his'n arter I die—but I'll live a hundred jest t' fool ye all—an' he'll be growed then—yewr age a'most! (EBEN *laughs again his sardonic "Ha." This drives* CABOT *into a fury.*) Ha? Ye think ye kin git 'round that someways, do ye? Waal, it'll be her'n, too—Abbie's—ye won't git 'round her—she knows yer tricks—she'll be too much fur ye—she wants the farm her'n —she was afeerd o' ye—she told me ye was sneakin' 'round tryin' t' make love t' her t' git her on yer side ... ye ... ye mad fool, ye! (*He raises his clenched fists threateningly.*)

EBEN (*is confronting him choking with rage*). Ye lie, ye old skunk! Abbie never said no sech thing!

CABOT (*suddenly triumphant when he sees how shaken* EBEN *is*). She did. An' I says, I'll blow his brains t' the top o' them elums—an' she says no, that hain't sense, who'll ye git t' help ye on the farm in his place—an' then she says yew'n me ought t' have a son—I know we kin, she says—an' I says, if we do, ye kin have anythin' I've got ye've a mind t'. An' she says, I wants Eben cut off so's this farm'll be mine when ye die! (*With terrible gloating*) An' that's what's happened, hain't it? An' the farm's her'n! An' the dust o' the road—that's you'rn! Ha! Now who's hawin'?

EBEN (*has been listening, petrified with grief and rage—suddenly laughs wildly and brokenly*). Ha-ha-ha! So that's her sneakin' game—all along!—like I suspicioned at fust—t' swaller it all—an' me, too ... ! (*Madly*) I'll murder her! (*He springs toward the porch but* CABOT *is quicker and gets in between.*)

CABOT. No, ye don't!

EBEN. Git out o' my road! (*He tries to throw* CABOT *aside. They grapple in what becomes immediately a murderous struggle. The old man's concentrated strength is too much for* EBEN. CABOT *gets one hand on his throat and presses him back across the stone wall. At the same moment,* ABBIE *comes out on the porch. With a stifled cry she runs toward them.*)

ABBIE. Eben! Ephraim! (*She tugs at the hand on* EBEN'S *throat.*) Let go, Ephraim! Ye're chokin' him!

CABOT (*removes his hand and flings* EBEN *sideways full length on the grass, gasping and choking. With a cry,* ABBIE *kneels beside him, trying to take his head on her lap, but he pushes her away.* CABOT *stands looking down with fierce triumph*). Ye needn't t've fret, Abbie, I wa'n't aimin' t' kill him. He hain't wuth hangin' fur—not by a hell of a sight! (*More and more triumphantly*) Seventy-six an' him not thirty yit—an' look whar he be fur thinkin' his Paw was easy! No, by God, I hain't easy! An' him upstairs, I'll raise him t' be like me! (*He turns to leave them.*) I'm goin' in an' dance! —sing an' celebrate! (*He walks to the porch—then turns with a great grin.*) I don't calc'late it's left in him, but if he gits pesky, Abbie, ye jest sing out. I'll come a-runnin' an' by the Etarnal, I'll put him across my knee an' birch him! Ha-ha-ha! (*He goes into the house laughing. A moment later his loud "whoop" is heard.*)

ABBIE (*tenderly*). Eben. Air ye hurt? (*She tries to kiss him but he pushes her violently away and struggles to a sitting position.*)

EBEN (*gaspingly*). T'hell—with ye!

ABBIE (*not believing her ears*). It's me, Eben—Abbie—don't ye know me?

EBEN (*glowering at her with hatred*). Ay-eh—I know ye—now! (*He suddenly breaks down, sobbing weakly.*)

ABBIE (*fearfully*). Eben—what's happened t' ye—why did ye look at me 's if ye hated me?

EBEN (*violently, between sobs and gasps*). I do hate ye! Ye're a whore—a damn trickin' whore!

ABBIE (*shrinking back horrified*). Eben! Ye don't know what ye're sayin'!

EBEN (*scrambling to his feet and following her—accusingly*). Ye're nothin' but a stinkin' passel o' lies! Ye've been lyin' t' me every word ye spoke, day an' night, since we fust—done it. Ye've kept sayin' ye loved me. . . .

ABBIE (*frantically*). I do love ye! (*She takes his hand but he flings hers away.*)

EBEN (*unheeding*). Ye've made a fool o' me—a sick, dumb fool—a-purpose! Ye've been on'y playin' yer sneakin', stealin' game all along—gittin' me t' lie with ye so's ye'd hev a son he'd think was his'n, an' makin' him promise he'd give ye the farm and let me eat dust, if ye did git him a son! (*Staring at her with anguished, bewildered eyes*) They must be a devil livin' in ye! 'Tain't human t' be as bad as that be!

ABBIE (*stunned—dully*). He told yew . . . ?

EBEN. Hain't it true? It hain't no good in yew lyin'.

ABBIE (*pleadingly*). Eben, listen—ye must listen—it was long ago—afore we done nothin'—yew was scornin' me—goin' t' see Min—when I was lovin' ye—an' I said it t' him t' git vengeance on ye!

EBEN (*unheedingly. With tortured passion*). I wish ye was dead! I wish I was dead along with ye afore this come! (*Ragingly*) But I'll git my vengeance too! I'll pray Maw t' come back t' help me—t' put her cuss on yew an' him!

ABBIE (*brokenly*). Don't ye, Eben! Don't ye! (*She throws herself on her knees before him, weeping.*) I didn't mean t' do bad t'ye! Fergive me, won't ye?

EBEN (*not seeming to hear her—fiercely*). I'll git squar' with the old skunk—an' yew! I'll tell him the truth 'bout the son he's so proud o'! Then I'll leave ye here t' pizen each other—with Maw comin' out o' her grave at nights—an' I'll go t' the gold fields o' Californi-a whar Sim an' Peter be!

ABBIE (*terrified*). Ye won't—leave me? Ye can't!

EBEN (*with fierce determination*). I'm a-goin', I tell ye! I'll git rich thar an' come back an' fight him fur the farm he stole—an' I'll kick ye both out in the road—t' beg an' sleep in the woods—an' yer son along with ye—t' starve an' die! (*He is hysterical at the end.*)

ABBIE (*with a shudder—humbly*). He's yewr son, too, Eben.

EBEN (*torturedly*). I wish he never was born! I wish he'd die this minit! I wish I'd never sot eyes on him! It's him—yew havin' him—a-purpose t' steal —that's changed everythin'!

ABBIE (*gently*). Did ye believe I loved ye—afore he come?

EBEN. Ay-eh—like a dumb ox!

ABBIE. An' ye don't believe no more?

EBEN. B'lieve a lyin' thief! Ha!

ABBIE (*shudders—then humbly*). An' did ye r'ally love me afore?

EBEN (*brokenly*). Ay-eh—an' ye was trickin' me!

ABBIE. An' ye don't love me now!

EBEN (*violently*). I hate ye, I tell ye!

ABBIE. An' ye're truly goin' West—goin' t' leave me—all account o' him being born?

EBEN. I'm a-goin' in the mornin'—or may God strike me t' hell!

ABBIE (*after a pause—with a dreadful cold intensity—slowly*). If that's what his comin's done t' me—killin' yewr love—takin' yew away—my on'y joy—the on'y joy I've ever knowed—like heaven t' me —purtier'n heaven—then I hate him, too, even if I be his Maw!

EBEN (*bitterly*). Lies! Ye love him! He'll steal the farm fur ye! (*Brokenly*) But 'tain't the farm so much—not no more—it's yew foolin' me—gittin' me t' love ye—lyin' yew loved me—jest t' git a son t' steal!

ABBIE (*distractedly*). He won't steal! I'd kill him fust! I do love ye! I'll prove t' ye . . . !

EBEN (*harshly*). 'Tain't no use lyin' no more. I'm deaf t' ye! (*He turns away.*) I hain't seein' ye agen. Good-by!

ABBIE (*pale with anguish*). Hain't ye even goin' t' kiss me—not once—arter all we loved?

EBEN (*in a hard voice*). I hain't wantin' t' kiss ye never agen! I'm wantin' t' forgit I ever sot eyes on ye!

ABBIE. Eben!—ye mustn't—wait a spell— I want t' tell ye. . . .

EBEN. I'm a-goin' in t' git drunk. I'm a-goin' t' dance.

ABBIE (*clinging to his arm—with passionate earnestness*). If I could make it —'s if he'd never come up between us— if I could prove t' ye I wa'n't schemin' t' steal from ye—so's everythin' could be jest the same with us, lovin' each other jest the same, kissin' an' happy the same's we've been happy afore he come—if I could do it—ye'd love me agen, wouldn't ye? Ye'd kiss me agen? Ye wouldn't never leave me, would ye?

EBEN (*moved*). I calc'late not. (*Then shaking her hand off his arm—with a bitter smile*) But ye hain't God, be ye?

ABBIE (*exultantly*). Remember ye've promised! (*Then with strange intensity*) Mebbe I kin take back one thin' God does!

EBEN (*peering at her*). Ye're gittin' cracked, hain't ye? (*Then going towards door*) I'm a-goin' t' dance.

ABBIE (*calls after him intensely*). I'll prove t' ye! I'll prove I love ye better'n. . . . (*He goes in the door, not seeming to hear. She remains standing where she is, looking after him— then she finishes desperately:*) Better'n everythin' else in the world!

Scene III

(*Just before dawn in the morning— shows the kitchen and* CABOT'S *bedroom. In the kitchen, by the light of a tallow candle on the table,* EBEN *is sitting, his chin propped on his hands, his drawn face blank and expressionless. His carpetbag is on the floor beside him. In the bedroom, dimly lighted by a small whale-oil lamp,* CABOT *lies asleep.* ABBIE *is bending over the cradle, listening, her face full of terror yet with an undercurrent of desperate triumph. Suddenly, she breaks down and sobs, appears about to throw herself on her knees beside the cradle; but the old man turns restlessly, groaning in his sleep, and she controls herself, and shrinking away from the cradle with a gesture of horror, backs swiftly toward the door in rear and goes out. A moment later she comes into the kitchen and, running to* EBEN, *flings her arms about his neck and kisses him wildly. He hardens himself, he remains unmoved and cold, he keeps his eyes straight ahead.*)

ABBIE (*hysterically*). I done it, Eben! I told ye I'd do it! I've proved I love ye —better'n everythin'—so's ye can't never doubt me no more!

EBEN (*dully*). Whatever ye done, it hain't no good now.

ABBIE (*wildly*). Don't ye say that! Kiss me, Eben, won't ye? I need ye t' kiss me arter what I done! I need ye t' say ye love me!

EBEN (*kisses her without emotion— dully*). That's fur good-by. I'm a-goin' soon.

ABBIE. No! No! Ye won't go—not now!

EBEN (*going on with his own thoughts*). I been a-thinkin'—an' I hain't goin' t' tell Paw nothin'. I'll leave Maw t' take vengeance on ye. If I told him, the old skunk'd jest be stinkin' mean enuf to take it out on that baby. (*His voice showing emotion in spite of him*) An' I don't want nothin' bad t' happen t' him. He hain't t' blame fur yew. (*He adds with a certain queer pride:*) An' he looks like me! An' by God, he's mine! An' some day I'll be a-comin' back an' . . . !

ABBIE (*too absorbed in her own thoughts to listen to him—pleadingly*). They's no cause fur ye t' go now—they's no sense—it's all the same's it was— they's nothin' come b'tween us now— arter what I done!

EBEN (*something in her voice arouses him. He stares at her a bit frightenedly*). Ye look mad, Abbie. What did ye do?

ABBIE. I—I killed him, Eben.

EBEN (*amazed*). Ye killed him?

ABBIE (*dully*). Ay-eh.

EBEN (*recovering from his astonishment—savagely*). An' serves him right! But we got t' do somethin' quick t' make it look s'if the old skunk'd killed himself when he was drunk. We kin prove by 'em all how drunk he got.

ABBIE (*wildly*). No! No! Not him! (*Laughing distractedly*) But that's what I ought t' done, hain't it? I oughter killed him instead! Why didn't ye tell me?

EBEN (*appalled*). Instead? What d'ye mean?

ABBIE. Not him.

EBEN (*his face grown ghastly*). Not— not that baby!

ABBIE (*dully*). Ay-eh!

EBEN (*falls to his knees as if he'd been struck—his voice trembling with horror*). Oh, God A'mighty! A'mighty God! Maw, whar was ye, why didn't ye stop her?

ABBIE (*simply*). She went back t' her grave that night we fust done it, remember? I hain't felt her about since. (*A pause.* EBEN *hides his head in his hands, trembling all over as if he had the ague. She goes on dully:*) I left the piller over his little face. Then he killed himself. He stopped breathin'. (*She begins to weep softly.*)

EBEN (*rage beginning to mingle with grief*). He looked like me. He was mine, damn ye!

ABBIE (*slowly and brokenly*). I didn't want t' do it. I hated myself fur doin' it. I loved him. He was so purty—dead spit 'n' image o' yew. But I loved yew more —an' yew was goin' away—far off whar I'd never see ye agen, never kiss ye, never feel ye pressed agin me agen—an' ye said ye hated me fur havin' him—ye said ye hated him an' wished he was dead—ye said if it hadn't been fur him comin' it'd be the same's afore between us.

EBEN (*unable to endure this, springs to his feet in a fury, threatening her, his twitching fingers seeming to reach out for her throat*). Ye lie! I never said—I never dreamed ye'd—I'd cut off my head afore I'd hurt his finger!

ABBIE (*piteously, sinking on her knees*). Eben, don't ye look at me like that—hatin' me—not after what I done fur ye—fur us—so's we could be happy agen—

EBEN (*furiously now*). Shut up, or I'll kill ye! I see yer game now—the same old sneakin' trick—ye're aimin' t' blame me fur the murder ye done!

ABBIE (*moaning—putting her hands over her ears*). Don't ye, Eben! Don't ye! (*She grasps his legs.*)

EBEN (*his mood suddenly changing to horror, shrinks away from her*). Don't ye tech me! Ye're pizen! How could ye —t' murder a pore little critter—Ye must've swapped yer soul t' hell! (*Sudden raging*) Ha! I kin see why ye done it! Not the lies ye jest told—but 'cause ye wanted t' steal agen—steal the last thin' ye'd left me—my part o' him—no, the hull o' him—ye saw he looked like me —ye knowed he was all mine—an' ye

couldn't b'ar it—I know ye! Ye killed him fur bein' mine! (*All this has driven her almost insane. He makes a rush past her for the door—then turns—shaking both fists at her, violently.*) But I'll take vengeance now! I'll git the Sheriff! I'll tell him everythin'! Then I'll sing "I'm off to Californi-a!" an' go—gold—Golden Gate—gold sun—fields o' gold in the West! (*This last he half shouts, half croons incoherently, suddenly breaking off passionately.*) I'm a-goin' fur the Sheriff t' come an' git ye! I want ye tuk away, locked up from me! I can't stand t' luk at ye! Murderer an' thief 'r not, ye still tempt me! I'll give ye up t' the Sheriff! (*He turns and runs out, around the corner of house, panting and sobbing, and breaks into a swerving sprint down the road.*)

ABBIE (*struggling to her feet, runs to the door, calling after him*). I love ye, Eben! I love ye! (*She stops at the door weakly, swaying, about to fall.*) I don't care what ye do—if ye'll on'y love me agen— (*She falls limply to the floor in a faint.*)

Scene IV

(*About an hour later. Same as Scene III. Shows the kitchen and* CABOT'S *bedroom. It is after dawn. The sky is brilliant with the sunrise. In the kitchen,* ABBIE *sits at the table, her body limp and exhausted, her head bowed down over her arms, her face hidden. Upstairs,* CABOT *is still asleep but awakens with a start. He looks toward the window and gives a snort of surprise and irritation—throws back the covers and begins hurriedly pulling on his clothes. Without looking behind him, he begins talking to* ABBIE, *whom he supposes beside him.*)

CABOT. Thunder 'n' lightnin', Abbie! I hain't slept this late in fifty year! Looks 's if the sun was full riz a'most. Must've been the dancin' an' likker. Must be gittin' old. I hope Eben's t'wuk. Ye might've tuk the trouble t' rouse me, Abbie. (*He turns—sees no one there— surprised.*) Waal—whar air she? Gittin' vittles, I calc'late. (*He tiptoes to the cradle and peers down—proudly*) Mornin', sonny. Purty's a picter! Sleepin' sound. He don't beller all night like most o' 'em. (*He goes quietly out the door in rear—a few moments later enters kitchen —sees* ABBIE—*with satisfaction*) So thar ye be. Ye got any vittles cooked?

ABBIE (*without moving*). No.

CABOT (*coming to her, almost sympathetically*). Ye feelin' sick?

ABBIE. No.

CABOT (*pats her on shoulder. She shudders*). Ye'd best lie down a spell. (*Half jocularly*) Yer son'll be needin' ye soon. He'd ought t' wake up with a gnashin' appetite, the sound way he's sleepin'.

ABBIE (*shudders—then in a dead voice*). He ain't never goin' to wake up.

CABOT (*jokingly*). Takes after me this mornin'. I ain't slept so late in . . .

ABBIE. He's dead.

CABOT (*stares at her—bewilderedly*). What . . .

ABBIE. I killed him.

CABOT (*stepping back from her— aghast*). Air ye drunk—'r crazy—'r . . . !

ABBIE (*suddenly lifts her head and turns on him—wildly*). I killed him, I tell ye! I smothered him. Go up an' see if ye don't b'lieve me! (CABOT *stares at her a second, then bolts out the rear door, can be heard bounding up the stairs, and rushes into the bedroom and over to the cradle,* ABBIE *has sunk back lifelessly into her former position.* CABOT *puts his hand down on the body in the crib. An expression of fear and horror comes over his face.*)

CABOT (*shrinking away—tremblingly*). God A'mighty! God A'mighty! (*He stumbles out the door—in a short while returns to the kitchen—comes to* ABBIE, *the stunned expression still on his face— hoarsely*) Why did ye do it? Why? (*As she doesn't answer, he grabs her violently by the shoulder and shakes her.*) I ax ye why ye done it! Ye'd better tell me 'r . . . !

ABBIE (*gives him a furious push which sends him staggering back and springs to her feet—with wild rage and hatred*). Don't ye dare tech me! What right hev ye t' question me 'bout him? He wa'n't yewr son! Think I'd have a son by yew? I'd die fust! I hate the sight o' ye an' allus did! It's yew I should've murdered, if I'd had good sense! I hate ye! I love Eben. I did from the fust. An' he was Eben's son—mine an' Eben's—not your'n.

CABOT (*stands looking at her dazedly —a pause—finding his words with an effort—dully*). That was it—what I felt —pokin' round the corners—while ye lied—holdin' yerself from me—sayin' ye'd a'ready conceived— (*He lapses into crushed silence—then with a strange emotion*) He's dead, sart'n. I felt his heart. Pore little critter! (*He blinks back one tear, wiping his sleeve across his nose.*)

ABBIE (*hysterically*). Don't ye! Don't ye! (*She sobs unrestrainedly.*)

CABOT (*with a concentrated effort that stiffens his body into a rigid line and hardens his face into a stony mask —through his teeth to himself*). I got t' be—like a stone—a rock o' jedgment! (*A pause. He gets complete control over himself—harshly*) If he was Eben's, I be glad he air gone! An' mebbe I suspicioned it all along. I felt they was somethin' onnateral—somewhars—the house got so lonesome—an' cold—drivin' me down t' the barn—t' the beasts o' the field. . . . Ay-eh. I must've suspicioned —somethin'. Ye didn't fool me—not altogether, leastways—I'm too old a bird— growin' ripe on the bough. . . . (*He becomes aware he is wandering, straightens again, looks at* ABBIE *with a cruel grin.*) So ye'd liked t' hev murdered me 'stead o' him, would ye? Waal, I'll live to a hundred! I'll live t' see ye hung! I'll deliver ye up t' the jedgment o' God an' the law! I'll git the Sheriff now. (*Starts for the door.*)

ABBIE (*dully*). Ye needn't. Eben's gone fur him.

CABOT (*amazed*). Eben—gone fur the Sheriff?

ABBIE. Ay-eh.

CABOT. T' inform agen ye?

ABBIE. Ay-eh.

CABOT (*considers this—a pause—then in a hard voice*). Waal, I'm thankful fur him savin' me the trouble. I'll git t' wuk. (*He goes to the door—then turns—in a voice full of strange emotion*) He'd ought t' been my son, Abbie. Ye'd ought t' loved me. I'm a man. If ye'd loved me, I'd never told no Sheriff on ye no matter what ye did, if they was t' brile me alive!

ABBIE (*defensively*). They's more to it nor yew know, makes him tell.

CABOT (*dryly*). Fur yewr sake, I hope they be. (*He goes out—comes around to the gate—stares up at the sky. His con-*

trol relaxes. For a moment he is old and weary. He murmurs despairingly:) God A'mighty, I be lonesomer'n ever! (*He hears running footsteps from the left, immediately is himself again.* EBEN *runs in, panting exhaustedly, wild-eyed and mad looking. He lurches through the gate.* CABOT *grabs him by the shoulder.* EBEN *stares at him dumbly.*) Did ye tell the Sheriff?

EBEN (*nodding stupidly*). Ay-eh.

CABOT (*gives him a push away that sends him sprawling—laughing with withering contempt*). Good fur ye! A prime chip o' yer Maw ye be! (*He goes toward the barn, laughing harshly.* EBEN *scrambles to his feet. Suddenly* CABOT *turns—grimly threatening*) Git off this farm when the Sheriff takes her—or, by God, he'll have t' come back an' git me fur murder, too! (*He stalks off.* EBEN *does not appear to have heard him. He runs to the door and comes into the kitchen.* ABBIE *looks up with a cry of anguished joy.* EBEN *stumbles over and throws himself on his knees beside her —sobbing brokenly.*)

EBEN. Fergive me!

ABBIE (*happily*). Eben! (*She kisses him and pulls his head over against her breast.*)

EBEN. I love ye! Fergive me!

ABBIE (*ecstatically*). I'd fergive ye all the sins in hell fur sayin' that! (*She kisses his head, pressing it to her with a fierce passion of possession.*)

EBEN (*brokenly*). But I told the Sheriff. He's comin' fur ye!

ABBIE. I kin b'ar what happens t' me —now!

EBEN. I woke him up. I told him. He says, wait 'til I git dressed. I was waiting. I got to thinkin' o' yew. I got to thinkin' how I'd loved ye. It hurt like somethin' was bustin' in my chest an' head. I got t' cryin'. I knowed sudden I loved ye yet, an' allus would love ye!

ABBIE (*caressing his hair—tenderly*). My boy, hain't ye?

EBEN. I begun t' run back. I cut across the fields an' through the woods. I thought ye might have time t' run away—with me—an' . . .

ABBIE (*shaking her head*). I got t' take my punishment—t' pay fur my sin.

EBEN. Then I want t' share it with ye.

ABBIE. Ye didn't do nothin'.

EBEN. I put it in yer head. I wisht he was dead! I as much as urged ye t' do it!

ABBIE. No. It was me alone!

EBEN. I'm as guilty as yew be! He was the child o' our sin.

ABBIE (*lifting her head as if defying God*). I don't repent that sin! I hain't askin' God t' fergive that!

EBEN. Nor me—but it led up t' the other—an' the murder ye did, ye did 'count o' me—an' it's my murder, too, I'll tell the Sheriff—an' if ye deny it, I'll say we planned it t'gether—an' they'll all b'lieve me, fur they suspicion everythin' we've done, an' it'll seem likely an' true to 'em. An' it is true—way down. I did help ye—somehow.

ABBIE (*laying her head on his—sobbing*). No! I dont want yew t' suffer!

EBEN. I got t' pay fur my part o' the sin! An' I'd suffer wuss leavin' ye, goin' West, thinking' o' ye day an' night, bein' out when yew was in—(*lowering his voice*)—'r bein' alive when yew was dead. (*A pause.*) I want t' share with ye, Abbie —prison 'r death 'r hell 'r anythin'! (*He looks into her eyes and forces a trembling smile.*) If I'm sharin' with ye, I won't feel lonesome, leastways.

ABBIE (*weakly*). Eben! I won't let ye! I can't let ye!

EBEN (*kissing her—tenderly*). Ye can't he'p yerself. I got ye beat fur once!

ABBIE (*forcing a smile—adoringly*). I hain't beat—s'long's I got ye!

EBEN (*hears the sound of feet outside*). Ssshh! Listen! They've come t' take us!

ABBIE. No, it's him. Don't give him no chance to fight ye, Eben. Don't say nothin' —no matter what he says. An' I won't neither. (*It is* CABOT. *He comes up from the barn in a great state of excitement and strides into the house and then into the kitchen.* EBEN *is kneeling beside* ABBIE, *his arm around her, hers around him. They stare straight ahead.*)

CABOT (*stares at them, his face hard. A long pause—vindictively*). Ye make a slick pair o' murderin' turtle doves! Ye'd ought t' be both hung on the same limb an' left thar t' swing in the breeze an' rot—a warnin' t' old fools like me t' b'ar their lonesomeness alone—an' fur young fools like ye t' hobble their lust. (*A pause. The excitement returns to his face, his eyes snap, he looks a bit crazy.*)

I couldn't work today. I couldn't take no interest. T' hell with the farm! I'm leavin' it! I've turned the cows an' other stock loose! I've druv 'em into the woods whar they kin be free! By freein' 'em, I'm freein' myself! I'm quittin' here today! I'll set fire t'house an' barn an' watch 'em burn, an I'll leave yer Maw t' haunt the ashes, an' I'll will the fields back t' God, so that nothin' human kin never touch 'em! I'll be a-goin' to Californi-a —t' jine Simeon an' Peter—true sons o' mine if they be dumb fools—an' the Cabots'll find Solomon's Mines t'gether! (*He suddenly cuts a mad caper*) Whoop! What was the song they sung? "Oh, Californi-a! That's the land fur me." (*He sings this—then gets on his knees by the floorboard under which the money was hid.*) An' I'll sail thar on one o' the finest clippers I kin find! I've got the money! Pity ye didn't know whar this was hidden so's ye could steal . . . (*He has pulled up the board. He stares—feels —stares again. A pause of dead silence. He slowly turns, slumping into a sitting position on the floor, his eyes like those of a dead fish, his face the sickly green of an attack of nausea. He swallows pain- fully several times—forces a weak smile at last.*) So—ye did steal it!

EBEN (*emotionlessly*). I swapped it t' Sim an' Peter fur their share o' the farm—t' pay their passage t' Californi-a.

CABOT (*with one sardonic*) Ha! (*He begins to recover. Gets slowly to his feet —strangely*). I calc'late God give it to 'em—not yew! God's hard, not easy! Mebbe they's easy gold in the West but it hain't God's gold. It hain't fur me. I kin hear His voice warnin' me agen t' be hard an' stay on my farm. I kin see his hand usin' Eben t' steal t' keep me from weakness. I kin feel I be in the palm o' His hand, His fingers guidin' me. (*A pause—then he mutters sadly:*) It's a-goin' t' be lonesomer now than ever it war afore—an' I'm gittin' old, Lord— ripe on the bough. . . . (*Then stiffen- ing*) Waal—what d'ye want? God's lone- some, hain't He? God's hard an' lone-

some! (*A pause. The* SHERIFF *with two men comes up the road from the left. They move cautiously to the door. The* SHERIFF *knocks on it with the butt of his pistol.*)

SHERIFF. Open in the name o' the law! (*They start.*)

CABOT. They've come fur ye. (*He goes to the rear door.*) Come in, Jim! (*The three men enter.* CABOT *meets them in doorway.*) Jest a minit, Jim. I got 'em safe here. (*The* SHERIFF *nods. He and his companions remain in the doorway.*)

EBEN (*suddenly calls*). I lied this mornin', Jim. I helped her to do it. Ye kin take me, too.

ABBIE (*brokenly*). No!

CABOT. Take 'em both. (*He comes forward—stares at* EBEN *with a trace of grudging admiration*) Purty good—fur yew! Waal, I got t' round up the stock. Good-by.

EBEN. Good-by.

ABBIE. Good-by. (CABOT *turns and strides past the men—comes out and around the corner of the house, his shoul- ders squared, his face stony, and stalks grimly toward the barn. In the mean- time the* SHERIFF *and men have come into the room.*)

SHERIFF (*embarrassedly*). Waal—we'd best start.

ABBIE. Wait. (*Turns to* EBEN.) I love ye, Eben.

EBEN. I love ye, Abbie. (*They kiss. The three men grin and shuffle em- barrassedly.* EBEN *takes* ABBIE'S *hand. They go out the door in rear, the men following, and come from the house, walking hand in hand to the gate.* EBEN *stops there and points to the sunrise sky.*) Sun's a-risin'. Purty, hain't it?

ABBIE. Ay-eh. (*They both stand for a moment looking up raptly in attitudes strangely aloof and devout.*)

SHERIFF (*looking around at the farm enviously—to his companion*). It's a jim-dandy farm, no denyin'. Wished I owned it!

Curtain

JOSEPH WOOD KRUTCH: *Eugene O'Neill, the Lonely Revolutionary*

From *Theatre Arts*, April, 1952. Copyright 1952 by *Theatre Arts*. Reprinted by permission of the publisher and author.

IN RECENT YEARS IT HAS BECOME FASHIONABLE TO POINT OUT THAT the most important American writers have been lonely men. Poe, Hawthorne, Melville, Thoreau, and Henry Adams all rejected the ideals of the society into which they were born. So too in his different way did Henry James. Not one of them gave the public what the public was supposed to want, not one of them participated in what was supposed to be the spirit of the age. Each felt himself rejected, each retired into himself, each inhabited a spiritual world which seemed to him a private one. Americans are supposed to be gregarious and yet the literature most admired at the present moment was produced by a group of hermits whose sympathy, even with one another, was decidedly imperfect.

No one, so far as I know, has ever pointed out the obvious fact that Eugene O'Neill, commonly regarded as the most considerable playwright our country has ever produced, fits into this same pattern. Most of his plays were written during the cheerful, confident twenties but they were far from being cheerful or optimistic, and O'Neill's attitudes were also as different from those of other critics of our society as they were from popular optimism and complacency. At a time when naturalism was the literary norm he wrote plays which were symbolic in method and mystical in intention. While other dissenters were busy with attacks on Main Street, Comstockery, or the worship of Mr. Babbitt, he was concerning himself with primitive passions and with dark Gods.

Sometimes, to be sure, his themes seemed to have an ambiguous relation to those commonly developed. Thus *The Hairy Ape* could be interpreted as liberal sociological protest, *Strange Interlude* could be interpreted as a psychoanalytical study, *Desire Under the Elms* could be, in fact sometimes was, taken as an attempt to debunk our Puritan ancestors.

But this last misinterpretation is only a little more palpably absurd than the others and it was possible only because O'Neill's contemporaries found it so difficult to understand precisely what it was that he was getting at. Sinclair Lewis and H. L. Mencken were dissenters but they were not lonely men. Neither for that matter were Sidney Howard or, in the twenties, Maxwell Anderson. They understood one another, and they soon had a large public which understood them. But O'Neill was lonely in the sense that Hawthorne and Thoreau and Melville were lonely.

In his case as in theirs, this loneliness, this isolation from both the prevailing spirit and from that of others who criticized or rejected it, was the result of a sense that the rebels, hardly less than the complacent majority, missed the point, failed to go deeply enough. In O'Neill, as in Hawthorne and Melville, the protest was not merely rational but had instead a daemonic element. Their premises were almost too far from those of any considerable audience to make communication possible. All had to depend for such attention as they got upon the simple fact that they were obviously strange and powerful rather than upon any fundamental sympathy or understanding.

One consequence of this is that O'Neill's plays, considered simply as plays, are even more revolutionary than they are commonly thought to be. Because what he wanted to communicate was something radically different from what most of his fellow playwrights, either of Europe or America, wanted to communicate, his whole conception of what a play should be was radically different from the prevailing one. Almost alone among considerable modern playwrights he attempted Tragedy—with a capital T—and it may very well turn out to be that this single fact sums up better than anything else his ultimate influence and importance.

In this connection it must be remembered that if the modern drama began with Ibsen it began as an intellectual protest against old fashioned moral and political ideas rather than as either Tragedy or Comedy. Behind *A Doll's House* and even behind *Ghosts* lies the assumption that the fundamental human problems are solvable by reason and by reasonableness. It is true that in later plays Ibsen receded from this simple optimism and that Strindberg, whom O'Neill has called his master, rejected it utterly. But it was the simplest part of Ibsen's doctrine that his most esteemed second-rate followers—Bjornston, Brieux, Galsworthy and the rest—took up. Shaw, the only other real giant, moved away from them in a direction the opposite from that to be taken by O'Neill. He pursued rational optimism until it reached a *reductio ad absurdum* in which human beings become mere talking and arguing machines so completely devoid of passions or even irrationalities that they lose all semblance of humanity and become nothing except the counters in a delightful comic game which is often as irrelevant to human life as a puppet show.

What the lonely O'Neill soon discovered was that neither modern optimism nor modern pessimism corresponded to either his own experience or his own vision. On the one hand, man's unhappiness was not simply the result of "social maladjustment." "The sorrows of our proud and angry dust are from eternity and shall not fail." On the other hand those sorrows are not merely the ignoble thing which pessimistic naturalism makes of them. What obsessed O'Neill was a tragic sense of life not to be expressed either in the mere play of social significance or in the mere drama with an unhappy ending which was the nearest the modern convention ever approached to tragedy. He needed something more passionate, and more mystical than that. He needed a form which acknowledged man's relevance, not merely to society, but to the universe which is larger than man and larger than human society. And the only form which does presuppose what he presupposed is Tragedy in a sense of the term almost lost.

That he succeeded at all in the popular theatre is evidence of his extraordinary power. That he has seldom been revived despite both his original success and the esteem in which he has been held is evidence of the fundamental resistance which the unfamiliarity of his preoccupations and his attitudes arouses. His best plays always demand of the audience that it enter a world which that audience is afraid of. His universe is one ruled by powers which the comfortable rationalism of the average spectator does not want to acknowledge. His characters are in the grip of passions stronger and more primitive than that same spectator wants to believe possible.

Because of these facts one's first impulse is to discover some way of escaping from or of neutralizing his effect. The most radical method of achieving these ends is simply to refuse to take him seriously. Who is O'Neill that he should venture to attempt what most moderns have given up attempting? What makes him think that he can write Tragedy when it is generally acknowledged that our age is incapable of it? Why should he undertake to deal with man and the universe when the rest of us have decided to confine ourselves to man and society? Why should he defy the Gods when no one else raises his eyes above capitalism, communism, democracy, or the evils of racial discrimination? The other way of refusing to consider what he asks us to consider is to explain away both him and his plays. *Anna Christie* is "nothing but" a melodrama about a prostitute who tries to go straight. *Desire Under the Elms* is nothing but a dirty melodrama about Puritan repressions and Puritan lust. *Strange Interlude* is nothing but an amateur attempt to exploit the popular interest in Freudianism.

This season, and for the first time in many years, New York audiences have been offered an opportunity to see two of his major plays, *Anna Christie* and *Desire Under the Elms,* and thus to expose themselves to the experience which they afford. Both received critical acclaim and attracted audiences sufficiently large to justify at least the kind of non-commercial productions which were given them. But it is of course too soon to say whether or not this is the beginning of a more general recognition of O'Neill's claim to be regarded as our contribution to enduring dramatic literature. Many, perhaps most, writers destined to permanence go through a dubious period during which they have ceased to be contemporary but have not yet become established. Ibsen went through such a period during which it seemed as though he might gradually recede until he had become a mere historical figure. Shaw stayed more continuously alive, but even in his case there was a time when it seemed possible to say that he had "outlived the day he was born too soon for." Yet that time was the time immediately before his sudden emergence into a popularity greater than any he enjoyed during what had seemed his heyday. Many works have been for a time merely outmoded before they came to be classic.

Whether or not O'Neill's appearance on Broadway for the first time in some years marks the beginning of a general revival, the two plays presented give a taste of his quality, and of the two *Desire Under the Elms* is more difficult either to dismiss or to misinterpret. *Anna Christie* can be taken as no more than a realistic if highly colored love story. *Desire Under the Elms* is preposterous unless it be taken as the Tragedy which was intended. It is a play about extraordinarily violent passions whose intensity is possible because they are assumed to arise not merely out of the relation of man to man but out of man's relation to two irrational forces—belief in the puritan God and a commitment to the land which is as irrational as the commitment to God. At the end O'Neill neatly defines the nature of the commitment to the land when the sheriff looks about at the scene of the tragedy and remarks:

"It's a jim dandy farm, no denyin'. Wished I owned it!"

The chief significance of this remark does not lie in the irony of the wish to own something which has cursed the others who wished to own it. It lies in the fact that the sheriff has no conception of what owning or wanting to own meant to the protagonists in the drama. To him the farm represents merely having a negotiable cash value. It is a piece of saleable real estate. The use which he could have for it is a rational use. And therefore he could never own it or be owned by it in the sense that Eben and Abbie owned and were owned.

O'Neill is not defending or recommending the kind of relationship with either land or a puritan God which the Cabots had achieved or fallen victim to. He is saying merely that it is a type, as the ambiguous love of the sea in *Anna Christie* was also a type, of the kind of relationship to something outside one's self which makes for passions great enough to make tragedy possible. He is saying that it is from such things that the sorrows of our proud and angry dust arise and he is warning a complacent modern audience that it has not as permanently or as completely freed itself from them as it likes to think. In *Strange Interlude,* for example, Nina Leeds, a modern rationalist, falls similarly a victim to what she can call only her fixation. But whatever we call the irrational, it lies in wait for us.

At least one thing O'Neill will have achieved if he has achieved nothing else. He has won for the American dramatist the right to be as serious as he wants to be and to aim as high as he can. Whatever they may or may not think they learned from him, Tennessee Williams and Arthur Miller, for example, have reason to be grateful. Because of his example it is no longer deemed necessarily absurd for a modern—and an American to boot—to aim high.

ERIC BENTLEY: *Trying to Like O'Neill*

Reprinted from *In Search of Theatre* by Eric Bentley, by permission of
Alfred A. Knopf, Inc. Copyright 1952 by Eric Bentley.

IT WOULD BE NICE TO LIKE O'NEILL. HE IS THE LEADING AMERICAN
playwright; damn him, damn all; and damning all is a big responsibility. It is tempting
to damn the rest and make of O'Neill an exception. He *is* an exception in so many

ways. He has cared less for temporary
publicity than for lasting and deserved
fame. When he was successful on Broadway he was not sucked in by Broadway.
The others have vanity; O'Neill has self-
respect. No dickering with the play-
doctors in Manhattan hotel rooms. He
had the guts to go away and the guts to
stay away. O'Neill has always had the
grown-up writer's concern for that continuity and development which must take
place quietly and from within. In a
theater that chiefly attracts idiots and
crooks he was a model of good sense and
honor.

In 1946 he was raised to the American
peerage: his picture was on the cover of
Time. The national playwright was inter-
viewed by the nationalist press. It was
his chance to talk rot and be liked for it.
It was his chance to spout optimistic uplift and play the patriotic pundit. O'Neill
said:

> I'm going on the theory that the United
> States, instead of being the most suc-
> cessful country in the world, is the
> greatest failure . . . because it was
> given everything more than any other
> country. Through moving as rapidly as
> it has, it hasn't acquired any real roots.
> Its main idea is that everlasting game
> of trying to possess your own soul by
> the possession of something outside it
> too. . . .

Henry Luce possesses a good many things
besides his own soul. He possesses *Life* as
well as *Time,* and in the former he published an editorial complaining of the
lack of inspiration to be found in the
national playwright. In *The Iceman
Cometh* there were no princes and heroes,
only bums and drunks. This was "demo-
cratic snobbism." Henry Luce was evidently in favor of something more aristocratic (the pin-up girls in his magazine
notwithstanding). Inevitably, though,

what the aristocrats of *Time Inc.* objected
to in O'Neill was his greatest virtue: his
ability to stay close to the humbler forms
of American life as he had seen them. It
is natural that his claim to be a national
playwright should rest chiefly on a critical
and realistic attitude to American life
which they reject. Like the three great
Irish playwrights, O'Neill felt his "belonging" to his country so deeply that
he took its errors to heart, and though
admittedly he wished his plays to be
universal, they all start at home; they
are specifically a criticism of American life. *Marco Millions* is only the
bluntest of his critical studies. Interest
in the specifically American pattern of
living sustains his lightest work, *Ah,
Wilderness!* New England patterns are
integral to *Desire under the Elms* and
Mourning Becomes Electra, the latter being an attempt at an *Oresteia* in terms of
American history, with the Civil War as
an equivalent of the Trojan War. The
protagonist of *The Iceman Cometh* is a
product of Hoosier piety, a study much
more deeply rooted in American life than
Arthur Miller's of a salesman going to his
death. It would be nice to like O'Neill
because the Luce magazines *dis*like him—
that is, because he is opposed to everything they stand for.

Last autumn, when I was invited to
direct the German-language *première* of
The Iceman, along with Kurt Hirschfeld,
I decided I should actually succeed in
liking O'Neill. I reminded myself that
he had been honored with prefaces by
Joseph Wood Krutch and Lionel Trilling,
that he had aroused enthusiasm in the
two hardest-to-please of the New York
critics, Stark Young and George Jean
Nathan, and so forth. I even had a personal motive to aid and abet the pressure
of pure reason. My own published strictures on O'Neill had always been taken

as a display of gratuitous pugnacity, amusing or reprehensible according to my reader's viewpoint. Now, it is a fallacy that drama critics are strongly attached to their own opinions; actually they would far rather be congratulated on having the flexibility to change their minds. Under a rain of dissent one begins to doubt one's opinions and to long for the joy that is not confined to heaven when a sinner repenteth. In short, I should have been glad to write something in praise of O'Neill, and I actually did lecture—and speak on the Swiss radio—as an O'Neill-ite. If this seems disingenuous, I can only plead that I spoke as a director, not as critic, and that it is sometimes a great relief to do so. There is something too godlike about criticism; it is a defiance of the injunction to men: "Judge not, that ye be not judged"; it is a strain. And if it would be subhuman to give up the critical attitude for mere liking and disliking, the directorial, interpretative attitude seems a more mature and challenging alternative.

Both critic and director are aware of faults, but whereas it is the critic's job to point them out, it is the director's job to cover them up, if only by strongly bringing out a play's merits. It is not true that a director accepts a play with its faults on its head, that he must follow the playwright even into what he believes to be error. He cannot be a self-respecting interpreter without following his own taste and judgment. Thus, Hirschfeld and I thought we were doing our best by O'Neill in toning certain things down and playing others full blast. Specifically, there seemed to us to be in The Iceman Cometh a genuine and a non-genuine element, the former, which we regarded as the core, being realistic, the latter, which we took as inessential excrescence, being expressionistic. I had seen what came of author-worshipping direction in the Theatre Guild production, where all O'Neill's faults were presented to the public with careful reverence. In order to find the essential—or at least the better—O'Neill we agreed to forgo much O'Neillism. . . .

To get at the core of reality in The Iceman—which is also its artistic, its dramatic core—you have to cut away the rotten fruit of unreality around it. More plainly stated: you have to cut. The play is far too long—not so much in asking that the audience sit there so many hours as on sheer internal grounds. The main story is meant to have suspense, but we are suspended so long we forget all about it. One can cut a good many of Larry's speeches since he is forever rephrasing a pessimism that is by no means hard to understand the first time. One can cut down the speeches of Hugo since they are both too long and too pretentious. It is such a pretentiousness, replete with obvious and unimaginative symbols, that constitutes the expressionism of the play. . . .

We cut about an hour out of the play. It wasn't always easy. Not wishing to cut out whole characters, we mutilated a few till they had, I'm afraid, no effective existence. But we did not forget that some of the incidental details of The Iceman are among O'Neill's finest achievements. Nothing emerged more triumphantly from our shortened, crisper version than the comic elements. With a dash of good humor O'Neill can do more than with all his grandiloquent lugubriousness. Nothing struck my fancy more, in our production, than the little comedy of the Boer general and the English captain. O'Neill is also very good at a kind of homely genre painting. Harry's birthday party with its cake and candles and the whores singing his late wife's favorite song, "She Is the Sunshine of Paradise Alley," is extremely well done; and no other American playwright could do it without becoming either too sentimental or too sophisticated. . . .

A systematic underlining of all that is realistic in the play did, as we hoped it would, bring the locale—Jimmy the Priest's—to successful theatrical realization, despite the loss of much of O'Neill's detail. It gave body and definition to what otherwise would have remained insubstantial and shapeless; the comedy was sharpened, the sentiment purified.

And yet it was not a greater success with the public than the New York production, and whereas some New York critics were restrained by awe before the national playwright, the Swiss critics, when they were bored, said so. My newly won liking for O'Neill would perhaps have been unshaken by the general opinion—except that in the end I couldn't help sharing it.

I enjoyed the rehearsal period—unreservedly. I didn't have to conceal my reservations about O'Neill out of tact. They ceased to exist. They were lost in the routine, the tension, and the delight of theater work. I don't mean to suggest that you could lose yourself thus in any script, however bad; there are scripts that bear down on a director with all the dead weight of their fatuity. But in an O'Neill script there are problems, technical and intellectual, and every one a challenge. I gladly threw myself headlong into that mad joy of the theater in which the world and its atomic bombs recede and one's own first night seems to be the goal toward which creation strives.

The shock of the first night was the greater. It was not one of those catastrophic first nights when on all faces you can see expectancy fading into ennui or lack of expectancy freezing into a smug I Told You So. But, theatrically speaking, mild approval is little better. Theatrical art is a form of aggression. Like the internal-combustion engine it proceeds by a series of explosions. Because it is in the strictest sense the most shocking of the arts, it has failed most utterly when no shock has been felt, and it has failed in a large measure when the shock is mild. *The Iceman* aroused mild interest, and I had to agree that *The Iceman* was only mildly interesting. When I read the critics, who said about my O'Neill production precisely what I as critic had said about other O'Neill productions, my period of liking O'Neill was over.

Of course there were shortcomings that O'Neill could not be blamed for. We were presenting him in German, and in addition to the normal translation problems there were two special ones: that of translating contrasting dialects and that of reproducing the tone of American, semi-gangster, hard-boiled talk. There was little the translator could do about the dialects. She wisely did not lay under contribution the various regions of Germany or suggest foreign accents, and her idea of using a good deal of Berlin slang had to be modified for our Swiss public. One simply forwent many of O'Neill's effects or tried to get them by non-verbal means—and by that token one realized how much O'Neill does in the original with the various forms of the vernacular (real or histrionic). One also realizes how much he uses the peculiarly American institution of Tough Talk, now one of the conventions of the American stage, a lingo that the young playwright learns, just as at one time the young poet learned Milton's poetic diction. In German there seems to be no real equivalent of this lingo, because there is no equivalent of the psychology from which it springs and to which it caters. And there is no teaching the actors how to speak their lines in the hard-boiled manner. Irony is lost, and the dialogue loses its salt. This loss and that of dialect flavor were undoubtedly great deficiencies.

But not the greatest. I saw the production several times and, in addition to the flaws for which we of the Schauspielhaus were responsible, there stood out clearer each time the known, if not notorious, faults of O'Neill. True, he is a man of the theater and, true, he is an eloquent writer composing, as his colleagues on Broadway usually do not, under the hard compulsion of something he has to say. But his gifts are mutually frustrating. His sense of theatrical form is frustrated by an eloquence that decays into mere repetitious garrulousness. His eloquence is frustrated by the extreme rigidity of the theatrical mold into which it is poured—jelly in an iron jar. Iron. Study, for example, the stage directions of *The Iceman,* and you will see how carefully O'Neill has drawn his ground plan. There everyone sits—a row of a dozen and a half men. And as they sit, the plot progresses; as each new stage is reached, the bell rings, and the curtain comes down. Jelly. Within the tyrannically, mechanically rigid scenes, there is an excessive amount of freedom. The order of speeches can be juggled without loss, and almost any speech can be cut in half.

The eloquence might of course be regarded as clothing that is necessary to cover a much too mechanical man. Certainly, though we gained more by abridging the play than we lost, the abridgment did call attention rather cruelly to the excessively schematic character of the play. Everything is contrived, *voulu,* drawn on the blackboard, thought out beforehand, imposed on the material by the dead hand of calculation. We had started out from the realization that the most lifeless schemata in this overschematic play are the expressionistic ones, but we had been too sanguine in hoping to conceal or cancel them. . . .

It would perhaps be churlish to press the point, were O'Neill's ambition . . . not symptomatic both of his whole endeavor as a playwright and of the endeavor of many other serious playwrights in our time. It is the ambition to transcend realism. O'Neill spoke of it nearly thirty years ago in a program note on Strindberg:

> It is only by means of some form of "super-naturalism" that we may express in the theatre what we comprehend intuitively of that self-obsession which is the particular discount we moderns have to pay for the loan of life. The old naturalism—or realism if you will (I wish to God some genius were gigantic enough to define clearly the separateness of these terms once and for all!)—no longer applies. It represents our fathers' daring aspirations towards self-recognition by holding the family kodak up to ill-nature. But to us their audacity is blague, we have taken too many snapshots of each other in every graceless position. We have endured too much from the banality of surfaces.

So far, so good. This is a warning against that extreme and narrow form of realism generally known as naturalism. Everyone agrees. The mistake is to talk as if it followed that one must get away from realism altogether, a mistake repeated by every poetaster who thinks he can rise above Ibsen by writing flowerily (for example, Christopher Fry as quoted and endorsed by *Time*). Wherever O'Neill tries to clarify his non-realistic theory the only thing that is clear is lack of clarity. For example:

> It was far from my idea in writing *The Great God Brown* that the background pattern of conflicting tides in the soul of man should ever overshadow and thus throw out of proportion the living drama of the recognizable human beings. . . . I meant *it* always to be mystically within and behind them, giving them a significance beyond themselves, forcing itself through them to expression in mysterious words, symbols, actions they do not themselves comprehend. And that is as clearly as I wish an audience to comprehend *it*. *It* is Mystery—the mystery any one man or woman can feel but not understand as the meaning of any event—or accident—in any life on earth. And it is this mystery which I want to realize in the theatre.

I have italicized the word *it* to underline the shift in reference that takes place. The first two times "it" is "the background pattern of conflicting tides in the soul of man." The third time "it" is just a blur, meaning nothing in particular, exemplifying rather than clearing up the mystery that O'Neill finds important. An event can be mysterious, but how can its mystery be its meaning? And how can we know that its mystery is its meaning if we do "not understand" it? And what would constitute a "realization" of such a phenomenon in the theater?

In a letter to Thomas Hobson Quinn, O'Neill tries again. He has been seeking to be a poet, he says,

> and to see the transfiguring nobility of tragedy, in as near the Greek sense as one can grasp it, in seemingly the most ignoble, debased lives. And just here is where I am a most confirmed mystic too, for I'm always, always trying *to interpret Life in terms of lives, never just lives in terms of characters.* I'm always acutely conscious of the Force behind (Fate, God, our biological past creating our present, whatever one calls it—Mystery certainly) and of the one eternal tragedy of Man in his glorious, self-destructive struggle *to make the Force express him instead of being, as an animal is, an infinitesimal incident in its expression.* And my profound conviction is that this is the only subject worth writing about and that it is possible—or can be— to develop a tragic expression in terms of transfigured modern values and symbols in the theatre which may to some degree bring home to members of a modern audience their ennobling identity with the tragic figures on the stage. Of course, this is very much of a dream, but where theatre is concerned, one must have a dream and the Greek dream in tragedy is the noblest ever!

This time I have italicized phrases where we expect O'Neill to say something, where we even think for a moment that he *has* said something. Reading them several times over, we find that we could give them a meaning—but without any assurance that it is O'Neill's. What is interpreting "Life in terms of lives" and what is "mystical" about it? What does it mean to be "expressed" by a Force—as against being an incident in "its expression"? Isn't O'Neill comforting himself with verbiage? For what connection is there—beyond the external ones of *Mourning Becomes Electra*—between his kind of drama and the Greek? How could one be ennobled by identifying oneself with any of his characters?

It is no use wanting to get away from realism (or anything else) unless you know what you want to get away *to*. Raising a dust of symbols and poeticisms is not to give artistic expression to a sense of mystery. It is merely, in O'Neill's case, to take your eye off the object. (Cf. Ibsen: "To be a poet is chiefly to see.") . . .

Most of O'Neill's plays have big intentions written all over them. He has written of

> the death of an old God and the failure of science and materialism to give any satisfying new one for the surviving primitive religious instinct to find a meaning for life in, and to comfort its fears of death with. It seems to me (he adds) anyone trying to do big work nowadays must have this subject behind all the little subjects of his plays or novels.

In other words, O'Neill's intentions as a writer are no less vast than Dostoyevsky's. . . . What is surprising is not that his achievements fall below Dostoyevsky's but that critics—including some recent rehabilitators—have taken the will for the deed and find O'Neill's nobler "conception" of theater enough. "Conception" is patently a euphemism for "intention" and they are applauding O'Neill for strengthening the pavement of hell. In this they are not disingenuous; their own intentions are also good; they are simply a party to a general gullibility. People believe what they are told, and in our time a million units of human energy are spent on the telling to every one that is spent on examining what is told; reason is swamped by propaganda and publicity. Hence it is that an author's professions and intentions, broadcast not only by

himself but by an army of interested and even disinterested parties, determine what people think his work is. The realm of false culture thus created is not all on one level; brows here, as elsewhere, may be high or low. No brows are higher indeed than those of the subintelligentsia. They spend their time seeking sublimities, works that provide the answers to the crying questions of our time, impassioned appeals for justice, daring indictments of tyranny, everything sure-fire. Seek and you shall find: a writer like O'Neill does not give them the optimism of an "American century," but he provides profundities galore, and technical innovations, and (as he himself says) Mystery. Now, there is a large contingent of the subintelligentsia in the theater world. They are seen daily at the Algonquin and nightly at Sardi's. They don't all like O'Neill, yet his "profound" art is inconceivable without them. O'Neill doesn't like *them*, but he needs them, and could never have dedicated himself to "big work" had their voices not been in his ears telling him he was big. The man who could not be bribed by the Broadway tycoons was seduced by the Broadway intelligentsia.

At one time he performed a historic function, that of helping the American theater to grow up. In all his plays an earnest attempt is made to interpret life; this fact in itself places O'Neill above his predecessors in American drama and beside his colleagues in the novel and poetry. He was a good playwright in so far as he kept within the somewhat narrow range of his own sensibility. When he stays close to a fairly simple reality and when, by way of technique, he uses fairly simple forms of realism or fairly simple patterns of melodrama, he can render the bite and tang of reality or, alternatively, he can startle and stir us with his effects. If he is never quite a poet, he is occasionally able—as we have seen in *The Iceman*—to create the striking theatric image.

But the more he attempts, the less he achieves. *Lazarus Laughed* and *The Great God Brown* and *Days without End* are inferior to *The Emperor Jones* and *Anna Christie* and *Ah, Wilderness!* O'Neill has never learned this lesson. The idea of "big work" lured him out into territory

where his sensibility is entirely inopera-
tive. Even his most ardent admirers have
little to say in favor of *Dynamo,* the only
play where he frontally assails the problem of "the death of an old God and the
failure of science." A hundred novelists
have dealt more subtly with hidden
motives than O'Neill did in his famous
essay in psychological subtlety, *Strange
Interlude,* a play that is equally inferior
as a study of upper-class Americans. Then
there is his desire to re-create ancient
tragedy. Although no one is more conscious than he that America is not an
Athens, the "Greek dream"—the desire
to be an Æschylus—has been his nightmare.

The classic and notorious problem
about tragedy in modern dress has been
that the characters, not being over life-
size but rather below it, excite pity without admiration and therefore without
terror. Though O'Neill has talked of an
"ennobling identification" with protagonists, he has only once tried to do anything about it: only in *Mourning Becomes Electra* are the characters over life-
size. Unhappily this is not because of the
size of their bones but, as it were, by
inflation with gas, cultural and psychological.

The cultural gas is the classic story.
The use of classic stories has been customary for so long, and has recently come
into such vogue again, that writers have
forgotten their obligation to make the
stories their own. They figure that the
Æschylean names will themselves establish the dignity and identity of the subject, while they—the modern adapters—
get the credit and draw the royalties.
They are not necessarily conscious op-
portunists. They probably assume, with
some psychologists and anthropologists,
that archetypal patterns of myth elicit
profound responses of themselves, irrespective of presentation; if this were
true, the poet would be unnecessary; it is
a belief not to be discussed by a critic
since the very fact of criticism presup-
poses its falsity. If we ask what difference
it makes that Orin and Lavinia are ver-
sions of Orestes and Electra, the answer
is that they thereby acquire an artificial
prestige. They have become more important without any creative work on the
author's part. We now associate them

with the time-honored and sublime. They
are inflated with cultural gas. It's like
finding out that your girl friend is the
daughter of a duke. If you are impres-
sionable, you are impressed; she will
seem different from now on, clad in all
your illusions about nobility.

We are told that myth is useful because
the audience knows the plot already and
can turn its attention to the how and
why. To this I would not protest that all
adapters, including O'Neill, change the
mythic plots, though this is true; what I
have in mind is, rather, that they do not
always change them enough. Events in
their works have often no organic place
there, they are fossilized vestiges of the
older version. We ask: why does this
character do that? And the answer is:
because his Greek prototype did it. In
Mourning Becomes Electra the myth
makes it hard for O'Neill to let his
people have their own identity at all,
yet to the extent that they do have one,
it is, naturally, a modern and American
identity, and this in turn makes their
ancient and Greek actions seem wildly
improbable. Heaven knows that murders
take place today as in ancient times; but
the murders in O'Neill are not given
today's reality.

Instead, the characters are blown up
with psychological gas. O'Neill has
boasted his ignorance of Freud, but such
ignorance is not enough. He should be
ignorant also of the watered-down Freudianism of Sardi's and the Algonquin, the
Freudianism of all those who are ignorant
of Freud, the Freudianism of the subintelligentsia. It is through this Freudianism, and through it alone, that O'Neill
has made the effort, though a vain one,
to assimilate the myth to modern life.
Now, what is it that your subintellectual
knows about Freud? That he "put everything down to sex." Precisely; and that
is what O'Neill does with the myth. Instead of reverent family feeling to unite
an Orestes and an Electra we have incest.
Mourning Becomes Electra is all sex talk.
Sex *talk*—not sex lived and embodied,
but sex talked of and fingered. The sex
talk of the subintelligentsia. It is the only
means by which some sort of eloquence
and urgency gets into the play, the source
of what is meant to be its poetry. The
Civil War never gains the importance it

might have had in this telling of the story, it is flooded out by sex. "New England," surely a cultural conception with wider reference than this, stands only, in O'Neill, for the puritanic (that is, sexually repressive) attitude.

O'Neill is an acute case of what D. H. Lawrence called "sex in the head." Sex is almost the only idea he has—has insistently—and it is for him only an idea. Looking back on what I wrote about him a few years ago, I still maintain that O'Neill is no thinker. He is so little a thinker, it is dangerous for him to think. To prove this you have only to look at the fruits of his thinking; his comparatively thoughtless plays are better. For a non-thinker he thinks too much. Almost as bad as sex in the head is tragedy in the head, for tragedy too can decline into a doctrine and dwindle into an idea. And when the thing is absent, its "idea" is apt to go soft. Tragedy is hard, but the idea of tragedy ("the tragic view of life," "the tragic sense of life," and so forth) is seldom evoked without nostalgic longing. And the most decadent of longings is the longing for barbarism, *nostalgie de la boue,* such as is voiced by our tragedy-loving poets:

> Poetry is not a civilizer, rather the reverse, for great poetry appeals to the most primitive instincts. . . .
> Tragedy has been regarded, ever since Aristotle, as a moral agent, a purifier of the mind and emotions. But the story of *Medea* is about a criminal adventurer and his gun-moll; it is no more moral than the story of Frankie and Johnny; only more ferocious. And so with the yet higher summits of Greek Tragedy, the Agamemnon series and the *Oedipus Rex;* they all tell primitive horror stories, and the con-

ventional pious sentiments of the chorus are more than balanced by the bad temper and wickedness, or folly, of the principal characters. What makes them noble is the poetry; the poetry and the beautiful shapes of the plays, and the extreme violence born of extreme passion. . . . These are stories of disaster and death, and it is not in order to purge the mind of passions but because death and disaster are exciting. People love disaster, if it does not touch them too nearly—as we run to see a burning house or a motor crash. . . .

Aristotle's view of tragedy is humane; this one—that of Robinson Jeffers—is barbaric without the innocence of barbarism; it is neo-barbaric, decadent. O'Neill is too simple and earnest to go all the way with Jeffers. Puritanism and a rough-hewn honesty keep him within the realm of the human. But *Mourning Becomes Electra* does belong, so to speak, to the same world as Jeffers's remarks, a world that titillates itself with tragedy in the head. Your would-be tragedian despises realism, the problem play, liberalism, politics in general, optimism, and what not. Hence *Mourning Becomes Electra* is unrealistic, unsocial, illiberal, unpolitical, and pessimistic. What of the *Oresteia?* It celebrates the victory of law over arbitrary violence, of the community over the individual. It is optimistic, political, social, and with permissible license might be called liberal and realistic as well. *O tempora, o mores!* If one does not like O'Neill, it is not really he that one dislikes: it is our age—of which like the rest of us he is more the victim than the master.

(1951)

LORCA, BORN IN THE SPANISH PROVINCE OF GRANADA

Federico García Lorca 1889-1936

to prosperous, cultivated parents, was a sickly child. The resulting close contact with the women of the household may explain Lorca's extraordinary ability to identify with the feminine sex. From a peasant servant he learned the folk legends and songs of his people, and even in early life he showed his inclination towards drama by staging plays for his friends. Some years later his family moved into the city of Granada, where Lorca began his university studies in law. At the same time he was writing poetry, studying folk music, and participating in the intellectual life of Granada. On the advice of a friend, Lorca abandoned his studies in Granada and moved into the cosmopolitan intellectual circle in Madrid. In 1928 he published, to great critical acclaim, *Romancero Gitano,* a collection of poems based on gypsy chants and ballads. Lorca then became interested in surrealism. In 1929 he left Spain, passed through Paris and London, and went on to New York, where he stayed at Columbia University and spent some time in the Catskill Mountains, writing poems which were published posthumously as *Poeta in Neuva York.* The following year he returned to Spain; his experiments with folk forms and surrealism were now succeeded by poems and plays which fused popular and cultivated styles. In 1932 he formed a theatrical troupe, La Barraca, which traveled throughout Spain and presented the Spanish classics as well as Lorca's own plays, which gave passionate and somber voice to the sufferings of his people and to the themes of love and death. Still, he could display a lighter side in his puppet plays, e.g., *The Shoemaker's Marvelous Wife. Blood Wedding,* the first of his rural tragedies, was produced in 1933; *Yerma* followed in 1934. Two years later he completed *The House of Bernarda Alba.* But on July 18, 1936, the Spanish Civil War broke out. Lorca tended to be apolitical, but he was associated with left-wing intellectuals, and though a Falangist friend offered to hide him he was seized by a group of Fascist terrorists. Along with other Republican prisoners, he was shot.

THE HOUSE OF BERNARDA ALBA

❧ BY FEDERICO GARCÍA LORCA

A DRAMA ABOUT WOMEN IN THE VILLAGES OF SPAIN
Translated by James Graham-Luján and Richard L. O'Connell

CHARACTERS

BERNARDA, *age 60.*
MARIA JOSEFA, *Bernarda's mother, age 80.*
ANGUSTIAS. *Bernarda's daughter, age 39.*
MAGDALENA, *Bernarda's daughter, age 30.*
AMELIA, *Bernarda's daughter, age 27.*

MARTIRIO, *Bernarda's daughter, age 24.*
ADELA, *Bernarda's daughter, age 20.*
A MAID, *age 50.*
LA PONCIA, *a maid, age 60.*
PRUDENCIA, *age 50.*
WOMEN IN MOURNING.

The writer states that these Three Acts are intended as a photographic document.

❧ Act I

A very white room in Bernarda Alba's house. The walls are white. There are arched doorways with jute curtains tied back with tassels and ruffles. Wicker chairs. On the walls, pictures of unlikely landscapes full of nymphs or legendary kings.

It is summer. A great brooding silence fills the stage. It is empty when the curtain rises. Bells can be heard tolling outside.

FIRST SERVANT (*Entering*). The tolling of those bells hits me right between the eyes.

PONCIA (*She enters, eating bread and sausage*). More than two hours of mumbo jumbo. Priests are here from all the towns. The church looks beautiful. At the first responsory for the dead, Magdalena fainted.

FIRST SERVANT. She's the one who's left most alone.

PONCIA. She's the only one who loved her father. Ay! Thank God we're alone for a little. I came over to eat.

FIRST SERVANT. If Bernarda sees you . . . !

PONCIA. She's not eating today so she'd just as soon we'd all die of hunger! Dom-

ineering old tyrant! But she'll be fooled! I opened the sausage crock.

FIRST SERVANT (*With an anxious sadness*). Couldn't you give me some for my little girl, Poncia?

PONCIA. Go ahead! and take a fistful of peas too. She won't know the difference today.

VOICE (*Within*). Bernarda!

PONCIA. There's the grandmother! Isn't she locked up tight?

FIRST SERVANT. Two turns of the key.

PONCIA. You'd better put the crossbar up too. She's got the fingers of a lock-picker!

VOICE (*Within*). Bernarda!

PONCIA (*Shouting*). She's coming! (*To* THE SERVANT). Clean everything up good. If Bernarda doesn't find things shining, she'll pull out the few hairs I have left.

SERVANT. What a woman!

PONCIA. Tyrant over everyone around her. She's perfectly capable of sitting on your heart and watching you die for a whole year without turning off that cold little smile she wears on her wicked face. Scrub, scrub those dishes!

SERVANT. I've got blood on my hands from so much polishing of everything.

PONCIA. She's the cleanest, she's the decentest, she's the highest everything! A good rest her poor husband's earned!

(*The bells stop.*)

SERVANT. Did all the relatives come?

The House of Bernarda Alba by Federico García Lorca. From *Three Tragedies of Federico García Lorca.* Copyright 1947 by New Directions. Reprinted by permission of New Directions, Publishers.

PONCIA. Just hers. His people hate her. They came to see him dead and make the sign of the cross over him; that's all.

SERVANT. Are there enough chairs?

PONCIA. More than enough. Let them sit on the floor. When Bernarda's father died people stopped coming under this roof. She doesn't want them to see her in her "domain." Curse her!

SERVANT. She's been good to you.

PONCIA. Thirty years washing her sheets. Thirty years eating her leftovers. Nights of watching when she had a cough. Whole days peeking through a crack in the shutters to spy on the neighbors and carry her the tale. Life without secrets one from the other. But in spite of that—curse her! May the "pain of the piercing nail"[1] strike her in the eyes.

SERVANT. Poncia!

PONCIA. But I'm a good watchdog! I bark when I'm told and bite beggars' heels when she sics me on 'em. My sons work in her fields—both of them already married, but one of these days I'll have enough.

SERVANT. And then . . . ?

PONCIA. Then I'll lock myself up in a room with her and spit in her face—a whole year. "Bernarda, here's for this, that and the other!" Till I leave her—just like a lizard the boys have squashed. For that's what she is—she and her whole family! Not that I envy her her life. Five girls are left her, five ugly daughters—not counting Angustias the eldest, by her first husband, who has money—the rest of them, plenty of eyelets to embroider, plenty of linen petticoats, but bread and grapes when it comes to inheritance.

SERVANT. Well, *I'd* like to have what they've got!

PONCIA. All we have is our hands and a hole in God's earth.

SERVANT. And that's the only earth they'll ever leave to us—to us who have nothing!

PONCIA (*At the cupboard*). This glass has some specks.

SERVANT. Neither soap nor rag will take them off.

(*The bells toll.*)

PONCIA. The last prayer! I'm going over and listen. I certainly like the way our priest sings. In the Pater Noster his voice went up, and up—like a pitcher filling with water little by little. Of course, at the end his voice cracked, but it's glorious to hear it. No, there never was anybody like the old Sacristan—Tronchapinos. At my mother's Mass, may she rest in peace, he sang. The walls shook—and when he said "Amen," it was as if a wolf had come into the church. (*Imitating him*). A-a-a-a-men! (*She starts coughing.*)

SERVANT. Watch out—you'll strain your windpipe!

PONCIA. I'd rather strain something else! (*Goes out laughing.*)

(THE SERVANT *scrubs. The bells toll*).

SERVANT (*Imitating the bells*). Dong, dong, dong. Dong, dong, dong. May God forgive him!

BEGGAR WOMAN (*At the door, with a little girl*). Bléssed be God![2]

SERVANT. Dong, dong, dong. I hope he waits many years for us! Dong, dong, dong.

BEGGAR (*Loudly, a little annoyed*). Bléssed be God!

SERVANT (*Annoyed*). Forever and ever!

BEGGAR. I came for the scraps.

(*The bells stop tolling.*)

SERVANT. You can go right out the way you came in. Today's scraps are for me.

BEGGAR. But you have somebody to take care of you—and my little girl and I are all alone!

SERVANT. Dogs are alone too, and they live.

BEGGAR. They always give them to me.

SERVANT. Get out of here! Who let you in anyway? You've already tracked up the place. (THE BEGGAR WOMAN *and* LITTLE GIRL *leave*. THE SERVANT *goes on scrubbing*). Floors finished with oil, cupboards, pedestals, iron beds—but us servants, we can suffer in silence—and live in mud huts with a plate and a spoon. I hope someday not a one will be left to tell it. (*The bells sound again.*) Yes, yes—ring away. Let them put you in a coffin with gold inlay and brocade to carry it on—you're no less dead than I'll be, so

---

[1] "pain of the piercing nail" i.e. pain of the cross.

[2] "Blessed be God": a ritual phrase to which the expected answer is—in this case—"Forever and ever!"

take what's coming to you, Antonio
María Benavides—stiff in your broad-
cloth suit and your high boots—take
what's coming to you! You'll never again
lift my skirts behind the corral door!

(*From the rear door, two by two,
women in mourning with large shawls
and black skirts and fans begin to enter.
They come in slowly until the stage is
full.*)

SERVANT (*Breaking into a wail*). Oh,
Antonio María Benavides, now you'll
never see these walls, nor break bread in
this house again! I'm the one who loved
you most of all your servants. (*Pulling
her hair*). *Must* I live on after you've
gone? Must I go on living?

(*The two hundred women finish coming in, and Bernarda and her five daughters enter.* BERNARDA *leans on a cane.*)

BERNARDA (*To* THE SERVANT). Silence!

SERVANT (*Weeping*). Bernarda!

BERNARDA. Less shrieking and more
work. You should have had all this cleaner
for the wake. Get out. This isn't your
place.

(THE SERVANT *goes off crying.*)

The poor are like animals—they seem
to be made of different stuff.

FIRST WOMAN. The poor feel their sorrows too.

BERNARDA. But they forget them in
front of a plateful of peas.

FIRST GIRL (*Timidly*). Eating is necessary for living.

BERNARDA. At your age one doesn't
talk in front of older people.

FIRST WOMAN. Be quiet, child.

BERNARDA. I've never taken lessons
from anyone. Sit down. Magdalena, don't
cry. If you want to cry, get under your
bed. Do you hear me?

SECOND WOMAN (*To* BERNARDA).
Have you started to work the fields?

BERNARDA. Yesterday.

THIRD WOMAN. The sun comes down
like lead.

FIRST WOMAN. I haven't known heat
like this for years.

(*Pause. They all fan themselves.*)

BERNARDA. Is the lemonade ready?

PONCIA. Yes, Bernarda.

(*She brings in a large tray full of little
white jars, which she distributes.*)

BERNARDA. Give the men some.

PONCIA. They're already drinking in
the patio.

BERNARDA. Let them get out the way
they came in. I don't want them walking
through here.

A GIRL (*To* ANGUSTIAS). Pepe el Romano was with the men during the service.

ANGUSTIAS. There he was.

BERNARDA. His mother was there. She
saw his mother. Neither she nor I saw
Pepe . . .

GIRL. I thought . . .

BERNARDA. The one who *was* there
was Darajalí, the widower. Very close
to your Aunt. We all of us saw him.

SECOND WOMAN (*Aside, in a low
voice*). Wicked, worse than wicked
woman!

THIRD WOMAN. A tongue like a knife!

BERNARDA. Women in church shouldn't
look at any man but the priest—and him
only because he wears skirts. To turn
your head is to be looking for the warmth
of corduroy.

FIRST WOMAN. Sanctimonious old
snake!

PONCIA (*Between her teeth*). Itching
for a man's warmth.

BERNARDA (*Beating with her cane on
the floor*). Blesséd be God![3]

ALL (*Crossing themselves*). Forever
blesséd and praised.

BERNARDA. Rest in peace with holy
company at your head.

ALL. Rest in peace!

BERNARDA. With the Angel Saint Michael, and his sword of justice.

ALL. Rest in peace!

BERNARDA. With the key that opens,
and the hand that locks.

ALL. Rest in peace!

BERNARDA. With the most blesséd, and
the little lights of the field.

ALL. Rest in peace!

BERNARDA. With our holy charity, and
all souls on land and sea.

ALL. Rest in peace!

BERNARDA. Grant rest to your servant,
Antonio María Benavides, and give him
the crown of your blesséd glory.

ALL. Amen.

BERNARDA (*She rises and chants*). Requiem aeternam donat eis domine.

ALL (*Standing and chanting in the

---

3 "Blesséd be God"; the passage which follows is in part litany and in part folk phrase.

Gregorian fashion). Et lux perpetua luce ab eis.[4]

(*They cross themselves.*)

FIRST WOMAN. May you have health to pray for his soul.

(*They start filing out.*)

THIRD WOMAN. You won't lack loaves of hot bread.

SECOND WOMAN. Nor a roof for your daughters.

(*They are all filing in front of* BERNARDA *and going out.* ANGUSTIAS *leaves by the door to the patio.*)

FOURTH WOMAN. May you go on enjoying your wedding wheat.

PONCIA (*She enters, carrying a money bag*). From the men—this bag of money for Masses.

BERNARDA. Thank them—and let them have a glass of brandy.

GIRL (*To* MAGDALENA). Magdalena . . .

BERNARDA (*To* MAGDALENA, *who is starting to cry*). Sh-h-h-h! (*She beats with her cane on the floor.*)

(*All the women have gone out.*)

BERNARDA (*To the women who have just left*). Go back to your houses and criticize everything you've seen! I hope it'll be many years before you pass under the archway of my door again.

PONCIA. You've nothing to complain about. The whole town came.

BERNARDA. Yes, to fill my house with the sweat from their wraps and the poison of their tongues.

AMELIA. Mother, don't talk like that.

BERNARDA. What other way is there to talk about this curséd village with no river—this village full of wells where you drink water always fearful it's been poisoned?

PONCIA. Look what they've done to the floor!

BERNARDA. As though a herd of goats had passed through. (PONCIA *cleans the floor.*) Adela, give me a fan.

ADELA. Take this one. (*She gives her a round fan with green and red flowers.*)

BERNARDA (*Throwing the fan on the floor*). Is that the fan to give to a widow? Give me a black one and learn to respect your father's memory.

_____
[4] "Requiem aeternam . . . ab eis" Bernarda and the others misquote a passage from the Burial Mass. "Requiem aeternam dona eis Domine: et lux perpetua luceat eis." "Eternal rest give unto them, O Lord: and let perpetual light shine upon them."

MARTIRIO. Take mine.

BERNARDA. And you?

MARTIRIO. I'm not hot.

BERNARDA. Well, look for another, because you'll need it. For the eight years of mourning, not a breath of air will get in this house from the street. We'll act as if we'd sealed up doors and windows with bricks. That's what happened in my father's house—and in my grandfather's house. Meantime, you can all start embroidering your hope-chest linens. I have twenty bolts of linen in the chest from which to cut sheets and coverlets. Magdalena can embroider them.

MAGDALENA. It's all the same to me.

ADELA (*Sourly*). If you don't want to embroider them—they can go without. That way yours will look better.

MAGDALENA. Neither mine nor yours. I know I'm not going to marry. I'd rather carry sacks to the mill. Anything except sit here day after day in this dark room.

BERNARDA. That's what a woman is for.

MAGDALENA. Cursed be all women.

BERNARDA. In this house you'll do what I order. You can't run with the story to your father any more. Needle and thread for women. Whiplash and mules for men. That's the way it has to be for people who have certain obligations.

(ADELA *goes out.*)

VOICE. Bernarda! Let me out!

BERNARDA (*Calling*). Let her out now!

(THE FIRST SERVANT *enters.*)

FIRST SERVANT. I had a hard time holding her. In spite of her eighty years, your mother's strong as an oak.

BERNARDA. It runs in the family. My grandfather was the same way.

SERVANT. Several times during the wake I had to cover her mouth with an empty sack because she wanted to shout out to you to give her dishwater to drink at least, and some dogmeat, which is what she says you feed her.

MARTIRIO. She's mean!

BERNARDA (*To* SERVANT). Let her get some fresh air in the patio.

SERVANT. She took her rings and the amethyst earrings out of the box, put them on, and told me she wants to get married.

(*The daughters laugh.*)

BERNARDA. Go with her and be careful she doesn't get near the well.

SERVANT. You don't need to be afraid she'll jump in.

BERNARDA. It's not that—but the neighbors can see her there from their windows.

(THE SERVANT *leaves.*)

MARTIRIO. We'll go change our clothes.

BERNARDA. Yes, but don't take the 'kerchiefs from your heads.

(ADELA *enters.*)

And Angustias?

ADELA (*Meaningfully*). I saw her looking out through the cracks of the back door. The men had just gone.

BERNARDA. And you, what were *you* doing at the door?

ADELA. I went there to see if the hens had laid.

BERNARDA. But the men had already gone!

ADELA (*Meaningfully*). A group of them were still standing outside.

BERNARDA (*Furiously*). Angustias! Angustias!

ANGUSTIAS (*Entering*). Did you want something?

BERNARDA. For what—and at whom—were you looking?

ANGUSTIAS. Nobody.

BERNARDA. Is it decent for a woman of your class to be running after a man the day of her father's funeral? Answer me! Whom were you looking at?

(*Pause.*)

ANGUSTIAS. I . . .

BERNARDA. Yes, you!

ANGUSTIAS. Nobody.

BERNARDA. Soft! Honeytongue! (*She strikes her.*)

PONCIA (*Running to her*). Bernarda, calm down! (*She holds her.* ANGUSTIAS *weeps.*)

BERNARDA. Get out of here, all of you!

(*They all go out.*)

PONCIA. She did it not realizing what she was doing—although it's bad, of course. It really disgusted me to see her sneak along to the patio. Then she stood at the window listening to the men's talk which, as usual, was not the sort one should listen to.

BERNARDA. That's what they come to funerals for. (*With curiosity.*) What were they talking about?

PONCIA. They were talking about Paca la Roseta. Last night they tied her husband up in a stall, stuck her on a horse

behind the saddle, and carried her away to the depths of the olive grove.

BERNARDA. And what did she do?

PONCIA. She? She was just as happy—they say her breasts were exposed and Maximiliano held on to her as if he were playing a guitar. Terrible!

BERNARDA. And what happened?

PONCIA. What had to happen. They came back almost at daybreak. Paca la Roseta with her hair loose and a wreath of flowers on her head.

BERNARDA. She's the only bad woman we have in the village.

PONCIA. Because she's not from here. She's from far away. And those who went with her are the sons of outsiders too. The men from here aren't up to a thing like that.

BERNARDA. No, but they like to see it, and talk about it, and suck their fingers over it.

PONCIA. They were saying a lot more things.

BERNARDA (*Looking from side to side with a certain fear*). What things?

PONCIA. I'm ashamed to talk about them.

BERNARDA. And my daughter heard them?

PONCIA. Of course!

BERNARDA. That one takes after her Aunts: white and mealy-mouthed and casting sheep's eyes at any little barber's compliment. Oh, what one has to go through and put up with so people will be decent and not too wild!

PONCIA. It's just that our daughters are of an age when they ought to have husbands. Mighty little trouble they give you. Angustias must be much more than thirty now.

BERNARDA. Exactly thirty-nine.

PONCIA. Imagine. And she's never had a beau . . .

BERNARDA (*Furiously*). None of them has ever had a beau and they've never needed one! They get along very well.

PONCIA. I didn't mean to offend you.

BERNARDA. For a hundred miles around there's no one good enough to come near them. The men in this town are not of their class. Do you want me to turn them over to the first shepherd?

PONCIA. You should have moved to another town.

BERNARDA. That's it. To sell them!

PONCIA. No, Bernarda, to change. . . . Of course, any place else, they'd be the poor ones.

BERNARDA. Hold your tormenting tongue!

PONCIA. One can't even talk to you. Do we, or do we not share secrets?

BERNARDA. We do not. You're a servant and I pay you. Nothing more.

PONCIA. But . . .

SERVANT (*Entering*). Don Arturo's here. He's come to see about dividing the inheritance.

BERNARDA. Let's go. (*To the* SERVANT). You start whitewashing the patio. (*To* LA PONCIA.) And you start putting all the dead man's clothes away in the chest.

PONCIA. We could give away some of the things.

BERNARDA. Nothing—not a button even! Not even the cloth we covered his face with.

(*She goes out slowly, leaning on her cane. At the door she turns to look at the two servants. They go out. She leaves.*)

(AMELIA *and* MARTIRIO *enter.*)

AMELIA. Did you take the medicine?

MARTIRIO. For all the good it'll do me.

AMELIA. But you took it?

MARTIRIO. I do things without any faith, but like clockwork.

AMELIA. Since the new doctor came you look livelier.

MARTIRIO. I feel the same.

AMELIA. Did you notice? Adelaida wasn't at the funeral.

MARTIRIO. I know. Her sweetheart doesn't let her go out even to the front doorstep. Before, she was gay. Now, not even powder on her face.

AMELIA. These days a girl doesn't know whether to have a beau or not.

MARTIRIO. It's all the same.

AMELIA. The whole trouble is all these wagging tongues that won't let us live. Adelaida has probably had a bad time.

MARTIRIO. She's afraid of our mother. Mother is the only one who knows the story of Adelaida's father and where he got his lands. Every time she comes here, Mother twists the knife in the wound. Her father killed his first wife's husband in Cuba so he could marry her himself. Then he left her there and went off with another woman who already had one daughter, and then he took up with this other girl, Adelaida's mother, and married her after his second wife died insane.

AMELIA. But why isn't a man like that put in jail?

MARTIRIO. Because men help each other cover up things like that and no one's able to tell on them.

AMELIA. But Adelaida's not to blame for any of that.

MARTIRIO. No. But history repeats itself. I can see that everything is a terrible repetition. And she'll have the same fate as her mother and grandmother—both of them wife to the man who fathered her.

AMELIA. What an awful thing!

MARTIRIO. It's better never to look at a man. I've been afraid of them since I was a little girl. I'd see them in the yard, yoking the oxen and lifting grain sacks, shouting and stamping, and I was always afraid to grow up for fear one of them would suddenly take me in his arms. God has made me weak and ugly and has definitely put such things away from me.

AMELIA. Don't say that! Enrique Humanas was after you and he liked you.

MARTIRIO. That was just people's ideas! One time I stood in my nightgown at the window until daybreak because he let me know through his shepherd's little girl that he was going to come, and he didn't. It was all just talk. Then he married someone else who had more money than I.

AMELIA. And ugly as the devil.

MARTIRIO. What do men care about ugliness? All they care about is lands, yokes of oxen, and a submissive bitch who'll feed them.

AMELIA. Ay!

(MAGDALENA *enters.*)

MAGDALENA. What are you doing?

MARTIRIO. Just here.

AMELIA. And you?

MAGDALENA. I've been going through all the rooms. Just to walk a little, and look at Grandmother's needlepoint pictures—the little woolen dog, and the black man wrestling with the lion—which we liked so much when we were children. Those were happier times. A wedding lasted ten days and evil tongues weren't in style. Today people are more refined. Brides wear white veils, just as in the cities, and we drink bottled wine, but we rot inside because of what people might say.

MARTIRIO. Lord knows what went on then!

AMELIA (*To* MAGDALENA). One of your shoelaces has come untied.

MAGDALENA. What of it?

AMELIA. You'll step on it and fall.

MAGDALENA. One less!

MARTIRIO. And Adela?

MAGDALENA. Ah! She put on the green dress she made to wear for her birthday, went out to the yard, and began shouting: "Chickens! Chickens, look at me!" I had to laugh.

AMELIA. If Mother had only seen her!

MAGDALENA. Poor little thing! She's the youngest one of us and still has her illusions. I'd give something to see her happy.

(*Pause.* ANGUSTIAS *crosses the stage, carrying some towels.*)

ANGUSTIAS. What time is it?

MAGDALENA. It must be twelve.

ANGUSTIAS. So late?

AMELIA. It's about to strike.

(ANGUSTIAS *goes out.*)

MAGDALENA (*Meaningfully*). Do you know what? (*Pointing after* ANGUSTIAS.)

AMELIA. No.

MAGDALENA. Come on!

MARTIRIO. I don't know what you're talking about!

MAGDALENA. Both of you know it better than I do, always with your heads together, like two little sheep, but not letting anybody else in on it. I mean about Pepe el Romano!

MARTIRIO. Ah!

MAGDALENA (*Mocking her*). Ah! The whole town's talking about it. Pepe el Romano is coming to marry Angustias. Last night he was walking around the house and I think he's going to send a declaration soon.

MARTIRIO. I'm glad. He's a good man.

AMELIA. Me too. Angustias is well off.

MAGDALENA. Neither one of you is glad.

MARTIRIO. Magdalena! What do you mean?

MAGDALENA. If he were coming because of Angustias' looks, for Angustias as a woman, I'd be glad too, but he's coming for her money. Even though Angustias is our sister, we're her family here and we know she's old and sickly, and always has been the least attractive one of us! Because if she looked like a dressed-up stick at twenty, what can she look like now, now that she's forty?

MARTIRIO. Don't talk like that. Luck comes to the one who least expects it.

AMELIA. But Magdalena's right after all! Angustias has all her father's money; she's the only rich one in the house and that's why, now that Father's dead and the money will be divided, they're coming for her.

MAGDALENA. Pepe el Romano is twenty-five years old and the best looking man around here. The natural thing would be for him to be after you, Amelia, or our Adela, who's twenty—not looking for the least likely one in this house, a woman who, like her father, talks through her nose.

MARTIRIO. Maybe he likes that!

MAGDALENA. I've never been able to bear your hypocrisy.

MARTIRIO. Heavens!

(ADELA *enters.*)

MAGDALENA. Did the chickens see you?

ADELA. What did you want me to do?

AMELIA. If Mother sees you, she'll drag you by your hair!

ADELA. I had a lot of illusions about this dress. I'd planned to put it on the day we were going to eat watermelons at the well. There wouldn't have been another like it.

MARTIRIO. It's a lovely dress.

ADELA. And one that looks very good on me. It's the best thing Magdalena's ever cut.

MAGDALENA. And the chickens, what did they say to you?

ADELA. They presented me with a few fleas that riddled my legs.

(*They laugh.*)

MARTIRIO. What you can do is dye it black.

MAGDALENA. The best thing you can do is give it to Angustias for her wedding with Pepe el Romano.

ADELA (*With hidden emotion*). But Pepe el Romano . . .

AMELIA. Haven't you heard about it?

ADELA. No.

MAGDALENA. Well, now you know!

ADELA. But it can't be!

MAGDALENA. Money can do anything.

ADELA. Is that why she went out after

the funeral and stood looking through the door? (*Pause.*) And that man would . . .

MAGDALENA. Would do anything.

(*Pause.*)

MARTIRIO. What are you thinking, Adela?

ADELA. I'm thinking that this mourning has caught me at the worst moment of my life for me to bear it.

MAGDALENA. You'll get used to it.

ADELA (*Bursting out, crying with rage*). I will not get used to it! I can't be locked up. I don't want my skin to look like yours. I don't want my skin's whiteness lost in these rooms. Tomorrow I'm going to put on my green dress and go walking in the streets. I want to go out!

(THE FIRST SERVANT *enters.*)

MAGDALENA (*In a tone of authority*). Adela!

SERVANT. The poor thing! How she misses her father. . . .

(*She goes out.*)

MARTIRIO. Hush!

AMELIA. What happens to one will happen to all of us.

(ADELA *grows calm.*)

MAGDALENA. The servant almost heard you.

SERVANT (*Entering*). Pepe el Romano is coming along at the end of the street.

(AMELIA, MARTIRIO *and* MAGDALENA *run hurriedly.*)

MAGDALENA. Let's go see him!

(*They leave rapidly.*)

SERVANT (*To* ADELA). Aren't you going?

ADELA. It's nothing to me.

SERVANT. Since he has to turn the corner, you'll see him better from the window of your room.

(THE SERVANT *goes out.* ADELA *is left on the stage, standing doubtfully; after a moment, she also leaves rapidly, going toward her room.* BERNARDA *and* LA PONCIA *come in.*)

BERNARDA. Damned portions and shares.

PONCIA. What a lot of money is left to Angustias!

BERNARDA. Yes.

PONCIA. And for the others, considerably less.

BERNARDA. You've told me that three times now, when you know I don't want it mentioned! Considerably less; a lot less!

Don't remind me any more. (ANGUSTIAS *comes in, her face heavily made up.*) Angustias!

ANGUSTIAS. Mother.

BERNARDA. Have you dared to powder your face? Have you dared to wash your face on the day of your father's death?

ANGUSTIAS. He wasn't my father. Mine died a long time ago. Have you forgotten that already?

BERNARDA. You owe more to this man, father of your sisters, than to your own. Thanks to him, your fortune is intact.

ANGUSTIAS We'll have to see about that first!

BERNARDA. Even out of decency! Out of respect!

ANGUSTIAS. Let me go out, Mother!

BERNARDA. Let you go out? After I've taken that powder off your face, I will. Spineless! Painted hussy! Just like your Aunts! (*She removes the powder violently with her handkerchief.*) Now get out!

PONCIA. Bernarda, don't be so hateful!

BERNARDA. Even though my mother is crazy, I still have my five senses and I know what I'm doing.

(*They all enter.*)

MAGDALENA. What's going on here?

BERNARDA. Nothing's "going on here"!

MAGDALENA (*To* ANGUSTIAS). If you're fighting over the inheritance, you're the richest one and can hang on to it all.

ANGUSTIAS. Keep your tongue in your pocketbook!

BERNARDA (*Beating on the floor*). Don't fool yourselves into thinking you'll sway me. Until I go out of this house feet first I'll give the orders for myself and for you!

(*Voices are heard and* MARIA JOSEFA, BERNARDA'S *mother, enters. She is very old and has decked out her head and breast with flowers.*)

MARIA JOSEFA. Bernarda, where is my mantilla? Nothing, nothing of what I own will be for any of you. Not my rings nor my black moiré dress. Because not a one of you is going to marry—not a one. Bernarda, give me my necklace of pearls.

BERNARDA (*To* THE SERVANT). Why did you let her get in here?

SERVANT (*Trembling*). She got away from me!

MARIA JOSEFA. I ran away because I

want to marry—I want to get married to a beautiful manly man from the shore of the sea. Because here the men run from women.

BERNARDA. Hush, hush, Mother!

MARIA JOSEFA. No, no—I won't hush. I don't want to see these single women, longing for marriage, turning their hearts to dust; and I want to go to my home town. Bernarda, I want a man to get married to and be happy with!

BERNARDA. Lock her up!

MARIA JOSEFA. Let me go out, Bernarda!

(THE SERVANT *seizes* MARIA JOSEFA.)

BERNARDA. Help her, all of you!

(*They all grab the old woman.*)

MARIA JOSEFA. I want to get away from here! Bernarda! To get married by the shore of the sea—by the shore of the sea!

Quick Curtain

❦ Act II

A white room in BERNARDA'S *house. The doors on the left lead to the bedrooms.*

BERNARDA'S DAUGHTERS *are seated on low chairs, sewing.* MAGDALENA *is embroidering.* LA PONCIA *is with them.*

ANGUSTIAS. I've cut the third sheet.

MARTIRIO. That one goes to Amelia.

MAGDALENA. Angustias, shall I put Pepe's initials here too?

ANGUSTIAS (*Dryly*). No.

MAGDALENA (*Calling*). Adela, aren't you coming?

AMELIA. She's probably stretched out on the bed.

PONCIA. Something's wrong with that one. I find her restless, trembling, frightened—as if a lizard were between her breasts.

MARTIRIO. There's nothing, more or less, wrong with her than there is with all of us.

MAGDALENA. All of us except Angustias.

ANGUSTIAS. I feel fine, and anybody who doesn't like it can pop.

MAGDALENA. We all have to admit the nicest things about you are your figure and your tact.

ANGUSTIAS. Fortunately, I'll soon be out of this hell.

MAGDALENA. Maybe you won't get out!

MARTIRIO. Stop this talk!

ANGUSTIAS. Besides, a good dowry is better than dark eyes in one's face!

MAGDALENA. All you say just goes in one ear and out the other.

AMELIA (*To* LA PONCIA). Open the patio door and see if we can get a bit of a breeze.

(LA PONCIA *opens the door.*)

MARTIRIO. Last night I couldn't sleep because of the heat.

AMELIA. Neither could I.

MAGDALENA. I got up for a bit of air. There was a black storm cloud and a few drops even fell.

PONCIA. It was one in the morning and the earth seemed to give off fire. I got up too. Angustias was still at the window with Pepe.

MAGDALENA (*With irony*). That late? What time did he leave?

ANGUSTIAS. Why do you ask, if you saw him?

AMELIA. He must have left about one-thirty.

ANGUSTIAS. Yes. How did you know?

AMELIA. I heard him cough and heard his mare's hoofbeats.

PONCIA. But I heard him leave around four.

ANGUSTIAS. It must have been someone else!

PONCIA. No, I'm sure of it!

AMELIA. That's what it seemed to me, too.

MAGDALENA. That's very strange.

(*Pause.*)

PONCIA. Listen, Angustias, what did he say to you the first time he came by your window?

ANGUSTIAS. Nothing. What should he say? Just talked.

MARTIRIO. It's certainly strange that two people who never knew each other should suddenly meet at a window and be engaged.

ANGUSTIAS. Well, I didn't mind.

AMELIA. I'd have felt very strange about it.

ANGUSTIAS. No, because when a man comes to a window he knows, from all the busybodies who come and go and fetch and carry, that he's going to be told "yes."

MARTIRIO. All right, but he'd have to ask you.

ANGUSTIAS. Of course!

AMELIA (*Inquisitively*). And how did he ask you?

ANGUSTIAS. Why, no way:—"You know I'm after you. I need a good, well brought up woman, and that's you—if it's agreeable."

AMELIA. These things embarrass me!

ANGUSTIAS. They embarrass me too, but one has to go through it!

PONCIA. And did he say anything more?

ANGUSTIAS. Yes, he did all the talking.

MARTIRIO. And you?

ANGUSTIAS. I couldn't have said a word. My heart was almost coming out of my mouth. It was the first time I'd ever been alone at night with a man.

MAGDALENA. And such a handsome man.

ANGUSTIAS. He's not bad looking.

PONCIA. Those things happen among people who have an idea how to do things, who talk and say and move their hand. The first time my husband, Evaristo the Short-tailed, came to my window . . . Ha! Ha! Ha!

AMELIA. What happened?

PONCIA. It was very dark. I saw him coming along and as he went by he said, "Good evening." "Good evening," I said. Then we were both silent for more than half an hour. The sweat poured down my body. Then Evaristo got nearer and nearer as if he wanted to squeeze in through the bars and said in a very low voice—"Come here and let me feel you!"

(*They all laugh.* AMELIA *gets up, runs, and looks through the door.*)

AMELIA. Ay, I thought Mother was coming!

MAGDALENA. What she'd have done to us!

(*They go on laughing.*)

AMELIA. Sh-h-h! She'll hear us.

PONCIA. Then he acted very decently. Instead of getting some other idea, he went to raising birds, until he died. You aren't married but it's good for you to know, anyway, that two weeks after the wedding a man gives up the bed for the table, then the table for the tavern, and the woman who doesn't like it can just rot, weeping in a corner.

AMELIA. You liked it.

PONCIA. I learned how to handle him!

MARTIRIO. Is it true that you sometimes hit him?

PONCIA. Yes, and once I almost poked out one of his eyes!

MAGDALENA. All women ought to be like that!

PONCIA. I'm one of your mother's school. One time I don't know what he said to me, and then I killed all his birds —with the pestle!

(*They laugh.*)

MAGDALENA. Adela, child! Don't miss this.

AMELIA. Adela!

(*Pause.*)

MAGDALENA. I'll go see!

(*She goes out.*)

PONCIA. That child is sick!

MARTIRIO. Of course. She hardly sleeps!

PONCIA. What *does* she do, then?

MARTIRIO. How do I know what she does?

PONCIA. You probably know better than we do, since you sleep with just a wall between you.

ANGUSTIAS. Envy gnaws on people.

AMELIA. Don't exaggerate.

ANGUSTIAS. I can tell it in her eyes. She's getting the look of a crazy woman.

MARTIRIO. Don't talk about crazy women. This is one place you're not allowed to say that word.

(MAGDALENA *and* ADELA *enter.*)

MAGDALENA. Didn't you say she was asleep?

ADELA. My body aches.

MARTIRIO (*With a hidden meaning*). Didn't you sleep well last night?

ADELA. Yes.

MARTIRIO. Then?

ADELA (*Loudly*). Leave me alone. Awake or asleep, it's no affair of yours. I'll do whatever I want to with my body.

MARTIRIO. I was just concerned about you!

ADELA. Concerned?—curious! Weren't you sewing? Well, continue! I wish I were invisible so I could pass through a room without being asked where I was going!

SERVANT (*Entering*). Bernarda is calling you. The man with the laces is here.

(*All but* ADELA *and* LA PONCIA *go out, and as* MARTIRIO *leaves, she looks fixedly at* ADELA.)

ADELA. Don't look at me like that! If

you want, I'll give you my eyes, for they're younger, and my back to improve that hump you have, but look the other way when I go by.

PONCIA. Adela, she's your sister, and the one who most loves you besides!

ADELA. She follows me everywhere. Sometimes she looks in my room to see if I'm sleeping. She won't let me breathe, and always, "Too bad about that face!" "Too bad about that body! It's going to waste!" But I won't let that happen. My body will be for whomever I choose.

PONCIA (*Insinuatingly, in a low voice*). For Pepe el Romano, no?

ADELA (*Frightened*). What do you mean?

PONCIA. What I said, Adela!

ADELA. Shut up!

PONCIA (*Loudly*). Don't you think I've noticed?

ADELA. Lower your voice!

PONCIA. Then forget what you're thinking about!

ADELA. What do you know?

PONCIA. We old ones can see through walls. Where do you go when you get up at night?

ADELA. I wish you were blind!

PONCIA. But my head and hands are full of eyes, where something like this is concerned. I couldn't possibly guess your intentions. Why did you sit almost naked at your window, and with the light on and the window open, when Pepe passed by the second night he came to talk with your sister?

ADELA. That's not true!

PONCIA. Don't be a child! Leave your sister alone. And if you like Pepe el Romano, keep it to yourself. (ADELA *weeps*.) Besides, who says you can't marry him? Your sister Angustias is sickly. She'll die with her first child. Narrow waisted, old—and out of my experience I can tell you she'll die. Then Pepe will do what all widowers do in these parts: he'll marry the youngest and most beautiful, and that's you. Live on that hope, forget him, anything; but don't go against God's law.

ADELA. Hush!

PONCIA. I won't hush!

ADELA. Mind your own business. Snooper, traitor!

PONCIA. I'm going to stick to you like a shadow!

ADELA. Instead of cleaning the house and then going to bed and praying for the dead, you root around like an old sow about goings on between men and women —so you can drool over them.

PONCIA. I keep watch; so people won't spit when they pass our door.

ADELA. What a tremendous affection you've suddenly conceived for my sister.

PONCIA. I don't have any affection for any of you. I want to live in a decent house. I don't want to be dirtied in my old age!

ADELA. Save your advice. It's already too late. For I'd leap not over you, just a servant, but over my mother to put out this fire I feel in my legs and my mouth. What can you possibly say about me? That I lock myself in my room and will not open the door? That I don't sleep? I'm smarter than you! See if you can catch the hare with your hands.

PONCIA. Don't defy me, Adela, don't defy me! Because I can shout, light lamps, and make bells ring.

ADELA. Bring four thousand yellow flares and set them about the walls of the yard. No one can stop what has to happen.

PONCIA. You like him that much?

ADELA. That much! Looking in his eyes I seem to drink his blood in slowly.

PONCIA. I won't listen to you.

ADELA. Well, you'll have to! I've been afraid of you. But now I'm stronger than you!

(ANGUSTIAS *enters*.)

ANGUSTIAS. Always arguing!

PONCIA. Certainly. She insists that in all this heat I have to go bring her I don't know what from the store.

ANGUSTIAS. Did you buy me the bottle of perfume?

PONCIA. The most expensive one. And the face powder. I put them on the table in your room.

(ANGUSTIAS *goes out*.)

ADELA. And be quiet!

PONCIA. We'll see!

(MARTIRIO *and* AMELIA *enter*.)

MARTIRIO (*To* ADELA). Did you see the laces?

AMELIA. Angustias', for her wedding sheets, are beautiful.

ADELA (*To* MARTIRIO, *who is carrying some lace*). And these?

MARTIRIO. They're for me. For a nightgown.

ADELA (*With sarcasm*). One needs a sense of humor around here!

MARTIRIO (*Meaningfully*). But only for me to look at. I don't have to exhibit myself before anybody.

PONCIA. No one ever sees us in our nightgowns.

MARTIRIO (*Meaningfully, looking at* ADELA). Sometimes they don't! But I love nice underwear. If I were rich, I'd have it made of Holland Cloth. It's one of the few tastes I've left.

PONCIA. These laces are beautiful for babies' caps and christening gowns. I could never afford them for my own. Now let's see if Angustias will use them for hers. Once she starts having children, they'll keep her running night and day.

MAGDALENA. I don't intend to sew a stitch on them.

AMELIA. And much less bring up some stranger's children. Look how our neighbors across the road are—making sacrifices for four brats.

PONCIA. They're better off than you. There at least they laugh and you can hear them fight.

MARTIRIO. Well, you go work for them, then.

PONCIA. No, fate has sent me to this nunnery!

(*Tiny bells are heard distantly as though through several thicknesses of wall.*)

MAGDALENA. It's the men going back to work.

PONCIA. It was three o'clock a minute ago.

MARTIRIO. With this sun!

ADELA (*Sitting down*). Ay! If only we could go out in the fields too!

MAGDALENA (*Sitting down*). Each class does what it has to!

MARTIRIO (*Sitting down*). That's it!

AMELIA (*Sitting down*). Ay!

PONCIA. There's no happiness like that in the fields right at this time of year. Yesterday morning the reapers arrived. Forty or fifty handsome young men.

MAGDALENA. Where are they from this year?

PONCIA. From far, far away. They came from the mountains! Happy! Like weathered trees! Shouting and throwing stones! Last night a woman who dresses in se-

quins and dances, with an accordion, arrived, and fifteen of them made a deal with her to take her to the olive grove. I saw them from far away. The one who talked with her was a boy with green eyes—tight knit as a sheaf of wheat.

AMELIA. Really?

ADELA. Are you sure?

PONCIA. Years ago another one of those women came here, and I myself gave my eldest son some money so he could go. Men need things like that.

ADELA. Everything's forgiven *them*.

AMELIA. To be born a woman's the worst possible punishment.

MAGDALENA. Even our eyes aren't our own.

(*A distant song is heard, coming nearer.*)

PONCIA. There they are. They have a beautiful song.

AMELIA. They're going out to reap now.

CHORUS.
The reapers have set out
Looking for ripe wheat;
They'll carry off the hearts
Of any girls they meet.

(*Tambourines and carrañacas[5] are heard. Pause. They all listen in the silence cut by the sun.*)

AMELIA. And they don't mind the sun!

MARTIRIO. They reap through flames.

ADELA. How I'd like to be a reaper so I could come and go as I pleased. Then we could forget what's eating us all.

MARTIRIO. What do you have to forget?

ADELA. Each one of us has something.

MARTIRIO (*Intensely*). Each one!

PONCIA. Quiet! Quiet!

CHORUS (*Very distantly*).
Throw wide your doors and windows,
You girls who live in the town.
The reaper asks you for roses
With which to deck his crown.

PONCIA. What a song!

MARTIRIO (*With nostalgia*).
Throw wide your doors and windows,
You girls who live in the town.

ADELA (*Passionately*).
The reaper asks you for roses
With which to deck his crown.

(*The song grows more distant.*)

PONCIA. Now they're turning the corner.

ADELA. Let's watch them from the window of my room.

[5] "Carrañacas": rattles, noisemakers.

PONCIA. Be careful not to open the shutters too much because they're likely to give them a push to see who's looking.

(*The three leave.* MARTIRIO *is left sitting on the low chair with her head between her hands.*)

AMELIA (*Drawing near her*). What's wrong with you?

MARTIRIO. The heat makes me feel ill.

AMELIA. And it's no more than that?

MARTIRIO. I was wishing it were November, the rainy days, the frost—anything except this unending summertime.

AMELIA. It'll pass and come again.

MARTIRIO. Naturally. (*Pause.*) What time did you go to sleep last night?

AMELIA. I don't know. I sleep like a log. Why?

MARTIRIO. Nothing. Only I thought I heard someone in the yard.

AMELIA. Yes?

MARTIRIO. Very late.

AMELIA. And weren't you afraid?

MARTIRIO. No. I've heard it other nights.

AMELIA. We'd better watch out! Couldn't it have been the shepherds?

MARTIRIO. The shepherds come at six.

AMELIA. Maybe a young, unbroken mule?

MARTIRIO (*To herself, with double meaning*). That's it! That's it. An unbroken little mule.

AMELIA. We'll have to set a watch.

MARTIRIO. No. No. Don't say anything. It may be I've just imagined it.

AMELIA. Maybe.

(*Pause.* AMELIA *starts to go.*)

MARTIRIO. Amelia!

AMELIA (*At the door*). What?

(*Pause.*)

MARTIRIO. Nothing.

(*Pause.*)

AMELIA. Why did you call me?

(*Pause.*)

MARTIRIO. It just came out. I didn't mean to.

(*Pause.*)

AMELIA. Lie down for a little.

ANGUSTIAS (*She bursts in furiously, in a manner that makes a great contrast with previous silence*). Where's that picture of Pepe I had under my pillow? Which one of you has it?

MARTIRIO: No one.

AMELIA. You'd think he was a silver St. Bartholomew.

ANGUSTIAS. Where's the picture?

(PONCIA, MAGDALENA *and* ADELA *enter.*)

ADELA. What picture?

ANGUSTIAS. One of you has hidden it on me.

MAGDALENA. Do you have the effrontery to say that?

ANGUSTIAS. I had it in my room, and now it isn't there.

MARTIRIO. But couldn't it have jumped out into the yard at midnight? Pepe likes to walk around in the moonlight.

ANGUSTIAS. Don't joke with me! When he comes I'll tell him.

PONCIA. Don't do that! Because it'll turn up. (*Looking at* ADELA.)

ANGUSTIAS. I'd like to know which one of you has it.

ADELA. (*Looking at* MARTIRIO). Somebody has it! But not me!

MARTIRIO (*With meaning*). Of course not you!

BERNARDA (*Entering, with her cane*). What scandal is this in my house in the heat's heavy silence? The neighbors must have their ears glued to the walls.

ANGUSTIAS. They've stolen my sweetheart's picture!

BERNARDA (*Fiercely*). Who? Who?

ANGUSTIAS. They have!

BERNARDA. Which one of you? (*Silence.*) Answer me! (*Silence.*) (*To* LA PONCIA.) Search their rooms! Look in their beds. This comes of not tying you up with shorter leashes. But I'll teach you now! (*To* ANGUSTIAS.) Are you sure?

ANGUSTIAS. Yes.

BERNARDA. Did you look everywhere?

ANGUSTIAS. Yes, Mother.

(*They all stand in an embarrassed silence.*)

BERNARDA. At the end of my life—to make me drink the bitterest poison a mother knows. (*To* PONCIA.) Did you find it?

PONCIA. Here it is.

BERNARDA. Where did you find it?

PONCIA. It was . . .

BERNARDA. Say it! Don't be afraid.

PONCIA. (*Wonderingly*). Between the sheets in Martirio's bed.

BERNARDA (*To* MARTIRIO). Is that true?

MARTIRIO. It's true.

BERNARDA (*Advancing on her, beating her with her cane*). You'll come to a bad end yet, you hypocrite! Trouble maker!

MARTIRIO (*Fiercely*). Don't hit me, Mother!

BERNARDA. All I want to!

MARTIRIO. If I let you! You hear me? Get back!

PONCIA. Don't be disrespectful to your mother!

ANGUSTIAS (*Holding* BERNARDA). Let her go, please!

BERNARDA. Not even tears in your eyes.

MARTIRIO. I'm not going to cry just to please you.

BERNARDA. Why did you take the picture?

MARTIRIO. Can't I play a joke on my sister? What else would I want it for?

ADELA (*Leaping forward, full of jealousy*). It wasn't a joke! You never liked to play jokes. It was something else bursting in her breast—trying to come out. Admit it openly now.

MARTIRIO. Hush, and don't make me speak; for if I should speak the walls would close together one against the other with shame.

ADELA. An evil tongue never stops inventing lies.

BERNARDA. Adela!

MAGDALENA. You're crazy.

AMELIA. And you stone us all with your evil suspicions.

MARTIRIO. But some others do things more wicked!

ADELA. Until all at once they stand forth stark naked and the river carries them along.

BERNARDA. Spiteful!

ANGUSTIAS. It's not my fault Pepe el Romano chose me!

ADELA. For your money.

ANGUSTIAS. Mother!

BERNARDA. Silence!

MARTIRIO. For your fields and your orchards.

MAGDALENA. That's only fair.

BERNARDA. Silence, I say! I saw the storm coming but I didn't think it'd burst so soon. Oh, what an avalanche of hate you've thrown on my heart! But I'm not old yet—I have five chains for you, and this house my father built, so not even the weeds will know of my desolation. Out of here! (*They go out.* BERNARDA *sits down desolately.* LA PONCIA *is standing close to the wall.* BERNARDA *recovers herself, and beats on the floor.*) I'll have to let them feel the weight of my hand! Bernarda, remember your duty!

PONCIA. May I speak?

BERNARDA. Speak. I'm sorry you heard. A stranger is always out of place in a family.

PONCIA. What I've seen, I've seen.

BERNARDA. Angustias must get married right away.

PONCIA. Certainly. We'll have to get her away from here.

BERNARDA. Not her, him!

PONCIA. Of course. He's the one to get away from here. You've thought it all out.

BERNARDA. I'm not thinking. There are things that shouldn't and can't be thought out. I give orders.

PONCIA. And you think he'll be satisfied to go away?

BERNARDA (*Rising*). What are you imagining now?

PONCIA. He will, of course, marry Angustias.

BERNARDA. Speak up! I know you well enough to see that your knife's out for me.

PONCIA. I never knew a warning could be called murder.

BERNARDA. Have you some "warning" for me?

PONCIA. I'm not making any accusations, Bernarda. I'm only telling you to open your eyes and you'll see.

BERNARDA. See what?

PONCIA. You've always been smart, Bernarda. You've seen other people's sins a hundred miles away. Many times I've thought you could read minds. But, your children are your children, and now you're blind.

BERNARDA. Are you talking about Martirio?

PONCIA. Well, yes—about Martirio . . . (*With curiosity.*) I wonder why she hid the picture?

BERNARDA (*Shielding her daughter*). After all, she says it was a joke. What else could it be?

PONCIA (*Scornfully*). Do you believe that?

BERNARDA (*Sternly*). I don't merely believe it. It's so!

PONCIA. Enough of this. We're talking about your family. But if we were talking about your neighbor across the way, what would it be?

BERNARDA. Now you're beginning to pull the point of the knife out.

PONCIA (*Always cruelly*). No, Bernarda. Something very grave is happening here. I don't want to put the blame on your shoulders, but you've never given your daughters any freedom. Martirio is lovesick, I don't care what you say. Why didn't you let her marry Enrique Humanas? Why, on the very day he was coming to her window, did you send him a message not to come?

BERNARDA (*Loudly*). I'd do it a thousand times over! My blood won't mingle with the Humanas' while I live! His father was a shepherd.

PONCIA. And you see now what's happening to you with these airs!

BERNARDA. I have them because I can afford to. And you don't have them because you know where you came from!

PONCIA (*With hate*). Don't remind me! I'm old now. I've always been grateful for your protection.

BERNARDA (*Emboldened*). You don't seem so!

PONCIA (*With hate, behind softness*). Martirio will forget this.

BERNARDA. And if she doesn't—the worse for her. I don't believe this is that "very grave thing" that's happening here. Nothing's happening here. It's just that you wish it would! And if it should happen one day, you can be sure it won't go beyond these walls.

PONCIA. I'm not so sure of that! There are people in town who can also read hidden thoughts, from afar.

BERNARDA. How you'd like to see me and my daughters on our way to a whorehouse!

PONCIA. No one knows her own destiny!

BERNARDA. I know my destiny! And my daughters'! The whorehouse was for a certain woman, already dead. . . .

PONCIA (*Fiercely*). Bernarda, respect the memory of my mother!

BERNARDA. Then don't plague me with your evil thoughts!

(*Pause.*)

PONCIA. I'd better stay out of everything.

BERNARDA. That's what you ought to do. Work and keep your mouth shut. The duty of all who work for a living.

PONCIA. But we can't do that. Don't you think it'd be better for Pepe to marry Martirio or . . . yes! . . . Adela?

BERNARDA. No, I don't think so.

PONCIA (*With meaning*). Adela! She's Romano's real sweetheart!

BERNARDA. Things are never the way we want them!

PONCIA. But it's hard work to turn them from their destined course. For Pepe to be with Angustias seems wrong to me—and to other people—and even to the wind. Who knows if they'll get what they want?

BERNARDA. There you go again! Sneaking up on me—giving me bad dreams. But I won't listen to you, because if all you say should come to pass—I'd scratch your face.

PONCIA. Frighten someone else with that.

BERNARDA. Fortunately, my daughters respect me and have never gone against my will!

PONCIA. That's right! But, as soon as they break loose they'll fly to the rooftops!

BERNARDA. And I'll bring them down with stones!

PONCIA. Oh, yes! You were always the bravest one!

BERNARDA. I've always enjoyed a good fight!

PONCIA. But aren't people strange. You should see Angustias' enthusiasm for her lover, at her age! And he seems very smitten too. Yesterday my oldest son told me that when he passed by with the oxen at four-thirty in the morning they were still talking.

BERNARDA. At four-thirty?

ANGUSTIAS (*Entering*). That's a lie!

PONCIA. That's what he told me.

BERNARDA (*To* ANGUSTIAS). Speak up!

ANGUSTIAS. For more than a week Pepe has been leaving at one. May God strike me dead if I'm lying.

MARTIRIO (*Entering*). I heard him leave at four too.

BERNARDA. But did you see him with your eyes?

MARTIRIO. I didn't want to look out. Don't you talk now through the side window?

ANGUSTIAS. We talk through my bedroom window.

(ADELA *appears at the door.*)

MARTIRIO. Then . . .

BERNARDA. What's going on here?

PONCIA. If you're not careful, you'll find out! At least Pepe was at *one* of your windows—and at four in the morning too!

BERNARDA. Are you sure of that?

PONCIA. You can't be sure of anything in this life!

ADELA. Mother, don't listen to someone who wants us to lose everything we have.

BERNARDA. I know how to take care of myself! If the townspeople want to come bearing false witness against me, they'll run into a stone wall! Don't any of you talk about this! Sometimes other people try to stir up a wave of filth to drown us.

MARTIRIO. I don't like to lie.

PONCIA. So there must be something.

BERNARDA. There won't be anything. I was born to have my eyes always open. Now I'll watch without closing them 'til I die.

ANGUSTIAS. I have the right to know.

BERNARDA. You don't have any right except to obey. No one's going to fetch and carry for me. (*To* LA PONCIA.) And don't meddle in our affairs. No one will take a step without my knowing it.

SERVANT (*Entering*). There's a big crowd at the top of the street, and all the neighbors are at their doors!

BERNARDA (*To* PONCIA). Run see what's happening!

(*The Girls are about to run out*). Where are you going? I always knew you for window-watching women and breakers of your mourning. All of you, to the patio!

(*They go out.* BERNARDA *leaves. Distant shouts are heard.* MARTIRIO *and* ADELA *enter and listen, not daring to step farther than the front door*).

MARTIRIO. You can be thankful I didn't happen to open my mouth.

ADELA. I would have spoken too.

MARTIRIO. And what were you going to say? Wanting isn't doing!

ADELA. I do what I can and what happens to suit me. You've wanted to, but haven't been able.

MARTIRIO. You won't go on very long.

ADELA. I'll have everything!

MARTIRIO. I'll tear you out of his arms!

ADELA (*Pleadingly*). Martirio, let me be!

MARTIRIO. None of us will have him!

ADELA. He wants me for his house!

MARTIRIO. I saw how he embraced you!

ADELA. I didn't want him to. It's as if I were dragged by a rope.

MARTIRIO. I'll see you dead first!

(MAGDALENA *and* ANGUSTIAS *look in. The tumult is increasing.* THE SERVANT *enters with* BERNARDA. PONCIA *also enters from another door*.)

PONCIA. Bernarda!

BERNARDA. What's happening?

PONCIA. Librada's daughter, the unmarried one, had a child and no one knows whose it is!

ADELA. A child?

PONCIA. And to hide her shame she killed it and hid it under the rocks, but the dogs, with more heart than most Christians, dug it out and, as though directed by the hand of God, left it at her door. Now they want to kill her. They're dragging her through the streets—and down the paths and across the olive groves the men are coming, shouting so the fields shake.

BERNARDA. Yes, let them all come with olive whips and hoe handles—let them all come and kill her!

ADELA. No, not to kill her!

MARTIRIO. Yes—and let us go out too!

BERNARDA. And let whoever loses her decency pay for it!

(*Outside a woman's shriek and a great clamor are heard.*)

ADELA. Let her escape! Don't you go out!

MARTIRIO (*Looking at* ADELA). Let her pay what she owes!

BERNARDA (*At the archway*). Finish her before the guards come! Hot coals in the place where she sinned!

ADELA (*Holding her belly*). No! No!

BERNARDA. Kill her! Kill her!

Curtain

❧ *Act III*

Four white walls, lightly washed in blue, of the interior patio of BERNARDA ALBA's *house. The doorways, illumined*

*by the lights inside the rooms, give a
tenuous glow to the stage.*

*At the center there is a table with a
shaded oil lamp about which* BERNARDA
and her DAUGHTERS *are eating.* LA PONCIA
serves them. PRUDENCIA *sits apart. When
the curtain rises, there is a great silence
interrupted only by the noise of plates
and silverware.*

PRUDENCIA. I'm going. I've made you
a long visit. (*She rises.*)

BERNARDA. But wait, Prudencia. We
never see one another.

PRUDENCIA. Have they sounded the
last call to rosary?

PONCIA. Not yet.

(PRUDENCIA *sits down again.*)

BERNARDA. And your husband, how's
he getting on?

PRUDENCIA. The same.

BERNARDA. We never see him either.

PRUDENCIA. You know how he is.
Since he quarrelled with his brothers over
the inheritance, he hasn't used the front
door. He takes a ladder and climbs over
the back wall.

BERNARDA. He's a real man! And your
daughter?

PRUDENCIA. He's never forgiven her.

BERNARDA. He's right.

PRUDENCIA. I don't know what he told
you. I suffer because of it.

BERNARDA. A daughter who's disobe-
dient stops being a daughter and becomes
an enemy.

PRUDENCIA. I let water run. The only
consolation I've left is to take refuge in
the church, but since I'm losing my sight,
I'll have to stop coming so the children
won't make fun of me.

(*A heavy blow is heard against the
walls.*)
What's that?

BERNARDA. The stallion. He's locked
in the stall and he kicks against the wall
of the house. (*Shouting.*) Tether him
and take him out in the yard! (*In a
lower voice.*) He must be too hot.

PRUDENCIA. Are you going to put the
new mares to him?

BERNARDA. At daybreak.

PRUDENCIA. You've known how to increase your stock.

BERNARDA. By dint of money and
struggling.

PONCIA (*Interrupting*). And she has

the best herd in these parts. It's a shame
that prices are low.

BERNARDA. Do you want a little cheese
and honey?

PRUDENCIA. I have no appetite.

(*The blow is heard again.*)

PONCIA. My God!

PRUDENCIA. It quivered in my chest!

BERNARDA (*Rising, furiously*). Do I
have to say things twice? Let him out to
roll on the straw. (*Pause. Then, as though
speaking to the Stableman.*) Well, then
lock the mares in the corral, but let him
run free or he may kick down the walls.
(*She returns to the table and sits again.*)
Ay, what a life!

PRUDENCIA. You have to fight like a
man.

BERNARDA. That's it.

(ADELA *gets up from the table.*)
Where are you going?

ADELA. For a drink of water.

BERNARDA (*Raising her voice*). Bring
a pitcher of cool water. (*To* ADELA.)
You can sit down.

(ADELA *sits down.*)

PRUDENCIA. And Angustias, when will
she get married?

BERNARDA. They're coming to ask for
her within three days.

PRUDENCIA. You must be happy.

ANGUSTIAS. Naturally!

AMELIA (*To* MAGDALENA). You've
spilled the salt!

MAGDALENA. You can't possibly have
worse luck than you're having.

AMELIA. It always brings bad luck.

BERNARDA. That's enough!

PRUDENCIA (*To* ANGUSTIAS). Has he
given you the ring yet?

ANGUSTIAS. Look at it. (*She holds it
out.*)

PRUDENCIA. It's beautiful. Three
pearls. In my day, pearls signified tears.

ANGUSTIAS. But things have changed
now.

ADELA. I don't think so. Things go on
meaning the same. Engagement rings
should be diamonds.

PONCIA. The most appropriate.

BERNARDA. With pearls or without
them, things are as one proposes.

MARTIRIO. Or as God disposes.

PRUDENCIA. I've been told your furniture is beautiful.

BERNARDA. It cost sixteen thousand
reales.

PONCIA (*Interrupting*). The best is the wardrobe with the mirror.

PRUDENCIA. I never saw a piece like that.

BERNARDA. We had chests.

PRUDENCIA. The important thing is that everything be for the best.

ADELA. And that you never know.

BERNARDA. There's no reason why it shouldn't be.

(*Bells are heard very distantly.*)

PRUDENCIA. The last call. (*To* ANGUS-TIAS). I'll be coming back to have you show me your clothes.

ANGUSTIAS. Whenever you like.

PRUDENCIA. Good evening—God bless you!

BERNARDA. Good-bye, Prudencia.

ALL FIVE DAUGHTERS (*At the same time*). God go with you!

(*Pause,* PRUDENCIA *goes out.*)

BERNARDA. Well, we've eaten.

(*They rise.*)

ADELA. I'm going to walk as far as the gate to stretch my legs and get a bit of fresh air.

(MAGDALENA *sits down in a low chair and leans against the wall.*)

AMELIA. I'll go with you.

MARTIRIO. I too.

ADELA (*With contained hate*). I'm not going to get lost!

AMELIA. One needs company at night.

(*They go out.* BERNARDA *sits down.* ANGUSTIAS *is clearing the table*).

BERNARDA. I've told you once already! I want you to talk to your sister Martirio. What happened about the picture was a joke and you must forget it.

ANGUSTIAS. You know she doesn't like me.

BERNARDA. Each one knows what she thinks inside. I don't pry into anyone's heart, but I want to put up a good front and have family harmony. You understand?

ANGUSTIAS. Yes.

BERNARDA. Then that's settled.

MAGDALENA (*She is almost asleep*). Besides, you'll be gone in no time. (*She falls asleep.*)

ANGUSTIAS. Not soon enough for me.

BERNARDA. What time did you stop talking last night?

ANGUSTIAS. Twelve-thirty.

BERNARDA. What does Pepe talk about?

ANGUSTIAS. I find him absent-minded.

He always talks to me as though he were thinking of something else. If I ask him what's the matter, he answers—"We men have our worries."

BERNARDA. You shouldn't ask him. And when you're married, even less. Speak if he speaks, and look at him when he looks at you. That way you'll get along.

ANGUSTIAS. But, Mother, I think he's hiding things from me.

BERNARDA. Don't try to find out. Don't ask him, and above all, never let him see you cry.

ANGUSTIAS. I should be happy, but I'm not.

BERNARDA. It's all the same.

ANGUSTIAS. Many nights I watch Pepe very closely through the window bars and he seems to fade away—as though he were hidden in a cloud of dust like those raised by the flocks.

BERNARDA. That's just because you're not strong.

ANGUSTIAS. I hope so!

BERNARDA. Is he coming tonight?

ANGUSTIAS. No, he went into town with his mother.

BERNARDA. Good, we'll get to bed early. Magdalena!

ANGUSTIAS. She's asleep.

(ADELA, MARTIRIO *and* AMELIA *enter.*)

AMELIA. What a dark night!

ADELA. You can't see two steps in front of you.

MARTIRIO. A good night for robbers, for anyone who needs to hide.

ADELA. The stallion was in the middle of the corral. White. Twice as large. Filling all the darkness.

AMELIA. It's true. It was frightening. Like a ghost.

ADELA. The sky has stars as big as fists.

MARTIRIO. This one stared at them till she almost cracked her neck.

ADELA. Don't you like them up there?

MARTIRIO. What goes on over the roof doesn't mean a thing to me. I have my hands full with what happens under it.

ADELA. Well, that's the way it goes with you!

BERNARDA. And it goes the same for you as for her.

ANGUSTIAS. Good night.

ADELA. Are you going to bed now?

ANGUSTIAS. Yes, Pepe isn't coming tonight.

(*She goes out.*)

ADELA. Mother, why, when a star falls or lightning flashes, does one say:

Holy Barbara, blessed on high
May your name be in the sky
With holy water written high?

BERNARDA. The old people know many things we've forgotten.

AMELIA. I close my eyes so I won't see them.

ADELA. Not I. I like to see what's quiet and been quiet for years on end, running with fire.

MARTIRIO. But all that has nothing to do with us.

BERNARDA. And it's better not to think about it.

ADELA. What a beautiful night! I'd like to stay up till very late and enjoy the breeze from the fields.

BERNARDA. But we have to go to bed. Magdalena!

AMELIA. She's just dropped off.

BERNARDA. Magdalena!

MAGDALENA (*Annoyed*). Leave me alone!

BERNARDA. To bed!

MAGDALENA (*Rising, in a bad humor*). You don't give anyone a moment's peace! (*She goes off grumbling.*)

AMELIA. Good night! (*She goes out.*)

BERNARDA. You two get along, too.

MARTIRIO. How is it Angustias' sweetheart isn't coming tonight?

BERNARDA. He went on a trip.

MARTIRIO (*Looking at* ADELA). Ah!

ADELA. I'll see you in the morning! (*She goes out.* MARTIRIO *drinks some water and goes out slowly, looking at the door to the yard.* LA PONCIA *enters.*)

PONCIA. Are you still here?

BERNARDA. Enjoying this quiet and not seeing anywhere the "very grave thing" that's happening here—according to you.

PONCIA. Bernarda, let's not go any further with this.

BERNARDA. In this house there's no question of a yes or a no. My watchfulness can take care of anything.

PONCIA. Nothing's happening outside. That's true, all right. Your daughters act and are as though stuck in a cupboard. But neither you nor anyone else can keep watch inside a person's heart.

BERNARDA. My daughters breathe calmly enough.

PONCIA. That's your business, since you're their mother. I have enough to do just with serving you.

BERNARDA. Yes, you've turned quiet now.

PONCIA. I keep my place—that's all.

BERNARDA. The trouble is you've nothing to talk about. If there were grass in this house, you'd make it your business to put the neighbors' sheep to pasture here.

PONCIA. I hide more than you think.

BERNARDA. Do your sons still see Pepe at four in the morning? Are they still repeating this house's evil litany?

PONCIA. They say nothing.

BERNARDA. Because they can't. Because there's nothing for them to sink their teeth in. And all because my eyes keep constant watch!

PONCIA. Bernarda, I don't want to talk about this because I'm afraid of what you'll do. But don't you feel so safe.

BERNARDA. Very safe!

PONCIA. Who knows, lightning might strike suddenly. Who knows but what all of a sudden, in a rush of blood, your heart might stop.

BERNARDA. Nothing will happen here. I'm on guard now against all your suspicions.

PONCIA. All the better for you.

BERNARDA. Certainly, all the better!

SERVANT (*Entering*). I've just finished with the dishes. Is there anything else, Bernarda?

BERNARDA (*Rising*). Nothing. I'm going to get some rest.

PONCIA. What time do you want me to call you?

BERNARDA. No time. Tonight I intend to sleep well. (*She goes out.*)

PONCIA. When you're powerless against the sea, it's easier to turn your back on it and not look at it.

SERVANT. She's so proud! She herself pulls the blindfold over her eyes.

PONCIA. I can do nothing. I tried to head things off, but now they frighten me too much. You feel this silence?—in each room there's a thunderstorm—and the day it breaks, it'll sweep all of us along with it. But I've said what I had to say.

SERVANT. Bernarda thinks nothing can stand against her, yet she doesn't know the strength a man has among women alone.

PONCIA. It's not all the fault of Pepe el Romano. It's true last year he was running after Adela; and she was crazy about him—but she ought to keep her place and not lead him on. A man's a man.

SERVANT. And some there are who believe he didn't have to talk many times with Adela.

PONCIA. That's true. (*In a low voice.*) And some other things.

SERVANT. I don't know what's going to happen here.

PONCIA. How I'd like to sail across the sea and leave this house, this battleground, behind!

SERVANT. Bernarda's hurrying the wedding and it's possible nothing will happen.

PONCIA. Things have gone much too far already. Adela is set no matter what comes, and the rest of them watch without rest.

SERVANT. Martirio too . . . ?

PONCIA. That one's the worst. She's a pool of poison. She sees El Romano is not for her, and she'd sink the world if it were in her hand to do so.

SERVANT. How bad they all are!

PONCIA. They're women without men, that's all. And in such matters even blood is forgotten. Sh-h-h-h! (*She listens.*)

SERVANT. What's the matter?

PONCIA (*She rises*). The dogs are barking.

SERVANT. Someone must have passed by the back door.

(*ADELA enters wearing a white petticoat and corselet.*)

PONCIA. Aren't you in bed yet?

ADELA. I want a drink of water. (*She drinks from a glass on the table.*)

PONCIA. I imagined you were asleep.

ADELA. I got thirsty and woke up. Aren't you two going to get some rest?

SERVANT. Soon now.

(*ADELA goes out.*)

PONCIA. Let's go.

SERVANT. We've certainly earned some sleep. Bernarda doesn't let me rest the whole day.

PONCIA. Take the light.

SERVANT. The dogs are going mad.

PONCIA. They're not going to let us sleep.

(*They go out. The stage is left almost*

dark. MARIA JOSEFA *enters with a lamb in her arms.*)

MARIA JOSEFA (*Singing*).
Little lamb, child of mine,
Let's go to the shore of the sea,
The tiny ant will be at his doorway,
I'll nurse you and give you your bread.
Bernarda, old leopard-face,
And Magdalena, hyena-face,
Little lamb . . .
Rock, rock-a-bye,
Let's go to the palms at Bethlehem's gate.
(*She laughs.*)
Neither you nor I would want to sleep
The door will open by itself
And on the beach we'll go and hide
In a little coral cabin.
Bernarda, old leopard-face,
And Magdalena, hyena-face,
Little lamb . . .
Rock, rock-a-bye,
Let's go to the palms at Bethlehem's gate.
(*She goes off singing.*)

(*ADELA enters. She looks about cautiously and disappears out the door leading to the corral. MARTIRIO enters by another door and stands in anguished watchfulness near the center of the stage. She also is in petticoats. She covers herself with a small black scarf. MARIA JOSEFA crosses before her.*)

MARTIRIO. Grandmother, where are you going?

MARIA JOSEFA. You are going to open the door for me? Who are you?

MARTIRIO. How did you get out here?

MARIA JOSEFA. I escaped. You, who are you?

MARTIRIO. Go back to bed.

MARIA JOSEFA. You're Martirio. Now I see you. Martirio, face of a martyr. And when are you going to have a baby? I've had this one.

MARTIRIO. Where did you get that lamb?

MARIA JOSEFA. I know it's a lamb. But can't a lamb be a baby? It's better to have a lamb than not to have anything. Old Bernarda, leopard-face, and Magdalena, hyena-face!

MARTIRIO. Don't shout.

MARIA JOSEFA. It's true. Everything's very dark. Just because I have white hair you think I can't have babies, but I can —babies and babies and babies. This baby will have white hair, and I'd have this baby, and another, and this one other;

and with all of us with snow white hair we'll be like the waves—one, then another, and another. Then we'll all sit down and all of us will have white heads, and we'll be seafoam. Why isn't there any seafoam here? Nothing but mourning shrouds here.

MARTIRIO. Hush, hush.

MARIA JOSEFA. When my neighbor had a baby, I'd carry her some chocolate and later she'd bring me some, and so on —always and always and always. You'll have white hair, but your neighbors won't come. Now I have to go away, but I'm afraid the dogs will bite me. Won't you come with me as far as the fields? I don't like fields. I like houses, but open houses, and the neighbor women asleep in their beds with their little tiny tots, and the men outside sitting in their chairs. Pepe el Romano is a giant. All of you love him. But he's going to devour you because you're grains of wheat. No, not grains of wheat. Frogs with no tongues!

MARTIRIO (Angrily). Come, off to bed with you. (She pushes her.)

MARIA JOSEFA. Yes, but then you'll open the door for me, won't you?

MARTIRIO. Of course.

MARIA JOSEFA (Weeping).
Little lamb, child of mine,
Let's go to the shore of the sea,
The tiny ant will be at his doorway,
I'll nurse you and give you your bread.

(MARTIRIO locks the door through which MARIA JOSEFA came out and goes to the yard door. There she hesitates, but goes two steps farther.)

MARTIRIO (In a low voice). Adela! (Pause. She advances to the door. Then, calling.) Adela!

(ADELA enters. Her hair is disarranged.)

ADELA. And what are you looking for me for?

MARTIRIO. Keep away from him.

ADELA. Who are you to tell me that?

MARTIRIO. That's no place for a decent woman.

ADELA. How you wish you'd been there!

MARTIRIO (Shouting). This is the moment for me to speak. This can't go on.

ADELA. This is just the beginning. I've had strength enough to push myself forward—the spirit and looks you lack. I've seen death under this roof, and gone out to look for what was mine, what belonged to me.

MARTIRIO. That soulless man came for another woman. You pushed yourself in front of him.

ADELA. He came for the money, but his eyes were always on me.

MARTIRIO. I won't allow you to snatch him away. He'll marry Angustias.

ADELA. You know better than I he doesn't love her.

MARTIRIO. I know.

ADELA. You know because you've seen —he loves me, me!

MARTIRIO (Desperately). Yes.

ADELA (Close before her). He loves me, me! He loves me, me!

MARTIRIO. Stick me with a knife if you like, but don't tell me that again.

ADELA. That's why you're trying to fix it so I won't go away with him. It makes no difference to you if he puts his arms around a woman he doesn't love. Nor does it to me. He could be a hundred years with Angustias, but for him to have his arms around me seems terrible to you —because you too love him! You love him!

MARTIRIO (Dramatically). Yes! Let me say it without hiding my head. Yes! My breast's bitter, bursting like a pomegranate. I love him!

ADELA (Impulsively, hugging her). Martirio, Martirio, I'm not to blame!

MARTIRIO. Don't put your arms around me! Don't try to smooth it over. My blood's no longer yours, and even though I try to think of you as a sister, I see you as just another woman. (She pushes her away.)

ADELA. There's no way out here. Whoever has to drown—let her drown. Pepe is mine. He'll carry me to the rushes along the river bank. . . .

MARTIRIO. He won't!

ADELA. I can't stand this horrible house after the taste of his mouth. I'll be what he wants me to be. Everybody in the village against me, burning me with their fiery fingers; pursued by those who claim they're decent, and I'll wear, before them all, the crown of thorns that belongs to the mistress of a married man.

MARTIRIO. Hush!

ADELA. Yes, yes. (In a low voice.) Let's go to bed. Let's let him marry

Angustias. I don't care any more, but I'll go off alone to a little house where he'll come to see me whenever he wants, whenever he feels like it.

MARTIRIO. That'll never happen! Not while I have a drop of blood left in my body.

ADELA. Not just weak you, but a wild horse I could force to his knees with just the strength of my little finger.

MARTIRIO. Don't raise that voice of yours to me. It irritates me. I have a heart full of a force so evil that, without my wanting to be, I'm drowned by it.

ADELA. You show us the way to love our sisters. God must have meant to leave me alone in the midst of darkness, because I can see you as I've never seen you before.

(*A whistle is heard and* ADELA *runs toward the door, but* MARTIRIO *gets in front of her.*)

MARTIRIO. Where are you going?

ADELA. Get away from that door!

MARTIRIO. Get by me if you can!

ADELA. Get away!

(*They struggle.*)

MARTIRIO (*Shouts*). Mother! Mother!

ADELA. Let me go.

(BERNARDA *enters. She wears petticoats and a black shawl.*)

BERNARDA. Quiet! Quiet! How poor I am without even a man to help me!

MARTIRIO (*Pointing to* ADELA). She was with him. Look at those skirts covered with straw!

BERNARDA (*Going furiously toward* ADELA). That's the bed of a bad woman!

ADELA (*Facing her*). There'll be an end to prison voices here!

(ADELA *snatches away her mother's cane and breaks it in two.*)

This is what I do with the tyrant's cane. Not another step. No one but Pepe commands me!

(MAGDALENA *enters.*)

MAGDALENA. Adela!

(LA PONCIA *and* ANGUSTIAS *enter.*)

ADELA. I'm his. (*To* ANGUSTIAS.) Know that—and go out in the yard and tell him. He'll be master in this house.

ANGUSTIAS. My God!

BERNARDA. The gun! Where's the gun?

(*She rushes out,* MARTIRIO *following.*

AMELIA *enters and looks on frightened, leaning her head against the wall.*)

ADELA. No one can hold me back! (*She tries to go out.*)

ANGUSTIAS (*Holding her*). You're not getting out of here with your body's triumph! Thief! Disgrace of this house!

MAGDALENA. Let her go where we'll never see her again!

(*A shot is heard.*)

BERNARDA (*Entering*). Just try looking for him now!

MARTIRIO (*Entering*). That does away with Pepe el Romano.

ADELA. Pepe! My God! Pepe!

(*She runs out.*)

PONCIA. Did you kill him?

MARTIRIO. No. He raced away on his mare!

BERNARDA. It was my fault. A woman can't aim.

MAGDALENA. Then, why did you say . . . ?

MARTIRIO. For her! I'd like to pour a river of blood over her head!

PONCIA. Curse you!

MAGDALENA. Devil!

BERNARDA. Although it's better this way!

(*A thud is heard.*) Adela! Adela!

PONCIA (*At her door*). Open this door!

BERNARDA. Open! Don't think the walls will hide your shame!

SERVANT (*Entering*). All the neighbors are up!

BERNARDA (*In a low voice, but like a roar*). Open! Or I'll knock the door down! (*Pause. Everything is silent.*) Adela! (*She walks away from the door.*) A hammer!

(LA PONCIA *throws herself against the door. It opens and she goes in. As she enters, she screams and backs out.*) What is it?

PONCIA. (*She puts her hands to her throat.*) May we never die like that!

(THE SISTERS *fall back.* THE SERVANT *crosses herself.* BERNARDA *screams and goes forward.*) Don't go in!

BERNARDA. No, not I! Pepe, you're running now, alive, in the darkness, under the trees, but another day you'll fall. Cut her down! My daughter died a virgin. Take her to another room and dress her as though she were a virgin. No one will say anything about this! She died a virgin. Tell them, so that at dawn, the bells will ring twice.

MARTIRIO. A thousand times happy she, who had him.

BERNARDA. And I want no weeping. Death must be looked at face to face. Silence! (*To one daughter.*) Be still, I said! (*To another daughter.*) Tears when you're alone! We'll drown ourselves in a sea of mourning. She, the youngest daughter of Bernarda Alba, died a virgin. Did you hear me? Silence, silence, I said. Silence!

Curtain

ARTURO BAREA: *The Poet and Sex*

FEDERICO GARCÍA LORCA, WHO NEVER WANTED TO FACE POLITICS, did face the problems of sex with the greatest clarity. Now, sexual life has in every nation its definite characteristics, traditions, and rites, even though the sexual problems are universal and non-national. In every nation there exists a cultured, sophisticated minority which shares its rules of behavior and its conscious ideals with similar minorities of all other nations within the same sphere of civilization; and there exists the great mass of people following their national sexual code, their peculiar unwritten but unviolable sexual laws. Lorca felt and expressed the problems of sex such as they had been shaped and transformed by the complex conventions of his people. He felt the emotions at the root of the Spanish sexual code so deeply that in his art he magnified them until traditional values stood out with a perturbing significance.

His three rural tragedies, *Bodas de Sangre, Yerma,* and *La Casa de Bernarda Alba,* show these traditions and the problems behind them with the greatest force.

Bodas de Sangre, "Blood Wedding," has a simple pattern of love, honor, and vengeance. The only son of a widow, whose husband and first-born son were killed by the men of a neighboring family, is in love with the daughter of a widower, a rich farmer like himself. A marriage is arranged in which the father's greed for more land and the mother's wish to bury the memory of bloodshed and see new life created have as much part as the son's love. The girl, however, has long been in love with the son of the man who had killed her betrothed's father and brother. Neither of the young men wants to carry on the feud which is ever present in the mind of the mother. The girl has been fighting against her passion for years and intends to fulfill her contract. The man she loves has even married to escape from his forbidden desire for her. But neither he nor the girl can bear the idea that she should deliver herself to another; they elope on her wedding day. There is only one thing to be done. "The hour of blood has struck again." The mother knows that she now has lost her hope of grandchildren and will lose her only remaining son, but she sends him in pursuit of the couple, because the murderer of her hope must be killed—the blood of the son of her husband's murderer must be shed. The two men meet, fight, and kill each other.

The outline of this triangle-and-vendetta story is familiar. But Lorca has filled it with an essentially Spanish tragedy.

The mother is the incarnation of this tragedy. A strong woman who enjoyed life with her husband, she has become dominated by the fear of the extinction of her blood—fear of death, not for herself but for the seed—and by an anxiety to see her physical existence continued, perpetuated by her son's children. This constant fear fills her with a sense of doom. Vengeance of her "blood" follows from her possessive, death-haunted love: to let the enemy's seed survive one's own would mean final death.

Centuries of Moorish and medieval-Catholic breeding, centuries of a social order in which women were valued only for the sons they produced, created this attitude. The code which sprang from it is still valid in Spain. Lorca's "mother," who likes men to be lusty and wild because it means more sons, is deeply convinced that procreation and fecundity are the object, not the correlate, of married sexual love. Her son must marry to give her, the mother, grandchildren: ". . . and see to it that you make me happy by giving me six grandchildren, or as many as you like, since your father did not have the time to make me more sons."

She glories in man's procreative strength: "Your grandfather left a son at every corner," she says proudly to her son. But she believes that a man must not only beget children but also engender life around him, be fecund in every sense.

Mother and son talk about this while they are walking over the land of his betrothed:

SON. These are dry lands.

MOTHER. Your father would have covered them with trees.

SON. Without water—?

MOTHER. He would have found it. In the three years he lived with me, he planted ten cherry trees, the three walnut trees by the mill, a whole vineyard, and the plant called Jupiter which had scarlet flowers and withered.

This moral conviction that men and women must be fecund and that the man and husband is the master because he is the instrument of fecundation has the deepest possible psychological and social roots. In peasant communities it is kept alive in its ancient form by a powerful economic fact: there must be sons to work the land and to defend the property. In Spain this law was reinforced by the rules of the Moorish harem, rules which influenced the non-Moorish society of the country and survived the expulsion of the Moors. It was adjusted, exalted, and perpetuated in the stern teachings of the Church, which made it sinful for husband and wife to enjoy each other, but righteous to multiply. The code of honor which demands the taking of life and the preservation of virginity, not for the sake of "virtue" or love but for the sake of the purity of the "blood," is part of this tradition; it provides the sanctions against sexual offenses and protects the property of the family.

This code and the elements that went into its making were by no means confined to Spain. But the interesting point is that the code is still real to Spaniards, including those who have rationally repudiated it. Even in the towns, the same men and women who will look unmoved at the display of an exaggerated "point of honor" in some of the plays of Calderón and Lope de Vega are stirred by the sterner, simpler justice of the *Alcalde de Zalamea,* the village mayor who kills the violator of his daughter and earns the approval of the King for his act. And they are moved in the recesses of their consciousness by the ancient popular emotions crystallized in Lorca's images.

In fact, blood feud and its code of honor are things of this age, not merely of the past, to Spaniards. The modern laws have prosecuted and suppressed vendettas, but they were powerless against family feuds which lasted through generations and destroyed generations. The same fierce possessive love and haunting fear of extinction which drive the mother in Lorca's tragedy, drove many women during the Spanish Civil War and, through children steeped in hatred against the murderers of their "blood," threaten to breed relentless feuds for generations to come.

On this hard soil, the code of the blood is stronger than love. The mother in *Bodas de Sangre* admits no justification for the betrayal of the law of purity. A woman must have no lover. Contemptuously she says of the girl who followed her beloved: "Honest women, clean women, go into the water. But not she." This rule is accepted by the girl herself. She knows that she did wrong in following the other man, whom she could never marry, and in wanting to live with him. She accepts the law that the honor of the family and her own honor are safe only if her virginity is left intact for her husband to convert it into maternity.

When the two dead bodies have been carried back to the village the unfaithful bride goes to the house of her dead bridegroom's mother and faces her curses. The mother cries out: "But his honor—what about his honor?" The bride then justifies her "crime," not by her love but by the other man's fatal erotic attraction. Fiercely she defends her "intact" honor, ready to pass through an ordeal by fire to prove it:

I want her to know that I am pure. That I may be mad, but that if they were to bury me now, no man would have seen himself in the whiteness of my breasts. . . . For I went away with the other one. I went. You would have done the same. I was a seared woman, covered with sores within and without, and your son was a trickle of water from which I hoped to get children, land, and health. But the other was a dark leaf-grown river, he overcame me with the sounds of reeds, singing through his teeth. And I went along with your son who was like a little child of cold water, and the other sent me hundreds of birds which would not let me walk and which left white frost on my wounds, the wounds of a poor

blighted woman, of a girl kissed by fire.
. . . But what you say—no. I am clean and
honest as a newborn girl child, and I am
strong enough to prove it to you. Light the
fire. We shall put our hands in the flame.
You for your son, I for my body. And you
will be the first to drop your hands.

The lyrical language is the poet's, but
the images come from the speech people of the Andalusian countryside use in
emotional moments, describing their passions and half-comprehended thoughts in
ageless, occult metaphors, as though in
magic formulas. . . .

In reshaping the old, familiar, half-
forgotten tale Lorca thus made visible not
merely the behavior of people possessed
by their blood code, but the "dark root
of the cry" in a ritual in which sex is
possession of life and salvation from
death, but death the final, ordained frustration. To this ritual all Spaniards respond. . . .

There is an ascending scale of frustration in the plays which Lorca wrote in
the last three years of his life, and in
each of them women are destroyed by
their acceptance of the somber moral
code of their social world. In his last
play, *La Casa de Bernarda Alba,* published
nine years after his death and in a version
he may not have considered final, he exposed this code in its most sinister shape.
He called his play "Drama of Women in
the Villages of Spain," to announce its
bitter general significance, and a foot-
note says: "The poet warns the public
that these three acts are meant as a
photographic documentary," thus leaving
no doubt of the typical and, within these
limits, realistic character of the scenes.
Lorca's friend Angel del Río reports that
the raw material of the tragedy was provided by "a family which really used to
live near Fuentevaqueros," in the district
of the poet's home; another friend, Adolfo
Salazar, recalls that Lorca, reading his
play aloud, proudly exclaimed after each
scene: "Not a drop of poetry! Reality!
Realism!"

The personages of the play are all
women. It is set in the country house
of Bernarda Alba, a caste-proud and
wealthy widow with five daughters, one
of them rich in her own right as the sole
child and heir of the first husband. The
village itself lies in a hot plain. It is far

from the river, its inhabitants drink their
water from wells and live a life as stag-
nant as that water. Its women, as far as
they are not in domestic service or on the
verge of beggary, live and die within the
walls of their whitewashed houses. To
go to church is their main diversion.
There the young girls may see the men
of the neighborhood, spied upon by the
eyes of all the older women. The men
have more freedom. They are at least in
the fields during the day. Even if they
break out from their domestic confines
and find their pleasure with the one "bad
woman" of the village, or with a married
woman, or with a stranger from the outside world, they are forgiven because they
are men. But their women pay for it.
None of the families of the village are
accepted as equals by Bernarda Alba, who
sits in the house she inherited from her
father as in a castle. Even during the lifetime of her easygoing second husband
she had imposed her steely will on her
household. After his death—this is the
starting point of the play—she enjoys her
sole possession of power and property,
determined not to let it be frittered away
by the marriage of her daughters, except
that of the eldest, the heiress in her own
right. Bernarda condemns the girls to
nunlike seclusion during the traditional
eight years of mourning for their father:
"For the eight years of the mourning
not even the wind of the street may enter
this house. We must think of the windows and doors as being blocked up with
bricks. So it was done in my father's and
my grandfather's house. During the time,
you can begin with the embroidery for
your dowry."

But the four know only too well that
there is little chance of their getting husbands. Their shares in the estate are
small, not tempting for suitors, and no
man can even come to see them now.
It is particularly bitter for all of them
that Angustias, the wealthy stepsister,
should be betrothed to the handsome
Pepe Romano, the only man of the social
class whom they used to see. It is hardest
for young Adela, who is passionately in
love with him and knows that he has
desired her, even though he is willing to
marry the money and lands of her ugly,
aged sister. Adela is proud of her young
body, afraid of withering away behind

the bleak, whitewashed walls of the house, and willing to fight for her right to love. Every night, after Pepe Romano has paid a dutiful call to his betrothed, Angustias (a call which consists in the traditional conversation through the wrought-iron grille of her window), he lingers on outside Adela's window rails until the small hours of the morning—and their encounter is passionate. Adela can hide her love and desperate determination from her mother, but not from her sister Martirio. Martirio is the second youngest, a hunchback with an ardent body, racked by suppressed desire. Once, only once, a man had wanted to court her, but because his father used to be a common laborer, Bernarda had driven him off. Martirio had been waiting for him in vain behind her barred window, with nothing but a nightdress to clothe her deformity and her desire. Then she had been kindled by the sight of Pepe Romano, and his daily visit to the windows of her sisters is now driving her crazy. Hiding her hatred and longing under a meek submission, she spies on Adela. She might resign herself to the conventional marriage between the man and Angustias, because there would never be any joy and love in it, but she cannot bear the thought that Adela should have what would always be denied to herself. Of the remaining two sisters, one, Amelia, is spared suffering by her almost infantile, brainless vacuity, while the other, Magdalena, saves her sanity by desperate cynicism and a clear-sighted resignation to her fate. Neither of them can do anything to halt the currents of passion released by the invisible presence of the male.

These currents are clearly seen by an old family retainer, half beggarwoman, half servant, who is the only person to speak openly to Bernarda. Old Poncia brings a breath of vulgar gaiety and shrewdness into the cloistered house; she speaks to the girls of the normal, brutal, gusty life shared by men and women outside. But even this sturdy, warm-blooded woman has been warped by her thirty years' bondage in Bernarda's house; she has turned sly and malicious, resentful of the arrogant contempt with which she is treated. For Bernarda's pride of caste kills every human approach. Though she likes

hearing village gossip from Poncia, she grants her no right of companionship. "Poor folk are like beasts, they seem to be made from another stuff than we." Poncia rebels against Bernarda's rule, but she half accepts her rules. She would like to prevent a catastrophe which she sees coming when Angustias' impending wedding drives Adela to a reckless decision, but has not the courage and selflessness to act. The only soul in the house who is beyond the reach of Bernarda's soulless code is her old mother—who is a madwoman. She escapes from her room and tells her crazy truth: "I want fields. I want houses, but open houses where the women lie in bed with their little children and the men sit in the open on their chairs. Pepe Romano is a giant. All of you want him. But he will devour you because you are nothing but grains of corn. No, not grains of corn. You are frogs without tongues." Her lunacy reveals the suppressed madness in these women's unnatural life, but it does not help the other prisoners of Bernarda's house.

In a sultry summer night, when the stallion of the farmyard drums with his hooves on the stable door until he is let out, Adela commits her final act of revolt. She meets her sister's betrothed out in the open. When Martirio surprises her on her return to the house, she cries out that she will never again stay in their "prison." She will brave the opinion of their world —the world of the village which hounds rebels to death—and she will live in freedom where her lover will be able to see her at his pleasure, after his barren marriage with her sister. Martirio is mad with rage and envy of Adela's "triumphant body." She rouses Bernarda and denounces Adela: "She's been with him! Look, her petticoat is covered with straw." The impassioned girl tells the whole house that she is his "wife" and that he is outside in the garden, "strong as a lion." Bernarda takes a rifle and goes on the chase, followed by Martirio. The other women hear a shot; Martirio comes back to tell them that Pepe Romano is finished. This is a lie. Bernarda has missed him, he has escaped on his horse. But Adela does not stay to hear this. Her lover has been killed: she goes and hangs herself. And now Bernarda's stony conviction of the rightness of her code is stronger than any feeling. She orders her daughters to lay out Adela in her room, in a virgin's shroud. For this is to be the truth and the story which the world will hear: "We shall bury ourselves in a sea of mourning. She, the youngest daughter of Bernarda Alba, has died a virgin. Have you heard me? Silence, I tell you, silence. Silence!" The honor of the house of Bernarda Alba is saved. Nothing else matters. Death is stronger than rebellious life.

In black on white—the black of sterile mourning set against the dead white of a prisonhouse—Lorca's play shows the working of the old Spanish code of honor and caste in its deadly extremes, valid and fatal in a sector of society where there is no outlet, no hope of sanity and freedom, for the hysteria of frustrated women. Erotic frustration and perverted power are certainly not specifically Spanish; but their tragic fatality that seems so inevitable to its victims is a characteristic element of the Spanish world from which Lorca took his characters and his plot. It was the "black" Spain which killed Lorca himself, two months after the day —June 19, 1936—when he finished the "Drama of Women in the Villages of Spain."

The exceptional sensitiveness to feminine reactions which fills Lorca's plays runs through the whole of his poetry, wherever it touches themes of love, and even when the man appears as the actor and conqueror. Perhaps it was this power to identify himself with both men and women which made it possible for Lorca to capture and express all the main elements in Spanish sexual consciousness, including those subtly entangled with the religious life of the people.

Spanish children first learn about the supreme value of chastity in men and virginity in women through the stories of saints and martyrs on which religious tuition centers during the early years of childhood. Except for St. Anna, the mother of the Virgin—of the "Immaculate Conception"—most of the female saints in Spanish hagiology and martyrology are virgins. In popular language "virgin" and "martyr" are always coupled. Through their religious instruction and

their studies of classical literature Spanish boys are forced to visualize the female body as a "sack of uncleanliness" and to imagine its putrefaction in slow, loathsome stages. They are shown the virginal martyrs in the clean loveliness of their young flesh and in the horror of their mutilated bodies. Perversely, a deeper exaltation and a deeper compassion are produced when the breasts hacked off by the executioner are described as young and virginal than when they are the good tired breasts of a mother of many children. Young boys and girls are taught to long for a martyr's death which, in the midst of unbearable pain, contains the searing joy of union with the Savior, the felicity of a transition to a better life. This educational process breeds, particularly in the girls, the ideas and ideals of Lust through Pain, Holiness through Horror, and Virginity triumphant over Violence and crowned by the Heavenly Bridegroom. Juvenile sadomasochism is cultivated by those unimpeachable legends and developed by the terrifying, grimly naturalistic paintings of martyred saints in Spanish churches, where the air is thick with sensuous exaltation, cruel and cloying. . . .

There is another important side to religious eroticism as it exists in Spain today. The terrible realism of the old, stern images of Christ on the Cross and of tortured saints was followed in Renaissance and Baroque art by the sensuous idealization of beauty in the paintings or sculptures of beings "in the Glory," the Virgin, the beatified saints, the archangels—including the fallen Lucifer— and the hosts of the angels. The sinless, disembodied subjects gave the artists liberty to create stainless, "immaculate" bodies, and justified, indeed demanded, adoring contemplation. It is impossible not to feel the bodily warmth of Murillo's glowing, oversweet Virgins and female saints. Less obvious, but of greater psychological importance, is the physical fascination of the images of juvenile male martyrs—such as St. Sebastian—and above all of the angels. In them women who had been taught to renounce all sensual thoughts of the masculine body found "innocent," concrete shapes on which their imagination was allowed to dwell. The traditional images of the arch-angels are androgynous, and the Baroque artists particularly created ideal forms of an ambiguous beauty which is not sexless, but belongs to neither sex, and to both. In Murcia there is a polychrome wood sculpture of the archangel Gabriel, by the eighteenth-century monk Salzillo, in which feminine and masculine elements are inextricably fused to a gentle, perfect, and seductive shape of great purity. . . .

Yet there runs a pagan streak through Spanish eroticism even if, in the traditional moral code guarded by the Church, it is banned from married life and altogether from the life of the women. It emerges in the man's delight in the body of a woman or another man. It breaks loose, unexpectedly, in the almost orgiastic mass festivals which transform ecclesiastic holidays or pilgrimages, such as that which Lorca brought into his story of Yerma. It is strong and joyful in some of the folk songs and folk sayings, diluted in sensuous romantic poetry, and perverted to "adulterous" passion in conventional drama. But it exists, a dark and powerful undertow, and Lorca had to give it form, just as he uncovered the other currents in the sex life of his people. And what he shows is not so much the joyous freedom or the physical delight, but rather the frightening, ruthless force of lust.

Jean Giraudoux 1882-1944

JEAN GIRAUDOUX WAS BORN IN A SMALL FRENCH town into a lower-middle-class family. Giraudoux was a brilliant student and seemed headed for an academic career in philology—his specialty was Germanic studies. Although he taught for a time (he was once an instructor in French at Harvard), he eventually decided not to become a professor and entered the French diplomatic service. He traveled widely in the course of his work, but he also wrote—short stories at first, later an attempt at a novel. Then World War I broke out, and Giraudoux joined the infantry; during his service he was cited three times for bravery and received the cross of the Legion of Honor. After the war Giraudoux returned to the diplomatic service and also resumed his writing; a series of novels followed. In 1928, at the suggestion of the distinguished actor-director Louis Jouvet, Giraudoux, then forty-six, turned to the drama and triumphed with his play *Siegfried*. Thereafter, drama remained his chief literary medium and his plays established Giraudoux as one of France's important dramatists. In 1929 came his version of the classical myth of Amphitrion, *Amphitrion 38*; in the 1930's a series of major plays appeared, including *Judith* (1931), *Intermezzo* (1933), *The Trojan War Will Not Take Place* (1935; translated as *Tiger at the Gates*), *Electra* (1937), and *Ondine* (1939). During World War II Giraudoux headed the French propaganda ministry until shortly before the German occupation of France under the Vichy regime. Giraudoux's mind was highly cultivated, elegant, and versatile; his plays weave a world of fancy about the antinomies of human existence: love and lust, war and peace, the real and the ideal, man and woman, the mortal and the supernatural. His last important plays were *The Madwoman of Chaillot* (1943) and *For Lucrece* (1944; translated as *Duel of Angels*).

ONDINE ❧ BY JEAN GIRAUDOUX

Adapted by Maurice Valency

CHARACTERS
(IN ORDER OF APPEARANCE)

AUGUSTE	MATHO
EUGENIE	SALAMMBO
RITTER HANS	A LORD
ONDINE	A LADY
THE ONDINES	THE ILLUSIONIST, *The Old One*
THE OLD ONE	THE KING
THE LORD CHAMBERLAIN	A SERVANT
THE SUPERINTENDENT OF THE THEATRE	THE FIRST FISHERMAN
THE TRAINER OF SEALS	THE SECOND FISHERMAN, *The Old One*
BERTHA	THE FIRST JUDGE
BERTRAM	THE SECOND JUDGE
VIOLANTE	THE EXECUTIONER
ANGELIQUE	THE KITCHEN MAID
VENUS	

ACT ONE: *A Fisherman's Cottage*
ACT TWO: *A Hall in the King's Palace*
ACT THREE: *The Courtyard in the Castle of the Wittenstein*
TIME: *The Middle Ages*

❧ Act I

A fisherman's hut near a lake in the forest. The living room has a fireplace, a door that leads into the kitchen, and a door that leads out into the forest. The windows are shuttered. There is a table near the fireplace, with a bench next to it and a heavy wooden chair next to the fire, which is blazing. It is night. A storm is raging.

Two old people, AUGUSTE and EUGENIE, are in the room. EUGENIE is setting the table. AUGUSTE is at the window. He has opened the shutters and is peering out into the storm.

AUGUSTE. What can she be doing out there at this hour?

EUGENIE. Don't worry about her. She can see in the dark.

AUGUSTE. In this storm!

EUGENIE. She's quite safe. The rain doesn't wet her.

AUGUSTE. She's singing. Is it she that's singing? You think that's her voice?

EUGENIE. Whose else? There is no other house within twenty leagues.

AUGUSTE. Now it comes from the top of the waterfall and now from the middle of the lake.

EUGENIE. Because now she's on top of the waterfall and now in the middle of the lake.

AUGUSTE. It's all so simple, isn't it? But did you, by any chance, ever amuse yourself by diving down the waterfalls in the nude when you were her age?

EUGENIE. Yes. Once. They fished me out by the feet. Every girl tries just once to do what Ondine does fifty times a day. I jumped into the whirlpool once, and I tried to catch the waterfall once in a bowl, and once I tried to walk on the water. It seems very long ago.

AUGUSTE. You've spoiled her, Eugenie. A girl of sixteen has no business running around in the forest in the dark in a storm. A well-brought-up girl does not insist on doing her sewing on the brink of a waterfall. She doesn't insist on saying her prayers under water. Where would we be today if you had been brought up like that?

EUGENIE. She's very helpful with the housework.

AUGUSTE. That brings up another question.

EUGENIE. Doesn't she wash the dishes? Doesn't she clean your boots?

AUGUSTE. I don't know. Does she?

EUGENIE. It's not clean, this dish?

AUGUSTE. That's not the point. Have you ever, in all her life, seen her cleaning or washing anything?

EUGENIE. What difference does it make whether or not I've seen her? She gets it done.

AUGUSTE. Yes. But explain this—three dishes or twelve, one shoe or eight, it takes her exactly the same time to do them. She takes them out; she's hardly gone a minute, and she's back. The dish-cloth is dry. The shoe polish hasn't been used. But everything is clean, everything sparkles. And that affair of the golden plates on her birthday—did you ever get to the bottom of that? And her hands. Why are they never soiled, like anyone else's?

EUGENIE. Because she's not like anyone else. She's never been like anyone else.

AUGUSTE. Today she lifted the gate of the trout pond. All the trout are gone. All but the one I brought home for supper. Are you going to broil it? (*The windows spring open suddenly.*) Who did that?

EUGENIE. The wind, Auguste.

AUGUSTE. I hope she doesn't start that performance again with the lightning, and those horrible heads that peer in at the window out of the storm. The old man with the crown—oh!

EUGENIE. I love the woman with the pearls. Well, bar the window if you're afraid.

(AUGUSTE *crosses to close the window. There is a flash of lightning. The head of an old man with a crown and a streaming beard appears in the window frame.*)

THE HEAD. No use, Auguste. No lock so strong, no bar so stout will serve to keep the old one out!

(*He vanishes, laughing, in a clap of thunder.*)

AUGUSTE. I'll show you if it's too late, Ondine.

(*He closes the window. It immediately bursts open. There appears, in another lightning flash, a charming naiad's head with a necklace of pearls.*)

THE NAIAD. Good evening, Eugenie! (*It vanishes.*)

EUGENIE. Ondine, you're annoying your father. It's time to come in.

AUGUSTE. Ondine, I'm going to count up to three. If you're not inside when I finish, I'll bolt the door. And you can sleep out.

(*There is a roar of thunder*).

EUGENIE. You're not serious?

AUGUSTE. You'll see if I'm serious. Ondine, one!

(*A roar of thunder.*)

EUGENIE. Stop it, Auguste. It's deafening.

AUGUSTE. Am I doing it?

EUGENIE. Well, then, hurry. We all know you can count up to three.

AUGUSTE. Ondine, two! (*Thunder.* EUGENIE *covers her ears.*)

EUGENIE. Really, Auguste, I don't see the use—

AUGUSTE. Ondine, three!

EUGENIE (*Waiting for the thunder.*) Well, well, finish, Auguste, finish—

(*There is no thunder.*)

AUGUSTE. I've finished. (*He bolts the door.*) There. I'd like to see anyone come in now.

(*The door springs open. They turn in terror. A knight in full armor stands on the threshold. He holds his helmet under his arm.*)

RITTER HANS (*Clicking his heels*). Ritter Hans von Wittenstein zu Wittenstein.

AUGUSTE (*Bows*). My name is Auguste. I am a fisherman.

RITTER HANS. I took the liberty of putting my horse in your shed. The horse, as we know, is the most important part of the knight-errant. And the most sensitive.

AUGUSTE. I'll go and rub him down at once, my lord.

HANS. Thanks very much. I've already

done it. I make it an invariable rule, away from home, to rub down my horse myself. In these parts, you rub horses down Swabian fashion, against the grain—the coat soon loses its luster. May I sit down?

AUGUSTE. The house is yours, my lord.

HANS (*Sets down his helmet and puts by his sword*). What a storm! The water has been running down my neck steadily since noon. Of course it doesn't stay. It runs out again through the blood gutters. But once it gets in, the damage is done. (*He sits down ponderously.*) That's what we fear most, we knights-errant, the rain. The water. And, of course, a flea. Once a flea gets in here—

AUGUSTE. Would you care to remove your armor, my lord?

HANS. My dear Auguste, have you ever watched a lobster shed his carapace? Then you know it's not the affair of a moment. I will rest first. You said your name was Auguste, I believe?

AUGUSTE. And my wife, Eugenie.

HANS (*Bows to* EUGENIE). Ah. Auguste and Eugenie. Charming names.

EUGENIE. Excuse them, my lord. They are not names for knights-errant.

HANS. Dear Eugenie, when a knight-errant has spent a month in the forest, searching in vain for Osmond and Pharamond, you cannot imagine his joy when he comes suddenly at dinner time upon Auguste and Eugenie.

EUGENIE. Thank you, my lord. It's ill-mannered, I know, to annoy a guest with questions, but perhaps you will forgive this one: are you hungry?

HANS. I am hungry. I am extremely hungry. It will give me great pleasure to share your meal.

EUGENIE. We have already supped, my lord. But there is a trout. Would you honor us by eating it?

HANS. With the greatest pleasure.

EUGENIE. Would you like it broiled or fried?

HANS. Poached, if you please.

(AUGUSTE *and* EUGENIE *make a gesture of fear.*)

EUGENIE. Poached? I really do them best *sautée, meunière,* with a little white butter. It's very good.

HANS. Since you ask my preference—

AUGUSTE. *Gratinée,* perhaps with fresh cream? Eugenie's specialty.

HANS. When we say poached—that's when the fish is thrown into the boiling water alive?

EUGENIE. Yes. Alive.

HANS. So that the fish retains all its tenderness because the heat takes it by surprise?

AUGUSTE. Surprise is the word, my lord.

HANS. Then that's it. I'll have it poached.

EUGENIE (*Walks slowly to the kitchen. She turns at the door*). Broiled, they're very nice, with a slice of lemon—

HANS. Poached, if you please. (EUGENIE *goes into the kitchen.* HANS *makes himself comfortable in the chair by the fireside.*) I'm happy to see, Auguste, that knights-errant are not unwelcome in these parts . . . ?

AUGUSTE. Much more welcome than armies, my lord. When the winter is over, the robins come; when the wars are over, the knights. A knight-errant is a sign of peace.

HANS. I love war.

AUGUSTE. Each to his taste, my lord.

HANS. Don't misunderstand me. (*Expansively.*) If I love war, it's because by nature I'm a friendly person. I love company. Now in a war, you always have someone to talk to. If your comrades don't feel like chatting, there's always the enemy—you can always get yourself a prisoner. He shows you his wife's picture. You tell him about your sister. That's what I call living. But a knight-errant . . . ! Would you believe it, in all the time I've spent riding about this enchanted forest, I haven't so much as heard a human voice.

AUGUSTE. But isn't it true that knights-errant can understand the language of animals?

HANS. Ah, yes, that's true enough—they speak to us, the animals. And we understand them very well. But it's not quite what you think, the language of animals. For us every animal is a symbol, naturally, and its message is written indelibly on our souls. But that's it, you see, the animals write—they don't speak.

AUGUSTE. They don't speak?

HANS. They speak without speaking. What they say is important, of course. The stag speaks to us of nobility. The unicorn, of chastity. The lion, of courage.

It's stimulating—but you don't call that a conversation.

AUGUSTE. But the birds . . . ?

HANS. To tell you the truth, Auguste, I'm a little disappointed in the birds. They chatter incessantly. But they're not good listeners. They're always preaching.

AUGUSTE. That surprises me. Especially with the lark. I should have thought the lark would love to confide in one.

HANS. The knight's headgear does not permit him to converse with larks.

AUGUSTE. But what sent you, if I may ask, into the Black Forest?

HANS. What do you suppose? A woman.

AUGUSTE. I ask no more questions, my lord.

HANS. Please, Auguste! It's thirty days since I've said a word about her to a living soul. No, no, ask me questions. Ask me anything. Ask me her name.

AUGUSTE. My lord—I wouldn't dare.

HANS. Ask me. Ask me.

AUGUSTE. What is her name, my lord?

HANS. Bertha. Bertha! Tell me, fisherman, have you ever heard such a beautiful name? Bertha!

AUGUSTE. It's beautiful, my lord.

HANS. There are those who are called Angelique, Diane, Violante. Anybody can be called Angelique, Diane, Violante. But she alone deserves a name so solemn, vibrating, passionate: Bertha! (EUGENIE *comes in with a loaf of bread.*) And now, Eugenie, you will ask me is she beautiful?

EUGENIE. Is she beautiful?

AUGUSTE. We are speaking of Bertha, the Princess Bertha, Eugenie.

EUGENIE. Ah, yes, of course. And is she beautiful?

HANS. Eugenie, it is I who am entrusted with the purchase of horses for the king. You understand, then, my eye is sharp. No blemish, however slight, ever escapes me. The Angelique in question is not bad, but she has a ridge in her left thumbnail. Violante has a fleck of gold in her eye. Bertha is flawless.

AUGUSTE. That must be a lovely thing to see, a fleck of gold in a woman's eye.

EUGENIE. Stick to your fishing, Auguste.

HANS. A fleck of gold? Don't deceive yourself, my dear fellow. That might amuse you, a thing like that, for a day, two days at the most—

AUGUSTE. What is it like, exactly?

HANS. Well, it sparkles.

AUGUSTE. Like a grain of mica?

EUGENIE. Come, Auguste—you're getting on our nerves with your gold and your mica. Let the knight speak.

HANS. Yes, my dear Auguste, why this sudden partiality for Violante? Violante, when she joins with us in the hunt, crowns a white mare. And it's a pretty sight, a red-headed girl on a white mare, there's no denying it. And Violante, when she brings the queen the three-branched candlestick, always bears it high in both hands, like the celebrant approaching the altar. But Violante, when the old Duke takes her hand and tells her a spicy story, never laughs. She cries.

AUGUSTE. Violante cries?

HANS. I know. You are going to ask me what happens to these flecks of gold when they are drowned in tears—

EUGENIE. He's surely thinking of it, my lord. Once he gets his mind on anything . . . !

HANS. Yes, he will think of it till the day when he sees Bertha. For you shall certainly come to our wedding, both of you. You are invited. The condition Bertha made to our marriage was that I should come back alive after spending a month in the forest. And if I do come back, it will be thanks to you, my friends. And so, you shall see your Violante, fisherman, with her little red mouth and her pink ears and her little straight nose, you shall see what effect she makes next to my great dark angel! And now, fetch me my poached trout, Eugenie, or it will be overdone.

(*The door opens slowly.* ONDINE *appears on the threshold. She stands there motionless for a moment.*)

AUGUSTE. Ondine!

ONDINE. How beautiful he is!

AUGUSTE. What did she say?

ONDINE. I said, how beautiful he is!

AUGUSTE. It is our daughter, my lord. She has no manners.

ONDINE. It's thrilling to know that men are so beautiful. My heart is racing.

AUGUSTE. Will you keep still?

ONDINE. I'm trembling from head to foot.

AUGUSTE. She's only sixteen, my lord.

ONDINE. I knew there must be some reason for being a girl. The reason is that men are so beautiful.

AUGUSTE. You are embarrassing our guest, Ondine.

ONDINE. I'm not embarrassing him. He likes me. What's your name?

AUGUSTE. That's not the way to speak to a knight, my child.

ONDINE (*Coming closer*). Look at his ear, Father. It's a perfect little shell. Do you expect me to treat it like a stranger? To whom do you belong, little shell? What is his name?

HANS. His name is Hans.

ONDINE. I should have guessed it. When people are happy and they open their mouths, they say Hans.

HANS. Hans von Wittenstein.

ONDINE. When there is sun in the morning, and the cloud of sadness lifts from your soul, when you sigh, you say Hans.

HANS. Hans von Wittenstein zu Wittenstein.

ONDINE. How lovely when a name makes its own echo! Why have you come, Hans? To take me away?

AUGUSTE. That will do, Ondine. Go to your room now.

ONDINE. Very well, take me. Take me with you.

(EUGENIE *comes in with the trout on a platter.*)

EUGENIE. Here is your trout, my lord.

ONDINE. His trout!

HANS. It looks magnificent.

ONDINE. You dared to poach a trout, Mother?

EUGENIE. Be quiet. In any case, it's done.

ONDINE. Oh, my poor darling trout! You who loved the cold water! What have they done to you?

AUGUSTE. You're not going to make a scene before our guest, Ondine?

ONDINE. They caught you—and they quenched your life in boiling water!

HANS. It was I, my girl, who asked them to.

ONDINE. You? I should have known. When one looks closely at your face, it all becomes clear. You're not very bright, are you? No. You are stupid.

EUGENIE. She doesn't know what she's saying, my lord.

ONDINE. That's chivalry! That's cour-

age! You run about looking for giants who don't exist, and when you come upon a little joyous creature springing in the clear water, you boil it alive.

HANS. And I eat it. And I find it delicious.

ONDINE. You shall see how delicious it is! (*She snatches up the dish and throws it out of the window.*) Now eat it! (*She runs to the door.*)

AUGUSTE. Ondine!

EUGENIE. Where are you going, child?

ONDINE. There is someone out there who knows about men. So far I have refused to listen to him. Now that's over. I shall listen.

AUGUSTE. Ondine!

ONDINE. In a moment, I shall know. I shall know what they are, what they do, what they become. And so much the worse for you!

AUGUSTE. You're not going out. (*She springs aside.*)

ONDINE. I already know that they lie, that their beauty is ugliness, that their courage is cowardice. And I already know that I hate them.

HANS. And they already know that they love you.

ONDINE (*Stops at the door, without turning*). What did he say?

HANS. Nothing.

ONDINE. Say it once more, just to see.

HANS. They already know that they love you.

ONDINE. I hate them! (*She runs out into the darkness.*)

HANS. My compliments. You've brought her up well.

AUGUSTE. God knows I scold her often enough.

HANS. You should beat her.

EUGENIE. Beat her? Try and catch her.

HANS. You should send her to bed without supper.

AUGUSTE. What good would that do? She's never hungry.

HANS. I'm starved.

AUGUSTE. That was the last of the trout, my lord. But we have smoked a ham. Eugenie will go down and cut you some slices.

HANS. Then she permits you to kill her poor darling pigs?

AUGUSTE. She has no interest in pigs.

HANS. That's a mercy.

(EUGENIE *goes out for the ham.*)

AUGUSTE. You are annoyed with the girl, my lord.

HANS. I'm annoyed because I'm vain just as she said. When she said I was handsome, though I know I'm not handsome, I was pleased. And when she said I was a coward, though I know I'm no coward, I was hurt. I'm annoyed with myself.

AUGUSTE. You're very kind to take it so well.

HANS. Oh, I don't take it well at all. I'm furious.

(EUGENIE *comes in.*)

EUGENIE. Where is the ham, Auguste? I can't find it.

AUGUSTE. The ham? Why, the ham is hanging in the cellar. Excuse me, my lord, I'll go and get it. (*He goes out with* EUGENIE. HANS *turns to the fire and warms his hands.* ONDINE *comes in noiselessly and stands just behind him. He doesn't hear her till she speaks.*)

ONDINE. My name is Ondine.

HANS (*Without turning*). It's a pretty name.

ONDINE. Hans and Ondine. There are no more beautiful names in the world, are there?

HANS. Yes. Ondine and Hans.

ONDINE. Oh no. Hans first. He is the man. He commands. Ondine is the girl. She is always one step behind. She keeps quiet.

HANS. She keeps quiet? Now how the devil does she manage that?

ONDINE. Hans is always one step ahead. In the processions—before the king—before all the world, he goes first. He is the first to age. He is the first to die. It's terrible! But Ondine follows at once. She kills herself.

HANS. What are you talking about?

ONDINE. There is the little moment of agony to live through. The moment that comes after the death of Hans. But it is short.

HANS. At your age, luckily, it doesn't mean much to talk about death.

ONDINE. At my age? Is that what you think? Very well, try—(*She pulls his dagger from its sheath.*) Here, kill yourself. You'll see if I am not dead the next moment.

HANS (*Takes the dagger from her hand*). I never felt less like killing myself.

ONDINE. Say you don't love me. You'll see if I don't die.

HANS. Fifteen minutes ago, you didn't even know I existed. And now you want to kill yourself on my account. I thought we had quarreled on account of the trout.

ONDINE. Oh, I can't be bothered with the trout. They're not very clever, the trout. If they don't like to be caught, all they have to do is to keep away from men. It's different with me. I want to be caught.

HANS. In spite of your mysterious friend outside?

ONDINE. I learned nothing from him that I didn't already know.

HANS. Naturally not. You asked the questions. You gave the answers.

ONDINE. Don't joke. He's very near. And he's very dangerous.

HANS. Who?

ONDINE. The Old One.

HANS. The Old One?

ONDINE. The King of the Sea. I'm afraid, Hans.

HANS (*Smiles*). You're afraid of what?

ONDINE. I'm afraid you will deceive me. That's what he said. He also said you were not handsome. But you are!

HANS. Do you know that you're beautiful?

ONDINE. No, I don't know it yet. I would prefer to be beautiful. But I can be beautiful only if I love you.

HANS. You're a little liar. You were just as beautiful a moment ago when you hated me. Is that all he told you?

ONDINE. He said that if ever I kissed you, I would be lost. That was silly of him. I hadn't even thought of it till then.

HANS. And now you are thinking of it?

ONDINE. Very much.

HANS. Well, there is no harm in thinking.

ONDINE. Oh no. It's good to think about it. Of course, in the end I shall do it. But first we shall wait a long time, as long as possible. We shall wait an hour. Then in after years we shall have this hour always to remember. The hour before you kissed me.

HANS. My little Ondine—

ONDINE. The hour before you said you loved me. Hans, I can't wait an hour. There isn't time. Tell me now.

HANS. You think that's something one says—just like that?

ONDINE. No? Well, then speak, command. What must I do? What is the appropriate posture? Do I sit in your lap, is that it?

HANS. In my lap in full armor?

ONDINE. Oh. Take it off quickly.

HANS. Do you know what you're saying? It takes me fifteen minutes to unbolt the shoulder-plates alone.

ONDINE. I have a way of removing armor. (*The armor falls to the floor.*)

HANS. Well!

ONDINE. Sit down. (*He sits. She springs into his lap.*)

HANS. You're mad, Ondine!

ONDINE. Yes. That's what he said.

HANS. And my arms—do you think they open to the first comer?

ONDINE. I have a way of opening arms —(HANS *opens his arms, with an expression of surprise.*) And of closing them. (*He closes them. A woman's voice is heard outside the window.*)

THE VOICE. Ondine!

ONDINE (*Turns furiously to the window*). No! Go away. Nobody called you.

THE VOICE. Ondine! Be careful!

ONDINE. Do I meddle in your affairs? Did you consult me about your husband?

THE VOICE. Ondine!

ONDINE. A fine handsome husband you found yourself, wasn't it? A seal with nostrils like rabbit holes and no nose. He gave you a string of pearls and you were his. And not even matched pearls.

HANS. To whom are you speaking, Ondine?

ONDINE. Oh, one of the neighbors.

HANS. But I saw no other house in the forest. Do you have neighbors?

ONDINE. Thousands. And all jealous.

A SECOND VOICE. Ondine! Be careful!

ONDINE. Oh, you're a fine one to speak! You were careful, weren't you? A narwhal dazzled you with his jet of water, and you gave yourself to him without a word.

THE SECOND VOICE. Ondine!

HANS. Their voices are charming.

ONDINE. My name is charming, not their voices. Kiss me, Hans, Kiss me.

A MAN'S VOICE. Ondine!

ONDINE. It's too late, Old One. Let me alone.

HANS. Is that the friend?

ONDINE. I'm sitting in his lap. He loves me.

THE MAN'S VOICE. Ondine!

ONDINE. It's too late, I say. It's finished. I'm already his mistress. Yes, his mistress. You don't understand? That's another word they have for a wife.

(*There is a noise at the kitchen door.*)

HANS (*Pushing* ONDINE *gently from his lap*). That's your father, Ondine.

ONDINE. Oh. I didn't think I had taught you that.

HANS. What?

ONDINE. My way of opening arms.

(AUGUSTE *and* EUGENIE *come in.*)

EUGENIE. Your supper is almost ready, my lord.

AUGUSTE. I can't imagine who put the ham in the attic.

ONDINE. I did. So I could be alone with Hans.

AUGUSTE. Ondine! Have you no shame?

ONDINE. I've not wasted my time. He's going to marry me.

AUGUSTE. You might help your mother with the table instead of talking nonsense.

ONDINE. You're right. Give me the silver, Mother. From now on, it's I who will serve Hans.

AUGUSTE. I brought up a bottle of wine, my lord. If you permit, we shall drink a glass with you. The glasses, Ondine.

ONDINE. You will have to teach me everything, my lord Hans. From morning to night, I shall be your handmaid. In the morning, I shall wake you. . . .

HANS. You won't find that easy. I sleep very soundly.

ONDINE (*Sits down next to him and looks at him closely*). Tell me, what does one do to awaken you?

(EUGENIE *comes out with a platter.*)

EUGENIE. The glasses, Ondine.

ONDINE. Oh Mother, you set the table. Hans is teaching me how to awaken him. Let's see, Hans. Make believe you're asleep.

HANS. With this wonderful odor of cooking? Out of the question.

ONDINE. Wake up, little Hans. It's dawn. Take this kiss in your darkness and this in your day . . .

HANS (*Accepting a slice of ham*). Thank you.

AUGUSTE. Pay no attention to the child,

my lord. She doesn't know what she's saying.

ONDINE. I love you.

EUGENIE. She's young. She becomes attached. It's nothing.

ONDINE. I love you, Hans.

HANS (*Eating*). This is what I call ham!

AUGUSTE. It's smoked with juniper.

HANS. Marvelous.

ONDINE. It was a mistake to awaken you, Hans. We should never awaken the man we love. In his sleep, he's ours completely. But the moment he opens his eyes, he escapes. Sleep again, little Hans—

HANS (*Accepting another slice*). Yes, thank you. Simply wonderful.

ONDINE. You don't want to be loved, you want to be stuffed.

HANS. Everything in its place, my dear.

EUGENIE. Ah, you'd make a fine wife, you would!

ONDINE. I?

AUGUSTE. Silence, Ondine. I want to say a word. (*He lifts his glass.*)

ONDINE. I shall certainly make a fine wife. You think you're a wife because you know how to cook a ham? That's not being a wife.

HANS. No? What else is it?

ONDINE. It's to be everything your husband is and everything he loves. It's to be the humblest part of him and the noblest. I shall be the shoes of your feet, my husband. I shall be the breath of your lungs. I shall be the hilt of your sword and the pommel of your saddle. I shall be your tears, your laughter and your dreams. What you are eating there, it's I.

HANS. It's seasoned to perfection.

ONDINE. Eat me, Hans. Eat me all.

(AUGUSTE *clears his throat.*)

EUGENIE. Your father wishes to speak, Ondine. Quiet.

AUGUSTE (*Lifting his glass again*). Quiet! My lord, since you are doing us the honor of spending the night under our humble roof—

ONDINE. A hundred nights. A thousand nights—

AUGUSTE. Permit me to drink to the lady of your heart—

ONDINE. How nice of you, Father!

AUGUSTE. She who is even now trembling for your safety—

ONDINE. She's not trembling now. He's safe enough.

AUGUSTE. She whom you rightly call the most beautiful of women, although for my part, I am a little partial to Violante on account of—

EUGENIE. Yes, yes, we know. Go on.

AUGUSTE. I drink, then, to the most beautiful and noblest of women, to your dark angel, to your betrothed, the Princess Bertha.

ONDINE (*Rising to her feet*). What name did you say?

AUGUSTE. The name the knight told me.

ONDINE. Since when am I called Bertha?

EUGENIE. We were not speaking of you, dear.

AUGUSTE. The knight is going to marry the Princess Bertha, Ondine, as soon as he returns to court. Isn't that so, my lord?

ONDINE. It's not so at all!

HANS. My little Ondine—

ONDINE. Ah, he's emerging from the ham at last, that one. Well, speak, since your mouth is no longer full—is there a Bertha? Yes or no?

HANS. Let me explain—

ONDINE. Is there a Bertha? Yes or no?

HANS. Yes. There is a Bertha. No. There was a Bertha.

ONDINE. So it's true, what he told me about men! They're all deceivers. They draw you to them with a thousand tricks, they seat you in their laps, they pass their hands all over your body and kiss you till you can't breathe—and all the time they are thinking of a dark angel called Bertha!

HANS. I did nothing like that to you, Ondine!

ONDINE. You did. Don't you dare deny it. And you hurt me, too. (*She bites her arm.*) Look at that, Father. See how he bit me? Let him deny it, if he dares!

HANS. You don't believe this nonsense, I hope?

ONDINE. I shall be the humblest part of you and the noblest, he said. I am your bare feet. I am the wine you drink. I am the bread you eat. Those were his words, Mother! And the things one has to do for him! One has to spend the whole morning waking him up. One has to kill oneself the moment he dies. Yes!

And all the time, in their secret hearts, they are nursing the thought of a dark angel called Bertha!

HANS. Ondine, on my word—

ONDINE. I despise you! I detest you!

HANS. Nevertheless, you might listen to me—

ONDINE. I can see her from here, the dark angel, with her little shadowy mustache and her plucked eyebrows.

HANS. Now, Ondine, really . . . !

ONDINE. Don't come near me! Or I'll throw myself into the lake. (*She opens the door. It is raining heavily.*) So her name is Bertha!

HANS. I think there is no longer any Bertha, Ondine.

ONDINE. Leave this house at once, or I shall never enter it again! (*She turns suddenly.*) What did you say?

HANS. I said, I think there is no longer any Bertha, Ondine.

ONDINE. You lie! Farewell. (*She runs out into the rain.*)

HANS. Ondine! (*He runs to the door.*)

AUGUSTE. My lord, my lord—you'll get drenched! (*To* EUGENIE.) There's a pretty kettle of fish.

EUGENIE. Yes, there's a pretty kettle of fish.

AUGUSTE. I might as well tell him everything now.

EUGENIE. Yes, you might as well tell him everything now. (HANS *turns.*)

HANS. She's not your daughter, is she?

EUGENIE. No, my lord.

AUGUSTE. We had a daughter. She was stolen from the cradle.

HANS. Who left Ondine with you?

AUGUSTE. We found her at the edge of the lake the day our daughter disappeared.

HANS. These things happen only in fairy tales.

AUGUSTE. Yes, my lord. But it happened to us.

HANS. Then it is you who must be asked for her hand?

AUGUSTE. She calls us her parents, my lord.

HANS. Then, my friends, I have the honor of asking you for the hand of your daughter.

AUGUSTE. My lord, are you in your right mind?

HANS. Do you think that little wine of yours would turn my head?

AUGUSTE. The wine? Oh, never. It's a little Moselle, very modest, very reliable.

HANS. I assure you, I have never been more sober in my life. I ask you for the hand of Ondine with nothing in mind but the hand of Ondine. I want to hold this hand in mine. I want it to lead me to church, to war, and when the time comes, to death.

AUGUSTE. But, my lord, you already have a hand for that. This would be a hand too many.

HANS. A hand? Whose hand?

AUGUSTE. The lady Bertha.

HANS. Bertha? Do you know Bertha? I know her. I know her, that is, now that I know Ondine—

AUGUSTE. But is not a knight, above all, required to be loyal?

HANS. To his quest, yes. And I shall be loyal, above all, to my quest. Because, you know, up to now, we knights have been fools, all of us. We've been exploited; they take us for imbeciles. When we kill a monster, we're expected to vanish gracefully. When we find a treasure, we give it away. Well, that's finished. From now on I shall try to profit a little by my exploits. I have found a treasure and I shall keep it. Whether or not I knew it, my quest was Ondine, and I have found Ondine, and I shall marry Ondine. And nobody else in this world.

EUGENIE. You are making a mistake, my lord.

HANS. Eugenie—there was once a knight and his quest was to find something wonderful. And one night in a forest on the edge of a lake, he found a girl called Ondine. In her hands, tin turned to gold and water to jewels. The rain did not wet her. Her eyes were full of joy and her manner was royal. And not only was she the most wonderful creature he had ever seen, but he knew also that she would bring him all the delight and tenderness and goodness he would ever know in this world. Whereupon he bowed to her and went off to marry a girl called Bertha. Tell me, Eugenie, what sort of knight was this?

AUGUSTE. You don't put the question properly, my lord.

HANS. I ask you what sort of knight this would be. You don't dare to answer, but you know as well as I do. He would be a sort of idiot, would he not?

EUGENIE. But, my lord, since you have given your word to another—

HANS. He would be an idiot!

EUGENIE. Speak, Auguste.

HANS. Yes, speak. If there is any reason why I should not have Ondine, tell it to me now.

AUGUSTE. My lord, you are asking us for the hand of Ondine. It's a great honor for us—but she's not ours to give.

HANS. You must have some idea who her parents may be?

AUGUSTE. With Ondine it's not a question of parents. If we had not adopted Ondine, she would have grown up just the same. Ondine is strange. You saw her tonight in the storm. You understand, my lord, it's not that she's in the storm. She is the storm. She's a beautiful child, my lord, there's no denying it. But there is more than beauty in Ondine. There is power.

HANS. It's because she's young.

EUGENIE. It's true, she's young—

AUGUSTE. When I first married you, my poor Eugenie, you too were young. But your youth had no effect on the lake. You were beautiful. But the lake remained what it had always been, selfish and rude. And the floods were brutal and senseless as always, and the storm was a beast of prey. But since Ondine came to us, everything has changed. The water has become gentle.

HANS. It's because you're old.

AUGUSTE. It's true I'm no longer young. But a lake that counts into your net each day exactly the same twelve fish, a lake that never enters your boat, not even if it happens to have a hole in the bottom —I think you will agree that is a remarkably courteous lake.

HANS. Well, suppose it is. What do you suggest? That I apply to the lake for permission to marry?

AUGUSTE. I wouldn't joke about the lake. The lake has ears.

HANS. And what's it to me if the lake has ears? I have no designs on the lake.

AUGUSTE. We are speaking of Ondine, my lord. Ondine belongs to the lake. Ondine is the lake, my lord.

HANS. Then I shall gladly take the lake to my bosom, and with it all the water in the world. The rivers shall be my brothers, the sea my mother, and the ocean itself my father-in-law. I love the water.

AUGUSTE. Beware of the water, my lord!

HANS. But why, Auguste? Why?

AUGUSTE. That's all I know, my lord.

HANS. Give me Ondine, Auguste.

AUGUSTE. Give you Ondine! And who am I to give you Ondine? Where is she now, Ondine? Oh, I remember, naturally, having seen her once, the little Ondine. I remember her voice, her laughter, I remember she threw your trout out of the window, a twelve-inch trout, the only one I had left. But we shall never see her again, she will never again come to us except in tender little lightnings, in little storms; she will never again tell us she loves us except with the waves lapping at our feet, or the rain on our cheeks, or perhaps, suddenly one day with a great salt-water fish in my pike-weir. That wouldn't surprise me a bit.

EUGENIE. Auguste, you're tired. It's time you came to bed.

AUGUSTE. Do you remember the morning we found her, Eugenie?

EUGENIE. Permit us to retire, my lord.

AUGUSTE. There wasn't a mark on the sand, not a footprint—nothing—to show how the child got there. Only the wind and the sun and the lake staring at us fixedly with its eye—

EUGENIE. I will show you to your room.

HANS. Thank you. I shall sit here by the fire a little longer, if I may.

EUGENIE. Come, Auguste. Tomorrow we shall speak of Ondine.

AUGUSTE. If there is an Ondine. (*He shakes his head.*)

EUGENIE. Good night, my lord.

HANS. Good night. Good night.

(AUGUSTE *and* EUGENIE *go out.* HANS *sits down by the fire and closes his eyes for a moment. The wall of the hut slowly becomes transparent, and through it appear the lake and the forest. In the half-light there rises the figure of an* ONDINE, *blonde and nude.*)

THE ONDINE. Take me, handsome knight.

HANS (*Looking up with a start*). What?

THE ONDINE. Kiss me.

HANS. I beg pardon?

THE ONDINE. Take me. Kiss me.

HANS. What are you talking about?

THE ONDINE. Am I too bold, handsome knight? Do I frighten you?

HANS. Not in the least.

THE ONDINE. Would you rather I were clothed? Shall I put on a dress?

HANS. A dress? What for?

THE ONDINE. Come to me. Take me. I am yours.

(*She vanishes. Another* ONDINE *appears. She is dark and clothed.*)

THE SECOND ONDINE. Don't look at me, handsome knight.

HANS. Why not?

THE SECOND ONDINE. Don't come near me. I'm not that sort. If you touch me, I'll scream.

HANS. Don't worry.

THE SECOND ONDINE. If you touch my hair, if you touch my breasts, if you kiss my lips, I swear, I'll kill myself. I will not take off my dress!

HANS. As you please.

THE SECOND ONDINE. Don't come out, handsome knight. Don't come near me. I am not for you, handsome knight. (*She vanishes.* HANS *shrugs his shoulders. The* TWO ONDINES *appear together at opposite sides of the room.*)

FIRST ONDINE. Take me.

SECOND ONDINE. Don't touch me.

FIRST ONDINE. I am yours.

SECOND ONDINE. Keep your distance.

FIRST ONDINE. I want you.

SECOND ONDINE. You frighten me.

ONDINE (*Appears suddenly*). Oh how silly you look, both of you!

(*The* TWO ONDINES *vanish.*)

HANS (*Takes* ONDINE *in his arms*). Little Ondine! What is this nonsense? Who are those women?

ONDINE. My friends. They don't want me to love you. They say anyone can have you for the asking. But they're wrong.

HANS. They're very nice, your friends. Are those the prettiest?

ONDINE. The cleverest. Kiss me, Hans.

FIRST ONDINE (*Reappears*). Kiss me, Hans—

ONDINE. Look at that fool! Oh, how silly a woman looks when she offers herself! Go away! Don't you know when you've lost? Hans—

SECOND ONDINE (*Appears again next to the first*). Hans—

ONDINE. Go away, I say! Hans—

A THIRD ONDINE (*Appears next to the others*). Hans—

ONDINE. It's not fair! No!

HANS. Let them speak, Ondine.

ONDINE. No. It's the Song of the Three Sisters. I'm afraid.

HANS. Afraid? Of them?

ONDINE. Cover your ears, Hans.

HANS. But I love music.

THE FIRST ONDINE (*Sings*).
Hans Wittenstein zu Wittenstein,
Without you life is but a fever.
Alles was ist mein ist dein,
Love me always, leave me never.

HANS. Bravo! That's charming.

ONDINE. In what way is that charming?

HANS. It's simple. It's direct. It's charming. The song of the sirens must have been about like that.

ONDINE. It was exactly like that. They copied it. They're going to sing again. Don't listen.

THE THREE ONDINES (*Sing*).
Heed no more the west wind's urging,
Slack your sail and rest your oar.
Drift upon the current surging
Powerfully toward our shore.

HANS. The tune is not bad.

ONDINE. Don't listen, Hans.

THE THREE ONDINES (*Sing*).
Sorrow once for all forsaking,
Take our laughter for your sighs.
These are yours but for the taking,
Tender breasts and wanton thighs.

ONDINE. If you think it's pleasant to hear others singing the things one feels and can't express. . . .

THE THREE ONDINES (*Sing*).
Come and take your fill of pleasure,
Taste delight and drink it deep.
We shall give you beyond measure
Joy and rest and love and sleep.

HANS. That's wonderful! Sing it again! Sing it again!

ONDINE. Don't you understand? They don't mean a word of it. They're just trying to take you away from me.

THE FIRST ONDINE. You've lost, Ondine, you've lost!

HANS. What have you lost?

ONDINE. Your song means nothing to him!

FIRST ONDINE. He holds you in his arms, Ondine, but he looks at me!

SECOND ONDINE. He speaks your name, Ondine, but he thinks of me!

THIRD ONDINE. He kisses your lips, Ondine, but he smiles at me!

THE THREE ONDINES. He deceives you! He deceives you! He deceives you!

HANS. What are they talking about?

ONDINE. He may look at you and smile at you and think of you as much as he pleases. He loves me. And I shall marry him.

THE FIRST ONDINE. Then you agree? You make the pact?

HANS. What pact?

ONDINE. Yes, I agree. I make the pact.

(*The words are taken up mysteriously. They echo and re-echo from every quarter.*)

THE FIRST ONDINE. I am to tell them?

ONDINE. Yes. Tell them. Tell them all. Those who sit and those who swim, those who float in the sunlight and those who crawl in darkness on the ocean floor.

HANS. What the devil are you saying?

ONDINE. Tell them I said yes. (*The word "yes" is taken up by a thousand whispering voices.*)

THE FIRST ONDINE. And the Old One? Shall we tell him also?

ONDINE. Tell him I hate him! Tell him he lies!

THE FIRST ONDINE. Yes?

ONDINE. Yes! Yes! Yes!

(*Again the sound is taken up. The mysterious voices whisper through the darkness until the air is filled with echoes. There is a climax of sound, then silence.* THE ONDINES *vanish. The walls of the hut regain their solidity.*)

HANS. What a fuss! What a racket!

ONDINE. Naturally. It's the family. (HANS *sits in the armchair.* ONDINE *sits at his feet*). You're caught, my little Hans?

HANS. Body and soul.

ONDINE. You don't wish to struggle a little more? Just a little more?

HANS. I'm too happy to struggle.

ONDINE. So it takes twenty minutes to catch a man. It takes longer to catch a bass.

HANS. Don't flatter yourself. It took thirty years to catch me. All my life. Ever since I was a child, I've felt something drawing me toward this forest and this lake. It was you?

ONDINE. Yes. And now after thirty years, would it be too much if you told me at last that you love me?

HANS. I love you.

ONDINE. You say it easily. You've said it before.

HANS. I've said something like it that meant something else.

ONDINE. You've said it often?

HANS. I've said it to every woman I didn't love. And now at last I know what it means.

ONDINE. Why didn't you love them? Were they ugly?

HANS. No. They were beautiful. But they no longer exist.

ONDINE. Oh, Hans, I meant to give you everything in the world, and I begin by taking everything away. Some day you will hate me for it.

HANS. Never, Ondine.

ONDINE. Shall I ever see them, these women you don't love?

HANS. Of course.

ONDINE. Where?

HANS. Everywhere. In their castles. In their gardens. At the court.

ONDINE. At the court? I?

HANS. Of course. We leave in the morning.

ONDINE. Oh, Hans, am I to leave my lake so soon?

HANS. I want to show the world the most perfect thing it possesses. Did you know you were the most perfect thing the world possessed?

ONDINE. I suspected it. But will the world have eyes to see it?

HANS. When the world sees you, it will know. It's really very nice, Ondine, the world.

ONDINE. Tell me, Hans. In this world of yours, do lovers live together always?

HANS. Together? Of course.

ONDINE. No. You don't understand. When a man and a woman love each other are they ever separate?

HANS. Separate? Of course.

ONDINE. No, you still don't understand. Take the dogfish, for instance. Not that I'm especially fond of dogfish, mind you. But, once the dogfish couples with its mate, he never leaves her, never as long as he lives, did you know that? Through storm and calm they swim together, thousands and thousands of miles, side by side, two fingers apart, as if an invisible link held them together. They are no longer two. They become one.

HANS. Well?

ONDINE. Do lovers live like that in your world?

HANS. It would be a little difficult for lovers to live like that in our world, Ondine. In our world, each has his own life, his own room, his own friends—

ONDINE. What a horrible word that is, each.

HANS. Each has his work—his play—

ONDINE. But the dogfish too have their work and their play. They have to hunt, you know, in order to live. And sometimes they come upon a school of herrings which scatter before them in a thousand flashes, and they have a thousand reasons to lose each other, to swerve one to the right, the other to the left. But they never do. As long as they live, not even a sardine can come between them.

HANS. In our world, Ondine, a whale can come between a husband and wife twenty times a day, no matter how much they love each other.

ONDINE. I was afraid of that.

HANS. The man looks to his affairs; the woman to hers. They swim in different currents.

ONDINE. But the dogfish have to swim through different currents also. There are cold currents and warm currents. And sometimes the one likes the cold and the other the warm. And sometimes they swim into currents so powerful that they can divide a fleet, and yet they cannot divide these fish by the breadth of a nail.

HANS. That merely proves that men and fish are not the same.

ONDINE. And you and I, we are the same?

HANS. Oh yes, Ondine.

ONDINE. And you swear that you will never leave me, not even for a moment?

HANS. Yes, Ondine.

ONDINE. Because now that I love you, two steps away from you my loneliness begins.

HANS. I will never leave you, Ondine.

ONDINE. Hans, listen to me seriously. I know someone who can join us forever, someone very powerful. And if I ask him, he will solder us together with a band of flesh so that nothing but death can separate us. Would you like me to call him?

HANS. No, Ondine.

ONDINE. But, Hans, the more I think of it, the more I see there is no other way to keep lovers together in your world.

HANS. And your dogfish? Do they need to be soldered like that?

ONDINE. It's true. But they don't live among men. Let me call him. You'll see. It's a very practical arrangement.

HANS. No. Let's try this way first. Later, we'll see.

ONDINE. I know what you're thinking. Of course, she's right, you're thinking, the little Ondine, and naturally I shall be with her always, but once in a while, for just a little moment perhaps I shall go and take a turn by myself, I shall go and visit my friend.

HANS. Or my horse.

ONDINE. Or your horse. When this angel falls asleep, you're thinking, this angel whom I shall never leave not even for a moment, then, at last, I shall have a chance to go and spend a good half hour with my horse.

HANS. As a matter of fact, I had better go and have a look at him now, don't you think? We're leaving at dawn, you know, and I ought to see if he's bedded properly. Besides I always tell him everything.

ONDINE. Ah yes. Well, tonight you shall tell him nothing.

HANS. But why, Ondine?

ONDINE. Because tonight you're going to sleep, my little Hans. (*And with a gesture, she throws sleep into his eyes.*) Good night, my love. (*He falls asleep.*)

THE FIRST ONDINE (*Her voice seems very far away*). Good-bye, Ondine.

ONDINE. Look after my lake!

THE SECOND ONDINE. Good-bye, Ondine.

ONDINE. Take care of my stream!

THE KING OF THE SEA. Ondine!

ONDINE. Farewell, Old One.

THE KING OF THE SEA. Don't leave us, Ondine.

ONDINE. I have left you, Old One.

THE KING OF THE SEA. The world of men is not your world, Ondine. It will bring you sorrow.

ONDINE. It will bring me joy.

THE KING OF THE SEA. The man will deceive you. He will abandon you.

ONDINE. Never! Never!

THE KING OF THE SEA. And when he deceives you? When he abandons you? You will remember our pact?

ONDINE. I shall remember our pact.

THE KING OF THE SEA (*His voice recedes*). Remember, Ondine.

THE ONDINES (*Their voices are like the murmur of water*). Remember, Ondine.

HANS (*Turning in his sleep*). Remember, Ondine—

ONDINE. Oh dear, from this time on, how much I shall have to remember!

Curtain

🌿 Act II

The hall of honor of the king's palace. It is a large vaulted loggia of Gothic design. The roof is supported by columns. The upstage side opens on the palace gardens, in which may be seen three jets of water playing in marble basins in the sunshine. To the left is a dais with the king's throne, and above the throne a mural depicting one of the labors of Hercules. There are arched doorways.

THE LORD CHAMBERLAIN *and* THE SUPERINTENDENT OF THE ROYAL THEATRES *are engaged in a conference. To one side stand respectfully* THE TRAINER OF THE SEALS *and* THE ILLUSIONIST.

THE CHAMBERLAIN. My dear Superintendent, this is a matter that will require all your skill, and all your inventiveness. The Knight of Wittenstein has at last been persuaded to present his bride at court. His Majesty has asked me to provide an amusing interlude with which to grace the occasion. But the reception is to take place immediately.

THE SUPERINTENDENT. The time is short, my Lord Chamberlain.

THE CHAMBERLAIN. It couldn't be shorter. Well? As Superintendent of the Royal Theatres, what do you propose?

THE SUPERINTENDENT. *Salammbo.*

(*At this word* MATHO *and* SALAMMBO *appear and begin at once to sing.*)

THE CHAMBERLAIN (*Striking the floor with his staff for silence*). But you played *Salammbo* only last night for the Margrave's birthday. Besides, *Salammbo* is sad.

THE SUPERINTENDENT. It's sad. But it's ready. (*He signs to his actors, who burst at once into their duet.*)

THE CHAMBERLAIN (*Stops them*

again). I don't see why it is any more ready than *Orpheus,* which has only one character. Or the *Interlude of Adam and Eve,* which requires no costumes.

THE SUPERINTENDENT. Excellency, my success in the theatre is based solely on the discovery that each particular stage has its likes and dislikes which it is useless to combat.

THE CHAMBERLAIN. Time presses, my good man.

THE SUPERINTENDENT. Each theatre, Excellency, is built for one play and one play only. The whole secret of management is to discover what play that is. It's not easy, especially when the play is not yet written. And so, a thousand disasters —until that happy day when the play for which it was intended comes to its proper theatre and gives it its life, its soul, and, if I may say so, its sex.

THE CHAMBERLAIN. Superintendent—

THE SUPERINTENDENT. For years I managed a theatre which bumbled along miserably with the classics until suddenly one night it found its joy in a bawdy farce with sailors. It was a female theatre. I knew another which tolerated only *Othello.* It was male. Last year I was forced to close the Royal Ballet. Impossible to determine its sex.

THE CHAMBERLAIN. And you believe the Royal Auditorium—

THE SUPERINTENDENT. Exists only for *Salammbo,* yes, your Excellency. At the word *Salammbo,* the tightness of throat with which the royal chorus is normally afflicted suddenly relaxes, and the hall resounds with voices full of resonance and joy. (MATHO *and* SALAMMBO *begin singing, at first softly, crescendo to the end of the speech.*) I tell you, my Lord Chamberlain, sometimes when I play a German opera, I notice one of my singers, brimming with happiness, making magnificent gestures, sending out full-throated tones which fill the audience with such joy and comfort that it breaks into spontaneous applause—Why? Because among his fellow-actors, who are merely grinding out their parts by rote, this actor in the general confusion is blissfully singing his role in *Salammbo.*

THE CHAMBERLAIN (*Silencing the singers*). No. It would hardly do to entertain a newly married couple with a tragedy of unhappy love. *Salammbo* is out of the question. (THE SUPERINTENDENT *waves his singers away. They go reluctantly.* THE CHAMBERLAIN *turns to* THE TRAINER OF SEALS.) Who are you?

THE TRAINER. I am the Trainer of Seals, Your Excellency.

THE CHAMBERLAIN. What do they do, your seals?

THE TRAINER. They don't sing *Salammbo.*

THE CHAMBERLAIN. That's a pity. A chorus of seals singing *Salammbo* would constitute a very appropriate entertainment. Besides, I am told that your head seal has a beard that makes him look like his Majesty's father-in-law. Is that true?

THE TRAINER. I could shave him, Excellency.

THE CHAMBERLAIN. By a regrettable coincidence, his Majesty's father-in-law shaved his beard only yesterday. We had best avoid even the shadow of a scandal. And who are you?

THE ILLUSIONIST. I am an illusionist, Excellency.

THE CHAMBERLAIN. Where is your apparatus?

THE ILLUSIONIST. I am an illusionist without apparatus.

THE CHAMBERLAIN. Now what do you take us for? You don't produce claps of thunder and lightning without apparatus.

THE ILLUSIONIST. Yes.

(*There is a clap of thunder and lightning.*)

THE CHAMBERLAIN (*Cowering with fear*). Nonsense. You can't produce sudden clouds of smoke which leave the stage covered with flowers without apparatus?

(*There is a sudden cloud of smoke, and flowers fall from the ceiling.*)

THE ILLUSIONIST. Yes.

THE CHAMBERLAIN. What stubbornness! You don't suddenly produce before the eyes of the Lord Chamberlain—

BERTRAM (*Comes in*). Your Excellency—

THE CHAMBERLAIN. Just a moment.— Venus completely nude—without apparatus.

THE ILLUSIONIST. Yes.

BERTRAM. Excellency—(*A nude* VENUS *appears.* BERTRAM *bows.*) Madame. (VENUS *disappears.*)

THE CHAMBERLAIN. I've always wondered who these Venuses are that magicians produce out of thin air? Relatives?

THE ILLUSIONIST. Or Venus herself. It depends on the magician.

BERTRAM. Excellency, his Majesty is unavoidably detained by the African envoy. The reception is postponed for an hour.

THE CHAMBERLAIN. Excellent. That gives us time to think of something. (*To* the SUPERINTENDENT.) Have you thought of something?

THE SUPERINTENDENT. Yes, Excellency.

THE CHAMBERLAIN. Ah. Splendid. What?

THE SUPERINTENDENT. *Salammbo.*

(*The two singers appear, only to be waved off peremptorily by* THE CHAMBERLAIN.)

THE CHAMBERLAIN (*To* THE ILLUSIONIST). And how do you propose to amuse his Majesty?

THE ILLUSIONIST. If Your Excellency permits, I shall do what the occasion inspires.

THE CHAMBERLAIN. That's asking a great deal. After all, we have never seen your work.

THE ILLUSIONIST. I shall be happy, while we are waiting, to offer a little private entertainment by way of demonstration.

THE CHAMBERLAIN. Ah. Very good.

THE ILLUSIONIST. What would Your Excellency like to see?

THE CHAMBERLAIN. I should very much like to see—

THE ILLUSIONIST. Splendid. I shall bring them together at once.

THE CHAMBERLAIN. You are also a mind-reader?

THE ILLUSIONIST. Yes. Excellency, I can, if you wish, bring together before your eyes a man and a woman who have been carefully avoiding each other for the past three months.

THE CHAMBERLAIN. Here? Now?

THE ILLUSIONIST. Here and now. If you will be so good as to conceal yourselves—

THE CHAMBERLAIN. But it's impossible, my dear fellow. Consider that the gentleman in question is at this very moment in the royal apartments supervising the last details of his wife's costume. A tornado could not draw him from her. The injured lady, on the other hand, is locked up in her room. She has sworn she will under no circumstances appear. These two cannot possibly meet.

THE ILLUSIONIST. Yes. But suppose that a dog were to steal the bride's glove and run out into the garden with it? And suppose that the lady's pet bullfinch should fly out of its cage and come to perch on the edge of the fountain?

THE CHAMBERLAIN. That will get you nowhere. It is the halberdier's high duty to divert all dogs from the royal apartments. And as for the bird—the king has just loosed a falcon in the garden. It is hovering over the bullfinch's cage.

THE ILLUSIONIST. Yes. But suppose that the halberdier slips on a banana peel? And suppose a gazelle distracts the falcon's attention?

THE CHAMBERLAIN. Bananas and gazelles are unknown in these parts.

THE ILLUSIONIST. Yes. But the African envoy peeled a banana while waiting for his morning audience. And among the gifts sent by his government, there was a gazelle which is at this moment feeding in the garden.

THE CHAMBERLAIN. Quite resourceful, you magicians.

THE ILLUSIONIST. Yes. Take your places. In a moment you shall see the Princess Bertha and the Knight of Wittenstein come together in this hall.

(VIOLANTE *and* ANGELIQUE *come in from the garden. They hear the last words.*)

VIOLANTE. Really?

ANGELIQUE. Really?

THE CHAMBERLAIN (*Beckoning to the ladies to join him behind a column*). Sh! Come here.

BERTRAM. But, Excellency, why are we doing this evil thing?

THE CHAMBERLAIN. Sooner or later it would have to happen. That's life.

BERTRAM. Then why not let life take its course?

THE CHAMBERLAIN. My dear Bertram, you are young and you are a poet. When you have reached my age, you will understand that life is a very poorly constructed play. As a rule, the curtain goes up in the wrong places, the climaxes don't come off, the denouement is interminably postponed, so that those who should die at once of a broken heart die instead of a kidney ailment at an advanced age. If

this excellent illusionist can make us see a life unfold for once with the concision and logic that a good play requires—(*To* THE ILLUSIONIST.) Can you?

THE ILLUSIONIST. Perhaps.

THE CHAMBERLAIN. Just one little scene, then. Just one little scene.

BERTRAM. But, Excellency, the poor girl—

THE CHAMBERLAIN. The girl has caused a knight to be false to his word. She deserves to suffer.

BERTRAM. But why should we . . . ?

THE CHAMBERLAIN. Don't excite yourself, my boy. Six months from now, in the normal course of events, Hans and Bertha would meet. Six months after that, they would kiss. A year after that, beyond a shadow of a doubt, they would—it's inevitable. And if we spare ourselves these delays, and bring their hands together at once; and, ten minutes later, their lips; and five minutes after that, whatever else is necessary—will we be changing their story, really, in any way? We shall just be giving it a little pace, a little tempo— Magician!—What's that noise?

THE TRAINER. The halberdier. He slipped on a banana peel.

THE CHAMBERLAIN. Splendid.

BERTRAM. Excellency, I beg of you, let's carry this no further. It's a mischievous thing. Left to themselves, perhaps these two would never meet again. (*There is a scream from the garden.*) What's that scream?

THE SUPERINTENDENT. The gazelle. The falcon struck it.

THE CHAMBERLAIN. Perfect. You think you can bring off the whole thing at this pace, Magician?

THE ILLUSIONIST. Perhaps.

(*The bird appears, perched on the fountain.*)

THE SUPERINTENDENT. The bird!

THE TRAINER (*Looking out into the garden*). The dog!

VIOLANTE. The knight!

(HANS *is seen running after the dog in the garden.*)

THE SUPERINTENDENT. The lady!

(BERTHA *runs in and catches the bird.*)

HANS. Ah! There you are, you rascal! At last I've caught you!

BERTHA. Ah! There you are, you rascal! At last I've found you!

(*Each goes off without seeing the other. The spectators poke their heads out of their hiding places. They hiss.*)

BERTRAM. (*Sighs with relief*). Thank heaven!

THE CHAMBERLAIN. What's this, Magician? Are you making fun of us?

THE ILLUSIONIST. Sorry, sir. A fault in direction.

THE CHAMBERLAIN. Are they going to meet or are they not?

THE ILLUSIONIST. They are going to meet. And this time there will be no mistake about it. I'll knock their heads together. (*The spectators hide once more.*) Now!

(*The dog runs across the garden, glove in mouth, with* HANS *in pursuit. The bird flies in and settles on the fountain.* BERTHA *runs in from the right and catches it.*)

BERTHA. Again! What a bad bird you are!

HANS. Again! What an obstinate beast! (*He enters the room with the glove in his hand, just as* BERTHA *runs up with the bird. They collide.* HANS *takes her hands to keep her from falling. They recognize each other.*) Oh! I beg your pardon, Bertha.

BERTHA. Oh! I'm sorry, Hans.

HANS. Did I hurt you?

BERTHA. Not a bit.

HANS. I'm a clumsy brute, Bertha.

BERTHA. Yes. You are. (*There is a moment of embarrassed silence. Then each turns and walks off slowly.* BERTHA *stops.*) Pleasant honeymoon?

HANS. Marvelous.

BERTHA. A blonde, I believe?

HANS. Blonde, like the sun.

BERTHA. Sunlit nights! I prefer the darkness.

HANS. Each to his taste.

BERTHA. It was dark that night under the oak tree. My poor Hans! You must have suffered!

HANS. Bertha!

BERTHA. I didn't suffer. I loved it.

HANS. Bertha, my wife is coming in at any moment.

BERTHA. I was happy that night in your arms. I thought it was for always.

HANS. And so it could have been, had you not insisted on sending me into the forest on a wild-goose chase. Why didn't you keep me with you, if you wanted me?

BERTHA. One takes off a ring sometimes to show to one's friends. Even an engagement ring.

HANS. I'm sorry. The ring didn't understand.

BERTHA. No. And so it rolled, as rings do, under the nearest bed.

HANS. I beg your pardon!

BERTHA. Forgive me. I shouldn't have mentioned a bed. Among peasants, you sleep in the straw, I believe? You pick it out of your hair the morning after. Is it fun?

HANS. One day you will see.

BERTHA. No, I don't think so. Black hair and straw don't go well together. That's for blondes.

HANS. You may be right. Although in love, these details don't seem to matter. But, of course, you've never had that experience.

BERTHA. You think?

HANS. When you're in love, you don't think of yourself so much. You think of the other. You will see one day. But when it happens to you, don't let your lover go.

BERTHA. No?

HANS. Don't send him into senseless danger and loneliness and boredom.

BERTHA. One would say you had a bad time in the Black Forest.

HANS. You are haughty. But when you meet the man you love, take my advice—pocket your pride, throw your arms around his neck and tell him, before all the world, that you love him.

BERTHA (*She throws her arms around his neck*). I love you. (*She kisses him, then tries to run off. But he holds her by the hands.*)

HANS. Bertha!

BERTHA. Let me go, Hans.

HANS. What game are you playing with me now, Bertha?

BERTHA. Be careful, Hans. I have a bird in my hand.

HANS. I love another woman, Bertha.

BERTHA. The bird!

HANS. You should have done that before, Bertha.

BERTHA. Hans, don't squeeze my hand so. You're going to kill it.

HANS. Let the bird go, Bertha.

BERTHA. No. Its little heart is beating

with fear. And just now I need this little heart next to mine.

HANS. What is it you want of me, Bertha?

BERTHA. Hans—Oh! (*Opening her hand and showing the bird.*) There. You've killed it.

HANS. Oh, Bertha! (*Taking the bird.*) Forgive me, Bertha. Forgive me.

(BERTHA *looks at him a long moment. He is completely contrite.*)

BERTHA. Give it to me. I'll take the poor little thing away. (*She takes it from him.*)

HANS. Forgive me.

BERTHA. I want nothing of you now, Hans. But once, I wanted something for you, and that was my mistake. I wanted glory—for the man I loved. The man I had chosen when I was a little girl, and whom I led one night under the oak tree on which long ago I had carved his name. I thought it was a woman's glory to lead her lover not only to his table and his bed, but to whatever in the world is hardest to find and most difficult to conquer. I was wrong.

HANS. No, Bertha. No, Bertha.

BERTHA. I am dark. I thought that in the darkness of the forest this man would see my face in every shadow. I am dark, I trusted my love to the darkness. How could I have known that in those shadows he would come one night upon a head of gold?

HANS. How could anyone have known it?

BERTHA. That was my error. I have confessed it. And that's the end of it. I shall carve no more initials in the bark of trees. A man alone in a dream of glory —that's already foolish. But a woman alone in a dream of glory is completely ridiculous. So much the worse for me.

HANS. Forgive me, Bertha?

BERTHA. Farewell, Hans.

(*She goes out, right. He goes out, left. The spectators appear, crying "Bravo!"*)

THE ILLUSIONIST. There it is, Your Excellency. The scene that would have taken place, without my assistance, next winter. I have brought it about, as you see, here and now. It has happened.

BERTRAM. It is amply sufficient. We can stop here, can we not?

THE CHAMBERLAIN. No. No. No. No.

I'm dying to see the next. The next, Magician, the next!

THE ILLUSIONIST. The next scene?

VIOLANTE. The next!

ANGELIQUE. The next!

THE ILLUSIONIST. At your service, ladies. Which one?

VIOLANTE. The one in which Hans unlaces the helmet of the knight he has killed and it is the Lady Bertha . . . ?

THE ILLUSIONIST. That scene is in another play, Mademoiselle.

THE SUPERINTENDENT. The scene in which the knight in the nick of time saves Bertha from the dragon . . . ?

THE TRAINER. The scene in which the knight, while twirling a ball on his nose—

THE ILLUSIONIST. Please!

THE CHAMBERLAIN. The scene in which Bertha and Hans first speak of Ondine.

THE ILLUSIONIST. Very well, Excellency. That takes place next spring.

THE CHAMBERLAIN. So much the better. I love the spring. (*He goes behind his column. The lights dim.* BERTHA *and* HANS *come in slowly from opposite directions.*)

HANS (*Calls*). Bertha.

BERTHA (*Calls*). Hans. (*They catch sight of each other.*) I was looking for you, Hans.

HANS. I was looking for you, Bertha.

(THE CHAMBERLAIN *comes out suddenly.*)

THE CHAMBERLAIN. Magician! What does this mean? What have you done to me?

THE ILLUSIONIST. It is one of the inconveniences of my system. You have grown an eight months' beard. You see, it is now next spring.

THE CHAMBERLAIN. Ah— (*He disappears. The scene continues.*)

BERTHA. Hans, must there be this awful cloud between us? Can't we be friends?

HANS. I wish we could be, Bertha. But—

BERTHA. I know. We can't be friends without Ondine. But it's your fault, Hans. You haven't let me see her since that awful day of the king's reception. And that's eight months ago, and quite forgotten. Send her to me this evening, Hans. I am illuminating a manuscript of the *Aeneid* for the king. Ondine can draw in the initials, and I shall teach her the secret of the gold leaf.

HANS. Thanks, Bertha. But I doubt very much—

BERTHA. Ondine doesn't letter?

HANS. Ondine doesn't write.

BERTHA. How lucky she is! When you write, it takes away half the pleasure of reading. She has a charming voice. I'm sure she reads aloud beautifully?

HANS. Ondine doesn't read.

BERTHA. How I envy her! How wonderful among all these pedants to be able to give oneself up to the luxury of not reading. But she dances, I know—

HANS. Never.

BERTHA. You're joking, Hans! You don't mean to say that she neither reads, nor writes, nor dances?

HANS. Yes. And she doesn't recite. And she doesn't play the rote. Nor the harp, nor the lute. And she won't go hunting. She can't bear to see things killed.

BERTHA. But what then does she do, in heaven's name?

HANS. Oh, she swims. Occasionally.

BERTHA. That's nice. Though it's not by swimming that a girl advances her husband's interests at court. And yet, let's be just, Hans. After all, these accomplishments mean nothing. A pretty woman has the right to be ignorant of everything, provided she knows when to keep still.

HANS. It is this point precisely, Bertha, that worries me the most. Ondine does not know when to keep still. Quite the contrary. She says whatever comes into her head—and the things that come into that girl's head! Bertha, you know, the jousting season opens this week. And the thought of the phrases which will issue from Ondine as she watches these tournaments in which every step and pass-at-arms has its appropriate term—it makes me shudder.

BERTHA. She can learn.

HANS. I spent the morning trying to teach her the rudiments. Each time I give her a new term, she thanks me with a kiss. Now in the first position of the horseman alone there are thirty-three points to identify—

BERTHA. Thirty-six.

HANS. God, that's true! What am I thinking of? I tell you, I'm losing my wits, Bertha!

BERTHA. Send her to me, Hans. I'll see that she learns what she needs to know.

HANS. Thanks. But, what she needs to know above all is the special signs and prerogatives of the Wittenstein. And those are a family secret.

BERTHA. You forget, Hans. I was almost one of the Wittenstein. Ask me a question.

HANS. If you can answer this, I shall owe you a forfeit. What device does a Wittenstein bear on his shield when he enters the lists?

BERTHA. On a field azure, a squirrel passant, gules.

HANS. Does he bear this device into combat?

BERTHA. Never. At the moment he lowers his visor, his squire hands him a shield on which are emblazoned three lions rampant or, on a field sable. That is his device of war.

HANS. Bertha! You're incredible! And how does a Wittenstein approach the barrier?

BERTHA. Lance squared, charger collected, slow trot.

HANS. Ah, Bertha, what a lucky man the knight will be who marries you! (*He kisses her hand. She snatches it away. They go off in opposite directions.*)

THE CHAMBERLAIN (*No beard*). Bravo! Bravo! Bravo! And how right he is! The Princess Bertha knows everything. She does everything. She is the ideal woman, beyond a doubt. You have us on pins and needles, Magician. The third scene! Quickly!

VIOLANTE. The scene in which Bertha sees Ondine dancing in the moonlight with her fairies.

THE ILLUSIONIST. You appear to be still a little confused, Mademoiselle.

THE CHAMBERLAIN. The first quarrel of Hans and Ondine.

BERTRAM. Couldn't we let that, at least, take care of itself?

THE CHAMBERLAIN. No, no. We'd never get to see it. Magician—

BERTRAM. But Excellency! His Majesty will be here in a moment.

THE CHAMBERLAIN. By heaven, that's true. I will just have time to give this young lady the customary words of advice before the reception begins. You're not planning to do anything more till I get back, Magician?

THE ILLUSIONIST. Just one tiny scene, perhaps.

THE CHAMBERLAIN. In connection with what?

THE ILLUSIONIST. In connection with nothing at all. Just a trifle to please an old fisherman whom I love. But Your Excellency needn't leave.

THE CHAMBERLAIN. Oh no, I must. It is the Lord Chamberlain's duty to instruct all those who are presented at court. And in this particular case—

THE ILLUSIONIST. If Your Excellency wishes, I can save you the trouble of going. Take your place and you shall see yourself speaking to her.

THE CHAMBERLAIN. You can't do it!

THE ILLUSIONIST. Nothing simpler.

THE CHAMBERLAIN (*He backs away in astonishment until he is lost from sight*). What an extraordinary illusion!

THE ILLUSIONIST. Yes. But first, the Lady Violante. (VIOLANTE *steps forward.* AUGUSTE *walks in from the garden. He looks in bewilderment at* THE ILLUSIONIST.) The fleck of gold, Auguste.

AUGUSTE (*He sees* VIOLANTE). Are you the Lady Violante?

VIOLANTE. Yes. What do you wish?

AUGUSTE (*Looking into her eyes*). I was right! It's marvelous!

THE VOICE OF EUGENIE. Auguste! Stick to your fishing!

(AUGUSTE *makes a gesture of resignation, bows and goes.*)

THE ILLUSIONIST. Thank you, my lady. Here you come, Your Excellency.

(VIOLANTE *goes behind the column.* THE CHAMBERLAIN *comes in leading* ONDINE *by the hand.*)

THE CHAMBERLAIN. Absolutely out of the question, dear lady!

ONDINE. But it would make me so happy—

THE CHAMBERLAIN. I regret deeply. To change the court reception, third class, into a water festival is entirely out of the question. The Minister of Finance would never hear of such a thing. Every time we turn the water into the pool, it costs us a fortune.

ONDINE. But this will cost you nothing.

THE CHAMBERLAIN. Please don't insist. There is absolutely no precedent for a court reception in the water.

ONDINE. But I am so much more at ease in the water.

THE CHAMBERLAIN. I am not.

ONDINE. You would be. You especially. Your palm is damp. In the water, it wouldn't show.

THE CHAMBERLAIN. I beg your pardon. My palm is not damp.

ONDINE. Oh, it is. Touch it and you will see.

THE CHAMBERLAIN. Madame, do you feel strong enough to listen for a moment to a word of advice which will help you to avoid a great deal of trouble in the future?

ONDINE. Oh yes.

THE CHAMBERLAIN. To listen without interrupting?

ONDINE. Oh, I shouldn't dream of interrupting.

THE CHAMBERLAIN. Splendid. Now, in the first place—the court is a sacred precinct—

ONDINE. Excuse me just one moment. (*She goes to the place where* BERTRAM *is hidden and fetches him out.*) What is your name? You?

BERTRAM. Bertram.

ONDINE. You are the poet, are you not?

BERTRAM. So they say.

ONDINE. You are not beautiful.

BERTRAM. They say that too. But usually they whisper it.

ONDINE. Writing doesn't improve the appearance?

BERTRAM. Oh yes. I used to be much uglier.

(ONDINE *laughs and goes back to* THE CHAMBERLAIN. BERTRAM *stands by.*)

ONDINE. Excuse me.

THE CHAMBERLAIN (*Controlling himself*). As I was saying. The court is a sacred precinct in which it is necessary for a man at all times to control—his face and his tongue. Here, when a man is afraid, he seems brave. When he lies, he seems frank. It is quite appropriate also, if by chance one is telling the truth, to appear to be lying. It inspires confidence.

ONDINE. I see.

THE CHAMBERLAIN. Let us take the example that you in your innocence bring up. It is true, my palm perspires. Ever since I was a child it has caused me infinite embarrassment. But damp as my hand is, my arm is long. It reaches to the throne. To displease me is to put oneself in jeopardy—and it does not please me to hear any mention of my physical shortcomings, to be precise, of my sole physical shortcoming. And now, lovely Ondine, tell me, as a sophisticated court lady, how is my hand, damp or dry?

ONDINE. Damp. Like your feet.

THE CHAMBERLAIN. What?

ONDINE. Just a moment. Do you mind?

THE CHAMBERLAIN. I mind very much!

(ONDINE *crosses once more to the poet, who comes this time to meet her.*)

ONDINE. What was the first poem you ever wrote?

BERTRAM. The most beautiful.

ONDINE. The most beautiful of your poems?

BERTRAM. The most beautiful of all poems. It so far surpassed the others as you, Ondine, surpass all women.

ONDINE. Tell it to me quickly.

BERTRAM. I don't remember it. It came to me in a dream. When I awoke, it was gone.

ONDINE. You should have written it down sooner.

BERTRAM. I did. Even a little too soon. I was still dreaming when I wrote it.

(ONDINE *smiles and leaves him. She joins* THE CHAMBERLAIN, *who is fuming.*)

ONDINE. Yes, Your Excellency?

THE CHAMBERLAIN (*With a prodigious effort*). My lady, let us admit that the Lord Chamberlain's palm is damp, and let's admit that he admits it. But tell me this—would you tell his Majesty that his hand was damp?

ONDINE. Oh no!

THE CHAMBERLAIN. Ah, bravo! And why not?

ONDINE. Because it's not.

THE CHAMBERLAIN. But I put you a case where it is! Look here, my girl, suppose his Majesty should question you about the wart on his nose. And his Majesty, believe me, has a wart on his nose. And for heaven's sake don't make me shout. It is death to mention it. No one ever has. Now—suppose he asked you what his wart resembled?

ONDINE. Is it usual for a monarch who meets a lady for the first time to ask her what his wart resembles?

THE CHAMBERLAIN. My dear girl, I am putting you a hypothetical case. In the event that you had a wart on your nose—

ONDINE. I shall never have a wart on my nose.

THE CHAMBERLAIN. The girl is impossible!

ONDINE. Warts come from touching frogs. Did you know that?

THE CHAMBERLAIN. No.

BERTRAM (*Coming forward*). Madame, the Lord Chamberlain is merely trying to tell you that it is inconsiderate to remind people of their ugliness.

ONDINE. It is inconsiderate of them to be ugly. Why should they be ugly?

THE CHAMBERLAIN. Courtesy is an investment, my dear girl. When you grow old, in your turn, people will tell you, out of courtesy, that you look distinguished. When you grow ugly, they will say that you look interesting. And all this in return for a tiny payment on your part now.

ONDINE. I don't need to make it. I shall never grow old.

THE CHAMBERLAIN. What a child you are!

ONDINE. Yes. Excuse me a moment. (*She goes to* BERTRAM.)

THE CHAMBERLAIN (*Exasperated*). Ondine!

ONDINE. I like you, Bertram.

BERTRAM. I'm delighted. But the Chamberlain is annoyed.

ONDINE. Oh dear. (*She goes back to* THE CHAMBERLAIN.) I'm sorry.

THE CHAMBERLAIN (*A bit stiffly*). There is just time now for me to instruct you on the question that his Majesty asks of every debutante at court. It has to do with the sixth labor of Hercules. Hercules, as you know, is his Majesty's name—he is Hercules the Sixth. Now listen carefully.

ONDINE (*Taking a little step toward* BERTRAM). If I could just—

THE CHAMBERLAIN. Madame, his Majesty is almost here. When he asks you about the sixth labor of Hercules—(*A flourish of trumpets at some little distance.*) Too late.

(HANS *enters angrily.*)

HANS. Excellency—

ONDINE. Don't interrupt, Hans. His Excellency is speaking.

HANS. What does this mean, Excellency? Have you put me below the Margrave of Salm?

THE CHAMBERLAIN. Yes, Knight.

HANS. I am entitled to the third rank below the king and the silver fork.

THE CHAMBERLAIN. You were. And even to the first, and even to the golden fork, if a certain project had materialized as we expected. But your present marriage assigns you to the fourteenth place and the pewter spoon.

HANS. The fourteenth place!

ONDINE. What difference does it make, Hans? I've been to the kitchen. I'm sure there's enough for all. (BERTRAM *laughs.*)

HANS. And why are you laughing, Bertram?

BERTRAM. I am laughing because my heart is gay.

ONDINE. You don't wish to stop him from laughing, Hans?

HANS. He's laughing at you.

ONDINE. He's laughing at me because he likes me.

BERTRAM. That's very true, Madame.

HANS. My wife must provoke no laughter of any description.

THE CHAMBERLAIN. Gentlemen! Gentlemen!

ONDINE. He won't laugh if you don't like it. He has no desire to displease me. Have you, Bertram?

BERTRAM. My only wish is to please you, Madame.

ONDINE. Don't be angry with my husband, Bertram. It's flattering that he should be so scrupulous on my account. Don't you think so?

BERTRAM. We all envy him the privilege.

HANS (*Belligerently*). Thanks very much.

ONDINE. Don't show your nervousness, Hans. Be like me. I'm trembling. But an earthquake could not shake this smile from my lips.

(*Meanwhile people have streamed in from all sides.* THE ILLUSIONIST *comes up to* ONDINE.)

THE ILLUSIONIST. Ondine—

ONDINE. What are you doing here?

THE ILLUSIONIST. I am furnishing the entertainment. Pardon the intrusion.

ONDINE. Yes. On one condition. Go away.

THE ILLUSIONIST. If you like. But in a little while, you will call me back, Ondine.

(*He walks off. There is another flourish of trumpets near at hand.* THE CHAMBERLAIN *takes his place at the door. He strikes the floor with his staff three times.*)

THE CHAMBERLAIN. His Majesty, the King!

(THE KING *enters, bowing.*)

THE KING. Hail, Knight von Wittenstein.

HANS. Your Majesty. (THE KING *mounts his throne.*)

THE CHAMBERLAIN (*Advancing with* ONDINE). Your Majesty, with your gracious permission, may I present the Lady von Wittenstein zu Wittenstein.

THE KING. Madame.

ONDINE. My name is Ondine.

(BERTHA *takes her place on the lower step of the dais.* ONDINE *looks at no one else.*)

THE CHAMBERLAIN (*Whispers*). Your curtsey, Madame.

(ONDINE *curtseys, with her eyes still on* BERTHA.)

THE KING. We receive you with pleasure, dear child, in this gallery which is called the Hall of Hercules. I love Hercules. Of all my many names, his is by far my favorite, and of course the one by which I am known. The resemblance between Hercules and myself has been noticed by everyone, ever since I was a little child, and I must confess that at work or at play I have tried to emulate him in everything. And speaking of work—you know, I presume, how many labors Hercules brought to a successful conclusion?

THE CHAMBERLAIN (*Whispers*). Twelve.

ONDINE (*Without taking her eyes from* BERTHA'S *face*). Twelve.

THE KING. Twelve. Exactly. The Lord Chamberlain prompts a little loudly, but your voice is delightful. It will be a little more difficult for him to whisper in your ear the complete description of the sixth labor, but he won't have to. If you lift your eyes, you will see it depicted on the wall. Look. Who is this woman who is trying to seduce Hercules, with a smile on her lips and a lie in her heart? Her name, my dear?

ONDINE. Bertha.

THE KING. I beg pardon?

ONDINE (*Taking a step toward* BERTHA). You shall never have him, Bertha!

BERTHA. What?

ONDINE. He will never be yours, Bertha. Never!

THE KING. Is the girl quite well?

THE CHAMBERLAIN. Madame, His Majesty is addressing you.

ONDINE. If you say a word to him, if you dare to touch him, I'll kill you!

HANS. Ondine!

BERTHA. The girl is mad!

ONDINE. Majesty, I'm frightened! I I beg you, save us!

THE KING. Save you from what, my child?

HANS. Your Majesty, she's not used to the court.

ONDINE. You, be quiet. You don't see what's happening? Oh, King, isn't it a pity? You have a husband for whose sake you'd give up anything in the world. He's strong—he's brave—he's handsome—

HANS. Ondine, for heaven's sake!

ONDINE. I know what I'm saying. You're stupid, but you're handsome. It's no secret—all the women know it. And they say, what a lucky thing it is for us that being so handsome, he's so stupid! Because he's so handsome, how sweet it will be to take him in our arms. And how easy—since he's so stupid. Because he's so handsome, he will give us such joy as our husbands can never give us. And this, without the slightest danger to ourselves —since he's so stupid.

BERTRAM. Bravo!

ONDINE. I am right, am I not, Bertram?

HANS. Ondine, please! And you— what do you mean by saying Bravo?

BERTRAM. When I say Bravo, Knight, I mean Bravo.

THE KING. That's quite enough, Count Bertram.

THE CHAMBERLAIN (*Intervening suavely*). Your Majesty, I had hoped to offer by way of interlude a little diversion—

BERTHA. His Majesty is sufficiently diverted. His adopted daughter has been insulted before all the court by a peasant!

HANS. Majesty, permit us to take our leave. I have an adorable wife, but she is not like other women. She is very innocent, and she says whatever comes into her head. I humbly beg your forgiveness.

ONDINE. You see, King? You see what's happening?

THE KING. Bertha is the soul of sweetness. She wants only to be your friend—

ONDINE. You're entirely mistaken!

HANS. Ondine!

ONDINE. You think it's sweet to kill a bird!

THE KING. Bird? What bird? Why should Bertha kill a bird?

ONDINE. To trouble Hans. To bring him to his knees. To make him beg her pardon.

BERTHA. The bird was in my hand, Majesty. He pressed my hand so hard that the bird was killed.

ONDINE. He did not. A woman's hand, no matter how soft, becomes a shell of iron when it protects a living thing. If a bird were in my hand, Your Majesty, Hercules himself could press with all his strength and never hurt it. But Bertha knows men. These knights whom dragons cannot frighten grow faint at the death of a bird. The bird was alive in her hand. She killed it.

HANS. It was I who pressed her hand.

ONDINE. It was she who killed it.

THE KING. Ondine, my dear, I want you to be Bertha's friend.

ONDINE. If you wish. On condition she stops shouting.

HANS. But she hasn't said a word, Ondine.

THE KING. She really hasn't.

ONDINE. Are you deaf? Don't you hear? She says that a week of this foolishness will cost me my husband, and a month will cost me my life, that all she needs to do is to wait and I shall vanish. That's what your soul of sweetness is saying. Oh, Hans, take me in your arms, here, now, before her eyes, or we are lost forever!

HANS. You forget where you are, Ondine.

ONDINE. The bird is alive, Hans. I wouldn't let it die.

BERTHA. She is out of her mind. The bird is dead.

ONDINE. Go and see if you don't believe me. You killed it. I brought it to life. Which of us is out of her mind?

THE KING. You brought the bird back to life, you say?

ONDINE. Yes, King. Now do you see what a hypocrite she is?

THE KING. Bertha is no hypocrite, Ondine.

ONDINE. She is. She calculates her every word. She flatters you constantly.

THE KING. Nonsense, my dear.

ONDINE. Has she ever dared to speak to you about—

THE KING. About my descent from Hercules on the sinister side? Do you think that makes me blush?

ONDINE. No. About the wart on your nose.

THE KING (*Rises*). What? (*General consternation.* VIOLANTE *faints and is carried out.*) Leave us, all of you.

THE CHAMBERLAIN. Clear the room! Clear the room!

(*All leave, with the exception of* THE KING *and* ONDINE.)

THE KING. Ondine!

ONDINE (*Desperately*). If you ask me what it resembles, it resembles a flower, a mountain. It resembles a cathedral. Hercules had two in exactly the same place, one alongside of the other. They were called the Pillars of Hercules.

THE KING. Ondine!

ONDINE. He got them by touching the Hydra. He had to touch the Hydra, naturally, in order to strangle it. It was his fifth labor.

THE KING (*Sitting down again.*) My little Ondine, I like you very much. It's a rare pleasure to hear a voice like yours at court, even when this voice insists on discussing my wart—which, incidentally, I do inherit from Hercules, precisely as you say. But, for your own sake—tell me the truth.

ONDINE. Yes. Yes, I shall tell you the truth.

THE KING. Who are you?

ONDINE. I belong to the water. I am an Ondine.

THE KING. How old are you?

ONDINE. Sixteen. But I was born many ages ago. And I shall never die.

THE KING. What are you doing here? Does our world attract you?

ONDINE. From the water it seems so beautiful.

THE KING. And from the land?

ONDINE. There are ways to have water before one's eyes always.

THE KING. It is in order to make the world seem beautiful that you are weeping?

ONDINE. No. It's because they wish to take Hans away from me.

THE KING. And suppose they do? Would that be so great a misfortune?

ONDINE. Oh yes. If he deceives me, he will die.

THE KING. Don't worry, my dear. Men have been known to survive under those conditions.

ONDINE. Not this one.

THE KING. And what makes you think that Hans will deceive you?

ONDINE. I don't know. But they knew it the moment they saw him. Isn't it strange? The lake had never known deceit, not even the sound of the word. Then one day there appeared on its banks a handsome man with a loyal face and an honest voice, and that very moment the word "deceit" thrilled through the depths.

THE KING. Poor Ondine!

ONDINE. It's because your world is inverted in ours. All the things that I trust in Hans—his straight look, his clear words—to the water they seem crooked and cunning. He said he would love me always—and the water said, he deceives you!

THE KING. The water speaks?

ONDINE. Everything in the universe speaks, even the fish. Each time I left the cottage that night, they spat the word at me. He is beautiful, I said. Yes, said the bass, he will deceive you. He is strong, I said. Yes, said the perch, he will deceive you. Are you fond of perch, by any chance?

THE KING. I have no particular feeling about them.

ONDINE. Spiteful little things! But I was proud of him. I decided to take the risk. I made the pact.

THE KING. The pact? What pact?

ONDINE. The king, my uncle, said to me, you agree that he shall die if he deceives you? What could I answer?

THE KING. But he hasn't deceived you —yet.

ONDINE. But he is a man. He will. And then he will die.

THE KING: A king's memory is short. Your uncle will forget.

ONDINE. No.

THE KING. But, after all, what power has your uncle over him? What danger is he in?

ONDINE. Whatever is wave or water is angry with him. If he goes near a well, the level rises. When it rains, the water drenches him to the skin. Wherever he goes, the water reaches after him.

THE KING. Will you take my advice, little Ondine?

ONDINE. Yes.

THE KING. Go away, my dear.

ONDINE. With Hans?

THE KING. Dive into the first river you come to, and vanish forever.

ONDINE. But he's so clumsy in the water.

THE KING. You have had three months of happiness with Hans. In our world, that is a lifetime. Go while there is time.

ONDINE. Without Hans?

THE KING. He's not for you. His soul is small.

ONDINE. I have no soul.

THE KING. Because you don't need one. You are a soul. But human souls are tiny. There is no man whose soul is great enough for you.

ONDINE. I wouldn't love him if there were. I have already seen men with great souls—they are completely wrapped up in them. No, the only men whom one can love are those who are just like other men, whose thoughts are the thoughts of other men, who are distinguished from other men only by being themselves and nothing more.

THE KING. You are describing Hans.

ONDINE. Yes. that is Hans.

THE KING. But don't you see, my dear, that Hans loves what is great in you only because he sees it small? You are the sunlight; he loves a blonde. You are grace itself; he loves a madcap. You are adventure; he loves an adventure. One day he will see his mistake—and at that moment, you will lose him.

ONDINE. He will never see it. If it were Bertram, he would see it. Not Hans.

THE KING. If you wish to save him, leave him.

ONDINE. But I cannot save him by leaving him. If I leave him, they will say he deceived me, and Hans will die. No, it's here that I must save him. Here.

THE KING. And how will you do that, my little Ondine?

ONDINE. I have the remedy. It came to me while I was quarreling with Bertha. Did you notice—each time I came between Hans and Bertha, I succeeded only in bringing them more closely together. The instant I said something against Bertha, he sprang to her defense. Very well, from now on I shall do exactly the opposite. I shall tell him twenty times a day how beautiful Bertha is, how right she is. Then she will be wrong. I shall manage so that they are always alone. Then they will no longer feel the slightest desire for each other. In that way, with Bertha always there, I shall have Hans completely to myself. Oh, how well I understand men! Don't I? (THE KING *rises and kisses her.*) Oh, Your Majesty! What are you doing?

THE KING. The king thanks you, my child.

ONDINE. Thanks me? For what?

THE KING. For a lesson in true love.

ONDINE. My idea is good?

THE KING. Stupendous.

(*Enter* THE CHAMBERLAIN.)

THE CHAMBERLAIN. Forgive me, Your Majesty, The court is in complete consternation. What is your will? Shall I tell them all to withdraw?

THE KING. By no means.

THE CHAMBERLAIN. The reception is to continue?

THE KING. Of course.

THE CHAMBERLAIN. And the interlude? You wish to see it?

THE KING. At once.

ONDINE. How wonderful! Now I shall be able to ask Bertha's pardon before everyone.

(THE CHAMBERLAIN *goes to the door and waves his staff.* THE COURT *comes in from all sides.* BERTHA *takes her place, haughtily.*)

THE KING. Princess Bertha, Ondine has something to say to you.

ONDINE. I ask your pardon, Bertha.

THE KING. Very nice, my child.

ONDINE. Yes. But she might answer me.

HANS. What?

ONDINE. I have asked her pardon, though I don't want it. She might at least answer me.

THE KING. Bertha, Ondine has acknowledged her error, whatever it was. I should like you to be friends.

BERTHA. Very well, Your Majesty. I pardon her.

ONDINE. Thank you, Bertha.

BERTHA. On condition that she admits publicly that I did not kill the bird.

ONDINE. I admit it publicly. She did not kill the bird. The bird is alive—you can hear it singing. But she tried to kill it.

BERTHA. You see, Your Majesty?

HANS. One doesn't speak like that to the royal princess, Ondine!

ONDINE. The royal princess? Would you like to know who she is, this royal princess? Shall I show you? Shall I?

HANS. Silence, Ondine.

ONDINE. I happen to know the father of this royal princess. He is not a king. He is a fisherman—

BERTHA. Hans!

HANS. Ondine. You've said enough. (*He takes* ONDINE *by the wrist.*) Come.

ONDINE. (*Resisting*). Not yet, Hans!

HANS. Come, I say!

ONDINE. Old One! Old One! Help me!

(THE ILLUSIONIST *appears. He is followed by* THE CHAMBERLAIN.)

THE ILLUSIONIST. Your Majesty, the interlude.

THE KING (*As they seat themselves*). Yes, Ondine, you have gone too far. Everyone knows there was a golden crown on Bertha's pillow when she was found.

ONDINE. The crown was mine!

(*The lights go out, and come up immediately on a little set on the garden level. It depicts the fisherman's cottage on the edge of the lake.* TWO ONDINES *are dancing in the waterfall. An* ONDINE *comes in with a child in its arms. The others join her as she puts the child into a basket which she cover with rich silks.*)

THE ONDINE (*Sings*).
Wrap the child in silk and lace
So the princess of the sea
May be nurtured in her place
By Auguste and Eugenie.

(*At this moment the burly tenor dressed as* MATHO *and the robust soprano dressed as* SALAMMBO *advance to either side of the set and begin singing loudly.* THE ONDINES *stop in astonishment.*)

MATHO (*Sings*). I am a soldier, that is all.

SALAMMBO (*Sings*). And I the niece of Hannibal. (THE ILLUSIONIST *steps forward.*)

THE ILLUSIONIST. Who are these people, Exellency? They have nothing to do with my show.

MATHO (*Sings*). I am a common mercenary.

SALAMMBO. I stand at the other pole.

MATHO. But I love this sacred person.

SALAMMBO. I adore this humble soul.

THE ILLUSIONIST. Where did they come from? What are they singing?

THE CHAMBERLAIN. *Salammbo.*

THE ILLUSIONIST. But they're spoiling the illusion. Tell them to stop.

THE CHAMBERLAIN. Impossible. Once they begin, nothing can stop them.

SALAMMBO (*Sings*). Take me, take me, and Carthage too.

THE ILLUSIONIST. Enough! (*He makes a gesture. The two singers continue singing and posturing, but without a sound.* THE ONDINES *resume.*)

FIRST ONDINE (*Sings*).
Set the little creature down,
Whom we stole from Eugenie,
And beside her set the crown
Of the princess of the sea.

SECOND ONDINE. (*Sings*).
Weep not, we shall not forsake you,
Helpless, human little thing,
Soon a knight will come and take you
To the palace of the king.

THIRD ONDINE. (*Sings*).
But lest it ever be forgotten
Who she is and whence begotten,
On her skin I draw the sign
Of her father's hook and line.

(THE ONDINES *turn toward* BERTHA *and sing together.*)

THE ONDINES.
Bertha, Bertha, if you dare,
Show the world your shoulder bare!

(*The lights go on suddenly; the fisherman's cottage and* THE ONDINES *vanish. Hubbub.* BERTHA *is on her feet.*)

ONDINE. Well, Bertha?

BERTHA. It's a lie!

ONDINE. Is it? (*She tears the dress from* BERTHA'S *shoulders. The sign is there.*) You see? (BERTHA *kneels before* THE KING.)

MATHO
SALAMMBO } (*Suddenly audible, they walk off together, singing*).

All is love beneath the stars,
Is love, is love, is love!

BERTHA. It's a lie! (*She kneels before* THE KING.) It's a lie, Your Majesty. (THE KING *glances at her shoulder on which the mark is visible.*)

THE KING. Is this true, Ondine?

ONDINE. Yes, King.

BERTHA (*Desperately*). Hans! (HANS *makes a protecting gesture.*)

ONDINE. Old One! Where are they? (THE ILLUSIONIST *lifts a hand.* AUGUSTE *and* EUGENIE *appear. They see* BERTHA.) Oh, my darlings!

THE KING. Bertha, it is your father. Have you no word to say to him, to your mother? (BERTHA *is silent.*) As you please . . . (AUGUSTE *and* EUGENIE *go.* THE KING *walks off. The court follows slowly.*) But—(*He stops.*)—until you have asked their pardon, I forbid you to show your face at court.

(*He goes off, followed by the court.* BERTHA *is left sobbing bitterly.*)

ONDINE. Forgive me, Bertha. (*There is no answer.*) You will see. The king will call you back in a moment. And they will all love you more than before. (BERTHA *says nothing.*) Ask her to come and stay with us, Hans.

HANS. Bertha. Come with us. (BERTHA *turns silently.*)

ONDINE. Oh, how difficult it is to live among you, where what has happened can never again not have happened! How terrible to live where a word can never be unspoken and a gesture can never be unmade! But I will undo it all. You will see.

HANS. Come with us, Bertha. My castle is large. You shall live with us always, in the wing that looks out on the lake.

ONDINE. A lake? Your castle has a lake, Hans?

HANS. It has a lake. The other side faces the Rhine.

ONDINE. The Rhine?

(THE CHAMBERLAIN *comes in.*)

THE CHAMBERLAIN. The king wishes to know whether the pardon has been asked.

ONDINE. It has been asked. From the heart.

THE CHAMBERLAIN. In that case, Princess—

ONDINE: Oh Hans, haven't you a castle in the plains, in the mountains far from the water?

THE CHAMBERLAIN. Princess Bertha, the king desires your presence. He forgives you.

ONDINE. You see?

HANS. Tell him we have asked you to come with us.

ONDINE. He already knows that.

(BERTHA *and* THE CHAMBERLAIN *go out.* HANS *and* ONDINE *cross in the direction of the garden.*)

HANS (*As they pass the fountain*). And why all this fear of the water? What is it that threatens you from the water?

ONDINE. Me? Nothing.

HANS. If I sit down at the edge of a brook, you drag me away. If I walk near a pond, you come between us. What is it you fear?

ONDINE. Nothing, Hans.

HANS. Yes, Ondine, my castle is surrounded by water. And in the mornings, I shall bathe under my waterfall, and at noon I shall fish in my lake, and in the evening I shall swim in the Rhine. You don't frighten me with these tales about water. What's water? Can it see? Can it hear?

(*As he passes, the jets of water rise high and threatening over their basins.* THE ILLUSIONIST *appears.*)

ONDINE. Yes, Hans.

(*They go.* THE CHAMBERLAIN *comes out from behind his column, and, a moment later,* THE SUPERINTENDENT, THE TRAINER, BERTRAM *and* THE TWO LADIES *come out of hiding.*)

THE CHAMBERLAIN. Wonderful! Wonderful! (*To* THE ILLUSIONIST.) Very nice indeed.

THE SUPERINTENDENT. Wonderful!

VIOLANTE. But is all this really going to happen?

THE ILLUSIONIST. My dear, it has happened.

THE CHAMBERLAIN. And what happens next, Magician?

THE COURT. Yes. What next?

THE CHAMBERLAIN: Does he decide to marry Bertha?

THE COURT. Does he?

THE CHAMBERLAIN. Does he deceive Ondine?

THE COURT. Does he?

THE ILLUSIONIST. Naturally.

THE CHAMBERLAIN. When can we see that?

THE ILLUSIONIST. At once, if you like.

THE CHAMBERLAIN. Splendid. Let's see it. (*He goes behind his column.*) Go on.

BERTRAM. No, Excellency. No.

THE CHAMBERLAIN. Yes, yes. Go on. Go on. But what's this? What's happened? (*He comes out.*) I'm bald?

THE ILLUSIONIST. Five years have passed.

THE CHAMBERLAIN. My teeth are gone? I'm stuttering?

THE ILLUSIONIST. Shall I continue?

THE CHAMBERLAIN. No. No, for heaven's sake! An intermission! An intermission!

Curtain

🌷 Act III

The courtyard of the castle of the Wittenstein. The yard is surrounded on three sides by the walls of the castle. Arched doorways lead into it. At one side there is a platform with a well.

It is the morning of the marriage of BERTHA *and* HANS. *There is a sound of church bells from the chapel.* HANS, *splendidly dressed, is sitting on the platform steps with his head in his hands. A* SERVANT *enters.*

THE SERVANT. My lord, the choir has filed into the chancel.

HANS. What did you say?

THE SERVANT. I refer to the choir which will sing at your wedding.

HANS. Do you have to use this pompous tone? Can't you talk like a human being?

(BERTHA *comes in. She too is dressed for a wedding.*)

THE SERVANT. Long life to the bride! To the Lady Bertha!

HANS. Oh. Go away!

BERTHA. But, Hans, why are you angry on the day of our wedding?

HANS. What? You too?

BERTHA. I had hoped that your face would be radiant with joy.

HANS. Stop it, stop it! Stop it!

BERTHA. Hans, really!

HANS. I'm lost, Bertha! I'm lost!

BERTHA. Hans, you frighten me. You're so strange today.

HANS. There is a tradition in our family, Bertha. Whenever misfortune threat-

ens, the servants feel it before anyone else, and they begin to speak all at once in solemn language. On the day of misfortune, the kitchen maids are filled with grandeur. The swineherds see what they never saw before. They speak of the curve of the stream; the shape of the flower fills them with awe; they exclaim with wonder at the honeycomb. They speak of nature, of the soul of man. They become poets. That day, misfortune strikes.

BERTHA. But the man wasn't speaking in poetry, Hans. There were no rhymes.

HANS. When I hear him speak in rhymes, I shall know that death is at hand.

BERTHA. Oh Hans, that's superstitious!

HANS. You think?

BERTHA. This is not the day of your death, Hans, Is it the day of your wedding.

HANS (*He calls*). Walter! (THE SERVANT *enters.*) Where is the swineherd?

THE SERVANT. Under a spreading oak—

HANS. Hold your tongue.

THE SERVANT. On a grassy bank he lies—

HANS. Go fetch him. Quickly.

(THE SERVANT *goes out.* BERTHA *takes* HANS *in her arms.*)

BERTHA. Oh Hans, my dear, I love you.

HANS (*Absently*). You're good to me, Bertha.

BERTHA. You are holding me in your arms, Hans, but you are not thinking of me. What are you thinking?

HANS. I was weak, Bertha. I should have made her confess. I should have made her suffer as she made me suffer.

BERTHA. Can't you put her out of your mind, Hans? Not even today?

HANS. Today less than any other. Oh, Bertha, you should have married a man full of joy and pride. And look at me; Oh Bertha, how she lied to me, that woman!

BERTHA. She never lied to you, Hans. She was no woman. You married a creature of another world. You married an Ondine. You must forget her.

HANS. If she would only let me forget

her! But that cry that awakened me the morning she left—"I have deceived you with Bertram!" Has it stopped echoing for even a moment? Does one hear anything else from the river, from the lake? Does the waterfall ever stop dinning it in my ears? Day and night, in the castle, in the city, from the fountains, from the wells—it's deafening! But why does she insist on proclaiming to the world that she deceived me with Bertram? (*An echo comes from the well.*)

THE ECHO. Deceived you with Bertram. (*Another echo whispers from the right.*) With Bertram. (*From the left.*) With Bertram.

HANS. You hear? You hear?

BERTHA. Let's be just, Hans. You had already deceived her with me. And of course she knew it. It was only in revenge that she deceived you with Bertram.

THE ECHOES (*Whisper back*). Deceived you with Bertram. With Bertram.

HANS. Where is she now, Bertha? What is she doing? In the six months since she left, every huntsman, every fisherman in the region has been trying to find her. You would say she had vanished. And yet she's not far off. This morning at dawn they found a wreath of starfish and sea urchins on the chapel door. She put it there, of course. You know that.

BERTHA. Oh, my darling, who would have thought that you of all men would have seen anything in a girl like Ondine? When I sent you into the forest, I thought, this man will surely come back. He will look carefully, right and left, but he will never find an enchanted lake, nor the cave of a dragon, he will never glimpse among the trees at twilight the white forehead of a unicorn. He has nothing to do in that world. He will follow the human path. He will not lose his way.

HANS. I lost it.

BERTHA. Yes, but you found it again. It was in the fifth year of your marriage, that night in the winter when you told me it was me you had always loved, and I ran away from you, and you followed my tracks in the snow. They were deep and wide. They spoke plainly of my distress. They were not the tracks of a spirit. They were human tracks, and you found

them, and once more you found your way. You carried me back in your arms that night.

HANS. Yes. Like Bertram when he carried away Ondine. (THE SERVANT *enters.*) Where is the swineherd?

THE SERVANT. In the shadow of an oak, by the banks of a stream—

HANS. Well?

THE SERVANT. I called him, but he did not answer. He is gazing at the sky. He is looking at the clouds.

HANS. Never mind. Fetch me the kitchen maid.

THE SERVANT. There is a fisherman to see you, my lord.

HANS. Get me the kitchen maid at once, do you hear, no matter what she's gazing at.

THE SERVANT. Yes, my lord. The fisherman.

(THE SERVANT *goes.* THE FISHERMAN *comes in.*)

FIRST FISHERMAN. My lord! My lord!

HANS. Say it twice more and it's poetry.

FIRST FISHERMAN. We have her. She's caught.

HANS. Ondine?

FIRST FISHERMAN. Yes. Yes. An Ondine!

BERTHA. Are you sure?

HANS. Where did you catch her?

FIRST FISHERMAN. In the Rhine. In my net.

HANS. You're sure it's she?

FIRST FISHERMAN. Positive. Her hair was over her face, but her voice was marvelous, her skin like velvet. She's wonderfully formed, the little monster.

(THE SECOND FISHERMAN *appears.*)

SECOND FISHERMAN. Prepare yourself. The judges are coming.

BERTHA. Judges?

HANS. What judges?

SECOND FISHERMAN. The Imperial and Episcopal judges who have jurisdiction over the supernatural.

BERTHA. So soon?

SECOND FISHERMAN. They were already holding assizes below in the city.

FIRST FISHERMAN. They came from Bingen, you see, to hang a werewolf. Now they will try the Ondine.

BERTHA. But why must they try her here?

FIRST FISHERMAN. Because an Ondine must be tried on a rock.

SECOND FISHERMAN. And besides, you are the complainant.

HANS. That's true.

BERTHA. Don't they know what day this is? Couldn't they try her another time?

SECOND FISHERMAN. My lady, the trial must be now.

HANS. They're right, Bertha. The trial must be now.

BERTHA. Hans—don't see her again, I beg you.

HANS. I shall never see her again. You heard what he said—he caught an Ondine in the Rhine. What I shall see won't even know me.

BERTHA. Don't look at her, Hans.

THE SERVANT (*Comes in*). The judges, my lord.

HANS. Just a few minutes more, Bertha, and we shall be at peace.

THE FISHERMAN. The judges.

(*The* JUDGES *come in, puffing a little. They are followed by an* ANCIENT CLERK *with a great book.*)

FIRST JUDGE. Marvelous! The exact altitude. Just above the realm of the water. Just below the realm of the air. It couldn't be better. (*He bows to* BERTHA.) My lady. Our felicitations.

SECOND JUDGE. Our compliments, my lord.

BERTHA. I shall be within call, Hans, if you want me.

(BERTHA *goes out.*)

HANS. You come in the nick of time, gentlemen. But how did you know there was work for you here?

FIRST JUDGE. Our work gives us a degree of insight unknown to our colleagues in the civil and criminal law.

SECOND JUDGE. It is also more difficult.

(*The* SERVANTS *arrange the court.* THE CLERK *sits down, opens his register and sharpens his quill.*)

FIRST JUDGE. To determine the line that divides two vineyards is easy. But to fix the proper boundaries between humanity and the spirits, *hoc opus, hic*— excuse me—*hic labor est.*

SECOND JUDGE. But in the case at hand, our task appears to be easy.

FIRST JUDGE. It is the first time we have tried an Ondine who does not deny being an Ondine.

SECOND JUDGE. All the more reason to be careful.

FIRST JUDGE. Quite right, my dear colleague.

SECOND JUDGE. You have no idea of the subterfuges these creatures use to elude our investigations. The salamanders pretend to be Ondines. The Ondines pretend to be salamanders. (*He sits down.*)

FIRST JUDGE. Excuse me.

SECOND JUDGE. You remember, my dear colleague, that affair at Kreiznach, when we tried the pretended Dorothea, the alderman's cook? She gave us every reason to believe she was a salamander. But we didn't jump at conclusions. We put her to the torch to make sure. She burnt to a crisp.

FIRST JUDGE (*Smiles reminiscently*). She was no more salamander than I am. (*He sits down.*)

SECOND JUDGE. She was an Ondine.

FIRST JUDGE. We had a similar case last week, the matter of a certain Gertrude, a blonde barmaid of Tübingen. It was clearly established that in her presence the beer glasses filled by themselves and, what is even more miraculous, without heads of foam. You would have been certain she was an Ondine. We threw her into the water with her hands tied—

SECOND JUDGE. She immediately drowned.

FIRST JUDGE. (*He shrugs*). A salamander.

HANS. Did you bring Ondine with you?

FIRST JUDGE. We have her in custody. But before we examine her, Knight, it would be extremely valuable for us to ascertain the exact nature of your complaint.

HANS. My complaint? My complaint is the complaint of all mankind. Is it so much after all that God has granted us, these few yards of air between hell and heaven? Is it so attractive, after all, this bit of life we have, with these hands that get dirty, these teeth that fall out, this hair that turns gray? Why must these creatures trespass on our little world? Gentlemen, on the morning of my marriage, I claim the right to be left in peace in a world that is free of these intrusions, these threats, these seductions, alone with myself, with my bride, alone at last.

FIRST JUDGE. That is a great deal to ask, Knight.

SECOND JUDGE. Yes. It may seem surprising that these creatures should derive all their satisfaction from staring at us while we wash our feet, kiss our wives, or beat our children. But that is the undeniable fact. Around each human gesture, the meanest, the noblest, a host of grotesque presences with tails and horns is constantly dancing its round. What's to be done? We must resign ourselves.

HANS. Has there never been an age when they did not infest us?

SECOND JUDGE. An age? To my knowledge, Knight, there has never been a moment.

FIRST JUDGE. Yes, once there was a moment. One only. It was late August, near Augsburg, in the harvest season when the peasants were dancing. I had stretched out under an apple tree. I looked up into the sky. And suddenly I felt that the whole world was free of these shadows that beset it. Above my head I saw a lark soaring in the heavens —without its usual twin, the raven. Our Swabia spread to the Alps, green and blue, without my seeing over it the Swabia of the air, peopled with blue angels, nor below it the Swabia of hell, teeming with green devils. On the road there trotted a horseman with a lance, unattended by the horseman with the scythe. By the river, in the sun, the mill wheel turned slowly, without dragging in its orbit that enormous shadowy wheel that grinds the souls of the damned. For that instant, the whole world was single-hearted, at work, at play, at peace—and yet I tasted for the first time a certain loneliness, the loneliness of humanity. But the next moment, the horseman was joined by Death, the clouds bristled as always with lances and brooms, and the customary fish-headed devils had joined the dancing couples. There they were, all back at their posts again just as before. Bring in the accused.

(ONDINE *is led in by* THE EXECUTIONER. *She is nude, but draped around her body is the net in which she was caught. She is made to stand on a little elevation opposite the* JUDGES. *A num-*

ber of people come in to witness the trial.)

SECOND JUDGE (*Peering at her*). Her hands are not webbed, apparently. She is wearing a ring.

HANS. Remove it.

ONDINE. No!

(THE EXECUTIONER *removes it by force and hands it to* HANS.)

HANS. It is my wedding ring. I shall need it presently.

FIRST JUDGE. Knight—

HANS. The necklace too. The locket has my picture in it.

ONDINE. No!

THE EXECUTIONER *takes it off.*)

FIRST JUDGE. Knight, with all respect, I must ask you not to interfere with the conduct of this trial. Your anger is doubtless justified, but we must avoid even the semblance of confusion. We will proceed with the identification.

HANS. It is she.

FIRST JUDGE. Beyond a doubt. But we must follow the indicated procedure. Where is the fisherman who caught her? Summon the fisherman to the bar.

(*The* FIRST FISHERMAN *takes the stand.*)

FIRST FISHERMAN. It's the first time I ever caught one, your honor. This is my lucky day!

FIRST JUDGE. Congratulations. Now— what was she doing when you caught her?

FIRST FISHERMAN. I knew that some day I'd catch one. I have known it every morning for the last thirty years. How often have I said—today I'm going to catch one. But this morning, I was certain.

FIRST JUDGE. I asked you what she was doing.

FIRST FISHERMAN. And, mind you, I caught her alive. The one they caught at Regensburg, they bashed its head in with an oar. But I was careful. I just knocked her head against the side of the boat a few times to stun her. Then I dragged her in.

HANS. You ox. You hurt her head.

FIRST JUDGE. Answer my questions. Was she swimming when you caught her?

FIRST FISHERMAN. She was swimming. She was showing her breasts, her buttocks. She can stay under a full fifteen minutes. I timed her.

FIRST JUDGE. Was she singing?

FIRST FISHERMAN. She was making a little sound, like a moan. If it was a dog, you'd call it a yelp, a bark. I remember what she was barking. She was barking: I deceived you with Bertram.

FIRST JUDGE. You're talking nonsense. Since when can you understand a bark?

FIRST FISHERMAN. As a rule, I don't. To me a bark is a bark, as a rule. But this one I understood. And what it said was—

FIRST JUDGE. She had an odor of sulphur when you pulled her out?

FIRST FISHERMAN. She had an odor of algae, of pine.

SECOND JUDGE. That's not the same thing. Did she have an odor of algae or an odor of pine?

FIRST FISHERMAN. She had an odor of algae, of pine.

FIRST JUDGE. Never mind, my dear colleague.

FIRST FISHERMAN. She had an odor that said plainly: I deceived you with Bertram.

FIRST JUDGE. Since when do odors speak?

FIRST FISHERMAN. Odors don't speak. But this one said—

FIRST JUDGE. She struggled, I presume?

FIRST FISHERMAN. No. Not at all. You might say, she let herself be caught. But when I had her in the boat, she shuddered. It was a sort of movement of the shoulders that said, as clear as clear can be: I deceived you with—

HANS. Have you quite finished, you idiot?

FIRST JUDGE. You must excuse the man, Knight. These simple souls are always imagining things. That is the origin of folklore.

FIRST FISHERMAN. I swear by all that's holy that that's one of them. I'm sorry about the tail. She didn't have it when I caught her. There's a double reward for catching them alive?

FIRST JUDGE. You may collect it after the trial. Very well, Fisherman. That's all.

FIRST FISHERMAN. And what about my net? Can I have my net back?

FIRST JUDGE. Your net is in evidence. It will be returned to you in due course.

SECOND JUDGE. Out you go.

(THE FISHERMAN goes out, grumbling.)

FIRST JUDGE. Proceed with the examination.

(THE SECOND JUDGE extends a very long telescope and focuses it on ONDINE.)

HANS. What are you doing?

SECOND JUDGE. I am going to examine the body of this girl—

HANS. No one is going to examine her body!

FIRST JUDGE. Calm your fears, Knight. My colleague is an experienced anatomist. It was he who personally established the physical integrity of the Electress Josepha in connection with the annulment of her marriage, and she commented especially on his tact.

HANS. I tell you, this is Ondine. That's enough.

SECOND JUDGE. Knight, I understand that it is painful for you to have me auscultate in public the body of someone who was once your wife. But I can, without touching her, study through the glass those parts which differentiate her species from the human race.

HANS. Never mind the glass. You can look at her from where you are.

SECOND JUDGE. To identify with the naked eye and from a distance the very subtle variations that distinguish an Ondine from a human being seems to me an extremely impractical operation. She could at least take off the net and walk a little. She could show us her legs?

HANS. She·will do nothing of the sort.

FIRST JUDGE. It would perhaps be in better taste not to insist, my dear colleague. In any case, the evidence is sufficient. Is there anyone present who denies that this is an Ondine?

SECOND FISHERMAN (Without moving). I deny it.

FIRST JUDGE. Who said that? Remove that man.

THE SERVANT. Don't kill her, your honor. She was good to us.

SECOND JUDGE (Shrugs his shoulders). She was a good Ondine, that's all.

THE SERVANT. She loved us.

SECOND JUDGE. There are affectionate varieties even among turtles.

FIRST JUDGE. Since we hear no objection, we declare that the supernatural character of the accused has been established beyond a reasonable doubt. We proceed to the second part of the trial. Knight, do you accuse this creature, by reason of her illegal intrusion into our world, of having caused disorder and confusion in your domain?

HANS. I? Certainly not.

FIRST JUDGE. But you do accuse her of being a sorceress?

HANS. Ondine, a sorceress?

FIRST JUDGE. We are merely trying to define her crime, Knight.

SECOND FISHERMAN (*Stepping forward*). Ondine, a sorceress?

FIRST JUDGE. Who is this man?

SECOND FISHERMAN. I am a witness.

ONDINE. He's lying!

FIRST JUDGE. Ah. In that case, you may speak.

SECOND FISHERMAN. This Ondine is no longer an Ondine. She has renounced her race and betrayed its interests. She has become a woman.

FIRST JUDGE. A sorceress.

SECOND FISHERMAN. This woman could call upon the earth and the heavens to do her bidding. The Rhine is her servant. But she gave up her power in favor of such human specialties as hay fever, headaches and cooking. Is that true, Knight, or is it false?

FIRST JUDGE. You accuse her, if I understand correctly, of having taken on a favorable appearance in order to ferret out the secrets of the human race?

HANS. Rubbish!

SECOND FISHERMAN. The human race has no secrets, your honor. It has only afflictions.

FIRST JUDGE. It also has treasures. Doubtless she stole your gold, Knight, your jewels?

HANS. She?

SECOND FISHERMAN. All the gold and the jewels of the world meant nothing to Ondine. Of the treasures of humanity, she preferred only the humblest—the stove, the kettle, the spoon. The elements loved Ondine, but she did not return their affection. She loved the fire because it was good for making omelettes, and the water because it made soup, and the wind because it dried the wash. Write this into your record, Judge—this Ondine was the most human being that ever lived. She was human by choice.

SECOND JUDGE. We are informed that the accused was in the habit of locking herself up for hours each day in order to practice her magic arts. What do you say to that?

SECOND FISHERMAN. It's true. And what was the result of her magic, you?

THE SERVANT. A meringue, your honor.

SECOND JUDGE. A meringue? What sort of meringue?

THE SERVANT. She worked for two months to discover the secret of a good meringue.

SECOND JUDGE. That is one of the deepest of human secrets. Did she succeed?

FIRST JUDGE. Fisherman, we thank you. We shall take account of these facts in considering our judgment. If these creatures envy us our pastry, our bric-a-brac, our ointments for eczema, it is hardly to be wondered at. It is only natural that they should recognize the pre-eminence of the human condition.

SECOND JUDGE. There's nothing in the world like a good meringue. You say she discovered the secret?

THE SERVANT. Her crust was pure magic, your honor.

SECOND JUDGE (*To the* FIRST JUDGE). You don't suppose that with a few turns on the rack we might perhaps induce her to—?

FIRST JUDGE. No, my dear colleague, no. (*He clears his throat.*) We come now to the heart of the matter. At last, Knight, I understand the full import of your complaint. Ondine, you are accused of having cheated this knight of the joys of marriage. In place of the loving companion to which every man is entitled, you foisted upon this knight a wearisome existence with a woman who cared for nothing but her kitchen. In this way—and this is the greatest of the crimes against the human spirit—you have robbed him of love. Naturally. An Ondine is incapable of love.

HANS. Ondine incapable of love?

FIRST JUDGE. Really, Knight, it is becoming a trifle difficult to follow you. Of what, precisely, do you accuse this woman?

HANS. I accuse this woman of adoring me beyond human endurance. I accuse her of thinking only of me, of dreaming only of me, of living only for me.

FIRST JUDGE. That is not a crime, exactly.

HANS. I was this woman's god, do you understand?

FIRST JUDGE. Now, now—

HANS. You don't believe me? Very well. Answer me, Ondine. Who was your god?

ONDINE. You.

HANS. You hear? She pushes love as far as blasphemy.

FIRST JUDGE. Oh, come, there's no need to complicate the issue. These creatures are not Christians. They cannot blaspheme. All she means is that she had a proper wifely reverence for you.

HANS. Who were your saints, Ondine?

ONDINE. You.

HANS. Who were your angels? Whose face did you see in the holy pictures in your Book of Hours?

ONDINE. Yours.

HANS. You see?

FIRST JUDGE. But where is all this leading us, Knight? We are here to try an Ondine, not to judge the nature of love.

HANS. Nevertheless, that is what you are required to judge. It is Love I am accusing. I accuse the highest love of being the foulest and the truest love of being the most false. This woman who lived only for me deceived me with Bertram.

FIRST JUDGE. You are heaping confusion on confusion, Knight. If what this woman says is true, she could not possibly have deceived you with anyone.

HANS. Answer, Ondine. Did you or did you not deceive me with Bertram?

ONDINE. With Bertram.

HANS. Swear it, then. Swear it before these judges.

ONDINE (*Rises to her feet*). I swear it before these judges.

FIRST JUDGE. If she deceived you, we shall see soon enough. My dear colleague, put the three canonical questions. The first?

SECOND JUDGE. Ondine, when you see this man running, what do you do?

ONDINE. I lose my breath.

FIRST JUDGE. Hm.

SECOND JUDGE. And when he snores in his sleep—excuse me, Knight—what do you hear?

ONDINE. I hear the sound of singing.

FIRST JUDGE. So far her answers are correct. The third question, if you please.

SECOND JUDGE. When he tells an amusing story for the twentieth time in your presence, how does it seem to you?

ONDINE. Twenty times funnier than before.

FIRST JUDGE. And nevertheless you deceived him with Bertram?

ONDINE. I deceived him with Bertram.

SECOND FISHERMAN. You needn't shout, Ondine. I heard you.

ONDINE (*Whispers*). I deceived him with Bertram.

HANS. There you have it.

FIRST JUDGE. Do you realize, young woman, what the punishment for adultery is? Do you realize that this is a crime that is never confessed, because the confession doubles the injury?

ONDINE. All the same—

SECOND FISHERMAN. You deceived him with Bertram?

ONDINE. Yes.

SECOND FISHERMAN. Answer me, now, Ondine. And see that you answer me truly. Where is Bertram now?

ONDINE. In Burgundy, where he is waiting for me to join him.

SECOND FISHERMAN. Where was it that you deceived your husband with Bertram?

ONDINE. In a forest.

SECOND FISHERMAN. In the morning? At noon?

ONDINE. At noon.

SECOND FISHERMAN. Was it cold? Was it warm?

ONDINE. It was icy. Bertram said: Our love will keep us warm. One doesn't forget such words.

SECOND FISHERMAN. Very good. And now, if you please, summon Bertram to the bar.

FIRST JUDGE. Bertram has been gone these six months, Fisherman. He is beyond the power of the law.

SECOND FISHERMAN. Its power seems limited. Here he is.

(BERTRAM *comes in*.)

HANS. Bertram!

FIRST JUDGE. Just a moment, Knight. You are the Count Bertram?

BERTRAM. Yes.

FIRST JUDGE. This woman says she deceived her husband with you.

BERTRAM. What?

FIRST JUDGE. Is it true?

BERTRAM. If she says it, it is true.

FIRST JUDGE. Where did it happen?

BERTRAM. In her room. In this castle.

FIRST JUDGE. In the morning? At night?

BERTRAM. At midnight.

FIRST JUDGE. Was it cold? Was it warm?

BERTRAM. The logs were blazing on the hearth. Ondine said: How hot it is, the way to hell! One doesn't forget such words.

SECOND FISHERMAN. Perfect. And now everything is clear.

ONDINE. And why is it so clear? Why should we remember these trifles? When people really love each other do you think they know whether it is warm or cold or noon or midnight?

SECOND FISHERMAN. Count Bertram, take this woman in your arms and kiss her lips.

BERTRAM. I take my orders only from her.

SECOND FISHERMAN. Ask him to kiss you, Ondine.

ONDINE. Before all these people? Never.

SECOND JUDGE. And yet you expect us to believe that you gave yourself to him?

ONDINE. Kiss me, Bertram.

BERTRAM. You really wish it?

ONDINE. Yes. I wish you to kiss me. Just for a moment. Just to prove that we can. And if I should shudder a little when you take me in your arms, Bertram, it's only because it's cold.

SECOND JUDGE. We are waiting, Ondine.

ONDINE. Couldn't I have something to cover myself with, at least?

SECOND JUDGE. No. As you are.

ONDINE. Very well. So much the better. I love to feel Bertram's hands on my body when he kisses me. Come, Bertram. But if I should scream a little, Bertram, when you take me in your arms, it's only because I'm frightened here before these people. Besides, I may not scream.

SECOND JUDGE. Make up your mind, Ondine.

ONDINE. Or if I should faint. But if I faint, Bertram, you may do whatever you please with me, whatever you please.

FIRST JUDGE. Well, Ondine?

ONDINE. Well, Bertram?

BERTRAM. Ondine! (*He takes her in his arms and kisses her.*)

ONDINE. Hans! Hans!

SECOND FISHERMAN. There's your proof, gentlemen. (*The* JUDGES *put on their hats.*)

ONDINE. But you don't understand. If I say Hans when I kiss Bertram, it is only to deceive him the better. If I loved Bertram with no thought of Hans, would that be deceit? No, but every moment that I love Bertram, I think of Hans and I deceive him. With Bertram.

SECOND FISHERMAN. We understand. The trial is over. You may go, Count Bertram.

BERTRAM. Must I go, Ondine?

ONDINE. Farewell, Bertram.

BERTRAM. Farewell. (BERTRAM *goes.*)

FIRST JUDGE. The court will now deliver its judgment.

SECOND JUDGE. Oyez! Oyez!

FIRST JUDGE. It is the judgment of this court that this Ondine has transgressed the boundaries of nature. However the evidence indicates that in so doing she brought with her nothing but kindness and love.

SECOND JUDGE. And even a little too much kindness and love.

FIRST JUDGE. Why she wished to make us believe that she deceived you with Bertram when in fact she did not, is a question beyond the scope of our inquiry. As she has done no great harm, it is our judgment that she shall be spared the humiliation of a public execution. She shall have her throat cut without witnesses this day directly after sunset. Until that time, we place her in the custody of the public executioner. (*Church bells begin to ring again.*) What's that?

SECOND JUDGE. Wedding bells, my dear colleague. The Knight is about to be married.

FIRST JUDGE. Ah, of course. The nuptial procession is forming in front of the chapel. Knight, permit us to join you in the hour of your happiness. (THE KITCHEN MAID *walks up to* HANS.)

HANS. Who is this?

FIRST JUDGE. Who?

HANS. This woman who walks toward me like a creature from the other world?

SECOND JUDGE. We don't know her.

FIRST JUDGE. She seems to be of this world.

THE SERVANT. It's the kitchen maid, my lord. You asked me to fetch her.

HANS. How beautiful she is!

FIRST JUDGE. Beautiful?

HANS. How very beautiful!

SECOND JUDGE. We shall not contradict you. Will you precede us?

HANS. No, no. I have to hear first what she says. She alone knows the end of this story. Speak! Speak! We are listening.

SECOND JUDGE. Is he out of his mind?

FIRST JUDGE. He has every reason.

HANS. Speak! Speak!

THE KITCHEN MAID.

My face is plain, my nature sour,
But, oh, my soul is like a flower.

HANS. That rhymes?

FIRST JUDGE. Rhymes? Not at all.

THE KITCHEN MAID.

Had I been free to choose my lot,
My hands had never touched a pot.

HANS. You're going to tell me these verses don't rhyme?

SECOND JUDGE. Verses?

FIRST JUDGE. What verses?

THE KITCHEN MAID.

My clothes are poor, my face is plain,
And yet of high rank is my pain;
There is as much salt in my tears
As in those shed by emperors.
And when the butler vents his spleen,
It hurts as if I were a queen.
Oh, when we two come to your city,
And, kneeling, ask for grace and pity,
Both bearing on our brows the same
Affronts and thorns and marks of shame,
Will you know us one from the other,
My Lord, my savior and my brother?

HANS. That's a poem, is it not? Would you call that a poem?

FIRST JUDGE. A poem? All I heard was a scullion complaining that she had been falsely accused of stealing a spoon.

SECOND JUDGE. She said her corns have been aching since November.

HANS. Is that a scythe she bears in her hand?

FIRST JUDGE. A scythe? No, that's a spindle.

SECOND JUDGE. It's a broom.

HANS. I thank you, kitchen maid. When next you come, I shall be ready. Come, gentlemen.

(THE KITCHEN MAID goes out. THE SERVANT crosses the stage solemnly. He turns.)

THE SERVANT. Your bride is in the chapel, my lord. The priest is waiting.

HANS. Go and say that I am coming.

(The wedding bells begin to toll as for a funeral. They all go out, except THE EXECUTIONER, THE SECOND FISHERMAN and ONDINE.)

THE EXECUTIONER (Taking hold of ONDINE). Now then, Mistress—

SECOND FISHERMAN. One moment, Executioner. (With a gesture of his hand, he turns THE EXECUTIONER into an automaton and waves him off the stage.) The end is near, Ondine.

ONDINE. Don't kill him, Old One.

SECOND FISHERMAN. You haven't forgotten our pact?

ONDINE. Don't judge men by our standards, Old One. Men don't deceive their wives unless they love them. When they love them most, they deceive them. It's a form of fidelity, their deceit.

SECOND FISHERMAN. Ah, Ondine, what a woman you are!

ONDINE. It's only because he wished to honor me that he deceived me. It was to show the world how pure I was, how true. I really don't see how else he could have done it.

SECOND FISHERMAN. You have always suffered from a lack of imagination.

ONDINE. When a man comes home in the evening with his eyes full of gratitude and his arms full of flowers, and he kisses our hands and calls us his savior and his angel—we all know what that means. It's scarcely an hour since he has deceived us. And is there anything more beautiful in marriage?

SECOND FISHERMAN. He has made you suffer, my little Ondine.

ONDINE. Yes. I have suffered. But remember we are speaking of humans. Among humans you are not unhappy when you suffer. On the contrary. To seek out in a world full of joy the one thing that is certain to give you pain, and to hug that to your bosom with all your strength—that's the greatest human happiness. People think you're strange if you don't do it. Save him, Old One.

SECOND FISHERMAN. He is going to die, Ondine.

ONDINE. Old One!

SECOND FISHERMAN. What does it matter to you, Ondine? You have only a few minutes left of human memory. Your sisters will call you three times, and you will forget everything.

ONDINE. Save him! Save him!

SECOND FISHERMAN. If you wish, I will let him die at the same moment that you forget him. That seems humane.

ONDINE. He is so young. So strong.

SECOND FISHERMAN. You have strained his heart, Ondine.

ONDINE. I? How could I?

SECOND FISHERMAN. Since you show such interest in dogfish, perhaps you remember a couple who broke their hearts one day while swimming together peacefully in a calm sea. They had crossed the entire width of the ocean side by side in winter, through a tempest, without the slightest difficulty. And then one day in a blue gulf, they swam against a little wave. All the steel of the sea was in that ripple of water, and the effort was too much for them. For a week their eyes grew pale, their lips drooped. But there was nothing wrong with them, they said . . . but they were dying. And so it is with men, Ondine. What breaks the woodsman's heart, or the knight's, is not the great oak, nor the battle with the dragon: It is a slender reed, it is a child who loves him.—He has only a few minutes left to live.

ONDINE. But he has everything to live for now. His life is in order.

SECOND FISHERMAN. His brain is full of the music of those who are dying. When the kitchen maid held forth just now on the price of eggs and cheese, you saw, it was all sheer poetry in his ears.

ONDINE. He has Bertha—

SECOND FISHERMAN. She is waiting for him in vain in the chapel. He is in the stable with his horse. His horse is speaking to him. Dear master, good-bye till we meet in the sky, his horse is saying. Today his horse has become a poet.

ONDINE. I can hear them singing in the chapel. He is being married.

SECOND FISHERMAN. What does this marriage mean to him now? The whole thing has slipped away from him like a ring too wide for the finger. He is wandering about by himself. He is talking to himself, he doesn't know what he's saying. It's a way men have of escaping when they come up suddenly against a reality. They become what is called mad. All at once they are logical. They don't compromise. They don't marry the woman they don't love. They reason simply and

clearly like the plants and the water. Like us.

ONDINE. Listen to him. He is cursing me.

(HANS *is heard speaking offstage.*)

SECOND FISHERMAN. He loves you. He's mad. He's here. (*He goes.* HANS *comes in slowly and stands behind* ON-DINE *for a moment.*)

HANS. My name is Hans.

ONDINE. It's a beautiful name.

HANS. Ondine and Hans. The most beautiful names in the world, are they not?

ONDINE. Yes. Hans and Ondine.

HANS. Oh, no. Ondine first. That's the title. Ondine. It will be called *Ondine,* this story in which I appear from time to time. And I don't play a very brilliant part in it, do I, because, as you said once, I'm not very bright; I'm just the man in the story. I loved Ondine because she wanted me; I deceived her because I had to. I didn't count for much. I was born to live between the stable and the kennels —such was my fate, and I might have been happy there. But I strayed from the appointed path, and I was caught between nature and destiny. I was trapped.

ONDINE. Forgive me, Hans.

HANS. But why do you make this error, all of you? Was I the man for love? Lovers are of a different stamp—little threadbare professors full of fury, stockbrokers with heavy glasses; such men have the time and capacity for enjoyment and suffering. But you never choose such men, never. Instead you fall with all your weight on some poor general called Antony, or some poor knight called Hans, ordinary men of action for whom love is a torment and a poison. And then it's all up with them. Between the wars and the chase and the tourneys and the hospital, did I ever have a spare moment in my life? But you had to add also the poison in my veins, the flame in my eyes, the gall in my mouth! And then, oh God, how they shook me between them and bruised me, and flayed me between hell and heaven! It wasn't very just of you, Ondine.

ONDINE. Farewell, Hans.

HANS. And then, you see? One day they leave you. The day when suddenly everything becomes clear, the day you realize that you would die if they left you—that day they leave you. The day when you find them again, and with them, everything that gives life its meaning, that day, they look you in the eye with a limpid glance, and they say farewell.

ONDINE. I am going to forget everything, Hans.

HANS. And a real farewell, a farewell forever! Not like those lovers who part on the threshold of death, but are destined to meet again in another world, to jostle each other eternally in the same heaven. These part only in order never to part again—you don't call that a parting. But Ondine and I will never meet again. We part for eternity, we go to different worlds. We must do this properly, Ondine. It is the first real farewell that has ever been said in this world.

ONDINE. Live, Hans. You too will forget.

HANS. Live! It's easy to say. If at least I could work up a little interest in living —but I'm too tired to make the effort. Since you left me, Ondine, all the things my body once did by itself, it does now only by special order. The grass doesn't look green to my eyes unless I order them to see it green. And it's not very gay, you know, when the grass is black. It's an exhausting piece of management I've undertaken. I have to supervise five senses, two hundred bones, a thousand muscles. A single moment of inattention, and I forget to breathe. He died, they will say, because it was a nuisance to breathe . . . (*He shakes his head.*) He died of love. Why did you let the fisherman catch you, Ondine? What did you wish to tell me?

ONDINE. That an Ondine will mourn for you always.

HANS. No. No one will mourn for me. I am the last of my house. I shall leave no trace behind me. There will be only an Ondine, and she will have forgotten.

ONDINE. No, Hans. I have taken my precautions. You used to laugh at me because I always made the same movements in your house. You said I counted my steps. It was true. It was because I knew the day would come when I would have to go back. I was training myself. And now, in the depths of the Rhine or the ocean, without knowing why, I shall go on forever making the movements that I

made when I lived with you. When I plunge to the bottom, I shall be going to the cellar—when I spring to the surface, I shall be going to the attic. I shall pass through doors in the water. I shall open windows. In this way I shall live a little with you always. Among the wild Ondines there will be one who will forever be your wife. Oh! What is it?

HANS. I forgot for a moment.

ONDINE. Forgot what?

HANS. To breathe. Go on, Ondine, go on.

ONDINE. Before I left, I took some of the things in our room. I threw them into the river. They seem strange to me in the water, these bits of wood and metal that speak to me of you, they float about aimlessly out of their element. It's because I'm not used to it yet: tomorrow they will seem as firm and stable as the currents in which they float. I shall not know what they mean, exactly, but I shall live among them, and it will be strange if I don't use them sometimes. I shall drink from your cup. I shall look into your mirror. Sometimes perhaps your clock will strike. Timeless, I shall not understand this sound but I shall hear it. And so, in my way, though death and the infinite come between us, I shall be true to you always.

HANS. Thank you, Ondine. And I—

THE FIRST VOICE. Ondine!

HANS. They are calling you, Ondine.

ONDINE. They will call me three times. I shall remember until the last. Hans, let us not waste these moments! Ask me something quickly. What is it, Hans? What is it? You're pale.

HANS. I too am being called, Ondine.

ONDINE. Speak! Question me!

HANS. What did you say, Ondine, when you came out of the storm, the first time I saw you?

ONDINE. I said: How beautiful he is!

HANS. And when you saw me eating the trout?

ONDINE. I said: How stupid he is!

HANS. And when I said: It does no harm to think?

ONDINE. I said: In after years we shall have this hour to remember. The hour before you kissed me.

HANS. I can't wait now, Ondine. Kiss me now.

THE SECOND VOICE. Ondine!

ONDINE. It's all whirling about in my head! Speak, Hans, speak!

HANS. I can't speak and kiss you at the same time.

ONDINE. I'll be quiet.

(*He kisses her.* THE KITCHEN MAID *comes in with her broom.*)

HANS. Look! Look! There she is!

ONDINE. Who?

HANS. Her face is plain, her nature sour. But oh, her soul is like a flower! (*He falls.*)

ONDINE. Help! Help!

HANS. Ondine—

THE THIRD VOICE. Ondine!

(HANS *dies.* ONDINE *looks about in surprise.*)

ONDINE. How did I get here? How strange! It's solid. It's empty. It's the earth?

(THE SECOND FISHERMAN *appears.*)

SECOND FISHERMAN. It is the earth, Ondine. It's no place for you.

ONDINE. No—

(THE ONDINES *are heard singing in the distance.*)

SECOND FISHERMAN. Come, little one, let us leave it.

ONDINE. Oh yes. Let us leave it. (*She takes a few steps, then stops before the body of* HANS, *which is lying on the platform steps.*) Wait. Why is this handsome young man lying here? Who is he?

SECOND FISHERMAN. His name is Hans.

ONDINE. What a beautiful name! But why doesn't he move? Is there something wrong with him?

SECOND FISHERMAN. He is dead.

FIRST ONDINE. Come, Ondine.

ONDINE. Oh, I like him so much! Can you bring him back to life, Old One?

SECOND FISHERMAN. Impossible.

ONDINE. What a pity! How I should have loved him!

Curtain

MAURICE VALENCY: *Giraudoux: An Introduction*

From *Jean Giraudoux: Four Plays*. Adapted and with an introduction by Maurice Valency. Copyright © 1958 by Hill and Wang, Inc. Reprinted by permission of Ashley-Steiner, Inc.

WHEN WE THINK OF GIRAUDOUX, WHAT COMES TO MIND FIRST OF all is his style; in fact it is very arguable that both his life and his work were patterned in conformity with an inexorable stylistic principle. He himself wrote: *"Sans style rien ne vit, et rien ne survit: tout est dans le style."*

What lies behind an attitude of this sort is clear enough. No man can establish title to an idea—at the most he can only claim possession. The stream of thought that irrigates the mind of each of us is a confluent of the intellectual river that drains the whole of the living universe. But a man's style is intrinsic and private with him like his voice or his gesture, partly a matter of inheritance, partly of cultivation. It is more than a pattern of expression. It is the pattern of the soul. This much, at any rate, seems evident: the ideas of Giraudoux may be traced without undue effort to the main intellectual and artistic preoccupations of his time, but the style of Giraudoux is Giraudoux.

By the time he was twenty-three, this style was formed. It was characteristic of the man that once he found a good thing he wasted no time splashing about for a better. The youth of twenty-three was simply an early model of the man of sixty-two. The style of his first book, *Provinciales,* is surprisingly similar to that of his last works. From first to last, his turn of thought and his turn of phrase are the same.

Like the generation of Baudelaire and Nerval, to which he owed a certain allegiance, Giraudoux greatly felt the need to be original. He had little desire to do what had been done before, no wish to say what had already been said. Perhaps for this reason he cultivated a manner which is deliberately provocative, enigmatic, and precious. It is a mannered style, certainly, but not decadent. On the contrary, it is fresh and bright, youthful and enthusiastic. Among French writers, he admired most of all those whose work is distinguished by a clear and precise outline—Racine, La Fontaine, Nerval, Émile Clermont, Charles-Louis Philippe. He was much impressed also by the German Romantics, particularly by Novalis, Jean Paul Richter, Chamisso, La Motte Fouqué; but in general his tastes inclined to the eighteenth century, that last refuge of common sense in our time. Gluck was his favorite composer, Deism his preferred religion. Passion embarrassed him. He constantly exploded whatever was unduly emotional in his work by an immediate *reductio ad absurdum.* His critics sometimes speak of the influence of Jules Renard, of Laforgue—they are illusions which do not seem particularly profitable to me. He has been called impressionist, pointillist, symbolist. There is undoubtedly something in his work which reflects each of these attitudes, but I am not sure that these terms really have much relation to his writing. In the drama, he had an uncanny ability to create, in a completely realistic décor, a theatre of the unreal. It is a theatre in which the natural order is the supernatural, and the nonhuman exhibits in its relations to humanity a calm assurance which makes highly questionable the reality to which we are accustomed. It is in terms of this question, mildly obsessional, that Giraudoux generally arranged his dramatic structure. I don't know that we have a word for this sort of thing. Magic, perhaps.

The plays that best characterize his mature style occupy a middle ground between comedy and tragedy. His characters are precisely observed, but this precision has nothing to do with naturalism. His situations are, on the whole, clearly and firmly based in the reality which we know, but Giraudoux has only a qualified interest in this reality. It is there only as a point of departure for an excursion into poetry. "Whatever I have written," Giraudoux once said, "I consider merely as a sort of poetic divagation."

Giraudoux does not view life with the analytic eye of the abstractionist. For him reality is what it is, so far as it goes. But he sees further; he adds a dimension, and is thus able to enjoy a degree of freedom with respect to his subject which the earthbound do not enjoy. With regard to the world we inhabit, he believes what good Frenchmen are expected to believe. But like many liberated souls who have endured an inordinate amount of instruction, he seems to have slipped early into the sort of polite skepticism which we associate with Montaigne. This skepticism of his does not in the least interfere with a well-bred acquiescence in the established order and its values, though it is clear that at bottom he distrusts them. Nor does it seriously deface the idealized world-picture which the bright *lycéen* carries away from school together with his diploma and his prizes. It merely distorts this picture a little in the direction of caricature. For Giraudoux, as for his more conventional contemporaries, history remains a volume of highly colored examples of virtue, and morality a system of precepts suitable for framing. But Giraudoux sees clearly, amid these idealizations, the comic plight of the civilized male. It is, above all, in this unfailing awareness of the droll aspects of mankind strutting with ceremonial solemnity before the uncomprehending stare of nature that his drama finds it characteristic expression.

Giraudoux felt himself to be, fundamentally, a moral writer. "In my opinion," he wrote, "the purpose of a book, the dominant idea of an author while he is writing a book, must be a moral idea." But while he had been trained in a school for teachers, and was in some sense a teacher all his life, he was far too much the artist to moralize in public. His style was occasionally forensic, but he had the blessed gift, not often accorded to orators, of listening to himself objectively, and, to a degree almost unknown among serious writers, he reserved the right to take himself not quite seriously. Like Shaw, Giraudoux was by nature a joyous man; he enjoyed frivolity. Unlike the Irish playwright, however, he resisted the temptation to syllogize, to

demonstrate, to preach. His theatre is not a laboratory. It is the tower of a sorcerer, full of uncertainties. With Giraudoux, it is impossible to disentangle the jest from the truth. He never tells us when to stop smiling. Nor is he in the least interested in the philosophic demonstration of the certainty of uncertainty that provides Pirandello with his dramatic formula. Giraudoux has neither the complacency of belief nor the torment of doubt. His work, like his life, reflects the pleasant adventure of a singular man, the unhurried exploration of a universe which he found, on the whole, enchanting. Even in the realms of death, his spirit botanizes: ". . . What has been said of the asphodels is true; the meadows are covered with them, and with cowslips as well."

Jean Giraudoux was born in 1882 in Bellac, a little town in the Limousin. Bellac is in no way different from any other of the 35,000 towns of France. It sits astride the main highway that leads from Limoges to Poitiers, a little cluster of houses, very decent, very taxable, grouped about a public square, very clean, dominated by the *Mairie,* very shabby. It is bounded geographically and, one might add, intellectually, on one side by the church, on another by the railway station, on a third by the barracks of the local gendarmerie. But Bellac has a fourth side, and on that side it is not bounded. On that side the fields begin, and beyond them is the sky. Bellac has no monuments, no palaces, no points of interest; one might easily drive through it without noticing. For Giraudoux it was always *la plus belle ville du monde.*

For Giraudoux, this world of his childhood was the world—first Bellac; then Cusset, near Vichy, where the family moved while he was still very young; after that, all sorts of places. His connections with the little world were intimate. His father was the local tax collector, his brother, a town physician in Vichy. When Giraudoux moved out into the great world, his relations with the little world remained intact. A good part of his life was spent among statesmen, major and minor; he came to know all the great writers of his time—but he kept his distance. He capitulated neither to the snobbishness nor the glamour of the most snobbish and glamorous capital in the world. He was a provincial by choice.

In time, his destiny bore him very far from home, to America, Greece, Africa, and Turkey. He knew all the great cities well, the great hotels, the wide avenues. But it is clear that for him the world and its problems were chiefly comprehensible in terms of the little town of his youth and, whatever name he gave it in his plays—and he gave it many names: Paris, Argos, Thebes, and Troy—it is in Bellac that all his plays are set. For him, this well-ordered little community, precise, respectable, and redolent of good bourgeois cooking, represented perfectly the *civitas terrena,* at once our mansion and our prison house. It is just so in his plays that Argos and Thebes are shaped. It is, without doubt, from the direction of the railway station, over the fields covered with buttercups, that Amphitryon gallops to visit Alcmena in the freshness of the morning. Near the lake beyond the barracks is the dwelling of Ondine's foster parents, with its mysterious presences. From Isabel's apartment, Place Denfert-Rochereau, one can see the enchanted clock on the façade of the *Mairie* which, under influences the nature of which one can only surmise, strikes thirteen at midnight.

Bellac is a modest concept, as cities go, but it is not simple. For above and in this little world, enfolding it at every point like a spiritual exhalation, one can sense another world, turbulent, beautiful, wild, and dangerous, a world full of irresistible urgencies, in which every rock harbors a mystery and every brook a nymph. Between the visible town and the invisible empire which surrounds and defines it there are infinite points of connection. The gates through which these worlds communicate are carefully locked, and for eternity, but the keys are under the mat; the doors open at the slightest touch; the signs that say *"Eintritt verboten"* also read "Enter without knocking."

The chief nexus, however, between the world of matter and the realm of the spirit is the young girl, a form of existence which perfectly combines these antithetical elements and which is, for this reason perhaps, completely absorbing to Giraudoux. It is at this point of junction between the two worlds that he ordinarily sets his stage, and from this viewpoint he unfolds a wonderful, if somewhat unsettling, perspective of the universe, a quasi-familiar region in which appearance and reality are indistinguishable, the true and the false merge in cordial friendship, the animate and inanimate join hands, and from the nearest jukebox comes the music of the spheres.

Giraudoux was a learned writer, the product of one of those formidable educations which only the French seem able to digest without suffering that intellectual dyspepsia which is the occupational disease of the lettered class. Germany fascinated him. At the *École normale,* he specialized in German literature, and on graduation he was awarded a scholarship which enabled him to carry on his studies in Munich. There was much about Germany that attracted him, much that repelled him. Somehow Germany took a significant position at one pole of the strange psychic pattern that he evolved. At the other extreme was France. On the side of France were ranged those adult qualities in which Frenchmen have faith —clarity, order, logic, the classics. On the other side stood the qualities which Giraudoux associated with Germany—the heroic, the rebellious, the unknowable, the romantic. Between these poles his fancy vibrated, and vibrates unceasingly, throughout his work. In some sense, this vibration constitutes the chief dynamic element in his life as an artist.

After his stay in Germany, Giraudoux spent a year at Harvard as a lecturer in French. Ten years later, during the First World War, he returned as a military instructor. Harvard appears to have made a lasting impression on him. Paul Morand tells us that for many years Giraudoux kept a Harvard pennant over the bed in his apartment, Rue de Condé, in Paris. He wore tweed jackets of an American cut, was indefatigable at tennis, and was a dedicated bridge player. In 1907, in Paris, he met a young editor who had just made a killing at the races and had rashly decided to put his winnings into the publishing business. It was Bernard Grasset. Giraudoux gave him three stories, and Grasset printed them that year under the title *Provinciales*. It was the beginning of Giraudoux's career as a writer.

By now he was twenty-five, a pleasant man with an earnest face and bright blue eyes behind thick glasses. His manner was calm, witty, good-humored, unhurried. He spoke quietly, without noise. He detested brutality, abrupt manners, direct questions, cigarettes. In his later life he made a good deal of money, but from first to last he loved simple things, an unpretentious hotel room, solitude, children, dogs. He seldom bothered to open his mail. A naturally mysterious nature, he liked to live withdrawn from society. At dinner it irked him to reveal where he had spent the day or with whom.

At twenty-seven, Giraudoux entered the French foreign service and was assigned to the Press Bureau. Twenty years later he had risen to the post of Chief of Press in the Foreign Ministry under Poincaré. Eventually he was made Minister of Propaganda in the ill-fated Daladier cabinet of 1939, a position which he held until the German occupation. He died in 1944. Thus in the course of half a lifetime he rose step by step in the civil service until he reached the very top of his possible trajectory. Meanwhile he was leading another life in another world. It was not easy. He had to steal time to write—a few hours after breakfast, an occasional hour at his desk at the office, an hour after dinner. Fortunately he had facility; though not as much facility as he would have us believe. He gave the impression of working at top speed, without effort and without revision. The truth is, he revised constantly and worked hard, as every writer must. But he avoided the appearance of work and, no matter how great the effort, he presented to the world a smooth brow and the joyous exterior of a man to whom everything is easy. In this manner, by the time he was forty-five, he had published a whole shelf of books—novels, short stories, essays—in all some thirty titles, and by this time his work had long been the subject of critical discussion.

At the age of forty-six he produced his first play, a dramatization of his novel, *Siegfried et le limousin*. In deference to public taste, this story was given a happy ending, and Jouvet put it on the stage in 1928 with Pierre Renoir in the title role. Its success was immediate. The consequence was the series of remarkable plays which forms the chief glory of the French theatre in our time.

The problem of *Siegfried* absorbed Giraudoux's attention for rather more than a decade. Out of it he made no less than six novels, to say nothing of a spectacular career in the theatre. Evidently, then, *Siegfried* represents a major investment of creative energy. It is, in fact, the obvious point of departure in any attempt to understand the life and work of the author.

Siegfried is a study of dual personality. The story is well known, I believe; in one form or another it has been exploited until by now it may be considered a dramatic stereotype. It has to do with a French soldier who suffers a severe traumatic amnesia on the battlefield. He is picked up by the Germans, naked, without any identification, and rehabilitated as a German. In this manner, the brilliant French writer Jacques Forestier becomes the brilliant German writer Siegfried Kleist, and the merger gives rise to an extraordinary personality, a fusion of opposites which amounts to genius. At a critical point of his life this man is made aware of his identity—by a woman, naturally—and the ensuing mental conflict as to who he is and what he must do is the substance of the play. It seems hardly necessary to insist on the autobiographical nature of this fantasy.

It was thus in a realistic and conventional setting that Giraudoux first exhibited in the theatre the conflict that was to entangle his interest in one way or another during the whole of his life as a dramatist. The profound psychic dualism which had already caused him to divide his life between two careers and two literatures flowered now into a series of remarkable works of art. He had begun by trying to explain the Germans to the French. He went on to fuller explanations. He undertook now to explain man to the universe, to the stars, to the water, to the spirits. It was no small task; but it was a mission that singularly suited a man who could be a citizen of one world only on condition that he belonged to another. He was, fortunately, not alone in his endeavor. Maeterlinck, in his time and in his way, had already explored the possibilities of the interworld, and there were those in the *théâtre d'entre deux guerres* who felt the need of expanding the horizons of the theatre as far as possible. Gaston Baty, for example, had written (*Masques. Quatrième cahier d'art dramatique,* p. 14): ". . . the universe is not simply made up of men and human groupings. Around these is all that lives, all that grows, all that has being. And all that has being is material for the dramatist: the animals, plants, things."

It was, in fact, to the animals, plants, and things of the universe, quite as much as to the human race, that Giraudoux addressed his poetic discourse. He was certainly not a mystic; he had too much humor and too much common sense for that type of self-absorption. But he had in a high degree that feeling of kinship with the universe which is characteristic of the romantic poets, and he permitted his fancy to range far beyond the limits of the naturalistic method which he habitually employed. The result is a drama of delightful surprises, somewhere between the art of the candid camera and the art of the fairy tale.

It is impossible to overestimate the contribution of Jouvet to the development of Giraudoux as a dramatist. Their partnership was legendary. In Jouvet, Giraudoux found an incomparable showman and a true friend. In Giraudoux, Jouvet found that indispensable adjunct of a creative theatre, a gifted writer who has something to say. Before long, Giraudoux came to think of himself not as a literary person with an occasional play to produce, but as a regular member of an acting company, the sort of person, he tells us, who may be seen in old engravings standing coyly at the side of a troupe of players with a roll of papers in his hand, the "poet," whose duty it is to keep a company supplied with plays.

Giraudoux in fact kept his company supplied with plays at the rate of about one a year for a considerable period. In return, Jouvet put at his disposal a unique playhouse and a company which Shakespeare might have envied, a company which included Valentine Tessier, Lucienne Bogaërt, Madeleine Ozeray, Pierre Renoir, Le Vigan, and, of course, Jouvet himself. He gave him a gift of even greater value to a playwright, the stimula-

tion of an enduring organization, constantly receptive to new ideas, willing to take any risk in the direction of the ideal, and none at all in the way of mediocrity. It was under these happy auspices that Giraudoux's phenomenal development as a dramatist took place. On the stage he found a freedom of expression that in the looser form of the novel he had not found. The stage did not greatly hamper his tendency to digression, but it kept it within the bounds of an organic structure. *Amphitryon 38* revealed his true genius. He entered at once upon his kingship. His Alcmena had taken the shape of Valentine Tessier; next, he gave his Judith the semblance of Elisabeth Bergner— "nothing helps you so much as to know the color of the hair and the shape of those whose drama you are writing." In this manner, with the greatest rapidity, he developed the style which distinguishes his great plays: *Intermezzo* (*The Enchanted*), 1933; *La Guerre de Troie n'aura pas Lieu* (*The Tiger at the Gates*), 1935; *Elèctre*, 1937; *Ondine*, 1939; *La Folle de Chaillot* (*The Madwoman of Chaillot*), 1945; and the incomparable one-acter, *L'Apollon de Bellac*, 1942.

What he evolved is basically a drama of the spoken word and the acted thought. He begins invariably with a poetic conception which is dramatically effective, a full and complete dramatic thought in terms of which the action is formulated. Within this frame the drama is developed with astonishing inventiveness and spontaneity, and without any of the engineering that is characteristic of the well-made play. The course of the action is gentle; there are no great climaxes, no sudden peripeties. The characters do not change; they simply live out their story. "The stage-play," wrote Giraudoux, "is a trial, not a deed of violence. The soul is opened, like the combination of a safe, by means of a word. You don't require an acetylene torch." Giraudoux's plays enter our lives chiefly through the mind. They do not blast their way into the viscera. They arouse emotion courteously and delicately through the understanding. His characters on every level are schooled in a gentle stoicism; they bear their roles with humor and dignity, without ostentation. From the lowest to the highest, they express themselves with the precision of trained conversationalists, all voluble, all witty, all a trifle precious, all Giraudoux. It is delightful theatre, elegant, but by no means bloodless, an evocation of power through poetry. It is a theatre that involves a good deal of discussion, but no shouting; a theatre in which the essential is spoken in a whisper.

Nevertheless these plays are mounted firmly on the solid structure of the *pièce bien faite*. Shaw did not scruple to borrow the clichés of Adelphi melodrama for the purposes of his theatre of ideas. In somewhat the same way, Giraudoux borrowed the stereotypes of the thesis play for his own poetic purpose. One does not immediately think of *Ondine* as domestic drama, but ultimately that is what it comes down to. *The Enchanted,* like *The Apollo of Bellac,* treats the pressing problem of a young girl's choice of a husband. *The Madwoman of Chaillot* offers a more or less practical solution to the problems of a world which is in danger of losing its joy. If these formulations seem overly simple, we have only to look at the plays themselves.

In *Ondine,* for example, a young man of good family is engaged to a girl of his own class. He suddenly becomes infatuated with a blonde of an inferior class and, impulsively, he marries this girl. But she doesn't make him happy, and after the vicissitudes usual in such cases of misalliance, the young man goes back to his first love, a brunette who is socially most acceptable. He is now in a predicament. He cannot live without the blonde; the brunette is indispensable to his happiness, and, torn apart by these two loves, the man dies. Obviously, this is class drama of the most conventional cut. The principal difference between this and the innumerable plays that have been written on the subject is that the blonde girl in this case is not a chorus girl or a waitress, but a fish.

It is in this difference, slight but decisive, that *Ondine* differs from the conventional play of miscegenation. Ondine belongs not to the demimonde but to the kingdom of the sea. She represents and is the elemental power of water, the spirit of the sea, a spirit, incidentally, which has seduced more than one man from a life of respectable domesticity. Thus *Ondine* is domestic drama—with a difference. It is the drama of nature which strives to domesticate itself out of love for man, the drama of man who, once he has caught a glimpse of the world beyond reality, can never more reconcile himself to the conventional life of his fellows. Of similar contexture are *The Enchanted,* the story of Isabel, and *The Apollo of Bellac,* the story of Agnes. Isabel yearns to reform the world by means of the spirit. She is adventurous. But her adventure bogs down invariably somewhere between Nice and Tours, and the world is never reformed. Agnes longs for a vision of the supreme beauty. But the supreme beauty, as every girl knows, is a terrifying thing. It is best to forget it in a vision of *Better Homes and Gardens.* These plays, diverse as they seem, are all made of the same material, just as the infinite patterns of the kaleidoscope are all made of the same bits of colored glass. The mystery which they share is the same mystery. It is the mystery of the human predicament. For Giraudoux, as I have said, it centers in the mystery of the young girl.

The young girl is Giraudoux's supreme achievement as a dramatist. She is, in his view, a point of incandescence in the darkness, a being through whom the two worlds communicate, in whom everything is possible and nothing ever happens. These young girls are not the overblown adolescents of Greuze or Pascin; they are the stately young ladies of Renoir, at once ethereal and robust. In their eyes the supreme light is reflected, we see in them the love that moves the sun and the other stars, but they have excellent appetites and are accustomed to put away a hearty breakfast. In them Giraudoux saw the riddle of the universe in its most tantalizing form.

The mystery of the young girl in whose eyes one sees the ineffable, and in whose arms one finds the cook, has troubled many a writer since the time of Dante. It resolves itself into the most common of literary stereotypes, the idea that the royal road to salvation is through the beauty of a woman one can never possess. There are two sides to our souls, it is very noticeable. There is the side that yearns for the infinite. There is the side that yearns for its dinner. The claims of the ideal are no more to be denied than the claims of the stomach, but their interests are not the same. These yearnings are of equal poignancy. The conflict is comic.

Man is a singular complex—the fact has often been remarked. He has created the music of Mozart and Beethoven. He aspires to break with his voice the silence of the interstellar spaces. But when at last he comes to break it, we may be sure he will bring to the ears of the astonished angels not the "Eroica" played by a Toscanini, but a sound truck hawking a patent medicine. Such is his nature. His soul longs for beauty, for the absolute, the transcendental. When he attains it, he has no use for it; it oppresses him. Such is the human condition—an endless aspiration and a constant betrayal. The conflict is tragic.

For Giraudoux the young girl is the living embodiment of this conflict in both its tragic and its comic aspects. In her we see the freshness of that marvelous instant in which life bursts into bloom in its most charming form. The moment is precious, but it is ephemeral: it is intolerable that it should endure. It marks the acme of our earthly existence, but we do not marry this moment. It does not cook, it does not bear children, it does not help us with our sums, or entertain our business acquaintances. For that we need another woman: we need Bertha. This is our dilemma. As men, we love Ondine always, but we cannot do without Bertha. We take Ondine into our arms, hoping to find Bertha. We marry Bertha, looking for Ondine. And so at every moment we deceive them, the ideal and the real, the one with the other. And in the end, between the two of them they destroy us. It is a sad story, but it makes us smile, perhaps because it is so utterly familiar. It is the story of marriage.

It is in his ability to tell a familiar story in terms of the highest poetic fantasy that Giraudoux most clearly demonstrates his control of the two worlds which it was his function as an artist to bring together. In the flight of his imagination he bears us very far, far beyond the world with which the theatre ordinarily concerns itself. But in the highest flight of this agile spirit we sense from first to last the strength of the anchoring thought which determines its course. It is all about something, something we can understand, something important, a truth which cannot, perhaps, be explored in any other way, and which, at any rate, nobody else has ever explored in this way.

Bertolt Brecht

1898-1956

BRECHT WAS BORN IN AUGSBURG, GERMANY, THE SON of a factory manager. Early in adult life he developed an antipathy toward militarism; he joined radical groups, and his writings and political activities earned him the enmity of the military and Fascist elements in Germany. As a student in Berlin and Munich he studied natural sciences and medicine, but Brecht's true interest lay in literature and particularly in drama. At one time he supported himself by singing in cabarets, but soon he scored a success with his play *Drums in the Night* (1922). Brecht joined the Deutsches Theater, where he produced Elizabethan, Spanish, and Chinese dramas along with his own works. He next accepted direction of the Schiffbauerdam Theater in Berlin, where he based his productions on his famous theory of "epic theatre" and gathered about him one of the outstanding acting troupes in Europe. Rather than lure the spectator into the play and give him an illusion of reality, Brecht attempted to place the audience at a distance from the play (the "alienation" principle) and to keep them from identifying emotionally with his characters. His use of naked staging, a commenting narrator, pantomime, songs, film projections, captions, and similar devices was intended to keep the audience aware that they were in a theatre, not participating in real life, and thus to compel them to a critical rather than a blindly emotional response. In 1928 Brecht triumphed with his *Three Penny Opera*, a bitingly satirical play with music by Kurt Weill. Other plays followed, in a variety of forms but all with a radical Marxist orientation. With Hitler's rise to power, Brecht was forced to leave Germany; he lived in France, Norway, the Soviet Union, and the United States. It was during this period of exile that Brecht wrote several of his most significant plays: *Mother Courage* (1939), *Galileo* (1939), *The Good Woman of Setzuan* (1940), and *Herr Puntila and His Servant Matti* (1941). Brecht was iconoclastic and bohemian, anti-bourgeois and revolutionary to the end. After the war he returned to Germany and settled in East Berlin, where until his death he directed the famous Berliner Ensemble. His last major play was *The Caucasian Chalk Circle* (1945).

THE GOOD WOMAN

OF SETZUAN ❧ BY BERTOLT BRECHT

English Version by Eric Bentley

CHARACTERS

WONG, *a water seller*
THREE GODS
SHEN TE, *a prostitute, later a shopkeeper*
MRS. SHIN, *former owner of* SHEN TE's *shop*
A FAMILY OF EIGHT (*husband,* *wife,* *brother,* *sister-in-law,* *grandfather,* *nephew, niece, boy*)
AN UNEMPLOYED MAN
A CARPENTER
MRS. MI TZU, SHEN TE's *landlady*

YANG SUN, *an unemployed pilot, later a factory manager*
AN OLD WHORE
A POLICEMAN
AN OLD MAN
AN OLD WOMAN, *his wife*
MR. SHU FU, *a barber*
MRS. YANG, *mother of* YANG SUN
GENTLEMEN, VOICES, CHILDREN (*three*), *etc.*

PROLOGUE

At the gates of the half-Westernized city of Setzuan.* Evening. WONG *the Water Seller introduces himself to the audience.*

WONG. I sell water here in the city of Setzuan. It isn't easy. When water is scarce, I have long distances to go in search of it, and when it is plentiful, I have no income. But in our part of the world there is nothing unusual about poverty. Many people think only the gods can save the situation. And I hear from a cattle merchant—who travels a lot—that some of the highest gods are on their way here at this very moment. Informed sources have it that heaven is quite disturbed at all the complaining. I've been coming out here to the city gates for three days now to bid these gods welcome. I want to be the first to greet them. What about those fellows over there? No, no, they *work*. And that one there has ink on his fingers, he's no god, he must be a clerk from the cement factory. *Those* two are another story. They look as though they'd like to beat you. But

gods don't need to beat you, do they? (THREE GODS *appear.*) What about those three? Old-fashioned clothes—dust on their feet—they *must* be gods! (*He throws himself at their feet.*) Do with me what you will, illustrious ones!

FIRST GOD (*with an ear trumpet*). Ah! (*He is pleased.*) So we were expected?

WONG (*giving them water*). Oh, yes. And I *knew* you'd come.

FIRST GOD. We need somewhere to stay the night. You know of a place?

WONG. The whole town is at your service, illustrious ones! What sort of a place would you like?

(*The* GODS *eye each other.*)

FIRST GOD. Just try the first house you come to, my son.

WONG. That would be Mr. Fo's place.

FIRST GOD. Mr. Fo.

WONG. One moment! (*He knocks at the first house.*)

VOICE FROM MR. FO's. No!

(WONG *returns a little nervously.*)

WONG. It's too bad. Mr. Fo isn't in. And his servants don't dare do a thing

* Thus the first MS of the play. Brecht later learned that Setzuan (Szechwan) is not a city but a province, and changed the script accordingly. But, as often, the solecism seems more appropriate than the fact. E. B.

without his consent. He'll have a fit when he finds out who they turned away, won't he?

FIRST GOD (*smiling*). He will, won't he?

WONG. One moment! The next house is Mr. Cheng's. Won't he be thrilled!

FIRST GOD. Mr. Cheng.

(WONG *knocks*.)

VOICE FROM MR. CHENG'S. Keep your gods. We have our own troubles!

WONG (*back with the* GODS). Mr. Cheng is very sorry, but he has a house-ful of relations. I think some of them are a bad lot, and naturally, he wouldn't like you to see them.

THIRD GOD. Are we so terrible?

WONG. Well, only with bad people, of course. Everyone knows the province of Kwan is always having floods.

SECOND GOD. Really? How's that?

WONG. Why, because they're so irre-ligious.

SECOND GOD. Rubbish. It's because they neglected the dam.

FIRST GOD (*to* SECOND). Sh! (*To* WONG.) You're still in hopes, aren't you, my son?

WONG. Certainly. All Setzuan is com-peting for the honor! What happened up to now is pure coincidence. I'll be back. (*He walks away, but then stands un-decided.*)

SECOND GOD. What did I tell you?

THIRD GOD. It *could* be pure co-incidence.

SECOND GOD. The same coincidence in Shun, Kwan, and Setzuan? People just aren't religious any more, let's face the fact. Our mission has failed!

FIRST GOD. Oh come, we might run into a good person any minute.

THIRD GOD. How did the resolution read? (*Unrolling a scroll and reading from it.*) "The world can stay as it is if enough people are found (*at the word "found" he unrolls it a little more*) living lives worthy of human beings." Good people, that is. Well, what about this Water Seller himself? *He's* good, or I'm very much mistaken.

SECOND GOD. You're very much mis-taken. When he gave us a drink, I had the impression there was something odd about the cup. Well, look! (*He shows the cup to the* FIRST GOD.)

FIRST GOD. A false bottom!

SECOND GOD. The man is a swindler.

FIRST GOD. Very well, count *him* out. That's one man among millions. And as a matter of fact, we only need one on *our* side. These atheists are saying, "The world must be changed because no one can *be* good and *stay* good." No one, eh? I say: let us find one—just one—and we have those fellows where we want them!

THIRD GOD (*to* WONG). Water Seller, is it so hard to find a place to stay?

WONG. Nothing could be easier. It's just me. I don't go about it right.

THIRD GOD. Really?

(*He returns to the others. A* GENTLE-MAN *passes by.*)

WONG. Oh dear, they're catching on. (*He accosts the* GENTLEMAN.) Excuse the intrusion, dear sir, but three gods have just turned up. Three of the very highest. They need a place for the night. Seize this rare opportunity—to have real gods as your guests!

GENTLEMAN (*laughing*). A new way of finding free rooms for a gang of crooks. (*Exit* GENTLEMAN.)

WONG (*shouting at him*). Godless rascal! Have you no religion, gentlemen of Setzuan? (*Pause.*) Patience, illustrious ones! (*Pause.*) There's only one person left. Shen Te, the prostitute. She *can't* say no. (*Calls up to a window*) Shen Te! (SHEN TE *opens the shutters and looks out.*)

WONG. Shen Te, it's Wong. *They're* here, and nobody wants them. Will you take them?

SHEN TE. Oh, no, Wong, I'm expecting a gentleman.

WONG. Can't you forget about him for tonight?

SHEN TE. The rent has to be paid by tomorrow or I'll be out on the street.

WONG. This is no time for calculation, Shen Te.

SHEN TE. Stomachs rumble even on the Emperor's birthday, Wong.

WONG. Setzuan is one big dung hill!

SHEN TE. Oh, very well! I'll hide till my gentleman has come and gone. Then I'll take them. (*She disappears.*)

WONG. They mustn't see her gentleman or they'll know what she is.

FIRST GOD (*who hasn't heard any of this*). I think it's hopeless.

(*They approach* WONG.)

WONG (*jumping, as he finds them be-*

hind him). A room has been found, illustrious ones! (*He wipes sweat off his brow.*)

SECOND GOD. Oh, good.

THIRD GOD. Let's see it.

WONG (*nervously*). Just a minute. It has to be tidied up a bit.

THIRD GOD. Then we'll sit down here and wait.

WONG (*still more nervous*). No, no! (*Holding himself back.*) Too much traffic, you know.

THIRD GOD (*with a smile*). Of course, if you *want* us to move.

(*They retire a little. They sit on a doorstep.* WONG *sits on the ground.*)

WONG (*after a deep breath*). You'll be staying with a single girl—the finest human being in Setzuan!

THIRD GOD. That's nice.

WONG (*to the audience*). They gave me such a look when I picked up my cup just now.

THIRD GOD. You're worn out, Wong.

WONG. A little, maybe.

FIRST GOD. Do people here have a hard time of it?

WONG. The good ones do.

FIRST GOD. What about yourself?

WONG. You mean I'm not good. That's true. And I don't have an easy time either!

(*During this dialogue, a* GENTLEMAN *has turned up in front of* SHEN TE's *house, and has whistled several times. Each time* WONG *has given a start.*)

THIRD GOD (*to* WONG, *softly*). Psst! I think he's gone now.

WONG (*confused and surprised*). Ye-e-es.

(*The* GENTLEMAN *has left now, and* SHEN TE *has come down to the street.*)

SHEN TE (*softly*). Wong!

(*Getting no answer, she goes off down the street.* WONG *arrives just too late, forgetting his carrying pole.*)

WONG (*softly*). Shen Te! Shen Te! (*To himself.*) So she's gone off to earn the rent. Oh dear, I can't go to the gods *again* with no room to offer them. Having failed in the service of the gods, I shall run to my den in the sewer pipe down by the river and hide from their sight!

(*He rushes off.* SHEN TE *returns, looking for him, but finding the* GODS. *She stops in confusion.*)

SHEN TE. You are the illustrious ones?

My name is Shen Te. It would please me very much if my simple room could be of use to you.

THIRD GOD. Where is the Water Seller, Miss . . . Shen Te?

SHEN TE. I missed him, somehow.

FIRST GOD. Oh, he probably thought you weren't coming, and was afraid of telling us.

THIRD GOD (*picking up the carrying pole*). We'll leave this with you. He'll be needing it.

(*Led by* SHEN TE, *they go into the house. It grows dark, then light. Dawn. Again escorted by* SHEN TE, *who leads them through the half-light with a little lamp, the* GODS *take their leave.*)

FIRST GOD. Thank you, thank you, dear Shen Te, for your elegant hospitality! We shall not forget! And give our thanks to the Water Seller—he showed us a good human being.

SHEN TE. Oh, *I'm* not good. Let me tell you something: when Wong asked me to put you up, I hesitated.

FIRST GOD. It's all right to hesitate if you then go ahead! And in giving us that room you did much more than you knew. You proved that good people still exist, a point that has been disputed of late— even in heaven. Farewell!

SECOND GOD. Farewell!

THIRD GOD. Farewell!

SHEN TE. Stop, illustrious ones! I'm not sure you're right. I'd like to be good, it's true, but there's the rent to pay. And that's not all: I sell myself for a living. Even so I can't make ends meet, there's too much competition. I'd like to honor my father and mother and speak nothing but the truth and not covet my neighbor's house. I should love to stay with one man. But how? How is it done? Even breaking a few of your commandments, I can hardly manage.

FIRST GOD (*clearing his throat*). These thoughts are but, um, the misgivings of an unusually good woman!

THIRD GOD. Good-bye, Shen Te! Give our regards to the Water Seller!

SECOND GOD. And above all: be good! Farewell!

FIRST GOD. Farewell!

THIRD GOD. Farewell!

(*They start to wave good-bye.*)

SHEN TE. But everything is so expensive, I don't feel sure I can do it!

SECOND GOD. That's not in our sphere. We never meddle with economics.

THIRD GOD. One moment. (*They stop.*) Isn't it true she might do better if she had more money?

SECOND GOD. Come, come! How could we ever account for it Up Above?

FIRST GOD. Oh, there are ways. (*They put their heads together and confer in dumb show. To* SHEN TE, *with embarrassment.*) As you say you can't pay your rent, well, um, we're not paupers, so of course we *insist* on paying for our room. (*Awkwardly thrusting money into her hands.*) There! (*Quickly.*) But don't tell anyone! The incident is open to misinterpretation.

SECOND GOD. It certainly is!

FIRST GOD (*defensively*). But there's no law against it! It was never decreed that a god mustn't pay hotel bills!

(*The* GODS *leave.*)

✥ 1

A small tobacco shop. The shop is not as yet completely furnished and hasn't started doing business.

SHEN TE (*to the audience*). It's three days now since the gods left. When they said they wanted to pay for the room, I looked down at my hand, and there was more than a thousand silver dollars! I bought a tobacco shop with the money, and moved in yesterday. I don't own the building, of course, but I can pay the rent, and I hope to do a lot of good here. Beginning with Mrs. Shin, who's just coming across the square with her pot. She had the shop before me, and yesterday she dropped in to ask for rice for her children. (*Enter* MRS. SHIN. *Both women bow.*) How do you do, Mrs. Shin.

MRS. SHIN. How do you do, Miss Shen Te. You like your new home?

SHEN TE. Indeed, yes. Did your children have a good night?

MRS. SHIN. In that hovel? The youngest is coughing already.

SHEN TE. Oh, dear!

MRS. SHIN. You're going to learn a thing or two in these slums.

SHEN TE. Slums? That's not what you said when you sold me the shop!

MRS. SHIN. Now don't start nagging! Robbing me and my innocent children

of their home and then calling it a slum! That's the limit! (*She weeps.*)

SHEN TE (*tactfully*). I'll get your rice.

MRS. SHIN. And a little cash while you're at it.

SHEN TE. I'm afraid I haven't sold anything yet.

MRS. SHIN (*screeching*). I've got to have it. Strip the clothes from my back and then cut my throat, will you? I know what I'll do: I'll dump my children on your doorstep! (*She snatches the pot out of* SHEN TE'S *hands.*)

SHEN TE. Please don't be angry. You'll spill the rice.

(*Enter an elderly* HUSBAND *and* WIFE *with their shabbily dressed* NEPHEW.)

WIFE. Shen Te, dear! You've come into money, they tell me. And we haven't a roof over our heads! A tobacco shop. We had one too. But it's gone. Could we spend the night here, do you think?

NEPHEW (*appraising the shop*). Not bad!

WIFE. He's our nephew. We're inseparable!

MRS. SHIN. And who are these . . . ladies and gentlemen?

SHEN TE. They put me up when I first came in from the country. (*To the audience.*) Of course, when my small purse was empty, they put me out on the street, and they may be afraid I'll do the same to them. (*To the newcomers, kindly.*) Come in, and welcome, though I've only one little room for you—it's behind the shop.

HUSBAND. That'll do. Don't worry.

WIFE (*bringing* SHEN TE *some tea*). We'll stay over here, so we won't be in your way. Did you make it a tobacco shop in memory of your first real home? We can certainly give you a hint or two! That's one reason we came.

MRS. SHIN (*to* SHEN TE). Very nice! As long as you have a few customers too!

HUSBAND. Sh! A customer!

(*Enter an* UNEMPLOYED MAN, *in rags.*)

UNEMPLOYED MAN. Excuse me. I'm unemployed.

(MRS. SHIN *laughs.*)

SHEN TE. Can I help you?

UNEMPLOYED MAN. Have you any damaged cigarettes? I thought there might be some damage when you're unpacking.

WIFE. What nerve, begging for tobacco! (*Rhetorically.*) Why don't they ask for bread?

UNEMPLOYED MAN. Bread is expensive. One cigarette butt and I'll be a new man.

SHEN TE (*giving him cigarettes*). That's very important—to be a new man. You'll be my first customer and bring me luck.

(*The* UNEMPLOYED MAN *quickly lights a cigarette, inhales, and goes off, coughing.*)

WIFE. Was that right, Shen Te, dear?

MRS. SHIN. If this is the opening of a shop, you can hold the closing at the end of the week.

HUSBAND. I bet he had money on him.

SHEN TE. Oh, no, he said he hadn't!

NEPHEW. How d'you know he wasn't lying?

SHEN TE (*angrily*). How do you know he was?

WIFE (*wagging her head*). You're too good, Shen Te, dear. If you're going to keep this shop, you'll have to learn to say no.

HUSBAND. Tell them the place isn't yours to dispose of. Belongs to . . . some relative who insists on all accounts being strictly in order . . .

MRS. SHIN. That's right! What do you think you are—a philanthropist?

SHEN TE (*laughing*). Very well, suppose I ask you for my rice back, Mrs. Shin?

WIFE (*combatively, at* MRS. SHIN). So that's *her* rice?

(*Enter the* CARPENTER, *a small man.*)

MRS. SHIN (*who, at the sight of him, starts to hurry away*). See you tomorrow, Miss Shen Te! (*Exit* MRS. SHIN.)

CARPENTER. Mrs. Shin, it's you I want!

WIFE (*to* SHEN TE). Has she some claim on you?

SHEN TE. She's hungry. That's a claim.

CARPENTER. Are you the new tenant? And filling up the shelves already? Well, they're not yours till they're paid for, ma'am. I'm the carpenter, so I should know.

SHEN TE. I took the shop "furnishings included."

CARPENTER. You're in league with that Mrs. Shin, of course. All right. I demand my hundred silver dollars.

SHEN TE. I'm afraid I haven't got a hundred silver dollars.

CARPENTER. Then you'll find it. Or I'll have you arrested.

WIFE (*whispering to* SHEN TE). That relative: make it a cousin.

SHEN TE. Can't it wait till next month?

CARPENTER. No!

SHEN TE. Be a little patient, Mr. Carpenter, I can't settle all claims at once.

CARPENTER. Who's patient with me? (*He grabs a shelf from the wall.*) Pay up—or I take the shelves back!

WIFE. Shen Te! Dear! Why don't you let your . . . cousin settle this affair? (*To* CARPENTER.) Put your claim in writing. Shen Te's cousin will see you get paid.

CARPENTER (*derisively*). Cousin, eh?

HUSBAND. Cousin, yes.

CARPENTER. I know these cousins!

NEPHEW. Don't be silly. He's a personal friend of mine.

HUSBAND. What a man! Sharp as a razor!

CARPENTER. All right. I'll put my claim in writing. (*Puts shelf on floor, sits on it, writes out bill.*)

WIFE (*to* SHEN TE). He'd tear the dress off your back to get his shelves. Never recognize a claim! That's my motto.

SHEN TE. He's done a job, and wants something in return. It's shameful that I can't give it to him. What will the gods say?

HUSBAND. You did your bit when you took *us* in.

(*Enter the* BROTHER, *limping, and the* SISTER-IN-LAW, *pregnant.*)

BROTHER (*to* HUSBAND *and* WIFE). So this is where you're hiding out! There's family feeling for you! Leaving us on the corner!

WIFE (*embarrassed, to* SHEN TE). It's my brother and his wife. (*To them:*) Now stop grumbling, and sit quietly in that corner. (*To* SHEN TE.) It can't be helped. She's in her fifth month.

SHEN TE. Oh yes. Welcome!

WIFE (*to the couple*). Say thank you. (*They mutter something.*) The cups are there. (*To* SHEN TE.) Lucky you bought this shop when you did!

SHEN TE (*laughing and bringing tea*). Lucky indeed!

(*Enter* MRS. MI TZU, *the landlady.*)

MRS. MI TZU. Miss Shen Te? I am Mrs. Mi Tzu, your landlady. I hope our relationship will be a happy one. I like to think I give my tenants modern, personalized service. Here is your lease. (*To the others, as* SHEN TE *reads the lease:*) There's nothing like the opening of a little shop, is there? A moment of true beauty! (*She is looking around.*) Not very much on the shelves, of course. But everything in the gods' good time! Where are your references, Miss Shen Te?

SHEN TE. Do I *have* to have references?

MRS. MI TZU. After all, I haven't a notion who you are!

HUSBAND. Oh, *we'd* be glad to vouch for Miss Shen Te! We'd go through fire for her!

MRS. MI TZU. And who may *you* be?

HUSBAND (*stammering*). Ma Fu, tobacco dealer.

MRS. MI TZU. Where is your shop, Mr. . . . Ma Fu?

HUSBAND. Well, um, I haven't got a shop—I've just sold it.

MRS. MI TZU. I see. (*To* SHEN TE:) Is there no one else that knows you?

WIFE (*whispering to* SHEN TE). Your cousin! Your cousin!

MRS. MI TZU. This is a respectable house, Miss Shen Te. I never sign a lease without certain assurances.

SHEN TE (*slowly, her eyes downcast*). I have . . . a cousin.

MRS. MI TZU. On the square? Let's go over and see him. What does he do?

SHEN TE (*as before*). He lives . . . in another city.

WIFE (*prompting*). Didn't you say he was in Shung?

SHEN TE. That's right. Shung.

HUSBAND (*prompting*). I had his name on the tip of my tongue. Mr. . . .

SHEN TE (*with an effort*). Mr. . . . Shui . . . Ta.

HUSBAND. That's it! Tall, skinny fellow!

SHEN TE. Shui Ta!

NEPHEW (*to* CARPENTER). *You* were in touch with him, weren't you? About the shelves?

CARPENTER (*surlily*). Give him this bill. (*He hands it over.*) I'll be back in the morning. (*Exit* CARPENTER.)

NEPHEW (*calling after him, but with his eyes on* MRS. MI TZU). Don't worry! Mr. Shui Ta pays on the nail!

MRS. MI TZU (*looking closely at* SHEN TE). I'll be happy to make his acquaintance, Miss Shen Te. (*Exit* MRS. MI TZU.) (*Pause.*)

WIFE. By tomorrow morning she'll know more about you than you do yourself.

SISTER-IN-LAW (*to* NEPHEW). This thing isn't built to last.

(*Enter* GRANDFATHER.)

WIFE. It's Grandfather! (*To* SHEN TE:) Such a good old soul!

(*The* BOY *enters.*)

BOY (*over his shoulder*). Here they are!

WIFE. And the boy, how he's grown! But he always could eat enough for ten.

(*Enter the* NIECE.)

WIFE (*to* SHEN TE). Our little niece from the country. There are more of us now than in your time. The less we had, the more there were of us; the more there were of us, the less we had. Give me the key. We must protect ourselves from unwanted guests. (*She takes the key and locks the door.*) Just make yourself at home. I'll light the little lamp.

NEPHEW (*a big joke*). I hope her cousin doesn't drop in tonight! The strict Mr. Shui Ta!

(SISTER-IN-LAW *laughs.*)

BROTHER (*reaching for a cigarette*). One cigarette more or less . . .

HUSBAND. One cigarette more or less. (*They pile into the cigarettes. The* BROTHER *hands a jug of wine round.*)

NEPHEW. Mr. Shui Ta'll pay for it!

GRANDFATHER (*gravely, to* SHEN TE). How do you do?

(SHEN TE, *a little taken aback by the belatedness of the greeting, bows. She has the* CARPENTER's *bill in one hand, the landlady's lease in the other.*)

WIFE. How about a bit of a song? To keep Shen Te's spirits up?

NEPHEW. Good idea. Grandfather: you start!

SONG OF THE SMOKE

GRANDFATHER.
I used to think (before old age beset me)
That brains could fill the pantry of the poor.
But where did all my cerebration get me?
I'm just as hungry as I was before.
So what's the use?
See the smoke float free

Into ever colder coldness!
It's the same with me.

HUSBAND.
The straight and narrow path leads to
     disaster
And so the crooked path I tried to tread.
That got me to disaster even faster
(They say we shall be happy when we're
     dead.)
So what's the use?
See the smoke float free
Into ever colder coldness!
It's the same with me.

NIECE.
You older people, full of expectation,
At any moment now you'll walk the
     plank!
The future's for the younger generation!
Yes, even if that future is a blank.
So what's the use?
See the smoke float free
Into ever colder coldness!
It's the same with me.

NEPHEW (*to the* BROTHER). Where'd
you get that wine?

SISTER-IN-LAW (*answering for the*
BROTHER). He pawned the sack of
tobacco.

HUSBAND (*stepping in*). What? That
tobacco was all we had to fall back on!
You pig!

BROTHER. *You'd* call a man a pig because your wife was frigid! Did you refuse to drink it?

(*They fight. The shelves fall over.*)

SHEN TE (*imploringly*). Oh don't!
Don't break everything! Take it, take it
all, but don't destroy a gift from the gods!

WIFE (*disparagingly*). This shop isn't
big enough. I should never have mentioned it to Uncle and the others. When
they arrive, it's going to be disgustingly
overcrowded.

SISTER-IN-LAW. And did you hear our
gracious hostess? She cools off quick!

(*Voices outside. Knocking at the
door.*)

UNCLE'S VOICE. Open the door!

WIFE. Uncle? Is that you, Uncle?

UNCLE'S VOICE. Certainly, it's me.
Auntie says to tell you she'll have the
children here in ten minutes.

WIFE (*to* SHEN TE). I'll have to let
him in.

SHEN TE (*who scarcely hears her*).
The little lifeboat is swiftly sent down
Too many men too greedily
Hold on to it as they drown.

❦ 1a

WONG's *den in a sewer pipe.*

WONG (*crouching there*). All quiet!
It's four days now since I left the city.
The gods passed this way on the second
day. I heard their steps on the bridge
over there. They must be a long way off
by this time, so I'm safe. (*Breathing a
sigh of relief, he curls up and goes to
sleep. In his dream the pipe becomes
transparent, and the* GODS *appear. Raising
an arm, as if in self-defense:*) I know, I
know, illustrious ones! I found no one
to give you a room—not in all Setzuan!
There, it's out. Please continue on your
way!

FIRST GOD (*mildly*). But you did find
someone. Someone who took us in for
the night, watched over us in our sleep,
and in the early morning lighted us down
to the street with a lamp.

WONG. It was . . . Shen Te that took
you in?

THIRD GOD. Who else?

WONG. And I ran away! "She isn't
coming," I thought, "she just can't afford
it."

GODS (*singing*).
O you feeble, well-intentioned, and yet
     feeble chap
Where there's need the fellow thinks
     there is no goodness!
When there's danger he thinks courage
     starts to ebb away!
Some people only see the seamy side!
What hasty judgment! What premature
     desperation!

WONG. I'm *very* ashamed, illustrious
ones.

FIRST GOD. Do us a favor, Water Seller.
Go back to Setzuan. Find Shen Te, and
give us a report on her. We hear that
she's come into a little money. Show interest in her goodness—for no one can
be good for long if goodness is not in
demand. Meanwhile we shall continue the
search, and find other good people. After

which, the idle chatter about the impossibility of goodness will stop!

(*The* GODS *vanish.*)

❦ 2

A knocking.

WIFE. Shen Te! Someone at the door. Where is she, anyway?

NEPHEW. She must be getting the breakfast. Mr. Shui Ta will pay for it.

(*The* WIFE *laughs and shuffles to the door. Enter* MR. SHUI TA *and the* CARPENTER.)

WIFE. Who is it?

SHUI TA. I am Miss Shen Te's cousin.

WIFE. What?

SHUI TA. My name is Shui Ta.

WIFE. Her cousin?

NEPHEW. Her cousin?

NIECE. But that was a joke. She hasn't got a cousin.

HUSBAND. So early in the morning?

BROTHER. What's all the noise?

SISTER-IN-LAW. This fellow says he's her cousin.

BROTHER. Tell him to prove it.

NEPHEW. Right. If you're Shen Te's cousin, prove it by getting the breakfast.

SHUI TA (*whose regime begins as he puts out the lamp to save oil; loudly, to all present, asleep or awake*). Would you all please get dressed! Customers will be coming! I wish to open my shop!

HUSBAND. *Your* shop? Doesn't it belong to our good friend Shen Te?

(SHUI TA *shakes his head.*)

SISTER-IN-LAW. So we've been cheated. Where *is* the little liar?

SHUI TA. Miss Shen Te has been delayed. She wishes me to tell you there will be nothing she can do—now I am here.

WIFE (*bowled over*). I thought she was good!

NEPHEW. Do you have to believe *him?*

HUSBAND. I don't.

NEPHEW. Then do something.

HUSBAND. Certainly! I'll send out a search party at once. You, you, you, and you, go out and look for Shen Te. (*As the* GRANDFATHER *rises and makes for the door:*) Not you, Grandfather, you and I will hold the fort.

SHUI TA. You won't find Miss Shen Te. She has suspended her hospitable activity for an unlimited period. There are too

many of you. She asked me to say: this is a tobacco shop, not a gold mine.

HUSBAND. Shen Te never said a thing like that. Boy, food! There's a bakery on the corner. Stuff your shirt full when they're not looking!

SISTER-IN-LAW. Don't overlook the raspberry tarts.

HUSBAND. And don't let the policeman see you.

(*The* BOY *leaves.*)

SHUI TA. Don't you depend on this shop now? Then why give it a bad name by stealing from the bakery?

NEPHEW. Don't listen to him. Let's find Shen Te. She'll give him a piece of her mind.

SISTER-IN-LAW. Don't forget to leave us some breakfast.

(BROTHER, SISTER-IN-LAW *and* NEPHEW *leave.*)

SHUI TA (*to the* CARPENTER). You see, Mr. Carpenter, nothing has changed since the poet, eleven hundred years ago, penned these lines:

A governor was asked what was needed
To save the freezing people in the city.
He replied:
"A blanket ten thousand feet long
To cover the city and all its suburbs."

(*He starts to tidy up the shop.*)

CARPENTER. Your cousin owes me money. I've got witnesses. For the shelves.

SHUI TA. Yes, I have your bill. (*He takes it out of his pocket.*) Isn't a hundred silver dollars rather a lot?

CARPENTER. No deductions! I have a wife and children.

SHUI TA. How many children?

CARPENTER. Three.

SHUI TA. I'll make you an offer. Twenty silver dollars.

(*The* HUSBAND *laughs.*)

CARPENTER. You're crazy. Those shelves are real walnut.

SHUI TA. Very well. Take them away.

CARPENTER. What?

SHUI TA. They cost too much. Please take them away.

WIFE. Not bad! (*And she, too, is laughing.*)

CARPENTER (*a little bewildered*). Call Shen Te, someone! (*To* SHUI TA:) She's *good!*

SHUI TA. Certainly. She's ruined.

CARPENTER (*provoked into taking*

some of the shelves). All right, you can keep your tobacco on the floor.

SHUI TA (*to the* HUSBAND). Help him with the shelves.

HUSBAND (*grins and carries one shelf over to the door where the* CARPENTER *now is*). Good-bye, shelves!

CARPENTER (*to the* HUSBAND). You dog! You want my family to starve?

SHUI TA. I repeat my offer. I have no desire to keep my tobacco on the floor. Twenty silver dollars.

CARPENTER (*with desperate aggressiveness*). One hundred!

(SHUI TA *shows indifference, looks through the window. The* HUSBAND *picks up several shelves.*)

CARPENTER (*to* HUSBAND). You needn't smash them against the doorpost, you idiot! (*To* SHUI TA:) These shelves were made to measure. They're no use anywhere else!

SHUI TA. Precisely.

(*The* WIFE *squeals with pleasure.*)

CARPENTER (*giving up, sullenly*). Take the shelves. Pay what you want to pay.

SHUI TA (*smoothly*). Twenty silver dollars.

(*He places two large coins on the table. The* CARPENTER *picks them up.*)

HUSBAND (*brings the shelves back in*). And quite enough too!

CARPENTER (*slinking off*). Quite enough to get drunk on.

HUSBAND (*happily*). Well, we got rid of *him!*

WIFE (*weeping with fun, gives a rendition of the dialogue just spoken*). "Real walnut," says he. "Very well, take them away," says his lordship. "I have three children," says he. "Twenty silver dollars," says his lordship. "They're no use anywhere else," says he. "Pre-cisely," said his lordship! (*She dissolves into shrieks of merriment.*)

SHUI TA. And now: go!

HUSBAND. What's that?

SHUI TA. You're thieves, parasites. I'm giving you this chance. Go!

HUSBAND (*summoning all his ancestral dignity*). That sort deserves no answer. Besides, one should never shout on an empty stomach.

WIFE. Where's that boy?

SHUI TA. Exactly. The boy. I want no stolen goods in this shop. (*Very loudly:*) I strongly advise you to leave! (*But they remain seated, noses in the air. Quietly:*) As you wish. (SHUI TA *goes to the door. A* POLICEMAN *appears.* SHUI TA *bows.*) I am addressing the officer in charge of this precinct?

POLICEMAN. That's right, Mr., um, what was the name, sir?

SHUI TA. Mr. Shui Ta.

POLICEMAN. Yes, of course, sir. (*They exchange a smile.*)

SHUI TA. Nice weather we're having.

POLICEMAN. A little on the warm side, sir.

SHUI TA. Oh, a little on the warm side.

HUSBAND (*whispering to the* WIFE). If he keeps it up till the boy's back, we're done for. (*Tries to signal* SHUI TA.)

SHUI TA (*ignoring the signal*). Weather, of course, is one thing indoors, another out on the dusty street!

POLICEMAN. Oh, quite another, sir!

WIFE (*to the* HUSBAND). It's all right as long as he's standing in the doorway— the boy will see him.

SHUI TA. Step inside for a moment! It's quite cool indoors. My cousin and I have just opened the place. And we attach the greatest importance to being on good terms with the, um, authorities.

POLICEMAN (*entering*). Thank you, Mr. Shui Ta. It *is* cool!

HUSBAND (*whispering to the* WIFE). And now the boy *won't* see him.

SHUI TA (*showing* HUSBAND *and* WIFE *to the* POLICEMAN). Visitors, I think my cousin knows them. They were just leaving.

HUSBAND (*defeated*). Ye-e-es, we were . . . just leaving.

SHUI TA. I'll tell my cousin you couldn't wait.

(*Noise from the street. Shouts of "Stop, Thief!"*)

POLICEMAN. What's that?

(*The* BOY *is in the doorway with cakes and buns and rolls spilling out of his shirt. The* WIFE *signals desperately to him to leave. He gets the idea.*)

POLICEMAN. No, you don't! (*He grabs the* BOY *by the collar.*) Where's all this from?

BOY (*vaguely pointing*). Down the street.

POLICEMAN (*grimly*). So that's it. (*Prepares to arrest the* BOY.)

WIFE (*stepping in*). And *we* knew

nothing about it. (*To the* BOY:) Nasty little thief!

POLICEMAN (*dryly*). Can you clarify the situation, Mr. Shui Ta? (SHUI TA *is silent.*)

POLICEMAN (*who understands silence*). Aha. You're all coming with me—to the station.

SHUI TA. I can hardly say how sorry I am that *my* establishment. . . .

THE WIFE. Oh, he saw the boy leave not ten minutes ago!

SHUI TA. And to conceal the theft asked a policeman in?

POLICEMAN. Don't listen to her, Mr. Shui Ta, I'll be happy to relieve you of their presence one and all! (*To all three:*) Out! (*He drives them before him.*)

GRANDFATHER (*leaving last, gravely*). Good morning!

POLICEMAN. Good morning!

(SHUI TA, *left alone, continues to tidy up.* MRS. MI TZU *breezes in.*)

MRS. MI TZU. *You're* her cousin, are you? Then have the goodness to explain what all this means—police dragging people from a respectable house! By what right does your Miss Shen Te turn my property into a house of assignation? —Well, as you see, I know all!

SHUI TA. Yes. My cousin has the worst possible reputation: that of being poor.

MRS. MI TZU. No sentimental rubbish, Mr. Shui Ta. Your cousin was a common. . . .

SHUI TA. Pauper. Let's use the uglier word.

MRS. MI TZU. I'm speaking of her conduct, not her earnings. But there must have *been* earnings, or how did she buy all this? Several elderly gentlemen took care of it, I suppose. I repeat: this is a respectable house! I have tenants who prefer not to live under the same roof with such a person.

SHUI TA (*quietly*). How much do you want?

MRS. MI TZU (*he is ahead of her now*). I beg your pardon.

SHUI TA. To reassure yourself. To reassure your tenants. How much will it cost?

MRS. MI TZU. You're a cool customer.

SHUI TA (*picking up the lease*). The rent is high. (*He reads on.*) I assume it's payable by the month?

MRS. MI TZU. Not in her case.

SHUI TA (*looking up*). What?

MRS. MI TZU. Six months rent payable in advance. Two hundred silver dollars.

SHUI TA. Six . . . ! Sheer usury! And where am I to find it?

MRS. MI TZU. You should have thought of that before.

SHUI TA. Have you no heart, Mrs. Mi Tzu? It's true Shen Te acted foolishly, being kind to all those people, but she'll improve with time. I'll see to it she does. She'll work her fingers to the bone to pay her rent, and all the time be as quiet as a mouse, as humble as a fly.

MRS. MI TZU. Her social background. . . .

SHUI TA. Out of the depths! She came out of the depths! And before she'll go back there, she'll work, sacrifice, shrink from nothing. . . . Such a tenant is worth her weight in gold, Mrs. Mi Tzu.

MRS. MI TZU. It's silver we were talking about, Mr. Shui Ta. Two hundred silver dollars or. . . .

(*Enter the* POLICEMAN)

POLICEMAN. Am I intruding, Mr. Shui Ta?

MRS. MI TZU. This tobacco shop is well-known to the police, I see.

POLICEMAN. Mr. Shui Ta has done us a service, Mrs. Mi Tzu. I am here to present our official felicitations!

MRS. MI TZU. That mean less than nothing to me, sir. Mr. Shui Ta, all I can say is: I hope your cousin will find my terms acceptable. Good day, gentlemen. (*Exit.*)

SHUI TA. Good day, ma'am.

(*Pause.*)

POLICEMAN. Mrs. Mi Tzu a bit of a stumbling block, sir?

SHUI TA. She wants six months' rent in advance.

POLICEMAN. And you haven't got it, eh? (SHUI TA *is silent.*) But surely you can get it, sir? A man like you?

SHUI TA. What about a woman like Shen Te?

POLICEMAN. You're not staying, sir?

SHUI TA. No, and I won't be back. Do you smoke?

POLICEMAN (*taking two cigars, and placing them both in his pocket*). Thank you, sir—I see your point. Miss Shen Te —let's mince no words—Miss Shen Te lived by selling herself. "What else could she have done?" you ask. "How else was she to pay the rent?" True. But the fact remains, Mr. Shui Ta, it is not respectable. Why not? A very deep question. But, in the first place, love—love isn't bought and sold like cigars, Mr. Shui Ta. In the second place, it isn't respectable to go waltzing off with someone that's paying his way, so to speak—it must be for love! Thirdly and lastly, as the proverb has it: not for a handful of rice but for love! (*Pause. He is thinking hard.*) "Well," you may say, "and what good is all this wisdom if the milk's already spilt?" Miss Shen Te is what she is. The question is *where* she is. We have to face the fact that if she doesn't get hold of six months' rent pronto, she'll be back on the streets. The question then as I see it—everything in this world is a matter of opinion—the question as I see it is: *how* is she to get hold of this rent? How? Mr. Shui Ta: I don't know. (*Pause.*) I take that back, sir. It's just come to me. A husband. We must find her a husband!

(*Enter a little* OLD WOMAN.)

OLD WOMAN. A good cheap cigar for my husband, we'll have been married forty years tomorrow and we're having a little celebration.

SHUI TA. Forty years? And you still want to celebrate?

OLD WOMAN. As much as we can afford to. We have the carpet shop across the square. We'll be good neighbors, I hope?

SHUI TA. I hope so too.

POLICEMAN (*who keeps making discoveries*). Mr. Shui Ta, you know what we need? We need capital. And how do we acquire capital? We get married.

SHUI TA (*to* OLD WOMAN). I'm afraid I've been pestering this gentleman with my personal worries.

POLICEMAN (*lyrically*). We can't pay six months' rent, so what do we do? We marry money.

SHUI TA. That might not be easy.

POLICEMAN. Oh, I don't know. She's a good match. Has a nice, growing business. (*To the* OLD WOMAN:) What do you think?

OLD WOMAN (*undecided*). Well—

POLICEMAN: Should she put an ad in the paper?

OLD WOMAN (*not eager to commit herself*). Well, if *she* agrees—

POLICEMAN. I'll write it for her. *You*

lend us a hand, and *we* write an ad for you! (*He chuckles away to himself, takes out his notebook, wets the stump of a pencil between his lips, and writes away.*)

SHUI TA (*slowly*). Not a bad idea.

POLICEMAN. "What . . . *respectable* . . . man . . . with small capital . . . widower . . . not excluded . . . desires . . . marriage . . . into flourishing . . . tobacco shop?" And now let's add: "Am . . . pretty . . ." No! . . . "Prepossessing appearance."

SHUI TA. If you don't think that's an exaggeration?

OLD WOMAN. Oh, not a bit. I've seen her.

(*The* POLICEMAN *tears the page out of his notebook, and hands it over to* SHUI TA.)

SHUI TA (*with horror in his voice*). How much luck we need to keep our heads above water! How many ideas! How many friends! (*To the* POLICEMAN:) Thank you, sir. I think I see my way clear.

☙ 3

Evening in the municipal park. Noise of a plane overhead. YANG SUN, *a young man in rags, is following the plane with his eyes: one can tell that the machine is describing a curve above the park.* YANG SUN *then takes a rope out of his pocket, looking anxiously about him as he does so. He moves toward a large willow. Enter two prostitutes, one old, the other the* NIECE *whom we have already met.*

NIECE. Hello. Coming with me?

YANG SUN (*taken aback*). If you'd like to buy me a dinner.

OLD WHORE. Buy you a dinner! (*To the* NIECE:) Oh, we know him—it's the unemployed pilot. Waste no time on him!

NIECE. But he's the only man left in the park. And it's going to rain.

OLD WHORE. Oh, how do you know?

(*And they pass by.* YANG SUN *again looks about him, again takes his rope, and this time throws it round a branch of the willow tree. Again he is interrupted. It is the two prostitutes returning —and in such a hurry they don't notice him.*)

NIECE. It's going to pour!

(*Enter* SHEN TE.)

OLD WHORE. There's that *gorgon* Shen Te! That *drove* your family out into the cold!

NIECE. It wasn't her. It was that cousin of hers. She offered to pay for the cakes. I've nothing against her.

OLD WHORE. I have, though. (*So that* SHEN TE *can hear:*) Now where could the little lady be off to? She may be rich now but that won't stop her snatching our young men, will it?

SHEN TE. I'm going to the tearoom by the pond.

NIECE. Is it true what they say? You're marrying a widower—with three children?

SHEN TE. Yes. I'm just going to see him.

YANG SUN (*his patience at breaking point*). Move on there! This is a park, not a whorehouse!

OLD WHORE. Shut your mouth!

(*But the two prostitutes leave.*)

YANG SUN. Even in the farthest corner of the park, even when it's raining, you can't get rid of them! (*He spits.*)

SHEN TE (*overhearing this*). And what right have you to scold them? (*But at this point she sees the rope.*) Oh!

YANG SUN. Well, what are you staring at?

SHEN TE. That rope. What is it for?

YANG SUN. Think! Think! I haven't a penny. Even if I had, I wouldn't spend it on you. I'd buy a drink of water.

(*The rain starts.*)

SHEN TE (*still looking at the rope*). What is the rope for? You mustn't!

YANG SUN. What's it to you? Clear out!

SHEN TE (*irrelevantly*). It's raining.

YANG SUN. Well, don't try to come under this tree.

SHEN TE. Oh, no. (*She stays in the rain.*)

YANG SUN. Now go away. (*Pause.*) For one thing, I don't like your looks, you're bowlegged.

SHEN TE (*indignantly*). That's not true!

YANG SUN. Well, don't show 'em to me. Look, it's raining. You better come under this tree.

(*Slowly, she takes shelter under the tree.*)

SHEN TE. Why did you want to do it?

YANG SUN. You really want to know? (*Pause.*) To get rid of you! (*Pause.*) You know what a flyer is?

SHEN TE. Oh yes, I've met a lot of pilots. At the tearoom.

YANG SUN. You call *them* flyers? Think they know what a machine is? Just 'cause they have leather helmets? They gave the airfield director a bribe, that's the way *those* fellows got up in the air! Try one of them out sometime. "Go up to two thousand feet," tell him, "then let it fall, then pick it up again with a flick of the wrist at the last moment." Know what he'll say to that? "It's not in my contract." Then again, there's the landing problem. It's like landing on your backside. It's no different, planes are human. Those fools don't understand. (*Pause.*) And I'm the biggest fool for reading the book on flying in the Peking school and skipping the page where it says: "We've got enough flyers and we don't need you." I'm a mail pilot with no mail. You understand that?

SHEN TE (*shyly*). Yes, I do.

YANG SUN. No, you don't. You'd never understand that.

SHEN TE. When we were little we had a crane with a broken wing. He made friends with us and was very good-natured about our jokes. He would strut along behind us and call out to stop us going too fast for him. But every spring and autumn when the cranes flew over the villages in great swarms, he got quite restless. (*Pause.*) I understand that. (*She bursts out crying.*)

YANG SUN. Don't!

SHEN TE (*quieting down*). No.

YANG SUN. It's bad for the complexion.

SHEN TE (*sniffing*). I've stopped.

(*She dries her tears on her big sleeve. Leaning against the tree, but not looking at her, he reaches for her face.*)

YANG SUN. You can't even wipe your own face. (*He is wiping it for her with his handkerchief. Pause.*)

SHEN TE (*still sobbing*). I don't know anything!

YANG SUN. You interrupted me! What for?

SHEN TE. It's such a rainy day. You only wanted to do . . . *that* because it's such a rainy day.

(*To the audience:*)

In our country
The evenings should never be somber
High bridges over rivers
The grey hour between night and morning
And the long, long winter:
Such things are dangerous
For, with all the misery,
A very little is enough
And men throw away an unbearable life.
(*Pause.*)
YANG SUN. Talk about yourself for a change.
SHEN TE. What about me? I have a shop.
YANG SUN (*incredulous*). You have a shop, have you? Never thought of walking the streets?
SHEN TE. I did walk the streets. Now I have a shop.
YANG SUN (*ironically*). A gift of the gods, I suppose!
SHEN TE. How did you know?
YANG SUN (*even more ironical*). One fine evening the gods turned up saying: here's some money!
SHEN TE (*quickly*). One fine morning.
YANG SUN (*fed up*). This isn't much of an entertainment.
(*Pause.*)
SHEN TE. I can play the zither a little. (*Pause.*) And I can mimic men. (*Pause.*) I got the shop, so the first thing I did was to give my zither away. I can be as stupid as a fish now, I said to myself, and it won't matter.
I'm rich now, I said
I walk alone, I sleep alone
For a whole year, I said
I'll have nothing to do with a man.
YANG SUN. And now you're marrying one! The one at the tearoom by the pond?
(SHEN TE *is silent.*)
YANG SUN. What do you know about love?
SHEN TE. Everything.
YANG SUN. Nothing. (*Pause.*) Or d'you just mean you enjoyed it?
SHEN TE. No.
YANG SUN (*again without turning to look at her, he strokes her cheek with his hand*). You like that?
SHEN TE. Yes.
YANG SUN (*breaking off*). You're easily satisfied, I must say. (*Pause.*) What a town!
SHEN TE. You have no friends?
YANG SUN (*defensively*). Yes, I have!

(*Change of tone.*) But they don't want to hear I'm still unemployed. "What?" they ask. "Is there still water in the sea?" You have friends?
SHEN TE (*hesitating*). Just a . . . cousin.
YANG SUN. Watch him carefully.
SHEN TE. He only came once. Then he went away. He won't be back. (YANG SUN *is looking away.*). But to be without hope, they say, is to be without goodness!
(*Pause.*)
YANG SUN. Go on talking. A voice is a voice.
SHEN TE. Once, when I was a little girl, I fell, with a load of brushwood. An old man picked me up. He gave me a penny too. Isn't it funny how people who don't have very much like to give some of it away? They must like to show what they can do, and how could they show it better than by being kind? Being wicked is just like being clumsy. When we sing a song, or build a machine, or plant some rice, we're being kind. You're kind.
YANG SUN. You make it sound easy.
SHEN TE. Oh, no. (*Little pause.*) Oh! A drop of rain!
YANG SUN. Where'd you feel it?
SHEN TE. Between the eyes.
YANG SUN. Near the right eye? Or the left?
SHEN TE. Near the left eye.
YANG SUN. Oh, good. (*He is getting sleepy.*) So you're through with men, eh?
SHEN TE (*with a smile*). But I'm not bowlegged.
YANG SUN. Perhaps not.
SHEN TE. Definitely not.
(*Pause.*)
YANG SUN (*leaning wearily against the willow*). I haven't had a drop to drink all day, I haven't eaten anything for *two* days. I couldn't love you if I tried.
(*Pause.*)
SHEN TE. I like it in the rain.
(*Enter* WONG *the Water Seller, singing.*)

THE SONG OF THE WATER SELLER IN THE RAIN

"Buy my water," I am yelling
And my fury restraining
For no water I'm selling

'Cause it's raining, 'cause it's raining!
I keep yelling: "Buy my water!"
But no one's buying
Athirst and dying
And drinking and paying!
Buy water!
Buy water, you dogs!

Nice to dream of lovely weather!
Think of all the consternation
Were there no precipitation
Half a dozen years together!
Can't you hear them shrieking: "Water!"
Pretending they adore me?
They all would go down on their knees
    before me!
Down on your knees!
Go down on your knees, you dogs!

What are lawns and hedges thinking?
What are fields and forests saying?
"At the cloud's breast we are drinking!
And we've no idea who's paying!"
I keep yelling: "Buy my water!"
But no one's buying
Athirst and dying
And drinking and paying!
Buy water!
Buy water, you dogs!

(*The rain has stopped now.* SHEN TE *sees* WONG *and runs toward him.*)
SHEN TE. Wong! You're back! Your carrying pole's at the shop.
WONG. Oh, thank you, Shen Te. And how is life treating *you?*
SHEN TE. I've just met a brave and clever man. And I want to buy him a cup of your water.
WONG (*bitterly*). Throw back your head and open your mouth and you'll have all the water you need—
SHEN TE (*tenderly*).

I want *your* water, Wong
The water that has tired you so
The water that you carried all this way
The water that is hard to sell because it's
    been raining.

I need it for the young man over there
—he's a flyer!

A flyer is a bold man:
Braving the storms
In company with the clouds

He crosses the heavens
And brings to friends in far-away lands
The friendly mail!

(*She pays* WONG, *and runs over to* YANG SUN *with the cup. But* YANG SUN *is fast asleep.*)
SHEN TE (*calling to* WONG, *with a laugh*). He's fallen asleep! Despair and rain and I have worn him out!

🌶 *3a*

WONG's *den. The sewer pipe is transparent, and the* GODS *again appear to* WONG *in a dream.*
WONG (*radiant*). I've seen her, illustrious ones! And she hasn't changed!
FIRST GOD. That's good to hear.
WONG. She loves someone.
FIRST GOD. Let's hope the experience gives her the strength to stay good!
WONG. It does. She's doing good deeds all the time.
FIRST GOD. Ah? What sort? What sort of good deeds, Wong?
WONG. Well, she has a kind word for everybody.
FIRST GOD (*eagerly*). And then?
WONG. Hardly anyone leaves her shop without tobacco in his pocket—even if he can't pay for it.
FIRST GOD. Not bad at all. Next?
WONG. She's putting up a family of eight.
FIRST GOD (*gleefully, to the* SECOND GOD). Eight! (*To* WONG.) And that's not all, of course!
WONG. She bought a cup of water from me even though it was raining.
FIRST GOD. Yes, yes, yes, all these smaller good deeds!
WONG. Even they run into money. A little tobacco shop doesn't make so much.
FIRST GOD (*sententiously*). A prudent gardener works miracles on the smallest plot.
WONG. She hands out rice every morning. That eats up half her earnings.
FIRST GOD (*a little disappointed*). Well, as a beginning . . .
WONG. They call her the Angel of the Slums—whatever the Carpenter may say!
FIRST GOD. What's this? A carpenter speaks ill of her?

WONG. Oh, he only says her shelves weren't paid for in full.

SECOND GOD (*who has a bad cold and can't pronounce his n's and m's*). What's this? Not paying a carpenter? Why was that?

WONG. I suppose she didn't have the money.

SECOND GOD (*severely*). One pays what one owes, that's in our book of rules! First the letter of the law, then the spirit!

WONG. But it wasn't Shen Te, illustrious ones, it was her cousin. She called *him* in to help.

SECOND GOD. Then her cousin must never darken her threshold again!

WONG. Very well, illustrious ones! But in fairness to Shen Te, let me say that her cousin is a businessman.

FIRST GOD. Perhaps we should enquire what is customary? I find business quite unintelligible. But everybody's doing it. Business! Did the Seven Good Kings do business? Did Kung the Just sell fish?

SECOND GOD. In any case, such a thing must not occur again!

(*The* GODS *start to leave.*)

THIRD GOD. Forgive us for taking this tone with you, Wong, we haven't been getting enough sleep. The rich recommend us to the poor, and the poor tell us they haven't enough room.

SECOND GOD. Feeble, feeble, the best of them!

FIRST GOD. No great deeds! No heroic daring!

THIRD GOD. On such a *small* scale!

SECOND GOD. Sincere, yes, but what is actually *achieved?*

(*One can no longer hear them.*)

WONG (*calling after them*). I've thought of something, illustrious ones: Perhaps you shouldn't ask—too—much—all—at—once!

🌷 4

The square in front of SHEN TE's *tobacco shop. Besides* SHEN TE's *place, two other shops are seen: the carpet shop and a barber's. Morning. Outside* SHEN TE's *the* GRANDFATHER, *the* SISTER-IN-LAW, *the* UNEMPLOYED MAN, *and* MRS. SHIN *stand waiting.*

SISTER-IN-LAW. She's been out all night again.

MRS. SHIN. No sooner did we get rid of that crazy cousin of hers than Shen Te herself starts carrying on! Maybe she does give us an ounce of rice now and then, but can you depend on her?

(*Loud voices from the Barber's.*)

VOICE OF SHU FU. What are you doing in my shop? Get out—at once!

VOICE OF WONG. But sir. They all let me sell . . .

(WONG *comes staggering out of the Barber's shop pursued by* MR. SHU FU, *the Barber, a fat man carrying a heavy curling iron.*)

SHU FU. Get out, I said! Pestering my customers with your slimy old water! Get out! Take your cup!

(*He holds out the cup.* WONG *reaches for it.* MR. SHU FU *strikes his hand with the curling iron, which is hot.* WONG *howls.*)

SHU FU. You had it coming, my man!

(*Puffing, he returns to his shop. The* UNEMPLOYED MAN *picks up the cup and gives it to* WONG.)

UNEMPLOYED MAN. You can report that to the police.

WONG. My hand! It's smashed up!

UNEMPLOYED MAN. Any bones broken?

WONG. I can't move my fingers.

UNEMPLOYED MAN. Sit down. I'll put some water on it.

(WONG *sits.*)

MRS. SHIN. The water won't cost you anything.

SISTER-IN-LAW. You might have got a bandage from Miss Shen Te till she took to staying out all night. It's a scandal.

MRS. SHIN (*despondently*). If you ask me, she's forgotten we ever existed!

(*Enter* SHEN TE *down the street, with a dish of rice.*)

SHEN TE (*to the audience*). How wonderful to see Setzuan in the early morning! I always used to stay in bed with my dirty blanket over my head, afraid to wake up. This morning I saw the newspapers being delivered by little boys, the streets being washed by strong men, and fresh vegetables coming in from the country on ox carts. It's a long walk from where Yang Sun lives, but I feel lighter at every step. They say you walk on air when you're in love, but it's even better walking on the rough earth, than on the hard cement. In the early morning, the old city looks like a great heap of rubbish! Nice, though, with all its little lights. And the sky, so pink, so transparent, before the dust comes and muddies it! What a lot you miss if you never see your city rising from its slumbers like an honest old craftsman pumping his lungs full of air and reaching for his tools, as the poet says! (*Cheerfully, to her waiting guests.*) Good morning, everyone, here's your rice! (*Distributing the rice, she comes upon* WONG.) Good morning, Wong, I'm quite lightheaded today. On my way over, I looked at myself in all the shop windows. I'd love to be beautiful.

(*She slips into the carpet shop.* MR. SHU FU *has just emerged from his shop.*)

SHU FU (*to the audience*). It surprises me how beautiful Miss Shen Te is looking today! I never gave her a passing thought before. But now I've been gazing upon her comely form for exactly three minutes! I begin to suspect I am in love with her. She is overpoweringly attractive! (*Crossly, to* WONG.) Be off with you, rascal!

(*He returns to his shop.* SHEN TE *comes back out of the carpet shop with the* OLD MAN, *its proprietor, and his wife—whom we have already met—the* OLD WOMAN. SHEN TE *is wearing a shawl. The* OLD MAN *is holding up a looking glass for her.*)

OLD WOMAN. Isn't it lovely? We'll give you a reduction because there's a little hole in it.

SHEN TE (*looking at another shawl on the* OLD WOMAN's *arm*). The other one's nice too.

OLD WOMAN (*smiling*). Too bad there's no hole in that!

SHEN TE. That's right. My shop doesn't make very much.

OLD WOMAN. And your good deeds eat it all up! Be more careful, my dear. . . .

SHEN TE (*trying on the shawl with the hole*). Just now, I'm lightheaded! Does the color suit me?

OLD WOMAN. You'd better ask a man.

SHEN TE (*to the* OLD MAN). Does the color suit me?

OLD MAN. You'd better ask your young friend.

SHEN TE. I'd like to have your opinion.

OLD MAN. It suits you very well. But wear it this way: the dull side out.

(SHEN TE *pays up.*)

OLD WOMAN. If you decide you don't like it, you can exchange it. (*She pulls* SHEN TE *to one side.*) Has he got money?

SHEN TE (*with a laugh*). Yang Sun? Oh, no.

OLD WOMAN. Then how're you going to pay your rent?

SHEN TE. I'd forgotten about that.

OLD WOMAN. And next Monday is the first of the month! Miss Shen Te, I've got something to say to you. After we (*indicating her husband*) got to know you, we had our doubts about that marriage ad. We thought it would be better if you'd let *us* help you. Out of our savings. We reckon we could lend you two hundred silver dollars. We don't need anything in writing—you could pledge us your tobacco stock.

SHEN TE. You're prepared to lend money to a person like me?

OLD WOMAN. It's folks like you that need it. We'd think twice about lending anything to your cousin.

OLD MAN (*coming up*). All settled, my dear?

SHEN TE. I wish the gods could have heard what your wife was just saying, Mr. Ma. They're looking for good people who're happy—and helping me makes you happy because you know it was love that got me into difficulties!

(*The* OLD COUPLE *smile knowingly at each other.*)

OLD MAN. And here's the money, Miss Shen Te.

(*He hands her an envelope.* SHEN TE *takes it. She bows. They bow back. They return to their shop.*)

SHEN TE (*holding up her envelope*). Look, Wong, here's six months' rent! Don't you believe in miracles now? And how do you like my new shawl?

WONG. For the young fellow I saw you with in the park?

(SHEN TE *nods.*)

MRS. SHIN. Never mind all that. It's time you took a look at his hand!

SHEN TE. Have you hurt your hand?

MRS. SHIN. That barber smashed it with his hot curling iron. Right in front of our eyes.

SHEN TE (*shocked at herself*). And I never noticed! We must get you to a doctor this minute or who knows what will happen?

UNEMPLOYED MAN. It's not a doctor he should see, it's a judge. He can ask for compensation. The barber's filthy rich.

WONG. You think I have a chance?

MRS. SHIN (with relish). If it's really good and smashed. But is it?

WONG. I think so. It's very swollen. Could I get a pension?

MRS. SHIN. You'd need a witness.

WONG. Well, you all saw it. You could all testify.

(He looks round. The UNEMPLOYED MAN, the GRANDFATHER, and the SISTER-IN-LAW are all sitting against the wall of the shop eating rice. Their concentration on eating is complete.)

SHEN TE (to MRS. SHIN). You saw it yourself.

MRS. SHIN. I want nothing to do with the police. It's against my principles.

SHEN TE (to SISTER-IN-LAW). What about you?

SISTER-IN-LAW. Me? I wasn't looking.

SHEN TE (to the GRANDFATHER, coaxingly). Grandfather, you'll testify, won't you?

SISTER-IN-LAW. And a lot of good that will do. He's simple-minded.

SHEN TE (to the UNEMPLOYED MAN). You seem to be the only witness left.

UNEMPLOYED MAN. My testimony would only hurt him. I've been picked up twice for begging.

SHEN TE.

Your brother is assaulted, and you shut your eyes?

He is hit, cries out in pain, and you are silent?

The beast prowls, chooses and seizes his victim, and you say:

"Because we showed no displeasure, he has spared us."

If no one present will be a witness, I will.

I'll say I saw it.

MRS. SHIN (solemnly). The name for that is perjury.

WONG. I don't know if I can accept that. Though maybe I'll have to. (Looking at his hand.) Is it swollen enough, do you think? The swelling's not going down?

UNEMPLOYED MAN. No, no, the swelling's holding up well.

WONG. Yes. It's more swollen, if anything. Maybe my wrist is broken after all. I'd better see a judge at once.

(Holding his hand very carefully, and fixing his eyes on it, he runs off. MRS. SHIN goes quickly into the Barber's shop.)

UNEMPLOYED MAN (seeing her). She is getting on the right side of Mr. Shu Fu.

SISTER-IN-LAW. You and I can't change the world, Shen Te.

SHEN TE. Go away! Go away all of you!

(The UNEMPLOYED MAN, the SISTER-IN-LAW, and the GRANDFATHER stalk off, eating and sulking.)

(To the audience.)

They've stopped answering

They stay put

They do as they're told

They don't care

Nothing can make them look up

But the smell of food.

(Enter MRS. YANG, YANG SUN's mother, out of breath.)

MRS. YANG. Miss Shen Te. My son has told me everything. I am Mrs. Yang, Sun's mother. Just think. He's got an offer. Of a job as a pilot. A letter has just come. From the director of the airfield in Peking!

SHEN TE. So he can fly again? Isn't that wonderful!

MRS YANG (less breathlessly all the time). They won't give him the job for nothing. They want five hundred silver dollars.

SHEN TE. We can't let money stand in his way, Mrs. Yang!

MRS. YANG. If only you could help him out!

SHEN TE. I have the shop. I can try! (She embraces MRS. YANG.) I happen to have two hundred with me now. Take it. (She gives her the OLD COUPLE's money.) It was a loan but they said I could repay it with my tobacco stock.

MRS. YANG. And they were calling Sun the Dead Pilot of Setzuan! A friend in need!

SHEN TE. We must find another three hundred.

MRS. YANG. How?

SHEN TE. Let me think. (Slowly.) I know someone who can help. I didn't want to call on his services again, he's hard and cunning. But a flyer must fly. And I'll make this the last time.

(Distant sound of a plane.)

MRS. YANG. If the man you mentioned can do it. . . . Oh, look, there's the morning mail plane, heading for Peking!

SHEN TE. The pilot can see us, let's wave!

(*They wave. The noise of the engine is louder.*)

MRS. YANG. You know that pilot up there?

SHEN TE. Wave, Mrs. Yang! I know the pilot who will be up there. He gave up hope. But he'll do it now. One man to raise himself above the misery, above us all.

(*To the audience.*)
Yang Sun, my lover:
Braving the storms
In company with the clouds
Crossing the heavens
And bringing to friends in far-away lands
The friendly mail!

 4a

In front of the inner curtain. Enter SHEN TE, *carrying* SHUI TA's *mask. She sings.*

THE SONG OF DEFENSELESSNESS

In our country
A useful man needs luck
Only if he finds strong backers
Can he prove himself useful.
The good can't defend themselves and
Even the gods are defenseless.

Oh, why don't the gods have their own ammunition
And launch against badness their own expedition
Enthroning the good and preventing sedition
And bringing the world to a peaceful condition?

Oh, why don't the gods do the buying and selling
Injustice forbidding, starvation dispelling
Give bread to each city and joy to each dwelling?
Oh, why don't the gods do the buying and selling?

(*She puts on* SHUI TA's *mask and sings in his voice.*)

You can only help one of your luckless brothers
By trampling down a dozen others.

Why is it the gods do not feel indignation
And come down in fury to end exploitation
Defeat all defeat and forbid desperation
Refusing to tolerate such toleration?

Why is it?

 5

SHEN TE's *tobacco shop. Behind the counter,* MR. SHUI TA, *reading the paper.* MRS. SHIN *is cleaning up. She talks and he takes no notice.*

MRS. SHIN. And when certain rumors get about, what *happens* to a little place like this? It goes to pot. *I* know. So, if you want my advice, Mr. Shui Ta, find out just what has been going on between Miss Shen Te and that Yang Sun from Yellow Street. And remember: a certain interest in Miss Shen Te has been expressed by the barber next door, a man with twelve houses and only one wife, who, for that matter, is likely to drop off at any time. A certain interest has been expressed. He was even enquiring about her means and, if *that* doesn't prove a man is getting serious, what would? (*Still getting no response, she leaves with her bucket.*)

YANG SUN'S VOICE. Is that Miss Shen Te's tobacco shop?

MRS. SHIN'S VOICE. Yes, it is, but it's Mr. Shui Ta who's here today.

(SHUI TA *runs to the mirror with the short, light steps of* SHEN TE, *and is just about to start primping, when he realizes his mistake, and turns away, with a short laugh. Enter* YANG SUN. MRS. SHIN *enters behind him and slips into the back room to eavesdrop.*)

YANG SUN. I am Yang Sun. (SHUI TA *bows.*) Is Shen Te in?

SHUI TA. No.

YANG SUN. I guess you know our relationship? (*He is inspecting the stock.*) Quite a place! And I thought she was just talking big. I'll be flying again, all right. (*He takes a cigar, solicits and receives a light from* SHUI TA.) You think we can squeeze the other three hundred out of the tobacco stock?

SHUI TA. May I ask if it is your intention to sell at once?

YANG SUN. It was decent of her to come out with the two hundred but they aren't much use with the other three hundred still missing.

SHUI TA. Shen Te was overhasty promising so much. She might have to sell the shop itself to raise it. Haste, they say, is the wind that blows the house down.

YANG SUN. Oh, she isn't a girl to keep a man waiting. For one thing or the other, if you take my meaning.

SHUI TA. I take your meaning.

YANG SUN (*leering*). Uh, huh.

SHUI TA. Would you explain what the five hundred silver dollars are for?

YANG SUN. Want to sound me out? Very well. The director of the Peking airfield is a friend of mine from flying school. I give him five hundred: he gets me the job.

SHUI TA. The price is high.

YANG SUN. Not as these things go. He'll have to fire one of the present pilots —for negligence. Only the man he has in mind isn't negligent. Not easy, you understand. You needn't mention that part of it to Shen Te.

SHUI TA (*looking intently at* YANG SUN). Mr. Yang Sun, you are asking my cousin to give up her possessions, leave her friends, and place her entire fate in your hands. I presume you intend to marry her?

YANG SUN. I'd be prepared to.

(*Slight pause.*)

SHUI TA. Those two hundred silver dollars would pay the rent here for six months. If you were Shen Te wouldn't you be tempted to continue in business?

YANG SUN. What? Can you imagine Yang Sun the Flyer behind a counter? (*In an oily voice.*) "A strong cigar or a mild one, worthy sir?" Not in this century!

SHUI TA. My cousin wishes to follow the promptings of her heart, and, from her own point of view, she may even have what is called the right to love. Accordingly, she has commissioned me to help you to this post. There is nothing here that I am not empowered to turn immediately into cash. Mrs. Mi Tzu, the landlady, will advise me about the sale.

(*Enter* MRS. MI TZU.)

MRS. MI TZU. Good morning, Mr. Shui Ta, you wish to see me about the rent? As you know it falls due the day after tomorrow.

SHUI TA. Circumstances have changed, Mrs. Mi Tzu: my cousin is getting married. Her future husband here, Mr. Yang Sun, will be taking her to Peking. I am interested in selling the tobacco stock.

MRS. MI TZU. How much are you asking, Mr. Shui Ta?

YANG SUN. Three hundred sil—

SHUI TA. Five hundred silver dollars.

MRS. MI TZU. How much did she pay for it, Mr. Shui Ta?

SHUI TA. A thousand. And very little has been sold.

MRS. MI TZU. She was robbed. But I'll make you a special offer if you'll promise to be out by the day after tomorrow. Three hundred silver dollars.

YANG SUN (*shrugging*). Take it, man, take it.

SHUI TA. It is not enough.

YANG SUN. Why not? Why not? Certainly, it's enough.

SHUI TA. Five hundred silver dollars.

YANG SUN. But why? We only need three!

SHUI TA (*to* MRS. MI TZU). Excuse me. (*Takes* YANG SUN *on one side.*) The tobacco stock is pledged to the old couple who gave my cousin the two hundred.

YANG SUN. Is it in writing?

SHUI TA. No.

YANG SUN (*to* MRS. MI TZU). Three hundred will do.

MRS. MI TZU. Of course, I need an assurance that Miss Shen Te is not in debt.

YANG SUN. Mr. Shui Ta?

SHUI TA. She is not in debt.

YANG SUN. When can you let us have the money?

MRS. MI TZU. The day after tomorrow. And remember: I'm doing this because I have a soft spot in my heart for young lovers!

(*Exit.*)

YANG SUN (*calling after her*). Boxes, jars and sacks—three hundred for the lot and the pain's over! (*To* SHUI TA.) Where else can we raise money by the day after tomorrow?

SHUI TA. Nowhere. Haven't you enough for the trip and the first few weeks?

YANG SUN. Oh, certainly.

SHUI TA. How much, exactly.

YANG SUN. Oh, I'll dig it up, even if I have to steal it.

SHUI TA. I see.

YANG SUN. Well, don't fall off the roof. I'll get to Peking somehow.

SHUI TA. Two people can't travel for nothing.

YANG SUN (*not giving* SHUI TA *a chance to answer*). I'm leaving *her* behind. No millstones round *my* neck!

SHUI TA. Oh.

YANG SUN. Don't look at me like that!

SHUI TA. How, precisely, is my cousin to live?

YANG SUN. Oh, you'll think of something.

SHUI TA. A small request, Mr. Yang Sun. Leave the two hundred silver dollars here until you can show me two tickets for Peking.

YANG SUN. You learn to mind your own business, Mr. Shui Ta.

SHUI TA. I'm afraid Miss Shen Te may not wish to sell the shop when she discovers that . . .

YANG SUN. You don't know women. She'll want to. Even then.

SHUI TA (*a slight outburst*). She is a human being, sir! And not devoid of common sense!

YANG SUN. Shen Te is a woman: she *is* devoid of common sense. I only have to lay my hand on her shoulder, and church bells ring.

SHUI TA (*with difficulty*). Mr. Yang Sun!

YANG SUN. Mr. Shui Whatever-it-is!

SHUI TA. My cousin is devoted to you . . . because . . .

YANG SUN. Because I have my hands on her breasts. Give me a cigar. (*He takes one for himself, stuffs a few more in his pocket, then changes his mind and takes the whole box.*) Tell her I'll marry her, then bring me the three hundred. Or let her bring it. One or the other. (*Exit.*)

MRS. SHIN (*sticking her head out of the back room*). Well, he has your cousin under his thumb, and doesn't care if all Yellow Street knows it!

SHUI TA (*crying out*). I've lost my shop! And he doesn't love me! (*He runs berserk through the room, repeating these lines incoherently. Then stops suddenly, and addresses* MRS. SHIN.) Mrs. Shin, you grew up in the gutter, like me. Are we

lacking in hardness? I doubt it. If you steal a penny from me, I'll take you by the throat till you spit it out! You'd do the same to me. The times are bad, this city is hell, but we're like ants, we keep coming, up and up the walls, however smooth! Till bad luck comes. Being in love, for instance. One weakness is enough, and love is the deadliest.

MRS. SHIN (*emerging from the back room*). You should have a little talk with Mr. Shu Fu the Barber. He's a real gentleman and just the thing for your cousin. (*She runs off.*)

SHUI TA.
A caress becomes a stranglehold
A sigh of love turns to a cry of fear
Why are there vultures circling in the air?
A girl is going to meet her lover.
(SHUI TA *sits down and* MR. SHU FU *enters with* MRS. SHIN.)

SHUI TA. Mr. Shu Fu?

SHU FU. Mr. Shui Ta.

(*They both bow.*)

SHUI TA. I am told that you have expressed a certain interest in my cousin Shen Te. Let me set aside all propriety and confess: she is at this moment in grave danger.

SHU FU. Oh, dear!

SHUI TA. She has lost her shop, Mr. Shu Fu.

SHU FU. The charm of Miss Shen Te, Mr. Shui Ta, derives from the goodness, not of her shop, but of her heart. Men call her the Angel of the Slums.

SHUI TA. Yet her goodness has cost her two hundred silver dollars in a single day: we must put a stop to it.

SHU FU. Permit me to differ, Mr. Shui Ta. Let us, rather, open wide the gates to such goodness! Every morning, with pleasure tinged by affection. I watch her charitable ministrations. For they are hungry, and she giveth them to eat! Four of them, to be precise. Why only four? I ask. Why not four hundred? I hear she has been seeking shelter for the homeless. What about my humble cabins behind the cattle run? They are at her disposal. And so forth. And so on. Mr. Shui Ta, do you think Miss Shen Te could be persuaded to listen to certain ideas of mine? Ideas like these?

SHUI TA. Mr. Shu Fu, she would be honored.

(*Enter* WONG *and the* POLICEMAN. MR. SHU FU *turns abruptly away and studies the shelves.*)

WONG. Is Miss Shen Te here?

SHUI TA. No.

WONG. I am Wong the Water Seller. You are Mr. Shui Ta?

SHUI TA. I am.

WONG. I am a friend of Shen Te's.

SHUI TA. An intimate friend, I hear.

WONG (*to the* POLICEMAN). You see? (*To* SHUI TA.) It's because of my hand.

POLICEMAN. He hurt his hand, sir, that's a fact.

SHUI TA (*quickly*). You need a sling, I see. (*He takes a shawl from the back room, and throws it to* WONG.)

WONG. But that's ner new shawl!

SHUI TA. She has no more use for it.

WONG. But she bought it to please someone!

SHUI TA. It happens to be no longer necessary.

WONG (*making the sling*). She is my only witness.

POLICEMAN. Mr. Shui Ta, your cousin is supposed to have seen the Barber hit the Water Seller with a curling iron.

SHUI TA. I'm afraid my cousin was not present at the time.

WONG. But she was, sir! Just ask her! Isn't she in?

SHUI TA (*gravely*). Mr. Wong, my cousin has her own troubles. You wouldn't wish her to add to them by committing perjury?

WONG. But it was she that told me to go to the judge!

SHUI TA. Was the judge supposed to heal your hand?

(MR. SHU FU *turns quickly around.* SHUI TA *bows to* SHU FU, *and vice versa.*)

WONG (*taking the sling off, and putting it back*). I see how it is.

POLICEMAN. Well, I'll be on my way. (*To* WONG.) And you be careful. If Mr. Shu Fu wasn't a man who tempers justice with mercy, as the saying is, you'd be in jail for libel. Be off with you!

(*Exit* WONG, *followed by* POLICEMAN.)

SHUI TA. Profound apologies, Mr. Shu Fu.

SHU FU. Not at all, Mr. Shui Ta. (*Pointing to the shawl.*) The episode is over?

SHUI TA. It may take her time to recover. There are some fresh wounds.

SHU FU. We shall be discreet. Delicate. A short vacation could be arranged. . . .

SHUI TA. First of course, you and she would have to talk things over.

MR. SHU FU. At a small supper in a small, but high-class, restaurant.

SHUI TA. I'll go and find her. (*Exit into back room.*)

MRS. SHIN (*sticking her head in again*). Time for congratulations, Mr. Shu Fu?

SHU FU. Ah, Mrs. Shin! Please inform Miss Shen Te's guests they may take shelter in the cabins behind the cattle run!

(MRS. SHIN *nods, grinning.*)

SHU FU (*to the audience*). Well? What do you think of me, ladies and gentlemen? What could a man do more? Could he be less selfish? More farsighted? A small supper in a small but . . . Does that bring rather vulgar and clumsy thoughts into your mind? Ts, ts, ts. Nothing of the sort will occur. She won't even be touched. Not even accidentally while passing the salt. An exchange of ideas only. Over the flowers on the table— white chrysanthemums, by the way (*he writes down a note of this*)—yes, over the white chrysanthemums, two young souls will . . . shall I say "find each other"? We shall NOT exploit the misfortune of others. Understanding? Yes. An offer of assistance? Certainly. But quietly. Almost inaudibly. Perhaps with a single glance. A glance that could also —mean more.

MRS. SHIN (*coming forward*). Everything under control, Mr. Shu Fu?

SHU FU. Oh, Mrs. Shin, what do you know about this worthless rascal Yang Sun?

MRS. SHIN. Why, he's the most worthless rascal . . .

SHU FU. Is he really? You're sure? (*As she opens her mouth.*) From now on, he doesn't exist! Can't be found anywhere!

(*Enter* YANG SUN.)

YANG SUN. What's been going on here?

MRS. SHIN. Shall I call Mr. Shui Ta, Mr. Shu Fu? He wouldn't want strangers in here!

SHU FU. Mr. Shui Ta is in conference with Miss Shen Te. Not to be disturbed!

YANG SUN. Shen Te here? I didn't see her come in. What kind of conference?

SHU FU (*not letting him enter the back room*). Patience, dear sir! And if by chance I have an inkling who you are, pray take note that Miss Shen Te and I are about to announce our engagement.

YANG SUN. What?

MRS. SHIN. You didn't expect that, did you?

(YANG SUN *is trying to push past the barber into the back room when* SHEN TE *comes out.*)

SHU FU. My dear Shen Te, ten thousand apologies! Perhaps you . . .

YANG SUN. What is it, Shen Te? Have you gone crazy?

SHEN TE (*breathless*). My cousin and Mr. Shu Fu have come to an understanding. They wish me to hear Mr. Shu Fu's plans for helping the poor.

YANG SUN. Your cousin wants to part us.

SHEN TE. Yes.

YANG SUN. And you've agreed to it?

SHEN TE. Yes.

YANG SUN. They told you I was bad. (SHEN TE *is silent.*) And suppose I am. Does that make me need you less? I'm low, Shen Te, I have no money, I don't do the right thing but at least I put up a fight! (*He is near her now, and speaks in an undertone.*) Have you no eyes? Look at him. Have you forgotten already?

SHEN TE. No.

YANG SUN. How it was raining?

SHEN TE. No.

YANG SUN. How you cut me down from the willow tree? Bought me water? Promised me money to fly with?

SHEN TE (*shakily*). Yang Sun, what do you want?

YANG SUN. I want you to come with me.

SHEN TE (*in a small voice*). Forgive me, Mr. Shu Fu, I want to go with Mr. Yang Sun.

YANG SUN. We're lovers you know. Give me the key to the shop. (SHEN TE *takes the key from around her neck.* YANG SUN *puts it on the counter. To* MRS. SHIN:) Leave it under the mat when you're through. Let's go, Shen Te.

SHU FU. But this is rape! Mr. Shui Ta!!

YANG SUN (*to* SHEN TE). Tell him not to shout.

SHEN TE. Please don't shout for my cousin, Mr. Shu Fu. He doesn't agree with me, I know, but he's wrong.

(*To the audience.*)
I want to go with the man I love
I don't want to count the cost
I don't want to consider if it's wise
I don't want to know if he loves me
I want to go with the man I love.

YANG SUN. That's the spirit.

(*And the couple leave.*)

❦ 5a

In front of the inner curtain. SHEN TE *in her wedding clothes, on the way to her wedding.*

SHEN TE. Something terrible has happened. As I left the shop with Yang Sun, I found the old carpet dealer's wife waiting on the street, trembling all over. She told me her husband had taken to his bed—sick with all the worry and excitement over the two hundred silver dollars they lent me. She said it would be best if I gave it back now. Of course, I had to say I would. She said she couldn't quite trust my cousin Shui Ta or even my fiancé Yang Sun. There were tears in her eyes. With my emotions in an uproar, I threw myself into Yang Sun's arms, I couldn't resist him. The things he'd said to Shui Ta had taught Shen Te nothing. Sinking into his arms, I said to myself:

To let no one perish, not even oneself
To fill everyone with happiness, even oneself
Is so good.

How could I have forgotten those two old people? Yang Sun swept me away like a small hurricane. But he's not a bad man, and he loves me. He'd rather work in the cement factory than owe his flying to a crime. Though, of course, flying *is* a great passion with Sun. Now, on the way to my wedding, I waver between fear and joy.

❦ 6

The "private dining room" on the upper floor of a cheap restaurant in a poor section of town. With SHEN TE: *the* GRANDFATHER, *the* SISTER-IN-LAW, *the* NIECE, MRS. SHIN, *the* UNEMPLOYED MAN. *In a corner, alone, a* PRIEST. *A*

WAITER *pouring wine. Downstage,* YANG SUN *talking to his* MOTHER. *He wears a dinner jacket.*

YANG SUN. Bad news, Mamma. She came right out and told me she can't sell the shop for me. Some idiot is bringing a claim because he lent her the two hundred she gave you.

MRS. YANG. What did you say? Of course, you can't marry her now.

YANG SUN. It's no use saying anything to *her*. I've sent for her cousin, Mr. Shui Ta. He said there was nothing in writing.

MRS. YANG. Good idea. I'll go out and look for him. Keep an eye on things.

(*Exit* MRS. YANG. SHEN TE *has been pouring wine.*)

SHEN TE (*to the audience, pitcher in hand*). I wasn't mistaken in him. He's bearing up well. Though it must have been an awful blow—giving up flying. I do love him so. (*Calling across the room to him:*) Sun, you haven't drunk a toast with the bride!

YANG SUN. What do we drink to?

SHEN TE. Why, to the future!

YANG SUN. When the bridegroom's dinner jacket won't be a hired one!

SHEN TE. But when the bride's dress will still get rained on sometimes!

YANG SUN. To everything we ever wished for!

SHEN TE. May all our dreams come true!

(*They drink.*)

YANG SUN (*with loud conviviality*). And now, friends, before the wedding gets under way, I have to ask the bride a few questions. I've no idea what kind of a wife she'll make, and it worries me. (*Wheeling on* SHEN TE:) For example. Can you make five cups of tea with three tea leaves?

SHEN TE. No.

YANG SUN. So I won't be getting very much tea. Can you sleep on a straw mattress the size of that book? (*He points to the large volume the* PRIEST *is reading.*)

SHEN TE. The two of us?

YANG SUN. The one of you.

SHEN TE. In that case, no.

YANG SUN. What a wife! I'm shocked!

(*While the audience is laughing, his* MOTHER *returns. With a shrug of her shoulders, she tells* SUN *the expected guest hasn't arrived. The* PRIEST *shuts the book with a bang, and makes for the door.*)

MRS. YANG. Where are *you* off to? It's only a matter of minutes.

PRIEST (*watch in hand*). Time goes on, Mrs. Yang, and I've another wedding to attend to. Also a funeral.

MRS. YANG (*irately*). D'you think we planned it this way? I was hoping to manage with one pitcher of wine, and we've run through two already. (*Points to empty pitcher. Loudly:*) My dear Shen Te, I don't know where your cousin can be keeping himself!

SHEN TE. My cousin?!

MRS. YANG. Certainly. I'm old-fashioned enough to think such a close relative should attend the wedding.

SHEN TE. Oh, Sun, is it the three hundred silver dollars?

YANG SUN (*not looking her in the eye*). Are you deaf? Mother says she's old-fashioned. And I say I'm considerate. We'll wait another fifteen minutes.

HUSBAND. Another fifteen minutes.

MRS. YANG (*addressing the company*). Now you all know, don't you, that my son is getting a job as a mail pilot?

SISTER-IN-LAW. In Peking, too, isn't it?

MRS. YANG. In Peking, too! The two of us are moving to Peking!

SHEN TE. Sun, tell your mother Peking is out of the question now.

YANG SUN. Your cousin'll tell her. If he agrees. I don't agree.

SHEN TE (*amazed, and dismayed*). Sun!

YANG SUN. I hate this godforsaken Setzuan. What people! Know what they look like when I half close my eyes? Horses! Whinnying, fretting, stamping, screwing their necks up! (*Loudly:*) And what is it the thunder says? They are su-per-flu-ous! (*He hammers out the syllables.*) They've run their last race! They can go trample themselves to death! (*Pause.*) I've got to get out of here.

SHEN TE. But I've promised the money to the old couple.

YANG SUN. And since you always do the wrong thing, it's lucky your cousin's coming. Have another drink.

SHEN TE (*quietly*). My cousin can't be coming.

YANG SUN. How d'you mean?

SHEN TE. My cousin can't be where I am.

YANG SUN. Quite a conundrum!

SHEN TE (*desperately*). Sun, I'm the one that loves you. Not my cousin. He was thinking of the job in Peking when he promised you the old couple's money—

YANG SUN. Right. And that's why he's bringing the three hundred silver dollars. Here—to my wedding.

SHEN TE. He is not bringing the three hundred silver dollars.

YANG SUN. Huh? What makes you think that?

SHEN TE (*looking into his eyes*). He says you only bought one ticket to Peking.

(*Short pause.*)

YANG SUN. That was yesterday. (*He pulls two tickets part way out of his inside pocket, making her look under his coat.*) Two tickets. I don't want Mother to know. She'll get left behind. I sold her furniture to buy these tickets, so you see . . .

SHEN TE. But what's to become of the old couple?

YANG SUN. What's to become of me? Have another drink. Or do you believe in moderation? If I drink, I fly again. And if you drink, you may learn to understand me.

SHEN TE. You want to fly. But I can't help you.

YANG SUN. "Here's a plane, my darling —but it's only got one wing!"

(*The* WAITER *enters.*)

WAITER. Mrs. Yang!

MRS. YANG. Yes?

WAITER. Another pitcher of wine, ma'am?

MRS. YANG. We have enough, thanks. Drinking makes me sweat.

WAITER. Would you mind paying, ma'am?

MRS. YANG (*to everyone*). Just be patient a few moments longer, everyone, Mr. Shui Ta is on his way over! (*To the* WAITER:) Don't be a spoilsport.

WAITER. I can't let you leave till you've paid your bill, ma'am.

MRS. YANG. But they know me here!

WAITER. That's just it.

PRIEST (*ponderously getting up*). I humbly take my leave. (*And he does.*)

MRS. YANG (*to the others, desperately*). Stay where you are, everybody! The priest says he'll be back in two minutes!

YANG SUN. It's no good, Mamma. Ladies and gentlemen, Mr. Shui Ta still

hasn't arrived and the priest has gone home. We won't detain you any longer.

(*They are leaving now.*)

GRANDFATHER (*in the doorway, having forgotten to put his glass down*). To the bride! (*He drinks, puts down the glass, and follows the others.*)

(*Pause.*)

SHEN TE. Shall I go too?

YANG SUN. You? Aren't you the bride? Isn't this your wedding? (*He drags her across the room, tearing her wedding dress.*) If we can wait, you can wait. Mother calls me her falcon. She wants to see me in the clouds. But I think it may be St. Nevercome's Day before she'll go to the door and see my plane thunder by. (*Pause. He pretends the guests are still present.*) Why such a lull in the conversation, ladies and gentlemen? Don't you like it here? The ceremony is only slightly postponed—because an important guest is expected at any moment. Also because the bride doesn't know what love is. While we're waiting, the bridegroom will sing a little song. (*He does so:*)

THE SONG OF ST. NEVERCOME'S DAY

On a certain day, as is generally known,
One and all will be shouting: Hooray, hooray!
For the beggar maid's son has a solid-gold throne
And the day is St. Nevercome's Day
On St. Nevercome's, Nevercome's, Nevercome's Day
He'll sit on his solid-gold throne

Oh, hooray, hooray! That day goodness will pay!
That day badness will cost you your head!
And merit and money will smile and be funny
While exchanging salt and bread
On St. Nevercome's, Nevercome's, Nevercome's Day
While exchanging salt and bread

And the grass, oh, the grass will look down at the sky
And the pebbles will roll up the stream
And all men will be good without batting an eye
They will make of our earth a dream

On St. Nevercome's, Nevercome's, Nevercome's Day
They will make of our earth a dream

And as for me, that's the day I shall be
A flyer and one of the best
Unemployed man, you will have work
to do
Washerwoman, you'll get your rest
On St. Nevercome's, Nevercome's, Never-
come's Day
Washerwoman, you'll get your rest

MRS. YANG. It looks like he's not
coming.
(*The three of them sit looking at the
door.*)

🌼 6a

WONG's *den. The sewer pipe is again
transparent and again the* GODS *appear
to* WONG *in a dream.*
WONG. I'm so glad you've come, illustrious ones. It's Shen Te. She's in great
trouble from following the rule about
loving thy neighbor. Perhaps she's *too*
good for this world!
FIRST GOD. Nonsense! You are eaten
up by lice and doubts!
WONG. Forgive me, illustrious one, I
only meant you might deign to intervene.
FIRST GOD. Out of the question! My
colleague here intervened in some squabble or other only yesterday. (*He points
to the* THIRD GOD, *who has a black eye.*)
The results are before us!
WONG. She had to call on her cousin
again. But not even he could help. I'm
afraid the shop is done for.
THIRD GOD (*a little concerned*). Perhaps we should help after all?
FIRST GOD. The gods help those that
help themselves.
WONG. What if we *can't* help ourselves, illustrious ones?
(*Slight pause.*)
SECOND GOD. Try, anyway! Suffering
ennobles!
FIRST GOD. Our faith in Shen Te is
unshaken!
THIRD GOD. We certainly haven't found
any *other* good people. You can see
where we spend our nights from the
straw on our clothes.

WONG. You might help her find her
way by—
FIRST GOD. The good man finds his own
way here below!
SECOND GOD. The good woman too.
FIRST GOD. The heavier the burden, the
greater her strength!
THIRD GOD. We're only onlookers, you
know.
FIRST GOD. And everything will be all
right in the end, O ye of little faith!
(*They are gradually disappearing
through these last lines.*)

🌼 7

The yard behind SHEN TE's *shop. A
few articles of furniture on a cart.* SHEN
TE *and* MRS. SHIN *are taking the washing
off the line.*
MRS. SHIN. If you ask me, you should
fight tooth and nail to keep the shop.
SHEN TE. How can I? I have to sell
the tobacco to pay back the two hundred
silver dollars today.
MRS. SHIN. No husband, no tobacco,
no house and home! What are you going
to live on?
SHEN TE. I can work. I can sort tobacco.
MRS. SHIN. Hey, look, Mr. Shui Ta's
trousers! He must have left here stark
naked!
SHEN TE. Oh, he may have another
pair, Mrs. Shin.
MRS. SHIN. But if he's gone for good
as you say, why has he left his pants behind?
SHEN TE. Maybe he's thrown them
away.
MRS. SHIN. Can I take them?
SHEN TE. Oh, no.
(*Enter* MR. SHU FU, *running.*)
SHU FU. Not a word! Total silence! I
know all. You have sacrificed your own
love and happiness so as not to hurt a
dear old couple who had put their trust
in you! Not in vain does this district—
for all its malevolent tongues—call you
the Angel of the Slums! That young man
couldn't rise to your level, so you left
him. And now, when I see you closing
up the little shop, that veritable haven
of rest for the multitude, well, I cannot,
I cannot let it pass. Morning after morning I have stood watching in the door-

way not unmoved—while you graciously handed out rice to the wretched. Is that never to happen again? Is the good woman of Setzuan to disappear? If only you would allow *me* to assist you! Now don't say anything! No assurances, no exclamations of gratitude! (*He has taken out his check book.*) Here! A blank check. (*He places it on the cart.*) Just my signature. Fill it out as you wish. Any sum in the world. I herewith retire from the scene, quietly, unobtrusively, making no claims, on tiptoe, full of veneration, absolutely selflessly . . . (*He has gone.*)

MRS. SHIN. Well! You're saved. There's always some idiot of a man. . . . Now hurry! Put down a thousand silver dollars and let me fly to the bank before he comes to his senses.

SHEN TE. I can pay you for the washing without any check.

MRS. SHIN. What? You're not going to cash it just because you might have to marry him? Are you crazy? Men like him *want* to be led by the nose! Are you still thinking of that flyer? All Yellow Street knows how he treated you!

SHEN TE.
When I heard his cunning laugh, I was afraid
But when I saw the holes in his shoes, I loved him dearly.

MRS. SHIN. Defending that good-for-nothing after all that's happened!

SHEN TE (*staggering as she holds some of the washing*). Oh!

MRS. SHIN (*taking the washing from her, dryly*). So you feel dizzy when you stretch and bend? There couldn't be a little visitor on the way? If that's it, you can forget Mr. Shu Fu's blank check: it wasn't meant for a christening present!

(*She goes to the back with a basket.* SHEN TE'*s eyes follow* MRS. SHIN *for a moment. Then she looks down at her own body, feels her stomach, and a great joy comes into her eyes.*)

SHEN TE. O joy! A new human being is on the way. The world awaits him. In the cities the people will say: he's got to be reckoned with, this new human being! (*She imagines a little boy to be present, and introduces him to the audience.*) This is my son, the well-known flyer!
Say: Welcome
To the conquerer of unknown mountains
    and unreachable regions

Who brings us our mail across the impassable deserts!

(*She leads him up and down by the hand.*)

Take a look at the world, my son. That's a tree. Tree, yes. Say: "Hello, tree!" And bow. Like this. (*She bows.*) Now you know each other. And, look, here comes the Water Seller. He's a friend, give him your hand. A cup of fresh water for my little son, please. Yes, it *is* a warm day. (*Handing the cup.*) Oh dear, a policeman, we'll have to make a circle round *him.* Perhaps we can pick a few cherries over there in the rich Mr. Pung's garden. But we mustn't be seen. You want cherries? Just like children with fathers. No, no, you can't go straight at them like that. Don't pull. We must learn to be reasonable. Well, have it your own way. (*She has let him make for the cherries.*) Can you reach? Where to put them? Your mouth is the best place. (*She tries one herself.*) Mmm, they're good. But the policeman, we must run! (*They run.*) Yes, back to the street. Calm now, so no one will notice us. (*Walking the street with her child, she sings:*)
Once a plum—'twas in Japan—
Made a conquest of a man
But the man's turn soon did come
For he gobbled up the plum.

(*Enter* WONG, *with a* CHILD *by the hand. He coughs.*)

SHEN TE. Wong!

WONG. It's about the Carpenter, Shen Te. He's lost his shop, and he's been drinking. His children are on the streets. This is one. Can you help?

SHEN TE (*to the* CHILD). Come here, little man. (*Takes him down to the footlights. To the audience:*)
You there! A man is asking you for
    shelter!
A man of tomorrow says: what about
    today?
His friend the conqueror, whom you
    know,
Is his advocate!

(*To* WONG:) He can live in Mr. Shu Fu's cabins. I may have to go there myself. I'm going to have a baby. That's a secret—don't tell Yang Sun—we'd only be in his way. Can you find the Carpenter for me?

WONG. I knew you'd think of something. (*To the* CHILD:) Goodbye, son, I'm going for your father.

SHEN TE. What about your hand, Wong? I wanted to help, but my cousin. . . . .

WONG. Oh, I can get along with one hand, don't worry. (*He shows how he can handle his pole with his left hand alone.*)

SHEN TE. But your right hand! Look, take this cart, sell everything that's on it, and go to the doctor with the money. . . .

WONG. She's still good. But first I'll bring the Carpenter. I'll pick up the cart when I get back. (*Exit* WONG.)

SHEN TE (*To the* CHILD). Sit down over here, son, till your father comes.

(*The* CHILD *sits crosslegged on the ground. Enter the* HUSBAND *and* WIFE, *each dragging a large, full sack.*)

WIFE (*furtively*). You're alone, Shen Te, dear?

(SHEN TE *nods.*)

(*The* WIFE *beckons to the* NEPHEW *off stage. He comes on with another sack.*)

WIFE. Your cousin's away? (SHEN TE *nods.*) He's not coming back?

SHEN TE. No. I'm giving up the shop.

WIFE. That's why we're here. We want to know if we can leave these things in your new home. Will you do us this favor?

SHEN TE. Why, yes, I'd be glad to.

HUSBAND (*cryptically*). And if anyone asks about them, say they're yours.

SHEN TE. Would anyone ask?

WIFE (*with a glance back at her husband*). Oh, someone might. The police, for instance. They don't seem to like us. Where can we put it?

SHEN TE. Well, I'd rather not get in any more trouble. . . .

WIFE. Listen to her! The good woman of Setzuan!

(SHEN TE *is silent.*)

HUSBAND. There's enough tobacco in those sacks to give us a new start in life. We could have our own tobacco factory!

SHEN TE (*slowly*). You'll have to put them in the back room.

(*The sacks are taken offstage, while the* CHILD *is left alone. Shyly glancing about him, he goes to the garbage can, starts playing with the contents, and eating some of the scraps. The others return.*)

WIFE. We're counting on you, Shen Te!

SHEN TE. Yes. (*She sees the* CHILD *and is shocked.*)

HUSBAND. We'll see you in Mr. Shu Fu's cabins.

NEPHEW. The day after tomorrow.

SHEN TE. Yes. Now, go. Go! I'm not feeling well.

(*Exeunt all three, virtually pushed off.*)

He is eating the refuse in the garbage can!
Only look at his little grey mouth!

(*Pause. Music.*)

As this is the world *my* son will enter
I will study to defend him.
To be good to you, my son,
I shall be a tigress to all others
If I have to.
And I shall have to.

(*She starts to go.*)

One more time, then. I hope really the last.

(*Exit* SHEN TE, *taking* SHUI TA'S *trousers.* MRS. SHIN *enters and watches her with marked interest. Enter the* SISTER-IN-LAW *and the* GRANDFATHER.)

SISTER-IN-LAW. So it's true, the shop has closed down. And the furniture's in the back yard. It's the end of the road!

MRS. SHIN (*pompously*). The fruit of high living, selfishness, and sensuality! Down the primrose path to Mr. Shu Fu's cabins—with you!

SISTER-IN-LAW. Cabins? Rat holes! He gave them to us because his soap supplies only went moldy there!

(*Enter the* UNEMPLOYED MAN.)

UNEMPLOYED MAN. Shen Te is moving?

SISTER-IN-LAW. Yes. She was sneaking away.

MRS. SHIN. She's ashamed of herself, and no wonder!

UNEMPLOYED MAN. Tell her to call Mr. Shui Ta or she's done for this time!

SISTER-IN-LAW. Tell her to call Mr. Shui Ta or *we're* done for this time!

(*Enter* WONG *and* CARPENTER, *the latter with a* CHILD *on each hand.*)

CARPENTER. So we'll have a roof over our heads for a change!

MRS. SHIN. Roof? Whose roof?

CARPENTER. Mr. Shu Fu's cabins. And we have little Feng to thank for it. (*Feng, we find, is the name of the child already there; his father now takes him. To the other two:*) Bow to your little brother, you two!

(*The* CARPENTER *and the* TWO NEW ARRIVALS *bow to* FENG. *Enter* SHUI TA.)

UNEMPLOYED MAN. Sst! Mr. Shui Ta! (*Pause.*)

SHUI TA. And what is this crowd here for, may I ask?

WONG. How do you do, Mr. Shui Ta. This is the Carpenter. Miss Shen Te promised him space in Mr. Shu Fu's cabins.

SHUI TA. That will not be possible.

CARPENTER. We can't go there after all?

SHUI TA. All the space is needed for other purposes.

SISTER-IN-LAW. You mean we have to get out? But we've got nowhere to go.

SHUI TA. Miss Shen Te finds it possible to provide employment. If the proposition interests you, you may stay in the cabins.

SISTER-IN-LAW (*with distaste*). You mean *work?* Work for Miss Shen Te?

SHUI TA. Making tobacco, yes. There are three bales here already. Would you like to get them?

SISTER-IN-LAW (*trying to bluster*). We have our own tobacco! We were in the tobacco business before you were born!

SHUI TA (*to the* CARPENTER *and the* UNEMPLOYED MAN). You *don't* have your own tobacco. What about you?

(*The* CARPENTER *and the* UNEMPLOYED MAN *get the point, and go for the sacks. Enter* MRS. MI TZU.)

MRS. MI TZU. Mr. Shui Ta? I've brought you your three hundred silver dollars.

SHUI TA. I'll sign your lease instead. I've decided not to sell.

MRS. MI TZU. What? You don't need the money for that flyer?

SHUI TA. No.

MRS. MI TZU. And you can pay six months' rent?

SHUI TA (*takes the Barber's blank check from the cart and fills it out*). Here is a check for ten thousand silver dollars. On Mr. Shu Fu's account. Look! (*He shows her the signature on the check.*) Your six months' rent will be in your hands by seven this evening. And now, if you'll excuse me.

MRS. MI TZU. So it's Mr. Shu Fu now. The flyer has been given his walking papers. These modern girls! In my day they'd have said she was flighty. That poor, deserted Mr. Yang Sun!

(*Exit* MRS. MI TZU. *The* CARPENTER *and the* UNEMPLOYED MAN *drag the three sacks back on the stage.*)

CARPENTER (*to* SHUI TA). I don't know why I'm doing this for you.

SHUI TA. Perhaps your children want to eat, Mr. Carpenter.

SISTER-IN-LAW (*catching sight of the sacks*). Was my brother-in-law here?

MRS. SHIN. Yes, he was.

SISTER-IN-LAW. I thought as much. I know those sacks! That's our tobacco!

SHUI TA. Really? I thought it came from my back room! Shall we consult the police on the point?

SISTER-IN-LAW (*defeated*). No.

SHUI TA. Perhaps you will show me the way to Mr. Shu Fu's cabins?

(*Taking* FENG *by the hand,* SHUI TA *goes off, followed by the* CARPENTER *and his* TWO OLDER CHILDREN, *the* SISTER-IN-LAW, *the* GRANDFATHER, *and the* UNEMPLOYED MAN. *Each of the last three drags a sack.*)

(*Enter* OLD MAN *and* OLD WOMAN.)

MRS. SHIN. A pair of pants—missing from the clothes line one minute—and next minute on the honorable backside of Mr. Shui Ta.

OLD WOMAN. We thought Miss Shen Te was here.

MRS. SHIN (*preoccupied*). Well, she's not.

OLD MAN. There was something she was going to give us.

WONG. She was going to help me too, (*Looking at his hand:*) It'll be too late soon. But she'll be back. This cousin has never stayed long.

MRS. SHIN (*approaching a conclusion*). No, he hasn't, has he?

❦ 7a

The Sewer Pipe: WONG *asleep. In his dream, he tells the* GODS *his fears. The* GODS *seem tired from all their travels. They stop for a moment and look over their shoulders at the Water Seller.*

WONG. Illustrious ones. I've been having a bad dream. Our beloved Shen Te was in great distress in the rushes down by the river—the spot where the bodies of suicides are washed up. She kept staggering and holding her head down as if she was carrying something and it was dragging her down into the mud. When

I called out to her, she said she had to take your Book of Rules to the other side, and not get it wet, or the ink would all come off. You had talked to her about the virtues, you know, the time she gave you shelter in Setzuan.

THIRD GOD. Well, but what do you suggest, my dear Wong?

WONG. Maybe a little relaxation of the rules, Benevolent One, in view of the bad times.

THIRD GOD. As for instance?

WONG. Well, um, good-will, for instance, might do instead of love?

THIRD GOD. I'm afraid that would create new problems.

WONG. Or, instead of justice, good sportsmanship?

THIRD GOD. That would only mean more work.

WONG. Instead of honor, outward propriety?

THIRD GOD. Still more work! No, no! The rules will have to stand, my dear Wong!

(*Wearily shaking their heads, all three journey on.*)

🌻 8

SHUI TA's *tobacco factory in* SHU FU's *cabins. Huddled together behind bars, several families, mostly women and children. Among these people the* SISTER-IN-LAW, *the* GRANDFATHER, *the* CARPENTER *and his* THREE CHILDREN. *Enter* MRS. YANG *followed by* YANG SUN.

MRS. YANG (*to the audience*). There's something I just *have* to tell you: strength and wisdom are wonderful things. The strong and wise Mr. Shui Ta has transformed my son from a dissipated good-for-nothing into a model citizen. As you may have heard, Mr. Shui Ta opened a small tobacco factory near the cattle runs. It flourished. Three months ago—I shall never forget it—I asked for an appointment, and Mr. Shui Ta agreed to see us—me and my son. I can see him now as he came through the door to meet us. . . .

(*Enter* SHUI TA, *from a door.*)

SHUI TA. What can I do for you, Mrs. Yang?

MRS. YANG. This morning the police came to the house. We find you've brought action for breach of promise of marriage. In the name of Shen Te. You also claim that Sun came by two hundred silver dollars by improper means.

SHUI TA. That is correct.

MRS. YANG. Mr. Shui Ta, the money's all gone. When the Peking job didn't materialize, he ran through it all in three days. I know he's a good-for-nothing. He sold my furniture. He was moving to Peking without me. Miss Shen Te thought highly of him at one time.

SHUI TA. What do *you* say, Mr. Yang Sun?

YANG SUN. The money's gone.

SHUI TA (*to* MRS. YANG). Mrs. Yang, in consideration of my cousin's incomprehensible weakness for your son, I am prepared to give him another chance. He can have a job—here. The two hundred silver dollars will be taken out of his wages.

YANG SUN. So it's the factory or jail?

SHUI TA. Take your choice.

YANG SUN. May I speak with Shen Te?

SHUI TA. You may not.

(*Pause.*)

YANG SUN (*sullenly*). Show me where to go.

MRS. YANG. Mr. Shui Ta, you are kindness itself: the gods will reward you! (*To* YANG SUN:) And honest work will make a man of you, my boy. (YANG SUN *follows* SHUI TA *into the factory.* MRS. YANG *comes down again to the footlights.*) Actually, honest work didn't agree with him—at first. And he got no opportunity to distinguish himself till—in the third week—when the wages were being paid . . .

(SHUI TA *has a bag of money. Standing next to his foreman—the former* UNEMPLOYED MAN—*he counts out the wages. It is* YANG SUN's *turn.*)

UNEMPLOYED MAN (*reading*). Carpenter, six silver dollars. Yang Sun, six silver dollars.

YANG SUN (*quietly*). Excuse me, sir. I don't think it can be more than five. May I see? (*He takes the foreman's list.*) It says six working days. But that's a mistake, sir. I took a day off for court business. And I won't take what I haven't earned, however miserable the pay is!

UNEMPLOYED MAN. Yang Sun. Five silver dollars. (*To* SHUI TA:) A rare case, Mr. Shui Ta!

SHUI TA. How is it the book says six when it should say five?

UNEMPLOYED MAN. I must've made a mistake, Mr. Shui Ta. (*With a look at* YANG SUN:) It won't happen again.

SHUI TA (*taking* YANG SUN *aside*). You don't hold back, do you? You give your all to the firm. You're even honest. Do the foreman's mistakes always favor the workers?

YANG SUN. He does have . . . friends.

SHUI TA. Thank you. May I offer you any little recompense?

YANG SUN. Give me a trial period of one week, and I'll prove my intelligence is worth more to you than my strength.

MRS. YANG (*still down at the footlights*). Fighting words, fighting words! That evening, I said to Sun: "If you're a flyer, then fly, my falcon! Rise in the world!" And he got to be foreman. Yes, in Mr. Shui Ta's tobacco factory, he worked real miracles.

(*We see* YANG SUN *with his legs apart standing behind the* WORKERS *who are handing along a basket of raw tobacco above their heads.*)

YANG SUN. Faster! Faster! You, there, d'you think you can just stand around, now you're not foreman any more? It'll be your job to lead us in song. Sing!

(UNEMPLOYED MAN *starts singing. The others join in the refrain.*)

SONG OF THE EIGHTH ELEPHANT

Chang had seven elephants—all much the same—
But then there was Little Brother
The seven, they were wild, Little Brother, he was tame
And to guard them Chang chose Little Brother
Run faster!
Mr. Chang has a forest park
Which must be cleared before tonight
And already it's growing dark!

When the seven elephants cleared that forest park
Mr. Chang rode high on Little Brother
While the seven toiled and moiled till dark
On his big behind sat Little Brother
Dig faster!
Mr. Chang has a forest park
Which must be cleared before tonight
And already it's growing dark!

And the seven elephants worked many an hour
Till none of them could work another
Old Chang, he looked sour, on the seven he did glower
But gave a pound of rice to Little Brother
What was that?
Mr. Chang has a forest park
Which must be cleared before tonight
And already it's growing dark!

And the seven elephants hadn't any tusks
The one that had the tusks was Little Brother
Seven are no match for one, if the one has a gun!
How old Chang did laugh at Little Brother!
Keep on digging!
Mr. Chang has a forest park
Which must be cleared before tonight
And already it's growing dark!

(*Smoking a cigar,* SHUI TA *strolls by.* YANG SUN, *laughing, has joined in the refrain of the third stanza and speeded up the tempo of the last stanza by clapping his hands.*)

MRS. YANG. And that's why I say: strength and wisdom are wonderful things. It took the strong and wise Mr. Shui Ta to bring out the best in Yang Sun. A real superior man is like a bell. If you ring it, it rings, and if you don't, it don't, as the saying is.

9

SHEN TE'*s shop, now an office with club chairs and fine carpets. It is raining.* SHUI TA, *now fat, is just dismissing the* OLD MAN *and* OLD WOMAN. MRS. SHIN, *in obviously new clothes, looks on, smirking.*

SHUI TA. No! I can NOT tell you when we expect her back.

OLD WOMAN. The two hundred silver dollars came today. In an envelope. There was no letter, but it must be from Shen Te. We want to write and thank her. May we have her address?

SHUI TA. I'm afraid I haven't got it.

OLD MAN (*pulling* OLD WOMAN's *sleeve*). Let's be going.

OLD WOMAN. She's got to come back some time!

(*They move off, uncertainly, worried.* SHUI TA *bows.*)

MRS. SHIN. They lost the carpet shop because they couldn't pay their taxes. The money arrived too late.

SHUI TA. They could have come to me.

MRS. SHIN. People don't like coming to you.

SHUI TA (*sits suddenly, one hand to his head*). I'm dizzy.

MRS. SHIN. After all, you *are* in your seventh month. But old Mrs. Shin will be there in your hour of trial! (*She cackles feebly.*)

SHUI TA (*in a stifled voice*). Can I count on that?

MRS. SHIN. We all have our price, and mine won't be too high for the great Mr. Shui Ta! (*She opens* SHUI TA's *collar.*)

SHUI TA. It's for the child's sake. All of this.

MRS. SHIN. "All for the child," of course.

SHUI TA. I'm so fat. People must notice.

MRS. SHIN. Oh no, they think it's 'cause you're rich.

SHUI TA (*more feelingly*). What will happen to the child?

MRS. SHIN. You ask that nine times a day. Why, it'll have the best that money can buy!

SHUI TA. He must never see Shui Ta.

MRS. SHIN. Oh, no. Always Shen Te.

SHUI TA. What about the neighbors? There are rumors, aren't there?

MRS. SHIN. As long as Mr. Shu Fu doesn't find out, there's nothing to worry about. Drink this.

(*Enter* YANG SUN *in a smart business suit, and carrying a businessman's briefcase.* SHUI TA *is more or less in* MRS. SHIN's *arms.*)

YANG SUN (*surprised*). I guess I'm in the way.

SHUI TA (*ignoring this, rises with an effort*). Till tomorrow, Mrs. Shin.

(MRS. SHIN *leaves with a smile, putting her new gloves on.*)

YANG SUN. Gloves now! She couldn't be fleecing you? And since when did *you* have a private life? (*Taking a paper from the briefcase:*) You haven't been at your best lately, and things are getting out of hand. The police want to close us down. They say that at the most they can only permit twice the lawful number of workers.

SHUI TA (*evasively*). The cabins are quite good enough.

YANG SUN. For the workers maybe, not for the tobacco. They're too damp. We must take over some of Mrs. Mi Tzu's buildings.

SHUI TA. Her price is double what I can pay.

YANG SUN. Not unconditionally. If she has me to stroke her knees she'll come down.

SHUI TA. I'll never agree to that.

YANG SUN. What's wrong? Is it the rain? You get so irritable whenever it rains.

SHUI TA. Never! I will never . . .

YANG SUN. Mrs. Mi Tzu'll be here in five minutes. *You* fix it. And Shu Fu will be with her. . . . What's all that noise?

(*During the above dialogue,* WONG *is heard offstage, calling:* "The good Shen Te, where is she? Which of you has seen Shen Te, good people? Where is Shen Te?" *A knock. Enter* WONG.)

WONG. Mr. Shui Ta, I've come to ask when Miss Shen Te will be back, it's six months now. . . . There are rumors. People say something's happened to her.

SHUI TA. I'm busy. Come back next week.

WONG (*excited*). In the morning there was always rice on her doorstep—for the needy. It's been there again lately!

SHUI TA. And what do people conclude from this?

WONG. That Shen Te is still in Setzuan! She's been . . . (*He breaks off.*)

SHUI TA. She's been what? Mr. Wong, if you're Shen Te's friend, talk a little less about her, that's my advice to you.

WONG. I don't want your advice! Before she disappeared, Miss Shen Te told me something very important—she's pregnant!

YANG SUN. What? What was that?

SHUI TA (*quickly*). The man is lying.

WONG. A good woman isn't so easily forgotten, Mr. Shui Ta.

(*He leaves.* SHUI TA *goes quickly into the back room.*)

YANG SUN (*to the audience*). Shen Te pregnant? So that's why. Her cousin sent her away, so I wouldn't get wind of it. I have a son, a Yang appears on the scene, and what happens? Mother and child vanish into thin air! That scoundrel, that unspeakable . . . (*The sound of sobbing is heard from the back room.*) What was that? Someone sobbing? Who was it? Mr. Shui Ta the Tobacco King doesn't weep his heart out. And where does the rice come from that's on the doorstep in the morning? (SHUI TA *returns. He goes to the door and looks out into the rain.*) Where is she?

SHUI TA. Sh! It's nine o'clock. But the rain's so heavy, you can't hear a thing.

YANG SUN. What do you want to hear?

SHUI TA. The mail plane.

YANG SUN. What?!

SHUI TA. I've been told *you* wanted to fly at one time. Is that all forgotten?

YANG SUN. Flying mail is night work. I prefer the daytime. And the firm is very dear to me—after all it belongs to my ex-fiancée, even if she's not around. And she's not, is she?

SHUI TA. What do you mean by that?

YANG SUN. Oh, well, let's say I haven't altogether—lost interest.

SHUI TA. My cousin might like to know that.

YANG SUN. I might not be indifferent —if I found she was being kept under lock and key.

SHUI TA. By whom?

YANG SUN. By you.

SHUI TA. What could you do about it?

YANG SUN. I could submit for discussion—my position in the firm.

SHUI TA. You are now my Manager. In return for a more . . . appropriate position, you might agree to drop the enquiry into your ex-fiancée's whereabouts?

YANG SUN. I might.

SHUI TA. What position *would* be more appropriate?

YANG SUN. The one at the top.

SHUI TA. My own? (*Silence.*) And if I preferred to throw you out on your neck?

YANG SUN. I'd come back on my feet. With suitable escort.

SHUI TA. The police?

YANG SUN. The police.

SHUI TA. And when the police found no one?

YANG SUN. I might ask them not to overlook the back room. (*Ending the pretense:*) In short, Mr. Shui Ta, my interest in this young woman has not been officially terminated. I should like to see more of her. (*Into* SHUI TA's *face:*) Besides, she's pregnant and needs a friend. (*He moves to the door.*) I shall talk about it with the Water Seller.

(*Exit.* SHUI TA *is rigid for a moment, then he quickly goes into the back room. He returns with* SHEN TE's *belongings: underwear, etc. He takes a long look at the shawl of the previous scene. He then wraps the things in a bundle, which, upon hearing a noise, he hides under the table. Enter* MRS. MI TZU *and* MR. SHU FU. *They put away their umbrellas and galoshes.*)

MRS. MI TZU. I thought your Manager was here, Mr. Shui Ta. He combines charm with business in a way that can only be to the advantage of all of us.

SHU FU. You sent for us, Mr. Shui Ta?

SHUI TA. The factory is in trouble.

SHU FU. It always is.

SHUI TA. The police are threatening to close us down unless I can show that the extension of our facilities is imminent.

SHU FU. Mr. Shui Ta, I'm sick and tired of your constantly expanding projects. I place cabins at your cousin's disposal; you make a factory of them. I hand your cousin a check; you present it. Your cousin disappears: you find the cabins too small and start talking of yet more—

SHUI TA. Mr. Shu Fu, I'm authorized to inform you that Miss Shen Te's return is now imminent.

SHU FU. Imminent? It's becoming his favorite word.

MRS. MI TZU. Yes, what does it mean?

SHUI TA. Mrs. Mi Tzu, I can pay you exactly half what you asked for your buildings. Are you ready to inform the police that I am taking them over?

MRS. MI TZU. Certainly, if I can take over your manager.

SHU FU. What?

MRS. MI TZU. He's so efficient.

SHUI TA. I'm afraid I need Mr. Yang Sun.

MRS. MI TZU. So do I.

SHUI TA. He will call on you tomorrow

SHU FU. So much the better. With Shen Te likely to turn up at any moment, the presence of that young man is hardly in good taste.

SHUI TA. So we have reached a settlement. In what was once the good Shen Te's little shop we are laying the foundations for the great Mr. Shui Ta's twelve magnificent super tobacco markets. You will bear in mind that though they call me the Tobacco King of Setzuan, it is my cousin's interests that have been served . . .

VOICES (*off*). The police, the police! Going to the tobacco shop! Something must have happened!

(*Enter* YANG SUN, WONG, *and the* POLICEMAN.)

POLICEMAN. Quiet there, quiet, quiet! (*They quiet down.*) I'm sorry, Mr. Shui Ta, but there's a report that you've been depriving Miss Shen Te of her freedom. Not that I believe all I hear, but the whole city's in an uproar.

SHUI TA. That's a lie.

POLICEMAN. Mr. Yang Sun has testified that he heard someone sobbing in the back room.

SHU FU. Mrs. Mi Tzu and myself will testify that no one here has been sobbing.

MRS. MI TZU. We have been quietly smoking our cigars.

POLICEMAN. Mr. Shui Ta, I'm afraid I shall have to take a look at that room. (*He does so. The room is empty.*) No one there, of course, sir.

YANG SUN. But I heard sobbing. What's that? (*He finds the clothes.*)

WONG. Those are Shen Te's things. (*To crowd:*) Shen Te's clothes are here!

VOICES (*off, in sequence*).

Shen Te's clothes!
They've been found under the table!
Body of murdered girl still missing!
Tobacco King suspected!

POLICEMAN. Mr. Shui Ta, unless you can tell us where the girl is, I'll have to ask you to come along.

SHUI TA. I do not know.

POLICEMAN. I can't say how sorry I am, Mr. Shui Ta. (*He shows him the door.*)

MR. SHUI TA. Everything will be cleared up in no time. There are still judges in Setzuan.

YANG SUN. I heard sobbing!

9a

WONG'*s den. For the last time, the* GODS *appear to the Water Seller in his dream. They have changed and show signs of a long journey, extreme fatigue, and plenty of mishaps. The* FIRST *no longer has a hat; the* THIRD *has lost a leg; all three are barefoot.*

WONG. Illustrious ones, at last you're here. Shen Te's been gone for months and today her cousin's been arrested. They think he murdered her to get the shop. But I had a dream and in this dream Shen Te said her cousin was keeping her prisoner. You must find her for us, illustrious ones!

FIRST GOD. We've found very few good people anywhere, and even they didn't keep it up. Shen Te is still the only one that stayed good.

SECOND GOD. If she *has* stayed good.

WONG. Certainly she has. But she's vanished.

FIRST GOD. That's the last straw. All is lost!

SECOND GOD. A little moderation, dear colleague!

FIRST GOD (*plaintively*). What's the good of moderation now? If she can't be found, we'll have to resign! The world is a terrible place! Nothing but misery, vulgarity, and waste! Even the countryside isn't what it used to be. The trees are getting their heads chopped off by telephone wires, and there's such a noise from all the gunfire, and I can't stand those heavy clouds of smoke, and—

THIRD GOD. The place is absolutely unlivable! Good intentions bring people to the brink of the abyss, and good deeds push them over the edge. I'm afraid our book of rules is destined for the scrap heap—

SECOND GOD. It's people! They're a worthless lot!

THIRD GOD. The world is too cold!

SECOND GOD. It's people! They're too weak!

FIRST GOD. Dignity, dear colleagues, dignity! Never despair! As for this world, didn't we agree that we only have to find one human being who can stand the place? Well, we found her. True, we lost her again. We must find her again, that's all! And at once!

(*They disappear.*)

✹ 10

Courtroom. Groups: SHU FU *and* MRS.
MI TZU; YANG SUN *and* MRS. YANG;
WONG, *the* CARPENTER, *the* GRANDFA-
THER, *the* NIECE, *the* OLD MAN, *the* OLD
WOMAN; MRS. SHIN, *the* POLICEMAN;
the UNEMPLOYED MAN, *the* SISTER-IN-
LAW.

OLD MAN. So much power isn't good
for one man.

UNEMPLOYED MAN. And he's going
to open twelve super tobacco markets!

WIFE. One of the judges is a friend of
Mr. Shu Fu's.

SISTER-IN-LAW. Another one accepted
a present from Mr. Shui Ta only last
night. A fat goose.

OLD WOMAN (*to* WONG). And Shen
Te is nowhere to be found.

WONG. Only the gods will ever know
the truth.

POLICEMAN. Order in the court! My
lords the judges!

(*Enter the* THREE GODS *in judges'
robes. We overhear their conversation as
they pass along the footlights to their
bench.*)

THIRD GOD. We'll never get away with
it, our certificates were so badly forged.

SECOND GOD. My predecessor's "sudden indigestion" will certainly cause comment.

FIRST GOD. But he *had* just eaten a
whole goose.

UNEMPLOYED MAN. Look at that!
New judges!

WONG. New judges. And what good
ones!

(*The* THIRD GOD *hears this, and turns
to smile at* WONG. *The* GODS *sit. The*
FIRST GOD *beats on the bench with his
gavel. The* POLICEMAN *brings in* SHUI
TA *who walks with lordly steps. He is
whistled at.*)

POLICEMAN (*to* SHUI TA). Be prepared for a surprise. The judges have
been changed.

(SHUI TA *turns quickly round, looks
at them, and staggers.*)

NIECE. What's the matter now?

WIFE. The great Tobacco King nearly
fainted.

HUSBAND. Yes, as soon as he saw the
new judges.

WONG. Does *he* know who they are?

(SHUI TA *picks himself up, and the
proceedings open.*)

FIRST GOD. Defendant Shui Ta, you
are accused of doing away with your
cousin Shen Te in order to take possession
of her business. Do you plead guilty or
not guilty?

SHUI TA. Not guilty, my lord.

FIRST GOD (*thumbing through the
documents of the case*). The first witness
is the Policeman. I shall ask him to tell
us something of the respective reputations
of Miss Shen Te and Mr. Shui Ta.

POLICEMAN. Miss Shen Te was a young
lady who aimed to please, my lord. She
liked to live and let live, as the saying
goes. Mr. Shui Ta, on the other hand, is
a man of principle. Though the generosity
of Miss Shen Te forced him at times to
abandon half measures, unlike the girl,
he was always on the side of the law,
my lord. One time, he even unmasked a
gang of thieves to whom his too trustful
cousin had given shelter. The evidence,
in short, my lord, proves that Mr. Shui
Ta was *incapable* of the crime of which
he stands accused!

FIRST GOD. I see. And are there others
who could testify along, shall we say,
the same lines?

(SHU FU *rises.*)

POLICEMAN (*whispering to* GODS).
Mr. Shu Fu—a very important person.

FIRST GOD (*inviting him to speak*).
Mr. Shu Fu!

SHU FU. Mr. Shui Ta is a businessman, my lord. Need I say more?

FIRST GOD. Yes.

SHU FU. Very well, I will. He is Vice
President of the Council of Commerce
and is about to be elected a Justice of
the Peace.

(*He returns to his seat.* MRS. MI TZU
rises.)

WONG. Elected! *He* gave him the job!

(*With a gesture the* FIRST GOD *asks
who* MRS. MI TZU *is.*)

POLICEMAN. Another very important
person. Mrs. Mi Tzu.

FIRST GOD (*inviting her to speak*).
Mrs. Mi Tzu!

MRS. MI TZU. My lord, as Chairman of
the Committee on Social Work, I wish
to call attention to just a couple of eloquent facts: Mr. Shui Ta not only has
erected a model factory with model hous-
ing in our city, he is a regular contributor

to our home for the disabled. (*She returns to her seat.*)

POLICEMAN (*whispering*). And she's a great friend of the judge that ate the goose!

FIRST GOD (*to the* POLICEMAN). Oh, thank you. What next? (*To the Court, genially:*) Oh, yes. We should find out if any of the evidence is less favorable to the defendant.

(WONG, the CARPENTER, *the* OLD MAN, *the* OLD WOMAN, *the* UNEMPLOYED MAN, *the* SISTER-IN-LAW, *and the* NIECE *come forward.*)

POLICEMAN (*whispering*). Just the riffraff, my lord.

FIRST GOD (*addressing the "riffraff"*). Well, um, riffraff—do you know anything of the defendant, Mr. Shui Ta?

WONG. Too much, my lord.

UNEMPLOYED MAN. What don't we know, my lord?

CARPENTER. He ruined us.

SISTER-IN-LAW. He's a cheat.

NIECE. Liar.

WIFE. Thief.

BOY. Blackmailer.

BROTHER. Murderer.

FIRST GOD. Thank you. We should now let the defendant state his point of view.

SHUI TA. I only came on the scene when Shen Te was in danger of losing what I had understood was a gift from the gods. Because I did the filthy jobs which someone had to do, they hate me. My activities were restricted to the minimum, my lord.

SISTER-IN-LAW. He had us arrested!

SHUI TA. Certainly. You stole from the bakery!

SISTER-IN-LAW. Such concern for the bakery! You didn't want the shop for yourself, I suppose!

SHUI TA. I didn't want the shop overrun with parasites.

SISTER-IN-LAW. We had nowhere else to go.

SHUI TA. There were too many of you.

WONG. What about this old couple: Were *they* parasites?

OLD MAN. We lost our shop because of you!

OLD WOMAN. And we gave your cousin money!

SHUI TA. My cousin's fiancé was a flyer. The money had to go to *him.*

WONG. Did you care whether he flew or not? Did you care whether she married him or not? You wanted her to marry someone else! (*He points at* SHU FU.)

SHUI TA. The flyer unexpectedly turned out to be a scoundrel.

YANG SUN (*jumping up*). Which was the reason you made him your Manager?

SHUI TA. Later on he improved.

WONG. And when he improved, you sold him to her? (*He points out* MRS. MI TZU.)

SHUI TA. She wouldn't let me have her premises unless she had him to stroke her knees!

MRS. MI TZU. What? The man's a pathological liar. (*To him:*) Don't mention my property to me as long as you live! Murderer! (*She rustles off, in high dudgeon.*)

YANG SUN (*pushing in*). My lord, I wish to speak for the defendant.

SISTER-IN-LAW. Naturally. He's your employer.

UNEMPLOYED MAN. And the worst slave driver in the country.

MRS. YANG. That's a lie! My lord, Mr. Shui Ta is a great man. He . . .

YANG SUN. He's this and that, but he is not a murderer, my lord. Just fifteen minutes before his arrest I heard Shen Te's voice in his own back room.

FIRST GOD. Oh? Tell us more!

YANG SUN. I heard sobbing, my lord!

FIRST GOD. But lots of women sob, we've been finding.

YANG SUN. Could I fail to recognize her voice?

SHU FU. No, you made her sob so often yourself, young man!

YANG SUN. Yes, But I also made her happy. Till he (*pointing at* SHUI TA) decided to sell her to you!

SHUI TA. Because you didn't love her.

WONG. Oh, no: it was for the money, my lord!

SHUI TA. And what was the money for, my lord? For the poor! And for Shen Te so she could go on being good!

WONG. For the poor? That he sent to his sweatshops? And why didn't you let Shen Te be good when you signed the big check?

SHUI TA. For the child's sake, my lord.

CARPENTER. What about *my* children? What did he do about them?

(SHUI TA *is silent.*)

WONG. The shop was to be a fountain of goodness. That was the gods' idea. You came and spoiled it!

SHUI TA. If I hadn't, it would have run dry!

MRS. SHIN. There's a lot in that, my lord.

WONG. What have you done with the good Shen Te, bad man? She *was* good, my lords, she was, I swear it! (*He raises his hand in an oath.*)

THIRD GOD. What's happened to your hand, Water Seller?

WONG (*pointing to* SHUI TA). It's all his fault, my lord, *she* was going to send me to a doctor—(*To* SHUI TA:) You were her worst enemy!

SHUI TA. I was her only friend!

WONG. Where is she then? Tell us where your good friend is!

(*The excitement of this exchange has run through the whole crowd.*)

ALL. Yes, where is she? Where is Shen Te? (*Etc.*)

SHUI TA. Shen Te . . . had to go.

WONG. Where? Where to?

SHUI TA. I cannot tell you! I cannot tell you!

ALL. Why? Why did she have to go away? (*Etc.*)

WONG (*into the din with the first words, but talking on beyond the others*). Why not, why not? Why did she have to go away?

SHUI TA (*shouting*). Because you'd all have torn her to shreds, that's why! My lords, I have a request. Clear the court! When only the judges remain, I will make a confession.

ALL (*except* WONG, *who is silent, struck by the new turn of events*). So he's guilty? He's confessing! (*Etc.*)

FIRST GOD (*using the gavel*). Clear the court!

POLICEMAN. Clear the court!

WONG. Mr. Shui Ta has met his match this time.

MRS. SHIN (*with a gesture toward the judges*). You're in for a little surprise.

(*The court is cleared. Silence.*)

SHUI TA. Illustrious ones!

(*The* GODS *look at each other, not quite believing their ears.*)

SHUI TA. Yes, I recognize you!

SECOND GOD (*taking matters in hand, sternly*). What have you done with our good woman of Setzuan?

SHUI TA. I have a terrible confession to make: I am she! (*He takes off his mask, and tears away his clothes.* SHEN TE *stands there.*)

SECOND GOD. Shen Te!

SHEN TE. Shen Te, yes. Shui Ta *and* Shen Te. Both.

Your injunction
To be good and yet to live
Was a thunderbolt:
It has torn me in two
I can't tell how it was
But to be good to others
And myself at the same time
I could not do it
Your world is not an easy one, illustrious ones!
When we extend our hand to a beggar, he tears it off for us
When we help the lost, we are lost ourselves
And so
Since not to eat is to die
Who can long refuse to be bad?
As I lay prostrate beneath the weight of good intentions
Ruin stared me in the face
It was when I was unjust that I ate good meat
And hobnobbed with the mighty
Why?
Why are bad deeds rewarded?
Good ones punished?
I enjoyed giving
I truly wished to be the Angel of the Slums
But washed by a foster-mother in the water of the gutter
I developed a sharp eye
The time came when pity was a thorn in my side
And, later, when kind words turned to ashes in my mouth
And anger took over
I became a wolf.
Find me guilty, then, illustrious ones,
But know:
All that I have done I did
To help my neighbor
To love my lover
And to keep my little one from want.
For your great, godly deeds, I was too poor, too small.
(*Pause.*)

FIRST GOD (*shocked*). Don't go on making yourself miserable, Shen Te! We're overjoyed to have found you!

SHEN TE. I'm telling you I'm the bad man who committed all those crimes!

FIRST GOD (*using—or failing to use —his ear trumpet*). The good woman who did all those good deeds?

SHEN TE. Yes, but the bad man too!

FIRST GOD (*as if something had dawned*). Unfortunate coincidences! Heartless neighbors!

THIRD GOD (*shouting in his ear*). But how is she to continue?

FIRST GOD. Continue? Well, she's a strong, healthy girl . . .

SECOND GOD. You didn't hear what she said!

FIRST GOD. I heard every word! She is confused, that's all! (*He begins to bluster.*) And what about this book of rules —we can't renounce our rules, can we? (*More quietly.*) Should the world be changed? How? By whom? The world should *not* be changed! (*At a sign from him, the lights turn pink, and music plays.*)
And now the hour of parting is at hand.
Dost thou behold, Shen Te, yon fleecy cloud?
It is our chariot. At a sign from me
'Twill come and take us back from whence we came
Above the azure vault and silver stars. . . .

SHEN TE. No! Don't go, illustrious ones!

FIRST GOD.
Our cloud has landed now in yonder field
From whence it will transport us back to heaven.
Farewell, Shen Te, let not thy courage fail thee. . . .
(*Exeunt* GODS.)

SHEN TE. What about the old couple? They've lost their shop! What about the Water Seller and his hand? And I've got to defend myself against the Barber, because I don't love him! And against Sun, because I do love him! How? How?

(SHEN TE'S *eyes follow the* GODS *as they are imagined to step into a cloud which rises and moves forward over the orchestra and up beyond the balcony.*)

FIRST GOD (*from on high*). We have faith in you, Shen Te!

SHEN TE. There'll be a child. And he'll have to be fed. I can't stay here. Where shall I go?

FIRST GOD. Continue to be good, good woman of Setzuan!

SHEN TE. I need my bad cousin!

FIRST GOD. But not very often!

SHEN TE. Once a week at least!

FIRST GOD. Once a month will be quite enough!

SHEN TE (*shrieking*). No, no! Help!

(*But the cloud continues to recede as the* GODS *sing.*)

VALEDICTORY HYMN

What rapture, oh, it is to know
  A good thing when you see it
And having seen a good thing, oh,
  What rapture 'tis to flee it

Be good, sweet maid of Setzuan
  Let Shui Ta be clever
Departing, we forget the man
  Remember your endeavor

Because through all the length of days
  Her goodness faileth never
Sing hallelujah! Make Shen Te's
  Good name live on forever!

SHEN TE. Help!

MARTIN ESSLIN: *The Brechtian Theatre—Its Theory and Practice*

From BRECHT by Martin Esslin. Copyright © 1959, 1960 by Martin Esslin. Reprinted by permission of Doubleday & Company, Inc.

TERMS LIKE "EPIC THEATRE," "NON-ARISTOTELIAN DRAMA," "*VER-fremdungseffekt*" (alienation effect, abbreviated into V-effect), and other catch phrases from Brecht's theoretical writings have become more widely known than any of his creative work (with the possible exception of the song "Mac the Knife"). Taken up by enthusiasts of theatre reform on both sides of the Atlantic, they have found their way into the currency of daily and weekly theatrical criticism and must have puzzled countless readers who have never heard of Brecht, let alone seen any of his plays.

Such Teutonic neologisms seem to exercise a powerful spell even on Anglo-Saxon minds, not excluding those who appreciate their usefulness in the sphere of lifemanship; from Kant to Marx down to our own times the difficulty and obscurity of a specialized and impenetrable jargon has contributed much to the success and influence of German ideologies. Brecht, unwittingly, achieved a similar result in his own, more modest theorizing. Even he, the clearest and most concrete of writers in his poetry and plays, often succumbed to the ponderous tradition of German aesthetic philosophy when he tried to expound the underlying principles of his work.

Basically these principles are neither very complicated nor very new, however stimulating and revivifying their influence may yet prove in the present-day theatre. Towards the end of his life Brecht made repeated efforts to dissipate the fog of the Brechtian theories he himself had created in his youth.

> The accounts (of my theatre) and many of the assessments based on them are applicable not to the theatre that I myself produce, but to the theatre that my critics imagine from reading my treatises. . . . My theories are altogether far more naïve than one might think—more naïve than my way of expressing them might allow one to suspect.[1]

Brecht has always acknowledged his debt to a wide range of old theatrical conventions and traditions: the Elizabethan, Chinese, Japanese and Indian theatre, the use of the chorus in Greek tragedy, the techniques of clowns and fair-ground entertainers, the Austrian and Bavarian folk play, and many others. Yet he somehow created the impression that he was advocating something radically new and entirely revolutionary—perhaps by the dogmatic and didactic tone of his earlier pronouncements, perhaps by his often excessive insistence that *his* was the only stage theory to meet the needs of a new, revolutionary, scientific age.

What perhaps adds to the confusion is that the Brechtian theory of the drama was not a single, homogeneous body of doctrine. Throughout his life it changed, developed, and finally mellowed in accordance with the changes in his styles of writing and stage production. The primary factor was always his creative work; the theories he put forward were postscripts to plays or poems rather than *a priori* principles on which these had been based. The rationalist Brecht deeply distrusted inspirations and intuitions. So he constructed his theories as rationalizations of changes in his style, taste, or stage practice. That is why so much of the discussion of these theories as general principles has proved barren and unreal. It is yet to be proved that they have any validity apart from Brecht's own works—and productions—which they were intended to explain and justify.

Brecht was a rebel. The Brechtian theatre can be understood only in the light of what he rebelled against: the theatre as he found it in Germany around 1920 and as it still remains in many parts

[1] Brecht, "Gespraech der Probe" (1953), *Schriften zum Theater*, pp. 285–86.

of the world to this day—a theatre in which bombastic productions of the classics alternate with empty photographic replicas of everyday life, whether in melodrama or drawing-room comedy; a theatre that oscillates between emotional uplift and after-dinner entertainment.

We are so used to the concept of the stage as a faithful representation of the world that we tend to forget how recent a growth the naturalistic theatre really is. Before the second half of the nineteenth century, before the introduction of modern lighting techniques and stage machinery, historically accurate costumes, and three-dimensional properties, the theatre could not even pretend to create a complete illusion of actual life, observed through a missing fourth wall. On the earlier stage styles of acting had to be kept openly theatrical to match the surrounding scenery and lighting. Declamation, asides and monologues formed part of a convention never intended to convey the illusion of real happenings on which the audience was merely eavesdropping.

So great was the effect of the new stage techniques that emerged from the efforts of directors like the Duke of Saxe-Meiningen, Stanislavsky, Antoine, Brahm, Granville-Barker, and Reinhardt, that the naturalistic theatre in the widest sense had become accepted as the only possible stage convention by the time Brecht was born. The previous convention survived only in the form of parody (as it does to this day in the skits on Shakespeare and Victorian melodrama one still sees in English music halls).

The reaction against this theatrical convention, which had to come, is entirely analogous to the reaction against representational painting that came at the same time. For centuries painters had tried to get nearer and nearer to reality; the Impressionists had finally captured the very flicker of daylight, just as the naturalistic stage could simulate the changing light from the blazing sun of noon to the bluish tints of the moon at night. Such perfection having been attained, the next step *had* to be a new beginning, the initiation of an entirely different line of development—in painting away from nature into the realms of the primitive and the abstract, in the theatre away from the illusion of eavesdropping on real events.

Brecht belonged to the generation which had to make this new beginning, and his solution is one of many that were put forward by his contemporaries. German Expressionism, the poetic drama of T. S. Eliot, the satires of Mayakovsky, the Russian theatre of Meyerhold and Tairov, the monster pantomimes of Max Reinhardt, Piscator's political theatre with its use of film and posters are all part of the same striving to overcome the limitations of the "theatre of illusion."

When Brecht began to formulate his ideas in the late twenties he had already experimented with a variety of techniques. He had written plays that showed the influence of the Expressionist trend in their loose construction, their treatment of the characters as types rather than individuals, and their highly concentrated, poetic language; and he had worked in close collaboration with Erwin Piscator, whose stage made use of every new technique in order to turn the theatre into a forum for the discussion of current affairs.

Brecht's theories show the influence of all these experiments. He, too, was convinced that the theatre must become a tool of social engineering, a laboratory of social change.

> Today (he wrote in 1931) when human character must be understood as the "totality of all social conditions" the epic form is the only one that can comprehend all the processes which could serve the drama as materials for a fully representative picture of the world.[2]

Why did Brecht consider the existing stage convention incapable of providing such a picture of the world? His objections against the theatre of illusion concern both the means employed and the uses to which these means are put.

According to Brecht the "Aristotelian" drama (as he calls it—not very aptly) strives to create terror and pity in the spectator, to purge his emotions, so that he emerges relieved and refreshed. It achieves this by conjuring up before the public's eyes an illusion of real events,

2 Brecht, "Anmerkungen zur Dreigroschenoper" (1931), *Schriften zum Theater*, p. 35.

drawing each individual member of the audience into the action by causing him to identify himself with the hero to the point of complete self-oblivion. The magical effect of the stage illusion hypnotizes the audience into a state of trance, which Brecht regarded as physically disgusting and downright obscene:

> looking around, one discovers more or less motionless bodies in a curious state—they seem to be contracting their muscles in a strong physical effort, or else to have relaxed them after violent strain . . . they have their eyes open, but they don't look, they stare . . . they stare at the stage as if *spellbound,* which is an expression from the Middle Ages, an age of witches and obscurantists. . . .[3]

Identification with the characters on the stage appeared equally indecent to Brecht:

> How long are our souls going to have to leave our "gross" bodies under cover of darkness to penetrate into those dream figures up there on the rostrum, in order to share their transports that would otherwise be denied to us?[4]

Such an audience, Brecht argues, may indeed leave the theatre purged by its vicarious emotions, but it will have remained uninstructed and unimproved. For them the theatre will be a means of mental refreshment in the same sense as a good meal, which is consumed with enjoyment, provides physical refreshment, but leaves no lasting trace behind. Brecht regarded the art of the theatre as more than a mere article of consumption and despised what he called the "culinary theatre," the theatre which merely provides mental foodstuffs, to be gobbled up and then forgotten. The audience in his view should not be made to feel emotions, they should be made to *think.* But identification with the characters of the play makes thinking almost impossible; the audience whose souls have crept into that of the hero will see the action entirely from *his* point of view, and as they are breathlessly following a course of events which, in suspension of disbelief, they accept as really happening before their very eyes, they have neither the time nor the detachment to sit back and reflect in

a truly critical spirit on the social and moral implications of the play. And all this because the author, the director and the actors have conspired to create so powerful an illusion of reality!

Brecht's answer is clear: the theatre must do its best to destroy in the bud any illusion of reality, which will continuously, and mischievously, tend to arise.

It must at all times be made apparent to the spectators that they are not witnessing real events happening before their very eyes at *this very moment,* but that they are sitting in a theatre, listening to an account (however vividly presented) of things that have happened in the *past* at a certain time in a certain place. They are to sit back, relax, and reflect on the lessons to be learned from those events of long ago, like the audience of the bards who sang of the deeds of heroes in the houses of Greek kings or Saxon earls, while the guests ate and drank. Hence the term *epic* theatre. While the theatre of illusion is trying to re-create a spurious present by pretending that the events of the play are actually taking place at the time of each performance, the "epic" theatre is strictly *historical;* it constantly reminds the audience that they are merely getting a report of past events.

Morever, the audience must be *discouraged* from losing their critical detachment by *identification* with one or more of the characters. The opposite of identification is the maintenance of a separate existence by being kept apart, alien, strange—therefore the director must strive to produce by all the means at his disposal effects that will keep the audience separate, estranged, alienated from the action. That is the meaning of the famous "*Verfremdungseffekt,*" a term that has never been successfully rendered in English because terms like alienation or estrangement have entirely different, and unfortunate, emotional overtones. In French, *distantiation* is a happier term.

The abolition of the old theatre of illusion, which Brecht once described as having sunk to the level of a "branch of the bourgeois drug traffic," frees the critical faculty of the audience and absolves the playwright from being cramped by the narrow and rigid conventions that the

[3] Brecht, "Kleines Organon fuer das Theater" (1948), *Versuche 12,* p. 119.
[4] Ibid., p. 122.

pretense of presenting real happenings imposes. In the realistic convention one can show only the action of the characters themselves; it is quite impossible to supply the sociological background of their actions or to comment on them from a higher viewpoint than their own. In the "epic" theatre the author is able to dispense with the tedious ritual of the naturalist exposition through which the characters laboriously have to establish their names and relationships in the framework of seemingly casual, "natural" conversation; he can now make them introduce themselves directly to the audience, or flash their names on a screen. He can go further: he can tell the audience in advance how the play will end, freeing their minds from the distraction of suspense; he can supply background material of all kinds by letting a narrator describe the thoughts and motives of the characters or, as in Brecht's adaptation of Gorky's *The Mother,* by flashing the prices of basic foodstuffs onto the backdrop during a scene in which the cost of living is mentioned in the dialogue. Brecht claimed that the "epic" theatre alone could present the complexity of the human condition in an age in which the life of individuals could no longer be understood in isolation from the powerful trend of social, economical and historical forces affecting the lives of millions.

By abandoning the pretense that the audience is eavesdropping on actual events, by openly admitting that the theatre is a theatre and not the world itself, the Brechtian stage approximates the lecture hall, to which audiences come in the expectation that they will be informed, and also the circus arena, where an audience, without identification or illusion, watches performers exhibit their special skills. What distinguishes the theatre from the lecture room or the circus, however, is the fact that it "produces living illustrations of historical or imaginary happenings among human beings."[5]

To what purpose are these happenings re-created? It is in this respect that

Brecht's thought changed most radically between his earlier and later periods. In the beginning Brecht proclaimed his conviction that the theatre had to be strictly didactic; he saw it as his task "to develop the article of consumption into a teaching aid and to refashion certain institutions from places of entertainment into organs of information."[6] In this period of the didactic plays and school operas the austerity of Brecht's conception was such that he wrote plays that were to serve for the instruction of the *participants alone.* "They need no audience."[7]

By 1948 he had mellowed to the extent of openly repudiating much of this severity of approach:

> Let us therefore recant . . . our intention of emigrating from the realm of the pleasing and let us . . . proclaim our intention of settling in this realm. Let us treat the theatre as a place of entertainment. . . . But let us inquire what kind of entertainment we regard as acceptable.[8]

Brecht answered this question by rejecting the old idea of entertainment through emotional catharsis. The pleasure that his theatre was now permitted to give was the pleasure we feel when we discover new truths, the exhilaration we experience when we enlarge our understanding. In this scientific age Brecht wanted his audience to experience some of the exaltation felt by the scientist who has uncovered one of the mysteries of the universe. For Brecht, whose own curiosity and thirst for knowledge were boundless, regarded the "instinct of inquiry as a social phenomenon not less pleasurable, nor less imperious, than the instinct of procreation."[9]

To keep the audience relaxed and yet receptive, to stimulate their critical faculties, and to make them think, the "epic" theatre employs a variety of means. In Brecht's view, the abolition of the dramatic illusion alone removes a good many of the less desirable implications of the "Aristotelian" theatre. The very fact that the action was each time assumed to be happening anew before the eyes of the

5 Ibid., p. 110.
6 Brecht, "Anmerkungen zur Oper *Aufsteig und Fall der Stadt Mahagonny*" (1930), *Schriften zum Theater,* p. 28.
7 Brecht, "Anmerkung zu den Lehrstuecken," *Stuecke V,* p. 276.
8 Brecht, "Kleines Organon fuer das Theater; Vorrede" (1948), *Versuche 12,* p. 109.
9 Brecht, "Anmerkungen zu *Leben des Galilei,*" *Stuecke VIII,* p. 205.

audience implied that the passions and attitudes of the characters were unchangeable expressions of a fixed "human nature"; the dynamic, tautly logical construction of such plays indicated the relentless course of fate and made it appear unfathomable and incapable of being influenced by human initiative. In the "epic" theatre, therefore, there is no attempt to create fixed, highly individualized characters. Character emerges from the social function of the individual and changes with that function. As Brecht once put it, character

> should not be regarded like a stain of grease on a pair of trousers, which, however much you try to rub and wipe it away, will always come up again. In actual fact the question is always how a given person is going to act in a specified set of circumstances and conditions.[10]

The plays of the "epic" theatre, which rejects the logically built, well-made drama, are free from the need of creating suspense, loosely knit, and episodic; instead of mounting to a dynamic climax, the story unfolds in a number of separate situations, each rounded and complete in itself. The total effect of the play is built up through the juxtaposition and "montage" of contrasting episodes. While the "Aristotelian" drama can be understood only as a whole, the "epic" drama can be cut into slices that will continue to make sense and give pleasure, like the favorite chapters of a novel that can be read by themselves, or the extracts from plays of great length that are performed as self-contained units in the Chinese classical theatre.

Just as isolated episodes of the play retain their individual significance even if taken out of the context of the play as a whole, the non-literary elements of the production—décor, music, and choreography—also retain their independence; instead of serving as mere auxiliaries of the text, reinforcing it by stressing some of its features, and painting in atmosphere, mood, or descriptive details, they are raised to the level of autonomous elements; instead of pulling in the same direction as the words, they enter into a dialectical, contrapuntal relationship with them. The musical numbers are no longer smuggled in at the point when the emotional charge of a scene rises to a climax and speech merges into song, but are introduced as entirely distinct ingredients of the play, which interrupt its flow, break the illusion, and thereby render the action "strange." And within the musical numbers themselves the music does not merely express the mood of the words; it often stands in contradiction to them, comments on them, or reveals the falsity of the sentiments they express.

The stage designer, who is no longer bound by the necessity of trying to create the illusion of a real locality in which the action takes place, is now free to supply his own, independent contribution to the play by providing background material of all kinds (in *Galileo* Caspar Neher backed the action by projections of maps, documents, and works of art of the Renaissance) or even by duplicating the action by showing it from a different angle (in the first production of *Mahagonny* the scene in which greedy Jakob eats himself to death was played in front of a backdrop showing a large portrait of Jakob eating, so that the audience saw the episode split in two).

Thus the "epic" theatre does not use décor and music to produce a Wagnerian *Gesamtkunstwerk* with its, in Brecht's view, diabolically strong narcotic and hypnotic effect and concerted onslaught on the senses, but to destroy the illusion of reality. As Brecht put it, "*Sie verfremden sich gegenseitig*" ("they mutually make each other appear strange").

The destruction of stage illusion, however, is not an end in itself. The *Verfremdungseffekt* has its positive side. By inhibiting the process of identification between the spectator and the characters, by creating a distance between them and enabling the audience to look at the action in a detached and critical spirit, familiar things, attitudes and situations appear in a new and strange light and create, through astonishment and wonder, a new understanding of the human situation. The great discoveries of mankind, Brecht points out, were made by men who looked at familiar things as if they had never seen them before—Newton at the falling apple, Galileo at the swinging chandelier—and in the same way the

[10] H. Bunge, "Brecht probiert," *Sinn und Form*, Second Special Brecht Issue, 1957, p. 324.

theatre public should be taught to look at the relationships between men with the critical "estranged" eye of the discoverer. "The natural must be made to look surprising."[11]

This is how Brecht has summed up the distinction between the old convention and his own conception of the theatre:

The spectator of the *dramatic* theatre says: "Yes, I have felt the same.—I am just like this.—This is only natural. —It will always be like this.—This human being's suffering moves me, because there is no way out for him.— This is great art: it bears the mark of the inevitable.—I am weeping with those who weep on the stage, laughing with those who laugh."

The spectator of the *epic* theatre says: "I should never have thought so.— That is not the way to do it.—This is most surprising, hardly credible.— This will have to stop.—This human being's suffering moves me, because there would have been a way out for him. This is great art: nothing here seems inevitable—I am laughing about those who weep on the stage, weeping about those who laugh."[12]

Brecht has written a great deal about the methods of production and the technique of acting he required to translate these theories into practice. And he has left detailed records of some of his most successful productions in the form of "model books"—scene-by-scene descriptions of the performances illustrated by photographs of every movement on the stage.

11 Brecht, "Vergnuegungstheater oder Lehrtheater" (1936), *Schriften zum Theater*, p. 63.
12 Ibid., pp. 63–64.

BORN IN MISSISSIPPI, THOMAS LANIER WILLIAMS

Tennessee

Williams

1911-

(he later adopted the name Tennessee) moved with his family to a slum section of St. Louis when he was eight. His father was a traveling shoe salesman; his mother the daughter of an Episcopal clergyman. Adaptation to St. Louis was difficult for him: his mother's illnesses, the tauntings of playmates who called him Sissy, his deepened insecurity when a younger brother was born, his resentment at the family's poverty were among the factors that drove Williams to seek comfort in a private dream-world. He began writing at fourteen and became an incessant movie-goer, finding compassionate understanding in his sister Rose, a shy and fragile girl who was the model for Laura in *The Glass Menagerie*. Williams' attendance at the University of Missouri was interrupted by the depression. For two painful years he worked in a shoe warehouse, then suffered a nervous collapse and went South to his grandparents. Some success with writing made possible his return to school, and in 1938 he graduated from the University of Iowa. For a time he drifted about the United States and Mexico, working at odd jobs, and writing all the while: poetry, stories, plays. An award in a playwriting contest brought him to the attention of a New York agent, Audrey Wood, who helped to launch Williams as a dramatist with his *Battle of Angels* (1940). The play was a luckless failure and soon closed, but with *The Glass Menagerie* (1944) Williams' fortunes took a decisive turn toward success, sensationally confirmed by *A Streetcar Named Desire* (1947), which ushered in a series of dark plays projecting a world of violent passions and actions, of brutality and madness, a world sex-obsessed and destructive of the delicate and sensitive. Williams is essentially a Southern Gothic writer. At their best, his plays reflect his gift for poetic theatre, imaginative staging, radiant language, robust humor, vivid characterization, and a humane, if detached, understanding of weakness and failure. Among his plays are *Summer and Smoke* (1948), *The Rose Tattoo* (1951), *Camino Real* (1953), *Cat on a Hot Tin Roof* (1955), *Suddenly Last Summer* (1957), and *Period of Adjustment* (1960).

THE GLASS MENAGERIE

❧ BY TENNESSEE WILLIAMS

AUTHOR'S PRODUCTION NOTES FOR
THE GLASS MENAGERIE

Being a "memory play," *The Glass Menagerie* can be presented with unusual freedom of convention. Because of its considerably delicate or tenuous material, atmospheric touches and subtleties of direction play a particularly important part. Expressionism and all other unconventional techniques in drama have only one valid aim, and that is a closer approach to truth. When a play employs unconventional techniques, it is not, or certainly shouldn't be, trying to escape its responsibility of dealing with reality, or interpreting experience, but is actually or should be attempting to find a closer approach, a more penetrating and vivid expression of things as they are. The straight realistic play with its genuine frigidaire and authentic ice-cubes, its characters that speak exactly as its audience speaks, corresponds to the academic landscape and has the same virtue of a photographic likeness. Everyone should know nowadays the unimportance of the photographic in art: that truth, life, or reality is an organic thing which the poetic imagination can represent or suggest, in essence, only through transformation, through changing into other forms than those which were merely present in appearance.

These remarks are not meant as a preface only to this particular play. They have to do with a conception of a new, plastic theatre which must take the place of the exhausted theatre of realistic conventions if the theatre is to resume vitality as a part of our culture.

THE SCREEN DEVICE

There is *only one important difference between the original and acting version of the play* and that is the *omission* in the latter of the device which I tentatively included in my *original* script. This device was the use of a screen on which were projected magic-lantern slides bearing images or titles. I do not regret the omission of this device from the present Broadway production. The extraordinary power of Miss Taylor's performance made it suitable to have the utmost simplicity in the physical production. But I think it may be interesting to some readers to see how this device was conceived. So I am putting it into the published manuscript. These images and legends, projected from behind, were cast on a section of wall between the front-room and dining-room areas, which should be indistinguishable from the rest when not in use.

The purpose of this will probably be apparent. It is to give accent to certain values in each scene. Each scene contains a particular point (or several) which is structurally the most important. In an episodic play, such as this, the basic structure or narrative line may be obscured from the audience; the effect may seem fragmentary rather than architectural. This may not be the fault of the play so much as a lack of attention in the audience. The legend or image upon the screen will strengthen the effect of what is merely allusion in the writing and allow the primary point to be made more simply and lightly than if the entire responsibility were on the spoken lines. Aside from this structural value, I think the screen will have a definite emotional appeal, less definable but just as important. An imaginative producer or director may invent many other uses for this device than those indicated in the present script. In fact the possibilities of the device seem much larger to me than the instance of this play can possibly utilize.

THE MUSIC

Another extra-literary accent in this play is provided by the use of music. A single recurring tune, "The Glass Menagerie," is used to give emotional emphasis to suitable passages. This tune is like circus music, not when you are on the grounds or in the immediate vicinity of the parade, but when you are at some distance and very likely thinking of something else. It seems under those circumstances to continue almost interminably and it weaves in and out of your preoccupied consciousness; then it is the lightest, most delicate music in the world and perhaps the saddest. It expresses the surface vivacity of life with the underlying strain of immutable and inexpressible sorrow. When you look at a piece of delicately spun glass you think of two things: how beautiful it is and how easily it can be broken. Both of those ideas should be woven into the recurring tune, which dips in and out of the play as if it were carried on a wind that changes. It serves as a thread of connection and allusion between the narrator with his separate point in time and space and the subject of his own story. Between each episode it returns as reference to the emotion, nostalgia, which is the first condition of the play. It is primarily Laura's music and therefore comes out most clearly when the play focuses upon her and the lovely fragility of glass which is her image.

THE LIGHTING

The lighting in the play is not realistic. In keeping with the atmosphere of memory, the stage is dim. Shafts of light are focused on selected areas or actors, sometimes in contradistinction to what is the apparent center. For instance, in the quarrel scene between Tom and Amanda, in which Laura has no active part, the clearest pool of light is on her figure. This is also true of the supper scene, when her silent figure on the sofa should remain the visual center. The light upon Laura should be distinct from the others, having a peculiar pristine clarity such as light used in early religious portraits of female saints or madonnas. A certain correspondence to light in religious paintings, such as El Greco's, where the figures are radiant in atmosphere that is relatively dusky, could be effectively used throughout the play. (It will also permit a more effective use of the screen.) A free, imaginative use of light can be of enormous value in giving a mobile, plastic quality to plays of a more or less static nature.

CHARACTERS

AMANDA WINGFIELD, the mother.

A little woman of great but confused vitality clinging frantically to another time and place. Her characterization must be carefully created, not copied from type. She is not paranoiac, but her life is paranoia. There is much to admire in AMANDA, and as much to love and pity as there is to laugh at. Certainly she has endurance and a kind of heroism, and though her foolishness makes her unwittingly cruel at times, there is tenderness in her slight person.

LAURA WINGFIELD, her daughter.

AMANDA, having failed to establish contact with reality, continues to live vitally in her illusions, but LAURA's situation is even graver. A childhood illness has left her crippled, one leg slightly shorter than the other, and held in a brace. This defect need not be more than suggested on the stage. Stemming from this, LAURA's separation increases till she is like a piece of her own glass collection, too exquisitely fragile to move from the shelf.

TOM WINGFIELD, her son, and the narrator of the play.

A poet with a job in a warehouse. His nature is not remorseless, but to escape from a trap he has to act without pity.

JIM O'CONNOR, the gentleman caller.

A nice, ordinary, young man.

Scene I

The Wingfield apartment is in the rear of the building, one of those vast hive-like conglomerations of cellular living-units that flower as warty growths in overcrowded urban centers of lower middle-class population and are symptomatic of the impulse of this largest and fundamentally enslaved section of American society to avoid fluidity and differentiation and to exist and function as one interfused mass of automatism.

The apartment faces an alley and is entered by a fire-escape, a structure whose name is a touch of accidental poetic truth, for all of these huge buildings are always burning with the slow and implacable fires of human desperation. The fire-escape is included in the set—that is, the landing of it and steps descending from it.

The scene is memory and is therefore nonrealistic. Memory takes a lot of poetic license. It omits some details; others are exaggerated, according to the emotional value of the articles it touches, for memory is seated predominantly in the heart. The interior is therefore rather dim and poetic.

At the rise of the curtain, the audience is faced with the dark, grim rear wall of the Wingfield tenement. This building, which runs parallel to the footlights, is flanked on both sides by dark, narrow alleys which run into murky canyons of tangled clotheslines, garbage cans, and the sinister lattice-work of neighboring fire-escapes. It is up and down these side alleys that exterior entrances and exits are made, during the play. At the end of TOM's opening commentary, the dark tenement wall slowly reveals (by means of a transparency) the interior of the ground floor Wingfield apartment.

Downstage is the living room, which also serves as a sleeping room for LAURA, the sofa unfolding to make her bed. Upstage, center, and divided by a wide arch or second proscenium with transparent faded portieres (or second curtain), is the dining room. In an old-fashioned what-not in the living room are seen scores of transparent glass animals. A blown-up photograph of the father hangs on the wall of the living room, facing the audience, to the left of the archway. It is the face of a very handsome young man in a doughboy's First World War cap. He is gallantly smiling, ineluctably smiling, as if to say, "I will be smiling forever."

The audience hears and sees the opening scene in the dining room through both the transparent fourth wall of the building and the transparent gauze portieres of the dining-room arch. It is during this revealing scene that the fourth wall slowly ascends, out of sight. This transparent exterior wall is not brought down again until the very end of the play, during TOM's final speech.

The narrator is an undisguised convention of the play. He takes whatever license with dramatic convention is convenient to his purposes.

(TOM enters dressed as a merchant sailor from alley, stage left, and strolls across the front of the stage to the fire-escape. There he stops and lights a cigarette. He addresses the audience.)

TOM. Yes, I have tricks in my pocket, I have things up my sleeve. But I am the opposite of a stage magician. He gives you illusion that has the appearance of truth. I give you truth in the pleasant disguise of illusion.

To begin with, I turn back time. I reverse it to that quaint period, the thirties, when the huge middle class of America was matriculating in a school for the blind. Their eyes had failed them, or they had failed their eyes, and so they were having their fingers pressed forcibly down on the fiery Braille alphabet of a dissolving economy.

In Spain there was revolution. Here there was only shouting and confusion.

In Spain there was Guernica. Here there were disturbances of labor, sometimes pretty violent, in otherwise peaceful cities such as Chicago, Cleveland, Saint Louis. . . .

This is the social background of the play. (*Music.*)

The play is memory.

Being a memory play, it is dimly lighted, it is sentimental, it is not realistic.

In memory everything seems to happen to music. That explains the fiddle in the wings.

I am the narrator of the play, and also a character in it.

The other characters are my mother, Amanda, my sister, Laura, and a gentleman caller who appears in the final scenes.

He is the most realistic character in the play, being an emissary from a world of reality that we were somehow set apart from.

But since I have a poet's weakness for symbols, I am using this character also as a symbol; he is the long delayed but always expected something that we live for.

There is a fifth character in the play who doesn't appear except in this larger-than-life-size photograph over the mantel.

This is our father who left us a long time ago.

He was a telephone man who fell in love with long distances; he gave up his job with the telephone company and skipped the light fantastic out of town. . . .

The last we heard of him was a picture post-card from Mazatlan, on the Pacific coast of Mexico, containing a message of two words——

"Hello——Good-bye!" and no address.

I think the rest of the play will explain itself. . . .

(AMANDA's *voice becomes audible through the portieres.* LEGEND ON SCREEN: "OÙ SONT LES NEIGES?" *He divides the portieres and enters the upstage area.* AMANDA *and* LAURA *are seated at a drop-leaf table. Eating is indicated by gestures without food or utensils.* AMANDA *faces the audience.* TOM *and* LAURA *are seated in profile. The interior has lit up softly and through the scrim we see* AMANDA *and* LAURA *seated at the table in the upstage area.*)

AMANDA (*calling*). Tom?

TOM. Yes, Mother.

AMANDA. We can't say grace until you come to the table!

TOM. Coming, Mother. (*He bows slightly and withdraws, reappearing a few moments later in his place at the table.*)

AMANDA (*to her son*). Honey, don't *push* with your *fingers.* If you have to push with something, the thing to push with is a crust of bread. And chew—chew! Animals have sections in their stomachs which enable them to digest food without mastication, but human beings are supposed to chew their food before they swallow it down. Eat food leisurely, son, and really enjoy it. A well-cooked meal has lots of delicate flavors that have to be held in the mouth for appreciation. So chew your food and give your salivary glands a chance to function! (TOM *deliberately lays his imaginary fork down and pushes his chair back from the table.*)

TOM. I haven't enjoyed one bite of this dinner because of your constant directions on how to eat it. It's you that make me rush through meals with your hawk-like attention to every bite I take. Sickening —spoils my appetite—all this discussion of—animals' secretion—salivary glands—mastication!

AMANDA (*lightly*). Temperament like a Metropolitan star! (*He rises and crosses downstage.*) You're not excused from the table.

TOM. I'm getting a cigarette.

AMANDA. You smoke too much. (LAURA *rises.*)

LAURA. I'll bring in the blanc mange. (*He remains standing with his cigarette by the portieres during the following.*)

AMANDA (*rising*). No, sister, no, sister —you be the lady this time and I'll be the darky.

LAURA. I'm already up.

AMANDA. Resume your seat, little sister —I want you to stay fresh and pretty— for gentlemen callers!

LAURA. I'm not expecting any gentlemen callers.

AMANDA (*crossing out to kitchenette. Airily*). Sometimes they come when they are least expected! Why, I remember one Sunday afternoon in Blue Mountain— (*Enters kitchenette.*)

TOM. I know what's coming!

LAURA. Yes. But let her tell it.

TOM. Again?

LAURA. She loves to tell it. (AMANDA *returns with bowl of dessert.*)

AMANDA. One Sunday afternoon in Blue Mountain—your mother received— *seventeen!*—gentlemen callers! Why, sometimes there weren't chairs enough to accommodate them all. We had to send the nigger over to bring in folding chairs from the parish house.

TOM (*remaining at portieres*). How did you entertain those gentlemen callers?

AMANDA. I understood the art of conversation!

TOM. I bet you could talk.

AMANDA. Girls in those days *knew* how to talk, I can tell you.

TOM. Yes?

(IMAGE: AMANDA AS A GIRL ON A PORCH, GREETING CALLERS.)

AMANDA. They knew how to entertain their gentlemen callers. It wasn't enough for a girl to be possessed of a pretty face and a graceful figure—although I wasn't slighted in either respect. She also needed to have a nimble wit and a tongue to meet all occasions.

TOM. What did you talk about?

AMANDA. Things of importance going on in the world! Never anything coarse or common or vulgar. (*She addresses* TOM *as though he were seated in the vacant chair at the table though he remains by portieres. He plays this scene as though he held the book.*) My callers were gentlemen—all! Among my callers were some of the most prominent young planters of the Mississippi Delta— planters and sons of planters! (TOM *motions for music and a spot of light on* AMANDA. *Her eyes lift, her face glows, her voice becomes rich and elegiac.* SCREEN LEGEND: "ÒU SONT LES NEIGES?")

There was young Champ Laughlin, who later became vice-president of the Delta Planters Bank.

Hadley Stevenson, who was drowned in Moon Lake and left his widow one hundred and fifty thousand in Government bonds.

There were the Cutrere brothers, Wesley and Bates. Bates was one of my bright particular beaux! He got in a quarrel with that wild Wainwright boy. They shot it out on the floor of Moon Lake Casino. Bates was shot through the stomach. Died in the ambulance on his way to Memphis. His widow was also well-provided for, came into eight or ten thousand acres, that's all. She married him on the rebound—never loved her —carried my picture on him the night he died!

And there was that boy that every girl in the Delta had set her cap for! That beautiful, brilliant young Fitzhugh boy from Greene County!

TOM. What did he leave his widow?

AMANDA. He never married! Gracious, you talk as though all of my old admirers had turned up their toes to the daisies!

TOM. Isn't this the first you've mentioned that still survives?

AMANDA. That Fitzhugh boy went North and made a fortune—came to be known as the Wolf of Wall Street! He had the Midas touch, whatever he touched turned to gold!

And I could have been Mrs. Duncan J. Fitzhugh, mind you! But—I picked your *father!*

LAURA (*rising*). Mother, let me clear the table.

AMANDA. No, dear, you go in front and study your typewriter chart. Or practice your shorthand a little. Stay fresh and pretty!—It's almost time for our gentlemen callers to start arriving. (*She flounces girlishly toward the kitchenette.*) How many do you suppose we're going to entertain this afternoon? (TOM *throws down the paper and jumps up with a groan.*)

LAURA (*alone in the dining room*). I don't believe we're going to receive any, Mother.

AMANDA (*reappearing, airily*). What? No one—not one? You must be joking! (LAURA *nervously echoes her laugh. She slips in a fugitive manner through the half-open portieres and draws them gently behind her. A shaft of very clear light is thrown on her face against the faded tapestry of the curtains.* MUSIC: "THE GLASS MENAGERIE" UNDER FAINTLY. *Lightly.*) Not one gentleman caller? It can't be true! There must be a flood, there must have been a tornado!

LAURA. It isn't a flood, it's not a tornado, Mother. I'm just not popular like you were in Blue Mountain. . . .

(TOM *utters another groan.* LAURA *glances at him with a faint, apologetic*

smile. Her voice catching a little.)
Mother's afraid I'm going to be an old
maid.

THE SCENE DIMS OUT WITH "GLASS
MENAGERIE" MUSIC.

Scene II

LEGEND: "LAURA, HAVEN'T YOU EVER
LIKED SOME BOY?"
*On the dark stage the screen is lighted
with the image of blue roses.*
Gradually LAURA's *figure becomes apparent and the screen goes out. The music
subsides.*
LAURA *is seated in the delicate ivory
chair at the small claw-foot table.*
*She wears a dress of soft violet material
for a kimono—her hair tied back from
her forehead with a ribbon.*
*She is washing and polishing her col-
lection of glass.*
(AMANDA *appears on the fire-escape
steps. At the sound of her ascent,* LAURA
*catches her breath, thrusts the bowl of
ornaments away and seats herself stiffly
before the diagram of the typewriter keyboard as though it held her spellbound.*
Something has happened to AMANDA.
*It is written in her face as she climbs to
the landing: a look that is grim and hopeless and a little absurd.*
*She has on one of those cheap or imi-
tation velvety-looking cloth coats with
imitation fur collar. Her hat is five or six
years old, one of those dreadful cloche
hats that were worn in the late twenties,
and she is clasping an enormous black
patent-leather pocketbook with nickel
clasps and initials. This is her full-dress
outfit, the one she usually wears to the
D.A.R.*
*Before entering she looks through the
door.*
*She purses her lips, opens her eyes very
wide, rolls them upward and shakes her
head.*
*Then she slowly lets herself in the door.
Seeing her mother's expression* LAURA
touches her lips with a nervous gesture.)
LAURA. Hello, Mother, I was—— (*She
makes a nervous gesture toward the chart
on the wall.* AMANDA *leans against the
shut door and stares at* LAURA *with a
martyred look.*)

AMANDA. Deception? Deception? (*She
slowly removes her hat and gloves, continuing the sweet suffering stare. She
lets the hat and gloves fall on the floor
—a bit of acting.*)
LAURA (*shakily*). How was the D.A.R.
meeting? (AMANDA *slowly opens her
purse and removes a dainty white handkerchief which she shakes out delicately
and delicately touches to her lips and
nostrils.*) Didn't you go to the D.A.R.
meeting, Mother?
AMANDA (*faintly, almost inaudibly*).
—No.—No. (*Then more forcibly.*) I
did not have the strength—to go to the
D.A.R. In fact, I did not have the courage!
I wanted to find a hole in the ground and
hide myself in it forever! (*She crosses
slowly to the wall and removes the diagram of the typewriter keyboard. She
holds it in front of her for a second,
staring at it sweetly and sorrowfully—
then bites her lips and tears it in two
pieces.*)
LAURA (*faintly*). Why did you do that,
Mother? (AMANDA *repeats the same procedure with the chart of the Gregg Alphabet.*) Why are you——
AMANDA. Why? Why? How old are
you, Laura?
LAURA. Mother, you know my age.
AMANDA. I thought that you were an
adult; it seems that I was mistaken. (*She
crosses slowly to the sofa and sinks down
and stares at* LAURA.)
LAURA. Please don't stare at me,
Mother. (AMANDA *closes her eyes and
lowers her head. Count ten.*)
AMANDA. What are we going to do,
what is going to become of us, what is
the future? (*Count ten.*)
LAURA. Has something happened,
Mother? (AMANDA *draws a long breath
and takes out the handkerchief again.
Dabbing process.*) Mother, has—some-
thing happened?
AMANDA. I'll be all right in a minute,
I'm just bewildered—(*Count five.*)—by
life. . . .
LAURA. Mother, I wish that you would
tell me what's happened!
AMANDA. As you know, I was sup-
posed to be inducted into my office at the
D.A.R. this afternoon. (IMAGE: A SWARM
OF TYPEWRITERS.) But I stopped off at
Rubicam's Business College to speak to
your teachers about your having a cold

and ask them what progress they thought you were making down there.

LAURA. Oh. . . .

AMANDA. I went to the typing instructor and introduced myself as your mother. She didn't know who you were. Wingfield, she said. We don't have any such student enrolled at the school!

I assured her she did, that you had been going to classes since early in January.

"I wonder," she said, "if you could be talking about that terribly shy little girl who dropped out of school after only a few days' attendance?"

"No," I said, "Laura, my daughter, has been going to school every day for the past six weeks!"

"Excuse me," she said. She took the attendance book out and there was your name, unmistakably printed, and all the dates you were absent until they decided that you had dropped out of school.

I still said, "No, there must have been some mistake! There must have been some mix-up in the records!"

And she said, "No—I remember her perfectly now. Her hands shook so that she couldn't hit the right keys! The first time we gave a speed-test, she broke down completely—was sick at the stomach and almost had to be carried into the washroom! After that morning she never showed up any more. We phoned the house but never got any answer"—while I was working at Famous and Barr, I suppose, demonstrating those——Oh!

I felt so weak I could barely keep on my feet!

I had to sit down while they got me a glass of water!

Fifty dollars' tuition, all of our plans —my hopes and ambitions for you—just gone up the spout, just gone up the spout like that. (LAURA draws a long breath and gets awkwardly to her feet. She crosses to the victrola and winds it up.)

What are you doing?

LAURA. Oh! (She releases the handle and returns to her seat.)

AMANDA. Laura, where have you been going when you've gone out pretending that you were going to business college?

LAURA. I've just been going out walking.

AMANDA. That's not true.

LAURA. It is. I just went walking.

AMANDA. Walking? Walking? In winter? Deliberately courting pneumonia in that light coat? Where did you walk to, Laura?

LAURA. All sorts of places—mostly in the park.

AMANDA. Even after you'd started catching that cold?

LAURA. It was the lesser of two evils, Mother. (IMAGE: WINTER SCENE IN PARK.) I couldn't go back up. I—threw up—on the floor!

AMANDA. From half past seven till after five every day you mean to tell me you walked around the park, because you wanted to make me think that you were still going to Rubicam's Business College?

LAURA. It wasn't as bad as it sounds. I went inside places to get warmed up.

AMANDA. Inside where?

LAURA. I went in the art museum and the bird-houses at the Zoo. I visited the penguins every day! Sometimes I did without lunch and went to the movies. Lately I've been spending most of my afternoons in the Jewel-box, that big glass house where they raise the tropical flowers.

AMANDA. You did all this to deceive me, just for deception? (LAURA looks down.) Why?

LAURA. Mother, when you're disappointed, you get that awful suffering look on your face, like the picture of Jesus' mother in the museum!

AMANDA. Hush!

LAURA. I couldn't face it. (Pause. A whisper of strings. LEGEND: "THE CRUST OF HUMILITY.")

AMANDA (hopelessly fingering the huge pocketbook). So what are we going to do the rest of our lives? Stay home and watch the parades go by? Amuse ourselves with the glass menagerie, darling? Eternally play those worn-out phonograph records your father left as a painful reminder of him?

We won't have a business career— we've given that up because it gave us nervous indigestion! (Laughs wearily.) What is there left but dependency all our lives? I know so well what becomes of unmarried women who aren't prepared to occupy a position. I've seen such pitiful cases in the South—barely tolerated spinsters living upon the grudging patronage of sister's husband or brother's wife!— stuck away in some little mouse-trap of a room—encouraged by one in-law to visit another—little birdlike women without any nest—eating the crust of humility all their life!

Is that the future that we've mapped out for ourselves?

I swear it's the only alternative I can think of!

It isn't a very pleasant alternative, is it? Of course—some girls *do marry*. (LAURA *twists her hands nervously*.) Haven't you ever liked some boy?

LAURA. Yes. I liked one once. (*Rises*.) I came across his picture a while ago.

AMANDA (*with some interest*). He gave you his picture?

LAURA. No, it's in the year-book.

AMANDA (*disappointed*). Oh—a high-school boy.

(SCREEN IMAGE: JIM AS HIGH-SCHOOL HERO BEARING A SILVER CUP.)

LAURA. Yes. His name was Jim. (LAURA *lifts the heavy annual from the claw-foot table*.) Here he is in *The Pirates of Penzance*.

AMANDA (*absently*). The what?

LAURA. The operetta the senior class put on. He had a wonderful voice and we sat across the aisle from each other Mondays, Wednesdays, and Fridays in the Aud. Here he is with the silver cup for debating! See his grin?

AMANDA (*absently*). He must have had a jolly disposition.

LAURA. He used to call me—Blue Roses. (IMAGE: BLUE ROSES.)

AMANDA. Why did he call you such a name as that?

LAURA. When I had that attack of pleurosis—he asked me what was the matter when I came back. I said pleurosis —he thought that I said Blue Roses! So that's what he always called me after that. Whenever he saw me, he'd holler, "Hello, Blue Roses!" I didn't care for the girl that he went out with. Emily Meisenbach. Emily was the best-dressed girl at Soldan. She never struck me, though, as being sincere . . . It says in the Personal Section—they're engaged. That's—six years ago! They must be married by now.

AMANDA. Girls that aren't cut out for business careers usually wind up married to some nice man. (*Gets up with a spark of revival*.) Sister, that's what you'll do! (LAURA *utters a startled, doubtful laugh*.

She reaches quickly for a piece of glass.)

LAURA. But, Mother——

AMANDA. Yes? (*Crossing to photograph*.)

LAURA (*in a tone of frightened apology*). I'm—crippled! (IMAGE: SCREEN.)

AMANDA. Nonsense! Laura, I've told you never, never to use that word. Why, you're not crippled, you just have a little defect—hardly noticeable, even! When people have some slight disadvantage like that, they cultivate other things to make up for it—develop charm and vivacity —and *charm!* That's all you have to do! (*She turns again to the photograph*.) One thing your father had *plenty of*— was *charm!* (TOM *motions to the fiddle in the wings*.)

THE SCENE FADES OUT WITH MUSIC.

Scene III

(LEGEND ON SCREEN: "AFTER THE FIASCO——" TOM *speaks from the fire-escape landing*.)

TOM. After the fiasco at Rubicam's Business College, the idea of getting a gentleman caller for Laura began to play a more and more important part in Mother's calculations.

It became an obsession. Like some archetype of the universal unconscious, the image of the gentleman caller haunted our small apartment. . . .

(IMAGE: YOUNG MAN AT DOOR WITH FLOWERS.)

An evening at home rarely passed without some allusion to this image, this spectre, this hope. . . .

Even when he wasn't mentioned, his presence hung in Mother's preoccupied look and in my sister's frightened, apologetic manner—hung like a sentence passed upon the Wingfields!

Mother was a woman of action as well as words.

She began to take logical steps in the planned direction.

Late that winter and in the early spring —realizing that extra money would be needed to properly feather the nest and plume the bird—she conducted a vigorous campaign on the telephone, roping in subscribers to one of those magazines for matrons called *The Home-maker's Companion,* the type of journal that features the serialized sublimations of ladies of letters who think in terms of delicate cup-like breasts, slim, tapering waists, rich, creamy thighs, eyes like wood-smoke in autumn, fingers that soothe and caress like strains of music, bodies as powerful as Etruscan sculpture.

(SCREEN IMAGE: GLAMOR MAGAZINE COVER. AMANDA *enters with phone on long extension cord. She is spotted in the dim stage.*)

AMANDA. Ida Scott? This is Amanda Wingfield!

We *missed* you at the D.A.R. last Monday!

I said to myself: She's probably suffering with that sinus condition! How is that sinus condition?

Horrors! Heaven have mercy!—You're a Christian martyr, yes, that's what you are, a Christian martyr!

Well, I just now happened to notice that your subscription to the *Companion's* about to expire! Yes, it expires with the next issue, honey!—just when that wonderful new serial by Bessie Mae Hopper is getting off to such an exciting start. Oh, honey, it's something that you can't miss! You remember how *Gone With the Wind* took everybody by storm? You simply couldn't go out if you hadn't read it. All everybody *talked* was Scarlett O'Hara. Well, this is a book that critics already compare to *Gone With the Wind.* It's the *Gone With the Wind* of the post-World War generation!—What?—Burning?—Oh, honey, don't let them burn, go take a look in the oven and I'll hold the wire! Heavens—I think she's hung up!

DIM OUT

(LEGEND ON THE SCREEN: "YOU THINK I'M IN LOVE WITH CONTINENTAL SHOEMAKERS?" *Before the stage is lighted the violent voices of* TOM *and* AMANDA *are heard. They are quarreling behind the portieres. In front of them stands* LAURA *with clenched hands and panicky expression. A clear pool of light on her figure throughout this scene.*)

TOM. What in Christ's name am I——

AMANDA (*shrilly*). Don't you use that——

TOM. Supposed to do!

AMANDA. Expression! Not in my——

TOM. Ohhh!

AMANDA. Presence! Have you gone out of your senses?

TOM. I have, that's true, *driven* out!

AMANDA. What is the matter with you, you—big—big—IDIOT!

TOM. Look!—I've got *no thing,* no single thing——

AMANDA. Lower your voice!

TOM. In my life here that I can call my OWN! Everything is——

AMANDA. Stop that shouting!

TOM. Yesterday you confiscated my books! You had the nerve to——

AMANDA. I took that horrible novel back to the library—yes! That hideous book by that insane Mr. Lawrence. (TOM *laughs wildly.*) I cannot control the output of diseased minds or people who cater to them—(TOM *laughs still more wildly.*) BUT I WON'T ALLOW SUCH FILTH BROUGHT INTO MY HOUSE! No, no, no, no, no!

TOM. House, house! Who pays rent on it, who makes a slave of himself to——

AMANDA (*fairly screeching*). Don't you DARE to——

TOM. No, no, *I* mustn't say things! *I've* got to just——

AMANDA. Let me tell you——

TOM. I don't want to hear any more! (*He tears the portieres open. The upstage area is lit with a turgid smoky red glow.* AMANDA's *hair is in metal curlers and she wears a very old bathrobe, much too large for her slight figure, a relic of the faithless Mr. Wingfield. An upright typewriter and a wild disarray of manuscripts are on the drop-leaf table. The quarrel was probably precipitated by* AMANDA's *interruption of his creative labor. A chair lying overthrown on the floor. Their gesticulating shadows are cast on the ceiling by the fiery glow.*)

AMANDA. You *will* hear more, you——

TOM. No, I won't hear more, I'm going out!

AMANDA. You come right back in——

TOM. Out, out, out! Because I'm——

AMANDA. Come back here, Tom Wingfield! I'm not through talking to you!

TOM. Oh go——

LAURA (*desperately*).—Tom!

AMANDA. You're going to listen, and no more insolence from you! I'm at the end of my patience! (*He comes back toward her.*)

TOM. What do you think I'm at? Aren't I supposed to have any patience to reach the end of, Mother? I know, I know. It seems unimportant to you, what I'm *doing*—what I *want* to do—having a little *difference* between them! You don't think that——

AMANDA. I think you've been doing things that you're ashamed of. That's why you act like this. I don't believe that you go every night to the movies. Nobody goes to the movies night after night. Nobody in their right minds goes to the movies as often as you pretend to. People don't go to the movies at nearly midnight, and movies don't let out at two A.M. Come in stumbling. Muttering to yourself like a maniac! You get three hours' sleep and then go to work. Oh, I can picture the way you're doing down there. Moping, doping, because you're in no condition.

TOM (*wildly*). No, I'm in no condition!

AMANDA. What right have you got to jeopardize your job? Jeopardize the security of us all? How do you think we'd manage if you were——

TOM. Listen! You think I'm crazy *about* the *warehouse?* (*He bends fiercely toward her slight figure.*) You think I'm in love with the Continental Shoemakers? You think I want to spend fifty-five *years* down there in that—*celotex interior!* with—*fluorescent*—*tubes!* Look! I'd rather somebody picked up a crowbar and battered out my brains—than go back mornings! I *go!* Every time you come in yelling that God damn *"Rise and Shine!"* *"Rise and Shine!"* I say to myself, "How *lucky dead* people are!" But I get up. I *go!* For sixty-five dollars a month I give up all that I dream of doing and being *ever!* And you say self—*self's* all I ever think of. Why, listen, if self is what I thought of, Mother, I'd be where he is —GONE! (*Pointing to father's picture.*) As far as the system of transportation reaches! (*He starts past her. She grabs his arm.*) Don't grab at me, Mother!

AMANDA. Where are you going?

TOM. I'm going to the *movies!*

AMANDA. I don't believe that lie!

TOM (*crouching toward her, overtowering her tiny figure. She backs away, gasping*). I'm going to opium dens! Yes, opium dens, dens of vice and criminals' hang-outs, Mother. I've joined the Hogan gang, I'm a hired assassin, I carry a tommy-gun in a violin case! I run a string of cat-houses in the Valley! They call me Killer, Killer Wingfield, I'm leading a double-life: a simple, honest warehouse worker by day, by night a dynamic *czar* of the *underworld*, *Mother.* I go to gambling casinos, I spin away fortunes on the roulette table! I wear a patch over one eye and a false mustache; sometimes I put on green whiskers. On those occasions they call me—*El Diablo!* Oh, I could tell you things to make you sleepless! My enemies plan to dynamite this place. They're going to blow us all sky-high some night! I'll be glad, very happy, and so will you! You'll go up, up on a broomstick, over Blue Mountain with seventeen gentlemen callers! You ugly—babbling old—*witch.* . . . (*He goes through a series of violent, clumsy movements, seizing his overcoat, lunging to the door, pulling it fiercely open. The* WOMEN *watch him, aghast. His arm catches in the sleeve of the coat as he struggles to pull it on. For a moment he is pinioned by the bulky garment. With an outraged groan he tears the coat off again, splitting the shoulder of it, and hurls it across the room. It strikes against the shelf of* LAURA's *glass collection, there is a tinkle of shattering glass.* LAURA *cries out as if wounded.* MUSIC. LEGEND: "THE GLASS MENAGERIE.")

LAURA (*shrilly*). My glass!—menagerie. . . . (*She covers her face and turns away. But* AMANDA *is still stunned and stupefied by the "ugly witch" so that she barely notices this occurrence. Now she recovers her speech.*)

AMANDA (*in an awful voice*). I won't speak to you—until you apologize! (*She crosses through portieres and draws them together behind her.* TOM *is left with* LAURA. LAURA *clings weakly to the mantel with her face averted.* TOM *stares at her stupidly for a moment. Then he crosses to shelf. Drops awkwardly on his knees to collect the fallen glass, glancing at* LAURA *as if he would speak but couldn't.*)

"THE GLASS MENAGERIE" *steals in as*

THE SCENE DIMS OUT.

Scene IV

The interior is dark. Faint light in the alley. A deep-voiced bell in a church is tolling the hour of five as the scene commences. (TOM appears at the top of the alley. After each solemn boom of the bell in the tower, he shakes a little noise-maker or rattle as if to express the tiny spasm of man in contrast to the sustained power and dignity of the Almighty. This and the unsteadiness of his advance make it evident that he has been drinking.

As he climbs the few steps to the fire-escape landing, light steals up inside. LAURA appears in night-dress, observing TOM's empty bed in the front room.

TOM fishes in his pockets for door-key, removing a motley assortment of articles in the search, including a perfect shower of movie-ticket stubs and an empty bottle. At last he finds the key, but just as he is about to insert it, it slips from his fingers. He strikes a match and crouches below the door.)

TOM (*bitterly*). One crack—and it falls through! (LAURA *opens the door.*)

LAURA. Tom! Tom, what are you doing?

TOM. Looking for a door-key.

LAURA. Where have you been all this time?

TOM. I have been to the movies.

LAURA. All this time at the movies?

TOM. There was a very long program. There was a Garbo picture and a Mickey Mouse and a travelogue and a newsreel and a preview of coming attractions. And there was an organ solo and a collection for the milk-fund—simultaneously—which ended up in a terrible fight between a fat lady and an usher!

LAURA (*innocently*). Did you have to stay through everything?

TOM. Of course! And, oh, I forgot! There was a big stage show! The head-liner on this stage show was Malvolio the Magician. He performed wonderful tricks, many of them, such as pouring water back and forth between pitchers. First it turned to wine and then it turned to beer and then it turned to whiskey. I know it was whiskey it finally turned into because he needed somebody to come up out of the audience to help him, and I came up —both shows! It was Kentucky Straight Bourbon. A very generous fellow, he gave

souvenirs. (*He pulls from his back pocket a shimmering rainbow-colored scarf.*) He gave me this. This is his magic scarf. You can have it, Laura. You wave it over a canary cage and you get a bowl of gold-fish. You wave it over the gold-fish bowl and they fly away canaries. . . . But the wonderfullest trick of all was the coffin trick. We nailed him into a coffin and he got out of the coffin without removing one nail. (*He has come inside.*) There is a trick that would come in handy for me—get me out of this 2 by 4 situation! (*Flops onto bed and starts removing shoes.*)

LAURA. Tom—shhh!

TOM. What're you shushing me for?

LAURA. You'll wake up Mother.

TOM. Goody, goody! Pay 'er back for all those "Rise an' Shines." (*Lies down, groaning.*) You know it don't take much intelligence to get yourself into a nailed-up coffin, Laura. But who in hell ever got himself out of one without removing one nail? (*As if in answer, the father's grinning photograph lights up.*)

SCENE DIMS OUT.

(*Immediately following: The church bell is heard striking six. At the sixth stroke the alarm clock goes off in AMANDA's room, and after a few moments we hear her calling: "Rise and Shine! Rise and Shine! Laura, go tell your brother to rise and shine!"*)

TOM (*sitting up slowly*). I'll rise— but I won't shine. (*The light increases.*)

AMANDA. Laura, tell your brother his coffee is ready. (LAURA *slips into front room.*)

LAURA. Tom!—It's nearly seven. Don't make Mother nervous. (*He stares at her stupidly. Beseechingly.*) Tom, speak to Mother this morning. Make up with her, apologize, speak to her!

TOM. She won't to me. It's her that started not speaking.

LAURA. If you just say you're sorry she'll start speaking.

TOM. Her not speaking—is that such a tragedy?

LAURA. Please—please!

AMANDA (*calling from kitchenette.*) Laura, are you going to do what I asked you to do, or do I have to get dressed and go out myself?

LAURA. Going, going—soon as I get on my coat! (*She pulls on a shapeless felt hat with nervous, jerky movement, pleadingly glancing at* TOM. *Rushes awkwardly for coat. The coat is one of* AMANDA'S *inaccurately made-over, the sleeves too short for* LAURA.) Butter and what else?

AMANDA (*entering upstage*). Just butter. Tell them to charge it.

LAURA. Mother, they make such faces when I do that.

AMANDA. Sticks and stones can break our bones, but the expression on Mr. Garfinkel's face won't harm us! Tell your brother his coffee is getting cold.

LAURA (*at door*). Do what I asked you, will you, will you, Tom? (*He looks sullenly away.*)

AMANDA. Laura, go now or just don't go at all!

LAURA (*rushing out*). Going—going! (*A second later she cries out.* TOM *springs up and crosses to door.* AMANDA *rushes anxiously in.* TOM *opens the door.*)

TOM. Laura?

LAURA. I'm all right. I slipped, but I'm all right.

AMANDA (*peering anxiously after her*). If anyone breaks a leg on those fire-escape steps, the landlord ought to be sued for every cent he possesses! (*She shuts door. Remembers she isn't speaking and returns to other room. As* TOM *enters listlessly for his coffee, she turns her back to him and stands rigidly facing the window on the gloomy gray vault of the areaway. Its light on her face with its aged but childish features is cruelly sharp, satirical as a Daumier print.* MUSIC UNDER: "AVE MARIA." TOM *glances sheepishly but sullenly at her averted figure and slumps at the table. The coffee is scalding hot; he sips it and gasps and spits it back in the cup. At his gasp,* AMANDA *catches her breath and half turns. Then catches herself and turns back to window.* TOM *blows on his coffee, glancing sidewise at his mother. She clears her throat.* TOM *clears his. He starts to rise. Sinks back down again, scratches his head, clears his throat again.* AMANDA *coughs.* TOM *raises his cup in both hands to blow on it, his eyes staring over the rim of it at his mother for several moments. Then he slowly sets the cup down and awkwardly and hesitantly rises from the chair.*)

TOM (*hoarsely*). Mother. I—I apologize, Mother. (AMANDA *draws a quick, shuddering breath. Her face works grotesquely. She breaks into childlike tears.*) I'm sorry for what I said, for everything that I said, I didn't mean it.

AMANDA (*sobbingly*). My devotion has made me a witch and so I make myself hateful to my children!

TOM. *No, you don't.*

AMANDA. I worry so much, don't sleep, it makes me nervous!

TOM (*gently*). I understand that.

AMANDA. I've had to put up a solitary battle all these years. But you're my right-hand bower! Don't fall down, don't fail!

TOM (*gently*). I'll try, Mother.

AMANDA (*with great enthusiasm*). Try and you will SUCCEED! (*The notion makes her breathless.*) Why, you—you're just *full* of natural endowments! Both of my children—they're *unusual* children! Don't you think I know it? I'm so—*proud!* Happy and—feel I've—so much to be thankful for but—— Promise me one thing, Son!

TOM. What, Mother?

AMANDA. Promise, Son, you'll—never be a drunkard!

TOM (*turns to her, grinning*). I will never be a drunkard, Mother.

AMANDA. That's what frightened me so, that you'd be drinking! Eat a bowl of Purina!

TOM. Just coffee, Mother.

AMANDA. Shredded wheat biscuit?

TOM. No. No, Mother, just coffee.

AMANDA. You can't put in a day's work on an empty stomach. You've got ten minutes—don't gulp! Drinking too-hot liquids makes cancer of the stomach. . . . Put cream in.

TOM. No, thank you.

AMANDA. To cool it.

TOM. No! No, thank you, I want it black.

AMANDA. I know, but it's not good for you. We have to do all that we can to build ourselves up. In these trying times we live in, all that we have to cling to is—each other. . . . That's why it's so important to—— Tom, I—— I sent out your sister so I could discuss something with you. If you hadn't spoken I would have spoken to you. (*Sits down.*)

TOM (*gently*). What is it, Mother, that you want to discuss?

AMANDA. Laura! (TOM *puts his cup down slowly,* LEGEND ON SCREEN: "LAURA." MUSIC: "THE GLASS MENAGERIE.")

TOM. —Oh.—Laura. . . .

AMANDA (*touching his sleeve*). You know how Laura is. So quiet but—still water runs deep! She notices things and I think she—broods about them. (TOM *looks up.*) A few days ago I came in and she was crying.

TOM. What about?

AMANDA. You.

TOM. Me?

AMANDA. She has an idea that you're not happy here.

TOM. What gave her that idea?

AMANDA. What gives her any idea? However, you do act strangely. I—I'm not criticizing, understand *that!* I know your ambitions do not lie in the warehouse, that like everybody in the whole wide world—you've had to—make sacrifices, but—Tom—Tom—life's not easy, it calls for—Spartan endurance! There's so many things in my heart that I cannot describe to you! I've never told you but I—*loved* your father. . . .

TOM (*gently*). I know that, Mother.

AMANDA. And you—when I see you taking after his ways! Staying out late—and—well, you *had* been drinking the night you were in that—terrifying condition! Laura says that you hate the apartment and that you go out nights to get away from it! Is that true, Tom?

TOM. No. You say there's so much in your heart that you can't describe to me. That's true of me, too. There's so much in my heart that I can't describe to *you!* So let's respect each other's——

AMANDA. But, why—*why,* Tom—are you always so *restless?* Where do you go to, nights?

TOM. I—go to the movies.

AMANDA. Why do you go to the movies so much, Tom?

TOM. I go to the movies because—I like adventure. Adventure is something I don't have much of at work, so I go to the movies.

AMANDA. But, Tom, you go to the movies *entirely* too *much!*

TOM. I like a lot of adventure. (AMANDA *looks baffled, then hurt. As the familiar inquisition resumes he becomes hard and impatient again.* AMANDA *slips back into her querulous attitude toward him.* IMAGE ON SCREEN: SAILING VESSEL WITH JOLLY ROGER.)

AMANDA. Most young men find adventure in their careers.

TOM. Then most young men are not employed in a warehouse.

AMANDA. The world is full of young men employed in warehouses and offices and factories.

TOM. Do all of them find adventure in their careers?

AMANDA. They do or they do without it! Not everybody has a craze for adventure.

TOM. Man is by instinct a lover, a hunter, a fighter, and none of those instincts are given much play at the warehouse!

AMANDA. Man is by instinct! Don't quote instinct to me! Instinct is something that people have got away from! It belongs to animals! Christian adults don't want it!

TOM. What do Christian adults want, then, Mother?

AMANDA. Superior things! Things of the mind and the spirit! Only animals have to satisfy instincts! Surely your aims are somewhat higher than theirs! Than monkeys—pigs——

TOM. I reckon they're not.

AMANDA. You're joking. However, that isn't what I wanted to discuss.

TOM (*rising*). I haven't much time.

AMANDA (*pushing his shoulders*). Sit down.

TOM. You want me to punch in red at the warehouse, Mother?

AMANDA. You have five minutes. I want to talk about Laura.

(LEGEND: "PLANS AND PROVISIONS.")

TOM. All right! What about Laura?

AMANDA. We have to be making some plans and provisions for her. She's older than you, two years, and nothing has happened. She just drifts along doing nothing. It frightens me terribly how she just drifts along.

TOM. I guess she's the type that people call home girls.

AMANDA. There's no such type, and if there is, it's a pity! That is unless the home is hers, with a husband!

TOM. What?

AMANDA. Oh, I can see the handwriting on the wall as plain as I see the nose in front of my face! It's terrifying!

More and more you remind me of your father! He was out all hours without explanation!—Then *left! Good-bye!*

And me with the bag to hold. I saw that letter you got from the Merchant Marine. I know what you're dreaming of. I'm not standing here blindfolded.

Very well, then. Then *do* it!

But not till there's somebody to take your place.

TOM. What do you mean?

AMANDA. I mean that as soon as Laura has got somebody to take care of her, married, a home of her own, independent —why, then you'll be free to go wherever you please, on land, on sea, whichever way the wind blows you!

But until that time you've got to look out for your sister. I don't say me because I'm old and don't matter! I say for your sister because she's young and dependent.

I put her in business college—a dismal failure! Frightened her so it made her sick at the stomach.

I took her over to the Young People's League at the church. Another fiasco. She spoke to nobody, nobody spoke to her. Now all she does is fool with those pieces of glass and play those worn-out records. What kind of a life is that for a girl to lead?

TOM. What can I do about it?

AMANDA. Overcome selfishness!

Self, self, self is all that you ever think of! (TOM *springs up and crosses to get his coat. It is ugly and bulky. He pulls on a cap with earmuffs.*) Where is your muffler? Put your wool muffler on! (*He snatches it angrily from the closet and tosses it around his neck and pulls both ends tight.*) Tom! I haven't said what I had in mind to ask you.

TOM. I'm too late to——

AMANDA (*catching his arm—very importunately. Then shyly*). Down at the warehouse, aren't there some—nice young men?

TOM. No!

AMANDA. There *must* be—*some* . . .

TOM. Mother——(*Gesture.*)

AMANDA. Find out one that's clean-living—doesn't drink and—ask him out for sister!

TOM. What?

AMANDA. For *sister!* To *meet!* Get *acquainted!*

TOM (*stamping to door*). Oh, my go-osh!

AMANDA. Will you? (*He opens door. Imploringly.*) Will you? (*He starts down.*) Will you? *Will* you, dear?

TOM (*calling back*). YES! (AMANDA *closes the door hesitantly and with a troubled but faintly hopeful expression.* SCREEN IMAGE: GLAMOR MAGAZINE COVER. *Spot* AMANDA *at phone.*)

AMANDA. Ella Cartwright? This is Amanda Wingfield!

How are you, honey?

How is that kidney condition? (*Count five.*)

Horrors! (*Count five.*)

You're a Christian martyr, yes, honey, that's what you are, a Christian martyr!

Well, I just now happened to notice in my little red book that your subscription to the *Companion* has just run out! I knew that you wouldn't want to miss out on the wonderful serial starting in this new issue. It's by Bessie Mae Hopper, the first thing she's written since *Honeymoon for Three.*

Wasn't that a strange and interesting story? Well, this one is even lovelier, I believe. It has a sophisticated, society background. It's all about the horsey set on Long Island!

FADE OUT.

Scene V

LEGEND ON SCREEN: "ANNUNCIA-TION." *Fade with music.*

It is early dusk of a spring evening. Supper has just been finished in the Wingfield apartment. AMANDA *and* LAURA *in light-colored dresses are removing dishes from the table, in the upstage area, which is shadowy, their movements formalized almost as a dance or ritual, their moving forms as pale and silent as moths.*

(TOM, *in white shirt and trousers, rises from the table and crosses toward the fire-escape.*)

AMANDA (*as he passes her*). Son, will you do me a favor?

TOM. What?

AMANDA. Comb your hair! You look

so pretty when your hair is combed! (TOM *slouches on sofa with evening paper. Enormous caption "Franco Triumphs."*) There is only one respect in which I would like you to emulate your father.

TOM. What respect is that?

AMANDA. The care he always took of his appearance. He never allowed himself to look untidy. (*He throws down the paper and crosses to fire-escape.*) Where are you going?

TOM. I'm going out to smoke.

AMANDA. You smoke too much. A pack a day at fifteen cents a pack. How much would that amount to in a month? Thirty times fifteen is how much, Tom? Figure it out and you will be astounded at what you could save. Enough to give you a night-school course in accounting at Washington U! Just think what a wonderful thing that would be for you, Son! (TOM *is unmoved by the thought.*)

TOM. I'd rather smoke. (*He steps out on landing, letting the screen door slam.*)

AMANDA (*sharply*). I know! That's the tragedy of it. . . . (*Alone, she turns to look at her husband's picture.* DANCE MUSIC: "ALL THE WORLD IS WAITING FOR THE SUNRISE!")

TOM (*to the audience*). Across the alley from us was the Paradise Dance Hall. On evenings in spring the windows and doors were open and the music came outdoors. Sometimes the lights were turned out except for a large glass sphere that hung from the ceiling. It would turn slowly about and filter the dusk with delicate rainbow colors. Then the orchestra played a waltz or a tango, something that had a slow and sensuous rhythm. Couples would come outside, to the relative privacy of the alley. You could see them kissing behind ash-pits and telephone poles.

This was the compensation for lives that passed like mine, without any change or adventure.

Adventure and change were imminent in this year. They were waiting around the corner for all these kids.

Suspended in the mist over Berchtesgaden, caught in the folds of Chamberlain's umbrella——

In Spain there was Guernica!

But here there was only hot swing music and liquor, dance halls, bars, and movies, and sex that hung in the gloom like a chandelier and flooded the world with brief, deceptive rainbows. . . .

All the world was waiting for bombardments!

(AMANDA *turns from the picture and comes outside.*)

AMANDA (*sighing*). A fire-escape landing's a poor excuse for a porch. (*She spreads a newspaper on a step and sits down gracefully and demurely as if she were settling into a swing on a Mississippi veranda.*) What are you looking at?

TOM. The moon.

AMANDA. Is there a moon this evening?

TOM. It's rising over Garfinkel's Delicatessen.

AMANDA. So it is! A little silver slipper of a moon. Have you made a wish on it yet?

TOM. Um-hum.

AMANDA. What did you wish for?

TOM. That's a secret.

AMANDA. A secret, huh? Well, I won't tell mine either. I will be just as mysterious as you.

TOM. I bet I can guess what yours is.

AMANDA. Is my head so transparent?

TOM. You're not a sphinx.

AMANDA. No, I don't have secrets. I'll tell you what I wished for on the moon. Success and happiness for my precious children! I wish for that whenever there's a moon, and when there isn't a moon, I wish for it, too.

TOM. I thought perhaps you wished for a gentleman caller.

AMANDA. Why do you say that?

TOM. Don't you remember asking me to fetch one?

AMANDA. I remember suggesting that it would be nice for your sister if you brought home some nice young man from the warehouse. I think that I've made that suggestion more than once.

TOM. Yes, you have made it repeatedly.

AMANDA. Well?

TOM. We are going to have one.

AMANDA. *What?*

TOM. A gentleman caller! (*The anunciation is celebrated with music.* AMANDA *rises.* IMAGE ON SCREEN: CALLER WITH BOUQUET.)

AMANDA. You mean you have asked some nice young man to come over?

TOM. Yep. I've asked him to dinner.

AMANDA. You really did?

TOM. I did!

AMANDA. You did, and did he—*accept?*

TOM. He did!

AMANDA. Well, well—well, well! That's—lovely!

TOM. I thought that you would be pleased.

AMANDA. It's definite, then?

TOM. Very definite.

AMANDA. Soon?

TOM. Very soon.

AMANDA. For heaven's sake, stop putting on and tell me some things, will you?

TOM. What things do you want me to tell you?

AMANDA. *Naturally* I would like to know when he's *coming!*

TOM. He's coming tomorrow.

AMANDA. *Tomorrow?*

TOM. Yep. Tomorrow.

AMANDA. But, Tom!

TOM. Yes, Mother?

AMANDA. Tomorrow gives me no time!

TOM. Time for what?

AMANDA. Preparations! Why didn't you phone me at once, as soon as you asked him, the minute that he accepted? Then, don't you see, I could have been getting ready!

TOM. You don't have to make any fuss.

AMANDA. Oh, Tom, Tom, Tom, of course I have to make a fuss! I want things nice, not sloppy! Not thrown together. I'll certainly have to do some fast thinking, won't I?

TOM. I don't see why you have to think at all.

AMANDA. You just don't know. We can't have a gentleman caller in a pigsty! All my wedding silver has to be polished, the monogrammed table linen ought to be laundered! The windows have to be washed and fresh curtains put up. And how about clothes? We have to *wear* something, don't we?

TOM. Mother, this boy is no one to make a fuss over!

AMANDA. Do you realize he's the first young man we've introduced to your sister?

It's terrible, dreadful, disgraceful that poor little sister has never received a single gentleman caller! Tom, come inside! (*She opens the screen door.*)

TOM. What for?

AMANDA. I want to ask you some things.

TOM. If you're going to make such a fuss, I'll call it off, I'll tell him not to come!

AMANDA. You certainly won't do anything of the kind. Nothing offends people worse than broken engagements. It simply means I'll have to work like a Turk! We won't be brilliant, but we will pass inspection. Come on inside. (TOM *follows, groaning.*) Sit down.

TOM. Any particular place you would like me to sit?

AMANDA. Thank heavens I've got that new sofa! I'm also making payments on a floor lamp I'll have sent out! And put the chintz covers on, they'll brighten things up! Of course I'd hoped to have these walls repapered. . . . What is the young man's name?

TOM. His name is O'Connor.

AMANDA. That, of course, means fish—tomorrow is Friday! I'll have that salmon loaf—with Durkee's dressing! What does he do? He works at the warehouse?

TOM. Of course! How else would I——

AMANDA. Tom, he—doesn't drink?

TOM. Why do you ask me that?

AMANDA. Your father *did!*

TOM. Don't get started on that!

AMANDA. He *does* drink, then?

TOM. Not that I know of!

AMANDA. Make sure, be certain! The last thing I want for my daughter's a boy who drinks!

TOM. Aren't you being a little bit premature? Mr. O'Connor has not yet appeared on the scene!

AMANDA. But will tomorrow. To meet your sister, and what do I know about his character? Nothing! Old maids are better off than wives of drunkards!

TOM. Oh, my God!

AMANDA. Be still!

TOM (*leaning forward to whisper*). Lots of fellows meet girls whom they don't marry!

AMANDA. Oh, talk sensibly, Tom—and don't be sarcastic! (*She has gotten a hairbrush.*)

TOM. What are you doing?

AMANDA. I'm brushing that cow-lick down! What is this young man's position at the warehouse?

TOM (*submitting grimly to the brush*

and the interrogation). This young man's position is that of a shipping clerk, Mother.

AMANDA. Sounds to me like a fairly responsible job, the sort of a job *you* would be in if you just had more *get-up*.

What is his salary? Have you any idea?

TOM. I would judge it to be approximately eight-five dollars a month.

AMANDA. Well—not princely, but——

TOM. Twenty more than I make.

AMANDA. Yes, how well I know! But for a family man, eight-five dollars a month is not much more than you can just get by on. . . .

TOM. Yes, but Mr. O'Connor is not a family man.

AMANDA. He might be, mightn't he? Some time in the future?

TOM. I see. Plans and provisions.

AMANDA. You are the only young man that I know of who ignores the fact that the future becomes the present, the present the past, and the past turns into everlasting regret if you don't plan for it!

TOM. I will think that over and see what I can make of it.

AMANDA. Don't be supercilious with your mother! Tell me some more about this—what do you call him?

TOM. James D. O'Connor. The D. is for Delaney.

AMANDA. Irish on *both* sides! *Gracious!* And doesn't drink?

TOM. Shall I call him up and ask him right this minute?

AMANDA. The only way to find out about those things is to make discreet inquiries at the proper moment. When I was a girl in Blue Mountain and it was suspected that a young man drank, the girl whose attentions he had been receiving, if any girl *was,* would sometimes speak to the minister of his church, or rather her father would if her father was living, and sort of feel him out on the young man's character. That is the way such things are discreetly handled to keep a young woman from making a tragic mistake!

TOM. Then how did you happen to make a tragic mistake?

AMANDA. That innocent look of your father's had everyone fooled!

He *smiled*—the world was *enchanted!*

No girl can do worse than put herself at the mercy of a handsome appearance!

I hope that Mr. O'Connor is not too good-looking.

TOM. No, he's not too good-looking. He's covered with freckles and hasn't too much of a nose.

AMANDA. He's not right-down homely, though?

TOM. Not right-down homely. Just medium homely, I'd say.

AMANDA. Character's what to look for in a man.

TOM. That's what I've always said, Mother.

AMANDA. You've never said anything of the kind and I suspect you would never give it a thought.

TOM. Don't be so suspicious of me.

AMANDA. At least I hope he's the type that's up and coming.

TOM. I think he really goes in for self-improvement.

AMANDA. What reason have you to think so?

TOM. He goes to night school.

AMANDA (*beaming*). Splendid! What does he do, I mean study?

TOM. Radio engineering and public speaking!

AMANDA. Then he has visions of being advanced in the world!

Any young man who studies public speaking is aiming to have an executive job some day!

And radio engineering? A thing for the future!

Both of these facts are very illuminating. Those are the sort of things that a mother should know concerning any young man who comes to call on her daughter. Seriously or—not.

TOM. One little warning. He doesn't know about Laura. I didn't let on that we had dark ulterior motives. I just said, why don't you come and have dinner with us? He said okay and that was the whole conversation.

AMANDA. I bet it was! You're eloquent as an oyster.

However, he'll know about Laura when he gets here. When he sees how lovely and sweet and pretty she is, he'll thank his lucky stars he was asked to dinner.

TOM. Mother, you mustn't expect too much of Laura.

AMANDA. What do you mean?

TOM. Laura seems all those things to you and me because she's ours and we love her. We don't even notice she's crippled any more.

AMANDA. Don't say crippled! You know that I never allow that word to be used!

TOM. But face facts, Mother. She is and—that's not all——

AMANDA. What do you mean "not all"?

TOM. Laura is very different from other girls.

AMANDA. I think the difference is all to her advantage.

TOM. Not quite all—in the eyes of others—strangers—she's terribly shy and lives in a world of her own and those things make her seem a little peculiar to people outside the house.

AMANDA. Don't say peculiar.

TOM. Face the facts. She is.

(THE DANCE-HALL MUSIC CHANGES TO A TANGO THAT HAS A MINOR AND SOMEWHAT OMINOUS TONE.)

AMANDA. In what way is she peculiar —may I ask?

TOM (gently). She lives in a world of her own—a world of—little glass ornaments, Mother. . . . (Gets up. AMANDA remains holding brush, looking at him, troubled.) She plays old phonograph records and—that's about all—— (He glances at himself in the mirror and crosses to door.)

AMANDA (sharply). Where are you going?

TOM. I'm going to the movies. (Out screen door.)

AMANDA. Not to the movies, every night to the movies! (Follows quickly to screen door.) I don't believe you always go to the movies! (He is gone. AMANDA looks worriedly after him for a moment. Then vitality and optimism return and she turns from the door. Crossing to portieres.) Laura! Laura! (LAURA answers from kitchenette.)

LAURA. Yes, Mother.

AMANDA. Let those dishes go and come in front! (LAURA appears with dish towel. Gaily.) Laura, come here and make a wish on the moon! (SCREEN IMAGE: MOON.)

LAURA (entering). Moon—moon?

AMANDA. A little silver slipper of a moon.

Look over your left shoulder, Laura, and make a wish! (LAURA looks faintly puzzled as if called out of sleep. AMANDA seizes her shoulders and turns her at an angle by the door.)

Now!

Now, darling, wish!

LAURA. What shall I wish for, Mother?

AMANDA (her voice trembling and her eyes suddenly filling with tears). Happiness! Good fortune! (The violin rises and the stage dims out.)

Curtain

Scene VI

(IMAGE: HIGH-SCHOOL HERO.)

TOM. And so the following evening I brought Jim home to dinner. I had known Jim slightly in high school. In high school Jim was a hero. He had tremendous Irish good nature and vitality with the scrubbed and polished look of white chinaware. He seemed to move in a continual spotlight. He was a star in basketball, captain of the debating club, president of the senior class and the glee club and he sang the male lead in the annual light operas. He was always running or bounding, never just walking. He seemed always at the point of defeating the law of gravity. He was shooting with such velocity through his adolescence that you would logically expect him to arrive at nothing short of the White House by the time he was thirty. But Jim apparently ran into more interference after his graduation from Soldan. His speed had definitely slowed. Six years after he left high school he was holding a job that wasn't much better than mine.

(IMAGE: CLERK.)

He was the only one at the warehouse with whom I was on friendly terms. I was valuable to him as someone who could remember his former glory, who had seen him win basketball games and the silver cup in debating. He knew of my secret practice of retiring to a cabinet of the washroom to work on poems when business was slack in the warehouse. He called me Shakespeare. And while the other boys in the warehouse regarded me with suspicious hostility, Jim took a humorous attitude toward me. Gradually his attitude affected the others; their hostility wore off and they also began to smile at me as people smile at an oddly fashioned dog who trots across their path at some distance.

I knew that Jim and Laura had known each other at Soldan, and I had heard Laura speak admiringly of his voice. I didn't know if Jim remembered her or not. In high school Laura had been as unobtrusive as Jim had been astonishing. If he did remember Laura, it was not as my sister, for when I asked him to dinner, he grinned and said, "You know, Shakespeare, I never thought of you as having folks!"

He was about to discover that I did.
. . . (LIGHT UP STAGE. LEGEND ON SCREEN: "THE ACCENT OF A COMING FOOT." *Friday evening. It is about five o'clock of a late spring evening which comes "scattering poems in the sky." A delicate lemony light is in the Wingfield apartment. AMANDA has worked like a Turk in preparation for the gentleman caller. The results are astonishing. The new floor lamp with its rose-silk shade is in place, a colored paper lantern conceals the broken light fixture in the ceiling, new billowing white curtains are at the windows, chintz covers are on chairs and sofa, a pair of new sofa pillows make their initial appearance. Open boxes and tissue paper are scattered on the floor. LAURA stands in the middle with lifted arms while AMANDA crouches before her, adjusting the hem of the new dress, devout and ritualistic. The dress is colored and designed by memory. The arrangement of LAURA's hair is changed; it is softer and more becoming. A fragile, unearthly prettiness has come out in LAURA: she is like a piece of translucent glass touched by light, given a momentary radiance, not actual, not lasting.)*

AMANDA *(impatiently)*. Why are you trembling?

LAURA. Mother, you've made me so nervous!

AMANDA. How have I made you nervous?

LAURA. By all this fuss! You make it seem so important!

AMANDA. I don't understand you, Laura. You couldn't be satisfied with just sitting home, and yet whenever I try to arrange something for you, you seem to resist it. *(She gets up.)*

Now take a look at yourself.

No, wait! Wait just a moment—I have an idea!

LAURA. What is it now? *(AMANDA produces two powder puffs which she wraps in handkerchiefs and stuffs in LAURA's bosom.)*

LAURA. Mother, what are you doing?

AMANDA. They call them "Gay Deceivers"!

LAURA. I won't wear them!

AMANDA. You will!

LAURA. Why should I?

AMANDA. Because, to be painfully honest, your chest is flat.

LAURA. You make it seem like we were setting a trap.

AMANDA. All pretty girls are a trap, a pretty trap, and men expect them to be. *(LEGEND: "A PRETTY TRAP.")*

Now look at yourself, young lady. This is the prettiest you will ever be!

I've got to fix myself now! You're going to be surprised by your mother's appearance! *(She crosses through portieres, humming gaily. LAURA moves slowly to the long mirror and stares solemnly at herself. A wind blows the white curtains inward in a slow, graceful motion and with a faint, sorrowful sighing.)*

AMANDA *(off stage)*. It isn't dark enough yet. *(LAURA turns slowly before the mirror with a troubled look.* LEGEND ON SCREEN: "THIS IS MY SISTER: CELEBRATE HER WITH STRINGS!" MUSIC.)

AMANDA *(laughing, off)*. I'm going to show you something. I'm going to make a spectacular appearance!

LAURA. What is it, Mother?

AMANDA. Possess your soul in patience —you will see!

Something I've resurrected from that old trunk! Styles haven't changed so terribly much after all. . . . *(She parts the portieres.)*

Now just look at your mother! *(She wears a girlish frock of yellowed voile with a blue silk sash. She carries a bunch of jonquils—the legend of her youth is nearly revived. Feverishly.)*

This is the dress in which I led the cotillion. Won the cakewalk twice at Sunset Hill, wore one spring to the Governor's ball in Jackson!

See how I sashayed around the ballroom, Laura? *(She raises her skirt and does a mincing step around the room.)*

I wore it on Sundays for my gentlemen

callers! I had it on the day I met your father——

I had malaria fever all that spring. The change of climate from East Tennessee to the Delta—weakened resistance—I had a little temperature all the time—not enough to be serious—just enough to make me restless and giddy!—Invitations poured in—parties all over the Delta!—"Stay in bed," said Mother, "you have fever!"—but I just wouldn't.—I took quinine but kept on going, going!—Evenings, dances!—Afternoons, long, long rides! Picnics—lovely! So lovely, that country in May.—All lacy with dogwood, literally flooded with jonquils!—That was the spring I had the craze for jonquils. Jonquils became an absolute obsession. Mother said, "Honey, there's no more room for jonquils." And still I kept on bringing in more jonquils. Whenever, wherever I saw them, I'd say, "Stop! Stop! I see jonquils!" I made the young men help me gather the jonquils! It was a joke, Amanda and her jonquils! Finally there were no more vases to hold them; every available space was filled with jonquils. No vases to hold them? All right, I'll hold them myself! And then I—— (*She stops in front of the picture.* MU-SIC.) met your father!

Malaria fever and jonquils and then—this—boy. . . . (*She switches on the rose-colored lamp.*)

I hope they get here before it starts to rain. (*She crosses upstage and places the jonquils in bowl on table.*)

I gave your brother a little extra change so he and Mr. O'Connor could take the service car home.

LAURA (*with altered look*). What did you say his name was?

AMANDA. O'Connor.

LAURA. What is his first name?

AMANDA. I don't remember. Oh, yes, I do. It was—Jim. (LAURA *sways slightly and catches hold of a chair.* LEGEND ON SCREEN: "NOT JIM!")

LAURA (*faintly*). Not—Jim!

AMANDA. Yes, that was it, it was Jim! I've never known a Jim that wasn't nice! (MUSIC: OMINOUS.)

LAURA. Are you sure his name is Jim O'Connor?

AMANDA. Yes. Why?

LAURA. Is he the one that Tom used to know in high school?

AMANDA. He didn't say so. I think he just got to know him at the warehouse.

LAURA. There was a Jim O'Connor we both knew in high school—— (*Then, with effort.*) If that is the one that Tom is bringing to dinner—you'll have to excuse me, I won't come to the table.

AMANDA. What sort of nonsense is this?

LAURA. You asked me once if I'd ever liked a boy. Don't you remember I showed you this boy's picture?

AMANDA. You mean the boy you showed me in the year book?

LAURA. Yes, that boy.

AMANDA. Laura, Laura, were you in love with that boy?

LAURA. I don't know, Mother. All I know is I couldn't sit at the table if it was him!

AMANDA. It won't be him! It isn't the least bit likely. But whether it is or not, you will come to the table. You will not be excused.

LAURA. I'll have to be, Mother.

AMANDA. I don't intend to humor your silliness, Laura. I've had too much from you and your brother, both!

So just sit down and compose yourself till they come. Tom has forgotten his key so you'll have to let them in, when they arrive.

LAURA (*panicky*). Oh, Mother—*you* answer the door!

AMANDA (*lightly*). I'll be in the kitchen—busy!

LAURA. Oh, Mother, please answer the door, don't make me do it!

AMANDA (*crossing into kitchenette*). I've got to fix the dressing for the salmon. Fuss, fuss—silliness!—over a gentleman caller! (*Door swings shut.* LAURA *is left alone.* LEGEND: "TERROR!" *She utters a low moan and turns off the lamp—sits stiffly on the edge of the sofa, knotting her fingers together.* LEGEND ON SCREEN: "THE OPENING OF A DOOR!" TOM *and* JIM *appear on the fire-escape steps and climb to landing. Hearing their approach,* LAURA *rises with a panicky gesture. She retreats to the portieres. The doorbell.* LAURA *catches her breath and touches her throat. Low drums.*)

AMANDA (*calling*). Laura, sweetheart! The door! (LAURA *stares at it without moving.*)

JIM. I think we just beat the rain.

TOM. Uh-huh. (*He rings again, nervously.* JIM *whistles and fishes for a cigarette.*)

AMANDA (*very, very gaily*). Laura, that is your brother and Mr. O'Connor! Will you let them in, darling? (LAURA *crosses toward kitchenette door.*)

LAURA (*breathlessly*). Mother—you go to the door! (AMANDA *steps out of kitchenette and stares furiously at* LAURA. *She points imperiously at the door.*)

LAURA. Please, please!

AMANDA (*in a fierce whisper*). What is the matter with you, you silly thing?

LAURA (*desperately*). Please, you answer it, *please!*

AMANDA. I told you I wasn't going to humor you, Laura. Why have you chosen this moment to lose your mind?

LAURA. Please, please, please, you go!

AMANDA. You'll have to go to the door because I can't!

LAURA (*despairingly*). I can't either!

AMANDA. *Why?*

LAURA. I'm *sick!*

AMANDA. I'm sick, too—of your nonsense! Why can't you and your brother be normal people? Fantastic whims and behavior! (TOM *gives a long ring.*)

Preposterous goings on! Can you give me one reason— (*Calls out lyrically.*) COMING! JUST ONE SECOND!—why you should be afraid to open a door? Now you answer it, Laura!

LAURA. Oh, oh, oh . . . (*She returns through the portieres. Darts to the victrola and winds it frantically and turns it on.*)

AMANDA. Laura Wingfield, you march right to that door!

LAURA. Yes—yes, Mother! (*A faraway, scratchy rendition of "Dardanella" softens the air and gives her strength to move through it. She slips to the door and draws it cautiously open.* TOM *enters with the caller,* JIM O'CONNOR.)

TOM. Laura, this is Jim. Jim, this is my sister, Laura.

JIM (*stepping inside*). I didn't know that Shakespeare had a sister!

LAURA (*retreating stiff and trembling from the door*). How—how do you do?

JIM (*heartily extending his hand*). Okay! (*Laura touches it hesitantly with hers.*)

JIM. Your hand's *cold,* Laura!

LAURA. Yes, well—I've been playing the victrola. . . .

JIM. Must have been playing classical music on it! You ought to play a little hot swing music to warm you up!

LAURA. Excuse me—I haven't finished playing the victrola. . . . (*She turns awkwardly and hurries into the front room. She pauses a second by the victrola. Then catches her breath and darts through the portieres like a frightened deer.*)

JIM (*grinning*). What was the matter?

TOM. Oh—with Laura? Laura is—terribly shy.

JIM. Shy, huh? It's unusual to meet a shy girl nowadays. I don't believe you ever mentioned you had a sister.

TOM. Well, now you know. I have one. Here is the *Post Dispatch.* You want a piece of it?

JIM. Uh-huh.

TOM. What piece? The comics?

JIM. Sports! (*Glances at it.*) Ole Dizzy Dean is on his bad behavior.

TOM (*disinterested*). Yeah? (*Lights cigarette and crosses back to fire-escape door.*)

JIM. Where are *you* going?

TOM. I'm going out on the terrace.

JIM (*goes after him*). You know, Shakespeare—I'm going to sell you a bill of goods!

TOM. What goods!

JIM. A course I'm taking.

TOM. Huh?

JIM. In public speaking! You and me, we're not the warehouse type.

TOM. Thanks—that's good news. But what has public speaking got to do with it?

JIM. It fits you for—executive positions!

TOM. Awww.

JIM. I tell you it's done a helluva lot for me. (IMAGE: EXECUTIVE AT DESK.)

TOM. In what respect?

JIM. In every! Ask yourself what is the difference between you an' me and men in the office down front? Brains? —No!—Ability?—No! Then what? Just one little thing——

TOM. What is that one little thing?

JIM. Primarily it amounts to—social poise! Being able to square up to people and hold your own on any social level!

AMANDA (*off stage*). Tom?

TOM. Yes, Mother?

AMANDA. Is that you and Mr. O'Connor?

TOM. Yes, Mother.

AMANDA. Well, you just make yourselves comfortable in there.

TOM. Yes, Mother.

AMANDA. Ask Mr. O'Connor if he would like to wash his hands.

JIM. Aw, no—no—thank you—I took care of that at the warehouse. Tom——

TOM. Yes?

JIM. Mr. Mendoza was speaking to me about you.

TOM. Favorably?

JIM. What do you think?

TOM. Well——

JIM. You're going to be out of a job if you don't wake up.

TOM. I am waking up——

JIM. You show no signs.

TOM. The signs are interior. (IMAGE ON SCREEN: THE SAILING VESSEL WITH JOLLY ROGER AGAIN.)

TOM. I'm planning to change. (*He leans over the rail speaking with quiet exhilaration. The incandescent marquees and signs of the first-run movie houses light his face from across the alley. He looks like a voyager.*) I'm right at the point of committing myself to a future that doesn't include the warehouse and Mr. Mendoza or even a night-school course in public speaking.

JIM. What are you gassing about?

TOM. I'm tired of the movies.

JIM. Movies!

TOM. Yes, movies! Look at them——
(*A wave toward the marvels of Grand Avenue.*) All of those glamorous people —having adventures—hogging it all, gobbling the whole thing up! You know what happens? People go to the *movies* instead of *moving!* Hollywood characters are supposed to have all the adventures for everybody in America, while everybody in America sits in a dark room and watches them have them! Yes, until there's a war. That's when adventure becomes available to the masses! *Everyone's* dish, not only Gable's! Then the people in the dark room come out of the dark room to have some adventures themselves—Goody, goody!—It's our turn now, to go to the South Sea Islands—to make a safari—to be exotic, far-off!— But I'm not patient. I don't want to wait till then. I'm tired of the *movies* and I am *about* to *move!*

JIM (*incredulously*). Move?

TOM. Yes.

JIM. When?

TOM. Soon!

JIM. Where? Where? (THEME THREE MUSIC SEEMS TO ANSWER THE QUESTION, WHILE TOM THINKS IT OVER. HE SEARCHES AMONG HIS POCKETS.)

TOM. I'm starting to boil inside. I know I seem dreamy, but inside—well, I'm boiling!—Whenever I pick up a shoe, I shudder a little thinking how short life is and what I am doing!— Whatever that means, I know it doesn't mean shoes—except as something to wear on a traveler's feet! (*Finds paper.*) Look——

JIM. What?

TOM. I'm a member.

JIM (*reading*). The Union of Merchant Seamen.

TOM. I paid my dues this month, instead of the light bill.

JIM. You will regret it when they turn the lights off.

TOM. I won't be here.

JIM. How about your mother?

TOM. I'm like my father. The bastard son of a bastard! See how he grins? And he's been absent going on sixteen years!

JIM. You're just talking, you drip. How does your mother feel about it?

TOM. Shhh!—Here comes Mother! Mother is not acquainted with my plans!

AMANDA (*enters portieres*). Where are you all?

TOM. On the terrace, Mother. (*They start inside. She advances to them.* TOM *is distinctly shocked at her appearance. Even* JIM *blinks a little. He is making his first contact with girlish Southern vivacity and in spite of the night-school course in public speaking is somewhat thrown off the beam by the unexpected outlay of social charm. Certain responses are attempted by* JIM *but are swept aside by* AMANDA's *gay laughter and chatter.* TOM *is embarrassed but after the first shock* JIM *reacts very warmly. Grins and chuckles, is altogether won over.* IMAGE: AMANDA AS A GIRL.)

AMANDA (*coyly smiling, shaking her girlish ringlets*). Well, well, well, so this is Mr. O'Connor. Introductions entirely unnecessary. I've heard so much about you from my boy. I finally said to him, Tom—good gracious!—why don't you bring this paragon to supper? I'd like to meet this nice young man at the warehouse!—Instead of just hearing him sing your praises so much!

I don't know why my son is so stand-offish—that's not Southern behavior!

Let's sit down and—I think we could stand a little more air in here! Tom, leave the door open. I felt a nice fresh breeze a moment ago. Where has it gone to?

Mmm, so warm already! And not quite summer, even. We're going to burn up when summer really gets started.

However, we're having—we're having a very light supper. I think light things are better fo' this time of year. The same as light clothes are. Light clothes an' light food are what warm weather calls fo'. You know our blood gets so thick during th' winter—it takes a while fo' us to *adjust* ou'selves!—when the season changes ...

It's come so quick this year. I wasn't prepared. All of a sudden—heavens! Already summer!—I ran to the trunk an' pulled out this light dress— Terribly old! Historical almost! But feels so good—so good an' co-ol, y'know. . . .

TOM. Mother——

AMANDA. Yes, honey?

TOM. How about—supper?

AMANDA. Honey, you go ask Sister if supper is ready! You know that Sister is in full charge of supper!

Tell her you hungry boys are waiting for it. (*To* JIM.)

Have you met Laura?

JIM. She——

AMANDA. Let you in? Oh, good, you've met already! It's rare for a girl as sweet an' pretty as Laura to be domestic. But Laura is, thank heavens, not only pretty but also very domestic. I'm not at all. I never was a bit. I never could make a thing but angel-food cake. Well, in the South we had so many servants. Gone, gone, gone. All vestige of gracious living! Gone completely! I wasn't prepared for what the future brought me. All of my gentlemen callers were sons of planters and so of course I assumed that I would be married to one and raise my family on a large piece of land with plenty of servants. But man proposes—and woman accepts the proposal!—To vary that old, old saying a little bit—I married no planter! I married a man who worked for the telephone company!—That gallantly smiling gentleman over there! (*Points to the picture.*) A telephone man who—fell in love with long-distance!—Now he travels and I don't even know where!—But what am I going on for about my—tribulations?

Tell me yours—I hope you don't have any!

Tom?

TOM (*returning*). Yes, Mother?

AMANDA. Is supper nearly ready?

TOM. It looks to me like supper is on the table.

AMANDA. Let me look— (*She rises prettily and looks through portieres.*) Oh, lovely!—But where is Sister?

TOM. Laura is not feeling well and she says that she thinks she'd better not come to the table.

AMANDA. What?—Nonsense!—Laura? Oh, Laura!

LAURA (*off stage, faintly*). Yes, Mother.

AMANDA. You really must come to the table. We won't be seated until you come to the table!

Come in, Mr. O'Connor. You sit over there, and I'll——

Laura? Laura Wingfield!

You're keeping us waiting, honey! We can't say grace until you come to the table! (*The back door is pushed weakly open and* LAURA *comes in. She is obviously quite faint, her lips trembling, her eyes wide and staring. She moves unsteadily toward the table.* LEGEND: "TERROR!" *Outside a summer storm is coming abruptly. The white curtains billow inward at the windows and there is a sorrowful murmur and deep blue dusk.* LAURA *suddenly stumbles—she catches at a chair with a faint moan.*)

TOM. Laura!

AMANDA. Laura! (*There is a clap of thunder.* LEGEND: "AH!" *Despairingly.*)

Why, Laura, you *are* sick, darling! Tom, help your sister into the living room, dear!

Sit in the living room, Laura—rest on the sofa.

Well! (*To the gentleman caller.*)

Standing over the hot stove made her ill!—I told her that it was just too warm this evening, but—— (TOM *comes back in.* LAURA *is on the sofa.*)

Is Laura all right now?

TOM. Yes.

AMANDA. What *is* that? Rain? A nice cool rain has come up! (*She gives the gentleman caller a frightened look.*)

I think we may—have grace—now . . . (TOM *looks at her stupidly.*)

Tom, honey—you say grace!

TOM. Oh . . .

"For these and all thy mercies——

(*They bow their heads,* AMANDA *stealing a nervous glance at* JIM. *In the living room* LAURA, *stretched on the sofa, clenches her hand to her lips, to hold back a shuddering sob.*)

God's Holy Name be praised"——

THE SCENE DIMS OUT.

Scene VII

LEGEND: A SOUVENIR.

Half an hour later. Dinner is just being finished in the upstage area which is concealed by the drawn portieres.

As the curtain rises LAURA *is still huddled upon the sofa, her feet drawn under her, her head resting on a pale blue pillow, her eyes wide and mysteriously watchful. The new floor lamp with its shade of rose-colored silk gives a soft, becoming light to her face, bringing out the fragile, unearthly prettiness which usually escapes attention. There is a steady murmur of rain, but it is slackening and stops soon after the scene begins; the air outside becomes pale and luminous as the moon breaks out.*

A moment after the curtain rises, the lights in both rooms flicker and go out.

JIM. Hey, there, Mr. Light Bulb!

(AMANDA *laughs nervously.* LEGEND: "SUSPENSION OF A PUBLIC SERVICE.")

AMANDA. Where was Moses when the lights went out? Ha-ha. Do you know the answer to that one, Mr. O'Connor?

JIM. No, Ma'am, what's the answer?

AMANDA. In the dark! (JIM *laughs appreciatively.*)

Everybody sit still. I'll light the candles. Isn't it lucky we have them on the table? Where's a match? Which of you gentlemen can provide a match?

JIM. Here.

AMANDA. Thank you, sir.

JIM. Not at all, Ma'am!

AMANDA. I guess the fuse has burnt out. Mr. O'Connor, can you tell a burnt-out fuse? I know I can't and Tom is a total loss when it comes to mechanics.

(SOUND: GETTING UP: VOICES RECEDE A LITTLE TO KITCHENETTE.)

Oh, be careful you don't bump into something. We don't want our gentleman caller to break his neck. Now wouldn't that be a fine howdy-do?

JIM. Ha-ha!

Where is the fuse-box?

AMANDA. Right here next to the stove. Can you see anything?

JIM. Just a minute.

AMANDA. Isn't electricity a mysterious thing?

Wasn't it Benjamin Franklin who tied a key to a kite?

We live in such a mysterious universe, don't we? Some people say that science clears up all the mysteries for us. In my opinion it only creates more!

Have you found it yet?

JIM. No, Ma'am. All these fuses look okay to me.

AMANDA. Tom!

TOM. Yes, Mother?

AMANDA. That light bill I gave you several days ago. The one I told you we got the notices about? (LEGEND: "HA!")

TOM. Oh.—Yeah.

AMANDA. You didn't neglect to pay it by any chance?

TOM. Why, I——

AMANDA. Didn't! I might have known it!

JIM. Shakespeare probably wrote a poem on that light bill, Mrs. Wingfield.

AMANDA. I might have known better than to trust him with it! There's such a high price for negligence in this world!

JIM. Maybe the poem will win a ten-dollar prize.

AMANDA. We'll just have to spend the remainder of the evening in the nineteenth century, before Mr. Edison made the Mazda lamp!

JIM. Candlelight is my favorite kind of light.

AMANDA. That shows you're romantic! But that's no excuse for Tom.

Well, we got through dinner. Very considerate of them to let us get through dinner before they plunged us into ever-lasting darkness, wasn't it, Mr. O'Connor?

JIM. Ha-ha!

AMANDA. Tom, as a penalty for your carelessness you can help me with the dishes.

JIM. Let me give you a hand.

AMANDA. Indeed you will not!

JIM. I ought to be good for something.

AMANDA. Good for something? (*Her tone is rhapsodic.*)

You? Why, Mr. O'Connor, nobody, *nobody's* given me this much entertain-ment in years—as you have!

JIM. Aw, now, Mrs. Wingfield!

AMANDA. I'm not exaggerating, not one bit! But Sister is all by her lonesome. You go keep her company in the parlor! I'll give you this lovely old candela-brum that used to be on the altar at the Church of the Heavenly Rest. It was melted a little out of shape when the church burnt down. Lightning struck it one spring. Gypsy Jones was holding a revival at the time and he intimated that the church was destroyed because the Episcopalians gave card parties.

JIM. Ha-ha.

AMANDA. And how about you coaxing Sister to drink a little wine? I think it would be good for her! Can you carry both at once?

JIM. Sure. I'm Superman!

AMANDA. Now, Thomas, get into this apron! (*The door of kitchenette swings closed on* AMANDA's *gay laughter; the flickering light approaches the portieres.* LAURA *sits up nervously as he enters. Her speech at first is low and breathless from the almost intolerable strain of being alone with a stranger.* (THE LEGEND: "I DON'T SUPPOSE YOU REMEMBER ME AT ALL!") *In her first speeches in this scene, before* JIM's *warmth overcomes her para-lyzing shyness,* LAURA's *voice is thin and breathless as though she has just run up a steep flight of stairs.* JIM's *attitude is gently humorous. In playing this scene it should be stressed that while the incident is apparently unimportant, it is to* LAURA *the climax of her secret life.*)

JIM. Hello, there, Laura.

LAURA (*faintly*). Hello. (*She clears her throat.*)

JIM. How are you feeling now? Better?

LAURA. Yes. Yes, thank you.

JIM. This is for you. A little dandelion wine. (*He extends it toward her with extravagant gallantry.*)

LAURA. Thank you.

JIM. Drink it—but don't get drunk! (*He laughs heartily.* LAURA *takes the glass uncertainly, laughs shyly.*) Where shall I set the candles?

LAURA. Oh—oh, anywhere . . .

JIM. How about here on the floor? Any objections?

LAURA. No.

JIM. I'll spread a newspaper under to catch the drippings. I like to sit on the floor. Mind if I do?

LAURA. Oh, no.

JIM. Give me a pillow?

LAURA. What?

JIM. A pillow!

LAURA. Oh . . . (*Hands him one quickly.*)

JIM. How about you? Don't you like to sit on the floor?

LAURA. Oh—yes.

JIM. Why don't you, then?

LAURA. I—will.

JIM. Take a pillow! (LAURA *does. Sits on the other side of the candelabrum.* JIM *crosses his legs and smiles engag-ingly at her.*) I can't hardly see you sit-ting way over there.

LAURA. I can—see you.

JIM. I know, but that's not fair; I'm in the limelight. (LAURA *moves her pillow closer.*) Good! Now I can see you! Comfortable?

LAURA. Yes.

JIM. So am I. Comfortable as a cow! Will you have some gum?

LAURA. No, thank you.

JIM. I think that I will indulge, with your permission. (*Musingly unwraps it and holds it up.*) Think of the fortune made by the guy that invented the first piece of chewing gum. Amazing, huh? The Wrigley Building is one of the sights of Chicago.—I saw it summer be-fore last when I went up to the Century of Progress. Did you take in the Century of Progress?

LAURA. No, I didn't.

JIM. Well, it was quite a wonderful exposition. What impressed me most was the Hall of Science. Gives you an idea of what the future will be in America, even more wonderful than the present time is! (*Pause. Smiling at her.*) Your brother tells me you're shy. Is that right, Laura?

LAURA. I—don't know.

JIM. I judge you to be an old-fashioned type of girl. Well, I think that's a pretty good type to be. Hope you don't think I'm being too personal—do you?

LAURA (*hastily, out of embarrassment*). I believe I *will* take a piece of gum, if you—don't mind. (*Clearing her throat.*) Mr. O'Connor, have you—kept up with your singing?

JIM. Singing? Me?

LAURA. Yes. I remember what a beautiful voice you had.

JIM. When did you hear me sing?

(VOICE OFF STAGE IN THE PAUSE.)

VOICE (*off stage*).

O blow, ye winds, heigh-ho,
A-roving I will go!
I'm off to my love
With a boxing glove—
Ten thousand miles away!

JIM. You say you've heard me sing?

LAURA. Oh, yes! Yes, very often . . . I—don't suppose—you remember me—at all?

JIM (*smiling doubtfully*). You know I have an idea I've seen you before. I had that idea soon as you opened the door. It seemed almost like I was about to remember your name. But the name that I started to call you—wasn't a name! And so I stopped myself before I said it.

LAURA. Wasn't it—Blue Roses?

JIM (*springs up. Grinning*). Blue Roses!—My gosh, yes—Blue Roses! That's what I had on my tongue when you opened the door!

Isn't it funny what tricks your memory plays? I didn't connect you with high school somehow or other.

But that's where it was; it was high school. I didn't even know you were Shakespeare's sister!

Gosh, I'm sorry.

LAURA. I didn't expect you to. You—barely knew me!

JIM. But we did have a speaking acquaintance, huh?

LAURA. Yes, we—spoke to each other.

JIM. When did you recognize me?

LAURA. Oh, right away!

JIM. Soon as I came in the door?

LAURA. When I heard your name I thought it was probably you. I knew that

Tom used to know you a little in high school. So when you came in the door——

Well, then I was—sure.

JIM. Why didn't you *say* something, then?

LAURA (*breathlessly*). I didn't know what to say, I was—too surprised!

JIM. For goodness' sake! You know, this sure is funny!

LAURA. Yes! Yes, isn't it, though . . .

JIM. Didn't we have a class in something together?

LAURA. Yes, we did.

JIM. What class was that?

LAURA. It was—singing—Chorus!

JIM. Aw!

LAURA. I sat across the aisle from you in the Aud.

JIM. Aw.

LAURA. Mondays, Wednesdays, and Fridays.

JIM. Now I remember—you always came in late.

LAURA. Yes, it was so hard for me, getting upstairs. I had that brace on my leg—it clumped so loud!

JIM. I never heard any clumping.

LAURA (*wincing at the recollection*). To me it sounded like—thunder!

JIM. Well, well, well, I never even noticed.

LAURA. And everybody was seated before I came in. I had to walk in front of all those people. My seat was in the back row. I had to go clumping all the way up the aisle with everyone watching!

JIM. You shouldn't have been self-conscious.

LAURA. I know, but I was. It was always such a relief when the singing started.

JIM. Aw, yes, I've placed you now! I used to call you Blue Roses. How was it that I got started calling you that?

LAURA. I was out of school a little while with pleurosis. When I came back you asked me what was the matter. I said I had pleurosis—you thought I said Blue Roses. That's what you always called me after that!

JIM. I hope you didn't mind.

LAURA. Oh, no—I liked it. You see, I wasn't acquainted with many—people. . . .

JIM. As I remember you sort of stuck by yourself.

LAURA. I—I—never have had much luck at—making friends.

JIM. I don't see why you wouldn't.

LAURA. Well, I—started out badly.

JIM. You mean being——

LAURA. Yes, it sort of—stood between me——

JIM. You shouldn't have let it!

LAURA. I know, but it did, and——

JIM. You were shy with people!

LAURA. I tried not to be but never could——

JIM. Overcome it?

LAURA. No, I—I never could!

JIM. I guess being shy is something you have to work out of kind of gradually.

LAURA (*sorrowfully*). Yes—I guess it——

JIM. Takes time!

LAURA. Yes——

JIM. People are not so dreadful when you know them. That's what you have to remember! And everybody has problems, not just you, but practically everybody has got some problems.

You think of yourself as having the only problems, as being the only one who is disappointed. But just look around you and you will see lots of people as disappointed as you are. For instance, I hoped when I was going to high school that I would be further along at this time, six years later, than I am now—— You remember that wonderful write-up I had in *The Torch?*

LAURA. Yes! (*She rises and crosses to table.*)

JIM. It said I was bound to succeed in anything I went into! (LAURA *returns with the annual.*) Holy Jeez! *The Torch!* (*He accepts it reverently. They smile across it with mutual wonder.* LAURA *crouches beside him and they begin to turn through it.* LAURA's *shyness is dissolving in his warmth.*)

LAURA. Here you are in *The Pirates of Penzance!*

JIM (*wistfully*). I sang the baritone lead in that operetta.

LAURA (*raptly*). So—*beautifully!*

JIM (*protesting*). Aw——

LAURA. Yes, yes—beautifully—beautifully!

JIM. You heard me?

LAURA. All three times!

JIM. No!

LAURA. Yes!

JIM. All three performances?

LAURA (*looking down*). Yes.

JIM. Why?

LAURA. I—wanted to ask you to—autograph my program.

JIM. Why didn't you ask me to?

LAURA. You were always surrounded by your own friends so much that I never had a chance to.

JIM. You should have just——

LAURA. Well, I—thought you might think I was——

JIM. Thought I might think you was—what?

LAURA. Oh——

JIM (*with reflective relish*). I was beleaguered by females in those days.

LAURA. You were terribly popular!

JIM. Yeah——

LAURA. You had such a—friendly way——

JIM. I was spoiled in high school.

LAURA. Everybody—liked you!

JIM. Including you?

LAURA. I—yes, I—I did, too—— (*She gently closes the book in her lap.*)

JIM. Well, well, well!—Give me that program, Laura. (*She hands it to him. He signs it with a flourish.*) There you are —better late than never!

LAURA. Oh, I—what a—surprise!

JIM. My signature isn't worth very much right now.

But some day—maybe—it will increase in value!

Being disappointed is one thing and being discouraged is something else. I am disappointed but I am not discouraged.

I'm twenty-three years old.

How old are you?

LAURA. I'll be twenty-four in June.

JIM. That's not old age!

LAURA. No, but——

JIM. You finished high school?

LAURA (*with difficulty*). I didn't go back.

JIM. You mean you dropped out?

LAURA. I made bad grades in my final examinations. (*She rises and replaces the book and the program. Her voice strained.*)

How is—Emily Meisenbach getting along?

JIM. Oh, that kraut-head!

LAURA. Why do you call her that?

JIM. That's what she was.

LAURA. You're not still—going with her?

JIM. I never see her.

LAURA. It said in the Personal Section that you were—engaged!

JIM. I know, but I wasn't impressed by that—propaganda!

LAURA. It wasn't—the truth?

JIM. Only in Emily's optimistic opinion!

LAURA. Oh—— (LEGEND: "WHAT HAVE YOU DONE SINCE HIGH SCHOOL?" JIM *lights a cigarette and leans indolently back on his elbows smiling at* LAURA *with a warmth and charm which lights her inwardly with altar candles. She remains by the table and turns in her hands a piece of glass to cover her tumult.*)

JIM (*after several reflective puffs on a cigarette*). What have you done since high school? (*She seems not to hear him.*) Huh? (LAURA *looks up.*) I said what have you done since high school, Laura?

LAURA. Nothing much.

JIM. You must have been doing something these six long years.

LAURA. Yes.

JIM. Well, then, such as what?

LAURA. I took a business course at business college——

JIM. How did that work out?

LAURA. Well, not very—well—I had to drop out, it gave me—indigestion—— (JIM *laughs gently.*)

JIM. What are you doing now?

LAURA. I don't do anything—much. Oh, please don't think I sit around doing nothing! My glass collection takes up a good deal of time. Glass is something you have to take good care of.

JIM. What did you say—about glass?

LAURA. Collection I said—I have one—— (*She clears her throat and turns away again, acutely shy.*)

JIM (*abruptly*). You know what I judge to be the trouble with you? Inferiority complex! Know what that is? That's what they call it when someone low-rates himself!

I understand it because I had it, too. Although my case was not so aggravated as yours seems to be. I had it until I took up public speaking, developed my voice, and learned that I had an aptitude for science. Before that time I never thought of myself as being outstanding in any way whatsoever!

Now I've never made a regular study of it, but I have a friend who says I can analyze people better than doctors that make a profession of it. I don't claim that to be necessarily true, but I can sure guess a person's psychology, Laura! (*Takes out his gum.*) Excuse me, Laura. I always take it out when the flavor is gone. I'll use this scrap of paper to wrap it in. I know how it is to get it stuck on a shoe.

Yep—that's what I judge to be your principal trouble. A lack of confidence in yourself as a person. You don't have the proper amount of faith in yourself. I'm basing that fact on a number of your remarks and also on certain observations I've made. For instance that clumping you thought was so awful in high school. You say that you even dreaded to walk into class. You see what you did? You dropped out of school, you gave up an education because of a clump, which as far as I know was practically non-existent! A little physical defect is what you have. Hardly noticeable even! Magnified thousands of times by imagination!

You know what my strong advice to you is? Think of yourself as *superior* in some way!

LAURA. In what way would I think?

JIM. Why, man alive, Laura! Just look about you a little. What do you see? A world full of common people! All of 'em born and all of 'em going to die!

Which of them has one-tenth of your good points? Or mine? Or anyone else's, as far as that goes——Gosh!

Everybody excels in some one thing. Some in many! (*Unconsciously glances at himself in the mirror.*)

All you've got to do is discover in *what!*

Take me, for instance. (*He adjusts his tie at the mirror.*)

My interest happens to lie in electro-dynamics. I'm taking a course in radio engineering at night school, Laura, on top of a fairly responsible job at the warehouse. I'm taking that course and studying public speaking.

LAURA. Ohhhh.

JIM. Because I believe in the future of television! (*Turning back to her.*)

I wish to be ready to go up right along with it. Therefore I'm planning to get in on the ground floor. In fact I've already made the right connections and all that remains is for the industry itself to get under way! Full steam—— (*His eyes are starry.*)

Knowledge—Zzzzzp! Money—Zzzzzzp! —Power!

That's the cycle democracy is built on! (*His attitude is convincingly dynamic. LAURA stares at him, even her shyness eclipsed in her absolute wonder. He suddenly grins.*)

I guess you think I think a lot of myself!

LAURA. No—o-o-o, I——

JIM. Now how about you? Isn't there something you take more interest in than anything else?

LAURA. Well, I do—as I said—have my —glass collection—(*A peal of girlish laughter from the kitchen.*)

JIM. I'm not right sure I know what you're talking about.

What kind of glass is it?

LAURA. Little articles of it, they're ornaments mostly!

Most of them are little animals made out of glass, the tiniest little animals in the world. Mother calls them a glass menagerie!

Here's an example of one, if you'd like to see it!

This one is one of the oldest. It's nearly thirteen (MUSIC: "THE GLASS MENAGERIE." *He stretches out his hand.*)

Oh, be careful—if you breathe, it breaks!

JIM. I'd better not take it. I'm pretty clumsy with things.

LAURA. Go on, I trust you with him! (*Places it in his palm.*)

There now—you're holding him gently!

Hold him over the light, he loves the light! You see how the light shines through him?

JIM. It sure does shine!

LAURA. I shouldn't be partial, but he is my favorite one.

JIM. What kind of a thing is this one supposed to be?

LAURA. Haven't you noticed the single horn on his forehead?

JIM. A unicorn, huh?

LAURA. Mmm-hmmm!

JIM. Unicorns, aren't they extinct in the modern world?

LAURA. I know!

JIM. Poor little fellow, he must feel sort of lonesome.

LAURA (*smiling*). Well, if he does he doesn't complain about it. He stays on a shelf with some horses that don't have horns and all of them seem to get along nicely together.

JIM. How do you know?

LAURA (*lightly*). I haven't heard any arguments among them!

JIM (*grinning*). No arguments, huh? Well, that's a pretty good sign!

Where shall I set him?

LAURA. Put him on the table. They all like a change of scenery once in a while!

JIM (*stretching*). Well, well, well, well ——

Look how big my shadow is when I stretch!

LAURA. Oh, oh, yes—it stretches across the ceiling!

JIM (*crossing to door*). I think it's stopped raining. (*Opens fire-escape door.*) Where does the music come from?

LAURA. From the Paradise Dance Hall across the alley.

JIM. How about cutting the rug a little, Miss Wingfield?

LAURA. Oh, I——

JIM. Or is your program filled up? Let me have a look at it. (*Grasps imaginary card.*) Why, every dance is taken! I'll just have to scratch some out. (WALTZ MUSIC: "LA GOLONDRINA.") Ahh, a waltz! (*He executes some sweeping turns by himself then holds his arms toward LAURA.*)

LAURA (*breathlessly*). I—can't dance!

JIM. There you go, that inferiority stuff!

LAURA. I've never danced in my life!

JIM. Come on, try!

LAURA. Oh, but I'd step on you!

JIM. I'm not made out of glass.

LAURA. How—how—how do we start?

JIM. Just leave it to me. You hold your arms out a little.

LAURA. Like this?

JIM. A little bit higher. Right. Now don't tighten up, that's the main thing about it—relax.

LAURA (*laughing breathlessly.*) It's hard not to.

JIM. Okay.

LAURA. I'm afraid you can't budge me.

JIM. What do you bet I can't? (*He swings her into motion.*)

LAURA. Goodness, yes, you can!

JIM. Let yourself go, now, Laura, just let yourself go.

LAURA. I'm——

JIM. Come on!

LAURA. Trying!

JIM. Not so stiff—— Easy does it!

LAURA. I know but I'm——

JIM. Loosen th' backbone! There now, that's a lot better.

LAURA. Am I?

JIM. Lots, lots better! (*He moves her about the room in a clumsy waltz.*)

LAURA. Oh, my!

JIM. Ha-ha!

LAURA. Oh, my goodness!

JIM. Ha-ha-ha! (*They suddenly bump in to the table.* JIM *stops.*) What did we hit on?

LAURA. Table.

JIM. Did something fall off it? I think ——

LAURA. Yes.

JIM. I hope that it wasn't the little glass horse with the horn!

LAURA. Yes.

JIM. Aw, aw, aw. Is it broken?

LAURA. Now it is just like all the other horses.

JIM. It's lost its——

LAURA. Horn!

It doesn't matter. Maybe it's a blessing in disguise.

JIM. You'll never forgive me. I bet that that was your favorite piece of glass.

LAURA. I don't have favorites much. It's no tragedy, Freckles. Glass breaks so easily. No matter how careful you are. The traffic jars the shelves and things fall off them.

JIM. Still I'm awfully sorry that I was the cause.

LAURA (*smiling*). I'll just imagine he had an operation.

The horn was removed to make him feel less—freakish! (*They both laugh.*)

Now he will feel more at home with the other horses, the ones that don't have horns . . .

JIM. Ha-ha, that's very funny! (*Suddenly serious.*)

I'm glad to see that you have a sense of humor.

You know—you're—well—very different!

Surprisingly different from anyone else I know! (*His voice becomes soft and hesitant with a genuine feeling.*)

Do you mind me telling you that? (LAURA *is abashed beyond speech.*)

I mean it in a nice way . . . (LAURA *nods shyly, looking away.*)

You make me feel sort of—I don't know how to put it!

I'm usually pretty good at expressing things, but——

This is something that I don't know how to say! (LAURA *touches her throat and clears it—turns the broken unicorn in her hands. Even softer.*)

Has anyone ever told you that you were pretty? (PAUSE: MUSIC. LAURA *looks up slowly, with wonder, and shakes her head.*)

Well, you are! In a very different way from anyone else.

And all the nicer because of the difference, too. (*His voice becomes low and husky.* LAURA *turns away, nearly faint with the novelty of her emotions.*)

I wish that you were my sister. I'd teach you to have some confidence in yourself. The different people are not like other people, but being different is nothing to be ashamed of. Because other people are not such wonderful people. They're one hundred times one thousand. You're one times one! They walk all over the earth. You just stay here. They're common as—weeds, but—you—well, you're—*Blue Roses*! (IMAGE ON SCREEN: BLUE ROSES. MUSIC CHANGES.)

LAURA. But blue is wrong for—roses. . . .

JIM. It's right for you!—You're—pretty!

LAURA. In what respect am I pretty?

JIM. In all respects—believe me! Your eyes—your hair—are pretty! Your hands are pretty! (*He catches hold of her hand.*)

You think I'm making this up because I'm invited to dinner and have to be nice. Oh, I could do that! I could put on an act for you, Laura, and say lots of things without being very sincere. But this time I am. I'm talking to you sincerely. I happened to notice you had this inferiority complex that keeps you from feeling comfortable with people. Somebody needs to build your confidence up and make you proud instead of shy and turning away and—blushing——

Somebody—ought to——

Ought to—kiss you, Laura! (*His hand slips slowly up her arm to her shoulder.* MUSIC SWELLS TUMULTUOUSLY. *He sud-*

denly turns her about and kisses her on the lips. When he releases her, LAURA *sinks on the sofa with a bright, dazed look.* JIM *backs away and fishes in his pocket for a cigarette.* LEGEND ON SCREEN: "SOUVENIR.")

Stumble-john! (*He lights the cigarette, avoiding her look. There is a peal of girlish laughter from* AMANDA *in the kitchen.* LAURA *slowly raises and opens her hand. It still contains the little broken glass animal. She looks at it with a tender, bewildered expression.*)

Stumble-john!

I shouldn't have done that—— That was way off the beam.

You don't smoke, do you? (*She looks up, smiling, not hearing the question. He sits beside her a little gingerly. She looks at him speechlessly—waiting. He coughs decorously and moves a little farther aside as he considers the situation and senses her feelings, dimly, with perturbation. Gently.*)

Would you—care for a—mint? (*She doesn't seem to hear him but her look grows brighter even.*)

Peppermint—Life-Saver?

My pocket's a regular drug store—wherever I go . . .

(*He pops a mint in his mouth. Then gulps and decides to make a clean breast of it. He speaks slowly and gingerly.*)

Laura, you know, if I had a sister like you, I'd do the same thing as Tom. I'd bring out fellows and—introduce her to them. The right type of boys of a type to —appreciate her.

Only—well—he made a mistake about me.

Maybe I've got no call to be saying this. That may not have been the idea in having me over. But what if it was?

There's nothing wrong about that. The only trouble is that in my case—I'm not in a situation to—do the right thing.

I can't take down your number and say I'll phone.

I can't call up next week and—ask for a date.

I thought I had better explain the situation in case you—misunderstood it and—hurt your feelings. . . . (*Pause. Slowly, very slowly,* LAURA's *look changes, her eyes returning slowly from his to the ornament in her palm.* AMANDA *utters another gay laugh in the kitchen.*)

LAURA (*faintly*). You—won't—call again?

JIM. No, Laura, I can't. (*He rises from the sofa.*)

As I was just explaining, I've—got strings on me.

Laura, I've—been going steady!

I go out all of the time with a girl named Betty. She's a home-girl like you, and Catholic, and Irish, and in a great many ways we—get along fine.

I met her last summer on a moonlight boat trip up the river to Alton, on the *Majestic*.

Well—right away from the start it was —love! (LEGEND: LOVE! LAURA *sways slightly forward and grips the arm of the sofa. He fails to notice, now enrapt in his own comfortable being.*)

Being in love has made a new man of me! (*Leaning stiffly forward, clutching the arm of the sofa,* LAURA *struggles visibly with her storm. But* JIM *is oblivious; she is a long way off.*)

The power of love is really pretty tremendous!

Love is something that—changes the whole world, Laura! (*The storm abates a little and* LAURA *leans back. He notices her again.*)

It happened that Betty's aunt took sick; she got a wire and had to go to Centralia. So Tom—when he asked me to dinner —I naturally just accepted the invitation, not knowing that you—that he—that I—— (*He stops awkwardly.*)

Huh—I'm a stumble-john! (*He flops back on the sofa. The holy candles in the altar of* LAURA's *face have been snuffed out. There is a look of almost infinite desolation.* JIM *glances at her uneasily.*)

I wish that you would—say something. (*She bites her lip which was trembling and then bravely smiles. She opens her hand again on the broken glass ornament. Then she gently takes his hand and raises it level with her own. She carefully places the unicorn in the palm of his hand, then pushes his fingers closed upon it.*) What are you—doing that for? You want me to have him?—Laura? (*She nods.*) What for?

LAURA. A—souvenir . . . (*She rises unsteadily and crouches beside the victrola to wind it up.* LEGEND ON SCREEN: "THINGS HAVE A WAY OF TURNING OUT

SO BADLY!" OR IMAGE: "GENTLEMAN CALLER WAVING GOOD-BYE!—GAILY." *At this moment* AMANDA *rushes brightly back in the front room. She bears a pitcher of fruit punch in an old-fashioned cut-glass pitcher and a plate of macaroons. The plate has a gold border and poppies painted on it.*)

AMANDA. Well, well, well! Isn't the air delightful after the shower?

I've made you children a little liquid refreshment. (*Turns gaily to the gentleman caller.*)

Jim, do you know that song about lemonade?

"Lemonade, lemonade
Made in the shade and stirred with a spade——
Good enough for any old maid!"

JIM (*uneasily*). Ha-ha! No—I never heard it.

AMANDA. Why, Laura! You look so serious!

JIM. We were having a serious conversation.

AMANDA. Good! Now you're better acquainted!

JIM (*uncertainly*). Ha-ha! Yes.

AMANDA. You modern young people are much more serious-minded than my generation. I was so gay as a girl!

JIM. You haven't changed, Mrs. Wingfield.

AMANDA. Tonight I'm rejuvenated! The gaiety of the occasion, Mr. O'Connor! (*She tosses her head with a peal of laughter. Spills lemonade.*)

Oooo! I'm baptizing myself!

JIM. Here—let me——

AMANDA (*setting the pitcher down*). There now. I discovered we had some maraschino cherries. I dumped them in, juice and all!

JIM. You shouldn't have gone to that trouble, Mrs. Wingfield.

AMANDA. Trouble, trouble? Why, it was loads of fun!

Didn't you hear me cutting up in the kitchen? I bet your ears were burning! I told Tom how outdone with him I was for keeping you to himself so long a time! He should have brought you over much, much sooner! Well, now that you've found your way, I want you to be a very frequent caller! Not just occasional but all the time.

Oh, we're going to have a lot of gay times together! I see them coming!

Mmm, just breathe that air! So fresh, and the moon's so pretty!

I'll skip back out—I know where my place is when young folks are having a—serious conversation!

JIM. Oh, don't go out, Mrs. Wingfield. The fact of the matter is I've got to be going.

AMANDA. Going, now? You're joking! Why, it's only the shank of the evening, Mr. O'Connor!

JIM. Well, you know how it is.

AMANDA. You mean you're a young workingman and have to keep workingmen's hours. We'll let you off early tonight. But only on the condition that next time you stay later.

What's the best night for you? Isn't Saturday night the best night for you workingmen?

JIM. I have a couple of time-clocks to punch, Mrs. Wingfield. One at morning, another one at night!

AMANDA. My, but you *are* ambitious! You work at night, too?

JIM. No, Ma'am, not work but—Betty! (*He crosses deliberately to pick up his hat. The band at the Paradise Dance Hall goes into a tender waltz.*)

AMANDA. Betty? Betty? Who's—Betty? (*There is an ominous cracking sound in the sky.*)

JIM. Oh, just a girl. The girl I go steady with! (*He smiles charmingly. The sky falls.* LEGEND: "THE SKY FALLS.")

AMANDA (*a long-drawn exhalation*). Ohhhh . . . Is it a serious romance, Mr. O'Connor?

JIM. We're going to be married the second Sunday in June.

AMANDA. Ohhhh—how nice!

Tom didn't mention that you were engaged to be married.

JIM. The cat's not out of the bag at the warehouse yet.

You know how they are. They call you Romeo and stuff like that. (*He stops at the oval mirror to put on his hat. He carefully shapes the brim and the crown to give a discreetly dashing effect.*)

It's been a wonderful evening, Mrs. Wingfield. I guess this is what they mean by Southern hospitality.

AMANDA. It really wasn't anything at all.

JIM. I hope it don't seem like I'm rushing off. But I promised Betty I'd pick her up at the Wabash depot, an' by the time I get my jalopy down there her train'll be in. Some women are pretty upset if you keep 'em waiting.

AMANDA. Yes, I know——The tyranny of women! (*Extends her hand.*) Good-bye, Mr. O'Connor.

I wish you luck—and happiness—and success! All three of them, and so does Laura!—Don't you, Laura?

LAURA. Yes!

JIM (*taking her hand*). Good-bye, Laura. I'm certainly going to treasure that souvenir. And don't you forget the good advice I gave you. (*Raises his voice to a cheery shout.*)

So long, Shakespeare!

Thanks again, ladies—— Good night! (*He grins and ducks jauntily out. Still bravely grimacing,* AMANDA *closes the door on the gentleman caller. Then she turns back to the room with a puzzled expression. She and* LAURA *don't dare to face each other.* LAURA *crouches beside the victrola to wind it.*)

AMANDA (*faintly*). Things have a way of turning out so badly.

I don't believe that I would play the victrola.

Well, well—well——

Our gentleman caller was engaged to be married!

Tom!

TOM (*from back*). Yes, Mother?

AMANDA. Come in here a minute. I want to tell you something awfully funny.

TOM (*enters with macaroon and a glass of the lemonade*). Has the gentleman caller gotten away already?

AMANDA. The gentleman caller has made an early departure.

What a wonderful joke you played on us!

TOM. How do you mean?

AMANDA. You didn't mention that he was engaged to be married.

TOM. Jim? Engaged?

AMANDA. That's what he just informed us.

TOM. I'll be jiggered! I didn't know about that.

AMANDA. That seems very peculiar.

TOM. What's peculiar about it?

AMANDA. Didn't you call him your best friend down at the warehouse?

TOM. He is, but how did I know?

AMANDA. It seems extremely peculiar that you wouldn't know your best friend was going to be married!

TOM. The warehouse is where I work, not where I know things about people!

AMANDA. You don't know things anywhere! You live in a dream; you manufacture illusions! (*He crosses to the door.*)

Where are you going?

TOM. I'm going to the movies.

AMANDA. That's right, now that you've had us make such fools of ourselves. The effort, the preparations, all the expense! The new floor lamp, the rug, the clothes for Laura! All for what? To entertain some other girl's fiancé!

Go to the movies, go! Don't think about us, a mother deserted, an unmarried sister who's crippled and has no job! Don't let anything interfere with your selfish pleasure!

Just go, go, go—to the movies!

TOM. All right, I will! The more you shout about my selfishness to me the quicker I'll go, and I won't go to the movies!

AMANDA. Go, then! Then go to the moon—you selfish dreamer! (TOM *smashes his glass on the floor. He plunges out on the fire-escape, slamming the door.* LAURA *screams—cut off by the door. Dance-hall music up.* TOM *goes to the rail and grips it desperately, lifting his face in the chill white moonlight penetrating the narrow abyss of the alley.* LEGEND ON SCREEN: "AND SO GOOD-BYE . . ." TOM'S *closing speech is timed with the interior pantomime. The interior scene is played as though viewed through soundproof glass.* AMANDA *appears to be making a comforting speech to* LAURA *who is huddled upon the sofa. Now that we cannot hear the mother's speech, her silliness is gone and she has dignity and tragic beauty.* LAURA'S *dark hair hides her face until at the end of the speech she lifts it to smile at her mother.* AMANDA'S *gestures are slow and graceful, almost dancelike, as she comforts the daughter. At the end of her speech she glances a moment at the father's picture—then withdraws through the portieres. At close of* TOM'S *speech,* LAURA *blows out the candles, ending the play.*)

TOM. I didn't go to the moon, I went

much further—for time is the longest distance between two places——

Not long after that I was fired for writing a poem on the lid of a shoe-box.

I left Saint Louis. I descended the steps of this fire-escape for the last time and followed, from then on, in my father's footsteps, attempting to find in motion what was lost in space——

I traveled around a great deal. The cities swept about me like dead leaves, leaves that were brightly colored but torn away from the branches.

I would have stopped, but I was pursued by something.

It always came upon me unawares, taking me altogether by surprise. Perhaps it was a familiar bit of music. Perhaps it was only a piece of transparent glass——

Perhaps I am walking along a street at night, in some strange city, before I have found companions. I pass the lighted window of a shop where perfume is sold. The window is filled with pieces of colored glass, tiny transparent bottles in delicate colors, like bits of a shattered rainbow.

Then all at once my sister touches my shoulder. I turn around and look into her eyes . . .

Oh, Laura, Laura, I tried to leave you behind me, but I am more faithful than I intended to be!

I reach for a cigarette, I cross the street, I run into the movies or a bar, I buy a drink, I speak to the nearest stranger—anything that can blow your candles out! (LAURA *bends over the candles.*)—for nowadays the world is lit by lightning! Blow out your candles, Laura—and so good-bye. . . . (*She blows the candles out.*)

THE SCENE DISSOLVES.

KENNETH TYNAN: *Valentine to Tennessee Williams*

From *Curtains* by Kenneth Tynan. Copyright © 1961 by Kenneth Tynan. Reprinted by permission of Atheneum Publishers.

IN SPAIN, WHERE I SAW HIM LAST, HE LOOKED PROFOUNDLY SPANISH. He might have passed for one of those confidential street dealers who earn their living selling spurious Parker pens in the cafés of Málaga or Valencia. Like them, he wore a faded chalk-striped shirt, a coat slung over his shoulders, a trim, dark moustache, and a sleazy, fat-cat smile. His walk, like theirs, was a raffish saunter, and everything about him seemed slept in, especially his hair, a nest of small, wet serpents. Had we been in Seville and his clothes been more formal, he could have been mistaken for a pampered elder son idling away a legacy in dribs and on drabs, the sort you see sitting in windows along the Sierpes, apparently stuffed. In Italy he looks Italian; in Greece, Greek; wherever he travels on the Mediterranean coast, Tennessee Williams takes on a protective colouring which melts him into his background, like a lizard on a rock. In New York or London he seems out of place, and is best explained away as a retired bandit. Or a beachcomber: shave the beard off any of the self-portraits Gauguin painted in Tahiti, soften the features a little, and you have a sleepy outcast face that might well be Tennessee's.

It is unmistakably the face of a nomad. Wherever Williams goes he is a stranger, one who lives out of suitcases and has a trick of making any home he acquires resemble, within ten minutes, a hotel apartment. Like most hypochondriacs, he is an uneasy guest on earth. When he sold the film rights of his play *Cat on a Hot Tin Roof* for half a million dollars, he asked that the payment should be spread over ten years, partly out of prudence but mostly out of a mantic suspicion, buzzing in his ears, that in ten years' time he might be dead. He says justly of himself that he is "a driven person." The condemned tend always to be lonely, and one of Williams' favourite quotations is a line from a play which runs: "We're all of us sentenced to solitary confinement inside our own skins." He says such things quite blandly, with a thick chuckle which is as far from cynicism as it is from self-pity.

To be alone at forty is to be really alone, and Williams has passed forty. In a sense, of course, solitude is a condition of his trade. All writing is an anti-social act, since the writer is a man who can speak freely only when alone; to be himself he must lock himself up, to communicate he must cut himself off from all communication; and in this there is something always a little mad. Many writers loathe above all sounds the closing of the door which seals them up in their privacy. Williams, by contrast, welcomes it: it dispels the haze of uncertainty through which he normally converses, and releases for his pleasure the creatures who people his imaginings—desperate women, men nursing troublesome secrets, untouchables whom he touches with frankness and mercy, society's derelict rag dolls. The theatre, he once said, is a place where one has time for the problems of people to whom one would show the door if they came to one's office for a job. His best-loved characters are people like this, and they are all, in some way, trapped—Blanche DuBois, of *Streetcar,* beating her wings in a slum; Alma of *Summer and Smoke,* stricken with elephantiasis of the soul; Brick in *Cat,* sodden with remorse. As we shall see, much of what has happened to them has also happened to him. He is the most personal of playwrights. Incomplete people obsess him—above all, those who, like himself, have ideals too large for life to accommodate. There is another, opposed kind of incompleteness, that of materialists like the Polack in *Streetcar* and Big Daddy in *Cat;* and in most of Williams' work both kinds are to be found, staring blankly at each other, arguing from different premises and conversing without comprehension. In his mental battlefield the real is perpetually at war with the ideal; what is public wrestles with what is private, what drags men down fights with what draws them up. This struggle is an allegory, by which I mean that it reflects a conflict within Williams himself. He cannot bring himself to believe that the flesh and the spirit can be reconciled, or to admit that the highest emotion can spring from the basest source. As Aldous Huxley has put it: "Whether it's passion or the desire of the moth for the star, whether it's tenderness or adoration or romantic yearning—love is always accompanied by events in the nerve endings, the skin, the mucous membranes, the glandular and erectile tissue. . . . What we need is another set of words. Words that can express the natural togetherness of things." For Williams they remain stubbornly apart, and it is this that gives his writing its odd urgency, its note of unfinished exploration. Alone behind the door, sustained by what one critic called the "comradeship of his introspection," he seeks to bridge the gap between his two selves. His work is a pilgrimage in search of a truce. His typewriter stands on the glass top of a hotel table, and most likely neither he nor it will be there tomorrow.

Though he does not need company, he does not shun it. Leaning back on a bar stool, one of a crowd, he can simulate ease with a barely perceptible effort. Mostly he is silent, sucking on a hygienic cigarette holder full of absorbent crystals, with a vague smile painted on his face, while his mind swats flies in outer space. He says nothing that is not candid and little that is not trite. A mental deafness seems to permeate him, so that he will laugh spasmodically in the wrong places, tell you the time if you ask him the date, or suddenly reopen conversations left for dead three days before. Late at night, part of him may come to life: in shreds of old slang ("We're in like Flynn") or bursts of old songs, remembered from St. Louis in the twenties and unexpectedly proceeding, in a voice at once true and blue, from his slumped figure, which you had thought slumbering, in the back seat of somebody else's

car. This is Williams on holiday, and you may be sure that his mind is not far from a blank.

He longs for intimacy, but shrinks from its responsibilities. Somewhere in the past, before he became famous, lies the one perfect passion; its object parted from him and afterward died of cancer. Since then, too cautious to spoil perfection by trying to repeat it, he has kept all emotional relationships deliberately casual. He will incur no more emotional debts, nor extend any more emotional credit. His friendships are many and generous, ranging from Mediterranean remittance men to Carson McCullers; but love is a sickness which he will do anything to avoid. If his deeper instincts crave release, you may find him at a bullfight—or even writing a play.

He was born forty-four years ago in Columbus, Mississippi, the son of an itinerant shoe salesman known throughout the territory as a fiery and accomplished poker player. As a child he lived in Columbus with his mother, his elder sister, and his younger brother at the home of his maternal grandfather, a highly respected Episcopal rector. Here an image took root which has haunted much of his work: the South as a fading mansion of gentility. The first great wrench of his life occurred when he was still very young. His father took a desk job in St. Louis and the family left Columbus to join him. "We suddenly discovered," Williams says, "that there were two kinds of people, the rich and the poor, and that we belonged more to the latter." It was here, in a stuffy, backstreet apartment, that his world split, amoeba-like, into two irreconcilable halves —the soft, feminine world of the room that he and his sister filled with little glass animals, and the cruel, male world of the alley outside, where cats fought and coupled to a persistent screaming. He entered the University of Missouri and at the age of sixteen got a story into *Weird Tales,* but the depression sent him to work for three memorably detested years in a shoe factory. The result was a heart attack, followed by a complete physical breakdown. He returned to his studies and in 1938 took a B.A. at the University of Iowa. By now his imagination was alive with human voices, and two of his plays had been performed by the St. Louis Mummers. The future offered by his father meant going back to the shoe factory. Subjecting his life to its second great wrench, he left home.

"And it don't look like I'm ever gonna cease my wanderin'. . . ." He waited on table in New Orleans and worked on a pigeon ranch in California; then a one-act play won him a prize of a hundred dollars and attracted the attention of a Broadway agent, Audrey Wood. He sent her the script of *Battle of Angels,* an ambitious survey of "the sometimes conflicting desires of the flesh and the spirit." To his amazement, the Theatre Guild bought it. It opened in Boston in December 1940 and closed without reaching New York. On top of that, and perhaps because of it, Williams developed a cataract in his left eye. The next two years found him a vulnerable and myopic vagabond in Bohemia, always the victim of a hectic nervous system, which alarmed him by expressing its disquiet as often in illness as in imaginative visions. Back to New Orleans, living from pawnshop to mouth; then to Greenwich Village, where he worked as a waiter, wearing a black eyepatch which someone adorned with a surrealistic white eyeball.

In 1943 Audrey Wood got him a six-month contract in Hollywood. He spent most of it writing *The Glass Menagerie,* in which his twin worlds of fact and dream came out for the first time distinct and dovetailed. Its Broadway success a year later gave him security: but "security," he was soon writing, "is a kind of death. . . ." To escape it he returned to New Orleans, to cheap hotels and rented apartments. On a trip to Taos, New Mexico, he came down with what proved to be a ruptured appendix; but he heard a nun whisper that it might be cancer, and, spurred by the death sentence, he fled from the hospital. Feverishly he composed what was meant to be his last message to the world.

A new friendship helped him to obey Hemingway's dictum and "get it out whole." This was with Carson McCullers. In his own words: "Carson came to me in the summer of 1946 at the height of my imaginary dying, she came to Nantucket Island, which I had chosen to die on, and the moment she came down the gangplank of the ship from the mainland, in her baseball cap, with that enchantingly radiant crooked-toothed grin of hers, something very light happened in me. I dropped my preoccupation with the thought that I was doomed, and from then on there was a process of adjustment to the new situation, and by the late fall of 1947 I was able to release all the emotional content of the long crisis in *Streetcar.*" The play was produced in the same year and fully deserves Williams' description of it: "saturated with death."

More studies in desperation followed: *Summer and Smoke* and *The Rose Tattoo,* perhaps the fullest expression of Williams' special kind of romanticism, which is not pale or scented but earthy and robust, the product of a mind vitally infected with the rhythms of human speech. When overheated, however, it can give off lurid fumes, some of which clouded the air in his next play, *Camino Real.* This was Williams' gaudiest rebellion against materialism, conceived in terms of symbols and carried out mainly in italics. Directed by Elia Kazan in the spring of 1953, the play flopped. There ensued one of those low-energy spells from which Williams frequently suffers. Work became a depressant instead of a stimulant; he kept losing sight of the impulse that sent him to the typewriter and felt that his ideas were being smirched and dog-eared by the well-meaning interference of agents, producers, and directors. *Cat on a Hot Tin Roof* was eighteen months in the writing. I now think it his best work, but when I first saw it, it struck me as an edifice somehow tilted, like a giant architectural folly. It was august, all right, and turbulent, but there were moments of unaccountable wrongness, as if a kazoo had intruded into a string quartet. When I saw the published text and read, side by side, the original third act and the version that was presented on Broadway, I guessed at once what had happened. The kazoo was Kazan.

Cat is a birthday party about death. The birthday is that of Big Daddy, a Southern millionaire dying of cancer. His son Brick is a quiet, defeated drinker; and the cat of the title is Maggie, Brick's wife, whose frayed vivacity derives from the fact that she is sexually ignored by her husband. The play deals with the emotional lies that are shockingly exposed as people try to "reach" each other, to penetrate the inviolable cell in which the soul lives. Williams' trade-marks are all there: the spectre of disease, the imminence of death, the cheating implicit in all emotion, the guilt bound up with sex —plus the technical ability to make tragic characters immeasurably funny. But a play might have all these things and still be bad; what distinguishes *Cat* is the texture of its writing. This is dialogue dead to the eyes alone. It begs for speech so shrilly that you find yourself reading it aloud. "When you are gone from here," says Big Daddy, "you are long gone and no where!"—the words fall from the tongue like "snow from a bamboo leaf," the image by which Zen Buddhists teach their pupils that "artless art" which is the goal of contemplation.

But Kazan was not satisfied. He felt that Brick should undergo a change of heart after the showdown with his father; and into Brick's lines a certain hollowness began to creep. In a stage direction Williams had spoken of "the thundercloud of a common crisis"; with stupefying literalness, Kazan introduced a full-tilt symbolic thunderstorm. Maggie's big lie, uttered to win Big Daddy's inheritance, originally ran: "Brick and I are going to have a child." Inflated by Kazan, the line became: "A child is coming, sired by Brick and out of Maggie the Cat!" The bitterness of the final tableau, when Brick prepares to sleep with

Maggie to sustain her lie, was sweetened until the scene seemed to betoken a lasting reconciliation. Williams in no way resents these adjustments, which, he says, "did not violate the essential truth of the play." For him, Kazan is "a very big man, the biggest artist in the theatre of our time." He is at present working on a film script, which Kazan will direct; but some of his admirers feel that a less creative collaborator might, in the long run, be more helpful.

Discussing the incidence of genius, Somerset Maugham once remarked: "The lesson of anatomy applies: there is nothing so rare as the normal." Williams' view of life is always abnormal, heightened and spotlighted, and slashed with bogey shadows. The marvel is that he makes it touch ours, thereby achieving the miracle of communication between human beings which he has always held to be impossible.

Yet he looks anonymous. One ends, as one began, with the enigma. Arthur Miller, after all, looks Lincolnesque, and Anouilh looks hypersensitive, and Sartre looks crazy. Williams, alone of the big playwrights, seems miscast. From that round, rubbery face, those dazed eyes which nothing, no excess or enormity, can surprise—from here the message comes, the latest bulletin from the civil war between purity and squalor. It will always, however long or well I know him, seem wonderfully strange.

STARK YOUNG: Review: *The Glass Menagerie*

OF ALL OUR ACTORS, CERTAINLY OF ALL THOSE WHO HAVE BECOME known, Miss Laurette Taylor could not be called the most cultured, the most versatile in divers styles, the most gracious-minded, but few would deny that she is the most talented. She is the real and first talent of them all. She has been largely absent from the stage during so many years that her return is an event and everybody knows it. It turns out, in *The Glass Menagerie,* to be a triumph as well. So is the rôle she plays.

Miss Taylor's rôle in Mr. Williams' play is that of a frowsy, aging woman who lives with her son and daughter, in a flat off a St. Louis alley. It is a far cry from the Deep South, where her girlhood was spent and her memories dwell, and where she has refused the rich planters' sons because she lost her heart to a man who worked for the telephone company and whose smile misled everybody. The daughter is a cripple, too shy and hurt and vague ever to have got through school. She spends her time playing old phonograph records that her father had left behind when he abandoned her mother and went away for good, and collecting glass animals—hence the title of the play. The son is a failure, discontented with his job in the warehouse, vaguely itching to write poetry, and longing to roam the world. The mother worships, nags, scolds and tries to do her best by her children. Finally, when she thinks it is time her daughter got married, she plagues the son into bringing a man home with him; he brings a friend from the warehouse. The visitor, impressed though he is with the daughter, turns out to be already in love and engaged.

In the end the son follows his father's example and goes off to make his way wandering the world. The scheme of *The Glass Menagerie* includes a Narrator, who opens the play and appears between the scenes from time to time (to follow "the part of the sun"). If properly followed, which it is not in the production, this is a very imaginative motif on the dramatist's part, this subtle identification of the father with the son, the son with the father.

This rôle is played by the actor who takes the part of the son. The story, as we see it on the stage, all happens in the son's mind long afterward, and in the last narration, a kind of epilogue, we are told that in the midst of the years and in far, strange places, wherever he goes, he can never lose the image of his sister there at home; all things bring her back to him.

What Miss Laurette Taylor does with these matters can be at least partially imagined if you know the quality of her special gift. This, even after just seeing the play, is almost impossible to convey with anything like the full, wonderful truth. Hers is naturalistic acting of the most profound, spontaneous, unbroken continuity and moving life. There is an inexplicable rightness, moment by moment, phrase by phrase, endlessly varied in the transitions. Technique, which is always composed of skill and instinct working together, is in this case so overlaid with warmth, tenderness and wit that any analysis is completely baffled. Only a trained theatre eye and ear can tell what is happening, and then only at times. Miss Laurette Taylor is capable of a performance so right and perfect that you do not even think of it as a great performance. I do not mean to go into a kind of Seidletz hysterics to make my point about what she does with this rôle in *The Glass Menagerie,* I merely say that it has a characteristic of seeming beyond any contrivance and of a sort of changing rhythm of translucence rarely to be seen in the theatre. The one shortcoming about this portrayal of the mother is that Miss Taylor does not achieve the quality of the aristocrat, however broken down and wasted and lost, that Mr. Williams intended. She is astonishingly Southern, partly due to the writing and partly to her ready intuition of feeling, tone and climax; but in an elusive sense that would be impossible to convey, and that any Southerner of Mr. Williams' class would understand almost automatically, she is not what is implied in the play. No use in wasting time on that point; if she had been so, had been the broken-down aristocrat that Mr. Williams wrote, the effect would have been largely lost on most audiences, and as things went the play got on very well without it.

But true as all this may be of Miss Taylor, we must not let that blind us to the case of the play itself and of the whole occasion. The play gives every one of the four characters that it presents a glowing, rich opportunity, genuine emotional motivations, a rhythm of situations that are alive, and speech that is fresh, living, abundant and free of stale theatre diction. The author is not awed by the usual sterilities of our play-writing patterns. On the other hand he is too imaginative, genuine, or has too much good taste, to be coy about the free devices on which his play is built, a true, rich talent, unpredictable like all true talents, an astute stage sense, an intense, quivering clarity, all light and feeling once the intelligence of it is well anchored—a talent, too, I should say, that New York will buy tickets for in later plays, especially if enough of the sexy is added to things, but will never quite understand.

The Glass Menagerie appears to drag, or go slow, at times, though I am not sure about this and certainly found it less so than a number of people I have heard speak of it. These slow places occur in the Narrator portions and sometimes in the scenes between mother and son. In my opinion this may be almost entirely due to the fact that Mr. Eddie Dowling does not let himself go enough to make you believe that he is the son of such a mother or such a father. We have no ready, or vivid, sense that he longs to wander, to write poetry—I even forgot to remember what he was working at when he sat before the papers on the table, supposed, however, to be bent on a poem. Mr. Dowling speaks his Narrator scenes plainly and serviceably, with the result that they are made to seem to be a mistake on the playwright's part, a mis-

take to include them at all; for they seem extraneous and tiresome in the midst of the play's emotional current. And many critics will speak of them as such. This is not the case at all. It is curious that an actor of Mr. Dowling's experience and showmanship should pass up thus a rôle where the dramatist's invention is really so striking and, for that matter, so useful to the player. If these speeches were spoken with variety, impulse and intensity, as if the son himself were speaking—which is what happens really, since the play is a dream within his memory—if they were spoken as if they were from a born wanderer and adventurer, a chip off the old block, wild-headed like his father—and like his mother for that matter, for she too had wandered far from home indeed—the whole of the Narrator would be another matter entirely, it would be truly a part of the story. Thus Mr. Dowling does much harm to the play. The fact remains, nevertheless, that he is sure to be praised for his playing of the rôle, on the basis that it is poised and not exaggerated—such is the irony of the acting art and its observers.

To say, as Mr. Nichols does in his review in the New York *Times* that there are such unconnected things with the story as "snatches of talk about the war, bits of psychology, occasional moments of rather florid writing" is mistaken indeed. The part Miss Taylor plays is, quite aside from her rendering of it, the best written rôle that I have seen in a play for years. All the language and all the motifs are free and true; I recognized them inch by inch, and I should know, for I came from the same part of the country, the same locality and life, in fact, that Mr. Williams does. Such a response and attitude as that Mr. Nichols expresses is the kind of thing that helps to tie our theatre down. It is the application of Times Square practical knowledge, the kind of thing that makes, to take one instance, the writing, the talk, in *The Late George Apley* so sterile and so little like the Boston it assumes to be. One of the things most needed in the theatre is a sense of language, a sense of texture in speech, vibration and impulse in speech. Behind the Southern speech in the mother's part is the echo of great literature, or at least a respect for it. There is the sense in it of her having been born out of a tradition, not out of a box. It has echo and the music of it. The mother's characterization is both appalling and human, both cold and loving. No rôle could be more realistically written than this, but it has the variety, suddenness, passion and freedom, almost unconscious freedom perhaps, of true realism.

Miss Julie Haydon gave one of her translucent performances of a dreaming, wounded, half-out-of-this-world young girl. Mr. Anthony Ross, as the visitor, for whom the author has written a long and excellent scene, original and tender, with the girl, played admirably.

Mr. Jo Mielziner did the complicated setting for *The Glass Menagerie,* streets at the side, a front room, a back room, a wall shutting them off when needed. The scene is effectively ingenious. But even though the story happens in a dream and vagueness may be called for, I see no reason why the color should be quite so dull. For example, it was only by a most creditable leap of the imagination that one could make out that the enlarged photograph of the vanished father on the wall was really that of Mr. Dowling, the son. The result was that a notable motivation on the part of the dramatist, which is that the son, the Narrator and the father are all one and the same, was all but lost. Of all places the stage is one of economies in effect, the moment is brief and such a fault as this is serious, practically.

In the Narrator's opening speech Mr. Williams has provided an excuse for music by saying that the play all happens in the memory, and memory always seems to move in music. That idea, or motif, goes well back to the classics: Phoebus replied and touched my trembling ear is Milton, but that in turn was Horace— *aurem vellit*—for the ear was the seat of memory. For *The Glass Menagerie,* therefore, Mr. Paul Bowles has written music that runs in and out of the scenes, sometimes for a long interval, sometimes less. It seems to be a special gift of his, this writing music for a play that becomes a part of the play, strangely beautiful and strangely right.

EUGÈNE IONESCO, ONE OF FRANCE'S MOST CONTROVER-

Eugène sial dramatists, did not begin writing plays until he
was thirty-six. A failure at first, he finally achieved

Ionesco success in the late 1950's as an avant-garde drama-
tist and exemplar of the "theatre of the absurd."

_1912-_ Ionesco was born in Romania; his family moved to
France while he was a child, but later returned to

Romania where Ionesco became a teacher of French. During the late
1930's, the rise of native Fascism in Romania led Ionesco to return to France,
where he worked obscurely for a publishing firm and assumed French citizen-
ship. A turning-point in his career came in 1948, when Ionesco, studying a
primer of conversational English, was struck by the absurdity of the sentences he was memorizing and proceeded to write his first play, _The Bald
Soprano._ When produced in 1950 the play was quietly ignored. But Ionesco
continued to mine his original vein of surrealist fantasy in plays such as
The Lesson (1950), _Jack_ (1950), _The Chairs_ (1951), _Amédée_ (1953),
The Killer (1957), and _Rhinoceros_ (1958). By the end of the decade
Ionesco had achieved a commanding position with the anti-realist playwrights and critics. Based on ingenious theatrical metaphors, Ionesco's "anti-
plays" break completely with naturalistic theatre and present grotesque paro-
dies of what, to Ionesco, is the human condition: general absurdity of life,
sterility of bourgeois culture, animal stupidity of conformist man, and failure
of human communication. In Ionesco we find the "sadness and weariness of
a clown" who cloaks serious purpose beneath a mask of comedy.

THE BALD SOPRANO, An Antiplay

❧ BY EUGÈNE IONESCO

Translated by Donald M. Allen

CHARACTERS

MR. SMITH
MRS. SMITH
MR. MARTIN

MRS. MARTIN
MARY *the maid*
THE FIRE CHIEF

A middle-class English interior, with English armchairs. An English evening. MR. SMITH, *an Englishman, seated in his English armchair and wearing English slippers, is smoking his English pipe and reading an English newspaper, near an English fire. He is wearing English spectacles and a small gray English mustache. Beside him, in another English armchair,* MRS. SMITH, *an Englishwoman, is darning some English socks. A long moment of English silence. The English clock strikes seventeen English strokes.*

MRS. SMITH. There, it's nine o'clock. We've drunk the soup, and eaten the fish and chips, and the English salad. The children have drunk English water. We've eaten well this evening. That's because we live in the suburbs of London and because our name is Smith.

(MR. SMITH *continues to read, clicks his tongue.*)

MRS. SMITH. Potatoes are very good fried in fat; the salad oil was not rancid. The oil from the grocer at the corner is better quality than the oil from the grocer across the street. It is even better than the oil from the grocer at the bottom of the street. However, I prefer not to tell them that their oil is bad.

(MR. SMITH *continues to read, clicks his tongue.*)

MRS. SMITH. However, the oil from the grocer at the corner is still the best.

(MR. SMITH *continues to read, clicks his tongue.*)

MRS. SMITH. Mary did the potatoes very well, this evening. The last time she did not do them well. I do not like them when they are well done.

(MR. SMITH *continues to read, clicks his tongue.*)

MRS. SMITH. The fish was fresh. It made my mouth water. I had two helpings. No, three helpings. That made me go to the w.c. You also had three helpings. However, the third time you took less than the first two times, while as for me, I took a great deal more. I eat better than you this evening. Why is that? Usually, it is you who eats more. It is not appetite you lack.

(MR. SMITH *clicks his tongue.*)

MRS. SMITH. But still, the soup was perhaps a little too salt. It was saltier than you. Ha, ha, ha. It also had too many leeks and not enough onions. I regret I didn't advise Mary to add some aniseed stars. The next time I'll know better.

(MR. SMITH *continues to read, clicks his tongue.*)

MRS. SMITH. Our little boy wanted to drink some beer; he's going to love getting tiddly. He's like you. At table did you notice how he stared at the bottle? But I poured some water from the jug into his glass. He was thirsty and he drank it. Helen is like me: she's a good manager, thrifty, plays the piano. She never asks to drink English beer. She's like our little daughter who drinks only milk and eats only porridge. It's obvious that she's only two. She's named Peggy. The quince and bean pie was marvelous. It would have been nice, perhaps, to have had a small glass of Australian Burgundy with the sweet, but I did not bring the bottle to the table because I did not wish to set the children a bad example of gluttony. They must learn to be sober and temperate.

(MR. SMITH *continues to read, clicks his tongue.*)

MRS. SMITH. Mrs. Parker knows a Rumanian grocer by the name of Popesco Rosenfeld, who has just come from Constantinople. He is a great specialist in yogurt. He has a diploma from the school of yogurt-making in Adrianople. Tomorrow I shall buy a large pot of native Rumanian yogurt from him. One doesn't often find such things here in the suburbs of London.

(MR. SMITH *continues to read, clicks his tongue.*)

MRS. SMITH. Yogurt is excellent for the stomach, the kidneys, the appendicitis, and apotheosis. It was Doctor Mackenzie-King who told me that, he's the one who takes care of the children of our neighbors, the Johns. He's a good doctor. One can trust him. He never prescribes any medicine that he's not tried out on himself first. Before operating on Parker, he had his own liver operated on first, although he was not the least bit ill.

MR. SMITH. But how does it happen that the doctor pulled through while Parker died?

MRS. SMITH. Because the operation was successful in the doctor's case and it was not in Parker's.

MR. SMITH. Then Mackenzie is not a good doctor. The operation should have succeeded with both of them or else both should have died.

MRS. SMITH. Why?

MR. SMITH. A conscientious doctor must die with his patient if they can't get well together. The captain of a ship goes down with his ship into the briny deep, he does not survive alone.

MRS. SMITH. One cannot compare a patient with a ship.

MR. SMITH. Why not? A ship has its diseases too; moreover, your doctor is as hale as a ship; that's why he should have perished at the same time as his patient, like the captain and his ship.

MRS. SMITH. Ah! I hadn't thought of that . . . Perhaps it is true . . And then, what conclusion do you draw from this?

MR. SMITH. All doctors are quacks. And all patients too. Only the Royal Navy is honest in England.

MRS. SMITH. But not sailors.

MR. SMITH. Naturally. (*A pause. Still reading his paper*) Here's a thing I don't understand. In the newspaper they always give the age of deceased persons but never the age of the newly born. That doesn't make sense.

MRS. SMITH. I never thought of that!

(*Another moment of silence. The clock strikes seven times. Silence. The clock strikes three times. Silence. The clock doesn't strike.*)

MR. SMITH (*still reading his paper*). Tsk, it says here that Bobby Watson died.

MRS. SMITH. My God, the poor man! When did he die?

MR. SMITH. Why do you pretend to be astonished? You know very well that he's been dead these past two years. Surely you remember that we attended his funeral a year and a half ago.

MRS. SMITH. Oh yes, of course I do remember. I remembered it right away, but I don't understand why you yourself were so surprised to see it in the paper.

MR. SMITH. It wasn't in the paper. It's been three years since his death was announced. I remembered it through an association of ideas.

MRS. SMITH. What a pity! He was so well preserved.

MR. SMITH. He was the handsomest corpse in Great Britain. He didn't look his age. Poor Bobby, he'd been dead for four years and he was still warm. A veritable living corpse. And how cheerful he was!

MRS. SMITH. Poor Bobby.

MR. SMITH. Which poor Bobby do you mean?

MRS. SMITH. It is his wife that I mean. She is called Bobby too, Bobby Watson. Since they both had the same name, you could never tell one from the other when you saw them together. It was only after his death that you could really tell which was which. And there are still people today who confuse her with the deceased and offer their condolences to him. Do you know her?

MR. SMITH. I only met her once, by chance, at Bobby's burial.

MRS. SMITH. I've never seen her. Is she pretty?

MR. SMITH. She has regular features and yet one cannot say that she is pretty. She is too big and stout. Her features are not regular but still one can say that she is very pretty. She is a little too small and too thin. She's a voice teacher.

(*The clock strikes five times. A long silence.*)

MRS. SMITH. And when do they plan to be married, those two?

MR. SMITH. Next spring, at the latest.

MRS. SMITH. We shall have to go to their wedding, I suppose.

MR. SMITH. We shall have to give them a wedding present. I wonder what?

MRS. SMITH. Why don't we give them one of the seven silver salvers that were given us for our wedding and which have never been of any use to us?

(*Silence.*)

MRS. SMITH. How sad for her to be left a widow so young.

MR. SMITH. Fortunately, they had no children.

MRS. SMITH. That was all they needed! Children! Poor woman, how could she have managed!

MR. SMITH. She's still young. She might very well remarry. She looks so well in mourning.

MRS. SMITH. But who would take care of the children? You know very well that they have a boy and a girl. What are their names?

MR. SMITH. Bobby and Bobby like their parents. Bobby Watson's uncle, old Bobby Watson, is a rich man and very fond of the boy. He might very well pay for Bobby's education.

MRS. SMITH. That would be proper. And Bobby Watson's aunt, old Bobby Watson, might very well, in her turn, pay for the education of Bobby Watson, Bobby Watson's daughter. That way Bobby, Bobby Watson's mother, could re-marry. Has she anyone in mind?

MR. SMITH. Yes, a cousin of Bobby Watson's.

MRS. SMITH. Who? Bobby Watson?

MR. SMITH. Which Bobby Watson do you mean?

MRS. SMITH. Why, Bobby Watson, the son of old Bobby Watson, the late Bobby Watson's other uncle.

MR. SMITH. No, it's not that one, it's someone else. It's Bobby Watson, the son of old Bobby Watson, the late Bobby Watson's aunt.

MRS. SMITH. Are you referring to Bobby Watson the commercial traveler?

MR. SMITH. All the Bobby Watsons are commercial travelers.

MRS. SMITH. What a difficult trade! However, they do well at it.

MR. SMITH. Yes, when there's no competition.

MRS. SMITH. And when is there no competition?

MR. SMITH. On Tuesdays, Thursdays, and Tuesdays.

MRS. SMITH. Ah! Three days a week? And what does Bobby Watson do on those days?

MR. SMITH. He rests, he sleeps.

MRS. SMITH. But why doesn't he work those three days if there's no competition?

MR. SMITH. I don't know everything. I can't answer all your idiotic questions!

MRS. SMITH (*offended*). Oh! Are you trying to humiliate me?

MR. SMITH (*all smiles*). You know very well that I'm not.

MRS. SMITH. Men are all alike! You sit there all day long, a cigarette in your mouth, or you powder your nose and rouge your lips, fifty times a day, or else you drink like a fish.

MR. SMITH. But what would you say if you saw men acting like women do, smoking all day long, powdering, rouging their lips, drinking whisky?

MRS. SMITH. It's nothing to me! But if you're only saying that to annoy me . . . I don't care for that kind of joking, you know that very well!

(*She hurls the socks across the stage and shows her teeth.*[1] *She gets up.*)

MR. SMITH (*also getting up and going toward his wife, tenderly*). Oh, my little ducky daddles, what a little spitfire you are! You know that I only said it as a joke! (*He takes her by the waist and kisses her.*) What a ridiculous pair of old lovers we are! Come, let's put out the lights and go bye-byes.

MARY (*entering*). I'm the maid. I have spent a very pleasant afternoon. I've been to the cinema with a man and I've seen a film with some women. After the cinema, we went to drink some brandy and milk and then read the newspaper.

MRS. SMITH. I hope that you've spent a pleasant afternoon, that you went to the cinema with a man and that you drank some brandy and milk.

[1] In Nicolas Bataille's production, Mrs. Smith did not show her teeth, nor did she throw the socks very far.

MR. SMITH. And the newspaper.

MARY. Mr. and Mrs. Martin, your guests, are at the door. They were waiting for me. They didn't dare come in by themselves. They were supposed to have dinner with you this evening.

MRS. SMITH. Oh, yes. We were expecting them. And we were hungry. Since they didn't put in an appearance, we were going to start dinner without them. We've had nothing to eat all day. You should not have gone out!

MARY. But it was you who gave me permission.

MR. SMITH. We didn't do it on purpose.

MARY (*bursts into laughter, then she bursts into tears; then she smiles*). I bought me a chamber pot.

MRS. SMITH. My dear Mary, please open the door and ask Mr. and Mrs. Martin to step in. We will change quickly.

(MR. *and* MRS. SMITH *exit right.* MARY *opens the door at the left by which* MR. *and* MRS. MARTIN *enter.*)

MARY. Why have you come so late! You are not very polite. People should be punctual. Do you understand? But sit down there, anyway, and wait now that you're here. (*She exits.*)

(MR. *and* MRS. MARTIN *sit facing each other, without speaking. They smile timidly at each other. The dialogue which follows must be spoken in voices that are drawling, monotonous, a little singsong, without nuances.*[2]

MR. MARTIN. Excuse me, madam, but it seems to me, unless I'm mistaken, that I've met you somewhere before.

MRS. MARTIN. I, too, sir. It seems to me that I've met you somewhere before.

MR. MARTIN. Was it, by any chance, at Manchester that I caught a glimpse of you, madam?

MRS. MARTIN. That is very possible. I am originally from the city of Manchester. But I do not have a good memory, sir. I cannot say whether it was there that I caught a glimpse of you or not!

MR. MARTIN. Good God, that's curious! I, too, am originally from the city of Manchester, madam!

MRS. MARTIN. That is curious!

MR. MARTIN. Isn't that curious! Only, I,

madam, I left the city of Manchester about five weeks ago.

MRS. MARTIN. That is curious! What a bizarre coincidence! I, too, sir, I left the city of Manchester about five weeks ago.

MR. MARTIN. N   . I took the 8:30 morning train w..   es in London at 4:45.

MRS. MARTIN.   at is curious! How very bizarre! And what a coincidence! I took the same train, sir, I too.

MR. MARTIN. Good Lord, how curious! Perhaps then, madam, it was on the train that I saw you?

MRS. MARTIN. It is indeed possible; that is, not unlikely. It is plausible and, after all, why not!—But I don't recall it, sir!

MR. MARTIN. I traveled second class, madam. There is no second class in England, but I always travel second class.

MRS. MARTIN. That is curious! How very bizarre! And what a coincidence! I, too, sir, I traveled second class.

MR. MARTIN. How curious that is! Perhaps we did meet in second class, my dear lady!

MRS. MARTIN. That is certainly possible, and it is not at all unlikely. But I do not remember very well, my dear sir!

MR. MARTIN. My seat was in coach No. 8, compartment 6, my dear lady.

MRS. MARTIN. How curious that is! My seat was also in coach No. 8, compartment 6, my dear sir!

MR. MARTIN. How curious that is and what a bizarre coincidence! Perhaps we met in compartment 6, my dear lady?

MRS. MARTIN. It is indeed possible, after all! But I do not recall it, my dear sir!

MR. MARTIN. To tell the truth, my dear lady, I do not remember it either, but it is possible that we caught a glimpse of each other there, and as I think of it, it seems to me even very likely.

MRS. MARTIN. Oh! truly, of course, truly, sir!

MR. MARTIN. How curious it is! I had seat No. 3, next to the window, my dear lady.

MRS. MARTIN. Oh, good Lord, how curious and bizarre! I had seat No. 6, next to the window, across from you, my dear sir.

MR. MARTIN. Good God, how curious that is and what a coincidence! We were then seated facing each other, my dear lady! It is there that we must have seen each other!

MRS. MARTIN. How curious it is! It is possible, but I do not recall it, sir!

MR. MARTIN. To tell the truth, my dear lady, I do not recall it either. However, it is very possible that we saw each other on that occasion.

MRS. MARTIN. It is true, but I am not at all sure of it, sir.

MR. MARTIN. Dear madam, were you not the lady who asked me to place her suitcase in the luggage rack and who thanked me and gave me permission to smoke?

MRS. MARTIN. But of course, that must have been I, sir. How curious it is, how curious it is, and what a coincidence!

MR. MARTIN. How curious it is, how bizarre, what a coincidence! And well, well, it was perhaps at that moment that we came to know each other, madam?

MRS. MARTIN. How curious it is and what a coincidence! It is indeed possible, my dear sir! However, I do not believe that I recall it.

MR. MARTIN. Nor do I, madam.

(*A moment of silence. The clock strikes twice, then once.*)

MR. MARTIN. Since coming to London, I have resided in Bromfield Street, my dear lady.

MRS. MARTIN. How curious that is, how bizarre! I, too, since coming to London, I have resided in Bromfield Street, my dear sir.

MR. MARTIN. How curious that is, well then, well then, perhaps we have seen each other in Bromfield Street, my dear lady.

MRS. MARTIN. How curious that is, how bizarre! It is indeed possible, after all! But I do not recall it, my dear sir.

MR. MARTIN. I reside at No. 19, my dear lady.

MRS. MARTIN. How curious that is. I also reside at No. 19, my dear sir.

MR. MARTIN. Well then, well then, well then, well then, perhaps we have seen each other in that house, dear lady?

MRS. MARTIN. It is indeed possible but I do not recall it, dear sir.

MR. MARTIN. My flat is on the fifth floor, No. 8, my dear lady.

MRS. MARTIN. How curious it is, good Lord, how bizarre! And what a coinci-

dence! I too reside on the fifth floor, in flat No. 8, dear sir!

MR. MARTIN (*musing*). How curious it is, how curious it is, how curious it is, and what a coincidence! You know, in my bedroom there is a bed, and it is covered with a green eiderdown. This room, with the bed and the green eiderdown, is at the end of the corridor between the w.c. and the bookcase, dear lady!

MRS. MARTIN. What a coincidence, good Lord, what a coincidence! My bedroom, too, has a bed with a green eiderdown and is at the end of the corridor, between the w.c., dear sir, and the bookcase!

MR. MARTIN. How bizarre, curious, strange! Then, madam, we live in the same room and we sleep in the same bed, dear lady. It is perhaps there that we have met!

MRS. MARTIN. How curious it is and what a coincidence! It is indeed possible that we have met there, and perhaps even last night. But I do not recall it, dear sir!

MR. MARTIN. I have a little girl, my little daughter, she lives with me, dear lady. She is two years old, she's blonde, she has a white eye and a red eye, she is very pretty, her name is Alice, dear lady.

MRS. MARTIN. What a bizarre coincidence! I, too, have a little girl. She is two years old, has a white eye and a red eye, she is very pretty, and her name is Alice, too, dear sir!

MR. MARTIN (*in the same drawling, monotonous voice*). How curious it is and what a coincidence! And bizarre! Perhaps they are the same, dear lady!

MRS. MARTIN. How curious it is! It is indeed possible, dear sir.

(*A rather long moment of silence. The clock strikes twenty-nine times.* MR. MARTIN, *after having reflected at length, gets up slowly and, unhurriedly, moves toward* MRS. MARTIN, *who, surprised by his solemn air, has also gotten up very quietly.*)

MR. MARTIN (*in the same flat, monotonous voice, slightly sing-song*). Then, dear lady, I believe that there can be no doubt about it, we have seen each other before and you are my own wife . . . Elizabeth, I have found you again!

(MRS. MARTIN *approaches* MR. MARTIN *without haste. They embrace without expression. The clock strikes once, very loud. This striking of the clock must be so loud that it makes the audience jump. The* MARTINS *do not hear it.*)

MRS. MARTIN. Donald, it's you, darling!

(*They sit together in the same armchair, their arms around each other, and fall asleep. The clock strikes several more times.* MARY, *on tiptoe, a finger to her lips, enters quietly and addresses the audience.*)

MARY. Elizabeth and Donald are now too happy to be able to hear me. I can therefore let you in on a secret. Elizabeth is not Elizabeth, Donald is not Donald. And here is the proof: the child that Donald spoke of is not Elizabeth's daughter, they are not the same person. Donald's daughter has one white eye and one red eye like Elizabeth's daughter. Whereas Donald's child has a white right eye and a red left eye, Elizabeth's child has a red right eye and a white left eye! Thus all of Donald's system of deduction collapses when it comes up against this last obstacle which destroys his whole theory. In spite of the extraordinary coincidences which seem to be definitive proofs, Donald and Elizabeth, not being the parents of the same child, are not Donald and Elizabeth. It is in vain that he thinks he is Donald, it is in vain that she thinks she is Elizabeth. He believes in vain that she is Elizabeth. She believes in vain that he is Donald—they are sadly deceived. But who is the true Donald? Who is the true Elizabeth? Who has any interest in prolonging this confusion? I don't know. Let's not try to know. Let's leave things as they are. (*She takes several steps toward the door, then returns. To the audience*) My real name is Sherlock Holmes. (*She exits.*)

(*The clock strikes as much as it likes. After several seconds,* MR. *and* MRS. MARTIN *separate and take the chairs they had at the beginning.*)

MR. MARTIN. Darling, let's forget all that has not passed between us and, now that we have found each other again, let's try not to lose each other any more, and live as before.

MRS. MARTIN. Yes, darling.

(MR. *and* MRS. SMITH *enter from the right, wearing the same clothes.*)

MRS. SMITH. Good evening, dear friends! Please forgive us for having made you wait so long. We thought that we should extend you the courtesy to which you are entitled and as soon as we learned that you had been kind enough to give us the pleasure of coming to see us without prior notice we hurried to dress for the occasion.

MR. SMITH (*furious*). We've had nothing to eat all day. And we've been waiting four whole hours for you. Why have you come so late?

(MR. *and* MRS. SMITH *sit facing their guests. The striking of the clock underlines the speeches, more or less strongly, according to the case. The* MARTINS, *particularly* MRS. MARTIN, *seem embarrassed and timid. For this reason the conversation begins with difficulty and the words are uttered, at the beginning, awkwardly. A long embarrassed silence at first, then other silences and hesitations follow.*)

MR. SMITH. Hm. (*Silence.*)

MRS. SMITH. Hm, hm. (*Silence.*)

MRS. MARTIN. Hm, hm, hm. (*Silence.*)

MR. MARTIN. Hm, hm, hm, hm. (*Silence.*)

MRS. MARTIN. Oh, but definitely. (*Silence.*)

MR. MARTIN. We all have colds. (*Silence.*)

MR. SMITH. Nevertheless, it's not chilly. (*Silence.*)

MRS. SMITH. There's no draft. (*Silence.*)

MR. MARTIN. Oh no, fortunately. (*Silence.*)

MR. SMITH. Oh dear, oh dear, oh dear. (*Silence.*)

MR. MARTIN. Don't you feel well? (*Silence.*)

MRS. SMITH. No, he's wet his pants. (*Silence.*)

MRS. MARTIN. Oh, sir, at your age, you shouldn't. (*Silence.*)

MR. SMITH. The heart is ageless. (*Silence.*)

MR. MARTIN. That's true. (*Silence.*)

MRS. SMITH. So they say. (*Silence.*)

MRS. MARTIN. They also say the opposite. (*Silence.*)

MR. SMITH. The truth lies somewhere between the two. (*Silence.*)

MR. MARTIN. That's true. (*Silence.*)

MRS. SMITH (*to the* MARTINS). Since you travel so much, you must have many interesting things to tell us.

MR. MARTIN (*to his wife*). My dear, tell us what you've seen today.

MRS. MARTIN. It's scarcely worth the trouble, for no one would believe me.

MR. SMITH. We're not going to question your sincerity!

MRS. SMITH. You will offend us if you think that.

MR. MARTIN (*to his wife*). You will offend them, my dear, if you think that . . .

MRS. MARTIN (*graciously*). Oh well, today I witnessed something extraordinary. Something really incredible.

MR. MARTIN. Tell us quickly, my dear.

MR. SMITH. Oh, this is going to be amusing.

MRS. SMITH. At last.

MRS. MARTIN. Well, today, when I went shopping to buy some vegetables, which are getting to be dearer and dearer . . .

MRS. SMITH. Where is it all going to end!

MR. SMITH. You shouldn't interrupt, my dear, it's very rude.

MRS. MARTIN. In the street, near a café, I saw a man, properly dressed, about fifty years old, or not even that, who . . .

MR. SMITH. Who, what?

MRS. SMITH. Who, what?

MR. SMITH (*to his wife*). Don't interrupt, my dear, you're disgusting.

MRS. SMITH. My dear, it is you who interrupted first, you boor.

MR. SMITH (*to his wife*). Hush. (*To* MRS. MARTIN) What was this man doing?

MRS. MARTIN. Well, I'm sure you'll say that I'm making it up—he was down on one knee and he was bent over.

MR. MARTIN, MR. SMITH, MRS. SMITH. Oh!

MRS. MARTIN. Yes, bent over.

MR. SMITH. Not possible.

MRS. MARTIN. Yes, bent over. I went near him to see what he was doing . . .

MR. SMITH. And?

MRS. MARTIN. He was tying his shoe lace which had come undone.

MR. MARTIN, MR. SMITH, MRS. SMITH. Fantastic!

MR. SMITH. If someone else had told me this, I'd not believe it.

MR. MARTIN. Why not? One sees things even more extraordinary every day, when one walks around. For instance, today in the Underground I myself saw a man, quietly sitting on a seat, reading his newspaper.

MRS. SMITH. What a character!

MR. SMITH. Perhaps it was the same man!

(*The doorbell rings.*)

MR. SMITH. Goodness, someone is ringing.

MRS. SMITH. There must be somebody there. I'll go and see. (*She goes to see, she opens the door and closes it, and comes back.*) Nobody. (*She sits down again.*)

MR. MARTIN. I'm going to give you another example . . .

(*Doorbell rings again.*)

MR. SMITH. Goodness, someone is ringing.

MRS. SMITH. There must be somebody there. I'll go and see. (*She goes to see, opens the door, and comes back.*) No one. (*She sits down again.*)

MR. MARTIN (*who has forgotten where he was*). Uh . . .

MRS. MARTIN. You were saying that you were going to give us another example.

MR. MARTIN. Oh, yes . . .

(*Doorbell rings again.*)

MR. SMITH. Goodness, someone is ringing.

MRS. SMITH. I'm not going to open the door again.

MR. SMITH. Yes, but there must be someone there!

MRS. SMITH. The first time there was no one. The second time, no one. Why do you think that there is someone there now?

MR. SMITH. Because someone has rung!

MRS. MARTIN. That's no reason.

MR. MARTIN. What? When one hears the doorbell ring, that means someone is at the door ringing to have the door opened.

MRS. MARTIN. Not always. You've just seen otherwise!

MR. MARTIN. In most cases, yes.

MR. SMITH. As for me, when I go to visit someone, I ring in order to be admitted. I think that everyone does the same thing and that each time there is a ring there must be someone there.

MRS. SMITH. That is true in theory. But in reality things happen differently. You have just seen otherwise.

MRS. MARTIN. Your wife is right.

MR. MARTIN. Oh! You women! You always stand up for each other.

MRS. SMITH. Well, I'll go and see. You can't say that I am obstinate, but you will see that there's no one there (*She goes to look, opens the door and closes it.*) You see, there's no one there. (*She returns to her seat.*)

MRS. MARTIN. Oh, these men who always think they're right and who're always wrong!

(*The doorbell rings again.*)

MR. SMITH. Goodness, someone is ringing. There must be someone there.

MRS. SMITH (*in a fit of anger*). Don't send me to open the door again. You've seen that it was useless. Experience teaches us that when one hears the doorbell ring it is because there is never anyone there.

MRS. MARTIN. Never.

MR. MARTIN. That's not entirely accurate.

MR. SMITH. In fact it's false. When one hears the doorbell ring it is because there is someone there.

MRS. SMITH. He won't admit he's wrong.

MRS. MARTIN. My husband is very obstinate, too.

MR. SMITH. There's someone there.

MR. MARTIN. That's not impossible.

MRS. SMITH (*to her husband*). No.

MR. SMITH. Yes.

MRS. SMITH. I tell you *no*. In any case you are not going to disturb me again for nothing. If you wish to know, go and look yourself!

MR. SMITH. I'll go.

(MRS. SMITH *shrugs her shoulders.* MRS. MARTIN *tosses her head.*)

MR. SMITH (*opening the door*). Oh! how do you do? (*He glances at* MRS. SMITH *and the* MARTINS, *who are all surprise.*) It's the Fire Chief!

FIRE CHIEF (*he is of course in uniform and is wearing an enormous shining helmet*). Good evening, ladies and gentlemen. (*The* SMITHS *and the* MARTINS *are still slightly astonished.* MRS. SMITH *turns her head away, in a temper, and does not reply to his greeting.*) Good evening, Mrs. Smith. You appear to be angry.

MRS. SMITH. Oh!

MR. SMITH. You see it's because my wife is a little chagrined at having been proved wrong.

MR. MARTIN. There's been an argument between Mr. and Mrs. Smith, Mr. Fire Chief.

MRS. SMITH (*to* MR. MARTIN). This is no business of yours! (*To* MR. SMITH) I beg you not to involve outsiders in our family arguments.

MR. SMITH. Oh, my dear, this is not so serious. The Fire Chief is an old friend of the family. His mother courted me, and I knew his father. He asked me to give him my daughter in marriage if ever I had one. And he died waiting.

MR. MARTIN. That's neither his fault, nor yours.

FIRE CHIEF. Well, what is it all about?

MRS. SMITH. My husband was claiming . . .

MR. SMITH. No, it was you who was claiming.

MR. MARTIN. Yes, it was she.

MRS. MARTIN. No, it was he.

FIRE CHIEF. Don't get excited. You tell me, Mrs. Smith.

MRS. SMITH. Well, this is how it was. It is difficult for me to speak openly to you, but a fireman is also a confessor.

FIRE CHIEF. Well then?

MRS. SMITH. We were arguing because my husband said that each time the doorbell rings there is always someone there.

MR. MARTIN. It is plausible.

MRS. SMITH. And I was saying that each time the doorbell rings there is never anyone there.

MRS. MARTIN. It might seem strange.

MRS. SMITH. But it has been proved, not by theoretical demonstrations, but by facts.

MR. SMITH. That's false, since the Fire Chief is here. He rang the bell, I opened the door, and there he was.

MRS. MARTIN. When?

MR. MARTIN. But just now.

MRS. SMITH. Yes, but it was only when you heard the doorbell ring the fourth time that there was someone there. And the fourth time does not count.

MRS. MARTIN. Never. It is only the first three times that count.

MR. SMITH. Mr. Fire Chief, permit me in my turn to ask you several questions.

FIRE CHIEF. Go right ahead.

MR. SMITH. When I opened the door

and saw you, it was really you who had rung the bell?

FIRE CHIEF. Yes, it was I.

MR. MARTIN. You were at the door? And you rang in order to be admitted?

FIRE CHIEF. I do not deny it.

MR. SMITH (*to his wife, triumphantly*). You see? I was right. When you hear the doorbell ring, that means someone rang it. You certainly cannot say that the Fire Chief is not someone.

MRS. SMITH. Certainly not. I repeat to you that I was speaking of only the first three times, since the fourth time does not count.

MRS. MARTIN. And when the doorbell rang the first time, was it you?

FIRE CHIEF. No, it was not I.

MR. MARTIN. You see? The doorbell rang and there was no one there.

MR. MARTIN. Perhaps it was someone else?

MR. SMITH. Were you standing at the door for a long time?

FIRE CHIEF. Three-quarters of an hour.

MR. SMITH. And you saw no one?

FIRE CHIEF. No one. I am sure of that.

MRS. MARTIN. And did you hear the bell when it rang the second time?

FIRE CHIEF. Yes, and that wasn't I either. And there was still no one there.

MRS. SMITH. Victory! I was right.

MR. SMITH (*to his wife*). Not so fast. (*To the* FIRE CHIEF) And what were you doing at the door?

FIRE CHIEF. Nothing. I was just standing there. I was thinking of many things.

MR. MARTIN (*to the* FIRE CHIEF). But the third time—it was not you who rang?

FIRE CHIEF. Yes, it was I.

MR. SMITH. But when the door was opened nobody was in sight.

FIRE CHIEF. That was because I had hidden myself—as a joke.

MRS. SMITH. Don't make jokes, Mr. Fire Chief. This business is too sad.

MR. MARTIN. In short, we still do not know whether, when the doorbell rings, there is someone there or not!

MRS. SMITH. Never anyone.

MR. SMITH. Always someone.

FIRE CHIEF. I am going to reconcile you. You both are partly right. When the doorbell rings, sometimes there is someone, other times there is no one.

MR. MARTIN. This seems logical to me.

MRS. MARTIN. I think so too.

FIRE CHIEF. Life is very simple, really. (*To the* SMITHS) Go on and kiss each other.

MRS. SMITH. We just kissed each other a little while ago.

MR. MARTIN. They'll kiss each other tomorrow. They have plenty of time.

MRS. SMITH. Mr. Fire Chief, since you have helped us settle this, please make yourself comfortable, take off your helmet and sit down for a moment.

FIRE CHIEF. Excuse me, but I can't stay long. I should like to remove my helmet, but I haven't time to sit down. (*He sits down, without removing his helmet.*) I must admit that I have come to see you for another reason. I am on official business.

MRS. SMITH. And what can we do for you, Mr. Fire Chief?

FIRE CHIEF. I must beg you to excuse my indiscretion (*terribly embarrassed*) . . . uhm (*pointing a finger at the* MARTINS) . . . you don't mind . . . in front of them . . .

MRS. MARTIN. Say whatever you like.

MR. MARTIN. We're old friends. They tell us everything.

MR. SMITH. Speak.

FIRE CHIEF. Eh, well—is there a fire here?

MRS. SMITH. Why do you ask us that?

FIRE CHIEF. It's because—pardon me—I have orders to extinguish all the fires in the city.

MRS. MARTIN. All?

FIRE CHIEF. Yes, all.

MRS. SMITH (*confused*). I don't know . . . I don't think so. Do you want me to go and look?

MR. SMITH (*sniffing*). There can't be one here. There's no smell of anything burning.[3]

FIRE CHIEF (*aggrieved*). None at all? You don't have a little fire in the chimney, something burning in the attic or in the cellar? A little fire just starting, at least?

MRS. SMITH. I am sorry to disappoint you but I do not believe there's anything here at the moment. I promise that I will notify you when we do have something.

FIRE CHIEF. Please don't forget, it would be a great help.

MRS. SMITH. That's a promise.

[3] In Nicolas Bataille's production Mr. and Mrs. Martin sniffed too.

FIRE CHIEF (*to the* MARTINS). And there's nothing burning at your house either?

MRS. MARTIN. No, unfortunately.

MRS. MARTIN (*to the* FIRE CHIEF). Things aren't going so well just now?

FIRE CHIEF. Very poorly. There's been almost nothing, a few trifles—a chimney, a barn. Nothing important. It doesn't bring in much. And since there are no returns, the profits on output are very meager.

MR. SMITH. Times are bad. That's true all over. It's the same this year with business and agriculture as it is with fires, nothing is prospering.

MR. MARTIN. No wheat, no fires.

FIRE CHIEF. No floods either.

MRS. SMITH. But there is some sugar.

MR. SMITH. That's because it is imported.

MRS. MARTIN. It's harder in the case of fires. The tariffs are too high!

FIRE CHIEF. All the same, there's an occasional asphyxiation by gas, but that's unusual too. For instance, a young woman asphyxiated herself last week—she had left the gas on.

MRS. MARTIN. Had she forgotten it?

FIRE CHIEF. No, but she thought it was her comb.

MR. SMITH. These confusions are always dangerous!

MRS. SMITH. Did you go to see the match dealer?

FIRE CHIEF. There's nothing doing there. He is insured against fires.

MR. MARTIN. Why don't you go see the Vicar of Wakefield, and use my name?

FIRE CHIEF. I don't have the right to extinguish clergymen's fires. The Bishop would get angry. Besides they extinguish their fires themselves, or else they have them put out by vestal virgins.

MR. SMITH. Go see the Durands.

FIRE CHIEF. I can't do that either. He's not English. He's only been naturalized. And naturalized citizens have the right to have houses, but not the right to have them put out if they're burning.

MRS. SMITH. Nevertheless, when they set fire to it last year, it was put out just the same.

FIRE CHIEF. He did that all by himself. Clandestinely. But it's not I who would report him.

MR. SMITH. Neither would I.

MRS. SMITH. Mr. Fire Chief, since you are not too pressed, stay a little while longer. You would be doing us a favor.

FIRE CHIEF. Shall I tell you some stories?

MRS. SMITH. Oh, by all means, how charming of you. (*She kisses him.*)

MR. SMITH, MRS. MARTIN, MR. MARTIN. Yes, yes, some stories, hurrah!

(*They applaud.*)

MR. SMITH. And what is even more interesting is the fact that firemen's stories are all true, and they're based on experience.

FIRE CHIEF. I speak from my own experience. Truth, nothing but the truth. No fiction.

MR. MARTIN. That's right. Truth is never found in books, only in life.

MRS. SMITH. Begin!

MR. MARTIN. Begin!

MRS. MARTIN. Be quiet, he is beginning.

FIRE CHIEF (*coughs slightly several times*). Excuse me, don't look at me that way. You embarrass me. You know that I am shy.

MRS. SMITH. Isn't he charming! (*She kisses him.*)

FIRE CHIEF. I'm going to try to begin anyhow. But promise me that you won't listen.

MRS. MARTIN. But if we don't listen to you we won't hear you.

FIRE CHIEF. I didn't think of that!

MRS. SMITH. I told you, he's just a boy.

MR. MARTIN, MR. SMITH. Oh, the sweet child!

(*They kiss him.*[4])

MRS. MARTIN. Chin up!

FIRE CHIEF. Well, then! (*He coughs again in a voice shaken by emotion.*) "The Dog and the Cow," an experimental fable. Once upon a time another cow asked another dog: "Why have you not swallowed your trunk?" "Pardon me," replied the dog, "it is because I thought that I was an elephant."

MRS. MARTIN. What is the moral?

FIRE CHIEF. That's for you to find out.

MR. SMITH. He's right.

MRS. SMITH (*furious*). Tell us another.

FIRE CHIEF. A young calf had eaten too much ground glass. As a result, it was obliged to give birth. It brought forth a

---

[4] In Nicolas Bataille's production, they did not kiss the Fire Chief.

cow into the world. However, since the calf was male, the cow could not call him Mamma. Nor could she call him Papa, because the calf was too little. The calf was then obliged to get married and the registry office carried out all the details completely à la mode.

MR. SMITH. A la mode de Caen.

MR. MARTIN. Like tripes.

FIRE CHIEF. You've heard that one?

MRS. SMITH. It was in all the papers.

MRS. MARTIN. It happened not far from our house.

FIRE CHIEF. I'll tell you another: "The Cock." Once upon a time, a cock wished to play the dog. But he had no luck because everyone recognized him right away.

MRS. SMITH. On the other hand, the dog that wished to play the cock was never recognized.

MR. SMITH. I'll tell you one: "The Snake and the Fox." Once upon a time, a snake came up to a fox and said: "It seems to me that I know you!" The fox replied to him: "Me too." "Then," said the snake, "give me some money." "A fox doesn't give money," replied the tricky animal, who, in order to escape, jumped down into a deep ravine full of strawberries and chicken honey. But the snake was there waiting for him with a Mephistophelean laugh. The fox pulled out his knife, shouting: "I'm going to teach you how to live!" Then he took to flight, turning his back. But he had no luck. The snake was quicker. With a well-chosen blow of his fist, he struck the fox in the middle of his forehead, which broke into a thousand pieces, while he cried: "No! No! Four times no! I'm not your daughter."[5]

MRS. MARTIN. It's interesting.

MRS. SMITH. It's not bad.

MR. MARTIN (shaking MR. SMITH'S hand). My congratulations.

FIRE CHIEF (jealous). Not so good. And anyway, I've heard it before.

MR. SMITH. It's terrible.

MRS. SMITH. But it wasn't even true.

MRS. MARTIN. Yes, unfortunately.

MR. MARTIN (to MRS. SMITH). It's your turn, dear lady.

MRS. SMITH. I only know one. I'm going to tell it to you. It's called "The Bouquet."

MR. SMITH. My wife has always been romantic.

MR. MARTIN. She's a true Englishwoman.[6]

MRS. SMITH. Here it is: Once upon a time, a fiancé gave a bouquet of flowers to his fiancée, who said, "Thanks"; but before she had said "Thanks," he without saying a single word, took back the flowers he had given her in order to teach her a good lesson, and he said, "I take them back." He said, "Goodbye," and took them back and went off in all directions.

MR. MARTIN. Oh, charming! (He either kisses or does not kiss MRS. SMITH.)

MRS. MARTIN. You have a wife, Mr. Smith, of whom all the world is jealous.

MR. SMITH. It's true. My wife is intelligence personified. She's even more intelligent than I. In any case, she is much more feminine, everyone says so.

MRS. SMITH (to the FIRE CHIEF). Let's have another, Mr. Fire Chief.

FIRE CHIEF. Oh, no, it's too late.

MR. MARTIN. Tell us one, anyway.

FIRE CHIEF. I'm too tired.

MR. SMITH. Please do us a favor.

MR. MARTIN. I beg you.

FIRE CHIEF. No.

MRS. MARTIN. You have a heart of ice. We're sitting on hot coals.

MRS. SMITH (falls on her knees sobbing, or else she does not do this). I implore you!

FIRE CHIEF. Righto.

MR. SMITH (in MRS. MARTIN'S ear). He agrees! He's going to bore us again.

MRS. MARTIN. Shh.

MRS. SMITH. No luck. I was too polite.

FIRE CHIEF. "The Headcold." My brother-in-law had, on the paternal side, a first cousin whose maternal uncle had a father-in-law whose paternal grandfather had married as his second wife a young native whose brother he had met on one of his travels, a girl of whom he was enamored and by whom he had a son who married an intrepid lady pharmacist who was none other than the niece of an unknown fourth-class petty officer of the Royal Navy and whose adopted father

[5] This story was deleted in Nicolas Bataille's production. Mr. Smith went through the gestures only, without making a sound.

[6] These two speeches were repeated three times in the original production.

had an aunt who spoke Spanish fluently and who was, perhaps, one of the grand-daughters of an engineer who died young, himself the grandson of the owner of a vineyard which produced mediocre wine, but who had a second cousin, a stay-at-home, a sergeant-major, whose son had married a very pretty young woman, a divorcée, whose first husband was the son of a loyal patriot who, in the hope of making his fortune, had managed to bring up one of his daughters so that she could marry a footman who had known Rothschild, and whose brother, after having changed his trade several times, married and had a daughter whose stunted great-grandfather wore spectacles which had been given him by a cousin of his, the brother-in-law of a man from Portugal, natural son of a miller, not too badly off, whose foster-brother had married the daughter of a former country doctor, who was himself a foster-brother of the son of a forester, himself the natural son of another country doctor, married three times in a row, whose third wife . . .

MR. MARTIN. I knew that third wife, if I'm not mistaken. She ate chicken sitting on a hornet's nest.

FIRE CHIEF. It's not the same one.

MRS. SMITH. Shh!

FIRE CHIEF. As I was saying . . . whose third wife was the daughter of the best midwife in the region and who, early left a widow . . .

MR. SMITH. Like my wife.

FIRE CHIEF. . . . Had married a glazier who was full of life and who had had, by the daughter of a station master, a child who had burned his bridges . . .

MRS. SMITH. His britches?

MR. MARTIN. No, his bridge game.

FIRE CHIEF. And had married an oyster woman, whose father had a brother, mayor of a small town, who had taken as his wife a blonde schoolteacher, whose cousin, a fly fisherman . . .

MR. MARTIN. A fly by night?

FIRE CHIEF. . . . Had married another blonde schoolteacher, named Marie, too, whose brother was married to another Marie, also a blonde schoolteacher . . .

MR. SMITH. Since she's blonde, she must be Marie.

FIRE CHIEF. . . . And whose father had been reared in Canada by an old woman who was the niece of a priest whose grandmother, occasionally in the winter, like everyone else, caught a cold.

MRS. SMITH. A curious story. Almost unbelievable.

MR. MARTIN. If you catch a cold, you should get yourself a colt.

MR. SMITH. It's a useless precaution, but absolutely necessary.

MRS. MARTIN. Excuse me, Mr. Fire Chief, but I did not follow your story very well. At the end, when we got to the grandmother of the priest, I got mixed up.

MR. SMITH. One always gets mixed up in the hands of a priest.

MRS. SMITH. Oh yes, Mr. Fire Chief, begin again. Everyone wants to hear.

FIRE CHIEF. Ah, I don't know whether I'll be able to. I'm on official business. It depends on what time it is.

MRS. SMITH. We don't have the time, here.

FIRE CHIEF. But the clock?

MR. SMITH. It runs badly. It is contradictory, and always indicates the opposite of what the hour really is.

(*Enter* MARY.)

MARY. Madam . . . sir . . .

MRS. SMITH. What do you want?

MR. SMITH. What have you come in here for?

MARY. I hope madam and sir will excuse me . . . and these ladies and gentlemen too . . . I would like . . . to tell you a story, myself.

MRS. MARTIN. What is she saying?

MR. MARTIN. I believe that our friends' maid is going crazy . . . she wants to tell us a story, too.

FIRE CHIEF. Who does she think she is? (*He looks at her.*) Oh!

MRS. SMITH. Why are you butting in?

MR. SMITH. This is really uncalled for, Mary . . .

FIRE CHIEF. Oh! But it is she! Incredible!

MR. SMITH. And you?

MARY. Incredible! Here!

MRS. SMITH. What does all this mean?

MR. SMITH. You know each other?

FIRE CHIEF. And how!

(MARY *throws herself on the neck of the* FIRE CHIEF.)

MARY. I'm so glad to see you again . . . at last!

MR. AND MRS. SMITH. Oh!

MR. SMITH. This is too much, here, in our home, in the suburbs of London.

MRS. SMITH. It's not proper! . . .

FIRE CHIEF. It was she who extinguished my first fires.

MARY. I'm your little fire hose.

MR. MARTIN. If that is the case . . . dear friends . . . these emotions are understandable, human, honorable . . .

MRS. MARTIN. All that is human is honorable.

MRS. SMITH. Even so, I don't like to see it . . . here among us . . .

MR. SMITH. She's not been properly brought up . . .

FIRE CHIEF. Oh, you have too many prejudices.

MRS. MARTIN. What I think is that a maid, after all—even though it's none of my business—is never anything but a maid . . .

MR. MARTIN. Even if she can sometimes be a rather good detective.

FIRE CHIEF. Let me go.

MARY. Don't be upset! . . . They're not so bad really.

MR. SMITH. Hm . . . hm . . you two are very touching, but at the same time, a little . . . a little . . .

MR. MARTIN. Yes, that's exactly the word.

MR. SMITH. . . . A little too exhibitionistic . . .

MR. MARTIN. There is a native British modesty—forgive me for attempting, yet again, to define my thought—not understood by foreigners, even by specialists, thanks to which, if I may thus express myself . . . of course, I don't mean to refer to you . . .

MARY. I was going to tell you . . .

MR. SMITH. Don't tell us anything . . .

MARY. Oh yes!

MRS. SMITH. Go, my little Mary, go quietly to the kitchen and read your poems before the mirror . . .

MR. MARTIN. You know, even though I'm not a maid, I also read poems before the mirror.

MRS. MARTIN. This morning when you looked at yourself in the mirror you didn't see yourself.

MR. MARTIN. That's because I wasn't there yet . . .

MARY. All the same, I could, perhaps, recite a little poem for you.

MRS. SMITH. My little Mary, you are frightfully obstinate.

MARY. I'm going to recite a poem, then, is that agreed? It is a poem entitled "The Fire" in honor of the Fire Chief:

The polypoids were burning in the wood
A stone caught fire
The castle caught fire
The forest caught fire
The men caught fire
The women caught fire
The birds caught fire
The fish caught fire
The water caught fire
The sky caught fire
The ashes caught fire
The smoke caught fire
The fire caught fire
Everything caught fire
Caught fire, caught fire.

(She recites the poem while the SMITHS are pushing her off-stage.)

MRS. MARTIN. That sent chills up my spine . . .

MR. MARTIN. And yet there's a certain warmth in those lines . . .

FIRE CHIEF. I thought it was marvelous.

MRS. SMITH. All the same . . .

MR. SMITH. You're exaggerating . . .

FIRE CHIEF. Just a minute . . . I admit . . . all this is very subjective . . . but this is my conception of the world. My world. My dream. My ideal . . . And now this reminds me that I must leave. Since you don't have the time here, I must tell you that in exactly three-quarters of an hour and sixteen minutes, I'm having a fire at the other end of the city. Consequently, I must hurry. Even though it will be quite unimportant.

MRS. SMITH. What will it be? A little chimney fire?

FIRE CHIEF. Oh, not even that. A straw fire and a little heartburn.

MR. SMITH. Well, we're sorry to see you go.

MRS. SMITH. You have been very entertaining.

MRS. MARTIN. Thanks to you, we have passed a truly Cartesian quarter of an hour.

FIRE CHIEF (moving toward the door, then stopping). Speaking of that—the bald soprano?

(General silence, embarrassment.)

MRS. SMITH. She always wears her hair in the same style.

FIRE CHIEF. Ah! Then goodbye, ladies and gentlemen.

MR. MARTIN. Good luck, and a good fire!

FIRE CHIEF. Let's hope so. For everybody.

(FIRE CHIEF exits. *All accompany him to the door and then return to their seats.*)

MRS. MARTIN. I can buy a pocketknife for my brother, but you can't buy Ireland for your grandfather.

MR. SMITH. One walks on his feet, but one heats with electricity or coal.

MR. MARTIN. He who sells an ox today, will have an egg tomorrow.

MRS. SMITH. In real life, one must look out of the window.

MRS. MARTIN. One can sit down on a chair, when the chair doesn't have any.

MR. SMITH. One must always think of everything.

MR. MARTIN. The ceiling is above, the floor is below.

MRS. SMITH. When I say yes, it's only a manner of speaking.

MRS. MARTIN. To each his own.

MR. SMITH. Take a circle, caress it, and it will turn vicious.

MRS. SMITH. A schoolmaster teaches his pupils to read, but the cat suckles her young when they are small.

MRS. MARTIN. Nevertheless, it was the cow that gave us tails.

MR. SMITH. When I'm in the country, I love the solitude and the quiet.

MR. MARTIN. You are not old enough yet for that.

MRS. SMITH. Benjamin Franklin was right; you are more nervous than he.

MRS. MARTIN. What are the seven days of the week?

MR. SMITH. Monday, Tuesday, Wednesday, Thursday, Friday, Saturday, Sunday.[7]

MR. MARTIN. Edward is a clerk; his sister Nancy is a typist, and his brother William a shop-assistant.[7]

MRS. SMITH. An odd family!

MRS. MARTIN. I prefer a bird in the bush to a sparrow in a barrow.

MR. SMITH. Rather a steak in a chalet than gristle in a castle.

[7] In English in the original.—Translator's note.

MR. MARTIN. An Englishman's home is truly his castle.

MRS. SMITH. I don't know enough Spanish to make myself understood.

MRS. MARTIN. I'll give you my mother-in-law's slippers if you'll give me your husband's coffin.

MR. SMITH. I'm looking for a monophysite priest to marry to our maid.

MR. MARTIN. Bread is a staff, whereas bread is also a staff, and an oak springs from an oak every morning at dawn.

MRS. SMITH. My uncle lives in the country, but that's none of the midwife's business.

MR. MARTIN. Paper is for writing, the cat's for the rat. Cheese is for scratching.

MRS. SMITH. The car goes very fast, but the cook beats batter better.

MR. SMITH. Don't be turkeys; rather kiss the conspirator.

MR. MARTIN. Charity begins at home.[7]

MRS. SMITH. I'm waiting for the aqueduct to come and see me at my windmill.

MR. MARTIN. One can prove that social progress is definitely better with sugar.

MR. SMITH. To hell with polishing!

(*Following this last speech of* MR. SMITH, *the others are silent for a moment, stupefied. We sense that there is a certain nervous irritation. The strokes of the clock are more nervous too. The speeches which follow must be said, at first, in a glacial, hostile tone. The hostility and the nervousness increase. At the end of this scene, the four characters must be standing very close to each other, screaming their speeches, raising their fists, ready to throw themselves upon each other.*)

MR. MARTIN. One doesn't polish spectacles with black wax.

MRS. SMITH. Yes, but with money one can buy anything.

MR. MARTIN. I'd rather kill a rabbit than sing in the garden.

MR. SMITH. Cockatoos, cockatoos, cockatoos, cockatoos, cockatoos, cockatoos, cockatoos, cockatoos, cockatoos, cockatoos.

MRS. SMITH. Such caca, such caca, such caca, such caca, such caca, such caca, such caca, such caca, such caca.

MR. MARTIN. Such cascades of cacas, such cascades of cacas, such cascades of cacas, such cascades of cacas, such cascades of cacas, such cascades of cacas, such cascades of cacas, such cascades of cacas.

MR. SMITH. Dogs have fleas, dogs have fleas.

MRS. MARTIN. Cactus, coccyx! crocus! cockaded! cockroach!

MRS. SMITH. Incasker, you incask us.

MR. MARTIN. I'd rather lay an egg in a box than go and steal an ox.

MRS. MARTIN (*opening her mouth very wide*). Ah! oh! ah! oh! Let me gnash my teeth.

MR. SMITH. Crocodile.

MR. MARTIN. Let's go and slap Ulysses.

MR. SMITH. I'm going to live in my cabana among my cacao trees.

MRS. MARTIN. Cacao trees on cacao farms don't bear coconuts, they yield cocoa! Cacao trees on cacao farms don't bear coconuts, they yield cocoa! Cacao trees on cacao farms don't bear coconuts, they yield cocoa.

MRS. SMITH. Mice have lice, lice haven't mice.

MRS. MARTIN. Don't ruche my brooch!

MR. MARTIN. Don't smooch the brooch!

MR. SMITH. Groom the goose, don't goose the groom.

MRS. MARTIN. The goose grooms.

MRS. SMITH. Groom your tooth.

MR. MARTIN. Groom the bridegroom, groom the bridegroom.

MR. SMITH. Seducer seduced!

MRS. MARTIN. Scaramouche!

MRS. SMITH. Sainte-Nitouche!

MR. MARTIN. Go take a douche.

MR. SMITH. I've been goosed.

MRS. MARTIN. Sainte-Nitouche stoops to my cartouche.

MRS. SMITH. "Who'd stoop to blame? . . . and I never choose to stoop"[8]

MR. MARTIN. Robert!

MR. SMITH. Browning!

MRS. MARTIN, MR. SMITH. Rudyard.

MRS. SMITH, MR. MARTIN. Kipling.

MRS. MARTIN, MR. SMITH. Robert Kipling!

MRS. SMITH, MR. MARTIN. Rudyard Browning.

MRS. MARTIN. Silly gobblegobblers, silly gobblegobblers.

MR. MARTIN. Marietta, spot the pot!

MRS. SMITH. Krishnamurti, Krishnamurti, Krishnamurti!

MR. SMITH. The pope elopes! The pope's got no horoscope. The horoscope's bespoke.

MRS. MARTIN. Bazaar, Balzac, bazooka!

MR. MARTIN. Bizarre, beaux-arts, brassieres!

MR. SMITH. A, e, i, o, u, a, e, i, o, u, a, e, i, o, u, i!

MRS. MARTIN. B, c, d, f, g, l, m, n, p, r, s, t, v, w, x, z!

MR. MARTIN. From sage to stooge, from stage to serge!

MRS. SMITH (*imitating a train*). Choo, choo, choo, choo, choo, choo, choo, choo, choo, choo, choo!

MR. SMITH. It's!

MRS. MARTIN. Not!

MR. MARTIN. That!

MRS. SMITH. Way!

MR. SMITH. It's!

MRS. MARTIN. O!

MR. MARTIN. Ver!

MRS. SMITH. Here!

(*All together, completely infuriated, screaming in each other's ears. The light is extinguished.*)

ALL TOGETHER (*in the darkness, in increasingly rapid rhythm*). It's not that way, it's over here, it's not that way, it's over here, it's not that way, it's over here, it's not that way, it's over here![9]

(*The words cease abruptly. Again, the lights come on.* MR. *and* MRS. MARTIN *are seated like the* SMITHS *at the beginning of the play. The play begins again with the* MARTINS, *who say exactly the same lines as the* SMITHS *in the first scene, while the curtain softly falls.*)

---

8 Translator's note: in the French text these speeches read as follows:

MME SMITH. N'y touchez pas, elle est brisée.
M. MARTIN. Sully!
M. SMITH. Prudhomme!
MME MARTIN, M. SMITH. François.
MME SMITH, M. MARTIN. Coppée
MME MARTIN, M. SMITH. Coppée Sully!
MME SMITH, M. MARTIN. Prudhomme François.

9 When produced some of the speeches in this last scene were cut or shuffled. Moreover, the final beginning again, if one can call it that, still involved the Smiths, since the author did not have the inspired idea of substituting the Martins for the Smiths until after the hundredth performance.

EUGÈNE IONESCO: *The World of Ionesco*

From *International Theatre Annual* No. 2, 1957. Copyright © 1957 by International Theatre Annual. Reprinted by permission of John Calder Ltd.

THE "SOCIETY" I HAVE TRIED TO DEPICT IN *THE BALD PRIMA DONNA* is a society which is perfect, I mean where all social problems have been resolved. Unfortunately this has no effect upon life as it is lived. The play deals with a world where economic worries are a thing of the past, a universe without mystery, in which everything runs smoothly, for one section of humanity at least. I have no doubt that this is the world of tomorrow. In America, Russia, China, Africa, and so on, the march of science and industrialisation must finally arrive at stability and social contentment.

In *The Bald Prima Donna,* which is a completely unserious play where I was most concerned with solving purely theatrical problems, some people have seen a satire on bourgeois society, a criticism of life in England, and heaven knows what. In actual fact, if it is a criticism of anything, it must be of all societies, of language, of clichés—a parody of human behaviour, and therefore a parody of the theatre too. I am thinking both of the commercial theatre and the theatre of Brecht. In fact, I believe that it is precisely when we see the last of economic problems and class warfare (if I may avail myself of one of the most crashing clichés of our age) that we shall also see that this solves nothing, indeed that our problems are only beginning. We can no longer avoid asking ourselves what we are doing here on earth, and how, having no deep sense of our destiny, we can endure the crushing weight of the material world.

This is the *eternal problem* if ever there was one; for living means alienation. Other problems, even those of the Brechtian theatre, only confuse the real issue of alienation—that being Brecht's theme. When there is no more incentive to be wicked, and everyone is good, what shall we do with our goodness, or our non-wickedness, our non-greed, our ultimate neutrality? The people in *The Bald Prima Donna* have no hunger, no conscious desires; they are bored stiff. But people who are unconsciously alienated don't even know that they are bored. They feel it vaguely, hence the final explosion—which is quite useless, as the characters and situations are both static and interchangeable, and everything ends where it started.

In my play I have treated this comically, for the human drama is as absurd as it is painful. The second part of *The New Tenant* (which accompanied *The Bald Prima Donna* at the Arts Theatre, London) is perhaps less comic—or perhaps not, depending on the producer. It all comes to the same thing, anyway: comic and tragic are merely two aspects of the same situation, and I have now reached the stage when I find it hard to distinguish one from the other.

The non-metaphysical world of today has destroyed all mystery; and the so-called "scientific" theatre of the period, the theatre of politics and propaganda, anti-poetic and academic, has flattened mankind out, alienating the unfathomable third dimension which makes a whole man. The theatre of ideologies and theses, proposing political solutions and presuming to save humanity, actually saves no-one. I have no wish to save humanity—to wish to save it, is to kill it— and there are no solutions. To realise that, is the only healthy solution.

Some people have compared Brecht to Shakespeare, which seems to me pure madness. At this very moment, in France, there are several authors much more important than Brecht—I mean Ghelderode, Beckett, Jean Genet, Vauthier, and even the Sartre of "Huis-Clos"—because they question the whole state of man, and offer us clear proofs that man is more than merely a social animal; the great authors are tragic. And all great drama is unbearable; when Richard II is killed in his cell, I see the death of all kings on earth,

I witness the agonising desecration and downfall of all values and civilisations. It is beyond our control, and therefore it is true. I am myself a dying King.

There are no alternatives; if man is not tragic, he is ridiculous and painful, "comic" in fact, and by revealing his absurdity one can achieve a sort of tragedy. In fact I think that man must either be unhappy (metaphysically unhappy) or stupid.

I have often chosen to write plays about nothing, rather than about secondary problems (social, political, sexual, etc.). There is no action in *The Bald Prima Donna,* simply theatrical machinery functioning, as it were, in a void. It shows a hollow automatism being taken to pieces and put together in the wrong order, as well as automatic men speaking and behaving automatically; and to this extent it illustrates "comically" the emptiness of a world without metaphysics and a humanity without problems.

In *The Chairs* I have tried to deal more directly with the themes that obsess me; with emptiness, with frustration, with this world, at once fleeting and crushing, with despair and death. The characters I have used are not fully conscious of their spiritual rootlessness, but they feel it instinctively and emotionally. They feel "lost" in the world, something is missing which they cannot, to their grief, supply.

By "directly" I mean according to the rules of tragic construction (or comic and tragic at the same time)—but using what I might call pure theatre, which progresses not through a predetermined subject and plot, but through an increasingly intense and revealing series of emotional states.

Thus I have tried to give the play a classical form. I believe that the aim of the "avant-garde" should be to rediscover —not invent—in their purest state, the permanent forms and forgotten ideals of the theatre. We must cut through the clichés and break free of a hidebound "traditionalism"; we must rediscover the one true and living tradition. I make no claim to have succeeded in this. But others will succeed, and show that all truth and all reality is classical and eternal.

KENNETH TYNAN: *Ionesco: Man of Destiny*

From *The Observer*, June 22, 1958. Copyright 1958 by *The Observer*.
Reprinted by permission of publisher and author.

. . . EVER SINCE THE FRY-ELIOT "POETIC REVIVAL" CAVED IN ON them, the ostriches of our theatrical intelligentsia have been seeking another faith. Anything would do as long as it shook off what are known as "the fetters of realism."

Now the broad definition of a realistic play is that its characters and events have traceable roots in life. Gorki and Chekhov, Arthur Miller and Tennessee Williams, Brecht and O'Casey, Osborne and Sartre have all written such plays. They express one man's view of the world in terms of people we can all recognize. Like all hard disciplines, realism can easily be corrupted. It can sink into sentimentality . . . , half truth . . . , or mere photographic reproduction of the trivia of human behavior. Even so, those who have mastered it have created the lasting body of twentieth century drama; and I have been careful not to except Brecht, who employed stylized production techniques to set off eventually realistic characters.

That, for the ostriches, was what ruled him out of court. He was too real. Similarly, they preferred Beckett's "Endgame," in which the human element was minimal, to "Waiting for Godot," which not only contained two tramps of mephitic reality but even seemed to regard them, as human beings, with love. Veiling their disapproval, the ostriches seized on Beckett's more blatant verbal caprices and called them "authentic images of a disintegrated society." But it was only when M. Ionesco arrived that they hailed a messiah. Here at last was a self-proclaimed advocate of *anti-theatre*: explicitly anti-realist, and by implication anti-reality as well. Here was a writer ready to declare that words were meaningless and that all communication between human beings was impossible. The aged (as in "The Chairs") are wrapped in an impenetrable cocoon of hallucinatory memories; they can speak intelligibly neither to each other nor to the world. The teacher in "The Lesson" can "get through" to his pupil only by means of sexual assault, followed by murder. Words, the magic innovation of our species, are dismissed as useless and fraudulent.

Ionesco's is a world of isolated robots, conversing in cartoon-strip balloons of dialogue that are sometimes hilarious, sometimes evocative, and quite often neither, on which occasions they become profoundly tiresome. . . . This world is not mine, but I recognize it to be a valid personal vision, presented with great imaginative aplomb and verbal audacity. The peril arises when it is held up for general emulation as the gateway to the theatre of the future, that bleak new world from which the humanist heresies of faith in logic and belief in man will forever be banished.

M. Ionesco certainly offers an "escape from realism"; but an escape into what? A blind alley, perhaps, adorned with *tachiste* murals. Or a self-imposed vacuum, wherein the author ominously bids us observe the absence of air. Or, best of all, a funfair ride on a ghost train, all skulls and hooting waxworks, from which we emerge into the far more intimidating clamor of diurnal reality. M. Ionesco's theatre is pungent and exciting, but it remains a diversion. It is not on the main road; and we do him no good, nor the drama at large, to pretend that it is. . . .

EUGÈNE IONESCO: *A Reply to Kenneth Tynan: The Playwright's Role*

From *The Observer*, June 29, 1958. Copyright 1958 by *The Observer*. reprinted by permission of publisher and author.

I WAS OF COURSE HONORED BY THE ARTICLE MR. TYNAN DEVOTED to my two plays, "The Chairs" and "The Lesson," in spite of the strictures it contained, which a critic has a perfect right to make. However, since some of his objections seem to me to be based on premises that are not only false but, strictly speaking, outside the domain of the theatre, I think I have the right to make certain comments.

In effect, Mr. Tynan says that it has been claimed, and that I myself have approved or supported this claim, that I was a sort of "messiah" of the theatre. This is doubly untrue because I do not like messiahs and I certainly do not consider the vocation of the artist or the playwright to lie in that direction. I have a distinct impression that it is Mr. Tynan who is in search of messiahs. But to deliver a message to the world, to wish to direct its course, to save it, is the business of the founders of religions, of the moralists or the politicians who, incidentally, as we know only too well, make a pretty poor job of it. A playwright simply writes plays, in which he can offer only a testimony, not a didactic message, a personal, affective testimony of his anguish and the anguish of others or, which is rare, of his happiness—or he can express his feelings, comic or tragic, about life.

A work of art has nothing to do with doctrine. I have already written elsewhere that any work of art which was ideological and nothing else would be pointless, tautological, inferior to the doctrine it claimed to illustrate, which would already have been expressed in its proper language, that of discursive demonstration. An ideological play can be no more than the vulgarization of an ideology. In my view, a work of art has its own unique system of expression, its own means of directly apprehending the real.

Mr. Tynan seems to accuse me of being deliberately, explicitly, anti-realist; of having declared that words have no meaning and that all language is incommunicable. That is only partly true, for the very fact of writing and presenting plays is surely incompatible with such a view. I simply hold that it is difficult to make oneself understood, not absolutely impossible, and my play "The Chairs" is a plea, pathetic perhaps, for mutual understanding. As for the idea of reality, Mr. Tynan seems . . . to acknowledge only one plane of reality: what is called the "social" plane, which seems to me to be the most external, in other words, the most superficial. That is why I think that writers like Sartre. . . . , Osborne, Miller, Brecht, etc., are simply the new *auteurs du boulevard,* representatives of a left-wing conformism which is just as lamentable as the right-wing sort. These writers offer nothing that one does not know already, through books and political speeches.

But that is not all; it is not enough to be a social realist writer, one must also, apparently, be a militant believer in what is known as progress. The only worthwhile authors, those who are on the "main road" of the theatre, would be those who thought in a certain clearly defined way, obeying certain pre-established principles or directives. This would be to make the "main road" a very narrow one; it would considerably restrict the planes of reality (which are innumerable) and limit the field open to the investigation of artistic research and creation.

I believe that what separates us all from one another is simply society itself, or, if you like, politics. This is what raises barriers between men, this is what creates misunderstanding.

If I may be allowed to express myself paradoxically, I should say that the true society, the authentic human community, is extra-social—a wider, deeper society, that which is revealed by our common anxieties, our desires, our secret nostalgias. The whole history of the world has been governed by these nostalgias and anxieties, which political action does no more than reflect and interpret, very imperfectly. No society has been able to abolish human sadness, no political system can deliver us from the pain of living, from our fear of death, our thirst for the absolute; it is the human condition that directs the social condition, not vice versa.

This "reality" seems to me much vaster and more complex than the one to which Mr. Tynan and many others want to limit themselves. The problem is to get to the source of our malady, to find the non-conventional language of this anguish, perhaps by breaking down this "social" language which is nothing but clichés, empty formulas, and slogans. The "robot" characters Mr. Tynan disapproves of seem to me to be precisely those who belong *solely* to this or that *milieu* or social "reality," who are prisoners of it, and who—being no more than social, seeking a solution to their problems only by so-called social means—have become impoverished, alienated, empty. It is precisely the conformist, the *petit-bourgeois,* the ideologist of *every* society who is lost and dehumanized. If anything needs demystifying it is our ideologies, which offer ready-made solutions . . . in a language that congeals *as soon as it is formulated.* It is these ideologies which must be continually re-examined in the light of our anxieties and dreams, and their congealed language must be relentlessly split apart in order to find the living sap beneath.

To discover the fundamental problem common to all mankind, I must ask myself what *my* fundamental problem is, what *my* most ineradicable fear is. I am certain, then, to find the problems and fears of literally everyone. That is the true road, into my own darkness, our darkness, which I try to bring to the light of day.

It would be amusing to try an experiment, which I have no room for here but which I hope to carry out some day. I could take almost any work of art, any play, and guarantee to give it in turn a Marxist, a Buddhist, a Christian, an Existentialist, psycho-analytical interpretation and "prove" that the work subjected to each interpretation is a perfect and exclusive illustration of each creed, that it confirms this or that ideology beyond all doubt. For me this proves another thing: that every work of art (unless it is a pseudo-intellectualist work, a work already comprised in some ideology that it merely illustrates, as with Brecht) is outside ideology, is not reducible to ideology. Ideology circumscribes without penetrating it. The absence of ideology in a work does not mean an absence of ideas; on the contrary it fertilizes them. In other words, it was not Sophocles who was inspired by Freud but, obviously, the other way round. Ideology is not the source of art. A work of art is the source and the raw material of ideologies to come.

What, then, should the critic do? Where should he look for his criteria? Inside the work itself, its universe and its mythology. He must look at it, listen to it, and simply say whether it is true to its own nature. The best judgment is a careful exposition of the work itself. For that, the work must be allowed to speak, uncolored by preconceptions or prejudices.

Whether or not it is on the "main road"; whether or not it is what you would like it to be—to consider this is already to pass judgment, a judgment that is external, pointless and false. A work of art is the expression of an incommunicable reality that one tries to communicate—and which sometimes can be communicated. That is its paradox, and its truth.

KENNETH TYNAN: *Ionesco and the Phantom*

From *The Observer,* July 6, 1958. Copyright 1958 by *The Observer.*
Reprinted by permission of publisher and author.

M. IONESCO'S ARTICLE ON "THE PLAYWRIGHT'S ROLE" IS DISCUSSED elsewhere in these pages. . . . I want to add what I hope will not be a postscript, for this is a debate that should continue.

As I read the piece I felt first bewilderment, next admiration, and finally regret. Bewilderment at his assumption that I wanted drama to be forced to echo a particular political creed, when all I want is for drama to realize that it is a *part* of politics, in the sense that every human activity, even buying a packet of cigarettes, has social and political repercussions. Then admiration; no one could help admiring the sincerity and skill with which . . . M. Ionesco marshalled prose for his purposes. And ultimately, regret: regret that a man so capable of stating a positive attitude towards art should deny that there was any positive attitude worth taking towards life. Or even (which is essential) that there was an umbilical connection between the two.

The position towards which M. Ionesco is moving is that which regards art as if it were something different from and independent of everything else in the world; as if it not only did not but should not correspond to anything outside the mind of the artist. This position, as it happens, was reached some years ago by a French painter who declared that, since nothing in nature exactly resembled anything else, he proposed to burn all of his paintings which in any way resembled anything that already existed. The end of that line, of course, is Action Painting.

Mr. Ionesco has not yet gone so far. He is stuck, to pursue the analogy, in an earlier groove, the groove of cubism, which has fascinated him so much that he has begun to confuse ends and means. The Cubists employed distortion to make discoveries about the nature of objective reality. M. Ionesco, I fear, is on the brink of believing that his distortions are more valid and important than the external world it is their proper function to interpret. To adapt Johnson, I am not yet so lost in drama criticism as to forget that

plays are the daughters of the earth, and that things are the sons of heaven. But M. Ionesco is in danger of forgetting; of locking himself up in that hall of mirrors which in philosophy is known as solipsism.

Art is parasitic on life, just as criticism is parasitic on art. M. Ionesco and his followers are breaking the chain, applying the tourniquet, aspiring as writers to a condition of stasis. At their best, of course, they don't succeed; the alarming thing is that they try. As in physiology, note how quickly the brain, starved of blood, produces hallucinations and delusions of grandeur. "A work of art," says M. Ionesco, "is the source and the raw material of ideologies to come." O hubris! Art and ideology often interact on each other; but the plain fact is that they both spring from a common source. Both draw on human experience to explain mankind to itself; both attempt, in very different ways, to assemble coherence from seemingly unrelated phenomena; both stand guard for us against chaos. They are brothers, not child and parent. To say, as M. Ionesco does, that Freud was inspired by Sophocles is the direst nonsense. Freud merely found in Sophocles confirmation of a theory he had formed on a basis of empirical evidence. This does not make Sophocles a Freudian, or vice versa; it is simply a pleasing instance of fraternal corroboration.

You may wonder why M. Ionesco is so keen on this phantom notion of art as a world of its own, answerable to none but its own laws. Wonder no more: he is merely seeking to exempt himself from any kind of value judgment. His aim is to blind us to the fact that we are all in some sense critics, who bring to the theatre not only those "nostalgias and anxieties" by which, as he rightly says, world history has largely been governed, but also a whole series of new ideas—

moral, social, psychological, political—
through which we hope some day to free
ourselves from the rusty hegemony of
Angst. These fond ideas, M. Ionesco
quickly assures us, do not belong in the
theatre. Our job, as critics, is just to hear
the play and "simply say whether it is
true to its own nature." Not, you notice,
whether it is true to ours; or even relevant; for we, as an audience, have for-
feited our right to a hearing as conscious,
sentient beings. "Clear evidence of cancer here, sir." "Very well, leave it alone;
it's being true to its own nature."

Whether M. Ionesco admits it or not,
every play worth serious consideration is
a statement. It is a statement addressed
in the first person singular to the first
person plural; and the latter must retain
the right to dissent. I am rebuked in the
current *Encounter* for having disagreed
with the nihilistic philosophy expressed
in Strindberg's "Dream Play": "The important thing," says my interviewer,
"seems to me to be not the rightness of
Strindberg's belief, but rather how he has

expressed it. . . ." Strindberg expressed
it very vividly, but there are things
more important than that. If a man tells
me something I believe to be an un-
truth, am I forbidden to do more than
congratulate him on the brilliance of his
lying?

Cyril Connolly once said, once and
wanly, that it was closing time in the gardens of the West; but I deny the rest of
that suavely cadenced sentence, which as-
serts that "from now on an artist will be
judged only by the resonance of his solitude or the quality of his despair." Not
by me he won't. I shall, I hope, respond
to the honesty of such testimonies; but I
shall be looking for something more,
something harder: for evidence of the
artist who is not content with the passive
role of a symptom, but concerns himself, from time to time, with such things
as healing. M. Ionesco correctly says that
no ideology has as yet abolished fear, pain
or sadness. Nor has any work of art. But
both are in the business of trying. What
other business is there?

LIKE IONESCO, SAMUEL BECKETT CAME TO THE THEATRE

Samuel relatively late—he was forty-seven when his first play was produced. One of the most discussed of contemporary writers, Beckett is Irish by birth,
Beckett French by choice, a master of English who prefers to
1906- write in French and then translate into his native tongue, a leading figure in the "theater of the absurd." His well-to-do parents in Dublin gave him an excellent education, and he went on to distinguish himself as a student of French and Italian at Trinity College, Dublin. Upon graduation he received an appointment to teach English in Paris. While in Paris, Beckett moved in the literary circle that gathered about his compatriot James Joyce; he wrote an essay on Joyce, another on Proust, and published a long poem *Whoroscope* (1930). He then returned to Trinity College to lecture on French and to take his Master's degree, but he soon abandoned an academic career and went abroad, where for several years he wandered about Germany and France, doing odd jobs and writing short stories and poems. In 1937 he took up permanent residence in Paris, a city he found more congenial than Dublin. For years he wrote little and lived in relative obscurity. Several years after the war, however, he began writing in French, and in a burst of creativity produced a trilogy of novels (*Molloy,* 1951; *Malone Dies,* 1951; *The Unnamable,* 1953) and two major plays, *Waiting for Godot* (1952) and *Endgame* (1957). The decisive turn in Beckett's reputation came with *Waiting for Godot,* a complex tragi-comedy that defies conventional dramaturgy and expresses Beckett's dark view of man's condition. In 1956, at the invitation of the British Broadcasting Corporation, Beckett wrote—in English—a radio drama, *All That Fall,* a typical Beckett work and his most accessible play to date. Others of Beckett's plays are *Krapp's Last Tape* (1958) and *Happy Days* (1961) the radio drama *Embers* (1959), and two symbolic mimes, *Act Without Words I* and *Act Without Words II,* which carry to their logical extremes Beckett's tendencies to constrict the theatre to its ascetic essentials and to view man's lot as one of futility and impotence in a senseless world.

ALL THAT FALL, A Play for Radio

❧ BY SAMUEL BECKETT

CHARACTERS

MRS. ROONEY (MADDY), *a lady in her seventies*
CHRISTY, *a carter*
MR. TYLER, *a retired bill-broker*
MR. SLOCUM, *Clerk of the Racecourse*
TOMMY, *a porter*
MR. BARRELL, *a station-master*

MISS FITT, *a lady in her thirties*
A FEMALE VOICE
DOLLY, *a small girl*
MR. ROONEY (DAN), *husband of Mrs. Rooney, blind*
JERRY, *a small boy*

Rural sounds. Sheep, bird, cow, cock, severally, then together.
Silence.
MRS. ROONEY *advances along country road towards railway-station. Sound of her dragging feet.*
Music, faint from house by way. "Death and the Maiden." The steps slow down, stop.
MRS. ROONEY. Poor woman. All alone in that ruinous old house.
(*Music louder. Silence but for music playing.*
The steps resume. Music dies. MRS. ROONEY *murmurs melody. Her murmur dies.*
Sound of approaching cartwheels. The cart stops. The steps slow down, stop.)
MRS. ROONEY. Is that you, Christy?
CHRISTY. It is, Ma'am.
MRS. ROONEY. I thought the hinny was familiar. How is your poor wife?
CHRISTY. No better, Ma'am.
MRS. ROONEY. Your daughter then?
CHRISTY. No worse, Ma'am.
(*Silence.*)
MRS. ROONEY. Why do you halt? (*Pause.*) But why do I halt?
(*Silence.*)
CHRISTY. Nice day for the races, Ma'am.
MRS. ROONEY. No doubt it is. (*Pause.*) But will it hold up? (*Pause. With emotion.*) Will it hold up?
(*Silence.*)

CHRISTY. I suppose you wouldn't—
MRS. ROONEY. Hist! (*Pause.*) Surely to goodness that cannot be the up mail I hear already?
(*Silence. The hinny neighs. Silence.*)
CHRISTY. Damn the mail.
MRS. ROONEY. Oh thank God for that! I could have sworn I heard it, thundering up the track in the far distance. (*Pause.*) So hinnies whinny. Well, it is not surprising.
CHRISTY. I suppose you wouldn't be in need of a small load of dung?
MRS. ROONEY. Dung? What class of dung?
CHRISTY. Stydung.
MRS. ROONEY. Stydung . . . I like your frankness, Christy. (*Pause.*) I'll ask the master (*Pause.*) Christy.
CHRISTY. Yes, Ma'am.
MRS. ROONEY. Do you find anything . . . bizarre about my way of speaking? (*Pause.*) I do not mean the voice. (*Pause.*) No, I mean the words. (*Pause. More to herself.*) I use none but the simplest words, I hope, and yet I sometimes find my way of speaking very . . . bizarre. (*Pause.*) Mercy! What was that?
CHRISTY. Never mind her, Ma'am, she's very fresh in herself to-day.
(*Silence.*)
MRS. ROONEY. Dung? What would we want with dung, at our time of life? (*Pause.*) Why are you on your feet down on the road? Why do you not climb up

on the crest of your manure and let your-self be carried along? Is it that you have no head for heights?

(*Silence.*)

CHRISTY (*to the hinny*). Yep! (*Pause. Louder.*) Yep wiyya to hell owwa that!

(*Silence.*)

MRS. ROONEY. She does not move a muscle. (*Pause.*) I too should be getting along, if I do not wish to arrive late at the station. (*Pause.*) But a moment ago she neighed and pawed the ground. And now she refuses to advance. Give her a good welt on the rump. (*Sound of welt. Pause.*) Harder (*Sound of welt. Pause.*) Well! If someone were to do that for me I should not dally. (*Pause.*) How she gazes at me to be sure, with her great moist cleg-tormented eyes? Perhaps if I were to move on, down the road, out of her field of vision . . . (*Sound of welt.*) No, no, enough! Take her by the snaffle and pull her eyes away from me. Oh this is awful! (*She moves on. Sound of her dragging feet.*) What have I done to de-serve all this, what, what? (*Dragging feet.*) So long ago . . . No! No! (*Dragging feet. Quotes.*) "Sigh out a some-thing something tale of things, Done long ago and ill done." (*She halts.*) How can I go on, I cannot. Oh let me just flop down flat on the road like a big fat jelly out of a bowl and never move again! A great big slop thick with grit and dust and flies, they would have to scoop me up with a shovel. (*Pause.*) Heavens, there is that up mail again, what will become of me! (*The dragging steps resume.*) Oh I am just a hysterical old hag, I know, de-stroyed with sorrow and pining and gentility and church-going and fat and rheumatism and childlessness. (*Pause. Brokenly.*) Minnie! Little Minnie! (*Pause.*) Love, that is all I asked, a little love, daily, twice daily, fifty years of twice daily love like a Paris horse-butcher's regular, what normal woman wants affection? A peck on the jaw at morning, near the ear, and another at evening, peck, peck, till you grow whiskers on you. There is that lovely laburnum again.

(*Dragging feet. Sound of bicycle-bell. It is old* MR. TYLER *coming up behind her on his bicycle, on his way to the sta-*tion. *Squeak of brakes. He slows down and rides abreast of her.*)

MR. TYLER. Mrs. Rooney! Pardon me if I do not doff my cap, I'd fall off. Di-vine day for the meeting.

MRS. ROONEY. Oh, Mr. Tyler, you startled the life out of me stealing up be-hind me like that like a deer-stalker! Oh!

MR. TYLER. (*playfully*). I rang my bell, Mrs. Rooney, the moment I sighted you I started tinkling my bell, now don't you deny it.

MRS. ROONEY. Your bell is one thing, Mr. Tyler, and you are another. What news of your daughter?

MR. TYLER. Fair, fair. They removed everything, you know, the whole . . . er . . . bag of tricks. Now I am grand-childless.

(*Dragging feet.*)

MRS. ROONEY. Gracious how you wob-ble! Dismount, for mercy's sake, or ride on.

MR. TYLER. Perhaps if I were to lay my hand lightly on your shoulder, Mrs. Rooney, how would that be? (*Pause.*) Would you permit that?

MRS. ROONEY. No, Mr. Rooney, Mr. Tyler I mean, I am tired of light old hands on my shoulders and other sense-less places, sick and tired of them. Heavens, here comes Connolly's van! (*She halts. Sound of motor-van. It ap-proaches, passes with thunderous rattle, recedes.*) Are you all right, Mr. Tyler? (*Pause.*) Where is he? (*Pause.*) Ah there you are! (*The dragging steps re-sume.*) That was a narrow squeak.

MR. TYLER. I alit in the nick of time.

MRS. ROONEY. It is suicide to be abroad. But what is it to be at home, Mr. Tyler, what is it to be at home? A linger-ing dissolution. Now we are white with dust from head to foot. I beg your pardon?

MR. TYLER. Nothing, Mrs. Rooney, nothing, I was merely cursing, under my breath, God and man, under my breath, and the wet Saturday afternoon of my conception. My back tire has gone down again. I pumped it hard as iron before I set out. And now I am on the rim.

MRS. ROONEY. Oh what a shame!

MR. TYLER. Now if it were the front I should not so much mind. But the back. The back! The chain! The oil! The

grease! The hub! The brakes! The gear!
No! It is too much!

(*Dragging feet.*)

MRS. ROONEY. Are we very late, Mr.
Tyler, I have not the courage to look at
my watch.

MR. TYLER. (*bitterly*). Late! I on my
bicycle as I bowled along was already
late. Now therefore we are doubly late,
trebly, quadrupedly late. Would I had
shot by you, without a word.

(*Dragging feet.*)

MRS. ROONEY. Whom are you meeting, Mr. Tyler?

MR. TYLER. Hardy. (*Pause.*) We used
to climb together. (*Pause.*) I saved his
life once. (*Pause.*) I have not forgotten it.

(*Dragging feet. They stop.*)

MRS. ROONEY. Let us a halt a moment
and this vile dust fall back upon the viler
worms.

(*Silence. Rural sounds.*)

MR. TYLER. What sky! What light!
Ah in spite of all it is a blessed thing to
be alive in such weather, and out of hospital.

MRS. ROONEY. Alive?

MR. TYLER. Well half alive, shall we
say?

MRS. ROONEY. Speak for yourself, Mr.
Tyler. I am not half alive nor anything
approaching it. (*Pause.*) What are we
standing here for? This dust will not
settle in our time. And when it does some
great roaring machine will come and
whirl it all skyhigh again.

MR. TYLER. Well, shall we be getting
along in that case?

MRS. ROONEY. No.

MR. TYLER. Come, Mrs. Rooney—

MRS. ROONEY. Go, Mr. Tyler, go on
and leave me, listening to the cooing of
the ringdoves. (*Cooing.*) If you see my
poor blind Dan tell him I was on my
way to meet him when it all came over
me again, like a flood. Say to him, Your
poor wife, she told me to tell you it all
came flooding over her again and . . .
(*the voice breaks*) . . . she simply went
back home . . . straight back home . . .

MR. TYLER. Come, Mrs. Rooney, come,
the mail has not yet gone up, just take
my free arm and we'll be there with time
and to spare.

MRS. ROONEY. (*sobbing*). What?
What's all this now? (*Calmer.*) Can't

you see I'm in trouble? (*With anger.*)
Have you no respect for misery? (*Sobbing.*) Minnie! Little Minnie!

MR. TYLER. Come, Mrs. Rooney, come,
the mail has not yet gone up, just take my
free arm and we'll be there with time and
to spare.

MRS. ROONEY. (*brokenly*). In her
forties now she'd be, I don't know, fifty,
girding up her lovely little loins, getting
ready for the change . . .

MR. TYLER. Come, Mrs. Rooney, come,
the mail—

MRS. ROONEY. (*exploding*). Will you
get along with you, Mr. Rooney, Mr.
Tyler I mean, will you get along with you
now and cease molesting me? What kind
of a country is this where a woman can't
weep her heart out on the highways and
byways without being tormented by retired bill-brokers! (MR. TYLER *prepares
to mount his bicycle.*) Heavens, you're
not going to ride her flat! (MR. TYLER
mounts.) You'll tear your tube to rib-
bons! (MR. TYLER *rides off. Receding
sound of bumping bicycle. Silence. Cooing.*) Venus birds! Billing in the woods
all the long summer long. (*Pause.*) Oh
cursed corset! If I could let it out, without indecent exposure. Mr. Tyler! Mr.
Tyler! Come back and unlace me behind
the hedge! (*She laughs wildly, ceases.*)
What's wrong with me, what's wrong
with me, never tranquil, seething out of
my dirty old pelt, out of my skull, oh to
be in atoms, in atoms! (*Frenziedly.*)
ATOMS! (*Silence. Cooing. Faintly.*)
Jesus! (*Pause.*) Jesus!

(*Sound of car coming up behind her.
It slows down and draws up beside her,
engine running. It is* MR. SLOCUM, *the
Clerk of the Racecourse.*)

MR. SLOCUM. Is anything wrong, Mrs.
Rooney? You are bent all double. Have
you a pain in the stomach?

(*Silence.* MRS. ROONEY *laughs wildly.
Finally.*)

MRS. ROONEY. Well, if it isn't my old
admirer, the Clerk of the Course, in his
limousine.

MR. SLOCUM. May I offer you a lift,
Mrs. Rooney? Are you going in my direction?

MRS. ROONEY. I am, Mr. Slocum, we all
are. (*Pause.*) How is your poor mother?

MR. SLOCUM. Thank you, she is fairly

comfortable. We manage to keep her out of pain. That is the great thing, Mrs. Rooney, is it not?

MRS. ROONEY. Yes, indeed, Mr. Slocum, that is the great thing, I don't know how you do it. (*Pause. She slaps her cheek violently.*) Ah these wasps!

MR. SLOCUM. (*coolly*). May I then offer you a seat, Madam?

MRS. ROONEY. (*with exaggerated enthusiasm*). Oh that would be heavenly, Mr. Slocum, just simply heavenly. (*Dubiously.*) But would I ever get in, you look very high off the ground to-day, these new balloon tires, I presume. (*Sound of door opening and* MRS. ROONEY *trying to get in.*) Does this roof never come off? No? (*Efforts of* MRS. ROONEY.) No . . . I'll never do it . . . you'll have to get down, Mr. Slocum, and help me from the rear. (*Pause.*) What was that? (*Pause. Aggrieved.*) This is all your suggestion, Mr. Slocum, not mine. Drive on, Sir, drive on.

MR. SLOCUM. (*switching off the engine*). I'm coming, Mrs. Rooney, I'm coming, give me time, I'm as stiff as yourself.

(*Sound of* MR. SLOCUM *extracting himself from driver's seat.*)

MRS. ROONEY. Stiff! Well I like that! And me heaving all over back and front. (*To herself.*) The dry old reprobate!

MR. SLOCUM. (*in position behind her*). Now, Mrs. Rooney, how shall we do this?

MRS. ROONEY. As if I were a bale, Mr. Slocum, don't be afraid. (*Pause. Sounds of effort.*) That's the way! (*Effort.*) Lower! (*Effort.*) Wait! (*Pause.*) No, don't let go! (*Pause.*) Suppose I do get up, will I ever get down?

MR. SLOCUM. (*breathing hard*). You'll get down, Mrs. Rooney, you'll get down. We may not get you up, but I warrant you we'll get you down.

(*He resumes his efforts. Sound of these.*)

MRS. ROONEY. Oh! . . Lower! . . Don't be afraid! . . We're past the age when . . . There! . . Now! . . Get your shoulder under it . . . Oh! . . (*Giggles.*) Oh glory! . . Up! Up! . . Ah! . . I'm in! (*Panting of* MR. SLOCUM. *He slams the door. In a scream.*) My frock! You've nipped my frock! (MR. SLOCUM *opens the door.* MRS.

ROONEY *frees her frock.* MR. SLOCUM *slams the door. His violent unintelligible muttering as he walks round to the other door. Tearfully.*) My nice frock! Look what you've done to my nice frock! (MR. SLOCUM *gets into his seat, slams driver's door, presses starter. The engine does not start. He releases starter.*) What will Dan say when he sees me?

MR. SLOCUM. Has he then recovered his sight?

MRS. ROONEY. No, I mean when he knows, what will he say when he feels the hole? (MR. SLOCUM *presses starter. As before. Silence.*) What are you doing, Mr. Slocum?

MR. SLOCUM. Gazing straight before me, Mrs. Rooney, through the windscreen, into the void.

MRS. ROONEY. Start her up, I beseech you, and let us be off. This is awful!

MR. SLOCUM. (*dreamily*). All morning she went like a dream and now she is dead. That is what you get for a good deed. (*Pause. Hopefully.*) Perhaps if I were to choke her. (*He does so, presses the starter. The engine roars. Roaring to make himself heard.*) She was getting too much air!

(*He throttles down, grinds in his first gear, moves off, changes up in a grinding of gears.*)

MRS. ROONEY (*in anguish*). Mind the hen! (*Scream of brakes. Squawk of hen.*) Oh mother, you have squashed her, drive on, drive on! (*The car accelerates. Pause.*) What a death! One minute picking happy at the dung, on the road, in the sun, with now and then a dust bath, and then—bang!—all her troubles over. (*Pause.*) All the laying and the hatching. (*Pause.*) Just one great squawk and then . . . peace. (*Pause.*) They would have slit her weasand in any case. (*Pause.*) Here we are, let me down. (*The car slows down, stops, engine running.* MR. SLOCUM *blows his horn. Pause. Louder. Pause.*) What are you up to now, Mr. Slocum? We are at a standstill, all danger is past and you blow your horn. Now if instead of blowing it now you had blown it at that unfortunate—

(*Horn violently.* TOMMY *the porter appears at top of station steps.*)

MR. SLOCUM (*calling*). Will you come down, Tommy, and help this lady out,

she's stuck. (TOMMY *descends the steps.*)
Open the door, Tommy, and ease her out.
 (TOMMY *opens the door.*)
 TOMMY. Certainly, Sir. Nice day for
the races, Sir. What would you fancy
for—
 MRS. ROONEY. Don't mind me. Don't
take any notice of me. I do not exist.
The fact is well known.
 MR. SLOCUM. Do as you're asked,
Tommy, for the love of God.
 TOMMY. Yessir. Now, Mrs. Rooney.
 (*He starts pulling her out.*)
 MRS. ROONEY. Wait, Tommy, wait
now, don't bustle me, just let me wheel
round and get my feet to the ground. (*Her
efforts to achieve this.*) Now.
 TOMMY (*pulling her out*). Mind your
feather, Ma'am. (*Sounds of effort.*) Easy
now, easy.
 MRS. ROONEY. Wait, for God's sake,
you'll have me beheaded.
 TOMMY. Crouch down, Mrs. Rooney,
crouch down, and get your head in the
open.
 MRS. ROONEY. Crouch down! At my
time of life! This is lunacy!
 TOMMY. Press her down, Sir.
 (*Sounds of combined efforts.*)
 MRS. ROONEY. Merde!
 TOMMY. Now! She's coming! Straighten
up, Ma'am! There!
 (MR. SLOCUM *slams the door.*)
 MRS. ROONEY. Am I out?
 (*The voice of* MR. BARRELL, *the sta-
tion-master, raised in anger.*)
 MR. BARRELL. Tommy! Tommy! Where
the hell is he?
 (MR. SLOCUM *grinds in his gear.*)
 TOMMY (*hurriedly*). You wouldn't
have something for the Ladies Plate, Sir,
I was given Flash Harry.
 MR. SLOCUM (*scornfully*). Flash Harry!
That carthorse!
 MR. BARRELL (*at top of steps, roaring*).
Tommy! Blast your bleeding bloody—(*He
sees* MRS. ROONEY.) Oh, Mrs. Rooney . . .
(MR. SLOCUM *drives away in a grinding
of gears.*) Who's that crucifying his gear-
box, Tommy?
 TOMMY. Old Cissy Slocum.
 MRS. ROONEY. Cissy Slocum! That's a
nice way to refer to your betters. Cissy
Slocum! And you an orphan!
 MR. BARRELL (*angrily to* TOMMY).
What are you doing stravaging down here

on the public road? This is no place for
you at all! Nip up there on the platform
now and whip out the truck! Won't the
twelve thirty be on top of us before we
can turn round?
 TOMMY (*bitterly*). And that's the
thanks you get for a Christian act.
 MR. BARRELL (*violently*). Get on with
you now before I report you! (*Slow feet
of* TOMMY *climbing steps.*) Do you want
me to come down to you with the shovel?
(*The feet quicken, recede, cease.*) Ah,
God forgive me, it's a hard life. (*Pause.*)
Well, Mrs. Rooney, it's nice to see you up
and about again. You were laid up there
a long time.
 MRS. ROONEY. Not long enough, Mr.
Barrell. (*Pause.*) Would I were still in
bed, Mr. Barrell. (*Pause.*) Would I were
lying stretched out in my comfortable
bed, Mr. Barrell, just wasting slowly, pain-
lessly away, keeping up my strength with
arrowroot and calves-foot jelly, till in the
end you wouldn't see me under the blan-
kets any more than a board. (*Pause.*) Oh
no coughing or spitting or bleeding or
vomiting, just drifting gently down into
the higher life, and remembering, remembering . . . (*the voice breaks*) . . .
all the silly unhappiness . . . as though . . .
it had never happened . . . what did I do
with that handkerchief? (*Sound of handkerchief loudly applied.*) How long have
you been master of this station now, Mr.
Barrell?
 MR. BARRELL. Don't ask me, Mrs.
Rooney, don't ask me.
 MRS. ROONEY. You stepped into your
father's shoes, I believe, when he took
them off.
 MR. BARRELL. Poor Pappy! (*Reverent
pause.*) He didn't live long to enjoy his
ease.
 MRS. ROONEY. I remember him clearly.
A small ferrety purple-faced widower,
deaf as a doornail, very testy and snappy.
(*Pause.*) I suppose you'll be retiring soon
yourself, Mr. Barrell, and growing your
roses. (*Pause.*) Did I understand you to
say the twelve thirty would soon be upon
us?
 MR. BARRELL. Those were my words.
 MRS. ROONEY. But according to my
watch, which is more or less right—or
was—by the eight o'clock news, the time
is now coming up to twelve . . . (*pause

as she consults her watch) . . . thirty-six. (*Pause.*) And yet upon the other hand the up mail has not yet gone through. (*Pause.*) Or has it sped by unbeknown to me? (*Pause.*) For there was a moment there, I remember now, I was so plunged in sorrow I wouldn't have heard a steam roller go over me. (*Pause.* MR. BARRELL *turns to go.*) Don't go, Mr. Barrell! (MR. BARRELL *goes. Loud.*) Mr. Barrell! (*Pause. Louder.*) Mr. Barrell!

(MR. BARRELL *comes back.*)

MR. BARRELL (*testily*). What is it, Mrs. Rooney, I have my work to do.

(*Silence. Sound of wind.*)

MRS. ROONEY. The wind is getting up. (*Pause. Wind.*) The best of the day is over. (*Pause. Wind. Dreamily.*) Soon the rain will begin to fall and go on falling, all afternoon. (MR. BARRELL *goes.*) Then at evening the clouds will part, the setting sun will shine an instant, then sink, behind the hills. (*She realizes* MR. BARRELL *has gone.*) Mr. Barrell! Mr. Barrell! (*Silence.*) I estrange them all. They come towards me, uninvited, bygones bygones, full of kindness, anxious to help . . . (*the voice breaks*) . . . genuinely pleased . . . to see me again . . . looking so well . . . (*Handkerchief.*) A few simple words . . . from my heart . . . and I am all alone . . . once more . . . (*Handkerchief. Vehemently.*) I should not be out at all! I should never leave the grounds! (*Pause.*) Oh there is that Fitt woman, I wonder will she bow to me. (*Sound of* MISS FITT *approaching, humming a hymn. She starts climbing the steps.*) Miss Fitt! (MISS FITT *halts, stops humming.*) Am I then invisible, Miss Fitt? Is this cretonne so becoming to me that I merge into the masonry? (MISS FITT *descends a step.*) That is right, Miss Fitt, look closely and you will finally distinguish a once female shape.

MISS FITT. Mrs. Rooney! I saw you, but I did not know you.

MRS. ROONEY. Last Sunday we worshipped together. We knelt side by side at the same altar. We drank from the same chalice. Have I so changed since then?

MISS FITT (*shocked*). Oh but in church, Mrs. Rooney, in church I am alone with my Maker. Are not you? (*Pause.*) Why,

even the sexton himself, you know, when he takes up the collection, knows it is useless to pause before me. I simply do not see the plate, or bag, whatever it is they use, how could I? (*Pause.*) Why even when all is over and I go out into the sweet fresh air, why even then for the first furlong or so I stumble in a kind of daze as you might say, oblivious to my coreligionists. And they are very kind, I must admit—the vast majority—very kind and understanding. They know me now and take no umbrage. There she goes, they say, there goes the dark Miss Fitt, alone with her Maker, take no notice of her. And they step down off the path to avoid my running into them. (*Pause.*) Ah yes, I am distray, very distray, even on week-days. Ask Mother, if you do not believe me. Hetty, she says, when I start eating my doily instead of the thin bread and butter, Hetty, how can you be so distray? (*Sighs.*) I suppose the truth is I am not there, Mrs. Rooney, just not really there at all. I see, hear, smell, and so on, I go through the usual motions, but my heart is not in it, Mrs. Rooney, but heart is in none of it. Left to myself, with no one to check me, I would soon be flown . . . home. (*Pause.*) So if you think I cut you just now, Mrs Rooney, you do me an injustice. All I saw was a big pale blur, just another big pale blur. (*Pause.*) Is anything amiss, Mrs. Rooney, you do not look normal somehow. So bowed and bent.

MRS. ROONEY. (*ruefully*) Maddy Rooney, née Dunne, the big pale blur. (*Pause.*) You have piercing sight, Miss Fitt, if you only knew it, literally piercing.

(*Pause.*)

MISS FITT. Well . . . is there anything I can do, now that I am here?

MRS. ROONEY. If you would help me up the face of this cliff, Miss Fitt, I have little doubt your Maker would requite you, if no one else.

MISS FITT. Now now, Mrs. Rooney, don't put your teeth in me. Requite! I make these sacrifices for nothing—or not at all. (*Pause. Sound of her descending steps.*) I take it you want to lean on me, Mrs. Rooney.

MRS. ROONEY. I asked Mr. Barrell to give me his arm, just give me his arm.

(*Pause.*) He turned on his heel and strode away.

MISS FITT. Is it my arm you want then? (*Pause. Impatiently.*) Is it my arm you want, Mrs. Rooney, or what is it?

MRS ROONEY (*exploding*). Your arm! Any arm! A helping hand! For five seconds! Christ, what a planet!

MISS FITT. Really . . . Do you know what it is, Mrs. Rooney, I do not think it is wise of you to be going about at all.

MRS. ROONEY (*violently*). Come down here, Miss Fitt, and give me your arm, before I scream down the parish!

(*Pause. Wind. Sound of* MISS FITT *descending last steps.*)

MISS FITT (*resignedly*). Well, I suppose it is the Protestant thing to do.

MRS. ROONEY. Pismires do it for one another. (*Pause.*) I have seen slugs do it. (MISS FITT *proffers her arm.*) No, the other side, my dear, if it's all the same to you, I'm left-handed on top of everything else. (*She takes* MISS FITT'S *right arm.*) Heavens, child, you're just a bag of bones, you need building up. (*Sound of her toiling up steps on* MISS FITT'S *arm.*) This is worse than the Matterhorn, were you ever up the Matterhorn, Miss Fitt, great honeymoon resort. (*Sound of toiling.*) Why don't they have a handrail? (*Panting.*) Wait till I get some air (*Pause.*) Don't let me go! (MISS FITT *hums her hymn. After a moment* MRS. ROONEY *joins in with the words.*) . . . the encircling gloo-oom (MISS FITT *stops humming*) . . . tum tum me on. (*Forte.*) The night is dark and I am far from ho-ome, tum tum—

MISS FITT (*hysterically*). Stop it, Mrs. Rooney, stop it, or I'll drop you!

MRS. ROONEY. Wasn't it that they sung on the Lusitania? Or Rock of Ages? Most touching it must have been. Or was it the Titanic?

(*Attracted by the noise a group, including* MR. TYLER, MR. BARRELL *and* TOMMY, *gathers at top of steps.*)

MR. BARRELL. What the—

(*Silence.*)

MR. TYLER. Lovely day for the fixture.

(*Loud titter from* TOMMY *cut short by* MR. BARRELL *with backhanded blow in the stomach. Appropriate noise from* TOMMY.)

FEMALE VOICE (*shrill*). Oh look, Dolly, look!

DOLLY. What, Mamma?

FEMALE VOICE. They are stuck! (*Cackling laugh.*) They are stuck!

MRS. ROONEY. Now we are the laughing-stock of the twenty-six counties. Or is it thirty-six?

MR. TYLER. That is a nice way to treat your defenceless subordinates, Mr. Barrell, hitting them without warning in the pit of the stomach.

MISS FITT. Has anybody seen my mother?

MR. BARRELL. Who is that?

TOMMY. The dark Miss Fitt.

MR. BARRELL. Where is her face?

MRS. ROONEY. Now, deary, I am ready if you are. (*They toil up remaining steps.*) Stand back, you cads!

(*Shuffle of feet.*)

FEMALE VOICE. Mind yourself, Dolly!

MRS. ROONEY. Thank you, Miss Fitt, thank you, that will do, just prop me up against the wall like a roll of tarpaulin and that will be all, for the moment. (*Pause.*) I am sorry for all this ramdam, Miss Fitt, had I known you were looking for your mother I should not have importuned you, I know what it is.

MR. TYLER (*in marvelling aside*). Ramdam!

FEMALE VOICE. Come, Dolly darling, let us take up our stand before the first-class smokers. Give me your hand and hold me tight, one can be sucked under.

MR. TYLER. You have lost your mother, Miss Fitt?

MISS FITT. Good-morning, Mr. Tyler.

MR. TYLER. Good-morning, Miss Fitt.

MR. BARRELL. Good-morning, Miss Fitt.

MISS FITT. Good-morning, Mr. Barrell.

MR. TYLER. You have lost your mother, Miss Fitt?

MISS FITT. She said she would be on the last train.

MRS. ROONEY. Do not imagine, because I am silent, that I am not present, and alive, to all that is going on.

MR. TYLER (*to* MISS FITT). When you say the last train—

MRS. ROONEY. Do not flatter yourselves for one moment, because I hold aloof, that my sufferings have ceased. No. The entire scene, the hills, the plain, the race-course with its miles and miles of white rails and three red stands, the pretty little wayside station, even you yourselves, yes, I mean it, and over all the clouding blue, I see it all, I stand here and see it all with eyes . . . (*the voice breaks.*) . . . through eyes . . . oh, if you had my eyes . . . you would understand . . . the things they have seen . . . and not looked away . . . this is nothing . . . nothing . . . what did I do with that handkerchief?

(*Pause.*)

MR. TYLER (*to* MISS FITT). When you say the last train—(MRS. ROONEY *blows her nose violently and long*)—when you say the last train, Miss Fitt, I take it you mean the twelve thirty.

MISS FITT. What else could I mean, Mr. Tyler, what else could I *conceivably* mean?

MR. TYLER. Then you have no cause for anxiety, Miss Fitt, for the twelve thirty has not yet arrived. Look. (MISS FITT *looks.*) No, up the line. (MISS FITT *looks. Patiently.*) No, Miss Fitt, follow the direction of my index. (MISS FITT *looks.*) There. You see now. The signal. At the bawdy hour of nine. (*In rueful afterthought.*) Or three alas! (MR. BARRELL *stifles a guffaw.*) Thank you, Mr. Barrell.

MISS FITT. But the time is now getting on for—

MR. TYLER (*patiently*). We all know, Miss Fitt, we all know only too well what the time is now getting on for, and yet the cruel fact remains that the twelve thirty has not yet arrived.

MISS FITT. Not an accident, I trust! (*Pause.*) Do not tell me she has left the track! (*Pause.*) Oh darling mother! With the fresh sole for lunch!

(*Loud titter from* TOMMY, *checked as before by* MR. BARRELL.)

MR. BARRELL. That's enough old guff out of you. Nip up to the box now and see has Mr. Case anything for me.

(TOMMY *goes.*)

MRS. ROONEY (*sadly*). Poor Dan!

MISS FITT (*in anguish*). What terrible thing has happened?

MR. TYLER. Now now, Miss Fitt, do not—

MRS. ROONEY (*with vehement sadness*). Poor Dan!

MR. TYLER. Now now, Miss Fitt, do not give way . . . to despair, all will come right . . . in the end. (*Aside to* MR. BAR-

RELL.) What *is* the situation, Mr. Barrell? Not a collision, surely?

MRS. ROONEY (*enthusiastically*). A collision! Oh that would be wonderful!

MISS FITT (*horrified*). A collision! I knew it!

MR. TYLER. Come, Miss Fitt, let us move a little up the platform.

MRS. ROONEY. Yes, let us all do that. (*Pause.*) No? (*Pause.*) You have changed your mind? (*Pause.*) I quite agree, we are better here, in the shadow of the waiting-room.

MR. BARRELL. Excuse me a moment.

MRS. ROONEY. Before you slink away, Mr. Barrell, please, a statement of some kind, I insist. Even the slowest train on this brief line is not ten minutes and more behind its scheduled time without good cause, one imagines. (*Pause.*) We all know your station is the best kept of the entire network, but there are times when that is not enough, just not enough. (*Pause.*) Now, Mr. Barrell, leave off chewing your whiskers, we are waiting to hear from you—we, the unfortunate ticket-holders' nearest if not dearest.

(*Pause.*)

MR. TYLER (*reasonably*). I do think we are owed some kind of explanation, Mr. Barrell, if only to set our minds at rest.

MR. BARRELL. I know nothing. All I know is there has been a hitch. All traffic is retarded.

MRS. ROONEY (*derisively*). Retarded! A hitch! Ah these celibates! Here we are eating our hearts out with anxiety for our loved ones and he calls that a hitch! Those of us like myself with heart and kidney trouble may collapse at any moment and he calls that a hitch! In our ovens the Saturday roast is burning to a shrivel and he calls that—

MR. TYLER. Here comes Tommy, running! I am glad I have been spared to see this.

TOMMY (*excitedly, in the distance*). She's coming. (*Pause. Nearer.*) She's at the level-crossing!

(*Immediately exaggerated station sounds. Falling signals. Bells. Whistles. Crescendo of train whistle approaching. Sound of train rushing through station.*)

MRS. ROONEY (*above rush of train*). The up mail! The up mail! (*The up mail recedes, the down train approaches, enters*

*the station, pulls up with great hissing of
steam and clashing of couplings. Noise of
passengers descending, doors banging,*
MR. BARRELL *shouting "Boghill! Boghill!", etc. Piercingly.)* Dan! . . Are you
all right? . . Where is he? . . Dan! . . Did
you see my husband? . . Dan! . . (*Noise
of station emptying. Guard's whistle.
Train departing, receding. Silence.*) He
isn't on it! The misery I have endured, to
get here, and he isn't on it! . . Mr. Barrell! . . Was he not on it? (*Pause.*) Is
anything the matter, you look as if you
had seen a ghost. (*Pause.*) Tommy! . .
Did you see the master?

TOMMY. He'll be along, Ma'am, Jerry
is minding him.

(MR. ROONEY *suddenly appears on
platform, advancing on small boy* JERRY'S
*arm. He is blind, thumps the ground with
his stick and pants incessantly.*)

MRS. ROONEY. Oh, Dan! There you are!
(*Her dragging feet as she hastens towards
him. She reaches him. They halt.*) Where
in the world were you?

MR. ROONEY (*coolly.*) Maddy.

MRS. ROONEY. Where were you all this
time?

MR. ROONEY. In the men's.

MRS. ROONEY. Kiss me!

MR. ROONEY. Kiss you? In public? On
the platform? Before the boy? Have you
taken leave of your senses?

MRS. ROONEY. Jerry wouldn't mind.
Would you, Jerry?

JERRY. No, Ma'am.

MRS. ROONEY. How is your poor
father?

JERRY. They took him away, Ma'am.

MRS. ROONEY. Then you are all alone?

JERRY. Yes, Ma'am.

MR. ROONEY. Why are you here? You
did not notify me.

MRS. ROONEY. I wanted to give you a
surprise. For your birthday.

MR. ROONEY. My birthday?

MRS. ROONEY. Don't you remember? I
wished you your happy returns in the
bathroom.

MR. ROONEY. I did not hear you.

MRS. ROONEY. But I gave you a tie!
You have it on!

(*Pause.*)

MR. ROONEY. How old am I now?

MRS. ROONEY. Now never mind about
that. Come.

MR. ROONEY. Why did you not cancel
the boy? Now we shall have to give him a
penny.

MRS. ROONEY (*miserably*). I forgot! I
had such a time getting here! Such horrid
nasty people! (*Pause. Pleading.*) Be nice
to me, Dan, be nice to me today!

MR. ROONEY. Give the boy a penny.

MRS. ROONEY. Here are two halfpen-
nies, Jerry. Run along now and buy yourself a nice gobstopper.

JERRY. Yes, Ma'am.

MR. ROONEY. Come for me on Monday,
if I am still alive.

JERRY. Yessir.

(*He runs off.*)

MR. ROONEY. We could have saved
sixpence. We have saved fivepence. (*Pause.*) But at what cost?

(*They move off along platform arm
in arm. Dragging feet, panting, thudding
stick.*)

MRS. ROONEY. Are you not well?

(*They halt, on* MR. ROONEY'S *initiative.*)

MR. ROONEY. Once and for all, do not
ask me to speak and move at the same
time. I shall not say this in this life again.

(*They move off. Dragging feet, etc.
They halt at top of steps.*)

MRS. ROONEY. Are you not—

MR. ROONEY. Let us get this precipice
over.

MRS. ROONEY. Put your arm round me.

MR. ROONEY. Have you been drinking
again? (*Pause.*) You are quivering like a
blanc-mange. (*Pause.*) Are you in a condition to lead me? (*Pause.*) We shall fall
into the ditch.

MRS. ROONEY. Oh, Dan! It will be like
old times!

MR. ROONEY. Pull yourself together or
I shall send Tommy for the cab. Then,
instead of having saved sixpence, no, fivepence, we shall have lost . . . (*calculating
mumble*) . . . two and three less six one
and no plus one one and no plus three one
and nine and one ten and three two and
one . . . (*normal voice*) two and one, we
shall be the poorer to the tune of two and
one. (*Pause.*) Curse that sun, it has gone
in. What is the day doing?

(*Wind.*)

MRS. ROONEY. Shrouding, shrouding,
the best of it is past. (*Pause.*) Soon the

first great drops will fall splashing in the dust.

MR. ROONEY. And yet the glass was firm. (*Pause.*) Let us hasten home and sit before the fire. We shall draw the blinds. You will read to me. I think Effie is going to commit adultery with the Major. (*Brief drag of feet.*) Wait! (*Feet cease. Stick tapping at steps.*) I have been up and down these steps five thousand times and still I do not know how many there are. When I think there are six there are four or five or seven or eight and when I remember there are five there are three or four or six or seven and when finally I realize there are seven there are five or six or eight or nine. Sometimes I wonder if they do not change them in the night. (*Pause. Irritably.*) Well? How many do you make them to-day?

MRS. ROONEY. Do not ask me to count, Dan, not now.

MR. ROONEY. Not count! One of the few satisfactions in life?

MRS. ROONEY. Not steps, Dan, please, I always get them wrong. Then you might fall on your wound and I would have that on my manure-heap on top of everything else. No, just cling to me and all will be well.

(*Confused noise of their descent. Panting, stumbling, ejaculations, curses. Silence.*)

MR. ROONEY. Well! That is what you call well!

MRS. ROONEY. We are down. And little the worse. (*Silence. A donkey brays. Silence.*) That was a true donkey. Its father and mother were donkeys.

(*Silence.*)

MR. ROONEY. Do you know what, I think I shall retire.

MRS. ROONEY (*appalled*). Retire! And live at home? On your grant?

MR. ROONEY. Never tread these cursed steps again. Trudge this hellish road for the last time. Sit at home on the remnants of my bottom counting the hours—till the next meal. (*Pause.*) The very thought puts life in me! Forward, before it dies!

(*They move on. Dragging feet, panting, thudding stick.*)

MRS. ROONEY Now mind, here is the path . . . Up! . . Well done! Now we are in safety and a straight run home.

MR. ROONEY (*without halting, between gasps*). A straight . . . run! . . She calls that . . . a straight . . . run! . .

MRS. ROONEY. Hush! do not speak as you go along, you know it is not good for your coronary. (*Dragging steps, etc.*) Just concentrate on putting one foot before the next or whatever the expression is. (*Dragging feet, etc.*) That is the way, now we are doing nicely. (*Dragging feet, etc. They suddenly halt, on* MRS. ROONEY'S *initiative.*) Heavens! I knew there was something! With all the excitement! I forgot!

MR. ROONEY (*quietly*). Good God.

MRS. ROONEY. But you must know, Dan, of course, you were on it. What ever happened? Tell me!

MR. ROONEY. I have never known anything to happen.

MRS. ROONEY. But you must—

MR. ROONEY (*violently*). All this stopping and starting again is devilish, devilish! I get a little way on me and begin to be carried along when suddenly you stop dead! Two hundred pounds of unhealthy fat! What possessed you to come out at all? Let go of me!

MRS. ROONEY (*in great agitation*). No, I must know, we won't stir from here till you tell me. Fifteen minutes late! On a thirty minute run! It's unheard of!

MR. ROONEY. I know nothing. Let go of me before I shake you off.

MRS. ROONEY. But you must know! You were on it! Was it at the terminus? Did you leave on time? Or was it on the line? (*Pause.*) Did something happen on the line? (*Pause.*) Dan! (*Brokenly.*) Why won't you tell me!

(*Silence. They move off. Dragging feet, etc. They halt. Pause.*)

MR. ROONEY. Poor Maddy! (*Pause. Children's cries.*) What was that?

(*Pause for* MRS. ROONEY *to ascertain.*)

MRS. ROONEY. The Lynch twins jeering at us.

(*Cries.*)

MR. ROONEY. Will they pelt us with mud to-day, do you suppose?

(*Cries.*)

MRS. ROONEY. Let us turn and face them. (*Cries. They turn. Silence.*) Threaten them with your stick. (*Silence.*) They have run away.

(*Pause.*)

MR. ROONEY. Did you ever wish to kill

a child? (*Pause.*) Nip some young doom in the bud. (*Pause.*) Many a time at night, in winter, on the black road home, I nearly attacked the boy. (*Pause.*) Poor Jerry! (*Pause.*) What restrained me then? (*Pause.*) Not fear of man. (*Pause.*) Shall we go on backwards now a little?

MRS. ROONEY. Backwards?

MR. ROONEY. Yes. Or you forwards and I backwards. The perfect pair. Like Dante's damned, with their faces arsyversy. Our tears will water our bottoms.

MRS. ROONEY. What is the matter, Dan? Are you not well?

MR. ROONEY. Well! Did you ever know me to be well? The day you met me I should have been in bed. The day you proposed to me the doctors gave me up. You knew that, did you not? The night you married me they came for me with an ambulance. You have not forgotten that, I suppose? (*Pause.*) No, I cannot be said to be well. But I am no worse. Indeed I am better than I was. The loss of my sight was a great fillip. If I could go deaf and dumb I think I might pant on to be a hundred. Or have I done so? (*Pause.*) Was I a hundred to-day? (*Pause.*) Am I a hundred, Maddy?

(*Silence.*)

MRS. ROONEY. All is still. No living soul in sight. There is no one to ask. The world is feeding. The wind—(*brief wind*)—scarcely stirs the leaves and the birds—(*brief chirp*)—are tired singing. The cows—(*brief moo*)—and sheep—(*brief baa*)—ruminate in silence. The dogs—(*brief bark*)—are hushed and the hens—(*brief cackle*)—sprawl torpid in the dust. We are alone. There is no one to ask.

(*Silence.*)

MR. ROONEY (*clearing his throat, narrative tone*). We drew out on the tick of time, I can vouch for that. I was—

MRS. ROONEY. How can you vouch for it?

MR. ROONEY (*normal tone, angrily*). I can vouch for it, I tell you! Do you want my relation or don't you? (*Pause. Narrative tone.*) On the tick of time. I had the compartment to myself, as usual. At least I hope so, for I made no attempt to restrain myself. My mind—(*Normal tone.*) But why do we not sit down somewhere? Are we afraid we should never rise again?

MRS. ROONEY. Sit down on what?

MR. ROONEY. On a bench, for example.

MRS. ROONEY. There is no bench.

MR. ROONEY. Then on a bank, let us sink down upon a bank.

MRS. ROONEY. There is no bank.

MR. ROONEY. Then we cannot. (*Pause.*) I dream of other roads, in other lands. Of another home, another—(*he hesitates*)—another home. (*Pause.*) What was I trying to say?

MRS. ROONEY. Something about your mind.

MR. ROONEY (*startled*). My mind? Are you sure? (*Pause. Incredulous.*) My mind? . . (*Pause.*) Ah yes. (*Narrative tone.*) Alone in the compartment my mind began to work, as so often after office hours, on the way home, in the train, to the lilt of the bogeys. Your season-ticket, I said, costs you twelve pounds a year and you earn, on an average, seven and six a day, that is to say barely enough to keep you alive and twitching with the help of food, drink, tobacco and periodicals until you finally reach home and fall into bed. Add to this —or subtract from it—rent, stationery, various subscriptions, tramfares to and fro, light and heat, permits and licenses, hairtrims and shaves, tips to escorts, upkeep of premises and appearances, and a thousand unspecifiable sundries, and it is clear that by lying at home in bed, day and night, winter and summer, with a change of pyjamas once a fortnight, you would add very considerably to your income. Business, I said—(*A cry. Pause. Again. Normal tone.*) Did I hear a cry?

MRS. ROONEY. Mrs. Tully, I fancy. Her poor husband is in constant pain and beats her unmercifully.

(*Silence.*)

MR. ROONEY. That was a short knock. (*Pause.*) What was I trying to get at?

MRS. ROONEY. Business.

MR. ROONEY. Ah yes, business. (*Narrative tone.*) Business, old man, I said, retire from business, it has retired from you. (*Normal tone.*) One has these moments of lucidity.

MRS. ROONEY. I feel very cold and weak.

MR. ROONEY (*narrative tone*). On the

other hand, I said, there are the horrors of home life, the dusting, sweeping, airing, scrubbing, waxing, waning, washing, mangling, drying, mowing, clipping, raking, rolling, scuffling, shoveling, grinding, tearing, pounding, banging and slamming. And the brats, the happy little hearty little howling neighbours' brats. Of all this and much more the week-end, the Saturday intermission and then the day of rest, have given you some idea. But what must it be like on a working-day? A Wednesday? A Friday! What must it be like on a Friday! And I fell to thinking of my silent, back-street, basement office, with its obliterated plate, rest-couch and velvet hangings, and what it means to be buried there alive, if only from ten to five, with convenient to the one hand a bottle of light pale ale and to the other a long ice-cold fillet of hake. Nothing, I said, not even fully certified death, can ever take the place of that. It was then I noticed we were at a standstill. (*Pause. Normal tone. Irritably.*) Why are you hanging out of me like that? Have you swooned away?

MRS. ROONEY. I feel very cold and faint. The wind—(*whistling wind*)—is whistling through my summer frock as if I had nothing on over my bloomers. I have had no solid food since my elevenses.

MR. ROONEY. You have ceased to care. I speak—and you listen to the wind.

MRS. ROONEY. No no, I am agog, tell me all, then we shall press on and never pause, never pause, till we come safe to haven.

(*Pause.*)

MR. ROONEY. Never pause . . . safe to haven . . . Do you know, Maddy, sometimes one would think you were struggling with a dead language.

MRS. ROONEY. Yes indeed, Dan, I know full well what you mean, I often have that feeling, it is unspeakably excruciating.

MR. ROONEY. I confess I have it sometimes myself, when I happen to overhear what I am saying.

MRS. ROONEY. Well, you know, it will be dead in time, just like our own poor dear Gaelic, there is that to be said.

(*Urgent baa.*)

MR. ROONEY (*startled*). Good God!

MRS. ROONEY. Oh, the pretty little woolly lamb, crying to suck its mother! Theirs has not changed, since Arcady.

(*Pause.*)

MR. ROONEY. Where was I in my composition?

MRS. ROONEY. At a standstill.

MR. ROONEY. Ah yes. (*Clears his throat. Narrative tone.*) I concluded naturally that we had entered a station and would soon be on our way again, and I sat on, without misgiving. Not a sound. Things are very dull to-day, I said, nobody getting down, nobody getting on. Then as time flew by and nothing happened I realized my error. We had not entered a station.

MRS. ROONEY. Did you not spring up and poke your head out of the window?

MR. ROONEY. What good would that have done me?

MRS. ROONEY. Why to call out to be told what was amiss.

MR. ROONEY. I did not care what was amiss. No, I just sat on, saying, If this train were never to move again I should not greatly mind. Then gradually a—how shall I say—a growing desire to—er—you know—welled up within me. Nervous, probably. In fact now I am sure. You know, the feeling of being confined.

MRS. ROONEY. Yes yes, I have been through that.

MR. ROONEY. If we sit here much longer, I said, I really do not know what I shall do. I got up and paced to and fro between the seats, like a caged beast.

MRS. ROONEY. That is a help sometimes.

MR. ROONEY. After what seemed an eternity we simply moved off. And the next thing was Barrell bawling the abhorred name. I got down and Jerry led me to the men's, or Fir as they call it now, from Vir Viris I suppose, the *V* becoming *F,* in accordance with Grimm's Law. (*Pause.*) The rest you know. (*Pause.*) You say nothing? (*Pause.*) Say something, Maddy. Say you believe me.

MRS. ROONEY. I remember once attending a lecture by one of these new mind doctors, I forget what you call them. He spoke—

MR. ROONEY. A lunatic specialist?

MRS. ROONEY. No no, just the troubled mind, I was hoping he might shed a little light on my lifelong preoccupation with horses' buttocks.

MR. ROONEY. A neurologist.

MRS. ROONEY. No no, just mental distress, the name will come back to me in the night. I remember his telling us the story of a little girl, very strange and unhappy in her ways, and how he treated her unsuccessfully over a period of years and was finally obliged to give up the case. He could find nothing wrong with her, he said. The only thing wrong with her as far as he could see was that she was dying. And she did in fact die, shortly after he washed his hands of her.

MR. ROONEY. Well? What is there so wonderful about that?

MRS. ROONEY. No, it was just something he said, and the way he said it, that have haunted me ever since.

MR. ROONEY. You lie awake at night, tossing to and fro and brooding on it.

MRS. ROONEY. On it and other . . . wretchedness. (*Pause.*) When he had done with the little girl he stood there motionless for some time, quite two minutes I should say, looking down at his table. Then he suddenly raised his head and exclaimed, as if he had had a revelation, The trouble with her was she had never been really born! (*Pause.*) He spoke throughout without notes. (*Pause.*) I left before the end.

MR. ROONEY. Nothing about your buttocks? (MRS. ROONEY *weeps. In affectionate remonstrance.*) Maddy!

MRS. ROONEY. There is nothing to be done for those people.

MR. ROONEY. For which is there? (*Pause.*) That does not sound right somehow. (*Pause.*) What way am I facing?

MRS. ROONEY. What?

MR. ROONEY. I have forgotten what way I am facing.

MRS. ROONEY. You have turned aside and are bowed down over the ditch.

MR. ROONEY. There is a dead dog down there.

MRS. ROONEY. No no, just the rotting leaves.

MR. ROONEY. In June? Rotting leaves in June?

MRS. ROONEY. Yes dear, from last year, and from the year before last, and from the year before that again. (*Silence. Rainy wind. They move on. Dragging steps, etc.*) There is that lovely laburnum again. Poor thing, it is losing all its tassels. (*Dragging steps, etc.*) There are the first drops. (*Rain. Dragging feet, etc.*) Golden drizzle. (*Dragging steps, etc.*) Do not mind me, dear, I am just talking to myself. (*Rain heavier. Dragging steps, etc.*) Can hinnies procreate, I wonder.

(*They halt, on* MR. ROONEY'S *initiative.*)

MR. ROONEY. Say that again.

MRS. ROONEY. Come on, dear, don't mind me, we are getting drenched.

MR. ROONEY (*forcibly*). Can what what?

MRS. ROONEY. Hinnies procreate. (*Silence.*) You know, hinnies, or is it jinnies, aren't they barren, or sterile, or whatever it is? (*Pause.*) It wasn't an ass's colt at all, you know, I asked the Regius Professor. (*Pause.*)

MR. ROONEY. He should know.

MRS. ROONEY. Yes, it was a hinny, he rode into Jerusalem, or wherever it was, on a hinny. (*Pause.*) That must mean something. (*Pause.*) It's like the sparrows, than many of which we are of more value, they weren't sparrows at all.

MR. ROONEY. Than many of which . . . You exaggerate, Maddy.

MRS. ROONEY (*with emotion*). They weren't sparrows at all!

MR. ROONEY. Does that put our price up?

(*Silence. They move on. Wind and rain. Dragging feet, etc. They halt.*)

MRS. ROONEY. Do you want some dung? (*Silence. They move on. Wind and rain, etc. They halt.*) Why do you stop? Do you want to say something?

MR. ROONEY. No.

MRS. ROONEY. Then why do you stop?

MR. ROONEY. It is easier.

MRS. ROONEY. Are you very wet?

MR. ROONEY. To the buff.

MRS. ROONEY. The buff?

MR. ROONEY. The buff. From buffalo.

MRS. ROONEY. We shall hang up all our things in the hot-cupboard and get into our dressing-gowns. (*Pause.*) Put your arm round me. (*Pause.*) Be nice to me! (*Pause. Gratefully.*) Ah Dan! (*They move on. Wind and rain. Dragging feet, etc. Faintly same music as before. They halt. Music clearer. Silence but for music playing. Music dies.*) All day the same old record. All alone in that great empty house. She must be a very old woman now.

MR. ROONEY (*indistinctly*). Death and the Maiden.

(*Silence.*)

MRS. ROONEY. You are crying. (*Pause.*) Are you crying?

MR. ROONEY (*violently*). Yes! (*They move on. Wind and rain. Dragging feet, etc. They halt. They move on. Wind and rain. Dragging feet, etc. They halt.*) Who is the preacher to-morrow? The incumbent?

MRS. ROONEY. No.

MR. ROONEY. Thank God for that. Who?

MRS. ROONEY. Hardy.

MR. ROONEY. "How to be Happy though Married"?

MRS. ROONEY. No no, he died, you remember. No connexion.

MR. ROONEY. Has he announced the text?

MRS. ROONEY. "The Lord upholdeth all that fall and raiseth up all those that be bowed down." (*Silence. They join in wild laughter. They move on. Wind and rain. Dragging feet, etc.*) Hold me tighter, Dan! (*Pause.*) Oh yes!

(*They halt.*)

MR. ROONEY. I hear something behind us.

(*Pause.*)

MRS. ROONEY. It looks like Jerry. (*Pause.*) It is Jerry.

(*Sound of* JERRY'S *running steps approaching. He halts beside them, panting.*)

JERRY (*panting*). You dropped—

MRS. ROONEY. Take your time, my little man, you will burst a bloodvessel.

JERRY (*panting*). You dropped something, Sir, Mr. Barrell told me to run after you.

MRS. ROONEY. Show. (*She takes the object.*) What is it? (*She examines it.*) What is this thing, Dan?

MR. ROONEY. Perhaps it is not mine at all.

JERRY. Mr. Barrell said it was, Sir.

MRS. ROONEY. It looks like a kind of ball. And yet it is not a ball.

MR. ROONEY. Give it to me.

MRS. ROONEY (*giving it*). What *is* it, Dan?

MR. ROONEY. It is a thing I carry about with me.

MRS. ROONEY. Yes, but what—

MR. ROONEY (*violently*). It is a thing I carry about with me!

(*Silence.* MRS. ROONEY *looks for a penny.*)

MRS. ROONEY. I have no small money. Have you?

MR. ROONEY. I have none of any kind.

MRS. ROONEY. We are out of change, Jerry. Remind Mr. Rooney on Monday and he will give you a penny for your pains.

JERRY. Yes, Ma'am.

MR. ROONEY. If I am alive.

JERRY. Yessir.

(JERRY *starts running back towards the station.*)

MRS. ROONEY. Jerry! (JERRY *halts.*) Did you hear what the hitch was? (*Pause.*) Did you hear what kept the train so late?

MR. ROONEY. How would he have heard? Come on.

MRS. ROONEY. What was it, Jerry?

JERRY. It was a—

MR. ROONEY. Leave the boy alone, he knows nothing! Come on!

MRS. ROONEY. What was it, Jerry?

JERRY. It was a little child, Ma'am.

(MR. ROONEY *groans.*)

MRS. ROONEY. What do you mean, it was a little child?

JERRY. It was a little child fell out of the carriage. On to the line, Ma'am. (*Pause.*) Under the wheels, Ma'am.

(*Silence.* JERRY *runs off. His steps die away. Tempest of wind and rain. It abates. They move on. Dragging steps, etc. They halt. Tempest of wind and rain.*)

ROY WALKER: *Shagreen Shamrock*

From *The Listener*, Jan. 24, 1957. Copyright © 1957 by Roy Walker.
Reprinted by permission of the author.

SAMUEL BECKETT GAVE HIS FIRST RADIO PLAY A SARDONIC TITLE from the Psalms, "All That Fall." The partisans will all fall on it as they did on his "Waiting for Godot." A Third Programme don will see in the train that runs over

the child an intimation of the stern aspect of God the Father. A Sartrian sophist will seize on the allusion to blind man's buff. A literary specialist in word-complexes will distinguish forty-nine types of ambiguity and add an insult about broken-backed Irish Catholicism for good measure. The author will disappoint everybody by not replying to the debate. It will occur to almost no one that he has been left as incapable of comment as Pentheus when the wild women had done with him.

It has been amiably suggested—this is the alibi always handed out for substituting one's own ideology for Shakespeare's, too—that Mr. Beckett's quality lies in the fact that he can be interpreted in so many ways and on so many levels. Is it the business of criticism to pass round blank cheques on other people's creative work? Rushing in where nobody has feared to tread, I suggest that Mr. Beckett does his utmost to frustrate all this ideological imperialism. If we must retreat into our several shells (or shell-holes) at the approach of art, we cannot take the whole work in with us. Its subject is the thing itself, unaccommodated man. Man stumbling around in the waste land of immediate experience, trying ludicrously and tragically to thumb a lift in a miscellaneous dump of cultural bits and pieces, parts which deny and yet imply a comprehensible whole. "This dust will not settle in our time," says the old woman on the road, "and when it does, some great roaring machine will come and whirl it all skyhigh again."

"All That Fall" is a play of radioactive participles. It cannot be critically handled with safety. As in the work of Mr. Beckett's mentor, James Joyce, sounds and meanings suffer a series of associative but not haphazard metamorphoses. Even his

B.B.C. producer, Donald McWhinnie, who worked on the play with the author in Paris, is snared in the text. The piece is scarcely a dozen lines old when Maddy Rooney makes a mad rune with his unusual surname: "So hinnies whinny." Near the end she says—it is disquietingly vital to her—that it wasn't an ass on which "he rode into Jerusalem, or wherever it was, it was a hinny."

You could "interpret" this as a reflection that producers are sterile brutes. You could "interpret" it as a recognition that it is through producers that plays are born again. You might equally well deny that Mr. McWhinnie or his function are alluded to at all, though without him and it you would not be hearing the play. . . . There is the method in miniature. It is the complex of incommensurable meanings that is meant, the multiple irony. And the complex is comically cubed, as it were, if you recall that "hinny" may colloquially mean "mule" and may equally well mean "sweetheart." "I use none but the simplest words," says Maddy fearfully, surely speaking her author's apologia, "and yet I sometimes find my way of speaking very bizarre."

Mr. Beckett puns in counterpoint where possible, to help his players. In Maddy's early line, "Why do you halt? (*Pause.*) But why do I halt?," the first "halt" conveys "stop," the second—we have been listening to her dragging feet —adds "limp," a nightmare apprehension of struggling painfully on and yet somehow remaining at a standstill. If Mr. Beckett could be bounded in a nutshell, this might be it.

The point is that his style does work, it makes mysterious relativities imaginatively instantaneous. "All That Fall" is certainly—this is now being said on all sides—the most important piece of pure radio drama since "Under Milk Wood."[1] I burn my boats and admit that I rate it higher. Mr. Beckett's work comprehends a wider and deeper range of experience, goes further in making the blind man's theatre of radio an art form in its own right, is no less eloquent and evocative in monosyllabic brevities than was Thomas in his polychromatic 125-word periods.

Mary O'Farrell was a superb Maddy, J. G. Devlin's very fine performance was hardly harmed by two or three slight fluffs, and Donald McWhinnie's Third Programme production, with masterly pauses, human animal-noises, a railway that was Emmet made audible, and a wind that seemed to blow across miles of dreary bog, is something of a radio classic.

[1] [A radio play by the Welsh poet Dylan Thomas—*Ed.*]

TOM F. DRIVER: *Beckett by the Madeleine*

From *Columbia University Forum*, IV (Summer, 1961). Copyright
© 1961 by Tom F. Driver. Reprinted by permission of the author and
James Brown Associates, Inc.

NOTHING LIKE GODOT, HE ARRIVED BEFORE THE HOUR. HIS LETTER
had suggested we meet at my hotel at noon on Sunday, and I came into the lobby as
the clock struck twelve. He was waiting.

My wish to meet Samuel Beckett had
been prompted by simple curiosity and
interest in his work. American newspaper
reviewers like to call his plays nihilistic.
They find deep pessimism in them. Even
so astute a commentator as Harold Clurman of *The Nation* has said that "Waiting for Godot" is "the concentrate . . .
of the contemporary European . . . mood
of despair." But to me Beckett's writing
had seemed permeated with love for human beings and with a kind of humor
that I could reconcile neither with despair
nor with nihilism. Could it be that my
own eyes and ears had deceived me? Is
his a literature of defeat, irrelevant to the
social crises we face? Or is it relevant because it teaches us something useful to
know about ourselves?

I knew that a conversation with the
author would not settle such questions,
because a man is not the same as his writing: in the last analysis, the questions had
to be settled by the work itself. Nevertheless I was curious.

My curiosity was sharpened a day or
two before the interview by a conversation I had with a well-informed teacher
of literature, a Jesuit father, at a conference on religious drama near Paris. When
Beckett's name came into the discussion,
the priest grew loud and told me that
Beckett "hates life." That, I thought, is at
least one thing I can find out when we
meet.

Beckett's appearance is rough-hewn
Irish. The features of his face are distinct, but not fine. They look as if they
had been sculptured with an unsharpened
chisel. Unruly hair goes straight up from
his forehead, standing so high that the top
falls gently over, as if to show that it
really is hair and not bristle. One might
say it combines the man's own pride and
humility. For he has the pride that comes

of self-acceptance and the humility, perhaps of the same genesis, not to impose
himself upon another. His light blue eyes,
set deep within the face, are actively and
continually looking. He seems, by some
unconscious division of labor, to have
given them that one function and no
other, leaving communication to the rest
of the face. The mouth frequently breaks
into a disarming smile. The voice is light
in timbre, with a rough edge that corresponds to his visage. The Irish accent is,
as one would expect, combined with
slight inflections from the French. His
tweed suit was a baggy gray and green.
He wore a brown knit sports shirt with
no tie.

We walked down the Rue de L'Arcade,
thence along beside the Madeleine and
across to a sidewalk cafe opposite that
church. The conversation that ensued may
have been engrossing but it could hardly
be called world-shattering. For one thing,
the world that Beckett sees is already shattered. His talk turns to what he calls "the
mess," or sometimes "this buzzing confusion." I reconstruct his sentences made
from notes made immediately after our conversation. What appears here is shorter than
what he actually said but very close to his
own words.

"The confusion is not my invention.
We cannot listen to a conversation for
five minutes without being acutely aware
of the confusion. It is all around us and
our only chance now is to let it in. The
only chance of renovation is to open our
eyes and see the mess. It is not a mess
you can make sense of."

I suggested that one must let it in because it is the truth, but Beckett did not
take to the word truth.

"What is more true than anything else?
To swim is true, and to sink is true. One
is not more true than the other. One can-

not speak anymore of being, one must speak only of the mess. When Heidegger and Sartre speak of a contrast between being and existence, they may be right, I don't know, but their language is too philosophical for me. I am not a philosopher. One can only speak of what is in front of him, and that now is simply the mess."

Then he began to speak about the tension in art between the mess and form. Until recently, art has withstood the pressure of chaotic things. It has held them at bay. It realized that to admit them was to jeopardize form. "How could the mess be admitted, because it appears to be the very opposite of form and therefore destructive of the very thing that art holds itself to be?" But now we can keep it out no longer, because we have come into a time when "it invades our experience at every moment. It is there and it must be allowed in."

I granted this might be so, but found the result to be even more attention to form than was the case previously. And why not? How, I asked, could chaos be admitted to chaos? Would not that be the end of thinking and the end of art? If we look at recent art we find it preoccupied with form. Beckett's own work is an example. Plays more highly formalized than "Waiting for Godot," "Endgame," and "Krapp's Last Tape" would be hard to find.

"What I am saying does not mean that there will henceforth be no form in art. It only means that there will be new form, and that this form will be of such a type that it admits the chaos and does not try to say that the chaos is really something else. The form and the chaos remain separate. The latter is not reduced to the former. That is why the form itself becomes a preoccupation, because it exists as a problem separate from the material it accommodates. To find a form that accommodates the mess, that is the task of the artist now."

Yet, I responded, could not similar things be said about the art of the past? Is it not characteristic of the greatest art that it confronts us with something we cannot clarify, demanding that the viewer respond to it in his own never-predictable way? What is the history of criticism but the history of men attempting to make sense of the manifold elements in art that will not allow themselves to be reduced to a single philosophy or a single aesthetic theory? Isn't all art ambiguous?

"Not this," he said, and gestured toward the Madeleine. The classical lines of the church, which Napoleon thought of as a Temple of Glory, dominated all the scene where we sat. The Boulevard de la Madeleine, the Boulevard Malesherbes, and the Rue Royale ran to it with graceful flattery, bearing tidings of the Age of Reason. "Not this. This is clear. This does not allow the mystery to invade us. With classical art, all is settled. But it is different at Chartres. There is the unexplainable, and there art raises questions that it does not attempt to answer."

I asked about the battle between life and death in his plays. Didi and Gogo hover on the edge of suicide; Hamm's world is death and Clov may or may not get out of it to join the living child outside. Is this life-death question a part of the chaos?

"Yes. If life and death did not both present themselves to us, there would be no inscrutability. If there were only darkness, all would be clear. It is because there is not only darkness but also light that our situation becomes inexplicable. Take Augustine's doctrine of grace given and grace withheld: have you pondered the dramatic qualities in this theology? Two thieves are crucified with Christ, one saved and the other damned. How can we make sense of this division? In classical drama, such problems do not arise. The destiny of Racine's Phèdre is sealed from the beginning: she will proceed into the dark. As she goes, she herself will be illuminated. At the beginning of the play she has partial illumination and at the end she has complete illumination, but there has been no question but that she moves toward the dark. That is the play. Within this notion clarity is possible, but for us who are neither Greek nor Jansenist there is not such clarity. The question would also be removed if we believed in the contrary—total salvation. But where we have both dark and light we have also the inexplicable. The key word in my plays is 'perhaps.'"

Given a theological lead, I asked what he thinks about those who find a religious significance to his plays.

"Well, really there is none at all. I have no religious feeling. Once I had a religious emotion. It was at my first Communion. No more. My mother was deeply religious. So was my brother. He knelt down at his bed as long as he could kneel. My father had none. The family was Protestant, but for me it was only irksome and I let it go. My brother and mother got no value from their religion when they died. At the moment of crisis it had no more depth than an old-school tie. Irish Catholicism is not attractive, but it is deeper. When you pass a church on an Irish bus, all the hands flurry in the sign of the cross. One day the dogs of Ireland will do that too and perhaps also the pigs."

But do the plays deal with the same facets of experience religion must also deal with?

"Yes, for they deal with distress. Some people object to this in my writing. At a party an English intellectual—so-called —asked me why I write always about distress. As if it were perverse to do so! He wanted to know if my father had beaten me or my mother had run away from home to give me an unhappy childhood. I told him no, that I had had a very happy childhood. Then he thought me more perverse than ever. I left the party as soon as possible and got into a taxi. On the glass partition between me and the driver were three signs: one asked for help for the blind, another, help for orphans, and the third for relief for the war refugees. One does not have to look for distress. It is screaming at you even in the taxis of London."

Lunch was over, and we walked back to the hotel with the light and dark of Paris screaming at us.

The personal quality of Samuel Beckett is similar to qualities I had found in the plays. He says nothing that compresses experience within a closed pattern. "Perhaps" stands in place of commitment. At the same time, he is plainly sympathetic, clearly friendly. If there were only the mess, all would be clear; but there is also compassion.

As a Christian, I know I do not stand where Beckett stands, but I do see much of what he sees. As a writer on the theater, I have paid close attention to the plays. Harold Clurman is right to say that "Waiting for Godot" is a reflection (he calls it a distorted reflection) "of the impasse and disarray of Europe's present politics, ethic, and common way of life." Yet it is not only Europe the play refers to. "Waiting for Godot" sells even better in America than in France. The consciousness it mirrors may have come earlier to Europe than to America, but it is the consciousness that most "mature" societies arrive at when their successes in technological and economic systematization propel them into a time of examining the not-strictly-practical ends of culture. America is now joining Europe in this "mature" phase of development. Whether any of us remain in it long will depend on what happens as a result of the technological and economic revolutions now going on in the countries of Asia and Africa, and also of course on how long the cold war remains cold. At present no political party in Western Europe or America seems possessed of a philosophy of social change adequate to the pressures of current history.

In the Beckett plays, time does not go forward. We are always at the end, where events repeat themselves ("Waiting for Godot"), or hover at the edge of nothingness ("Endgame"), or turn back to the long-ago moment of genuine life ("Krapp's Last Tape"). This retreat from action may disappoint those of us who believe that the events of the objective world must still be dealt with. Yet it would be wrong to conclude that Beckett's work is "pessimistic." To say "perhaps," as the plays do, is not to say "no." The plays do not say that there is no future but that we do not see it, have no confidence about it, and approach it hopelessly. Apart from messianic Marxism, where is there today a faith asserting the contrary that succeeds in shaping a culture?

The walls that surround the characters of Beckett's plays are not walls that nature and history have built irrespective of the decisions of men. They are the walls of one's own attitude toward his situation. The plays are themselves evidence of a human capacity to see one's situation and by that very fact to transcend it. That is why Beckett can say that letting in "the mess" may bring with it a "chance of renovation." It is also why he is wrong, from philosophy's point of view, to say that there is *only* "the mess." If that were all there is, he could not recognize it as such. But the plays and the novels contain more, and that more is transcendence of the self and the situation.

In "Waiting for Godot" Beckett has a very simple and moving description of human self-transcendence. Vladimir and Estragon (Didi and Gogo) are discussing man, who bears his "little cross" until he dies and is forgotten. In a beautiful passage that is really a duet composed of short lines from first one pair of lips and then the other, the two tramps speak of their inability to keep slient. As Gogo says, "It's so we won't hear . . . all the dead voices." The voices of the dead make a noise like wings, sand, or leaves, all speaking at once, each one to itself, whispering, rustling, and murmuring.

VLADIMIR. What do they say?
ESTRAGON. They talk about their lives.
VLADIMIR. To have lived is not enough for them.
ESTRAGON. They have to talk about it.
VLADIMIR. To be dead is not enough for them.
ESTRAGON. It is not sufficient.
        (*Silence*)
VLADIMIR. They make a noise like feathers.
ESTRAGON. Like leaves.
VLADIMIR. Like ashes.
ESTRAGON. Like leaves.

In this passage, Didi and Gogo are like the dead, and the dead are like the living, because all are incapable of keeping silent.

The description of the dead voices is also a description of living voices. In either case, neither to live nor to die is "enough." One must talk about it. The human condition is self-reflection, self-transcendence. Beckett's plays are the whispering, rustling, and murmuring of man refusing merely to exist.

Is it not true that self-transcendence implies freedom, and that freedom is either the most glorious or the most terrifying of facts, depending on the vigor of the spirit that contemplates it? It is important to notice that the rebukes to Beckett's "despair" have mostly come from the dogmatists of humanist liberalism, who here reveal, as so often they do, that they desire the reassurance of certainty more than they love freedom. Having recognized that to live is not enough, they wish to fasten down in dogma the way that life ought to be lived. Beckett suggests something more free—that life is to be seen, to be talked about, and that the way it is to be lived cannot be stated unambiguously but must come as a response to that which one encounters in "the mess." He has devised his works in such a way that those who comment upon them actually comment upon themselves. One cannot say, "Beckett has said so and so," for Beckett has said, "Perhaps." If the critics and the public see only images of despair, one can only deduce that they are themselves despairing.

Beckett himself, or so I take it, has repented of the desire for certainty. There are therefore released in him qualities of affirmation that his interpreters often miss. That is why the laughter in his plays is warm, his concern for his characters affectionate. His warm humor and affection are not the attributes of defeatism but the consequences of what Paul Tillich has called "the courage to be."

Alexei Arbuzov

1908-

ALEXEI ARBUZOV HAS LONG BEEN ASSOCIATED WITH the Soviet Theatre, but he was virtually unknown in the West until 1960, when reports of the huge success of his play *It Happened in Irkutsk* suggested that the post-Stalin era might have borne some theatrical fruit. Actually, Arbuzov's play is entirely faithful to the principles of Socialist Realism, with its demands for the "positive hero," its optimistic faith in human nature, and its commitment to communist society. But Arbuzov does reveal an interest in formal experimentation—however mild and conservative by Western standards—and he attempts to break the rigidities of literal realism by the use of chorus, narration, and a fluid arrangement of scenes. By emphasizing the emotional aspects of his characters and their interpersonal relations, Arbuzov avoids narrowly political issues and militant social propaganda. Concerning his play he has written: "I have long been disturbed by the thought that we attach far too little significance to love, the kind of love that ennobles and uplifts. Yet I believe that a person who loves shapes to some extent the life and molds the character of his beloved. That is what my play is about." Arbuzov has been connected with the theatre since he became an actor at the age of sixteen. He later directed plays and finally turned to writing. His principal themes concern young people, their ambitions, dreams, mistakes, and accomplishments. Among his plays are *Tanya* (1938), *City at Dawn* (1940), and *Years of Wandering* (1953).

IT HAPPENED IN IRKUTSK

❦ BY ALEXEI ARBUZOV

Translated by Rose Prokofieva

CHARACTERS

CHORUS
VALYA—a cashier in a grocery store, 25
LARISA—salesclerk in the same store, 34
SERDYUK, STEPAN YEGOROVICH—foreman of the crew of a walking excavator, 51
SERGEI SERYOGIN—shift foreman and senior operator of the excavator, 26
VICTOR (VITYA) BOITSOV—electrician, first assistant to Seryogin, 25
RODION (RODIK)—hydraulic man, second assistant to Seryogin, 24
DENIS—oiler at the excavator, 25
AFANSY LAPCHENKO—helper, 20

ZINKA—Denis' wife, a concrete worker, 20
MAYA—Rodik's sister, schoolgirl from Moscow, 17
NYURA—electrician from Head Office, 22
TIPSY MAN
LITTLE GIRL
NURSE
FIRST YOUNG MAN
SECOND YOUNG MAN
ANTON—a boy of about 10
LERA—his friend, a girl of 9
PASSER-BY

❦ Part I

Enter CHORUS *and* CHARACTERS. *It might perhaps be best to allow them to settle themselves freely about the stage, for each will be engrossed in his own thoughts.*

One of them may perhaps be strumming a guitar, but very lightly and carelessly, as if tuning it. The faint sound of a lullaby, the mere suggestion of the melody that will recur later on, may be discerned. But, I repeat, all this musical accompaniment must be quite casual. . . . .

After a brief, reflective pause the dialogue begins.

FIRST YOUTH. Is it true that a man or woman who loves can blossom out like a flower in the sun?

GIRL (*thoughtfully*). Sometimes. . . .

SECOND YOUTH (*taking the girl's hand and looking into her eyes*). Could my love not transfigure you, make you wondrously beautiful so that I myself would not know you?

GIRL. Perhaps. . . .

CHORUS. This is the story of three young people who met on the banks of

the Angara River, not far from the city of Irkutsk, where in the middle of the twentieth century, a great hydroelectric station was being built.

— We shall leave it to you to judge these three young people. We shall not point any moral, for we have complete faith in your judgement.

— This story is—

VALYA. The story of my life.

SERGEI. And mine. . . .

VICTOR (*with a touch of defiance*). And mine too.

VALYA. My name is Valya.

VICTOR. Mine is Victor.

SERGEI (*thoughtfully*). They call me Sergei.

LARISA (*laying her hand on Valya's shoulder*). My name is Larisa. I am her friend, but this story is not about me. My part in it is only incidental, I'm sorry to say.

SERDYUK. Serdyuk's my name. I am over fifty. More's the pity. (*After a brief pause.*) There are several others involved in this story, but you will hear of them later.

CHORUS. This is how the story ends. It is a spring evening. A light shower is falling. Valya is standing on a small wooden

It Happened in Irkutsk, by Alexei Arbuzov. Translated by Rose Prokofieva. From *Three Soviet Plays*. Moscow, Foreign Languages Publishing House.

bridge overlooking the Angara, thinking of the future.

(*The outlines of a small wooden bridge emerge.* VALYA *is seen standing on the bridge under a dim street light, deep in thought.*)

And now Victor will appear. Here he comes.

VICTOR. Valya! (*Goes over to her.*) Look, it's raining!

VALYA. I don't care. . . . (*After a brief silence.*) Look at the lights on the dam. Aren't they lovely?

VICTOR. They say we will be damming up the river in two weeks' time.

VALYA (*nods*). Yes, and that will be the end.

VICTOR. Are you going home?

VALYA. Yes.

VICTOR. May I come with you?

VALYA. No.

VICTOR. Why not?

VALYA. I'd rather you didn't.

VICTOR. But you'll get wet. . . .

VALYA. It doesn't matter. (*Glances at him.*) Victor. . . .Victor, darling. Thank you.

VICTOR. What for?

VALYA. Look. . . . (*Shows him a roll of bills in her hand.*)

VICTOR. Your pay?

VALYA. Yes, my first. . . . (*Tears start to her eyes.*) If only he knew. . . . How glad he would be.

VICTOR. Yes.

VALYA (*presses her cheek to his sleeve*). Thank you.

VICTOR (*gently*). Silly girl.

VALYA (*smiling*). They say there's a girl at the Volga dam who's in charge of a whole section crew. Think it's possible?

VICTOR. Of course it is.

VALYA. Oh dear!

VICTOR. What is it?

VALYA (*smiling*). A raindrop went down my neck.

VICTOR. They say our excavator is going to Bratsk. Have you heard?

VALYA (*quickly*). Good-bye. I must go to the nursery, for the children.

VICTOR (*taking her hand*). Valya, darling. . . .

VALYA. No. . . . Don't say it.

VICTOR. Never?

VALYA. I'll be seeing you! (*Runs off.*)

VICTOR. She runs off, happy, her eyes glistening with tears. And I am alone.

CHORUS. Do you love her very much?

VICTOR (*thoughtfully*). Terribly. But I don't remember when the trouble began.

CHORUS. Trouble? Isn't it a wonderful thing to be in love?

VICTOR. Perhaps. . . . After all, I am not the same as I was when I first came here.

CHORUS. Most likely it all began that evening two years ago when you and Sergei went to the grocery store. . . . Remember? It stood not far from the hostel where you lived at the time.

— There it is, standing on a little hill, a stone's throw from the construction site.

— And here is Valya herself. She works in the store at the cash register.

— And that's her friend, Larisa. It is seven o'clock. Their working day is over.

VICTOR. Sergei and I were having dinner in the canteen, intending to drop over to the store afterwards.

CHORUS. Yes. You hadn't got there yet.

(VALYA *and* LARISA *are seen locking up the shop. The sky above them is clear. It is soon sundown.*)

VALYA. It gets dark much later now, doesn't it, Larisa?

LARISA. Yes, spring's coming. . . . I can't get the padlock into the rings, they're awfully small.

VALYA. Give it a few bangs with a stick. Here, let me. . . . (*Hits the padlock with a stick.*) There we are!

LARISA. Good for you!

VALYA (*looking about her with pleasure*). How jolly everything is! I do love the spring.

(A TIPSY MAN *hurries up to the shop.*)

TIPSY MAN. I say, girls, not shutting up shop, are you? Not before I've had another bottle of vodka.

LARISA. It's after seven. Shop's closed.

TIPSY MAN (*reproachfully*). Now then, girls. You can't do that to a fellow. What about that vodka?

VALYA. Nothing doing, we're through for the day.

TIPSY MAN. Think I'm a drunk, eh? Not me! Haven't tasted a drop in five months. Not since Christmas.

VALYA. Well, you've had more than a drop this time.

TIPSY MAN. My wife just gave birth to

a son. In Zlatoust. Got to celebrate, don't I?

VALYA. Of course. Let's dance. (*Seizes him and begins whirling him around, humming a tune.*) And now run along and sleep it off, Daddy.

TIPSY MAN. Listen, cashier girl. What's your name again?

VALYA. Valya.

TIPSY MAN. Thanks a lot, Valya girl. Thanks. This is a great day for me! Honest it is. Come on, let's go to town and make a night of it!

VALYA (*whirling him around again*). You go bye-bye—that's the best place for you, man.

TIPSY MAN. Thanks, Valya, I thank you on behalf of my wife. (*Goes off. Turns.*) I'll be all right if I don't meet anybody, but if I do. . . . Oh, the hell with it all! (*Goes off.*)

LARISA. Why did you do that?

VALYA. Just for the fun of it. Isn't it nice to know there's one more boy in the world? (*Laughs gaily.*)

(*Enter* SERGEI *and* VICTOR.)

VICTOR. Good-evening, girls. . . . Department store closed?

VALYA. You needn't laugh at our shop. Today's receipts were as big as at any big city shop. We had smoked herrings today. You ought to have seen the crush!

VICTOR. Meet Sergei. My boss. I've told you about him.

VALYA (*who has just noticed* SERGEI). How do you do.

VICTOR (*to* SERGEI). This is Valya—champion small change-ringer. And this is Larisa Petrovna, sales manager. Nice girls.

VALYA. So you are Sergei?

VICTOR (*to* VALYA). Seen him before?

VALYA. Yes, I've noticed him. He patronises our shop once in a while.

SERGEI: Occasionally. Tell the truth, I like crisp, well-baked loaves, not the pallid sort you sell here.

VALYA. Everybody prefers the crisp kind. But why do you always stare at me in such a queer way? As if I'd offended you in some way. . . .

SERGEI. Oh no, it's not that. (*Simply.*) I just think you're very nice to look at. So I look.

(*A brief silence.*)

VICTOR. Look, he's made her blush! It's not everybody that can do that.

(*A* LITTLE GIRL, *wrapped in a shawl, approaches the shop.*)

LITTLE GIRL. Oh, Auntie. . . . Is the shop closed already?

VALYA. I suppose you think we've got to sit here day and night! You try twirling the cash register handle eight hours on end!

LITTLE GIRL. I only want a loaf of bread, the 60-kopek kind. We need it for our hamburgers.

LARISA (*heatedly*). There they go! Every time you lock up someone's sure to appear.

LITTLE GIRL. Grandma's coming to supper. And we haven't enough bread.

VALYA. Here, take mine. (*Takes a loaf out of her string-bag and hands it to the child.*)

LITTLE GIRL. But don't you need it yourself?

VALYA. I can do without it. Mustn't put on weight. The boys won't like me if I get fat. See?

LITTLE GIRL. Thanks. (*Takes the bread.*) Do you want the 60 kopeks?

VALYA. Sure I do. Sixty kopeks will buy me two sodas.

LITTLE GIRL (*hands her a ruble*). Forty kopeks change, please.

VALYA. Here, take thirty. It's all I have. Ten kopeks commission. (*Turns to* VICTOR.) See how the co-operatives make money?

LITTLE GIRL. Thanks, Auntie. . . . (*Runs off.*)

VALYA (*calls after her*). Auntie yourself! (*To* SERGEI.) So you're the big noise on the excavator?

SERGEI. Not the biggest. That's old man Serdyuk. He's the chief of our crew. And I'm in charge of a shift. Senior operator.

LARISA. You don't look it.

SERGEI. Have you ever seen our ESA-75 at close range? Come over and have a look some time. She's a beauty.

LARISA. You seem to think so anyway.

SERGEI. We all do.

VICTOR. Works like blazes. Takes the place of 14,000 laborers.

VALYA. Senior operators make big money, too, I bet.

SERGEI (*hesitantly*). Sometimes.

VALYA. Excuse me for asking, but are you married?

SERGEI. No.

VALYA. Hear that, Larisa, here's our chance! (*Breaks into a little dance, humming a tune.*) Watch out. I'm making a play for you!

SERGEI (*looking at her*). You like to dance, don't you?

VALYA. Anything wrong with that?

SERGEI. No, you dance very well.

VALYA. You haven't taken a fancy to me, have you? Vitya dear, step aside, please. All is over between us.

VICTOR (*laughing*). You can't turn *his* head. He's made of the right stuff. There isn't a finer chap in existence.

SERGEI. Come on. Let's go. Good-bye, girls.

VALYA (*saucily*). Ta-ta. Be a good boy!

VICTOR (*to* VALYA, *in an undertone*). Come to the dance this evening. We'll take in a movie afterwards. Just in time for the last show.

VALYA (*winking*). Okay.

(SERGEI *and* VICTOR *go off.*)

VALYA (*after a pause*). Time we were off too. (*Looks back at the shop.*) Good-bye till morning, little shop. Oh dear, my head's in a whirl, Larisa . . . (*Leans against a tree.*) What a day we had with that fish! . . . I'm worn out.

LARISA. You talk too much.

VALYA. What do you care? We're only young once. (*Smiles.*) He's funny, that operator.

LARISA. See you don't fall in love with him.

VALYA. Not me. I wouldn't exchange my Victor for anyone.

LARISA. He's a good looker.

(VALYA, LARISA, *the shop and the trees fade out.*)

CHORUS. Ah, there goes Rodik, the operator's assistant. A nice lad.

— What are you thinking of, Rodik? Homesick for Moscow?

RODIK. I do get homesick sometimes. After all, I was born and brought up in Moscow. My mother and my two little sisters are there. They used to fuss over me frightfully. That's why I quit Moscow really. I wanted to learn to live on my own. It's an exciting experience for a spoiled youngster like me.

CHORUS. You ought to know!

RODIK. I always take my holiday around the New Year's, because I like Moscow best in January. In that month I take in enough of Moscow to last me for the rest of the year. Out here I am on my own. (*Looks around.*) I share a room in the hostel with four other fellows. There it is, on the hill overlooking the Angara.

CHORUS. Who is that sprawling on the bench?

RODIK. Just a minute, I'll look. (*Smiles.*) Oh, that's our helper, Lapchenko. Afanasy Lapchenko. A lazy sort of chap. (*Goes over to* LAPCHENKO.) What are you lying about here for, man?

LAPCHENKO. Because I like it, see?

(CHORUS *fades out.* RODIK *and* LAPCHENKO *in front of the hostel.* VICTOR *appears in the doorway.*)

VICTOR. Weather's clearing up . . . (*Sees* LAPCHENKO.) What're you doing on that bench?

LAPCHENKO. Taking it easy.

(DENIS *comes up. He has a letter in his hand.*)

RODIK. Who's it from?

DENIS. My old army pals. They don't forget me. (*With a broad grin.*) Listen to this, our captain's been promoted to major. Brainy chap, that. Couldn't be brainier.

RODIK. Don't say that. There's no limit to brain, you know.

SERGEI (*comes out of the hostel, sees* LAPCHENKO, *goes up to him*). Still on your back, Afanasy?

LAPCHENKO. I'm ruminating.

DENIS. My captain's been promoted, Sergei! He's a major now.

SERGEI. Congrats. . . . The Chief *was* in a temper today, wasn't he, Rodik?

RODIK. He's going to give us hell.

DENIS. What's holding Zinka up, I wonder? She'll be glad to hear the news.

VICTOR (*cleaning his teeth at the outdoor wash-stand*). What news?

DENIS. Haven't you heard? (*Showing the letter.*) My captain's been made a major.

(RODIK *chuckles.*)

My Zinka understands everything.

RODIK. You know why you two are such a happy couple? Because you live in different hostels. Wait till you get a room of your own. That'll be the end of domestic bliss.

SERGEI. That's a cheap bit of cynicism for an intelligent Muscovite like you, Rodik.

(SERDYUK *comes up. He looks like thunder.*)

SERDYUK. Everybody on deck? Where's Lapchenko? (*Notices him.*) On his back as usual. (*To* LAPCHENKO.) Come on, up with you!

(LAPCHENKO *springs up.*)
You'll get bed sores if you lie about so much. (*Bangs his fist on the table.*) What do you think this is, an old folks' home or a construction job? We're building a new future here, didn't you know that? It's an honour to be working on this job. . . . Quiet! Look here, Sergei, what damn fool brought this fellow to work on our excavator? Answer me, who was it?

SERGEI. You brought him yourself, Chief.

SERDYUK (*to* LAPCHENKO). Hear that? Thanks to you my assistant calls me a fool in public.

SERGEI. Now then, Chief, you're putting words into my mouth.

SERDYUK (*to* LAPCHENKO). Just because I want to do you a good turn I get myself called a fool, see? (*Sighs.*) Why do you think I've got the wind up? Because this shift means a lot to me. I was on it myself until last year when they made me crew foreman and put young Sergei here in my place at the controls. Victor was just an oiler then, but he finished an electricians' course and got shifted up to the job of first assistant. And look at Denis. Six months ago he was just a demobbed tankman. Now he's an oiler. That's what I call progress! It's what you expect on a big communist construction job like this one. See what I mean, Lapchenko? Now take yourself. Do you get the difference? A fellow who works on a machine, a marvel of modern engineering like this here walking excavator, has got to be something of a marvel himself, see? But what are you doing? Are you attending evening school? Are you studying? Are you improving your mind? Not you! You're marking time, getting nowhere. You're a stick-in-the-mud. (*Pauses a moment to let this sink in.*) Well, d'you get the point?

LAPCHENKO. Doing my best.

SERDYUK. Good. Now the next item on the agenda. Who was at the controls at ten o'clock this morning?

VICTOR. I was.

SERDYUK (*to* SERGEI). Where were you?

SERGEI. I was called out to the Komsomol Committee.

SERDYUK (*to* VICTOR). So you were the good-for-nothing who dropped a shovelful of earth on Babkin?

(LAPCHENKO *is unable to suppress a giggle.*)
That's right, laugh, Lapchenko. You ought to be crying! (*To* VICTOR.) Well, out with it!

VICTOR. You see, Chief, we're competing with Babkin. We've beat him on all counts. So the louse had the nerve to begin spying on us.

SERDYUK. What do you mean, spying on you?

VICTOR. Why do we have such a good showing? Because our shift works most efficiently. We save several seconds at each turn of the jib. And that runs up to a thousand cubic metres of earth every month.

SERDYUK (*cutting him short*). I didn't ask for a lecture on how to operate a walking excavator. Stick to the point.

VICTOR. Well, that Babkin wants to find out how we do it. So he keeps nosing around. Got himself a pair of powerful field-glasses, the vermin. I was at the controls this morning when I see him hiding behind a hump of earth, spying on us. So I accidentally opened up the scoop a bit too soon, and some of it emptied on Comrade Babkin, that's all.

SERDYUK (*to* SERGEI). Did you know about it?

SERGEI (*after a moment's hesitation*). Yes.

SERDYUK. What did you do about it?

SERGEI. Nothing.

SERDYUK. Well, you've earned yourself a reprimand.

VICTOR. He's not telling the truth. He didn't know anything about it.

SERDYUK. So you've begun to lie to me, Sergei? Protecting your comrades? Listen here, all of you. The crews on this job may be competing with one another, but we're all doing the same thing—building communism. So it's got to be clean, see? (*To* VICTOR.) You're in for a reprimand too. And if the big chief calls you in, don't expect me to defend you. (*Pauses.*) Not much, anyhow. What're you grinning about, you good-for-nothing? Tomorrow you'll get hold of that Babkin, take him up into the cab and show him all your trade secrets. Let him bring his notebook along, too. We're not so poor we can't give something away. (*Notices* ZINKA, *who has come up and is making signs to* DENIS.) You leave your husband alone. Can't you see he's in conference? Sit down over there and keep quiet. We'll be through soon.

DENIS (*bursting with his news*). Zinka. . . . My captain's been made a major!

ZINKA. Oo, isn't that nice!

SERDYUK. That'll do, ladybird. Sit quiet and listen to me give your husband a bawling out.

DENIS. Me, Chief? What for?

SERDYUK. Who put on the circus act with the match-boxes yesterday?

(LAPCHENKO *bursts out laughing.*) You ought to be crying, not laughing, Lapchenko. Answer, Denis.

RODIK. Stepan Yegorovich, let me answer. It was my idea. You see, the section wasn't ready when we reported for work, we had about ten minutes spare time. So I challenged Denis to take over the controls and try to lift up a box of matches with the scoop, but without picking up a scrap of earth.

SERDYUK. Not a scrap, you say?

RODIK. Not even the tiniest bit. Just the match-box. I showed him how to do it first.

SERGEI. Rodik does it very neatly, Chief.

SERDYUK (*interested*). Did Denis do it too?

DENIS. No, not once. It's damn hard, Chief.

RODIK. It's excavation elevated to a fine art.

SERDYUK. I ought to give you a reprimand for that sort of art. (*To* DENIS). And you too.

ZINKA (*pertly*). Why him? He didn't do it.

SERDYUK. You pipe down, ladybird.

ZINKA. You're awful grumpy, Chief. Time you got married.

SERDYUK. Nothing doing. This talk's been tried before. (*To* RODIK). If you weren't such a smart lad, I'd have your hide. So you can count yourself lucky. (*Turns.*) Hi, Victor, run over to the excavator. Get Vyatkin to look at the rectifier, it's not working properly.

VICTOR. Tomorrow, Chief. I've promised to go to the movies tonight.

SERDYUK. Promised who?

LAPCHENKO. Valya, the cashier girl. She goes with everybody . . . to the pictures.

SERGEI (*sharply*). Shut up, Lapchenko! (*After a pause.*) Valya's a nice girl. Clever, kind-hearted.

LAPCHENKO. Too kind-hearted for me! That's why everyone calls her Good-time Valya!

SERDYUK. Look here, Lapchenko. For the last time, are you going to behave decently or aren't you?

LAPCHENKO (*in mock despair*). It's no use, Stepan Yegorovich. The theatre's closed for repairs, the club's not working. There's no place for a fellow to imbibe culture.

SERDYUK (*losing his temper*). A club! Have you ever tried reading a good book? Ever stopped to think about anything? Ever looked up at the stars? Ever tried learning a foreign language? (*To* VICTOR.) So you'll go over to the excavator?

VICTOR. All right.

SERDYUK (*sheepishly*). I say, Rodik. When you get a spare moment, call me over, and we'll try that match-box trick. . . . (*To* LAPCHENKO). As for you, young fellow, you'd better look out! (*Hurries off.*)

ZINKA (*runs over to* DENIS, *and kisses him*). What did you eat for first course?

DENIS. Borsch.

ZINKA. Noodle soup would have been better.

VICTOR. Does he know any foreign languages himself?

RODIK. I doubt it, although I did see him buy a French grammar the other day.

ZINKA (*to* DENIS). Let's go for a walk, shall we? A long, long walk.

DENIS (*looks at her with a fond smile*). My little one. . . . (*Takes her arm and they walk off in the direction of the river.*)

LAPCHENKO (*calling after them*). See

the bears don't get you. (*Saunters off.*)

RODIK. The wind is blowing from Lake Baikal. (*After a pause.*) I'm going to write a letter to Mother. (*Thoughtfully.*) I can just see her there at home at Chistiye Prudy.

(VICTOR *and* SERGEI *remain alone.*)

VICTOR. Letters, letters. . . .

(*A pause.*)

SERGEI. Nothing from Leningrad?

VICTOR. No.

SERGEI (*softly*). Don't take it so hard, Victor.

VICTOR (*with a bitter smile*). Nice of you to try and comfort me.

SERGEI. Were you very fond of your father?

VICTOR. He was a wonderful man, kind, good-natured. Mother too. He was always telling her stories and making her laugh. I can still hear her laugh sometimes. (*He is silent for a few moments.*) When Mother died I thought Father would go mad. . . . But afterwards he met that woman. And that was the end of him for me. He's changed completely since she came. He's not the same man. He's miserable, frightened, bad-tempered. That's what love can do to people.

SERGEI. Don't you believe it. That's an ugly thought, Victor. Drive it out of your mind.

VICTOR. Yes, it's not a pleasant thought, you're right. (*Looks at* SERGEI.) Well, what else can you think of by way of consolation?

SERGEI (*smiles, takes a packet of biscuits out of his pocket*). Have some, they're not bad.

VICTOR. Thanks.

(*They eat the biscuits. There is a feeling of close comradeship between them at this moment.*)

SERGEI. Not bad at all. . . . I wonder how they get the filling into them? It must be quite a complicated process. I've been wondering about such things since I was a kid. Even an umbrella used to bother me—who invented it and how?

VICTOR. I could do with some soda water now. Well, I'm off. Can't let the Chief down. (*Takes movie tickets out of his pocket and hands them to* SERGEI.) Be a pal and give these to Valya. She'll be waiting for me outside the cinema. It's the eight-forty show. You explain the situation to her. Or better still, take her to the pictures yourself. You won't regret it, she's a nice girl.

SERGEI (*thoughtfully*). Perhaps Rodik ought to go?

VICTOR. I wouldn't trust him. (*Winks.*) Rodik's a gay young blade from the big city, don't forget. (*Looks at* SERGEI.) I'd rather it was you. (*Exit.*)

(SERGEI *looks at the tickets, smiles.*)

CHORUS. An Italian workingman has his bicycle stolen from him. Without it he is in danger of losing his job.

— The Italian has a wife and a small son, if he doesn't find his bicycle they will be left without bread. And so the Italian wanders about the streets of Rome searching for his bicycle.

— This foreign film is being shown in the little movie-house on the banks of the Angara. Outside the movie-house thousands of people are building for themselves—and the trials and sufferings of the people on the screen seem very remote. So remote that it is hard to believe in them.

— Sergei watches the picture in silence. He does not try to take Valya's hand and caress it under cover of darkness, which is what she is accustomed to expect from her movie escorts.

— The Italian worker did not find his bicycle. The picture ends.

— Poor Italian worker, what a sad life is yours!

(*A small garden outside the movie-house. The show is just over. A loudspeaker is blaring. The public disperses.* VALYA *and* SERGEI *stand beside a bench.*)

VALYA. Well, thanks for coming. And give my regards to Victor. It wasn't such a bad picture.

SERGEI. Shall I walk you home?

VALYA. No, thanks. If the boys in my house see us they'll make fun of you.

SERGEI. Would they make fun of Victor if he saw you home?

VALYA. No, they're used to him by now. You're new. They don't like to see me go out with different fellows.

SERGEI. Do you like it?

VALYA. Of course. It's much more fun. (*She is silent for a moment.*) I get tired of people very quickly.

SERGEI. How's that?

VALYA. I don't know really. But that's

how it is. We had a lecturer here once. He talked to us about literature. He said we ought to pattern ourselves after the heroes of books. Everyone ought to choose a hero and try to imitate him, he said. So I chose mine.

SERGEI. Who was that?

VALYA. Ever heard the opera *Carmen?* Well, I chose her.

SERGEI. I'm afraid the lecturer had good characters in mind.

VALYA. You think Carmen is bad? Well, you're all wrong. The composer wouldn't have written such good music about her if she was bad. (*Looks at* SERGEI *with disapproval.*) Well, good-bye, I must get going.

SERGEI. Good-bye. (*Sits down on the bench.*)

VALYA (*takes a few steps, then turns and looks at* SERGEI). Why aren't you going home?

SERGEI. I want to sit here for a while.

VALYA. It's nice here. You can see the Irkutsk bridge . . . And the city park. (*After a pause.*) Did you like the picture?

SERGEI. Yes, very much. I like Italian films. They give a very realistic picture of the poverty and suffering of the people there. It makes you appreciate what you've got all the more.

VALYA. Oh, so you don't think much of Soviet pictures, eh?

SERGEI. I wouldn't say that. We have some good pictures. But not very many. Most of them try to convince me of things I've taken for granted for a long time. And that's boring. I don't need convincing. I could convince others.

VALYA. That's very interesting. Though I'm not sure what you're talking about. By the way, how old are you?

SERGEI. Oh, I'm quite old. Soon be thirty. In four years from now.

VALYA. Twenty-six? I wouldn't have thought you a day over twenty-two.

SERGEI. Yes, I'm very well preserved.

VALYA. I have a piece of candy here. Shall we share it? I'll bite off a bit and you can have the other half.

SERGEI. Thanks. My favourite candy. (*He is about to put it into his mouth when he notices something.*)

VALYA. What's the matter?

SERGEI. It's got lipstick on it.

VALYA. Don't you like lipstick?

SERGEI. Not much. It's dye, after all.

VALYA. That's all the thanks we get for trying to please you men. Well, are you going to eat it?

SERGEI. Sure. (*Pops the sweet into his mouth.*)

VALYA. You *are* brave!

SERGEI. You bet I am.

VALYA. Why don't I ever see you at dances?

SERGEI. I'm always very busy. After all, I'm the Komsomol organiser and all that sort of thing. Do a bit of reading too.

VALYA. Yes, you're more serious than any of my other friends. (*Smiles.*) Are your parents living?

SERGEI. Yes. They live close by, in Cheremkhovo. Father is a mine foreman, Mother is . . . well, Mother is just a dear. I go to see them every other Sunday. It's not far from here.

VALYA (*with sudden brusqueness*). My dad was a sailor.

SERGEI. Was?

VALYA. Yes.

SERGEI. And your mother? Is she alive?

VALYA. I don't know. It doesn't matter.

SERGEI (*looks at her*). So you are all alone in the world?

VALYA. All alone? Certainly not. (*Laughs.*) If you want to know, I have a little daughter.

SERGEI. A daughter?

VALYA. Yes, in a children's home. So now you know, Sergei. Are you sorry for me?

SERGEI. Not at all. (*After a pause.*) But why do you work in the store? Do you like being a cashier?

VALYA. It's as good as anything else. I've tried all sorts of things. The store has its points.

SERGEI. What, for instance?

VALYA. Ah, you want to know too much. (*She is silent for a few moments.*) I don't know what's come over me to-day. Not my usual sparkling self, am I?

SERGEI. I don't know what you are like usually.

VALYA. No, you wouldn't. I like my character. I wish I could meet a boy like myself. I'd fall head over heels in love with him. (*Looks at* SERGEI.) Have you ever been married?

SERGEI. Yes, once. Why do you laugh?

VALYA. I don't know. What happened to your wife?

SERGEI. We parted.

VALYA. Why?

SERGEI (*thoughtfully*). Because we didn't need each other, I think. (*Apologetically.*) I suppose we didn't really love each other.

VALYA. (*softly*). Do you think there is such a thing?

SERGEI. What?

VALYA. Real love.

SERGEI (*after a moment*). Yes, I do.

VALYA (*softly*). I'm so glad.

SERGEI (*he does not hear*). What did you say?

VALYA. It's frightening sometimes to be alone.

SERGEI (*after a pause*). But what about Victor?

VALYA (*sharply*). Never mind Victor. Tell me about yourself. I want to know all about you. You haven't said anything. I've been doing all the talking.

SERGEI. There isn't much to tell. I haven't done anything worth mentioning, except for being born in Siberia. Don't smile! The whole second half of the twentieth century will belong to us Siberians. The heart of Russia is being shifted over here, believe me. Two hundred years ago Lomonosov said: "Russian might will grow through Siberia!" And this has come true in our time.

VALYA. Tell me about yourself. I've heard about Siberia, Sergei. Have you been on the construction job long?

SERGEI. This is my third year, which means I've been here since the very beginning. I finished technical school early and went to work on the excavator right away. I'll soon have a work record of eight years. True, I worked on Chelyabinsk excavators in the beginning, but they're small fry compared to this ten-cubic-metre baby of ours. I met Victor here and made friends with him. I suppose you know what a sad home life he's had. His mother died, and his father married again. Poor chap! His stepmother turned out to be a bad woman. They went back to Leningrad after the war but he stayed here. Became a Siberian. He misses his father terribly, but he can't forgive that woman . . . (*After a moment's silence.*) Do you know, he sometimes speaks your name in his sleep. Honestly. You must be kind to him, Valya, he also has nobody to love him. Nobody but you. And if he is a little brusque sometimes, you must forgive him . . .

(*Two* YOUNG MEN *come up to the bench.*)

FIRST YOUNG MAN. Who's this on the bench? Well, if it isn't Valya. Our little Valya.

SECOND YOUNG MAN. Who's she got this time? A brand-new boy friend!

FIRST YOUNG MAN (*to* SERGEI). Listen, you dope, you're wasting your breath on her. She doesn't like talk. She likes something else.

SECOND YOUNG MAN. Take her into the bushes, man. She won't mind.

(SERGEI *gets up slowly and knocks the* SECOND YOUNG MAN *down.*)

SECOND YOUNG MAN (*picking himself up*). Come on, pal, we'd better be off.

FIRST YOUNG MAN. The fellow's got a screw loose. (*Go off.*)

VALYA (*after a long silence*). I'm sorry, Sergei. (*Runs off.*)

(SERGEI *looks after her.*)

CHORUS. Night creeps slowly up to the Angara.

— The lights in the settlement go out one by one.

— And the cool breath of the night— rises over the river.

— It is very late but Valya is not yet home. Perhaps that is why Larisa cannot sleep.

LARISA (*in the* CHORUS). Thirty-four . . . Is that so much? Is my life really over?

CHORUS. But when Valya returns, Larisa will not ask her any questions. And the light in their window will go out at once. . . .

— But will Larisa go to sleep? The summer night is so warm . . .

LARISA. Is thirty-four so very much?

CHORUS. And in a few day's time on a Saturday evening, they will go down to the Angara together to where the forest comes right down to the water's edge.

(LARISA *and* VALYA *are lying under a tree on the bank of the Angara. It is late afternoon.*)

LARISA. Valya and I are lying on the bank of the Angara thinking our own thoughts. Valya must be thinking of Victor. I am remembering my childhood and youth. The blue sky on that Sunday morning of June twenty-second, nineteen forty-one.

VALYA. Larisa, let's have another dip.

LARISA (*without moving*). All right.

VALYA. Why are you so quiet today?

LARISA. I'm thinking.

VALYA. What about?

LARISA. About something that is gone for ever.

VALYA. What's that?

LARISA. My childhood.

VALYA. Imagine moping about that!

LARISA. I want to begin all over again.

VALYA. What, go back to school? Not me!

LARISA. You're silly, Valya.

VALYA. I like that! Why am I silly?

LARISA. My life is over. It's all right for you, you're only twenty-five.

VALYA. What of it?

LARISA. It's time you settled down, Valya. Though it isn't easy to get a husband nowadays.

VALYA. No, and especially for me. With my reputation. (*Tossing her head.*) I bet I could get married if I wanted to. There's plenty of fools about. Only marriage is so dull. (*Laughs.*) Why don't you get married yourself?

LARISA. Too late. My boy friend is probably lying in his grave somewhere near Berlin.

VALYA. Did you have a boy friend?

LARISA. I must have had. We just didn't meet, that's all.

VALYA (*with a sigh*). Yes, the war. . . . Let's have some beer, Larisa. Tomorrow's free day, after all. (*Opens a bottle.*) You can have the cup. I'll drink straight from the bottle. . . . Come on, let's toast, old girl. Here's to us.

LARISA (*drinking*). It's still cold.

VALYA. I kept it in the water.

LARISA (*suddenly*). Did you know that all my people were killed in Minsk on June 22?

VALYA (*quietly*). Shall I pour you some more?

LARISA. Go ahead.

VALYA. There, that's the last drop.

LARISA. Liza came home from the maternity home yesterday.

VALYA. She's crazy. What is it this time?

LARISA. A little boy. I saw him. Ugly little thing. But got eyes like two black berries. . . .

VALYA. I have another bottle of beer.

LARISA. That's enough.

VALYA (*after a pause*). I suppose they'll get a separate room now?

LARISA. They should. Her Pyotr is doing very well on the job.

VALYA. Don't envy them. . . . Diapers, wash-tubs, chamber-pots!

LARISA. You're just jealous, my girl.

VALYA (*tossing her head*). Rubbish! I could have a baby any time if I wanted. That's no problem. You know what I did, Larisa, I went and told a guy here that I've got a baby.

LARISA. You idiot. Whatever for?

VALYA. I just wanted to see how he would react.

LARISA. You're the limit.

VALYA. I suppose I am. (*Looks at her watch.*) Nearly eight. My Victor will be turning up soon.

LARISA (*lazily*). Like him?

VALYA. He's lots of fun.

(*They both fall silent.*)

LARISA (*suddenly*). God, I'm so sick of myself.

VALYA. Never mind, so long as the boys aren't sick of you.

LARISA. I'm getting mean and jealous.

VALYA. Stop it, Larisa. Listen, I received a letter today. From an unknown admirer. (*Takes out an envelope.*) See?

LARISA. What does it say?

VALYA (*reads*). "People are born into this world for a purpose, Valya. We must not waste our lives. And if a person can do something to beautify the world around him, he has made his life worth while. That is why no one can ever be happy alone. With best wishes."

LARISA. Is that all?

VALYA. Isn't it enough?

LARISA. Who wrote it? Any idea?

VALYA. "Who knows which way the wind blows?" But it's all nonsense. (*Tears up the note.*) Fly away, little paper birds.

LARISA. What did you do that for?

VALYA. I know who wrote that note.

LARISA. Who?

VALYA. Oh, some queer fellow.

(VICTOR *appears. He walks slowly over to the girls.*)

VICTOR. Greetings to the working

girls. How is your health today, Larisa Petrovna?

LARISA. No complaints, thanks. (*Gets up and walks off slowly along the bank of the river.*)

VALYA. Where're you going?

LARISA. Just for a stroll along the river. (*Exit.*)

VICTOR. Why did she go off like that?

VALYA. Thinks she's being tactful. (*A pause.*) Want some beer?

VICTOR. I don't mind.

VALYA. What's new?

VICTOR. We've been given a new plan. Going to be big doings on the dam soon. We'll have to work like blazes.

VALYA (*laughs*). Good-bye, glory!

VICTOR. That's where you're wrong. Sergei will think of something, you'll see. We're all right as long as we've got him.

VALYA. Always Sergei, Sergei. Anyone would think you were all babies. Can't you do anything without a nursemaid?

VICTOR. Sharp-tongued today, aren't you? Not like our gay old Valya a bit. What's up?

VALYA. Never you mind. Have some fried fish. Larisa and I got it at the market today.

VICTOR (*eating*). My mother used to make delicious soup out of this fish.

VALYA. Do you miss your father?

VICTOR (*does not reply at once*). He'll get along without me.

VALYA. Aren't you ever lonesome for Leningrad?

VICTOR. My home's here, on the Angara.

VALYA. You hate her terribly, don't you? . . . Your stepmother, I mean.

VICTOR. Who told you?

VALYA. I know all about it.

VICTOR. I'm sorry for Dad.

VALYA. Vitya, darling, is it true that you call to me in your sleep?

VICTOR. How the dickens should I know?

(*A pause.*)

VALYA. Shall we go boating today?

VICTOR. I can't. Chief's calling a meeting of the crew at eight o'clock this evening. Got to think up new ways of working faster and better.

VALYA. So we can kiss our evening good-bye?

VICTOR. Never mind, old girl, we'll make up for it another time.

(*They kiss.*)

VALYA (*after a pause, bursts out laughing*). Guess what, Victor? I'm going to get married.

VICTOR. Go on . . . Who's the lucky fellow?

VALYA (*defiantly*). What if it's you?

VICTOR. Me? That would be a good joke!

VALYA. What's so funny about it?

VICTOR. Oh, don't be a fool. What do you want to be hitched up for? Don't we have a nice time as it is? (*Embraces her*). I'll drop in to see you after the confab . . . Send your room-mate to the pictures—to the last show.

VALYA. All right.

VICTOR. Tell her it's a thriller . . . Will you?

VALYA. All right.

VICTOR. That's the girl. (*Pats her cheek.*) Well, I'd better be off, or I'll get it from the Chief (*Exit.*)

VALYA (*alone*). "That would be a good joke."

(*Larisa appears.*)

LARISA. Had a nice talk?

VALYA (*mechanically*). All right.

LARISA. Look, the sun's gone down.

(*Silence.*)

VALYA. Vitya's funny . . . Said he wants to marry me.

LARISA (*incredulous*). He didn't!

VALYA. Honest he did. Larisa, where did you want to go this evening?

LARISA. To the pictures. Thought I'd get a ticket for the last show.

VALYA. Well, don't.

LARISA. Why not?

VALYA. I hear it's a dull picture.

(*Fade-out. Gradually the* CHORUS *appears.*)

CHORUS. Outside your house little children are playing. Funny little things with grubby faces and hands. One of them has hurt his finger, another is staring with great concentration at a beetle, a third just slapped his playmate. You walk past them and not one of them calls out to you: "Mamma!"

— You return home alone, and there is no one to wake you in the morning.

— Your neighbours' radio is out of

order. Vasya comes home from work and begins to mend it. He turns the house upside down, but his wife is pleased: "My Vasya can fix anything." Late at night when they come home from their walk they will quarrel, sulk for a while and then make it up . . . Oh dear, they're kissing again!

— You have come home alone, no one will wake you in the morning.

(*The girls' room in the hostel. It is Sunday.* LARISA *and* VALYA *are laying the table.*)

LARISA. Did you tell Victor you had invited Sergei?

VALYA. No, I want it to be a surprise. It's my birthday, I can invite anyone I like.

LARISA. Valya, you're up to something.

VALYA. Now don't scold me. I'm going to be married.

LARISA. Don't be silly.

VALYA. Strange, everybody thinks it's a big joke. I don't care, you can laugh as much as you please. I'm sick of being alone. What's the matter, aren't I as good as anyone else?

LARISA. You mean . . . Did Victor really propose to you?

VALYA. Not yet, but he will. Only I might go and choose someone else.

LARISA. But you aren't in love with anyone.

VALYA. How do you know what it's like to be in love?

LARISA. I know. Only I don't remember whether it was real or only a dream.

VALYA. There you are. (*Gives her a hug.*) Run into the kitchen and wash the knives and forks, Larisa.

LARISA. All right. . . . (*Takes dishes from* VALYA *and goes out.*)

VALYA (*going over to the mirror and examining her reflection*). Ah, Valya, Valya. . . . You just show them.

(*A knock at the door.*)
Come in.

SERGEI (*entering*). Good-day, Valya. You sent me a note asking me to come. . . .

VALYA. That's right.

SERGEI. To tell the truth I was rather surprised. . . . We haven't seen each other since that trip to the movies.

VALYA. It's my birthday today.

SERGEI. Your birthday? Why didn't you tell me?

VALYA. I didn't want you to waste money on me.

SERGEI. That's a pity. (*Smiles.*) I'm quite well off, you know.

VALYA. All the more reason. It wouldn't mean anything to you.

SERGEI. But you could have let me know through Victor.

VALYA. Oh, I want it to be a surprise to him.

SERGEI. I see.

VALYA. You're his best friend, aren't you?

SERGEI. Yes.

VALYA. You told me he loves me very much, didn't you?

SERGEI. I did.

VALYA. Can you swear that you didn't make it all up? Ah, you won't answer. Go on, tell me another lie.

SERGEI (*quietly*). I think he does, Valya.

VALYA (*bitterly*). What else do you think? (*She is quiet for a moment, then she laughs.*) All right. I must go and help Larisa in the kitchen. (*Runs out.*)

(SERGEI *examines the girls' room with interest. There is a knock at the door.* VICTOR *comes in.*)

VICTOR. Sergei? What're you doing here?

SERGEI. Valya invited me . . . She wanted to make you a surprise.

VICTOR (*laughing*). She's marvellous, that girl! I was wondering what on earth I would do all evening with two girls on my hands. And here you are. Valya's a good sport, there's none better.

SERGEI (*presently*). Victor, I've been wanting to ask you. . . .

VICTOR. Yes?

SERGEI. I can't make out how things stand between you and Valya.

VICTOR. What's there to understand? I like her a lot.

SERGEI. You like her?

VICTOR. Yes. She's lots of fun. And she's a damn good dancer. Not to speak of anything else.

SERGEI (*noticing a parcel under* VICTOR's *arm*). A present for her?

VICTOR. I was wildly jealous when that photographer chap began hanging around her. (*Laughs wryly.*) Nearly went crazy.

SERGEI. You ought to marry her.

VICTOR. Why should I tie myself down? There's plenty of time for that. (*Pauses.*) Besides, there's too much gossip about Valya around here. I don't pay much attention to it, of course. Valya's a nice girl, only . . . in general, I don't trust them much, Sergei . . . women, I mean. They're mean at heart. They only pretend to be kind. Some are better, some worse. You ought to see what that woman did to my father. (*Takes a guitar off the wall.*)

SERGEI (*smiles*). My mother is a wonderful woman, that's why I think all women must be wonderful.

VICTOR. You're lucky. . . . (*Strumming and singing to himself.*)

(*Enter* VALYA *and* LARISA. *When they hear* VICTOR *singing, they stop in the doorway.*)

LARISA (*quietly*). How nicely you sing, Victor.

VICTOR. Thank you, ma'am. (*To* VALYA.) Congratulations, Valya. (*Hands her the parcel.*) Permit me to offer a small token of my esteem.

VALYA (*opening the parcel and taking out a pretty colored scarf*). Oh, Victor, how lovely! (*Throws the scarf around her shoulders.*)

SERGEI. It suits you, Valya.

VALYA. Sergei didn't bring me anything.

SERGEI. But I. . . .

LARISA. Never mind, Sergei. Forget it. (*Pause.*) What do you say to a game of cards?

SERGEI. I think playing cards is a fool's occupation.

LARISA. Why?

SERGEI. Because life is too short to waste time with cards.

VALYA. Maybe you'd like to give us a lecture on the international situation instead? That's more in your line, isn't it?

SERGEI (*smiles*). Guilty! I did give a talk on the situation in France the other day in the women's hostel. I even remember a note sent up asking me to explain the reasons for the decline in the birth rate in France. I had an idea you wrote that note, Valya.

VALYA. Why didn't you answer it?

SERGEI (*simply*). There wasn't any time.

VALYA. You mean you funked it!

SERGEI (*gaily*). That's right, I funked it.

VALYA. Anyway you needn't boast about getting notes. I also get notes sometimes.

VICTOR (*laughing*). Who from? Grateful customers?

VALYA. Most likely. You don't believe me. Here, I'll read one to you. What do you say, Sergei? (*Takes out a bundle of letters.*) Shall I read it?

SERGEI. Go ahead.

VICTOR. That's right. We'll have a good laugh.

VALYA (*reads*). "I think of you all the time, although you do not even know who I am. You're not living right, Valya. You have no interest either in yourself or in the people around you. In our day and age it is a disgrace to live like that. Think how awful it will be if you realise this too late." (*Looks up.*) Heart-breaking, isn't it?

VICTOR. Who wrote it?

VALYA. An unknown benefactor.

LARISA. You're making it all up.

VALYA. I'm not! Listen to this. . . . (*Takes another letter.*) "I am writing you again, please don't be angry with me. I believe you are very lonely. You must change your way of life, Valya. You must, you must. I do wish I could help you." (*Looks at* SERGEI.) Touching, aren't they?

(SERGEI *does not answer.*)

VICTOR. Maybe they're from some crazy Baptist?

VALYA. And here's the last one. (*Reads.*) "Valya, my darling, send your Victor to the devil and marry me. . . ."

SERGEI. That's not true. . . . There wasn't any letter like that.

VALYA. How do you know? (*Turns to* VICTOR.) Do you hear the advice I get about you? But it's you and not him I'm marrying, isn't it, Victor?

VICTOR. What sort of a joke is this?

LARISA. That's enough, Valya.

VALYA. Sergei tells me you call my name in your sleep.

VICTOR. Don't be funny.

VALYA. Perhaps your friend was lying to me? (*Looks at* VICTOR.) Do you want to know why he's backing out, Sergei? Because he doesn't want a wife with a reputation like mine. Remember what those fellows at the cinema said?

SERGEI. It's not true. . . . Tell her, Victor. . . .

VALYA. Taking his part, eh? It's very noble of you to take your friend's part. But why doesn't your friend speak up for himself? All right, now go away, all of you. The party's off. Besides, it isn't my birthday at all. I made it up. My birthday's in August . . .

SERGEI. I wrote those letters, Victor.

VICTOR. You?

SERGEI (simply). Yes. You see, I love Valya, I love her very much. I want to marry her. (To VALYA.) I don't know what I'll do if you refuse me.

LARISA. This is getting too complicated for me.

SERGEI (to VICTOR). I would never have spoken, Victor, if you hadn't given her up yourself.

VALYA (to VICTOR). Hear that? Now go away. I don't want you, get out!

VICTOR. Are you . . . serious?

VALYA (firmly). Yes. Now, go.

VICTOR. All right. I won't forget this. (Goes out slowly.)

(VALYA goes up to SERGEI and gives him a searching look.)

LARISA. Leave him alone. You hear, Valya?

VALYA (slowly). Why?

LARISA. You know you don't love him.

VALYA. How do you know? (Mockingly.) I'll find out when we're married. He earns good money, and he's not dull.

LARISA. I'm clearing out of here. I'm going to move to Tamara's. . . . You frighten me, Valya. (Hurries out.)

VALYA (after a brief silence). Well, and what do you say?

SERGEI. We'll take your little daughter out of the children's home, and we'll all live together.

VALYA. I haven't got a daughter. I made it all up. All of it, understand? And now go away, I want to be alone.

SERGEI (softly). I can't live without you. Can't you understand?

VALYA. Please . . . go.

(SERGEI goes slowly out of the room. VALYA drops on to the bed and bursts into tears.

Gradually the room fades, to be replaced by SERDYUK and the CHORUS.)

SERDYUK. I have a Ukranian name, but I'm a Siberian to the marrow of my bones.

CHORUS. What sort of a man are you, Stepan Serdyuk?

SERDYUK (thoughtfully). On the whole, I am a happy man.

CHORUS. What makes you happy?

SERDYUK (defiantly). I have found my place in life and I'm satisfied.

CHORUS (reproachfully). Yet you live alone.

SERDYUK. Women don't care for me.

CHORUS. Have you ever loved anyone, friend?

SERDYUK. Yes. A long time ago.

CHORUS. Whom?

A WOMAN'S VOICE. Me. . . . We met at Magnitogorsk. That was during the First Five-Year Plan years when the big steel mill was going up. The work was just beginning when we arrived. It was hard, harder than I can tell. We were in love with each other, but two years later I met Andrei, and I married him. He was the finest man I had ever met. I bore him three children. I know you took it very hard, Stepan, my dear, but I couldn't help it. Now I'm growing old. I have grandchildren. Yet sometimes when I sit alone in the evenings I like to remember my first love. . . .

SERDYUK (reflectively). I suppose I didn't know how to care for a woman.

CHORUS. There was another. . . . Have you forgotten her?

SERDYUK. No, I have not forgotten.

A GIRLISH VOICE. It was I. My name was Xenia. When the war broke out I volunteered as a nurse. I was very young then. We met in 1943. He was so strong, so brave, and so gentle. The war brought us together and we lived alone in a dugout for ten days. . . . When we parted I promised to write to him. He wept, I remember. But I never wrote him a line because two hours after we parted I was killed. He thinks I forgot him, that I was unfaithful to him, but it wasn't that at all. I was killed. . . . A shell burst near by— and that was the end.

SERDYUK. Yes, I was never very popular with the women, brother. But I've not been lonely, just the same. The lads on the excavator are all like my own sons. Especially the Seryogin shift. . . .

(*The men's hostel emerges. It is night.* RODIK *and* DENIS *are sitting at the table.* LAPCHENKO *appears at the window.*)

CHORUS. See, Stepan. It is night, but they aren't sleeping. . . .

— Perhaps something is wrong?

— Where's Sergei? Where's Victor?

SERDYUK. I don't know. I have gone to Slyudyanka to visit my father. But I'll soon be back. . . . Could something have happened?

(CHORUS *and* SERDYUK *gradually fade.*)

LAPCHENKO. Hello, fellows. . . . What's doing?

DENIS. Nothing.

LAPCHENKO. Victor back?

DENIS. No.

LAPCHENKO. Sergei's not back either?

DENIS. No.

LAPCHENKO. We're done for, fellows.

RODIK. Might as well curl up.

LAPCHENKO. Where's the Chief?

DENIS. Gone off to Slyudyanka. . . . He'll be back. . . . And he'll give it to us good and proper.

LAPCHENKO. You bet he will. (*Looks round.*) Here's Victor!

(VICTOR *comes in, pays no attention to anyone and throws himself on to the bed.*)

DENIS. Where've you been?

VICTOR (*hoarsely*). None of your business.

DENIS. Know what you'd get for that in the army?

VICTOR. To hell with the army!

DENIS. My major would teach you!

LAPCHENKO. Watch out, here's the Chief!

(*There is a commotion and the figure of* SERDYUK *appears in the doorway.*)

SERDYUK (*glares angrily at the group and seats himself on a stool*). Well, my fine fellows, what've you got to say for yourselves?

(*No one speaks, all avoid one another's eyes.*)

The model shift! Not a single dark spot on its record for the year! (*Bangs his fist on the table.*) How long did the excavator stand idle?

RODIK. Two hours.

SERDYUK. Two hours! (*Gets up and paces the room in a rage.*) Ten thousand people were idle for one hundred and twenty minutes because of your damn foolishness! Why did the machine break down? Come on! Out with it!

RODIK. The rectifier busted.

SERDYUK. I see. So the electrician's to blame.

VICTOR (*his face still hidden in his hands*). Yes, it's my fault.

SERDYUK. What's the great electrician doing lolling on his bed at this time of the day? Get up out of there. Come on, look at me, you good-for-nothing!

(VICTOR *sits up, and turns his face to* SERDYUK.)

SERDYUK. What's this! Tears? Have I wandered into the women's hostel by mistake? Now, speak up. How did this thing happen?

VICTOR. I wasn't sober.

SERDYUK. That's a lie. You're not the kind. What's the matter with you?

VICTOR. Don't ask me, Chief. I won't tell you anyway.

SERDYUK. Where's Sergei?

LAPCHENKO (*half out of the door*). He's out necking with Valya the cashier, down by the Angara.

VICTOR (*springing up in fury*). Shut up, you. . . .

SERDYUK. Quiet all of you! Now, Rodion, you tell me what's been going on here.

RODIK. There's not much to tell. Sergei and Victor quarrelled over a girl. It's that cashier girl Valya. She's got quite a reputation around here. . . . Well, no need to go into that. Victor lost his temper, and yesterday he and Sergei had words. Came to work this morning a little, er—under the weather, wasn't careful enough, and so it happened. (*To* VICTOR.) Right?

VICTOR. Right.

RODIK. I would like to say this. Ours was a damn good crew. We all got along splendidly. And now the first skirt that comes along has spoiled everything. I'm very fond of my sisters, not to speak of my mother, but I prefer to give women as such a wide berth. And I've been very glad to see that on the whole out here in Siberia women are less of a nuisance than in the centre.

DENIS. You pipe down, Rodion. I won't let you talk like that.

(SERGEI *appears in the doorway.*)

LAPCHENKO. Seryogin himself!

SERDYUK (*ironically*). 'Tenshun! The big chief!

SERGEI (*totally unaware of his surroundings*). Yes? . . . (*Goes over to his bed, sits down, stares into space with a blissful smile.*)

SERDYUK. Here, what's this?

SERGEI (*still smiling*). Yes, yes.

SERDYUK. Look at him! Loony, I swear! (*Shakes* SERGEI.) What's up, Sergei? Dropped from the moon, or what?

SERGEI. Hello, Chief! Back from Slyudyanka?

SERDYUK. What're you grinning about, you young lunatic?

SERGEI. I say, you must excuse us, me and Victor. I swear it won't happen again.

VICTOR. You leave me out of it.

SERDYUK. No, Chief, you're not getting off as easy as that.

SERGEI. Oh, no, it isn't easy at all. . . . Of course she may not love me just now, but in time she'll find that she needs me. . . . She has agreed at last. . . . We're getting married on Sunday, July 15. Ten days from now. You must all come to the wedding.

RODIK. The what?

VICTOR (*goes over to* SERGEI). You've got to clear out of here, Sergei. . . . Leave Valya alone. . . . I'm serious. . . . Go away.

SERGEI. No, I'm not going now. My conscience is quite clear as far as you are concerned, Victor. You gave her up yourself. Didn't you? You've nothing to say. You see, Chief, he's silent. (*Goes over to* VICTOR.) Let's forget it, Victor. For the sake of all of us let's be friends as before.

(VICTOR *does not respond.*)

On Sunday, the 15th. I invite all of you. Let's make it a happy day for her. . . . Just that one day, is it too much to ask? (*Looking at them with sudden fierceness.*) But if any one of you says a single nasty word about her. . . . You'd better take care. I'll never forgive you as long as I live. . . . So remember!

(*The scene fades out. Faint music sounds, and perhaps the patter of raindrops on a roof. Gradually the figure of* VALYA *emerges, seated on the bed. The* CHORUS *gathers round her.*)

CHORUS. Not sleeping, Valya? It has been raining all night long. The winds of summer are blowing over Lake Baikal, driving the low clouds this way.

— It will soon be morning, Valya. The morning of Sunday, the fifteenth of July. . . .

— Your last night alone in this room.

— What awaits you in that new life that begins tomorrow?

VALYA (*in a whisper*). I don't know.

CHORUS. What are you doing? Pause before it is too late. You know you don't love him.

VALYA (*softly*). Don't I? Who knows? I do not know for sure myself. Love. What is love anyway? What is it like? Who can tell me? (*Insistently.*) Why do I keep recalling the day I first met Sergei? He came up to me and paid me twenty kopeks for a box of matches. . . . And when we first spoke to each other I somehow felt sure he would say something wonderful.

CHORUS. How strange. . . .

VALYA. I was still going with Victor at that time, but I kept thinking of Sergei. He was always in my mind. I looked forward so much to his letters. I knew they were from him.

CHORUS. Then you must have been in love with him?

VALYA. Perhaps. No. . . . I don't know.

CHORUS. You don't know? Yet you want to be his wife?

VALYA (*sharply*). Yes, I do. What's wrong with that? He's so kind. . . . I am sick of being all alone. I'm so tired, so tired. . . . And all those nasty jokes. . . . Why am I worse than anyone else? But I will be all right with him, won't I?

CHORUS. What about Victor?

(*The figure of* VICTOR *is seen dimly in the background.*)

VICTOR. Remember, I came to you last evening. And you couldn't believe it when I told you. . . . (*Goes over to her and says quietly.*) Forgive me, Valya.

VALYA. I'm not angry.

VICTOR. I don't know what I'm going to do without you. . . . Let's go away from here together. We'll get married if you insist. I'm willing, if that's what you want.

VALYA. Too late, Victor. . . . Our song is ended. Good-bye. . . .

(She is alone again.)

CHORUS. It will soon be light, Valya. ... Look out of the window. It is a rainy morning.

— The morning of Sunday, July the 15th.

VALYA. Why do I feel so frightened? I am scared. ... His friends will never forgive me, they will turn away from us. We shall walk down the street and people will laugh as we go by. No, I must run away.

CHORUS. Too late! You hear? Someone is knocking at the door. It's Sergei. He has come for you. If you have made up your mind, open the door, Valya, and give him your hand.

VALYA. I have made up my mind. *(In a ringing voice.)* Is that you, Sergei?

SERGEI'S VOICE. Yes, I'm here!

(Strains of an organ. CHORUS throws a white bridal dress on VALYA.)

VALYA. Come in, Sergei.

(SERGEI stands on the threshold, his figure bathed in the light of the morning sun.)

SERGEI. I've come for you!

VALYA. Look, the sun is shining.

SERGEI. Yes, the rain has passed over.

VALYA. Shall we go?

SERGEI. I am not alone, Valya.

(The organ music dies, and in its place sound the clear pure notes of an accordion. Beside SERGEI, we see DENIS with his ZINKA, SERDYUK, LAPCHENKO, RODIK, his sister MAYA, and two or three other lads from the excavator crew, one of them has the accordion, another is strumming a guitar. They all carry flowers.)

SERGEI. Meet my friends, Valya. ... They all work on the excavator.

MAYA My name's Maya, I'm Rodik's sister. I came from Moscow yesterday. I've passed into the tenth form at school and I have come here for a visit. I've never been to a wedding before. ... I'm terribly thrilled. May I kiss you? *(Kisses VALYA.)*

SERGEI. Let's go.

(A thunderclap.)

Look, rain and sunshine, together. What strange company!

SERDYUK *(commanding)*. Umbrellas up!

PANTOMIME

To the accompaniment of music, the wedding procession marches gaily through the town, carrying umbrellas and stepping over puddles as it goes.

CHORUS. What a jolly company!

— Where are they going?

— And in the rain. ...

— Good friends, don't you know? There is a wonderful house on the outskirts of Irkutsk. You go in single and you come out married. Just like a fairytale, isn't it?

— So it is! Why, it's the only institution that issues you a paper complete with rubber stamp, hereby certifying that you are happy, happy as of such and such a day, month and year.

— The trouble is, though, some people forget that the house doesn't tolerate two things: hasty decisions and too sober calculation.

— Yes, if you overlook that, you are punished at once, for you come out of the house arm in arm with a woman, little suspecting how unhappy you have made yourself.

—What a pity I'm not an inventor. I would invent a machine that would determine how much couples really love each other, and decide whether they should be allowed to marry or not.

— Oh, won't someone invent such a machine? We need it badly, friends.

— But let us hasten to the wedding feast, to the new room where Valya and Sergei are to live. There have been many shouts of "bitter, bitter!" so much has been eaten and drunk that I am afraid there will be nothing left for you and me.

(The wedding scene emerges. Someone is playing an accordion and the guests are singing a Siberian song. It is not drunken singing, they sing clearly and tunefully. And when the song ends, they sit quietly, lost in the thoughts evoked by the song.)

SERDYUK. There's nothing like a song for stirring up old memories.

MAYA. Makes you think of the future, too.

DENIS. It's a good song. Gives you something to think about.

(A pause.)

LAPCHENKO. Songs are all right, but what about tackling some more of this good food?

RODIK. Second the motion. Carried unanimously.

(*All return gaily to their plates. There is much laughter and noisy conversation.*)

ZINKA. Hush, everyone. I want to say something.

(*Shouts of: "Speech! Speech!" The hubbub subsides a trifle.*)

(*Earnestly.*) Comrades! We, concrete mixers working on the foundation pit, have been watching you excavator chaps with admiration. We know it's far from easy to operate a huge machine like yours. We know how important it is for you to get proper rest and food. Now that's where a wife comes in, that's her job. And so I call on you, Valya, to bear that in mind and take proper care of Sergei.

RODIK. To three square meals a day! Hurrah!

(*General laughter, the clinking of glasses.*)

LAPCHENKO. Someone's knocking!

(*The gathering is hushed.*)

VALYA (*calling*). Come in!

LARISA (*on the threshold*). Am I welcome?

VALYA (*rushing over to her*). Larisa, darling. . . . I'm so glad you've come.

LARISA. You aren't angry with me?

VALYA. You're the one who ought to be angry. Forgive me. Don't think ill of me, will you?

LARISA. Let bygones be bygones. . . .

(*They kiss.*)

VALYA. Come and let me introduce you. This is my friend Larisa.

SERDYUK (*gaily*). The penalty for late-comers. (*Pours her out a full glass which she tosses off.*) Good for you! (*Introducing himself.*) Stepan Yegorovich Serdyuk. Come and sit by me.

LAPCHENKO. There's someone else knocking. More guests.

(*There is another tense silence.*)

VALYA. Come in.

(*Enter* VICTOR. *His eyes move slowly over the gathering, come to rest on* VALYA. *He goes over to her.*)

VICTOR (*in a low voice*). I wish you happiness.

VALYA (*softly*). Victor. . . .

VICTOR. Here's something . . . (*hands her a ring*) for remembrance.

VALYA. Thanks.

VICTOR (*goes over to* SERGEI, *embraces and kisses him and gives him a playful slap on the back*). And that's the end of that.

(*Accordion strikes up a Russian folk dance.*)

SERDYUK. Well, who wants to dance?

VALYA. Larisa. . . . Folk dancing is her speciality. Come on, Larisa, do your stuff!

(*Larisa enters the circle, begins to dance with passion and abandon.*)

VICTOR (*hoarsely*). Now then, make way! Give us a slow one, Lyosha. . . . With variations.

(VICTOR *begins with a slow step, then, tossing his head, he breaks into a wild and furious dance in which one senses a hint of despair. The shouting and clapping of the onlookers almost drown out the music, and* VICTOR *and* LARISA *finish the dance amid stormy applause.*)

ZINKA. That was wonderful, Larisa.

DENIS. Some lad, our Victor!

LAPCHENKO. That was showing them!

VICTOR (*to himself*). Good-bye, Valya.

SERDYUK (*to* LARISA). It will be a pleasure to drink to you. . . . That was a fine bit of dancing. You were like a flame.

LARISA. Not much fire left, I'm afraid.

SERDYUK. I'm fifty myself. Where've you been all this time?

LARISA. Everywhere and nowhere, Comrade Serdyuk.

MAYA. Oh, Valya, I shall never forget this day as long as I live. . . . You see, I'm just a plain Moscow schoolgirl, but I've always wanted to know how our Rodik lived here and who his friends were. Mama's dying to know all about it too. Forgive me for chattering so much, I'm afraid I've had a little too much to drink. . . . But we won't tell anyone, will we? I do love weddings! You must be very happy. It must be wonderful to know you've kept yourself for someone you love, kept yourself clean and pure, as pure and lovely as that wedding dress of yours. Why are you crying? Don't, don't cry, Valya. Look at your Sergei, see how his eyes are shining with love for you. I

do envy you for being so happy . . . .
(*She embraces* VALYA.)

(*Accordion strikes up an old-fashioned waltz. A few couples get up to dance to the music.*)

SERGEI (*going over to* VALYA). Don't cry, Valya. . . . You mustn't, really. . . .

VALYA. I . . . I can't help it. . . .

SERGEI. Yes, you can. All your troubles will soon be forgotten.

VALYA. Will they really?

SERGEI. Yes, you'll see.

VALYA. Thank you, Sergei. (*Embraces him.*)

(*They dance together.*)

SERDYUK. Now then, friends, make way. The newlyweds have the floor!

(*The dancers fall back, leaving the bride and bridegroom waltzing alone.* VALYA's *hand lies tenderly on* SERGEI's *shoulder. She dances in an ecstasy of love and tenderness, her head thrown back, her body swaying to the music.*)

CHORUS. The wedding waltz. . . . Will they ever forget it? The years will pass, much will be erased from their memory, but the simple, artless melody of the waltz they danced on their wedding night will for ever remind them both of that evening long ago.

— They may part, they may lose each other, or perhaps the flame of a new love will light their path—but whatever happens, whenever that waltz is played they will think of each other and their hearts will be flooded with gratitude and joy.

(*The guests disappear one by one from the room.*)

CHORUS. But now, while that waltz has yet to become a mere memory, this evening, this night is yours, and nothing else exists for you.

(*The melody of the waltz ceases.*)

CHORUS. Valya! Sergei! Do you hear? The door has closed behind the last guest. You are alone. Alone. . . .

(*It is night.* SERGEI *and* VALYA *are alone in the room.*)

VALYA. What time is it? Oh dear, my head is whirling.

SERGEI. It's half past one.

VALYA. In the morning? (*Laughs.*) Imagine asking such a silly question? (*She is silent for a few moments.*) Sergei . . . Sergei, what is your mother's name?

SERGEI. Pauline.

VALYA. I am going to love her very much. . . . May I?

SERGEI. Of course.

VALYA. And your sisters as well. There are two of them?

SERGEI. Yes.

VALYA. I shall love them both. Do you think they will like me?

SERGEI. I'm sure they will.

VALYA. I drank an awful lot of wine . . . that's why I'm talking so much. I want to talk. May I?

SERGEI. Fire away.

VALYA. I keep thinking—you haven't kissed me once yet. Why?

SERGEI (*in a whisper*). I shall kiss you.

VALYA (*also whispers*). When?

SERGEI. When you wake up.

VALYA. Like the sleeping beauty in the ballet? Music by Tchaikovsky.

SERGEI. Mhm.

VALYA. I heard it over the radio. (*Shivering in her chair.*) Yes . . . I'm terribly sleepy, you know. So silly of me, isn't it? Darling, don't speak, don't say another word. I'm so, so happy I'm your wife. . . . I am, aren't I? What wonderful friends you have. . . . May I go to sleep? You don't mind, do you, Sergei?

(*He takes her in his arms.*)

It will be morning soon, won't it? And then you'll kiss me. You will, won't you? Give me your handkerchief. . . .

SERGEI. What for?

VALYA. Look, I've wiped it all off . . . there's not a speck of lipstick left. So please, please you needn't be afraid of anything in the morning.

SERGEI (*lays her on the bed*). And now go to sleep.

VALYA. I'm asleep already. . . . I am even dreaming. I see you in a boat sailing towards me. (*Softly.*) We'll always be together, won't we, Sergei, even when we're old and feeble?

SERGEI. Even unto death.

VALYA. That's wonderful. . . .

(*The organ sounds again in the distance.* VALYA *falls asleep.* SERGEI *drops to his knees beside her and gazes at her. The* CHORUS *softly draws a curtain, as downy and white as a wedding veil.*)

CHORUS (*very softly*). The rain is pouring down as if it were about to flood the earth!

— Little streams are flowing past the houses, washing away the litter and refuse of yesterday.

— The rain is cleansing the earth. . . .

End of Part I

❧ Part II

Soft music, remotely resembling a lullaby. SERGEI *appears in a beam of light. He stands silent, his hands thrust into his pockets, lost in thought. A little apart is the* CHORUS.

CHORUS (*addressing the audience*). Do you remember how it was with you, Sergei? They took her away at dawn, and the rest of the day was a nightmare for you. . . .

— You could not put your mind to your work, you could think only of her, and you kept calling up the hospital to enquire. . . .

— After work you hurried straight there and stood under the windows, anxious and distressed. You ran in to ask the nurse on duty a hundred times over.

SERGEI (*in a hushed voice*). Well, how is she? No news?

CHORUS. Remember, Sergei?

(SERGEI *goes down the street, stops at a doorway, peers into windows. Presently he drops down on a bench and stares into the distance.* A BOY *of about ten comes up to him.*)

BOY (*after staring at him for a few minutes in silence*). Is your son being born?

SERGEI. I hope so. . . .

BOY. I live in the house over the road. I often see men sitting on this bench like you. I'm used to it. Some of them give me sweets.

SERGEI. Sorry, I haven't any with me.

BOY. Oh, that's all right. You know how many little babies have come out of this place? Thousands!

SERGEI. That's nice.

BOY. But isn't it queer? . . . One minute there's no one and suddenly there's someone—a boy or a girl.

SERGEI (*a trifle confused*). Well, yes. . . . That's how it is, brother. What's your name?

BOY. Anton. I'm from Chelyabinsk.

SERGEI. What do you want to be when you grow up, Anton?

BOY. A doctor.

SERGEI. Made up your mind already?

BOY. Yes, since last Saturday. Before that I wanted to be a passenger, so I could travel places. Guess what, there's a girl in our yard who doesn't believe there is such a person as Charlie Chaplin.

SERGEI (*absently*). Go on!

BOY. Well, here's wishing you good luck. (*Offers his hand to* SERGEI.)

SERGEI. Who taught you to say that?

BOY. My granny. She says if you see anyone sitting on that bench you wish them good luck.

SERGEI. Give my greetings to your granny, will you?

BOY. Thanks. (*Goes off.*)

(*Sergei gets up and goes over to the window.* A NURSE *appears at the entrance.*)

NURSE. Seryogin!

SERGEI (*springing up*). Yes?

NURSE. You can go in now. She's waiting for you.

SERGEI. Is it . . . is it all right?

NURSE (*smiling*). There's a surprise for you, my lad. Hurry up. (*Exit.*)

(SERGEI *hurries after her into the building.*)

CHORUS. A man is born!

(*There is soft, merry tinkling of tiny bells, like the bells in children's toys.*)

— A child is born. . . . No, two children, a girl and a boy. Their parents will call them Fyodor and Lena.

— The Seryogin twins. They will be dressed exactly alike. . . . Even their parents will have difficulty in telling them apart.

— And one day, hand in hand they will go to school, two little people, carrying bunches of flowers. . . .

— Let us wish them success. Good luck, Lena and Fyodor. But it is not the easy, smooth path in life we wish you.

(SERGEI *comes out of the building. He is bursting with pride and happiness. He looks about him, his face beaming.*)

SERGEI. Just think of it! Valya, my darling Valya!

(SERGEI *kisses the first person he meets, a complete stranger. He runs off. A violin and mandolin strike up a simple melody.*)

CHORUS. At last comes the day you have looked forward to so impatiently. . . . The day you will bring your family home.

— You are no longer alone, Sergei! There are two more Seryogins now.

— This is a day you will never forget. But now you must go, your friends are waiting for you. . . .

PANTOMIME

The excavator crew is on its way to the maternity hospital, each one carrying parcels. SERGEI *walks in front pushing a double pram. At the corner the procession is joined by* LARISA *and* ZINKA. *It is snowing, the last snow of winter, a soft April snow. The procession stops at the bench outside the hospital over which the boy* ANTON *presides like a guardian angel.* SERGEI *goes up to him and presents him with a box of sweets.* VALYA *appears in the doorway accompanied by a* NURSE. *There is a shy, radiant smile on her face.* SERGEI *gives her a bouquet of flowers. She kisses him and hands him one of the infants.* SERGEI *takes it gingerly and lays it carefully in the pram. Everyone crowds round* VALYA *to hug and kiss her. The* NURSE *hands the other baby to* SERGEI, *who gives it to* VICTOR *to hold while he makes room for it in the pram.* VICTOR *looks at it, then at* VALYA. SERGEI *puts the baby into the pram and goes over to* ANTON *and shakes hands with him solemnly. The procession then sets off for home with* SERGEI *and* VALYA *at the head, wheeling the pram together. At one corner* VICTOR, *unnoticed by the others, stops and lets his friends go on without him. Raising the collar of his coat, he watches the procession go. Now he is alone, the gay tune played by the violin and mandolin ceases.*

CHORUS. What's the matter, Victor?

VICTOR. The flame of life has burned out. (*Vanishes into the darkness.*)

(*The strains of a lullaby played by a single violin. The faintly illuminated figure of* VALYA, *bending over her sleeping twins, emerges gradually from the darkness.*)

CHORUS (*sternly*). Hush! Do not disturb these citizens, they are still very, very small. . . .

— It's all right for you who have already grown up and can do without much sleep. But these young citizens must sleep their fill.

— Do not disturb them, they are only one month old. . . .

— No, two months. . . .

— No, three. Hush. They must sleep and build up their strength. They are still very small, these little Seryogins.

(*The lullaby ceases.*)

— Someone is knocking at the door. But Valya has dozed off and doesn't hear.

— We must wake her.

— Wake up, Valya!

VALYA (*starting up*). What is it? Who's there?

(VALYA *runs to the door.* SERGEI *enters as the room takes shape.*)

SERGEI. Sleeping?

VALYA. Mm. (*Softly.*) See you don't make any noise.

SERGEI. I'm tired today. Amazing. (*Goes over to the sleeping twins.*) Fyodor's a funny little cuss.

VALYA (*disapprovingly*). What's funny about him?

SERGEI. He's getting awfully fat. Looks positively bourgeois.

VALYA. He isn't fat a bit. . . . Hungry?

SERGEI. Ravenous.

VALYA (*brings him food*). Here you are.

SERGEI. Mm. Delicious.

VALYA. Put some more butter in it.

SERGEI. Well, what've you been doing all day?

VALYA. Not twiddling my thumbs, you can be sure. Nursing twins is no joke.

SERGEI. I know that. (*Eating.*) Seen Adenauer's statement in the papers?

VALYA. No. . . . Lena has some kind of a rash on her tummy. Think we ought to call the doctor?

SERGEI. Perhaps we should. . . .

VALYA. I love taking them to the babies' clinic They're so much nicer than all the other children. . . . Fyodor is only going on four months and he weighs as much as a baby of six months. I know, because I compared the figures. And Lena is awfully intelligent. The doctor said so too. "That little girl of yours is very intelligent for her age," she said.

SERGEI. Lena is a darling.

VALYA. Some more stewed fruit?

SERGEI. Yes, please. . . . I like it with a fresh roll.

VALYA. Here you are . . . nice and crisp.

SERGEI. Remember?

VALYA (*kissing the back of his neck*). There! Get on with your supper.

SERGEI. Valya, shall I buy you a bicycle?

VALYA. Whatever for?

SERGEI. To ride, of course.

VALYA (*laughing*). You do have the funniest notions.

SERGEI. Want to hear a bit of news, Valya? Our excavator may have to stop working for a while.

VALYA. What's wrong?

SERGEI. The reducing gear needs repairing, and the scoop chains have to be changed. It's quite a job. Trouble is we can't afford the time to stand idle a minute.

VALYA. Serdyuk must be in a dither.

SERGEI. He's been acting queer these days.

VALYA. He's in love with Larisa. . . . (*Laughs.*) Your boss has disgraced himself. . . .

SERGEI. Why shouldn't he be in love? He's not so old.

VALYA. Depends how you look at it. (*After a pause.*) Why doesn't Victor ever come and see us?

SERGEI. That's his business, I suppose.

VALYA. Sergei. . . .

SERGEI. Yes?

VALYA. You're better than anyone else in the world.

SERGEI (*embracing her*). Valya, mine. . . . You're not bored or anything, are you?

VALYA. Silly thing, I've no time to be bored.

SERGEI. Stick it out for a bit. As soon as the kids are big enough we'll put them in a nursery and you can go to school or to work if you like.

VALYA (*coldly, after a slight pause*). What sort of work, may I ask?

SERGEI. Laying concrete. Concrete is most important at this stage.

VALYA (*scornfully*). Concrete! Give me a cash register any time!

SERGEI. No, Valya, you're wrong! (*With passion.*) What is it that makes a person happy? The satisfaction of knowing he's doing a worth-while job, that he's part of something bigger than himself.

VALYA. I don't know what you mean.

SERGEI. I don't quite know how to put it. I only know that there are jobs that do something to a man, make him bigger, better than he was before. (*Tenderly.*) If you don't want to work on concrete you could try the excavator. You could begin as a helper, and later on you could go to evening school. For all you know, you may have a gift for this sort of work and you'll end up as assistant foreman or something like that. They say there's a girl at the Volga dam who's in charge of a whole excavator crew. Isn't that wonderful?

VALYA (*angrily*). All right, if you insist on sending me out to earn my living I'll go right back to the store! Everybody knows me there. . . . I shan't be lonesome.

SERGEI. Valya!

VALYA. Don't shout, you'll wake the children.

SERGEI. Then stop talking like that!

VALYA. What's wrong with the store, I'd like to know? . . . I made as much as I wanted at that cash register.

SERGEI (*shocked*). What!

VALYA. Think I lived on my wages? Nothing doing! A little small change here and there amounts up to quite a bit by the end of the day.

SERGEI (*shouting*). Valya! (*Lowering his voice.*) Valya . . . darling. (*Strokes her hair.*)

VALYA (*softening*). Forgive me, Sergei. (*Drops on to her knees.*) Forgive me. . . .

SERGEI. Don't, Valya, darling. (*Raises her and embraces her tenderly.*) Don't.

VALYA. I'm so tired, Sergei. The children keep me busy all day. And there's dinner to be cooked, and all the washing and cleaning to do. And when you told me about that girl over there on the Volga. . . . Well, it hurt. . . .

SERGEI (*stroking her hair*) There, there. I shan't say another word. Don't cry. I'm an idiot, of course. But I love you so much, Valya. It's amazing.

VALYA (*smiling through her tears*). Amazing?

SERGEI. You mustn't cry. I don't want you ever to shed a single tear. People must be happy in this world, especially those who are building the future. You and me, for instance. (*Lays her gently on the couch.*) You're tired now. Go to sleep. I'll wash the dishes and tidy up. I'll do a beautiful job. And if Fyodor or Lena wake up I'll keep them quiet. Everything will be fine. So close your eyes and go to sleep.

(VALYA *falls asleep, and the room slowly fades.*)

CHORUS. Yet nearer and nearer comes the day you will never forget, Valya!

(VALYA *appears.*)

VALYA (*in a low voice*). I am here. . . .

CHORUS. This is the morning of July thirty-first. . . . It has come.

(VALYA *covers her face with her hands.*)

— Tell us how that morning began.

VALYA. We got up very early, I remember. Before leaving the house, Sergei stopped at the gate and took my hand. (*The little front garden and gate appear. Beyond it the dim outlines of a new two-storey house.* VALYA *and* SERGEI *are standing beside a bench.*)

VALYA (*looking at* SERGEI *and continuing her story*). If I had known what was going to happen I would have clung to him and not let him go. But I did not know. After all, it was just an ordinary morning, only hot. . . . Very hot. (*Addressing* SERGEI.) You ought to have stayed in bed a bit longer. It's Sunday today.

SERGEI. But it's so hot, Valya. I must have a dip in the river.

VALYA. Have you taken a towel?

SERGEI (*showing her the towel*). Here it is.

VALYA. Do you like my dress, Sergei?

SERGEI. It's amazing.

VALYA. Sergei, let's buy a leather coat for you, shall we?

SERGEI. Perhaps . . . later on.

VALYA. No, let's buy it now. You will look handsome in a leather coat. . . . (*Embraces him.*)

SERGEI. Watch out, here's the Chief.

VALYA. All dressed up, too.

(*Enter* SERDYUK. *He is more sprucely dressed than formerly.*)

SERGEI (*innocently*). Come to see us, Chief?

SERDYUK (*suspecting something*). Me? Oh, I'm just taking a little walk.

SERGEI (*barely suppressing a smile*). A walk, eh?

SERDYUK. By the way, I've heard that Larisa Petrovna lives here now.

SERGEI. Judging by your get-up I thought you might be going to pay a call on her. Haven't seen you looking so smart for a long time.

SERDYUK. Can't a man dress up on his free day?

SERGEI (*politely*). Excuse me, but did that handsome tie you are sporting actually come from our local emporium?

SERDYUK. Listen here, youngster. You were going for a swim, weren't you? Well, cut along.

SERGEI. Oh, I'm in no particular hurry. It's Sunday today.

SERDYUK. You're asking for trouble, my lad. (*Lamely.*) I have to see Larisa Petrovna on business.

(SERGEI *and* VALYA *laugh outright.*) You wait, my lad. . . . (*Shakes his finger.*) I'll get even with you. (*Goes off towards the house.*)

SERGEI. It's flat number three, Chief!

SERDYUK. Thanks for nothing. (*Disappears at entrance.*)

SERGEI (*chuckling*). He's a fine one.

VALYA. You weren't much better yourself once. Remember how you used to drop into the store for matches? (*With a little cry of dismay.*) Oh dear, I left the milk on the stove. It must have boiled over. (*Runs inside.*)

(*A* BOY *and a* GIRL *are walking down the road leading to the river. The* BOY *carries a fishing rod, the* GIRL, *a small pail.*)

SERGEI (*recognising the* BOY). Why, it's my old pal, Anton! Hello!

BOY. Hello! I remember you too. (*To the* GIRL.) He had two babies at one go.

GIRL. Imagine!

BOY. How are they? All right?

SERGEI. They're splendid, thanks. How are you, Anton? Still want to be a doctor?

BOY. Yes. We're going fishing.

SERGEI (*pointing to the* GIRL). Who's your friend?

BOY. This is Lera. I told you about her,

remember? She's the one who doesn't believe in Charlie Chaplin.

GIRL. Of course I don't.

BOY (*triumphantly*). See?

SERGEI. Amazing! Well, may I join you?

BOY. Of course. I've made us a raft.

SERGEI. Come on then.

(SERGEI *takes the children by the hand and they walk together towards the river. On the way they meet* VICTOR.)

VICTOR. Hello. Where are you going?

SERGEI. For a dip.

VICTOR. Yes, it's damn hot.

(*There is an awkward silence.*)

SERGEI (*to the children*). You go on, I'll catch up with you.

BOY. We'll be waiting for you.

(*Exeunt children.*)

SERGEI. Were you coming to see us?

VICTOR. No.

SERGEI. What's the matter with you, Victor?

VICTOR (*gruffly*). Nothing.

SERGEI (*lays his hand on the other's shoulder*). I. . . .

(VICTOR *pushes* SERGEI'S *hand away and raises his arm to strike him.*)

Victor. . . . What're you doing?

VICTOR. I can't forget her. And I never will. I don't know what to do. Perhaps you can tell me. (*Laughs bitterly.*) I look at you and feel hatred rise in me. I wish you were dead. You . . . you who were my best friend.

SERGEI (*his voice trembling*). Were? I still am. . . .

VICTOR. No, our friendship is finished. (*After a pause.*) All right, I'll go away. I'll leave this place and go to Leningrad, to my father. I'll get used to my stepmother, I suppose. (*In despair.*) I'm all alone now.

SERGEI. What about the Chief, Rodik, Denis? How can you think of leaving us all, Victor? Have you forgotten that first year, those nights on the job when we battled the frost and blizzards together? Can you cast aside a friendship like that so lightly?

VICTOR. I thought it would pass, I thought the pain would stop, that I'd forget her and it would be all over. But I was wrong. (*In a low voice.*) You took her away from me.

SERGEI. Can you truthfully say you loved her then?

VICTOR. Didn't I?

SERGEI (*quietly*). No, that was not love.

VICTOR (*after a silence*). I daresay you're right. (*Sharply.*) Well, good-bye! You won't see me again. I wish you happiness! (*Runs off.*)

SERGEI (*calls after him*). Victor, Victor. . . .

VALYA (*running out of the house*). Haven't you gone yet? Good. (*Coyly.*) I wanted to tell you something else.

SERGEI (*smiling*). Did you? Fire away.

VALYA (*softly*). I wanted to tell you that I love you very, very much, Sergei. Do you know why? Because the more I know you the more wonderful you are. See?

SERGEI. You're a great one, Valya. . . . (*Kisses her.*)

VALYA. He kisses me. I hold his hand and look at him. . . . I do not know I am looking at him for the last time. . . . For the last time I hold his warm hands in mine, for the last time I gaze into his eyes. Now he will go and he will never return. If only I had known! But I knew nothing. All I say to him in parting is— (*To* SERGEI). See you don't lose the towel. . . .

SERGEI. I'll be careful. (*Runs off.*)

VALYA. I watch him running down the road. I see him catch up with two children, take their hands and continue down the road to the river. I sit down on the bench to muse for a while. Then I decide I had better get on with my work while he is gone.

(VALYA *is hanging washing up on the line—*SERGEI'S *shirt and two undershirts.* LARISA *and* SERDYUK *come out of the house.*)

LARISA. Where shall we go, Stepan Yegorovich?

SERDYUK. Let's go down to the dam.

LARISA. But it's your free day today, isn't it?

SERDYUK. I just want to have a look at the machine. We have to lay up for repairs.

LARISA (*sighing*). All right, then.

SERDYUK. In the evening we'll take a trip out to Slyudyanka, shall we? To see my father. I want you to meet him.

LARISA. How old is he?

SERDYUK. Seventy-five. And he's still working in the fishing artel. Hardy old chap, he could still swim across the Angara if he had to. I think he'll like you. Oh dear! (*Steps back hastily from the door.*)

LARISA. What's the matter?

SERDYUK. The foreman's wife is out there hanging up laundry.

LARISA. Are you scared of her?

SERDYUK. Scared, no. . . . But . . . well, Larisa, I'm fifty-two, you know.

LARISA. What of it?

SERDYUK. People will laugh at me.

LARISA. There's nothing to laugh at so far. You haven't proposed to me yet. When you do, then people will have something to laugh at. (*Nods to* VALYA.) Hello, Valya!

VALYA. Going for a walk?

LARISA. Stepan Yegorovich is inviting me out for lunch. And we're going out dancing in the evening. I'm sure I don't know what to say.

SERDYUK (*to* LARISA *sotto voce*). You little devil! (*To* VALYA, *raising his cap politely.*) Good day to you. (*Exit with* LARISA.)

VALYA (*looking after them with a fond smile*). Funny pair.

(*Enter* VICTOR.)

VALYA. Victor? Hello.

VICTOR. Has Sergei gone?

VALYA. Yes. (*After a pause.*) Why don't you ever come to see us any more?

VICTOR (*brightly*). Too busy, too busy, old girl.

VALYA. You've grown thinner.

VICTOR (*gaily*). Too busy to eat sometimes.

VALYA (*scrutinising his face*). You've changed. You're better looking than you used to be.

VICTOR. Yes, so they tell me.

VALYA. Who do you go dancing with now?

VICTOR. I'm off dancing for a bit.

VALYA. Why?

VICTOR. Worn out all my shoes.

VALYA (*after a pause*). Did you want to see Sergei?

VICTOR. Yes, I came to say good-bye. I'm going away.

VALYA. Where to?

VICTOR. Leningrad.

VALYA. For long?

VICTOR. Depends how much I like it. I'll take a walk down Nevsky. I'll have a look at the Neva. I'll stand by the parapet and think of how you and I used to look at the Angara.

VALYA. You sound a little strange.

VICTOR. I was just wondering, Valya. Were we in love then or weren't we?

VALYA. No, Victor. That wasn't love. That was nothing. We were just fooling around.

VICTOR. Having a little fun, eh? I see.

VALYA. Oh, Victor, if only you knew how much heartache that fun gave me. No wonder they called me Good-time Valya, remember? But he, Sergei, really loved me, in spite of what I was. He made me his wife. And his love has saved me. (*Remembering herself, glances at* VICTOR.) Don't be hurt. . . .

VICTOR (*brightly*). Me? Hurt? Don't be silly. That's all over and done with.

(*From somewhere inside the house radio music is heard.* RODIK *appears. He walks slowly up the path and stops beside* VICTOR *and* VALYA, *but does not speak. The* CHORUS *appears, surrounding the little group.*)

VALYA: Hello, Rodik. . . . Have you come to see Sergei? He's gone.

RODIK. Yes.

(*The* CHORUS *moves closer.*)

VALYA. Come in and wait. He will be back soon.

RODIK. All right.

(*Silence. The* CHORUS *moves closer still.*)

VALYA. What's the matter, Rodik?

RODIK. Nothing.

VALYA (*with a sudden smile*). When Sergei comes back we'll all have tea. Victor too. Will you stay, Rodik? I'll go and add some water to the kettle. I'll be back in a jiffy.

(*Runs into the house.* CHORUS *surrounds* RODIK *and* VICTOR.)

VICTOR (*quietly*). Well, what is it?

RODIK. For God's sake keep calm, won't you!

VICTOR. What's happened?

RODIK (*in a whisper*). Sergei's drowned.

(*Someone raises his hands in despair. The* CHORUS *freezes in shocked silence.*)

VICTOR. Drowned! It can't be! Couldn't they save him?

(*A slight movement passes over the*

CHORUS, *which then subsides into immobility again.*)

VICTOR (*after a stunned pause*). How did it happen?

RODIK. There were a couple of kids, a boy and a girl, fishing from a homemade raft. Well, the raft overturned and there was nobody about except Sergei. He swam the girl ashore first and then went back for the boy . . . there was no sign of him. He must have searched for a long time. By the time he found the boy he was exhausted. He managed to get him safely on to the raft, but he hadn't any strength left to swim back to shore himself. The boy is all right.

VICTOR. Oh, Rodik. . . .

(*As if unable to bear the strain, the* CHORUS *recoils a few steps.*)

RODIK. Valya must be told.

VICTOR. No. . . . No!

RODIK. She will have to know some time.

VICTOR. That's true.

RODIK. Go and tell her.

VICTOR. I can't.

RODIK. Victor, please.

VICTOR. No, I can't do it.

RODIK. Very well, I'll have to do it. (*Goes into the house.*)

(CHORUS *moves towards the silent* VICTOR. VICTOR *glances around, goes towards the house, drops down on to the threshold and bursts into tears. The* CHORUS *stretches their hands out to him as if wishing to comfort him.* LARISA *and* SERDYUK *appear, returning from their walk.*)

SERDYUK (*furtively*). That's Victor sitting there.

LARISA. Why are you so scared of everybody, you big baby?

SERDYUK (*making up to* VICTOR). Look, I've bought my old man a pair of trousers. Not bad, eh?

VICTOR. What? (*Regarding* SERDYUK *with something like hatred.*)

CHORUS (*softly*). Don't say anything, Stepan Yegorovich.

— Don't say a word.

— This is a time for silence.

(VALYA *and* RODIK *come out of the house. The* CHORUS *makes a movement towards* VALYA.)

VALYA (*addressing* CHORUS). What have I done with my cap? (*Notices* SERGEI'S *shirt hanging on the line, stops and stares at it.*) Come, Rodik.

(*Exeunt.*)

VICTOR (*getting up*). Look after the children, Larisa. (*To* SERDYUK.) Yes, Chief. . . . Sergei's drowned.

SERDYUK (*cries out*). You're lying!

VICTOR. Sergei's dead. (*Goes out quickly.*)

(LARISA *enters the house.* SERDYUK *follows her.* CHORUS *spreads out until it occupies the whole stage. At last it stops and stands motionless.*

TWO LITTLE GIRLS *carrying flowers come down the road, singing merrily. The* CHORUS *does not move.*

The banks of the Angara River. A PASSER-BY *is seen on the path.*)

PASSER-BY. . . . And although it will soon be night, the sun gently caresses the russet leaves of the trees. I left Irkutsk this morning, travelling by motor-boat to the construction site, and now here I am strolling along the banks of the Angara beyond the houses of the workers' settlement.

They say a young man was drowned here ten days ago.

I see a group of five men sitting on the slope not far away. There is a girl with them. They sit talking quietly, each seemingly thinking his own thoughts. What can they be thinking of? A simple meal and a bottle of wine are laid out on a bright kerchief near by. The eldest member of the group pours out wine for everybody except the girl, and they drink in silence. I want to pass on. But I cannot. Why do these people interest me? What are they talking about? I try to listen but I cannot hear a word. And down below at the water's edge a woman is washing clothes. One of the men has seen her and says something to the others, and now they are all looking down to where she is. What is the connection between them? Why do these people interest me? This foolish professional craze for observing and listening to everything around me makes me pause and watch in the hope that something will occur to give me a clue to what is happening. . . .

(*The scene just described emerges.* SERDYUK *pours the wine into the tin mugs. Around him sit* VICTOR, RODIK,

DENIS *and* LAPCHENKO. ZINKA *sits a little apart.*)

SERDYUK. What remains after the death of a working man? (*With passion.*) His work. The memory of his work remains for ever. Under communism there will be no such thing as death, because the fruits of man's labours will be a hundred times finer than they are today. Sergei was closer to that time than any of us. He lived like a man, worked like a Communist and died like a hero. Eternal glory to his memory.

(*All raise their mugs and drink in silence.*)

It's two weeks today since it happened. We've got to think of the future. Sergei is lying in his grave, but we must go on living. That means we must carry on for him. (*After a pause.*) The excavator will soon be back in operation, and we're one man short in the crew now. What are we going to do about it?

RODIK. We don't want any outsiders.

ZINKA (*quickly*). Yes, that's what Denis said to me yesterday. . . .

SERDYUK (*severely*). Now then, ladybird, no one gave you the floor.

LAPCHENKO. We only brought you along out of respect for your husband, so you'd better keep quiet.

SERDYUK. Lapchenko, don't exceed your authority. (*To the others.*) Well, Victor, what do you say? You wanted to go away, I understand?

DENIS. You needn't take that seriously, Chief. He wouldn't leave his comrades in the lurch.

SERDYUK (*to* VICTOR). Is that right?

VICTOR (*after a moment's hesitation*). Yes, I've changed my mind.

SERDYUK. That's better.

ZINKA (*hastily*). He wouldn't ever leave you chaps, I'm telling you. . . . Why, I—

SERDYUK. Ladybird, must I warn you again?

DENIS. You're awful hard on her, Chief.

SERDYUK. You don't know these women, boy. Give them a little leeway and they'll be stepping on your neck.

ZINKA. Learned that by your own experience, eh, Comrade Serdyuk?

SERDYUK (*bristling*). What did you say? (*Calming down.*) All right, forget it. (*To* VICTOR.) What are you looking at down there?

VICTOR. Valya's down there, washing clothes.

(*All look down in silence.*)

LAPCHENKO. Babies' clothes.

RODIK. Stepan Yegorovich, I have a proposal to make. . . . Let's not take on another worker—we four will do the work of five. Victor can be the shift foreman. Denis, first assistant on electricity, I'll attend to the hydraulics, and Lapchenko will be oiler, he has been in reserve long enough. We won't need any extra help, we can manage ourselves. But I think we ought to keep the fifth man's wages.

SERDYUK. Whoa, man! What's this? You started out all right, Rodion, but now you're skidding. What do we want the fifth man's wages for?

RODIK. Stepan Yegorovich, the pension Valya will get for Sergei isn't very much. And they're used to living well. It will be hard for Valya to manage. I propose we pay out the fifth man's wages to Valya, just as if Sergei was still working with us.

(*No one speaks for a moment.*)

DENIS (*goes over to* RODIK). You're a genius, Rodik! That's a wonderful idea.

ZINKA (*ecstatically*). Oh, Rodik! (*Runs up to him and kisses him.*)

SERDYUK. Who gave you the floor, ladybird?

ZINKA. I didn't say anything. I only kissed him, and that's Denis' worry, not yours.

DENIS. Well, you could have said it just as well. But never mind. (*Pulls her ear.*)

SERDYUK. I see the majority is in favour. (*To* VICTOR.) Well, what do you say?

VICTOR. I second the motion.

SERDYUK. Are you willing to take over the shift? Can you cope with it?

VICTOR. With your help.

SERDYUK. And how about you, Lapchenko? Sure you won't let us down?

LAPCHENKO. That's not fair, Chief, you know. I'm a reformed man now. (*Pointing to* DENIS.) But he's undertaking a bit too much if you ask me. Year before last he was just a helper, and now he'll be a foreman's assistant.

DENIS. You take care of yourself. And stand up straight, man. What you need is army training.

VICTOR. Chief!

SERDYUK. Yes?

VICTOR. About Valya. . . .

SERDYUK. Well, what about her? (*A pause.*) Speak up! Or have you changed your mind?

VICTOR. Yes.

SERDYUK. Why?

VICTOR. It's no use.

SERDYUK. As you please. Zinka!

ZINKA (*eagerly*). Yes?

SERDYUK. Scoot down to the river, lass, and get Valya up here.

ZINKA. Right away! (*Dashes off.*)

(*The strains of the song "In Gorky's fair city . . ." sound in her wake.*)

VICTOR. Sergei liked that song.

SERDYUK. Well, boys, why are you so quiet?

VICTOR. What's there to talk about?

SERDYUK. Perhaps Denis will tell us about that major of his.

DENIS. He's not a major now, he was promoted to lieutenant-colonel last week.

RODIK (*with a grin*). We here work our heads off day after day and other folks get the promotions.

(ZINKA *appears, followed by* VALYA *carrying a basin of laundry.*)

VALYA (*an unseeing look in her eyes*). Hello.

SERDYUK (*lamely*). Been doing a bit of washing?

VALYA. Yes, I'm going home now.

SERDYUK. Why do you come all this way to wash clothes?

VALYA. The water is cleaner here.

SERDYUK. Who did you leave the children with?

VALYA. Larisa.

SERDYUK. Are you managing with money?

VALYA. I have enough so far.

SERDYUK. But what are you planning to do?

VALYA. I don't know, Chief.

SERDYUK. I'm glad you called me that. Remember, lass, everything has a beginning and an end. There is sadness in it, but there is joy in it too.

VALYA (*softly*). It's all the same to me now.

SERDYUK (*firmly*). You mustn't talk like that.

VALYA. Why not?

SERDYUK. You must think of your children.

VALYA (*thoughtfully*). I suppose I'll go back to the store.

SERDYUK. Now listen, girl. The boys have decided they'll work for Sergei, and his earnings will go to you. . . . In full.

VICTOR (*addressing the audience*). Valya does not speak. . . . She is silent for a long time. Why do I want her to refuse the offer? Why do I want it so badly? If only she would say: go away, I don't need your money. If only she would say that. . . .

VALYA. Thanks. (*With a faint smile.*) Thanks. . . .

(*The slope and the people on it disappear. Only the* PASSER-BY *is left standing on the path, looking into the distance.*)

PASSER-BY. They called the girl after all, but what they talked about will remain a mystery to me. Now they are getting up and going away, quietly, thoughtfully. And I stand here wondering what chord these people have struck in my heart. What has passed between them? (*He stands lost in thought for a few moments.*) Some foolish, trifling talk perhaps, which only appeared important to a bystander like myself. Strange. We are so often mistaken.

(*Fade-out. Gradually the* CHORUS *appears.*)

CHORUS. When a man dies, his possessions gradually disappear from their accustomed places. And within a few months the room he lived in tells us nothing of its former occupant.

— But this did not happen in Valya's room. Here everything has remained untouched. The only difference is that now Sergei's photograph hangs over the little couch, a snapshot enlarged by an Irkutsk photographer.

— It is warm and cosy in the room. The children are sound asleep. The ticking of the pendulum clock on the wall is the only sound.

— Are you very tired, Valya?

VALYA. Yes, very tired.

(*She is alone in her room. She has washed the dishes and laid aside the dishtowel.*)

Well, now the day is ended and I can have a little rest. (*Sits down on the couch and looks at Sergei's photograph.*) I'm going to tell you everything that happened today. Now wait a moment, let me think, what did I do today?

CHORUS. In the morning you went to the market. . . .

VALYA. Oh yes, and after that I took the children to the clinic. Fyodor was so naughty, Sergei, you can't imagine. You know I've been trying to get him used to doing without the pacifier, but he's so obstinate, he demands it. . . . But his doctor praised him as usual, she says he's a fine boy. Lena has suddenly started taking an interest in her food, she wasn't like that before at all. They are nearly seven months old already! Quite grown up, aren't they? When they went to sleep I ran down to the river to wash the clothes. But I was not very lucky today, it started to rain, I got soaked through. And a cold wind came up from Lake Baikal and tore all the leaves off the trees. So the last reminders of summer are gone. Well, it can't be helped, it is November already. As I passed the club I saw an announcement of a dance this evening. A dance. . . . How strange. (*Remembering.*) Oh yes, there was something else.

CHORUS. Serdyuk and Larisa came in for tea.

VALYA. They're such a funny pair, they are terribly in love with each other, but they're always quarrelling. Serdyuk talked about your excavator, he calls it the Seryogin excavator. He says they're having a hard time, the rain has turned the ground into mud. He is terribly worried. The other boys from the excavator drop in very often too, you know.

CHORUS. All except Victor. . . . Why?

VALYA. Yes, why doesn't he come? Oh, I forgot to tell you the main thing—today that boy came to see me, Anton, remember? He came with his mother. They brought all sorts of pretty toys for the children. Here they are, see? Anton still wants to be a doctor, he's a sweet boy. . . . (*She is silent for a while.*) Well, that's the whole day. (*Fervently.*) Now listen to me, listen, you are the only friend I ever had, the only one I ever loved. I miss you terribly, Sergei. Terribly. But when-

ever I think of you I feel a little better, a little easier.

VOICE FROM CHORUS. Valya, shall I buy you a bicycle?

VALYA. Whatever for?

VOICE FROM CHORUS. To ride on, of course. . . .

VALYA (*laughing softly*). You do have the funniest notions. . . .

VOICE FROM CHORUS. Have you read Adenauer's statement in the papers?

VALYA. No.

VOICE FROM CHORUS. Are you sure you're not bored?

VALYA. I haven't any time to be bored. (*With mounting desperation.*) Winter is coming, Sergei, and then there'll be spring and summer. What am I going to do? I keep thinking about it. How shall I manage, Sergei? (*Without waiting for an answer.*) Oh dear, I'm so tired. I didn't work so hard today, but I'm so, so tired. . . .

(*A violin plays the familiar lullaby. The melody is echoed faintly, first by women's voices, then men's.*)

VALYA (*half asleep*). You bustle about and fuss from one day to the next, and all the days are the same, and you go on bustling and fussing.

VOICE FROM CHORUS. You're tired, dear. Go to sleep, I'll wash the dishes and tidy up. I'll do a beautiful job. And if Fyodor or Lena wake up I'll keep them quiet. So go to sleep now and don't worry about anything.

CHORUS. Valya is asleep, and while she sleeps angry autumn gales blow from the Angara. Whistles sound near by.

— Valya sleeps, and while she sleeps the night shift crew of the big walking excavator are trudging through the rain to the job.

— Somewhere Anton, who is going to be a doctor, and Lera, his little friend Lera, the one who does not believe in Charlie Chaplin, are fast asleep. . . .

— Suddenly in the middle of the night Serdyuk wakes up with his heart aching at the thought of his age. . . . He cannot sleep, and so he pores over a French grammar until morning.

DENIS (*in* CHORUS). Zinka and I are fast asleep in our new room. . . . She sleeps with her head on my shoulder and I hold her tenderly in my arms as if I was afraid she would not be there when I wake up.

ZINKA (*in* CHORUS). Neither the roar of the engines at the cofferdam, nor the loud night whistles of the steam engines disturb our sleep. We are asleep and dreaming bright and beautiful dreams.

VICTOR (*in* CHORUS). No sleep for me! I go out on to the street and walk through the sleeping settlement. Now I stop under Valya's windows, but I do not knock at her door. How many times have I stood here like this at the dead of night and then wandered back home, without having come to any decision.

CHORUS. Now the night is fading and morning is dawning! Autumn is followed by winter, and then comes the spring.

— April! A cold, windy April, yet Spring nevertheless. The last snow-flakes melt rapidly in the sun!

(ZINKA *appears. She is very excited. She wears an apron over her best dress, and her arms are full of plates.*)

ZINKA. Congratulations! This is April thirtieth, Fyodor and Lena are one year old today! Think of it. A whole year already! We are having a birthday party for them. The whole Seryogin excavator crew are coming. After all, they're sort of godfathers. (*In a confidential whisper.*) Guess where they are, the babies I mean? We took them to Larisa Petrovna's room. It will be nice and quiet for them there. . . .

(*The* SERYOGIN *room emerges.* VALYA *and* LARISA *are busy setting the table.*)

ZINKA. When did Serdyuk and his army promise to come?

LARISA. Seven-thirty.

ZINKA (*throwing up her hands*). My goodness, it's nearly seven!

LARISA. Don't worry, we'll be ready. . . . (*To* VALYA.) What are you so thoughtful about?

VALYA. Nothing in particular.

(*A pause.*)

ZINKA. How many places shall we lay?

LARISA. Lay for the whole crew.

VALYA. You needn't count Victor. He never comes to see me.

ZINKA. Why?

VALYA. Oh, Victor believes in enjoying life. He gives trouble a wide berth.

ZINKA. I hear he's getting a premium for good work. A medal or a thousand rubles or something.

LARISA (*looking at* VALYA). What's the matter, dear?

VALYA. I feel numb and dead inside.

LARISA (*with compassion*). You'll forget in time.

VALYA. It's not that. . . . It's. . . . Apart from the children I have no interest in life. It frightens me sometimes.

ZINKA (*bustling at the table*). Girls, guess what? Our Lapchenko's gone and fallen in love.

LARISA. You don't say!

ZINKA. Honest to God. He's gone and bought himself a fancy Czech jacket too.

VALYA (*with a smile*). Lapchenko. . . .

ZINKA. Can't be helped. The Chief sets a bad example. (*Looks at* LARISA *and giggles.*)

LARISA. You leave my Serdyuk alone, child. (*Earnestly.*) He's a man in a million.

ZINKA (*embarrassed*). I didn't mean. . . . (*Timidly.*) Why don't you get married then?

LARISA. Married? He's too shy. He can't face people. Says he has no right to make himself look ridiculous.

ZINKA. He's awful bashful about such things. (*Proudly.*) He gave me hell for two years because me and Denis were in love.

VALYA. Larisa.

LARISA. Yes?

VALYA. Think I ought to go back to the store? Will you take me back?

LARISA. Too late, Valya. . . . I'm going to evening school to learn reinforcing work.

VALYA. What for?

LARISA. My hard-hearted Serdyuk's making me. You know him. (*Mimicking* SERDYUK.) Got to learn a proper trade, my girl!

ZINKA (*laughing*). That's him to a T. (*Exit.*)

LARISA. Truth is, Valya, I want to make a fresh start. (*Exit.*)

VALYA (*looking at some money lying on the table*). Sergei's pay. . . . (*Smiles.*) They're so punctual with it.

(VICTOR *appears in the doorway. A long silence.*)

Victor, you?

VICTOR. Yes, me. (*Laughs.*) Did I frighten you?

VALYA. I wasn't expecting you.

VICTOR. Well, here I am. Do you mind?

VALYA. No.

VICTOR. I came with the Chief. He stepped in to see the kids, and I came straight to you. . . . That Fyodor of yours is the image of Sergei. (*Hands Valya a parcel.*) Here's something for them.

VALYA. Take off your things, won't you. Is it snowing?

VICTOR. Yes, but it's spring just the same. (*Looks about him.*) It's very nice here. (*Sits down on a couch.*) I promised to go away. Remember? But I didn't keep my promise. Forgive me.

(*A pause.*)

VALYA (*softly*). Why didn't you come to see me?

VICTOR. I'm not a good consoler.

VALYA. You could have come anyway.

VICTOR (*his voice trembles*). I was afraid.

VALYA. Oh, Victor!

VICTOR (*unable to control his feelings any longer*). Did you think I'd forgotten? I remember everything. I think of you all the time. I see you before me wherever I look. I thought it was just foolishness between us, but I know better now. It's all my own fault, I know. I killed my happiness with my own hands. (*Despairingly.*) But how could I have known. . . . I didn't make it up. It was there. Remember White Hill, Valya? Remember the stars looking down at us?

VALYA. Stop, Victor.

VICTOR (*looking at her in fear*). You still love him?

(VALYA, *smiling, nods her head.*)

VICTOR (*his voice drops to almost a whisper*). Forgive me.

VALYA. I forgive you.

(VICTOR *lights a cigarette with shaking hands.* VALYA *fidgets with something to hide her embarrassment.*)

VICTOR (*without moving*). I'm going. I must go at once. It is such a long time since I saw her . . . that little line at her mouth wasn't there before. So she still loves Sergei. I don't remember that dress either. I shall get up and go. No, I cannot. It's no use.

VALYA (*without moving*). Strange. . . . Strange. So that's why he never came.

Sergei's death kept him away. He has changed. His eyes look quite different. Is it possible that I once danced with him in the park? No, this is a different Victor. But why doesn't he speak? How quiet he is! Poor Victor.

VICTOR. How are you getting along?

VALYA. I manage.

VICTOR. Lonely?

VALYA. Sometimes. I feel as if I too had died when Sergei went.

VICTOR. Don't talk like that.

VALYA. You needn't pity me! I have my joys. A widow's joys. I have the children to bring up, their happiness to think of.

VICTOR. But what about yourself? What about your own life? Home, children, is that quite enough, Valya?

VALYA. What more do I want? (*Laughs.*) I won't die of hunger. Thanks to you I have quite enough to live on.

VICTOR (*fervently*). Let me tell you something. I wish you hadn't agreed to take that money. And that's the truth!

VALYA. Really? But why!

VICTOR. Because I hate charity! You were always such a proud, independent creature. And now, just look at yourself. . . .

VALYA. Go on. Go on.

VICTOR. You've become a dependent.

VALYA (*looking at him with surprise and resentment*). Well, you certainly have changed, Victor.

VICTOR. That's what love has done to me.

VALYA. It's made you hard and callous!

VICTOR. You can call it that.

VALYA (*angrily*). Hard, hard.

(*Enter* LARISA.)

LARISA. What's all the noise about?

VALYA (*upset*). Nothing much. . . .

LARISA. Go to the children, Valya. Serdyuk can't handle them. They won't go to sleep without you.

(VALYA *runs out.*)

You're a fine one. You stay away for half a year and then you come and kick up a row!

VICTOR. So would you if you really loved her!

LARISA. What do you mean?

VICTOR. Nobody loves her.

LARISA. You're crazy.

(*Enter* SERDYUK, RODIK, DENIS *and* ZINKA.)

I say, Comrade Serdyuk, take your assistant here in hand. He's getting obstreperous. (*Exit.*)

SERDYUK. What's up, Victor?

VICTOR (*gruffly*). Nothing. . . .

ZINKA. Where's Lapchenko?

RODIK. Poor Lapchenko, he's lost to society.

DENIS. He's standing outside the cinema waiting for his Nyura.

RODIK. Victor, looks as if you and me are going to be the only bachelors left soon.

SERDYUK. I know what you're hinting at.

VICTOR (*with sudden brusqueness*). Now then, sit down all of you, and let's have this out once and for all. I've kept silent long enough, but I'm going to speak out now.

ZINKA. Look, he really is potty.

VICTOR. You keep out of this, Zinka.

SERDYUK. Silence, everybody! The shift boss has the floor.

VICTOR. This arrangement of ours with Valya. . . . It's all wrong. . . . She gets money regularly, but for what? For sitting at home doing nothing?

SERDYUK. Are you mad, boy?

ZINKA. Victor, how can you. . . .

RODIK. You ought to be ashamed of yourself!

VICTOR. Shut up, Rodik, it's you who's degrading her with those namby-pamby highbrow ideas of yours. . . .

DENIS. What on earth. . . .

RODIK (*huffily*). Look here, Victor. . . .

(*Enter* LAPCHENKO *with his girl* NYURA.)

LAPCHENKO (*gaily*). Hello, everybody. Birthday greetings to the babies! This is Nyura, she's from the Head Office. A big noise.

NYURA (*shyly*). Good evening.

LAPCHENKO (*to* NYURA). Meet my shift comrades. Great fellows, all of them. Best of pals.

VICTOR. Run along, Afanasy, we're busy at the moment.

DENIS. Why don't you say something, Chief? Didn't you hear what he said?

SERDYUK. Wait, I'll tell him. . . .

(*Shoves the bewildered* LAPCHENKO *out of his way and makes for* VICTOR.) Now then explain yourself, young man.

VICTOR. You've thought of Sergei and his children. But what about her? Isn't she a live human being?

LAPCHENKO (*good-naturedly*). Look here, fellows.

SERDYUK (*angrily*). Lapchenko, vanish. . . .

NYURA. I don't think much of your comrades. Looks like a fight to me.

VICTOR. Don't you see what your money is doing to her, Rodik? I can't stand it any more.

RODIK (*coldly*). You seem to have a personal interest in this, Victor.

VICTOR (*outraged*). What? (*Swings a chair at* RODIK.)

NYURA (*at the top of her voice*). No fighting, please!

VICTOR (*drops the chair*). Yes. I do have a personal interest. I happen to love Valya.

NYURA (*in awed whisper*). Oh, dear.

VICTOR. I don't see why I should hide it. You're my family, so you might as well know. I let my happiness slip through my fingers. . . . Why? Because I wasn't worth a damn. Valya became Sergei's wife, and that was the end of it. I thought I would forget the whole thing. But I couldn't. She bore him children, became a mother, and still I couldn't put her out of my mind. I loved her more than ever. I could have been in Sergei's place. I tried to run away from her, but I couldn't! It was enough for me to know that she was here, that's all I wanted. . . . That's my personal interest, Rodik. Now do you understand?

(*A long silence.*)

RODIK. I apologise, Victor.

NYURA (*in a whisper to* LAPCHENKO). Are you fellows always like this?

LAPCHENKO. Like what?

NYURA. Making a clean breast of everything.

LAPCHENKO. We try.

VICTOR (*noticing* NYURA *for the first time*). Hello, who's this?

LAPCHENKO. I told you, Nyura, from the Head Office.

VICTOR (*wearily*). Why did you bring her here?

LAPCHENKO. Well, she's my girl. . . . I wanted to introduce her to you fellows.

NYURA (*shyly to* VICTOR). How do you do.

VICTOR (*giving her a friendly hug*). Happy to meet you, Nyura from the Head Office.

NYURA. I've known you for a long time. We danced a slow fox trot together two years ago.

VICTOR (*with a slight smile*). So we did, Nyura. (*Banging his fist suddenly on the table.*) No! I don't want her to get money for nothing. Sergei put her on her feet. He believed in her and he taught her to believe in herself.

SERDYUK. What about the children. . . . Have you thought of them?

VICTOR (*finally taking the plunge*). Chief. . . . Let's take her to work on the excavator.

SERDYUK. Can't be done. . . . She hasn't any training.

VICTOR (*warmly*). Let her just come and watch—we'll do the work for her. And gradually we can begin to teach her things, in a year or two she'll get the hang of it. She'll have a real trade. And it won't be a hand-out she'll take home but real wages. She'll become a worker.

SERDYUK (*slowly*). So that's what all the fuss has been about. I must admit I didn't believe much in all your talk about love. But this is different. . . . (*Gives* VICTOR *a hug.*) Now I see you really do love her.

VICTOR. Chief. . . .

SERDYUK. But you weren't fair to Rodik. He made his offer with the best intentions. We had to think of some way of helping Valya in the first period when the children were small. But now I have an idea you're right. (*To* RODIK.) Don't you think so, Rodik?

RODIK. Yes, I believe he is right.

SERDYUK (*to the others*). What do you think?

DENIS. Victor's hit the nail on the head. My major, he's a colonel now, would have said the same.

LAPCHENKO. We've heard all about your major.

ZINKA. It won't do you any harm to hear some more about him, Lapchenko.

NYURA (*on the defensive*). Why, what's wrong with Lapchenko?

SERDYUK. Now, girls, there's three or four too many of you around here!

(*Enter* LARISA.)

LARISA. Does that include me?

SERDYUK (*fiercely*). Yes, it does. Just because I'm in love with you doesn't mean I've got to watch my step all the time, does it?

LARISA (*delighted*). He said it! . . . At last! In front of everybody.

SERDYUK. Well, what if I did? Now quiet everybody. Hush. How are we going to break it to Valya?

(VALYA *appears in the doorway.*)

VICTOR. Permit me, Chief. . . . I don't need to be afraid any more, I've told you everything. Let me tell her now.

VALYA. Yes, what is it you want to tell me, Victor?

(*All turn to look at* VALYA.)

VICTOR (*firmly*). It's time you started living your own life. Come and work with us on the excavator. We'll teach you the trade. It's the best there is.

VALYA (*levelly*). I see. You're sticking to your guns, aren't you, shift boss? (*Laughs.*) Only I don't see what right you have to protect my interests. (*To* SERDYUK.) Thanks for the offer, but I think I'll get along on my own somehow. (*Takes the money and places it in front of* SERDYUK.) Without charity. (*Surveying the gathering coldly.*) You think I won't manage? I'll go away from here. There's plenty of other places to go to.

DENIS (*flaring up*). You can't treat us like this, Valya. What have we done?

VALYA. I don't like your boss, soldier boy, that's why. He's a bit too vindictive. (*Goes up to* VICTOR, *looks him in the eyes.*) Evidently there are some things about me he simply can't forget.

VICTOR. Is that all you have to say, Valya? (*Goes to the door, puts on his coat.*) Good-bye. . . . (*Hurries out.*)

SERDYUK (*quietly, reproachfully*). You shouldn't have done that. . . .

RODIK (*goes over to* VALYA). He loves you (*gently*) very, very much.

ZINKA (*angrily*). You're all wrong, Valya. Why did you have to hurt Victor like that?

VALYA. Why, oh why, Sergei, darling?

(*The room and the people disappear, leaving* VALYA *alone in the limelight.*)

I'm so lost without you, dear. It's so hard.

What shall I do? I don't know, my head is reeling.

VOICE FROM CHORUS. Don't cry. I don't want you ever to shed a single tear. People must be happy in this world. That's the truth. Especially those who are building communism. You and me, for instance. And what does a person need to be happy? The satisfaction of knowing he's doing a worth-while job, that he's part of something bigger than himself.

VALYA. What do you mean by that?

VOICE FROM CHORUS. I don't quite know how to put it. I only know there are jobs that do something to a man, make him bigger, better than he was before. If you don't want to work on concrete you could try the excavator. You could begin as a helper and later on you could go to evening school. . . . They say there's a girl at the Volga dam who's in charge of a whole excavator crew. . . . Do you hear me, Valya?

VALYA. Oh, Sergei! Oh, my darling!

(*Lights go on again.* VALYA *is again in her own room, surrounded by her friends.*)

SERDYUK. Go and call Victor back. . . . Go and call him, Valya.

RODIK. Let me go, shall I?

VALYA. Thanks. But he won't come back. He's too stubborn. I know.

(*The door opens and* VICTOR *is seen standing on the threshold.*)

You? You've come back?

VICTOR. It's not like me, is it? You don't know me at all, Valya. (*Goes over to her.*) I shall never leave you. If you go away I'll follow you and I'll find you wherever you are. But don't make me give up my friends and comrades for your sake, Valya. . . . I am taking Sergei's place on the excavator; every screw, every rivet there is drenched with my sweat. . . . That machine is almost human, it has a soul, and without it I don't think I could ever be happy. I shall go down on my knees to you and beg you not to let me desert my comrades.

VALYA. Don't be silly, Victor. Don't!

VICTOR (*fiercely*). Then come and work with us on the excavator. Forget your hurts, forget my love for you, everything. After all, this is Sergei's machine, our Sergei. Your Sergei. He is not with us any more, but you and I, Valya, must

go on living. It is our duty to ourselves and to life.

CHORUS. And while everyone is waiting for Valya's answer, upstairs in Larisa's room the two young Seryogins, Fyodor and Lena, are fast asleep.

(*Darkness. The familiar lullaby is heard, and the voices humming the melody.*)

— They sleep and their dreams are such as you and I will never see again.

— Fyodor is dreaming of a little yellow flower he saw that day for the first time in his life, it was sticking up out of the ground beside his little boot.

— And Lena is dreaming of a bright blue ball which the boy Anton gave her this morning, the one who is going to be a doctor.

THE ACTOR WHO PLAYED THE PART OF SERGEI. I envy their dreams, their childhood. . . . But perhaps most of all I envy the day they will come of age. How different the world will be then! And how many wonderful things they will see in the world we have won for communism.

CHORUS. But now, on the threshold of future miracles, they are dreaming of a wonderful yellow flower and a bright blue ball.

(*And again the contours of a small wooden bridge appear. And on it, beside a street lamp, stand* VICTOR *and* VALYA. *It is raining.*)

VALYA. Victor, darling. . . . Thank you.

VICTOR. What for?

VALYA. Look. (*She shows him a roll of bills in her hand.*)

VICTOR. Your pay?

VALYA. Yes, my first. . . . (*Tears start to her eyes.*) If only he knew. . . . How glad he would be.

VICTOR. Yes.

VALYA (*presses her cheek to his sleeve*). Thank you.

VICTOR (*gently*). Silly girl.

VALYA (*smiling*). They say there's a girl at the Volga dam who's in charge of a whole excavator crew. Think it's possible?

VICTOR. Of course it is.

VALYA. Oh dear!

VICTOR. What is it?

VALYA (*smiling*). A raindrop went down my neck.

VICTOR. They say our excavator is going to Bratsk. Have you heard?

VALYA (*quickly*). Good-bye. I must go to the nursery, for the children.

VICTOR (*taking her hand*). Valya, darling. . . .

VALYA. No. . . . Don't say it.

VICTOR. Never?

VALYA. I'll be seeing you. . . . (*Runs off*).

VICTOR. With tears in her eyes and a smile on her lips she runs off the bridge into the night. . . . Will she ever be my wife, will she ever consent? Who knows! But that is another story, another tale. This one ends with me standing on the road, looking after her and thinking how dearly I love her.

CHORUS. Good luck, Victor! (*To audience.*) The end.

Curtain

ALEXANDER KORNEICHUK: *Soviet Drama*

From *The Current Digest of the Soviet Press*, VII, No. 5, published at Columbia University by the Joint Committee on Slavic Studies appointed by the American Council of Learned Societies and the Social Science Research Council. Copyright 1955, the Joint Committee on Slavic Studies. Reprinted by permission.

OUR GREAT COMMUNIST PARTY PRESENTS US WITH THE HIGH MISsion of making drama and the theater a genuine drama and theater of the people. This noble appeal, this constant demand is based on the principles of creating a new, unprecedented Soviet multinational art, national in form and socialist in content; it is based, moreover, on the centuries-long experience of development of world culture, in which the test of time has been met by those works which reflect most forcefully and ardently the people's life, struggle, aspirations and hopes.

How pitiful seem the efforts of all kinds of decadents and other enemies of our Soviet art when they try to discredit the lofty principles of our art and thereby to discredit all beautiful and great world art.

How ridiculous seem some of our muddleheads who swear by socialist realism at every step, yet try to inflict upon us their false esthetic criteria and champion plays and productions which are far removed from life and from the people.

These muddleheads accept gray naturalism but brand as formalism every fresh search for vivid stage form. They do not want to comprehend that we understand formalism to mean primarily lack of content, that formalism in art is determined not by vivid stage form but by lack of content, that formalism and naturalism are alike harmful and alien to our theater arts.

Some comrades may think that I am talking only of muddleheaded critics. There are muddleheads among playwrights, directors, actors and set designers, too.

Our drama and theater must endeavor to be rich in content in the same way as our life is rich in great deeds: Our drama and theater must be rich in variety of stage forms, just as our life is rich, full of color and infinitely bright.

Have we not heard innumerable speeches by muddleheads and read innumerable hypocritical articles, starting out with the declaration that we need vivid and sharp productions, and then proceeding to denounce the slightest fresh and vivid trace in acting, direction or stage sets? . . .

What genres do we need? What forms of stage art? Where can we find the answer?

If the dramatist has a deep understanding of his material and realizes his responsibility to the people; if the actor and director have the same understanding, from life, of what they should convey, then no one should stand in the way of a bold solution, bold selection of the form best enabling the artist to reveal the vital things which move men and to reach the very heart of his audience. . . .

From the beginning of the great patriotic war the Soviet dramatist was confronted with new tasks. The historic deeds of the Soviet people, who gained a great victory in the struggle against fascism, were recorded in the best plays written during those years. . . .

But after the war some playwrights and theater workers became complacent. They felt that they could rest on their laurels and still the militant voice of art. The stages of Soviet theaters were filled with the concoctions of bourgeois scribblers or empty plays by some of our writers. Such plays were based on empty, meaningless anecdotes, and distorted the images of Soviet people and made them appear stupid.

The Party could not ignore phenomena which were so alien to our art. The historic resolutions of the Party Central Committee on ideological problems marked the years 1946 to 1948. The decisions of the Party Central Committee, based on concrete cases in our arts, presented a clear outline for further development of Soviet literature and determined in the main its new, characteristic features in the epoch of building a communist society. The aim of Soviet art was to show to the whole world the moral beauty and might of victorious Soviet man. In order to disclose the remarkable spiritual qualities of our people more fully and clearly, Soviet artists were to expose bourgeois survivals in men's minds, to portray truthfully and to condemn unfavorable aspects of our life, and to show the best sides of the Soviet man's character in his struggle with negative forces.

In order to create a striking image of the positive hero, the writer must be able to view life with all its contradictions, to observe the true conflicts in life and to show how the new is strengthened in overcoming them.

Was all this done in our postwar drama? In the best plays, undoubtedly . . .

But, even in these good instances, it is interesting to note our playwrights' mistakes, which considerably impoverished their favorable characters.

The most important failure results from lack of understanding of the device of artistic emphasis, which is an indispensable requirement for creating a major typical character. In the portrayal of the hero, unfortunately, the playwright does not select and concentrate the best traits and qualities, but often contents himself with a simple, superficial imitation of a few character traits of the present-day man, an approach which impoverishes both the character, as compared with life, and the play.

Often when we meet writers in capitalist countries they reproach us for proclaiming as the basis of our drama and all literature the image of the positive hero.

It seems to me that the time has come for writers all over the world to give profound thought to the reasons why, over the centuries, many of the most truthful writers have told men: "Look how all your titanic efforts in fighting evil suffer defeat. No matter how it burns, the flame of your heart will never be able to light up the darkness of night for millions of people." They showed us the touching and noble love of a man for a woman, but always stupid and evil forces destroyed this love. What moving and noble feelings of friendship we find in the works of the past! But tears of joy do not form in the eyes of the readers when they close the book, or the audience when it comes out of the theater. Instead, one swallows bitter tears of regret for the doom, the inexorable destruction of great feelings of love and friendship crushed by terrible reality, by the harsh world of repression and force. The great writers of the past described profoundly the sufferings of the soul and stirring human dramas which, as a rule, ended in a break between lovers, between husband and wife, between children and parents or between friends, and the noblest feelings were trampled underfoot, broken and destroyed by the cruel conditions of life. Not knowing how to alter existing reality, writers of the world for centuries have given mankind not a bright "Hello, beloved!" but "Farewell!" not "Hello, friend!" but "Farewell!" not "Hello, father!" but "Farewell!" not "Hello, my native land!" but "Farewell!" Struggling for the future with their remarkable works, they poignantly sought a hero and courageously wrote about bright but still only isolated rays of light in the darkness.

Who, at the top of his voice, told all mankind: "No matter how hard it may be for you, no matter how difficult the struggle, you will be victorious, you will never be alone, you will meet friends and they will not forsake you"? . . .

Our Soviet literature said this, and joined itself openly and irrevocably with the victorious revolutionary proletariat.

Is there a more noble, humane and majestic task for a writer than to devote all his talent, all his efforts to the cause of uniting individuals, families and peoples, the cause of unbreakable friendship and love, the cause of man's victory over the dark forces of evil?

This is why we affirm with such passion the victory of the positive hero.

No doubt no one here would object to this. But is not this talk about idealizing the positive hero really a struggle against him? How can the partisans of whitewash fail to see the greatness of Soviet man today, the beauty of his soul, his heroic struggle on behalf of high ideals, and demand that we writers create contrived, artificial characters?

Our audience does not seek from us dramatists an idealized hero without blemish, a handsome, lofty babbler, but a fighter for the bright ideals of communism who overcomes not only the hostile forces which oppose the new world, but also the human weaknesses which are present to some degree in any man. The audience wants to see how our contemporary man tempers his soul in the heroic struggle for the bright happiness of his motherland and for all peoples of the world, how he serves as an example for those around him by his acts at any station he may occupy.

The no-conflict theory,[1] which has been so widespread in recent years, could only hamper the development of our drama and reduce the lifelike quality of its chief hero, the Soviet working man. If a play does not depict a major, vital conflict, it is obvious that the positive hero becomes inactive and deprived of intellect, since he is not fighting for anything in the play and his ideals cannot be pictured outside of an active struggle with evil.

In speaking of the necessity of portraying great social conflicts in our drama, however, we must not at the same time imagine that conflict is the sole end of a work of art, conflict no matter what, conflict for the sake of conflict. This unvoiced slogan has appeared in practice in a number of recent plays and leads to a distortion of life. Just as varnishing reality is a slander upon reality, so the attributing to it of contradictions which do not exist and cannot develop is also slander of the very foundations of our life. We criticize these plays not because the authors called them satires, but because, in pointing out some phenomena, the authors themselves descended to the level of shallow Philistinism and lost a clear, revolutionary perspective. A real, active fighter for communism is a man who hates evil which keeps people from living and working. But fearing evil and

exaggerating excessively its strength and importance means that one ceases to become a fighter for communism and is a defeatist. . . .

What makes a play not simply one among many good plays, but a first-class work, an innovation? Plays which show seeds of the new, where the typical is shown not only as an end result but in the process of birth, plays pointing the way, presenting new themes, new people, new facets of life—such plays are especially dear to our people.

One such, for example, was K. Simonov's "Alien Shadow." Simonov showed the danger of the influence of bourgeois ideology, he saw people influenced by it and he wrote a play permeated with lofty civic passion, a play in which the idea of Soviet patriotism was presented in brilliant artistic images. Success awaited the playwright when he portrayed not a full-blown character, but one in process of formation and change, a character in which a sharp psychological turn is taken under the influence of life—the character of Trubnikov. Simonov resisted the easy solution. The struggle is meaningful and the play has considerable educational impact because it is not easy to fight with Trubnikov. The educational force of the play is great also because the struggle is waged not only against but for Trubnikov, a struggle for his political enlightenment, a struggle for a man. The struggle for man has always been a mark of the best works of Russian and world literature. . . .

Important aspects of our life, previously poorly treated, were depicted in A. Arbuzov's "Years of Wandering."

A deep moral conflict is the basis of this play. The moral standards of Soviet man and his human, lofty morality form a new criterion for judging men's behavior and thoughts. The departures from this ethical standard which the character Vedernikov commits are not tried in court; they are judged by his comrades, they are condemned by society, the highest moral court. This new, typical phenomenon of our life, in which a man guilty not of a crime but of departure

---

[1] A theory, now discredited in Russia, maintaining that under Socialism drama can no longer realistically present conflicts between good and evil—since presumably evil disappears along with social conflicts—but only between various degrees of good.—*Ed.*

from Soviet morality must answer to those to whom such a departure is impossible, has been rightly noted by the playwright, and his play has shown it as a new norm of behavior in people's lives.

The public likes Arbuzov's play. But Arbuzov himself must ponder what is truly alive in his plays and what is a superficial effect calculated for an undemanding taste—one expressly contrived "intimate" note and pseudopsychological confusion which does not always clearly indicate the author's stand. Psychological drama, the form in which Arbuzov writes, must be developed in our plays, but its further development lies along the path of eliminating the shortcomings we have mentioned. . . .

The differing styles, modes of expression and artistic techniques of our dramatists are united in the single method of Soviet literature, the method of socialist realism. The full and brilliant development of genuine artistic individuality represents the guarantee and the immense emotional effectiveness of our drama, of its ideological content, vitality and beauty.

Along with full support for varied and fruitful tendencies, however, we must not slacken the struggle in our art against empty and dangerous eccentricities and against all attempts to sneak in bourgeois cosmopolitanism, formalism and naturalism under the guise of variety of forms in our art. We must not weaken our fight against these alien tendencies and must be able to recognize them under any camouflage. . . .

Selective Bibliography

SELECTIVE BIBLIOGRAPHY

I. Periodicals

Drama Survey
Educational Theatre Journal
Encore
Modern Drama

Theatre Arts
Tulane Drama Review
World Theatre

II. General Works on Drama and Theatre

FERGUSSON, FRANCIS, The Idea of a Theater, Princeton, 1949.

GASSNER, JOHN, Masters of the Drama, New York, 1954.

MACGOWAN, KENNETH, and WILLIAM MELNITZ, The Living Stage, New York, 1955.

MULLER, HERBERT J., The Spirit of Tragedy, New York, 1956.

STUART, DONALD CLIVE, The Development of Dramatic Art, New York, 1928.

III. Works on Modern Drama

BENTLEY, ERIC, The Playwright as Thinker, revised ed., New York, 1955.

DOWNER, ALAN, Fifty Years of American Drama, Chicago, 1951.

ESSLIN, MARTIN, The Theatre of the Absurd, Garden City, 1961.

GASSNER, JOHN, Form and Idea in Modern Theatre, New York, 1956.

GORELIK, MORDECAI, New Theatres for Old, New York, 1940.

KRUTCH, JOSEPH WOOD, "Modernism" in Modern Drama, Ithaca, 1953.

LEWIS, ALAN, The Contemporary Theatre, New York, 1962.

LUMLEY, FREDERICK, Trends in 20th Century Drama, revised ed., Fair Lawn, 1960.

WEALES, GERALD, American Drama Since World War II, New York, 1962.

WILLIAMS, RAYMOND, Drama from Ibsen to Eliot, London, 1952.

IV. Collections of Essays and Reviews

BENTLEY, ERIC, In Search of Theater, New York, 1953.

———, The Dramatic Event, New York, 1954.

———, What Is Theatre?, Boston, 1956.

BLOCK, HASKELL, and HERMAN SALINGER, eds., The Creative Vision, New York, 1960.

COLE, TOBY, ed., Playwrights on Playwriting, New York, 1960.

———, and HELEN CHINOY, eds., Actors on Acting, New York, 1949.

GASSNER, JOHN, Theatre at the Crossroads, New York, 1960.

———, Theatre in Our Times, New York, 1954.

MCCARTHY, MARY, Sights and Spectacles, New York, 1957.

TYNAN, KENNETH, Curtains, New York, 1961.

YOUNG, STARK, Immortal Shadows, New York, 1948.

V. Individual Authors

ALEXEI ARBUZOV

FROLOV, VLADIMIR, "The Theatre Today and Tomorrow," Soviet Literature, No. 4 (1961), 166–179.

LORDKIPANDZE, N., "Reflections on Happiness," Current Digest of the Soviet Press, XII (March 2, 1960), 29–30.

SURKOV, EVGENI, "Alexei Arbuzov," Soviet Literature, No. 10 (1960), 132–138.

SAMUEL BECKETT

Samuel Beckett Issue of Perspective, XI (Autumn, 1959).

COHN, RUBY, Samuel Beckett, New Brunswick, 1962.

ESSLIN, MARTIN, The Theatre of the Absurd, Garden City, 1961.

HOFFMAN, FREDERICK J., Samuel Beckett, Carbondale, 1962.

KENNER, HUGH, *Samuel Beckett*, New York, 1962.

BERTOLT BRECHT

Brecht Issue of *Tulane Drama Review*, VI (September, 1961).

ADLER, HENRY, "Bertolt Brecht's Theatre," *Twentieth Century*, CLX (August, 1956), 114–123.

BENTLEY, ERIC, *Playwright as Thinker*, New York, 1955.

BORNEMAN, ERNEST, "Credo Quia Absurdum: An Epitaph for Bertolt Brecht," *Kenyon Review*, XXI (Spring, 1959), 169–198.

BRECHT, BERTOLT, "Little Organum for the Theatre," *Playwrights on Playwriting*, ed., T. Cole, New York, 1960.

DEMETZ, PETER, ed., *Brecht* (Twentieth Century Views Series), Englewood Cliffs, 1962.

ESSLIN, MARTIN, *Brecht: The Man and His Work*, Garden City, 1960.

GRAY, RONALD, *Bertolt Brecht*, New York, 1961.

WILLET, JOHN, *The Theatre of Bertolt Brecht*, London, 1959.

ANTON CHEKHOV

BRUFORD, W. H., *Chekhov and His Russia*, New Haven, 1947.

GERHARDI, WILLIAM, *Anton Chekhov, A Critical Study*, New York, 1923.

FERGUSSON, FRANCIS, *The Idea of a Theater*, Princeton, 1949.

LAKSHIN, V., "The Literary Heritage of Chekhov," *Soviet Highlights*, II (March, 1960), 1–13.

MARGARSHAK, DAVID, *Chekhov the Dramatist*, London, 1952.

SIMMONS, ERNEST J., *Chekhov: A Biography*, Boston, 1962.

FEDERICO GARCÍA LORCA

BAREA, ARTURO, *Lorca, the Poet and His People*, New York, 1949.

BENTLEY, ERIC, "The Poet in Dublin," *In Search of Theater*, New York, 1953.

DURAN, MANUEL, ed., *Lorca* (Twentieth Century Views Series), Englewood Cliffs, 1962.

HONIG, EDWIN, *García Lorca*, New York, 1948.

JEAN GIRAUDOUX

Giraudoux Issue of *Tulane Drama Review*, III (Summer, 1959).

FOWLIE, WALLACE, *Dionysus in Paris*, New York, 1960.

INSKIP, DONALD, *Jean Giraudoux, The Making of a Dramatist*, Oxford, 1958.

LEEFMANS, BERT, "Giraudoux' Other Muse," *Kenyon Review*, XVI (Autumn, 1954), 611–627.

MAY, GEORGES, "Marriage vs. Love in the World of Giraudoux," *Yale French Studies*, No. 11 (1953), 106–115.

HENRIK IBSEN

BENTLEY, ERIC, "Ibsen, Pro and Con," *In Search of Theater*, New York, 1953.

BRADBROOK, MURIEL, *Ibsen, the Norwegian*, London, 1946.

BRUSTEIN, ROBERT, "Ibsen and Revolt," *Tulane Drama Review*, VII (Fall, 1962), 113–154.

DOWNS, BRIAN, *A Study of Six Plays by Ibsen*, Cambridge, 1950.

LUCAS, F. L., *Ibsen and Strindberg*, New York, 1962.

SHAW, GEORGE BERNARD, *The Quintessence of Ibsenism*, London, 1913.

EUGÈNE IONESCO

COE, RICHARD, *Eugène Ionesco*, New York, 1961.

CORRIGAN, ROBERT, "The Theatre in Search of a Fix," *Tulane Drama Review*, V (June, 1961), 21–35.

ESSLIN, MARTIN, *The Theatre of the Absurd*, Garden City, 1961.

IONESCO, EUGÈNE, "The Avant-Garde Theatre," *Tulane Drama Review*, V (December, 1960), 44–53.

———, "The Tragedy of Language: How an English Primer Became My First Play," *Tulane Drama Review*, IV (March, 1960), 10–13.

KITCHIN, LAURENCE, "Theatre—Nothing but Theatre," *Encounter*, X (April, 1958), 39–42.

EUGENE O'NEILL

ALEXANDER, DORIS, *The Tempering of Eugene O'Neill*, New York, 1962.

BOWEN, CROSWELL, *The Curse of the Misbegotten*, New York, 1959.

CARGILL, OSCAR, et al., eds., *O'Neill and His Plays*, New York, 1961.

ENGEL, EDWIN, *The Haunted Heroes of Eugene O'Neill*, Cambridge, Mass., 1953.

FALK, DORIS, *Eugene O'Neill and the Tragic Tension*, New Brunswick, 1958.

GELB, BARBARA and ARTHUR, *O'Neill*, New York, 1962.

LUIGI PIRANDELLO

BENTLEY, ERIC, *Playwright as Thinker*, New York, 1955.

FERGUSSON, FRANCIS, *The Idea of a Theater*, Princeton, 1949.

GASSNER, JOHN, "Pirandello and the 'Six Characters'," *The Theatre in Our Times*, New York, 1954.

KRUTCH, JOSEPH WOOD, *"Modernism" in Modern Drama*, Ithaca, 1953.

STARKIE, WALTER, *Luigi Pirandello*, New York, 1937.

VITTORINI, DOMENICO, *The Drama of Luigi Pirandello*. Philadelphia, 1935.

GEORGE BERNARD SHAW

BENTLEY, ERIC, *Bernard Shaw, 1856–1950*, New York, 1957.

CHESTERTON, G. K., *George Bernard Shaw*, London, 1909.

ERVINE, ST. JOHN, *Bernard Shaw, His Life, Works, and Friends*, New York, 1956.

HENDERSON, ARCHIBALD, *George Bernard Shaw: Man of the Century*, New York, 1956.

IRVINE, WILLIAM, *The Universe of G. B. S.*, New York, 1949.

KRONENBERGER, LOUIS, ed., *George Bernard Shaw, A Critical Survey*, Cleveland and New York, 1953.

MANDER, RAYMOND and JOE MITCHESON, *The Theatrical Companion to Shaw*, New York, 1955.

NETHERCOT, ARTHUR, *Men and Supermen: The Shavian Portrait Gallery*, Cambridge, Mass., 1954.

SHAW, BERNARD, *Sixteen Self-Sketches*, New York, 1949.

WEST, ALICK, *George Bernard Shaw: A Good Man Fallen Among Fabians*, New York, 1950.

WINSTEN, STEPHEN, ed., *G. B. S. 90*, New York, 1946.

AUGUST STRINDBERG

Strindberg Issue of *Modern Drama*, V (December, 1962).

BRUSTEIN, ROBERT, "Male and Female in August Strindberg," *Tulane Drama Review*, VII (Winter, 1962), 130–174.

CAMPBELL, GEORGE, *Strindberg*, New York, 1933.

McGILL, V.J., *August Strindberg: The Bedevilled Viking*, London, 1930.

MORTENSEN, BRITA, and BRIAN DOWNS, *Strindberg: An Introduction to His Life and Works*, Cambridge, 1949.

SPRIGGE, ELIZABETH, *The Strange Life of August Strindberg*, New York, 1949.

JOHN MILLINGTON SYNGE

Synge and O'Casey Issue of *Modern Drama*, IV (December, 1961).

BOURGEOIS, MAURICE, *John Millington Synge and the Irish Theatre*, London, 1913.

CORKERY, DANIEL, *Synge and Anglo-Irish Literature*, Oxford, 1947.

ELLIS-FERMOR, UNA, *The Irish Dramatic Movement*, London, 1954.

GREENE, DAVID H. and EDWARD M. STEPHENS, *J. M. Synge, 1871–1909*, New York, 1959.

MacLEAN, HUGH, "The Hero as Playboy," *The University of Kansas City Review*, XXI (Fall, 1954), 9–19.

PODHORETZ, NORMAN, "Synge's 'Playboy': Morality and Hero," *Essays in Criticism*, III (July, 1953), 337–344.

PRICE, ALAN, *Synge and Anglo-Irish Drama*, London, 1961.

YEATS, WILLIAM BUTLER, *Essays and Introductions*, New York, 1961.

TENNESSEE WILLIAMS

FALK, SIGNI, *Tennessee Williams*, New York, 1961.

GASSNER, JOHN, "Tennessee Williams: 1940–1960," *Theatre at the Crossroads*, New York, 1960.

NELSON, BENJAMIN, *Tennessee Williams*, New York, 1961.

POPKIN, HENRY, "The Plays of Tennessee Williams," *Tulane Drama Review*, IV (March, 1960).

TISCHLER, NANCY, *Tennessee Williams, Rebellious Puritan*, New York, 1961.

WILLIAMS, TENNESSEE, "Person to Person," *Cat on a Hot Tin Roof*, New York, 1955.

———, "The Catastrophe of Success," *The Glass Menagerie* (New Classics edition), New York, 1949.

———, "The World I Live In," *Observer*, April 7, 1957.